THE
USAGI
YOJIMBO
SAGA

D1501293

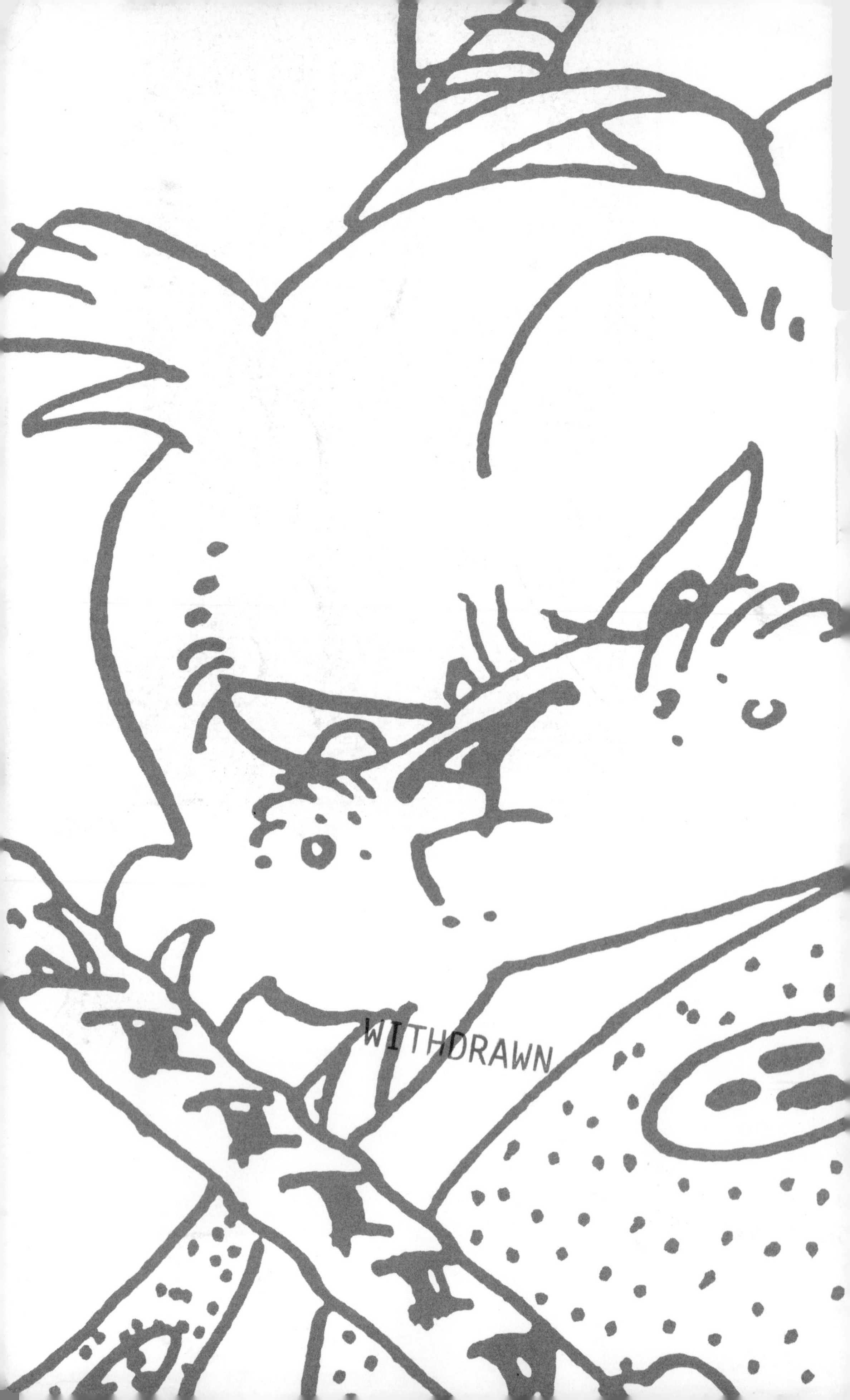

THE USAGI YOJIMBO™ SAGA

BOOK 3

Created, written,
and illustrated by

STAN SAKAI

"Tsuru" colored by
TOM LUTH

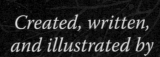

DARK HORSE BOOKS

Publisher
MIKE RICHARDSON

Series Editor
DIANA SCHUTZ

Collection Editor
BRENDAN WRIGHT

Assistant Editor
IAN TUCKER

Design and Digital Production
CARY GRAZZINI

THE USAGI YOJIMBO™ SAGA Book 3

This volume collects issues #31–#52 of the Dark Horse comic book series *Usagi Yojimbo Volume Three*, along with stories from issue #140 of *Dark Horse Presents*, *Dark Horse Presents Annual 1999*, *Dark Horse Maverick 2001*, and issues #20–#23 of *Dark Horse Extra*, all published by Dark Horse Comics; issue #97 of *Wizard: The Comics Magazine*, published by Gareb Shamus Enterprises, Inc.; and *Oni Double Feature* #11, published by Oni Press.

Visit the Usagi Yojimbo Dojo website:
UsagiYojimbo.com

Published by Dark Horse Books
A division of Dark Horse Comics, Inc.
10956 SE Main Street
Milwaukie, OR 97222
DarkHorse.com

To find a comics shop in your area, call the Comic Shop Locator Service toll-free at (888) 266-4226.
International Licensing: (503) 905-2377

Library of Congress Cataloging-in-Publication Data

Sakai, Stan, author, illustrator.
[Graphic novels. Selections]
The Usagi Yojimbo saga. Book 3 / created, written, and illustrated by Stan Sakai. -- First edition. Limited edition.
    pages cm
  Summary: "The latest tales of Miyamoto Usagi include the debut of Sasuké the Demon Queller, the history of ally Kitsune, the return of a friend long thought dead, and the final fate of the legendary sword Grasscutter"-- Provided by publisher.
  ISBN 978-1-61655-611-2 (pbk.) -- ISBN 978-1-61655-673-0 (limited hardcover edition)
1. Graphic novels. [1. Graphic novels. 2. Samurai--Fiction.] I. Title.

PZ7.7.S138Use 2015
741.5'973--dc23

                        2014031784

First edition: May 2015
ISBN 978-1-61655-611-2

Limited edition: May 2015
ISBN 978-1-61655-673-0

10 9 8 7 6 5 4 3 2 1

PRINTED IN CHINA

This one is for
Tone and April Rodriguez.
Love you guys.

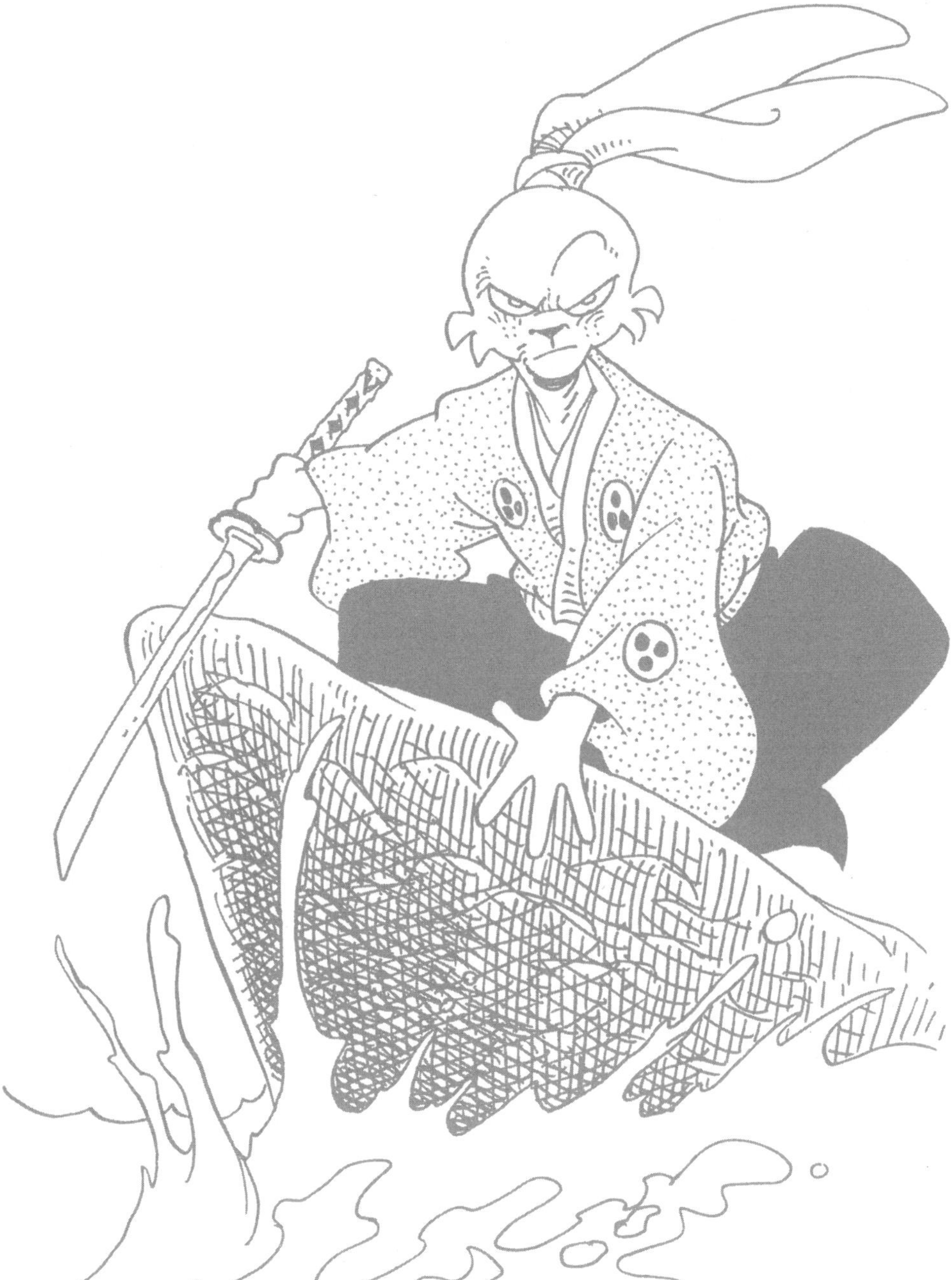

CONTENTS

DEMON MASK

GRASSCUTTER II: JOURNEY TO ATSUTA SHRINE

THE SHROUDED MOON

CAST OF CHARACTERS

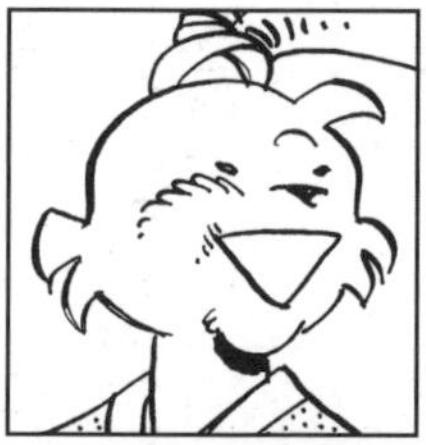

After the death of Lord Mifune in the battle of Adachi Plain, retainer **MIYAMOTO USAGI** chose the warrior's pilgrimage, becoming a wandering *ronin* in search of peace. Practicing the warrior code of *bushido*, Usagi avoids conflict whenever possible, but when called upon, his bravery and fighting prowess are unsurpassed.

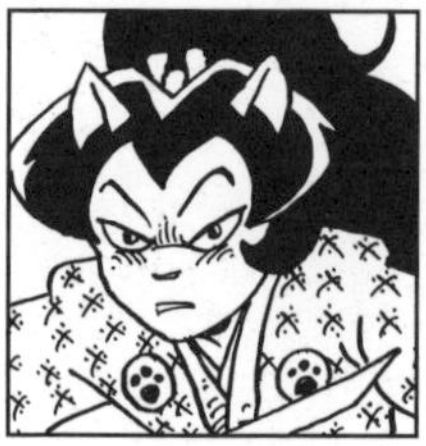

Trained in her father's Falling Rain school of swordsmanship, **TOMOE AME** serves as personal bodyguard and chief adviser to the young Lord Noriyuki of the Geishu clan. Tomoe is perhaps Usagi's equal as a fighter, with their duels to date ending in ties.

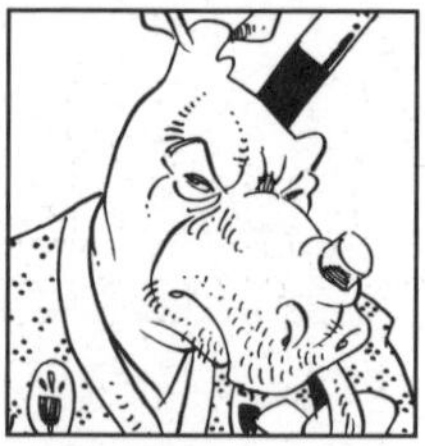

A descendant of samurai nobility, **MURAKAMI "GEN" GENNOSUKE** fell into poverty while his family pursued a vendetta and, vowing never to be poor again, turned to bounty hunting. Gen never fails to stick Usagi with the check for a meal or an inn and swears to be concerned only for himself, but his soft side sometimes briefly emerges.

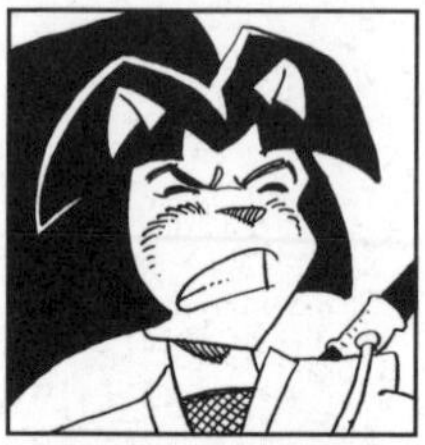

Upon the death of her brother Shingen, **KASHIRA CHIZU** became leader of the Neko ninja, a clan serving the dark lord Hikiji but often pursuing its own agendas. Though Chizu is a skilled leader, several clan members resent being commanded by a woman and seek to remove her.

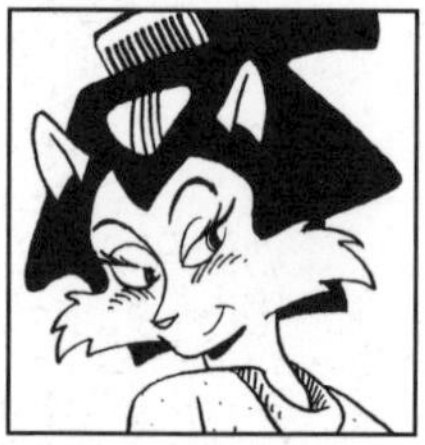

A street performer who believes "a girl has to do what she can to get by," **KITSUNE** makes extra money as a pickpocket, but steals only from those who deserve it. She and Usagi have been friends for many years, since the day she stole his purse and he stole it back.

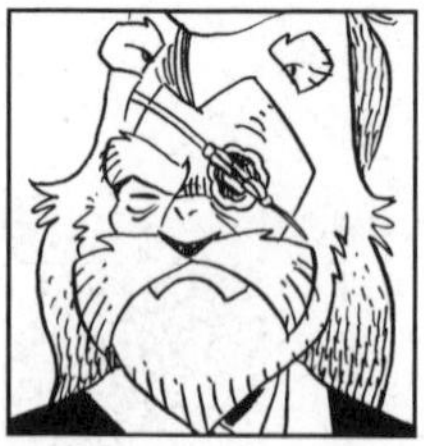

Once master of his own school of swordsmanship, **KATSUICHI SENSEI** lives as a hermit in the mountains near the village where Usagi grew up. Seeing Katsuichi defeat a gang of local toughs, a youthful Usagi begged to become his pupil, a request he eventually granted.

DEMON MASK

BEHIND THE RABBIT'S MASK

FROM THE ANCIENT FABLES OF AESOP to the contemporary cartoons of Bugs Bunny, the humble rabbit has long been a symbol of cleverness and survival. Even mythology's master strategist, the fox, routinely comes off the loser when he tries to match wits with his fleet-footed adversary, as the African American folktales of Br'er Rabbit readily attest. Whether he is called hare, cottontail, or jackrabbit, the little guy with the big ears and buck teeth is truly a timeless figure, and his legends have been told as long as there have been human beings around to tell them.

The storytelling tradition of ancient Japan holds friend rabbit in high esteem as well. As a child, one of my favorite bedtime stories was a rather ghoulish Japanese "fairy tale" telling of the murder of a farmer's kindly wife by a wicked *tanuki*, or raccoon dog. It seems the good wife fed and sheltered the little demon, who later repaid the woman for her generosity by murdering her and serving up her stewed remains to the farmer. Pretty gruesome behavior for old *tanuki*, a comical creature usually depicted wearing an oversized straw hat and toting a sake bottle. Maybe he drank too much sake and became unhinged, or maybe he was simply one seriously sociopathic raccoon dog; the story was vague on that point. What is known is that the grief-stricken farmer was horrified at the crime, as was his good friend, a rabbit who lived in the nearby woods. Playing on the *tanuki*'s greed, the rabbit lured the evil creature away on a treasure hunt, then secretly set fire to the *tanuki*'s backpack. When the nasty varmint jumped into a river to douse the flames, the rabbit clubbed him with a paddle and that was the end of that *tanuki*. In this story, as in many others told throughout the world, we witness the triumph of a small and traditionally meek character who has called upon his brains and bravery to defeat a larger, more aggressive enemy. It is a classic theme and one which writer/artist Stan Sakai weaves masterfully through his endlessly imaginative ongoing series, *Usagi Yojimbo*.

Stan often pits Usagi, a rabbit *ronin* of seventeenth-century Japan, in combat against a host of humanoid wolves, cats, bears, and other less easily defined carnivores. Far more than a funny-animal conceit, it always seemed to me that Stan was making a visual comment on the true natures of heroes and villains while perhaps referencing the great print maker Tsukioka Yoshitoshi. In his depictions of Japanese legends, Yoshitoshi often revealed the hidden, many times horrifying animalistic nature of his human subjects. A woman's shadow partially cast on a screen reveals the head of a fox. A samurai gazing into a dish of water sees not the pretty girl behind him but a reflection of her demonic inner being. In Yoshitoshi's world, the face of serenity masks the darker parts of the human id. It's only upon closer examination that we see the beast lurking within.

In the world of *Usagi*, the reverse is true. The animals' faces are their masks, while their humanity (or lack thereof) is revealed through their personalities, or to be more accurate, through Stan's deft characterizations. Whether he is armed with swords or not, Usagi is often perceived by many to be a physically weaker character. Ignorant enemies overlook his speed and skill, to say nothing of his courageous heart, and that is their inevitable undoing. Usagi also possesses the samurai's most valuable weapon: the wisdom of knowing when to fight and when to stand down. It's a trait that some might mistakenly read as cowardice (as the boy Eizo does in the short story "A Life of Mush"), but it subtly recalls the moral put forth in director Akira Kurosawa's samurai epic *Sanjuro* that the best swords are the ones that stay in their scabbards.

With the stories collected in this volume, Stan Sakai shows off every facet of Usagi's engaging and complex personality. We see him as Usagi the warrior certainly, but in "The Inn on Moon Shadow Hill" we also meet Usagi the trickster. After discovering the truth about a colony of *obakemono* (goblins) infesting the woods near a lonely inn, Usagi adds his own fantastic spin on the tale, preserving the legend of the creatures while slyly arranging a tidy profit for his efforts.

A much more serious encounter with demons is recounted in "*Kumo.*" Here Usagi joins forces with the mysterious demon hunter Sasuké to destroy a terrifying spider creature that has laid siege to a mountain village. The fox-like Sasuké is a terrific addition to *Usagi*'s extended cast of allies and enemies, and unlike the reluctant Usagi, I can't wait for the mystic to make a return appearance.

The collection's longest tale, "The Mystery of the Demon Mask," places Usagi in a situation that calls

on him to be as much detective as he is samurai. While searching for the masked fiend that has been killing masterless samurai, the rabbit *ronin* fights to stay alive in a tightening web of tragedy, betrayal, and madness. As with all good mysteries, the outcome is both surprising and satisfying, but Sakai goes a step further to add a final bitter, yet not inappropriate, twist to the epic. It's the sort of human touch that has placed *Usagi Yojimbo* far in front of every other "funny animal" book published since Carl Barks bid adieu to Duckburg thirty-five years ago.

It's the mark of a great storyteller. It's the stuff of legends.

PAUL DINI

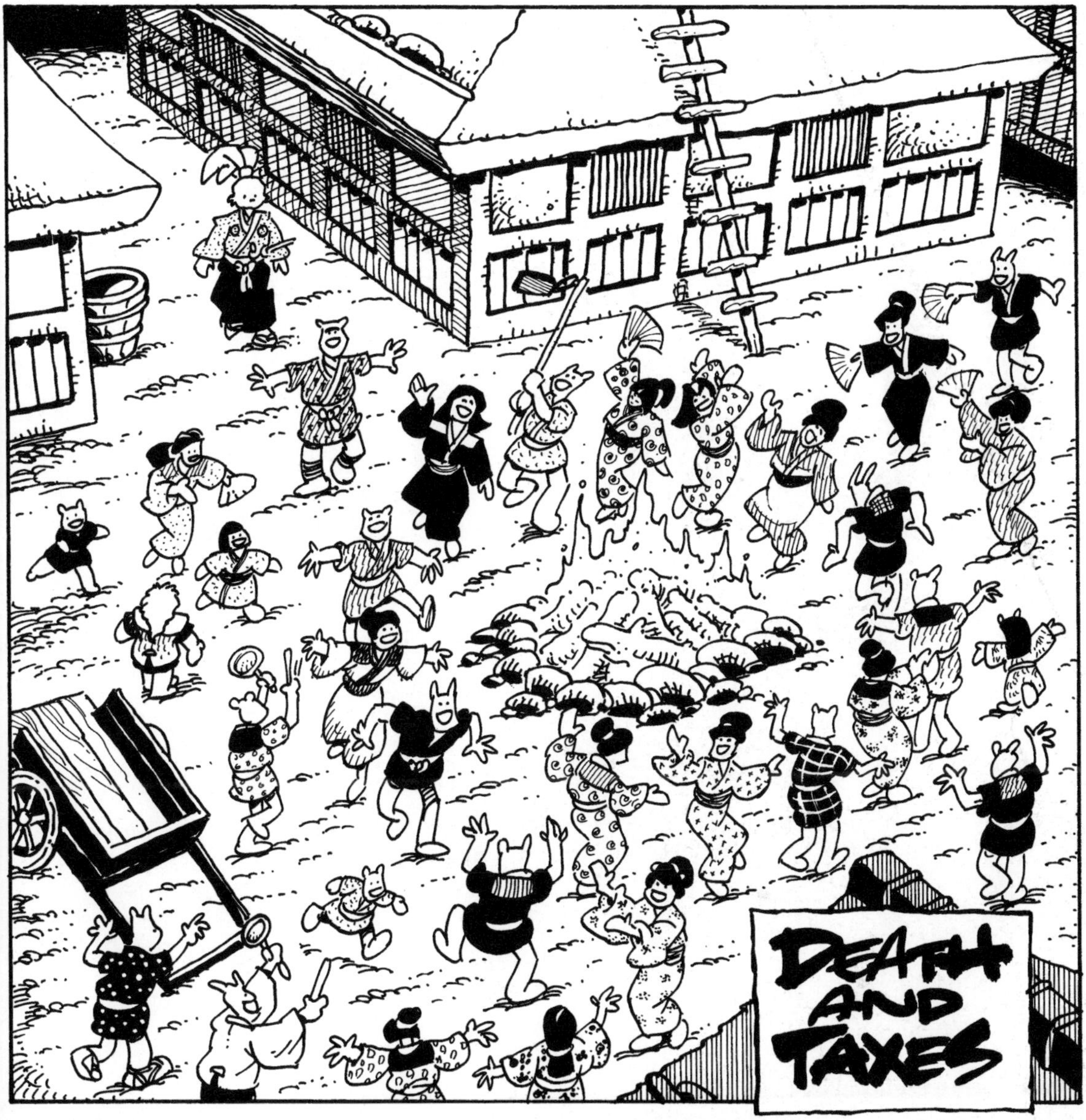
DEATH AND TAXES

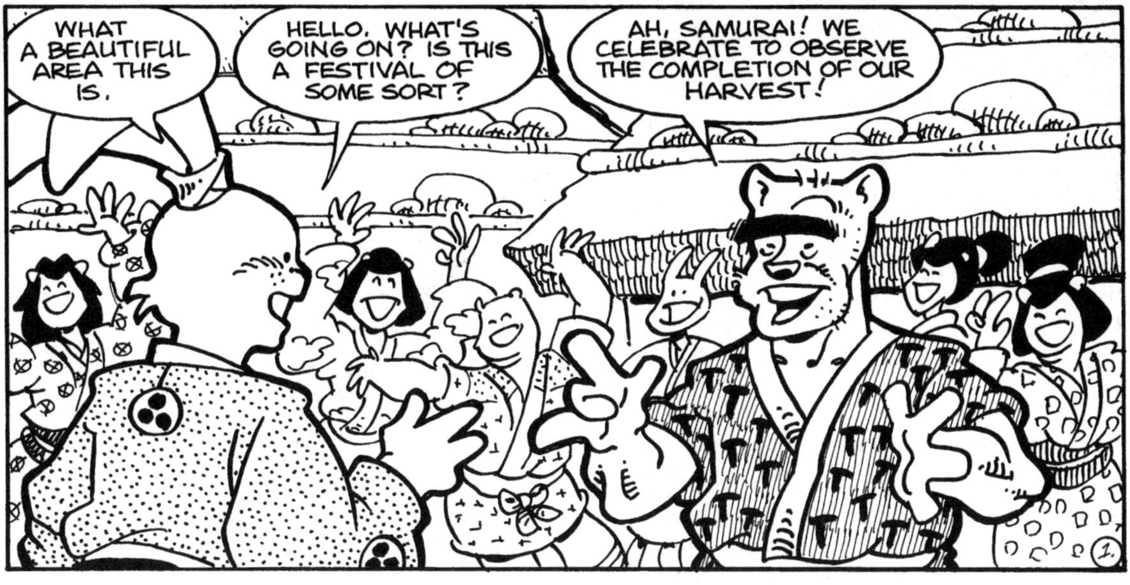
WHAT A BEAUTIFUL AREA THIS IS.
HELLO. WHAT'S GOING ON? IS THIS A FESTIVAL OF SOME SORT?
AH, SAMURAI! WE CELEBRATE TO OBSERVE THE COMPLETION OF OUR HARVEST!
1.

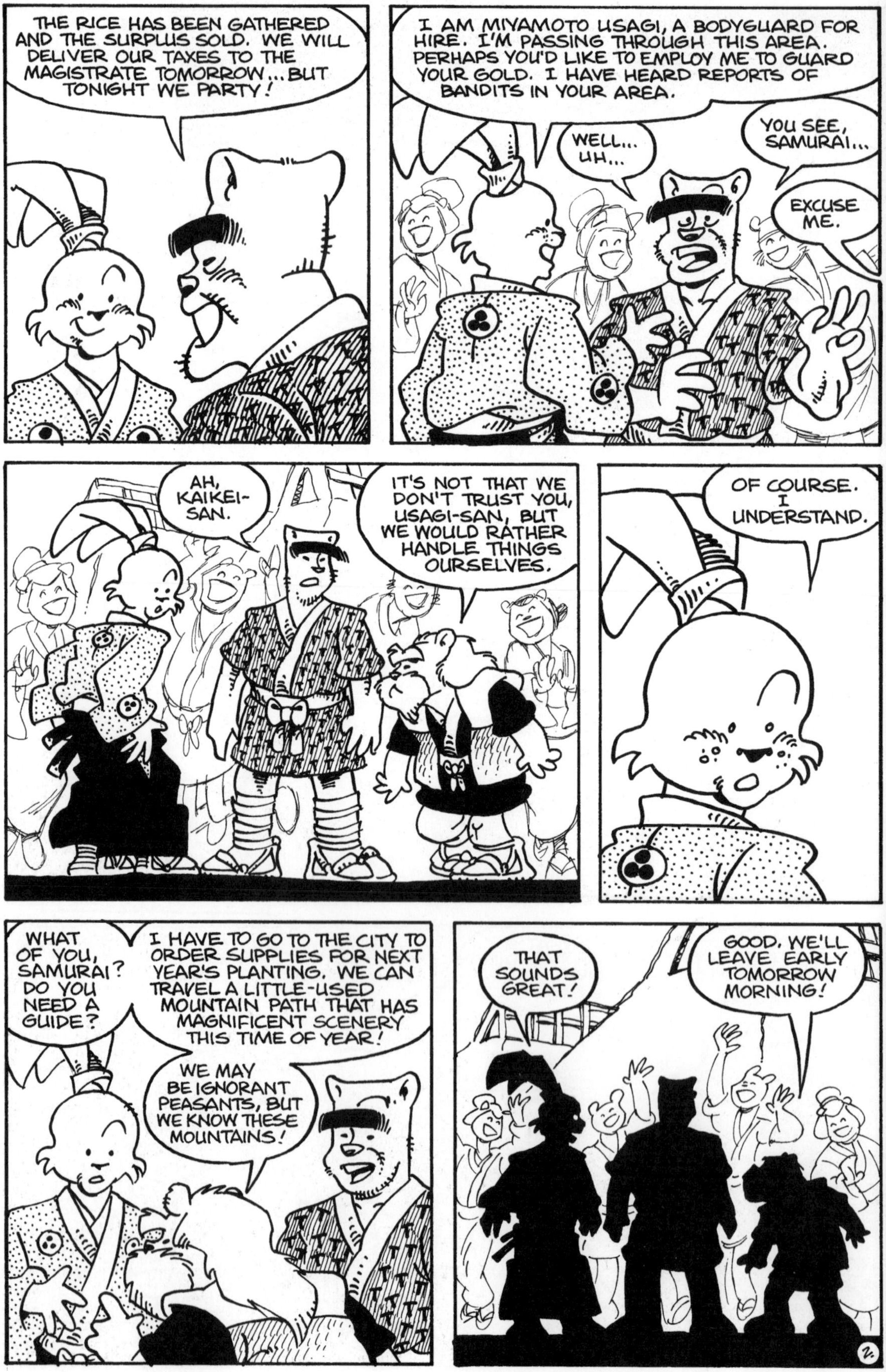

THE RICE HAS BEEN GATHERED AND THE SURPLUS SOLD. WE WILL DELIVER OUR TAXES TO THE MAGISTRATE TOMORROW... BUT TONIGHT WE PARTY!
I AM MIYAMOTO USAGI, A BODYGUARD FOR HIRE. I'M PASSING THROUGH THIS AREA. PERHAPS YOU'D LIKE TO EMPLOY ME TO GUARD YOUR GOLD. I HAVE HEARD REPORTS OF BANDITS IN YOUR AREA.
WELL... UH...
YOU SEE, SAMURAI...
EXCUSE ME.
AH, KAIKEI-SAN.
IT'S NOT THAT WE DON'T TRUST YOU, USAGI-SAN, BUT WE WOULD RATHER HANDLE THINGS OURSELVES.
OF COURSE. I UNDERSTAND.
WHAT OF YOU, SAMURAI? DO YOU NEED A GUIDE?
I HAVE TO GO TO THE CITY TO ORDER SUPPLIES FOR NEXT YEAR'S PLANTING. WE CAN TRAVEL A LITTLE-USED MOUNTAIN PATH THAT HAS MAGNIFICENT SCENERY THIS TIME OF YEAR!
WE MAY BE IGNORANT PEASANTS, BUT WE KNOW THESE MOUNTAINS!
THAT SOUNDS GREAT!
GOOD. WE'LL LEAVE EARLY TOMORROW MORNING!
2

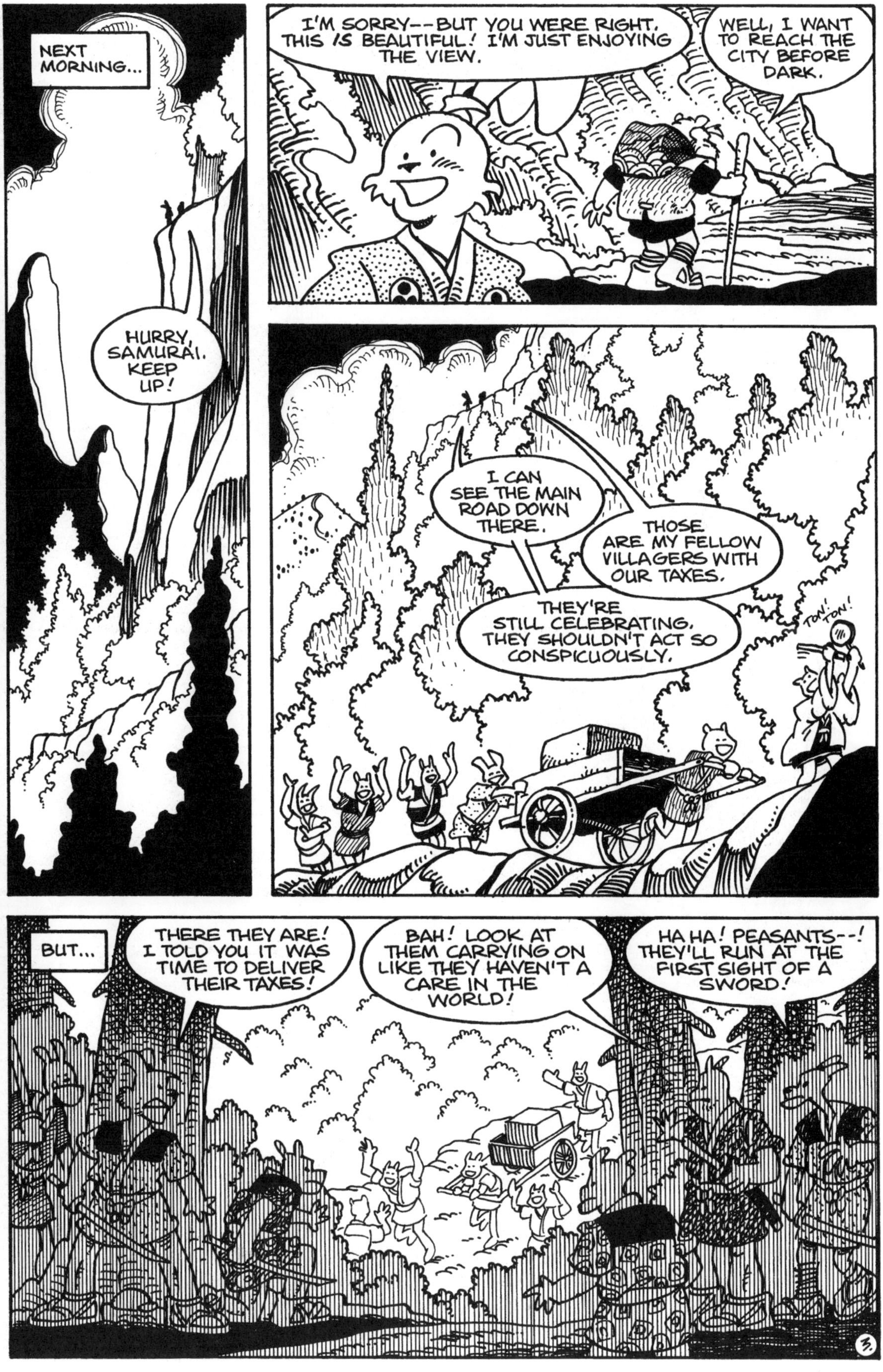
NEXT MORNING...
HURRY, SAMURAI. KEEP UP!
I'M SORRY--BUT YOU WERE RIGHT. THIS IS BEAUTIFUL! I'M JUST ENJOYING THE VIEW.
WELL, I WANT TO REACH THE CITY BEFORE DARK.
I CAN SEE THE MAIN ROAD DOWN THERE.
THOSE ARE MY FELLOW VILLAGERS WITH OUR TAXES.
THEY'RE STILL CELEBRATING. THEY SHOULDN'T ACT SO CONSPICUOUSLY.
TON! TON!
BUT...
THERE THEY ARE! I TOLD YOU IT WAS TIME TO DELIVER THEIR TAXES!
BAH! LOOK AT THEM CARRYING ON LIKE THEY HAVEN'T A CARE IN THE WORLD!
HA HA! PEASANTS--! THEY'LL RUN AT THE FIRST SIGHT OF A SWORD!
3.

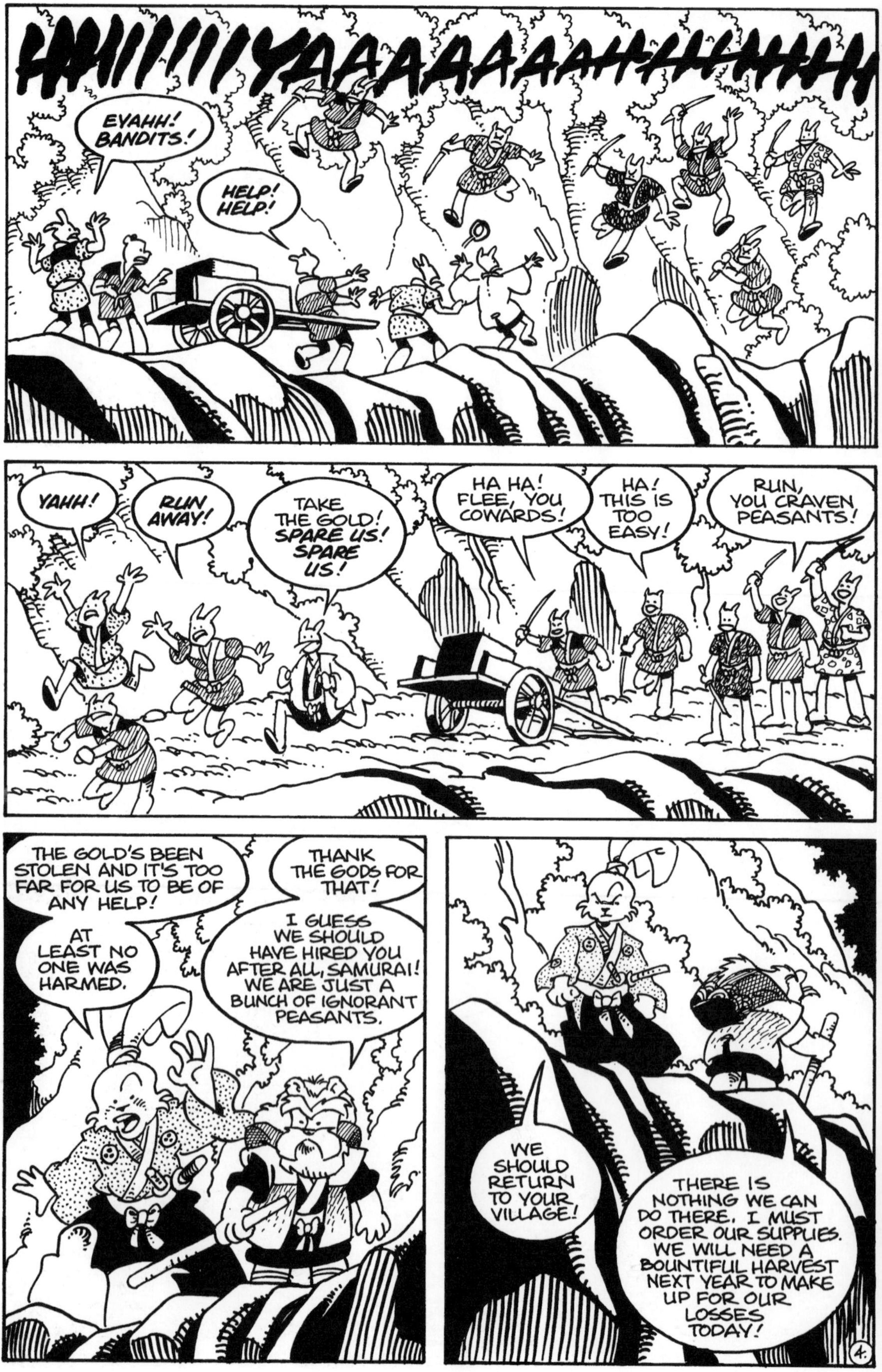
HAAIIIIIYAAAAAAAAHHHHHHH
EYAHH! BANDITS!
HELP! HELP!
YAHH!
RUN AWAY!
TAKE THE GOLD! SPARE US! SPARE US!
HA HA! FLEE, YOU COWARDS!
HA! THIS IS TOO EASY!
RUN, YOU CRAVEN PEASANTS!
THE GOLD'S BEEN STOLEN AND IT'S TOO FAR FOR US TO BE OF ANY HELP!
AT LEAST NO ONE WAS HARMED.
THANK THE GODS FOR THAT!
I GUESS WE SHOULD HAVE HIRED YOU AFTER ALL, SAMURAI! WE ARE JUST A BUNCH OF IGNORANT PEASANTS.
WE SHOULD RETURN TO YOUR VILLAGE!
THERE IS NOTHING WE CAN DO THERE. I MUST ORDER OUR SUPPLIES. WE WILL NEED A BOUNTIFUL HARVEST NEXT YEAR TO MAKE UP FOR OUR LOSSES TODAY!
4.

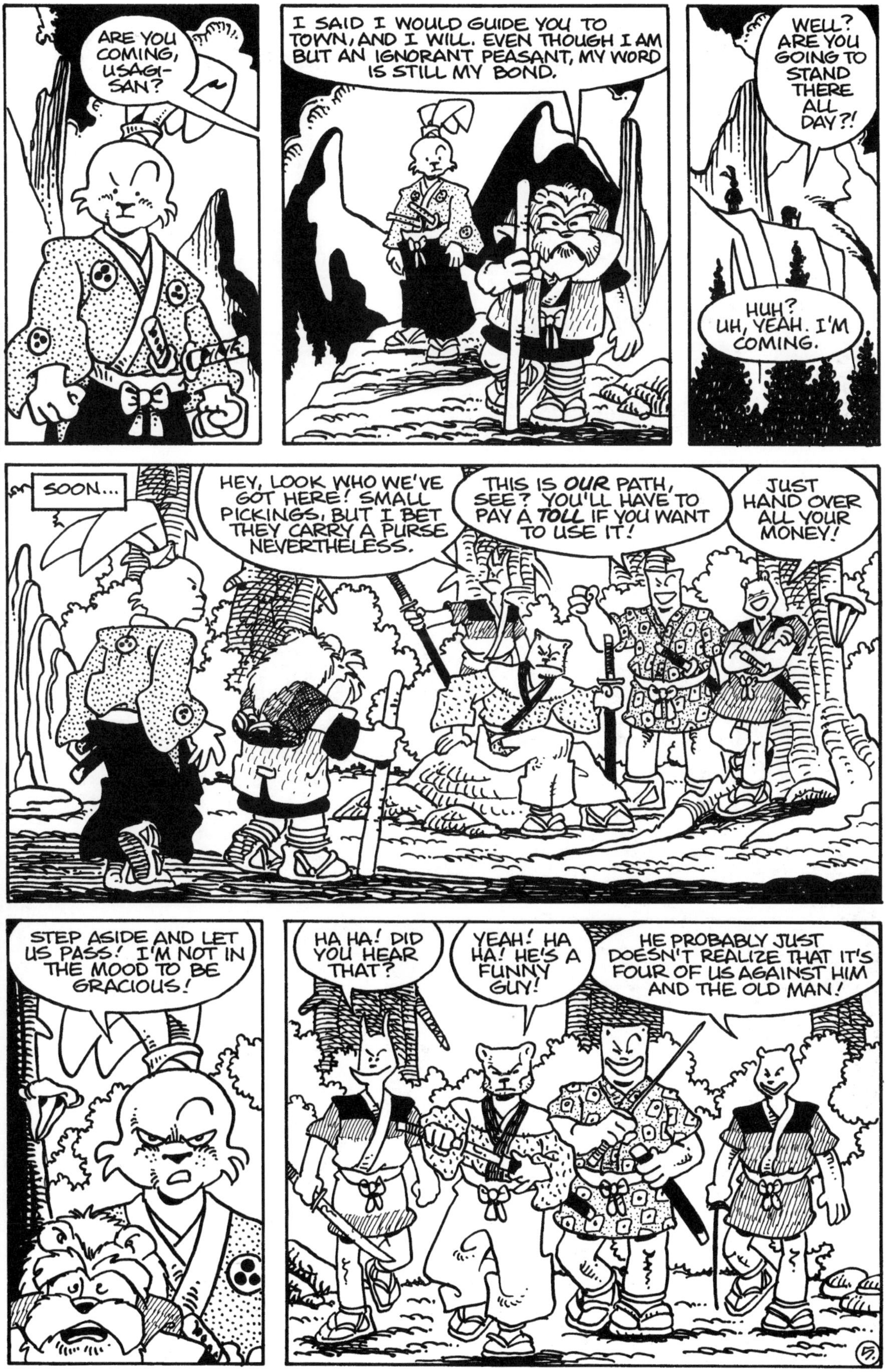
ARE YOU COMING, USAGI-SAN?
I SAID I WOULD GUIDE YOU TO TOWN, AND I WILL. EVEN THOUGH I AM BUT AN IGNORANT PEASANT, MY WORD IS STILL MY BOND.
WELL? ARE YOU GOING TO STAND THERE ALL DAY?!
HUH? UH, YEAH. I'M COMING.
SOON...
HEY, LOOK WHO WE'VE GOT HERE! SMALL PICKINGS, BUT I BET THEY CARRY A PURSE NEVERTHELESS.
THIS IS OUR PATH, SEE? YOU'LL HAVE TO PAY A TOLL IF YOU WANT TO USE IT!
JUST HAND OVER ALL YOUR MONEY!
STEP ASIDE AND LET US PASS! I'M NOT IN THE MOOD TO BE GRACIOUS!
HA HA! DID YOU HEAR THAT?
YEAH! HA HA! HE'S A FUNNY GUY!
HE PROBABLY JUST DOESN'T REALIZE THAT IT'S FOUR OF US AGAINST HIM AND THE OLD MAN!
5

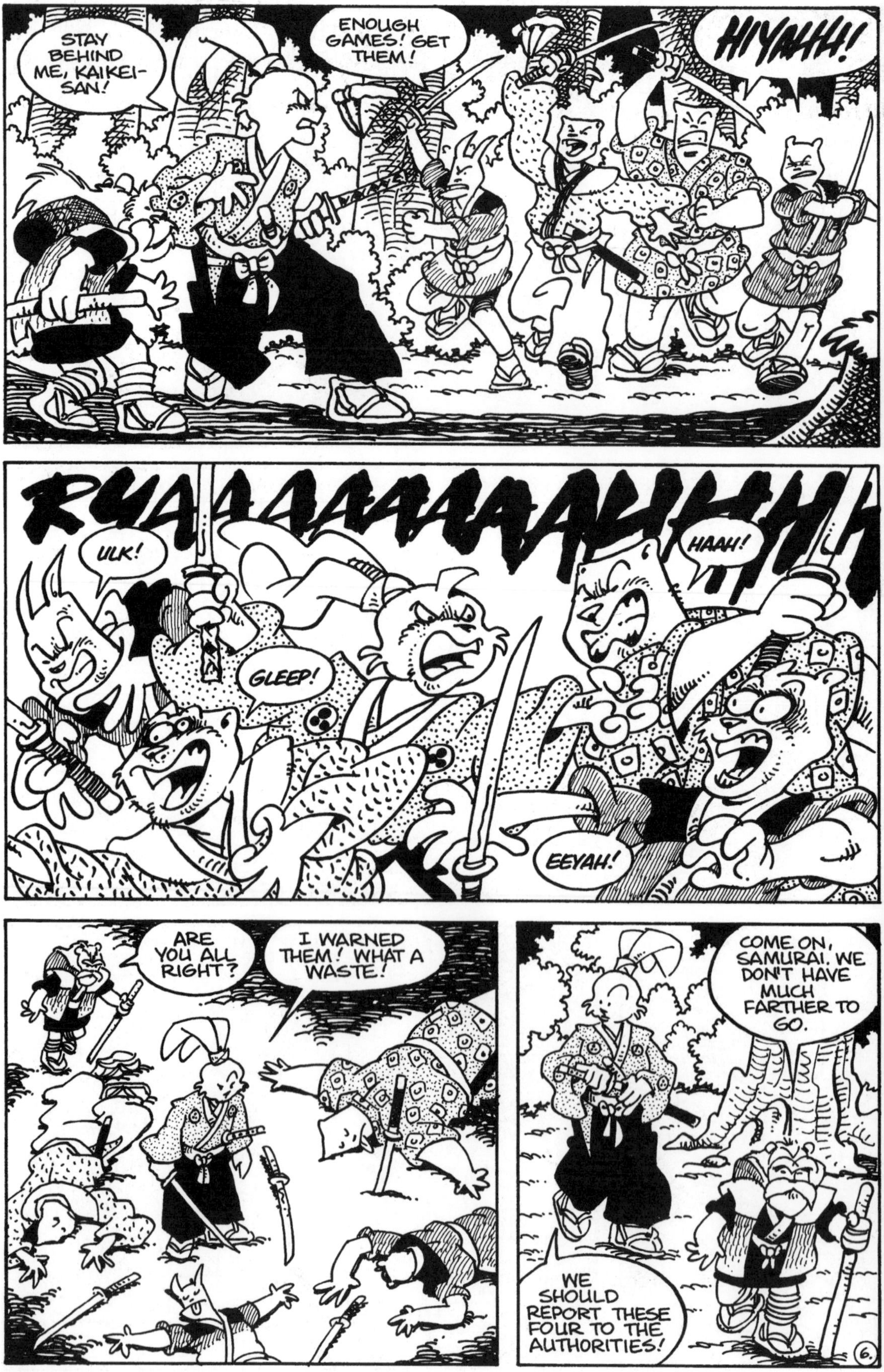
STAY BEHIND ME, KAIKEI-SAN!
ENOUGH GAMES! GET THEM!
HIYAHH!
RYAAAAAAAAAAHHHH
ULK!
HAAH!
GLEEP!
EEYAH!
ARE YOU ALL RIGHT?
I WARNED THEM! WHAT A WASTE!
COME ON, SAMURAI. WE DON'T HAVE MUCH FARTHER TO GO.
WE SHOULD REPORT THESE FOUR TO THE AUTHORITIES!
6.

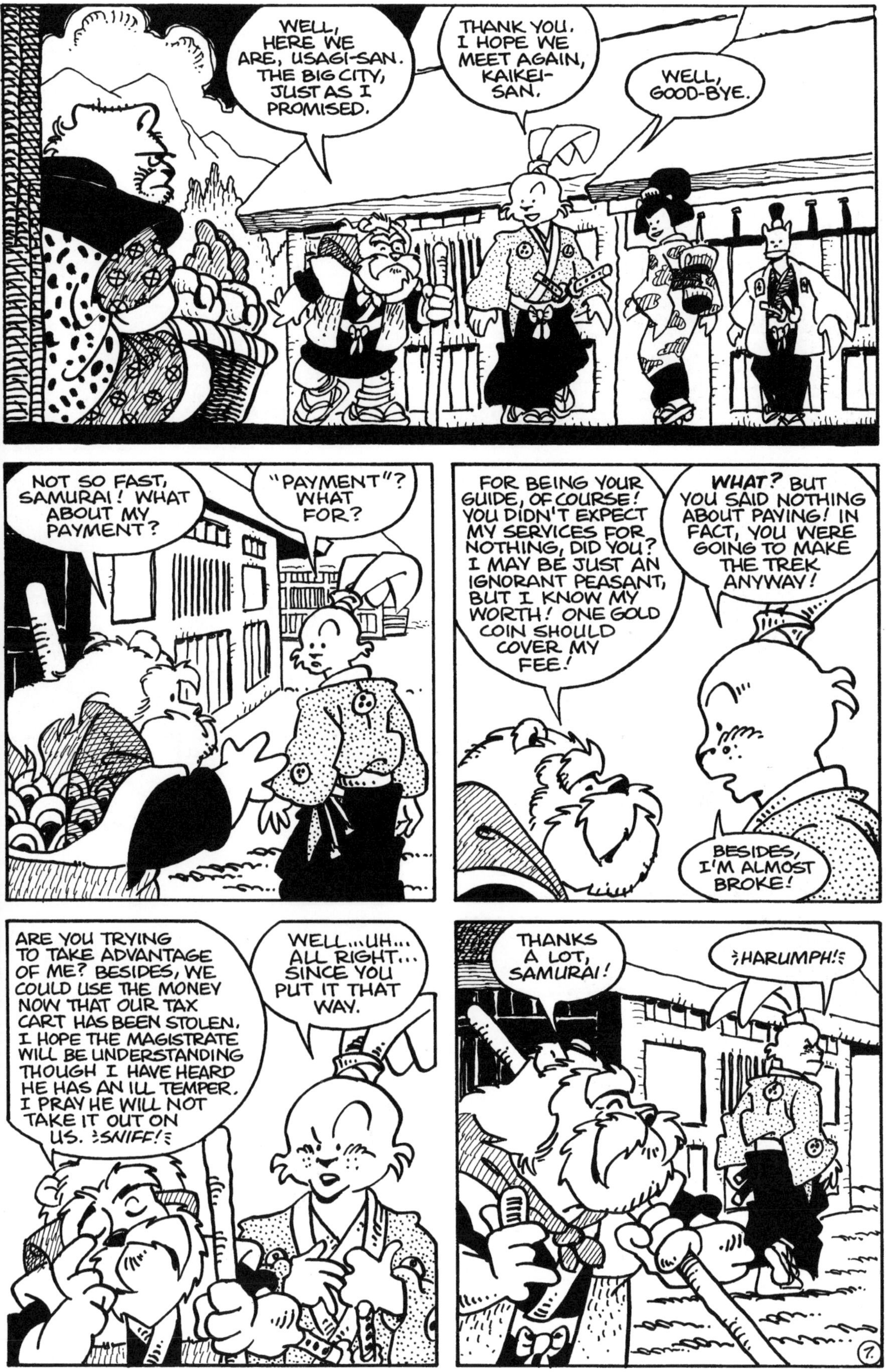
WELL, HERE WE ARE, USAGI-SAN. THE BIG CITY, JUST AS I PROMISED.
THANK YOU. I HOPE WE MEET AGAIN, KAIKEI-SAN.
WELL, GOOD-BYE.
NOT SO FAST, SAMURAI! WHAT ABOUT MY PAYMENT?
"PAYMENT"? WHAT FOR?
FOR BEING YOUR GUIDE, OF COURSE! YOU DIDN'T EXPECT MY SERVICES FOR NOTHING, DID YOU? I MAY BE JUST AN IGNORANT PEASANT, BUT I KNOW MY WORTH! ONE GOLD COIN SHOULD COVER MY FEE!
WHAT? BUT YOU SAID NOTHING ABOUT PAYING! IN FACT, YOU WERE GOING TO MAKE THE TREK ANYWAY!
BESIDES, I'M ALMOST BROKE!
ARE YOU TRYING TO TAKE ADVANTAGE OF ME? BESIDES, WE COULD USE THE MONEY NOW THAT OUR TAX CART HAS BEEN STOLEN. I HOPE THE MAGISTRATE WILL BE UNDERSTANDING THOUGH I HAVE HEARD HE HAS AN ILL TEMPER. I PRAY HE WILL NOT TAKE IT OUT ON US. SNIFF!
WELL...UH... ALL RIGHT... SINCE YOU PUT IT THAT WAY.
THANKS A LOT, SAMURAI!
HARUMPH!
7.

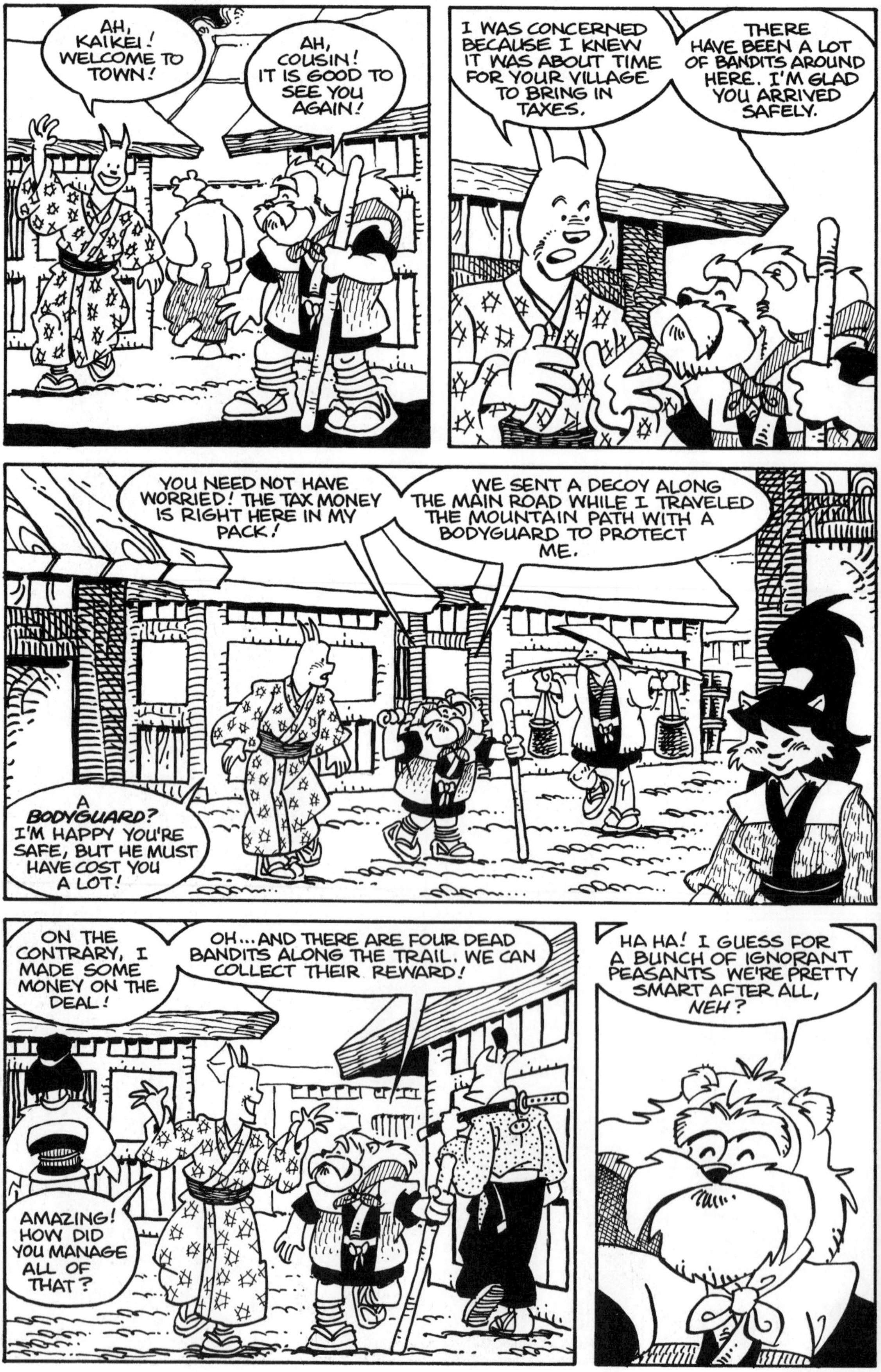
AH, KAIKEI! WELCOME TO TOWN!
AH, COUSIN! IT IS GOOD TO SEE YOU AGAIN!
I WAS CONCERNED BECAUSE I KNEW IT WAS ABOUT TIME FOR YOUR VILLAGE TO BRING IN TAXES.
THERE HAVE BEEN A LOT OF BANDITS AROUND HERE. I'M GLAD YOU ARRIVED SAFELY.
YOU NEED NOT HAVE WORRIED! THE TAX MONEY IS RIGHT HERE IN MY PACK!
WE SENT A DECOY ALONG THE MAIN ROAD WHILE I TRAVELED THE MOUNTAIN PATH WITH A BODYGUARD TO PROTECT ME.
A *BODYGUARD?* I'M HAPPY YOU'RE SAFE, BUT HE MUST HAVE COST YOU A LOT!
ON THE CONTRARY, I MADE SOME MONEY ON THE DEAL!
OH... AND THERE ARE FOUR DEAD BANDITS ALONG THE TRAIL. WE CAN COLLECT THEIR REWARD!
AMAZING! HOW DID YOU MANAGE ALL OF THAT?
HA HA! I GUESS FOR A BUNCH OF IGNORANT PEASANTS WE'RE PRETTY SMART AFTER ALL, *NEH?*

THE END

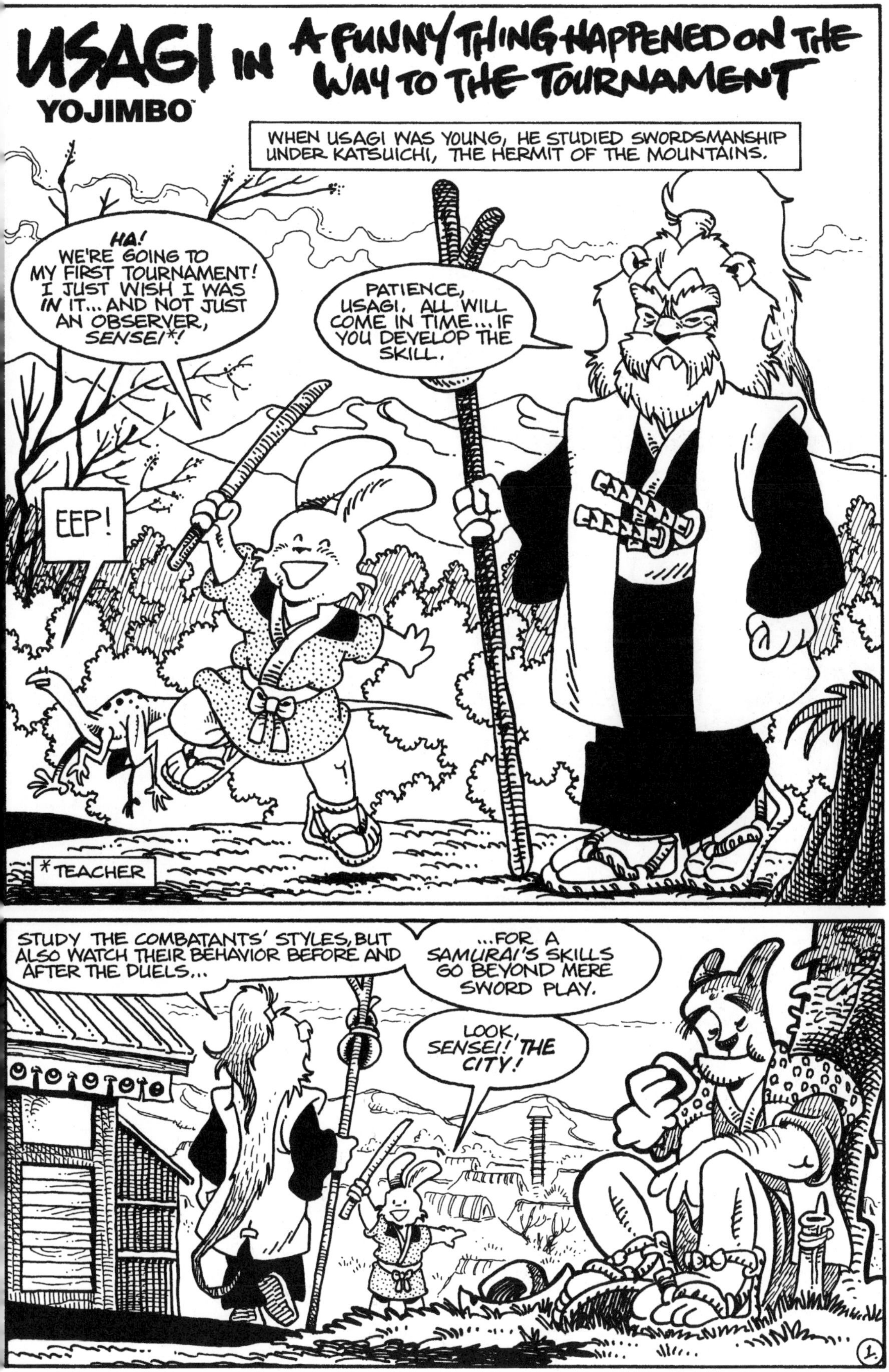
USAGI YOJIMBO IN A FUNNY THING HAPPENED ON THE WAY TO THE TOURNAMENT
WHEN USAGI WAS YOUNG, HE STUDIED SWORDSMANSHIP UNDER KATSUICHI, THE HERMIT OF THE MOUNTAINS.
HA! WE'RE GOING TO MY FIRST TOURNAMENT! I JUST WISH I WAS IN IT... AND NOT JUST AN OBSERVER, SENSEI*!
EEP!
PATIENCE, USAGI. ALL WILL COME IN TIME... IF YOU DEVELOP THE SKILL.
*TEACHER
STUDY THE COMBATANTS' STYLES, BUT ALSO WATCH THEIR BEHAVIOR BEFORE AND AFTER THE DUELS...
...FOR A SAMURAI'S SKILLS GO BEYOND MERE SWORD PLAY.
LOOK, SENSEI! THE CITY!
1.

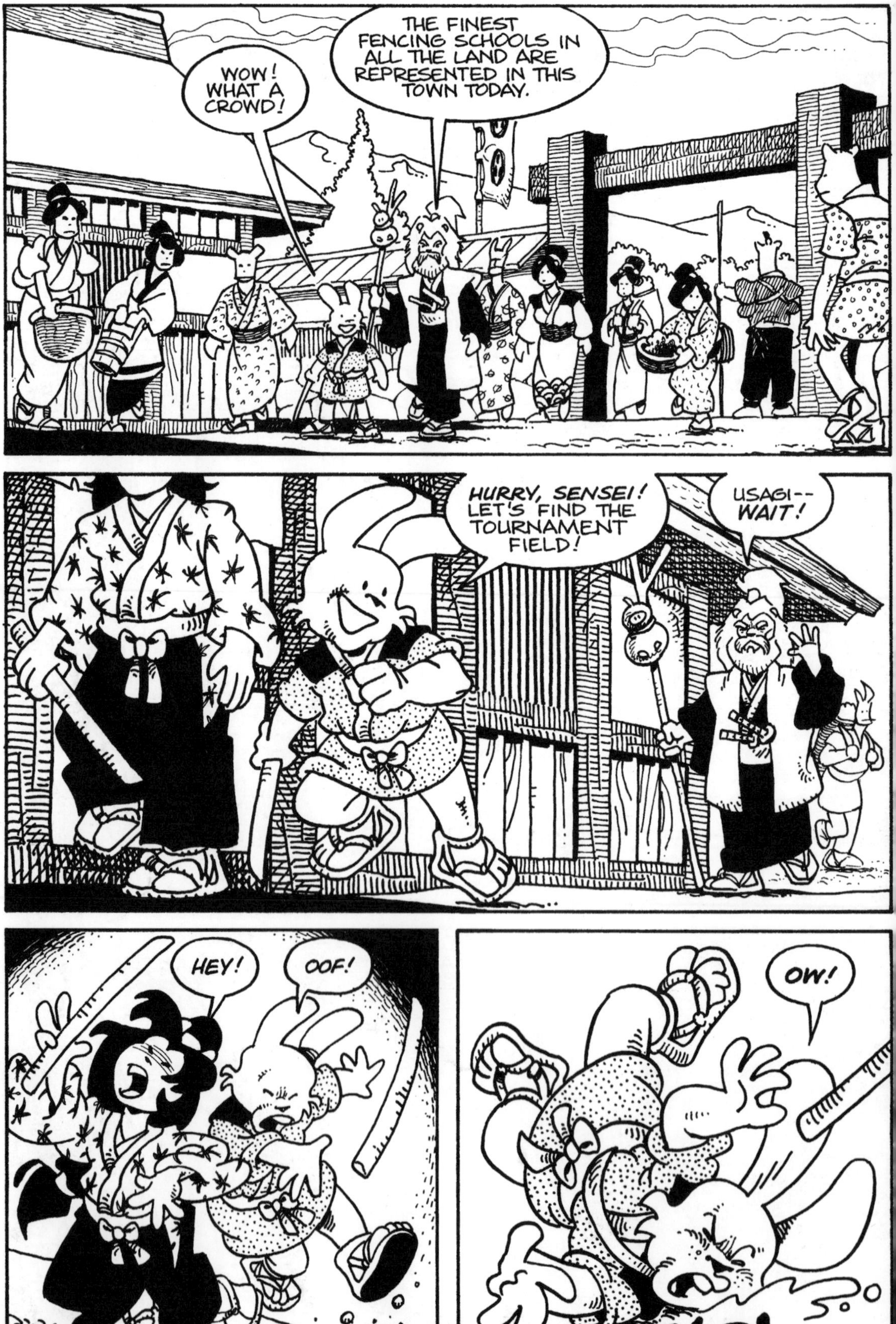
WOW! WHAT A CROWD!
THE FINEST FENCING SCHOOLS IN ALL THE LAND ARE REPRESENTED IN THIS TOWN TODAY.
HURRY, SENSEI! LET'S FIND THE TOURNAMENT FIELD!
USAGI-- WAIT!
HEY!
OOF!
OW!
THUD!

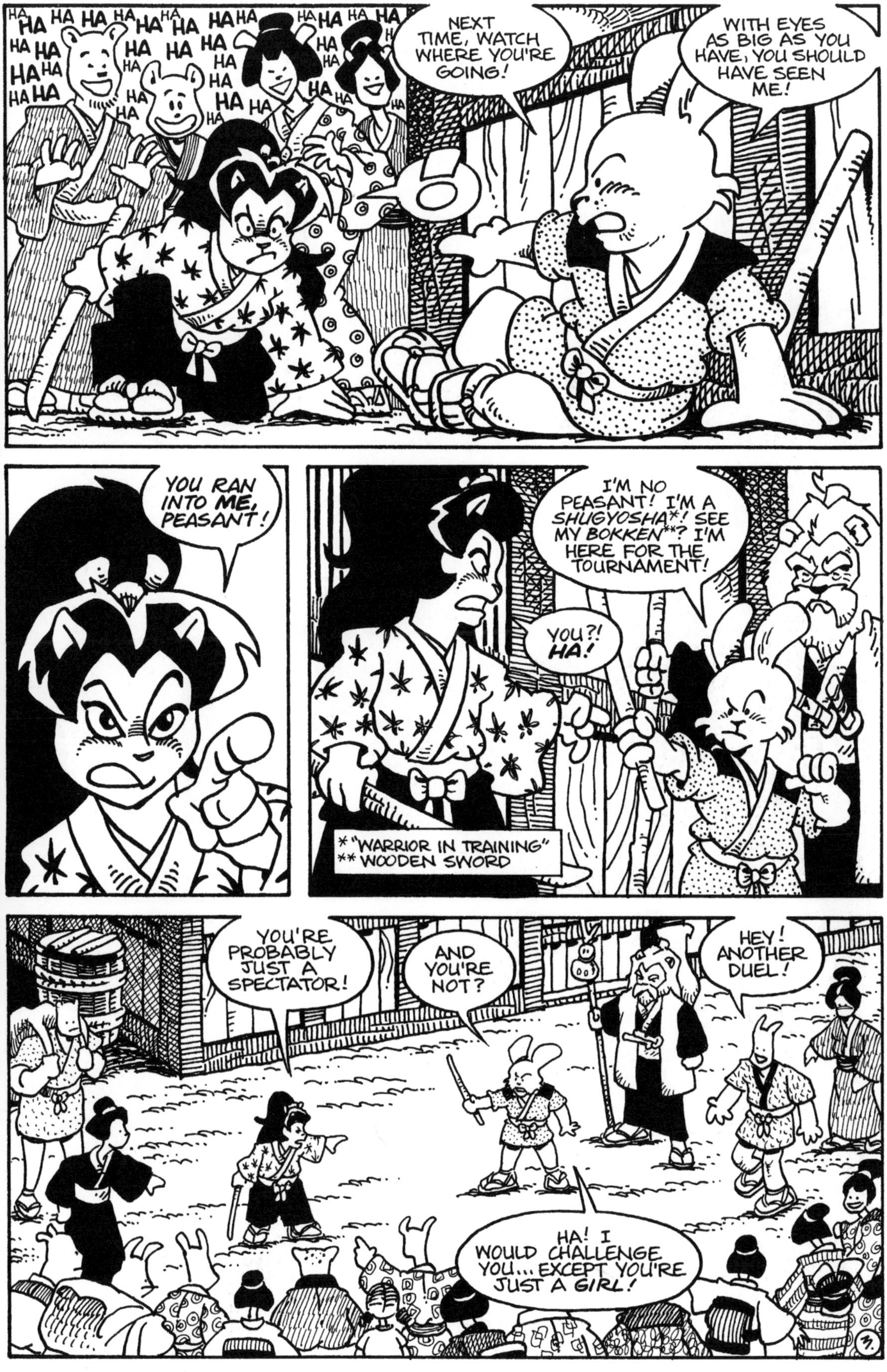
HA HA HA HA HA HA HA HA HA HA HA HA HA HA HA HA HA HA HA HA HA HA HA HA HA HA HA HA HA HA HA HA HA
NEXT TIME, WATCH WHERE YOU'RE GOING!
WITH EYES AS BIG AS YOU HAVE, YOU SHOULD HAVE SEEN ME!
YOU RAN INTO **ME**, PEASANT!
I'M NO PEASANT! I'M A *SHUGYOSHA**! SEE MY *BOKKEN***? I'M HERE FOR THE TOURNAMENT!
YOU?! **HA!**
* "WARRIOR IN TRAINING"
** WOODEN SWORD
YOU'RE PROBABLY JUST A SPECTATOR!
AND YOU'RE NOT?
HEY! ANOTHER DUEL!
HA! I WOULD CHALLENGE YOU... EXCEPT YOU'RE JUST A *GIRL*!

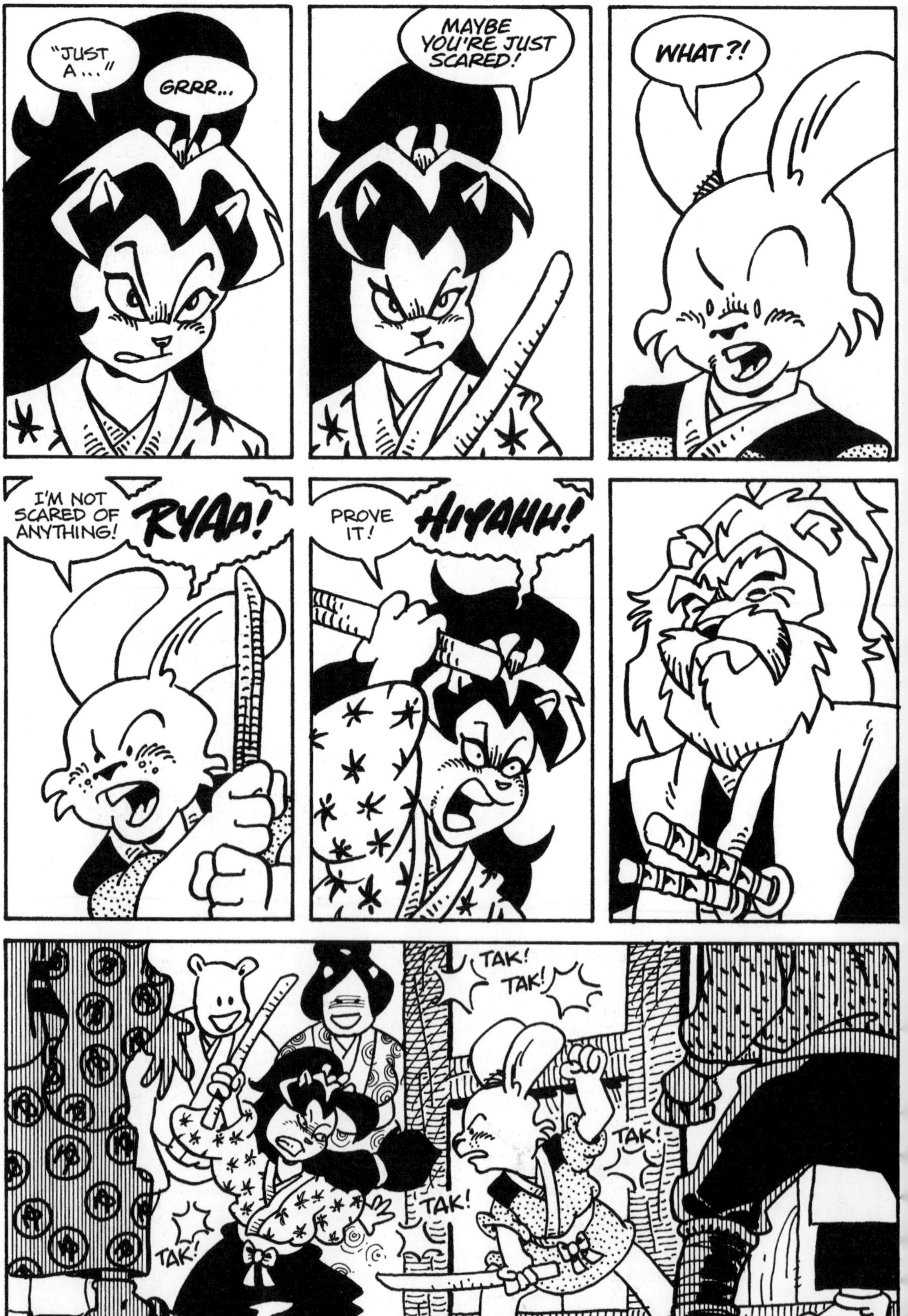
"JUST A..."
GRRR...
MAYBE YOU'RE JUST SCARED!
WHAT?!
I'M NOT SCARED OF ANYTHING!
RYAA!
PROVE IT!
HIYAHH!
TAK!
TAK!
TAK!
TAK!
TAK!
4.

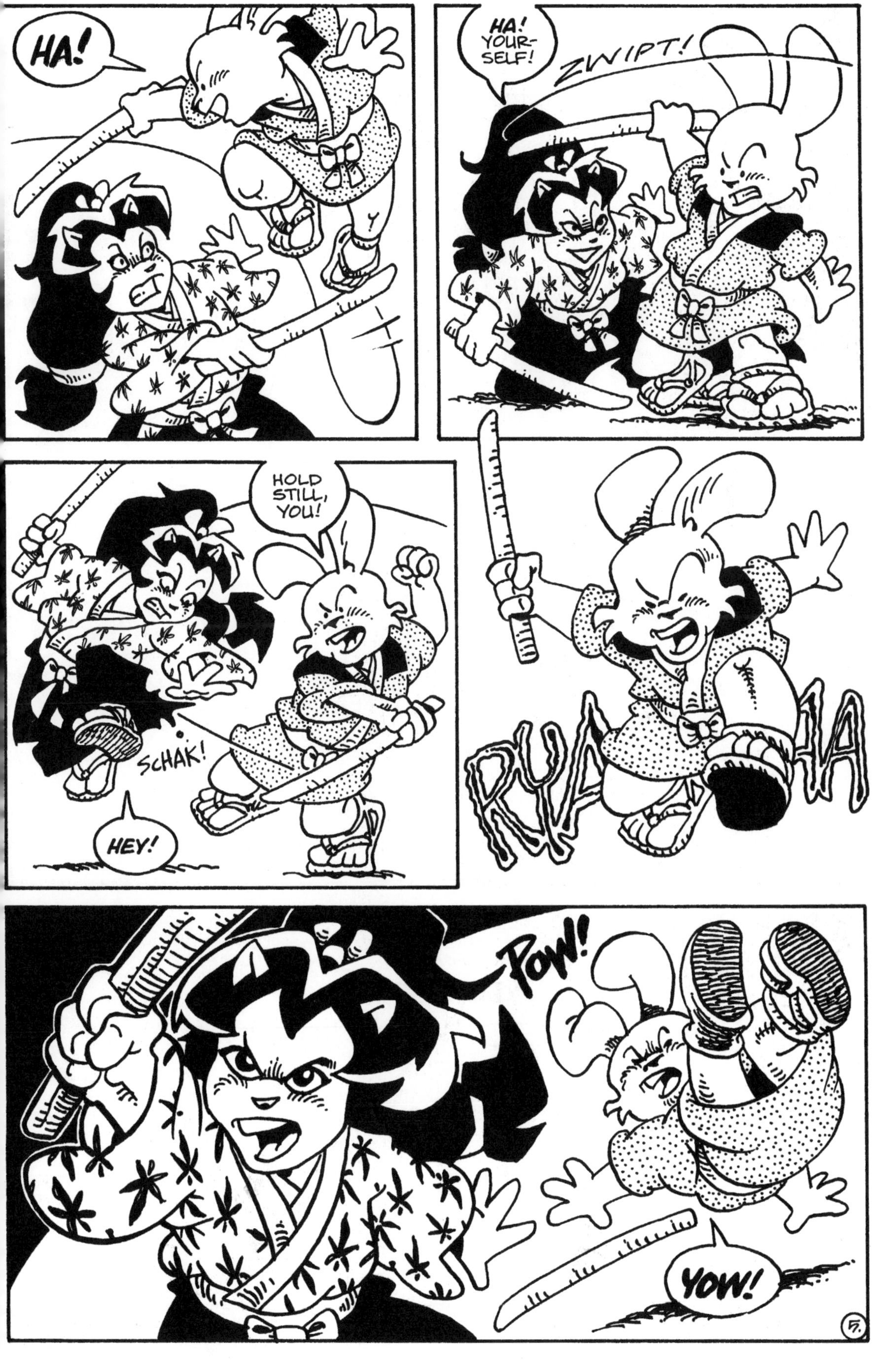
HA!
HA! YOUR-SELF!
ZWIPT!
HOLD STILL, YOU!
SCHAK!
HEY!
RYAAA
POW!
YOW!

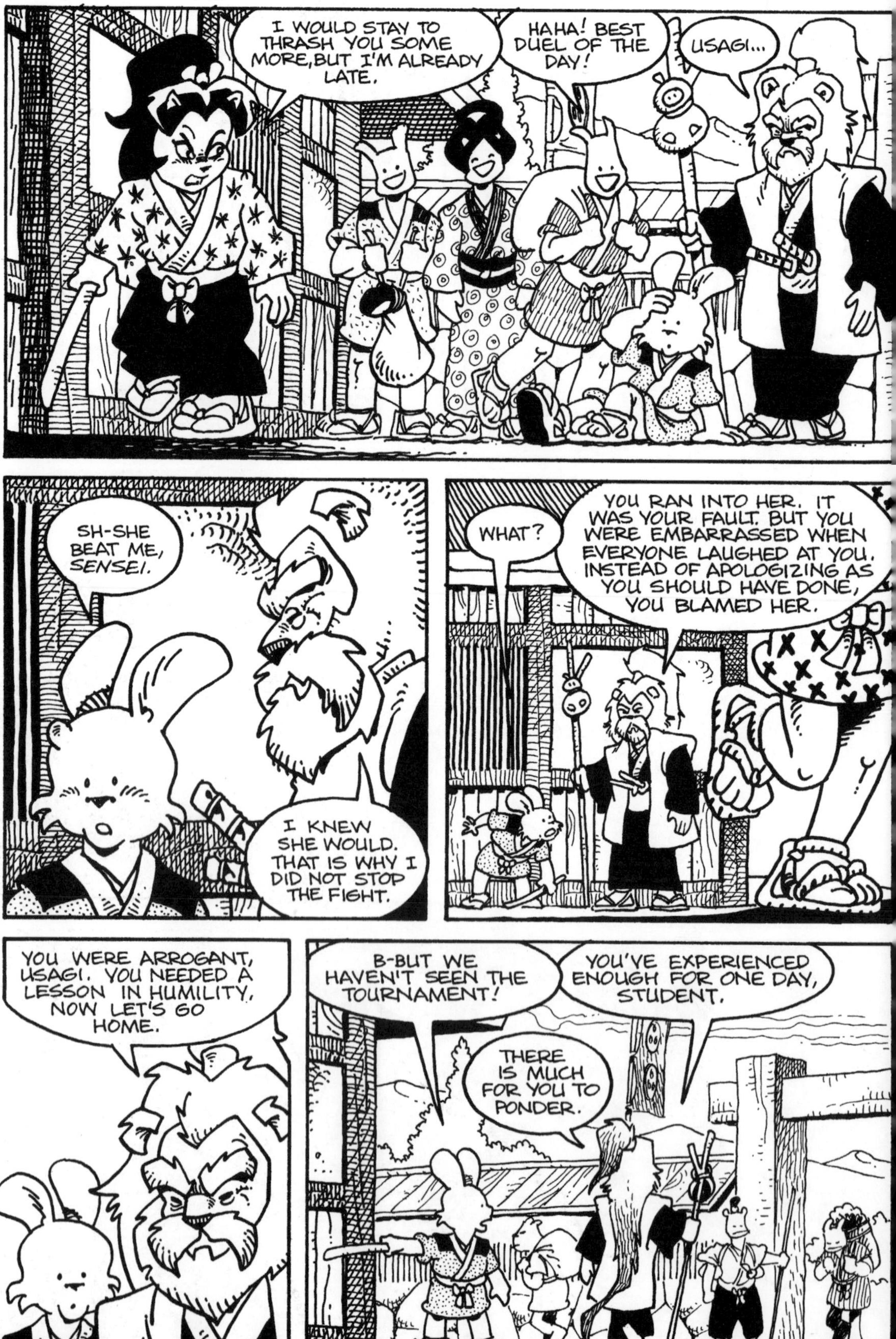
I WOULD STAY TO THRASH YOU SOME MORE, BUT I'M ALREADY LATE.
HAHA! BEST DUEL OF THE DAY!
USAGI...
SH-SHE BEAT ME, SENSEI.
I KNEW SHE WOULD. THAT IS WHY I DID NOT STOP THE FIGHT.
WHAT?
YOU RAN INTO HER. IT WAS YOUR FAULT. BUT YOU WERE EMBARRASSED WHEN EVERYONE LAUGHED AT YOU. INSTEAD OF APOLOGIZING AS YOU SHOULD HAVE DONE, YOU BLAMED HER.
YOU WERE ARROGANT, USAGI. YOU NEEDED A LESSON IN HUMILITY. NOW LET'S GO HOME.
B-BUT WE HAVEN'T SEEN THE TOURNAMENT!
YOU'VE EXPERIENCED ENOUGH FOR ONE DAY, STUDENT.
THERE IS MUCH FOR YOU TO PONDER.
6.

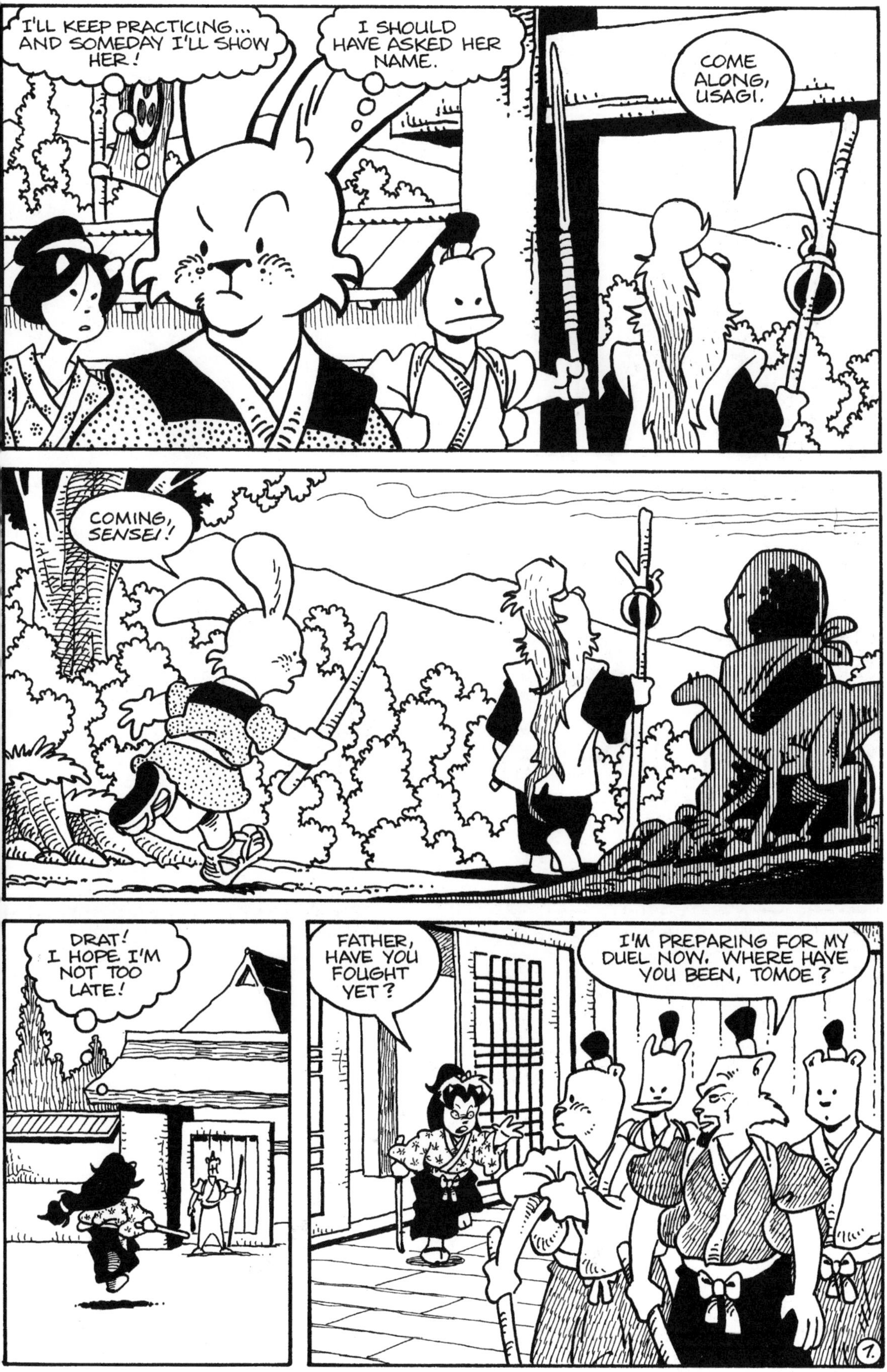
I'LL KEEP PRACTICING... AND SOMEDAY I'LL SHOW HER!
I SHOULD HAVE ASKED HER NAME.
COME ALONG, USAGI.
COMING, SENSEI!
DRAT! I HOPE I'M NOT TOO LATE!
FATHER, HAVE YOU FOUGHT YET?
I'M PREPARING FOR MY DUEL NOW. WHERE HAVE YOU BEEN, TOMOE?
7.

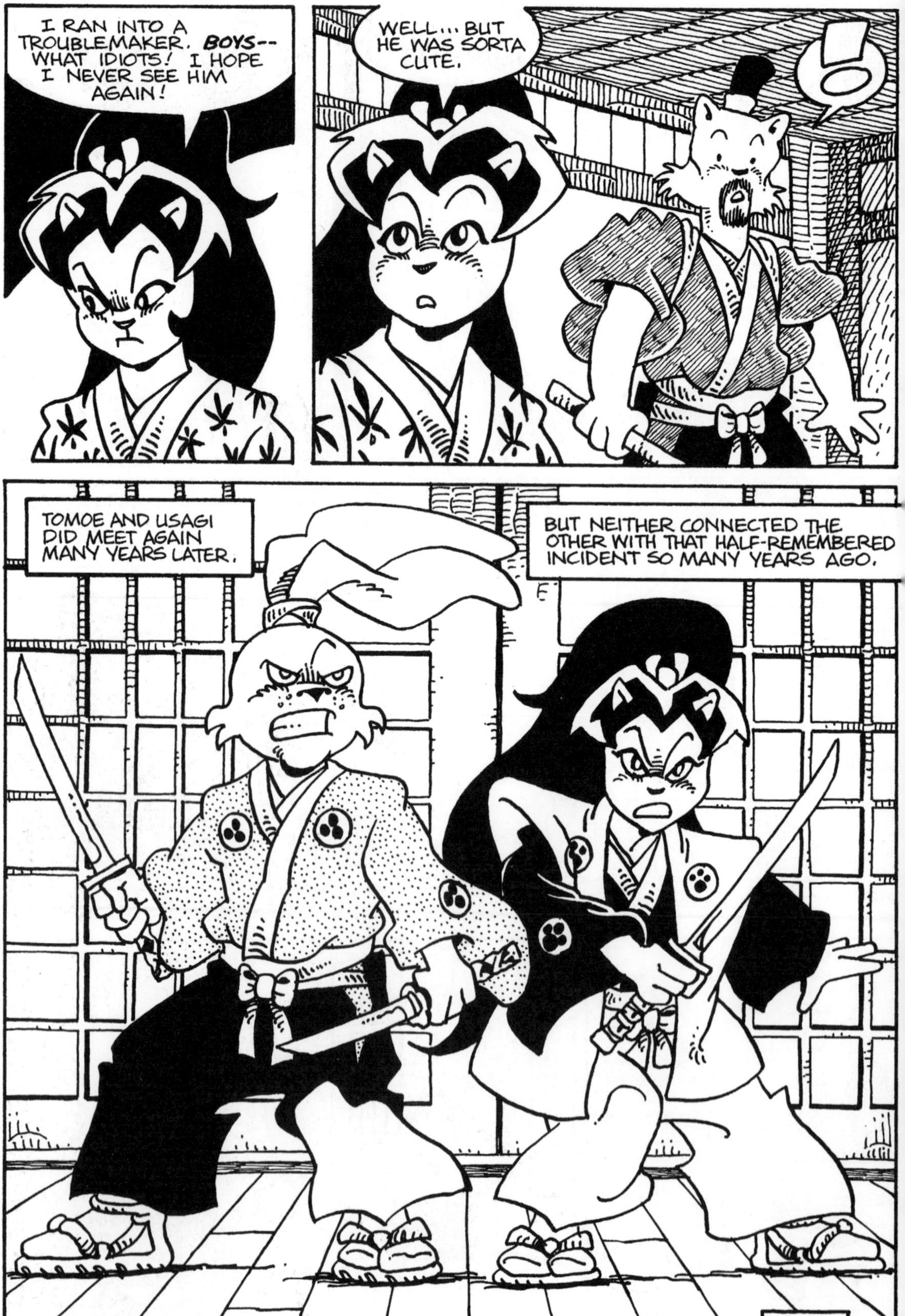
I RAN INTO A TROUBLEMAKER. **BOYS**-- WHAT IDIOTS! I HOPE I NEVER SEE HIM AGAIN!
WELL... BUT HE WAS SORTA CUTE.
!
TOMOE AND USAGI DID MEET AGAIN MANY YEARS LATER.
BUT NEITHER CONNECTED THE OTHER WITH THAT HALF-REMEMBERED INCIDENT SO MANY YEARS AGO.
END

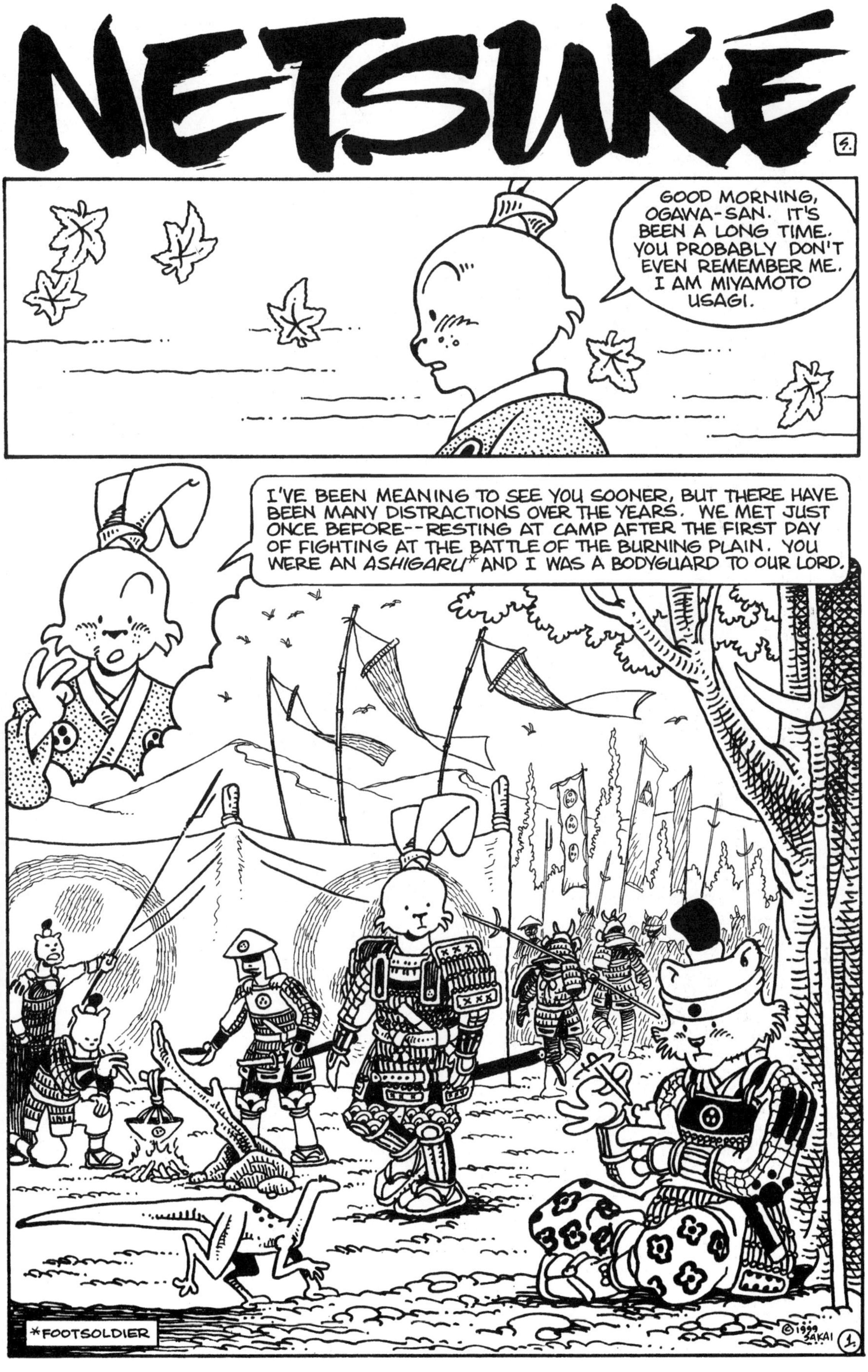
NETSUKÉ
GOOD MORNING, OGAWA-SAN. IT'S BEEN A LONG TIME. YOU PROBABLY DON'T EVEN REMEMBER ME. I AM MIYAMOTO USAGI.
I'VE BEEN MEANING TO SEE YOU SOONER, BUT THERE HAVE BEEN MANY DISTRACTIONS OVER THE YEARS. WE MET JUST ONCE BEFORE--RESTING AT CAMP AFTER THE FIRST DAY OF FIGHTING AT THE BATTLE OF THE BURNING PLAIN. YOU WERE AN *ASHIGARU** AND I WAS A BODYGUARD TO OUR LORD.
*FOOTSOLDIER
©1999 SAKAI
1.

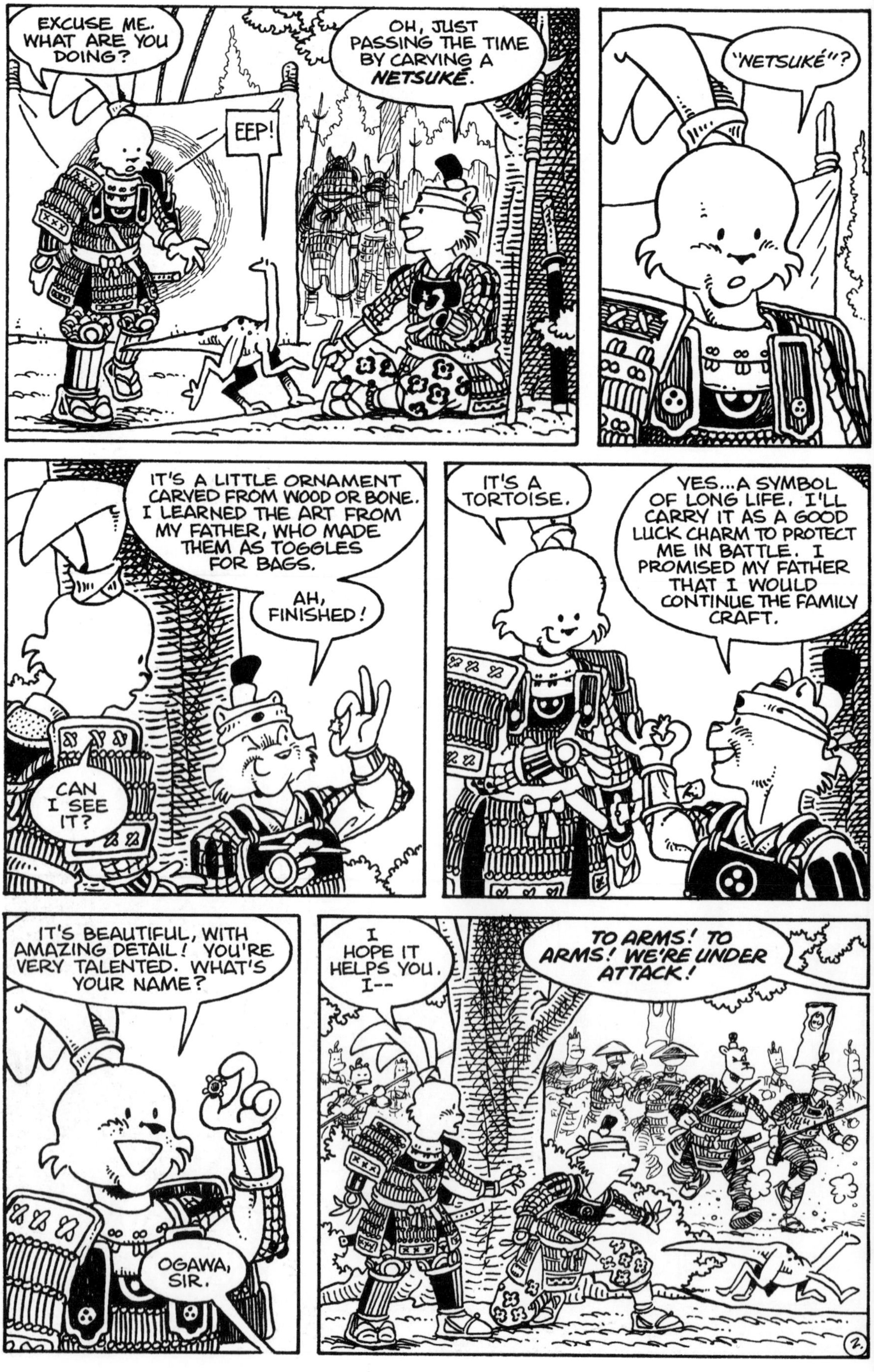
EXCUSE ME. WHAT ARE YOU DOING?
EEP!
OH, JUST PASSING THE TIME BY CARVING A NETSUKÉ.
"NETSUKÉ"?
IT'S A LITTLE ORNAMENT CARVED FROM WOOD OR BONE. I LEARNED THE ART FROM MY FATHER, WHO MADE THEM AS TOGGLES FOR BAGS.
AH, FINISHED!
CAN I SEE IT?
IT'S A TORTOISE.
YES...A SYMBOL OF LONG LIFE. I'LL CARRY IT AS A GOOD LUCK CHARM TO PROTECT ME IN BATTLE. I PROMISED MY FATHER THAT I WOULD CONTINUE THE FAMILY CRAFT.
IT'S BEAUTIFUL, WITH AMAZING DETAIL! YOU'RE VERY TALENTED. WHAT'S YOUR NAME?
OGAWA, SIR.
I HOPE IT HELPS YOU. I--
TO ARMS! TO ARMS! WE'RE UNDER ATTACK!
2.

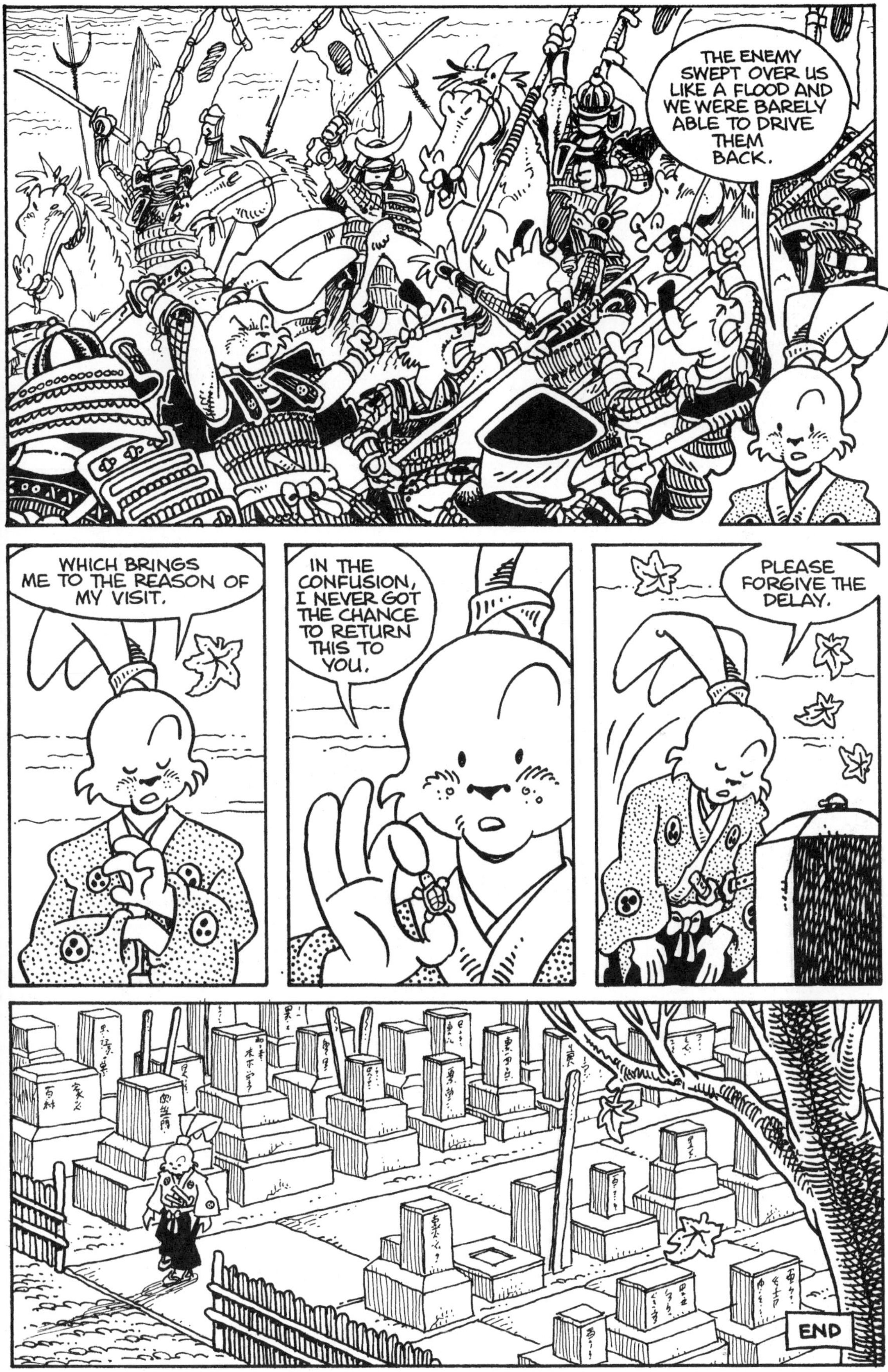
THE ENEMY SWEPT OVER US LIKE A FLOOD AND WE WERE BARELY ABLE TO DRIVE THEM BACK.
WHICH BRINGS ME TO THE REASON OF MY VISIT.
IN THE CONFUSION, I NEVER GOT THE CHANCE TO RETURN THIS TO YOU.
PLEASE FORGIVE THE DELAY.
END

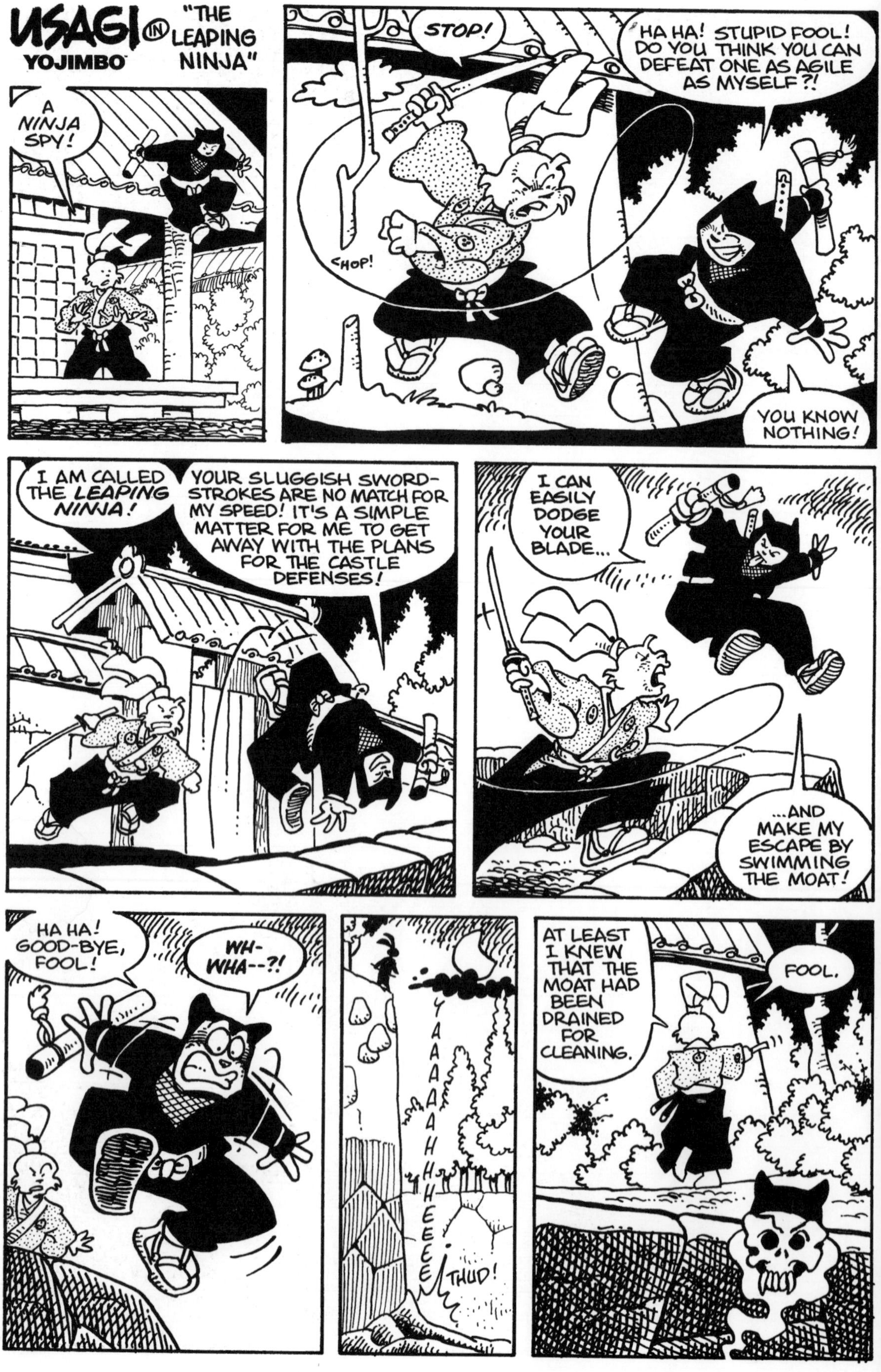
USAGI YOJIMBO
IN
"THE LEAPING NINJA"
A NINJA SPY!
STOP!
CHOP!
HA HA! STUPID FOOL! DO YOU THINK YOU CAN DEFEAT ONE AS AGILE AS MYSELF?!
YOU KNOW NOTHING!
I AM CALLED THE LEAPING NINJA!
YOUR SLUGGISH SWORD-STROKES ARE NO MATCH FOR MY SPEED! IT'S A SIMPLE MATTER FOR ME TO GET AWAY WITH THE PLANS FOR THE CASTLE DEFENSES!
I CAN EASILY DODGE YOUR BLADE...
...AND MAKE MY ESCAPE BY SWIMMING THE MOAT!
HA HA! GOOD-BYE, FOOL!
WH-WHA--?!
YAAAAAAHHHEEEE
THUD!
AT LEAST I KNEW THAT THE MOAT HAD BEEN DRAINED FOR CLEANING.
FOOL.

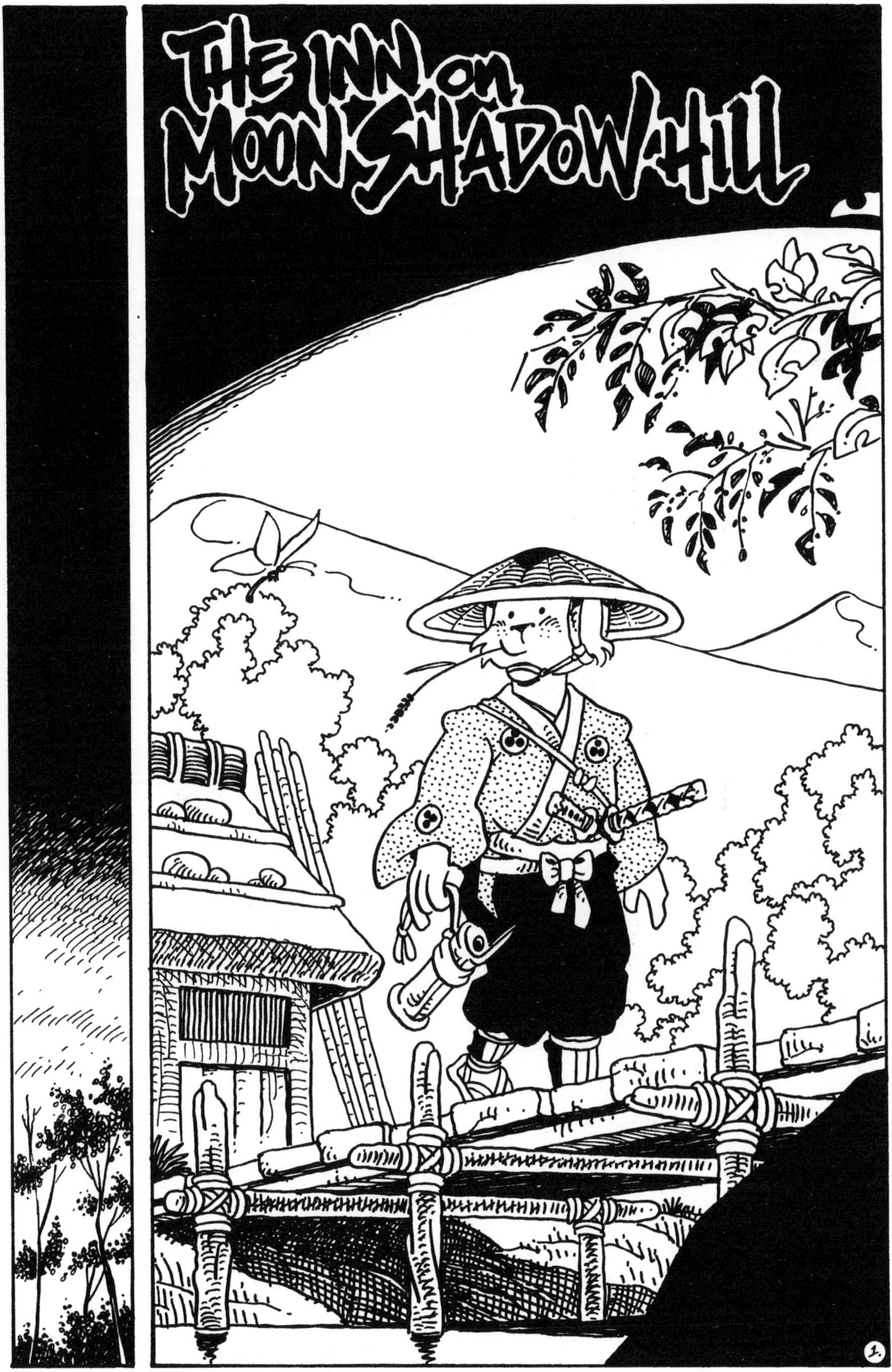
THE INN on MOON SHADOW HILL
1.

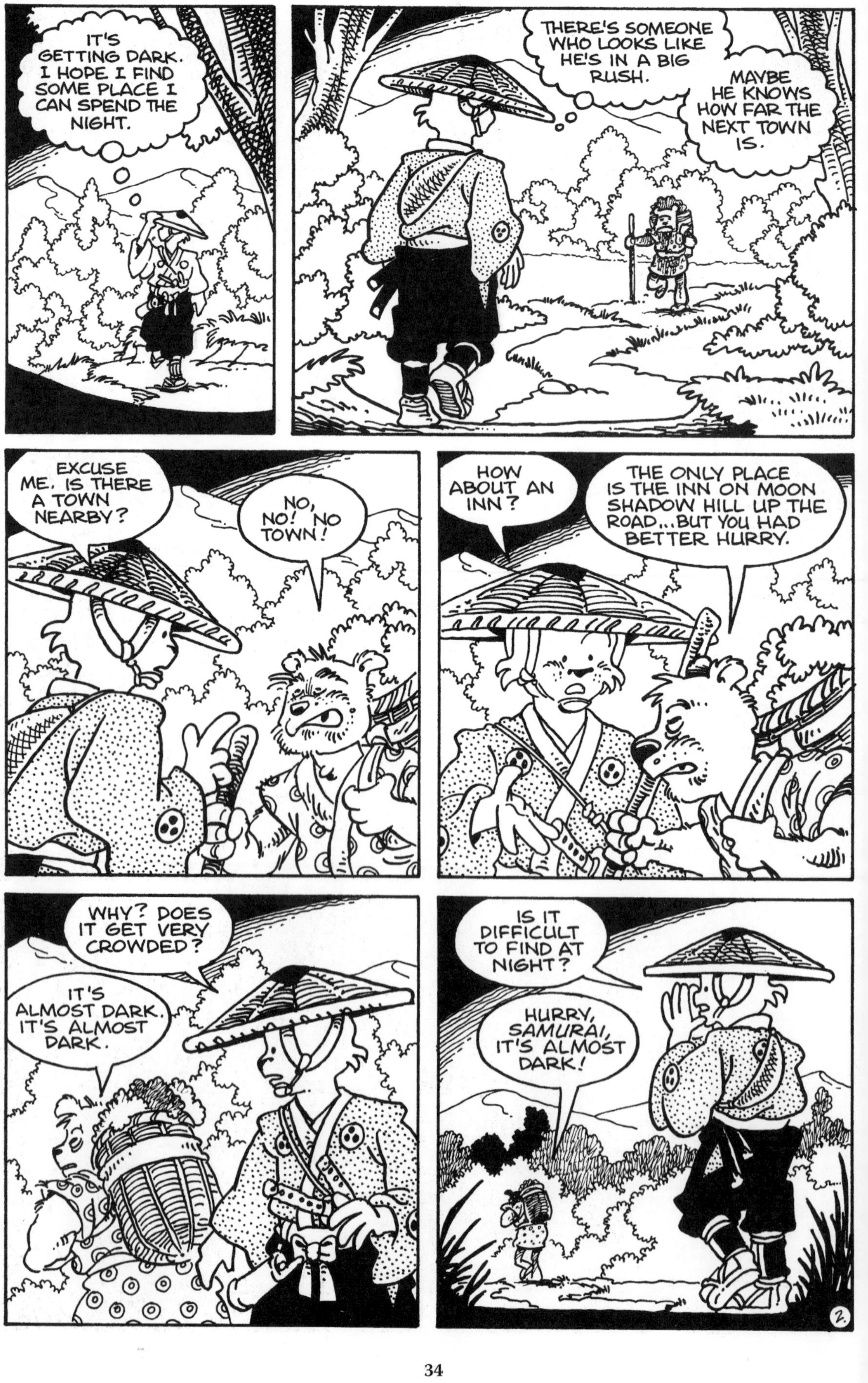
IT'S GETTING DARK. I HOPE I FIND SOME PLACE I CAN SPEND THE NIGHT.
THERE'S SOMEONE WHO LOOKS LIKE HE'S IN A BIG RUSH.
MAYBE HE KNOWS HOW FAR THE NEXT TOWN IS.
EXCUSE ME. IS THERE A TOWN NEARBY?
NO, NO! NO TOWN!
HOW ABOUT AN INN?
THE ONLY PLACE IS THE INN ON MOON SHADOW HILL UP THE ROAD...BUT YOU HAD BETTER HURRY.
WHY? DOES IT GET VERY CROWDED?
IT'S ALMOST DARK. IT'S ALMOST DARK.
IS IT DIFFICULT TO FIND AT NIGHT?
HURRY, SAMURAI, IT'S ALMOST DARK!
2.

HMM...WHAT A STRANGE FELLOW.

ALMOST DARK...ALMOST DARK...

BUT I HOPE HE WAS RIGHT ABOUT THERE BEING AN INN.

THERE'S A SIGN--PROBABLY DIRECTIONS TO THE INN.

WHAT THE--?

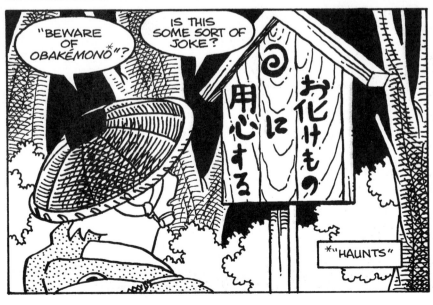

"BEWARE OF OBAKÉMONO*"?

IS THIS SOME SORT OF JOKE?

お化けもの に 用心する

*"HAUNTS"

JOKE OR NOT, I HAD BETTER HURRY ON TO THE INN.

35

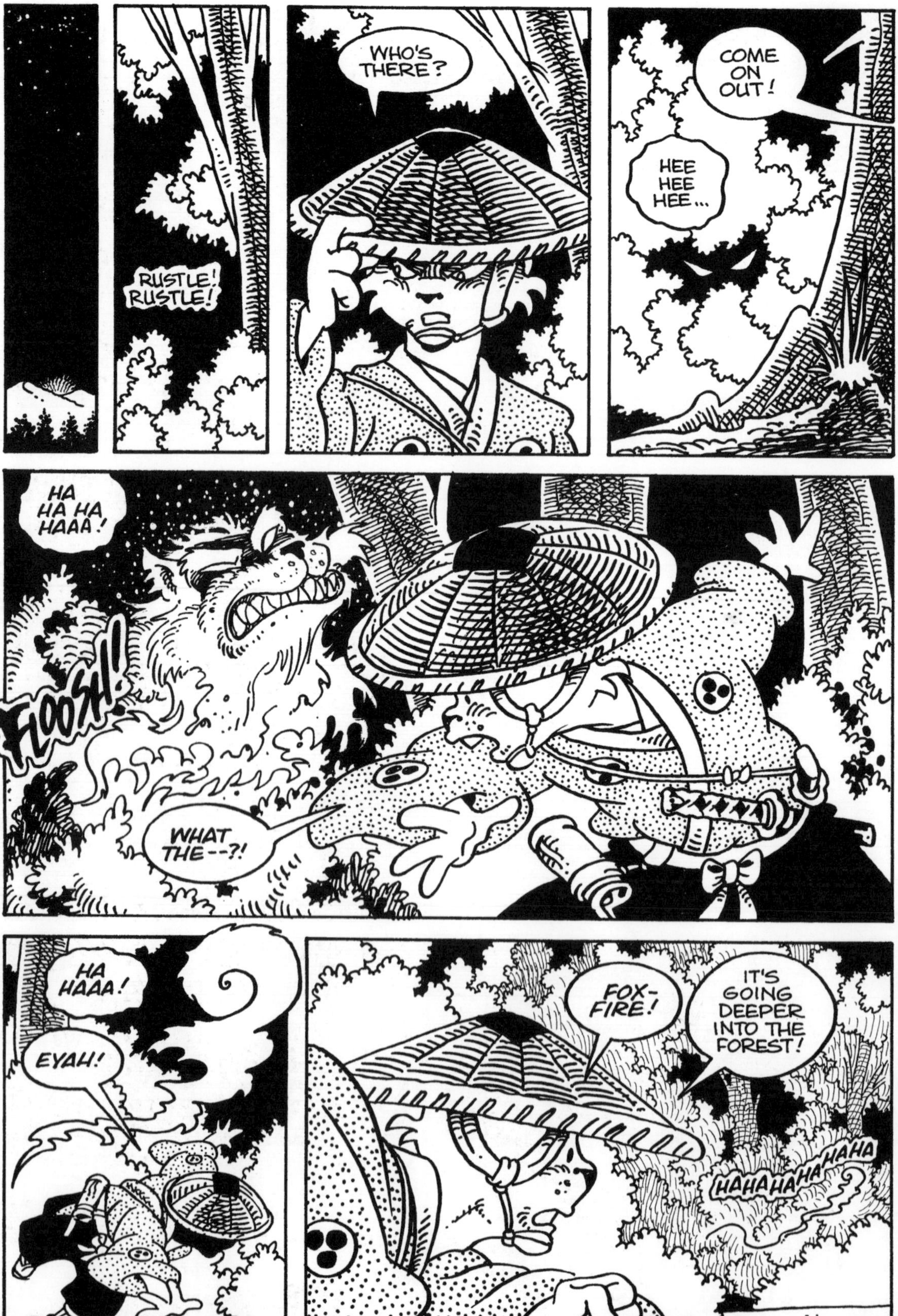
RUSTLE! RUSTLE!
WHO'S THERE?
COME ON OUT!
HEE HEE HEE...
HA HA HA HAAA!
FLOOSH!
WHAT THE--?!
HA HAAA!
EYAH!
FOX-FIRE!
IT'S GOING DEEPER INTO THE FOREST!
HAHAHAHAHAHA
4.

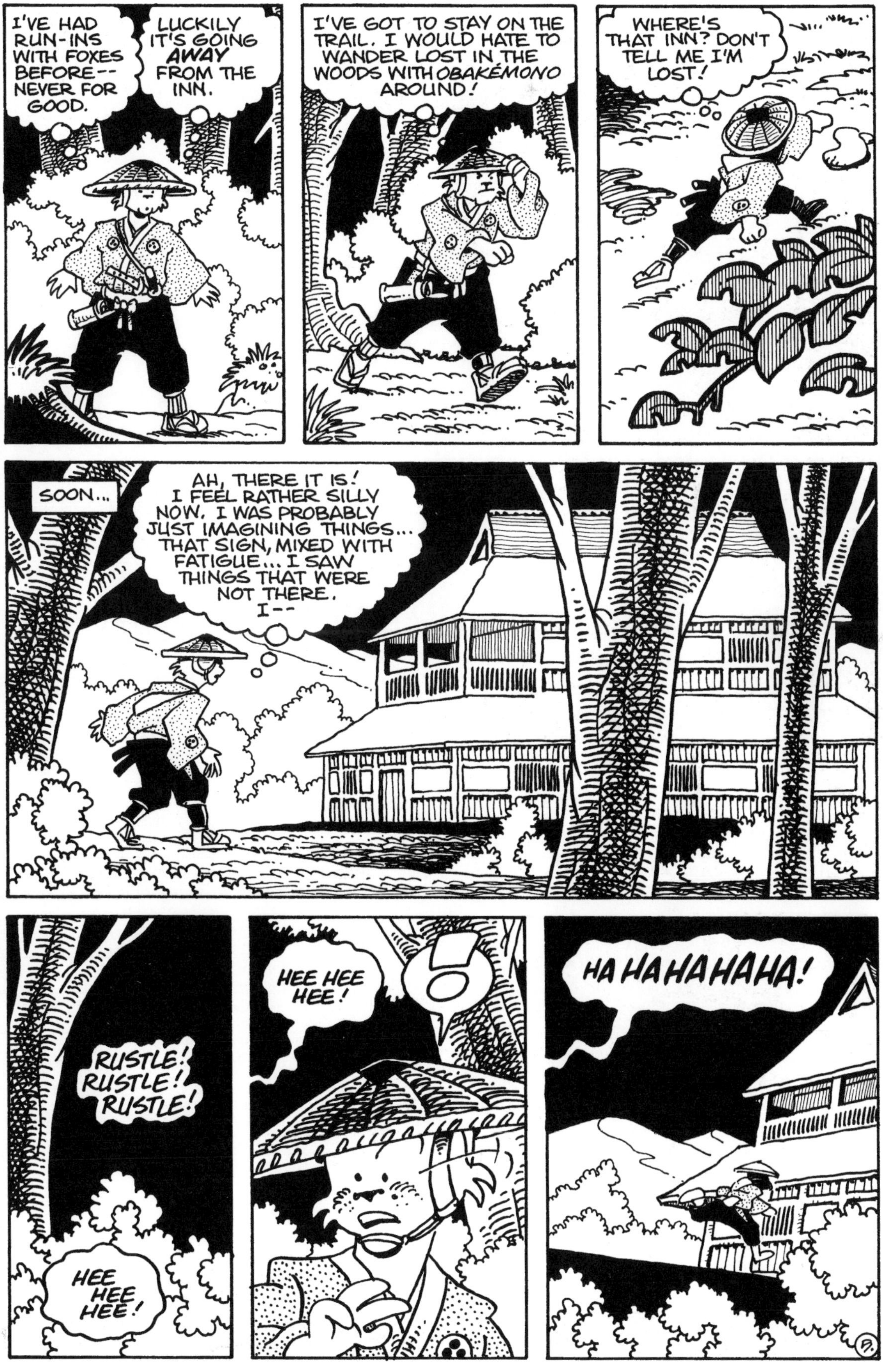
I'VE HAD RUN-INS WITH FOXES BEFORE-- NEVER FOR GOOD.
LUCKILY IT'S GOING **AWAY** FROM THE INN.
I'VE GOT TO STAY ON THE TRAIL. I WOULD HATE TO WANDER LOST IN THE WOODS WITH *OBAKÉMONO* AROUND!
WHERE'S THAT INN? DON'T TELL ME I'M LOST!
SOON...
AH, THERE IT IS! I FEEL RATHER SILLY NOW. I WAS PROBABLY JUST IMAGINING THINGS... THAT SIGN, MIXED WITH FATIGUE... I SAW THINGS THAT WERE NOT THERE. I--
RUSTLE! RUSTLE! RUSTLE!
HEE HEE HEE!
HEE HEE HEE!
!
HA HA HA HA HA HA!

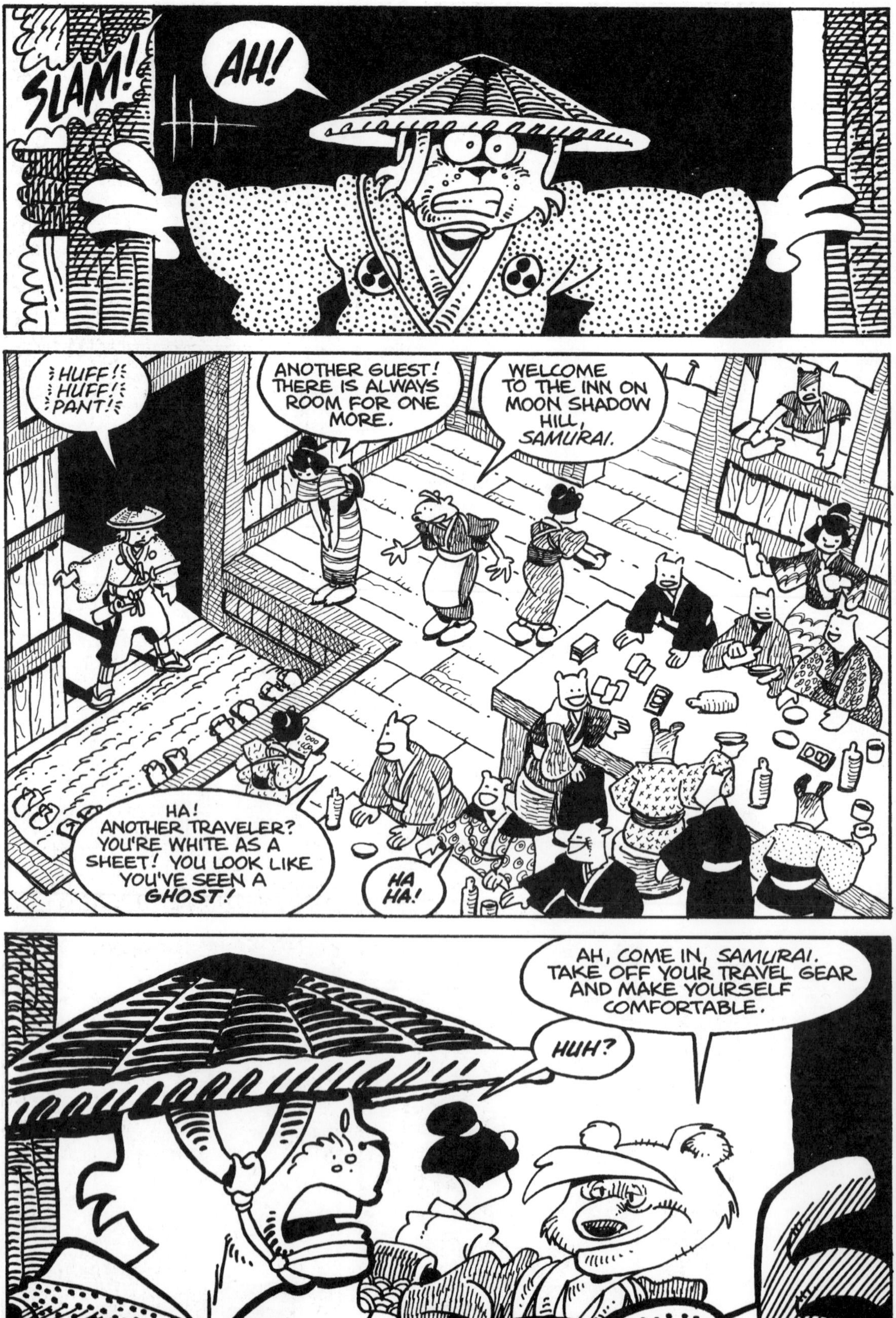
SLAM!
AH!
HUFF! HUFF! PANT!
ANOTHER GUEST! THERE IS ALWAYS ROOM FOR ONE MORE.
WELCOME TO THE INN ON MOON SHADOW HILL, SAMURAI.
HA! ANOTHER TRAVELER? YOU'RE WHITE AS A SHEET! YOU LOOK LIKE YOU'VE SEEN A GHOST!
HA HA!
HUH?
AH, COME IN, SAMURAI. TAKE OFF YOUR TRAVEL GEAR AND MAKE YOURSELF COMFORTABLE.
6.

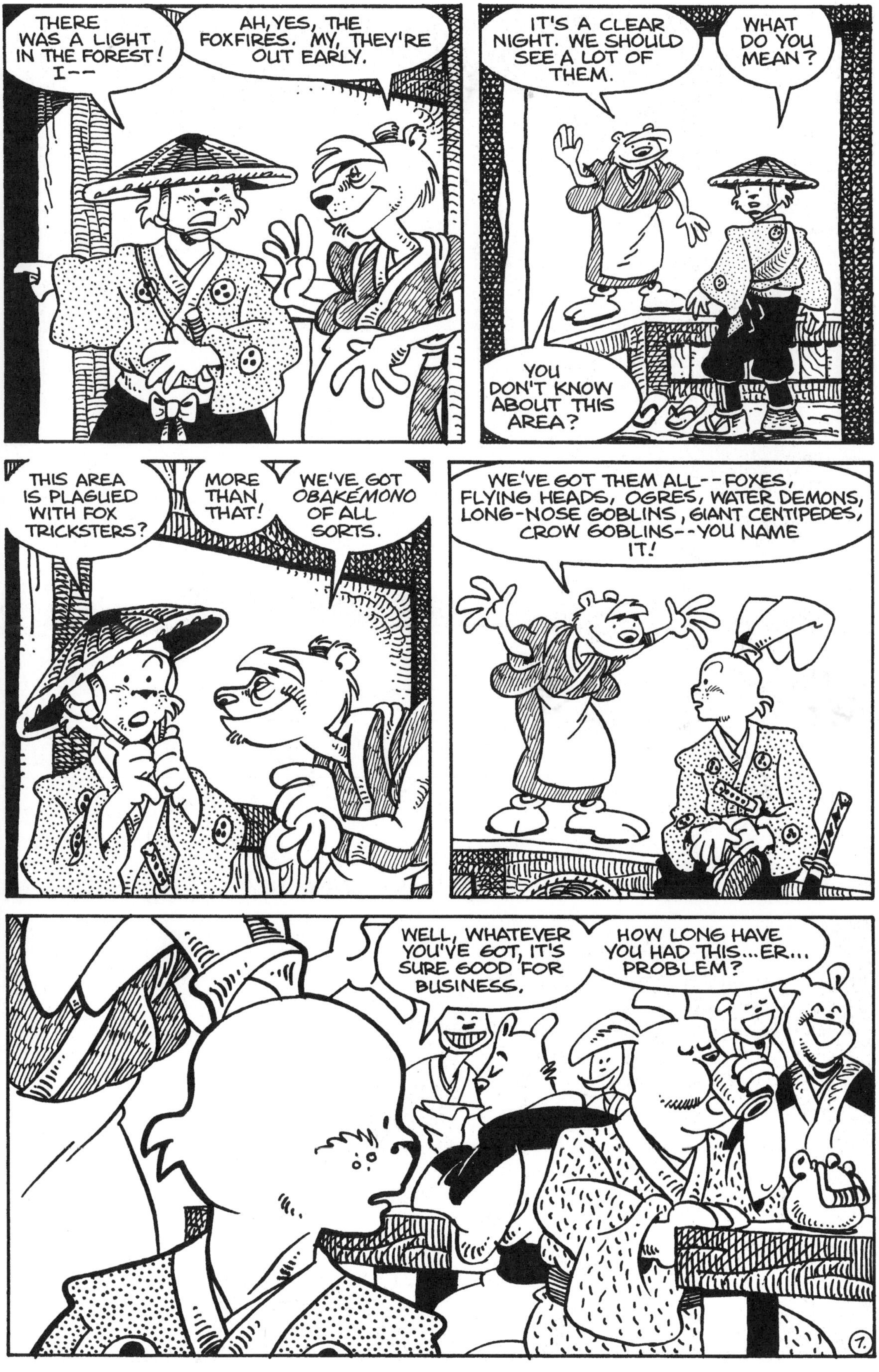
THERE WAS A LIGHT IN THE FOREST! I--
AH, YES, THE FOXFIRES. MY, THEY'RE OUT EARLY.
IT'S A CLEAR NIGHT. WE SHOULD SEE A LOT OF THEM.
WHAT DO YOU MEAN?
YOU DON'T KNOW ABOUT THIS AREA?
THIS AREA IS PLAGUED WITH FOX TRICKSTERS?
MORE THAN THAT!
WE'VE GOT *OBAKÉMONO* OF ALL SORTS.
WE'VE GOT THEM ALL--FOXES, FLYING HEADS, OGRES, WATER DEMONS, LONG-NOSE GOBLINS, GIANT CENTIPEDES, CROW GOBLINS--YOU NAME IT!
WELL, WHATEVER YOU'VE GOT, IT'S SURE GOOD FOR BUSINESS.
HOW LONG HAVE YOU HAD THIS...ER... PROBLEM?
7.

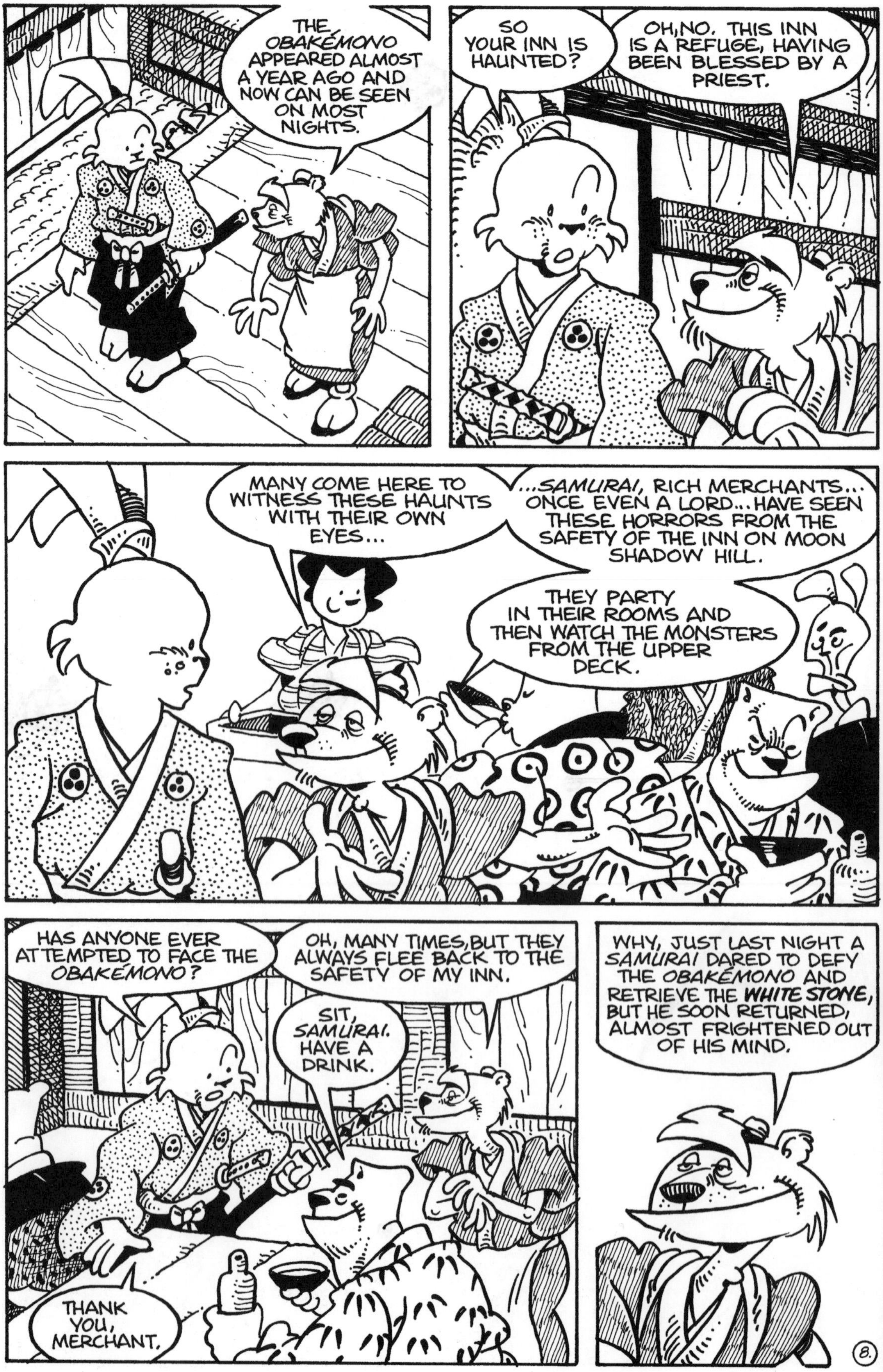
THE OBAKÉMONO APPEARED ALMOST A YEAR AGO AND NOW CAN BE SEEN ON MOST NIGHTS.
SO YOUR INN IS HAUNTED?
OH, NO. THIS INN IS A REFUGE, HAVING BEEN BLESSED BY A PRIEST.
MANY COME HERE TO WITNESS THESE HAUNTS WITH THEIR OWN EYES...
...SAMURAI, RICH MERCHANTS... ONCE EVEN A LORD... HAVE SEEN THESE HORRORS FROM THE SAFETY OF THE INN ON MOON SHADOW HILL.
THEY PARTY IN THEIR ROOMS AND THEN WATCH THE MONSTERS FROM THE UPPER DECK.
HAS ANYONE EVER ATTEMPTED TO FACE THE OBAKÉMONO?
OH, MANY TIMES, BUT THEY ALWAYS FLEE BACK TO THE SAFETY OF MY INN.
SIT, SAMURAI. HAVE A DRINK.
THANK YOU, MERCHANT.
WHY, JUST LAST NIGHT A SAMURAI DARED TO DEFY THE OBAKÉMONO AND RETRIEVE THE WHITE STONE, BUT HE SOON RETURNED, ALMOST FRIGHTENED OUT OF HIS MIND.
8.

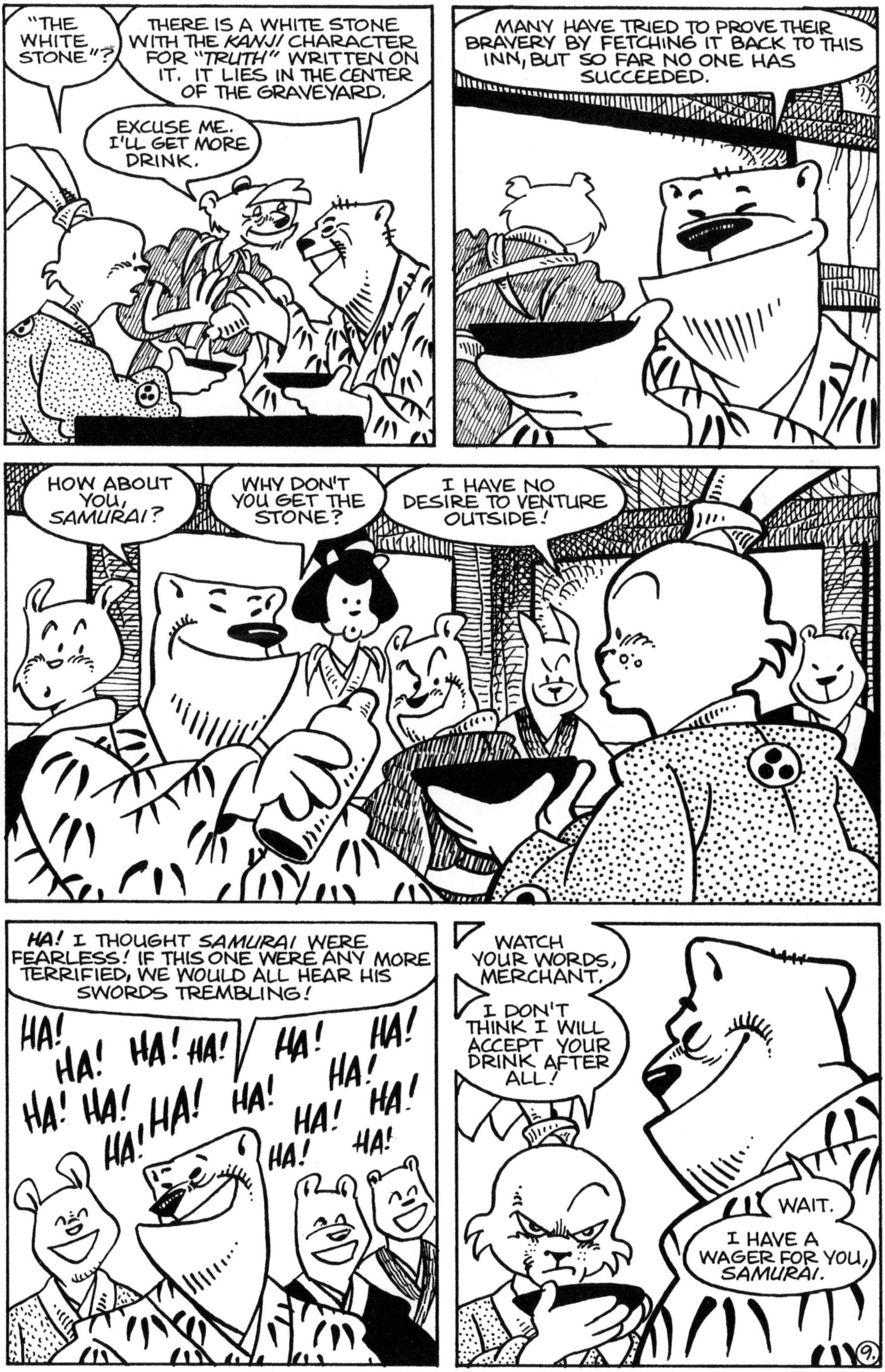
"THE WHITE STONE"?
THERE IS A WHITE STONE WITH THE KANJI CHARACTER FOR "TRUTH" WRITTEN ON IT. IT LIES IN THE CENTER OF THE GRAVEYARD.
EXCUSE ME. I'LL GET MORE DRINK.
MANY HAVE TRIED TO PROVE THEIR BRAVERY BY FETCHING IT BACK TO THIS INN, BUT SO FAR NO ONE HAS SUCCEEDED.
HOW ABOUT YOU, SAMURAI?
WHY DON'T YOU GET THE STONE?
I HAVE NO DESIRE TO VENTURE OUTSIDE!
HA! I THOUGHT SAMURAI WERE FEARLESS! IF THIS ONE WERE ANY MORE TERRIFIED, WE WOULD ALL HEAR HIS SWORDS TREMBLING!
HA! HA! HA! HA! HA! HA! HA! HA! HA! HA! HA! HA! HA! HA! HA! HA!
WATCH YOUR WORDS, MERCHANT.
I DON'T THINK I WILL ACCEPT YOUR DRINK AFTER ALL!
WAIT.
I HAVE A WAGER FOR YOU, SAMURAI.
9.

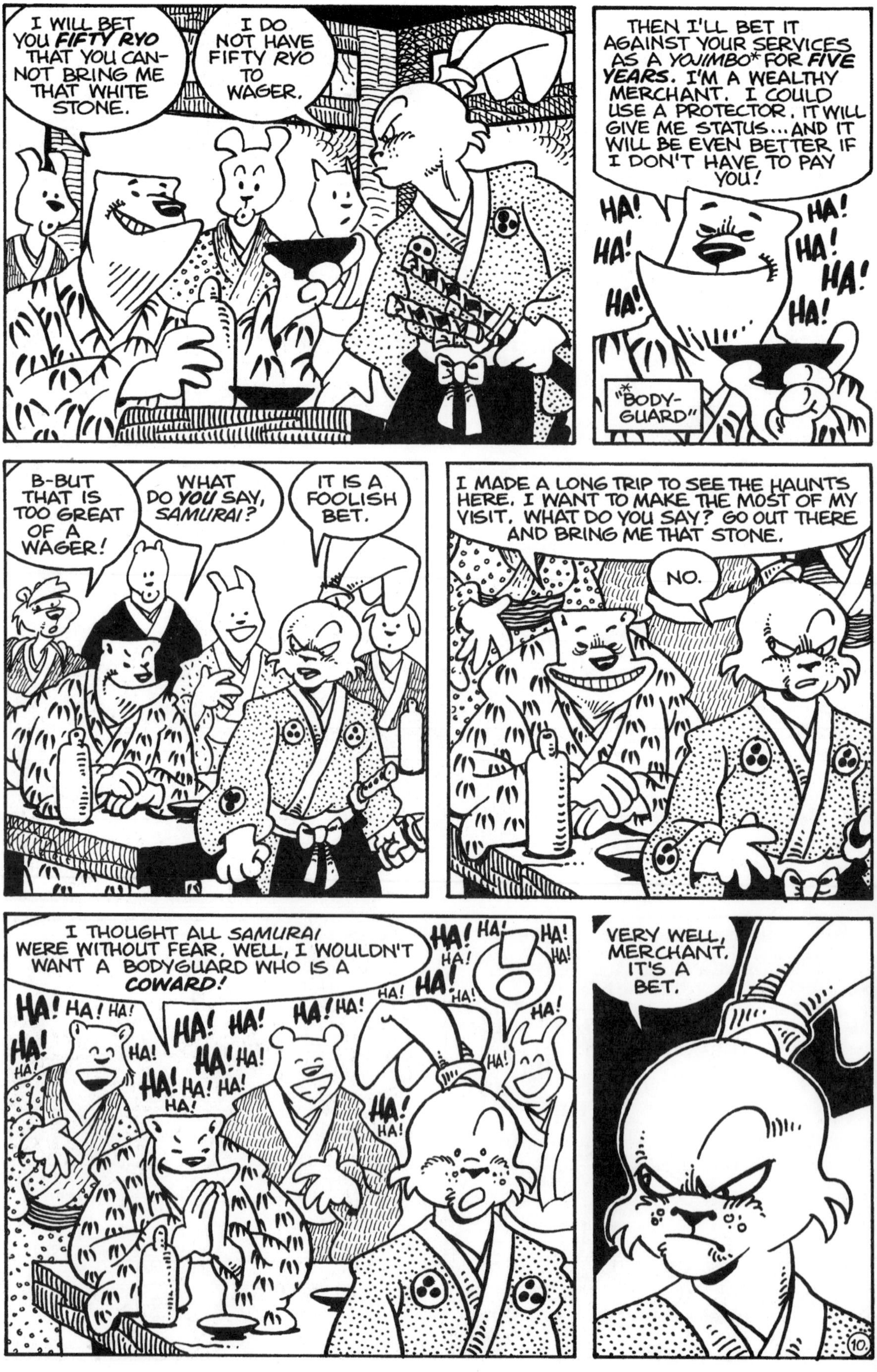
I WILL BET YOU FIFTY RYO THAT YOU CAN-NOT BRING ME THAT WHITE STONE.
I DO NOT HAVE FIFTY RYO TO WAGER.
THEN I'LL BET IT AGAINST YOUR SERVICES AS A YOJIMBO* FOR FIVE YEARS. I'M A WEALTHY MERCHANT. I COULD USE A PROTECTOR. IT WILL GIVE ME STATUS... AND IT WILL BE EVEN BETTER IF I DON'T HAVE TO PAY YOU!
HA! HA! HA! HA! HA! HA! HA!
*"BODY-GUARD"
B-BUT THAT IS TOO GREAT OF A WAGER!
WHAT DO YOU SAY, SAMURAI?
IT IS A FOOLISH BET.
I MADE A LONG TRIP TO SEE THE HAUNTS HERE. I WANT TO MAKE THE MOST OF MY VISIT. WHAT DO YOU SAY? GO OUT THERE AND BRING ME THAT STONE.
NO.
I THOUGHT ALL SAMURAI WERE WITHOUT FEAR. WELL, I WOULDN'T WANT A BODYGUARD WHO IS A COWARD!
HA! HA! HA! HA! HA! HA! HA! HA! HA! HA! HA! HA! HA! HA! HA!
!
VERY WELL, MERCHANT. IT'S A BET.
10.

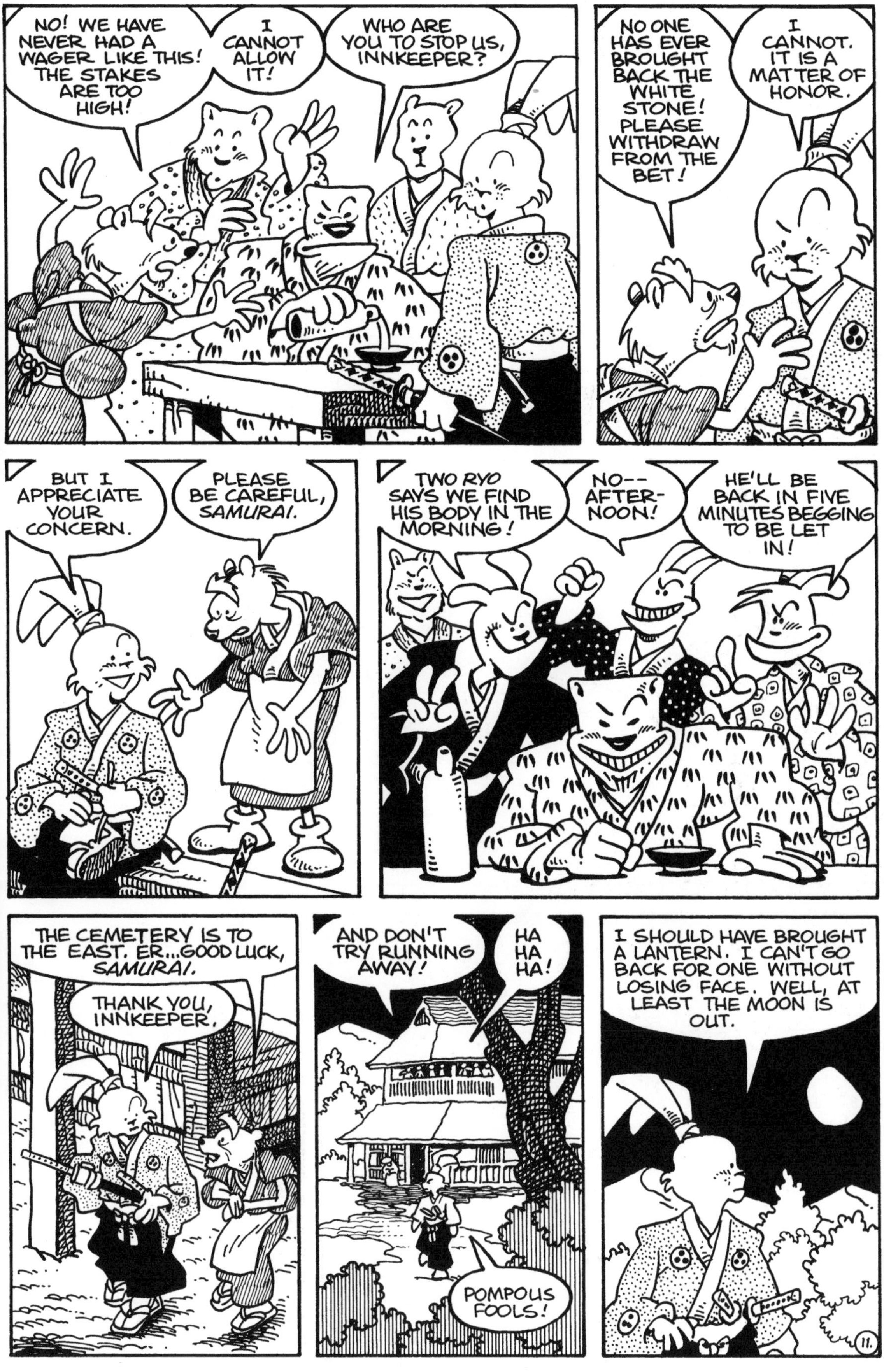
NO! WE HAVE NEVER HAD A WAGER LIKE THIS! THE STAKES ARE TOO HIGH!
I CANNOT ALLOW IT!
WHO ARE YOU TO STOP US, INNKEEPER?
NO ONE HAS EVER BROUGHT BACK THE WHITE STONE! PLEASE WITHDRAW FROM THE BET!
I CANNOT. IT IS A MATTER OF HONOR.
BUT I APPRECIATE YOUR CONCERN.
PLEASE BE CAREFUL, *SAMURAI*.
TWO *RYO* SAYS WE FIND HIS BODY IN THE MORNING!
NO-- AFTER-NOON!
HE'LL BE BACK IN FIVE MINUTES BEGGING TO BE LET IN!
THE CEMETERY IS TO THE EAST. ER...GOOD LUCK, *SAMURAI*.
THANK YOU, INNKEEPER.
AND DON'T TRY RUNNING AWAY!
HA HA HA!
POMPOUS FOOLS!
I SHOULD HAVE BROUGHT A LANTERN. I CAN'T GO BACK FOR ONE WITHOUT LOSING FACE. WELL, AT LEAST THE MOON IS OUT.
11.

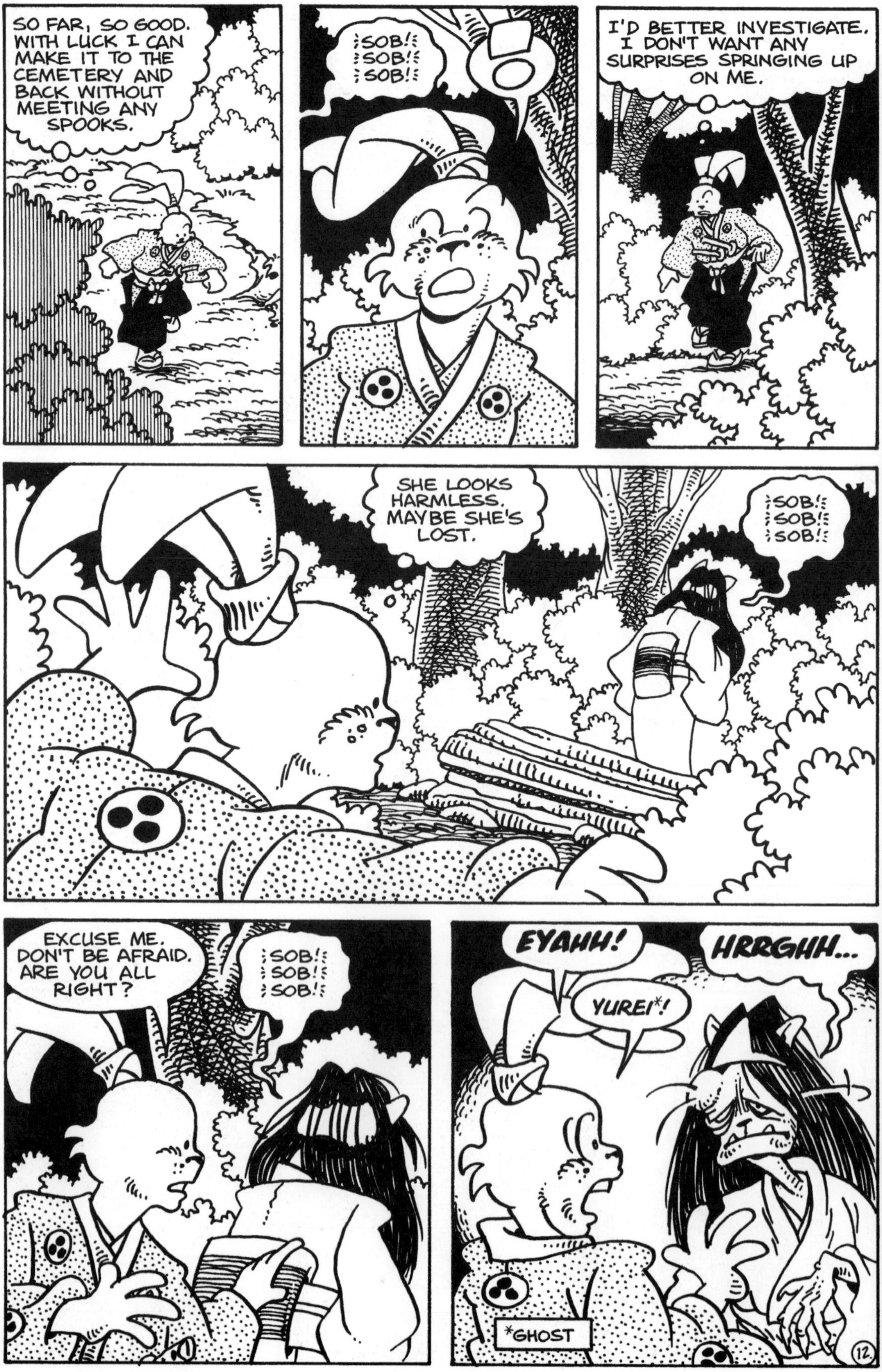
SO FAR, SO GOOD. WITH LUCK I CAN MAKE IT TO THE CEMETERY AND BACK WITHOUT MEETING ANY SPOOKS.
SOB! SOB! SOB!
I'D BETTER INVESTIGATE. I DON'T WANT ANY SURPRISES SPRINGING UP ON ME.
SHE LOOKS HARMLESS. MAYBE SHE'S LOST.
SOB! SOB! SOB!
EXCUSE ME. DON'T BE AFRAID. ARE YOU ALL RIGHT?
SOB! SOB! SOB!
EYAHH!
YUREI*!
HRRGHH...
*GHOST
12

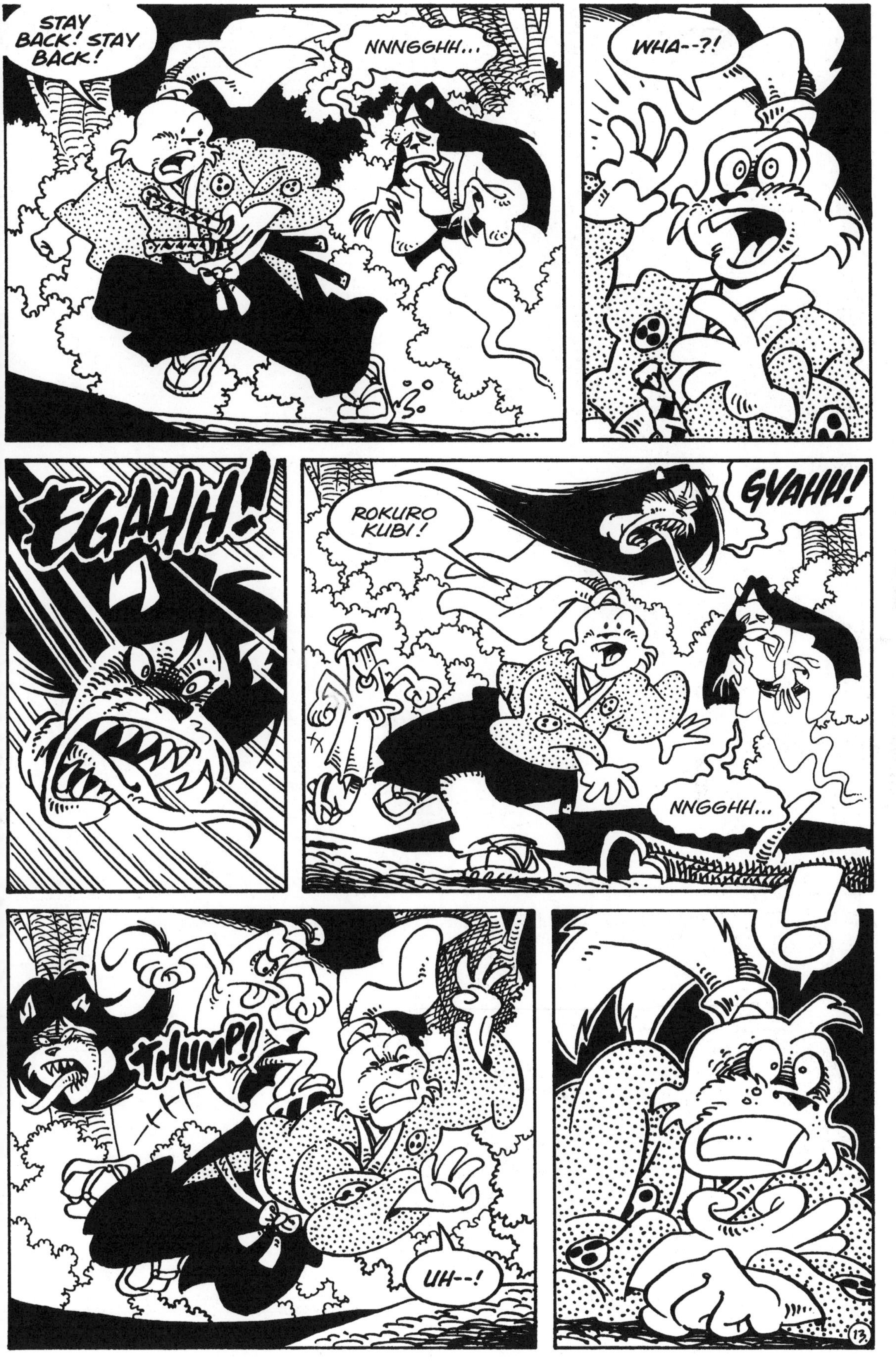
STAY BACK! STAY BACK!
NNNGGHH...
WHA--?!
EGAHH!
ROKURO KUBI!
GYAHH!
NNGGHH...
THUMP!
UH--!
!
13

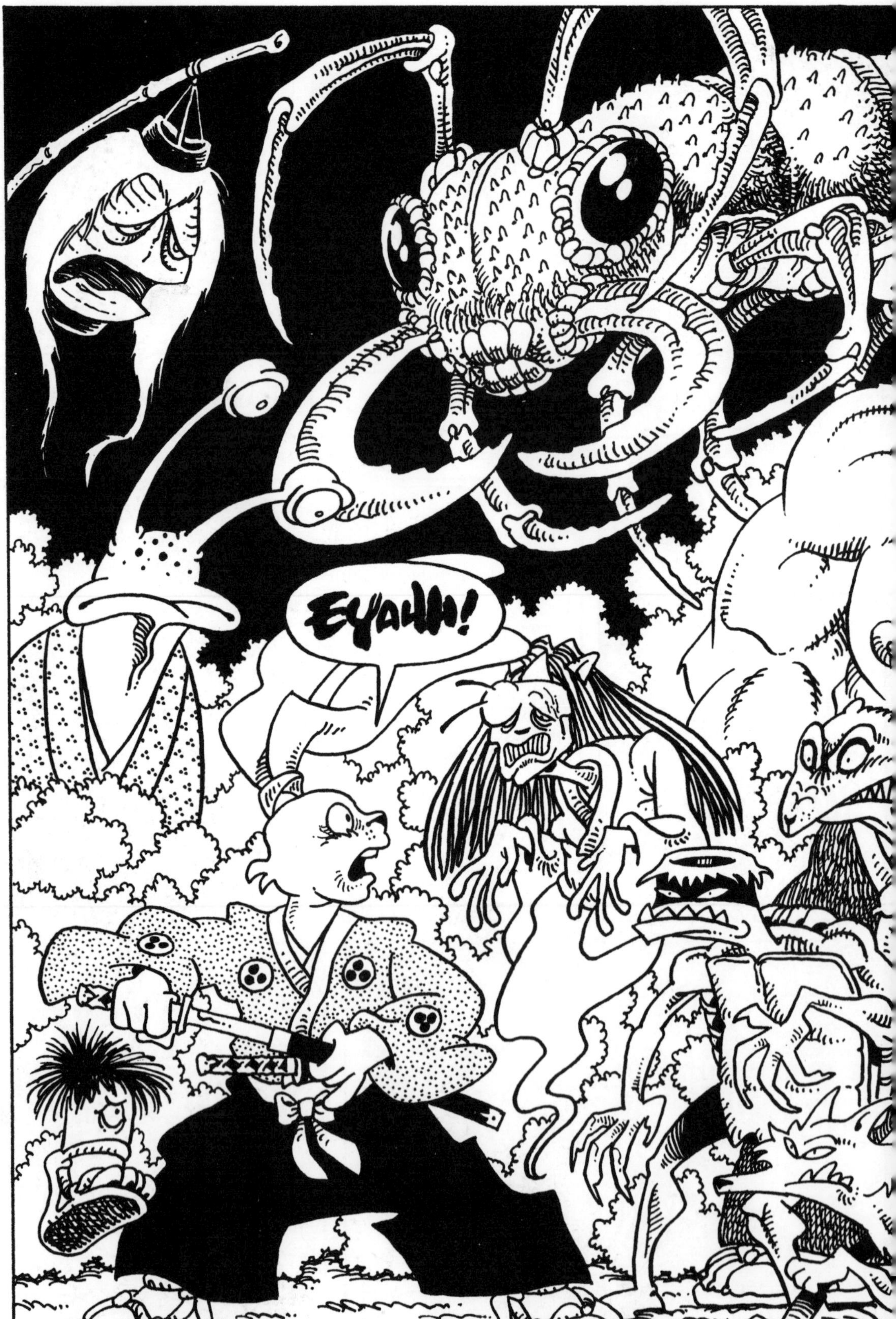
EYAHH!

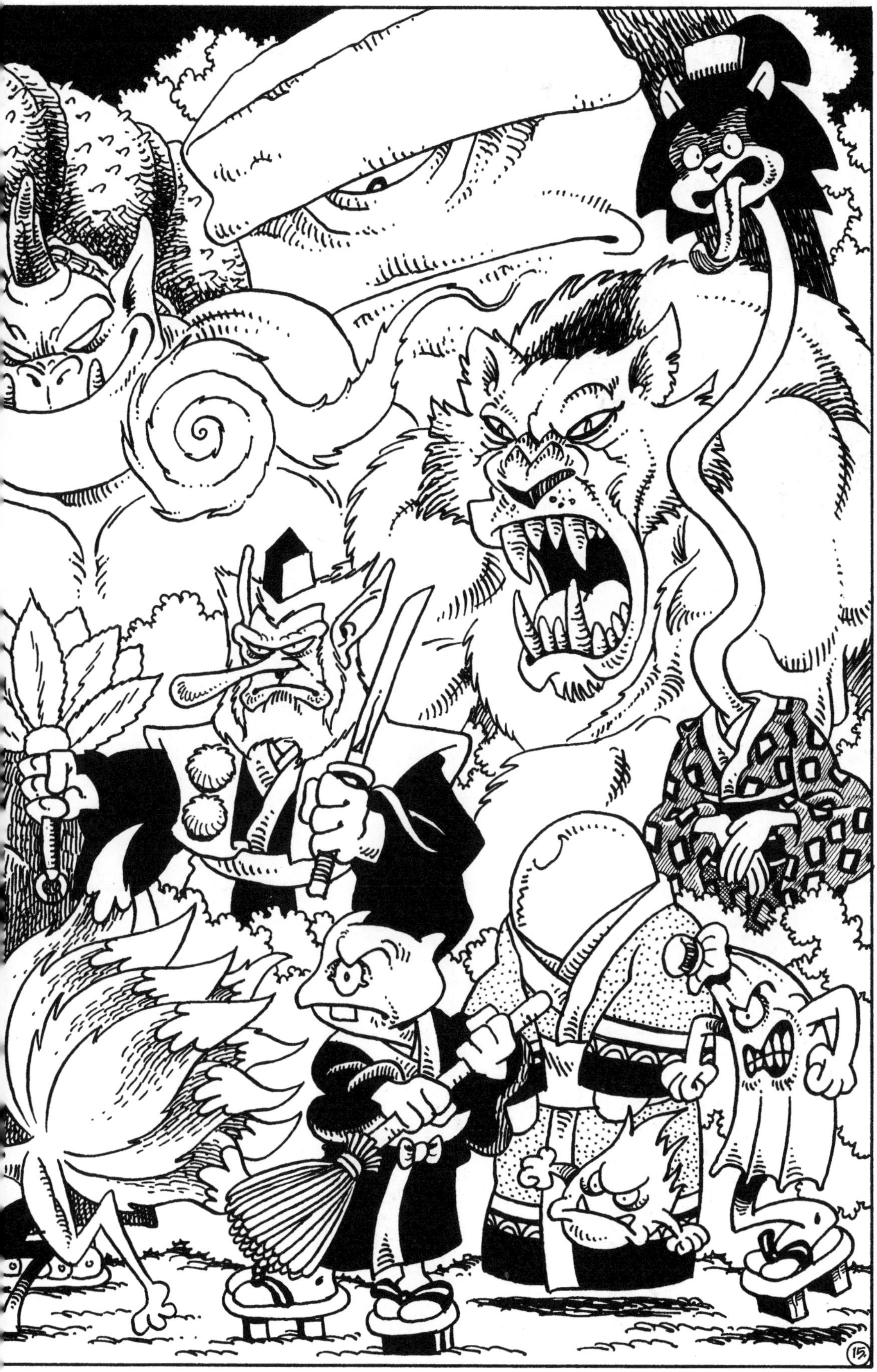

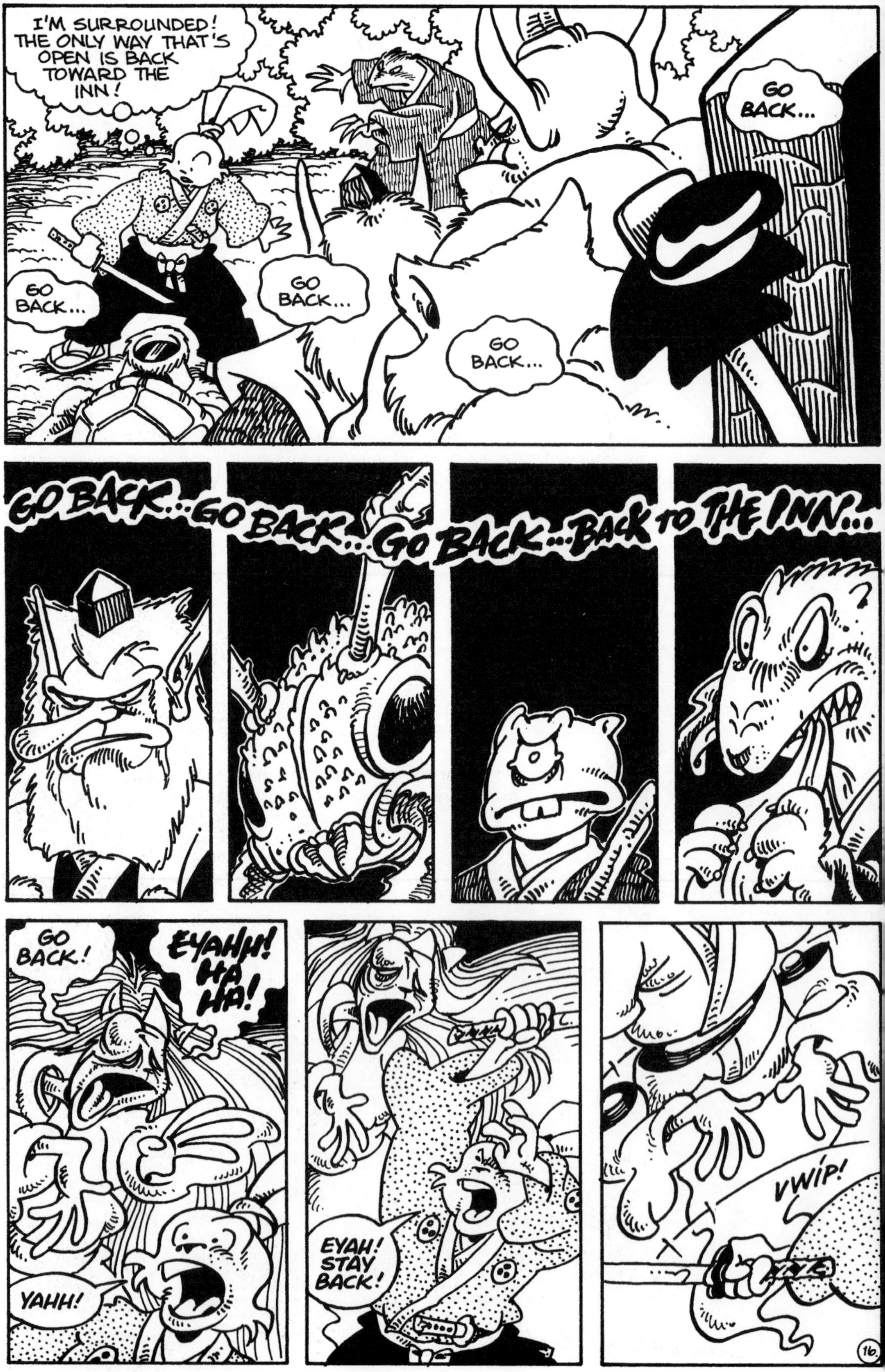

I'M SURROUNDED! THE ONLY WAY THAT'S OPEN IS BACK TOWARD THE INN!
GO BACK...
GO BACK...
GO BACK...
GO BACK...
GO BACK... GO BACK... GO BACK... BACK TO THE INN...
GO BACK!
EYAHH! HA HA!
YAHH!
EYAH! STAY BACK!
VWIP!
16.

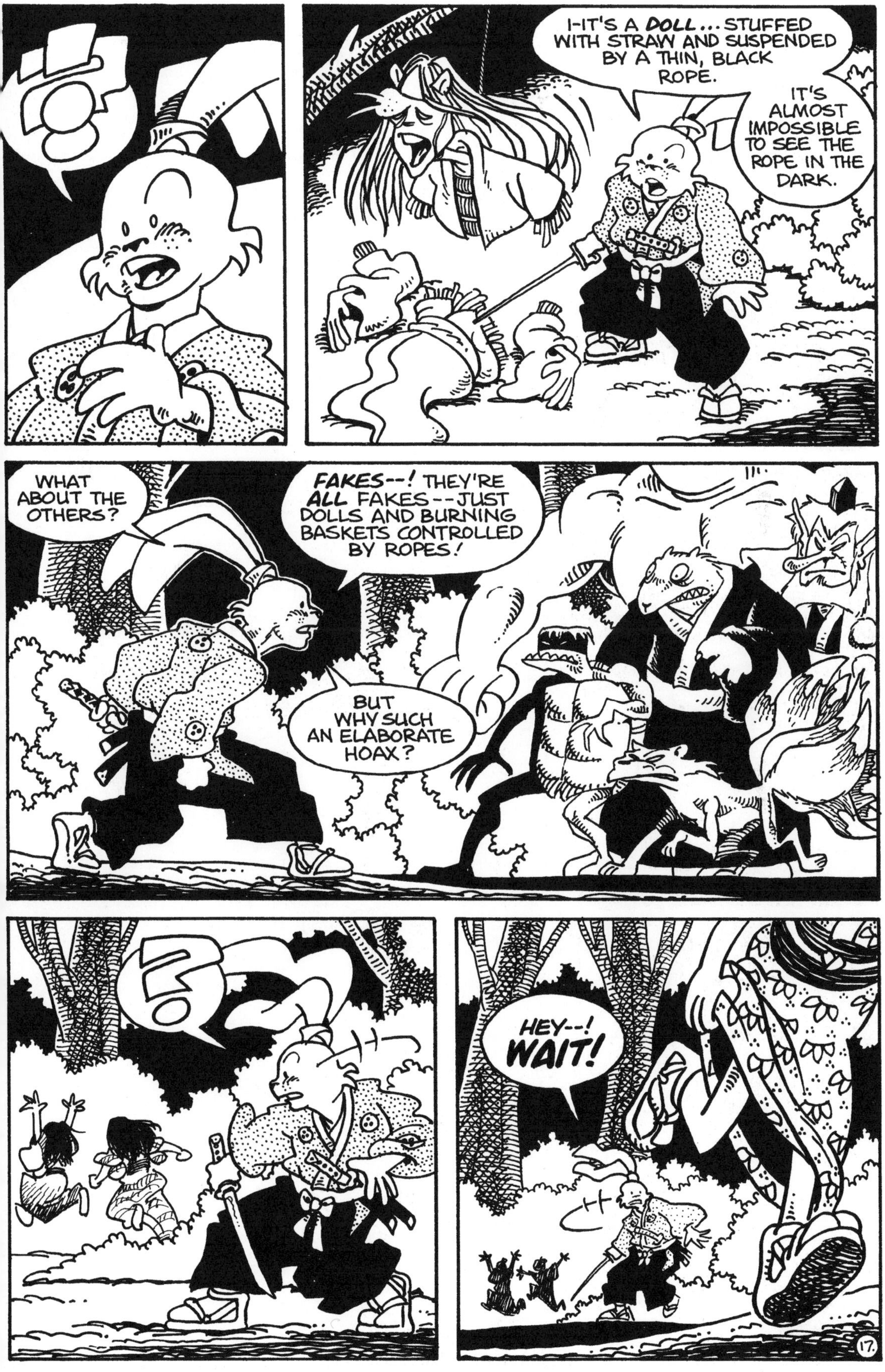
?!
I-IT'S A DOLL... STUFFED WITH STRAW AND SUSPENDED BY A THIN, BLACK ROPE.
IT'S ALMOST IMPOSSIBLE TO SEE THE ROPE IN THE DARK.
WHAT ABOUT THE OTHERS?
FAKES--! THEY'RE ALL FAKES--JUST DOLLS AND BURNING BASKETS CONTROLLED BY ROPES!
BUT WHY SUCH AN ELABORATE HOAX?
?!
HEY--! WAIT!
17.

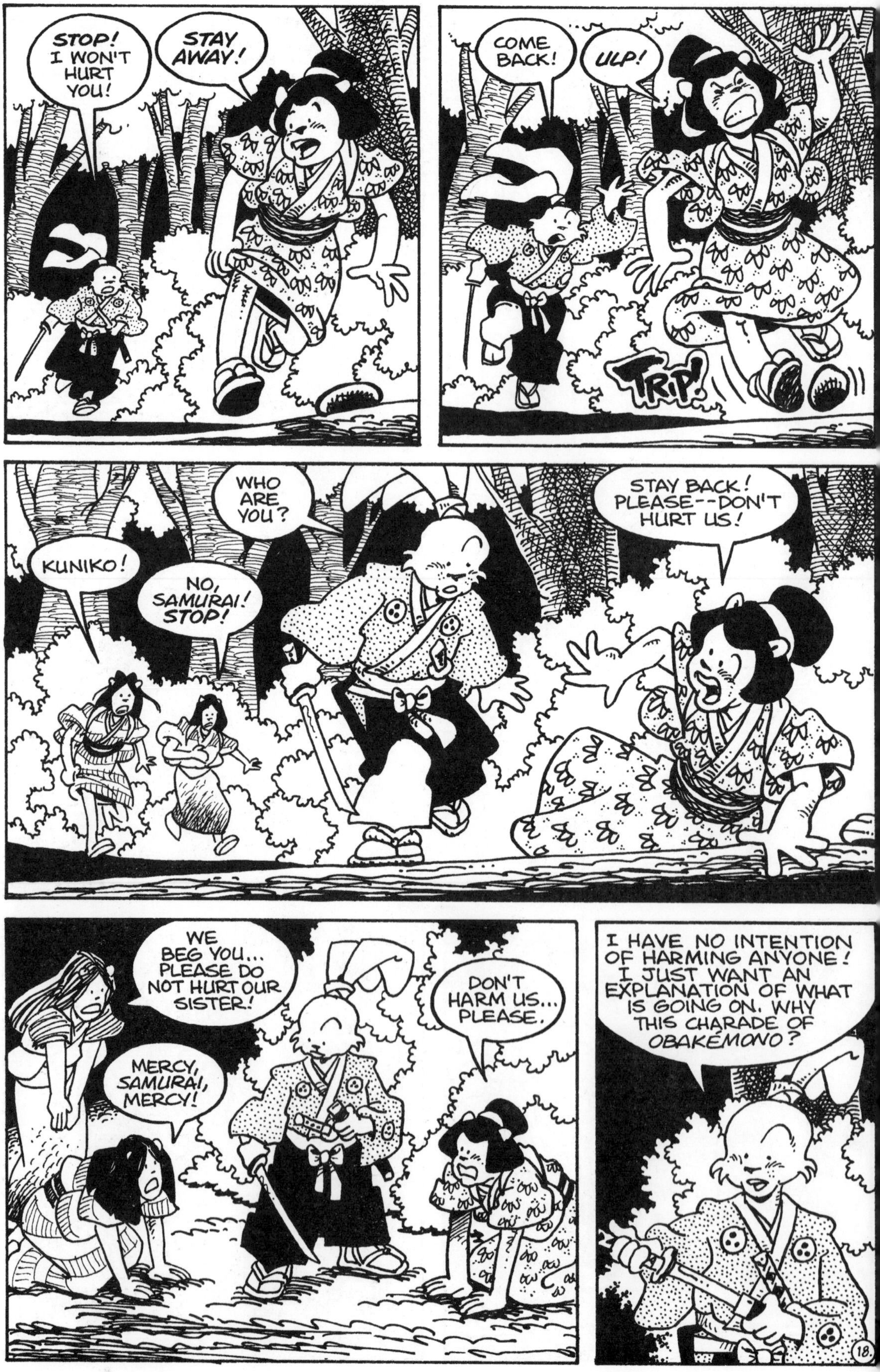
STOP! I WON'T HURT YOU!
STAY AWAY!
COME BACK!
ULP!
TRIP!
WHO ARE YOU?
STAY BACK! PLEASE--DON'T HURT US!
KUNIKO!
NO, SAMURAI! STOP!
WE BEG YOU... PLEASE DO NOT HURT OUR SISTER!
DON'T HARM US... PLEASE.
MERCY, SAMURAI, MERCY!
I HAVE NO INTENTION OF HARMING ANYONE! I JUST WANT AN EXPLANATION OF WHAT IS GOING ON. WHY THIS CHARADE OF *OBAKEMONO*?
18.

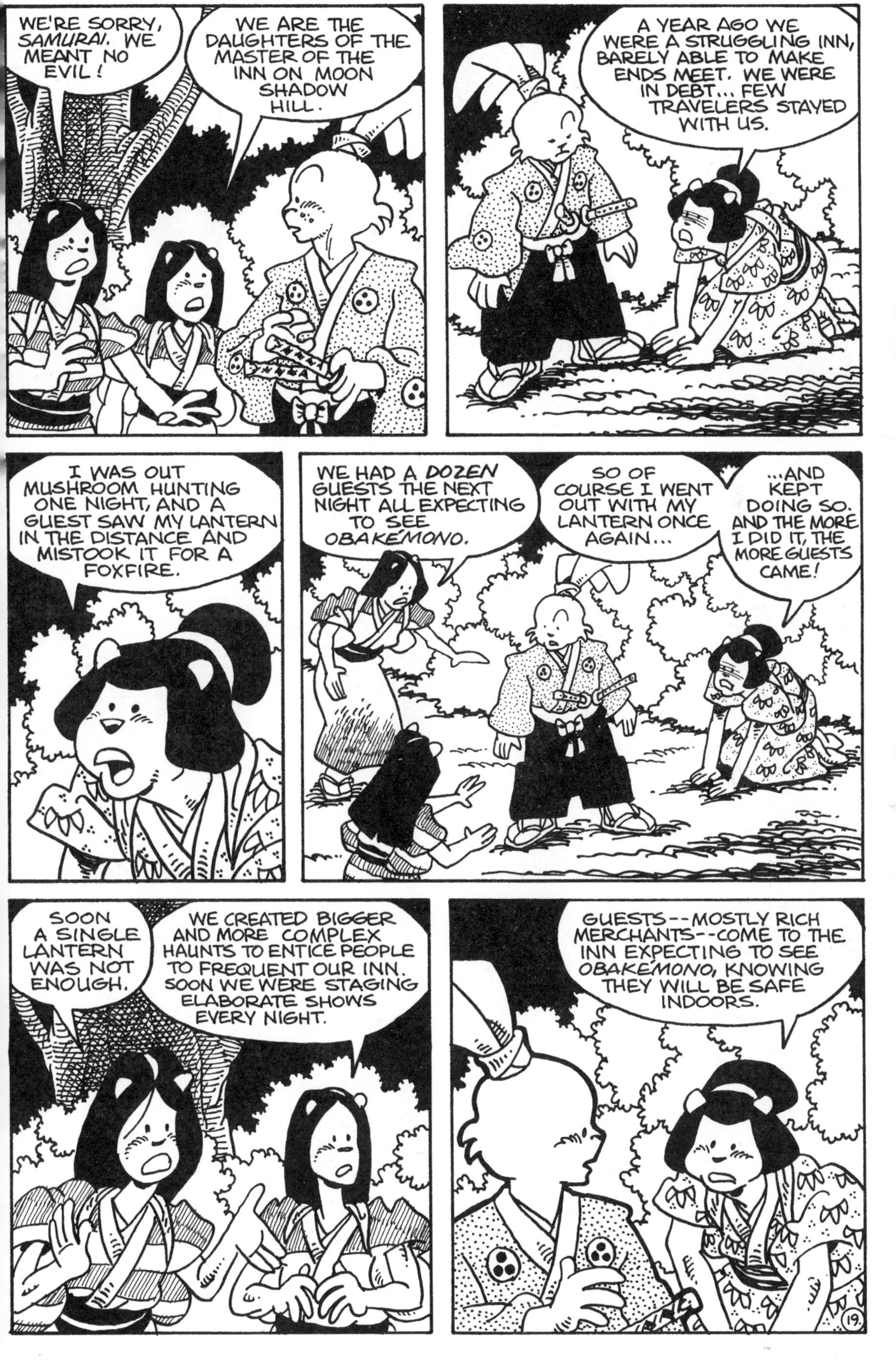
WE'RE SORRY, SAMURAI. WE MEANT NO EVIL!
WE ARE THE DAUGHTERS OF THE MASTER OF THE INN ON MOON SHADOW HILL.
A YEAR AGO WE WERE A STRUGGLING INN, BARELY ABLE TO MAKE ENDS MEET. WE WERE IN DEBT... FEW TRAVELERS STAYED WITH US.
I WAS OUT MUSHROOM HUNTING ONE NIGHT, AND A GUEST SAW MY LANTERN IN THE DISTANCE AND MISTOOK IT FOR A FOXFIRE.
WE HAD A DOZEN GUESTS THE NEXT NIGHT ALL EXPECTING TO SEE OBAKEMONO.
SO OF COURSE I WENT OUT WITH MY LANTERN ONCE AGAIN...
...AND KEPT DOING SO. AND THE MORE I DID IT, THE MORE GUESTS CAME!
SOON A SINGLE LANTERN WAS NOT ENOUGH.
WE CREATED BIGGER AND MORE COMPLEX HAUNTS TO ENTICE PEOPLE TO FREQUENT OUR INN. SOON WE WERE STAGING ELABORATE SHOWS EVERY NIGHT.
GUESTS--MOSTLY RICH MERCHANTS--COME TO THE INN EXPECTING TO SEE OBAKEMONO, KNOWING THEY WILL BE SAFE INDOORS.
19

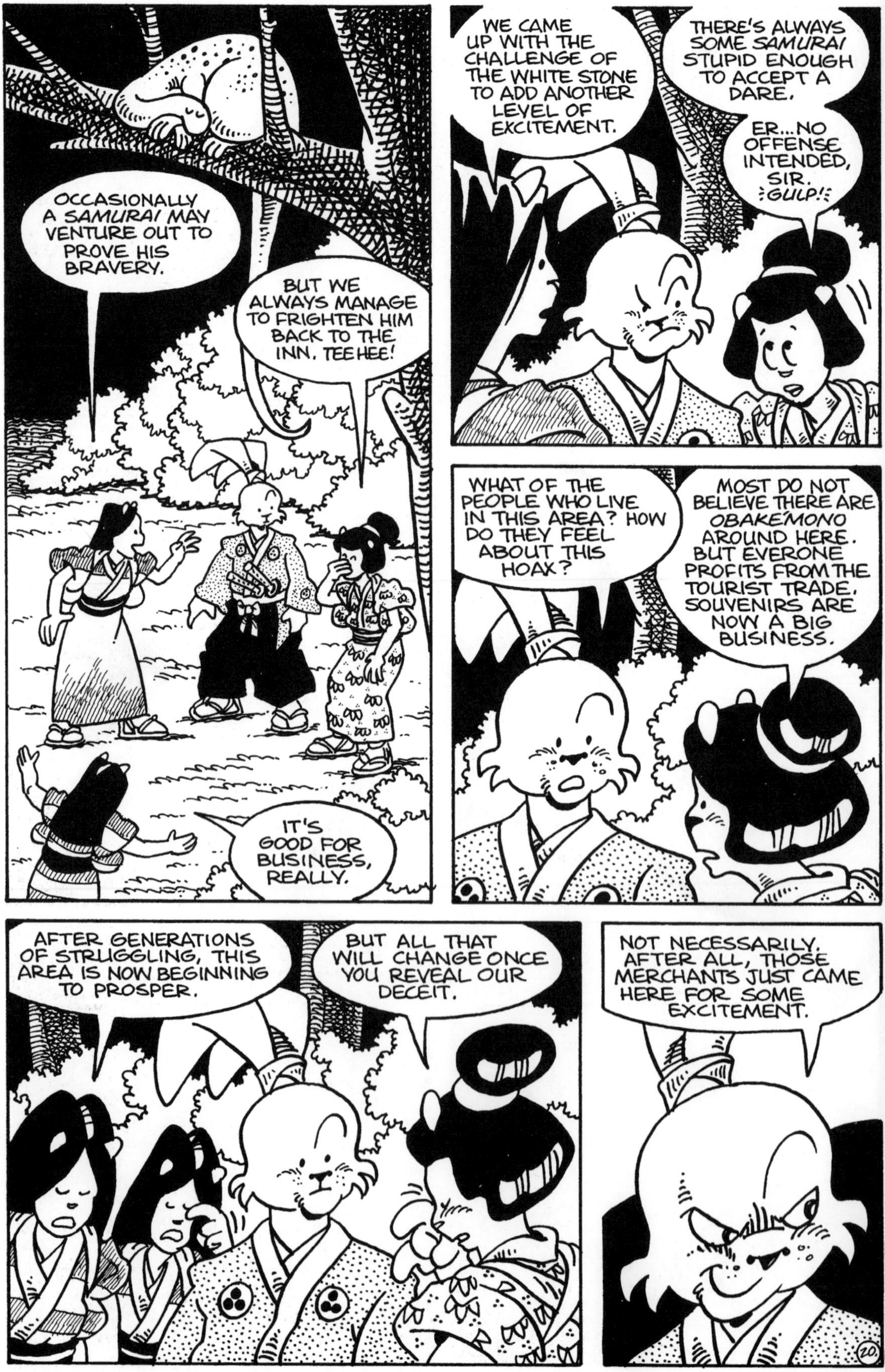
OCCASIONALLY A SAMURAI MAY VENTURE OUT TO PROVE HIS BRAVERY.
BUT WE ALWAYS MANAGE TO FRIGHTEN HIM BACK TO THE INN. TEE HEE!
IT'S GOOD FOR BUSINESS, REALLY.
WE CAME UP WITH THE CHALLENGE OF THE WHITE STONE TO ADD ANOTHER LEVEL OF EXCITEMENT.
THERE'S ALWAYS SOME SAMURAI STUPID ENOUGH TO ACCEPT A DARE.
ER...NO OFFENSE INTENDED, SIR.
GULP!
WHAT OF THE PEOPLE WHO LIVE IN THIS AREA? HOW DO THEY FEEL ABOUT THIS HOAX?
MOST DO NOT BELIEVE THERE ARE OBAKEMONO AROUND HERE. BUT EVERONE PROFITS FROM THE TOURIST TRADE. SOUVENIRS ARE NOW A BIG BUSINESS.
AFTER GENERATIONS OF STRUGGLING, THIS AREA IS NOW BEGINNING TO PROSPER.
BUT ALL THAT WILL CHANGE ONCE YOU REVEAL OUR DECEIT.
NOT NECESSARILY. AFTER ALL, THOSE MERCHANTS JUST CAME HERE FOR SOME EXCITEMENT.
20.

HE SHOULD HAVE BEEN BACK BY NOW!

HE'S DEAD FOR SURE!

OH, NO! I HOPE HE'S ALL RIGHT!

HE PROBABLY JUST RAN OFF TO SAVE FACE!

DO YOU THINK HE WOULD STAY OUT THERE UNTIL MORNING?

OF COURSE NOT!

I DECLARE MYSELF WINNER OF THE BET IF HE'S NOT BACK SOON!

LISTEN-- FOOTSTEPS... *RUNNING!*

SLAM!

EEYAHH--! IT'S TRUE! IT'S TRUE! I SAW THEM!

MONSTERS! GOBLINS! HAUNTS! DEMONS! THEY'RE ALL OUT THERE!

YAHH! HE'S CRAZED WITH FEAR!

THEY CLAWED AT ME... SCREAMED INTO MY EARS!

IT WAS COLD--SO COLD!

¡GASP!¡

¡GULP!¡

¡SHUDDER!¡

THERE WERE *HUNDREDS* OF THEM, IN ALL FORMS AND COLORS--EACH ONE THIRSTY FOR *BLOOD!*

EEP!

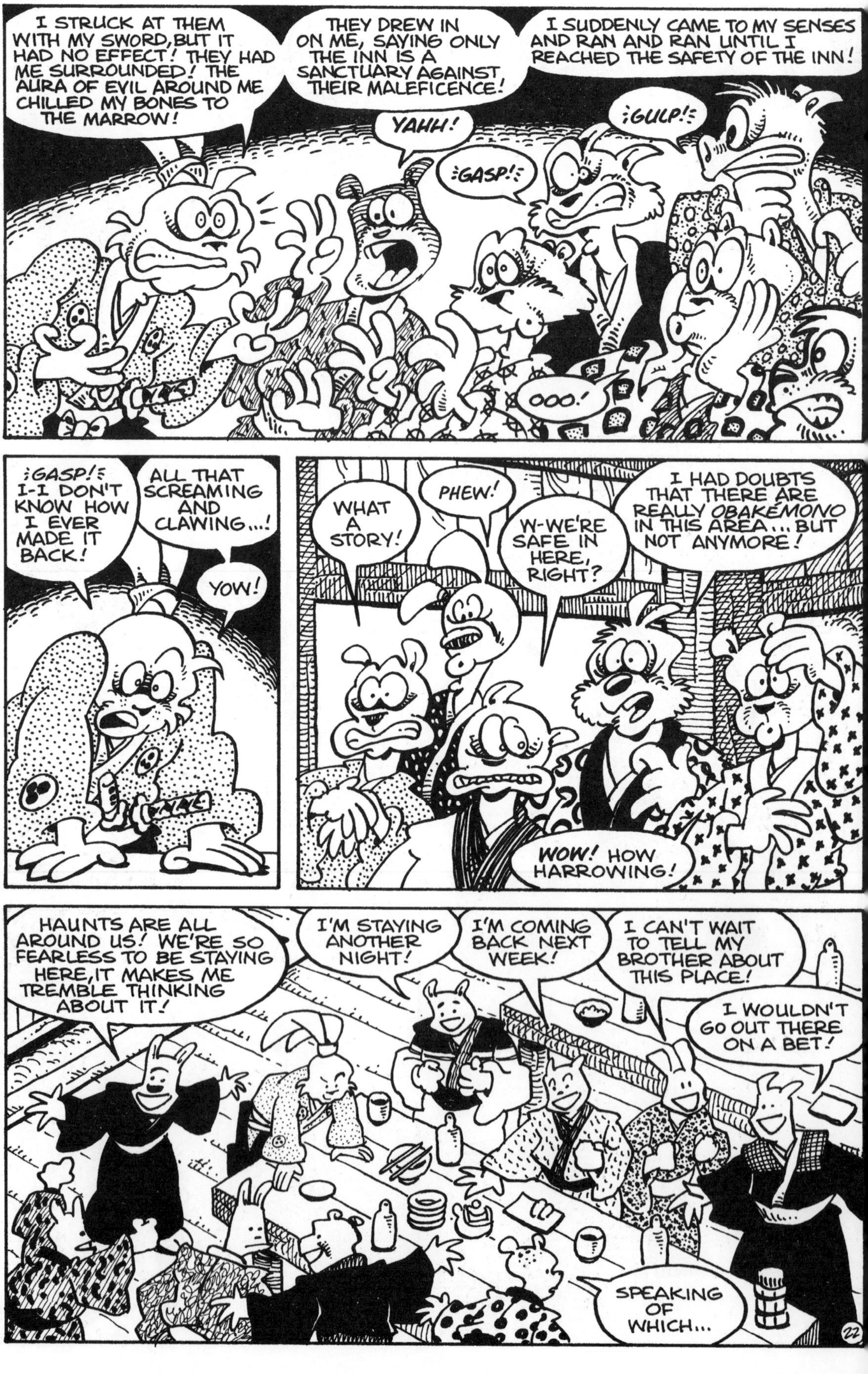

I STRUCK AT THEM WITH MY SWORD, BUT IT HAD NO EFFECT! THEY HAD ME SURROUNDED! THE AURA OF EVIL AROUND ME CHILLED MY BONES TO THE MARROW!
THEY DREW IN ON ME, SAYING ONLY THE INN IS A SANCTUARY AGAINST THEIR MALEFICENCE!
I SUDDENLY CAME TO MY SENSES AND RAN AND RAN UNTIL I REACHED THE SAFETY OF THE INN!
YAHH!
GASP!
GULP!
OOO!
GASP! I-I DON'T KNOW HOW I EVER MADE IT BACK!
ALL THAT SCREAMING AND CLAWING...!
YOW!
WHAT A STORY!
PHEW!
W-WE'RE SAFE IN HERE, RIGHT?
I HAD DOUBTS THAT THERE ARE REALLY OBAKEMONO IN THIS AREA... BUT NOT ANYMORE!
WOW! HOW HARROWING!
HAUNTS ARE ALL AROUND US! WE'RE SO FEARLESS TO BE STAYING HERE, IT MAKES ME TREMBLE THINKING ABOUT IT!
I'M STAYING ANOTHER NIGHT!
I'M COMING BACK NEXT WEEK!
I CAN'T WAIT TO TELL MY BROTHER ABOUT THIS PLACE!
I WOULDN'T GO OUT THERE ON A BET!
SPEAKING OF WHICH...
22

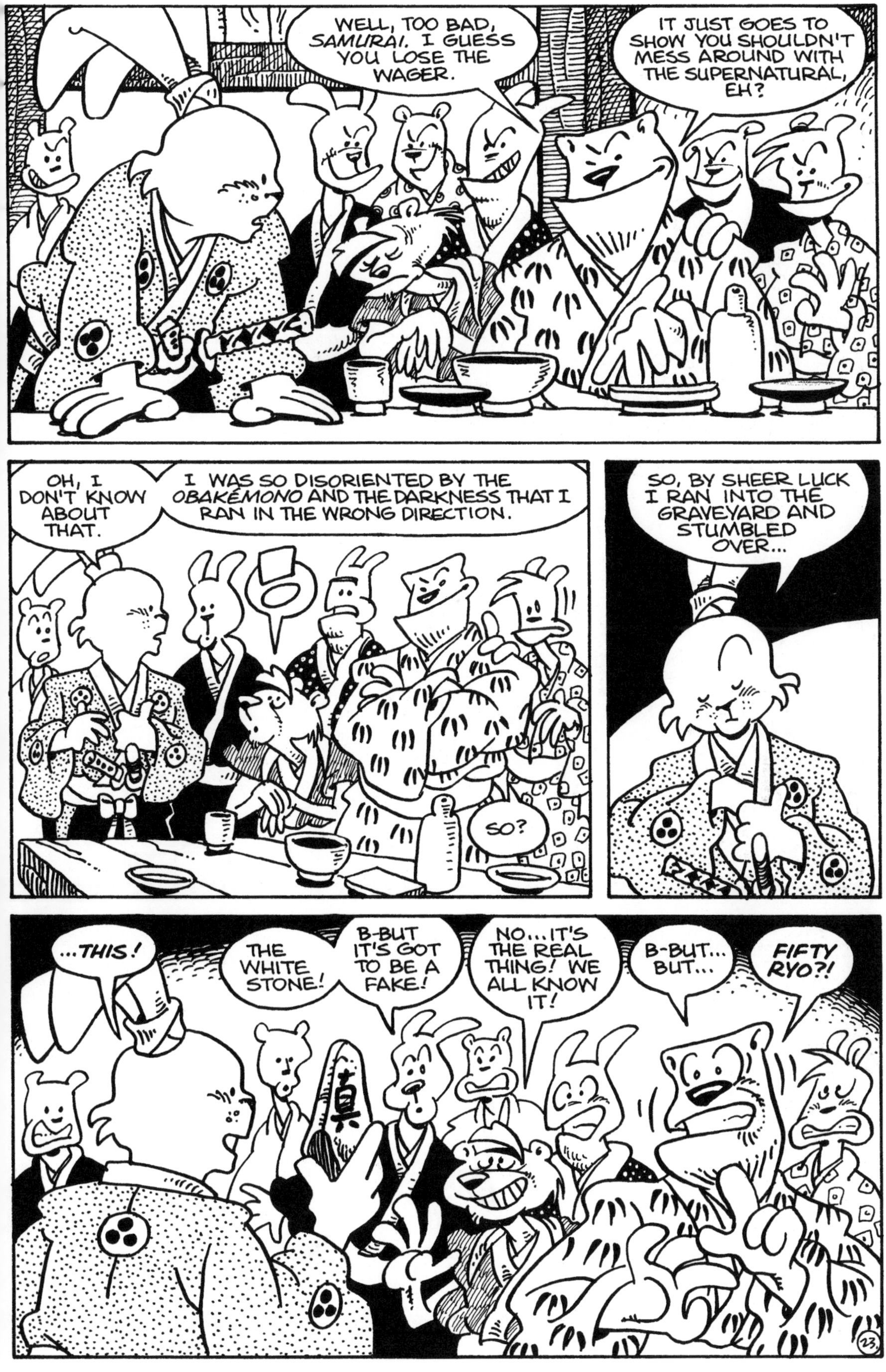
WELL, TOO BAD, *SAMURAI.* I GUESS YOU LOSE THE WAGER.
IT JUST GOES TO SHOW YOU SHOULDN'T MESS AROUND WITH THE SUPERNATURAL, EH?
OH, I DON'T KNOW ABOUT THAT.
I WAS SO DISORIENTED BY THE *OBAKEMONO* AND THE DARKNESS THAT I RAN IN THE WRONG DIRECTION.
SO?
SO, BY SHEER LUCK I RAN INTO THE GRAVEYARD AND STUMBLED OVER...
...*THIS!*
THE WHITE STONE!
B-BUT IT'S GOT TO BE A FAKE!
NO... IT'S THE REAL THING! WE ALL KNOW IT!
B-BUT... BUT...
FIFTY RYO?!
23

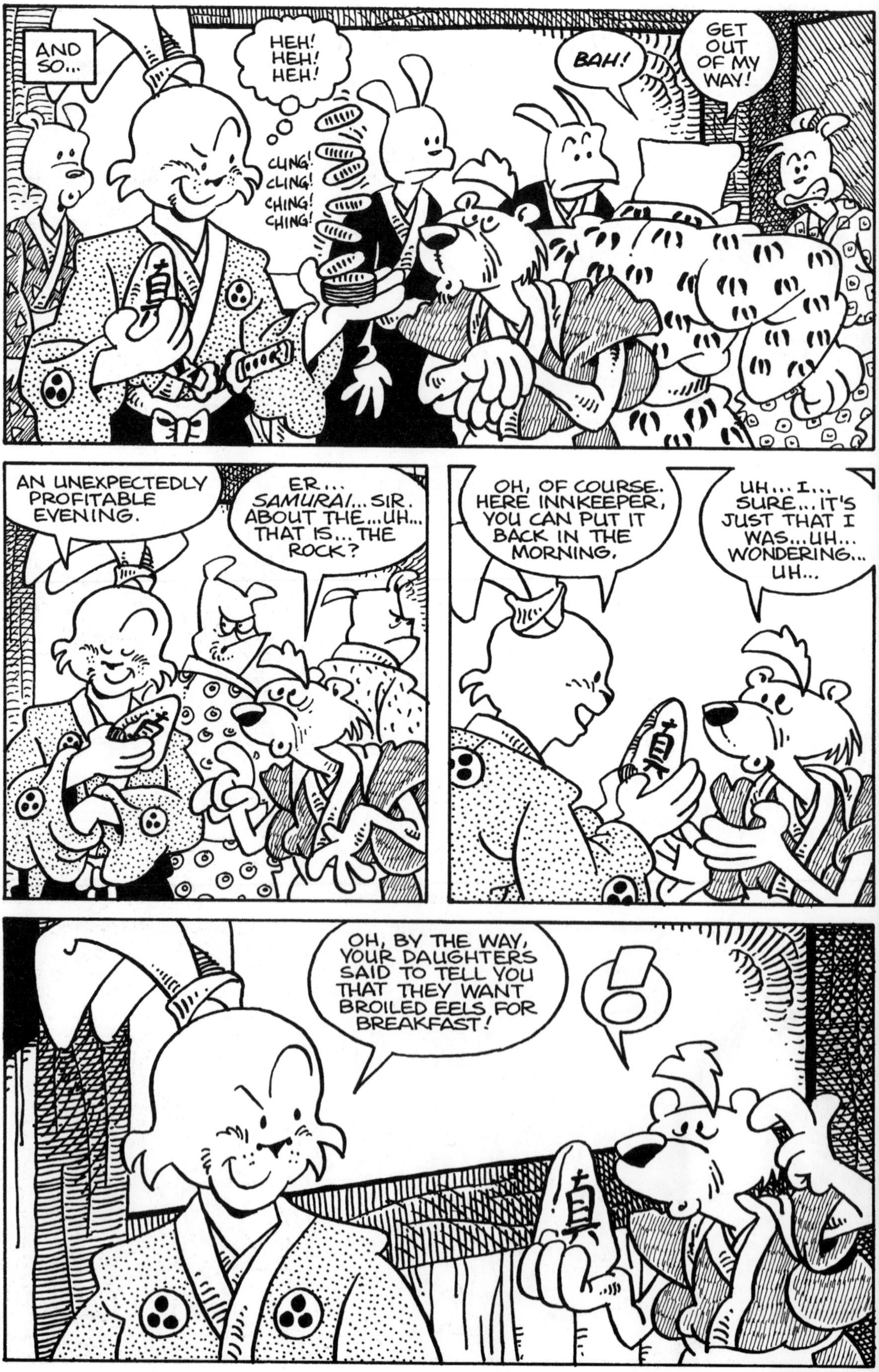
AND SO...
HEH! HEH! HEH!
CLING! CLING! CHING! CHING!
BAH!
GET OUT OF MY WAY!
AN UNEXPECTEDLY PROFITABLE EVENING.
ER... SAMURAI... SIR. ABOUT THE... UH... THAT IS... THE ROCK?
OH, OF COURSE. HERE INNKEEPER, YOU CAN PUT IT BACK IN THE MORNING.
UH... I... SURE... IT'S JUST THAT I WAS... UH... WONDERING... UH...
OH, BY THE WAY, YOUR DAUGHTERS SAID TO TELL YOU THAT THEY WANT BROILED EELS FOR BREAKFAST!
!

THE END

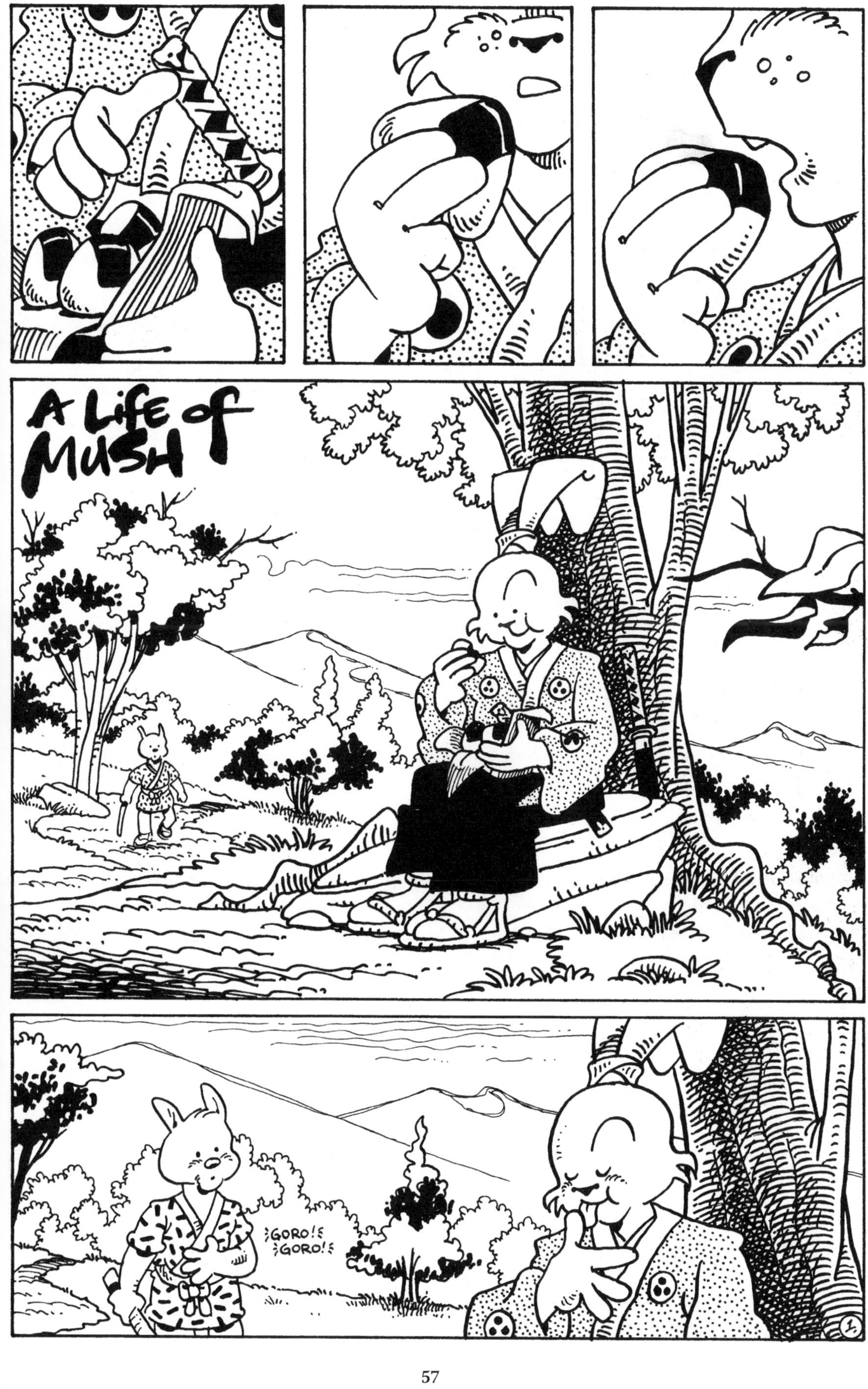
A Life of MUSH
GORO! GORO!
1.

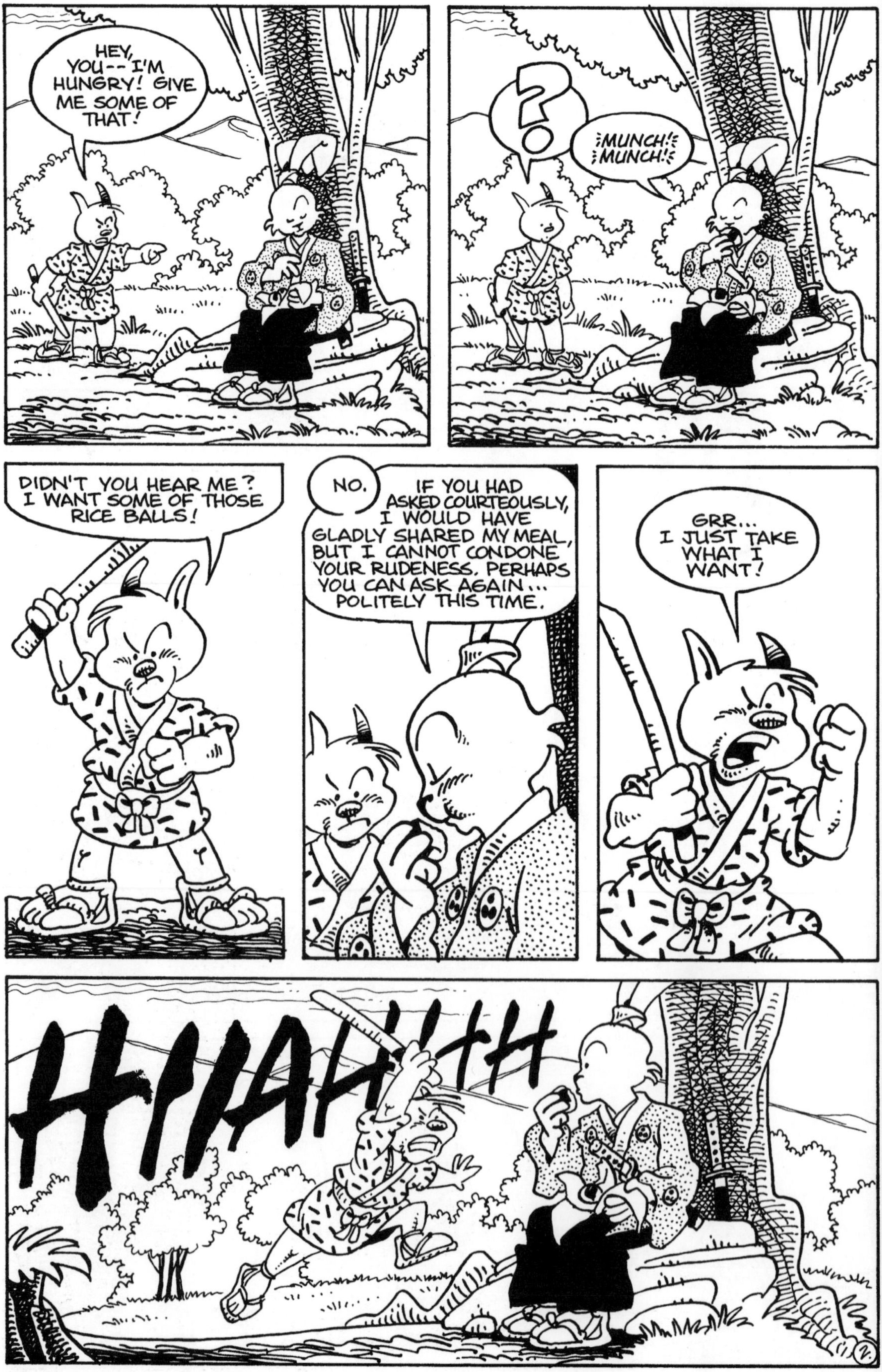
HEY, YOU-- I'M HUNGRY! GIVE ME SOME OF THAT!
?
!MUNCH! !MUNCH!
DIDN'T YOU HEAR ME? I WANT SOME OF THOSE RICE BALLS!
NO.
IF YOU HAD ASKED COURTEOUSLY, I WOULD HAVE GLADLY SHARED MY MEAL, BUT I CANNOT CONDONE YOUR RUDENESS. PERHAPS YOU CAN ASK AGAIN... POLITELY THIS TIME.
GRR... I JUST TAKE WHAT I WANT!
HIIAHHH

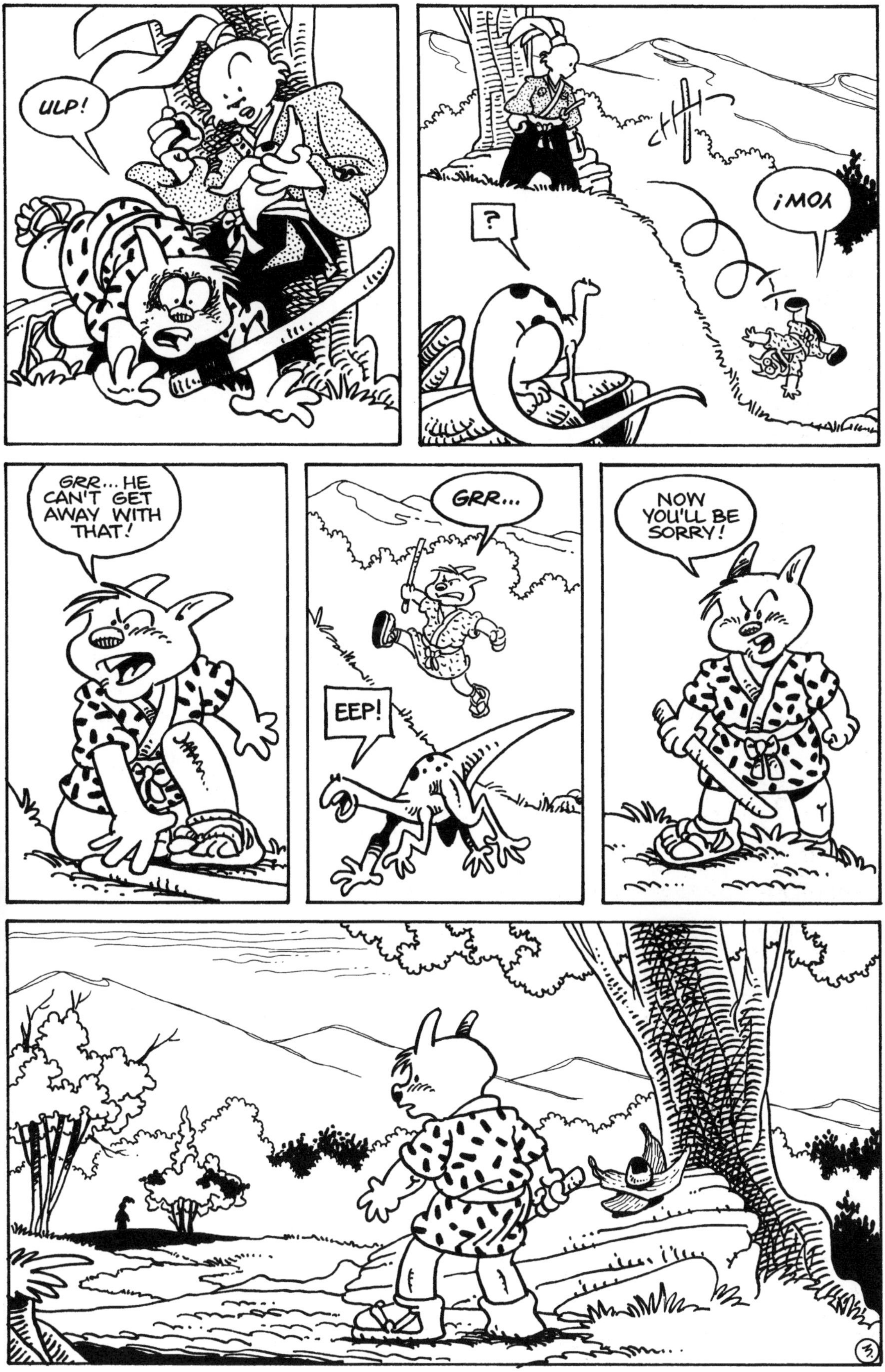
ULP!
?
YOW!
GRR... HE CAN'T GET AWAY WITH THAT!
GRR...
EEP!
NOW YOU'LL BE SORRY!

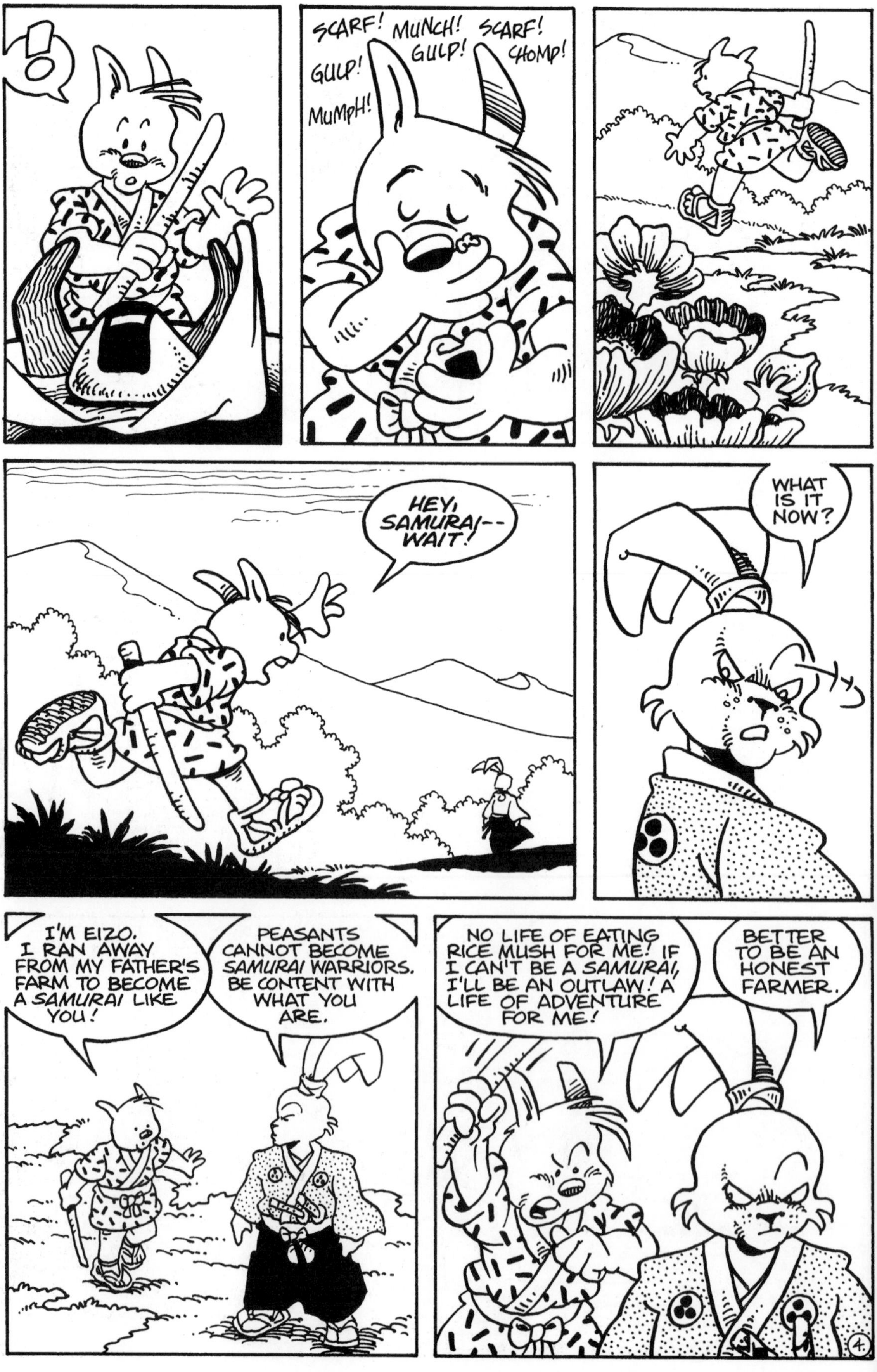
!
SCARF! MUNCH! SCARF!
GULP! GULP! CHOMP!
MUMPH!
HEY, SAMURAI-- WAIT!
WHAT IS IT NOW?
I'M EIZO. I RAN AWAY FROM MY FATHER'S FARM TO BECOME A *SAMURAI* LIKE YOU!
PEASANTS CANNOT BECOME *SAMURAI* WARRIORS. BE CONTENT WITH WHAT YOU ARE.
NO LIFE OF EATING RICE MUSH FOR ME! IF I CAN'T BE A *SAMURAI*, I'LL BE AN OUTLAW! A LIFE OF ADVENTURE FOR ME!
BETTER TO BE AN HONEST FARMER.
4.

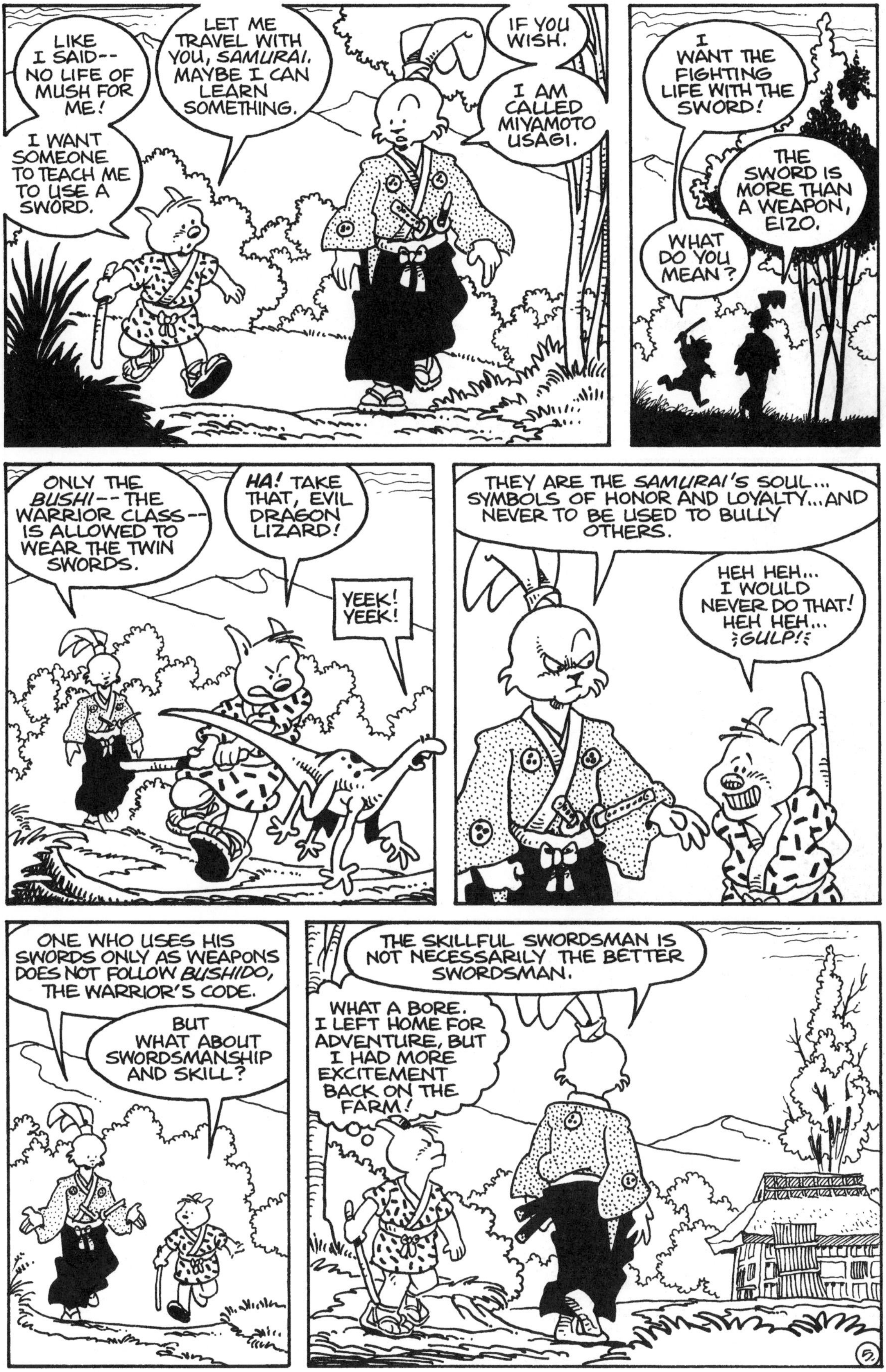
LIKE I SAID-- NO LIFE OF MUSH FOR ME!
I WANT SOMEONE TO TEACH ME TO USE A SWORD.
LET ME TRAVEL WITH YOU, *SAMURAI*. MAYBE I CAN LEARN SOMETHING.
IF YOU WISH.
I AM CALLED MIYAMOTO USAGI.
I WANT THE FIGHTING LIFE WITH THE SWORD!
THE SWORD IS MORE THAN A WEAPON, EIZO.
WHAT DO YOU MEAN?
ONLY THE *BUSHI*-- THE WARRIOR CLASS-- IS ALLOWED TO WEAR THE TWIN SWORDS.
HA! TAKE THAT, EVIL DRAGON LIZARD!
YEEK! YEEK!
THEY ARE THE *SAMURAI*'S SOUL... SYMBOLS OF HONOR AND LOYALTY... AND NEVER TO BE USED TO BULLY OTHERS.
HEH HEH... I WOULD NEVER DO THAT! HEH HEH... *GULP!*
ONE WHO USES HIS SWORDS ONLY AS WEAPONS DOES NOT FOLLOW *BUSHIDO*, THE WARRIOR'S CODE.
BUT WHAT ABOUT SWORDSMANSHIP AND SKILL?
THE SKILLFUL SWORDSMAN IS NOT NECESSARILY THE BETTER SWORDSMAN.
WHAT A BORE. I LEFT HOME FOR ADVENTURE, BUT I HAD MORE EXCITEMENT BACK ON THE FARM!
5

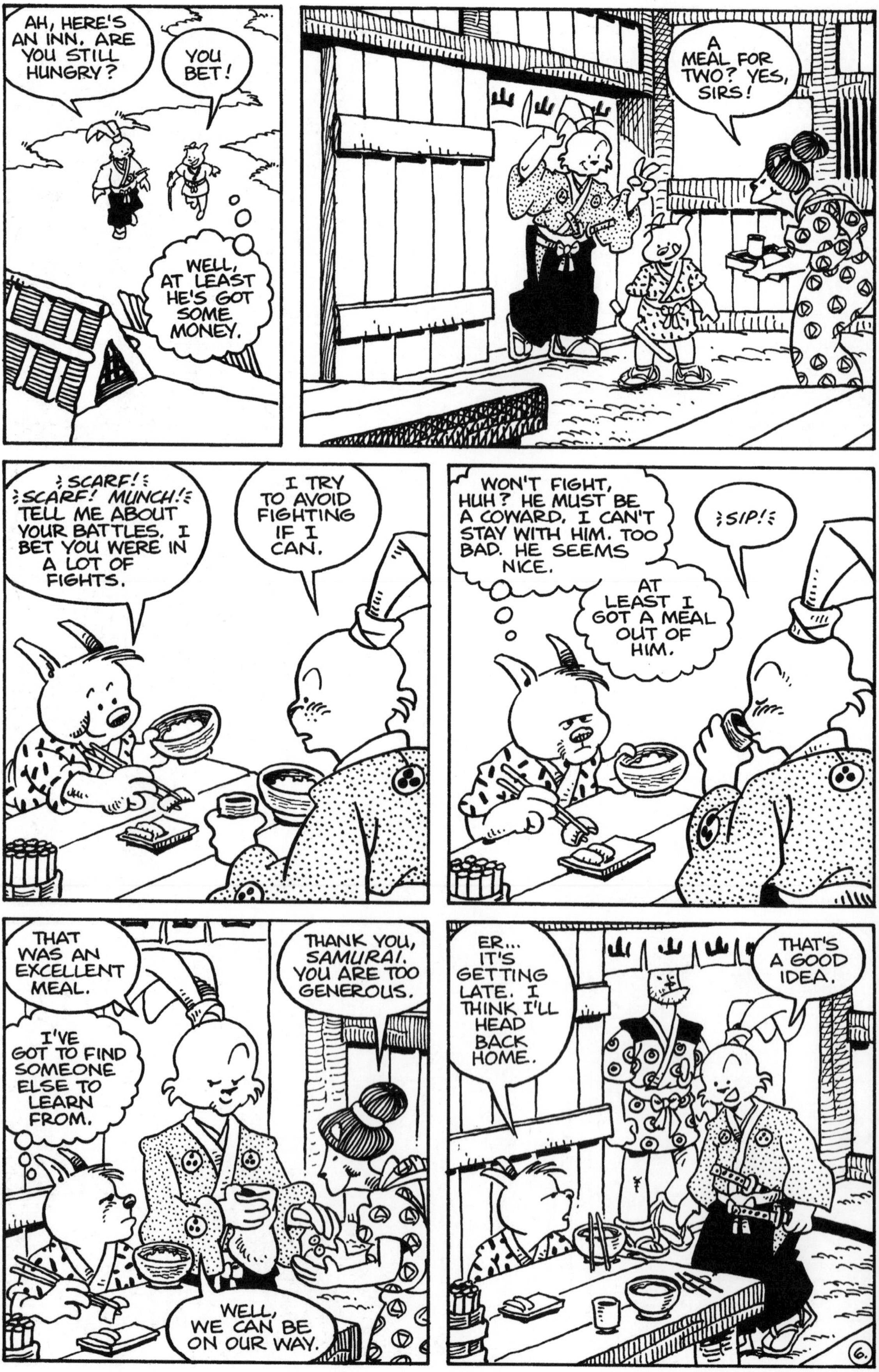
AH, HERE'S AN INN. ARE YOU STILL HUNGRY?
YOU BET!
WELL, AT LEAST HE'S GOT SOME MONEY.
A MEAL FOR TWO? YES, SIRS!
SCARF! SCARF! MUNCH! TELL ME ABOUT YOUR BATTLES. I BET YOU WERE IN A LOT OF FIGHTS.
I TRY TO AVOID FIGHTING IF I CAN.
WON'T FIGHT, HUH? HE MUST BE A COWARD. I CAN'T STAY WITH HIM. TOO BAD. HE SEEMS NICE.
AT LEAST I GOT A MEAL OUT OF HIM.
SIP!
THAT WAS AN EXCELLENT MEAL.
I'VE GOT TO FIND SOMEONE ELSE TO LEARN FROM.
THANK YOU, SAMURAI. YOU ARE TOO GENEROUS.
WELL, WE CAN BE ON OUR WAY.
ER... IT'S GETTING LATE. I THINK I'LL HEAD BACK HOME.
THAT'S A GOOD IDEA.
6.

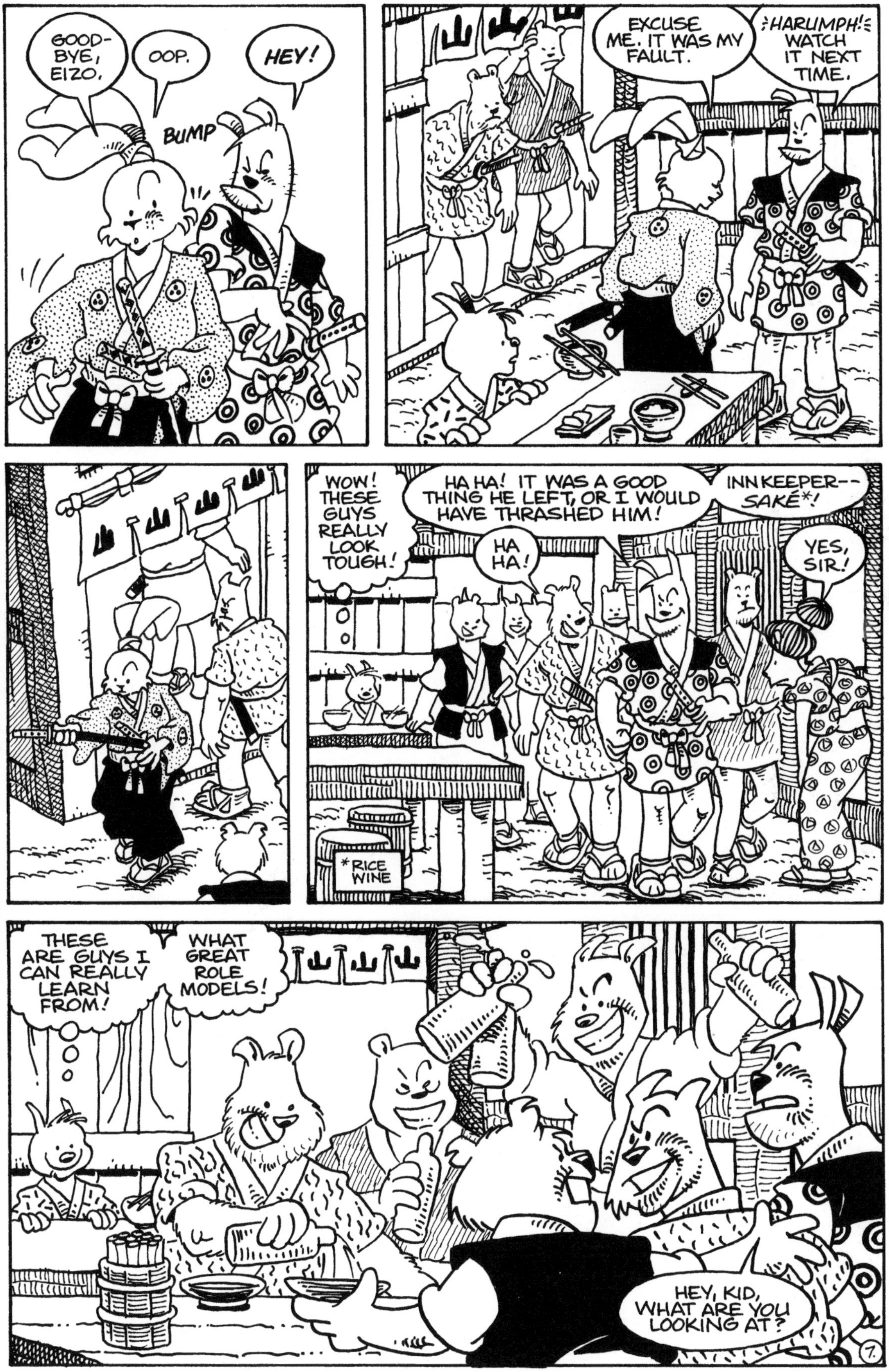
GOOD-BYE, EIZO.
OOP.
HEY!
BUMP
EXCUSE ME. IT WAS MY FAULT.
HARUMPH! WATCH IT NEXT TIME.
WOW! THESE GUYS REALLY LOOK TOUGH!
HA HA! IT WAS A GOOD THING HE LEFT, OR I WOULD HAVE THRASHED HIM!
HA HA!
INNKEEPER-- SAKÉ*!
YES, SIR!
*RICE WINE
THESE ARE GUYS I CAN REALLY LEARN FROM!
WHAT GREAT ROLE MODELS!
HEY, KID, WHAT ARE YOU LOOKING AT?
7.

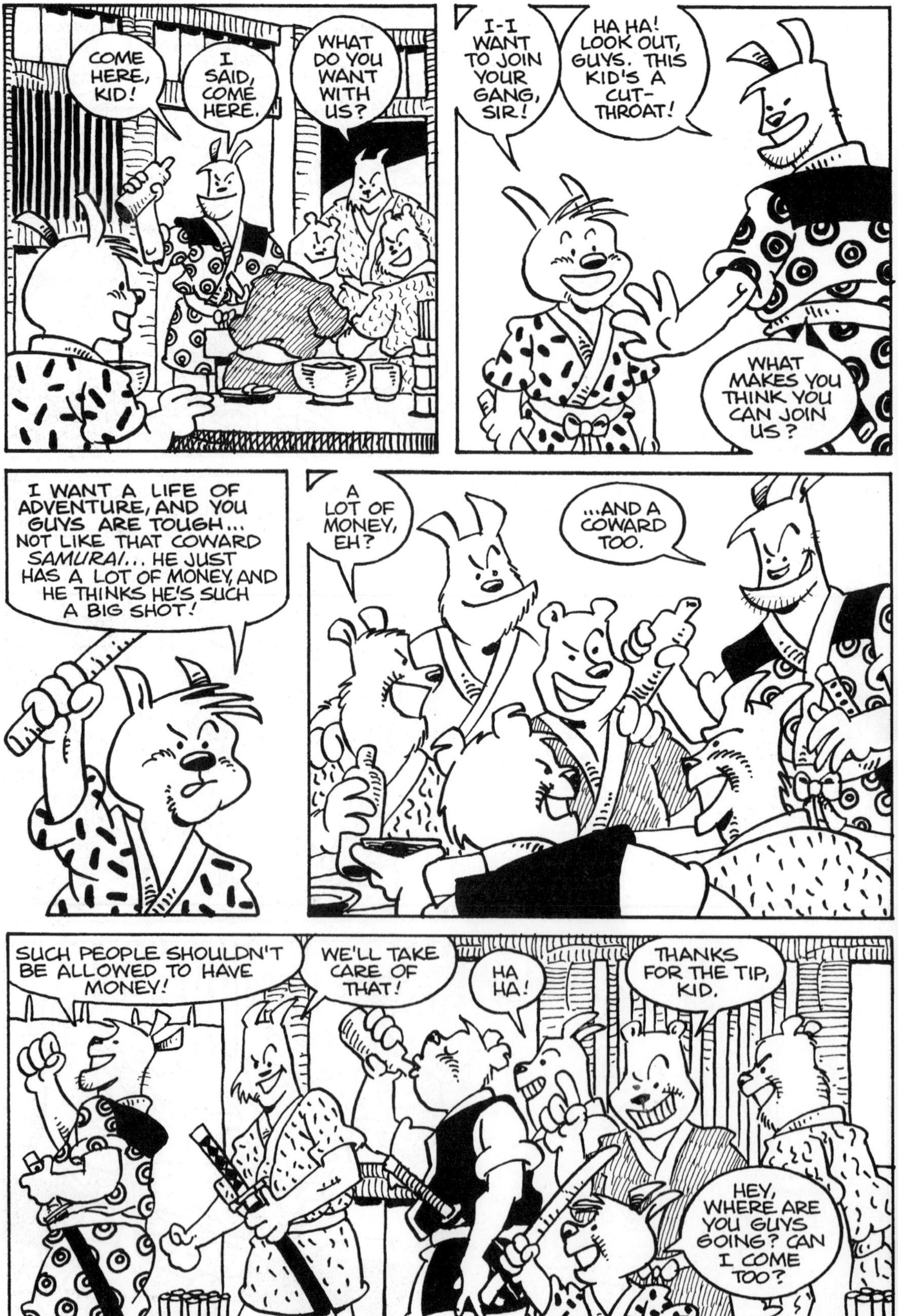
COME HERE, KID!
I SAID, COME HERE.
WHAT DO YOU WANT WITH US?
I-I WANT TO JOIN YOUR GANG, SIR!
HA HA! LOOK OUT, GUYS. THIS KID'S A CUT-THROAT!
WHAT MAKES YOU THINK YOU CAN JOIN US?
I WANT A LIFE OF ADVENTURE, AND YOU GUYS ARE TOUGH... NOT LIKE THAT COWARD *SAMURAI*... HE JUST HAS A LOT OF MONEY, AND HE THINKS HE'S SUCH A BIG SHOT!
A LOT OF MONEY, EH?
...AND A COWARD TOO.
SUCH PEOPLE SHOULDN'T BE ALLOWED TO HAVE MONEY!
WE'LL TAKE CARE OF THAT!
HA HA!
THANKS FOR THE TIP, KID.
HEY, WHERE ARE YOU GUYS GOING? CAN I COME TOO?
8.

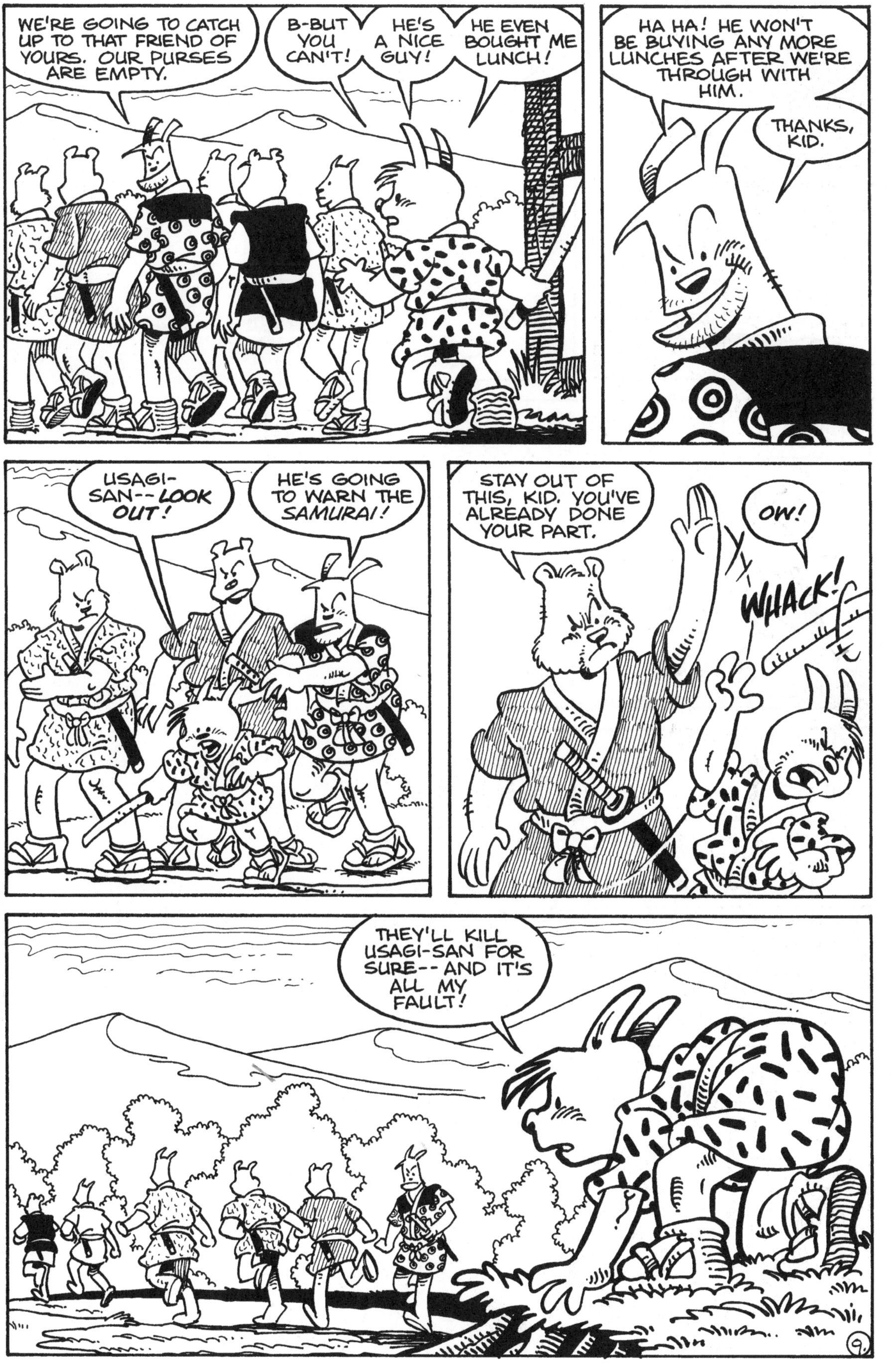
WE'RE GOING TO CATCH UP TO THAT FRIEND OF YOURS. OUR PURSES ARE EMPTY.
B-BUT YOU CAN'T!
HE'S A NICE GUY!
HE EVEN BOUGHT ME LUNCH!
HA HA! HE WON'T BE BUYING ANY MORE LUNCHES AFTER WE'RE THROUGH WITH HIM.
THANKS, KID.
USAGI-SAN--LOOK OUT!
HE'S GOING TO WARN THE SAMURAI!
STAY OUT OF THIS, KID. YOU'VE ALREADY DONE YOUR PART.
OW!
WHACK!
THEY'LL KILL USAGI-SAN FOR SURE--AND IT'S ALL MY FAULT!
9

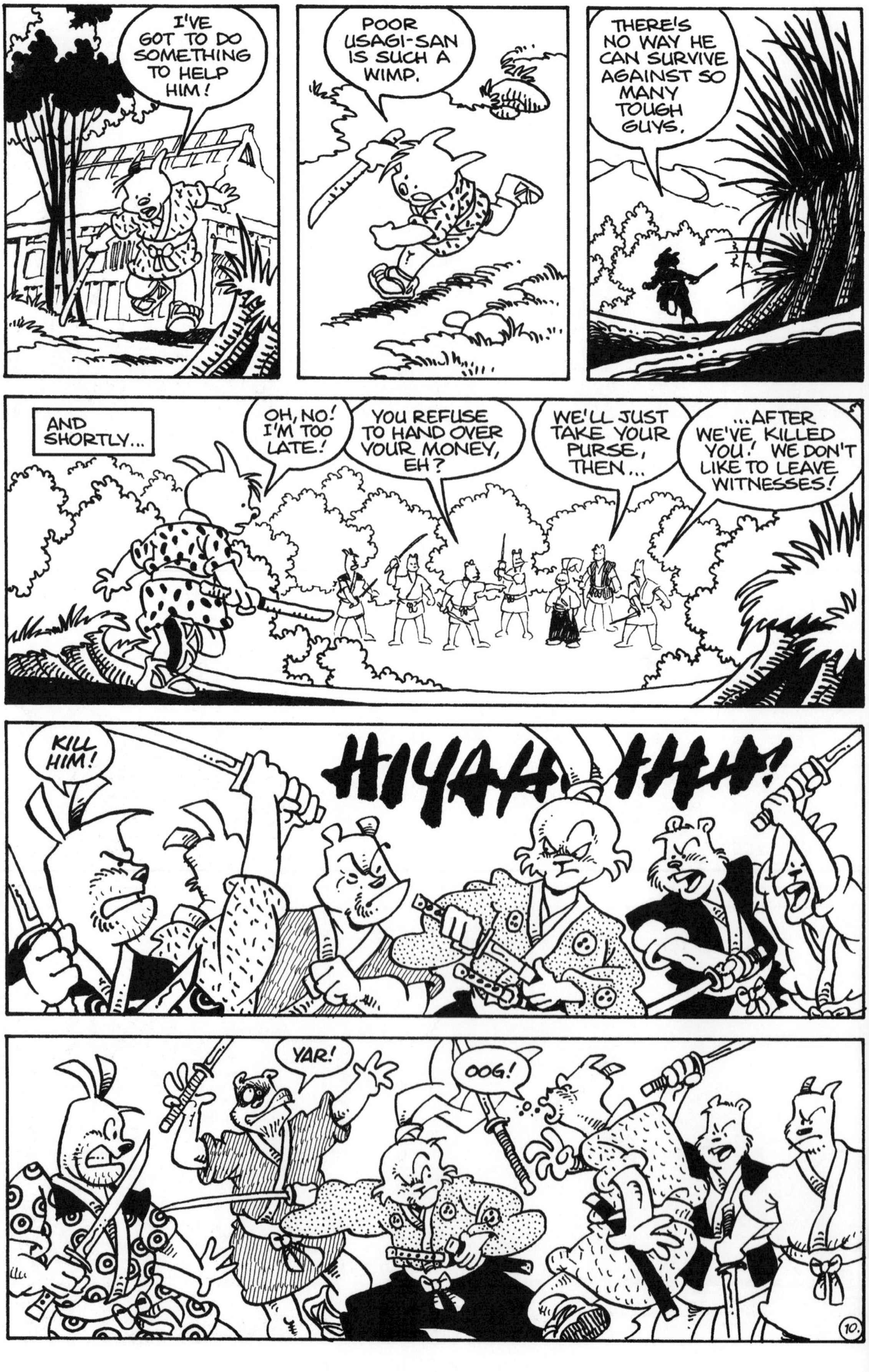
I'VE GOT TO DO SOMETHING TO HELP HIM!
POOR USAGI-SAN IS SUCH A WIMP.
THERE'S NO WAY HE CAN SURVIVE AGAINST SO MANY TOUGH GUYS.
AND SHORTLY...
OH, NO! I'M TOO LATE!
YOU REFUSE TO HAND OVER YOUR MONEY, EH?
WE'LL JUST TAKE YOUR PURSE, THEN...
...AFTER WE'VE KILLED YOU! WE DON'T LIKE TO LEAVE WITNESSES!
KILL HIM!
HIYAAAAAH!
YAR!
OOG!
10.

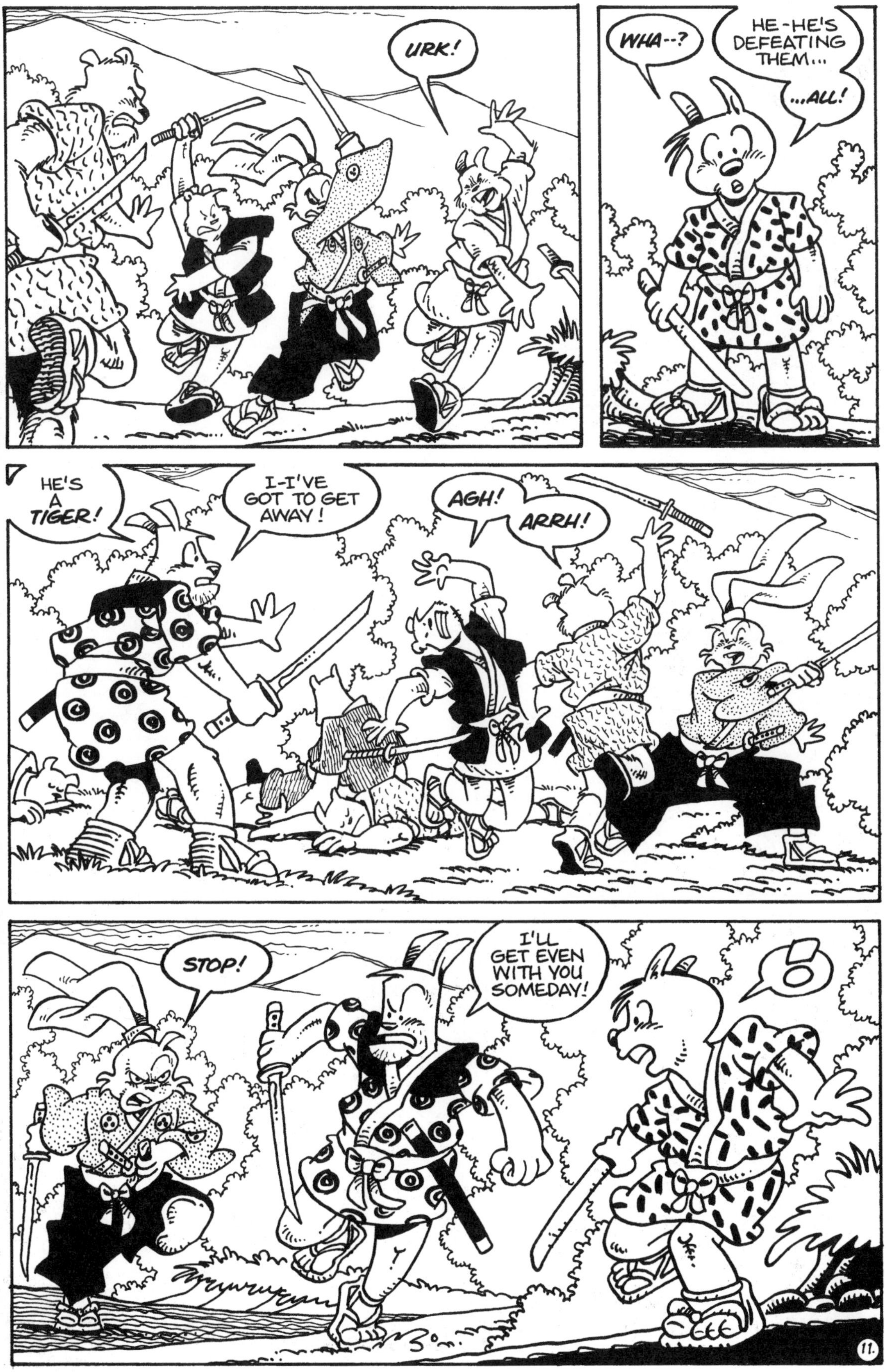
URK!
WHA--?
HE-HE'S DEFEATING THEM...
...ALL!
HE'S A TIGER!
I-I'VE GOT TO GET AWAY!
AGH!
ARRH!
STOP!
I'LL GET EVEN WITH YOU SOMEDAY!
11.

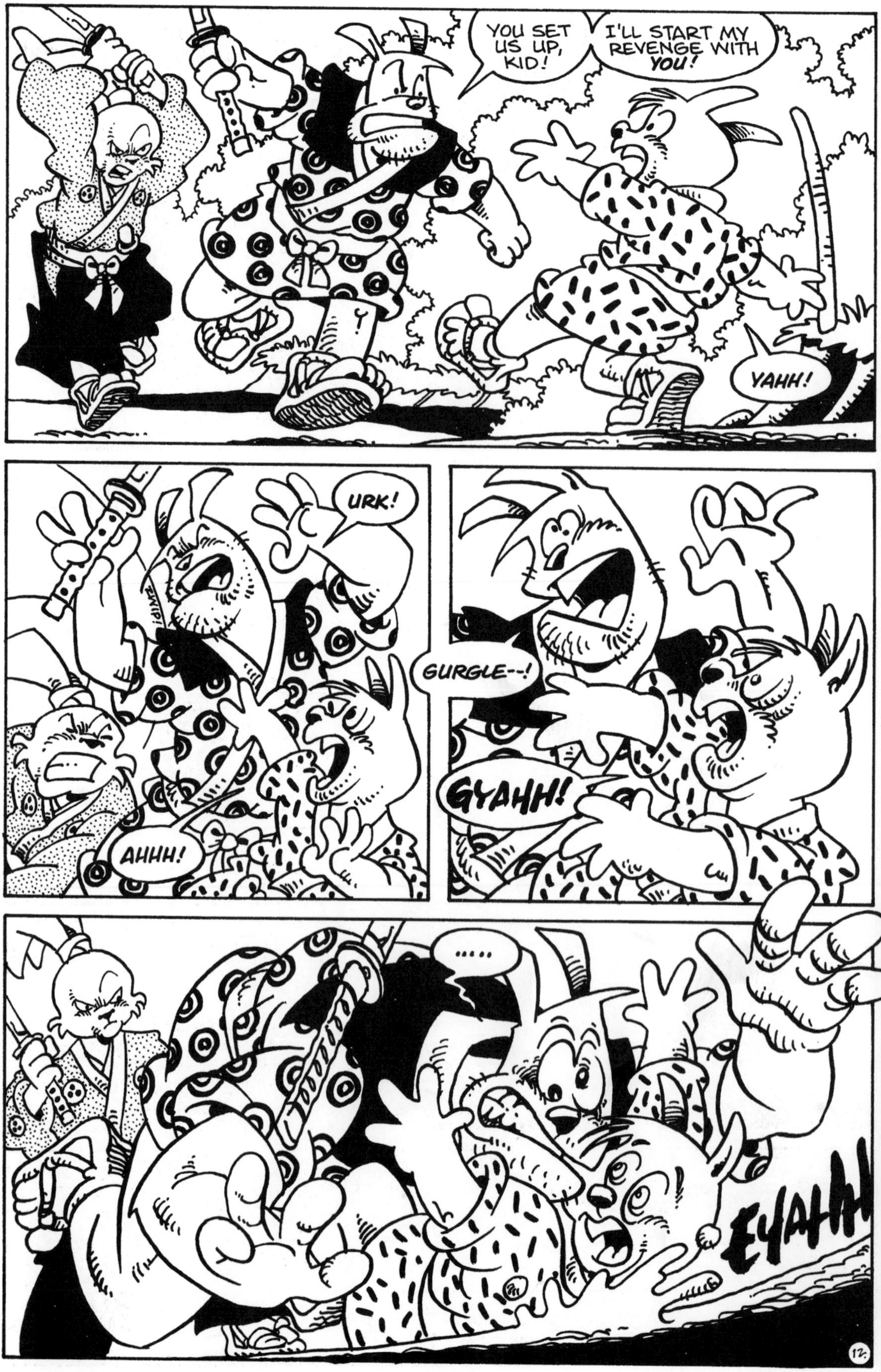

YOU SET US UP, KID!
I'LL START MY REVENGE WITH YOU!
YAHH!
ZWIP!
URK!
AHHH!
GURGLE--!
GYAHH!
.....
EYAHH
12.

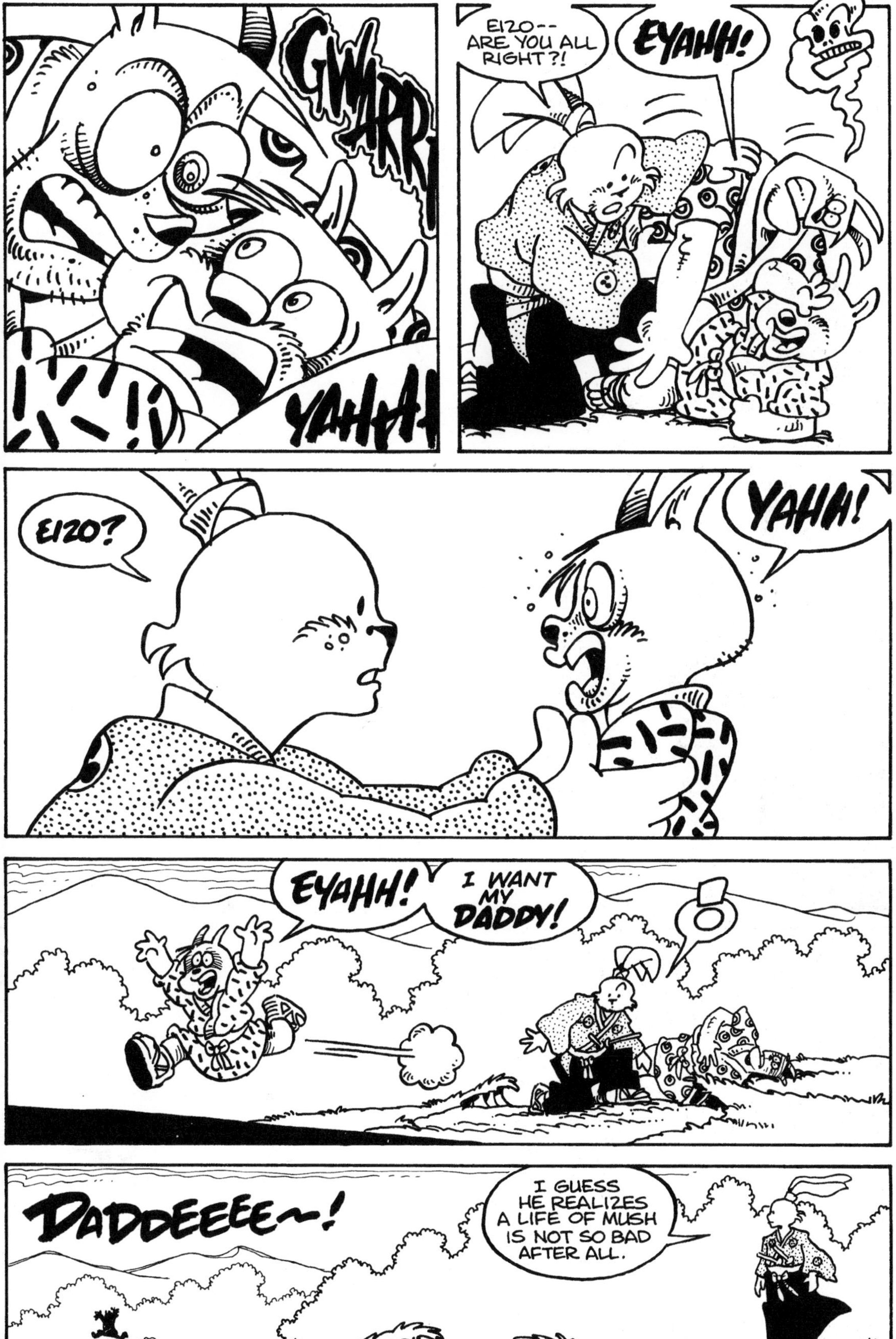
GWARR!
YAHHH
EIZO-- ARE YOU ALL RIGHT?!
EYAHH!
EIZO?
YAHH!
EYAHH!
I WANT MY DADDY!
DADDEEEE~!
I GUESS HE REALIZES A LIFE OF MUSH IS NOT SO BAD AFTER ALL.
THE END

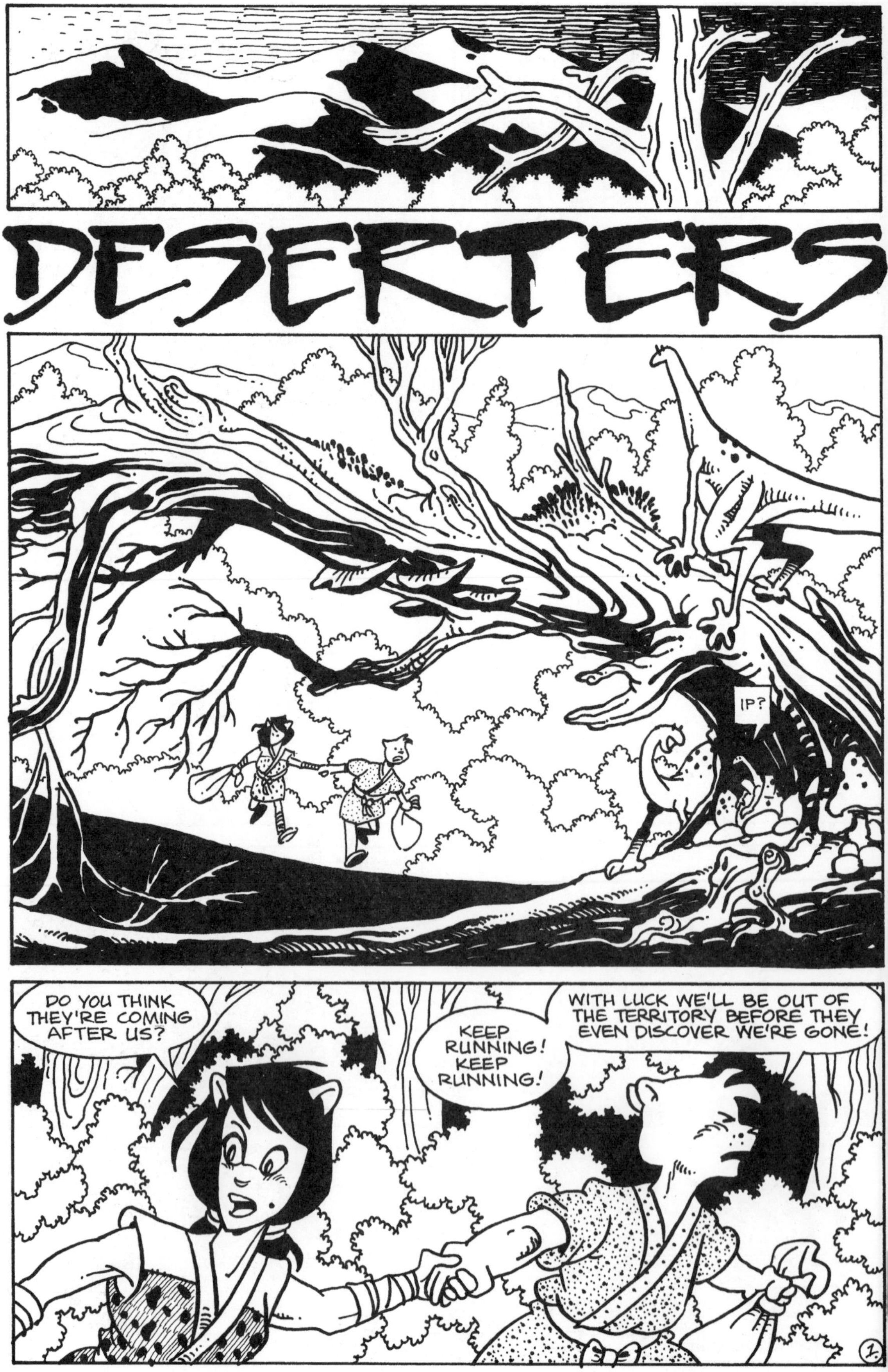
DESERTERS
IP?
DO YOU THINK THEY'RE COMING AFTER US?
KEEP RUNNING! KEEP RUNNING!
WITH LUCK WE'LL BE OUT OF THE TERRITORY BEFORE THEY EVEN DISCOVER WE'RE GONE!

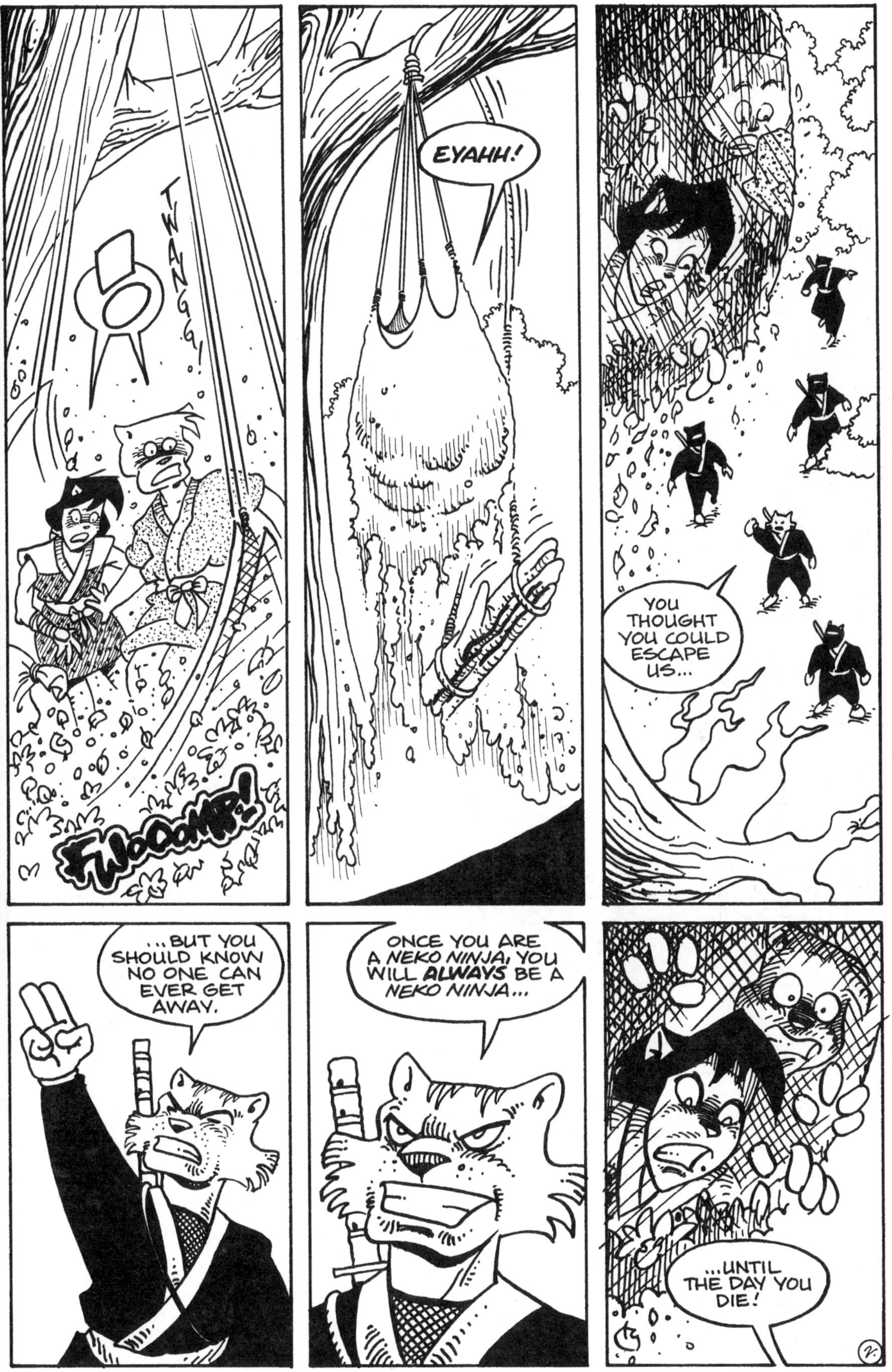
TWANGG!
FWOOOMP!
EYAHH!
YOU THOUGHT YOU COULD ESCAPE US...
...BUT YOU SHOULD KNOW NO ONE CAN EVER GET AWAY.
ONCE YOU ARE A *NEKO NINJA*, YOU WILL **ALWAYS** BE A *NEKO NINJA*...
...UNTIL THE DAY YOU DIE!

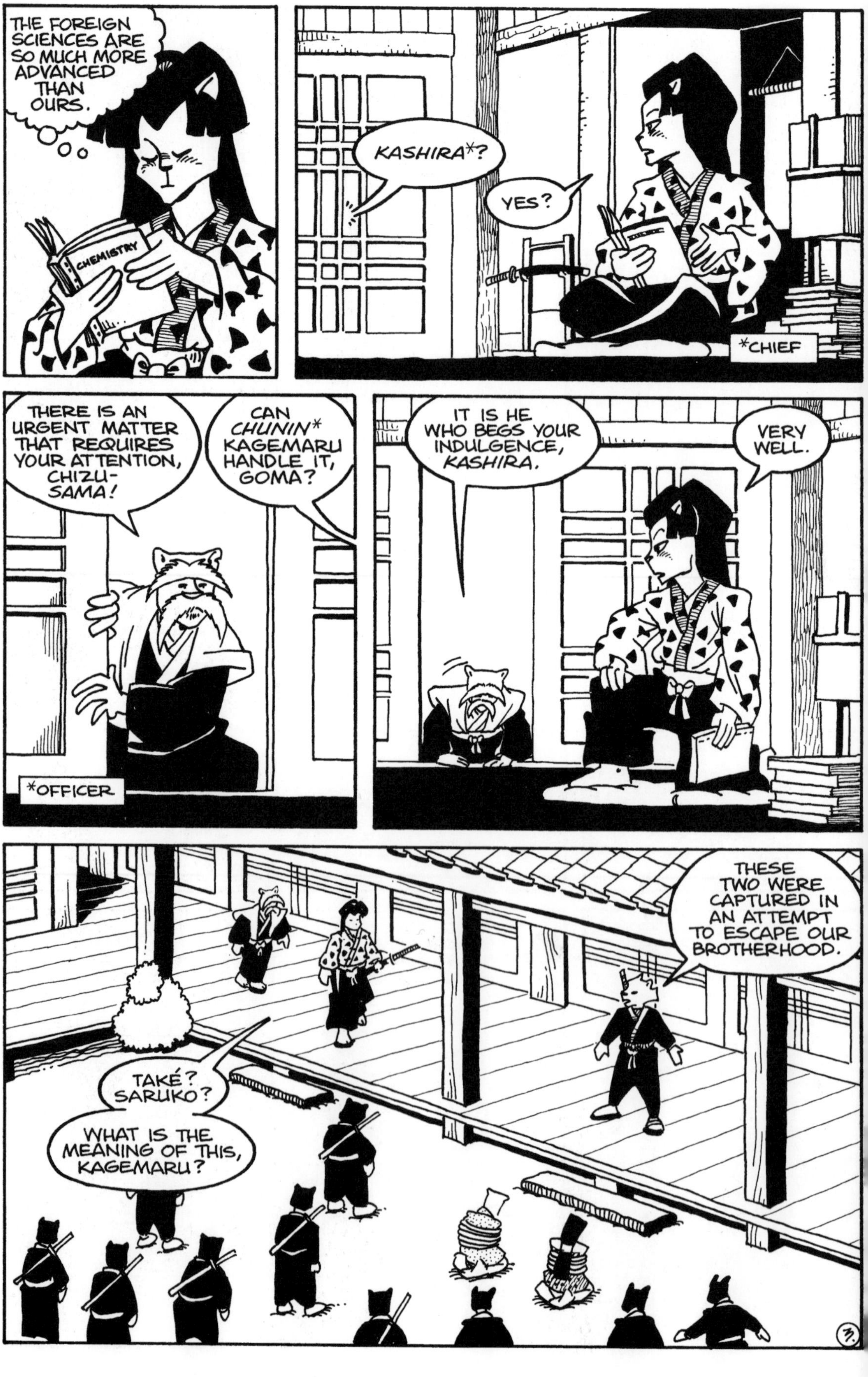
THE FOREIGN SCIENCES ARE SO MUCH MORE ADVANCED THAN OURS.
CHEMISTRY
KASHIRA*?
YES?
*CHIEF
THERE IS AN URGENT MATTER THAT REQUIRES YOUR ATTENTION, CHIZU-SAMA!
CAN CHUNIN* KAGEMARU HANDLE IT, GOMA?
*OFFICER
IT IS HE WHO BEGS YOUR INDULGENCE, KASHIRA.
VERY WELL.
THESE TWO WERE CAPTURED IN AN ATTEMPT TO ESCAPE OUR BROTHERHOOD.
TAKÉ? SARUKO?
WHAT IS THE MEANING OF THIS, KAGEMARU?

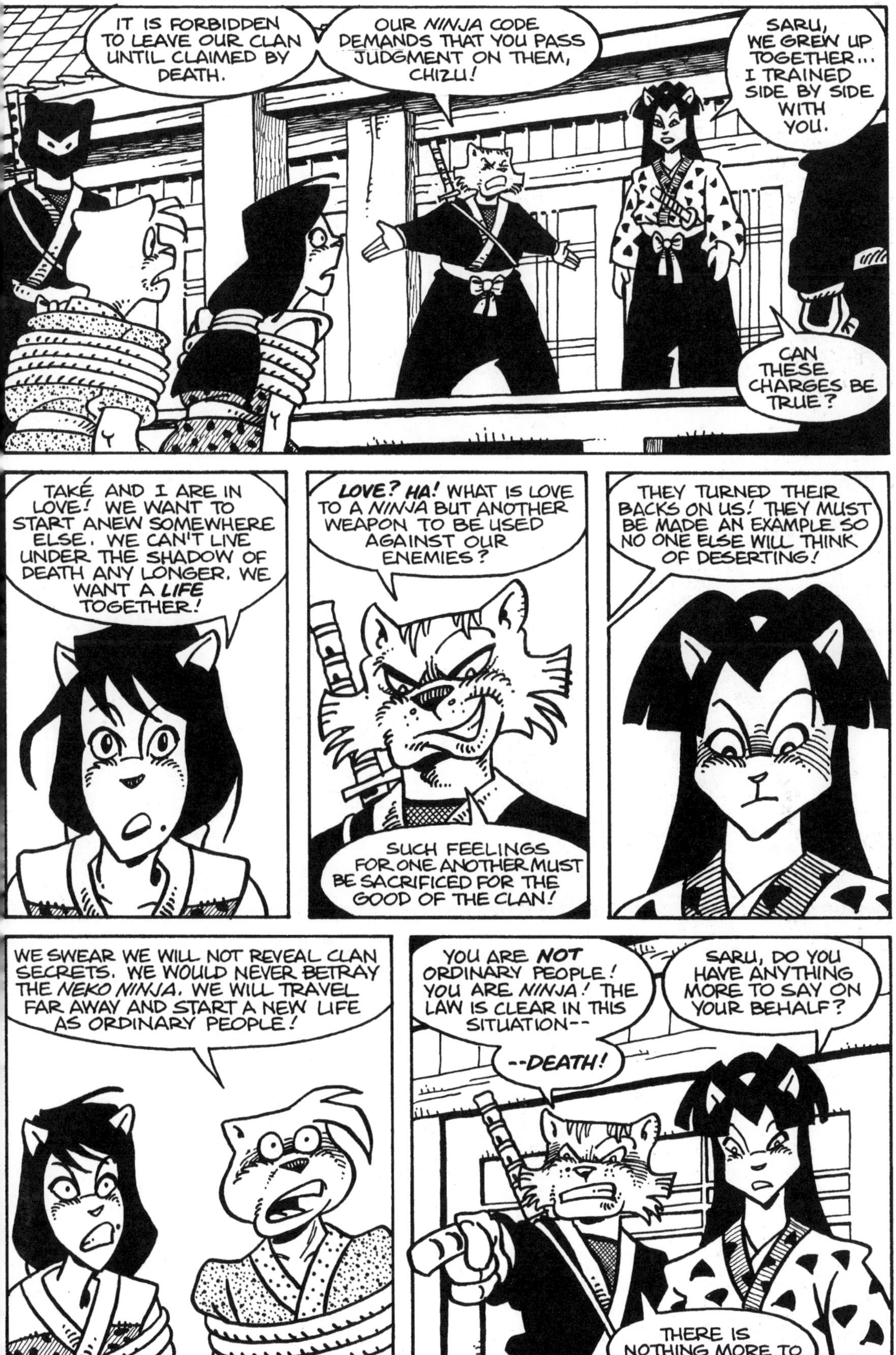
IT IS FORBIDDEN TO LEAVE OUR CLAN UNTIL CLAIMED BY DEATH.
OUR *NINJA* CODE DEMANDS THAT YOU PASS JUDGMENT ON THEM, CHIZU!
SARU, WE GREW UP TOGETHER... I TRAINED SIDE BY SIDE WITH YOU.
CAN THESE CHARGES BE TRUE?
TAKÉ AND I ARE IN LOVE! WE WANT TO START ANEW SOMEWHERE ELSE. WE CAN'T LIVE UNDER THE SHADOW OF DEATH ANY LONGER. WE WANT A ***LIFE*** TOGETHER!
LOVE? HA! WHAT IS LOVE TO A *NINJA* BUT ANOTHER WEAPON TO BE USED AGAINST OUR ENEMIES?
SUCH FEELINGS FOR ONE ANOTHER MUST BE SACRIFICED FOR THE GOOD OF THE CLAN!
THEY TURNED THEIR BACKS ON US! THEY MUST BE MADE AN EXAMPLE SO NO ONE ELSE WILL THINK OF DESERTING!
WE SWEAR WE WILL NOT REVEAL CLAN SECRETS. WE WOULD NEVER BETRAY THE *NEKO NINJA*. WE WILL TRAVEL FAR AWAY AND START A NEW LIFE AS ORDINARY PEOPLE!
YOU ARE ***NOT*** ORDINARY PEOPLE! YOU ARE *NINJA*! THE LAW IS CLEAR IN THIS SITUATION--
--***DEATH!***
SARU, DO YOU HAVE ANYTHING MORE TO SAY ON YOUR BEHALF?
THERE IS NOTHING MORE TO BE SAID!
4.

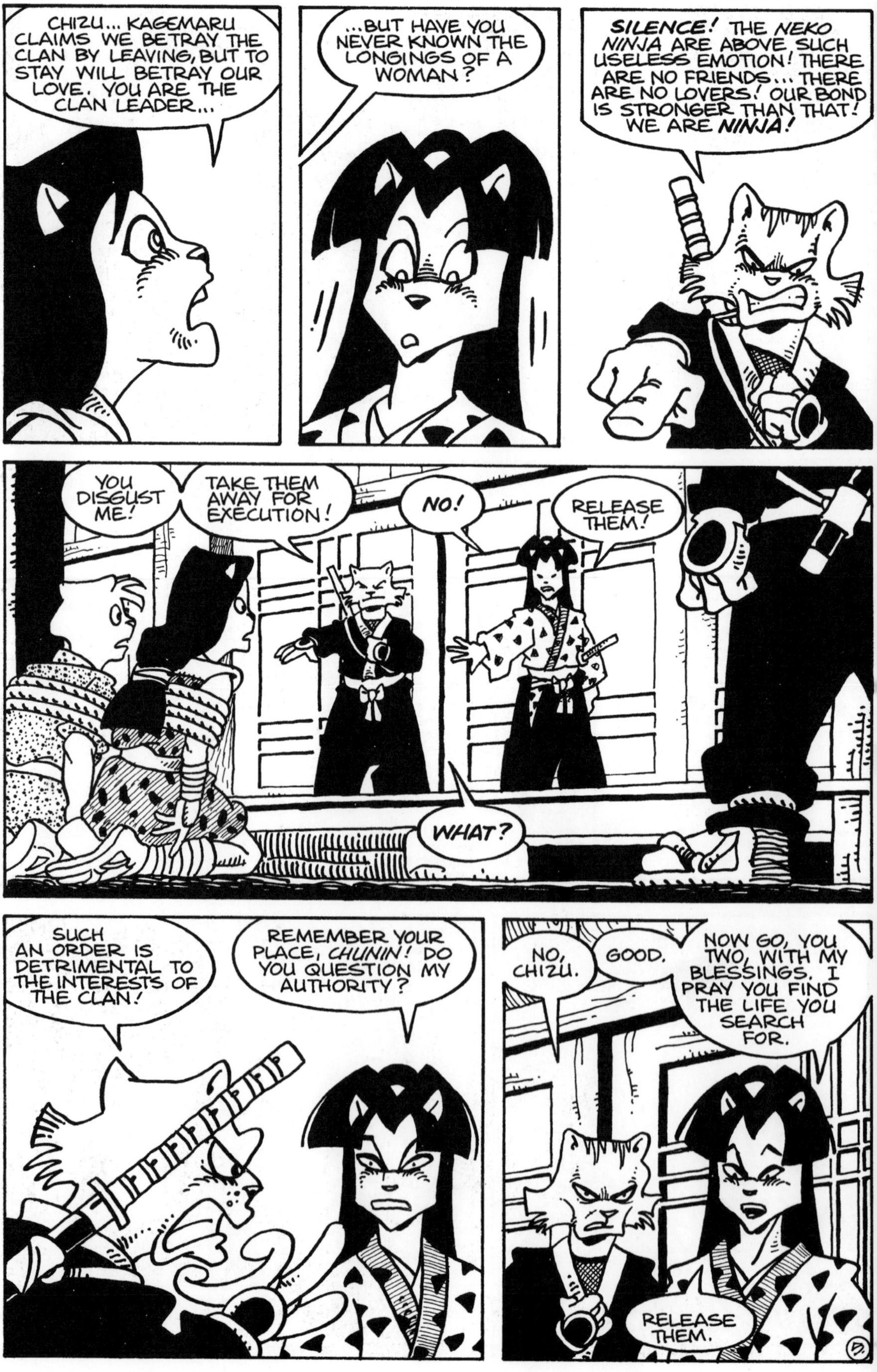
CHIZU... KAGEMARU CLAIMS WE BETRAY THE CLAN BY LEAVING, BUT TO STAY WILL BETRAY OUR LOVE. YOU ARE THE CLAN LEADER...
...BUT HAVE YOU NEVER KNOWN THE LONGINGS OF A WOMAN?
SILENCE! THE NEKO NINJA ARE ABOVE SUCH USELESS EMOTION! THERE ARE NO FRIENDS... THERE ARE NO LOVERS! OUR BOND IS STRONGER THAN THAT! WE ARE NINJA!
YOU DISGUST ME!
TAKE THEM AWAY FOR EXECUTION!
NO!
RELEASE THEM!
WHAT?
SUCH AN ORDER IS DETRIMENTAL TO THE INTERESTS OF THE CLAN!
REMEMBER YOUR PLACE, CHUNIN! DO YOU QUESTION MY AUTHORITY?
NO, CHIZU.
GOOD.
NOW GO, YOU TWO, WITH MY BLESSINGS. I PRAY YOU FIND THE LIFE YOU SEARCH FOR.
RELEASE THEM.

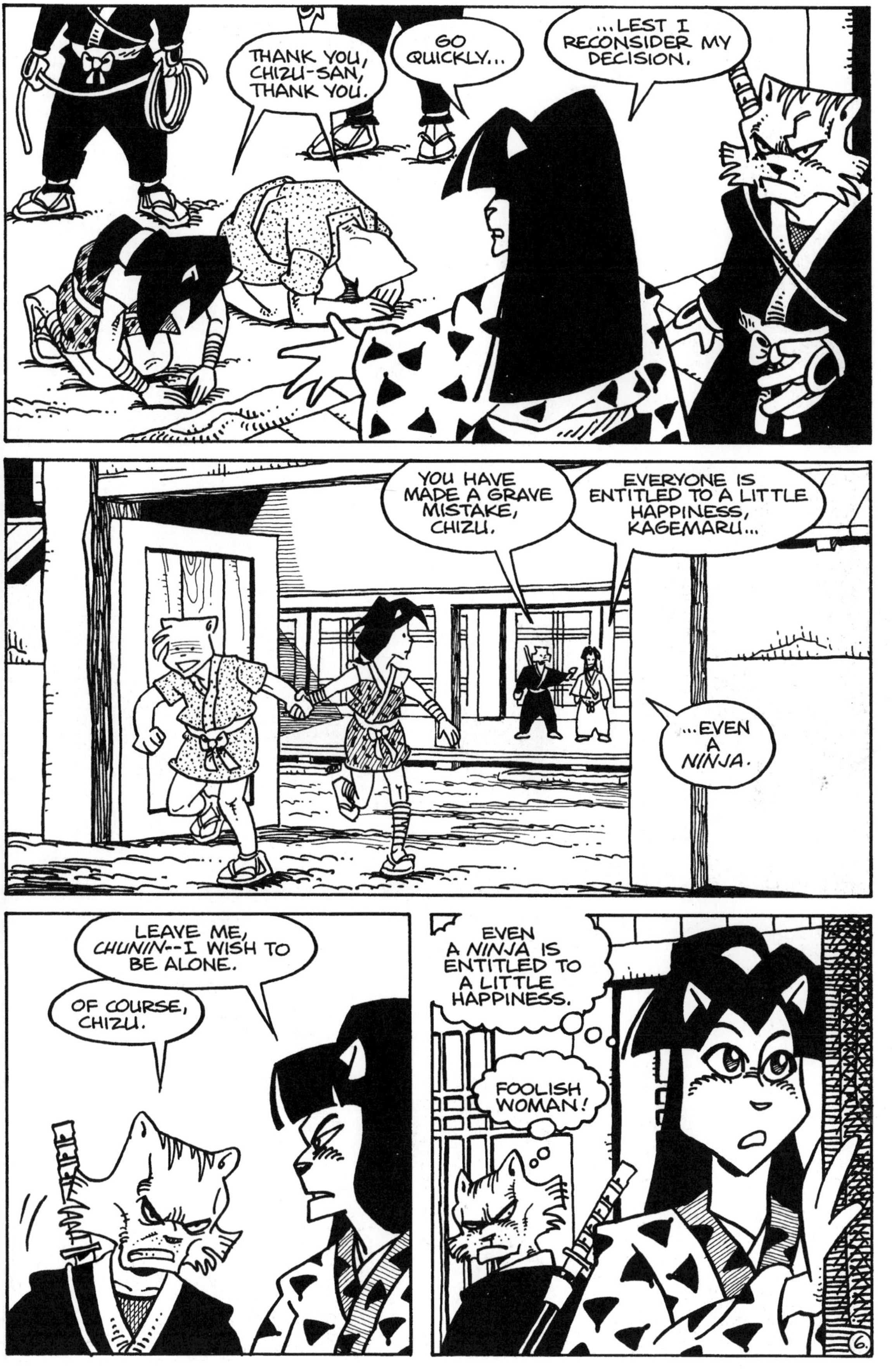
THANK YOU, CHIZU-SAN, THANK YOU.
GO QUICKLY...
...LEST I RECONSIDER MY DECISION.
YOU HAVE MADE A GRAVE MISTAKE, CHIZU.
EVERYONE IS ENTITLED TO A LITTLE HAPPINESS, KAGEMARU...
...EVEN A *NINJA*.
LEAVE ME, *CHUNIN*--I WISH TO BE ALONE.
OF COURSE, CHIZU.
EVEN A *NINJA* IS ENTITLED TO A LITTLE HAPPINESS.
FOOLISH WOMAN!
6.

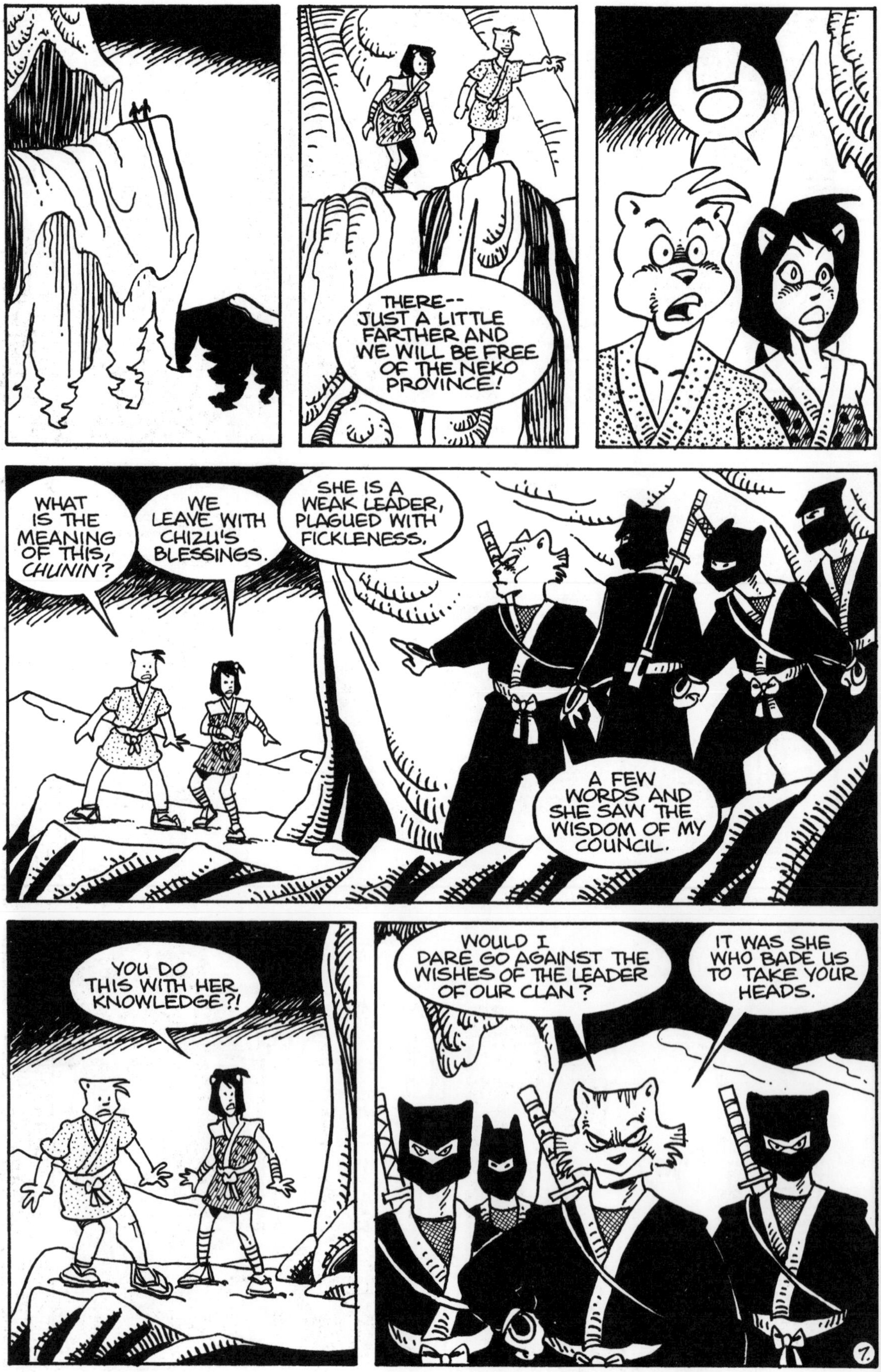
THERE-- JUST A LITTLE FARTHER AND WE WILL BE FREE OF THE NEKO PROVINCE!
!
WHAT IS THE MEANING OF THIS, CHUNIN?
WE LEAVE WITH CHIZU'S BLESSINGS.
SHE IS A WEAK LEADER, PLAGUED WITH FICKLENESS.
A FEW WORDS AND SHE SAW THE WISDOM OF MY COUNCIL.
YOU DO THIS WITH HER KNOWLEDGE?!
WOULD I DARE GO AGAINST THE WISHES OF THE LEADER OF OUR CLAN?
IT WAS SHE WHO BADE US TO TAKE YOUR HEADS.
7.

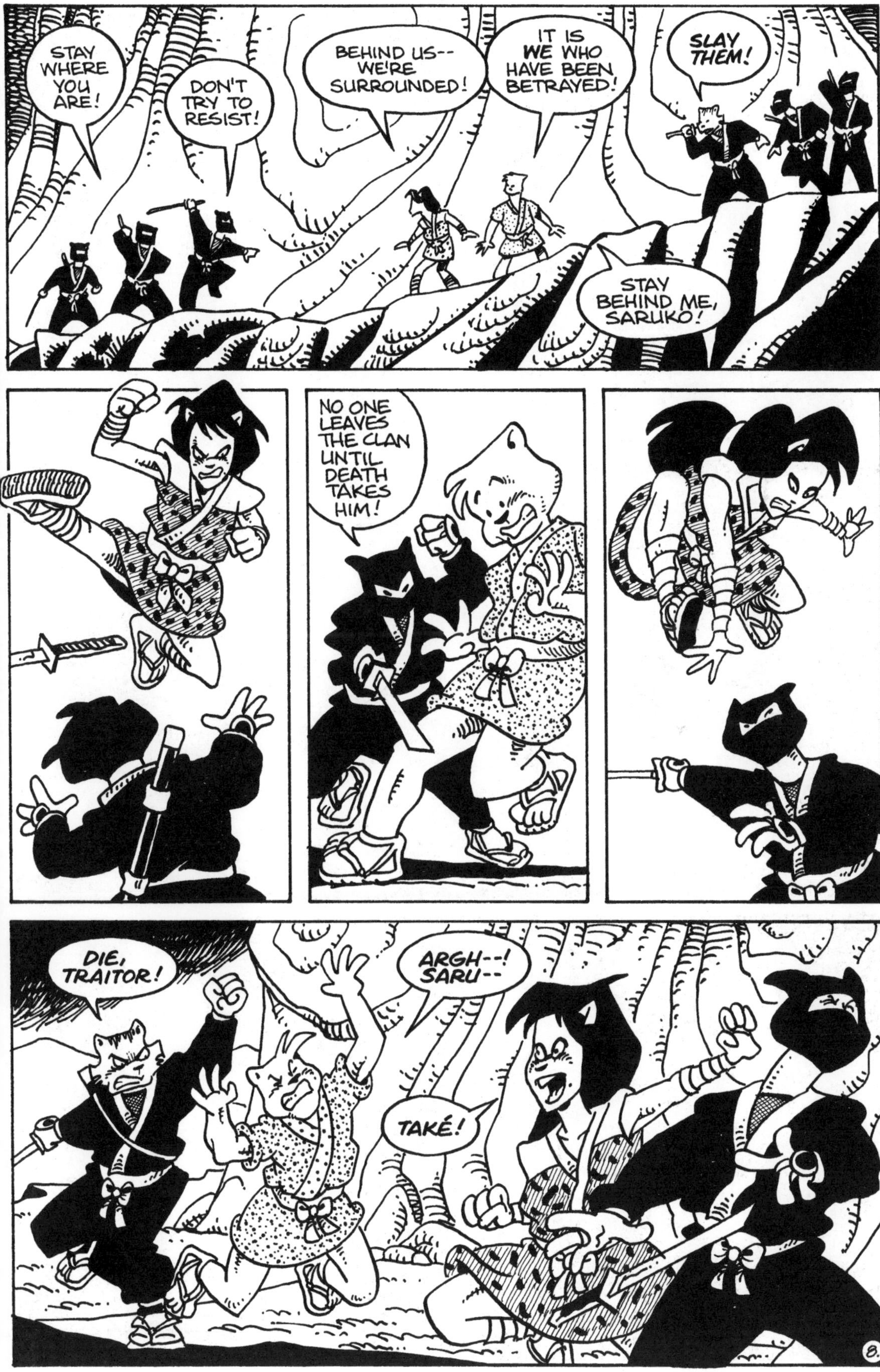
STAY WHERE YOU ARE!
DON'T TRY TO RESIST!
BEHIND US-- WE'RE SURROUNDED!
IT IS WE WHO HAVE BEEN BETRAYED!
SLAY THEM!
STAY BEHIND ME, SARUKO!
NO ONE LEAVES THE CLAN UNTIL DEATH TAKES HIM!
DIE, TRAITOR!
ARGH--! SARU--
TAKÉ!
8.

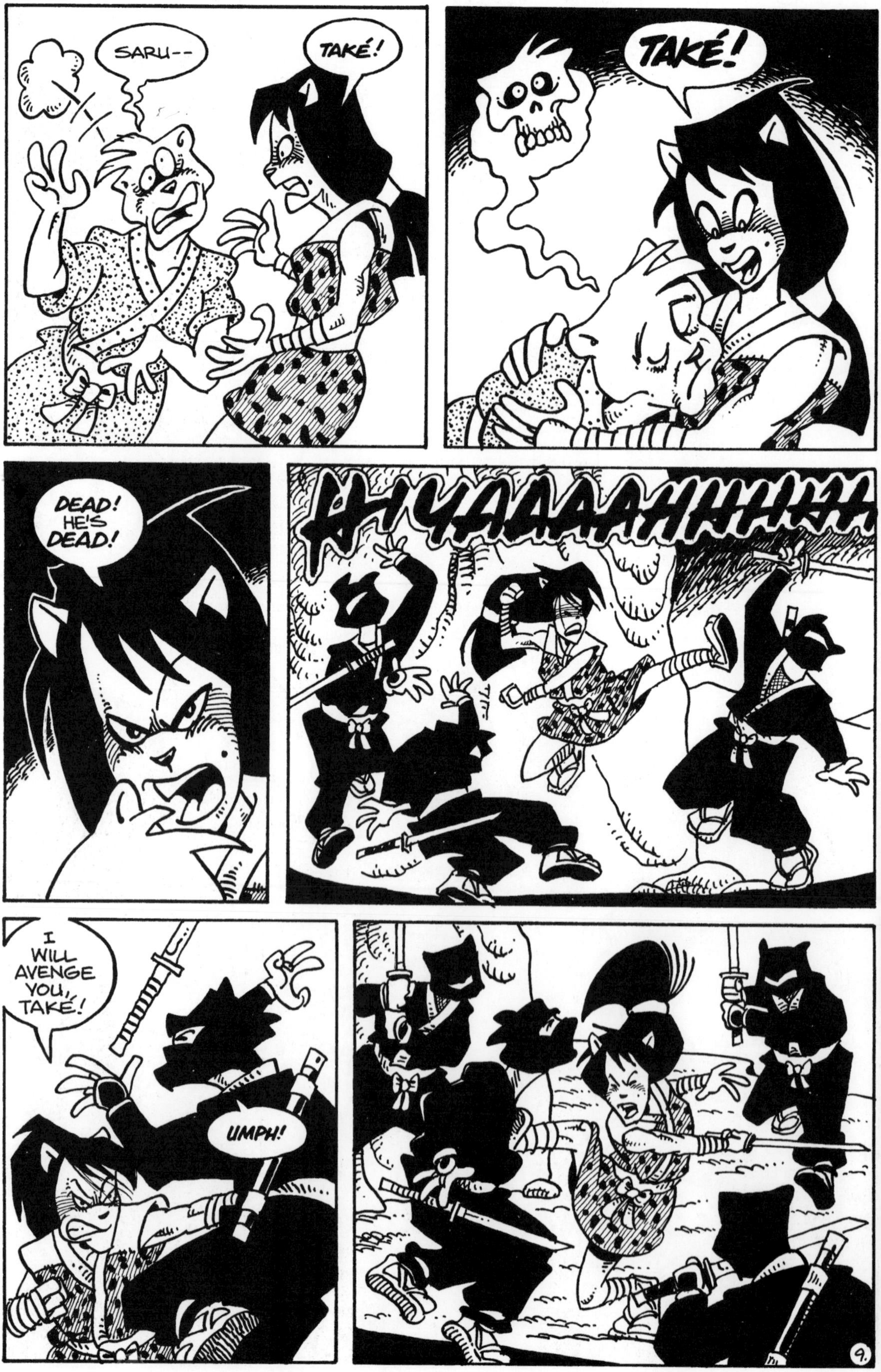
SARU--
TAKÉ!
TAKÉ!
DEAD! HE'S DEAD!
HIYAAAAAHHHHH
I WILL AVENGE YOU, TAKÉ!
UMPH!
9.

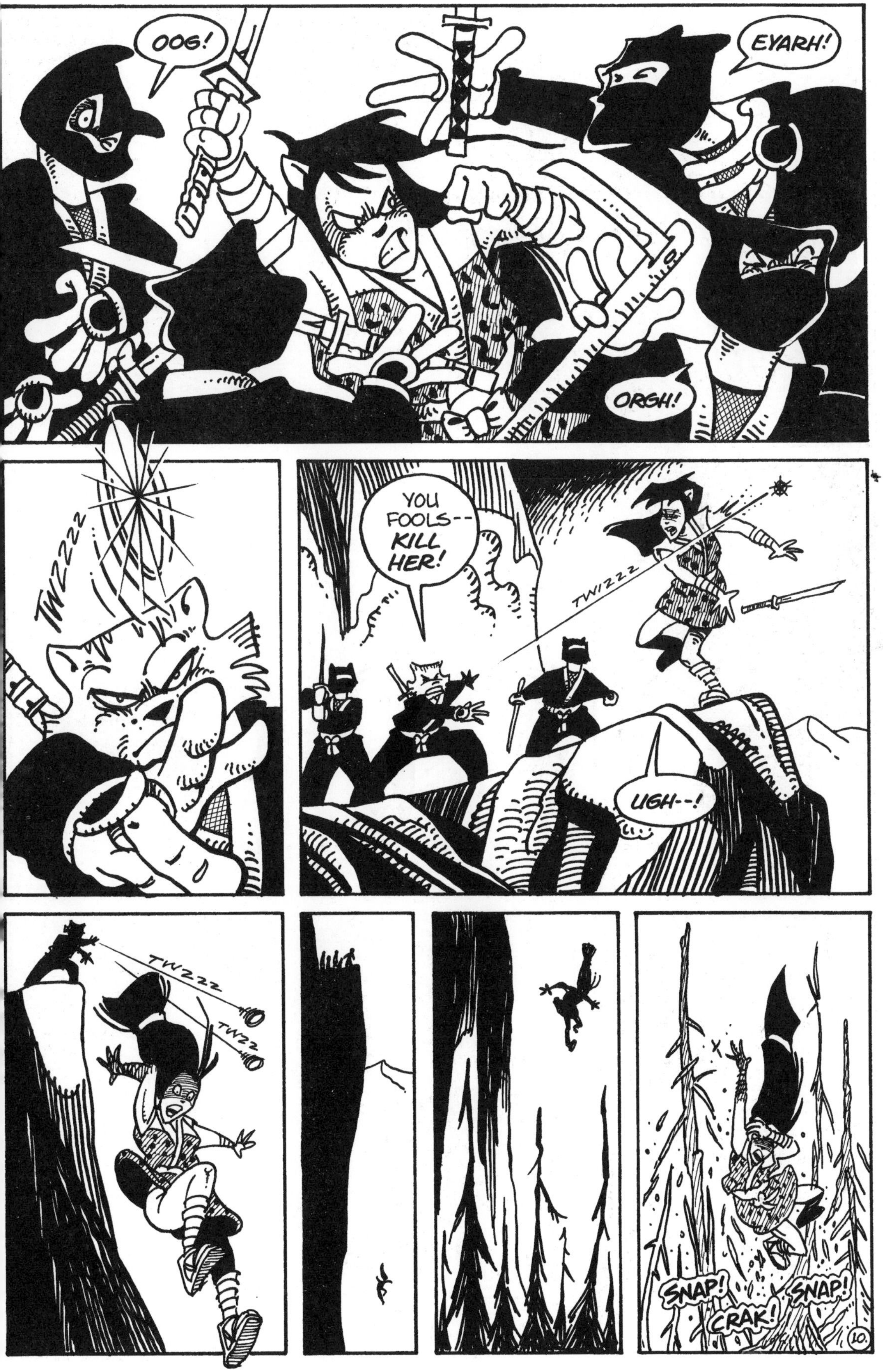

OOG!
EYARH!
ORGH!
TWZZZZZ
YOU FOOLS-- KILL HER!
TWIZZZ
UGH--!
TWZZZ
TWZZ
SNAP!
CRAK!
SNAP!
10.

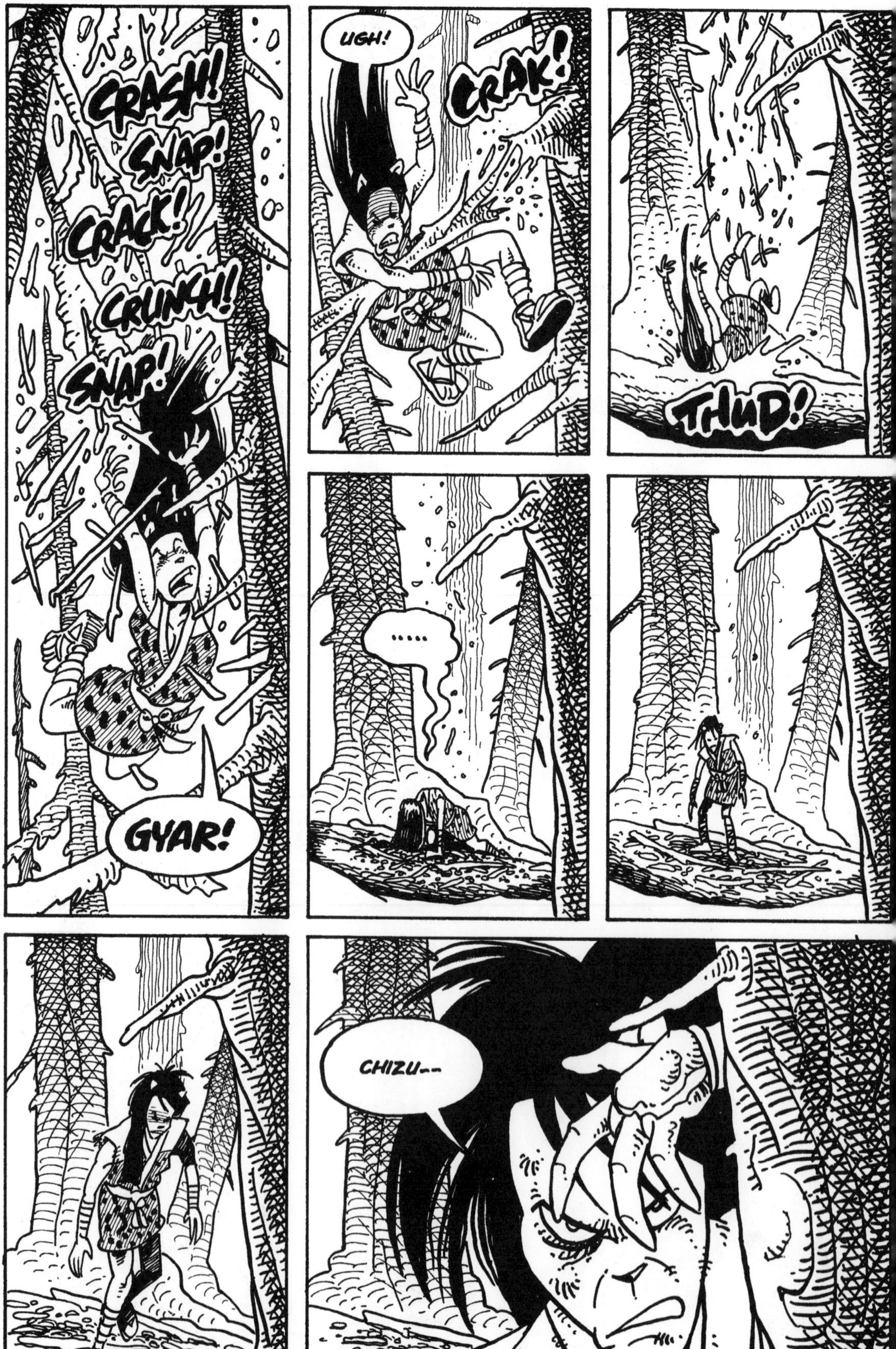
CRASH!
SNAP!
CRACK!
CRUNCH!
SNAP!
GYAR!
UGH!
CRAK!
THUD!
.....
CHIZU--
END

A POTTER'S TALE

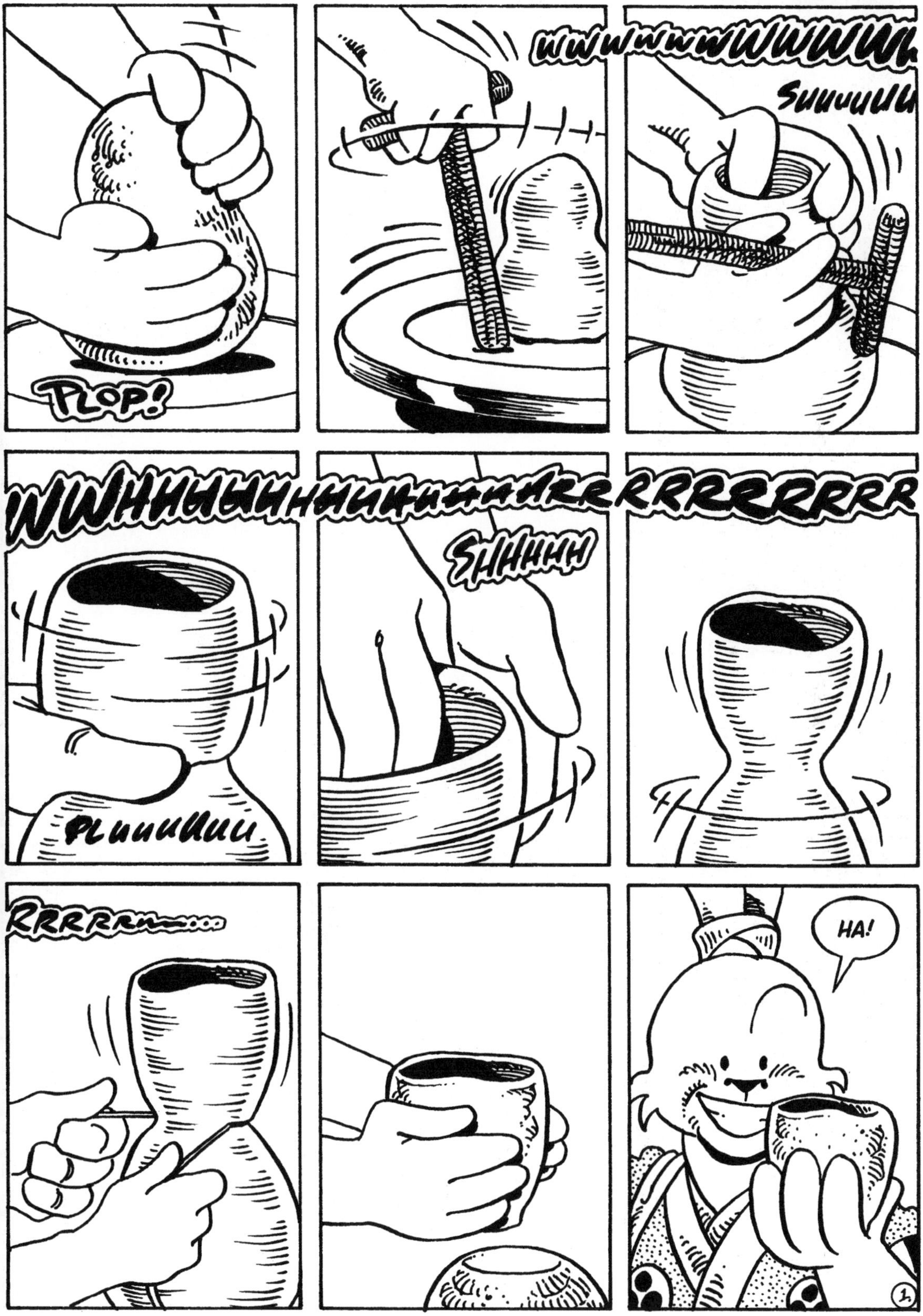
PLOP!
WWWWWWWWWWWWW
SWUUUUU
WWHHHHHHHHHHHHHHHHRRRRRRRRRRRRR
SHHHHH
PLUUUUUU
RRRRRN...
HA!
1

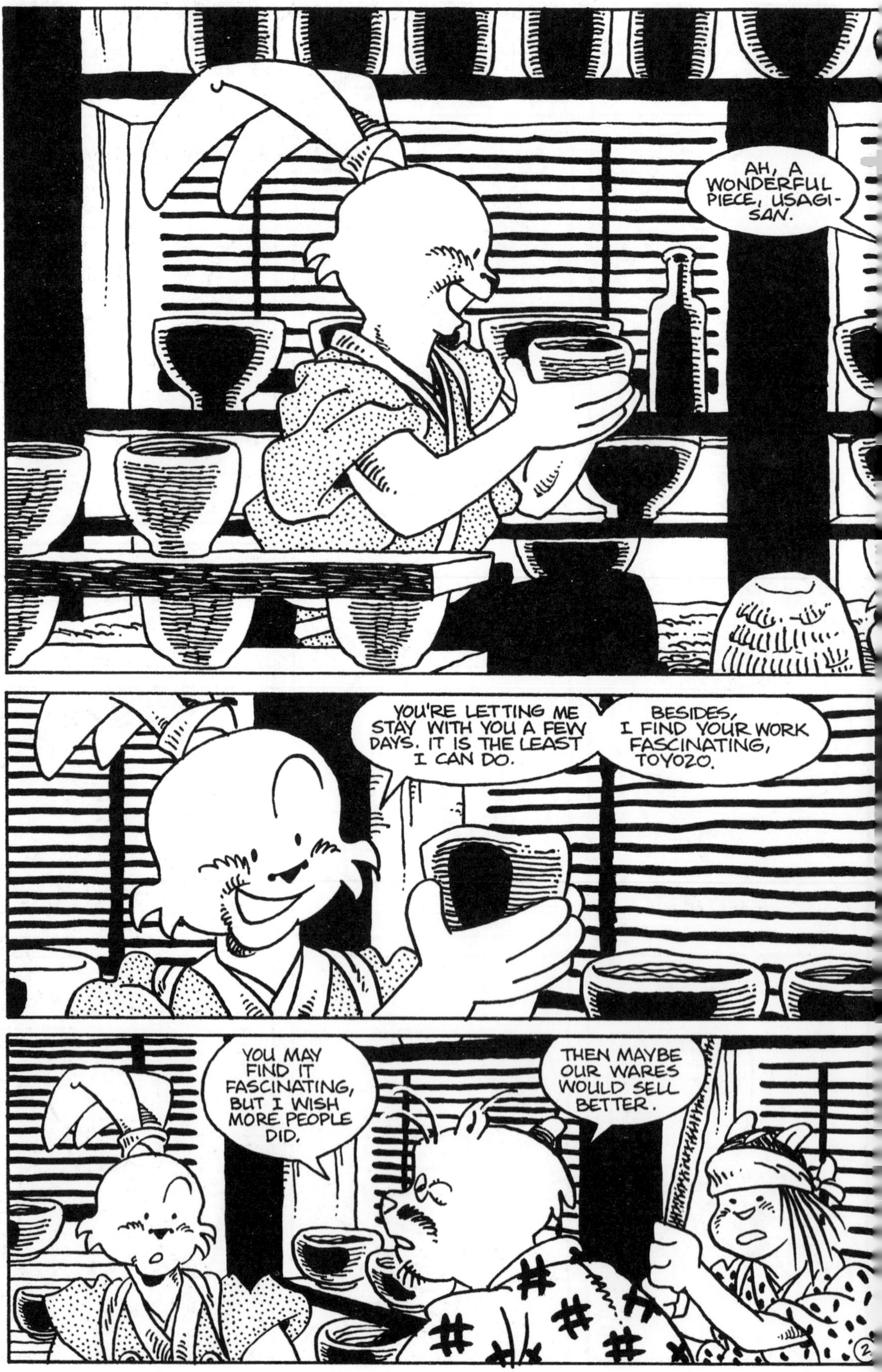
AH, A WONDERFUL PIECE, USAGI-SAN.
YOU'RE LETTING ME STAY WITH YOU A FEW DAYS. IT IS THE LEAST I CAN DO.
BESIDES, I FIND YOUR WORK FASCINATING, TOYOZO.
YOU MAY FIND IT FASCINATING, BUT I WISH MORE PEOPLE DID.
THEN MAYBE OUR WARES WOULD SELL BETTER.

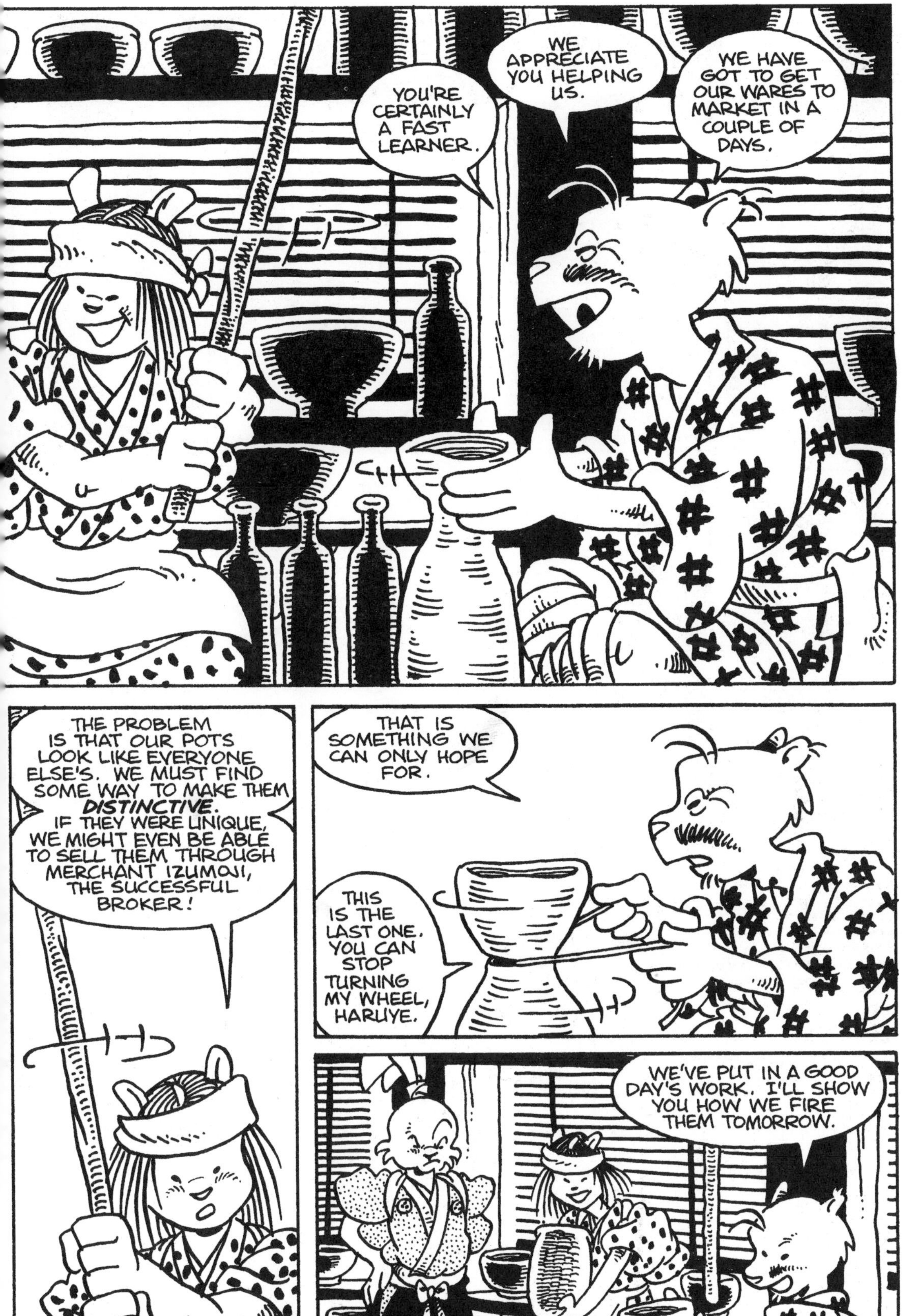
YOU'RE CERTAINLY A FAST LEARNER.
WE APPRECIATE YOU HELPING US.
WE HAVE GOT TO GET OUR WARES TO MARKET IN A COUPLE OF DAYS.
THE PROBLEM IS THAT OUR POTS LOOK LIKE EVERYONE ELSE'S. WE MUST FIND SOME WAY TO MAKE THEM ***DISTINCTIVE***. IF THEY WERE UNIQUE, WE MIGHT EVEN BE ABLE TO SELL THEM THROUGH MERCHANT IZUMOJI, THE SUCCESSFUL BROKER!
THAT IS SOMETHING WE CAN ONLY HOPE FOR.
THIS IS THE LAST ONE. YOU CAN STOP TURNING MY WHEEL, HARUYE.
WE'VE PUT IN A GOOD DAY'S WORK. I'LL SHOW YOU HOW WE FIRE THEM TOMORROW.

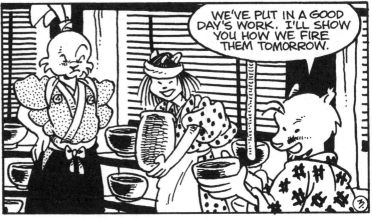

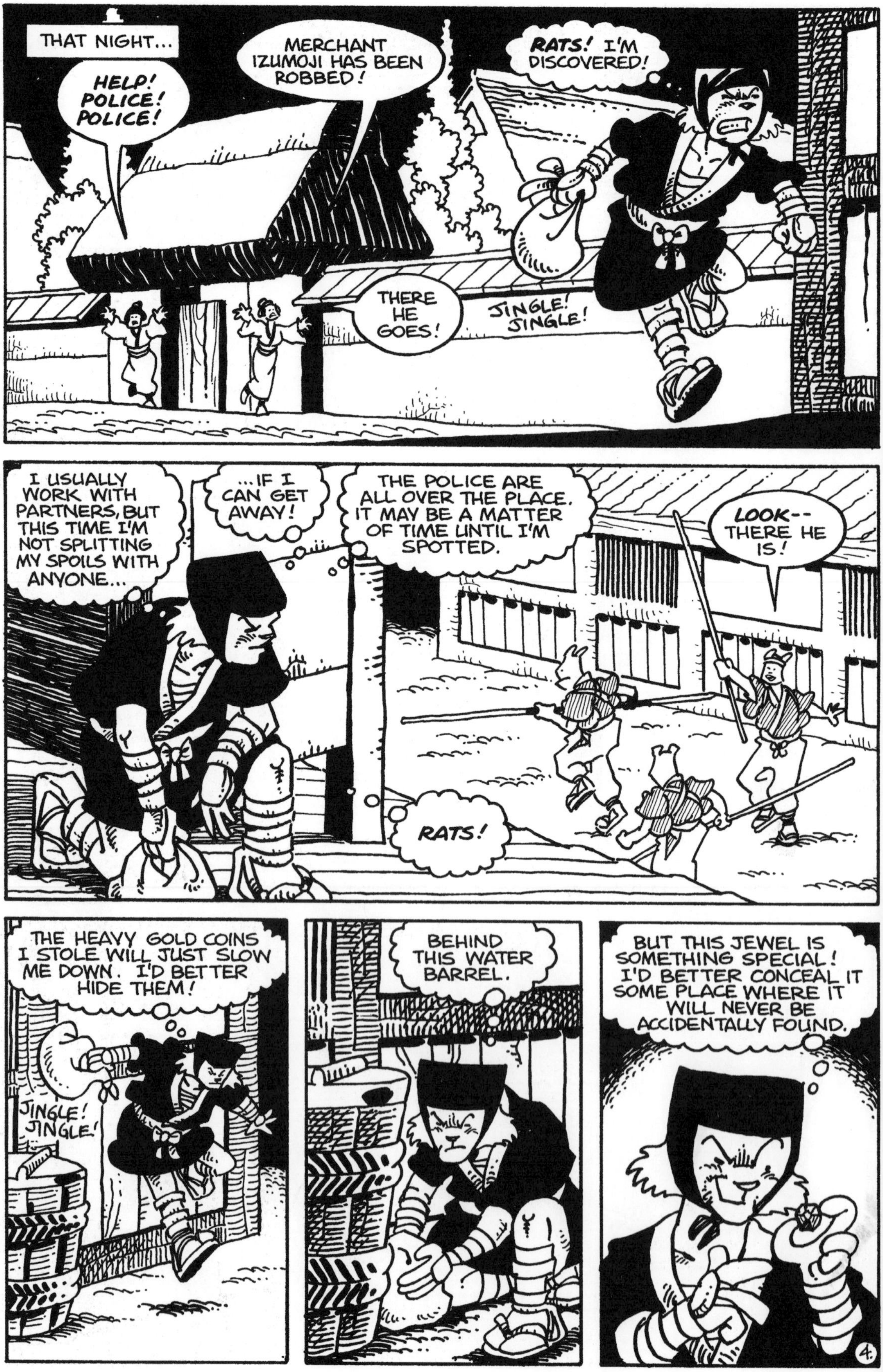
THAT NIGHT...
HELP! POLICE! POLICE!
MERCHANT IZUMOJI HAS BEEN ROBBED!
RATS! I'M DISCOVERED!
THERE HE GOES!
JINGLE! JINGLE!
I USUALLY WORK WITH PARTNERS, BUT THIS TIME I'M NOT SPLITTING MY SPOILS WITH ANYONE...
...IF I CAN GET AWAY!
THE POLICE ARE ALL OVER THE PLACE. IT MAY BE A MATTER OF TIME UNTIL I'M SPOTTED.
LOOK-- THERE HE IS!
RATS!
THE HEAVY GOLD COINS I STOLE WILL JUST SLOW ME DOWN. I'D BETTER HIDE THEM!
JINGLE! JINGLE!
BEHIND THIS WATER BARREL.
BUT THIS JEWEL IS SOMETHING SPECIAL! I'D BETTER CONCEAL IT SOME PLACE WHERE IT WILL NEVER BE ACCIDENTALLY FOUND.
4.

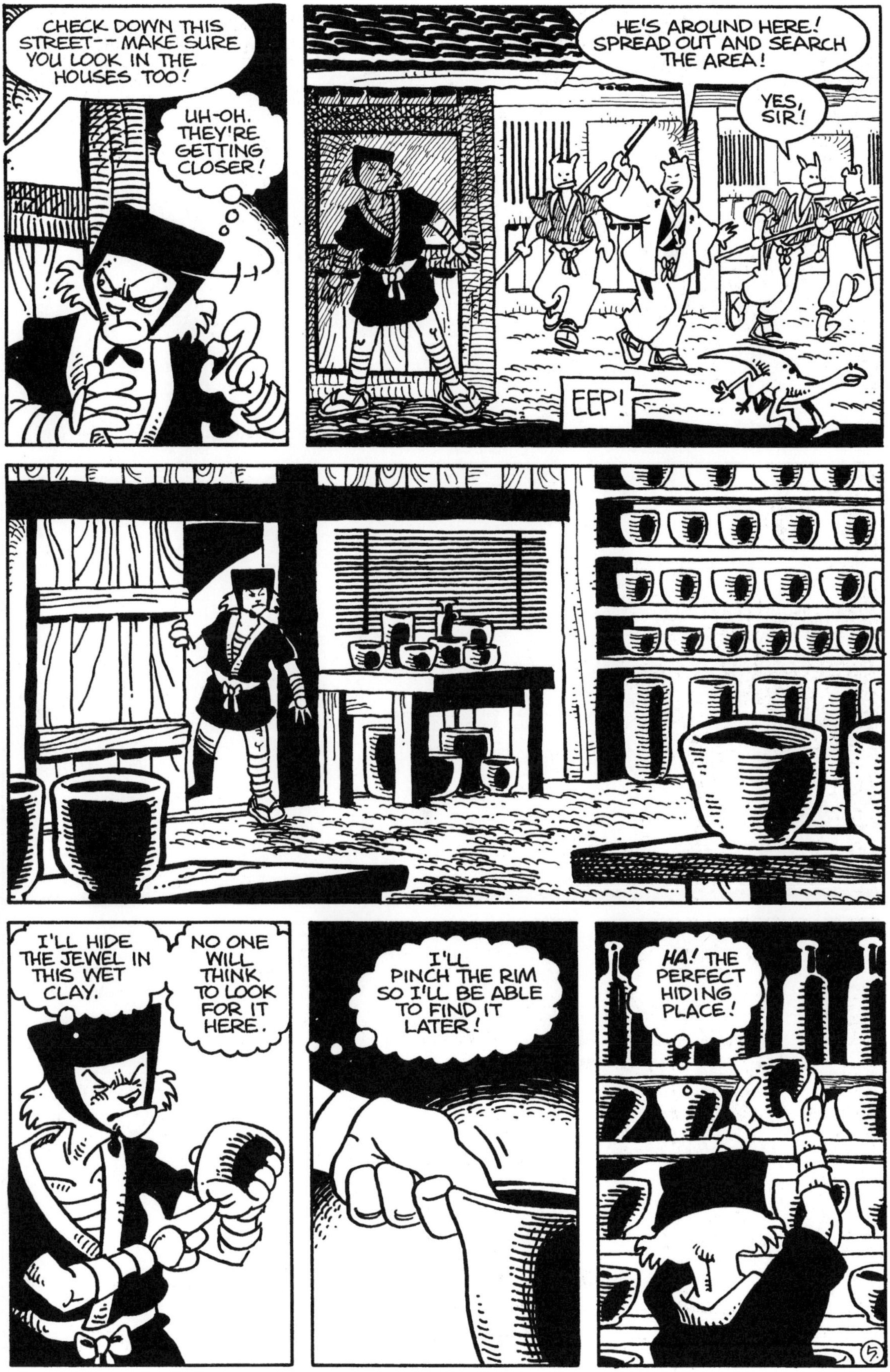
CHECK DOWN THIS STREET-- MAKE SURE YOU LOOK IN THE HOUSES TOO!
UH-OH. THEY'RE GETTING CLOSER!
HE'S AROUND HERE! SPREAD OUT AND SEARCH THE AREA!
YES, SIR!
EEP!
I'LL HIDE THE JEWEL IN THIS WET CLAY.
NO ONE WILL THINK TO LOOK FOR IT HERE.
I'LL PINCH THE RIM SO I'LL BE ABLE TO FIND IT LATER!
HA! THE PERFECT HIDING PLACE!
5

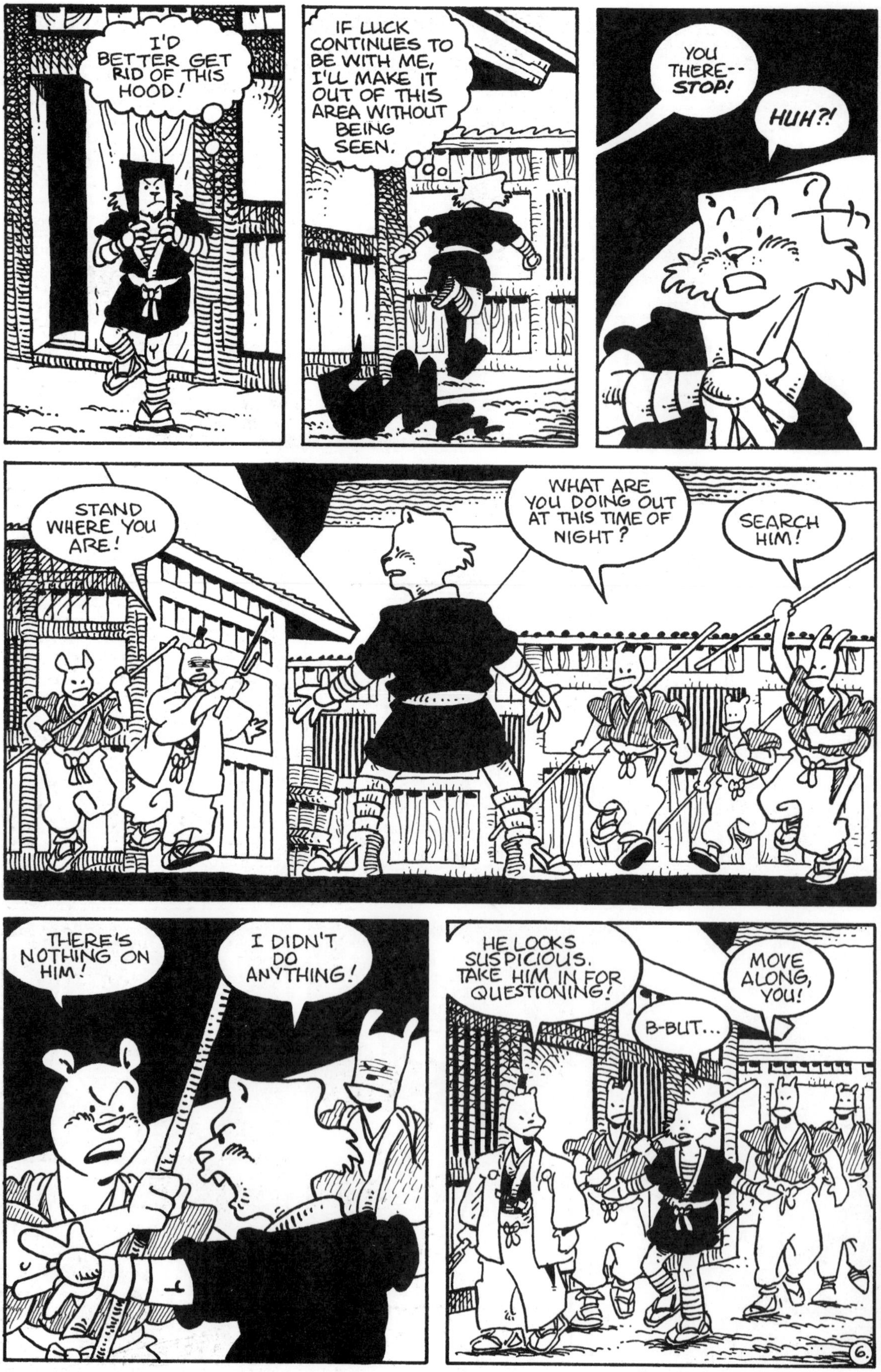
I'D BETTER GET RID OF THIS HOOD!
IF LUCK CONTINUES TO BE WITH ME, I'LL MAKE IT OUT OF THIS AREA WITHOUT BEING SEEN.
YOU THERE-- STOP!
HUH?!
STAND WHERE YOU ARE!
WHAT ARE YOU DOING OUT AT THIS TIME OF NIGHT?
SEARCH HIM!
THERE'S NOTHING ON HIM!
I DIDN'T DO ANYTHING!
HE LOOKS SUSPICIOUS. TAKE HIM IN FOR QUESTIONING!
B-BUT...
MOVE ALONG, YOU!
6.

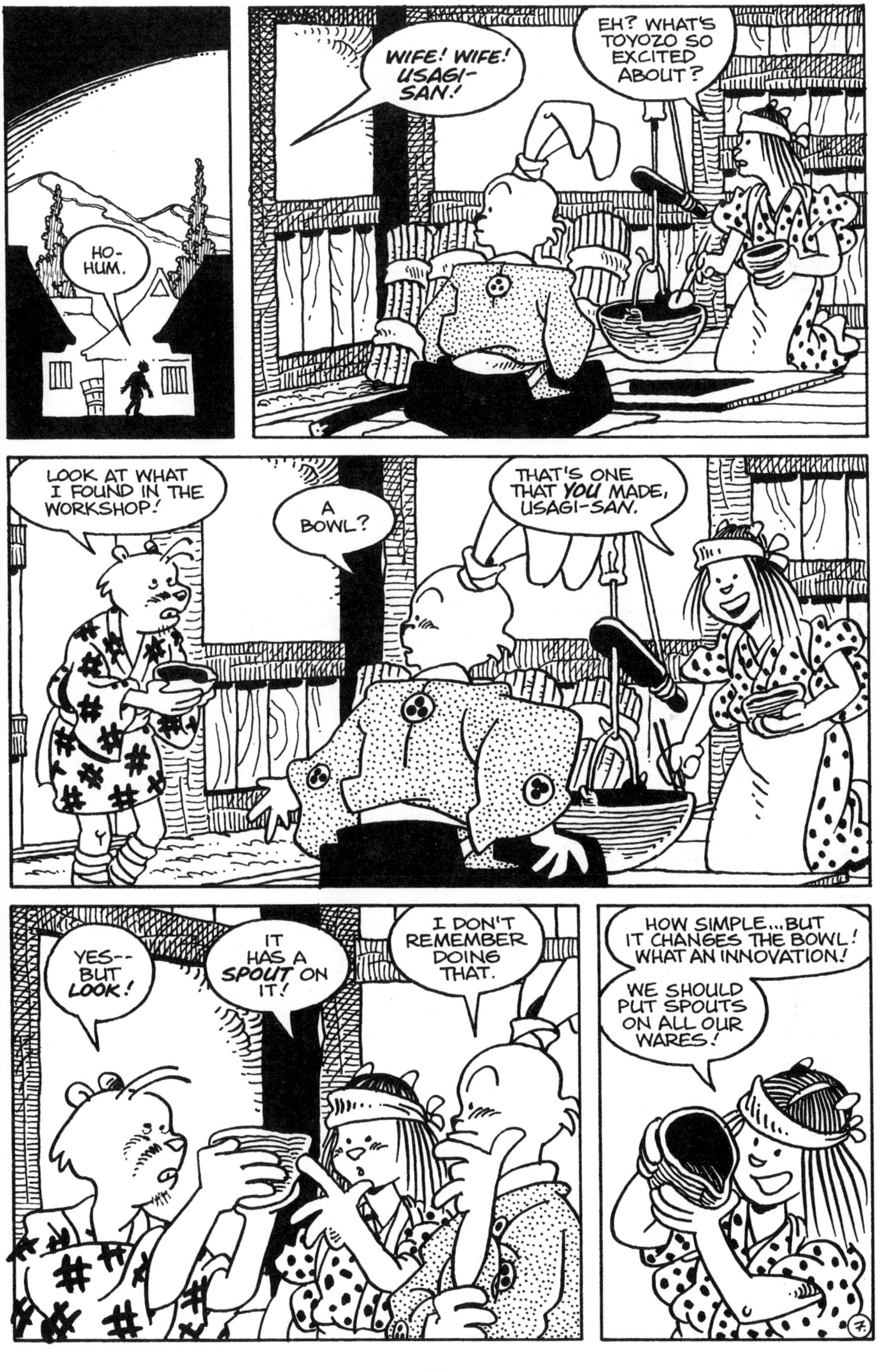
HO-HUM.
WIFE! WIFE! USAGI-SAN!
EH? WHAT'S TOYOZO SO EXCITED ABOUT?
LOOK AT WHAT I FOUND IN THE WORKSHOP!
A BOWL?
THAT'S ONE THAT YOU MADE, USAGI-SAN.
YES--BUT LOOK!
IT HAS A SPOUT ON IT!
I DON'T REMEMBER DOING THAT.
HOW SIMPLE...BUT IT CHANGES THE BOWL! WHAT AN INNOVATION!
WE SHOULD PUT SPOUTS ON ALL OUR WARES!
7.

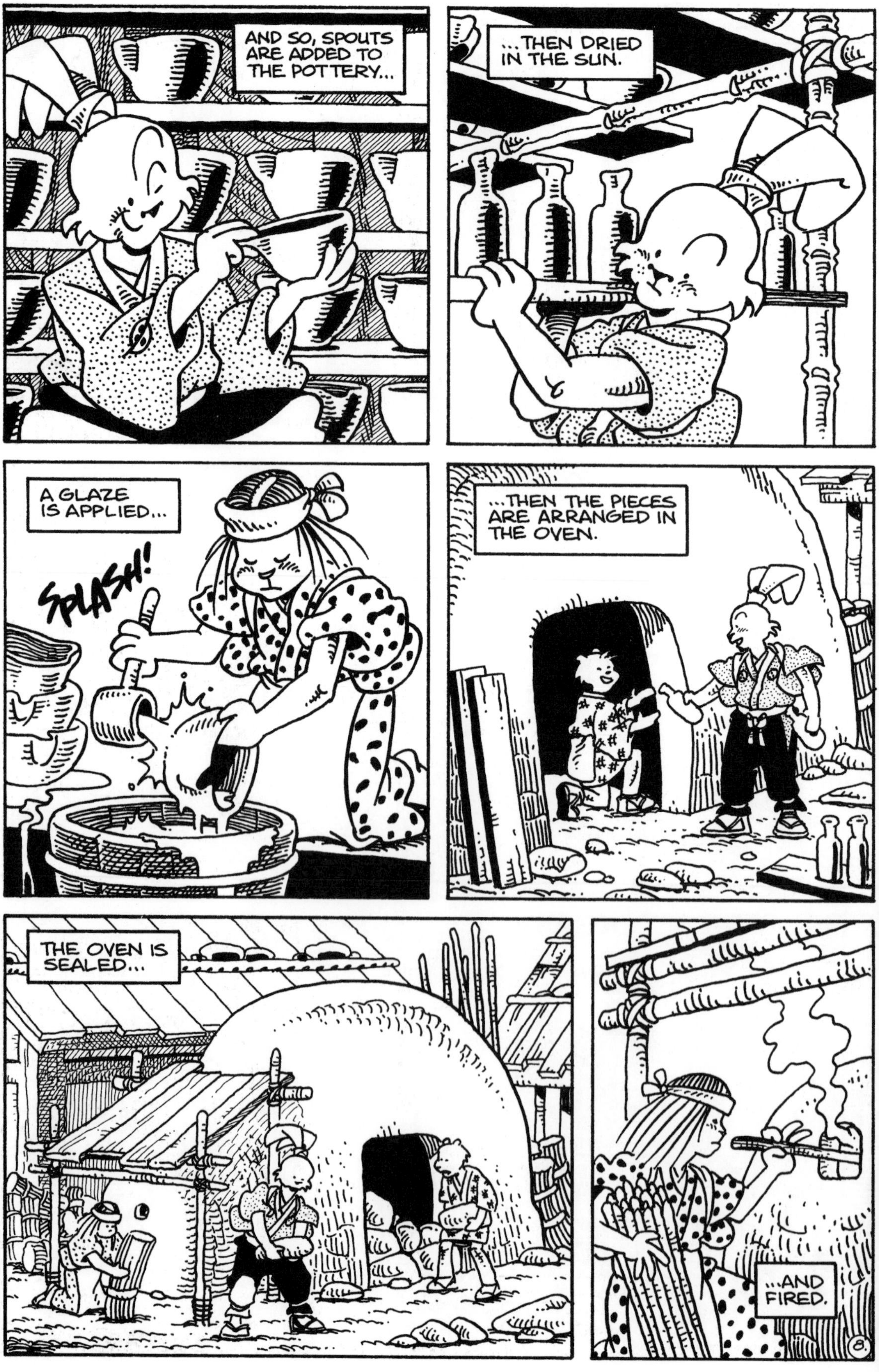
AND SO, SPOUTS ARE ADDED TO THE POTTERY...
...THEN DRIED IN THE SUN.
A GLAZE IS APPLIED...
SPLASH!
...THEN THE PIECES ARE ARRANGED IN THE OVEN.
THE OVEN IS SEALED...
...AND FIRED.
8

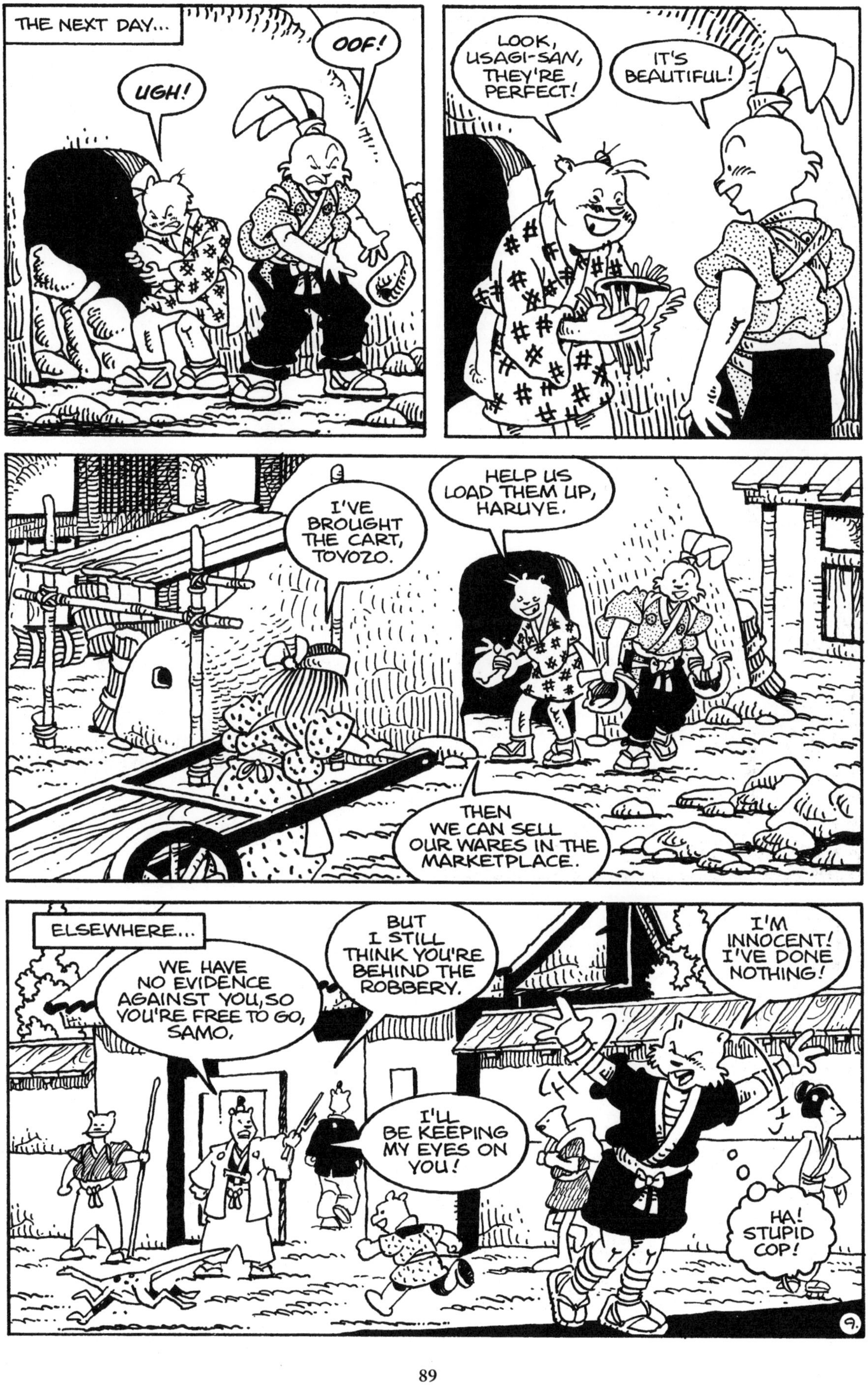
THE NEXT DAY...
UGH!
OOF!
LOOK, USAGI-SAN, THEY'RE PERFECT!
IT'S BEAUTIFUL!
I'VE BROUGHT THE CART, TOYOZO.
HELP US LOAD THEM UP, HARUYE.
THEN WE CAN SELL OUR WARES IN THE MARKETPLACE.
ELSEWHERE...
WE HAVE NO EVIDENCE AGAINST YOU, SO YOU'RE FREE TO GO, SAMO.
BUT I STILL THINK YOU'RE BEHIND THE ROBBERY.
I'LL BE KEEPING MY EYES ON YOU!
I'M INNOCENT! I'VE DONE NOTHING!
HA! STUPID COP!
9.

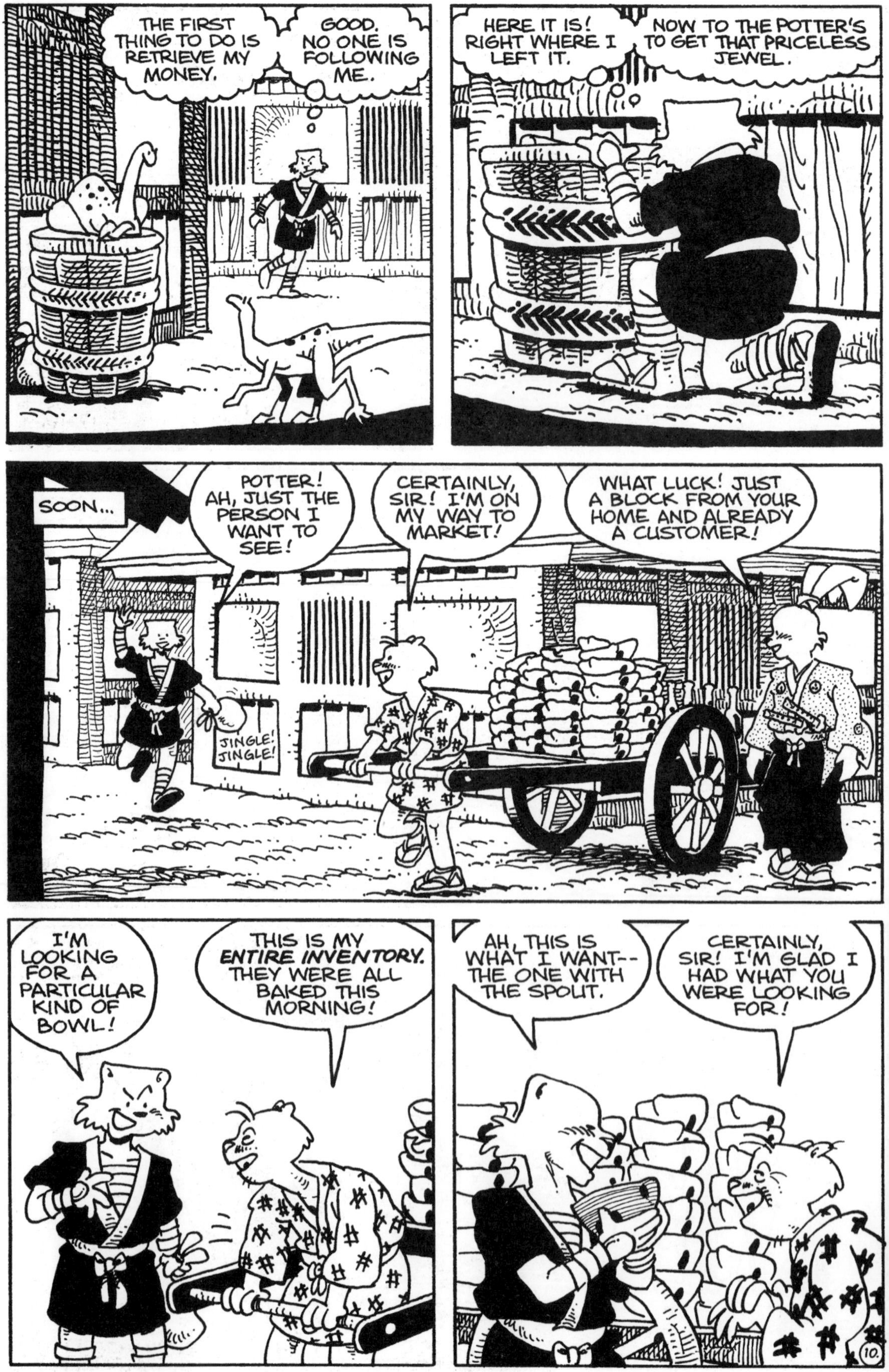
THE FIRST THING TO DO IS RETRIEVE MY MONEY.
GOOD. NO ONE IS FOLLOWING ME.
HERE IT IS! RIGHT WHERE I LEFT IT.
NOW TO THE POTTER'S TO GET THAT PRICELESS JEWEL.
SOON...
POTTER! AH, JUST THE PERSON I WANT TO SEE!
CERTAINLY, SIR! I'M ON MY WAY TO MARKET!
WHAT LUCK! JUST A BLOCK FROM YOUR HOME AND ALREADY A CUSTOMER!
JINGLE! JINGLE!
I'M LOOKING FOR A PARTICULAR KIND OF BOWL!
THIS IS MY ENTIRE INVENTORY. THEY WERE ALL BAKED THIS MORNING!
AH, THIS IS WHAT I WANT-- THE ONE WITH THE SPOUT.
CERTAINLY, SIR! I'M GLAD I HAD WHAT YOU WERE LOOKING FOR!
10.

WAIT A MINUTE-- *THAT ONE* HAS A SPOUT, TOO!

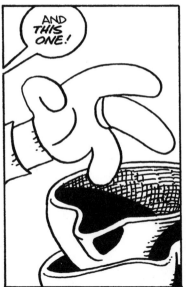

AND *THIS ONE!*

AND *THOSE!*

AN INTERESTING INNOVATION, ISN'T IT? THEY ALL HAVE SPOUTS.

A-ALL?!

WE ARE TRYING SOMETHING DIFFERENT WITH OUR MERCHANDISE.

THE JEWEL IS *PRICELESS!* I HAVE GOT TO GET IT BACK-- NO MATTER THE COST!

THE JEWEL IS IN ONE OF THESE CERAMIC PIECES. I'VE GOT TO SMASH THEM ALL-- BUT NOT WITH THAT *SAMURAI* STANDING THERE!

I-I'LL BUY *ALL* YOUR WARES, THIS SHOULD COVER THE COST.

A-ALL?!

IT'LL TAKE ALL THE MONEY I STOLE, BUT IT WILL BE WORTH IT!

WOW! SELLING THIS IS EASIER THAN I THOUGHT!

JINGLE! JINGLE!

11.

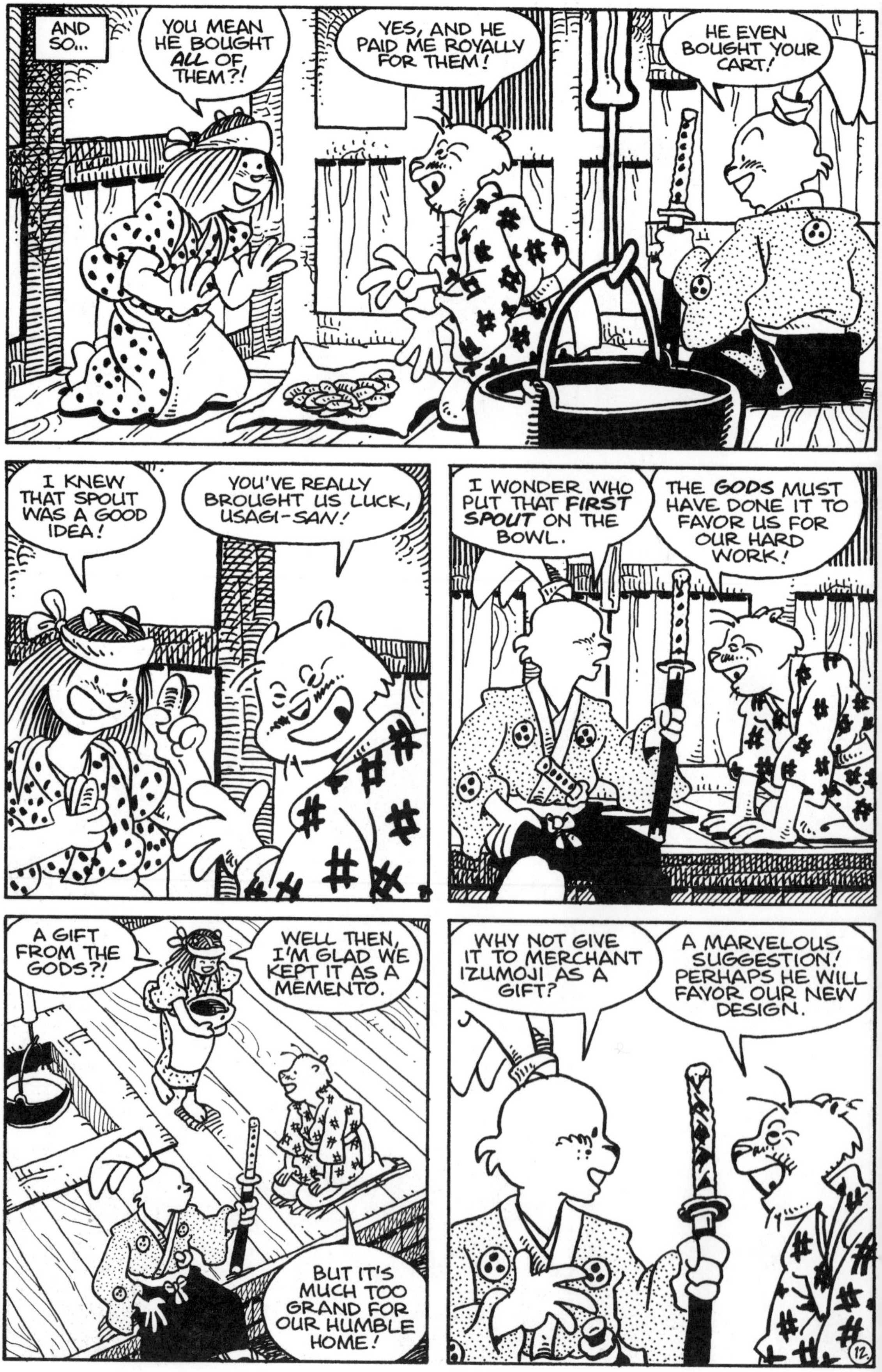
AND SO...
YOU MEAN HE BOUGHT ALL OF THEM?!
YES, AND HE PAID ME ROYALLY FOR THEM!
HE EVEN BOUGHT YOUR CART!
I KNEW THAT SPOUT WAS A GOOD IDEA!
YOU'VE REALLY BROUGHT US LUCK, USAGI-SAN!
I WONDER WHO PUT THAT FIRST SPOUT ON THE BOWL.
THE GODS MUST HAVE DONE IT TO FAVOR US FOR OUR HARD WORK!
A GIFT FROM THE GODS?!
WELL THEN, I'M GLAD WE KEPT IT AS A MEMENTO.
BUT IT'S MUCH TOO GRAND FOR OUR HUMBLE HOME!
WHY NOT GIVE IT TO MERCHANT IZUMOJI AS A GIFT?
A MARVELOUS SUGGESTION! PERHAPS HE WILL FAVOR OUR NEW DESIGN.
12

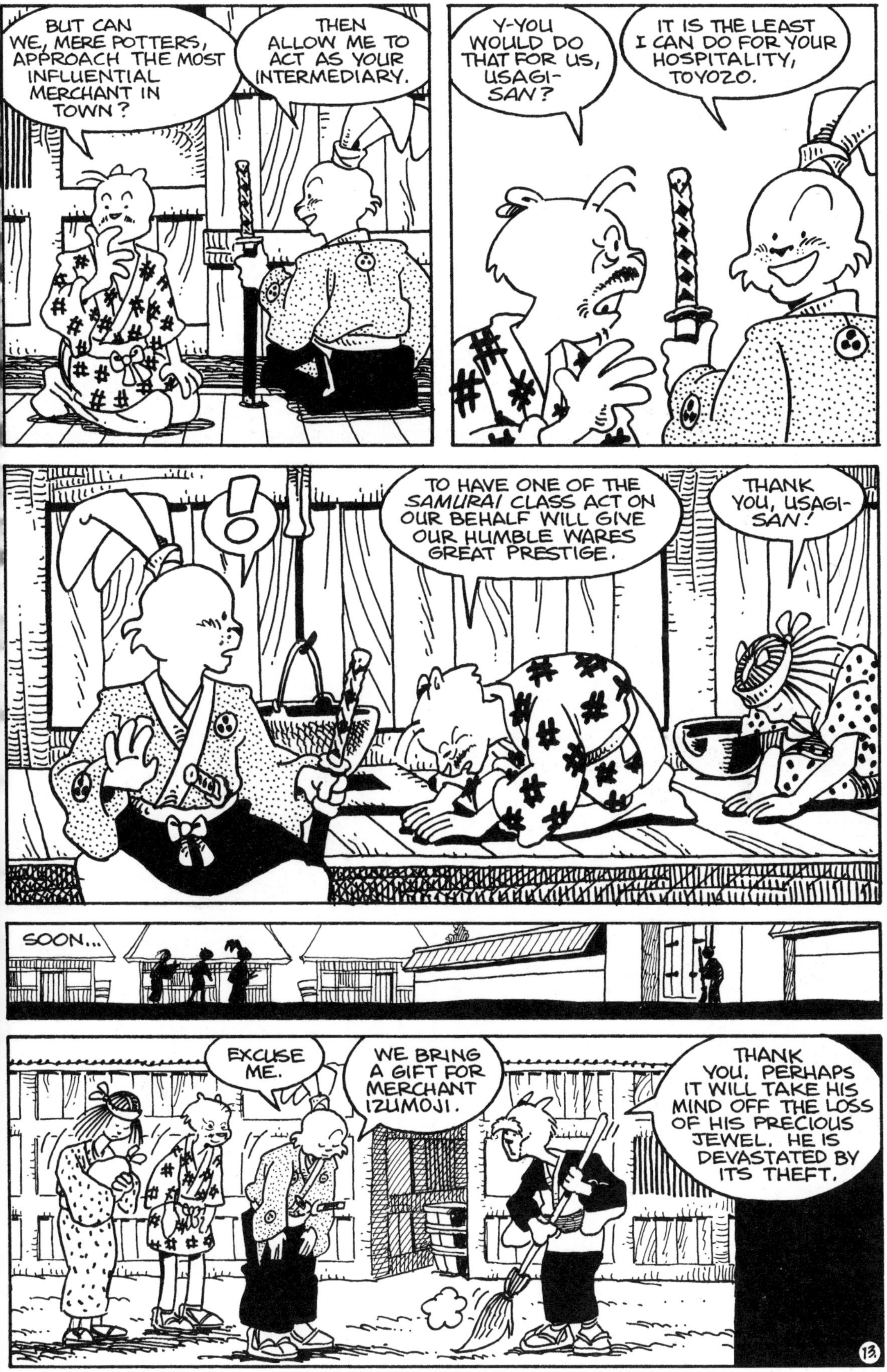

BUT CAN WE, MERE POTTERS, APPROACH THE MOST INFLUENTIAL MERCHANT IN TOWN?
THEN ALLOW ME TO ACT AS YOUR INTERMEDIARY.
Y-YOU WOULD DO THAT FOR US, USAGI-SAN?
IT IS THE LEAST I CAN DO FOR YOUR HOSPITALITY, TOYOZO.
!
TO HAVE ONE OF THE *SAMURAI* CLASS ACT ON OUR BEHALF WILL GIVE OUR HUMBLE WARES GREAT PRESTIGE.
THANK YOU, USAGI-SAN!
SOON...
EXCUSE ME.
WE BRING A GIFT FOR MERCHANT IZUMOJI.
THANK YOU. PERHAPS IT WILL TAKE HIS MIND OFF THE LOSS OF HIS PRECIOUS JEWEL. HE IS DEVASTATED BY ITS THEFT.
13

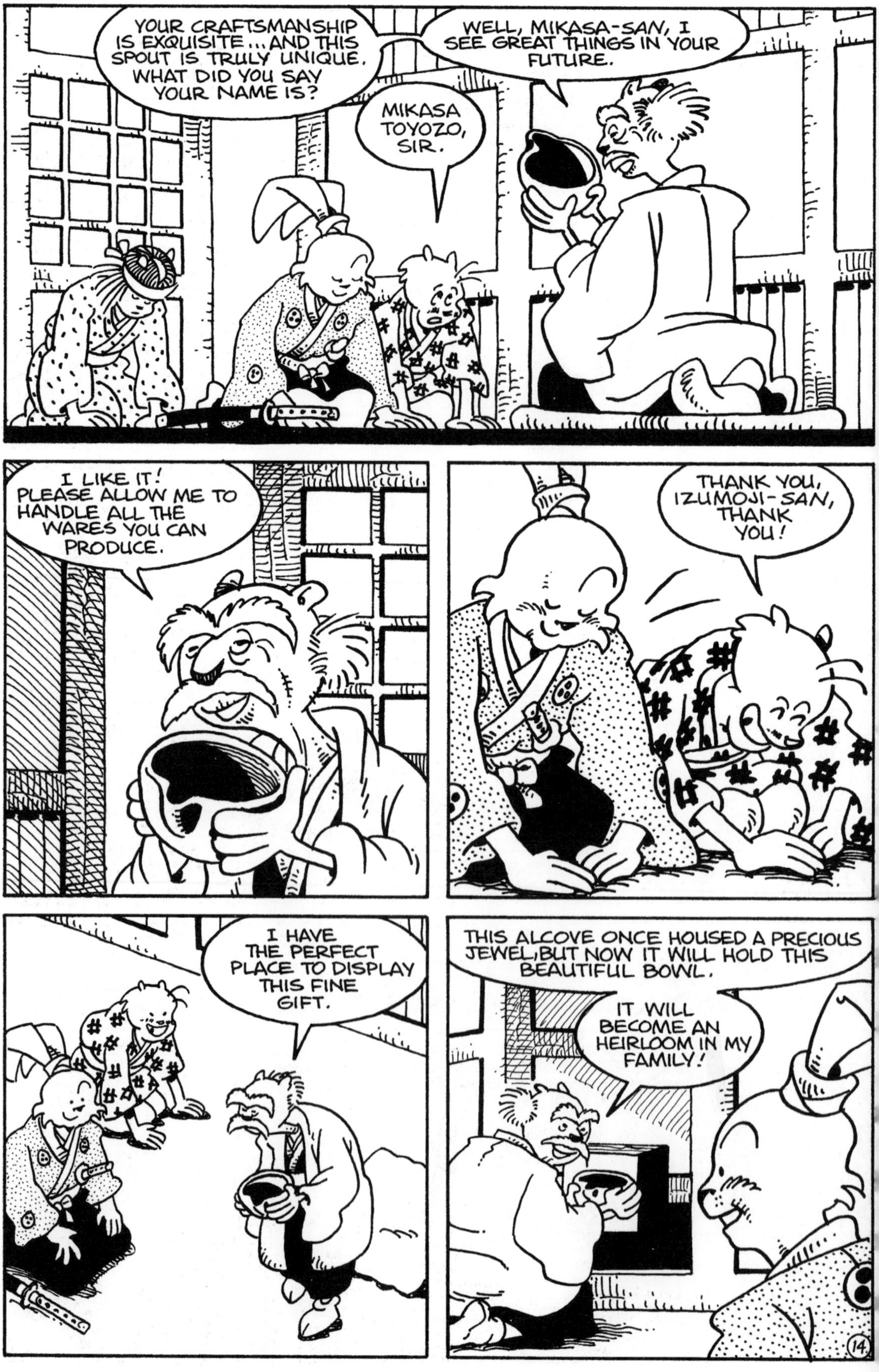
YOUR CRAFTSMANSHIP IS EXQUISITE...AND THIS SPOUT IS TRULY UNIQUE. WHAT DID YOU SAY YOUR NAME IS?
MIKASA TOYOZO, SIR.
WELL, MIKASA-SAN, I SEE GREAT THINGS IN YOUR FUTURE.
I LIKE IT! PLEASE ALLOW ME TO HANDLE ALL THE WARES YOU CAN PRODUCE.
THANK YOU, IZUMOJI-SAN, THANK YOU!
I HAVE THE PERFECT PLACE TO DISPLAY THIS FINE GIFT.
THIS ALCOVE ONCE HOUSED A PRECIOUS JEWEL, BUT NOW IT WILL HOLD THIS BEAUTIFUL BOWL.
IT WILL BECOME AN HEIRLOOM IN MY FAMILY!
14

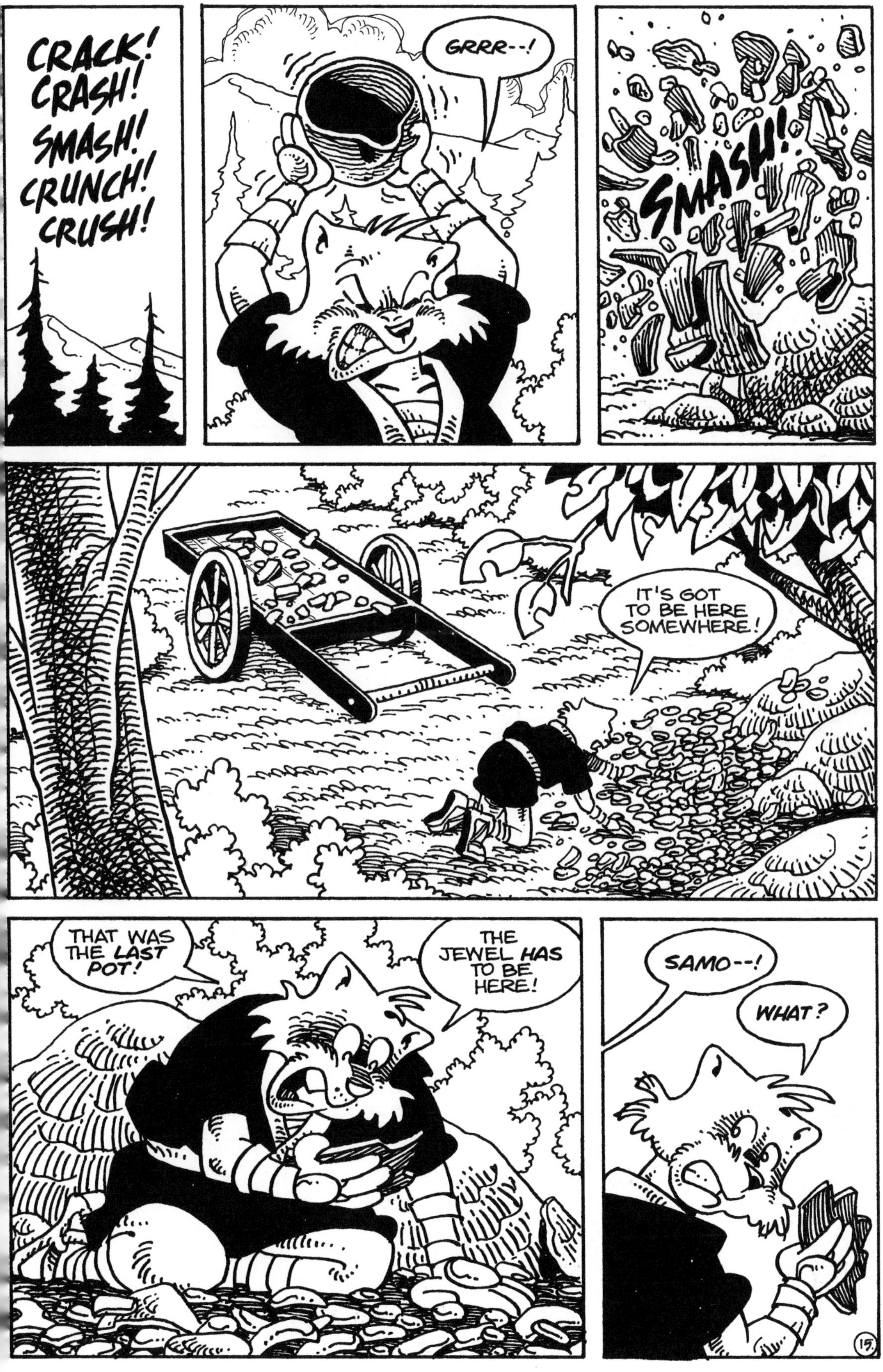
CRACK! CRASH! SMASH! CRUNCH! CRUSH!
GRRR--!
SMASH!
IT'S GOT TO BE HERE SOMEWHERE!
THAT WAS THE *LAST* POT!
THE JEWEL *HAS* TO BE HERE!
SAMO--!
WHAT?
15

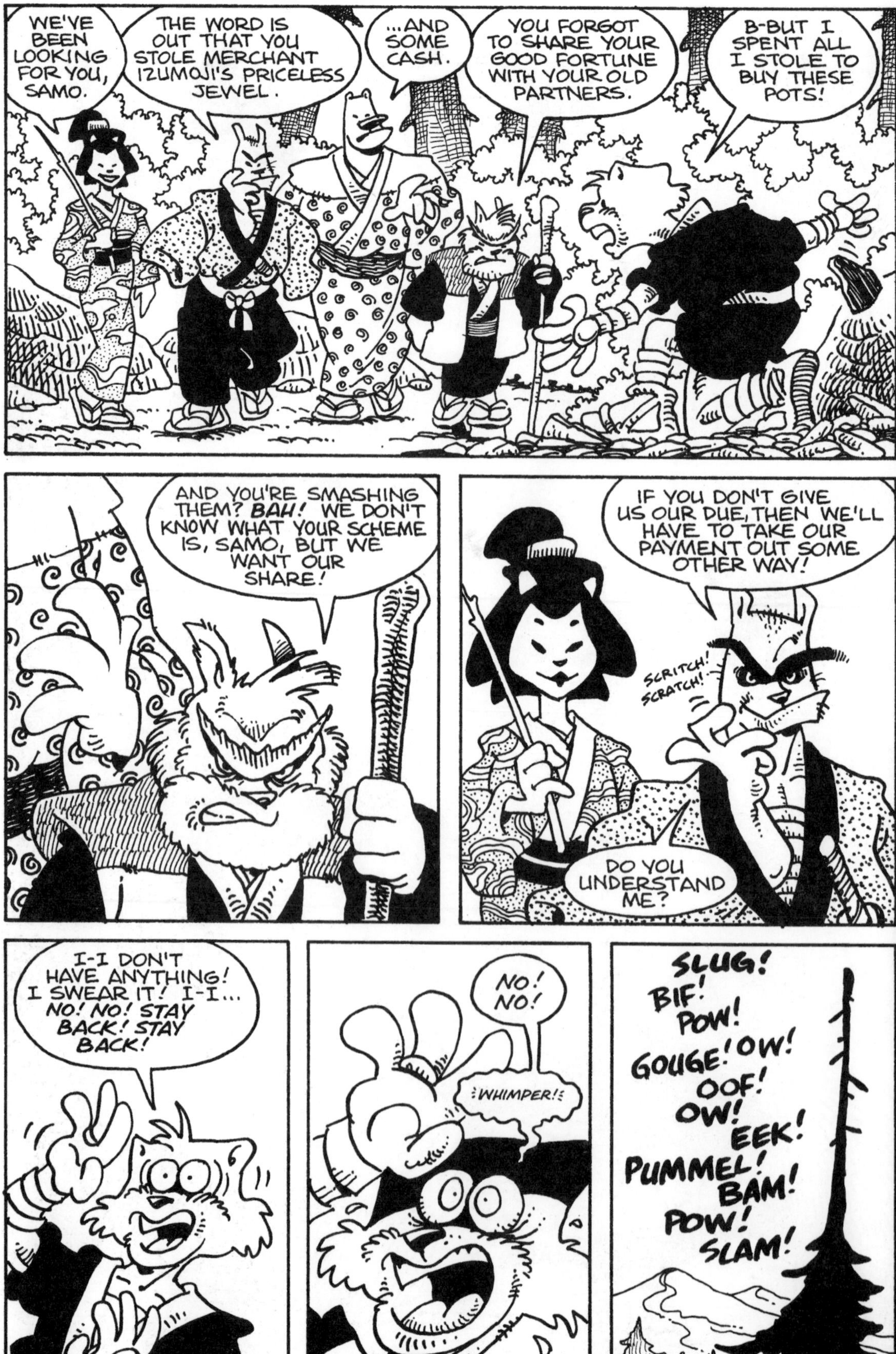
WE'VE BEEN LOOKING FOR YOU, SAMO.
THE WORD IS OUT THAT YOU STOLE MERCHANT IZUMOJI'S PRICELESS JEWEL.
...AND SOME CASH.
YOU FORGOT TO SHARE YOUR GOOD FORTUNE WITH YOUR OLD PARTNERS.
B-BUT I SPENT ALL I STOLE TO BUY THESE POTS!
AND YOU'RE SMASHING THEM? BAH! WE DON'T KNOW WHAT YOUR SCHEME IS, SAMO, BUT WE WANT OUR SHARE!
IF YOU DON'T GIVE US OUR DUE, THEN WE'LL HAVE TO TAKE OUR PAYMENT OUT SOME OTHER WAY!
SCRITCH! SCRATCH!
DO YOU UNDERSTAND ME?
I-I DON'T HAVE ANYTHING! I SWEAR IT! I-I... NO! NO! STAY BACK! STAY BACK!
NO! NO!
WHIMPER!
SLUG! BIF! POW! GOUGE! OW! OOF! OW! EEK! PUMMEL! BAM! POW! SLAM!
THE END

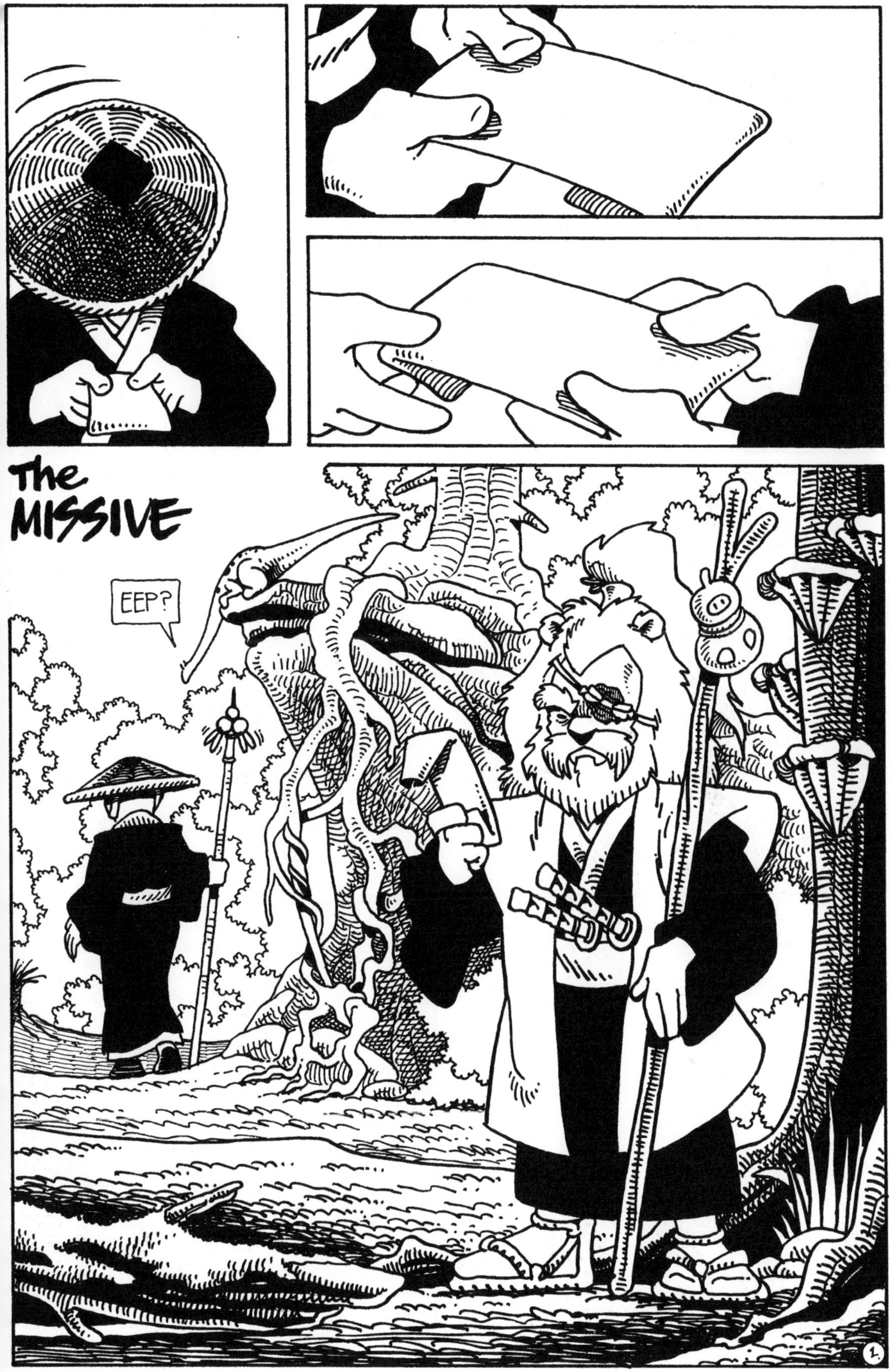
The MISSIVE
EEP?

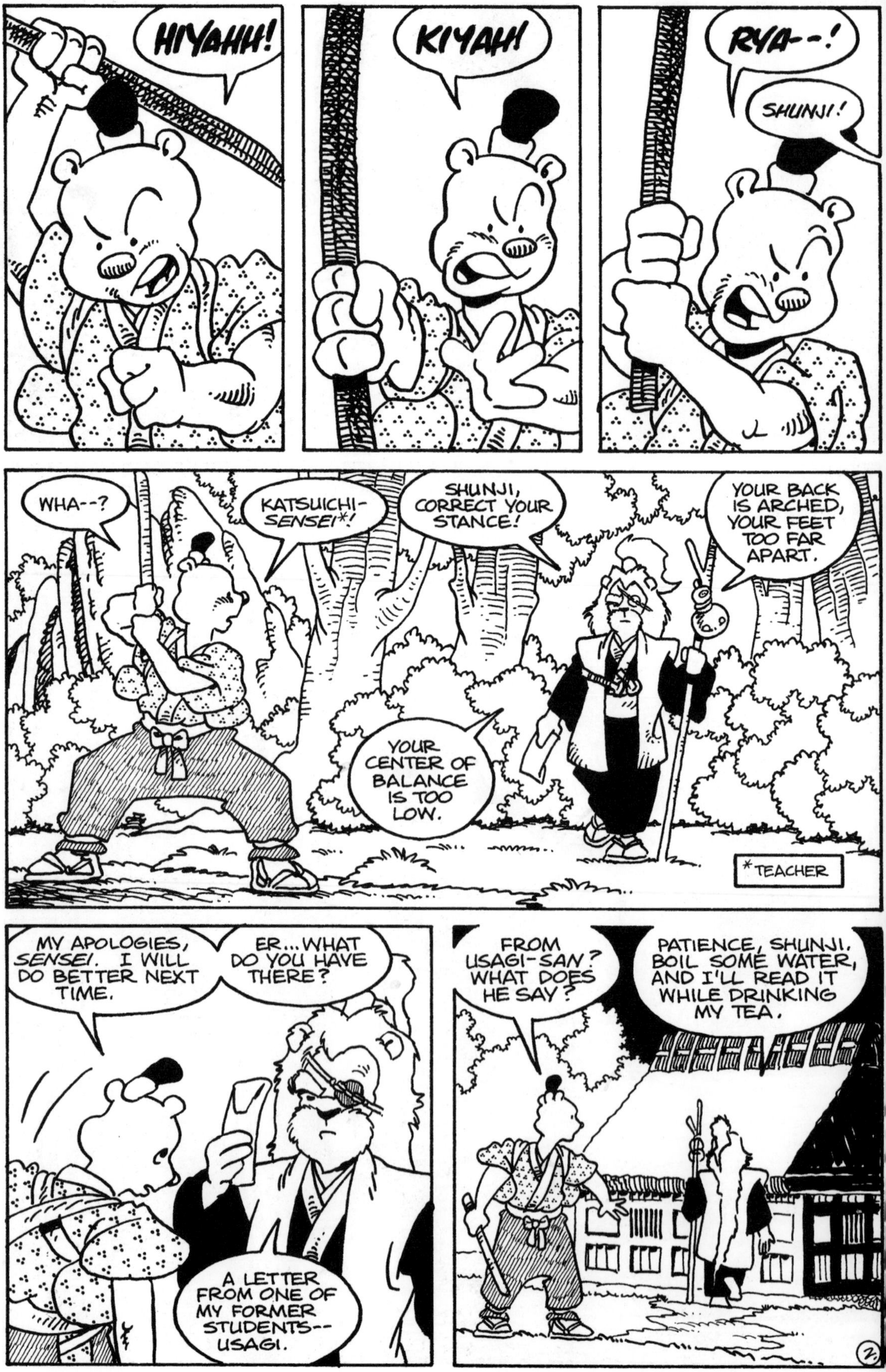
HIYAHH!
KIYAH!
RYA--!
SHUNJI!
WHA--?
KATSUICHI-SENSEI*!
SHUNJI, CORRECT YOUR STANCE!
YOUR BACK IS ARCHED, YOUR FEET TOO FAR APART.
YOUR CENTER OF BALANCE IS TOO LOW.
*TEACHER
MY APOLOGIES, SENSEI. I WILL DO BETTER NEXT TIME.
ER...WHAT DO YOU HAVE THERE?
A LETTER FROM ONE OF MY FORMER STUDENTS-- USAGI.
FROM USAGI-SAN? WHAT DOES HE SAY?
PATIENCE, SHUNJI. BOIL SOME WATER, AND I'LL READ IT WHILE DRINKING MY TEA.
2

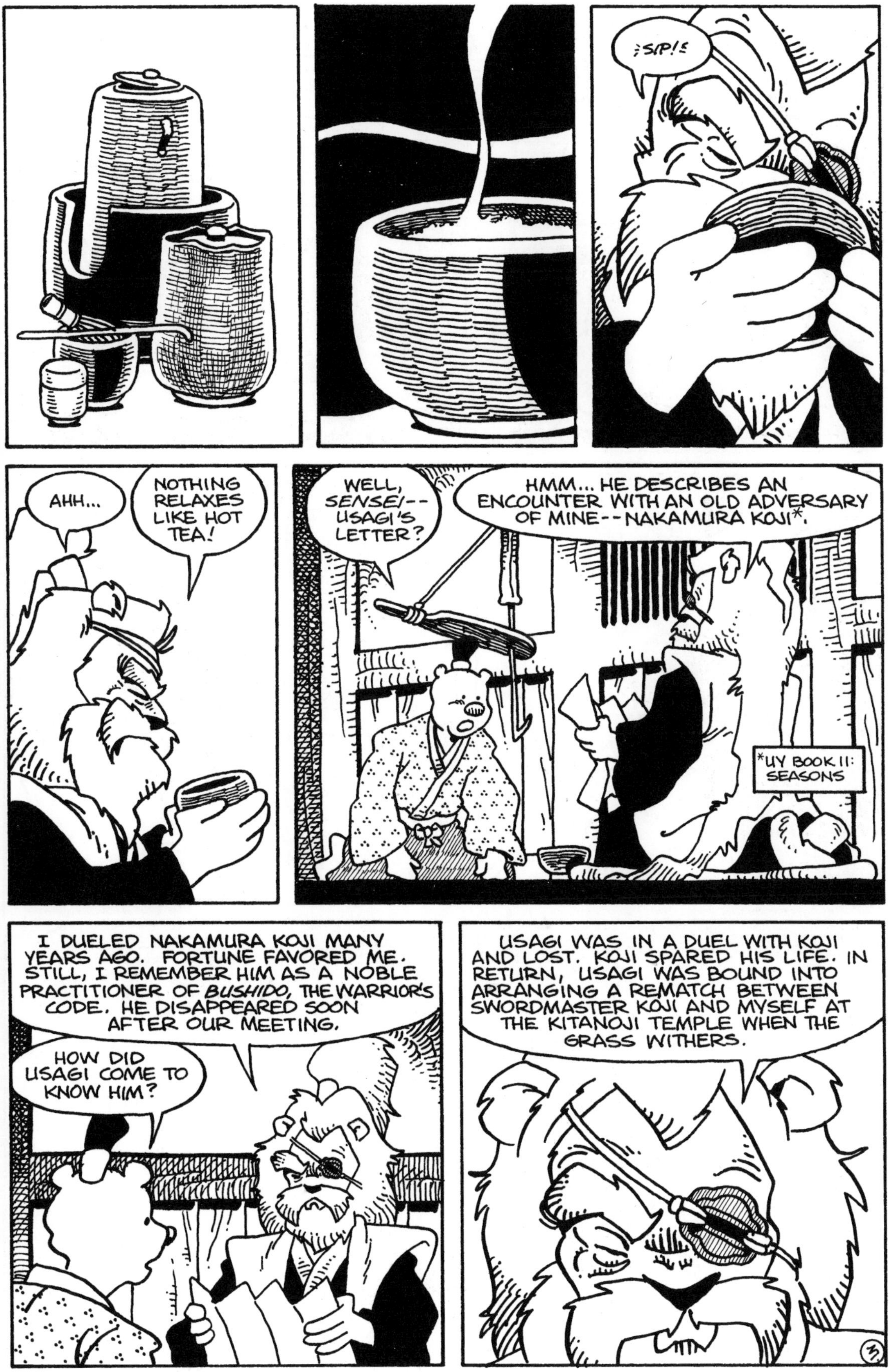
SIP!
AHH...
NOTHING RELAXES LIKE HOT TEA!
WELL, SENSEI-- USAGI'S LETTER?
HMM... HE DESCRIBES AN ENCOUNTER WITH AN OLD ADVERSARY OF MINE--NAKAMURA KOJI*.
*UY BOOK 11: SEASONS
I DUELED NAKAMURA KOJI MANY YEARS AGO. FORTUNE FAVORED ME. STILL, I REMEMBER HIM AS A NOBLE PRACTITIONER OF BUSHIDO, THE WARRIOR'S CODE. HE DISAPPEARED SOON AFTER OUR MEETING.
HOW DID USAGI COME TO KNOW HIM?
USAGI WAS IN A DUEL WITH KOJI AND LOST. KOJI SPARED HIS LIFE. IN RETURN, USAGI WAS BOUND INTO ARRANGING A REMATCH BETWEEN SWORDMASTER KOJI AND MYSELF AT THE KITANOJI TEMPLE WHEN THE GRASS WITHERS.
3

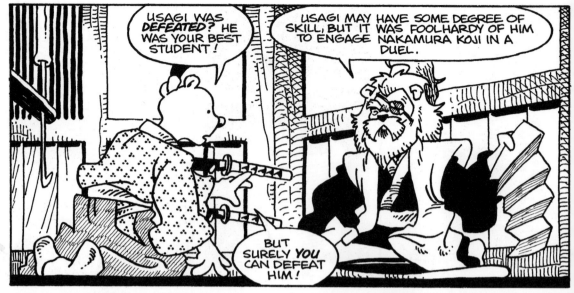

USAGI WAS **DEFEATED**? HE WAS YOUR BEST STUDENT!

USAGI MAY HAVE SOME DEGREE OF SKILL, BUT IT WAS FOOLHARDY OF HIM TO ENGAGE NAKAMURA KOJI IN A DUEL.

BUT SURELY *YOU* CAN DEFEAT HIM!

NEVER UNDERESTIMATE YOUR ADVERSARY, SHUNJI. NAKAMURA KOJI WAS A FORMIDABLE OPPONENT WHEN I WENT AGAINST HIM. HAS TIME DIMINISHED HIS SKILLS...

...OR ENHANCED THEM?

USAGI MUST HAVE BELIEVED HE COULD BEAT NAKAMURA KOJI, OR HE WOULD NOT HAVE FOUGHT HIM.

IF USAGI HAS A MAJOR FAILING, IT IS THAT HE IS RASH AND HEADSTRONG. HE IS IMPULSIVE AND RUSHES IN BEFORE HE UNDERSTANDS THE TRUE SITUATION.

I REMEMBER A TIME SO MANY YEARS AGO. WE WERE WALKING ALONG THE RIVER...

THE COUNTRY IS IN THE GRIP OF A CIVIL WAR, USAGI. EVEN PEASANTS ARE HARD PRESSED TO FIND SAFETY IN THEIR OWN HOMES.

BATTLES RAGE EVERYWHERE AS WARLORDS VIE FOR MORE LAND, MORE POWER.

YOW!

SPLASH! SPLASH! SPLASH!

SPASH!

4.

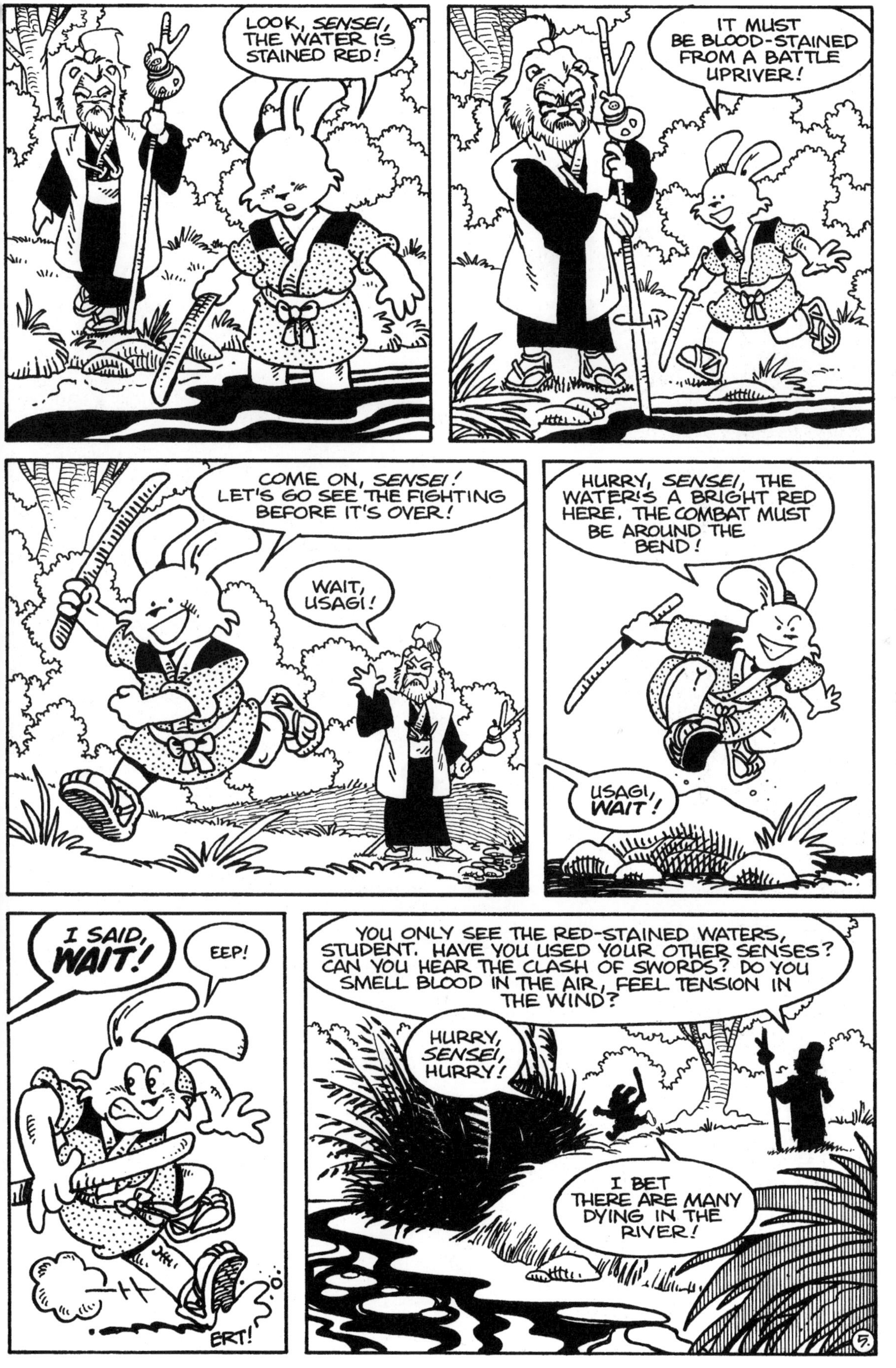
LOOK, *SENSEI*, THE WATER IS STAINED RED!
IT MUST BE BLOOD-STAINED FROM A BATTLE UPRIVER!
COME ON, *SENSEI*! LET'S GO SEE THE FIGHTING BEFORE IT'S OVER!
WAIT, USAGI!
HURRY, *SENSEI*, THE WATER'S A BRIGHT RED HERE. THE COMBAT MUST BE AROUND THE BEND!
USAGI, **WAIT**!
I SAID, **WAIT**!
EEP!
ERT!
YOU ONLY SEE THE RED-STAINED WATERS, STUDENT. HAVE YOU USED YOUR OTHER SENSES? CAN YOU HEAR THE CLASH OF SWORDS? DO YOU SMELL BLOOD IN THE AIR, FEEL TENSION IN THE WIND?
HURRY, *SENSEI*, HURRY!
I BET THERE ARE MANY DYING IN THE RIVER!
5.

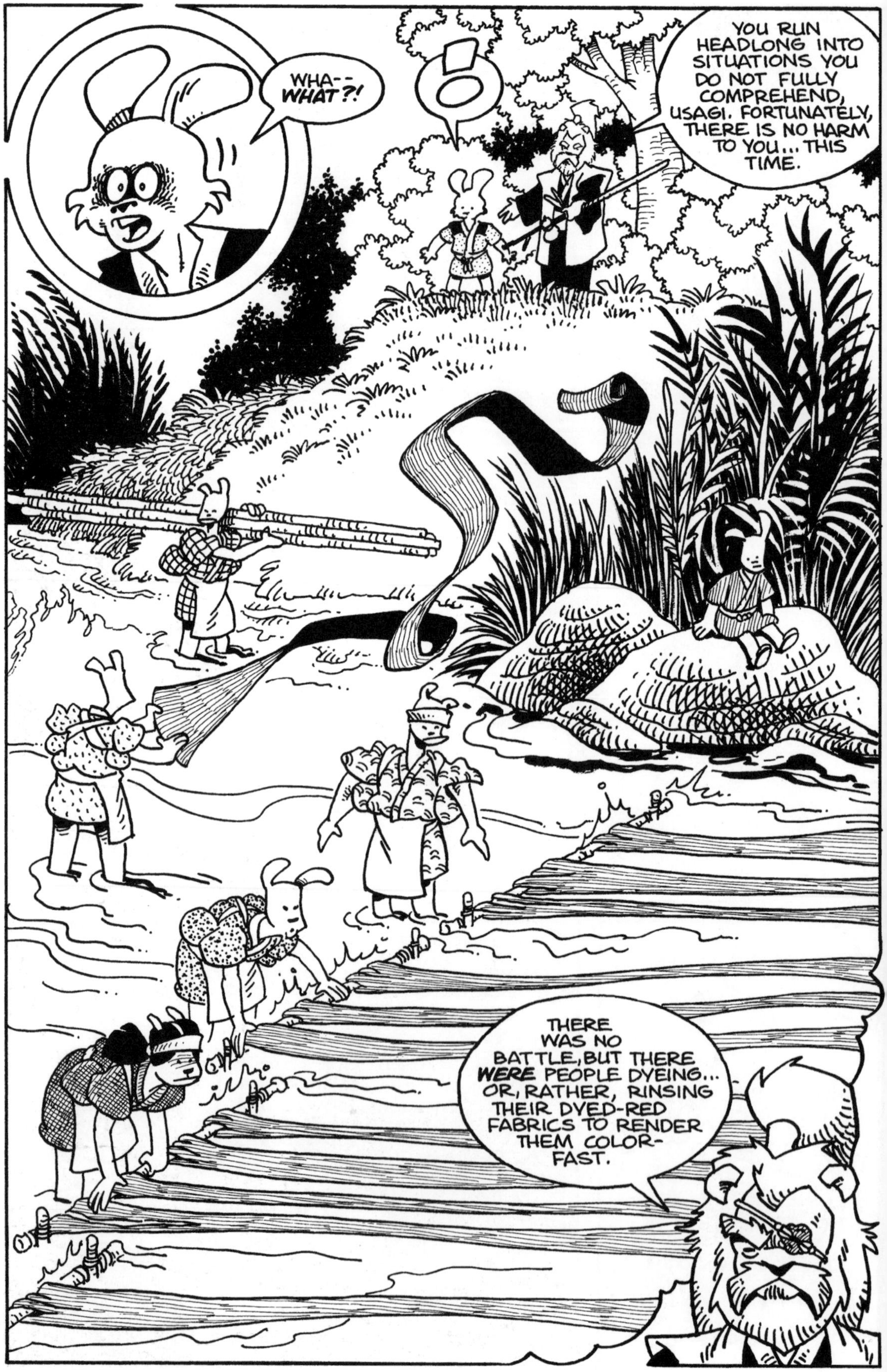
WHA--
WHAT?!
!
YOU RUN HEADLONG INTO SITUATIONS YOU DO NOT FULLY COMPREHEND, USAGI. FORTUNATELY, THERE IS NO HARM TO YOU... THIS TIME.
THERE WAS NO BATTLE, BUT THERE WERE PEOPLE DYEING... OR, RATHER, RINSING THEIR DYED-RED FABRICS TO RENDER THEM COLOR-FAST.

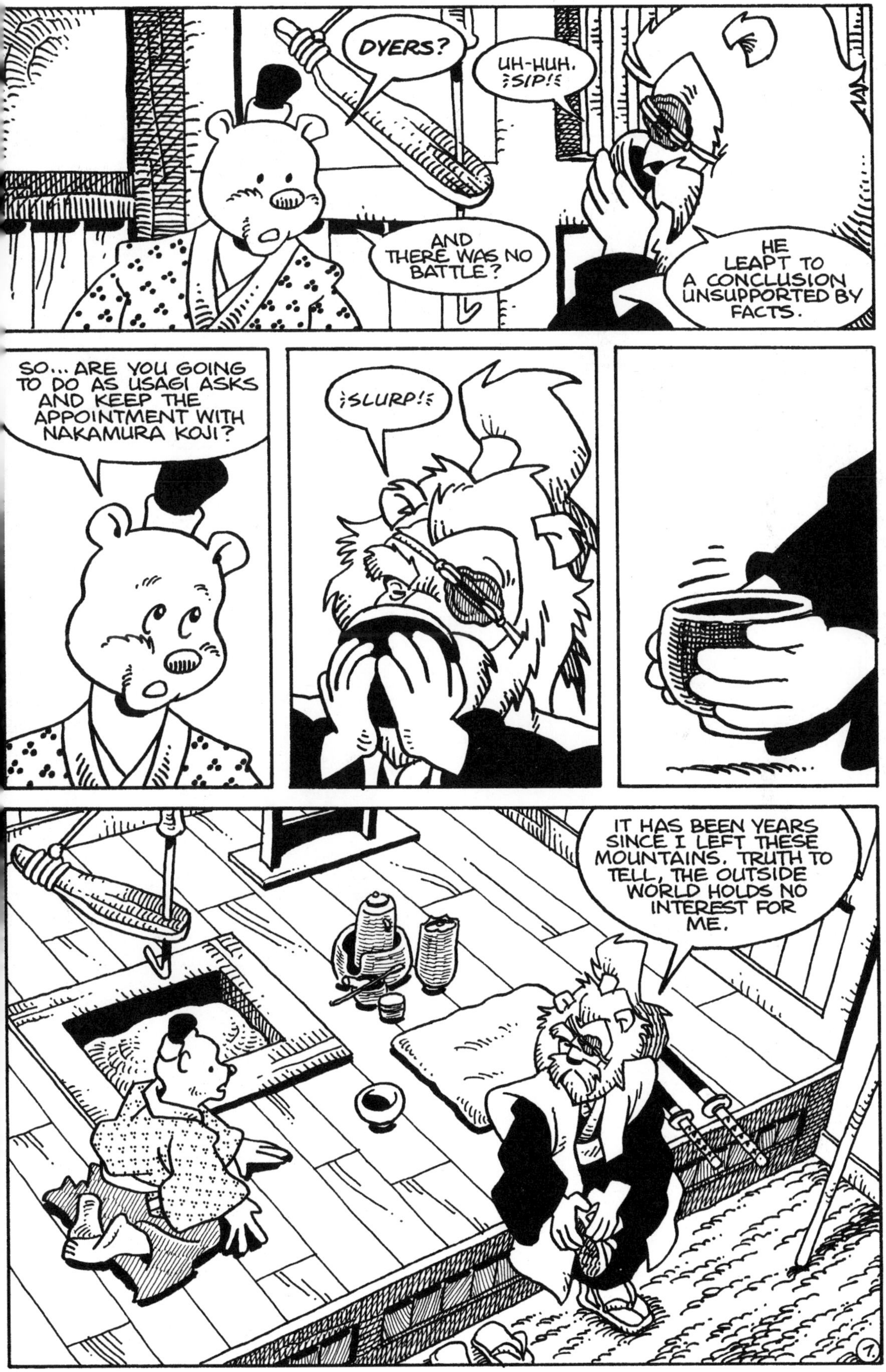
DYERS?
UH-HUH. ¡SIP!¡
AND THERE WAS NO BATTLE?
HE LEAPT TO A CONCLUSION UNSUPPORTED BY FACTS.
SO... ARE YOU GOING TO DO AS USAGI ASKS AND KEEP THE APPOINTMENT WITH NAKAMURA KOJI?
¡SLURP!¡
IT HAS BEEN YEARS SINCE I LEFT THESE MOUNTAINS. TRUTH TO TELL, THE OUTSIDE WORLD HOLDS NO INTEREST FOR ME.
7.

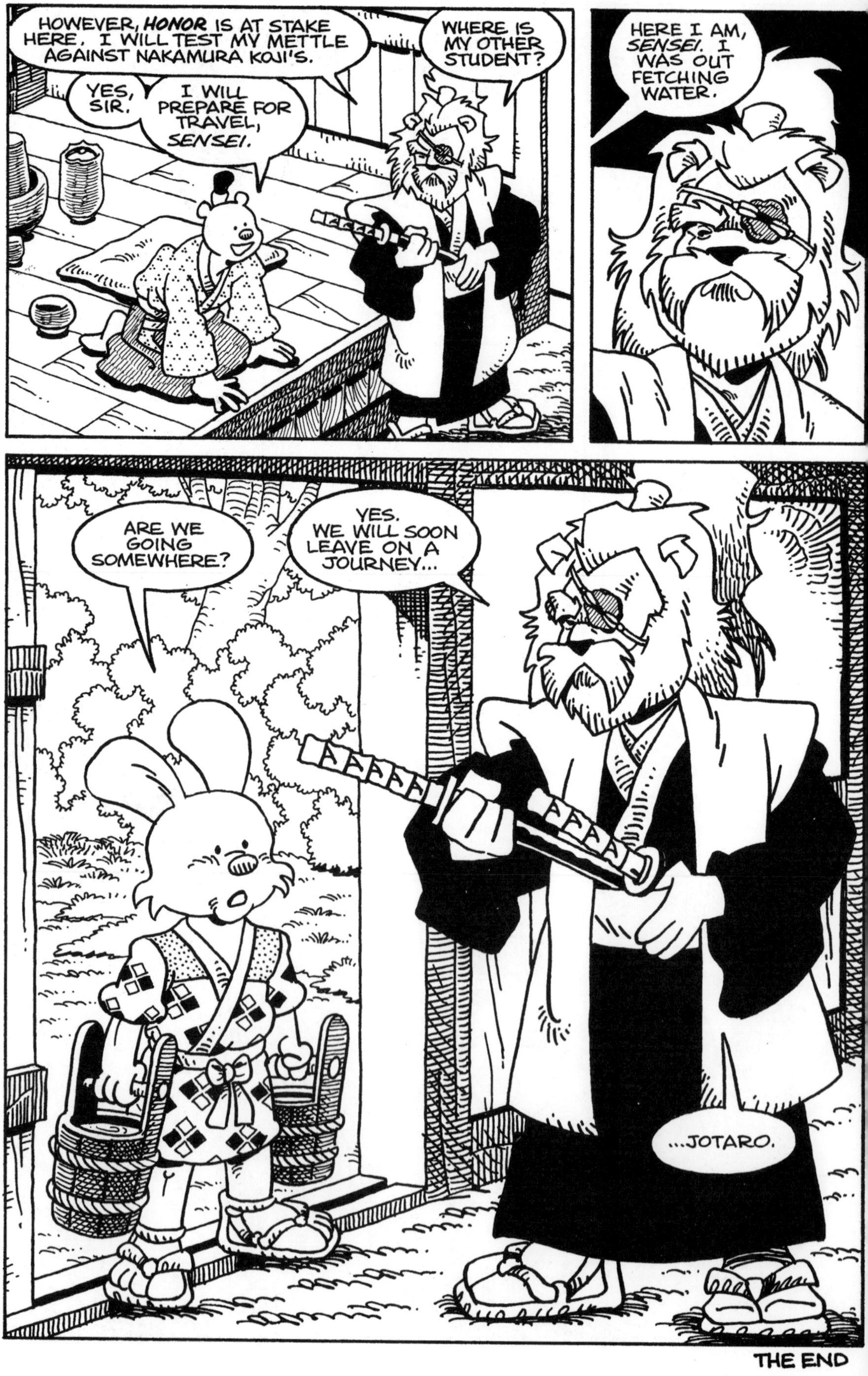
HOWEVER, **HONOR** IS AT STAKE HERE. I WILL TEST MY METTLE AGAINST NAKAMURA KOJI'S.
YES, SIR.
I WILL PREPARE FOR TRAVEL, *SENSEI.*
WHERE IS MY OTHER STUDENT?
HERE I AM, *SENSEI.* I WAS OUT FETCHING WATER.
ARE WE GOING SOMEWHERE?
YES. WE WILL SOON LEAVE ON A JOURNEY...
...JOTARO.
THE END

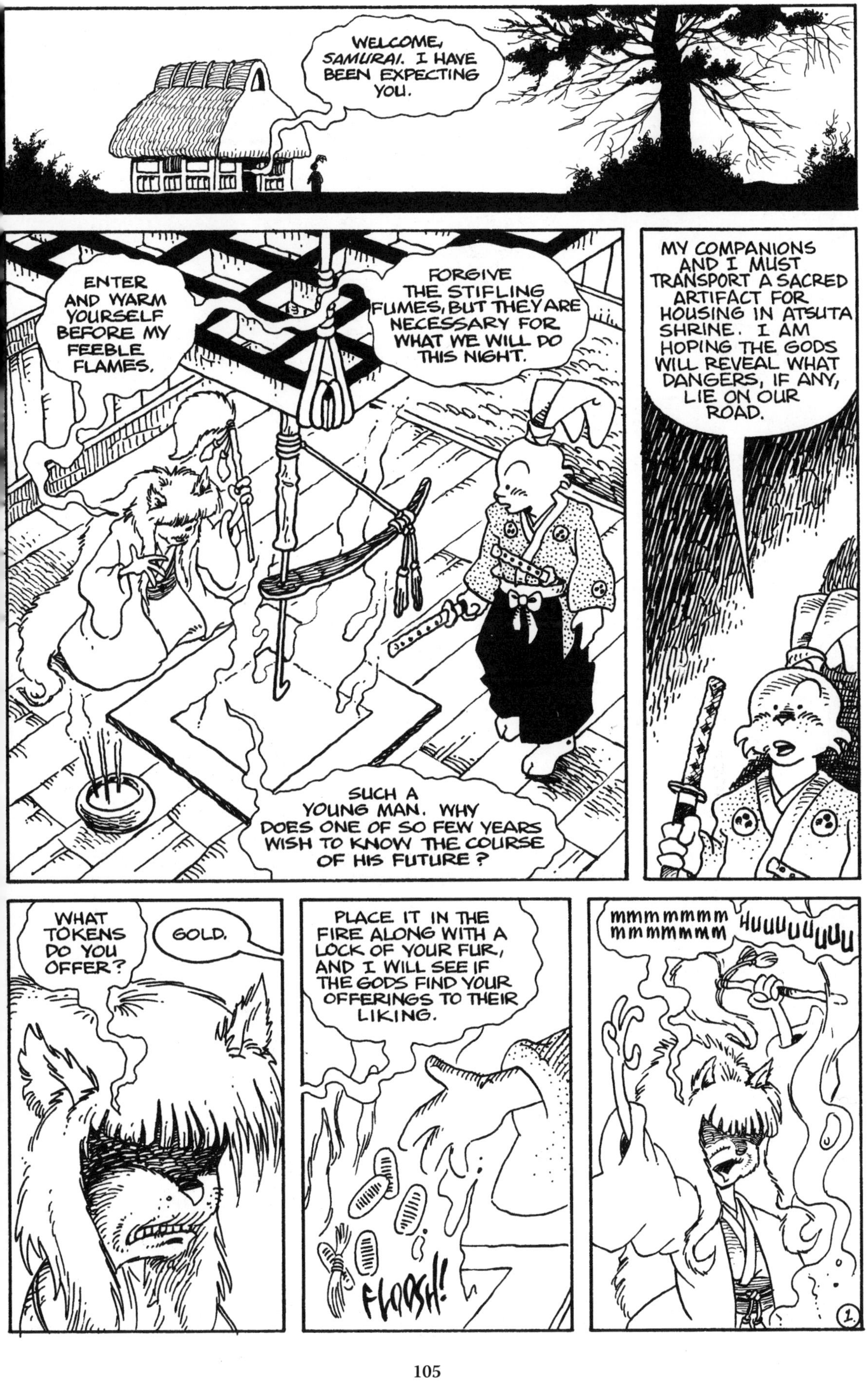
WELCOME, SAMURAI. I HAVE BEEN EXPECTING YOU.
ENTER AND WARM YOURSELF BEFORE MY FEEBLE FLAMES.
FORGIVE THE STIFLING FUMES, BUT THEY ARE NECESSARY FOR WHAT WE WILL DO THIS NIGHT.
SUCH A YOUNG MAN. WHY DOES ONE OF SO FEW YEARS WISH TO KNOW THE COURSE OF HIS FUTURE?
MY COMPANIONS AND I MUST TRANSPORT A SACRED ARTIFACT FOR HOUSING IN ATSUTA SHRINE. I AM HOPING THE GODS WILL REVEAL WHAT DANGERS, IF ANY, LIE ON OUR ROAD.
WHAT TOKENS DO YOU OFFER?
GOLD.
PLACE IT IN THE FIRE ALONG WITH A LOCK OF YOUR FUR, AND I WILL SEE IF THE GODS FIND YOUR OFFERINGS TO THEIR LIKING.
FLOOSH!
mmmmmmm mmmmmmm
HUUUUUUUU
1.

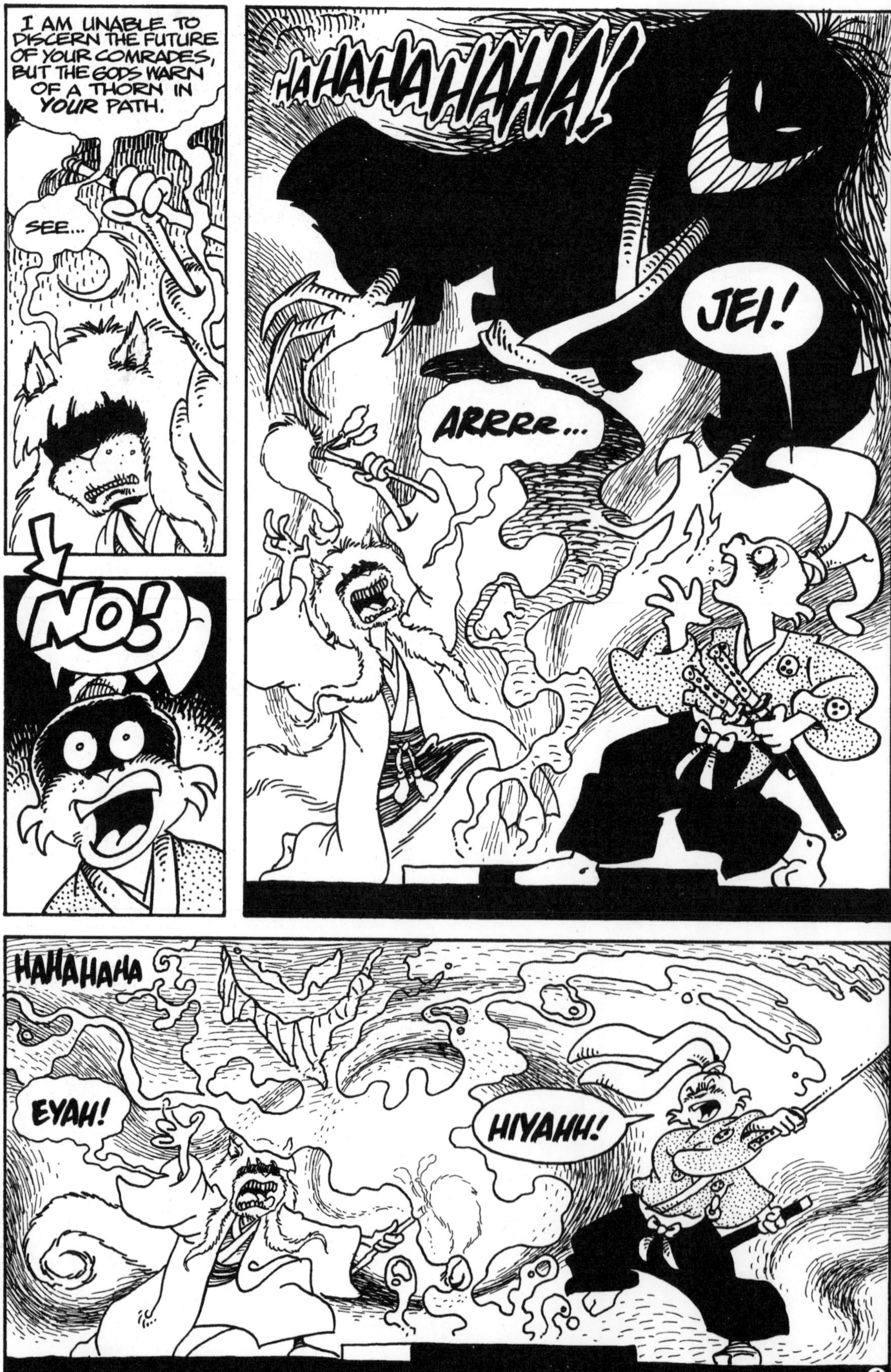

I AM UNABLE TO DISCERN THE FUTURE OF YOUR COMRADES, BUT THE GODS WARN OF A THORN IN YOUR PATH.
SEE...
NO!
HAHAHAHAHAHA!
JEI!
ARRRR...
HAHAHAHA
EYAH!
HIYAHH!
2

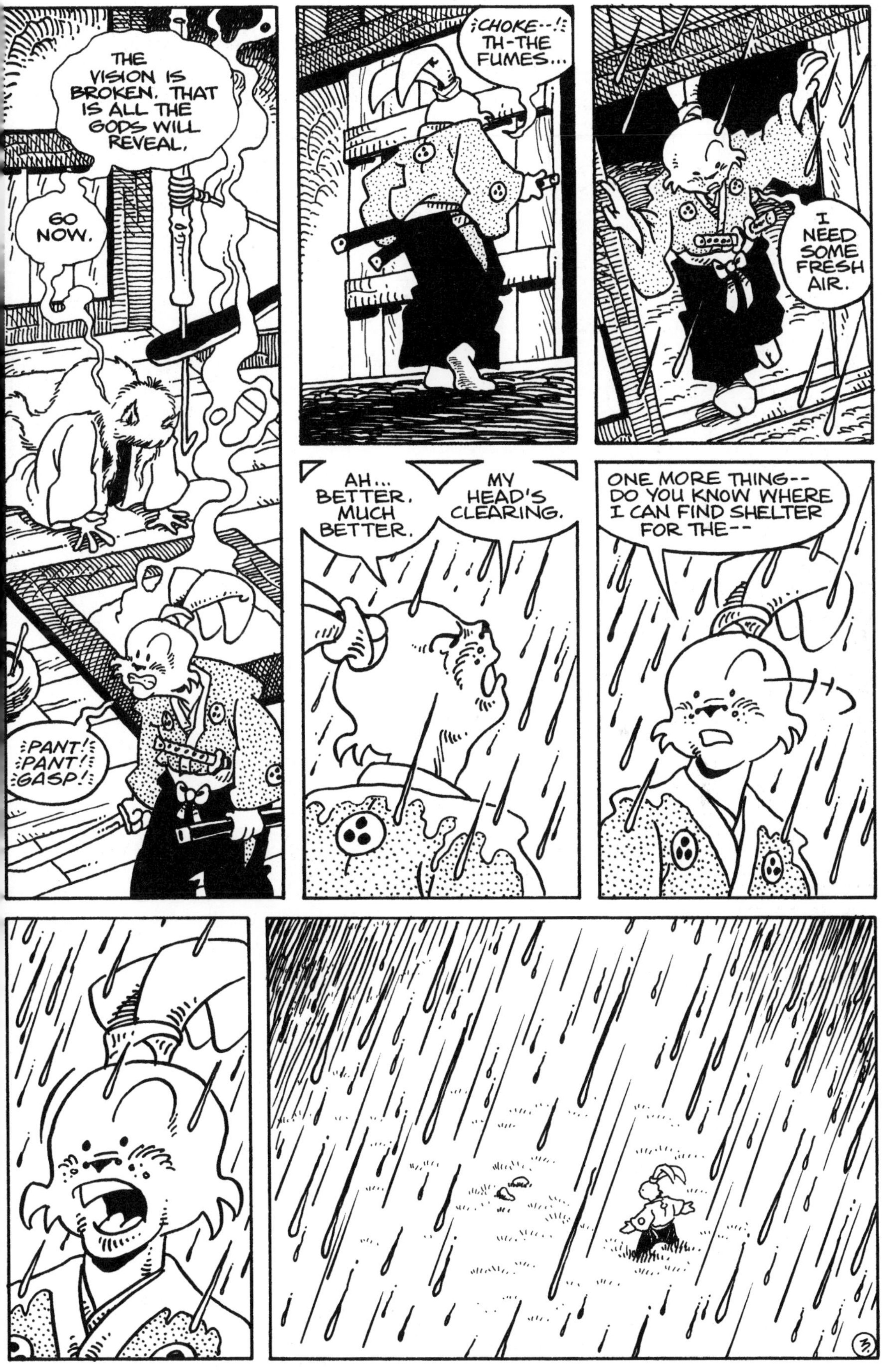
THE VISION IS BROKEN. THAT IS ALL THE GODS WILL REVEAL.
GO NOW.
PANT! PANT! GASP!
CHOKE--! TH-THE FUMES...
I NEED SOME FRESH AIR.
AH... BETTER. MUCH BETTER.
MY HEAD'S CLEARING.
ONE MORE THING-- DO YOU KNOW WHERE I CAN FIND SHELTER FOR THE--
3

THE MYSTERY OF THE DEMON MASK CHAPTER ONE

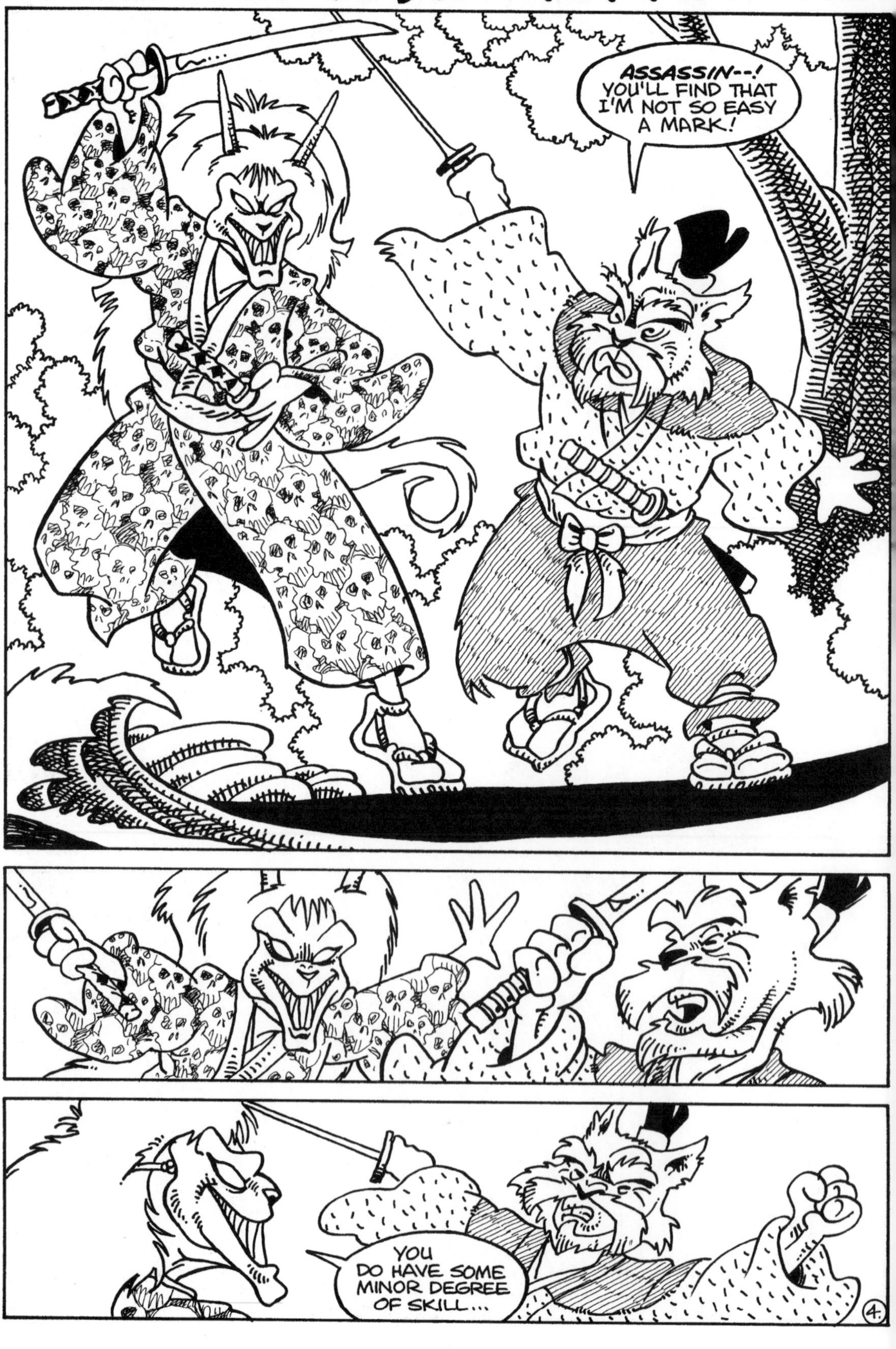
ASSASSIN--! YOU'LL FIND THAT I'M NOT SO EASY A MARK!
YOU DO HAVE SOME MINOR DEGREE OF SKILL...
4.

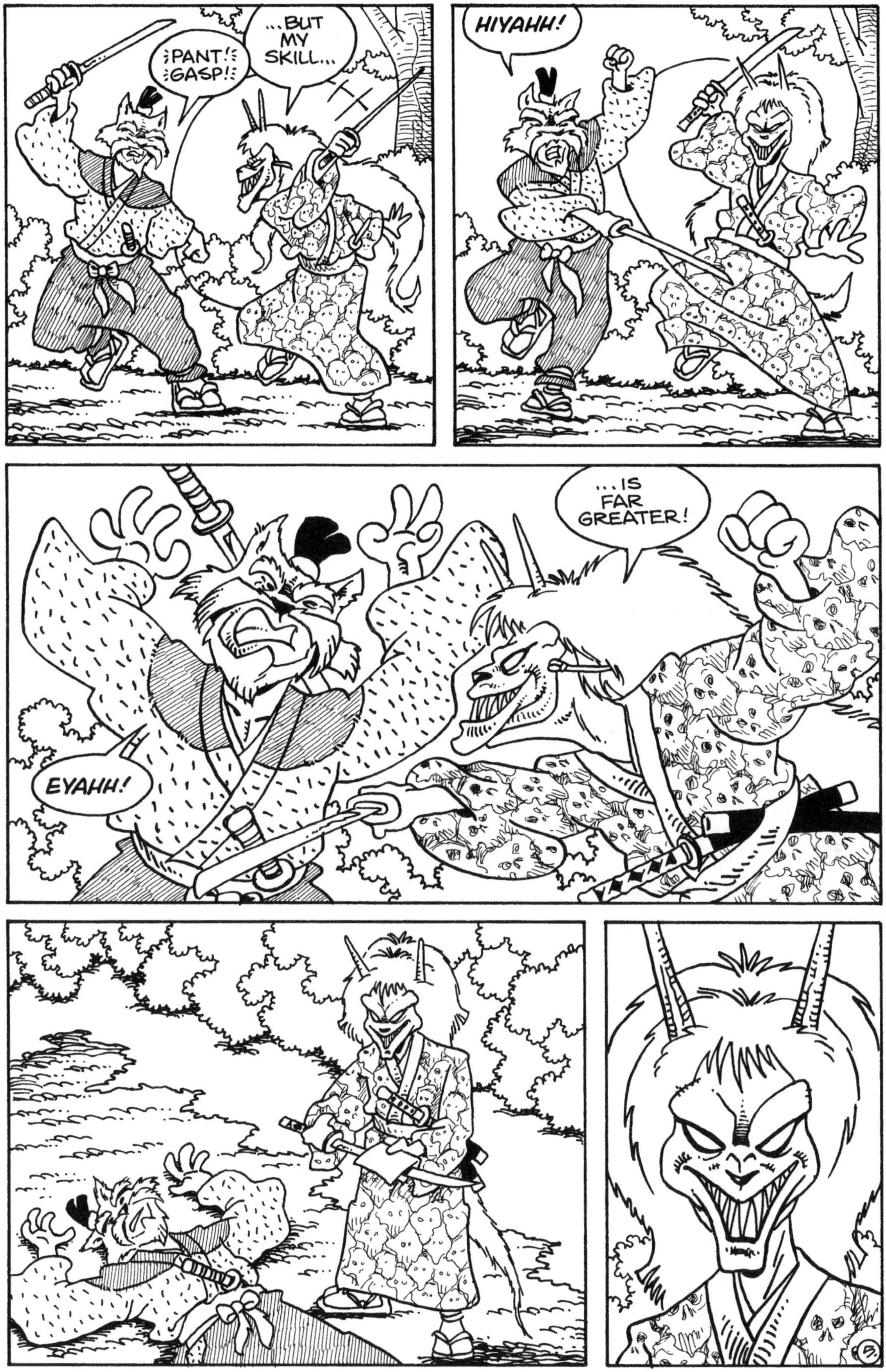

PANT! GASP!
...BUT MY SKILL...
HIYAHH!
...IS FAR GREATER!
EYAHH!
5

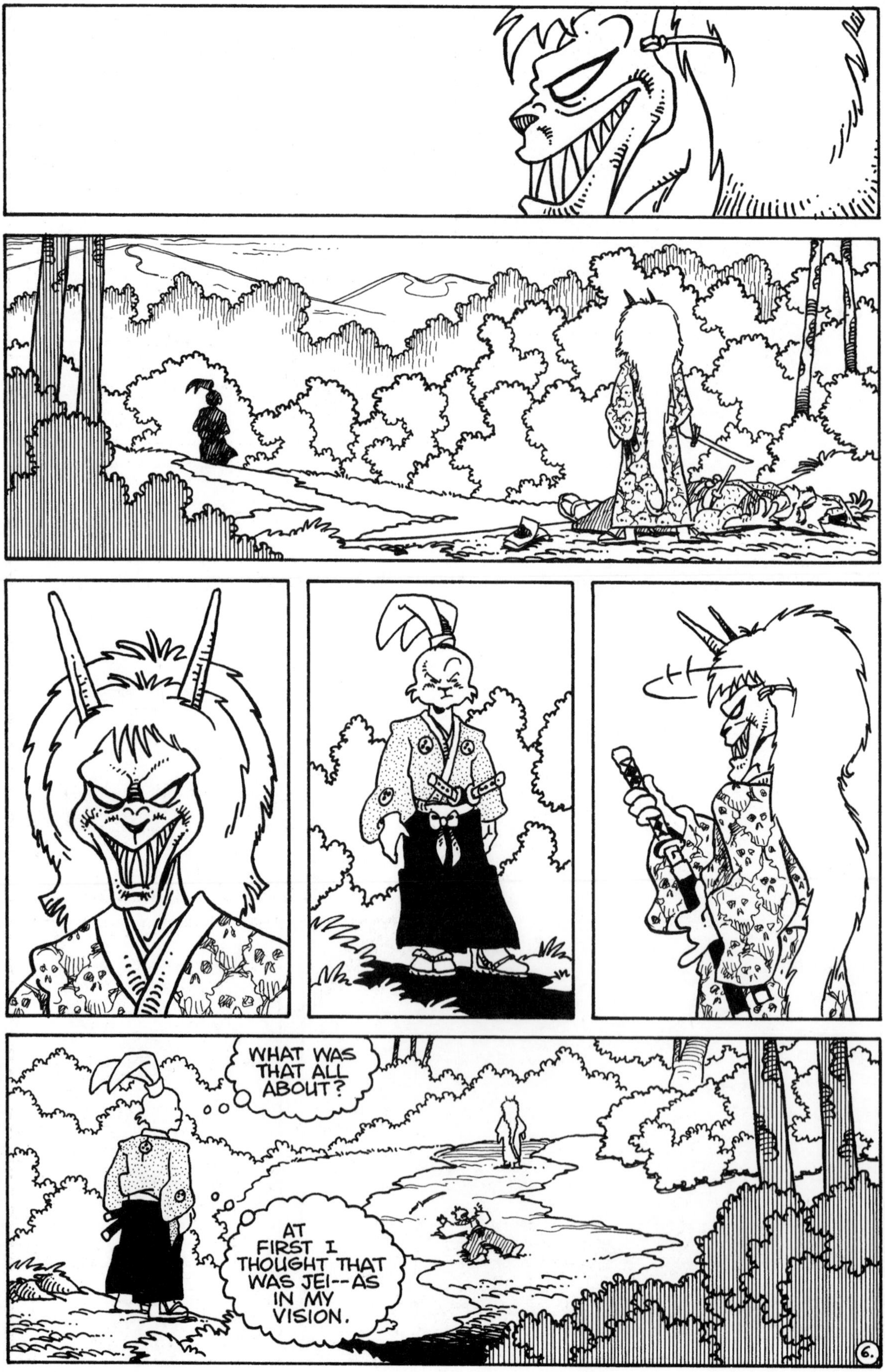

WHAT WAS THAT ALL ABOUT?
AT FIRST I THOUGHT THAT WAS JEI--AS IN MY VISION.
6.

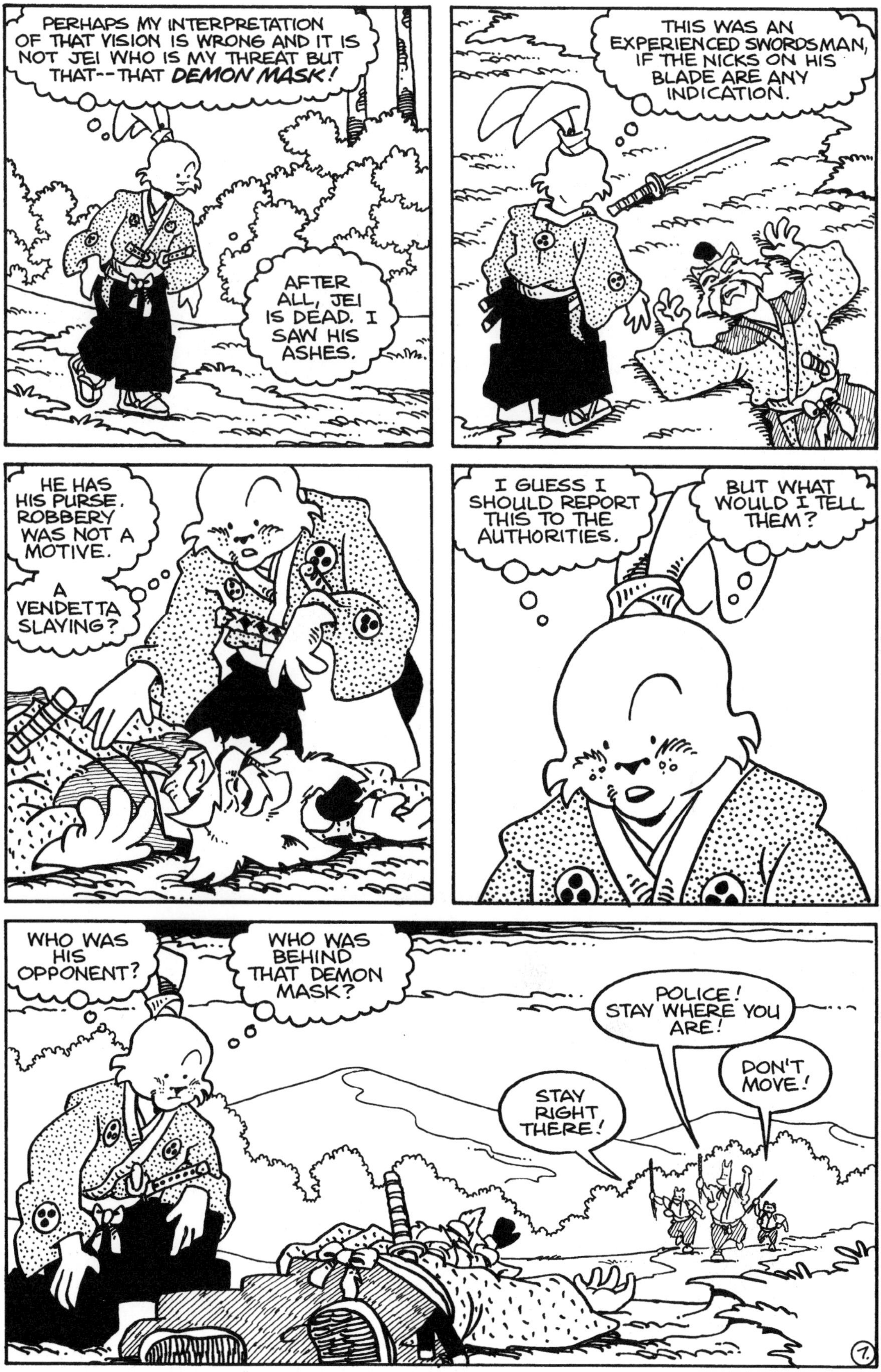
PERHAPS MY INTERPRETATION OF THAT VISION IS WRONG AND IT IS NOT JEI WHO IS MY THREAT BUT THAT--THAT DEMON MASK!
AFTER ALL, JEI IS DEAD. I SAW HIS ASHES.
THIS WAS AN EXPERIENCED SWORDSMAN, IF THE NICKS ON HIS BLADE ARE ANY INDICATION.
HE HAS HIS PURSE. ROBBERY WAS NOT A MOTIVE.
A VENDETTA SLAYING?
I GUESS I SHOULD REPORT THIS TO THE AUTHORITIES.
BUT WHAT WOULD I TELL THEM?
WHO WAS HIS OPPONENT?
WHO WAS BEHIND THAT DEMON MASK?
POLICE! STAY WHERE YOU ARE!
STAY RIGHT THERE!
DON'T MOVE!
7.

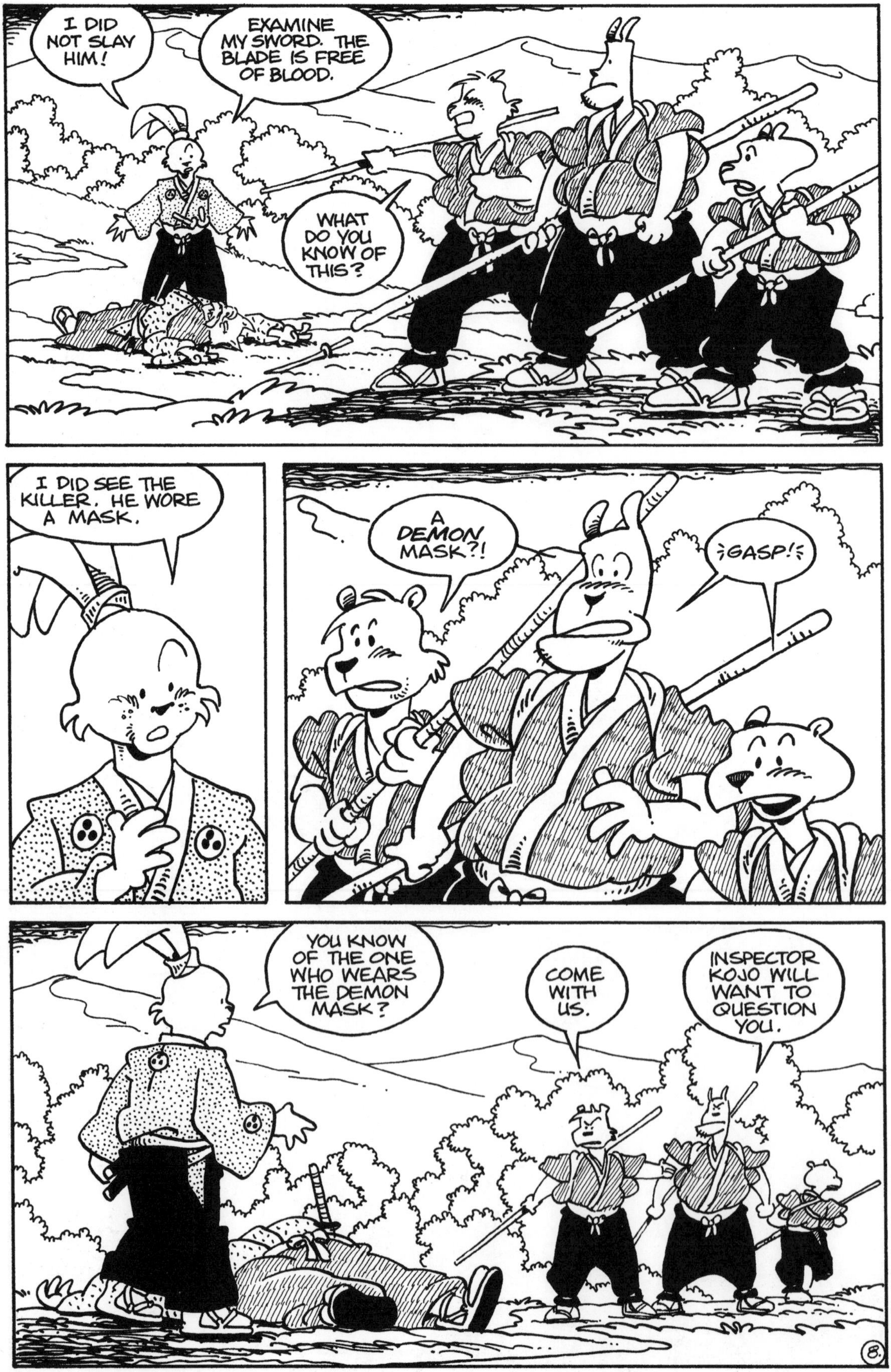
I DID NOT SLAY HIM!
EXAMINE MY SWORD. THE BLADE IS FREE OF BLOOD.
WHAT DO YOU KNOW OF THIS?
I DID SEE THE KILLER. HE WORE A MASK.
A DEMON MASK?!
GASP!
YOU KNOW OF THE ONE WHO WEARS THE DEMON MASK?
COME WITH US.
INSPECTOR KOJO WILL WANT TO QUESTION YOU.
8.

 CHOP!

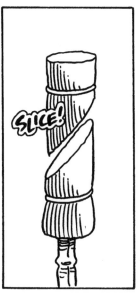 SLICE!

 CUT!

 SL'T!

SORRY TO INTERRUPT YOUR PRACTICE, ASSISTANT INSPECTOR NITTA, BUT THERE HAS BEEN A KILLING ON THE NORTH ROAD.

DEMON MASK?

YES, SIR.

WHO IS THIS?

THIS IS MIYAMOTO USAGI, A WITNESS WE ARE ESCORTING TO INSPECTOR KOJO FOR QUESTIONING.

ARE YOU A *RONIN**?

YES.

*MASTERLESS SAMURAI

PFFT.

ONE OF YOU, COME WITH ME TO INVESTIGATE THE CRIME SCENE.

YES, SIR.

9.

113

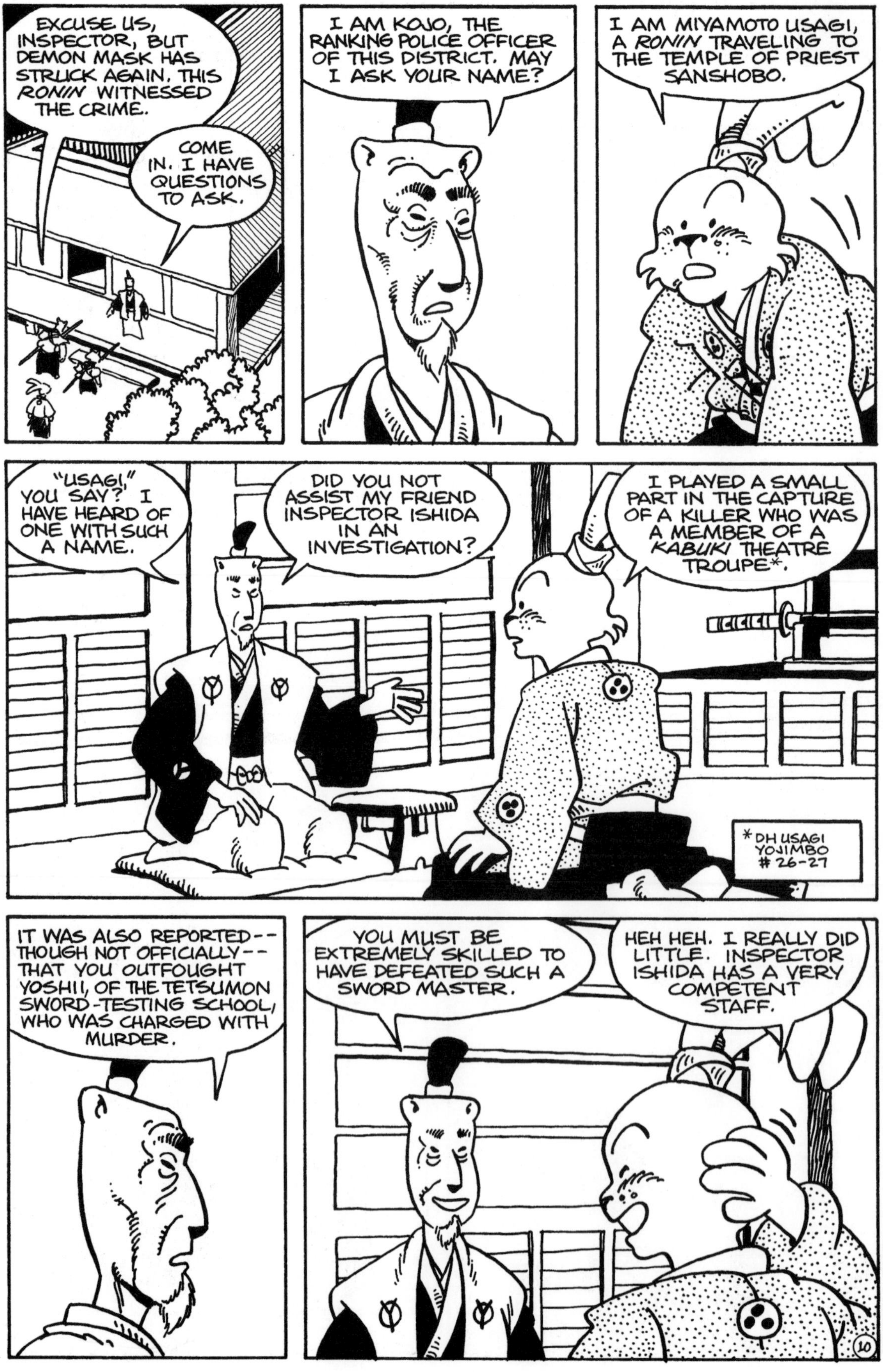
EXCUSE US, INSPECTOR, BUT DEMON MASK HAS STRUCK AGAIN. THIS *RONIN* WITNESSED THE CRIME.
COME IN. I HAVE QUESTIONS TO ASK.
I AM KOJO, THE RANKING POLICE OFFICER OF THIS DISTRICT. MAY I ASK YOUR NAME?
I AM MIYAMOTO USAGI, A *RONIN* TRAVELING TO THE TEMPLE OF PRIEST SANSHOBO.
"USAGI," YOU SAY? I HAVE HEARD OF ONE WITH SUCH A NAME.
DID YOU NOT ASSIST MY FRIEND INSPECTOR ISHIDA IN AN INVESTIGATION?
I PLAYED A SMALL PART IN THE CAPTURE OF A KILLER WHO WAS A MEMBER OF A *KABUKI* THEATRE TROUPE*.
*DH USAGI YOJIMBO # 26-27
IT WAS ALSO REPORTED-- THOUGH NOT OFFICIALLY-- THAT YOU OUTFOUGHT YOSHII, OF THE TETSUMON SWORD-TESTING SCHOOL, WHO WAS CHARGED WITH MURDER.
YOU MUST BE EXTREMELY SKILLED TO HAVE DEFEATED SUCH A SWORD MASTER.
HEH HEH. I REALLY DID LITTLE. INSPECTOR ISHIDA HAS A VERY COMPETENT STAFF.
10

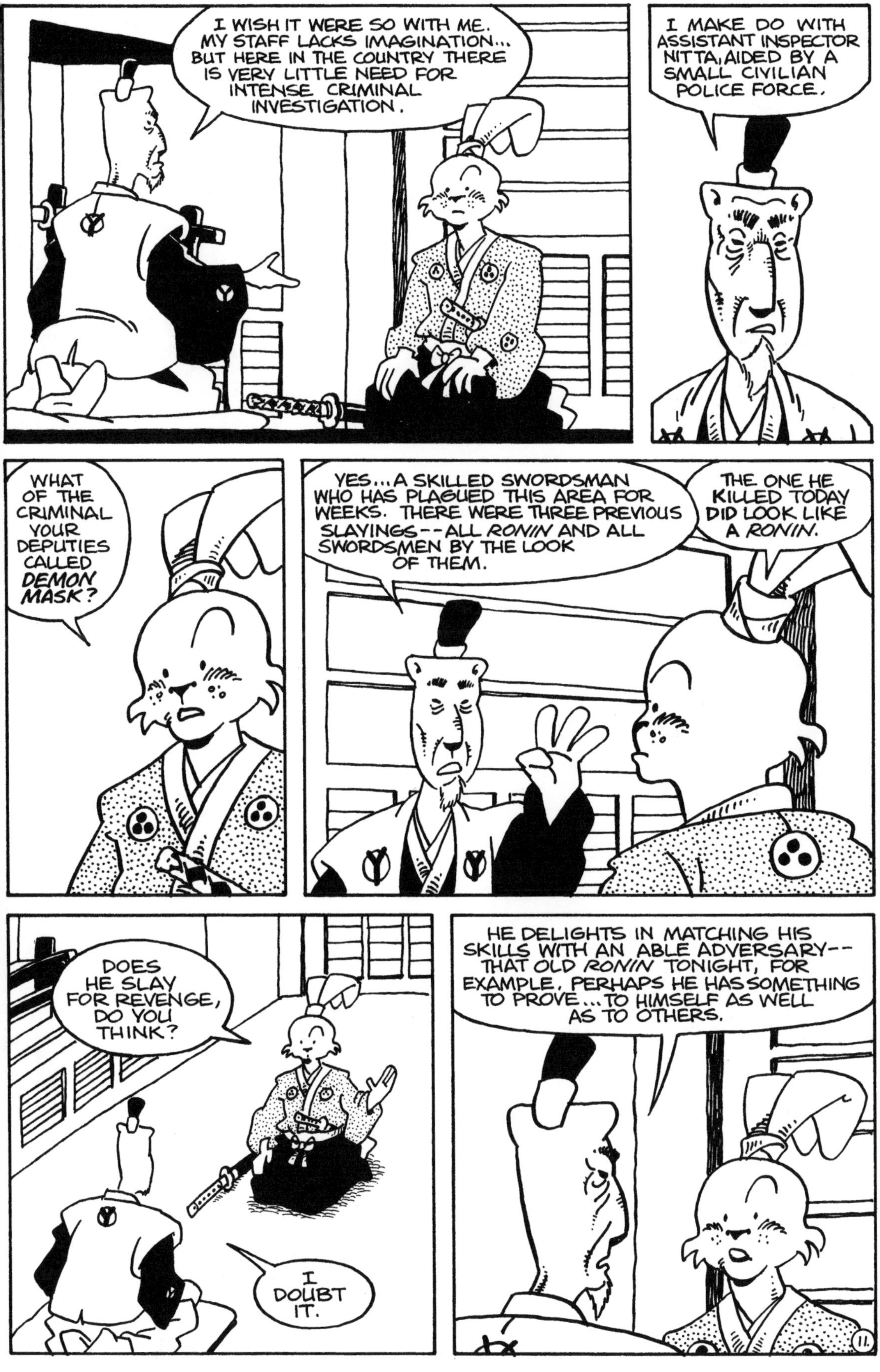
I WISH IT WERE SO WITH ME. MY STAFF LACKS IMAGINATION... BUT HERE IN THE COUNTRY THERE IS VERY LITTLE NEED FOR INTENSE CRIMINAL INVESTIGATION.
I MAKE DO WITH ASSISTANT INSPECTOR NITTA, AIDED BY A SMALL CIVILIAN POLICE FORCE.
WHAT OF THE CRIMINAL YOUR DEPUTIES CALLED *DEMON MASK*?
YES... A SKILLED SWORDSMAN WHO HAS PLAGUED THIS AREA FOR WEEKS. THERE WERE THREE PREVIOUS SLAYINGS--ALL *RONIN* AND ALL SWORDSMEN BY THE LOOK OF THEM.
THE ONE HE KILLED TODAY DID LOOK LIKE A *RONIN*.
DOES HE SLAY FOR REVENGE, DO YOU THINK?
I DOUBT IT.
HE DELIGHTS IN MATCHING HIS SKILLS WITH AN ABLE ADVERSARY--THAT OLD *RONIN* TONIGHT, FOR EXAMPLE. PERHAPS HE HAS SOMETHING TO PROVE... TO HIMSELF AS WELL AS TO OTHERS.
11.

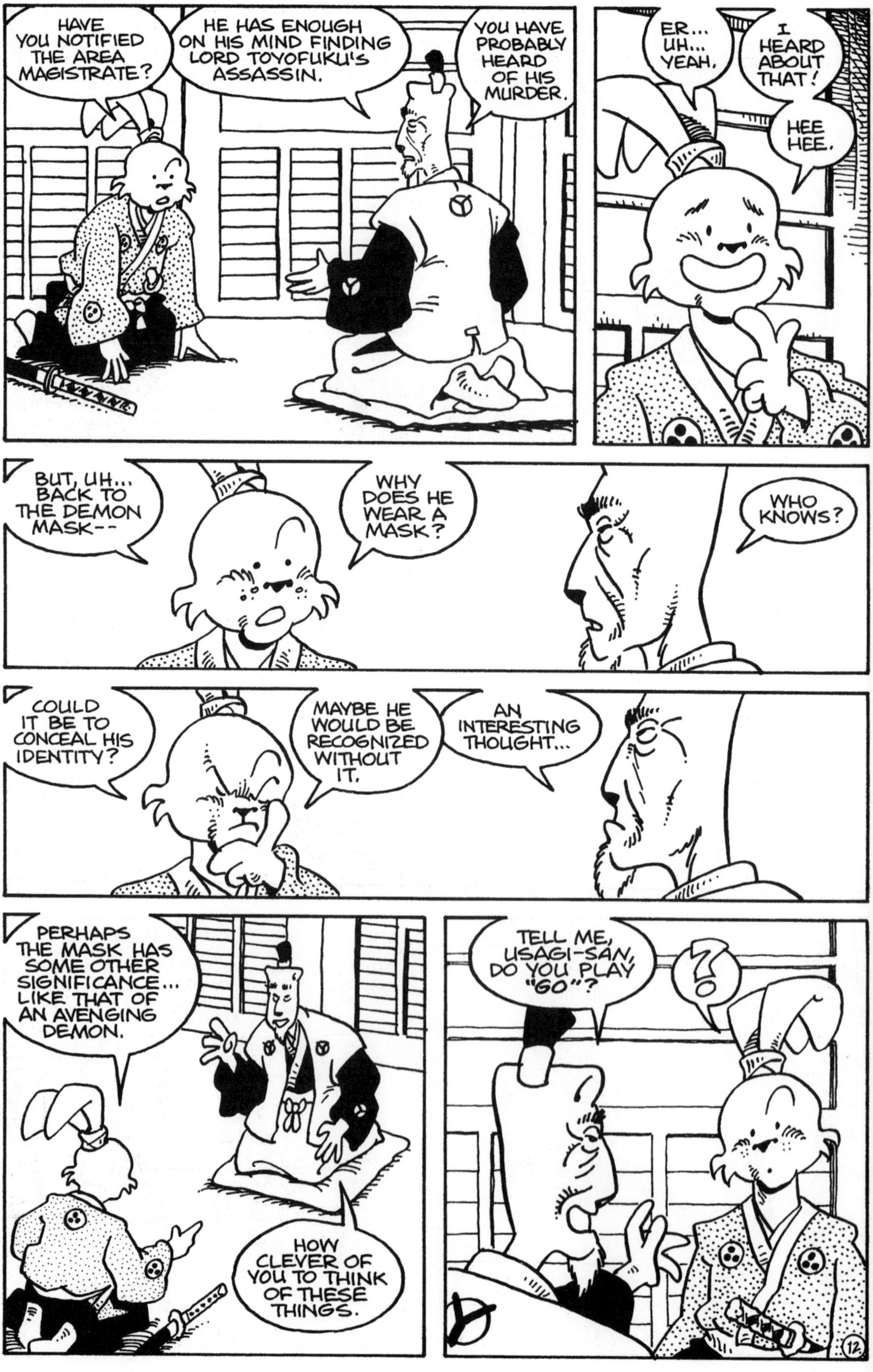
HAVE YOU NOTIFIED THE AREA MAGISTRATE?
HE HAS ENOUGH ON HIS MIND FINDING LORD TOYOFUKU'S ASSASSIN.
YOU HAVE PROBABLY HEARD OF HIS MURDER.
ER... UH... YEAH.
I HEARD ABOUT THAT!
HEE HEE.
BUT, UH... BACK TO THE DEMON MASK--
WHY DOES HE WEAR A MASK?
WHO KNOWS?
COULD IT BE TO CONCEAL HIS IDENTITY?
MAYBE HE WOULD BE RECOGNIZED WITHOUT IT.
AN INTERESTING THOUGHT...
PERHAPS THE MASK HAS SOME OTHER SIGNIFICANCE... LIKE THAT OF AN AVENGING DEMON.
HOW CLEVER OF YOU TO THINK OF THESE THINGS.
TELL ME, USAGI-SAN, DO YOU PLAY "GO"?
?
12

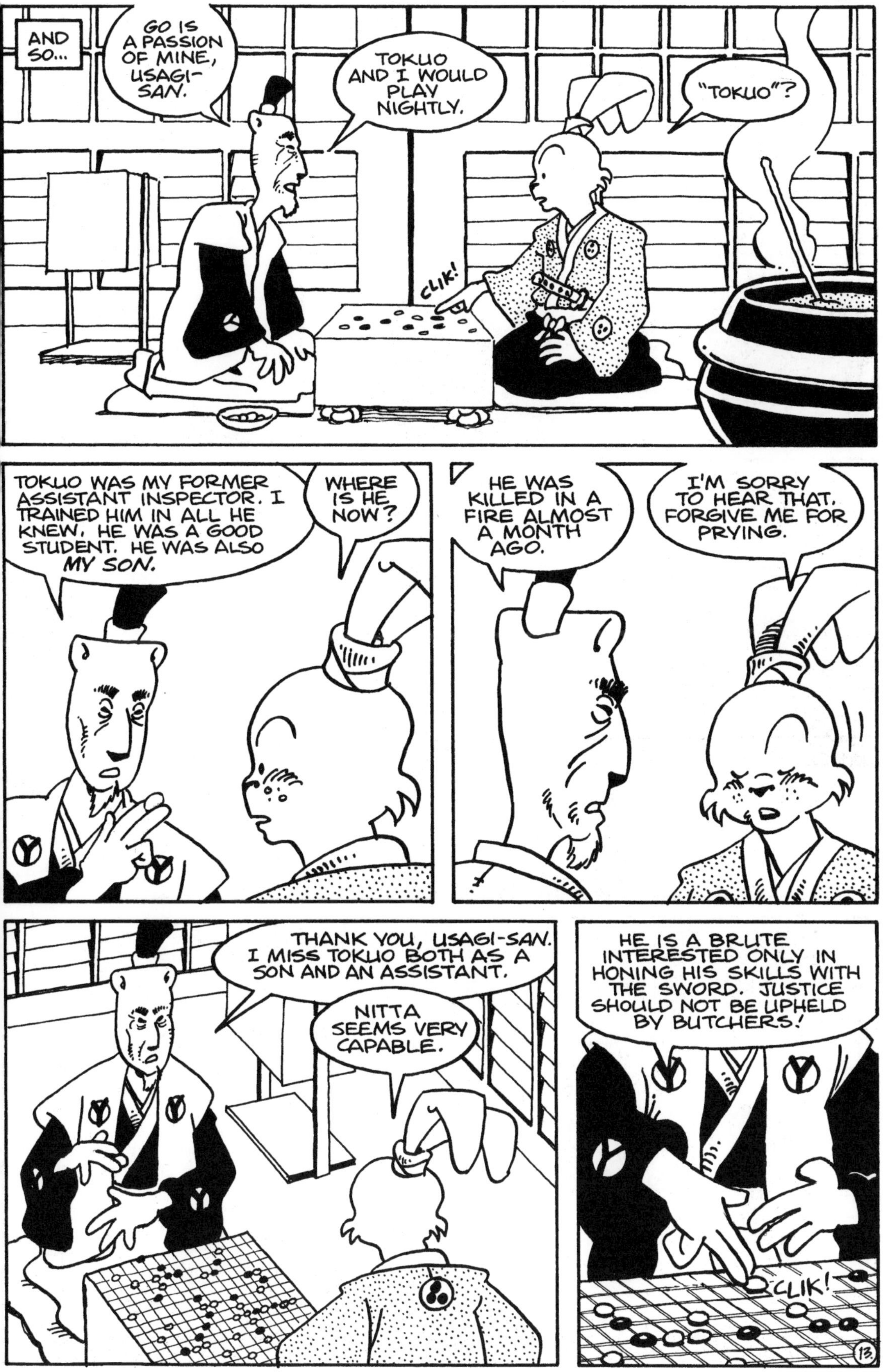
AND SO...
GO IS A PASSION OF MINE, USAGI-SAN.
TOKUO AND I WOULD PLAY NIGHTLY.
CLIK!
"TOKUO"?
TOKUO WAS MY FORMER ASSISTANT INSPECTOR. I TRAINED HIM IN ALL HE KNEW. HE WAS A GOOD STUDENT. HE WAS ALSO MY SON.
WHERE IS HE NOW?
HE WAS KILLED IN A FIRE ALMOST A MONTH AGO.
I'M SORRY TO HEAR THAT. FORGIVE ME FOR PRYING.
THANK YOU, USAGI-SAN. I MISS TOKUO BOTH AS A SON AND AN ASSISTANT.
NITTA SEEMS VERY CAPABLE.
HE IS A BRUTE INTERESTED ONLY IN HONING HIS SKILLS WITH THE SWORD. JUSTICE SHOULD NOT BE UPHELD BY BUTCHERS!
CLIK!
13.

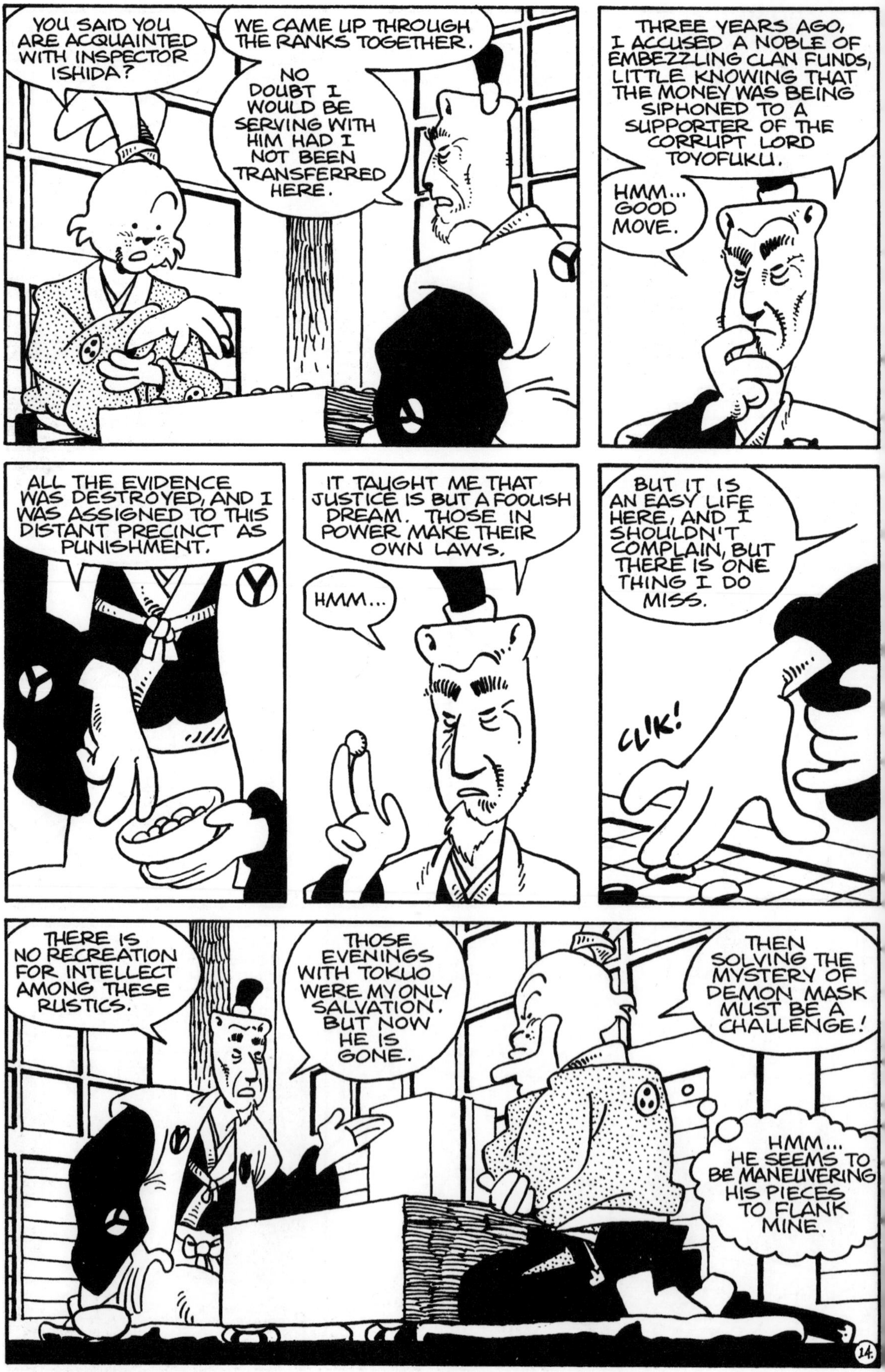
YOU SAID YOU ARE ACQUAINTED WITH INSPECTOR ISHIDA?
WE CAME UP THROUGH THE RANKS TOGETHER.
NO DOUBT I WOULD BE SERVING WITH HIM HAD I NOT BEEN TRANSFERRED HERE.
THREE YEARS AGO, I ACCUSED A NOBLE OF EMBEZZLING CLAN FUNDS, LITTLE KNOWING THAT THE MONEY WAS BEING SIPHONED TO A SUPPORTER OF THE CORRUPT LORD TOYOFUKU.
HMM... GOOD MOVE.
ALL THE EVIDENCE WAS DESTROYED, AND I WAS ASSIGNED TO THIS DISTANT PRECINCT AS PUNISHMENT.
IT TAUGHT ME THAT JUSTICE IS BUT A FOOLISH DREAM. THOSE IN POWER MAKE THEIR OWN LAWS.
HMM...
BUT IT IS AN EASY LIFE HERE, AND I SHOULDN'T COMPLAIN, BUT THERE IS ONE THING I DO MISS.
CLIK!
THERE IS NO RECREATION FOR INTELLECT AMONG THESE RUSTICS.
THOSE EVENINGS WITH TOKUO WERE MY ONLY SALVATION. BUT NOW HE IS GONE.
THEN SOLVING THE MYSTERY OF DEMON MASK MUST BE A CHALLENGE!
HMM... HE SEEMS TO BE MANEUVERING HIS PIECES TO FLANK MINE.
14.

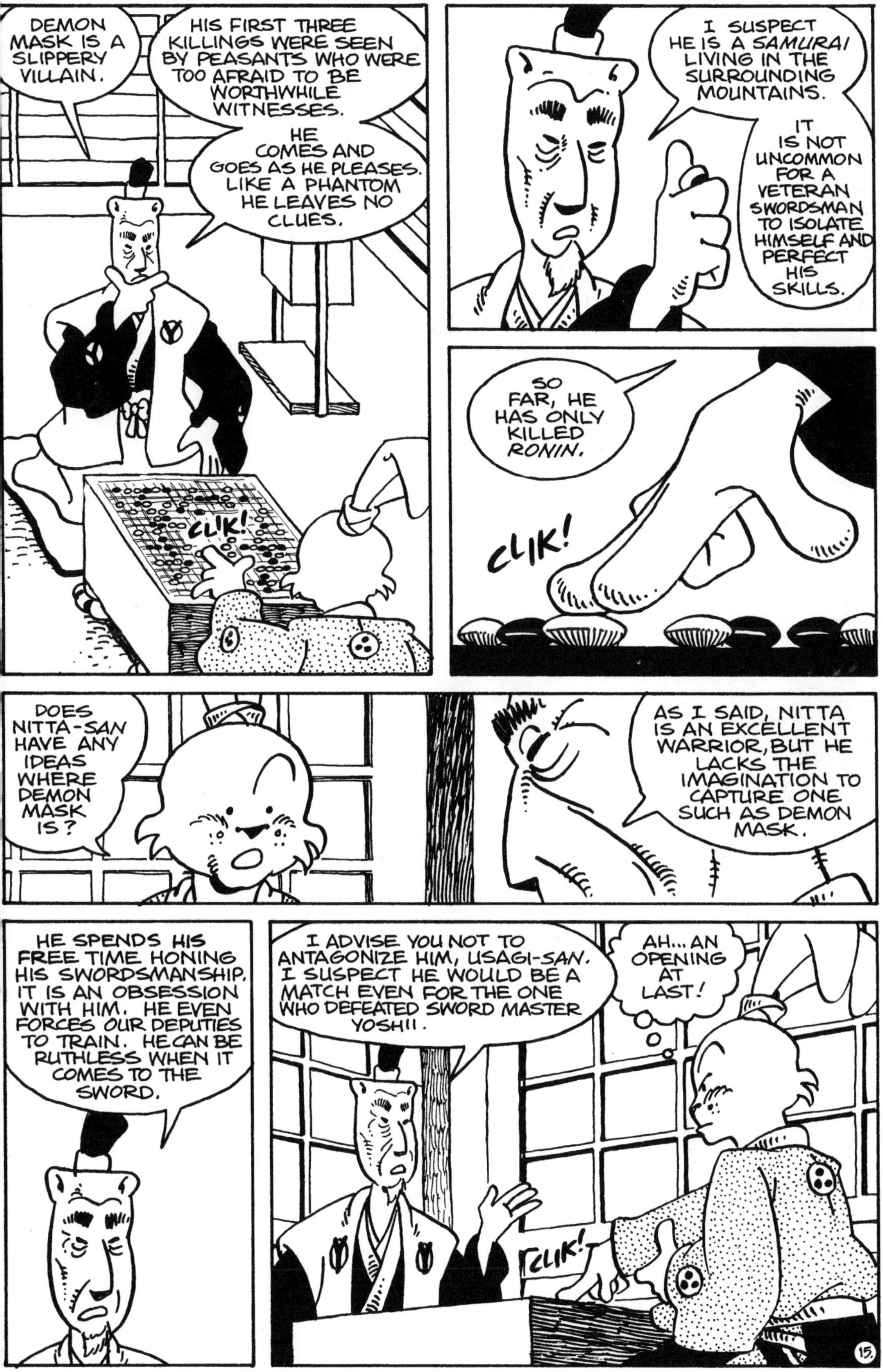
DEMON MASK IS A SLIPPERY VILLAIN.
HIS FIRST THREE KILLINGS WERE SEEN BY PEASANTS WHO WERE TOO AFRAID TO BE WORTHWHILE WITNESSES.
HE COMES AND GOES AS HE PLEASES. LIKE A PHANTOM HE LEAVES NO CLUES.
CLIK!
I SUSPECT HE IS A *SAMURAI* LIVING IN THE SURROUNDING MOUNTAINS.
IT IS NOT UNCOMMON FOR A VETERAN SWORDSMAN TO ISOLATE HIMSELF AND PERFECT HIS SKILLS.
SO FAR, HE HAS ONLY KILLED *RONIN*.
CLIK!
DOES NITTA-*SAN* HAVE ANY IDEAS WHERE DEMON MASK IS?
AS I SAID, NITTA IS AN EXCELLENT WARRIOR, BUT HE LACKS THE IMAGINATION TO CAPTURE ONE SUCH AS DEMON MASK.
HE SPENDS HIS FREE TIME HONING HIS SWORDSMANSHIP. IT IS AN OBSESSION WITH HIM. HE EVEN FORCES OUR DEPUTIES TO TRAIN. HE CAN BE RUTHLESS WHEN IT COMES TO THE SWORD.
I ADVISE YOU NOT TO ANTAGONIZE HIM, USAGI-*SAN*. I SUSPECT HE WOULD BE A MATCH EVEN FOR THE ONE WHO DEFEATED SWORD MASTER YOSHII.
AH... AN OPENING AT LAST!
CLIK!
15

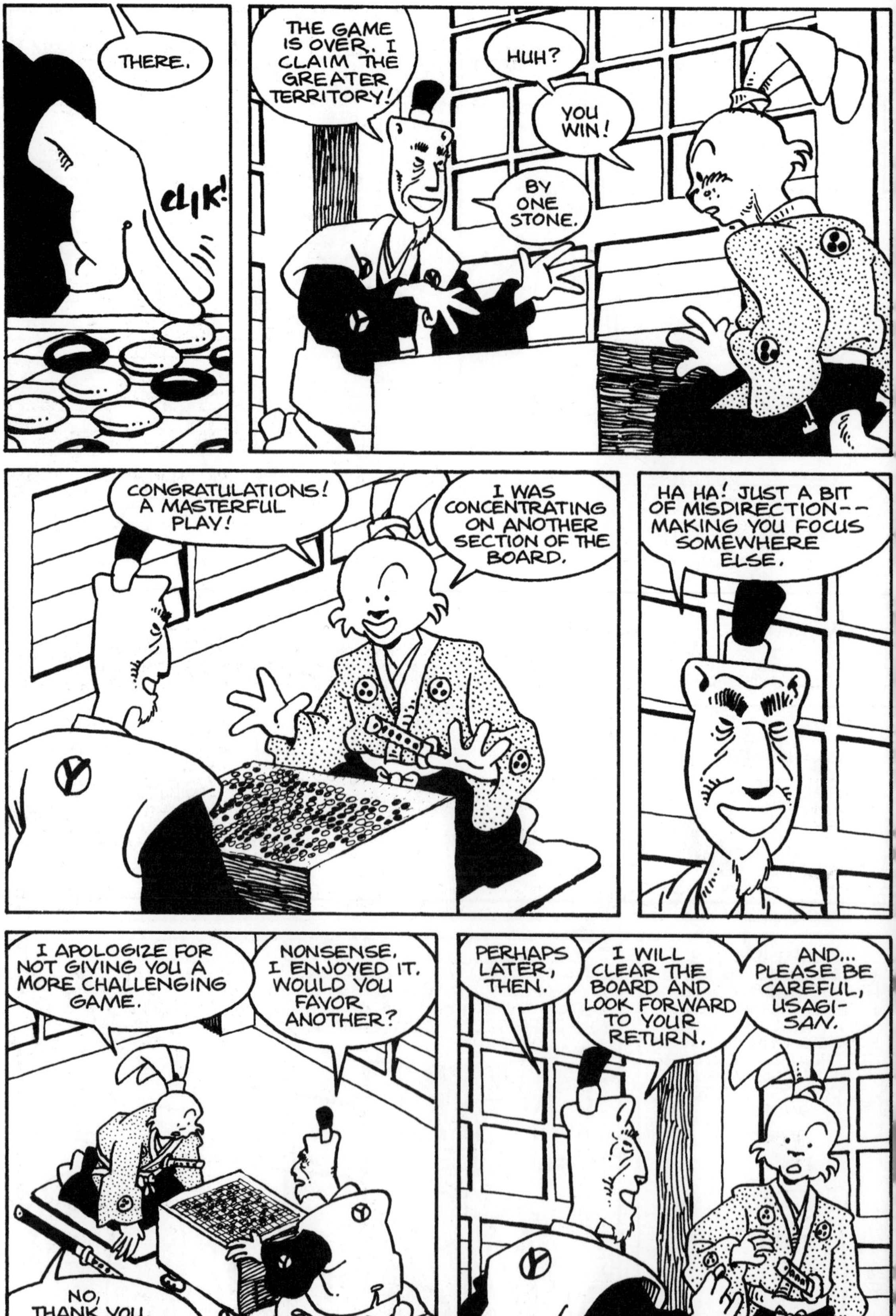
THERE.
CLIK!
THE GAME IS OVER. I CLAIM THE GREATER TERRITORY!
HUH?
YOU WIN!
BY ONE STONE.
CONGRATULATIONS! A MASTERFUL PLAY!
I WAS CONCENTRATING ON ANOTHER SECTION OF THE BOARD.
HA HA! JUST A BIT OF MISDIRECTION-- MAKING YOU FOCUS SOMEWHERE ELSE.
I APOLOGIZE FOR NOT GIVING YOU A MORE CHALLENGING GAME.
NONSENSE. I ENJOYED IT. WOULD YOU FAVOR ANOTHER?
NO, THANK YOU. I WOULD LIKE TO GET A MEAL AT AN INN.
PERHAPS LATER, THEN.
I WILL CLEAR THE BOARD AND LOOK FORWARD TO YOUR RETURN.
AND... PLEASE BE CAREFUL, USAGI-SAN.
16

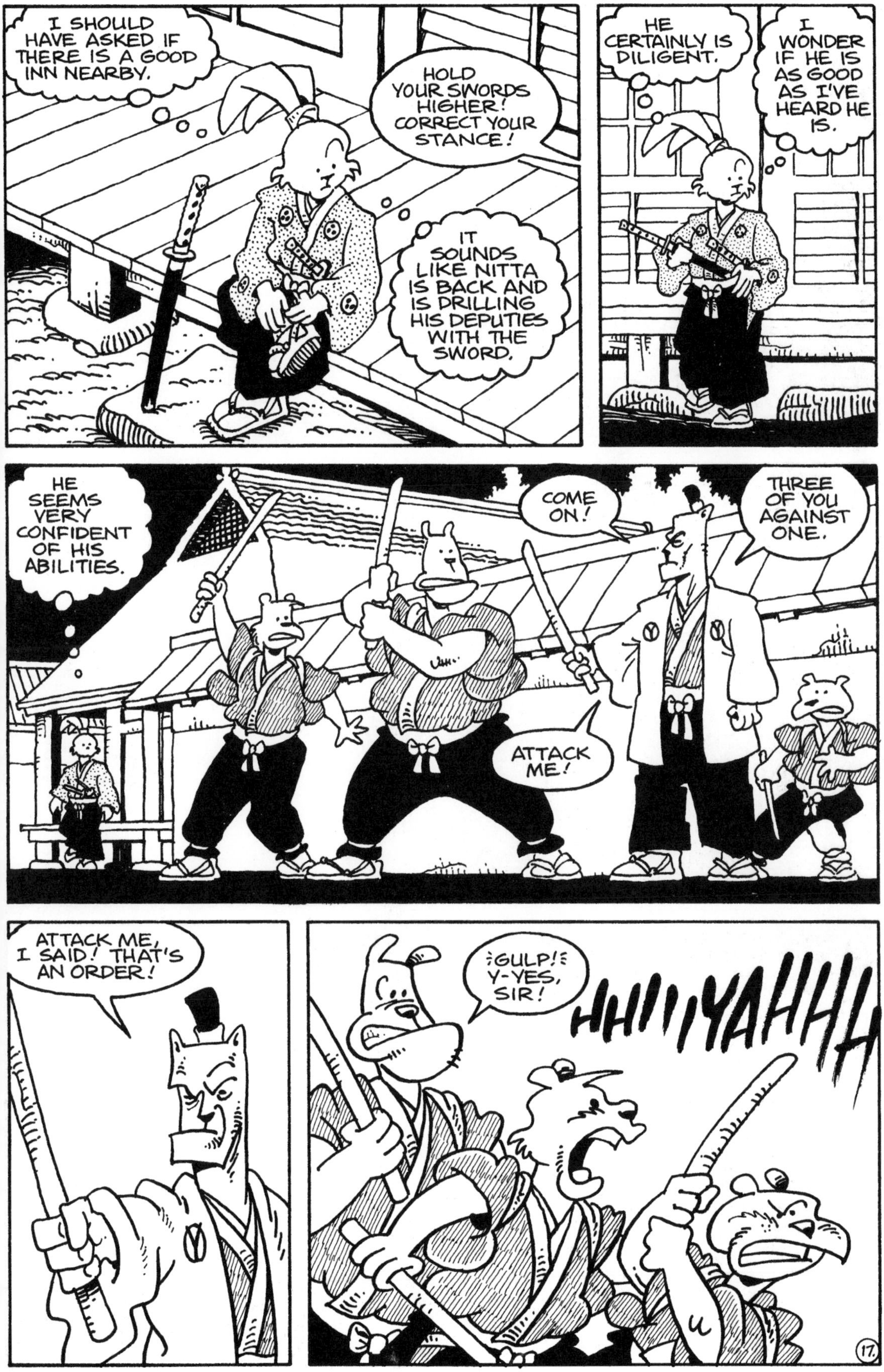
I SHOULD HAVE ASKED IF THERE IS A GOOD INN NEARBY.
HOLD YOUR SWORDS HIGHER! CORRECT YOUR STANCE!
IT SOUNDS LIKE NITTA IS BACK AND IS DRILLING HIS DEPUTIES WITH THE SWORD.
HE CERTAINLY IS DILIGENT.
I WONDER IF HE IS AS GOOD AS I'VE HEARD HE IS.
HE SEEMS VERY CONFIDENT OF HIS ABILITIES.
COME ON!
THREE OF YOU AGAINST ONE.
ATTACK ME!
ATTACK ME, I SAID! THAT'S AN ORDER!
GULP! Y-YES, SIR!
HHIIIYAHHH
17

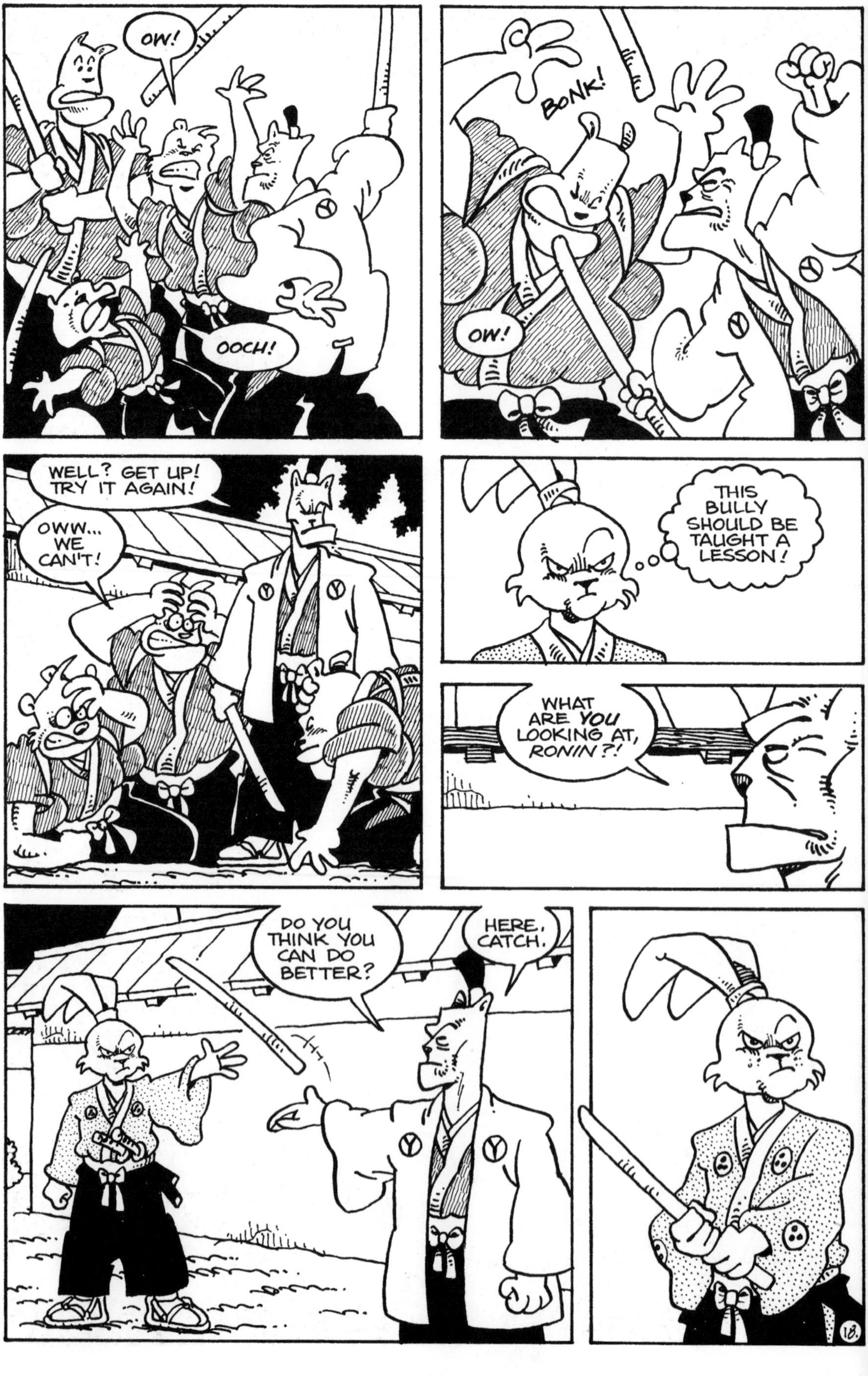
OW!
OOCH!
BONK!
OW!
WELL? GET UP! TRY IT AGAIN!
OWW... WE CAN'T!
THIS BULLY SHOULD BE TAUGHT A LESSON!
WHAT ARE YOU LOOKING AT, RONIN?!
DO YOU THINK YOU CAN DO BETTER?
HERE. CATCH.
18.

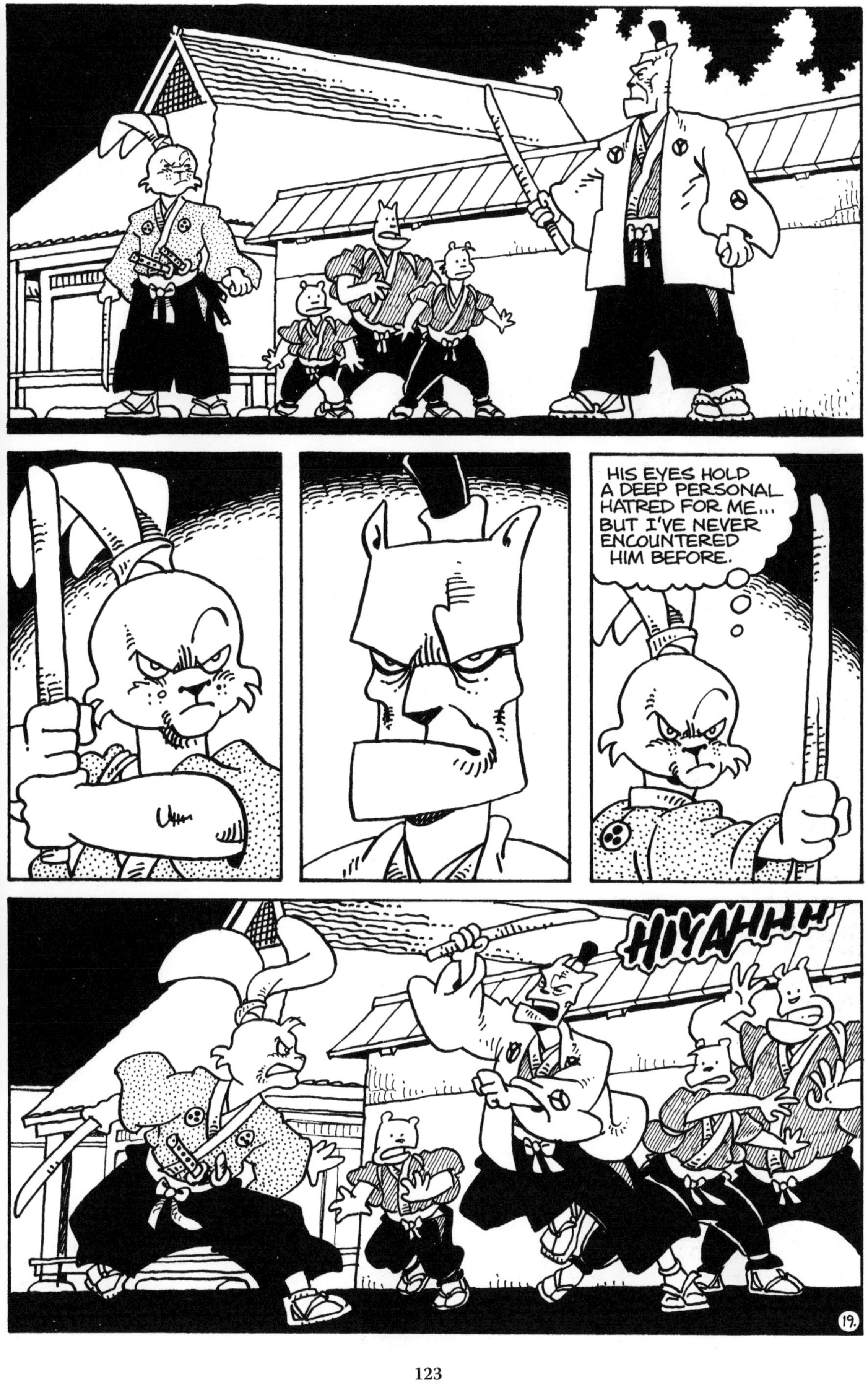
HIS EYES HOLD A DEEP PERSONAL HATRED FOR ME... BUT I'VE NEVER ENCOUNTERED HIM BEFORE.
HIYAHHH
19.

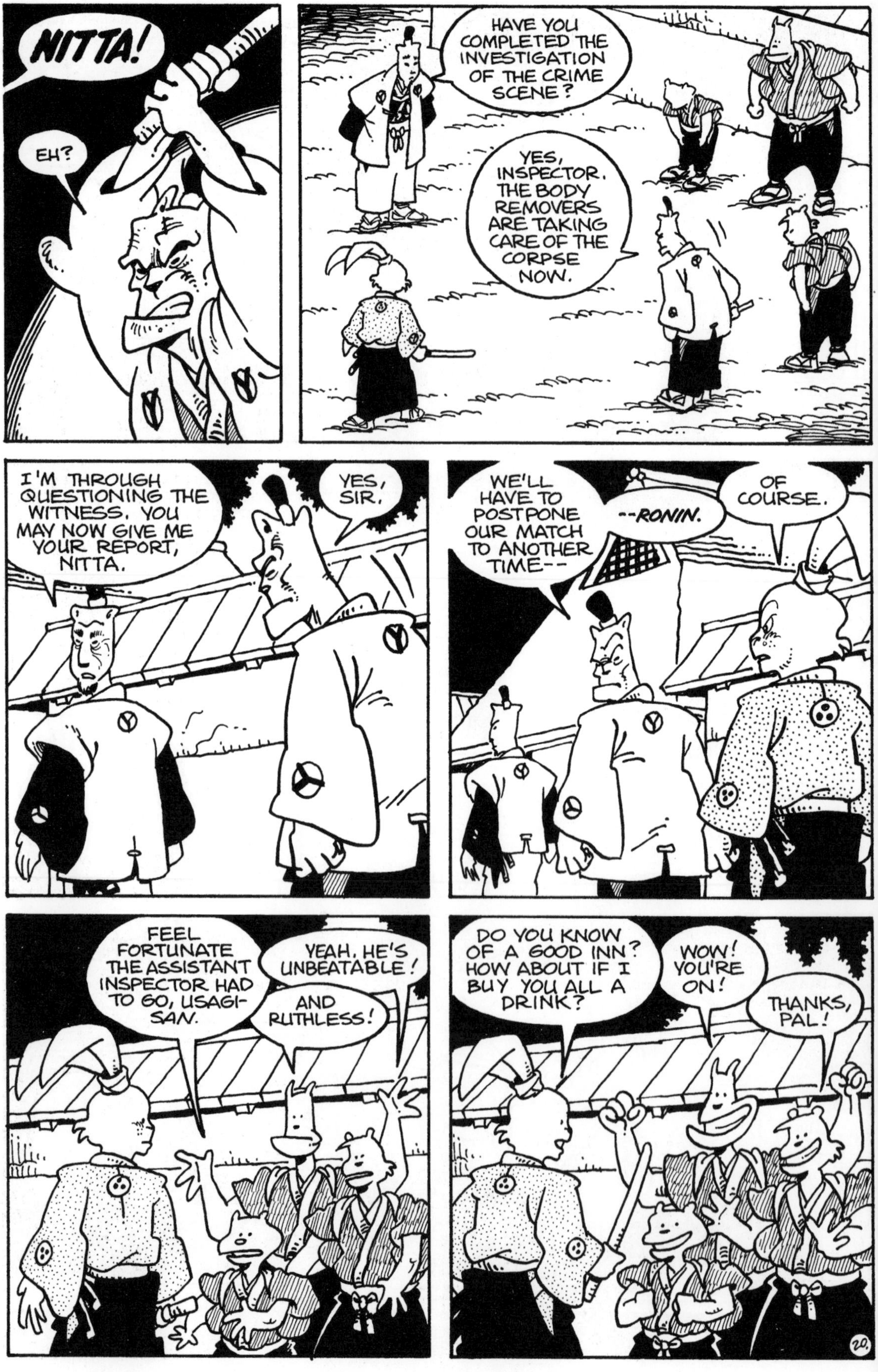
NITTA!
EH?
HAVE YOU COMPLETED THE INVESTIGATION OF THE CRIME SCENE?
YES, INSPECTOR. THE BODY REMOVERS ARE TAKING CARE OF THE CORPSE NOW.
I'M THROUGH QUESTIONING THE WITNESS. YOU MAY NOW GIVE ME YOUR REPORT, NITTA.
YES, SIR.
WE'LL HAVE TO POSTPONE OUR MATCH TO ANOTHER TIME--
--RONIN.
OF COURSE.
FEEL FORTUNATE THE ASSISTANT INSPECTOR HAD TO GO, USAGI-SAN.
YEAH, HE'S UNBEATABLE!
AND RUTHLESS!
DO YOU KNOW OF A GOOD INN? HOW ABOUT IF I BUY YOU ALL A DRINK?
WOW! YOU'RE ON!
THANKS, PAL!
20.

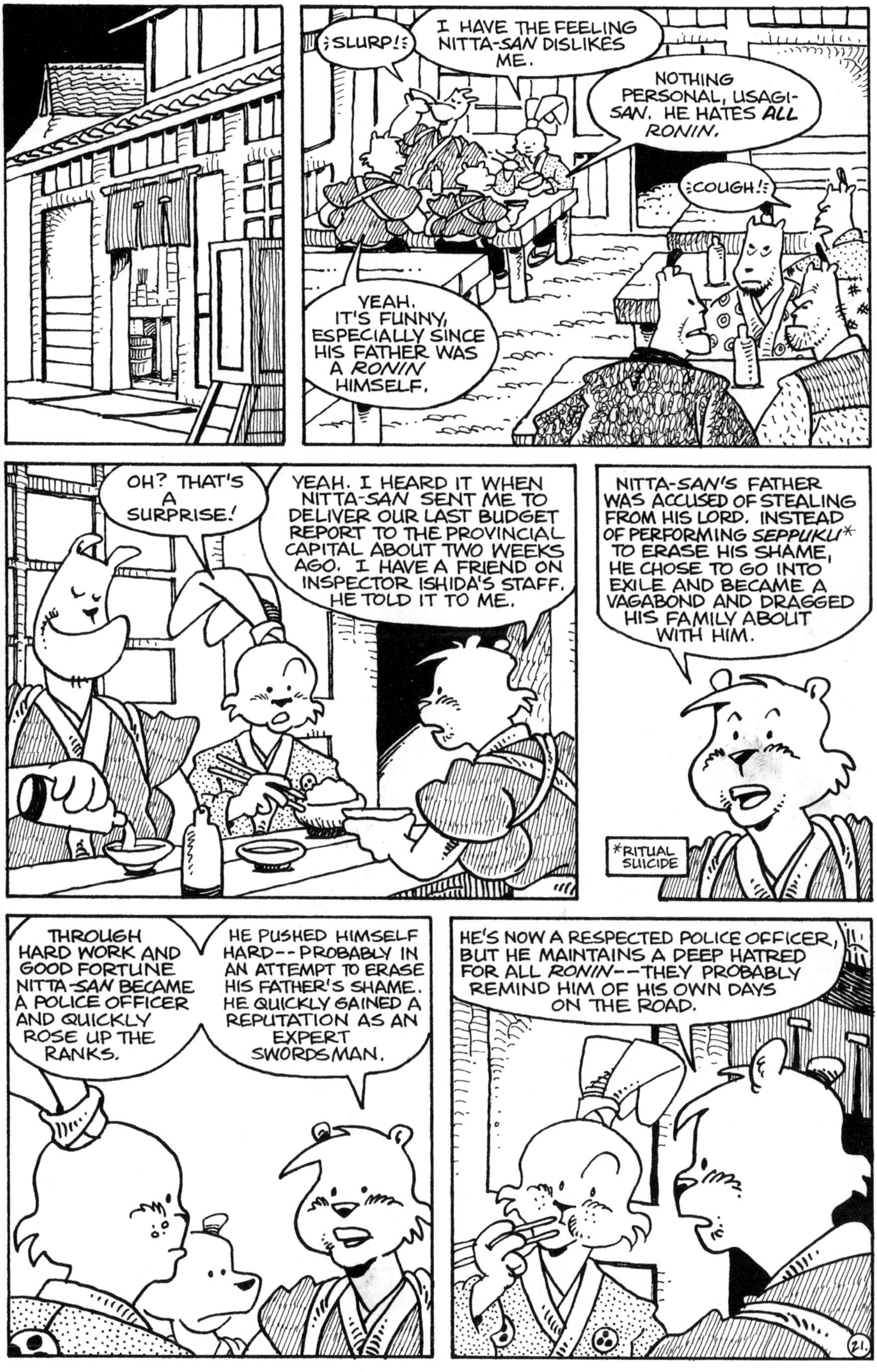
SLURP!
I HAVE THE FEELING NITTA-SAN DISLIKES ME.
NOTHING PERSONAL, USAGI-SAN. HE HATES ALL RONIN.
COUGH!
YEAH. IT'S FUNNY, ESPECIALLY SINCE HIS FATHER WAS A RONIN HIMSELF.
OH? THAT'S A SURPRISE!
YEAH. I HEARD IT WHEN NITTA-SAN SENT ME TO DELIVER OUR LAST BUDGET REPORT TO THE PROVINCIAL CAPITAL ABOUT TWO WEEKS AGO. I HAVE A FRIEND ON INSPECTOR ISHIDA'S STAFF. HE TOLD IT TO ME.
NITTA-SAN'S FATHER WAS ACCUSED OF STEALING FROM HIS LORD. INSTEAD OF PERFORMING SEPPUKU* TO ERASE HIS SHAME, HE CHOSE TO GO INTO EXILE AND BECAME A VAGABOND AND DRAGGED HIS FAMILY ABOUT WITH HIM.
*RITUAL SUICIDE
THROUGH HARD WORK AND GOOD FORTUNE NITTA-SAN BECAME A POLICE OFFICER AND QUICKLY ROSE UP THE RANKS.
HE PUSHED HIMSELF HARD--PROBABLY IN AN ATTEMPT TO ERASE HIS FATHER'S SHAME. HE QUICKLY GAINED A REPUTATION AS AN EXPERT SWORDSMAN.
HE'S NOW A RESPECTED POLICE OFFICER, BUT HE MAINTAINS A DEEP HATRED FOR ALL RONIN--THEY PROBABLY REMIND HIM OF HIS OWN DAYS ON THE ROAD.
21.

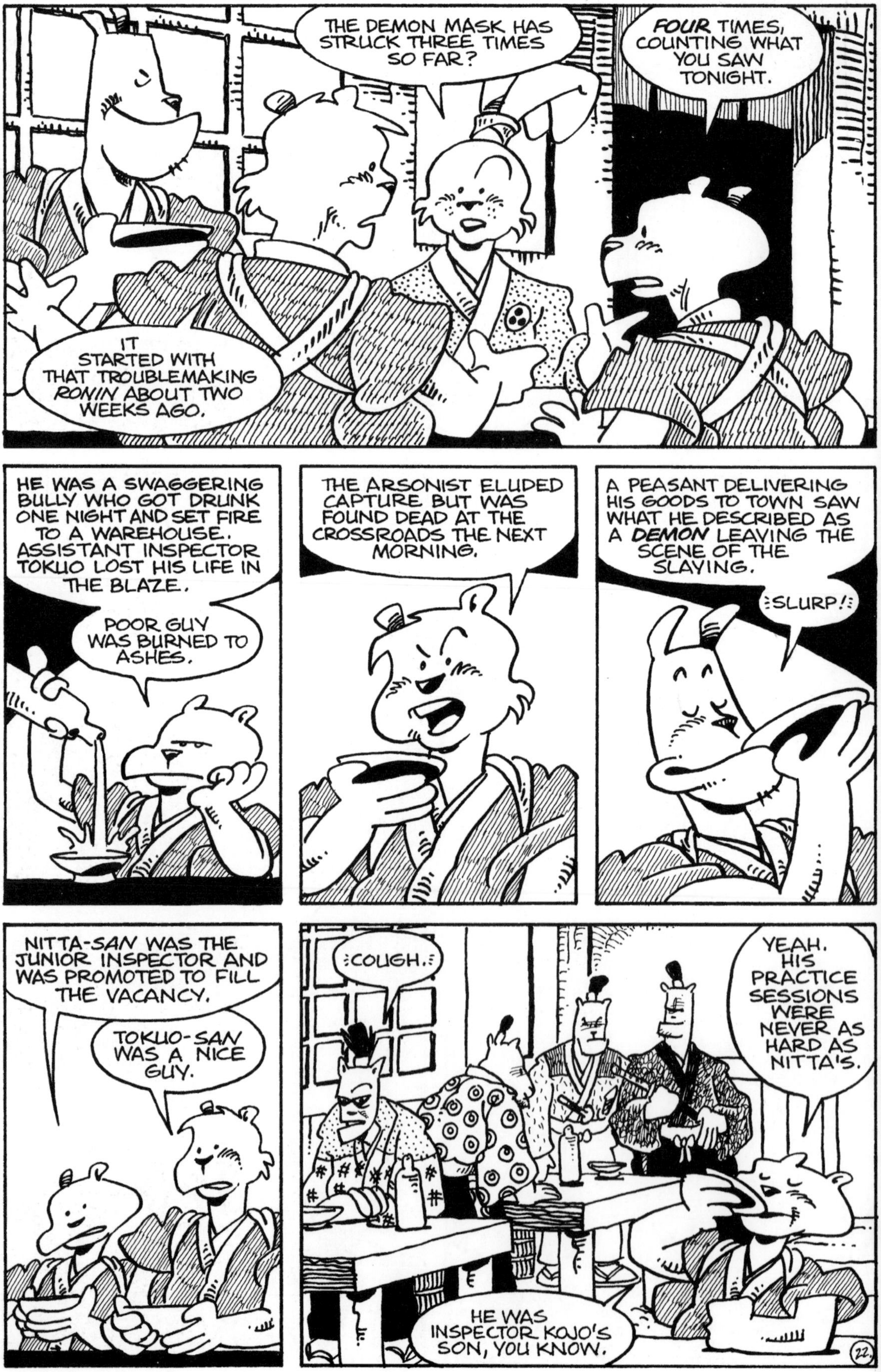
THE DEMON MASK HAS STRUCK THREE TIMES SO FAR?
FOUR TIMES, COUNTING WHAT YOU SAW TONIGHT.
IT STARTED WITH THAT TROUBLEMAKING RONIN ABOUT TWO WEEKS AGO.
HE WAS A SWAGGERING BULLY WHO GOT DRUNK ONE NIGHT AND SET FIRE TO A WAREHOUSE. ASSISTANT INSPECTOR TOKUO LOST HIS LIFE IN THE BLAZE.
POOR GUY WAS BURNED TO ASHES.
THE ARSONIST ELUDED CAPTURE BUT WAS FOUND DEAD AT THE CROSSROADS THE NEXT MORNING.
A PEASANT DELIVERING HIS GOODS TO TOWN SAW WHAT HE DESCRIBED AS A DEMON LEAVING THE SCENE OF THE SLAYING.
SLURP!
NITTA-SAN WAS THE JUNIOR INSPECTOR AND WAS PROMOTED TO FILL THE VACANCY.
TOKUO-SAN WAS A NICE GUY.
COUGH.
YEAH. HIS PRACTICE SESSIONS WERE NEVER AS HARD AS NITTA'S.
HE WAS INSPECTOR KOJO'S SON, YOU KNOW.
22

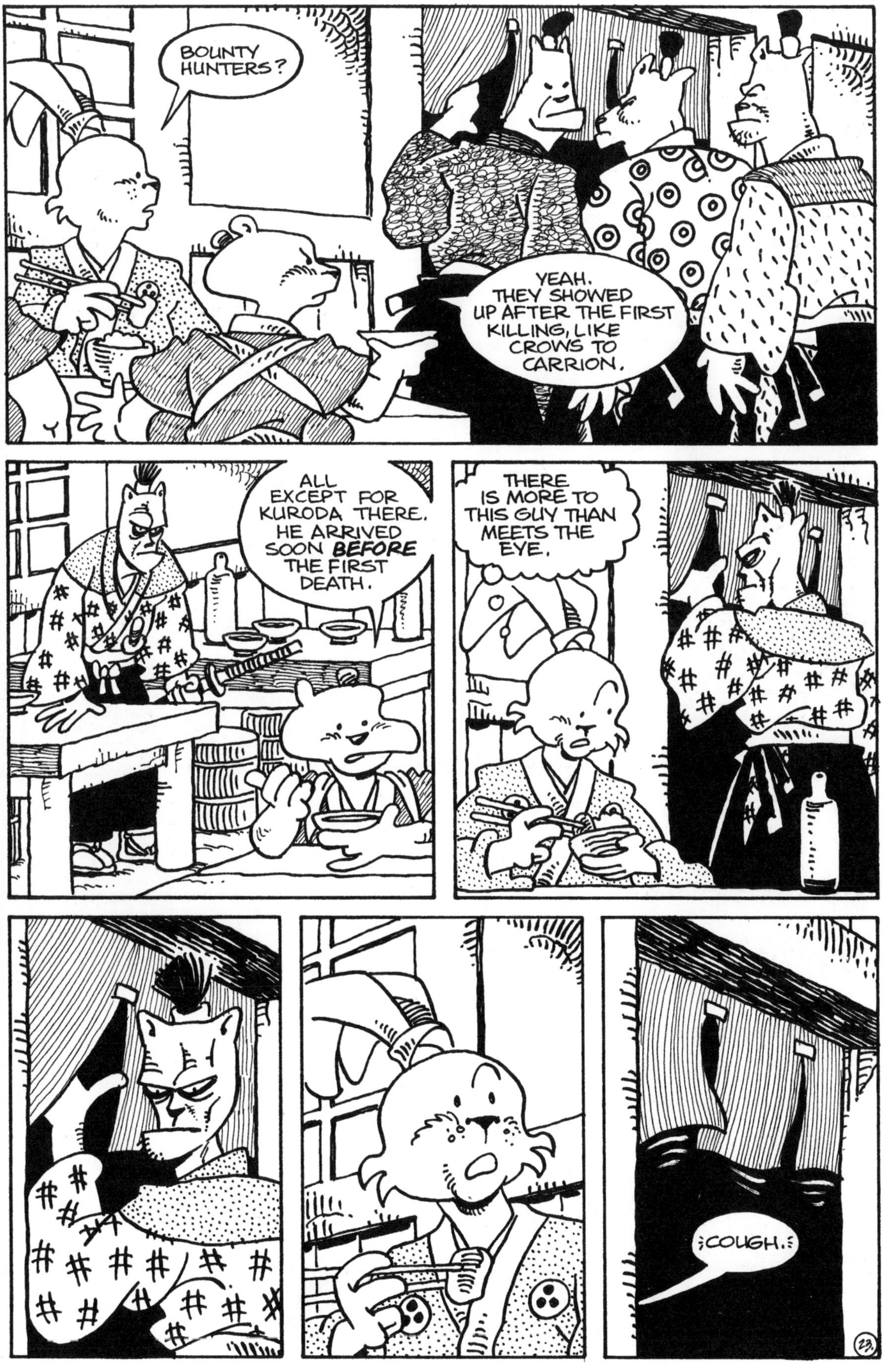
BOUNTY HUNTERS?
YEAH. THEY SHOWED UP AFTER THE FIRST KILLING, LIKE CROWS TO CARRION.
ALL EXCEPT FOR KURODA THERE. HE ARRIVED SOON **BEFORE** THE FIRST DEATH.
THERE IS MORE TO THIS GUY THAN MEETS THE EYE.
:COUGH:
23

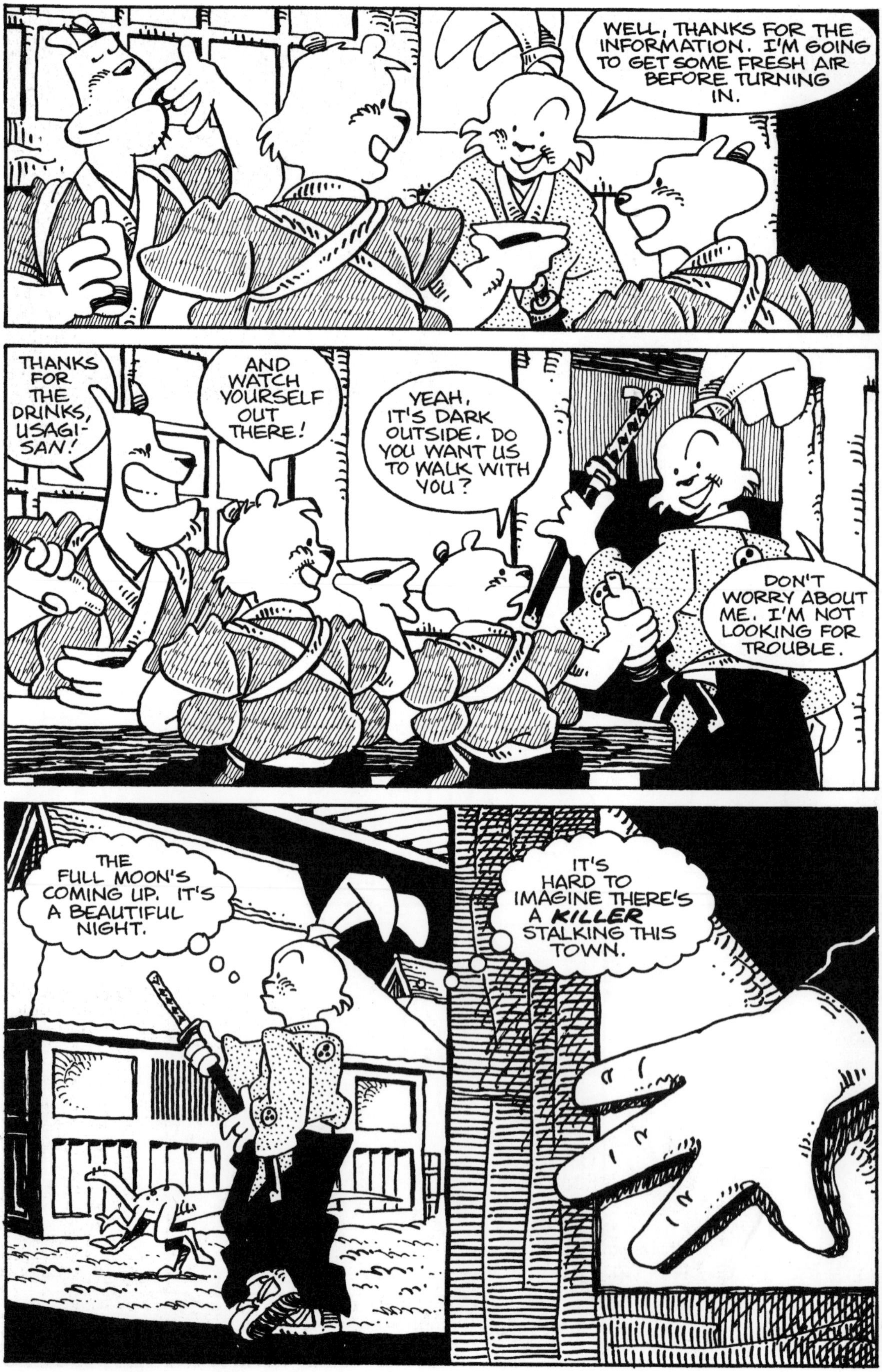

WELL, THANKS FOR THE INFORMATION. I'M GOING TO GET SOME FRESH AIR BEFORE TURNING IN.
THANKS FOR THE DRINKS, USAGI-SAN!
AND WATCH YOURSELF OUT THERE!
YEAH, IT'S DARK OUTSIDE. DO YOU WANT US TO WALK WITH YOU?
DON'T WORRY ABOUT ME. I'M NOT LOOKING FOR TROUBLE.
THE FULL MOON'S COMING UP. IT'S A BEAUTIFUL NIGHT.
IT'S HARD TO IMAGINE THERE'S A KILLER STALKING THIS TOWN.

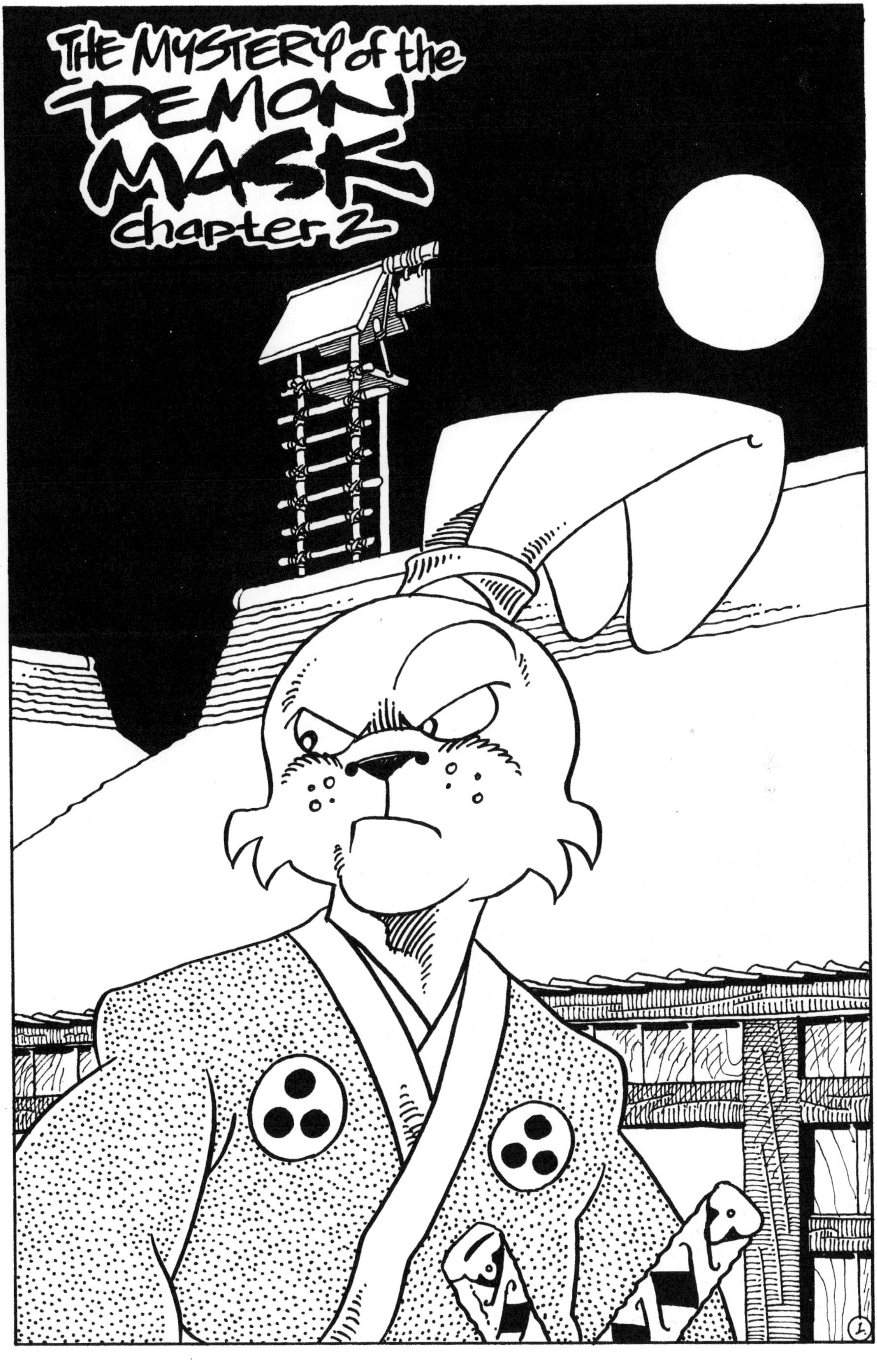
THE MYSTERY of the DEMON MASK chapter 2

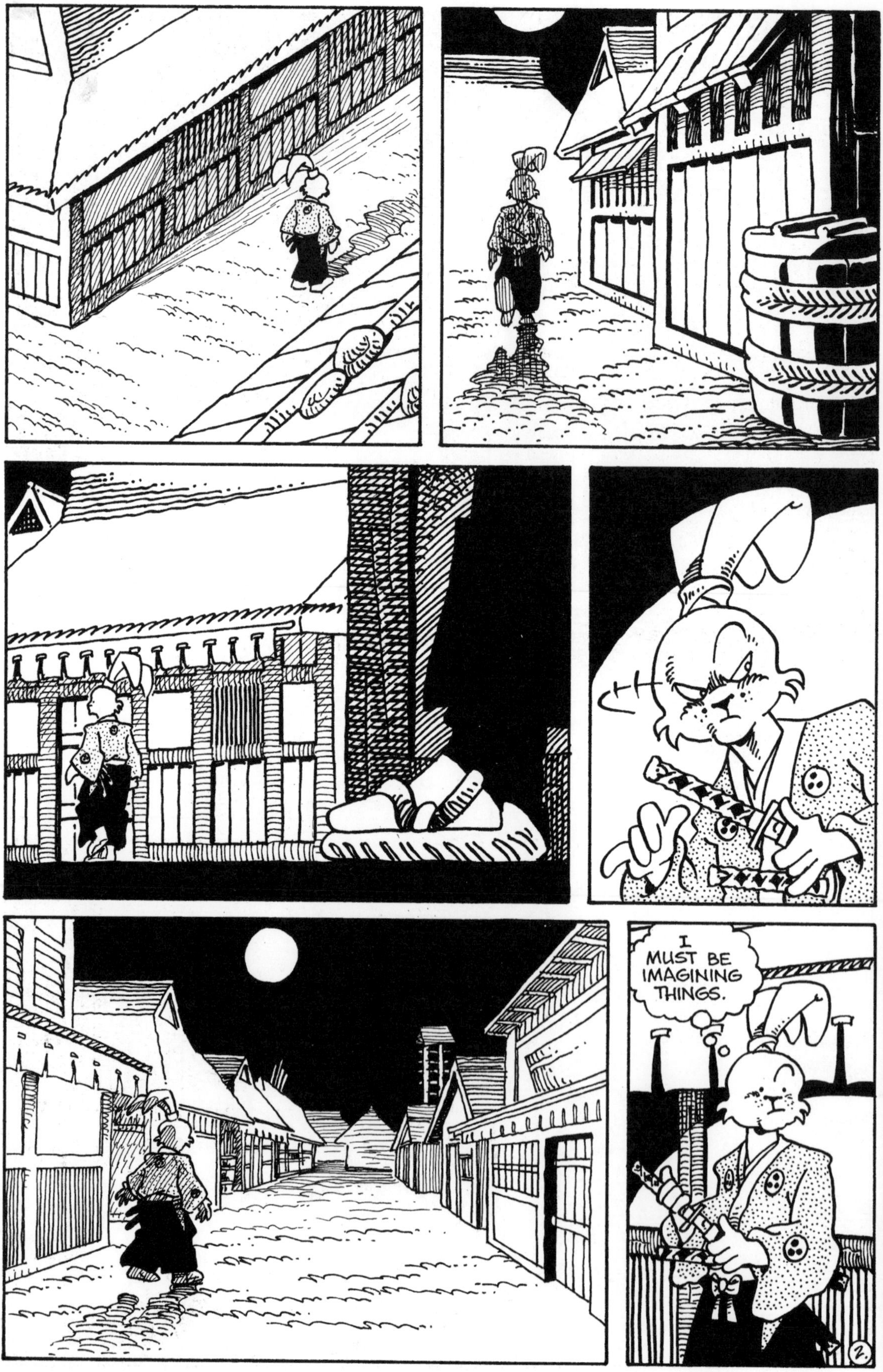
I MUST BE IMAGINING THINGS.

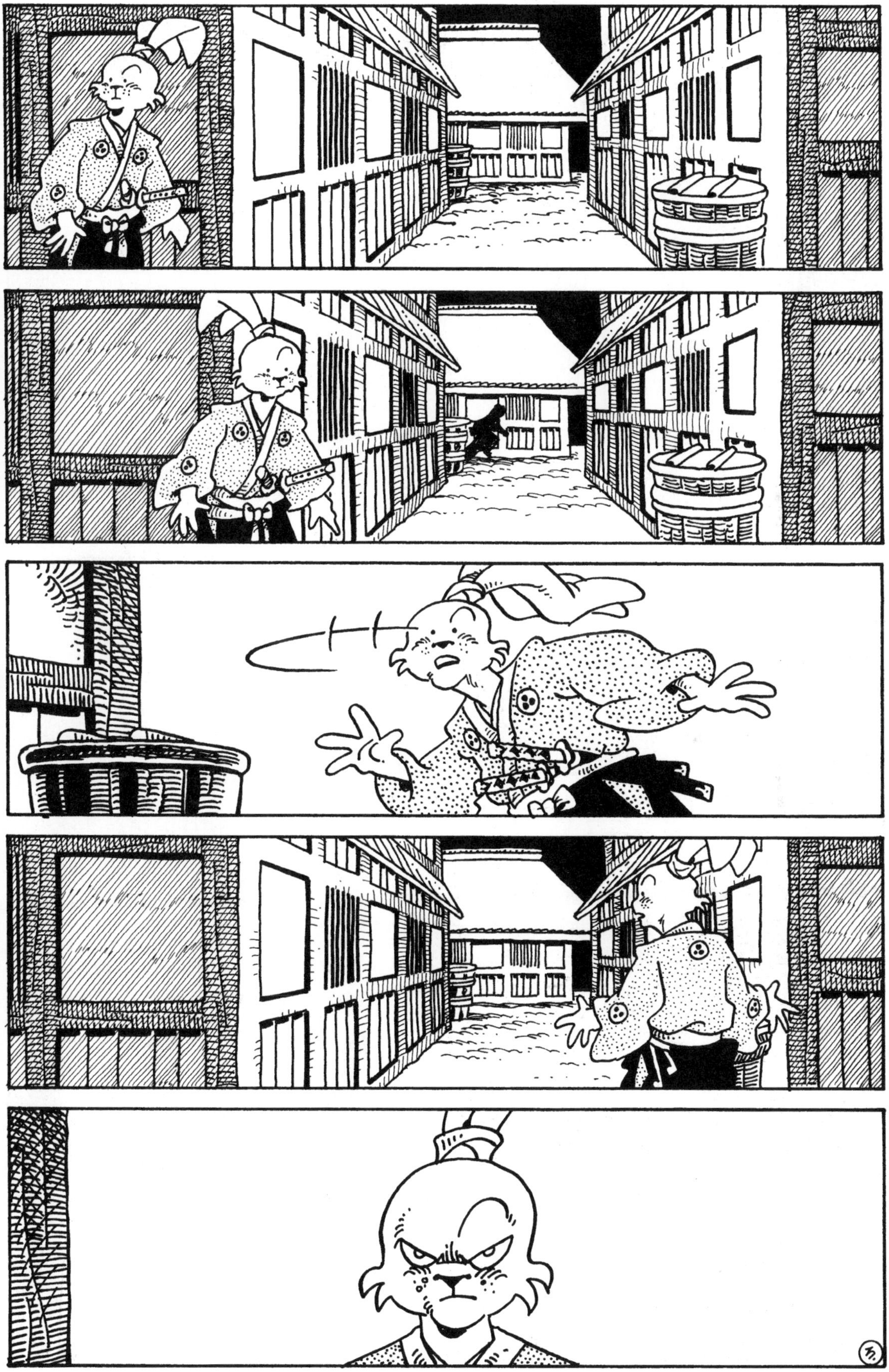

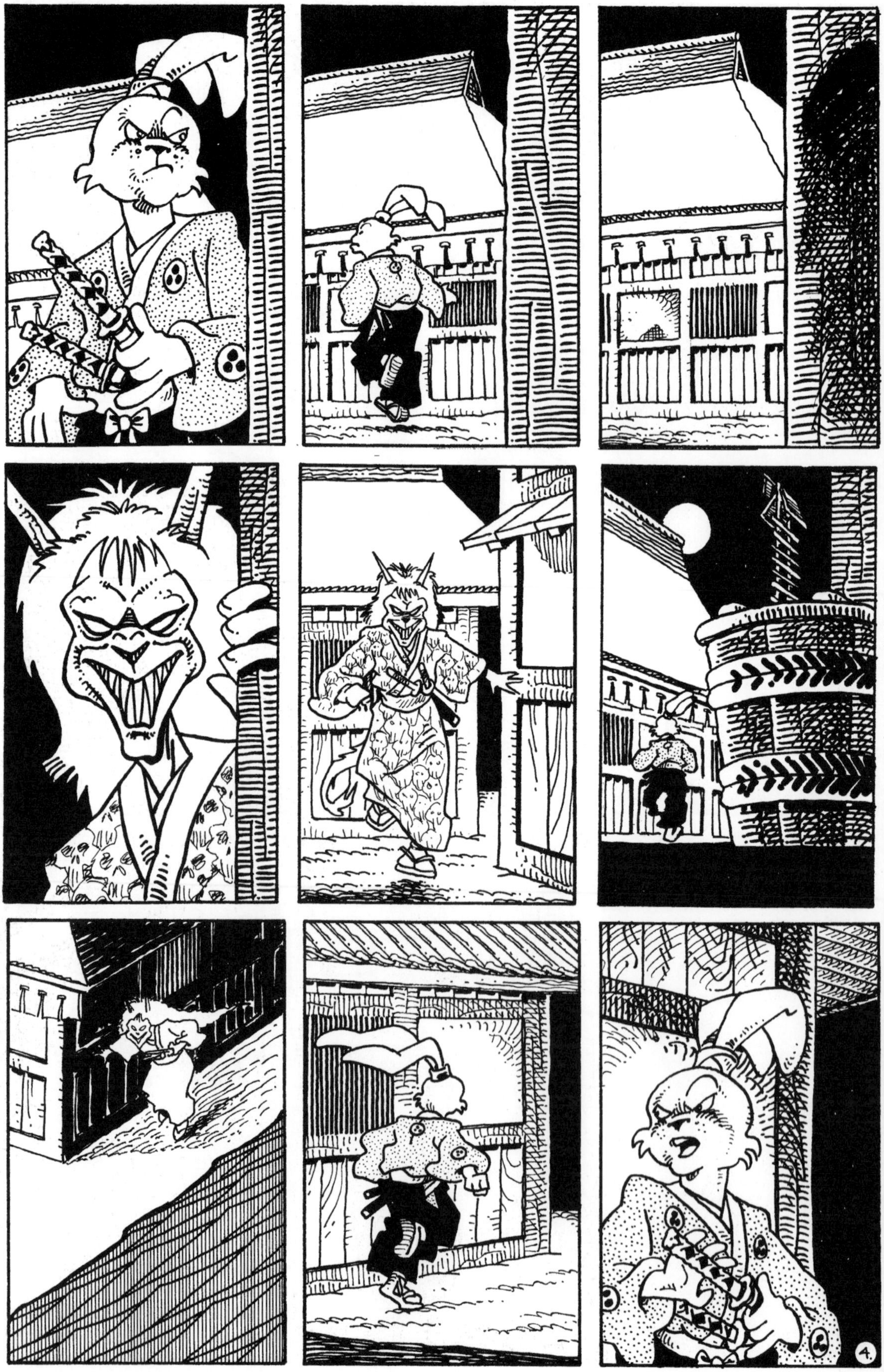
4.

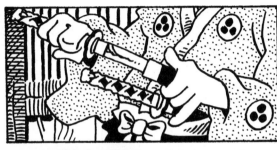

STOP!

WHY ARE YOU FOLLOWING ME, KURODA?

I SAY WE SPLIT UP. WE'LL NEVER GET THE KILLER IF WE STAY TOGETHER!

YEAH, HE'S ONLY ATTACKED LONE SWORDSMEN. HE'LL NEVER SHOW HIMSELF TO THREE OF US.

YOU'RE RIGHT ABOUT THAT!

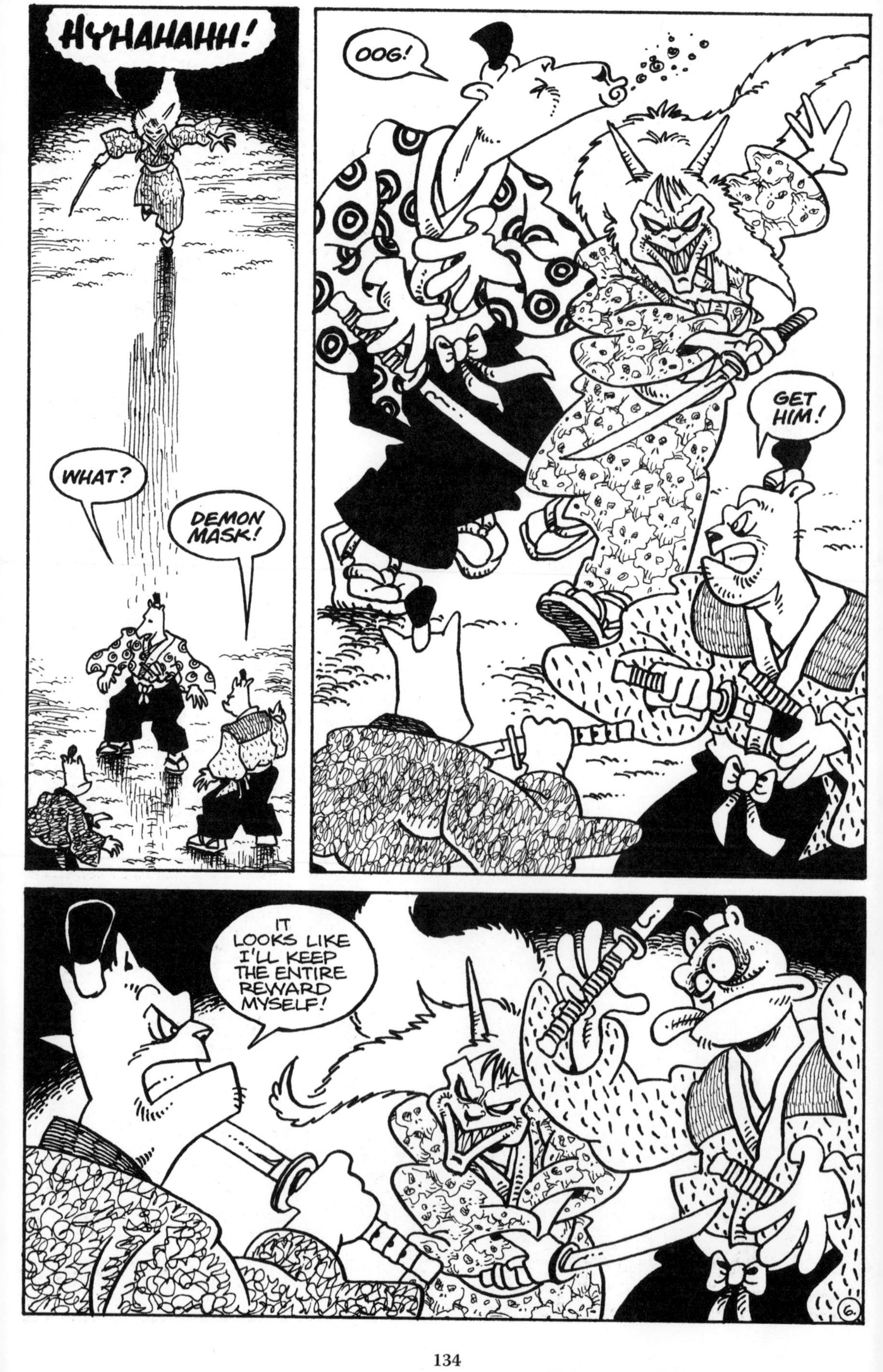
HYAHAHH!
WHAT?
DEMON MASK!
OOG!
GET HIM!
IT LOOKS LIKE I'LL KEEP THE ENTIRE REWARD MYSELF!
6.

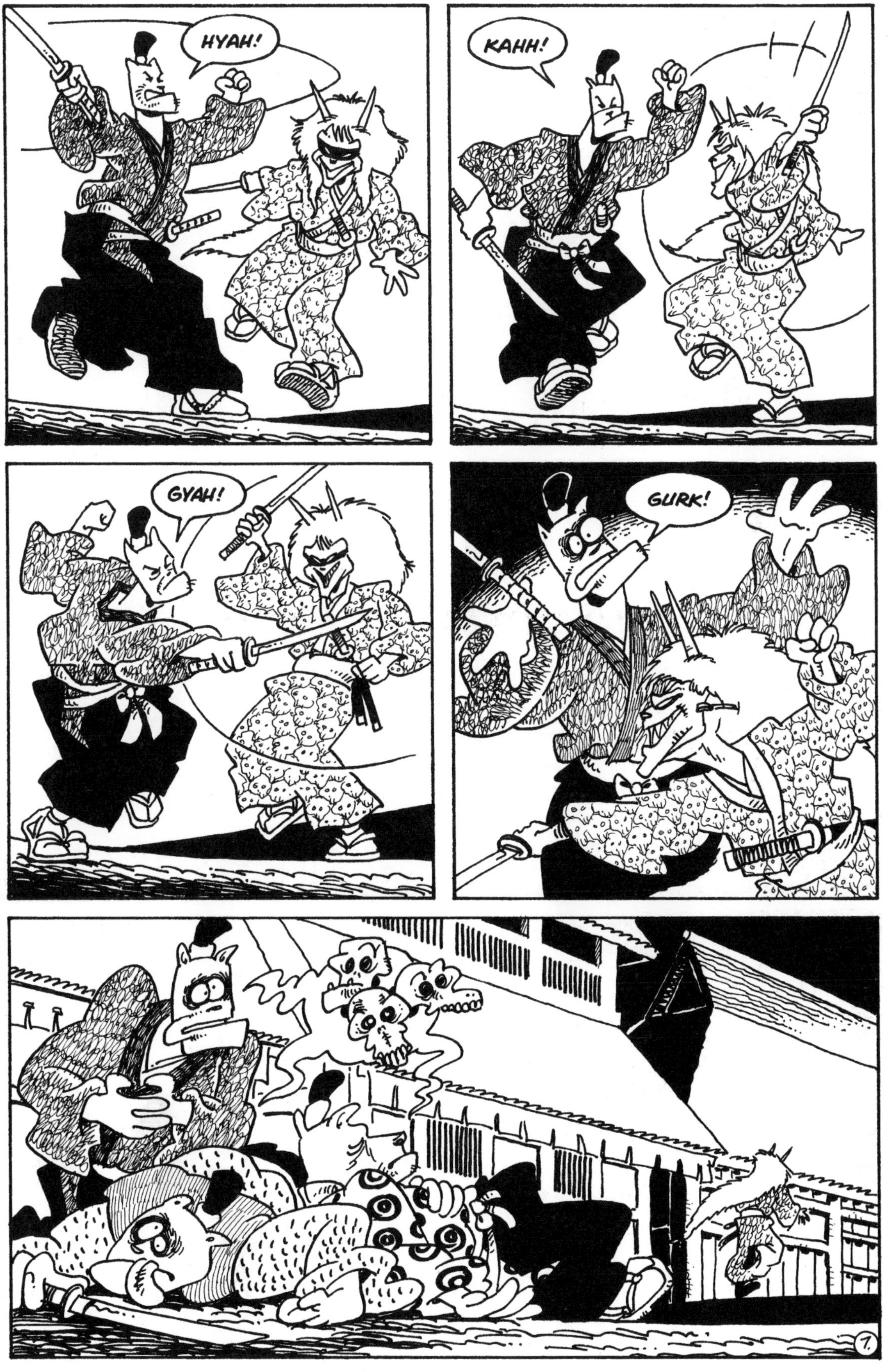
HYAH!
KAHH!
GYAH!
GURK!
7.

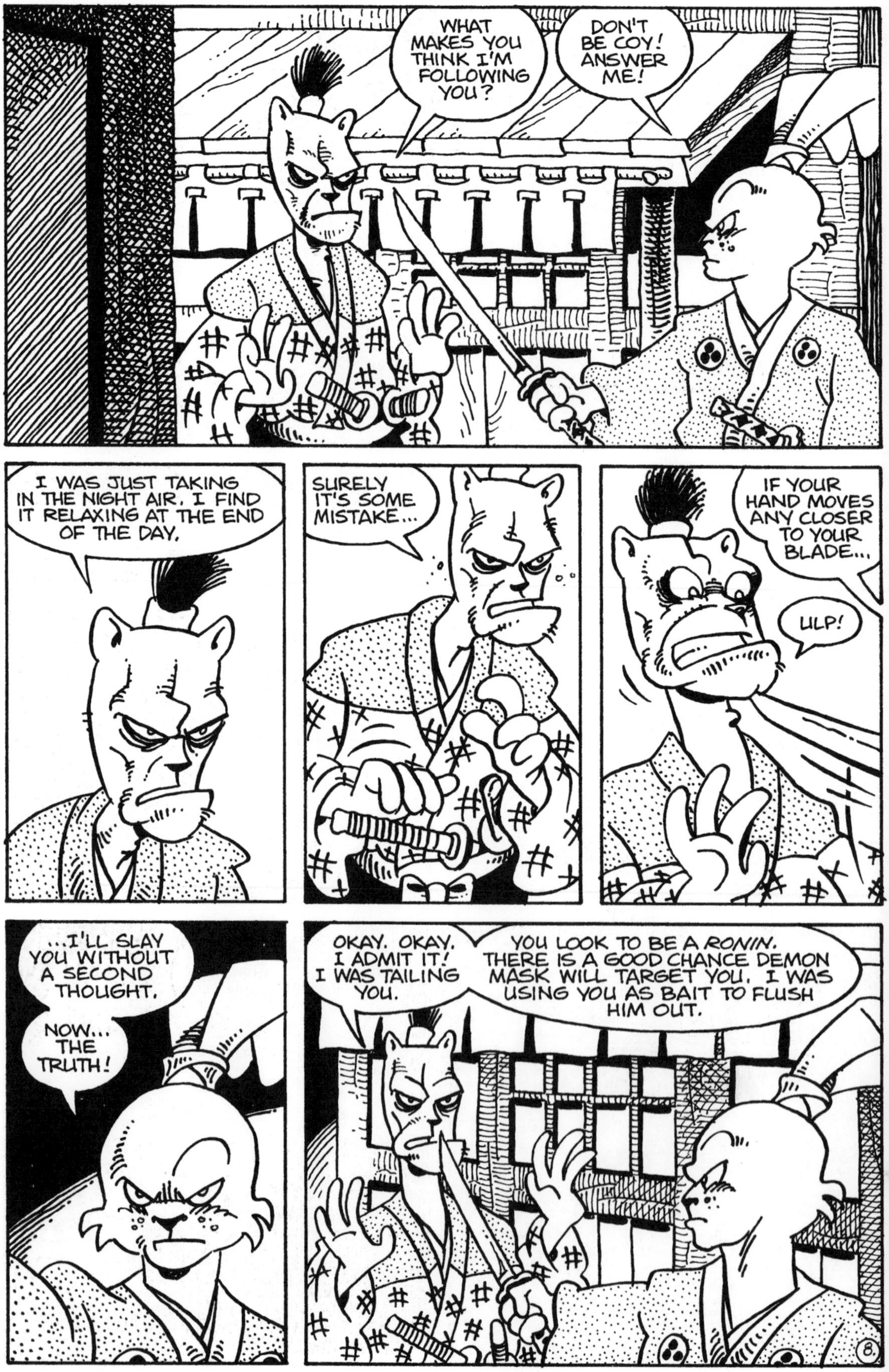
WHAT MAKES YOU THINK I'M FOLLOWING YOU?
DON'T BE COY! ANSWER ME!
I WAS JUST TAKING IN THE NIGHT AIR. I FIND IT RELAXING AT THE END OF THE DAY.
SURELY IT'S SOME MISTAKE...
IF YOUR HAND MOVES ANY CLOSER TO YOUR BLADE...
ULP!
...I'LL SLAY YOU WITHOUT A SECOND THOUGHT.
NOW... THE TRUTH!
OKAY. OKAY. I ADMIT IT! I WAS TAILING YOU.
YOU LOOK TO BE A *RONIN*. THERE IS A GOOD CHANCE DEMON MASK WILL TARGET YOU. I WAS USING YOU AS BAIT TO FLUSH HIM OUT.
8.

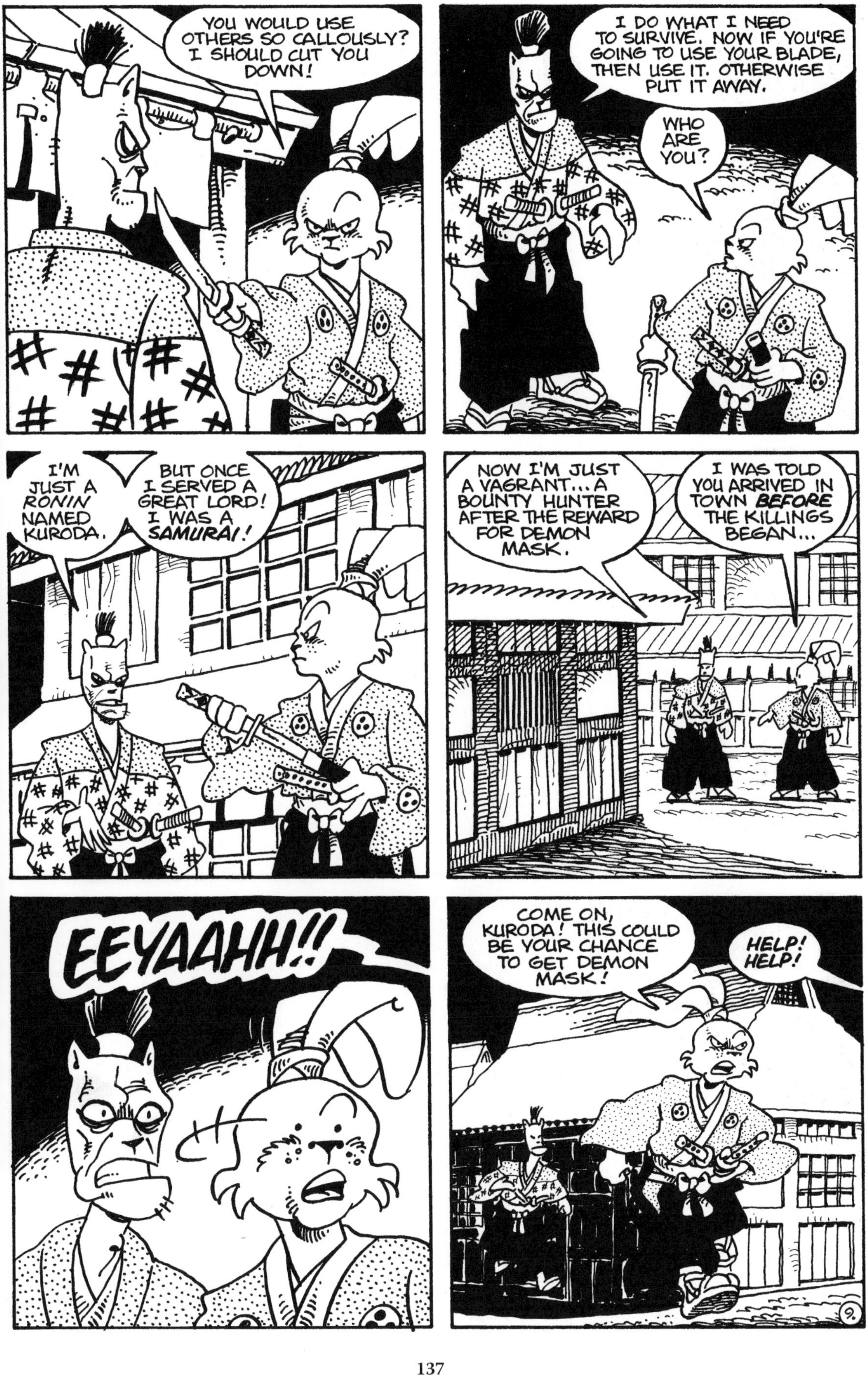
YOU WOULD USE OTHERS SO CALLOUSLY? I SHOULD CUT YOU DOWN!
I DO WHAT I NEED TO SURVIVE. NOW IF YOU'RE GOING TO USE YOUR BLADE, THEN USE IT. OTHERWISE PUT IT AWAY.
WHO ARE YOU?
I'M JUST A *RONIN* NAMED KURODA.
BUT ONCE I SERVED A GREAT LORD! I WAS A *SAMURAI*!
NOW I'M JUST A VAGRANT... A BOUNTY HUNTER AFTER THE REWARD FOR DEMON MASK.
I WAS TOLD YOU ARRIVED IN TOWN **BEFORE** THE KILLINGS BEGAN...
EEYAAHH!!
COME ON, KURODA! THIS COULD BE YOUR CHANCE TO GET DEMON MASK!
HELP! HELP!

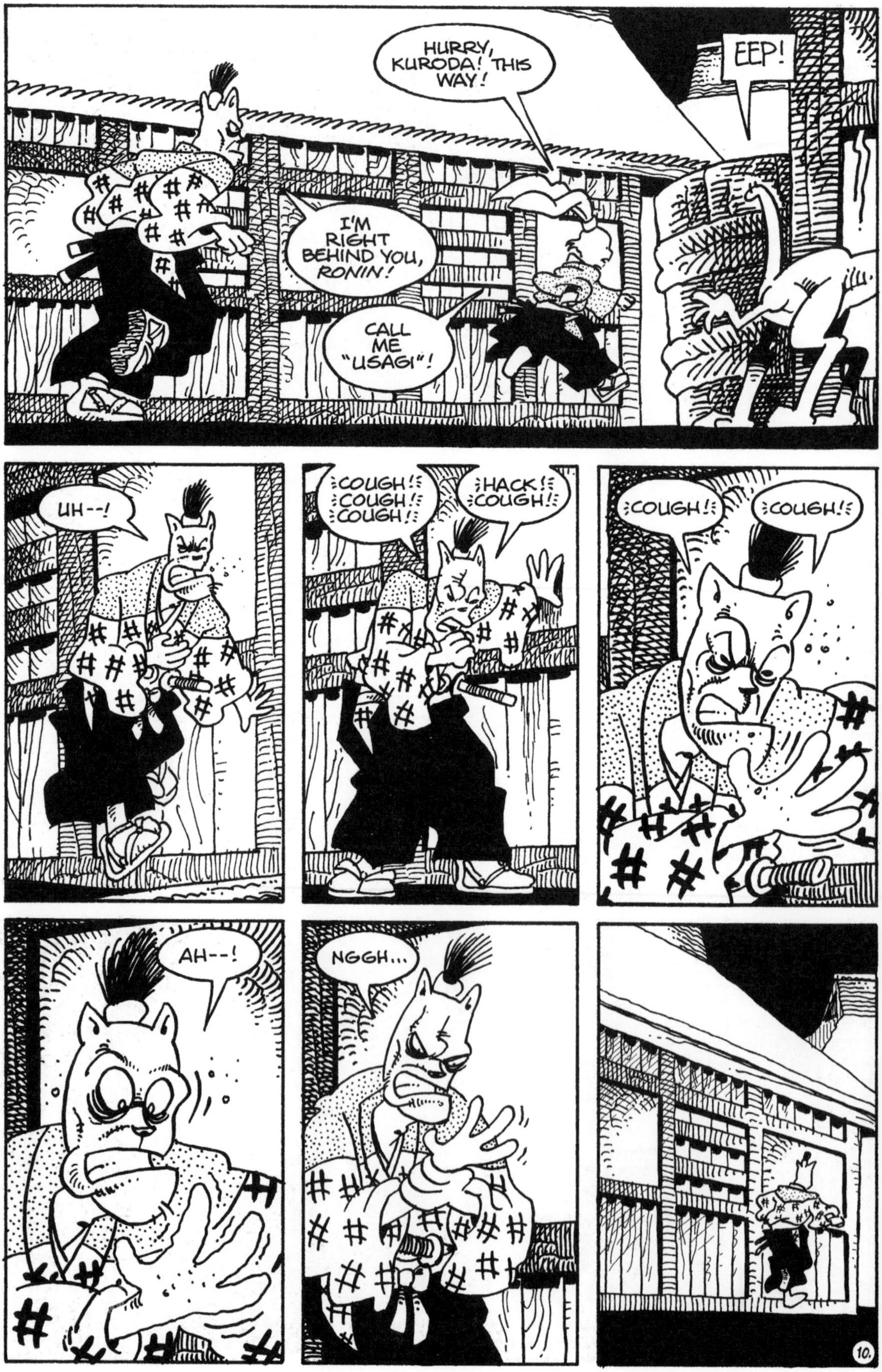
HURRY, KURODA! THIS WAY!
EEP!
I'M RIGHT BEHIND YOU, *RONIN!*
CALL ME "USAGI"!
UH--!
COUGH! COUGH! COUGH!
HACK! COUGH!
COUGH!
COUGH!
AH--!
NGGH...
10.

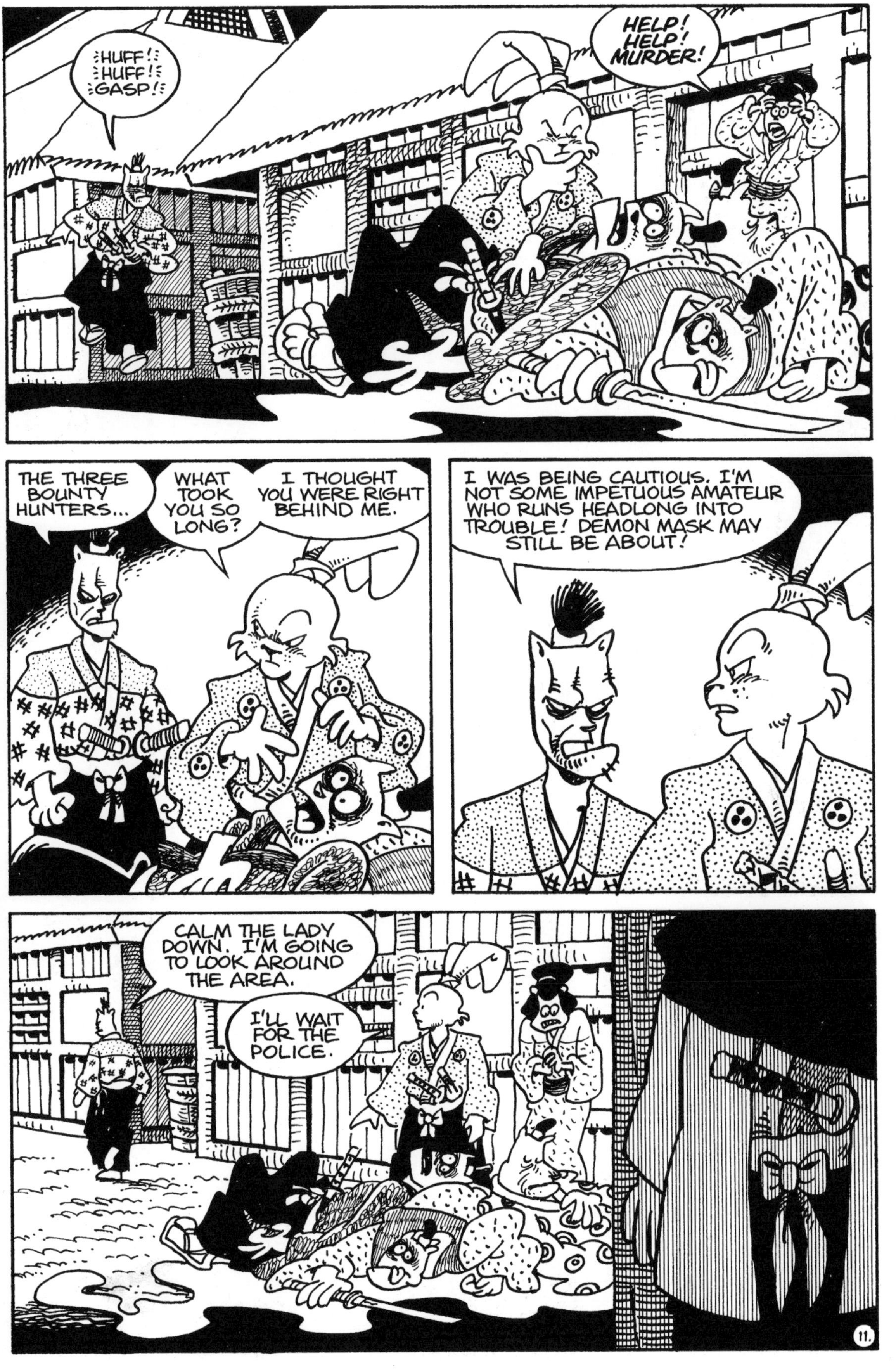
HUFF! HUFF! GASP!
HELP! HELP! MURDER!
THE THREE BOUNTY HUNTERS...
WHAT TOOK YOU SO LONG?
I THOUGHT YOU WERE RIGHT BEHIND ME.
I WAS BEING CAUTIOUS. I'M NOT SOME IMPETUOUS AMATEUR WHO RUNS HEADLONG INTO TROUBLE! DEMON MASK MAY STILL BE ABOUT!
CALM THE LADY DOWN. I'M GOING TO LOOK AROUND THE AREA.
I'LL WAIT FOR THE POLICE.
11.

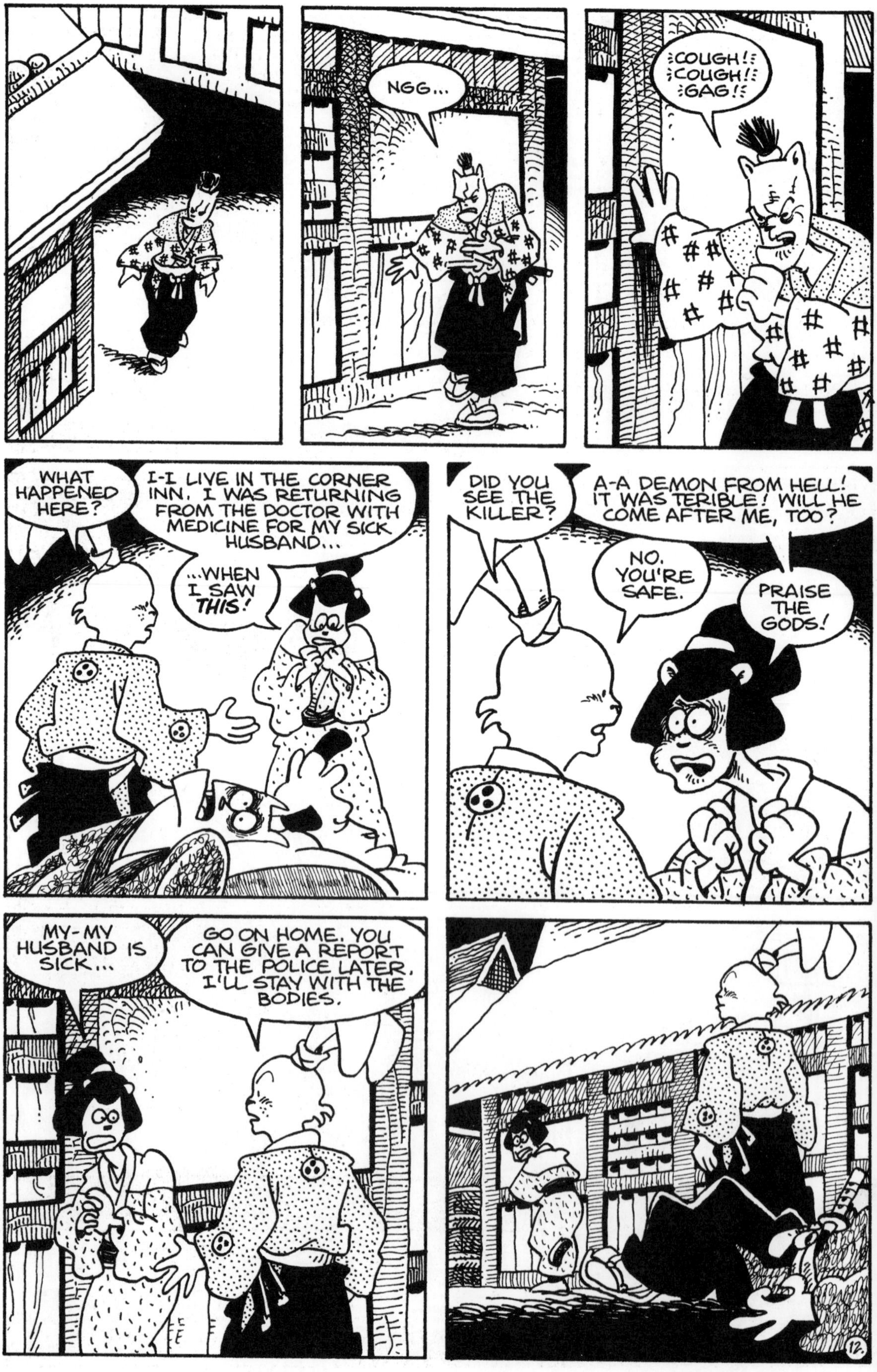
NGG...
COUGH! COUGH! GAG!
WHAT HAPPENED HERE?
I-I LIVE IN THE CORNER INN. I WAS RETURNING FROM THE DOCTOR WITH MEDICINE FOR MY SICK HUSBAND...
...WHEN I SAW THIS!
DID YOU SEE THE KILLER?
A-A DEMON FROM HELL! IT WAS TERIBLE! WILL HE COME AFTER ME, TOO?
NO. YOU'RE SAFE.
PRAISE THE GODS!
MY-MY HUSBAND IS SICK...
GO ON HOME. YOU CAN GIVE A REPORT TO THE POLICE LATER. I'LL STAY WITH THE BODIES.
12.

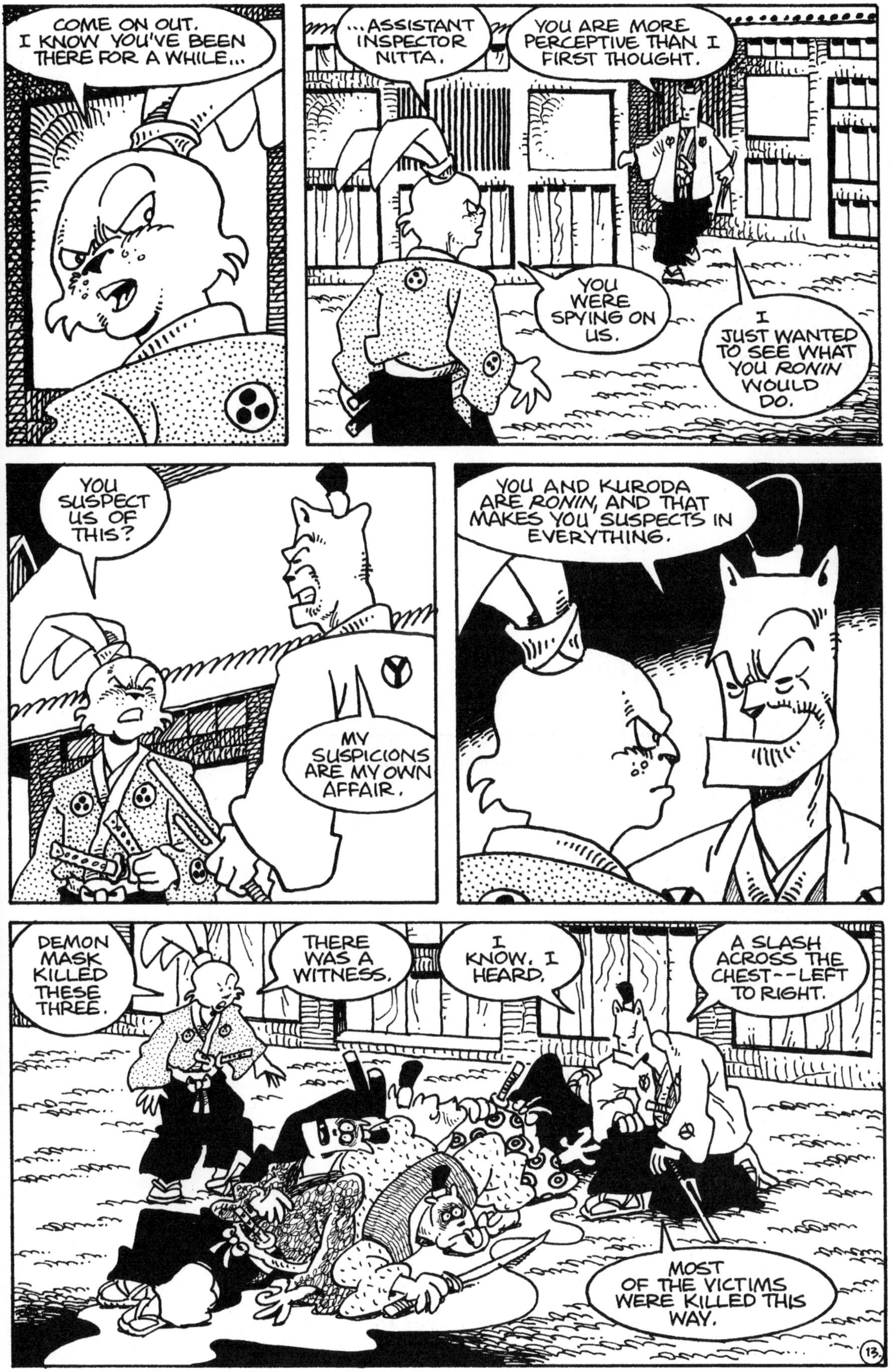
COME ON OUT. I KNOW YOU'VE BEEN THERE FOR A WHILE...
...ASSISTANT INSPECTOR NITTA.
YOU ARE MORE PERCEPTIVE THAN I FIRST THOUGHT.
YOU WERE SPYING ON US.
I JUST WANTED TO SEE WHAT YOU *RONIN* WOULD DO.
YOU SUSPECT US OF THIS?
MY SUSPICIONS ARE MY OWN AFFAIR.
YOU AND KURODA ARE *RONIN*, AND THAT MAKES YOU SUSPECTS IN EVERYTHING.
DEMON MASK KILLED THESE THREE.
THERE WAS A WITNESS.
I KNOW. I HEARD.
A SLASH ACROSS THE CHEST--LEFT TO RIGHT.
MOST OF THE VICTIMS WERE KILLED THIS WAY.
13

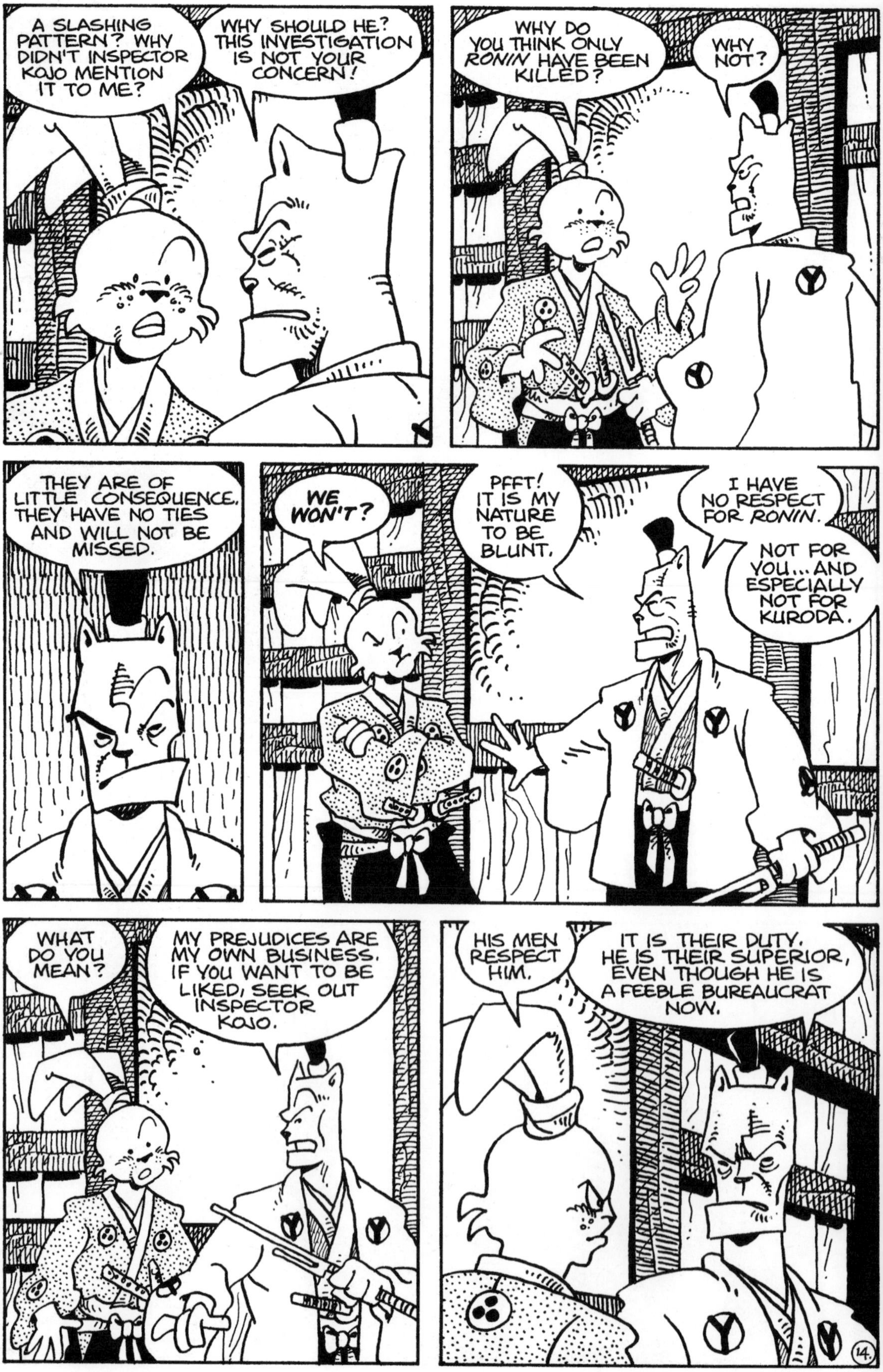
A SLASHING PATTERN? WHY DIDN'T INSPECTOR KOJO MENTION IT TO ME?
WHY SHOULD HE? THIS INVESTIGATION IS NOT YOUR CONCERN!
WHY DO YOU THINK ONLY *RONIN* HAVE BEEN KILLED?
WHY NOT?
THEY ARE OF LITTLE CONSEQUENCE. THEY HAVE NO TIES AND WILL NOT BE MISSED.
WE WON'T?
PFFT! IT IS MY NATURE TO BE BLUNT.
I HAVE NO RESPECT FOR *RONIN*.
NOT FOR YOU... AND ESPECIALLY NOT FOR KURODA.
WHAT DO YOU MEAN?
MY PREJUDICES ARE MY OWN BUSINESS. IF YOU WANT TO BE LIKED, SEEK OUT INSPECTOR KOJO.
HIS MEN RESPECT HIM.
IT IS THEIR DUTY. HE IS THEIR SUPERIOR, EVEN THOUGH HE IS A FEEBLE BUREAUCRAT NOW.
14.

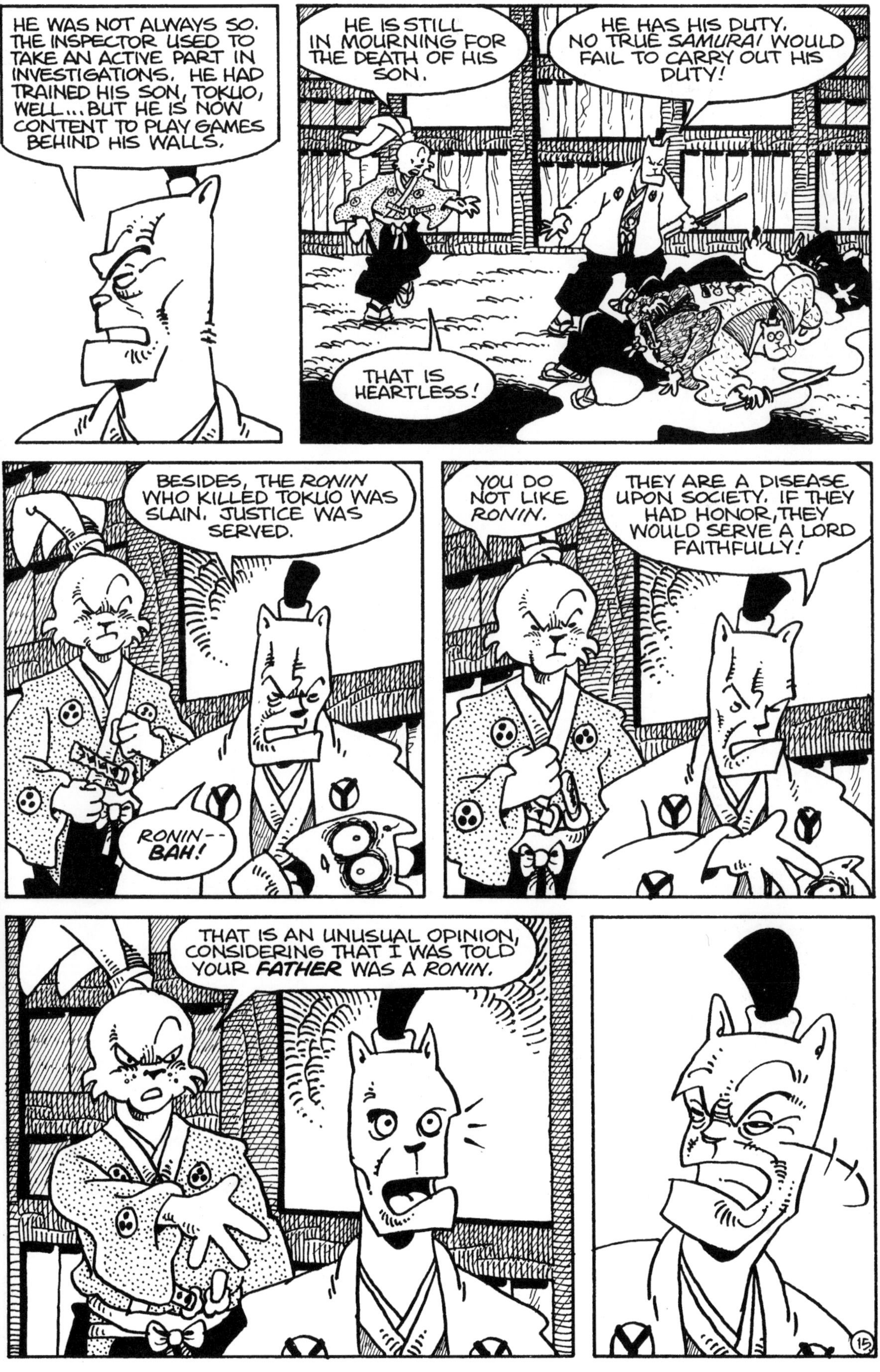
HE WAS NOT ALWAYS SO. THE INSPECTOR USED TO TAKE AN ACTIVE PART IN INVESTIGATIONS. HE HAD TRAINED HIS SON, TOKUO, WELL... BUT HE IS NOW CONTENT TO PLAY GAMES BEHIND HIS WALLS.
HE IS STILL IN MOURNING FOR THE DEATH OF HIS SON.
HE HAS HIS DUTY. NO TRUE SAMURAI WOULD FAIL TO CARRY OUT HIS DUTY!
THAT IS HEARTLESS!
BESIDES, THE RONIN WHO KILLED TOKUO WAS SLAIN. JUSTICE WAS SERVED.
RONIN-- BAH!
YOU DO NOT LIKE RONIN.
THEY ARE A DISEASE UPON SOCIETY. IF THEY HAD HONOR, THEY WOULD SERVE A LORD FAITHFULLY!
THAT IS AN UNUSUAL OPINION, CONSIDERING THAT I WAS TOLD YOUR FATHER WAS A RONIN.
15

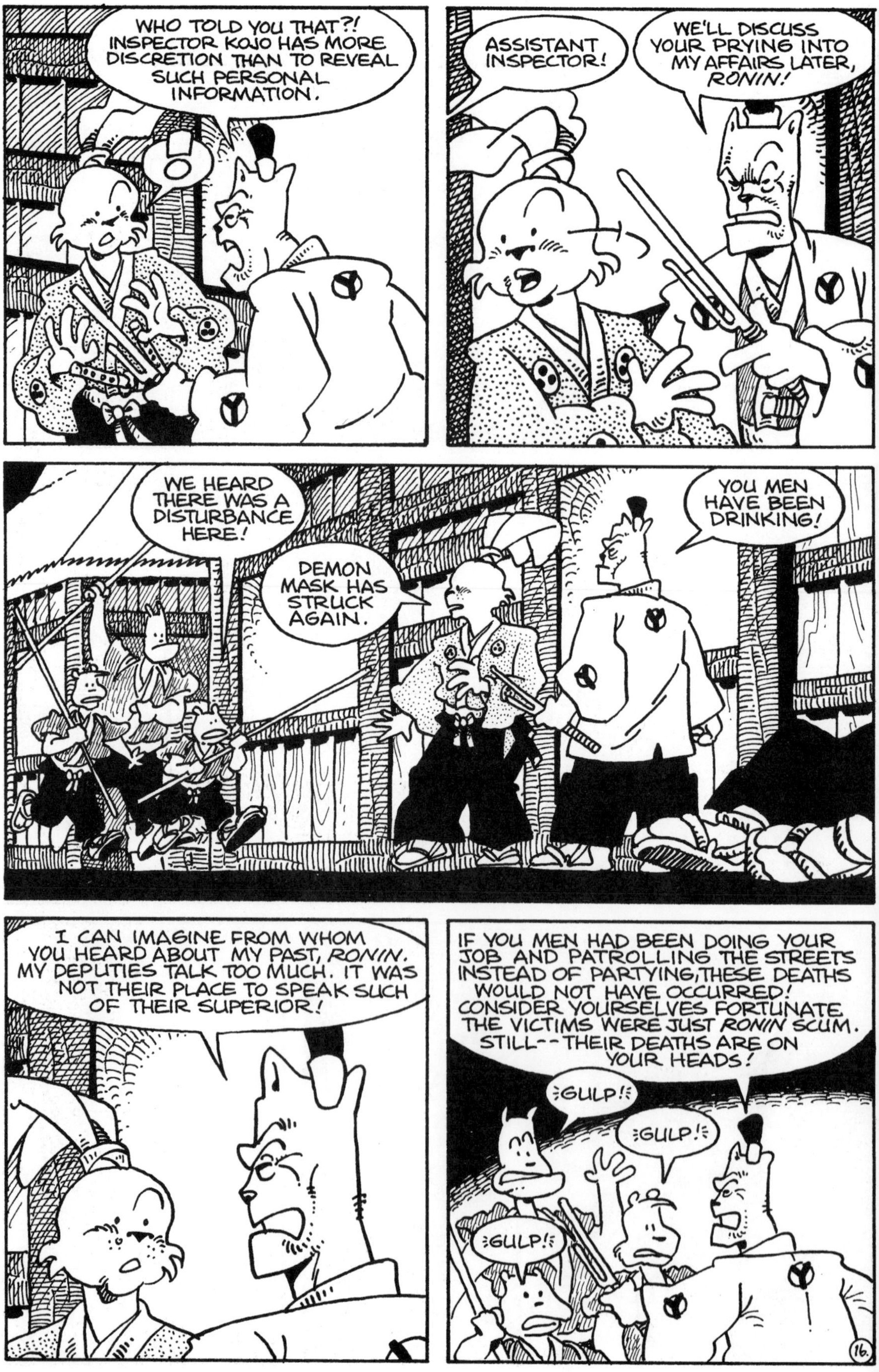
WHO TOLD YOU THAT?! INSPECTOR KOJO HAS MORE DISCRETION THAN TO REVEAL SUCH PERSONAL INFORMATION.
!
ASSISTANT INSPECTOR!
WE'LL DISCUSS YOUR PRYING INTO MY AFFAIRS LATER, RONIN!
WE HEARD THERE WAS A DISTURBANCE HERE!
DEMON MASK HAS STRUCK AGAIN.
YOU MEN HAVE BEEN DRINKING!
I CAN IMAGINE FROM WHOM YOU HEARD ABOUT MY PAST, RONIN. MY DEPUTIES TALK TOO MUCH. IT WAS NOT THEIR PLACE TO SPEAK SUCH OF THEIR SUPERIOR!
IF YOU MEN HAD BEEN DOING YOUR JOB AND PATROLLING THE STREETS INSTEAD OF PARTYING, THESE DEATHS WOULD NOT HAVE OCCURRED! CONSIDER YOURSELVES FORTUNATE THE VICTIMS WERE JUST RONIN SCUM. STILL--THEIR DEATHS ARE ON YOUR HEADS!
GULP!
GULP!
GULP!
16.

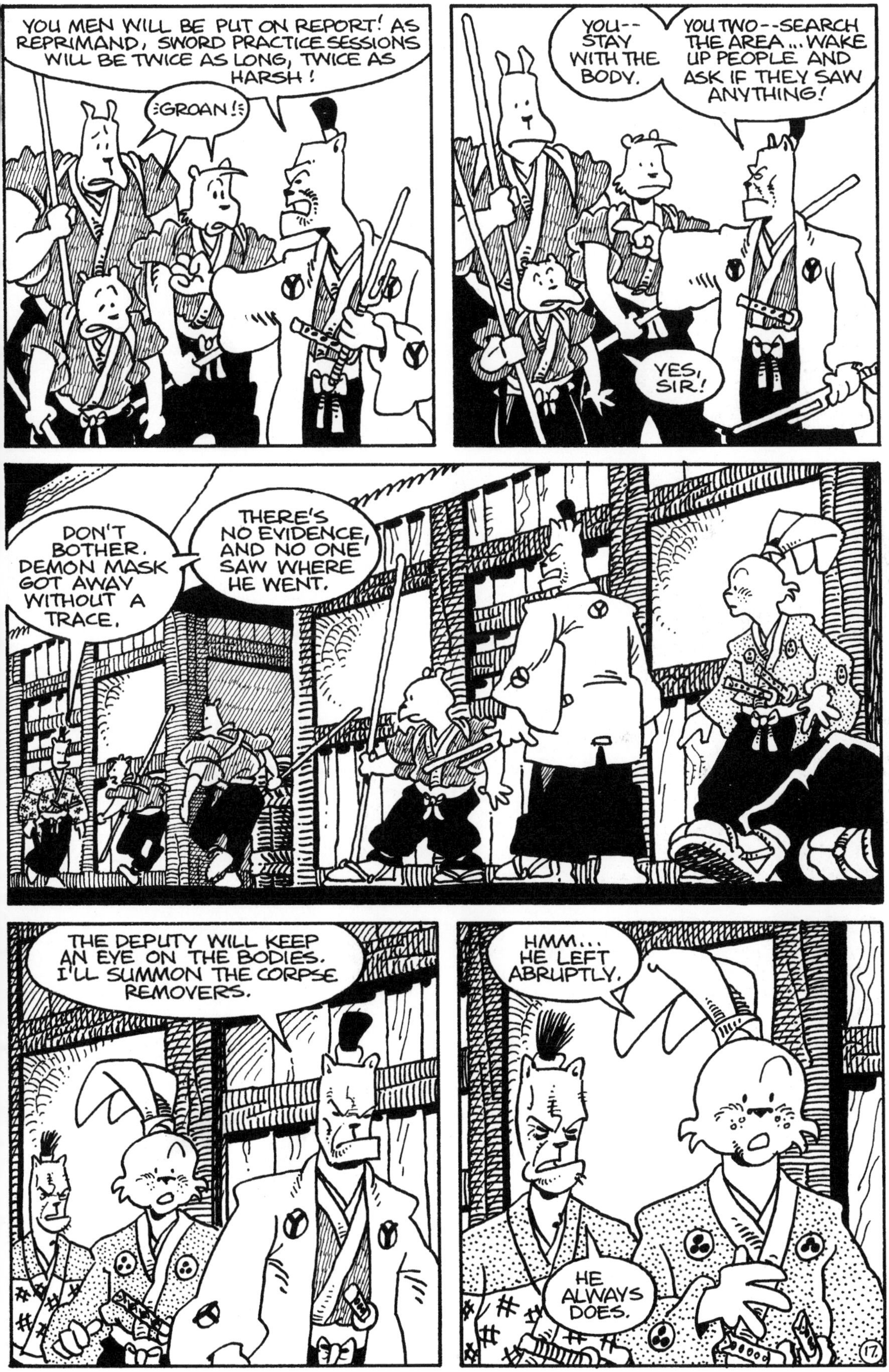
YOU MEN WILL BE PUT ON REPORT! AS REPRIMAND, SWORD PRACTICE SESSIONS WILL BE TWICE AS LONG, TWICE AS HARSH!
GROAN!
YOU-- STAY WITH THE BODY.
YOU TWO--SEARCH THE AREA... WAKE UP PEOPLE AND ASK IF THEY SAW ANYTHING!
YES, SIR!
DON'T BOTHER. DEMON MASK GOT AWAY WITHOUT A TRACE.
THERE'S NO EVIDENCE, AND NO ONE SAW WHERE HE WENT.
THE DEPUTY WILL KEEP AN EYE ON THE BODIES. I'LL SUMMON THE CORPSE REMOVERS.
HMM... HE LEFT ABRUPTLY.
HE ALWAYS DOES.
17.

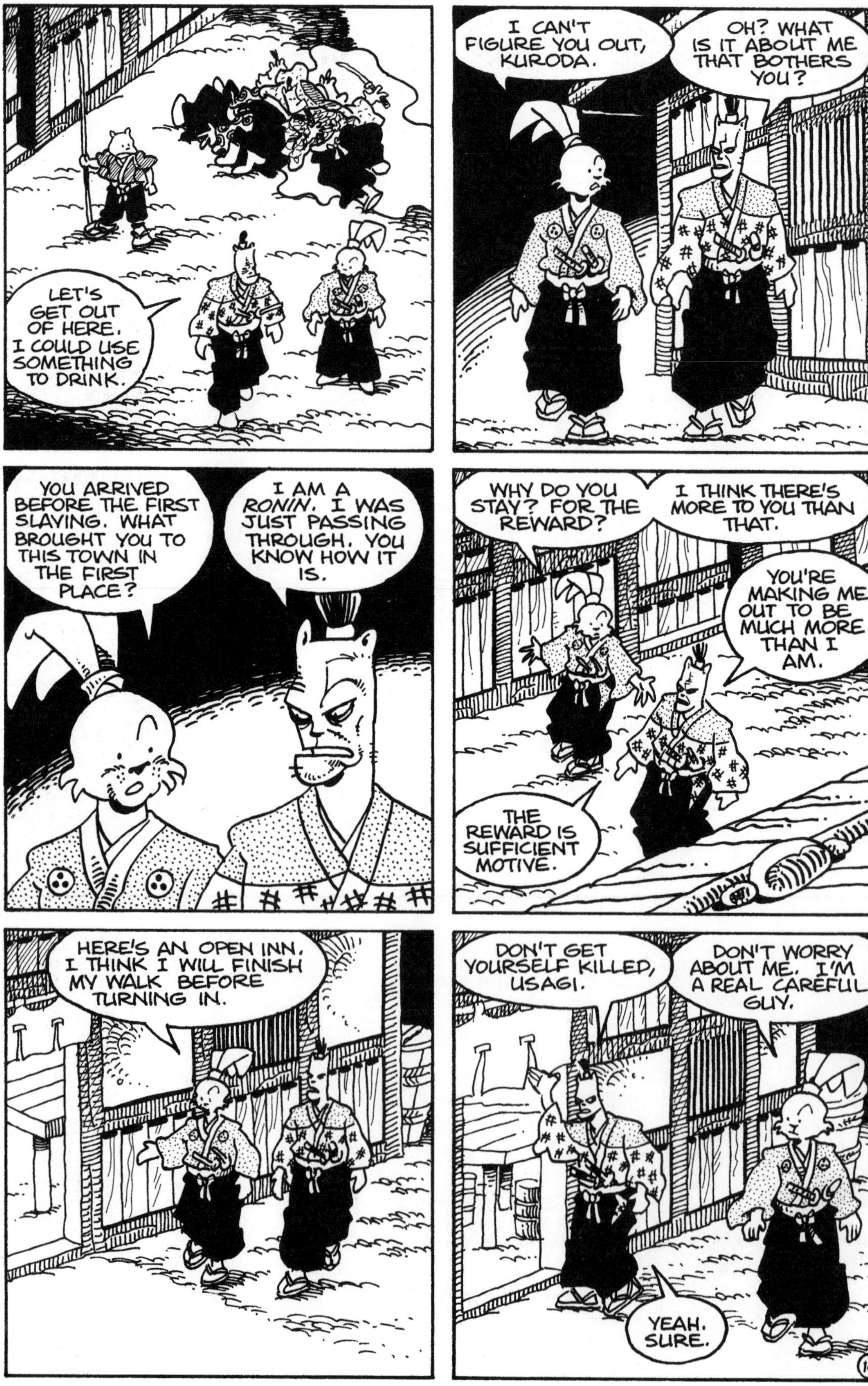
LET'S GET OUT OF HERE. I COULD USE SOMETHING TO DRINK.
I CAN'T FIGURE YOU OUT, KURODA.
OH? WHAT IS IT ABOUT ME THAT BOTHERS YOU?
YOU ARRIVED BEFORE THE FIRST SLAYING. WHAT BROUGHT YOU TO THIS TOWN IN THE FIRST PLACE?
I AM A *RONIN*. I WAS JUST PASSING THROUGH. YOU KNOW HOW IT IS.
WHY DO YOU STAY? FOR THE REWARD?
I THINK THERE'S MORE TO YOU THAN THAT.
YOU'RE MAKING ME OUT TO BE MUCH MORE THAN I AM.
THE REWARD IS SUFFICIENT MOTIVE.
HERE'S AN OPEN INN. I THINK I WILL FINISH MY WALK BEFORE TURNING IN.
DON'T GET YOURSELF KILLED, USAGI.
DON'T WORRY ABOUT ME. I'M A REAL CAREFUL GUY.
YEAH. SURE.
18.

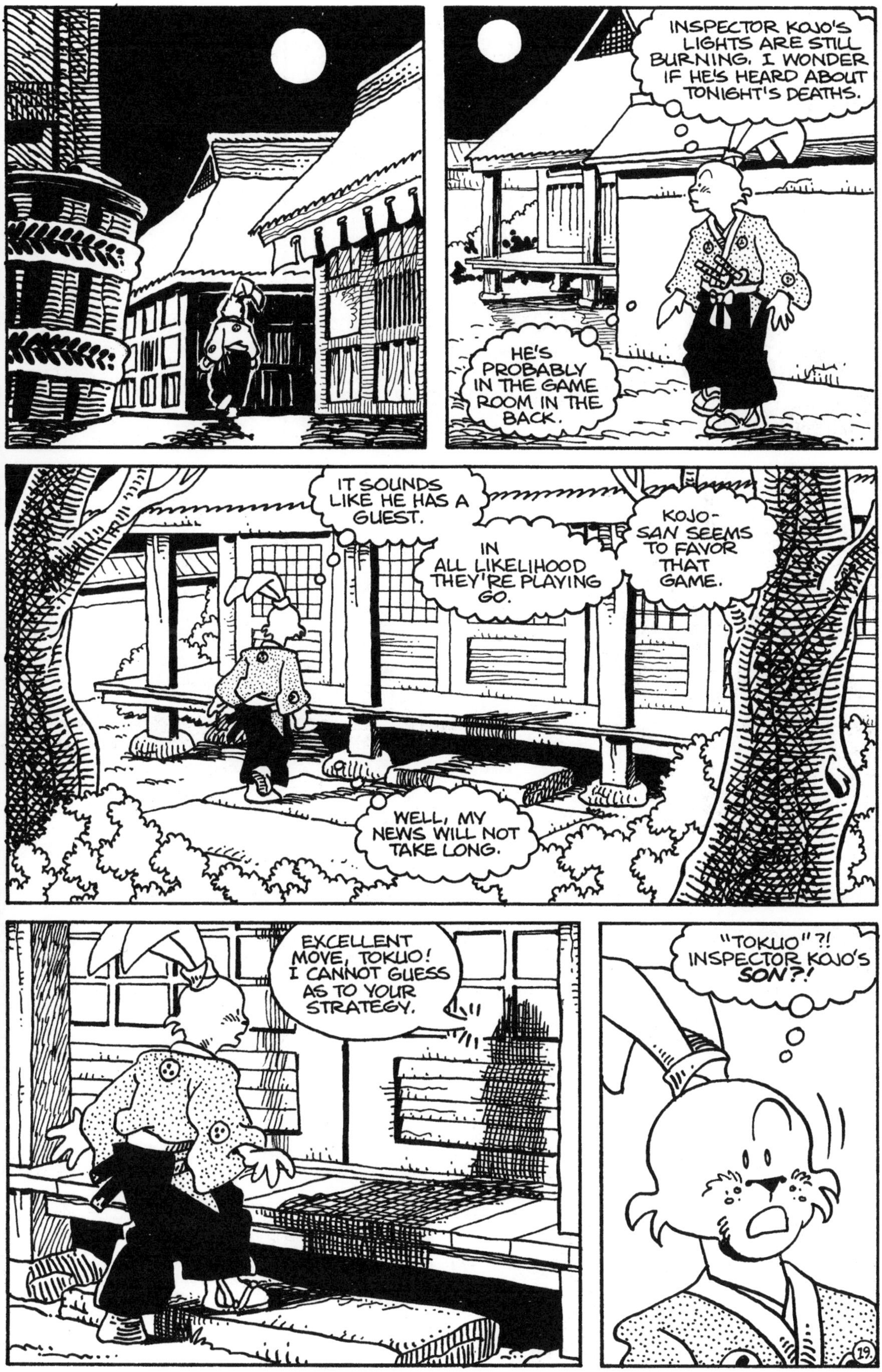
INSPECTOR KOJO'S LIGHTS ARE STILL BURNING. I WONDER IF HE'S HEARD ABOUT TONIGHT'S DEATHS.
HE'S PROBABLY IN THE GAME ROOM IN THE BACK.
IT SOUNDS LIKE HE HAS A GUEST.
IN ALL LIKELIHOOD THEY'RE PLAYING GO.
KOJO-SAN SEEMS TO FAVOR THAT GAME.
WELL, MY NEWS WILL NOT TAKE LONG.
EXCELLENT MOVE, TOKUO! I CANNOT GUESS AS TO YOUR STRATEGY.
"TOKUO"?! INSPECTOR KOJO'S SON?!
19.

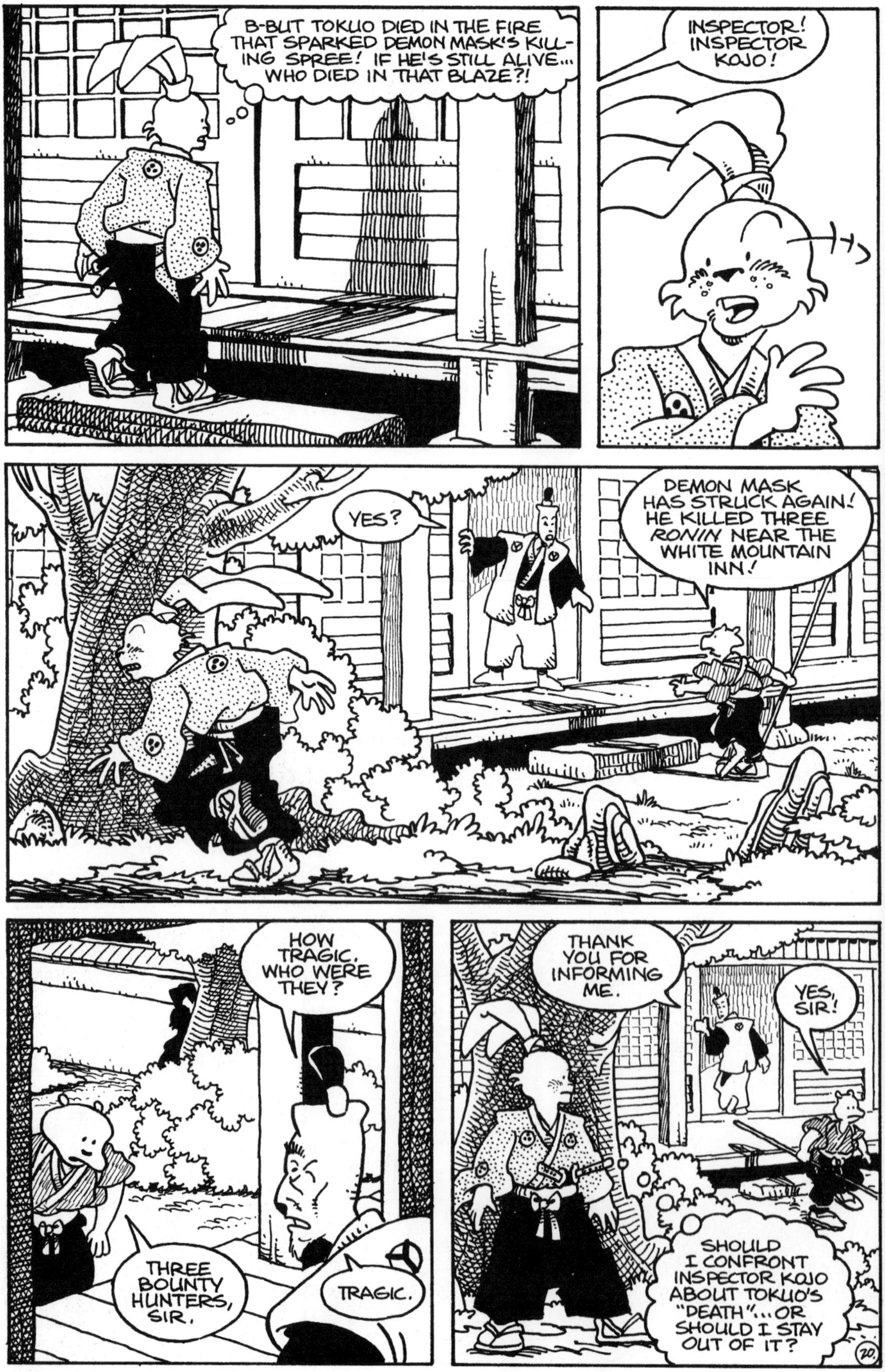
B-BUT TOKUIO DIED IN THE FIRE THAT SPARKED DEMON MASK'S KILLING SPREE! IF HE'S STILL ALIVE... WHO DIED IN THAT BLAZE?!
INSPECTOR! INSPECTOR KOJO!
YES?
DEMON MASK HAS STRUCK AGAIN! HE KILLED THREE *RONIN* NEAR THE WHITE MOUNTAIN INN!
HOW TRAGIC. WHO WERE THEY?
THREE BOUNTY HUNTERS, SIR.
TRAGIC.
THANK YOU FOR INFORMING ME.
YES, SIR!
SHOULD I CONFRONT INSPECTOR KOJO ABOUT TOKUIO'S "DEATH"...OR SHOULD I STAY OUT OF IT?
20.

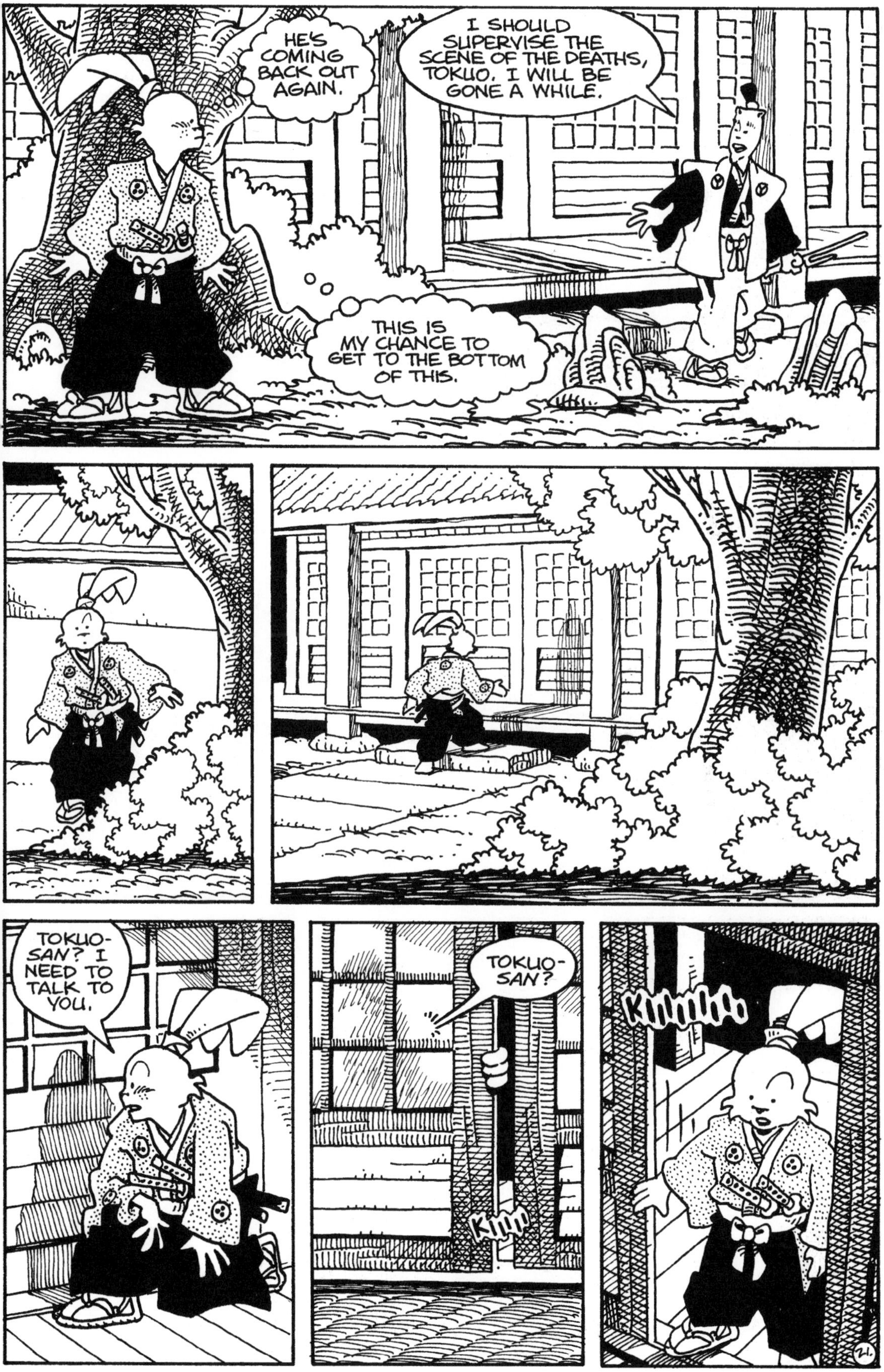
HE'S COMING BACK OUT AGAIN.
I SHOULD SUPERVISE THE SCENE OF THE DEATHS, TOKUO. I WILL BE GONE A WHILE.
THIS IS MY CHANCE TO GET TO THE BOTTOM OF THIS.
TOKUO-SAN? I NEED TO TALK TO YOU.
TOKUO-SAN?
KIII
KIIIIIII
21.

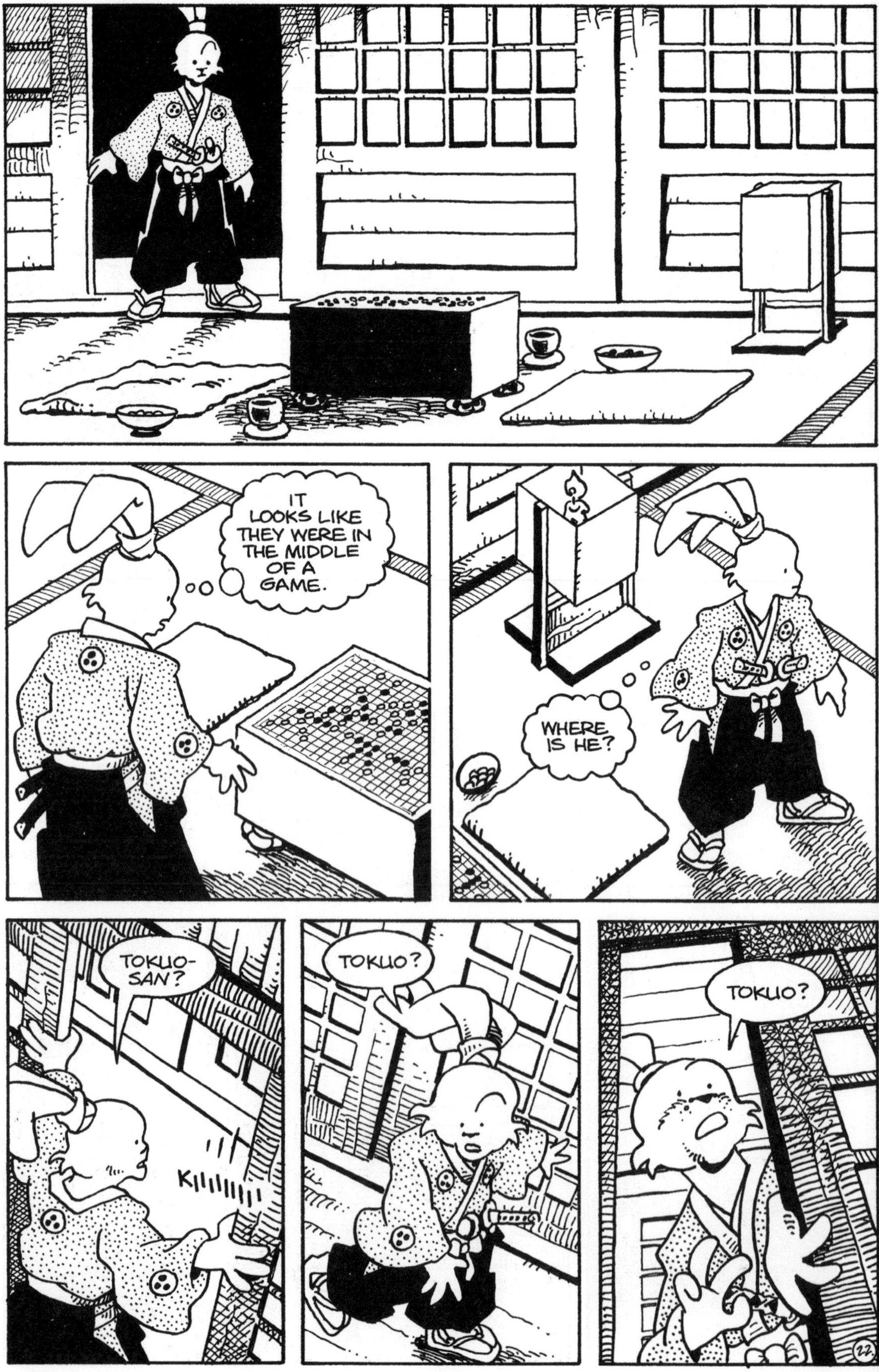
IT LOOKS LIKE THEY WERE IN THE MIDDLE OF A GAME.
WHERE IS HE?
TOKUO-SAN?
KIIIIIIII
TOKUO?
TOKUO?
22.

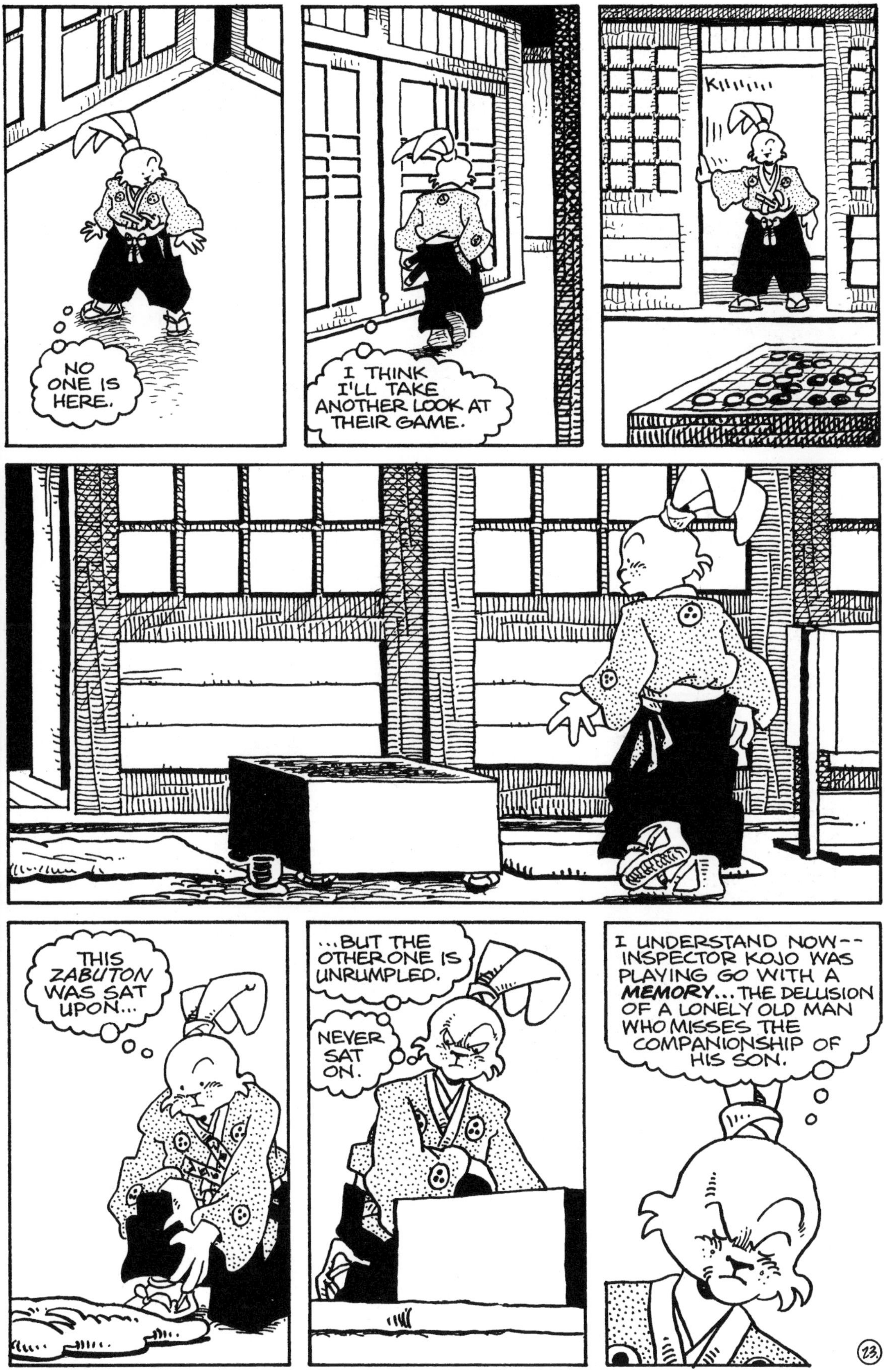
NO ONE IS HERE.
I THINK I'LL TAKE ANOTHER LOOK AT THEIR GAME.
KIIIII
THIS ZABUTON WAS SAT UPON...
...BUT THE OTHER ONE IS UNRUMPLED.
NEVER SAT ON.
I UNDERSTAND NOW-- INSPECTOR KOJO WAS PLAYING GO WITH A MEMORY... THE DELLUSION OF A LONELY OLD MAN WHO MISSES THE COMPANIONSHIP OF HIS SON.
23

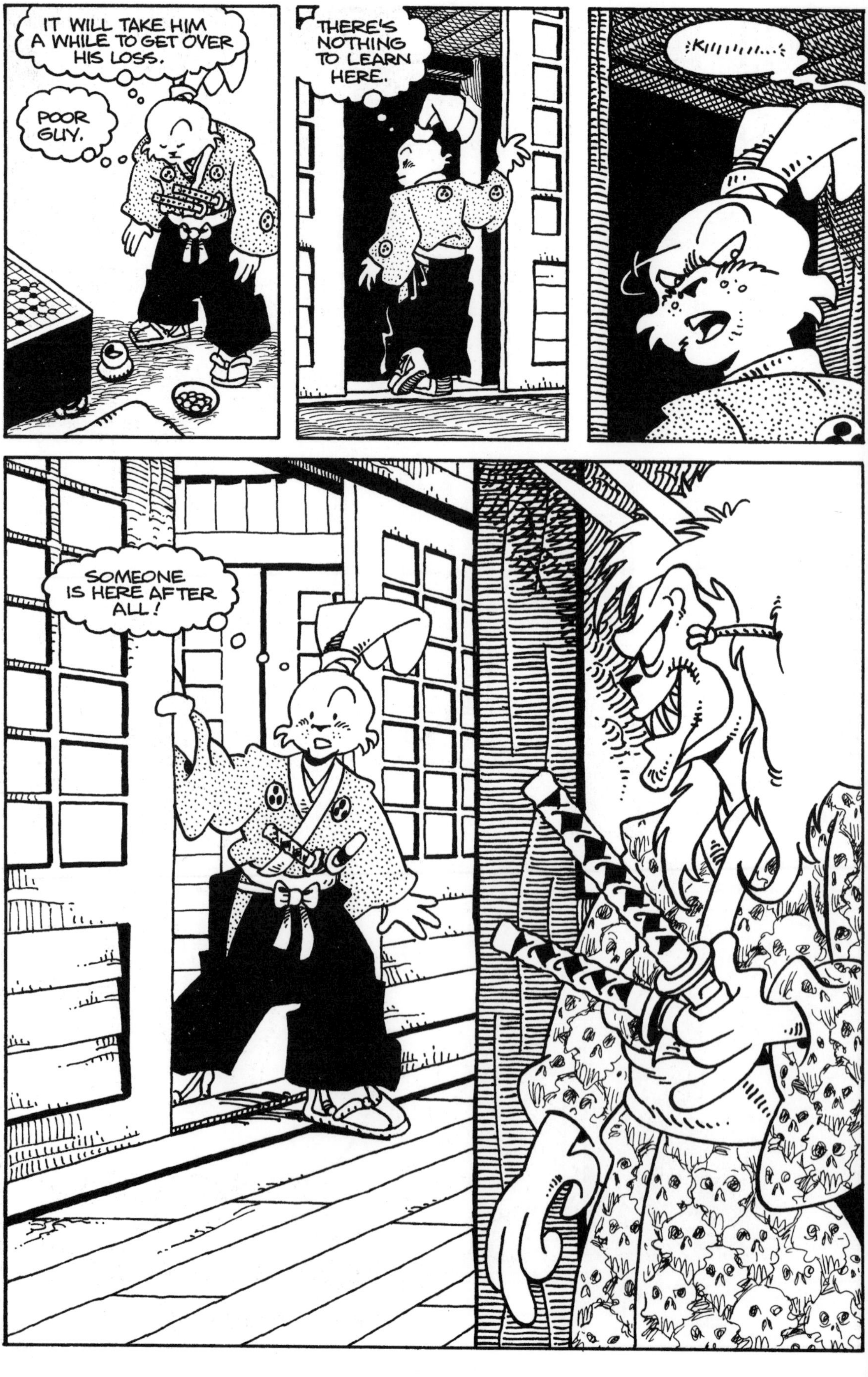
IT WILL TAKE HIM A WHILE TO GET OVER HIS LOSS.
POOR GUY.
THERE'S NOTHING TO LEARN HERE.
KIIIIIIII...
SOMEONE IS HERE AFTER ALL!

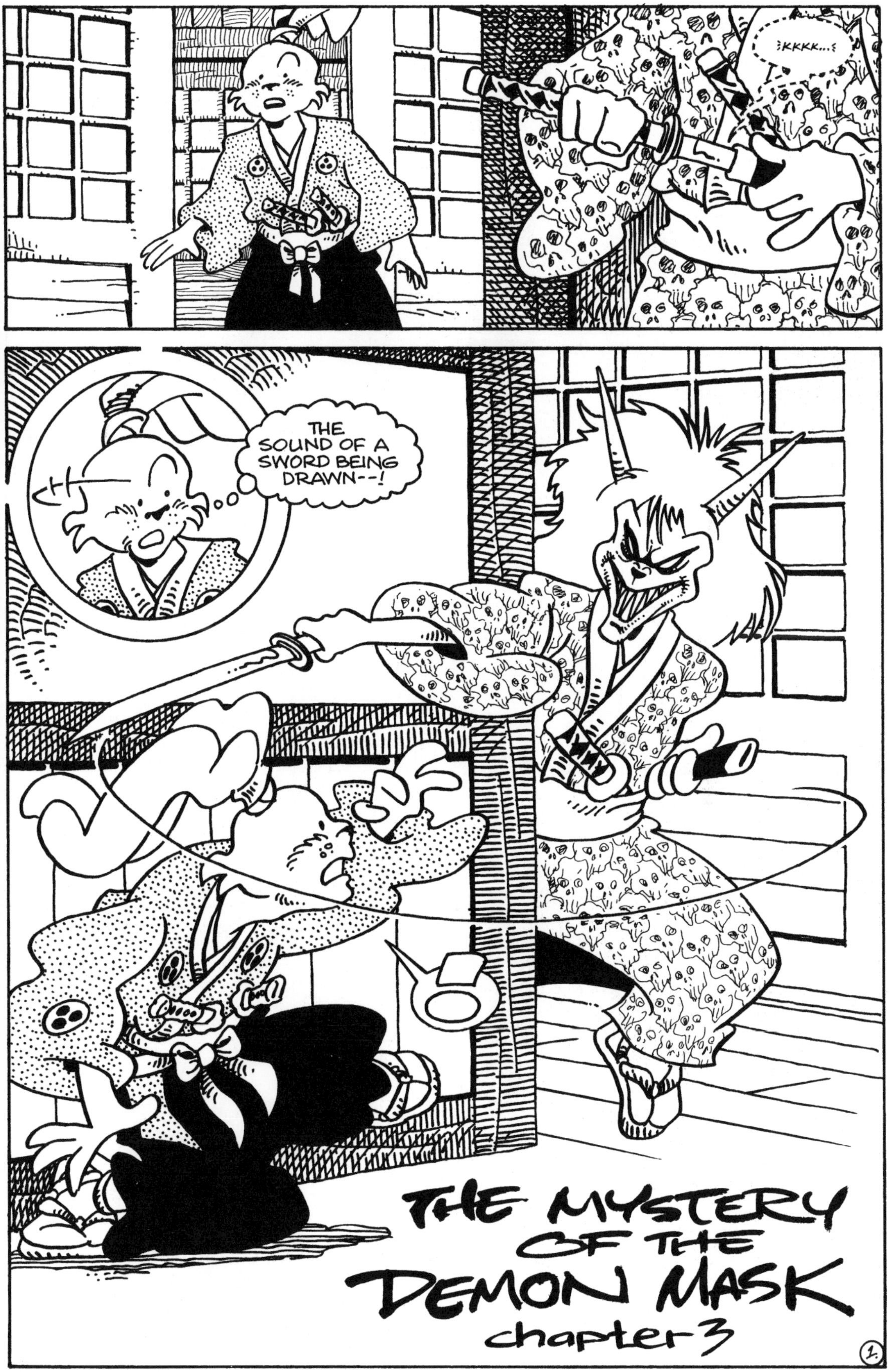
KKKK...
THE SOUND OF A SWORD BEING DRAWN--!
THE MYSTERY OF THE DEMON MASK
chapter 3
1.

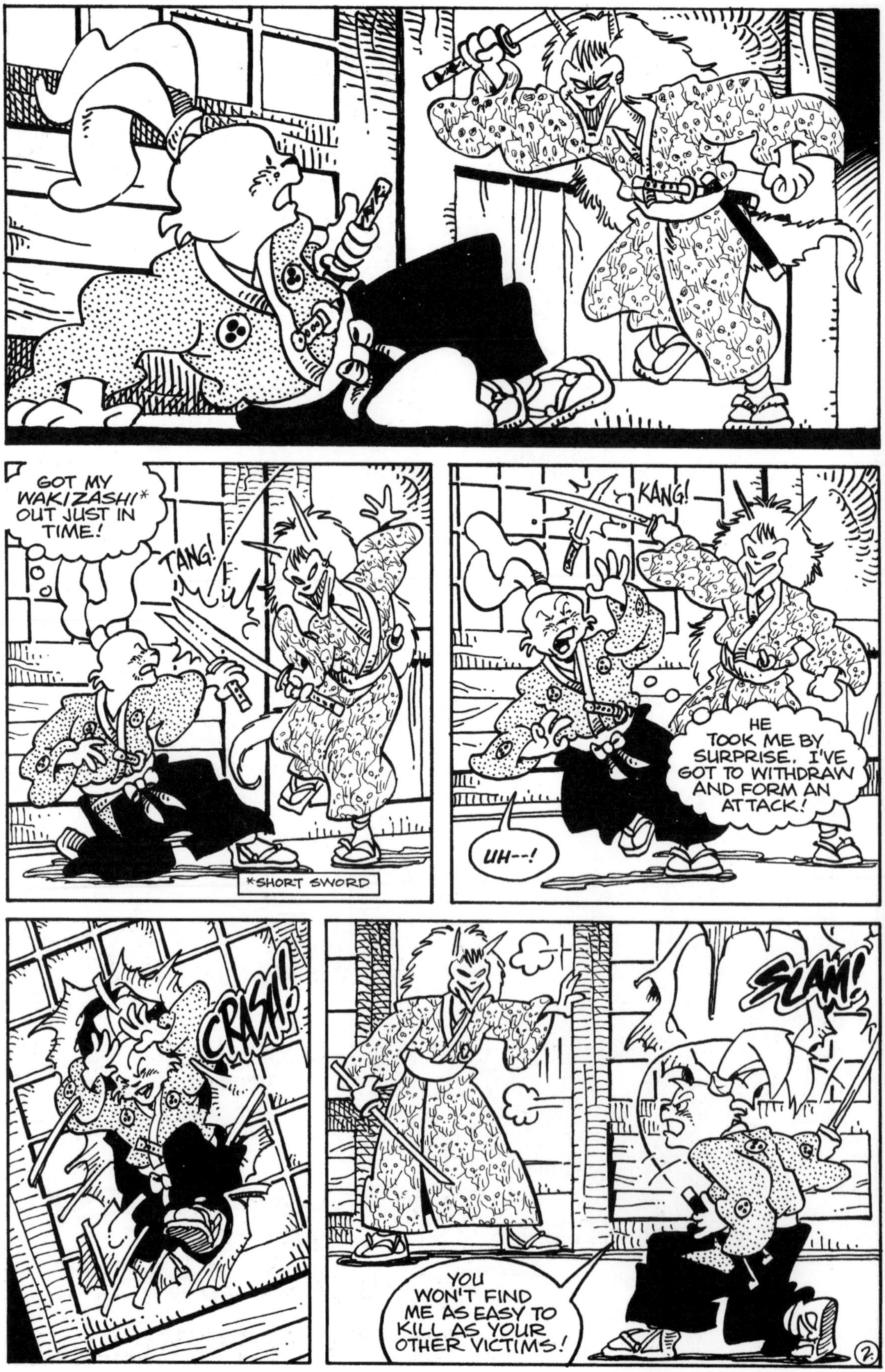
GOT MY WAKIZASHI* OUT JUST IN TIME!
TANG!
*SHORT SWORD
KANG!
UH--!
HE TOOK ME BY SURPRISE. I'VE GOT TO WITHDRAW AND FORM AN ATTACK!
CRASH!
SLAM!
YOU WON'T FIND ME AS EASY TO KILL AS YOUR OTHER VICTIMS!
2.

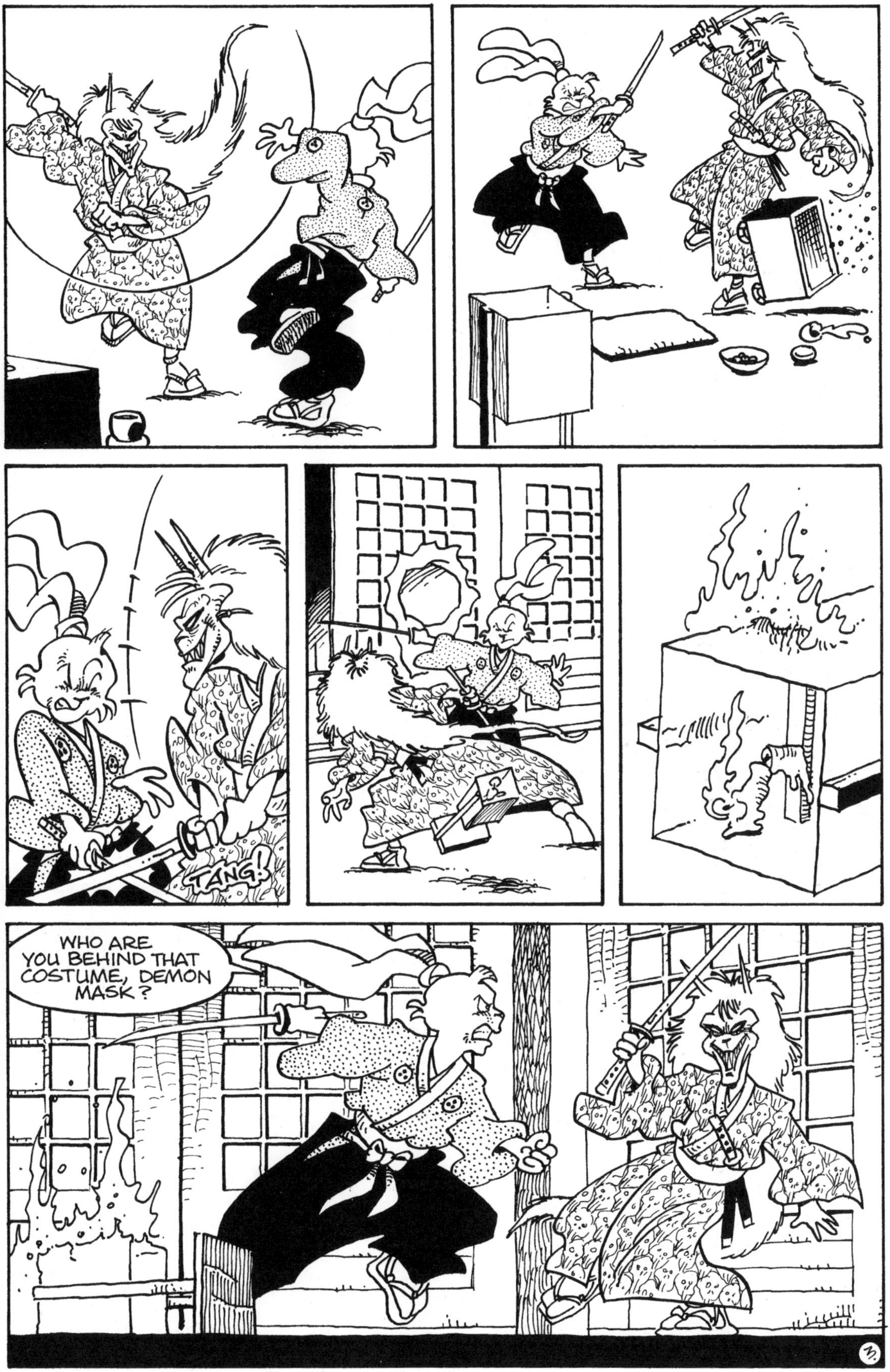
TANG!
WHO ARE YOU BEHIND THAT COSTUME, DEMON MASK?
3.

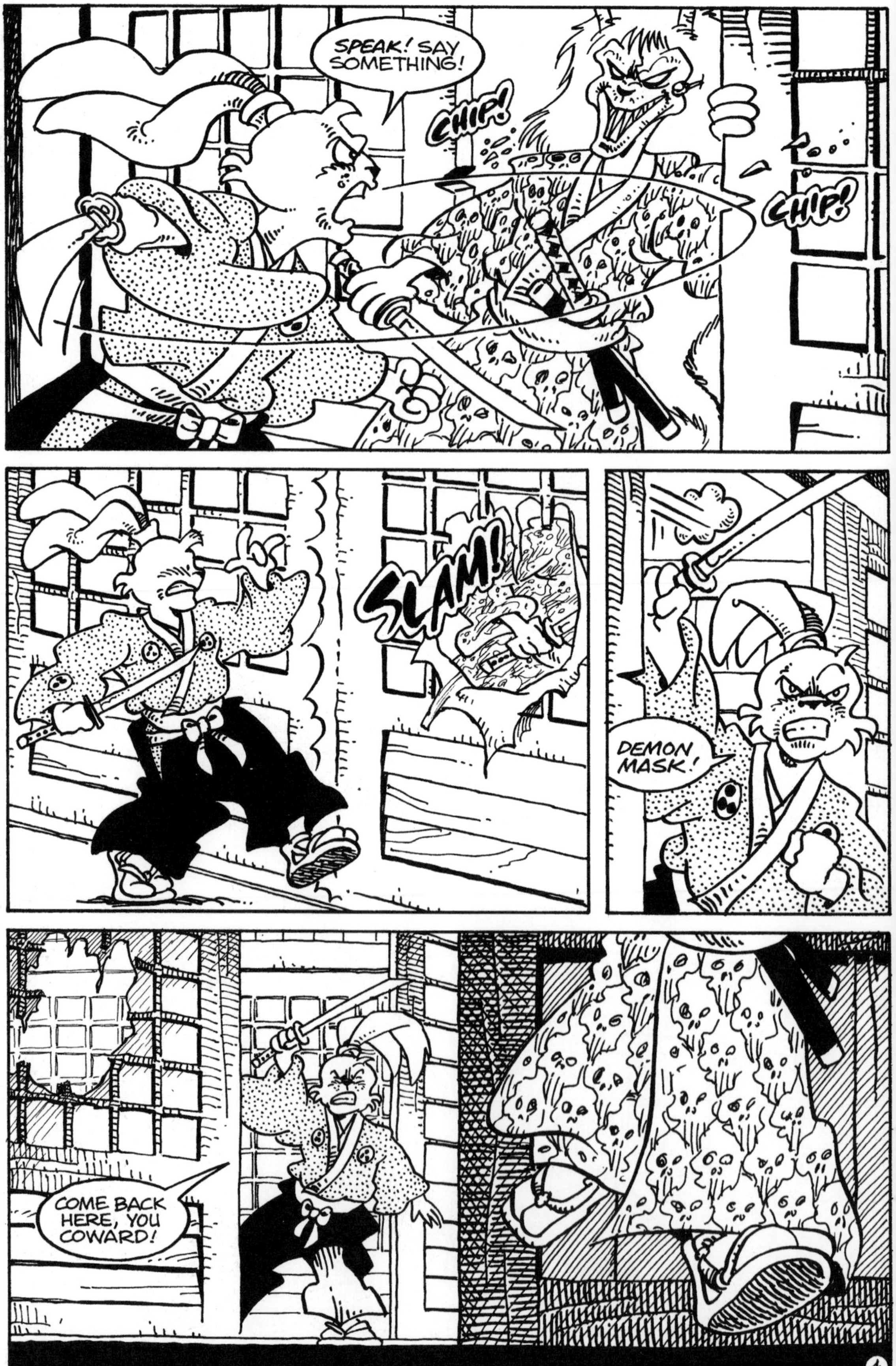
SPEAK! SAY SOMETHING!
CHIP!
CHIP!
SLAM!
DEMON MASK!
COME BACK HERE, YOU COWARD!
4.

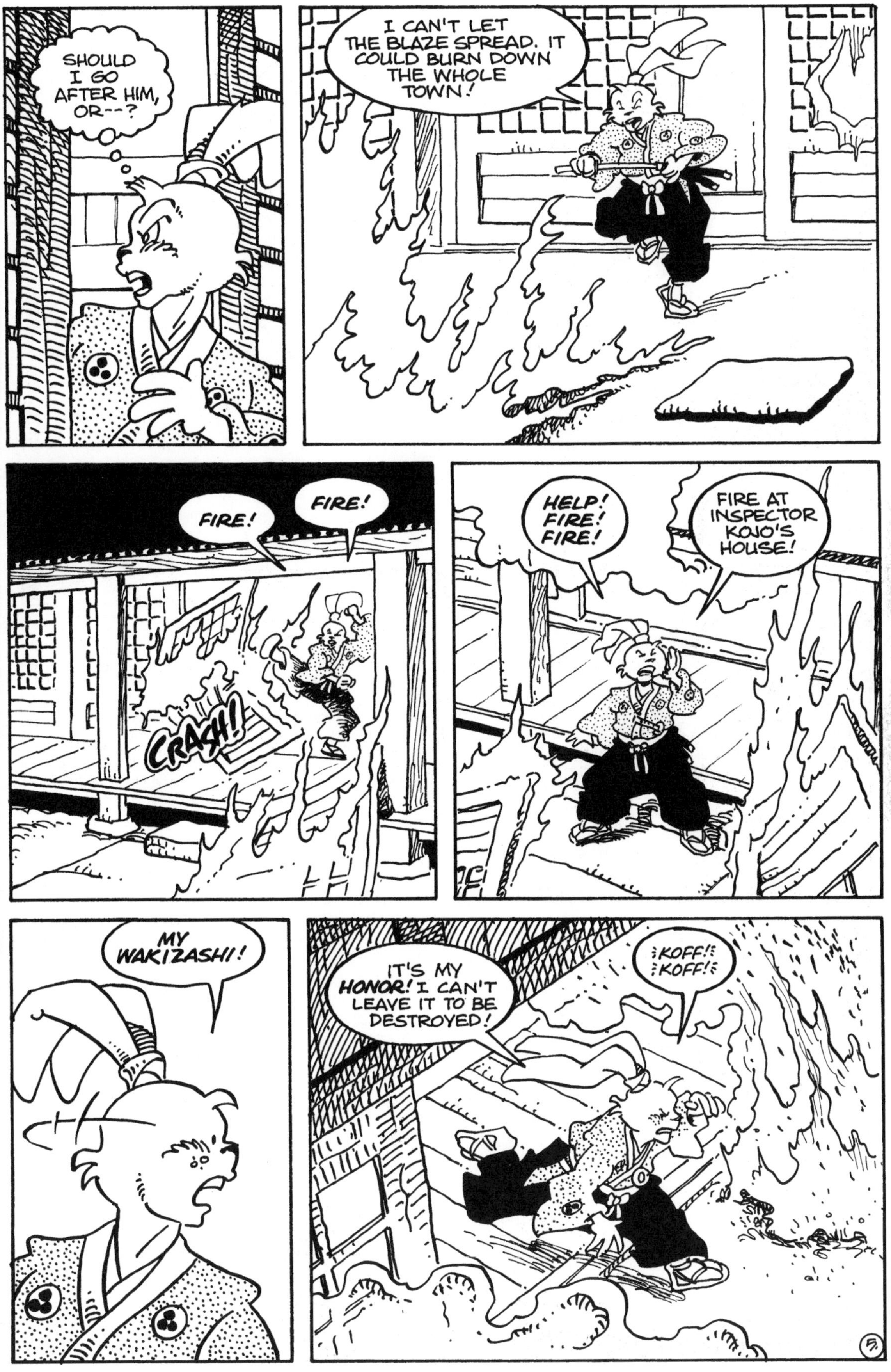
SHOULD I GO AFTER HIM, OR--?
I CAN'T LET THE BLAZE SPREAD. IT COULD BURN DOWN THE WHOLE TOWN!
FIRE!
FIRE!
CRASH!
HELP! FIRE! FIRE!
FIRE AT INSPECTOR KOJO'S HOUSE!
MY WAKIZASHI!
IT'S MY HONOR! I CAN'T LEAVE IT TO BE DESTROYED!
KOFF! KOFF!
5

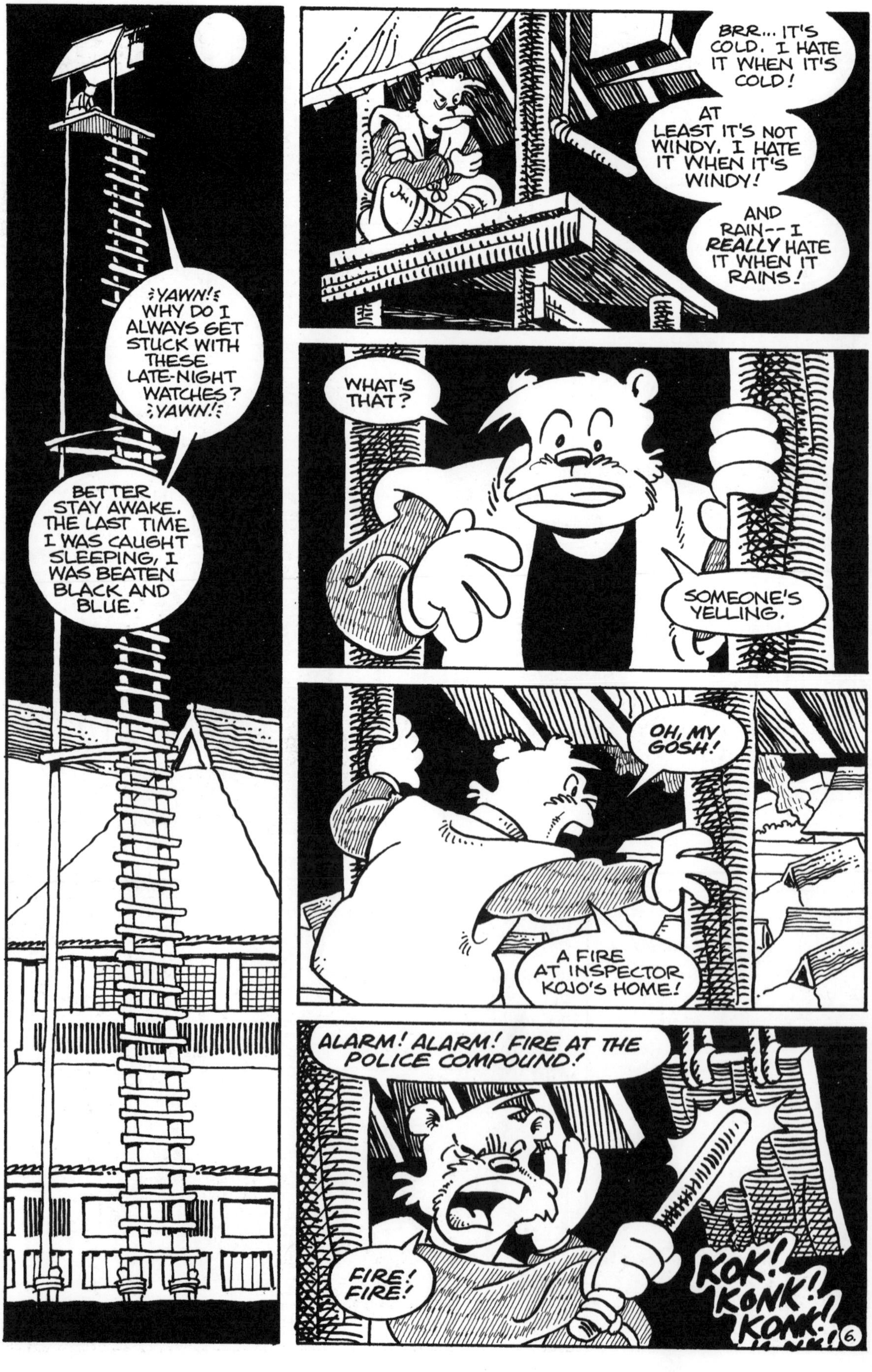

¡YAWN!¡ WHY DO I ALWAYS GET STUCK WITH THESE LATE-NIGHT WATCHES? ¡YAWN!¡
BETTER STAY AWAKE. THE LAST TIME I WAS CAUGHT SLEEPING, I WAS BEATEN BLACK AND BLUE.
BRR... IT'S COLD. I HATE IT WHEN IT'S COLD!
AT LEAST IT'S NOT WINDY. I HATE IT WHEN IT'S WINDY!
AND RAIN-- I REALLY HATE IT WHEN IT RAINS!
WHAT'S THAT?
SOMEONE'S YELLING.
OH, MY GOSH!
A FIRE AT INSPECTOR KOJO'S HOME!
ALARM! ALARM! FIRE AT THE POLICE COMPOUND!
FIRE! FIRE!
KOK! KONK! KONK!
6.

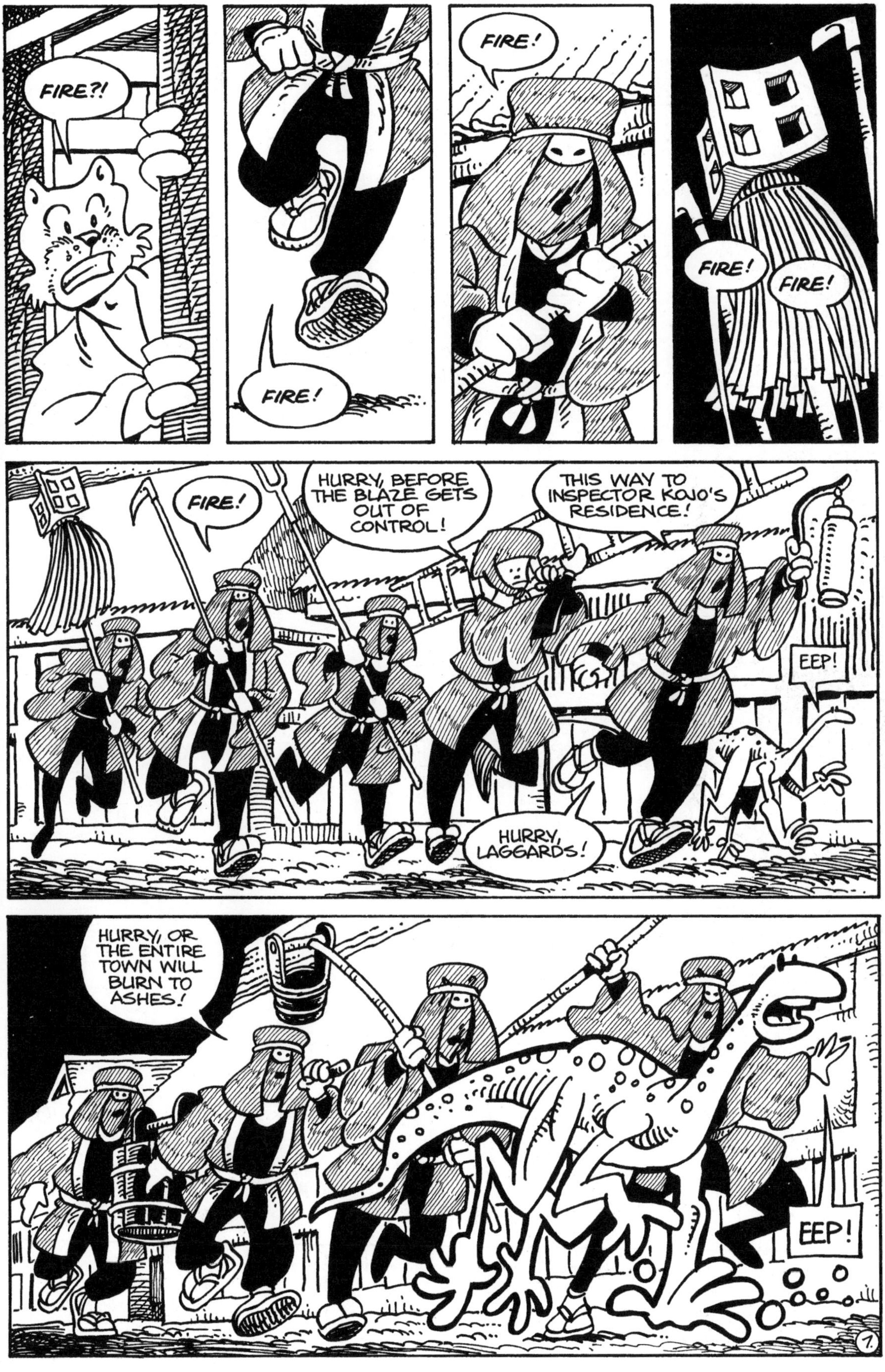
FIRE?!
FIRE!
FIRE!
FIRE!
FIRE!
FIRE!
HURRY, BEFORE THE BLAZE GETS OUT OF CONTROL!
THIS WAY TO INSPECTOR KOJO'S RESIDENCE!
EEP!
HURRY, LAGGARDS!
HURRY, OR THE ENTIRE TOWN WILL BURN TO ASHES!
EEP!
7.

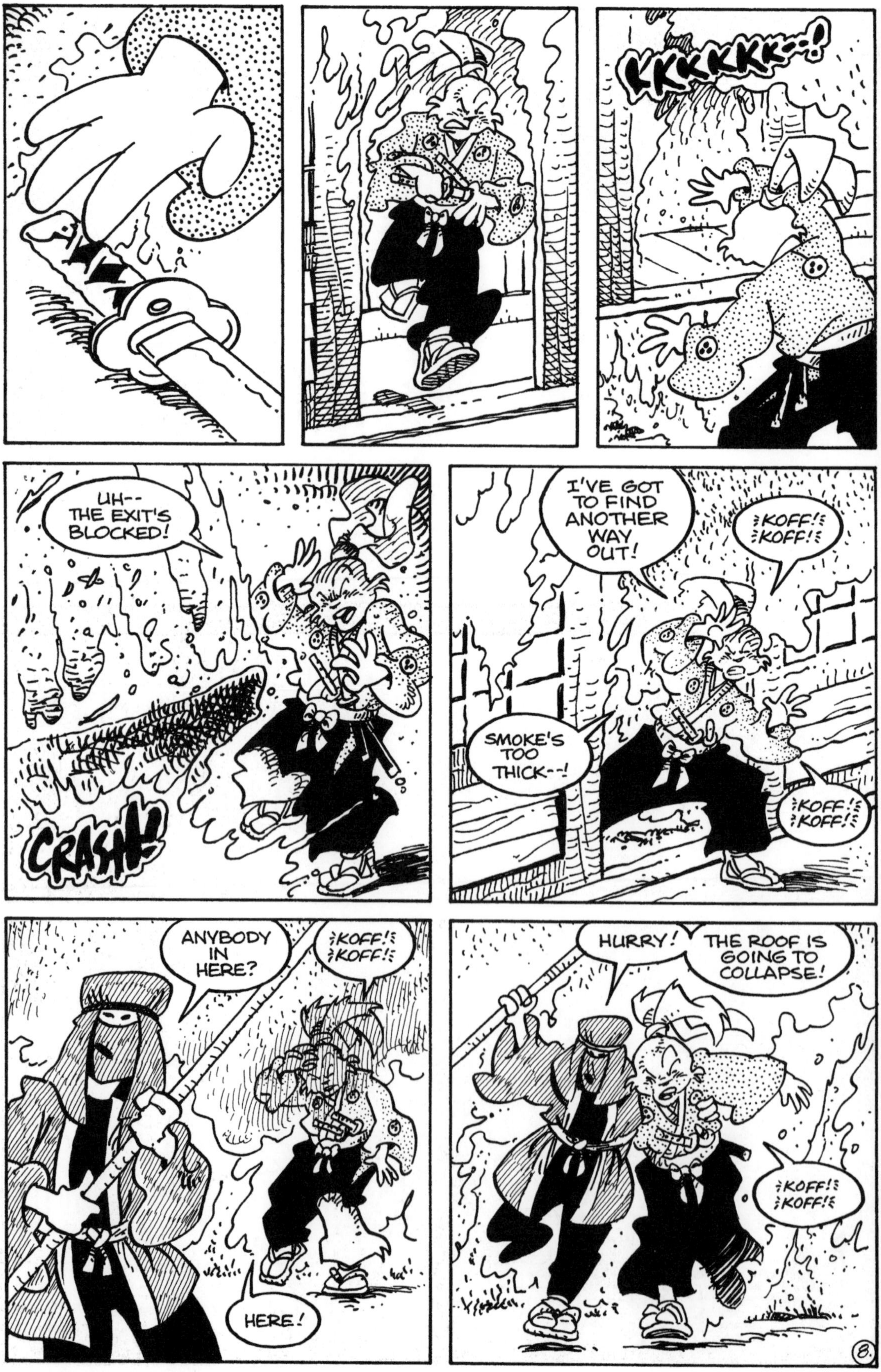
KKKKKK--!
UH-- THE EXIT'S BLOCKED!
CRASH!
I'VE GOT TO FIND ANOTHER WAY OUT!
KOFF! KOFF!
SMOKE'S TOO THICK--!
KOFF! KOFF!
ANYBODY IN HERE?
KOFF! KOFF!
HERE!
HURRY!
THE ROOF IS GOING TO COLLAPSE!
KOFF! KOFF!
8.

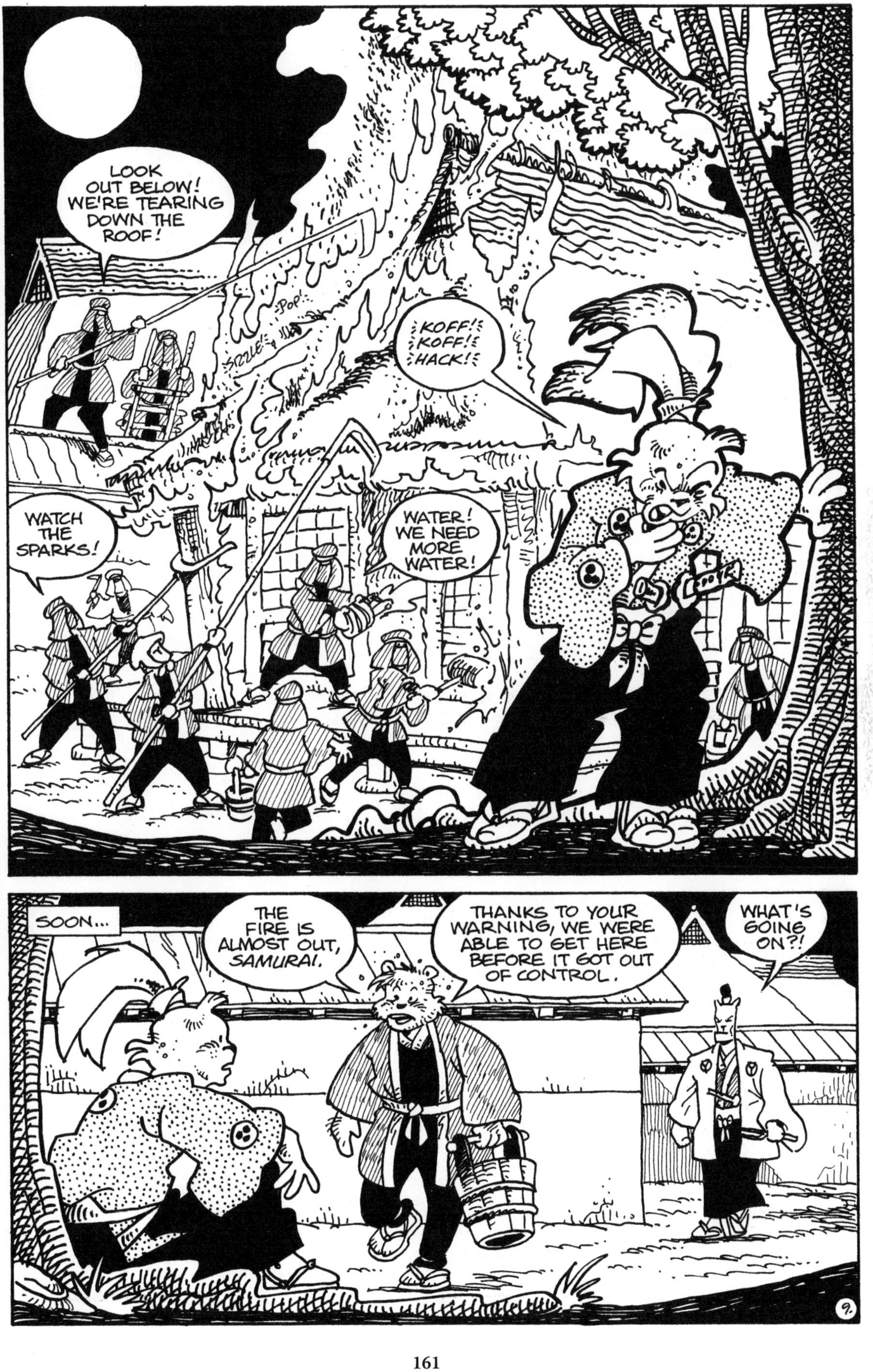
LOOK OUT BELOW! WE'RE TEARING DOWN THE ROOF!
SIZZLE!
POP!
KOFF! KOFF! HACK!
WATCH THE SPARKS!
WATER! WE NEED MORE WATER!
SOON...
THE FIRE IS ALMOST OUT, *SAMURAI.*
THANKS TO YOUR WARNING, WE WERE ABLE TO GET HERE BEFORE IT GOT OUT OF CONTROL.
WHAT'S GOING ON?!
9.

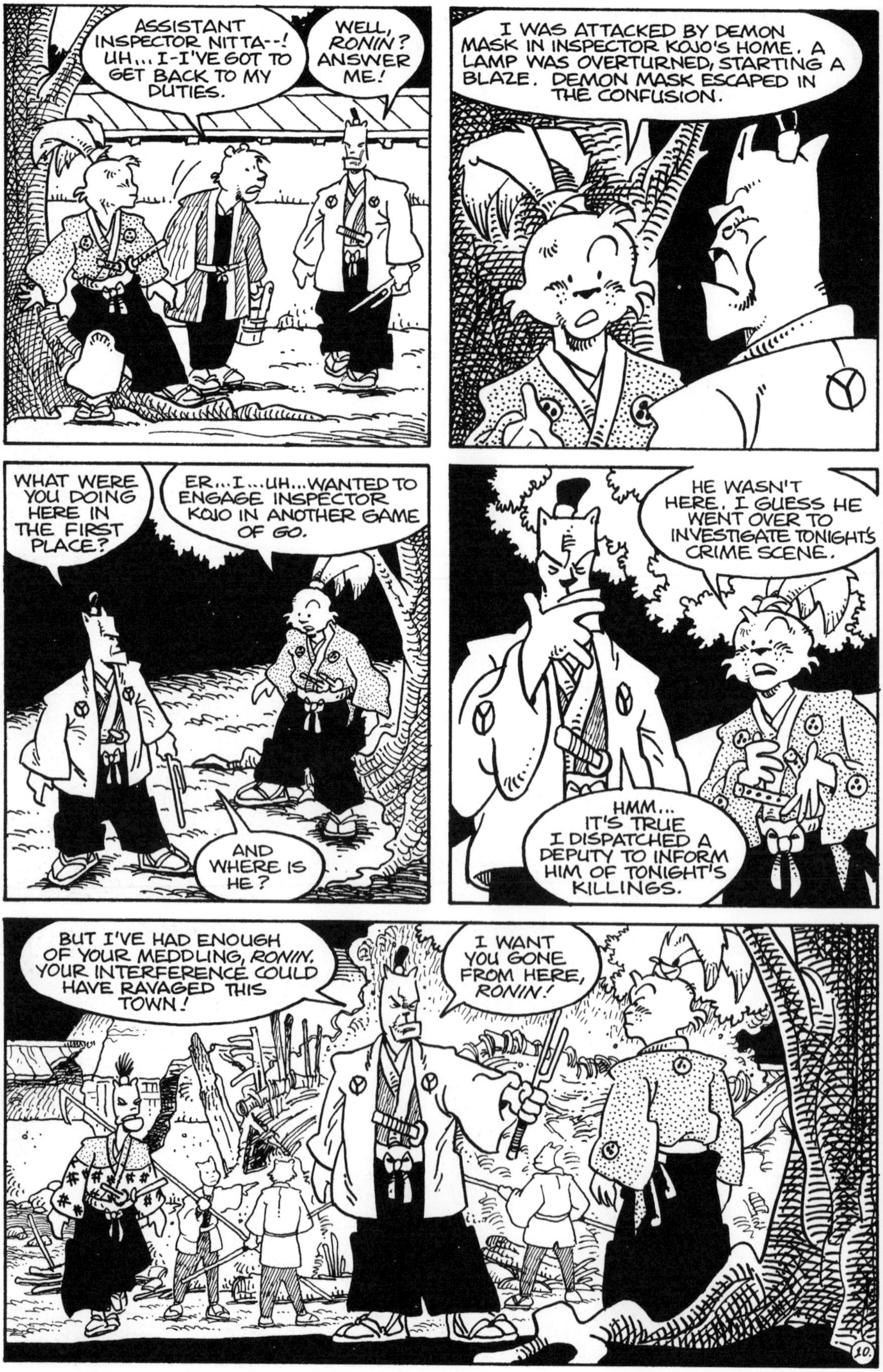
ASSISTANT INSPECTOR NITTA--! UH... I-I'VE GOT TO GET BACK TO MY DUTIES.
WELL, *RONIN*? ANSWER ME!
I WAS ATTACKED BY DEMON MASK IN INSPECTOR KOJO'S HOME. A LAMP WAS OVERTURNED, STARTING A BLAZE. DEMON MASK ESCAPED IN THE CONFUSION.
WHAT WERE YOU DOING HERE IN THE FIRST PLACE?
ER...I...UH...WANTED TO ENGAGE INSPECTOR KOJO IN ANOTHER GAME OF GO.
AND WHERE IS HE?
HE WASN'T HERE. I GUESS HE WENT OVER TO INVESTIGATE TONIGHT'S CRIME SCENE.
HMM... IT'S TRUE I DISPATCHED A DEPUTY TO INFORM HIM OF TONIGHT'S KILLINGS.
BUT I'VE HAD ENOUGH OF YOUR MEDDLING, *RONIN*. YOUR INTERFERENCE COULD HAVE RAVAGED THIS TOWN!
I WANT YOU GONE FROM HERE, *RONIN*!
10.

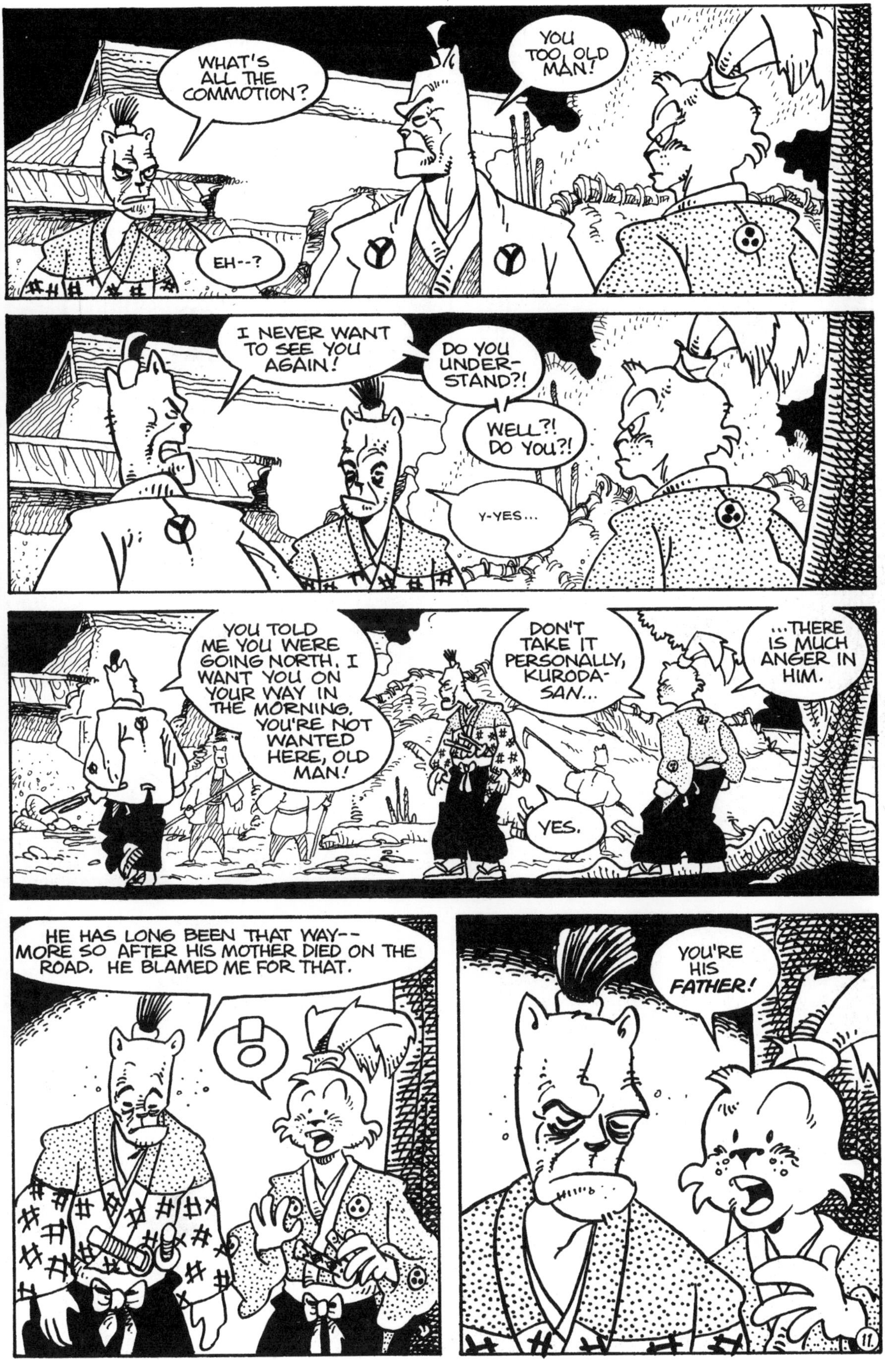
WHAT'S ALL THE COMMOTION?
EH--?
YOU TOO, OLD MAN!
I NEVER WANT TO SEE YOU AGAIN!
DO YOU UNDERSTAND?!
WELL?! DO YOU?!
Y-YES...
YOU TOLD ME YOU WERE GOING NORTH. I WANT YOU ON YOUR WAY IN THE MORNING. YOU'RE NOT WANTED HERE, OLD MAN!
YES.
DON'T TAKE IT PERSONALLY, KURODA-SAN...
...THERE IS MUCH ANGER IN HIM.
HE HAS LONG BEEN THAT WAY-- MORE SO AFTER HIS MOTHER DIED ON THE ROAD. HE BLAMED ME FOR THAT.
!
YOU'RE HIS ***FATHER!***
11

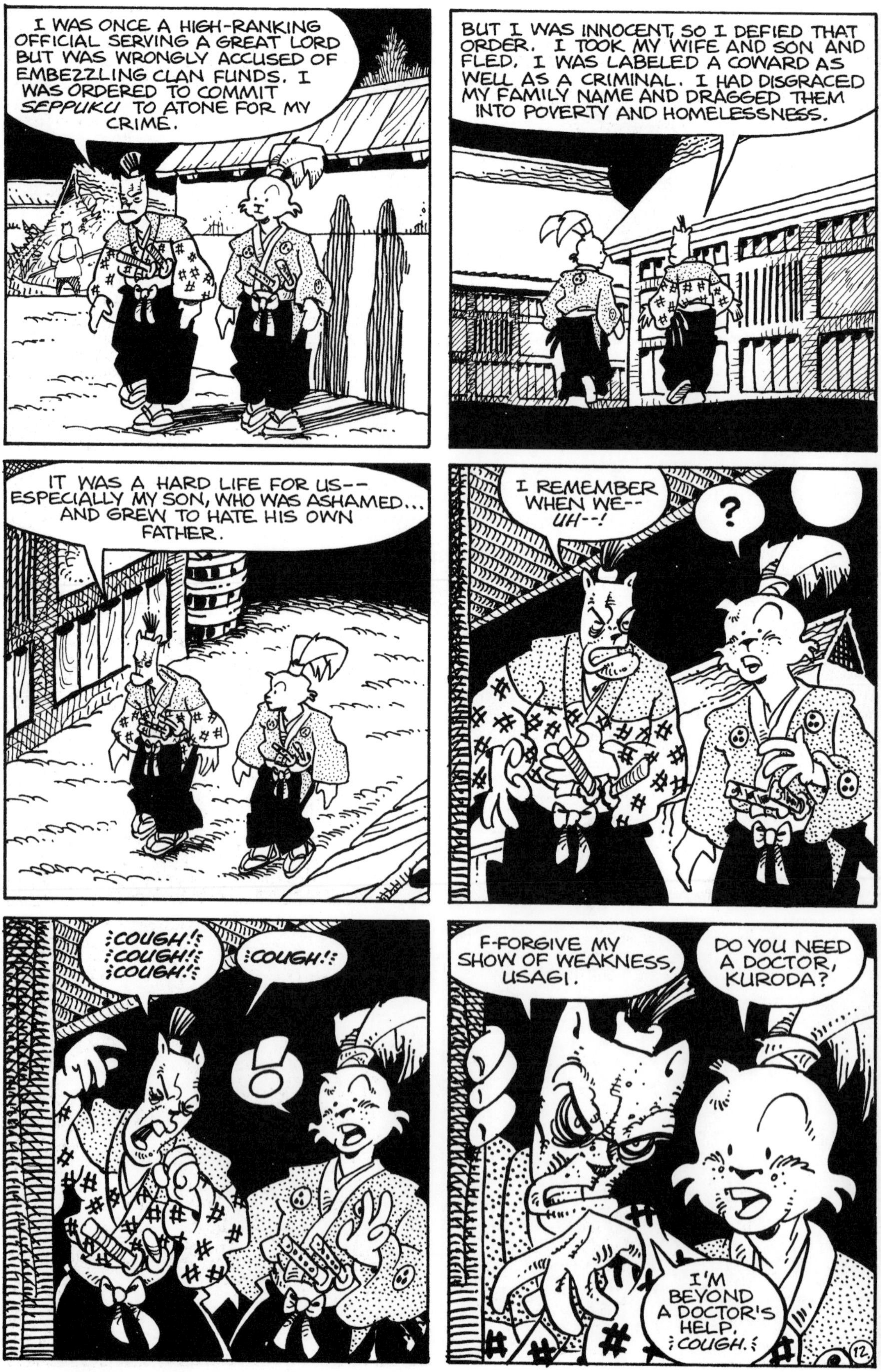
I WAS ONCE A HIGH-RANKING OFFICIAL SERVING A GREAT LORD BUT WAS WRONGLY ACCUSED OF EMBEZZLING CLAN FUNDS. I WAS ORDERED TO COMMIT *SEPPUKU* TO ATONE FOR MY CRIME.
BUT I WAS INNOCENT, SO I DEFIED THAT ORDER. I TOOK MY WIFE AND SON AND FLED. I WAS LABELED A COWARD AS WELL AS A CRIMINAL. I HAD DISGRACED MY FAMILY NAME AND DRAGGED THEM INTO POVERTY AND HOMELESSNESS.
IT WAS A HARD LIFE FOR US-- ESPECIALLY MY SON, WHO WAS ASHAMED... AND GREW TO HATE HIS OWN FATHER.
I REMEMBER WHEN WE-- *UH--!*
?
COUGH! COUGH! COUGH!
COUGH!
F-FORGIVE MY SHOW OF WEAKNESS, USAGI.
DO YOU NEED A DOCTOR, KURODA?
I'M BEYOND A DOCTOR'S HELP. COUGH.
12

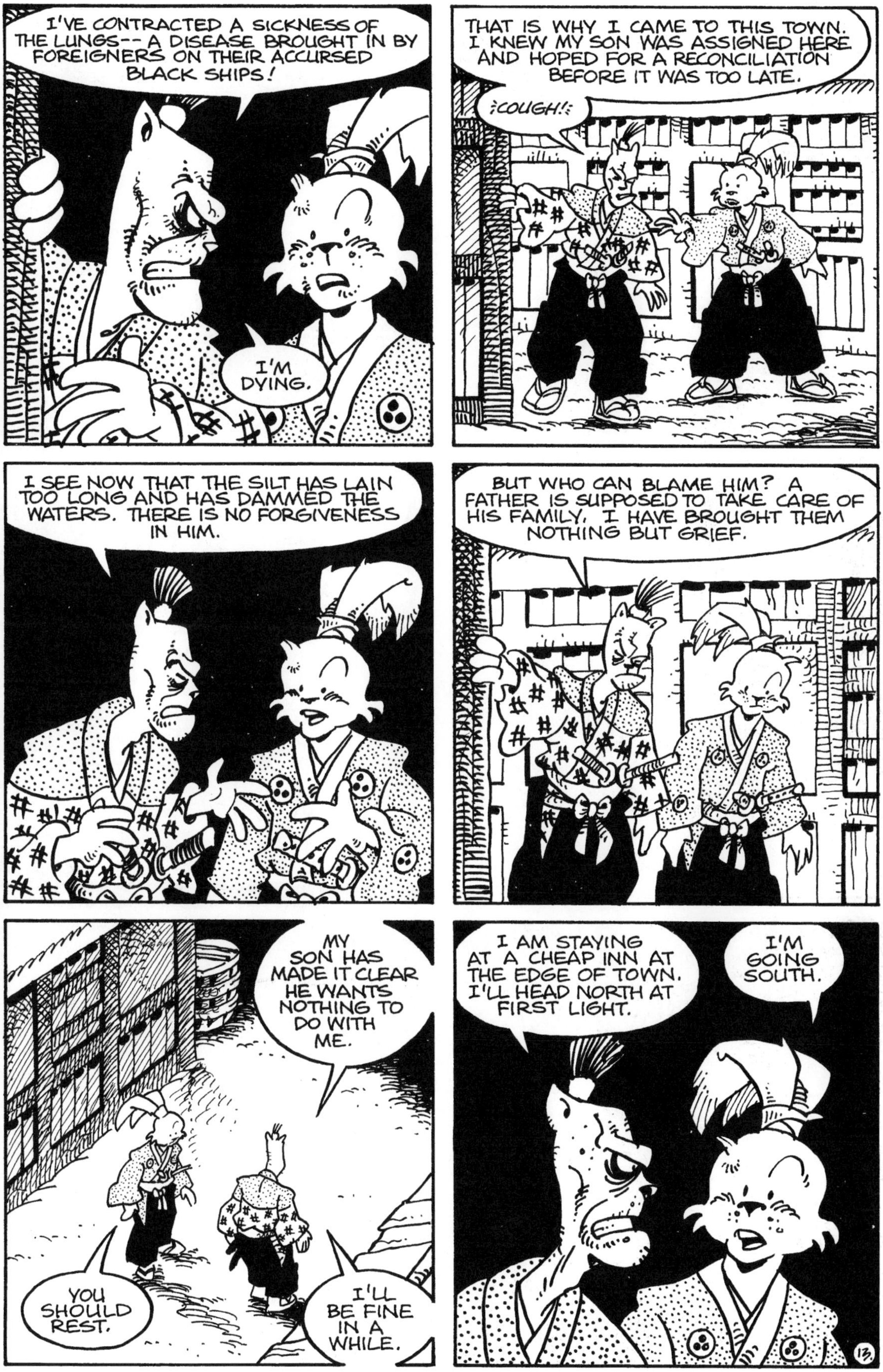
I'VE CONTRACTED A SICKNESS OF THE LUNGS-- A DISEASE BROUGHT IN BY FOREIGNERS ON THEIR ACCURSED BLACK SHIPS!
I'M DYING.
THAT IS WHY I CAME TO THIS TOWN. I KNEW MY SON WAS ASSIGNED HERE AND HOPED FOR A RECONCILIATION BEFORE IT WAS TOO LATE.
¡COUGH!¡
I SEE NOW THAT THE SILT HAS LAIN TOO LONG AND HAS DAMMED THE WATERS. THERE IS NO FORGIVENESS IN HIM.
BUT WHO CAN BLAME HIM? A FATHER IS SUPPOSED TO TAKE CARE OF HIS FAMILY. I HAVE BROUGHT THEM NOTHING BUT GRIEF.
MY SON HAS MADE IT CLEAR HE WANTS NOTHING TO DO WITH ME.
YOU SHOULD REST.
I'LL BE FINE IN A WHILE.
I AM STAYING AT A CHEAP INN AT THE EDGE OF TOWN. I'LL HEAD NORTH AT FIRST LIGHT.
I'M GOING SOUTH.
13

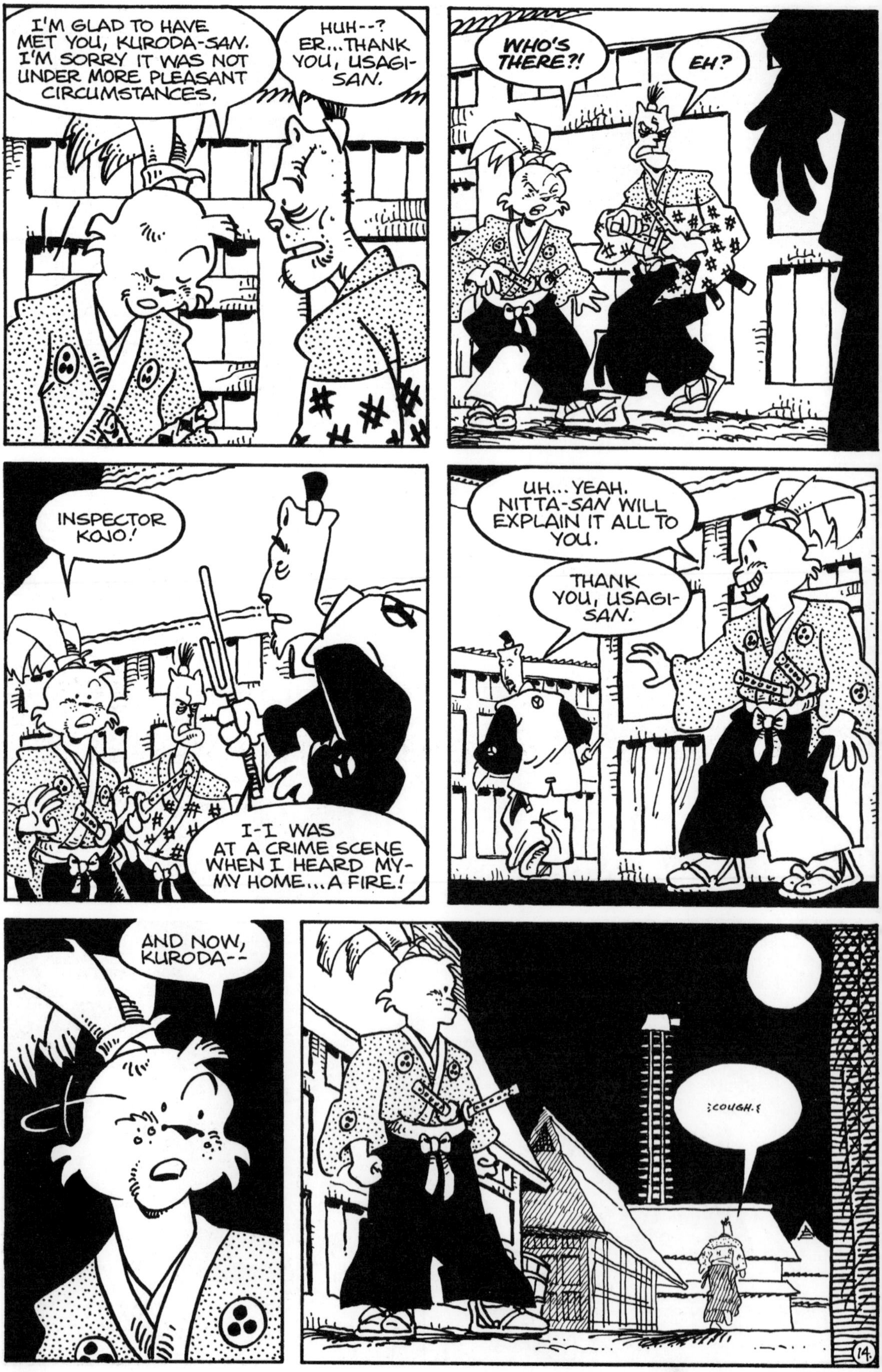
I'M GLAD TO HAVE MET YOU, KURODA-SAN. I'M SORRY IT WAS NOT UNDER MORE PLEASANT CIRCUMSTANCES.
HUH--? ER...THANK YOU, USAGI-SAN.
WHO'S THERE?!
EH?
INSPECTOR KOJO!
I-I WAS AT A CRIME SCENE WHEN I HEARD MY-MY HOME...A FIRE!
UH...YEAH. NITTA-SAN WILL EXPLAIN IT ALL TO YOU.
THANK YOU, USAGI-SAN.
AND NOW, KURODA--
COUGH.
14.

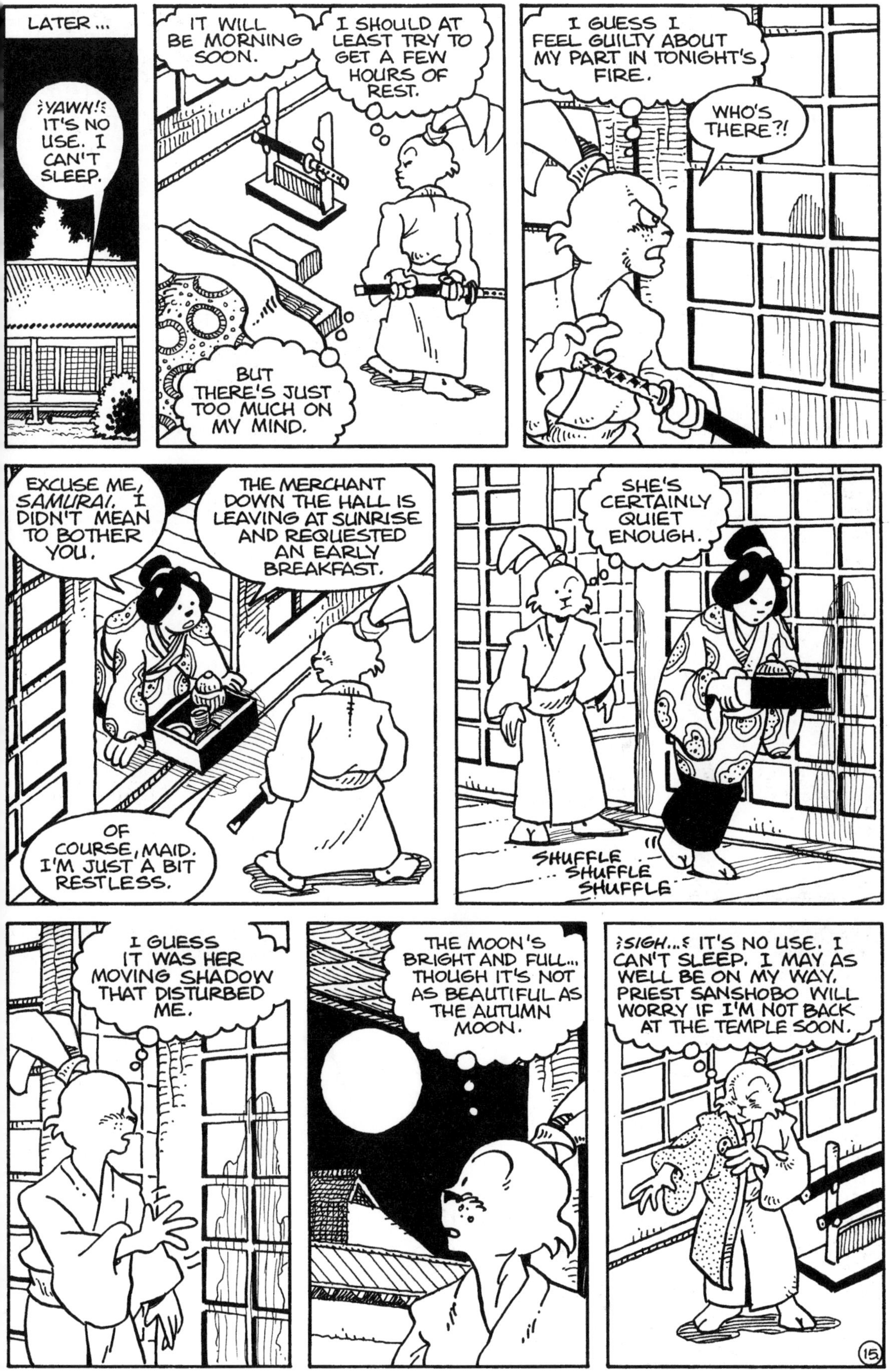

LATER...
¡YAWN!¡ IT'S NO USE. I CAN'T SLEEP.
IT WILL BE MORNING SOON.
I SHOULD AT LEAST TRY TO GET A FEW HOURS OF REST.
BUT THERE'S JUST TOO MUCH ON MY MIND.
I GUESS I FEEL GUILTY ABOUT MY PART IN TONIGHT'S FIRE.
WHO'S THERE?!
EXCUSE ME, SAMURAI. I DIDN'T MEAN TO BOTHER YOU.
THE MERCHANT DOWN THE HALL IS LEAVING AT SUNRISE AND REQUESTED AN EARLY BREAKFAST.
OF COURSE, MAID. I'M JUST A BIT RESTLESS.
SHE'S CERTAINLY QUIET ENOUGH.
SHUFFLE SHUFFLE SHUFFLE
I GUESS IT WAS HER MOVING SHADOW THAT DISTURBED ME.
THE MOON'S BRIGHT AND FULL... THOUGH IT'S NOT AS BEAUTIFUL AS THE AUTUMN MOON.
¡SIGH...¡ IT'S NO USE. I CAN'T SLEEP. I MAY AS WELL BE ON MY WAY. PRIEST SANSHOBO WILL WORRY IF I'M NOT BACK AT THE TEMPLE SOON.
15

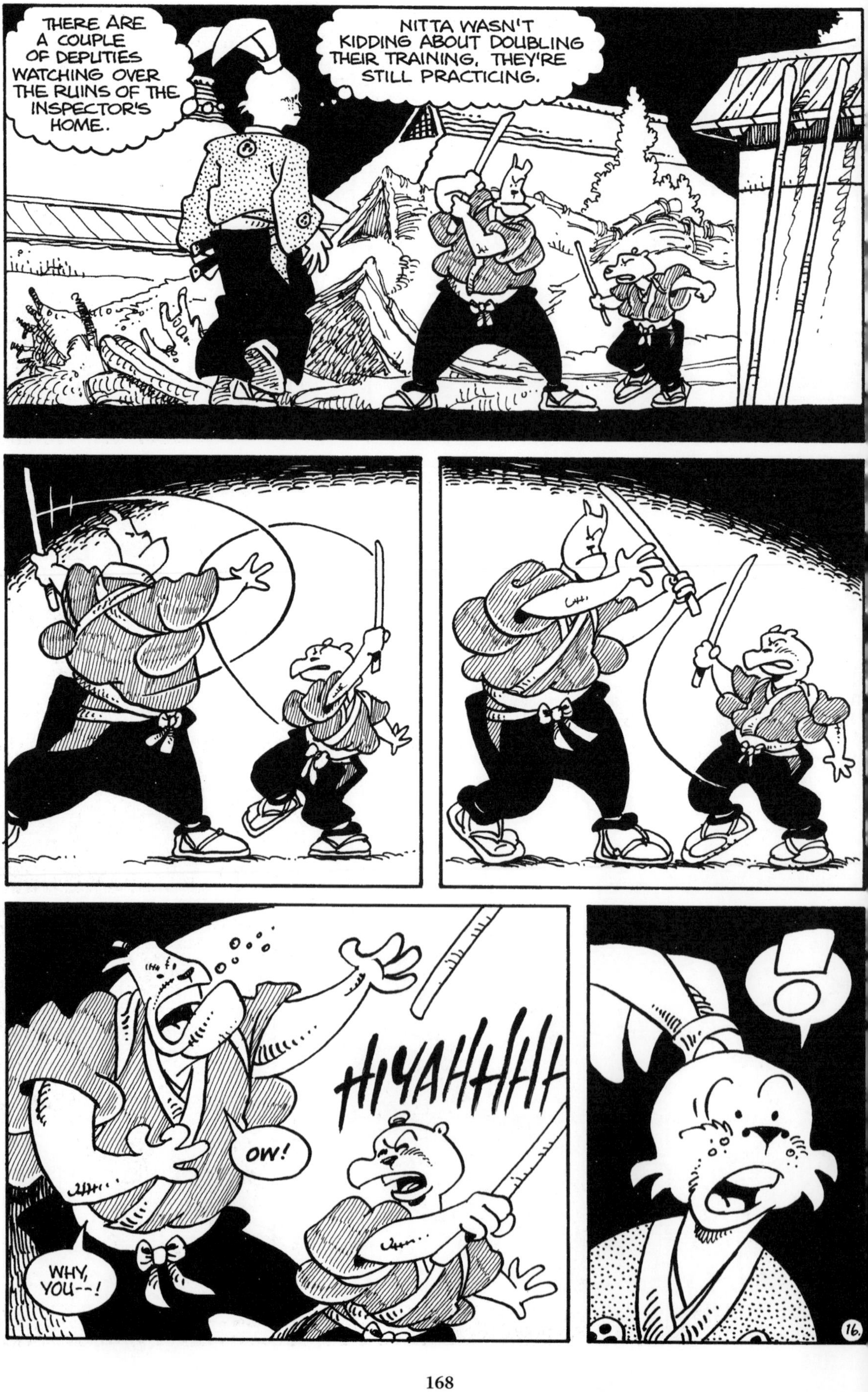
THERE ARE A COUPLE OF DEPUTIES WATCHING OVER THE RUINS OF THE INSPECTOR'S HOME.
NITTA WASN'T KIDDING ABOUT DOUBLING THEIR TRAINING. THEY'RE STILL PRACTICING.
HIYAHHHH
OW!
WHY, YOU--!
!
16.

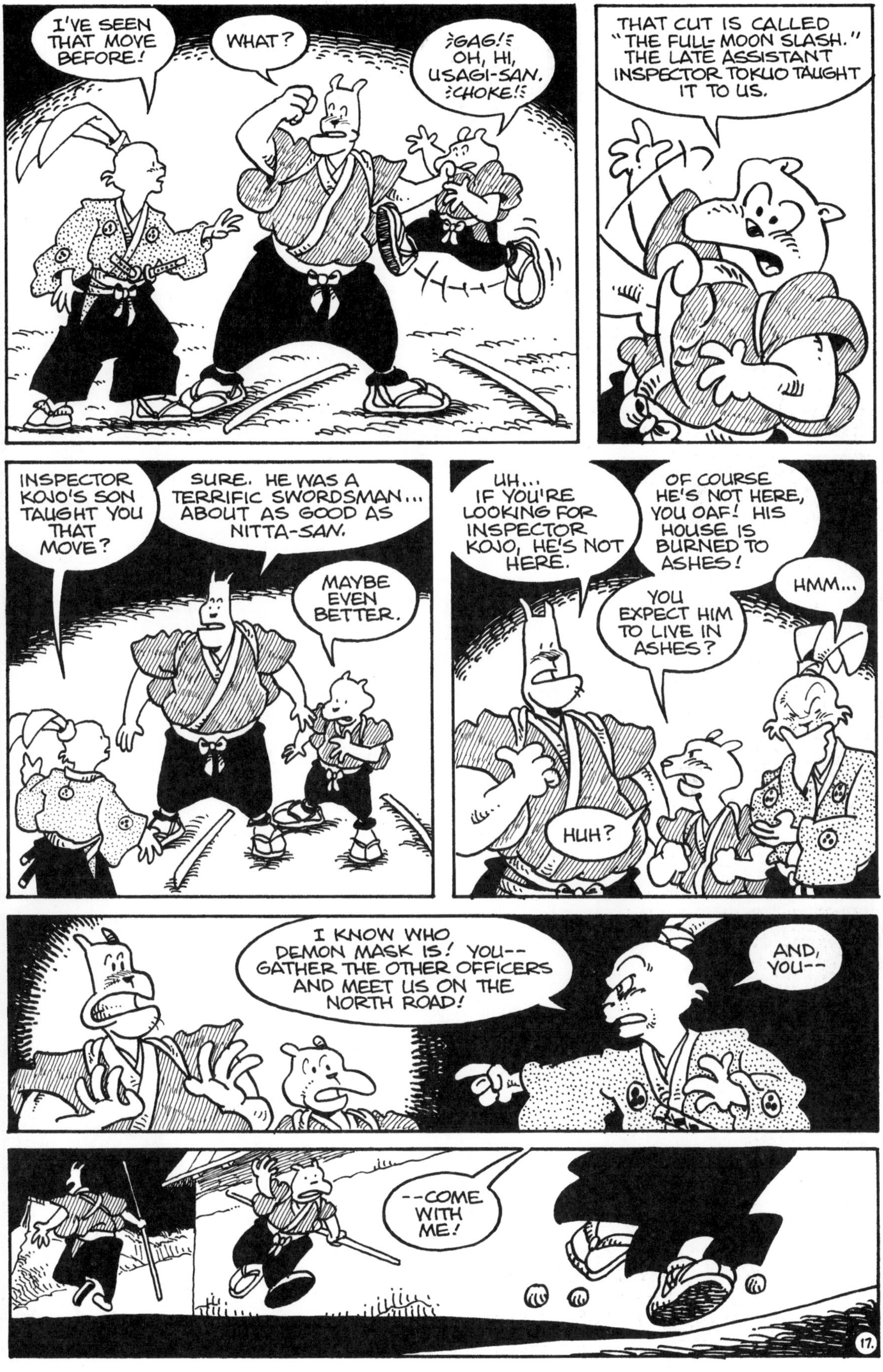
I'VE SEEN THAT MOVE BEFORE!
WHAT?
:GAG!: OH, HI, USAGI-SAN. :CHOKE!:
THAT CUT IS CALLED "THE FULL-MOON SLASH." THE LATE ASSISTANT INSPECTOR TOKUO TAUGHT IT TO US.
INSPECTOR KOJO'S SON TAUGHT YOU THAT MOVE?
SURE. HE WAS A TERRIFIC SWORDSMAN... ABOUT AS GOOD AS NITTA-SAN.
MAYBE EVEN BETTER.
UH... IF YOU'RE LOOKING FOR INSPECTOR KOJO, HE'S NOT HERE.
OF COURSE HE'S NOT HERE, YOU OAF! HIS HOUSE IS BURNED TO ASHES!
YOU EXPECT HIM TO LIVE IN ASHES?
HMM...
HUH?
I KNOW WHO DEMON MASK IS! YOU-- GATHER THE OTHER OFFICERS AND MEET US ON THE NORTH ROAD!
AND, YOU--
--COME WITH ME!
17.

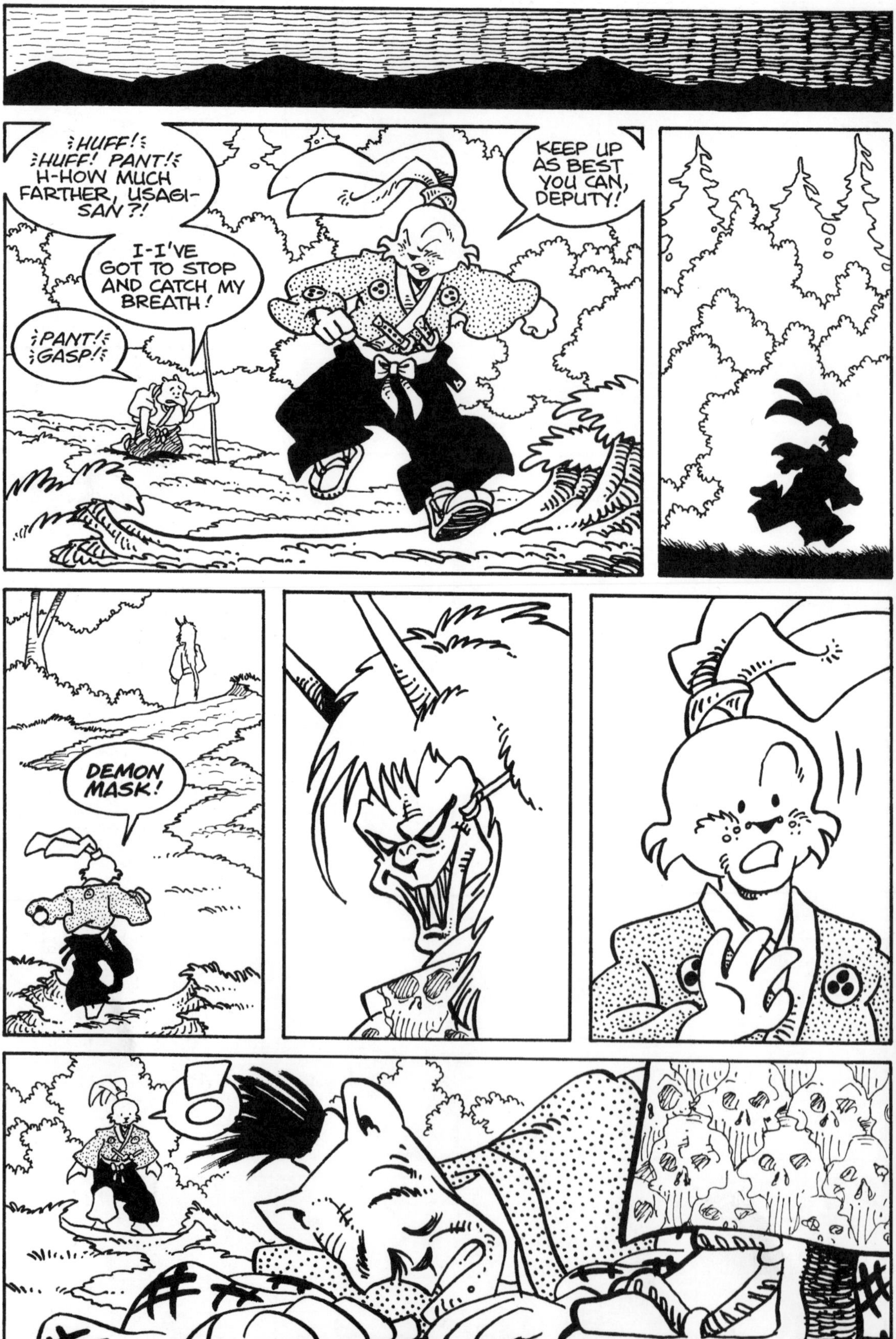
HUFF! HUFF! PANT! H-HOW MUCH FARTHER, USAGI-SAN?!
KEEP UP AS BEST YOU CAN, DEPUTY!
I-I'VE GOT TO STOP AND CATCH MY BREATH!
PANT! GASP!
DEMON MASK!
!
18.

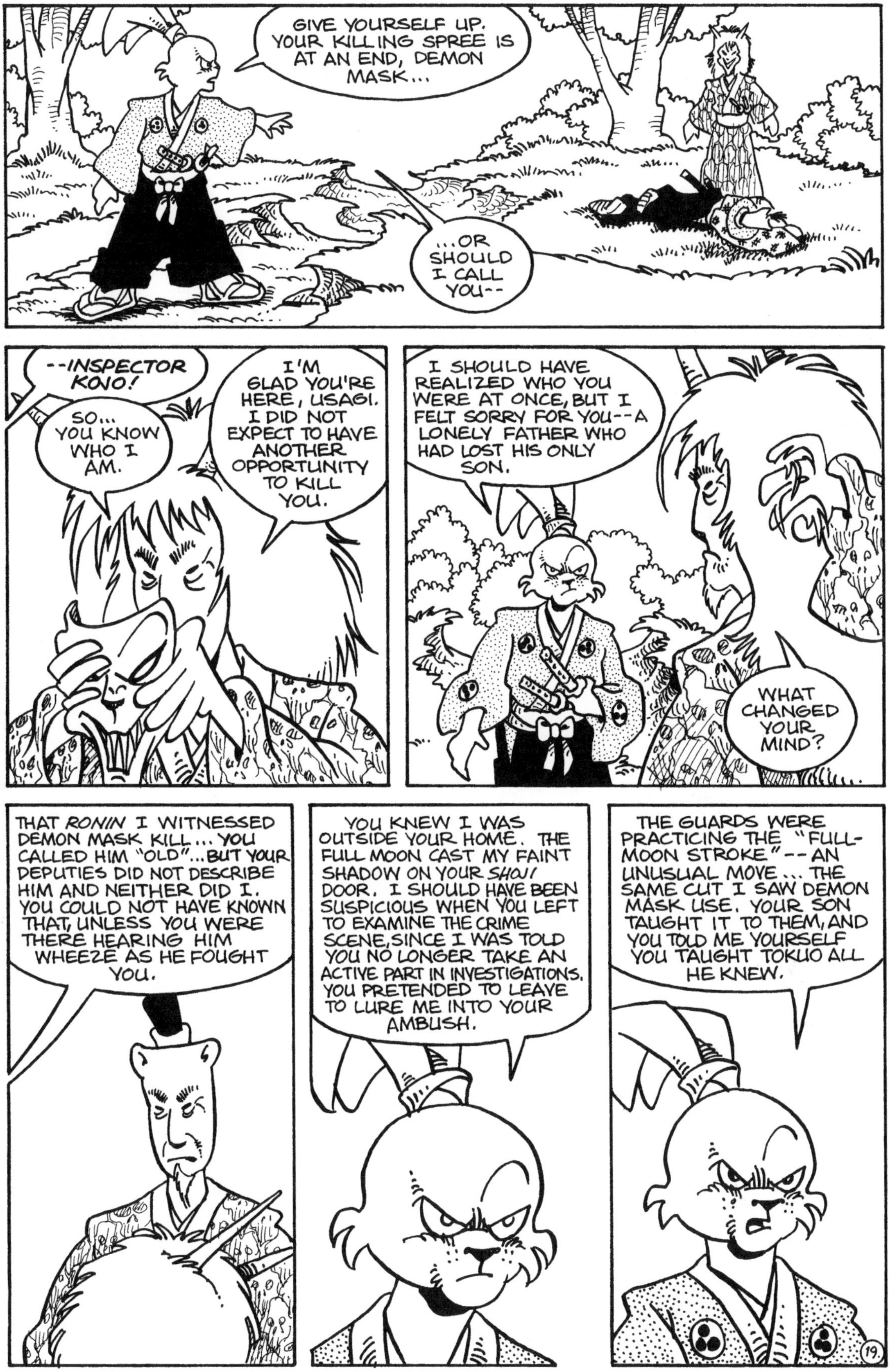
GIVE YOURSELF UP. YOUR KILLING SPREE IS AT AN END, DEMON MASK...
...OR SHOULD I CALL YOU--
--INSPECTOR KOJO!
SO... YOU KNOW WHO I AM.
I'M GLAD YOU'RE HERE, USAGI. I DID NOT EXPECT TO HAVE ANOTHER OPPORTUNITY TO KILL YOU.
I SHOULD HAVE REALIZED WHO YOU WERE AT ONCE, BUT I FELT SORRY FOR YOU--A LONELY FATHER WHO HAD LOST HIS ONLY SON.
WHAT CHANGED YOUR MIND?
THAT RONIN I WITNESSED DEMON MASK KILL... YOU CALLED HIM "OLD"... BUT YOUR DEPUTIES DID NOT DESCRIBE HIM AND NEITHER DID I. YOU COULD NOT HAVE KNOWN THAT, UNLESS YOU WERE THERE HEARING HIM WHEEZE AS HE FOUGHT YOU.
YOU KNEW I WAS OUTSIDE YOUR HOME. THE FULL MOON CAST MY FAINT SHADOW ON YOUR SHOJI DOOR. I SHOULD HAVE BEEN SUSPICIOUS WHEN YOU LEFT TO EXAMINE THE CRIME SCENE, SINCE I WAS TOLD YOU NO LONGER TAKE AN ACTIVE PART IN INVESTIGATIONS. YOU PRETENDED TO LEAVE TO LURE ME INTO YOUR AMBUSH.
THE GUARDS WERE PRACTICING THE "FULL-MOON STROKE"--AN UNUSUAL MOVE... THE SAME CUT I SAW DEMON MASK USE. YOUR SON TAUGHT IT TO THEM, AND YOU TOLD ME YOURSELF YOU TAUGHT TOKUO ALL HE KNEW.
19.

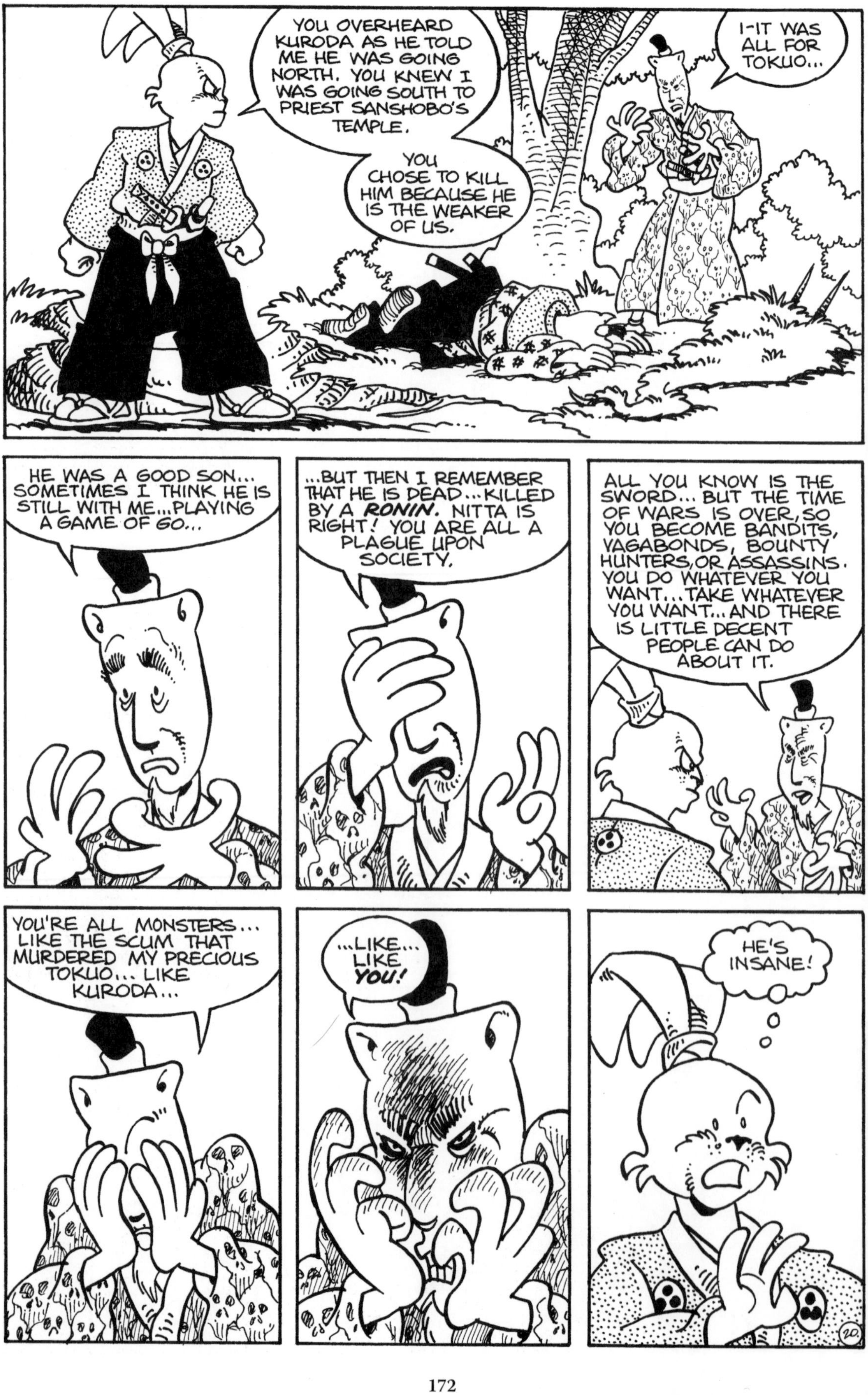
YOU OVERHEARD KURODA AS HE TOLD ME HE WAS GOING NORTH. YOU KNEW I WAS GOING SOUTH TO PRIEST SANSHOBO'S TEMPLE.
YOU CHOSE TO KILL HIM BECAUSE HE IS THE WEAKER OF US.
I-IT WAS ALL FOR TOKUO...
HE WAS A GOOD SON... SOMETIMES I THINK HE IS STILL WITH ME...PLAYING A GAME OF GO...
...BUT THEN I REMEMBER THAT HE IS DEAD...KILLED BY A RONIN. NITTA IS RIGHT! YOU ARE ALL A PLAGUE UPON SOCIETY.
ALL YOU KNOW IS THE SWORD... BUT THE TIME OF WARS IS OVER, SO YOU BECOME BANDITS, VAGABONDS, BOUNTY HUNTERS, OR ASSASSINS. YOU DO WHATEVER YOU WANT...TAKE WHATEVER YOU WANT...AND THERE IS LITTLE DECENT PEOPLE CAN DO ABOUT IT.
YOU'RE ALL MONSTERS... LIKE THE SCUM THAT MURDERED MY PRECIOUS TOKUO... LIKE KURODA...
...LIKE... LIKE YOU!
HE'S INSANE!
20.

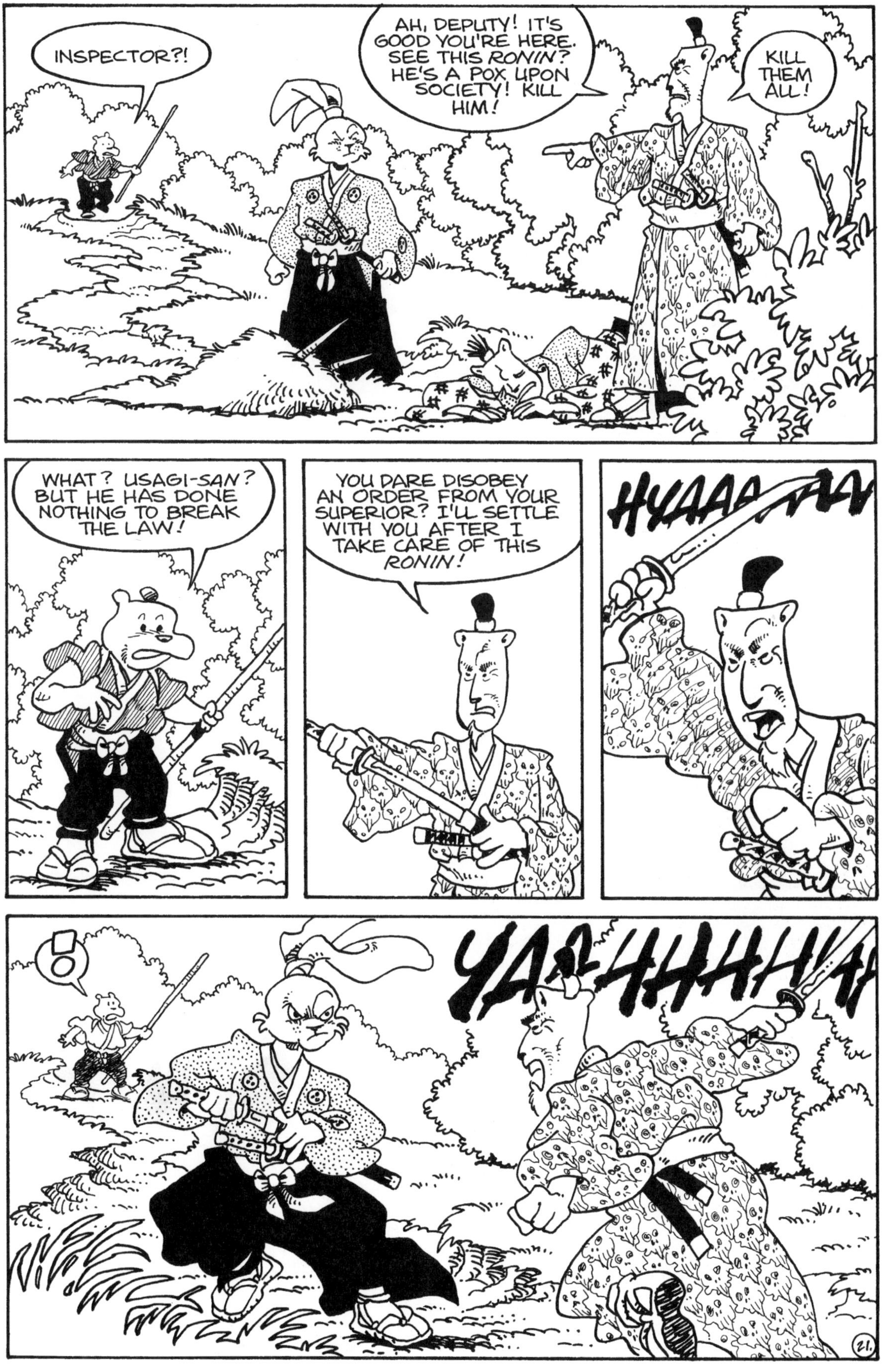
INSPECTOR?!
AH, DEPUTY! IT'S GOOD YOU'RE HERE. SEE THIS *RONIN*? HE'S A POX UPON SOCIETY! KILL HIM!
KILL THEM ALL!
WHAT? USAGI-*SAN*? BUT HE HAS DONE NOTHING TO BREAK THE LAW!
YOU DARE DISOBEY AN ORDER FROM YOUR SUPERIOR? I'LL SETTLE WITH YOU AFTER I TAKE CARE OF THIS *RONIN*!
HYAAAAAA
!
YAHHHHH!
21.

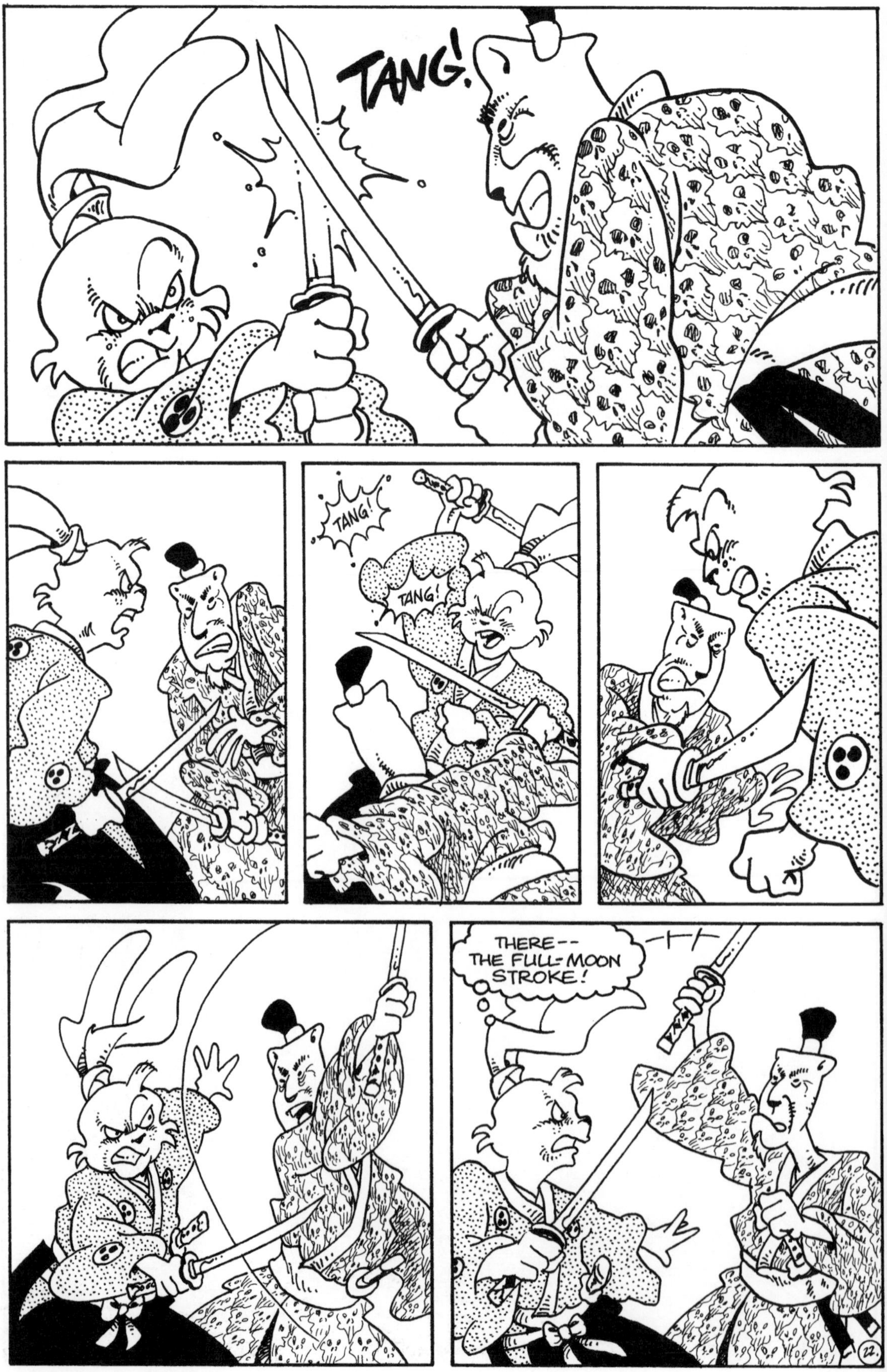

TANG!
TANG!
TANG!
THERE-- THE FULL-MOON STROKE!
22.

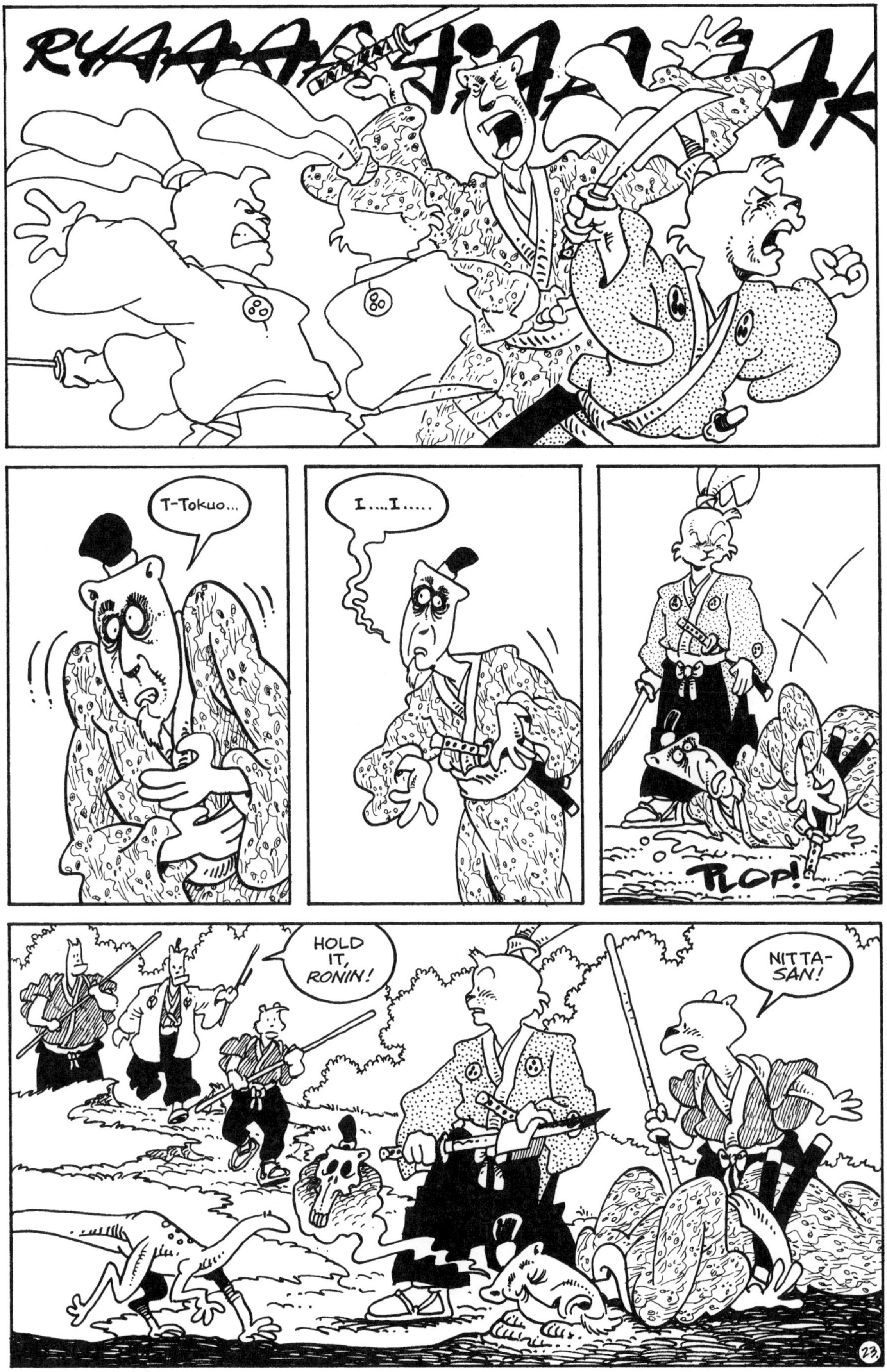
RYAAAAAAAAAAAAAK
T-Tokuo...
I....I.....
PLOP!
HOLD IT, RONIN!
NITTA-SAN!
23

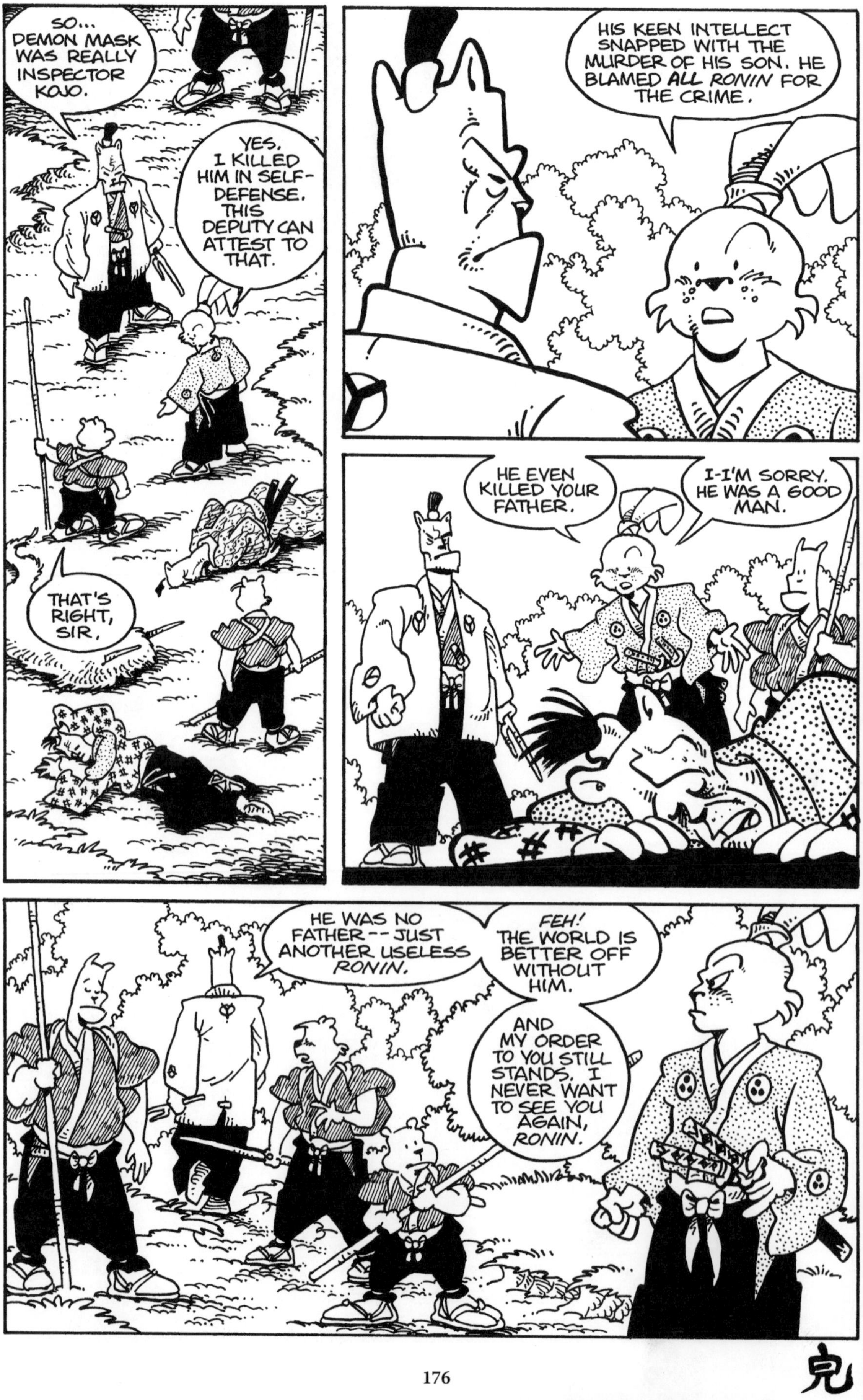
SO... DEMON MASK WAS REALLY INSPECTOR KOJO.
YES. I KILLED HIM IN SELF-DEFENSE. THIS DEPUTY CAN ATTEST TO THAT.
THAT'S RIGHT, SIR.
HIS KEEN INTELLECT SNAPPED WITH THE MURDER OF HIS SON. HE BLAMED ALL RONIN FOR THE CRIME.
HE EVEN KILLED YOUR FATHER.
I-I'M SORRY. HE WAS A GOOD MAN.
HE WAS NO FATHER--JUST ANOTHER USELESS RONIN.
FEH! THE WORLD IS BETTER OFF WITHOUT HIM.
AND MY ORDER TO YOU STILL STANDS. I NEVER WANT TO SEE YOU AGAIN, RONIN.

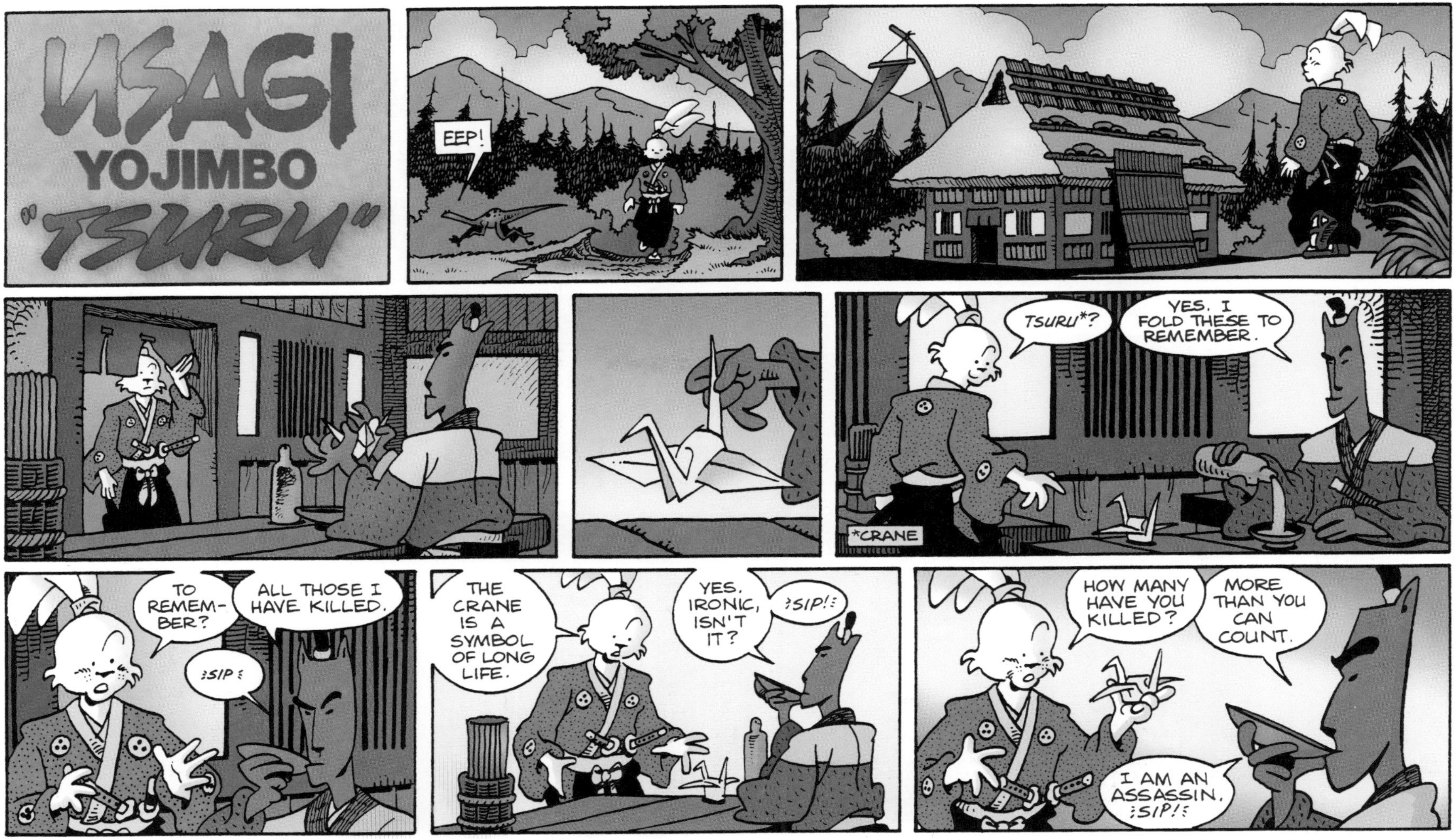
USAGI YOJIMBO
"TSURU"
EEP!
TSURU*?
YES. I FOLD THESE TO REMEMBER.
*CRANE
TO REMEM-BER?
ALL THOSE I HAVE KILLED.
¡SIP¡
THE CRANE IS A SYMBOL OF LONG LIFE.
YES. IRONIC, ISN'T IT?
¡SIP!¡
HOW MANY HAVE YOU KILLED?
MORE THAN YOU CAN COUNT.
I AM AN ASSASSIN. ¡SIP!¡

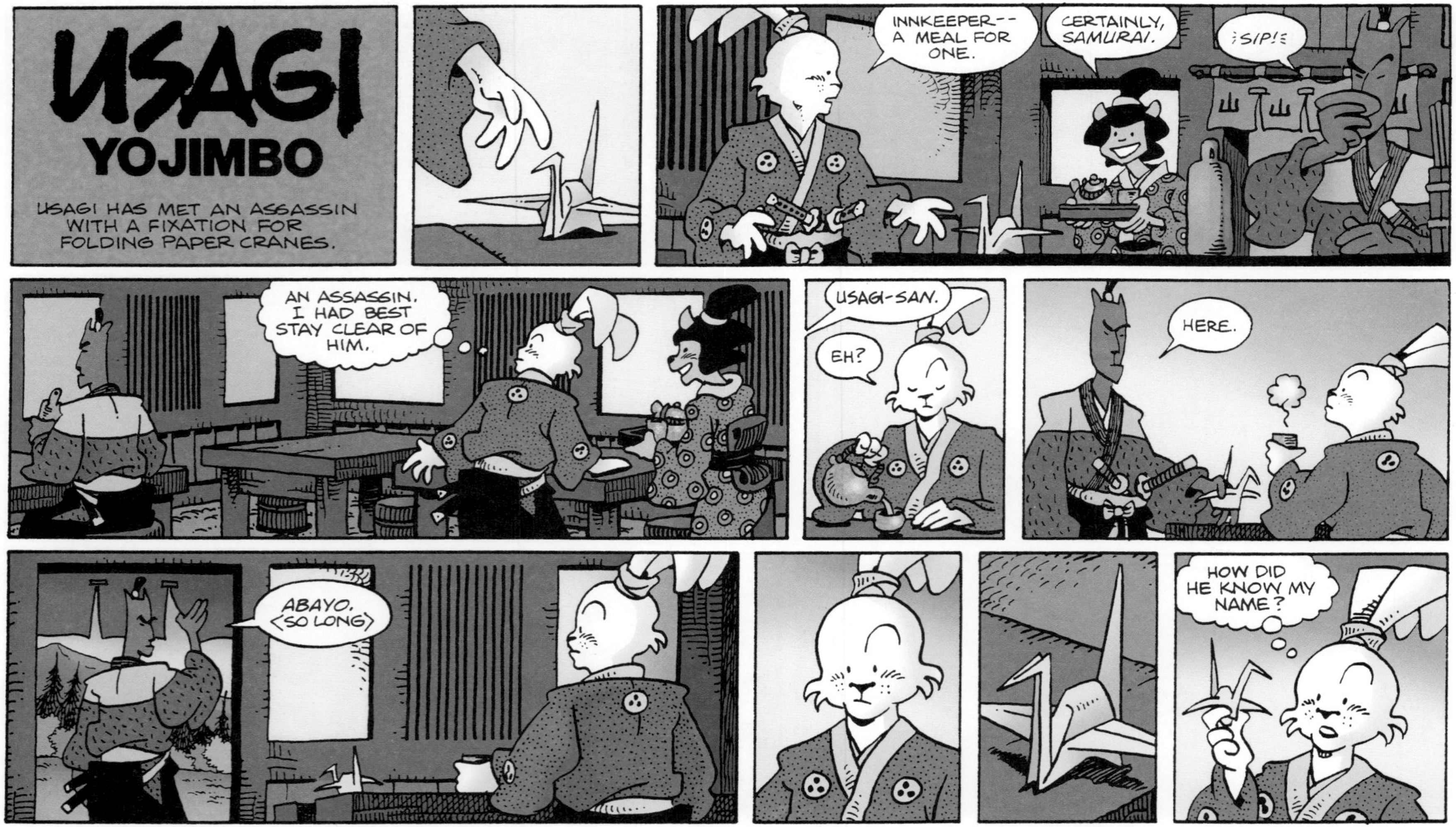
USAGI
YOJIMBO
USAGI HAS MET AN ASSASSIN WITH A FIXATION FOR FOLDING PAPER CRANES.
INNKEEPER-- A MEAL FOR ONE.
CERTAINLY, SAMURAI.
¡SIP!¡
AN ASSASSIN. I HAD BEST STAY CLEAR OF HIM.
USAGI-SAN.
EH?
HERE.
ABAYO. <SO LONG>
HOW DID HE KNOW MY NAME?

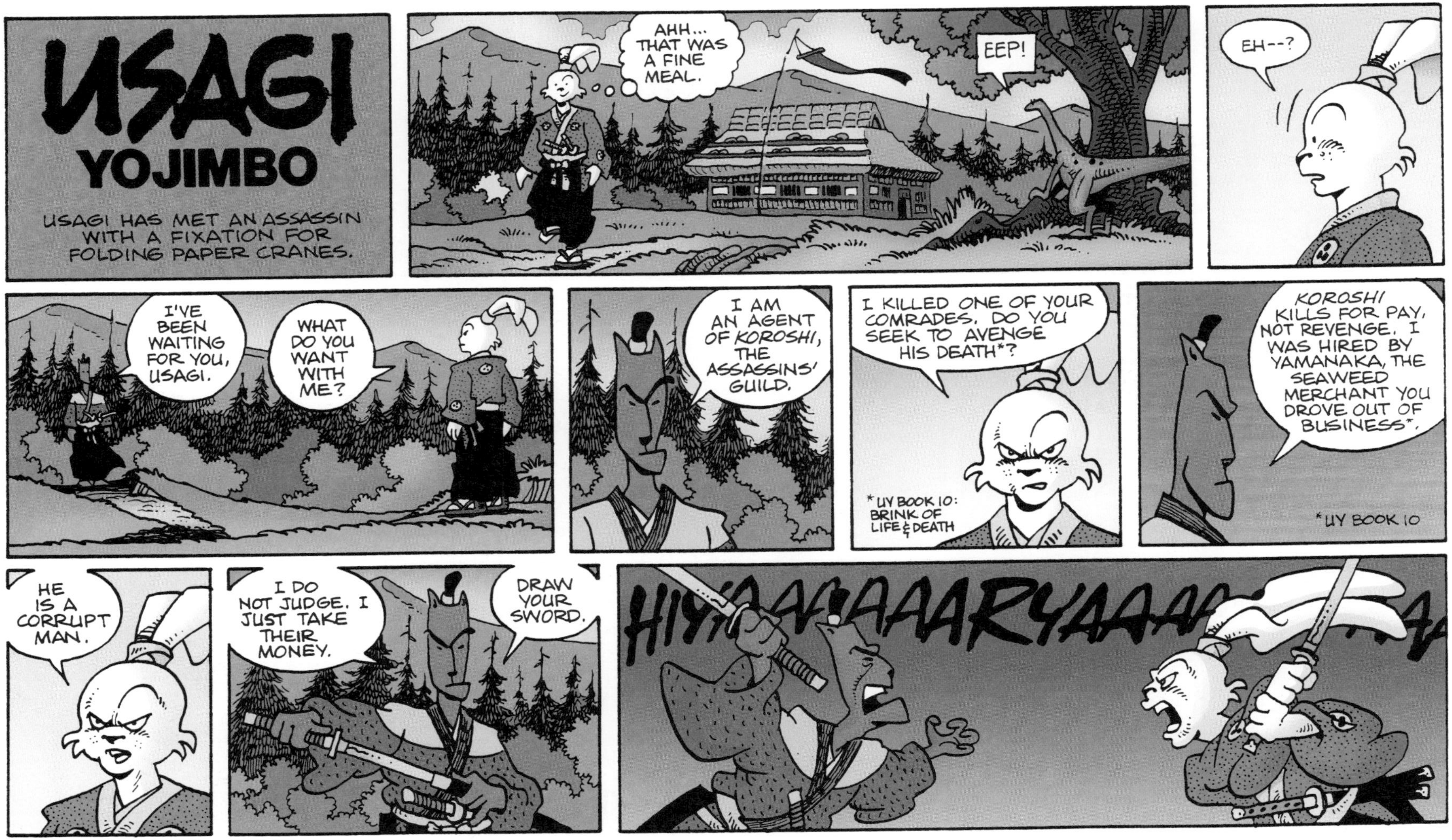
USAGI
YOJIMBO
USAGI HAS MET AN ASSASSIN WITH A FIXATION FOR FOLDING PAPER CRANES.
AHH... THAT WAS A FINE MEAL.
EEP!
EH--?
I'VE BEEN WAITING FOR YOU, USAGI.
WHAT DO YOU WANT WITH ME?
I AM AN AGENT OF KOROSHI, THE ASSASSINS' GUILD.
I KILLED ONE OF YOUR COMRADES. DO YOU SEEK TO AVENGE HIS DEATH*?
*UY BOOK 10: BRINK OF LIFE & DEATH
KOROSHI KILLS FOR PAY, NOT REVENGE. I WAS HIRED BY YAMANAKA, THE SEAWEED MERCHANT YOU DROVE OUT OF BUSINESS*.
*UY BOOK 10
HE IS A CORRUPT MAN.
I DO NOT JUDGE. I JUST TAKE THEIR MONEY.
DRAW YOUR SWORD.

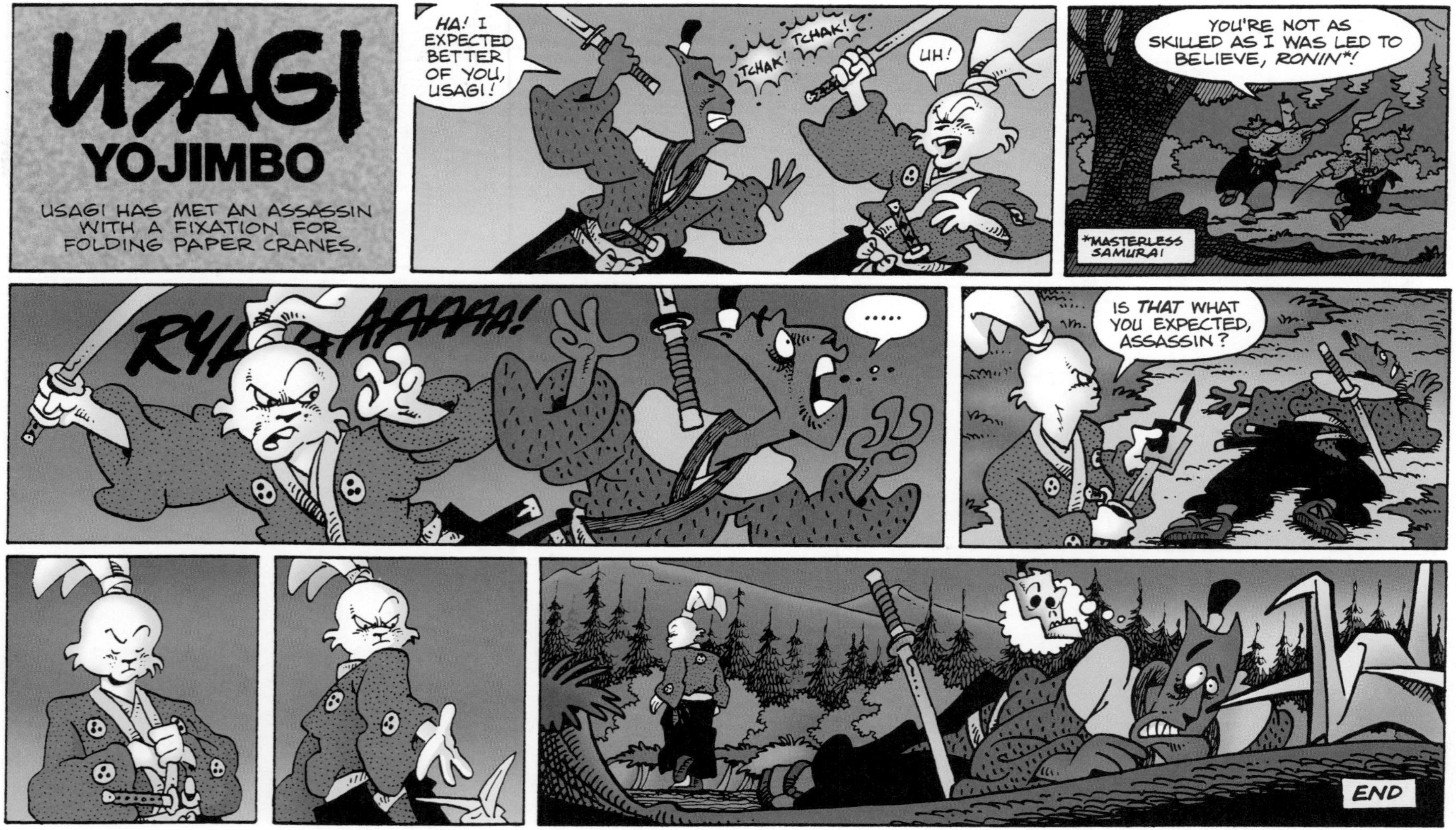
USAGI YOJIMBO
USAGI HAS MET AN ASSASSIN WITH A FIXATION FOR FOLDING PAPER CRANES.
HA! I EXPECTED BETTER OF YOU, USAGI!
TCHAK!
TCHAK!
UH!
YOU'RE NOT AS SKILLED AS I WAS LED TO BELIEVE, RONIN*!
*MASTERLESS SAMURAI
RYAAAAAA!
.....
IS THAT WHAT YOU EXPECTED, ASSASSIN?
END

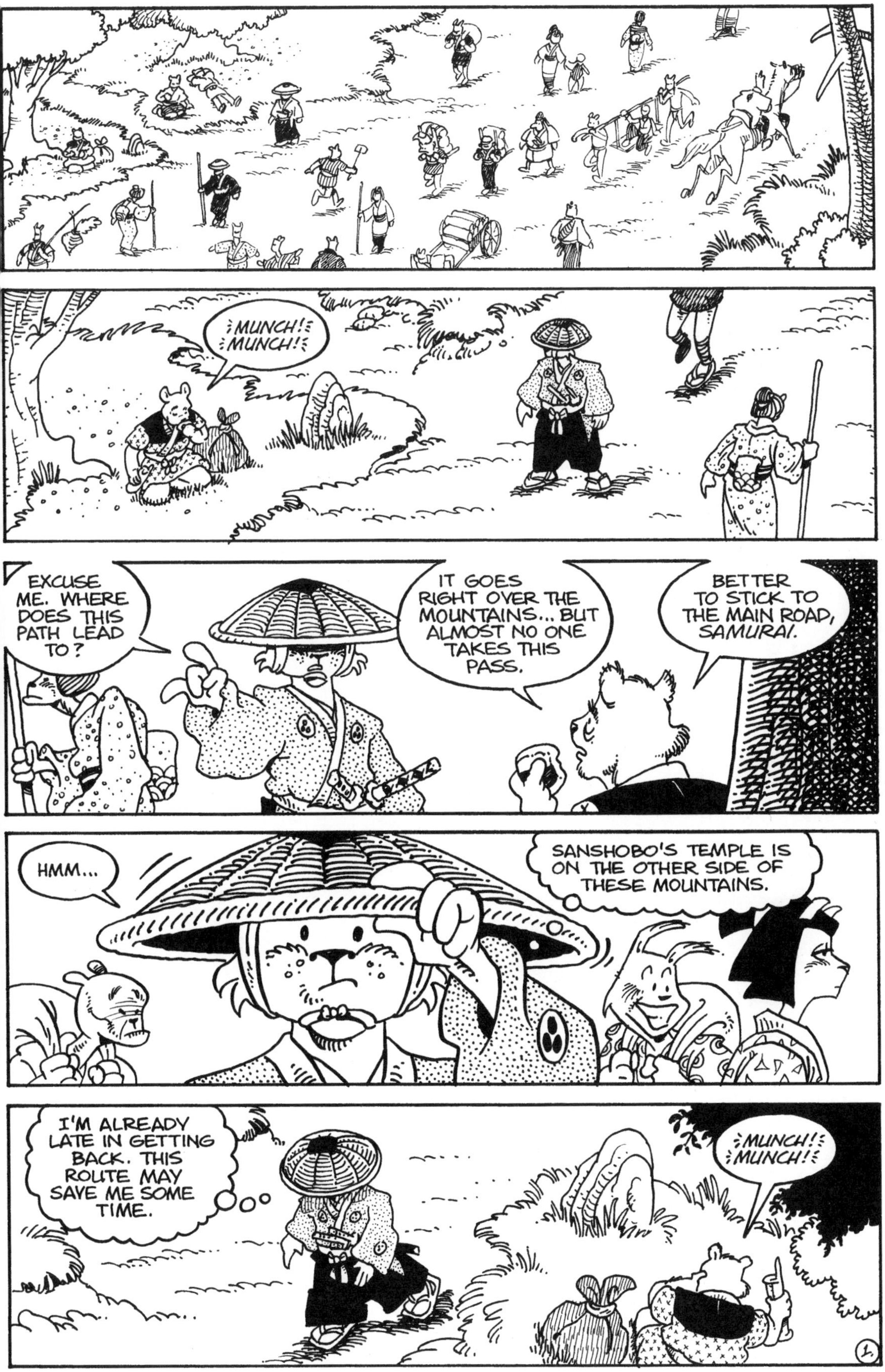
MUNCH! MUNCH!
EXCUSE ME. WHERE DOES THIS PATH LEAD TO?
IT GOES RIGHT OVER THE MOUNTAINS... BUT ALMOST NO ONE TAKES THIS PASS.
BETTER TO STICK TO THE MAIN ROAD, SAMURAI.
HMM...
SANSHOBO'S TEMPLE IS ON THE OTHER SIDE OF THESE MOUNTAINS.
I'M ALREADY LATE IN GETTING BACK. THIS ROUTE MAY SAVE ME SOME TIME.
MUNCH! MUNCH!
1.

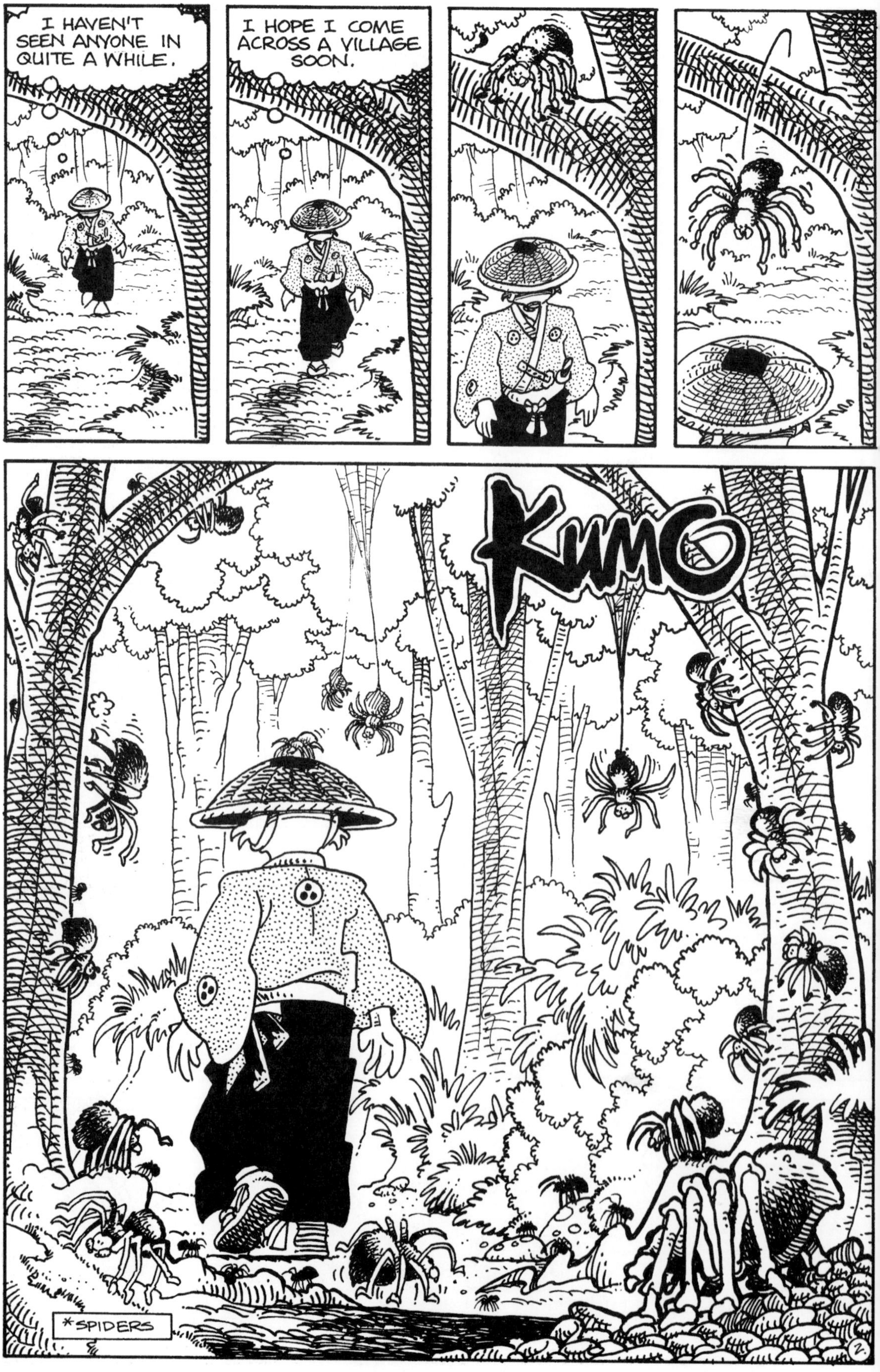
I HAVEN'T SEEN ANYONE IN QUITE A WHILE.
I HOPE I COME ACROSS A VILLAGE SOON.
KUMO*
*SPIDERS
2

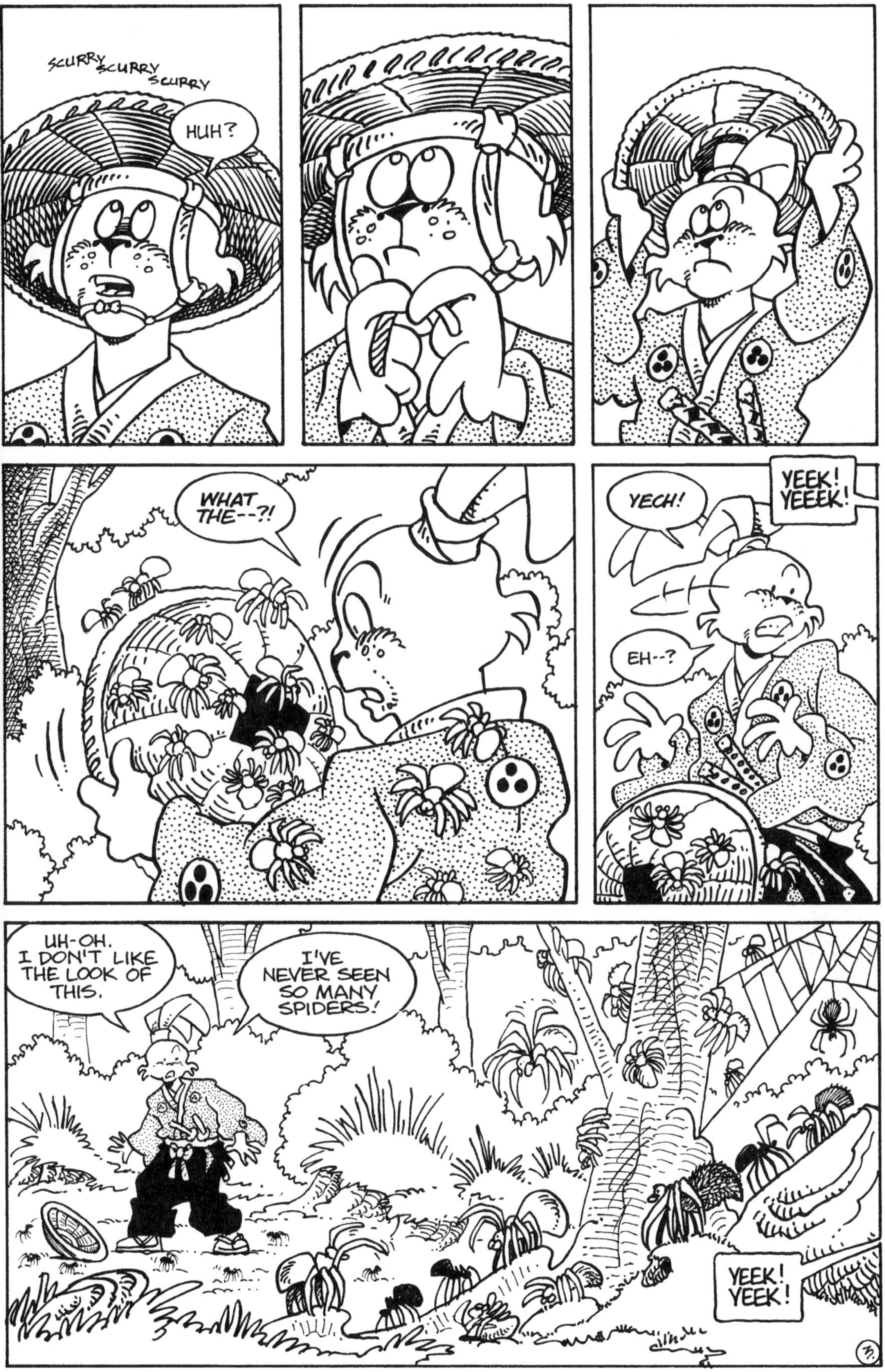
SCURRY SCURRY SCURRY
HUH?
WHAT THE--?!
YECH!
YEEK! YEEEK!
EH--?
UH-OH. I DON'T LIKE THE LOOK OF THIS.
I'VE NEVER SEEN SO MANY SPIDERS!
YEEK! YEEK!
3.

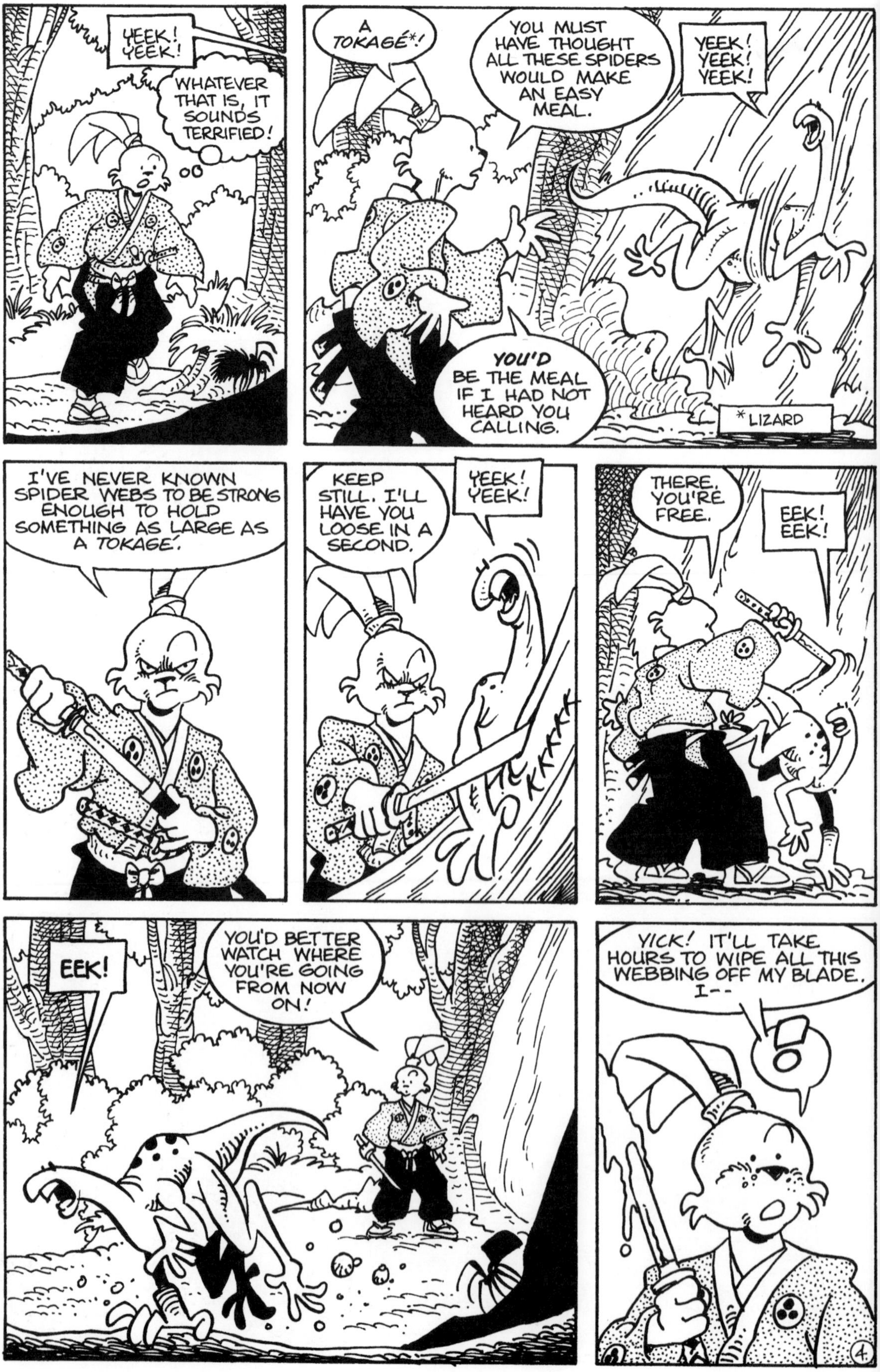
YEEK! YEEK!
WHATEVER THAT IS, IT SOUNDS TERRIFIED!
A TOKAGÉ*!
YOU MUST HAVE THOUGHT ALL THESE SPIDERS WOULD MAKE AN EASY MEAL.
YEEK! YEEK! YEEK!
YOU'D BE THE MEAL IF I HAD NOT HEARD YOU CALLING.
*LIZARD
I'VE NEVER KNOWN SPIDER WEBS TO BE STRONG ENOUGH TO HOLD SOMETHING AS LARGE AS A TOKAGÉ.
KEEP STILL. I'LL HAVE YOU LOOSE IN A SECOND.
YEEK! YEEK!
KKKKK
THERE. YOU'RE FREE.
EEK! EEK!
EEK!
YOU'D BETTER WATCH WHERE YOU'RE GOING FROM NOW ON!
YICK! IT'LL TAKE HOURS TO WIPE ALL THIS WEBBING OFF MY BLADE. I--
4.

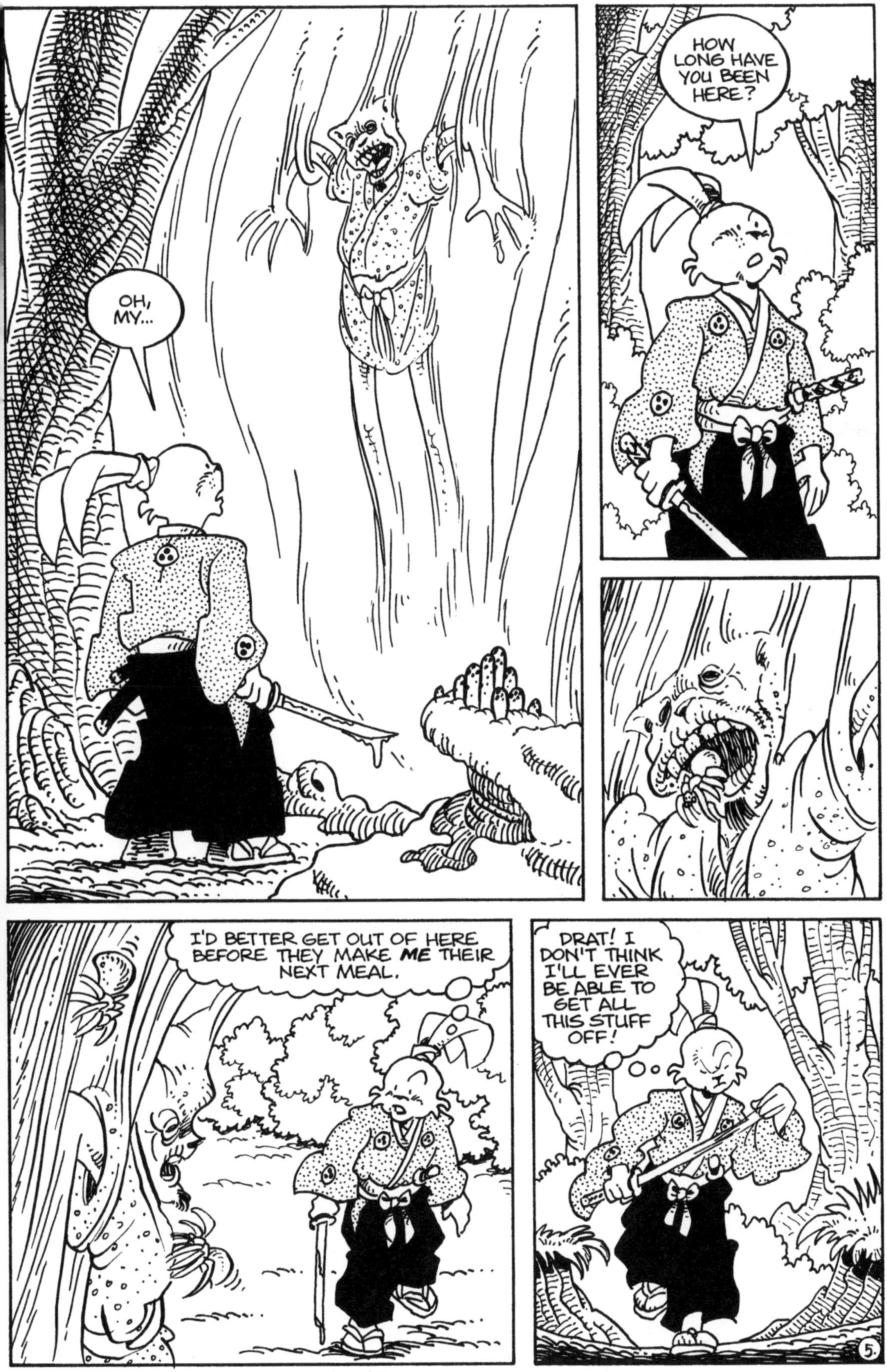
OH, MY...
HOW LONG HAVE YOU BEEN HERE?
I'D BETTER GET OUT OF HERE BEFORE THEY MAKE *ME* THEIR NEXT MEAL.
DRAT! I DON'T THINK I'LL EVER BE ABLE TO GET ALL THIS STUFF OFF!
5.

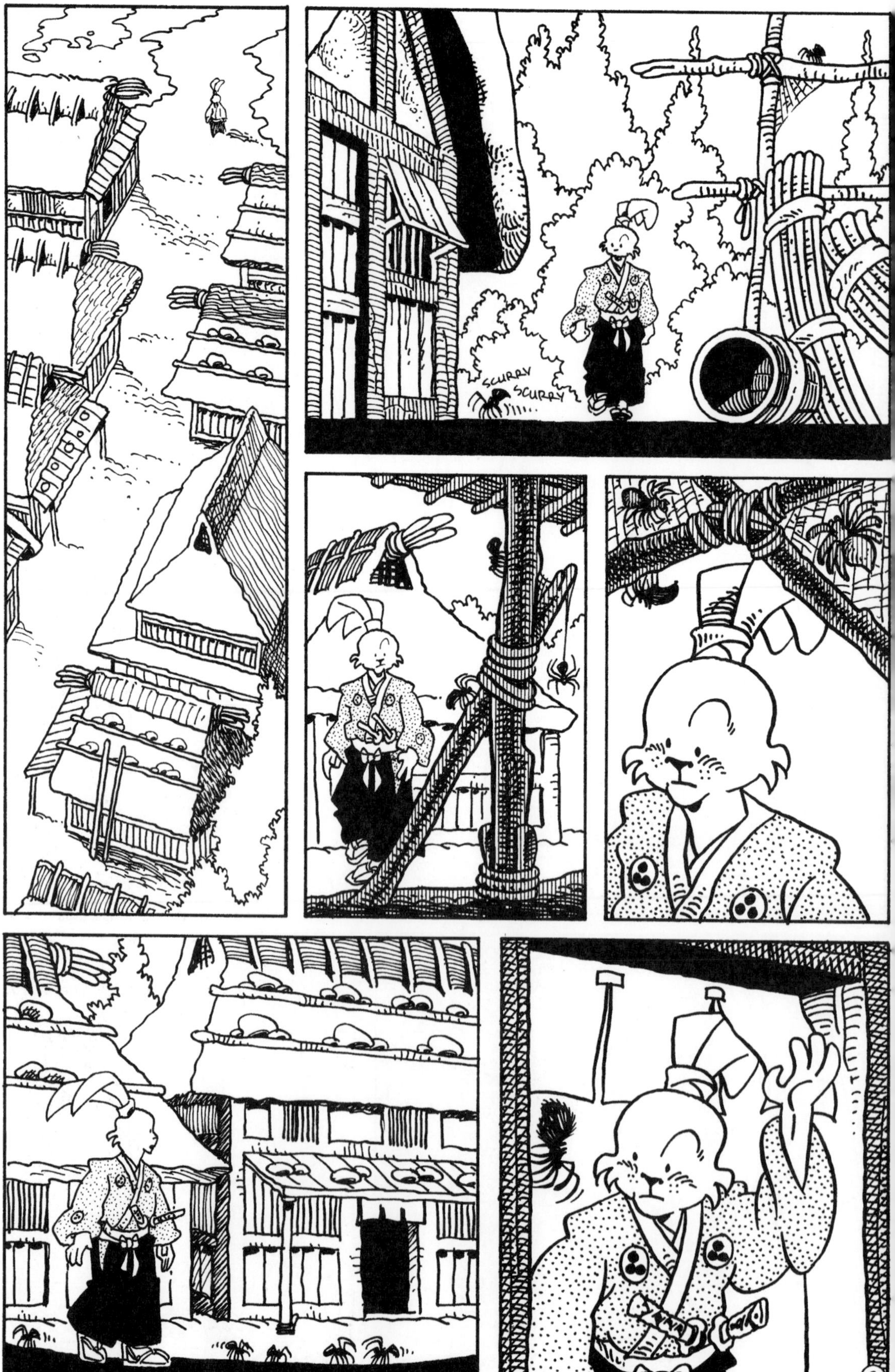
SCURRY
SCURRY
6.

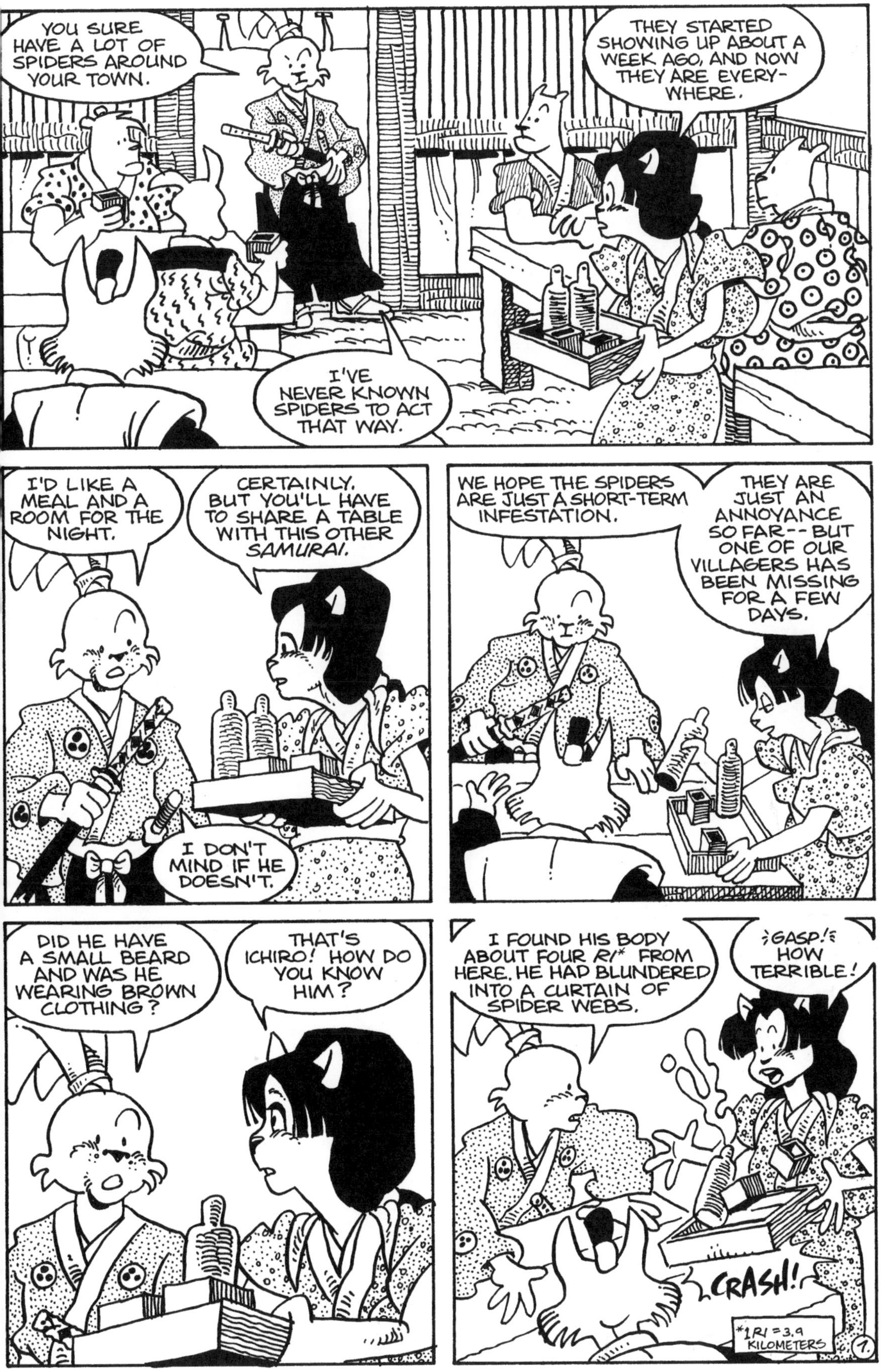
YOU SURE HAVE A LOT OF SPIDERS AROUND YOUR TOWN.
THEY STARTED SHOWING UP ABOUT A WEEK AGO, AND NOW THEY ARE EVERY-WHERE.
I'VE NEVER KNOWN SPIDERS TO ACT THAT WAY.
I'D LIKE A MEAL AND A ROOM FOR THE NIGHT.
CERTAINLY. BUT YOU'LL HAVE TO SHARE A TABLE WITH THIS OTHER *SAMURAI*.
I DON'T MIND IF HE DOESN'T.
WE HOPE THE SPIDERS ARE JUST A SHORT-TERM INFESTATION.
THEY ARE JUST AN ANNOYANCE SO FAR-- BUT ONE OF OUR VILLAGERS HAS BEEN MISSING FOR A FEW DAYS.
DID HE HAVE A SMALL BEARD AND WAS HE WEARING BROWN CLOTHING?
THAT'S ICHIRO! HOW DO YOU KNOW HIM?
I FOUND HIS BODY ABOUT FOUR *RI** FROM HERE. HE HAD BLUNDERED INTO A CURTAIN OF SPIDER WEBS.
GASP! HOW TERRIBLE!
CRASH!
*1 RI = 3.9 KILOMETERS
7.

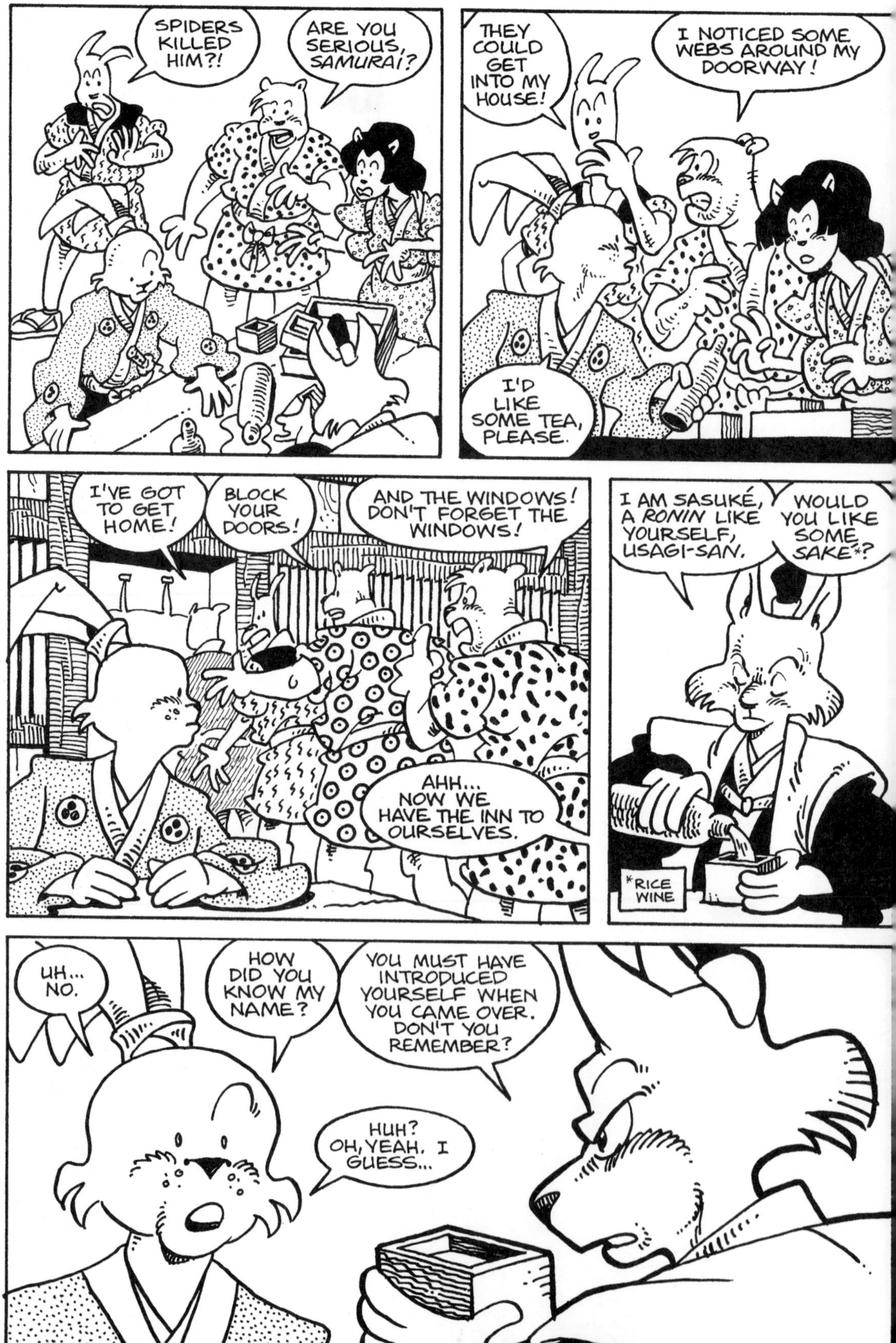
SPIDERS KILLED HIM?!
ARE YOU SERIOUS, *SAMURAI*?
THEY COULD GET INTO MY HOUSE!
I NOTICED SOME WEBS AROUND MY DOORWAY!
I'D LIKE SOME TEA, PLEASE.
I'VE GOT TO GET HOME!
BLOCK YOUR DOORS!
AND THE WINDOWS! DON'T FORGET THE WINDOWS!
AHH... NOW WE HAVE THE INN TO OURSELVES.
I AM SASUKÉ, A *RONIN* LIKE YOURSELF, USAGI-SAN.
WOULD YOU LIKE SOME *SAKE**?
*RICE WINE
UH... NO.
HOW DID YOU KNOW MY NAME?
YOU MUST HAVE INTRODUCED YOURSELF WHEN YOU CAME OVER. DON'T YOU REMEMBER?
HUH? OH, YEAH. I GUESS...
8.

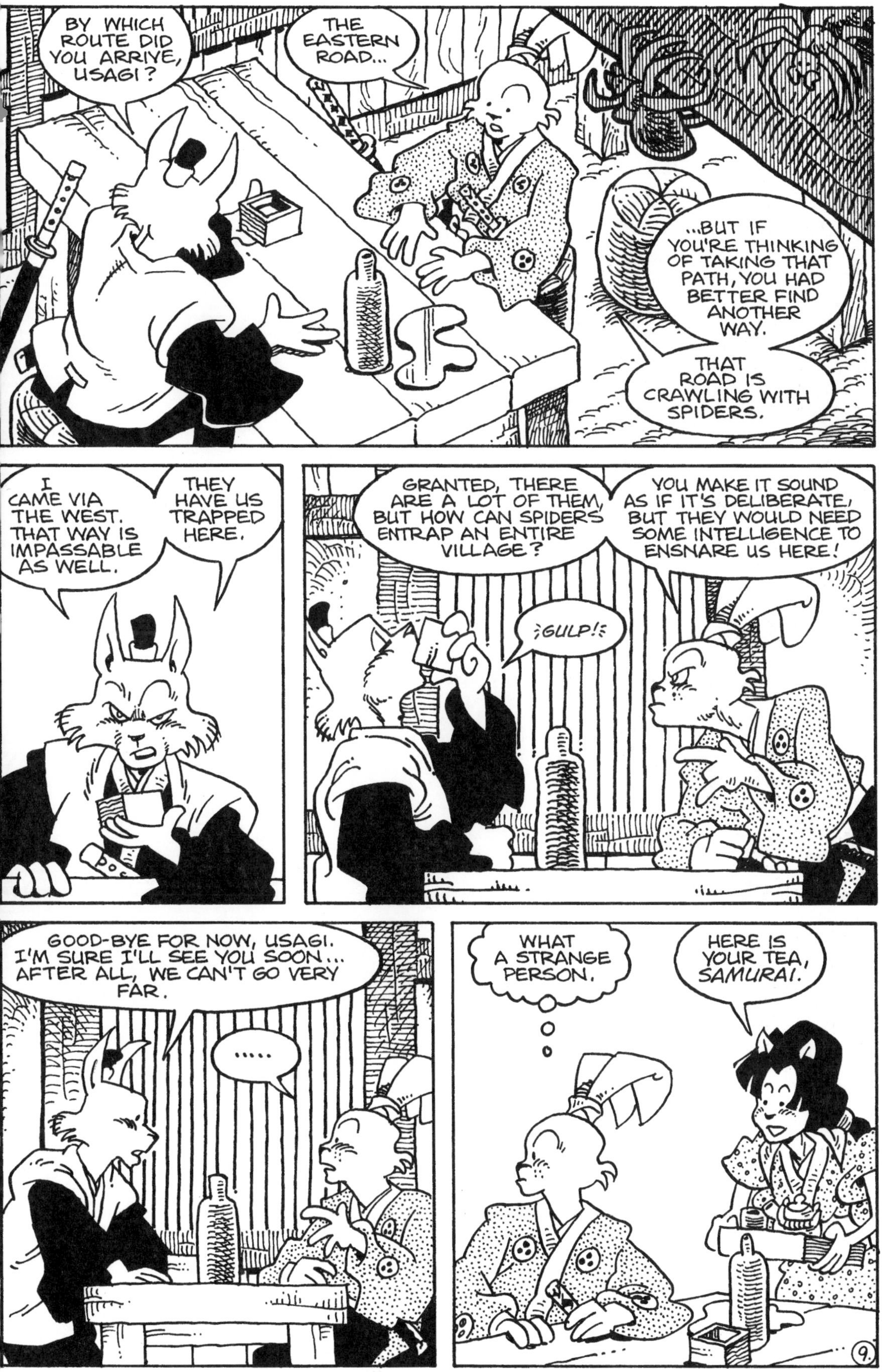
BY WHICH ROUTE DID YOU ARRIVE, USAGI?
THE EASTERN ROAD...
...BUT IF YOU'RE THINKING OF TAKING THAT PATH, YOU HAD BETTER FIND ANOTHER WAY.
THAT ROAD IS CRAWLING WITH SPIDERS.
I CAME VIA THE WEST. THAT WAY IS IMPASSABLE AS WELL.
THEY HAVE US TRAPPED HERE.
GRANTED, THERE ARE A LOT OF THEM, BUT HOW CAN SPIDERS ENTRAP AN ENTIRE VILLAGE?
YOU MAKE IT SOUND AS IF IT'S DELIBERATE, BUT THEY WOULD NEED SOME INTELLIGENCE TO ENSNARE US HERE!
GULP!
GOOD-BYE FOR NOW, USAGI. I'M SURE I'LL SEE YOU SOON... AFTER ALL, WE CAN'T GO VERY FAR.
.....
WHAT A STRANGE PERSON.
HERE IS YOUR TEA, SAMURAI.
9.

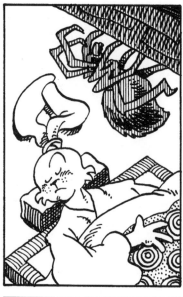

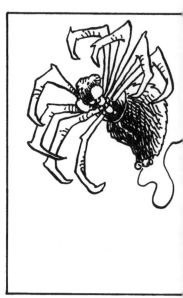

CHOMP!

OW!

YOW!

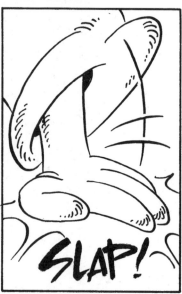

SLAP!

I HATE WAKING UP WITH BUGS!

KRASH! BAM!

EYAHH! HELP!

10.

190

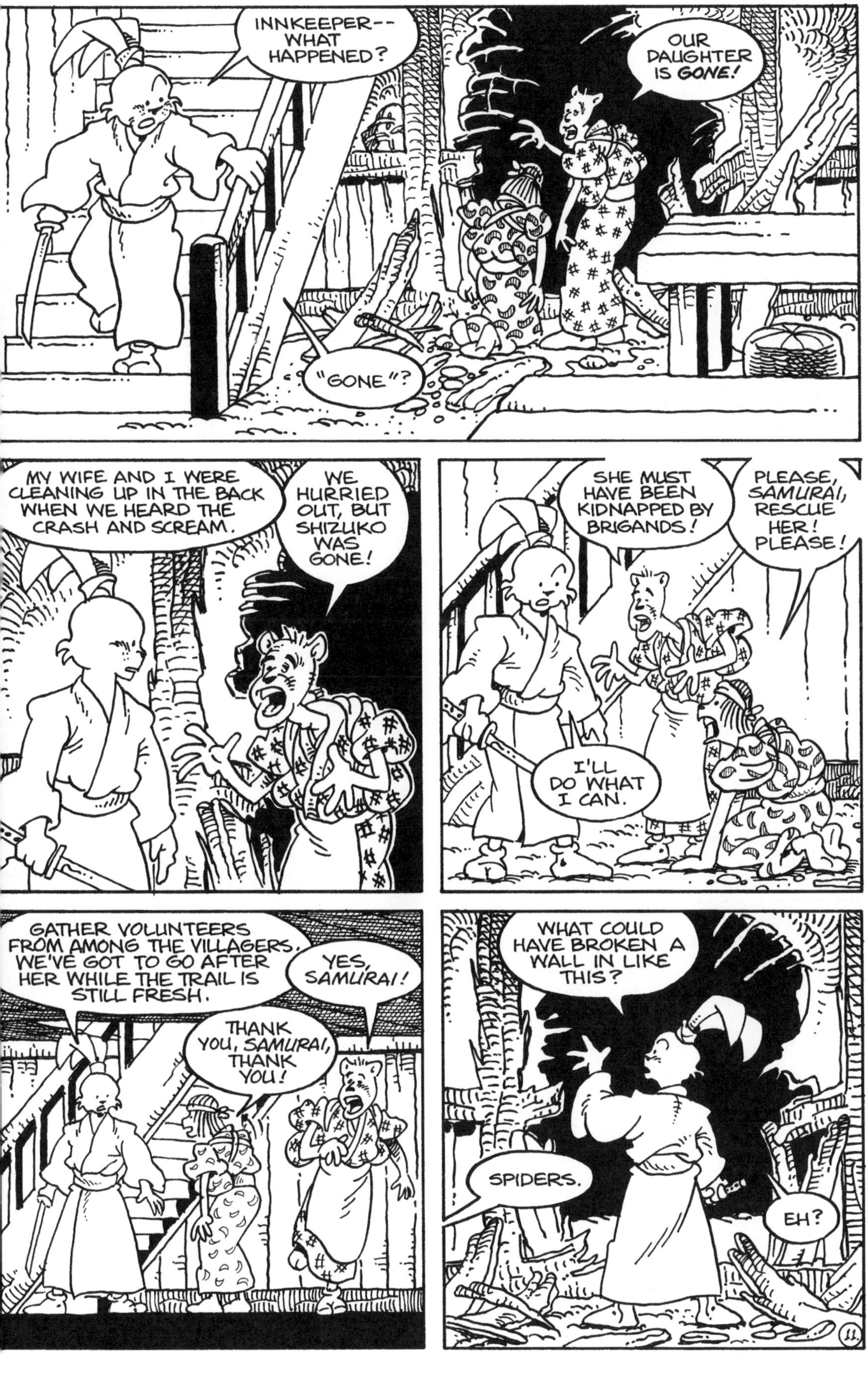
INNKEEPER-- WHAT HAPPENED?
OUR DAUGHTER IS GONE!
"GONE"?
MY WIFE AND I WERE CLEANING UP IN THE BACK WHEN WE HEARD THE CRASH AND SCREAM.
WE HURRIED OUT, BUT SHIZUKO WAS GONE!
SHE MUST HAVE BEEN KIDNAPPED BY BRIGANDS!
PLEASE, SAMURAI, RESCUE HER! PLEASE!
I'LL DO WHAT I CAN.
GATHER VOLUNTEERS FROM AMONG THE VILLAGERS. WE'VE GOT TO GO AFTER HER WHILE THE TRAIL IS STILL FRESH.
YES, SAMURAI!
THANK YOU, SAMURAI, THANK YOU!
WHAT COULD HAVE BROKEN A WALL IN LIKE THIS?
SPIDERS.
EH?
11

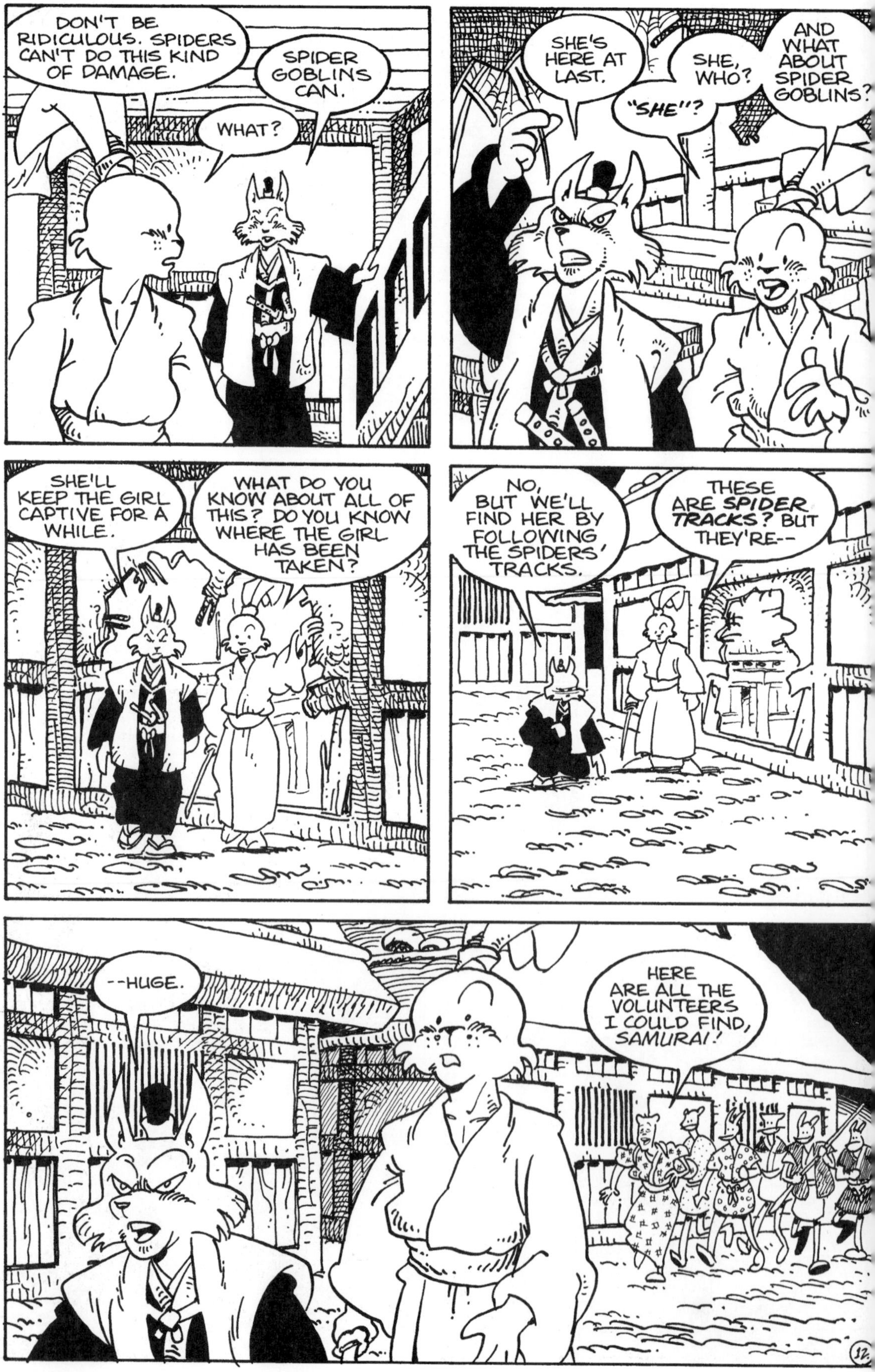

DON'T BE RIDICULOUS. SPIDERS CAN'T DO THIS KIND OF DAMAGE.
SPIDER GOBLINS CAN.
WHAT?
SHE'S HERE AT LAST.
SHE, WHO?
"SHE"?
AND WHAT ABOUT SPIDER GOBLINS?
SHE'LL KEEP THE GIRL CAPTIVE FOR A WHILE.
WHAT DO YOU KNOW ABOUT ALL OF THIS? DO YOU KNOW WHERE THE GIRL HAS BEEN TAKEN?
NO, BUT WE'LL FIND HER BY FOLLOWING THE SPIDERS' TRACKS.
THESE ARE SPIDER TRACKS? BUT THEY'RE--
--HUGE.
HERE ARE ALL THE VOLUNTEERS I COULD FIND, SAMURAI!
12

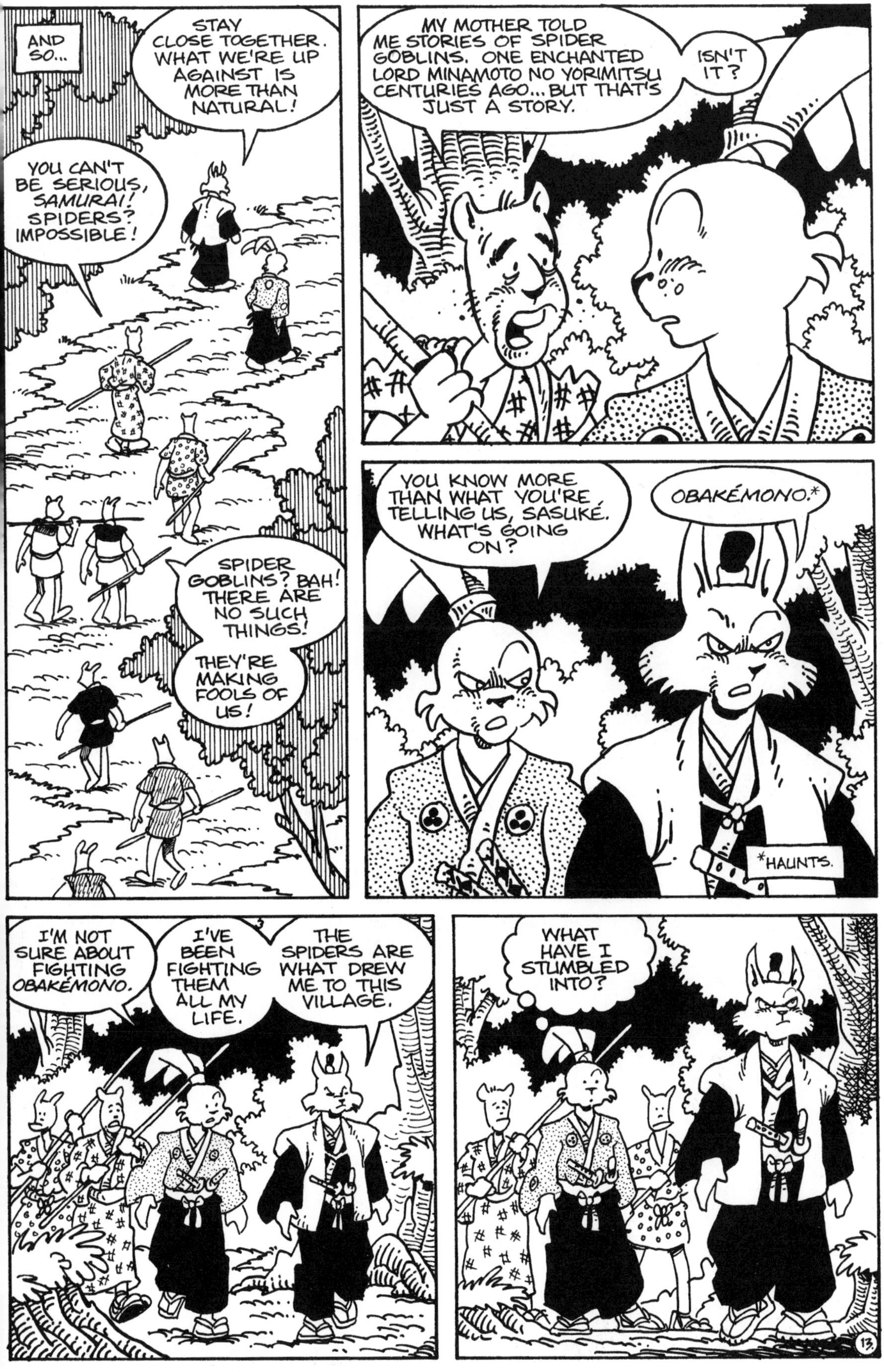
AND SO...
STAY CLOSE TOGETHER. WHAT WE'RE UP AGAINST IS MORE THAN NATURAL!
YOU CAN'T BE SERIOUS, SAMURAI! SPIDERS? IMPOSSIBLE!
SPIDER GOBLINS? BAH! THERE ARE NO SUCH THINGS!
THEY'RE MAKING FOOLS OF US!
MY MOTHER TOLD ME STORIES OF SPIDER GOBLINS. ONE ENCHANTED LORD MINAMOTO NO YORIMITSU CENTURIES AGO... BUT THAT'S JUST A STORY.
ISN'T IT?
YOU KNOW MORE THAN WHAT YOU'RE TELLING US, SASUKÉ. WHAT'S GOING ON?
OBAKÉMONO.*
*HAUNTS.
I'M NOT SURE ABOUT FIGHTING OBAKÉMONO.
I'VE BEEN FIGHTING THEM ALL MY LIFE.
THE SPIDERS ARE WHAT DREW ME TO THIS VILLAGE.
WHAT HAVE I STUMBLED INTO?
13

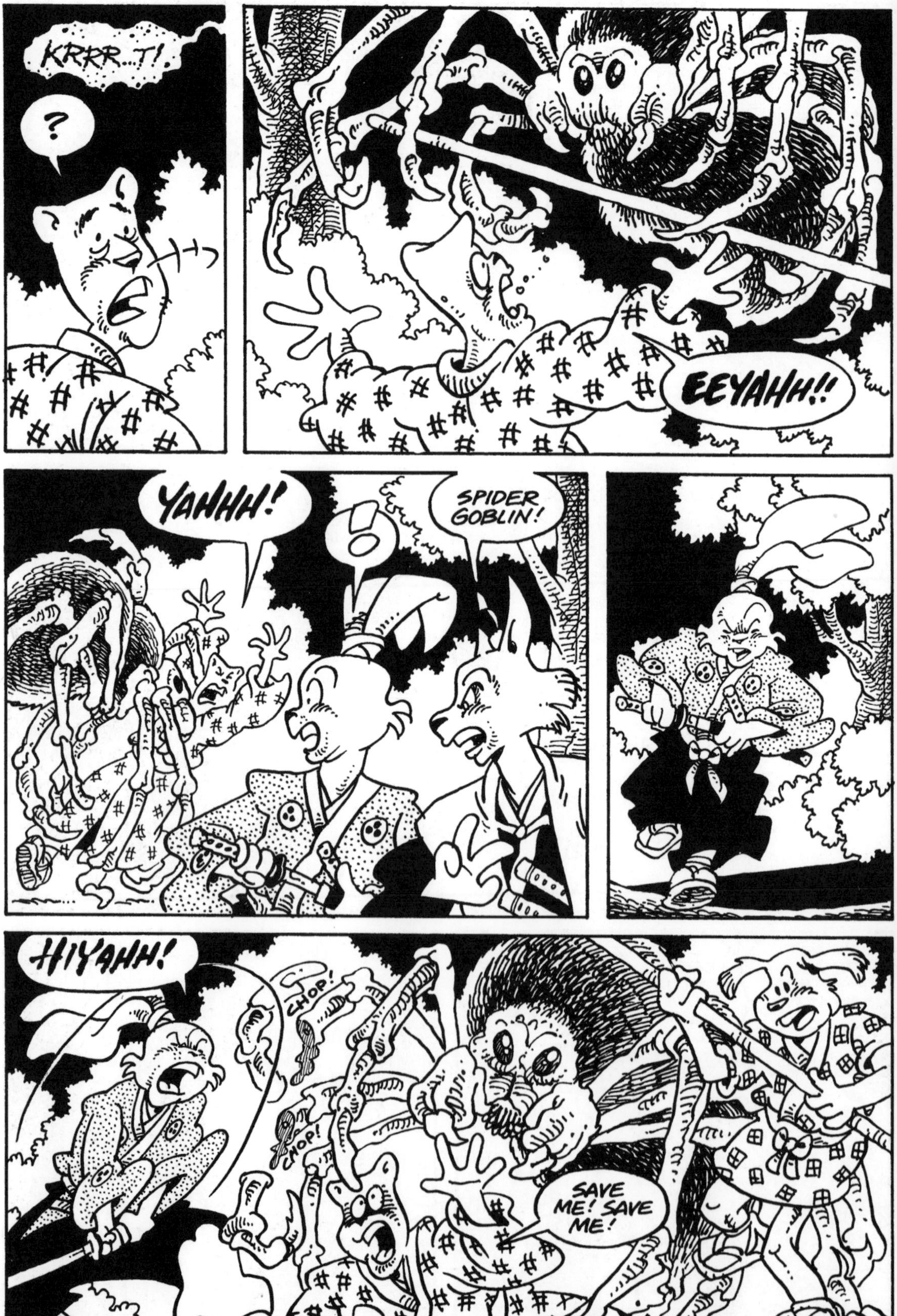
KRRR...T!
?
EEYAHH!!
YAHHH!
!
SPIDER GOBLIN!
HIYAHH!
CHOP!
CHOP!
SAVE ME! SAVE ME!
14.

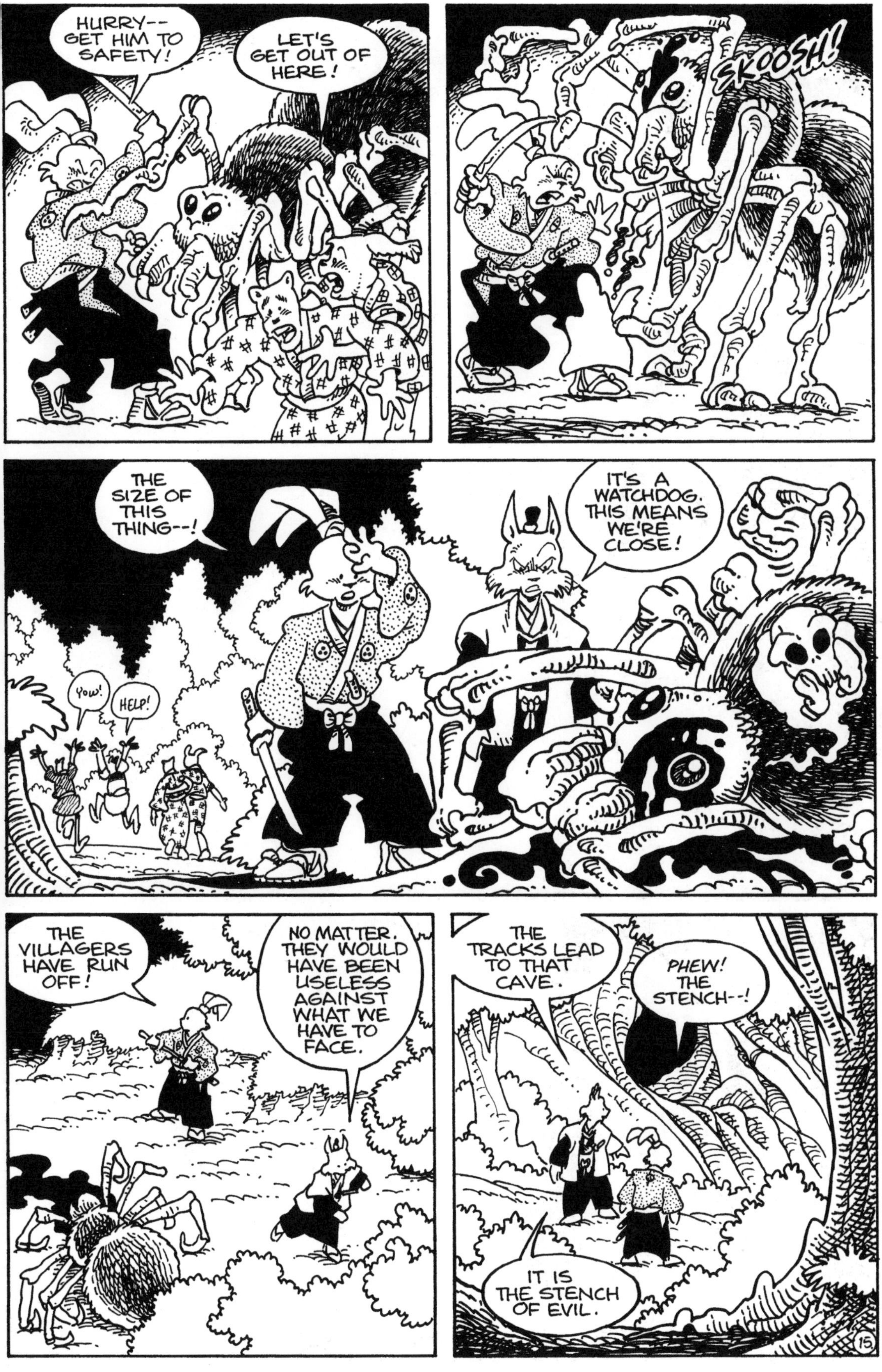
HURRY-- GET HIM TO SAFETY!
LET'S GET OUT OF HERE!
SKOOSH!
THE SIZE OF THIS THING--!
IT'S A WATCHDOG. THIS MEANS WE'RE CLOSE!
YOW!
HELP!
THE VILLAGERS HAVE RUN OFF!
NO MATTER. THEY WOULD HAVE BEEN USELESS AGAINST WHAT WE HAVE TO FACE.
THE TRACKS LEAD TO THAT CAVE.
PHEW! THE STENCH--!
IT IS THE STENCH OF EVIL.
15

WE SHOULD HAVE BROUGHT TORCHES.

GIVE ME A FEW MINUTES FOR MY EYES TO GET ACCUSTOMED TO THE DARK.

WE DON'T HAVE TIME FOR THAT.

DO YOU EXPECT US TO GROPE AROUND BLINDLY?

MAHO*!

*SORCERY

WELL, ARE YOU COMING OR ARE YOU STAYING THERE IN THE DARK?

WAIT FOR ME!

WHAT HAVE I GOTTEN INTO? I WOULD LEAVE HIM NOW IF IT WERE NOT FOR THE GIRL!

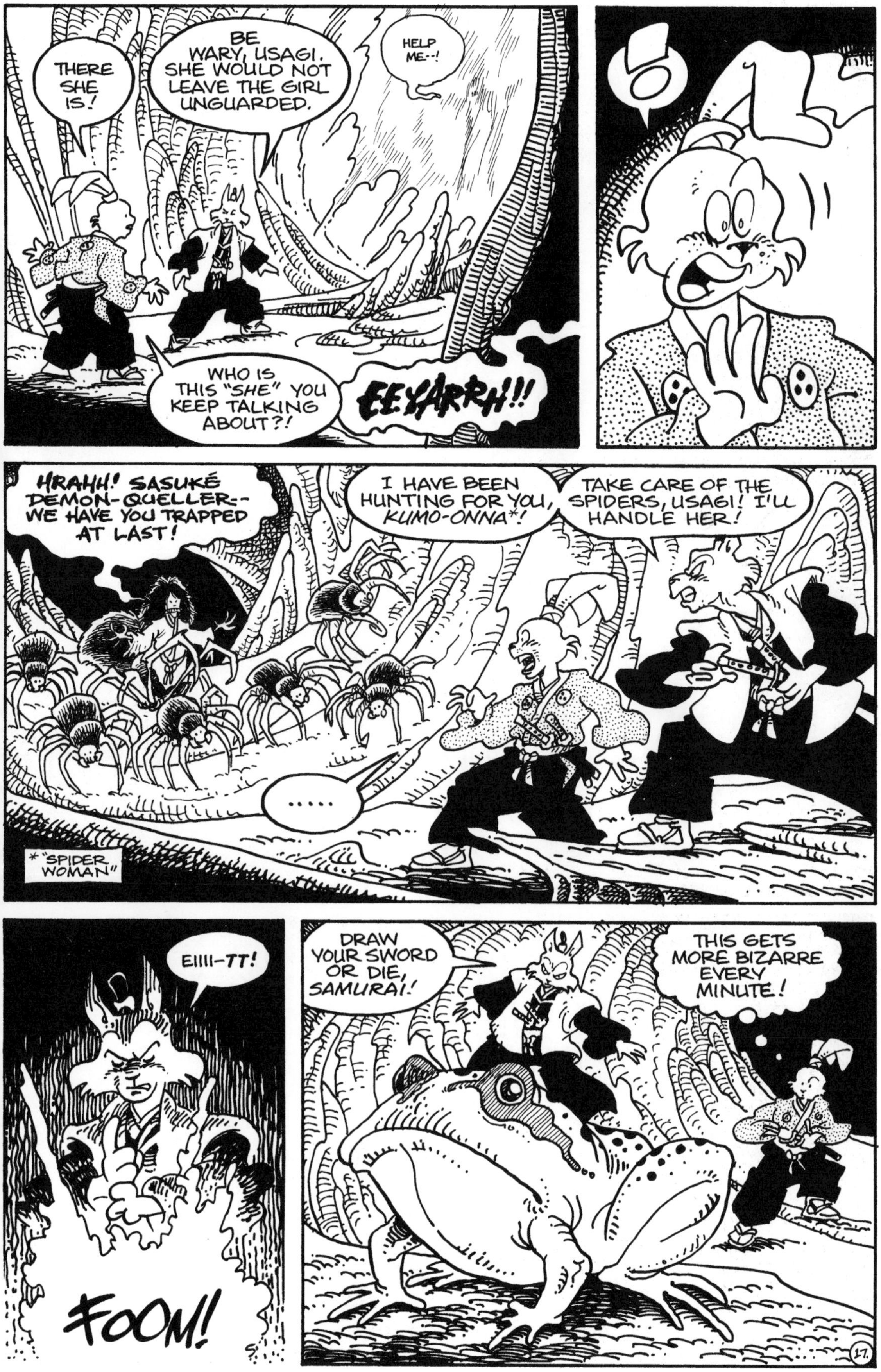
THERE SHE IS!
BE WARY, USAGI. SHE WOULD NOT LEAVE THE GIRL UNGUARDED.
HELP ME--!
WHO IS THIS "SHE" YOU KEEP TALKING ABOUT?!
EEYARRH!!!
HRAHH! SASUKÉ DEMON-QUELLER-- WE HAVE YOU TRAPPED AT LAST!
I HAVE BEEN HUNTING FOR YOU, KUMO-ONNA*!
TAKE CARE OF THE SPIDERS, USAGI! I'LL HANDLE HER!
.....
*"SPIDER WOMAN"
EIIII-TT!
FOOM!
DRAW YOUR SWORD OR DIE, SAMURAI!
THIS GETS MORE BIZARRE EVERY MINUTE!
17.

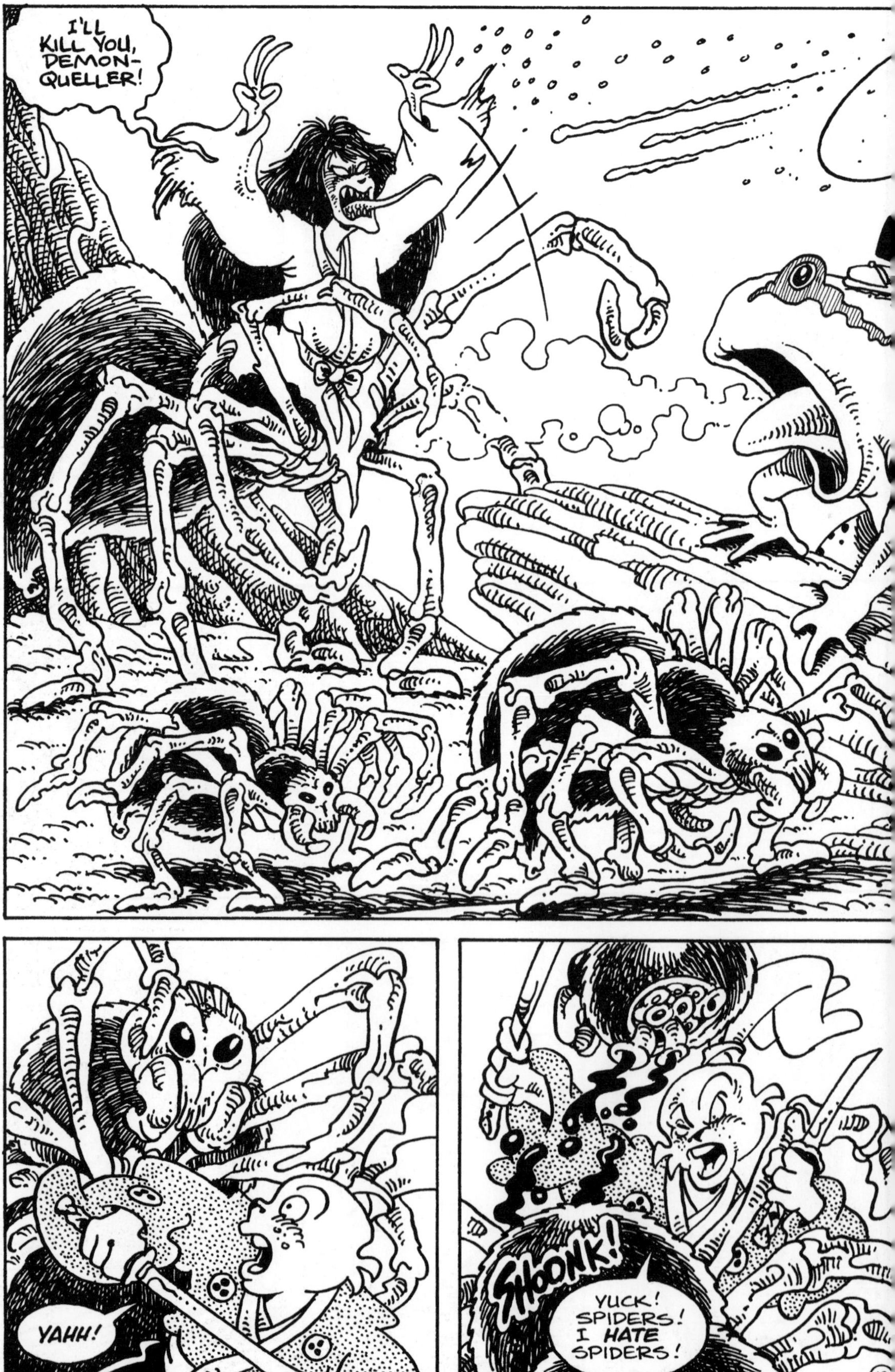
I'LL KILL YOU, DEMON-QUELLER!
YAHH!
SHOONK!
YUCK! SPIDERS! I HATE SPIDERS!
18.

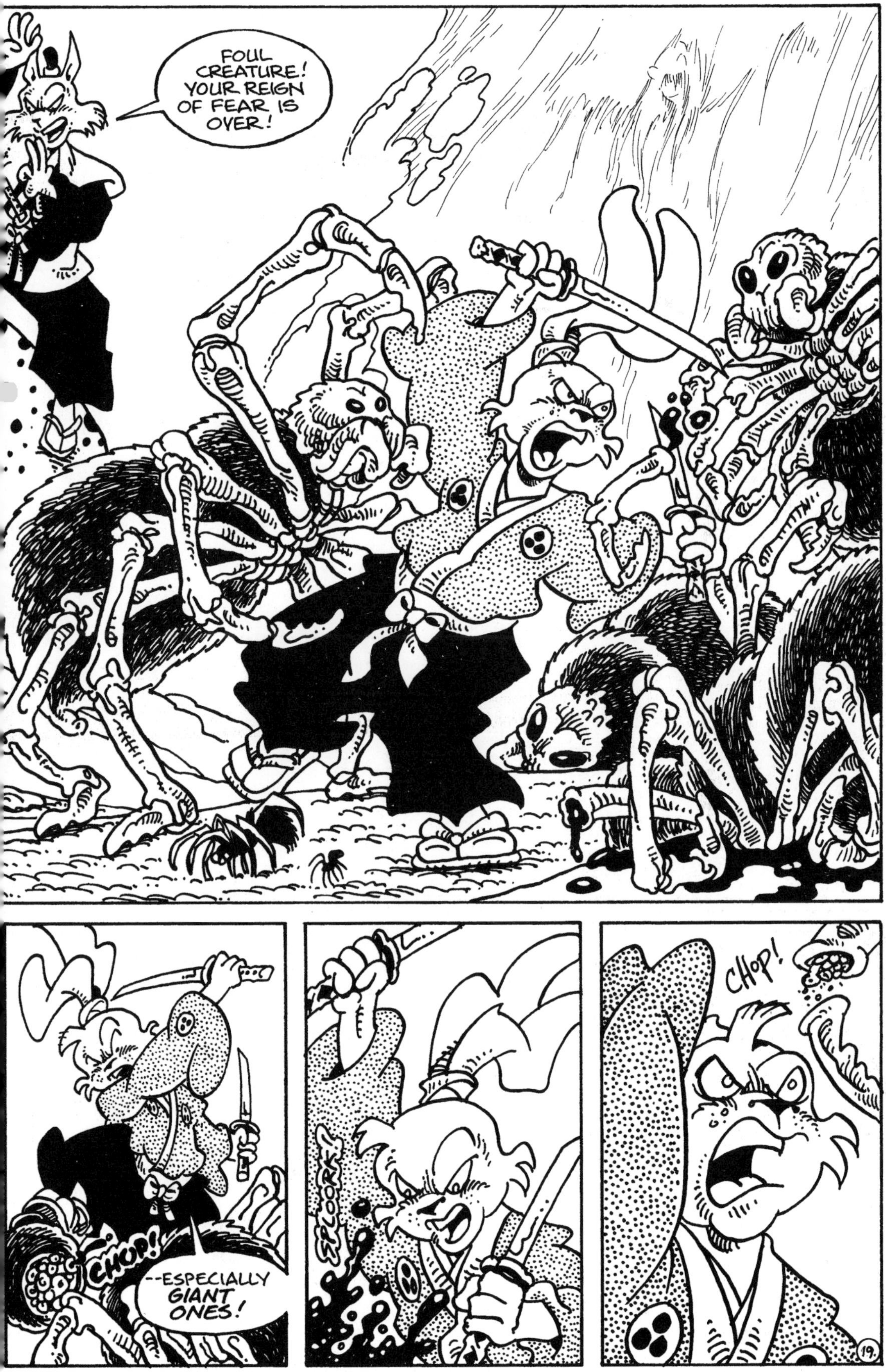
FOUL CREATURE! YOUR REIGN OF FEAR IS OVER!
CHOP!
--ESPECIALLY GIANT ONES!
SPLOORK!
CHOP!
19.

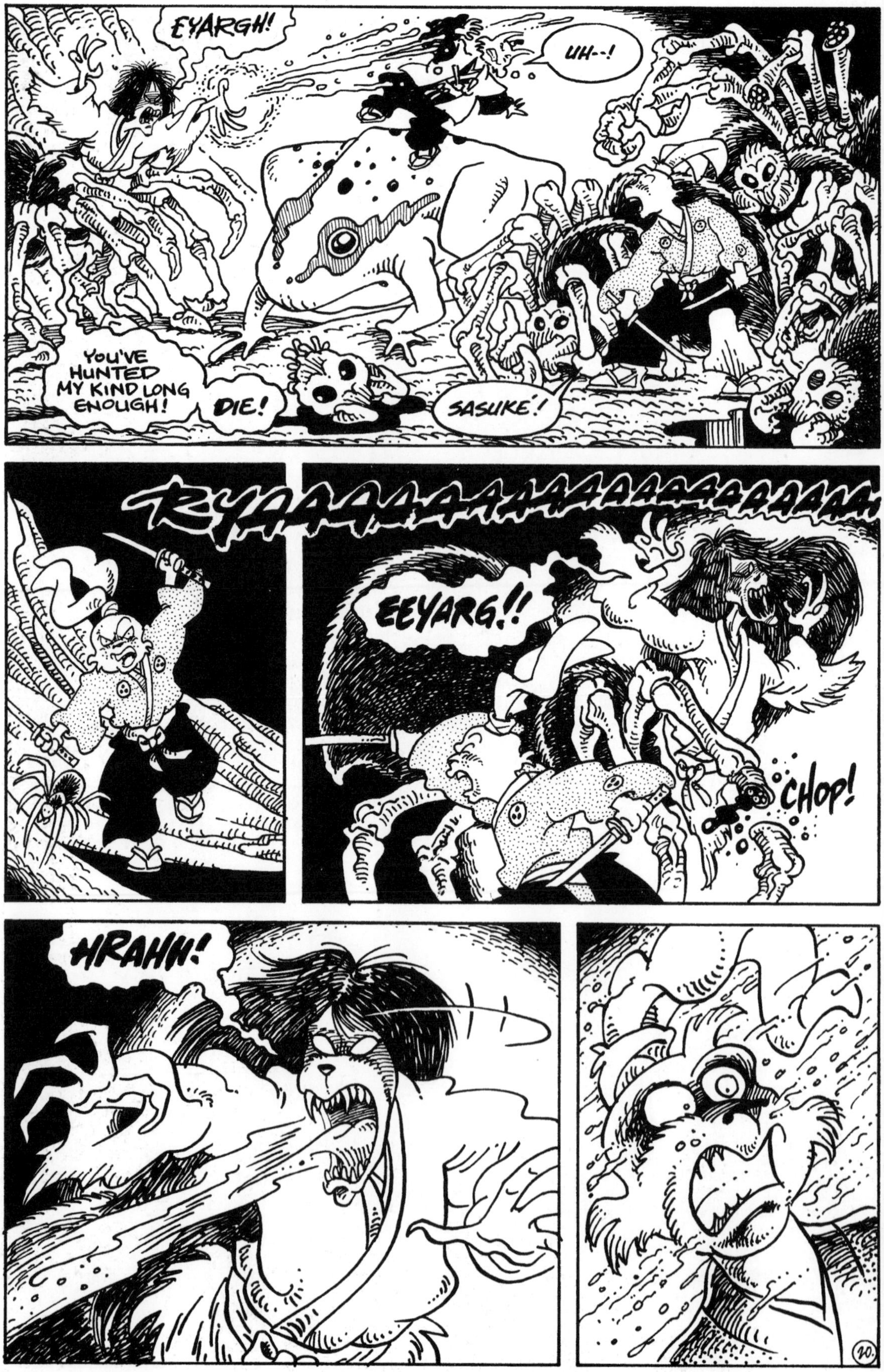
EYARGH!
UH--!
YOU'VE HUNTED MY KIND LONG ENOUGH!
DIE!
SASUKE!
RYAAAAAAAAAAAAAAAAAAAAAA
EEYARG!!
CHOP!
HRAHH!
20.

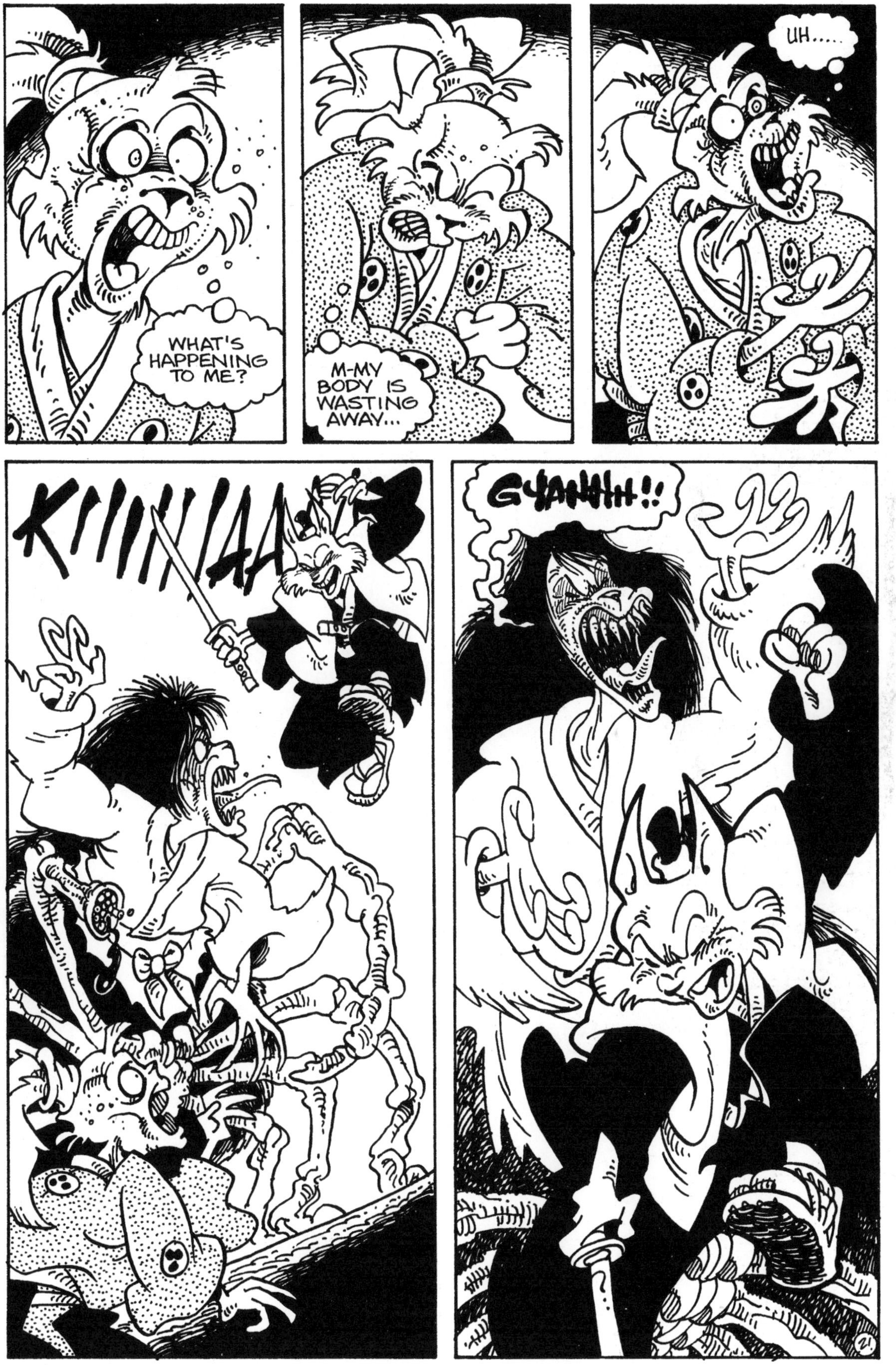
WHAT'S HAPPENING TO ME?
M-MY BODY IS WASTING AWAY...
UH.....
KIIIIIAAA
GYAHHH!!
21

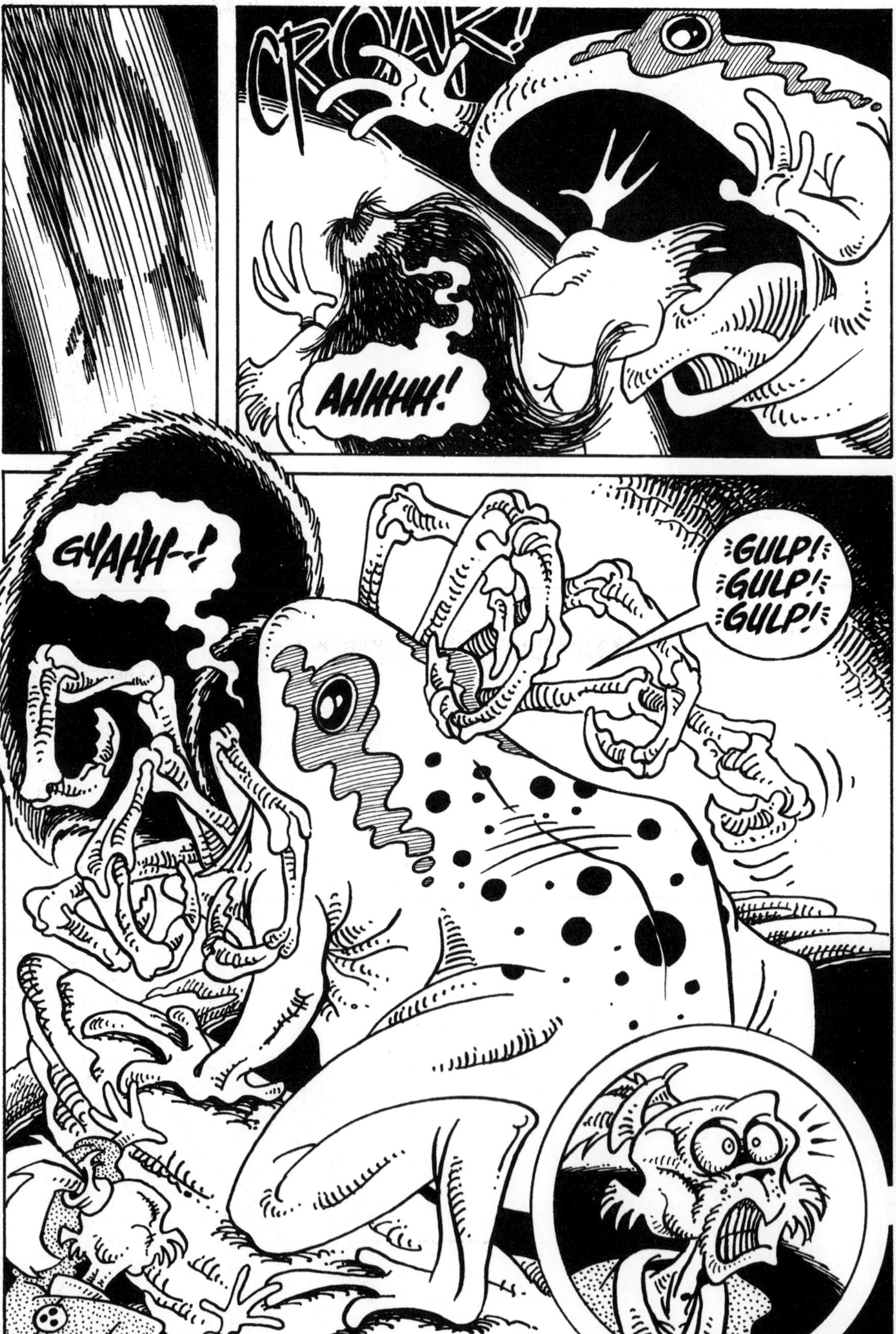
CROAK!
AHHHH!
GYAHH--!
GULP! GULP! GULP!
22

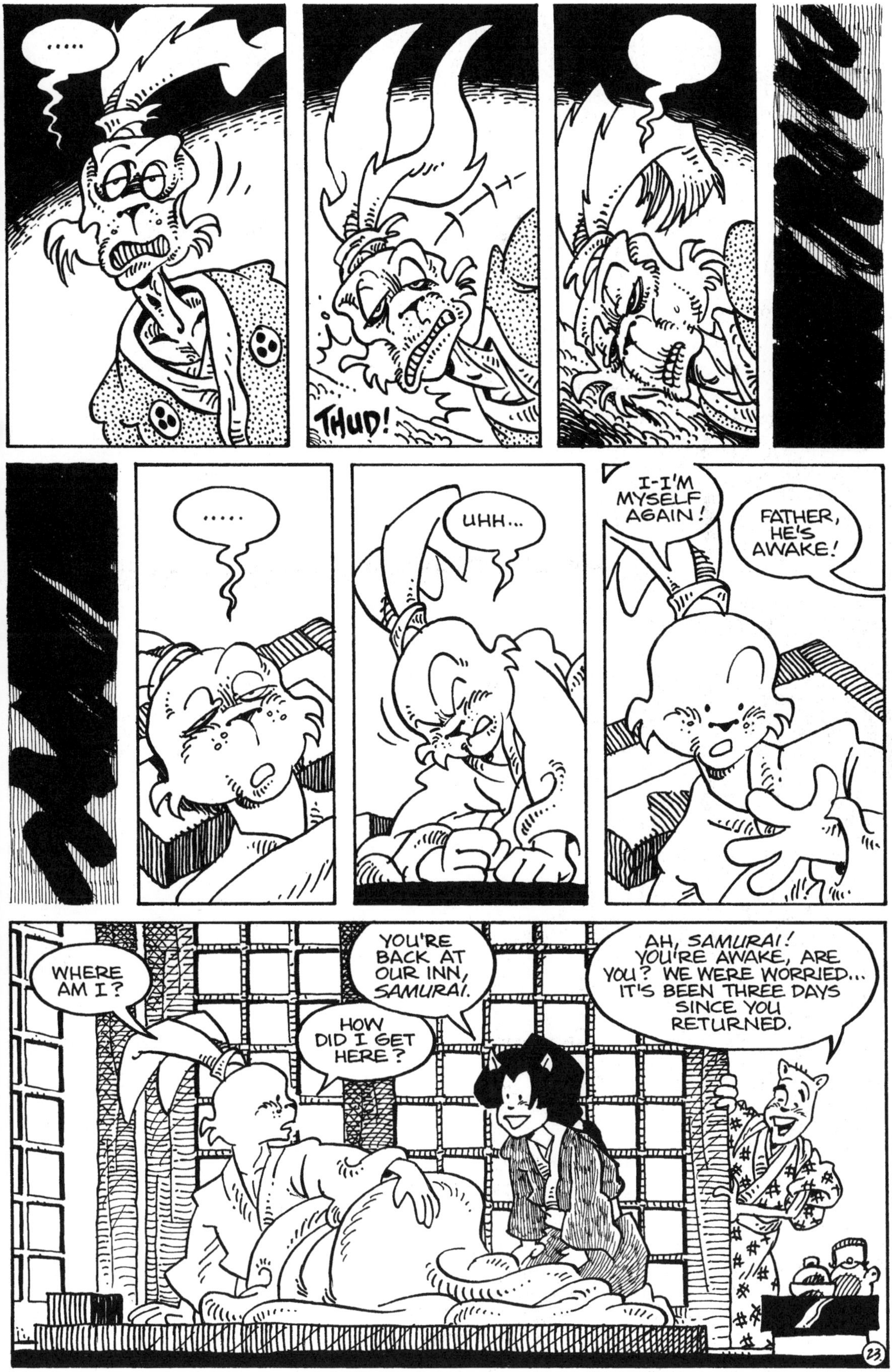
.....
THUD!
.....
UHH...
I-I'M MYSELF AGAIN!
FATHER, HE'S AWAKE!
WHERE AM I?
YOU'RE BACK AT OUR INN, *SAMURAI*.
HOW DID I GET HERE?
AH, *SAMURAI!* YOU'RE AWAKE, ARE YOU? WE WERE WORRIED... IT'S BEEN THREE DAYS SINCE YOU RETURNED.
23

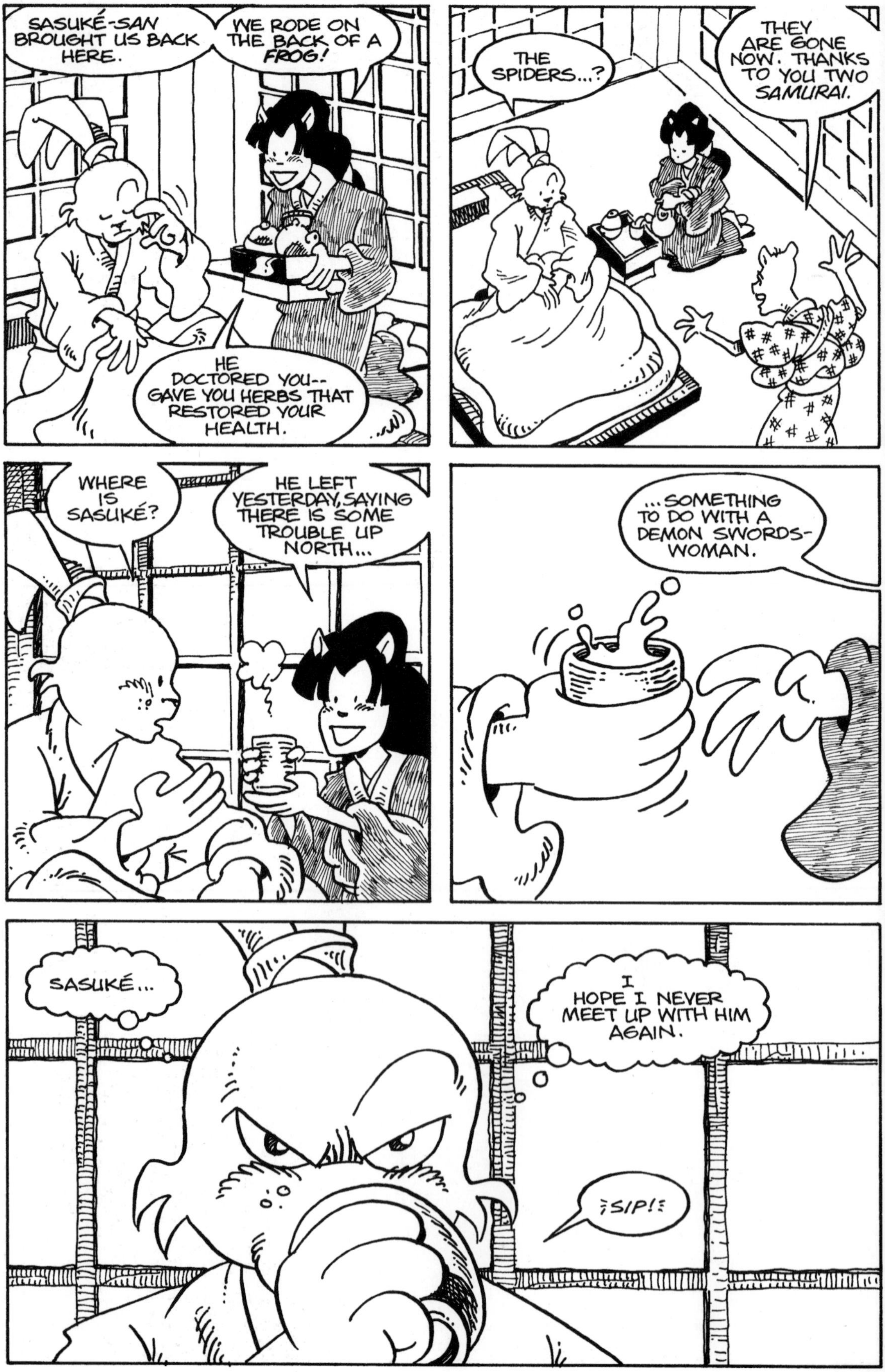
SASUKÉ-SAN BROUGHT US BACK HERE.
WE RODE ON THE BACK OF A *FROG*!
HE DOCTORED YOU-- GAVE YOU HERBS THAT RESTORED YOUR HEALTH.
THE SPIDERS...?
THEY ARE GONE NOW. THANKS TO YOU TWO *SAMURAI*.
WHERE IS SASUKÉ?
HE LEFT YESTERDAY, SAYING THERE IS SOME TROUBLE UP NORTH...
...SOMETHING TO DO WITH A DEMON SWORDS-WOMAN.
SASUKÉ...
I HOPE I NEVER MEET UP WITH HIM AGAIN.
¡SIP!¡
END

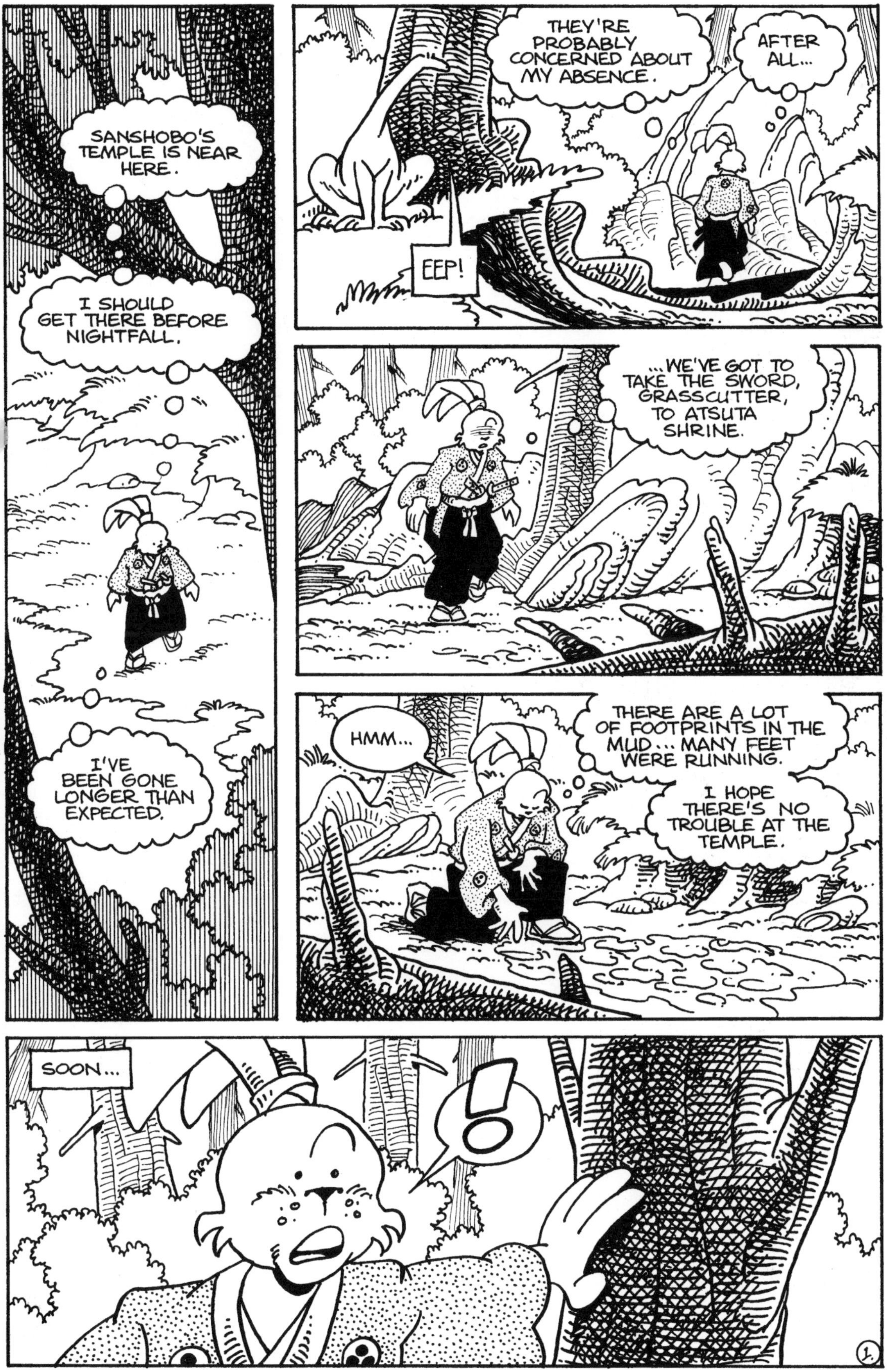
SANSHOBO'S TEMPLE IS NEAR HERE.
I SHOULD GET THERE BEFORE NIGHTFALL.
I'VE BEEN GONE LONGER THAN EXPECTED.
THEY'RE PROBABLY CONCERNED ABOUT MY ABSENCE.
AFTER ALL...
EEP!
...WE'VE GOT TO TAKE THE SWORD, GRASSCUTTER, TO ATSUTA SHRINE.
HMM...
THERE ARE A LOT OF FOOTPRINTS IN THE MUD... MANY FEET WERE RUNNING.
I HOPE THERE'S NO TROUBLE AT THE TEMPLE.
SOON...
!
1.

REUNION

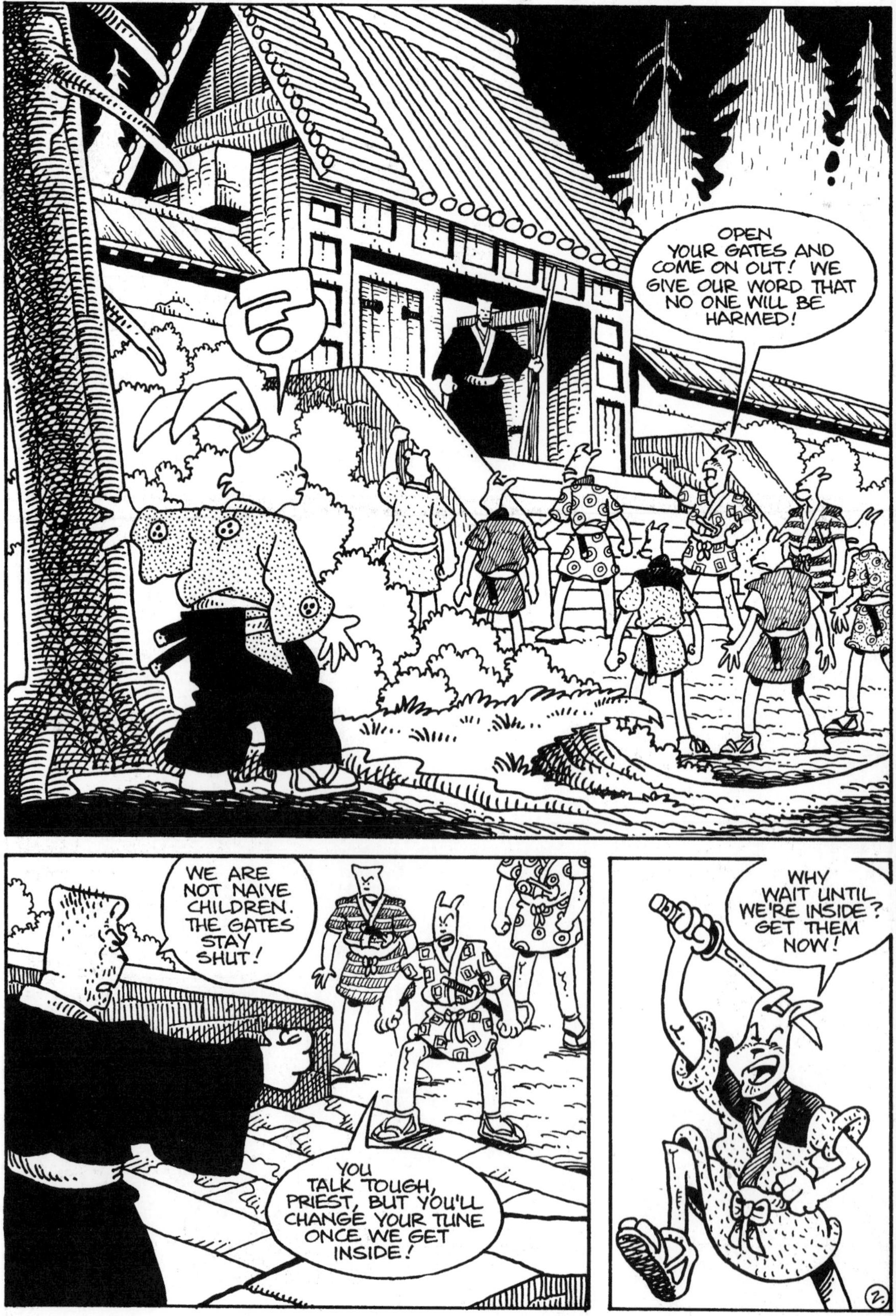
?
OPEN YOUR GATES AND COME ON OUT! WE GIVE OUR WORD THAT NO ONE WILL BE HARMED!
WE ARE NOT NAIVE CHILDREN. THE GATES STAY SHUT!
YOU TALK TOUGH, PRIEST, BUT YOU'LL CHANGE YOUR TUNE ONCE WE GET INSIDE!
WHY WAIT UNTIL WE'RE INSIDE? GET THEM NOW!

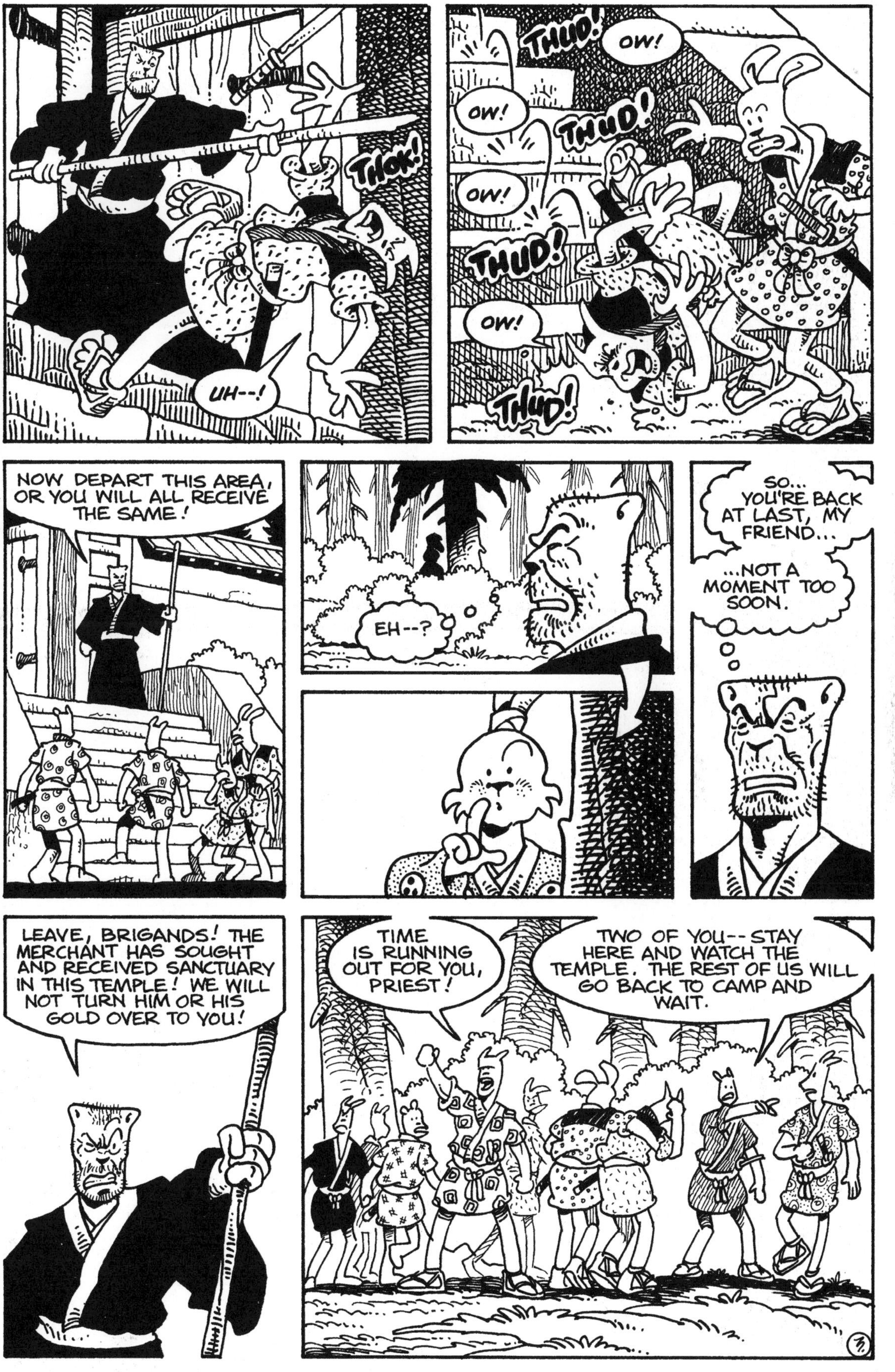
THOK!
UH--!
THUD!
OW!
OW!
THUD!
OW!
THUD!
OW!
THUD!
NOW DEPART THIS AREA, OR YOU WILL ALL RECEIVE THE SAME!
EH--?
SO... YOU'RE BACK AT LAST, MY FRIEND...
...NOT A MOMENT TOO SOON.
LEAVE, BRIGANDS! THE MERCHANT HAS SOUGHT AND RECEIVED SANCTUARY IN THIS TEMPLE! WE WILL NOT TURN HIM OR HIS GOLD OVER TO YOU!
TIME IS RUNNING OUT FOR YOU, PRIEST!
TWO OF YOU--STAY HERE AND WATCH THE TEMPLE. THE REST OF US WILL GO BACK TO CAMP AND WAIT.

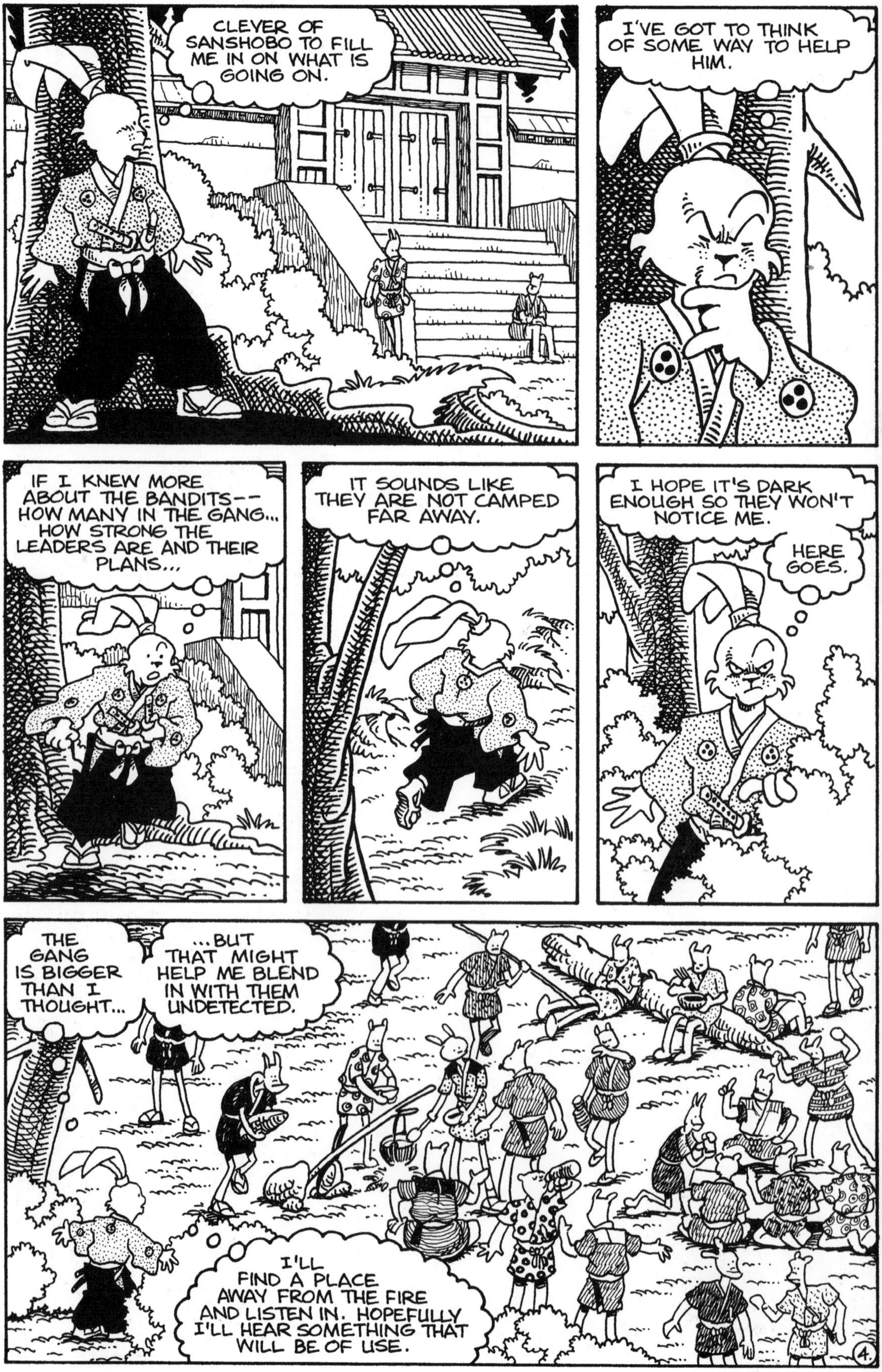
CLEVER OF SANSHOBO TO FILL ME IN ON WHAT IS GOING ON.
I'VE GOT TO THINK OF SOME WAY TO HELP HIM.
IF I KNEW MORE ABOUT THE BANDITS-- HOW MANY IN THE GANG... HOW STRONG THE LEADERS ARE AND THEIR PLANS...
IT SOUNDS LIKE THEY ARE NOT CAMPED FAR AWAY.
I HOPE IT'S DARK ENOUGH SO THEY WON'T NOTICE ME.
HERE GOES.
THE GANG IS BIGGER THAN I THOUGHT...
...BUT THAT MIGHT HELP ME BLEND IN WITH THEM UNDETECTED.
I'LL FIND A PLACE AWAY FROM THE FIRE AND LISTEN IN. HOPEFULLY I'LL HEAR SOMETHING THAT WILL BE OF USE.
4.

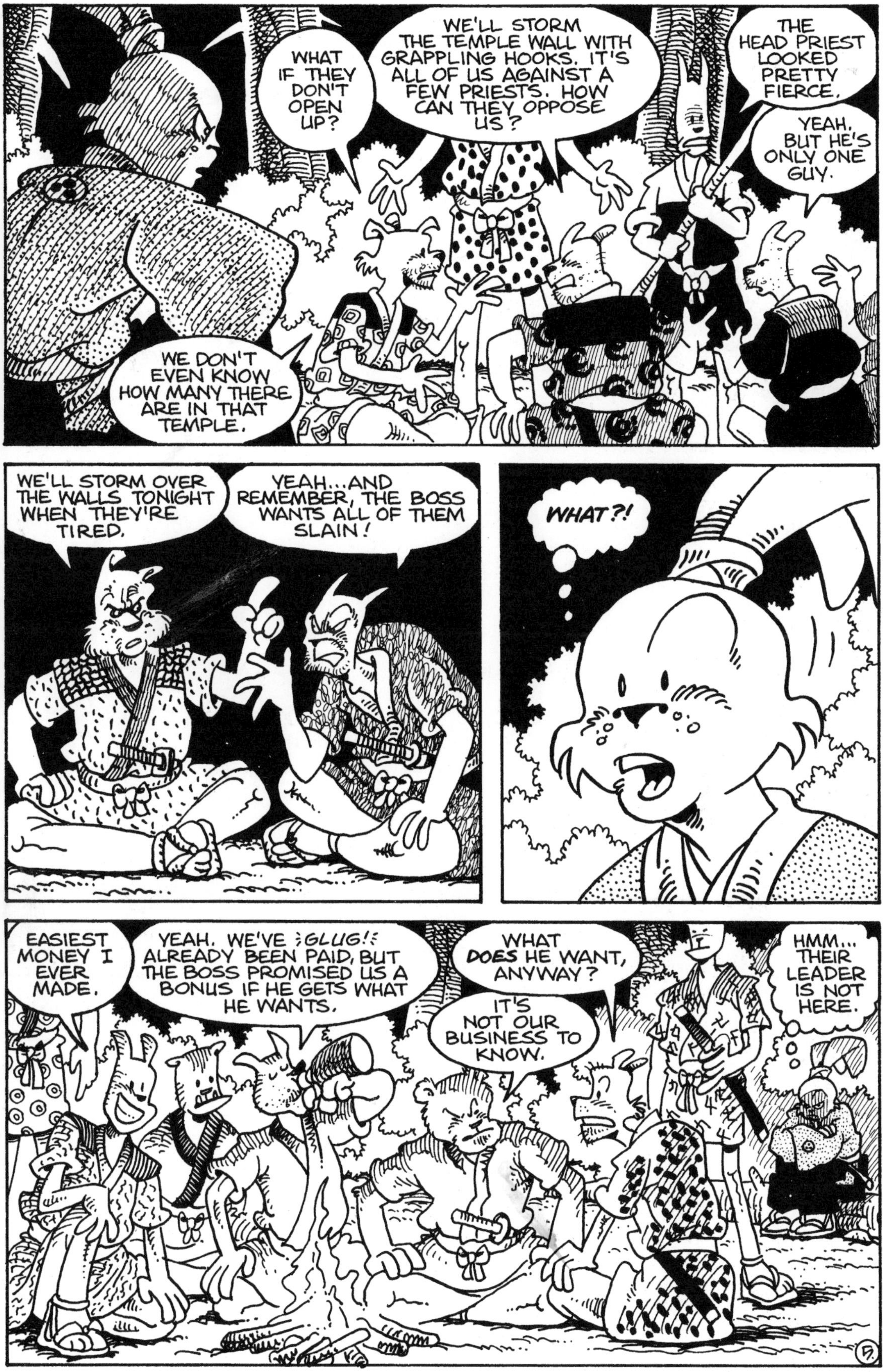
WHAT IF THEY DON'T OPEN UP?
WE'LL STORM THE TEMPLE WALL WITH GRAPPLING HOOKS. IT'S ALL OF US AGAINST A FEW PRIESTS. HOW CAN THEY OPPOSE US?
THE HEAD PRIEST LOOKED PRETTY FIERCE.
YEAH, BUT HE'S ONLY ONE GUY.
WE DON'T EVEN KNOW HOW MANY THERE ARE IN THAT TEMPLE.
WE'LL STORM OVER THE WALLS TONIGHT WHEN THEY'RE TIRED.
YEAH...AND REMEMBER, THE BOSS WANTS ALL OF THEM SLAIN!
WHAT?!
EASIEST MONEY I EVER MADE.
YEAH. WE'VE ;GLUG!; ALREADY BEEN PAID, BUT THE BOSS PROMISED US A BONUS IF HE GETS WHAT HE WANTS.
WHAT DOES HE WANT, ANYWAY?
IT'S NOT OUR BUSINESS TO KNOW.
HMM... THEIR LEADER IS NOT HERE.
5.

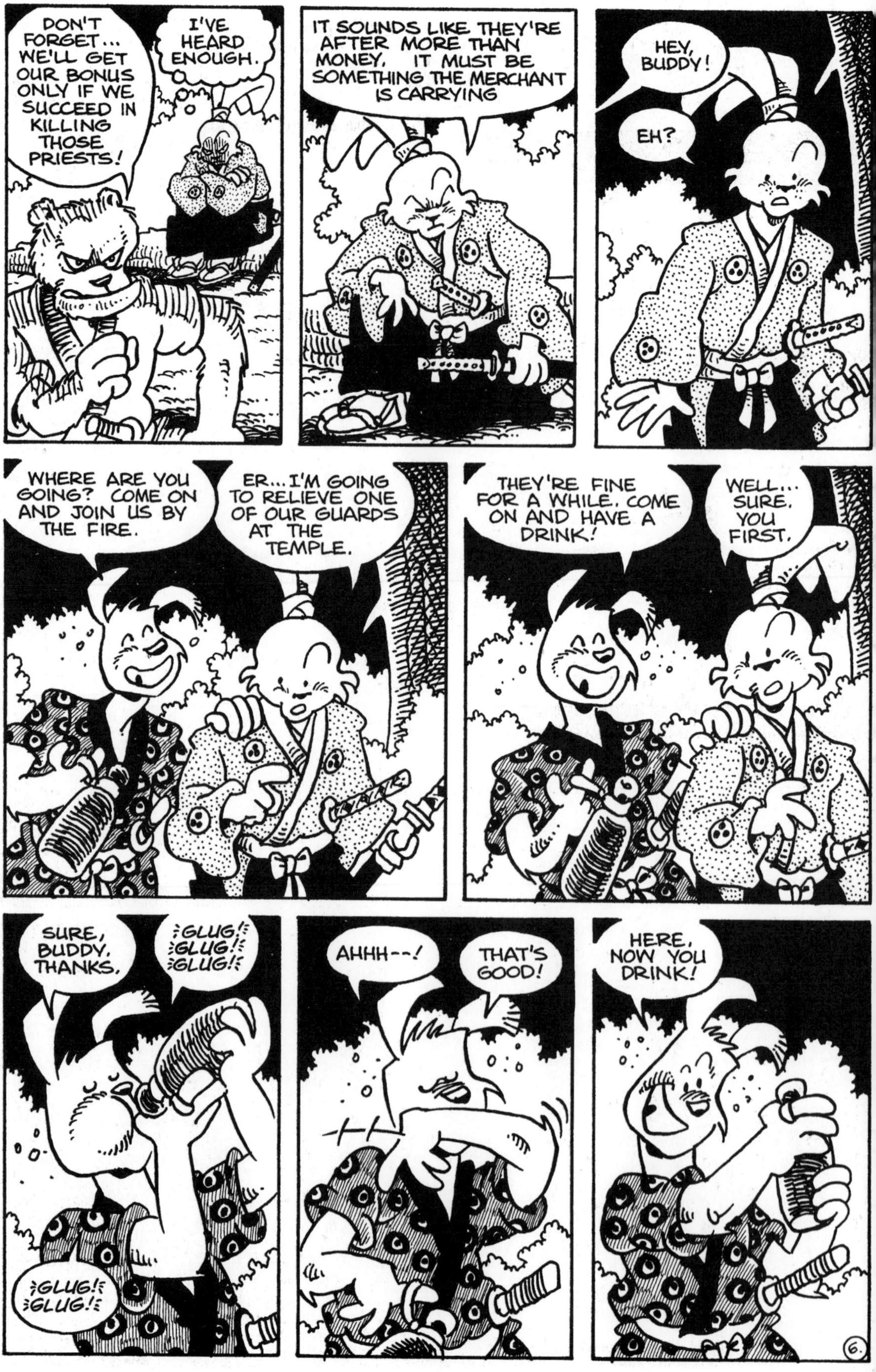
DON'T FORGET... WE'LL GET OUR BONUS ONLY IF WE SUCCEED IN KILLING THOSE PRIESTS!
I'VE HEARD ENOUGH.
IT SOUNDS LIKE THEY'RE AFTER MORE THAN MONEY. IT MUST BE SOMETHING THE MERCHANT IS CARRYING
HEY, BUDDY!
EH?
WHERE ARE YOU GOING? COME ON AND JOIN US BY THE FIRE.
ER... I'M GOING TO RELIEVE ONE OF OUR GUARDS AT THE TEMPLE.
THEY'RE FINE FOR A WHILE. COME ON AND HAVE A DRINK!
WELL... SURE. YOU FIRST.
SURE, BUDDY. THANKS.
GLUG! GLUG! GLUG!
GLUG! GLUG!
AHHH--!
THAT'S GOOD!
HERE, NOW YOU DRINK!
6.

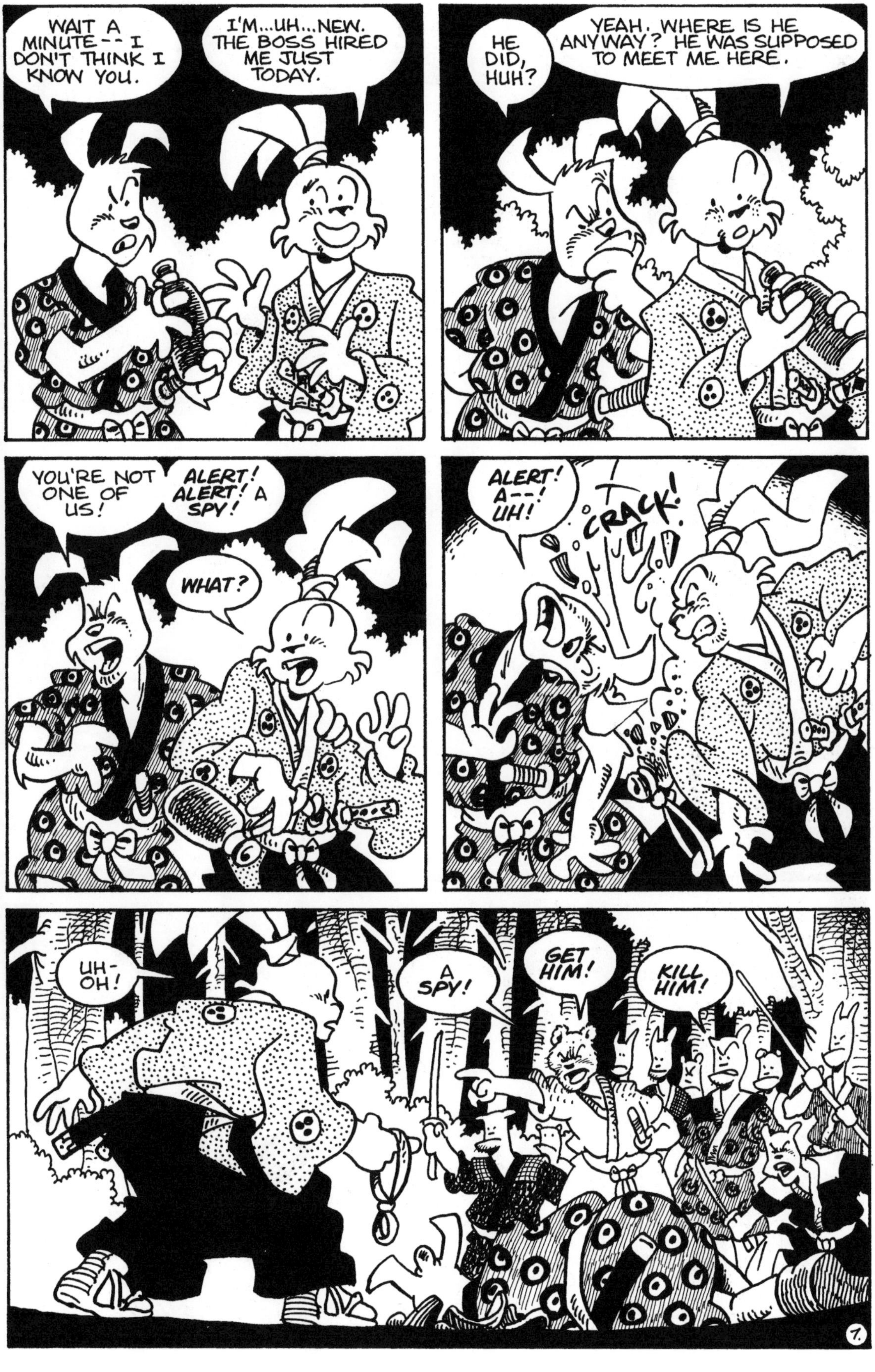
WAIT A MINUTE -- I DON'T THINK I KNOW YOU.
I'M...UH...NEW. THE BOSS HIRED ME JUST TODAY.
HE DID, HUH?
YEAH. WHERE IS HE ANYWAY? HE WAS SUPPOSED TO MEET ME HERE.
YOU'RE NOT ONE OF US!
ALERT! ALERT! A SPY!
WHAT?
ALERT! A--! UH!
CRACK!
UH-OH!
A SPY!
GET HIM!
KILL HIM!
7.

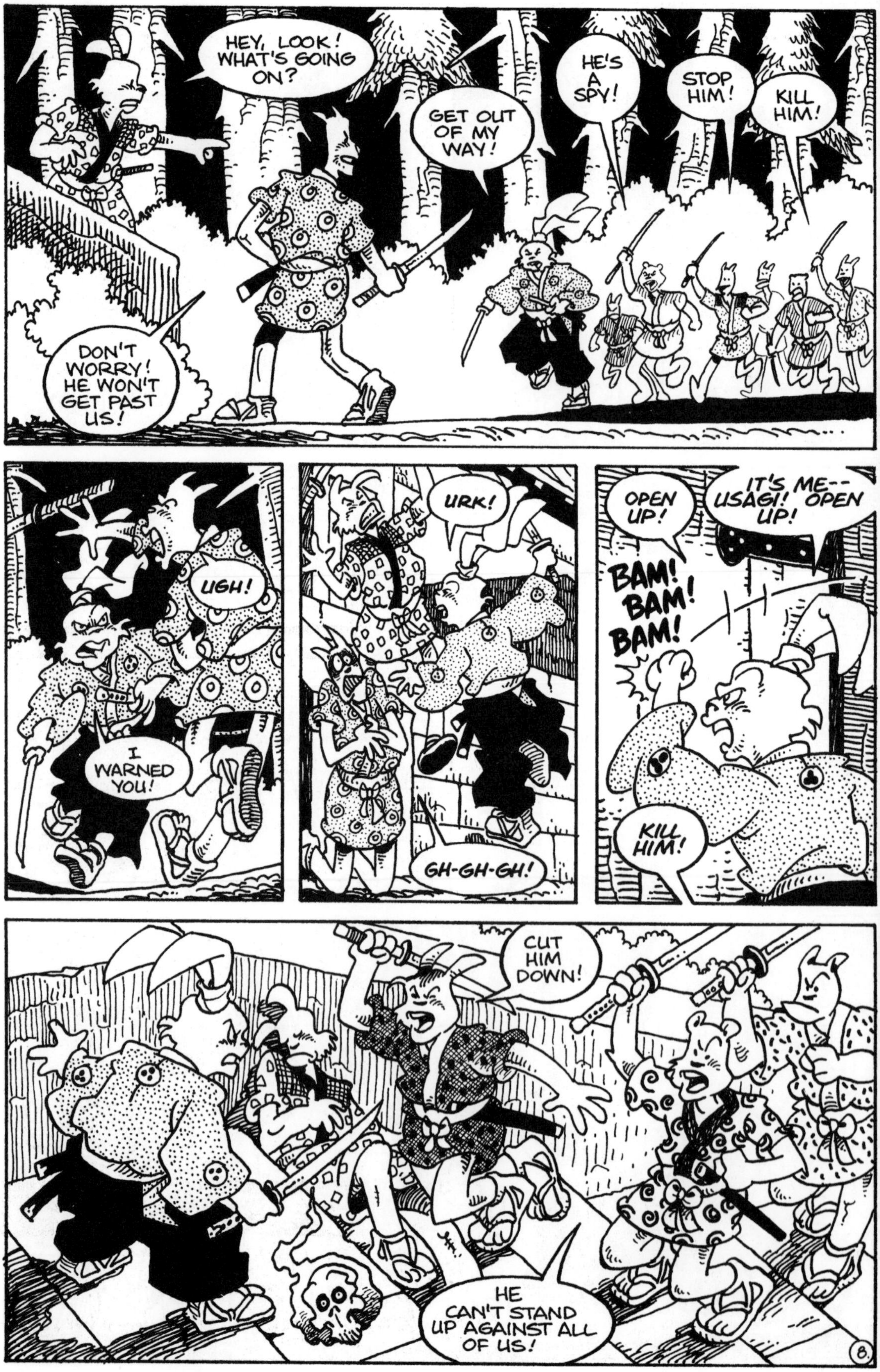
HEY, LOOK! WHAT'S GOING ON?
GET OUT OF MY WAY!
HE'S A SPY!
STOP HIM!
KILL HIM!
DON'T WORRY! HE WON'T GET PAST US!
UGH!
I WARNED YOU!
URK!
GH-GH-GH!
OPEN UP!
IT'S ME-- USAGI! OPEN UP!
BAM! BAM! BAM!
KILL HIM!
CUT HIM DOWN!
HE CAN'T STAND UP AGAINST ALL OF US!
8.

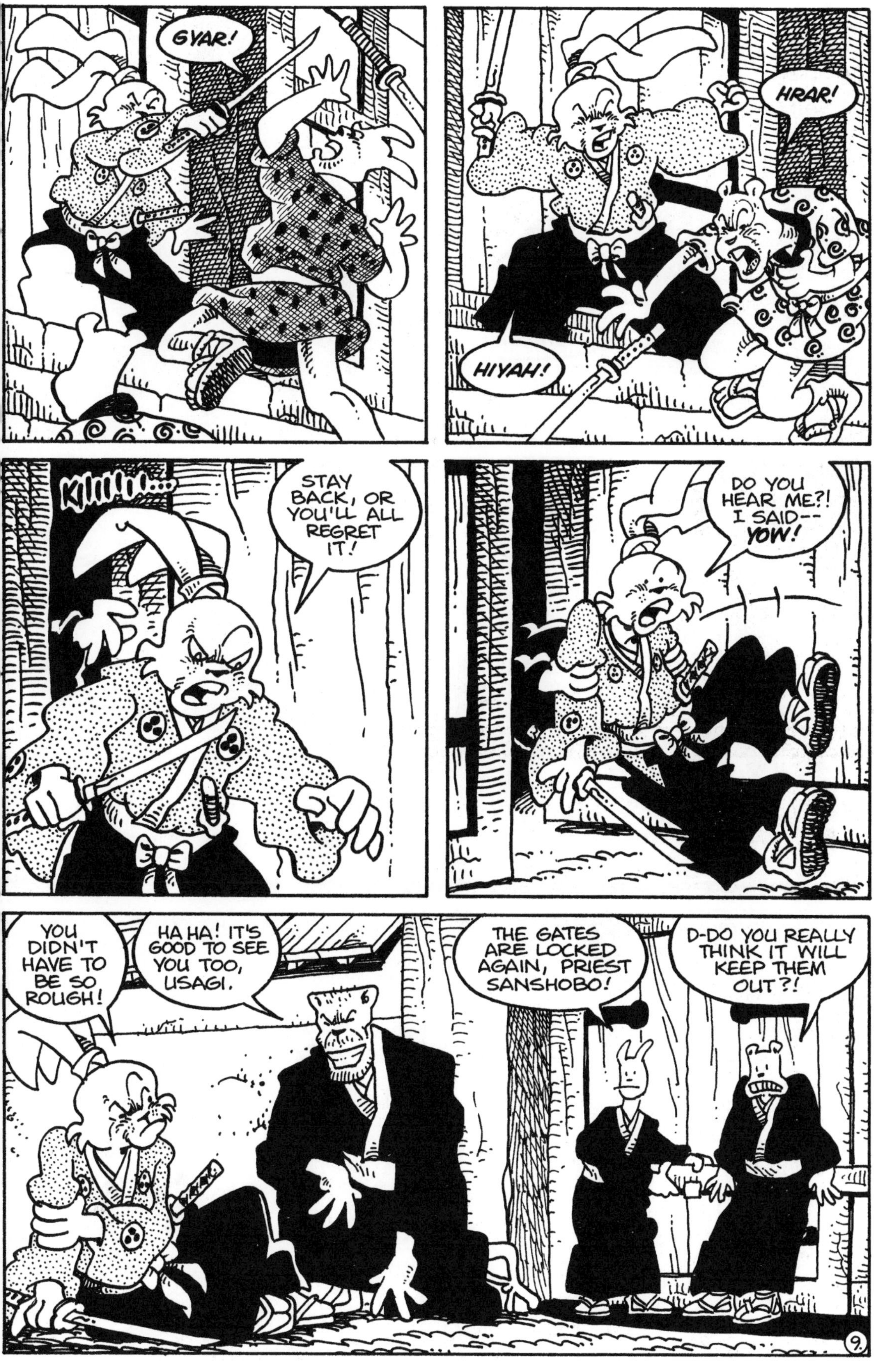
GYAR!
HRAR!
HIYAH!
KIIIIII...
STAY BACK, OR YOU'LL ALL REGRET IT!
DO YOU HEAR ME?! I SAID-- ***YOW!***
YOU DIDN'T HAVE TO BE SO ROUGH!
HA HA! IT'S GOOD TO SEE YOU TOO, USAGI.
THE GATES ARE LOCKED AGAIN, PRIEST SANSHOBO!
D-DO YOU REALLY THINK IT WILL KEEP THEM OUT?!
9

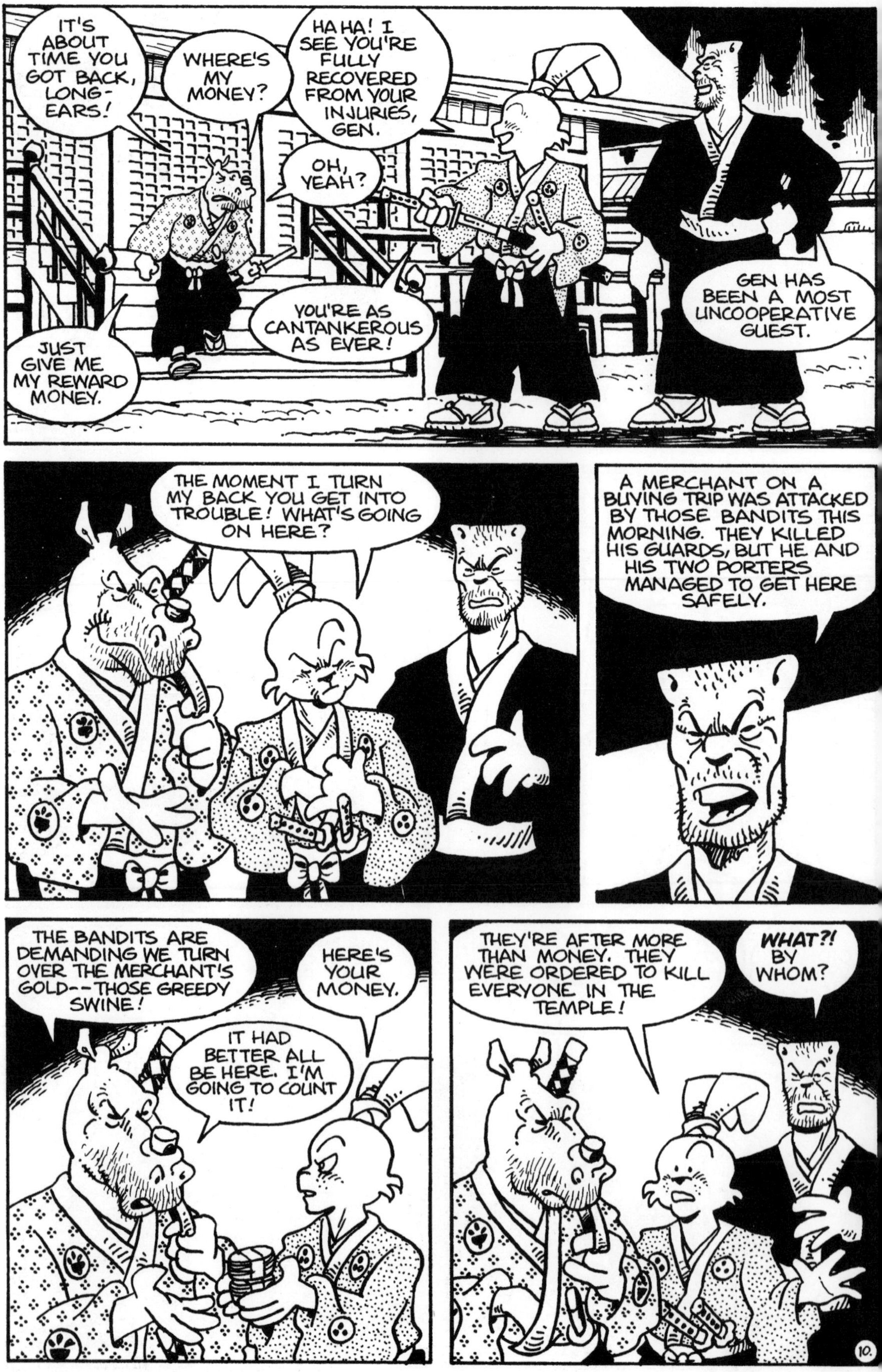
IT'S ABOUT TIME YOU GOT BACK, LONG-EARS!
WHERE'S MY MONEY?
HA HA! I SEE YOU'RE FULLY RECOVERED FROM YOUR INJURIES, GEN.
OH, YEAH?
JUST GIVE ME MY REWARD MONEY.
YOU'RE AS CANTANKEROUS AS EVER!
GEN HAS BEEN A MOST UNCOOPERATIVE GUEST.
THE MOMENT I TURN MY BACK YOU GET INTO TROUBLE! WHAT'S GOING ON HERE?
A MERCHANT ON A BUYING TRIP WAS ATTACKED BY THOSE BANDITS THIS MORNING. THEY KILLED HIS GUARDS, BUT HE AND HIS TWO PORTERS MANAGED TO GET HERE SAFELY.
THE BANDITS ARE DEMANDING WE TURN OVER THE MERCHANT'S GOLD--THOSE GREEDY SWINE!
HERE'S YOUR MONEY.
IT HAD BETTER ALL BE HERE. I'M GOING TO COUNT IT!
THEY'RE AFTER MORE THAN MONEY. THEY WERE ORDERED TO KILL EVERYONE IN THE TEMPLE!
WHAT?! BY WHOM?
10.

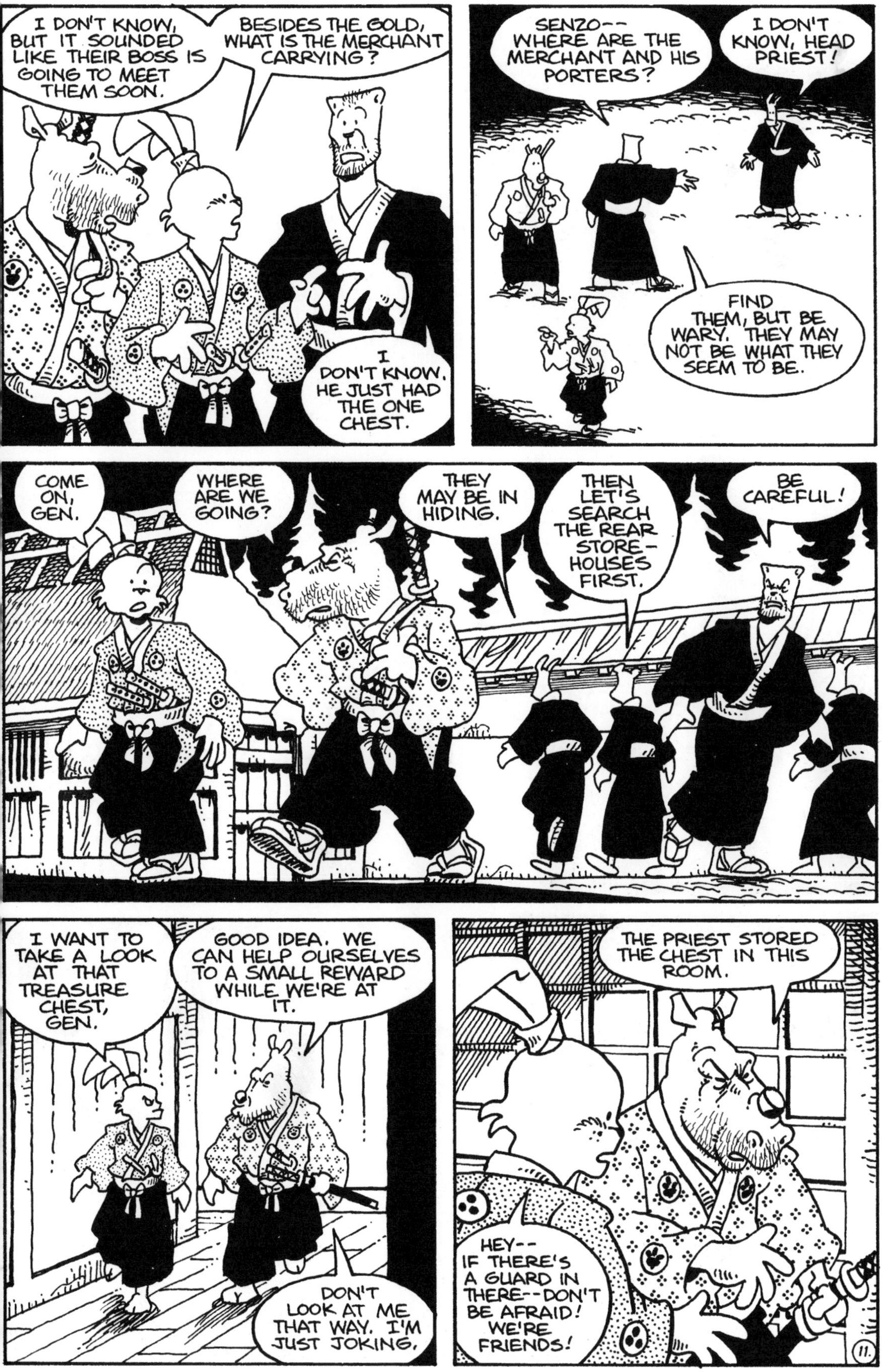
I DON'T KNOW, BUT IT SOUNDED LIKE THEIR BOSS IS GOING TO MEET THEM SOON.
BESIDES THE GOLD, WHAT IS THE MERCHANT CARRYING?
I DON'T KNOW. HE JUST HAD THE ONE CHEST.
SENZO-- WHERE ARE THE MERCHANT AND HIS PORTERS?
I DON'T KNOW, HEAD PRIEST!
FIND THEM, BUT BE WARY. THEY MAY NOT BE WHAT THEY SEEM TO BE.
COME ON, GEN.
WHERE ARE WE GOING?
THEY MAY BE IN HIDING.
THEN LET'S SEARCH THE REAR STORE-HOUSES FIRST.
BE CAREFUL!
I WANT TO TAKE A LOOK AT THAT TREASURE CHEST, GEN.
GOOD IDEA. WE CAN HELP OURSELVES TO A SMALL REWARD WHILE WE'RE AT IT.
DON'T LOOK AT ME THAT WAY. I'M JUST JOKING.
THE PRIEST STORED THE CHEST IN THIS ROOM.
HEY-- IF THERE'S A GUARD IN THERE--DON'T BE AFRAID! WE'RE FRIENDS!
11.

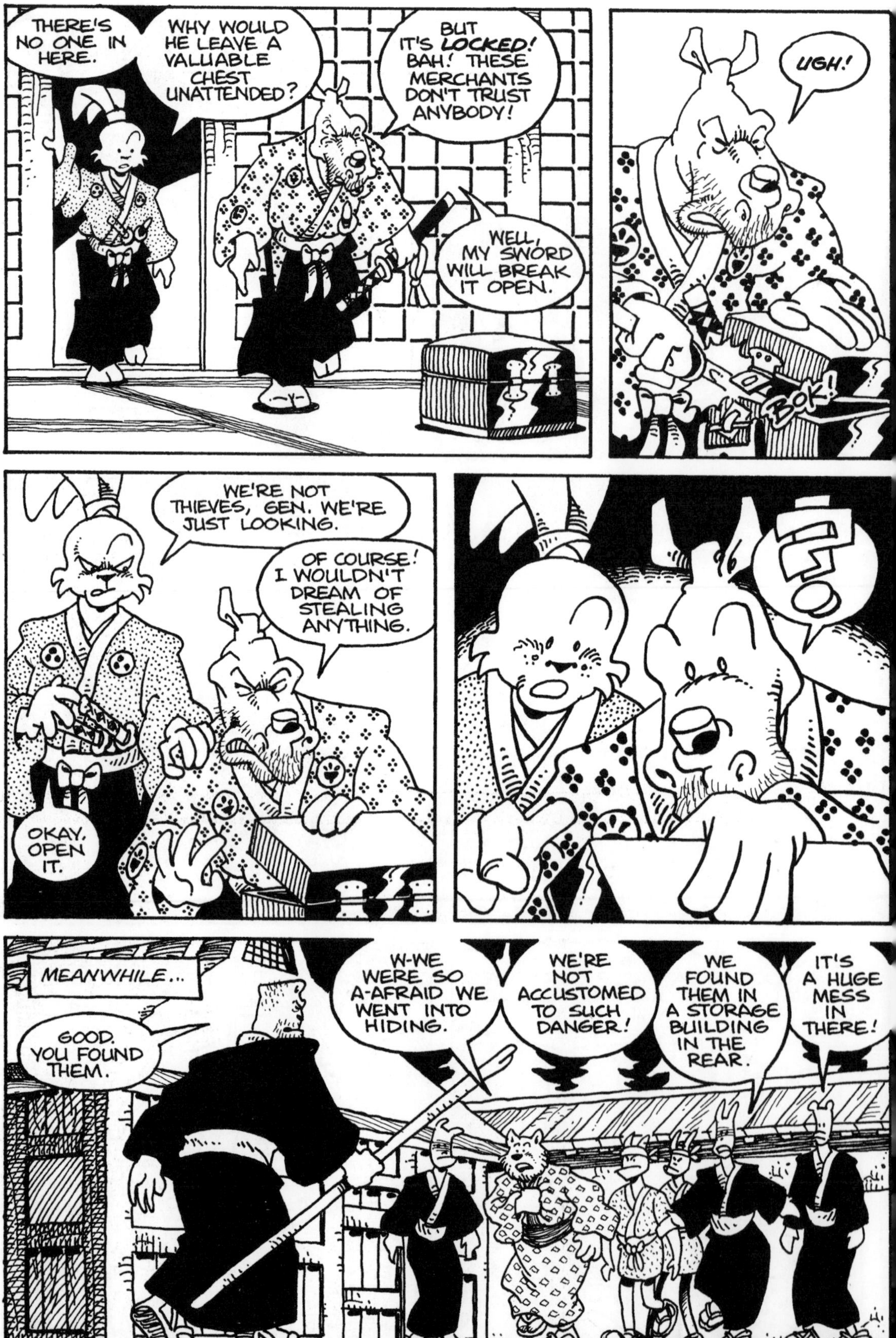
THERE'S NO ONE IN HERE.
WHY WOULD HE LEAVE A VALUABLE CHEST UNATTENDED?
BUT IT'S LOCKED! BAH! THESE MERCHANTS DON'T TRUST ANYBODY!
WELL, MY SWORD WILL BREAK IT OPEN.
UGH!
BOK!
WE'RE NOT THIEVES, GEN. WE'RE JUST LOOKING.
OF COURSE! I WOULDN'T DREAM OF STEALING ANYTHING.
OKAY. OPEN IT.
?
MEANWHILE...
GOOD. YOU FOUND THEM.
W-WE WERE SO A-AFRAID WE WENT INTO HIDING.
WE'RE NOT ACCUSTOMED TO SUCH DANGER!
WE FOUND THEM IN A STORAGE BUILDING IN THE REAR.
IT'S A HUGE MESS IN THERE!
12.

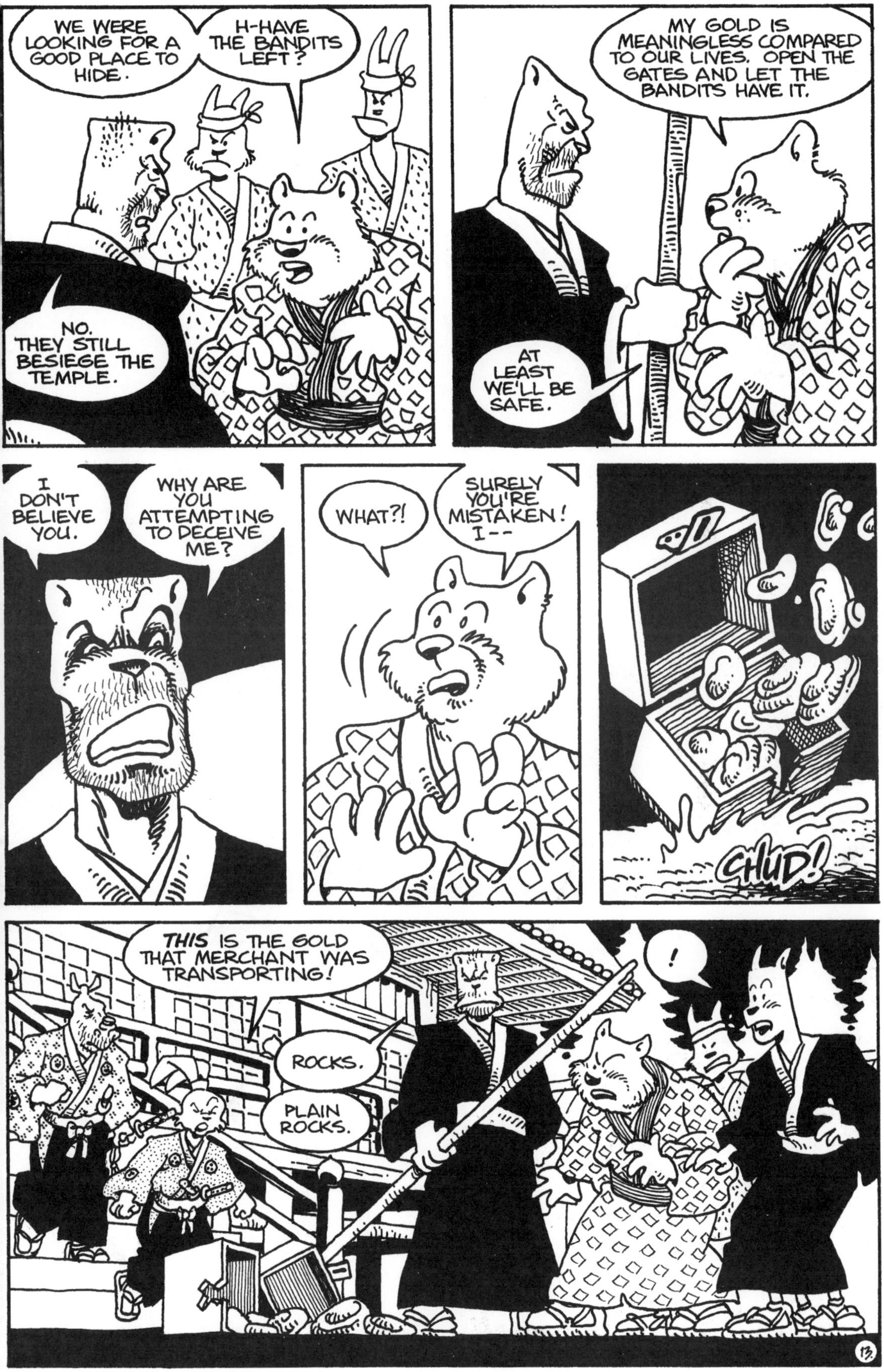

WE WERE LOOKING FOR A GOOD PLACE TO HIDE.
H-HAVE THE BANDITS LEFT?
NO. THEY STILL BESIEGE THE TEMPLE.
MY GOLD IS MEANINGLESS COMPARED TO OUR LIVES. OPEN THE GATES AND LET THE BANDITS HAVE IT.
AT LEAST WE'LL BE SAFE.
I DON'T BELIEVE YOU.
WHY ARE YOU ATTEMPTING TO DECEIVE ME?
WHAT?!
SURELY YOU'RE MISTAKEN! I--
CHUD!
THIS IS THE GOLD THAT MERCHANT WAS TRANSPORTING!
ROCKS.
PLAIN ROCKS.
!
13

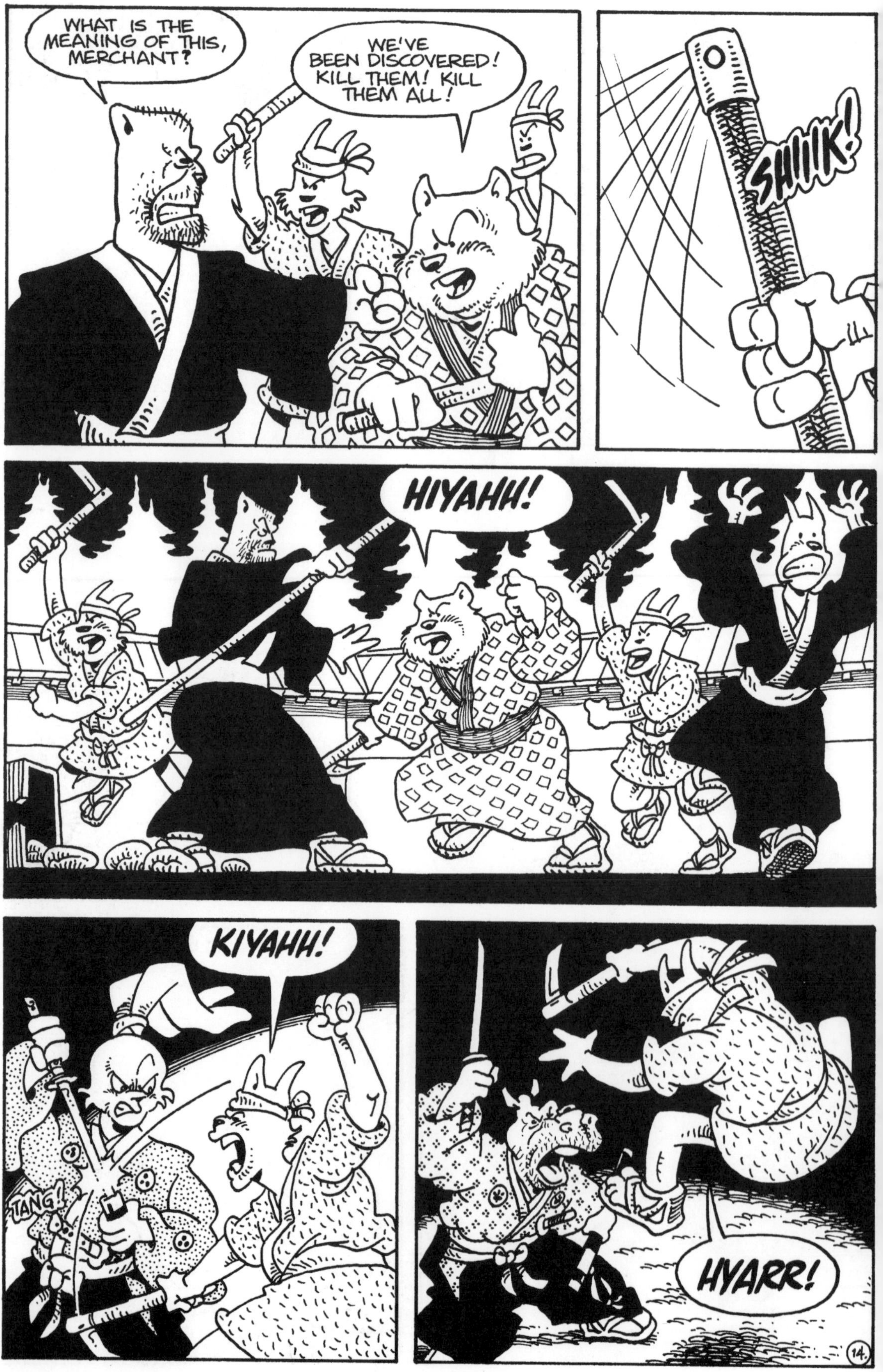

WHAT IS THE MEANING OF THIS, MERCHANT?
WE'VE BEEN DISCOVERED! KILL THEM! KILL THEM ALL!
SHIIIK!
HIYAHH!
KIYAHH!
TANG!
HYARR!
14.

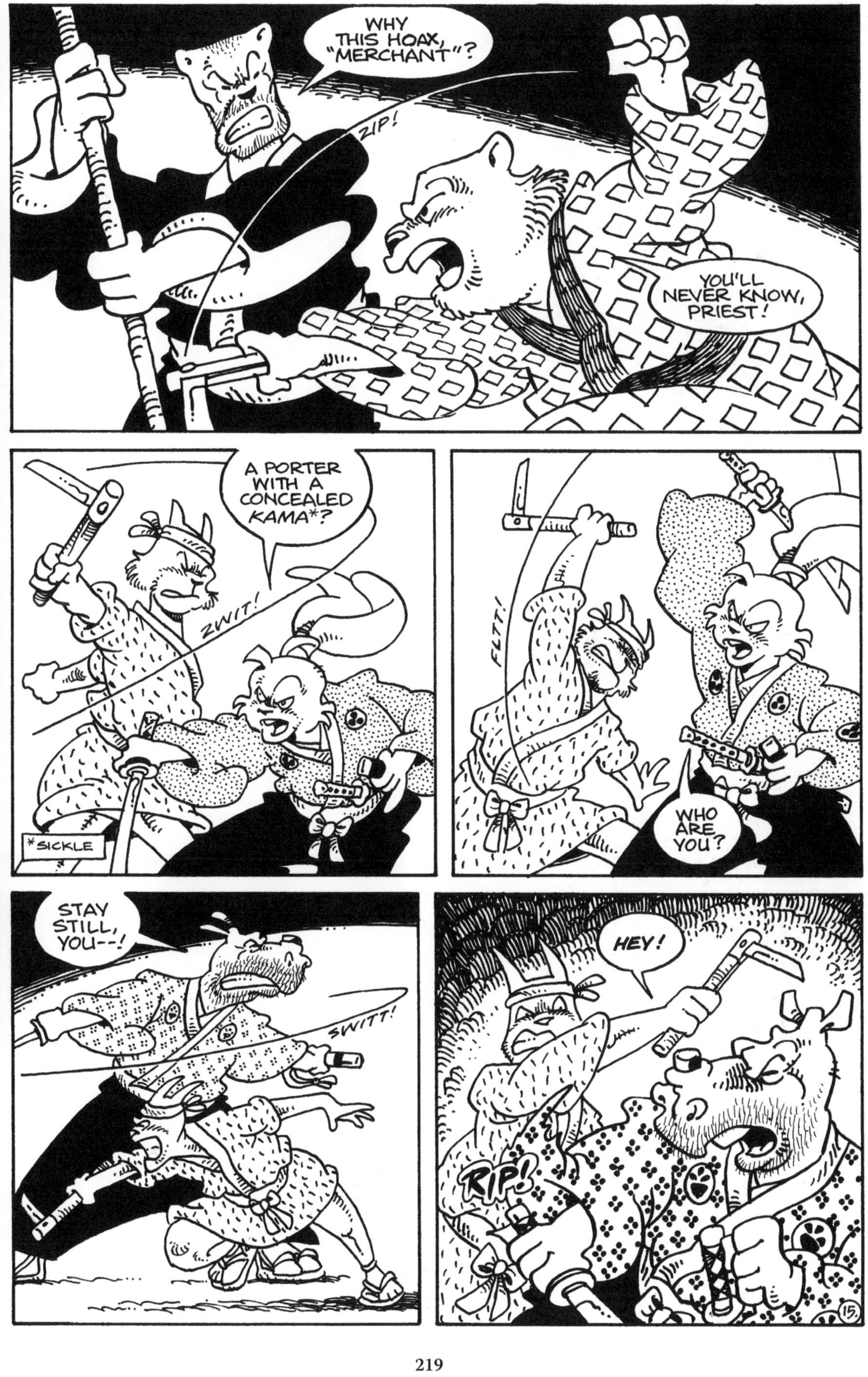
WHY THIS HOAX, "MERCHANT"?
ZIP!
YOU'LL NEVER KNOW, PRIEST!
A PORTER WITH A CONCEALED KAMA*?
ZWIT!
*SICKLE
FLTT!
WHO ARE YOU?
STAY STILL, YOU--!
SWITT!
HEY!
RIP!
15.

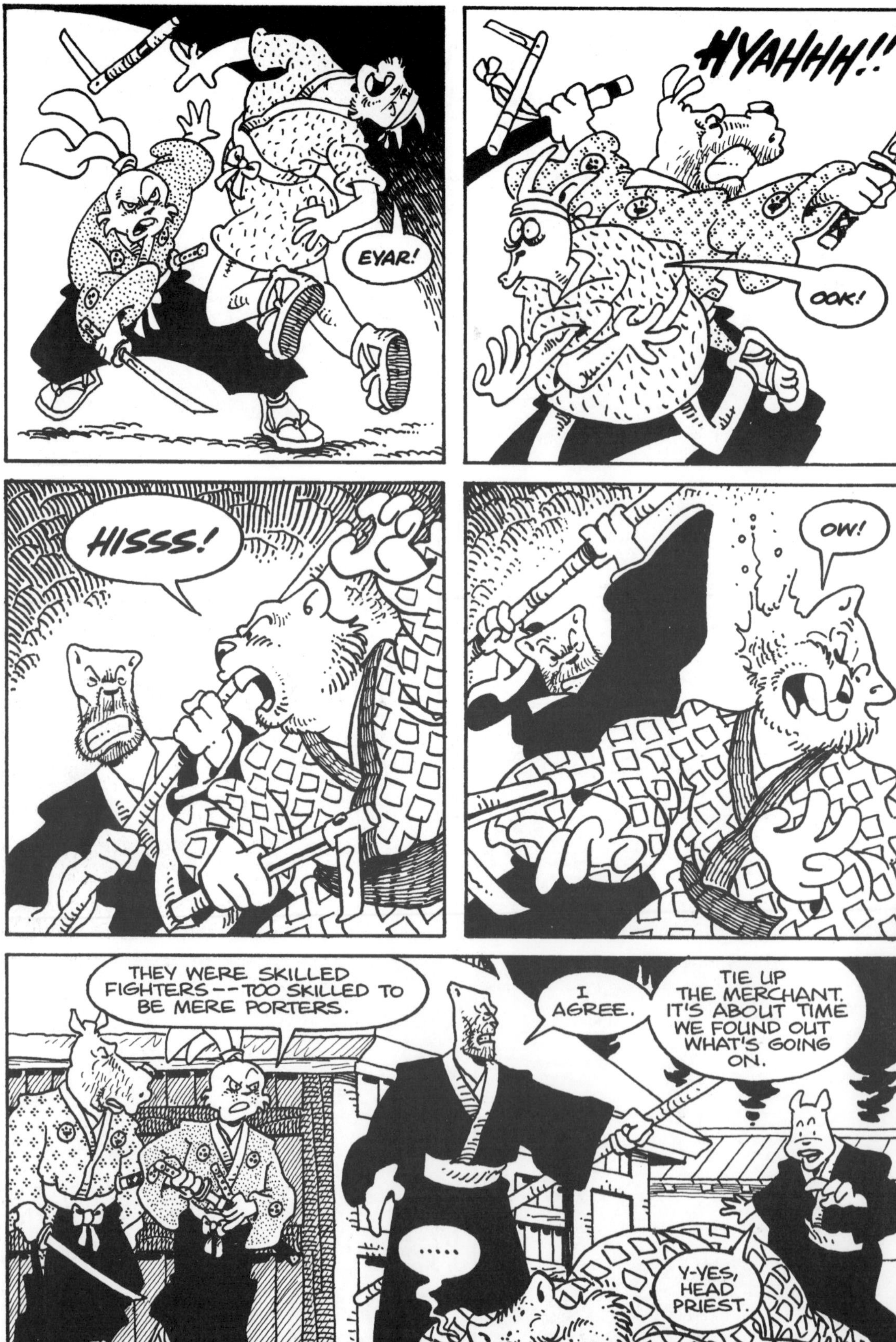
EYAR!
HYAHHH!!
OOK!
HISSS!
OW!
THEY WERE SKILLED FIGHTERS--TOO SKILLED TO BE MERE PORTERS.
I AGREE.
TIE UP THE MERCHANT. IT'S ABOUT TIME WE FOUND OUT WHAT'S GOING ON.
.....
Y-YES, HEAD PRIEST.
16.

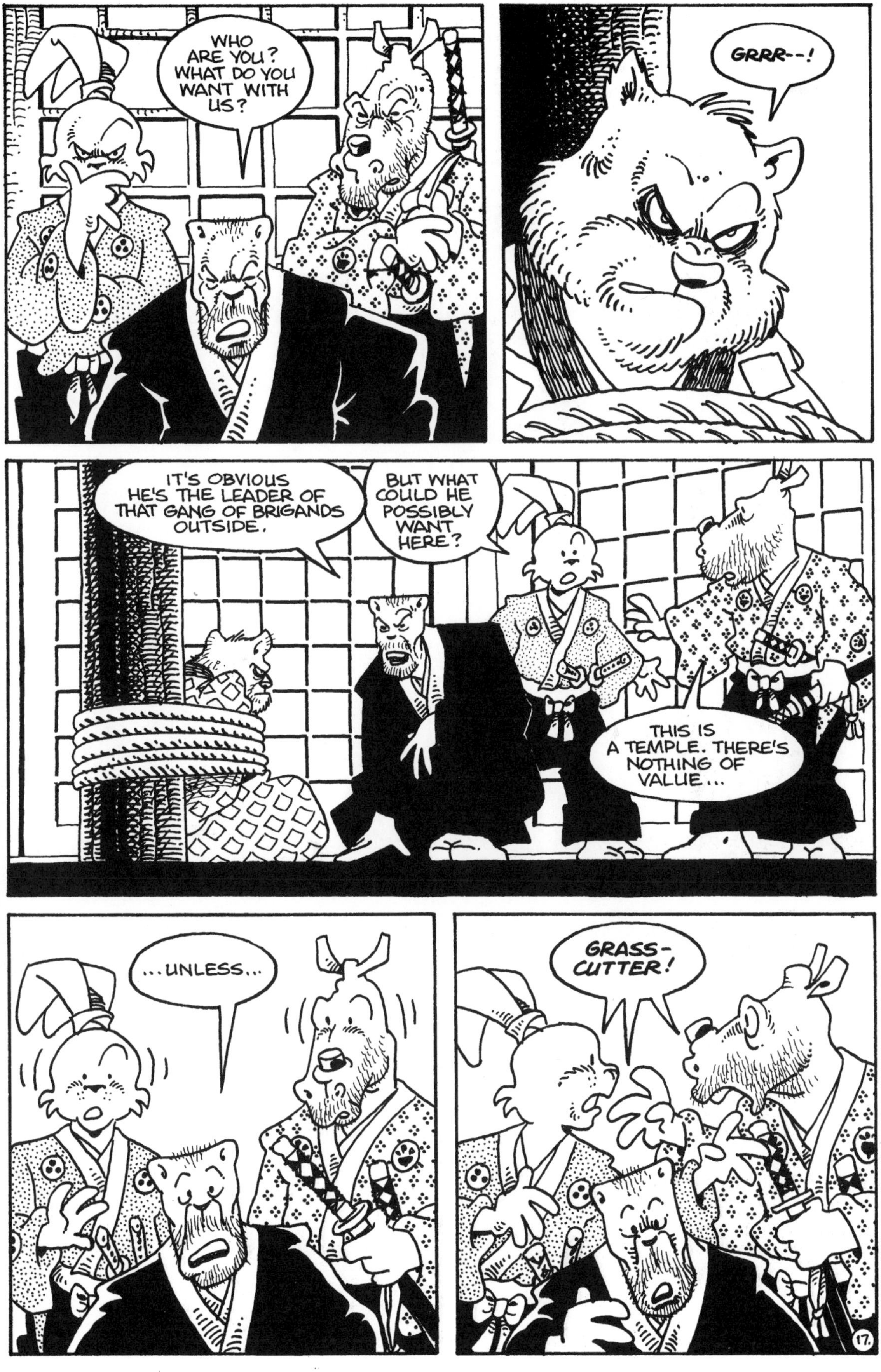
WHO ARE YOU? WHAT DO YOU WANT WITH US?
GRRR--!
IT'S OBVIOUS HE'S THE LEADER OF THAT GANG OF BRIGANDS OUTSIDE.
BUT WHAT COULD HE POSSIBLY WANT HERE?
THIS IS A TEMPLE. THERE'S NOTHING OF VALUE...
...UNLESS...
GRASS-CUTTER!
17.

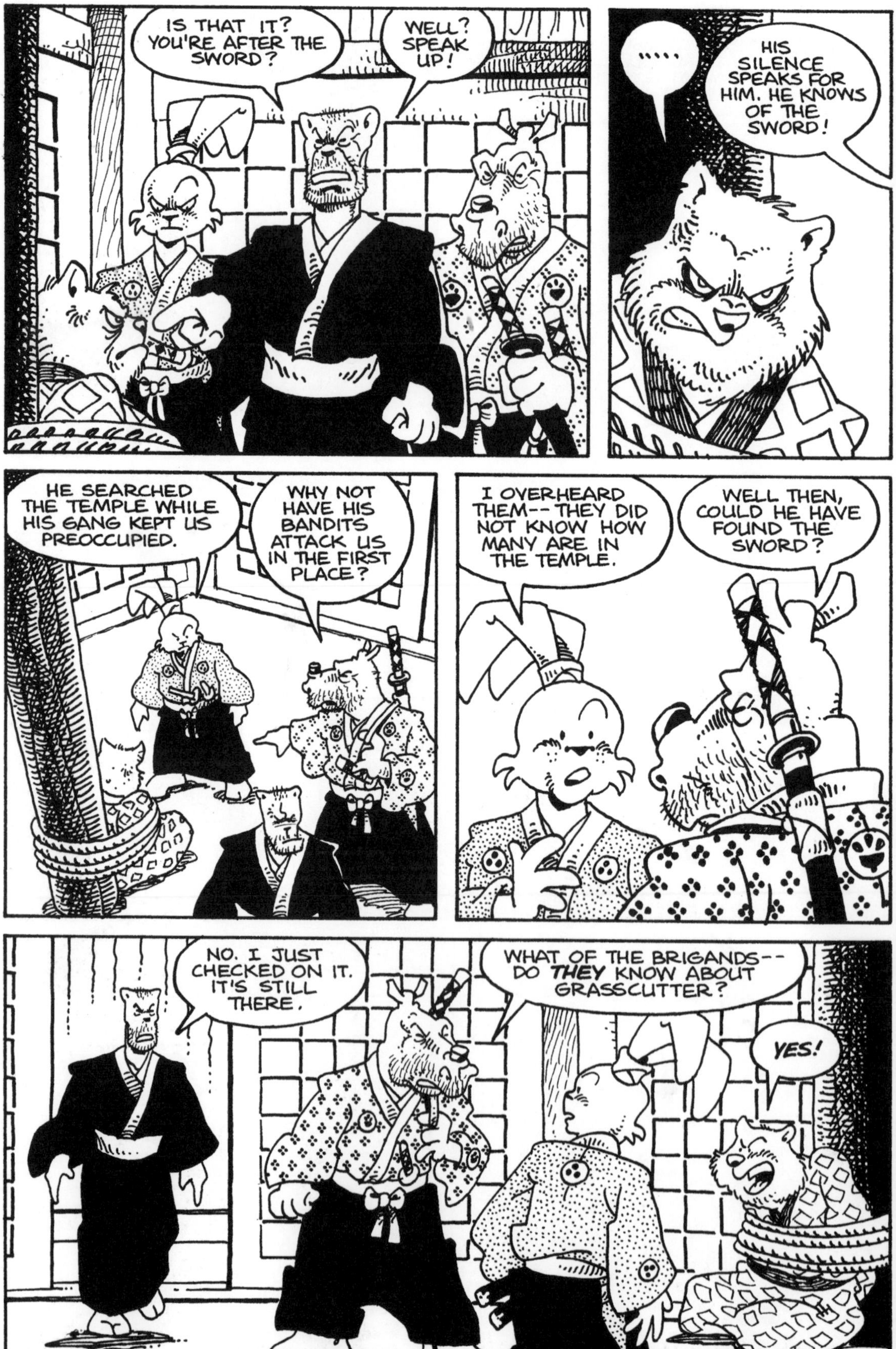
IS THAT IT? YOU'RE AFTER THE SWORD?
WELL? SPEAK UP!
.....
HIS SILENCE SPEAKS FOR HIM. HE KNOWS OF THE SWORD!
HE SEARCHED THE TEMPLE WHILE HIS GANG KEPT US PREOCCUPIED.
WHY NOT HAVE HIS BANDITS ATTACK US IN THE FIRST PLACE?
I OVERHEARD THEM-- THEY DID NOT KNOW HOW MANY ARE IN THE TEMPLE.
WELL THEN, COULD HE HAVE FOUND THE SWORD?
NO. I JUST CHECKED ON IT. IT'S STILL THERE.
WHAT OF THE BRIGANDS-- DO THEY KNOW ABOUT GRASSCUTTER?
YES!
18.

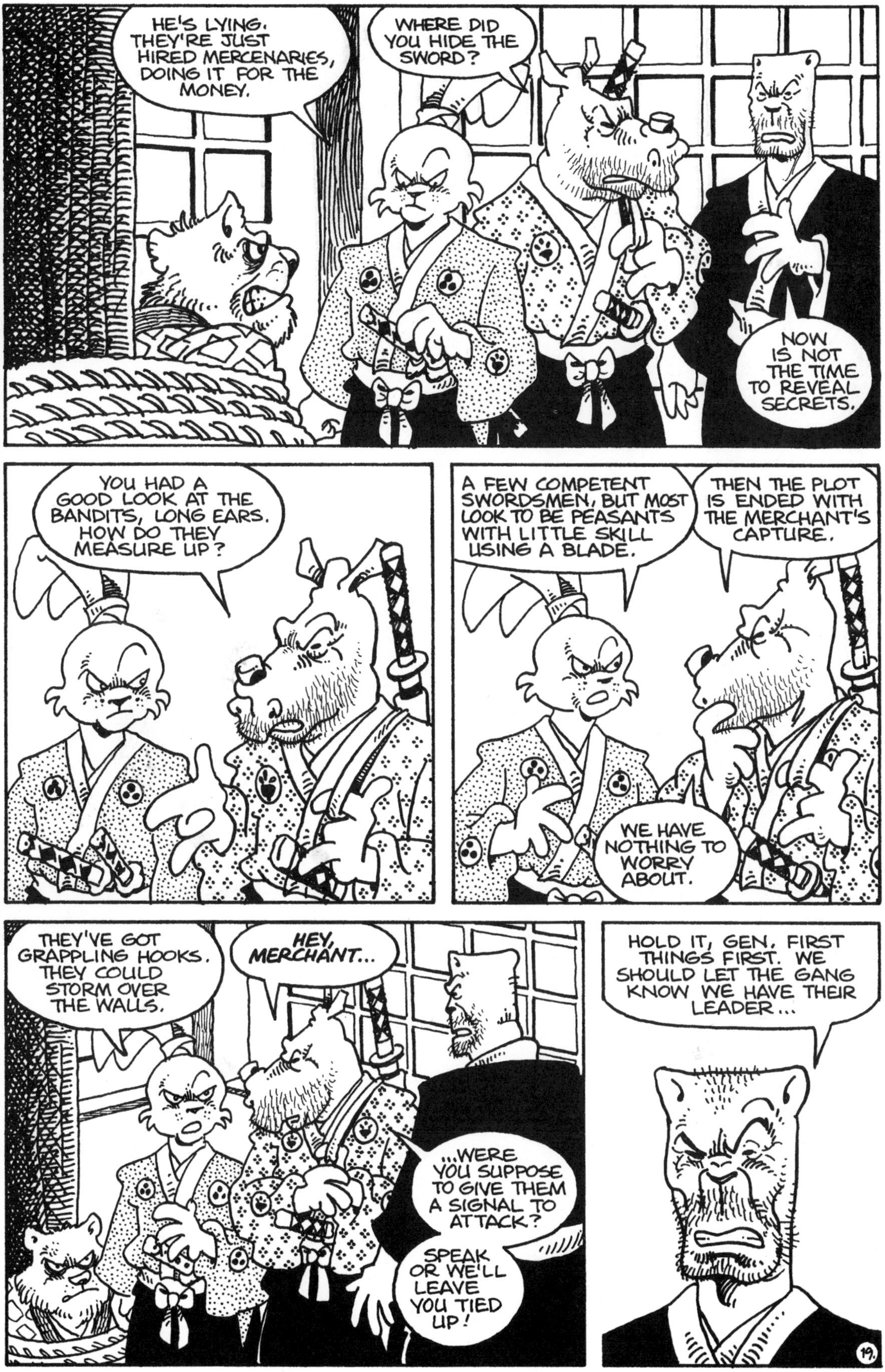
HE'S LYING. THEY'RE JUST HIRED MERCENARIES, DOING IT FOR THE MONEY.
WHERE DID YOU HIDE THE SWORD?
NOW IS NOT THE TIME TO REVEAL SECRETS.
YOU HAD A GOOD LOOK AT THE BANDITS, LONG EARS. HOW DO THEY MEASURE UP?
A FEW COMPETENT SWORDSMEN, BUT MOST LOOK TO BE PEASANTS WITH LITTLE SKILL USING A BLADE.
THEN THE PLOT IS ENDED WITH THE MERCHANT'S CAPTURE.
WE HAVE NOTHING TO WORRY ABOUT.
THEY'VE GOT GRAPPLING HOOKS. THEY COULD STORM OVER THE WALLS.
HEY, MERCHANT...
...WERE YOU SUPPOSE TO GIVE THEM A SIGNAL TO ATTACK?
SPEAK OR WE'LL LEAVE YOU TIED UP!
HOLD IT, GEN. FIRST THINGS FIRST. WE SHOULD LET THE GANG KNOW WE HAVE THEIR LEADER...
19.

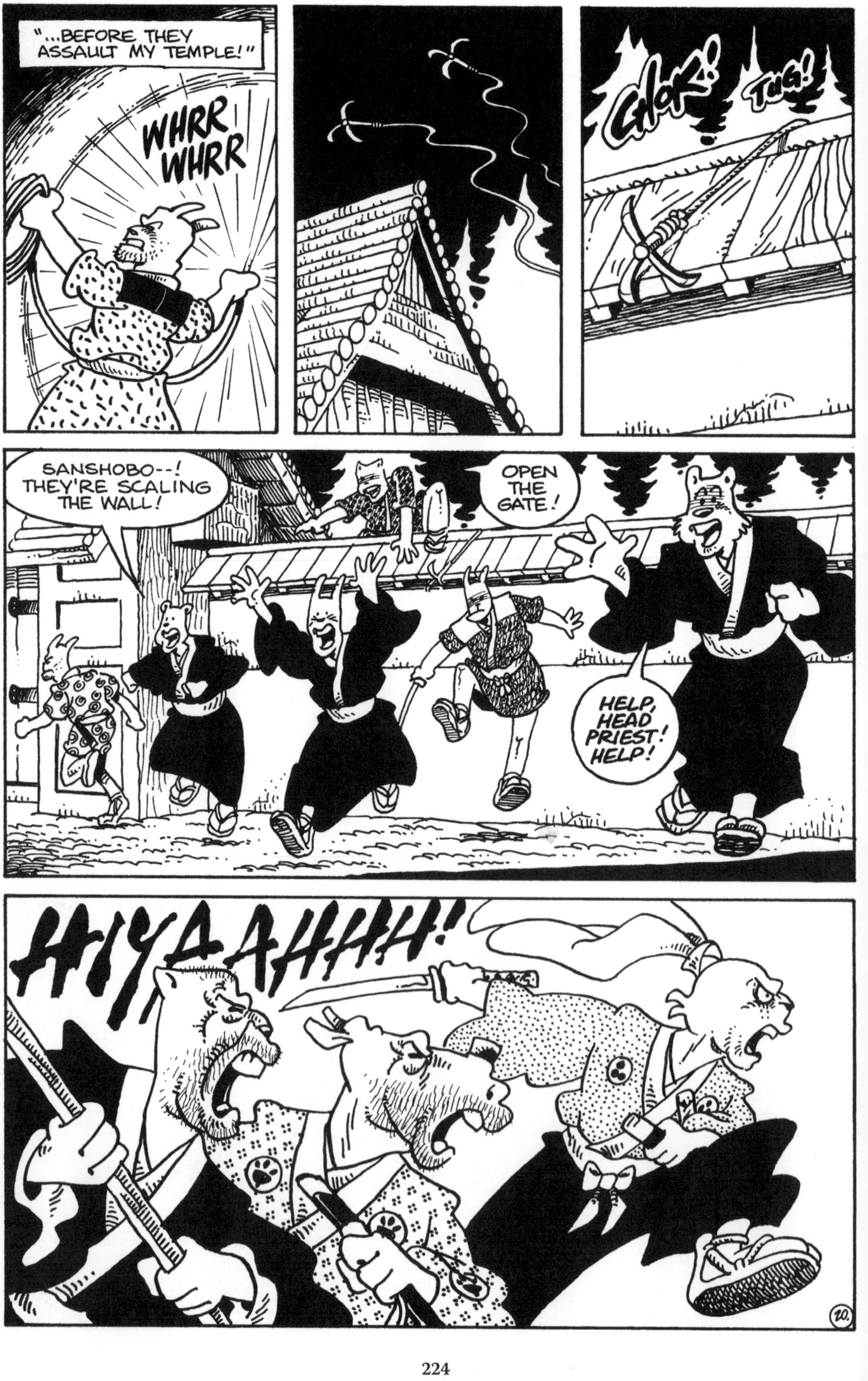
"...BEFORE THEY ASSAULT MY TEMPLE!"
WHRR WHRR
GLOK!
TUG!
SANSHOBO--! THEY'RE SCALING THE WALL!
OPEN THE GATE!
HELP, HEAD PRIEST! HELP!
HIYAAHHH!
20.

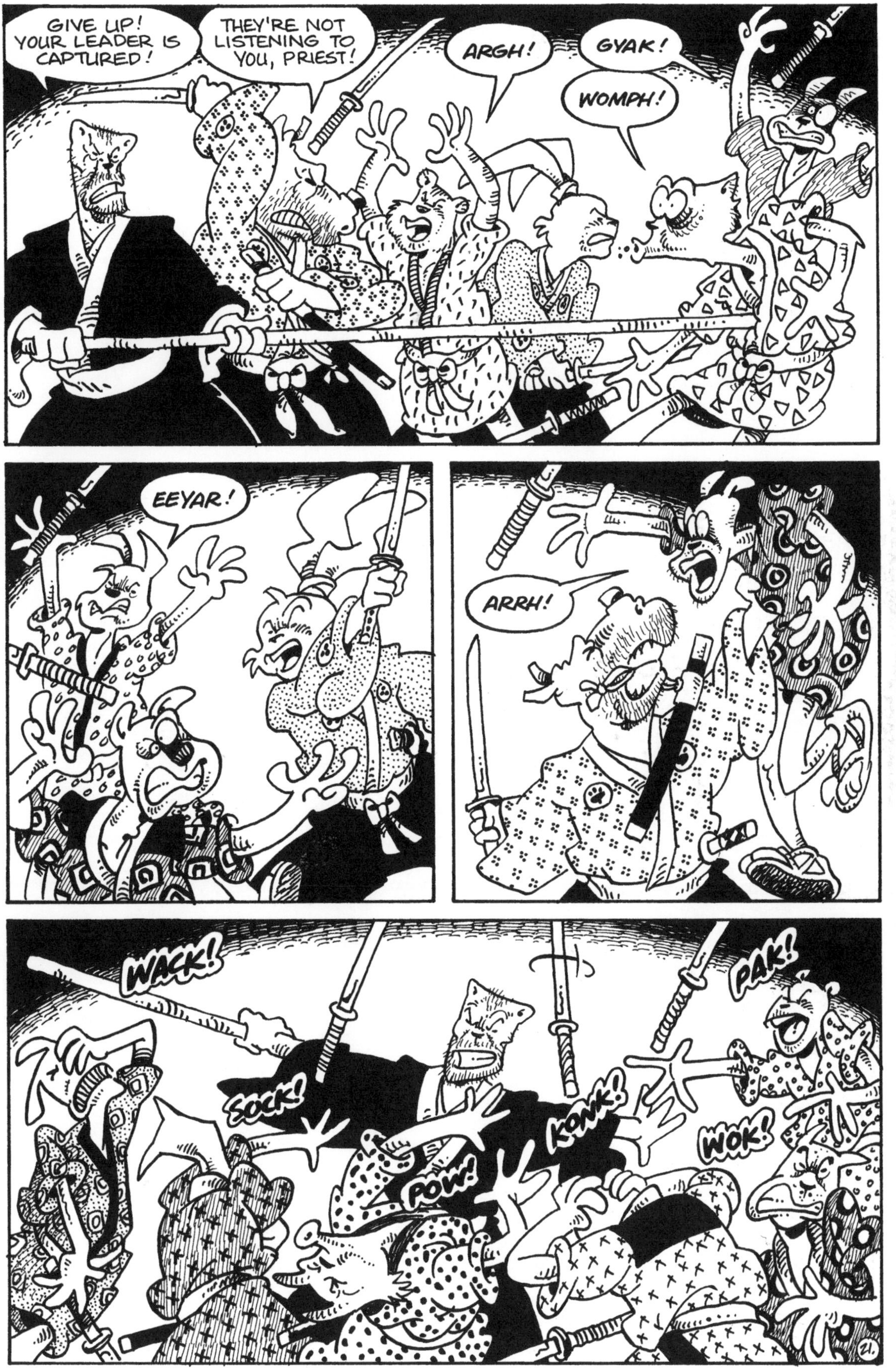
GIVE UP! YOUR LEADER IS CAPTURED!
THEY'RE NOT LISTENING TO YOU, PRIEST!
ARGH!
GYAK!
WOMPH!
EEYAR!
ARRH!
WACK!
PAK!
SOCK!
KONK!
WOK!
POW!
21.

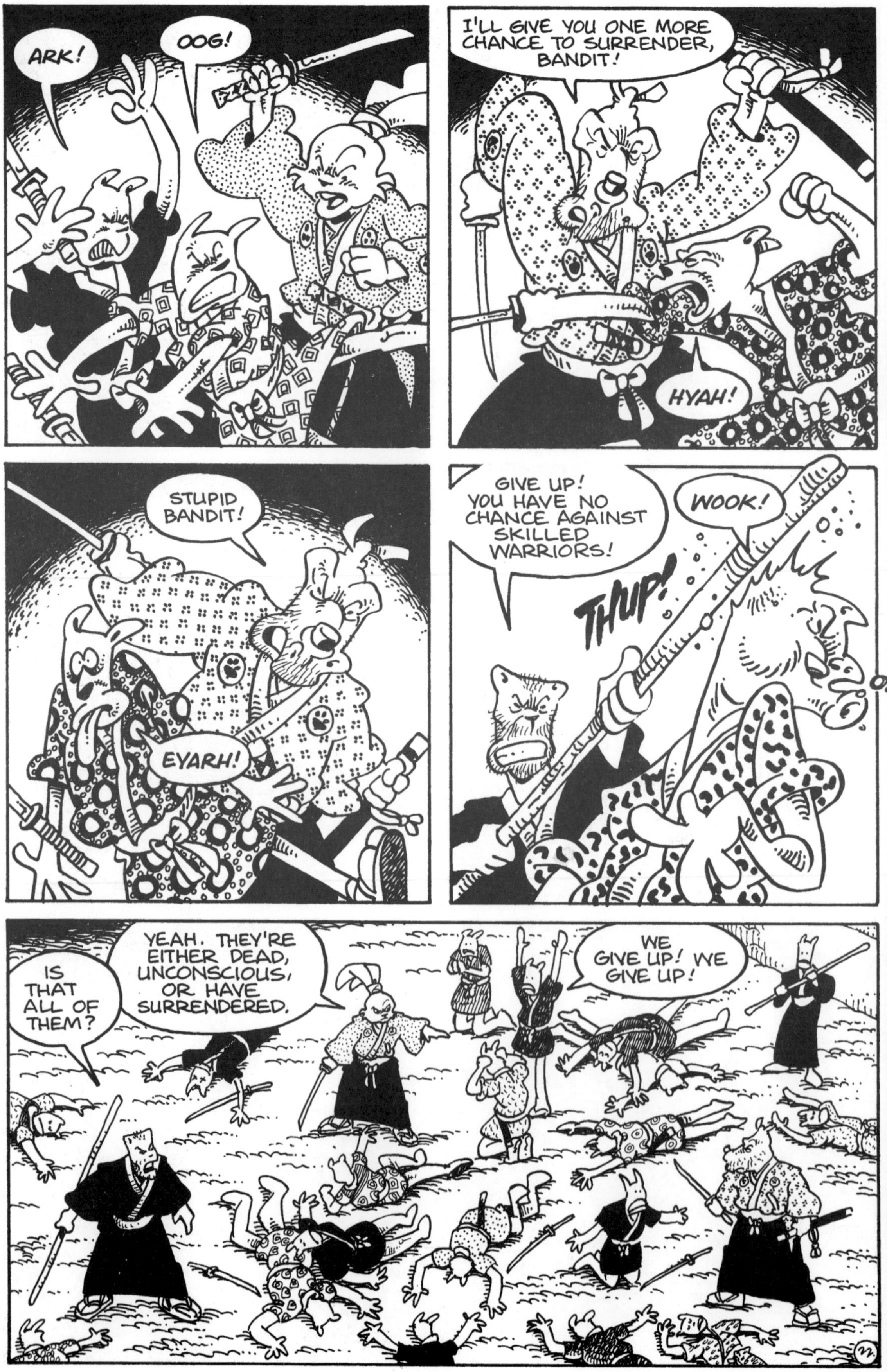
ARK!
OOG!
I'LL GIVE YOU ONE MORE CHANCE TO SURRENDER, BANDIT!
HYAH!
STUPID BANDIT!
EYARH!
GIVE UP! YOU HAVE NO CHANCE AGAINST SKILLED WARRIORS!
WOOK!
THUP!
IS THAT ALL OF THEM?
YEAH. THEY'RE EITHER DEAD, UNCONSCIOUS, OR HAVE SURRENDERED.
WE GIVE UP! WE GIVE UP!

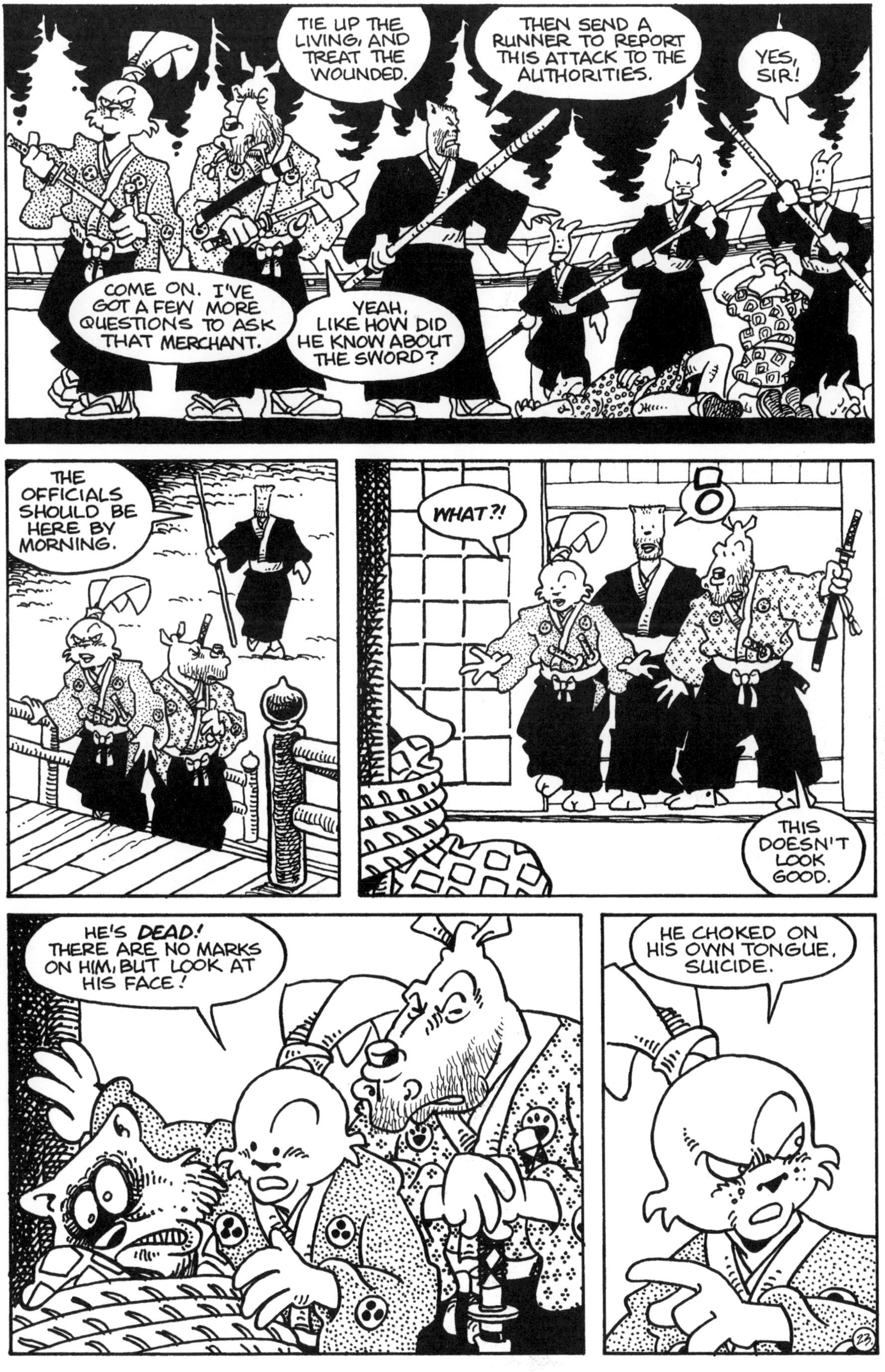
TIE UP THE LIVING, AND TREAT THE WOUNDED.
THEN SEND A RUNNER TO REPORT THIS ATTACK TO THE AUTHORITIES.
YES, SIR!
COME ON. I'VE GOT A FEW MORE QUESTIONS TO ASK THAT MERCHANT.
YEAH, LIKE HOW DID HE KNOW ABOUT THE SWORD?
THE OFFICIALS SHOULD BE HERE BY MORNING.
WHAT?!
THIS DOESN'T LOOK GOOD.
HE'S DEAD! THERE ARE NO MARKS ON HIM, BUT LOOK AT HIS FACE!
HE CHOKED ON HIS OWN TONGUE. SUICIDE.
23

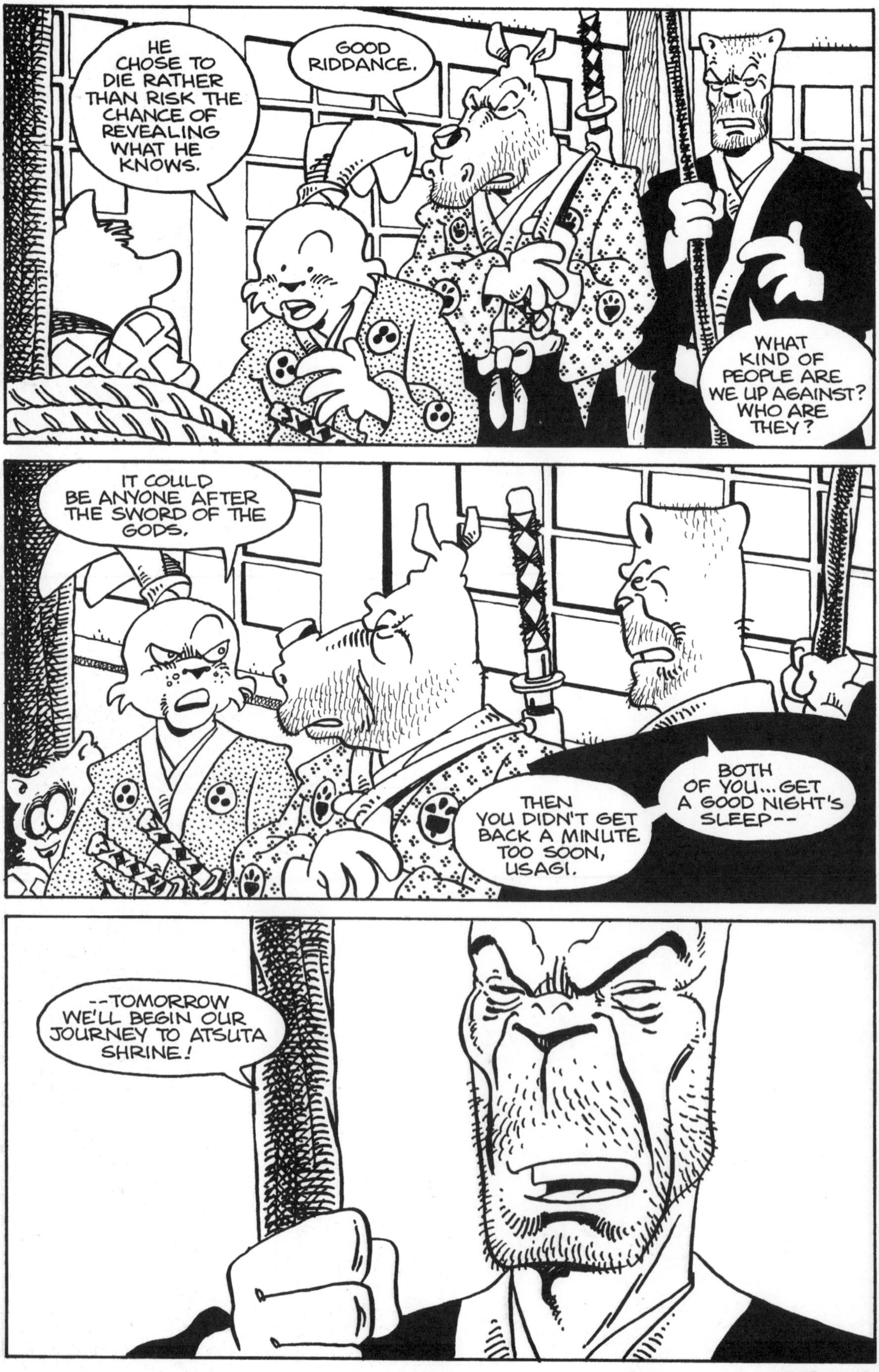
HE CHOSE TO DIE RATHER THAN RISK THE CHANCE OF REVEALING WHAT HE KNOWS.
GOOD RIDDANCE.
WHAT KIND OF PEOPLE ARE WE UP AGAINST? WHO ARE THEY?
IT COULD BE ANYONE AFTER THE SWORD OF THE GODS.
THEN YOU DIDN'T GET BACK A MINUTE TOO SOON, USAGI.
BOTH OF YOU...GET A GOOD NIGHT'S SLEEP--
--TOMORROW WE'LL BEGIN OUR JOURNEY TO ATSUTA SHRINE!

THE END

GRASSCUTTER II

INTRODUCTION

THERE'S A MARK TWAIN LINE that I'm fond of paraphrasing, one of those well-burnished pearls o' wisdom that I drop whenever someone comes to me and asks for advice on writing.

"I never use 'policeman' for a dime when I can get 'cop' for a nickel."

When pressed, I explain that—at least to me—Twain's talking about efficiency and economy, talking about the need of the artist to get out of the way of his or her work. He's cautioning against self-indulgence, something that every artist in every medium must guard against. The worst thing a storyteller can do is believe that he is more important than the story being told.

But I've said it so often, it's starting to sound a little hollow, even to me.

Then I pick up some of Stan Sakai's work, I read a tale of Usagi and Gen, and the truth of it comes back—the essence of storytelling, and perhaps even the essence of capital-*A* Art, is honesty. The resonance of the image, the power of the story, the emotional connection the audience makes with the work, all of it lives or dies on the basis of its honesty. Set your story in the far-flung reaches of the universe with great quantum-drive battle cruisers, set it in a superheroic, nihilistic future, hell, set it in feudal Japan with your cast portrayed as anthropomorphized rhinos and rabbits—it doesn't matter as long as the story is fundamentally *honest.*

Because there are things we all share. We've all been cold; we've all been hungry. We've all been betrayed, if not all of us on a grand scale. We've all loved.

We've all lost.

The best storyteller can hold those truths in one hand, and conjure the tale in the other. The best storyteller can mesh them seamlessly, creating a connection with his audience that at once is both fantastic and absolutely real. In the ideal, a tale is told that resonates long after the last word is read, the last image viewed.

Stan Sakai . . . Stan Sakai not only does this, but he does it consistently, issue after issue, executing with elegance and economy the epic of *Usagi Yojimbo.* This collection is Sakai at his best—not a word out of place, not a brushstroke laid in error.

Disguised as an adventure story of the most elementary kind—what can be more basic than a chase, after all?—*Grasscutter II* is so much more. From the foreshadowing prologue to the haunting first epilogue, Sakai teases out themes in word and image that first propel the narrative, then move the heart. His language, both in text and image, is succinct, deft, and ever precise.

Nothing in these pages is wasted.

In an age of self-indulgence, where more and more comics and their creators are enamored of flash and image, Stan Sakai never stands in the way of his own work. When we as a profession seem to be moving both forward and back all at the same time, that may be the highest praise anyone can offer.

Enjoy your journey to Atsuta.

Abayo!

Greg Rucka
Portland, Oregon
December 2001

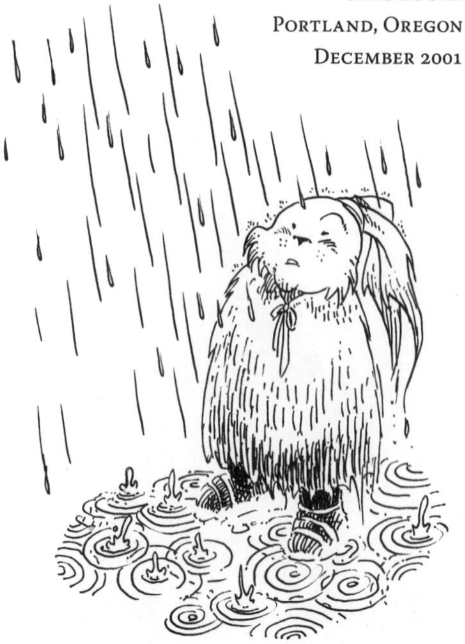

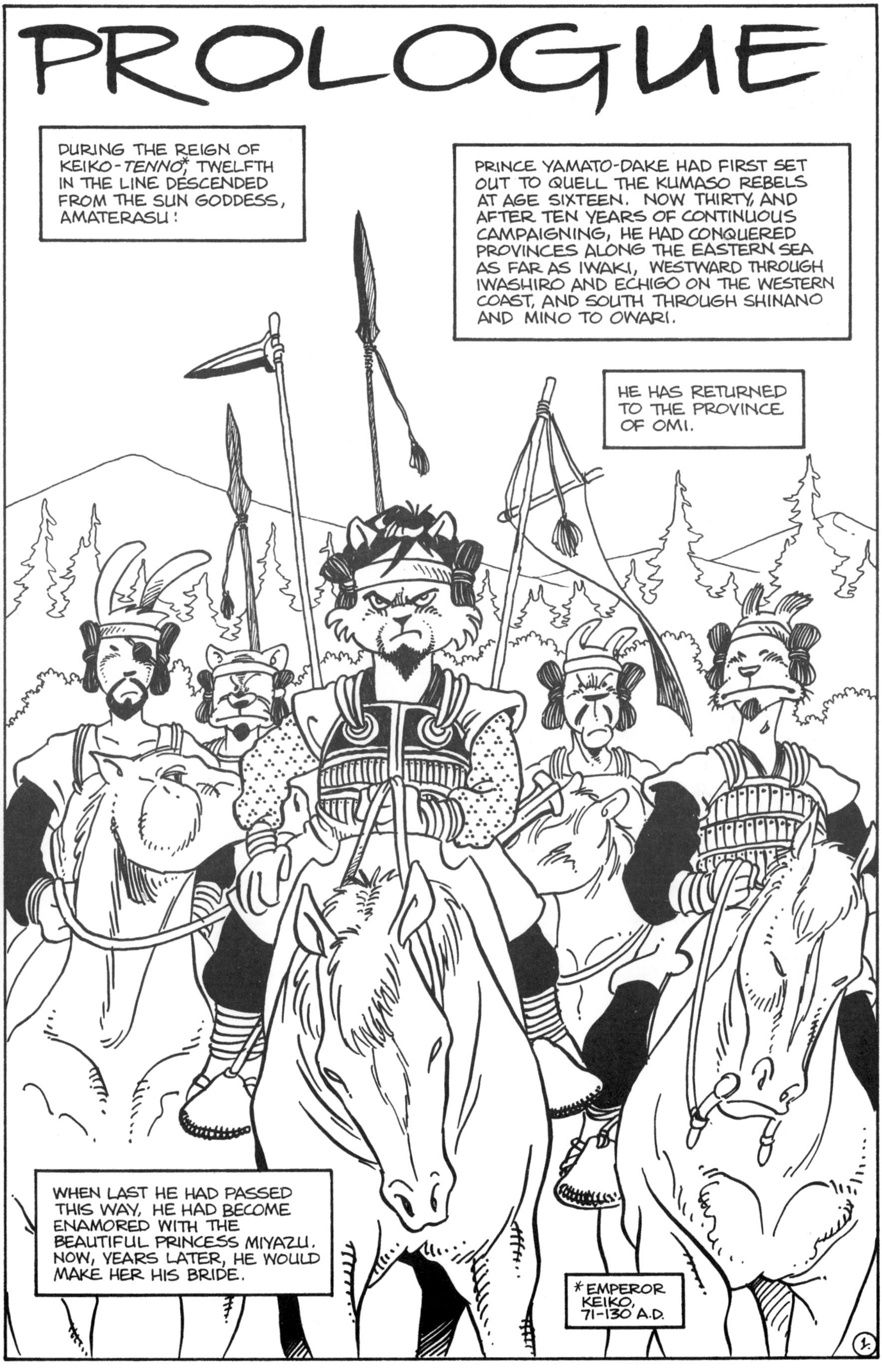
PROLOGUE
DURING THE REIGN OF KEIKO-*TENNO*,* TWELFTH IN THE LINE DESCENDED FROM THE SUN GODDESS, AMATERASU:
PRINCE YAMATO-DAKE HAD FIRST SET OUT TO QUELL THE KUMASO REBELS AT AGE SIXTEEN. NOW THIRTY, AND AFTER TEN YEARS OF CONTINUOUS CAMPAIGNING, HE HAD CONQUERED PROVINCES ALONG THE EASTERN SEA AS FAR AS IWAKI, WESTWARD THROUGH IWASHIRO AND ECHIGO ON THE WESTERN COAST, AND SOUTH THROUGH SHINANO AND MINO TO OWARI.
HE HAS RETURNED TO THE PROVINCE OF OMI.
WHEN LAST HE HAD PASSED THIS WAY, HE HAD BECOME ENAMORED WITH THE BEAUTIFUL PRINCESS MIYAZU. NOW, YEARS LATER, HE WOULD MAKE HER HIS BRIDE.
*EMPEROR KEIKO, 71-130 A.D.
1.

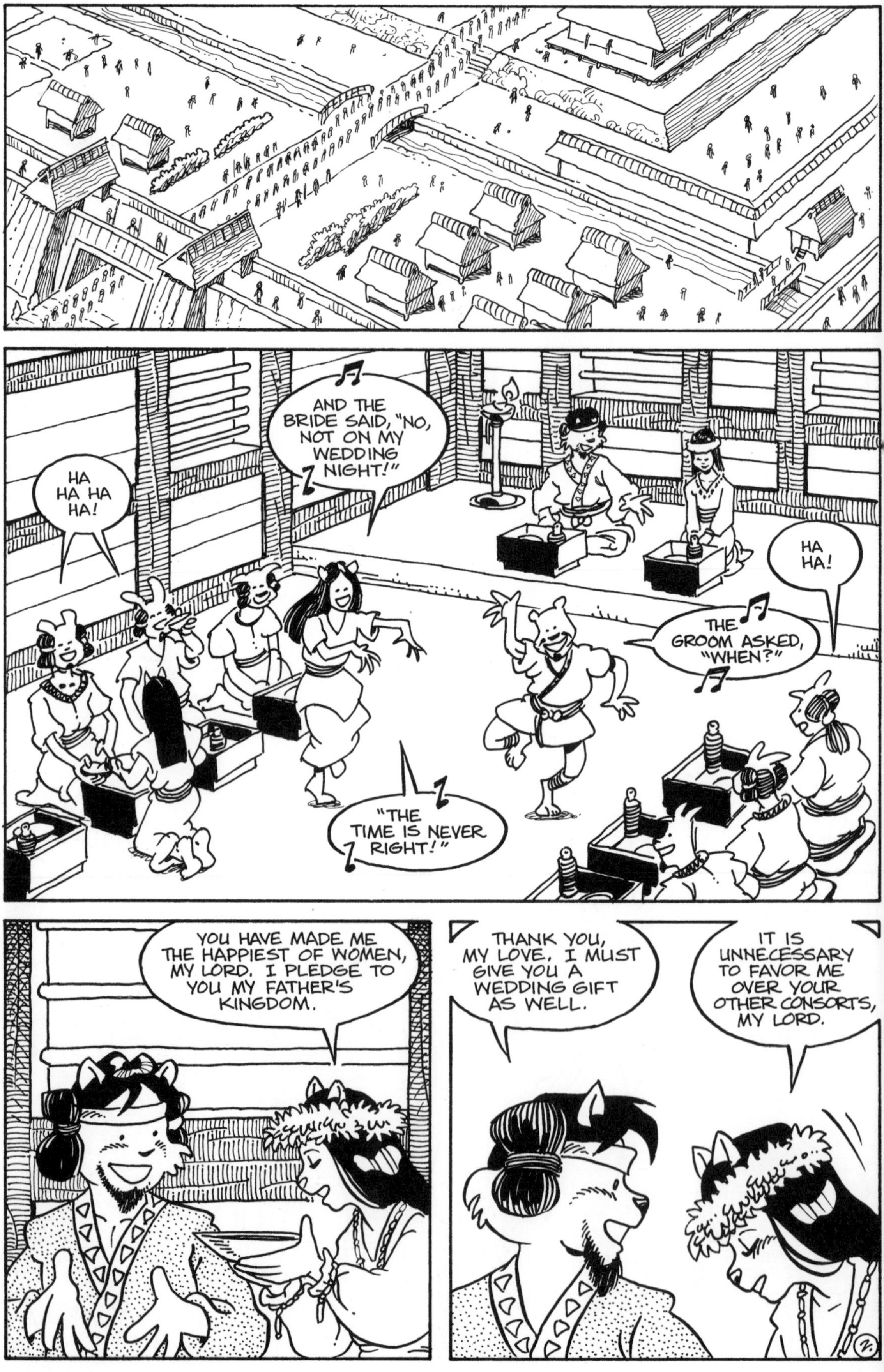
HA HA HA HA!
AND THE BRIDE SAID, "NO, NOT ON MY WEDDING NIGHT!"
THE GROOM ASKED, "WHEN?"
HA HA!
"THE TIME IS NEVER RIGHT!"
YOU HAVE MADE ME THE HAPPIEST OF WOMEN, MY LORD. I PLEDGE TO YOU MY FATHER'S KINGDOM.
THANK YOU, MY LOVE. I MUST GIVE YOU A WEDDING GIFT AS WELL.
IT IS UNNECESSARY TO FAVOR ME OVER YOUR OTHER CONSORTS, MY LORD.

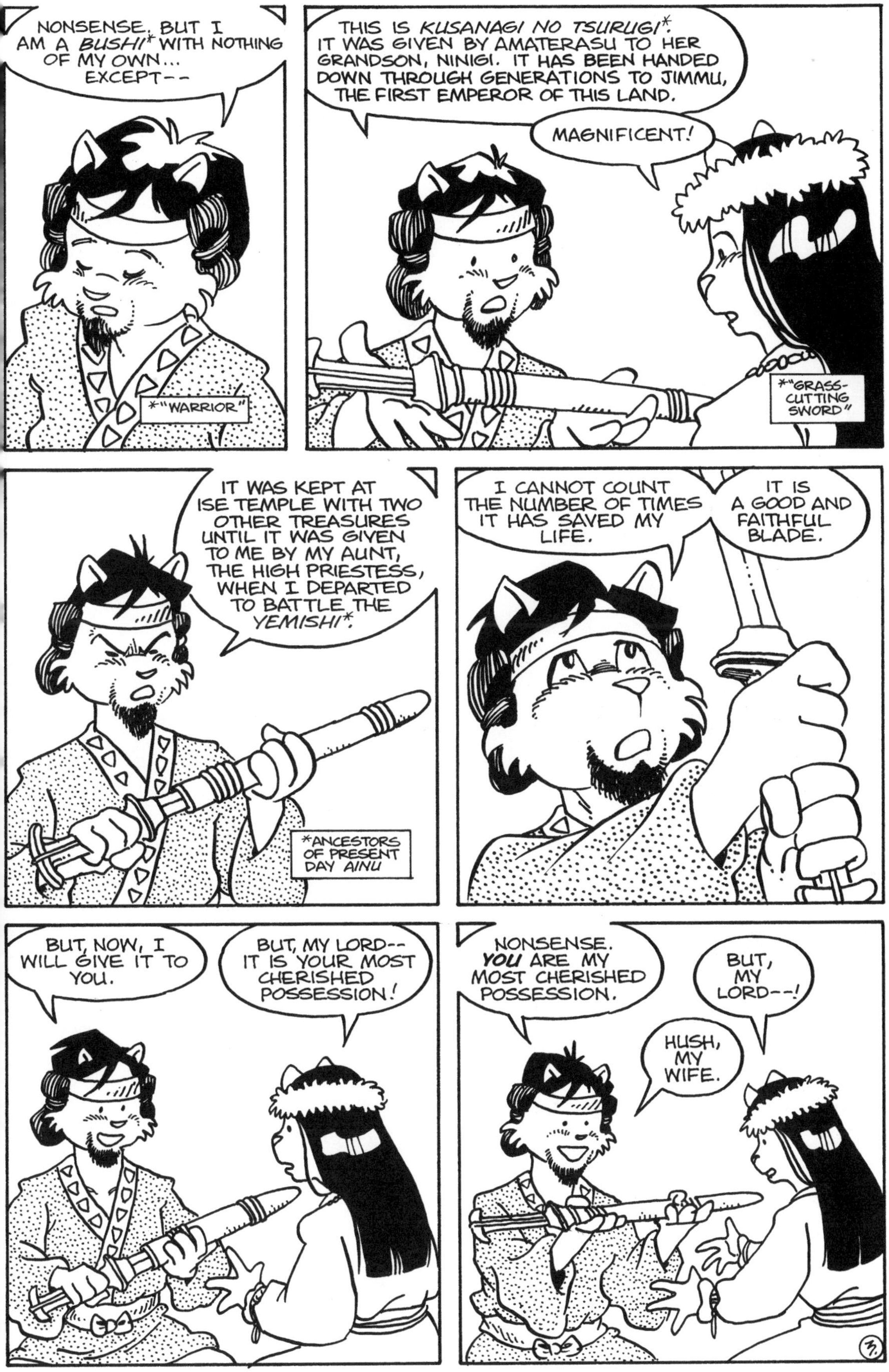
NONSENSE. BUT I AM A *BUSHI** WITH NOTHING OF MY OWN... EXCEPT--
*"WARRIOR"
THIS IS *KUSANAGI NO TSURUGI**. IT WAS GIVEN BY AMATERASU TO HER GRANDSON, NINIGI. IT HAS BEEN HANDED DOWN THROUGH GENERATIONS TO JIMMU, THE FIRST EMPEROR OF THIS LAND.
MAGNIFICENT!
*"GRASS-CUTTING SWORD"
IT WAS KEPT AT ISE TEMPLE WITH TWO OTHER TREASURES UNTIL IT WAS GIVEN TO ME BY MY AUNT, THE HIGH PRIESTESS, WHEN I DEPARTED TO BATTLE THE *YEMISHI**.
*ANCESTORS OF PRESENT DAY *AINU*
I CANNOT COUNT THE NUMBER OF TIMES IT HAS SAVED MY LIFE.
IT IS A GOOD AND FAITHFUL BLADE.
BUT, NOW, I WILL GIVE IT TO YOU.
BUT, MY LORD-- IT IS YOUR MOST CHERISHED POSSESSION!
NONSENSE. **YOU** ARE MY MOST CHERISHED POSSESSION.
BUT, MY LORD--!
HUSH, MY WIFE.
3.

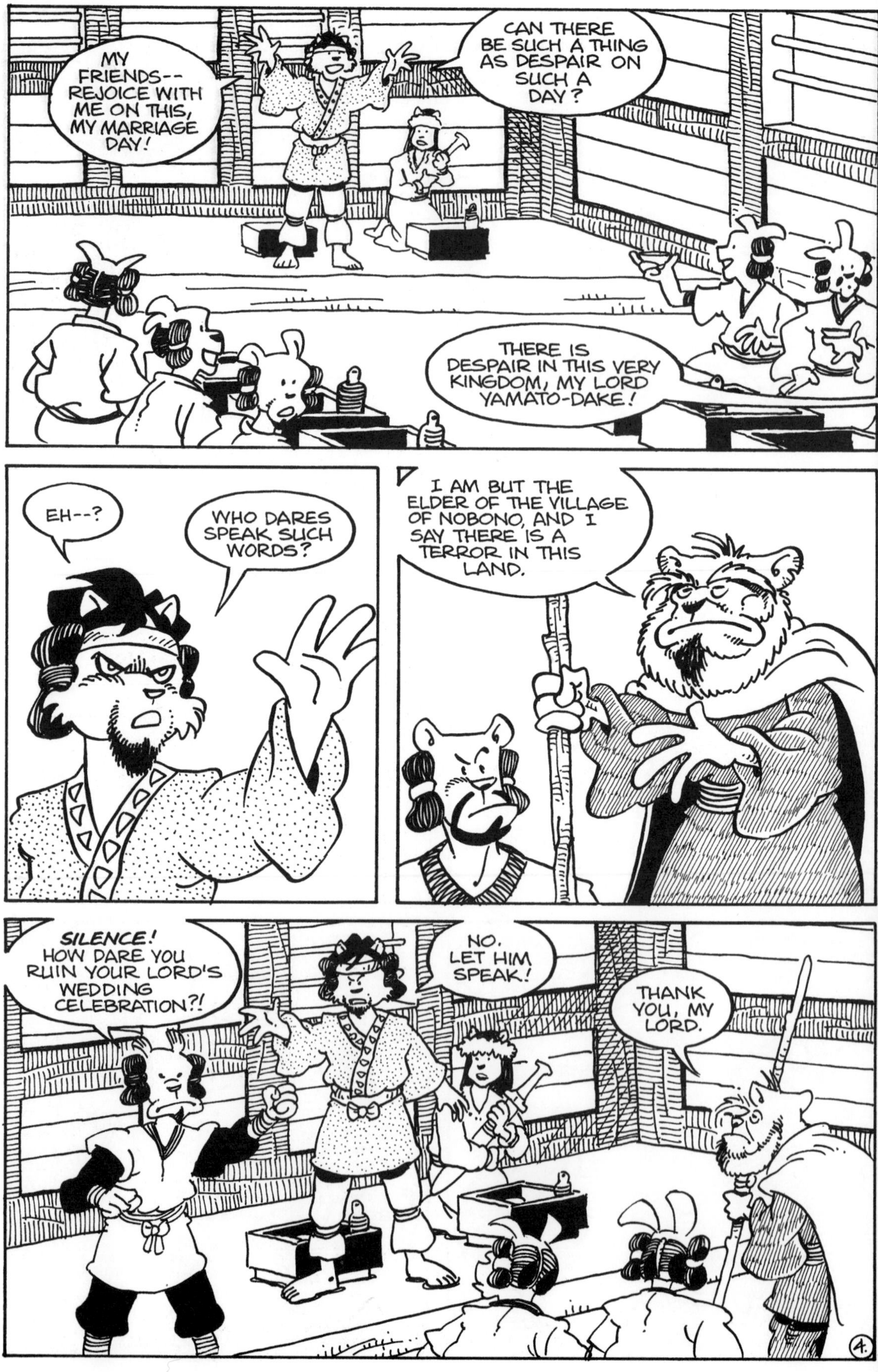
MY FRIENDS-- REJOICE WITH ME ON THIS, MY MARRIAGE DAY!
CAN THERE BE SUCH A THING AS DESPAIR ON SUCH A DAY?
THERE IS DESPAIR IN THIS VERY KINGDOM, MY LORD YAMATO-DAKE!
EH--?
WHO DARES SPEAK SUCH WORDS?
I AM BUT THE ELDER OF THE VILLAGE OF NOBONO, AND I SAY THERE IS A TERROR IN THIS LAND.
SILENCE! HOW DARE YOU RUIN YOUR LORD'S WEDDING CELEBRATION?!
NO. LET HIM SPEAK!
THANK YOU, MY LORD.
4.

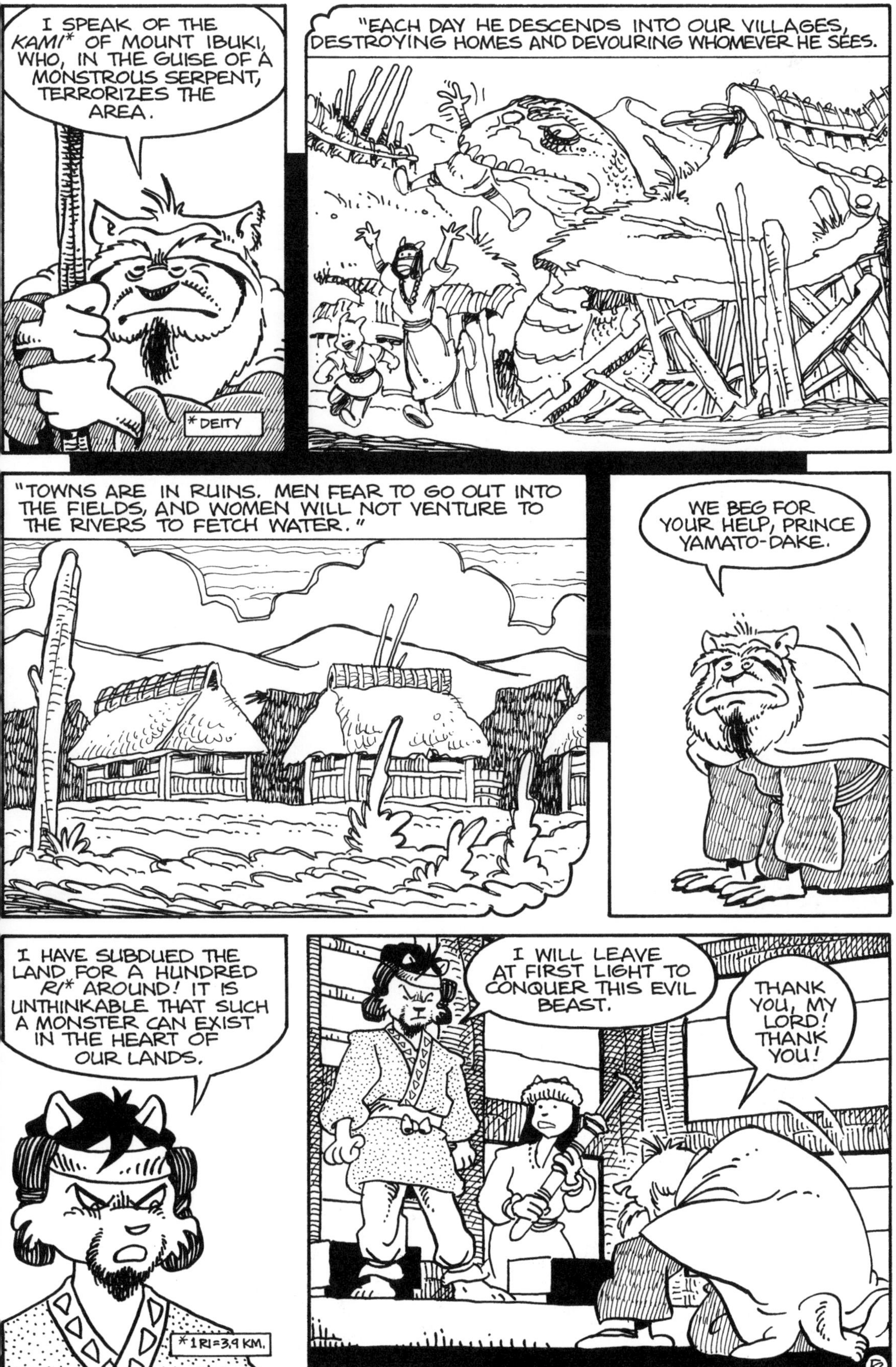
I SPEAK OF THE *KAMI** OF MOUNT IBUKI, WHO, IN THE GUISE OF A MONSTROUS SERPENT, TERRORIZES THE AREA.
*DEITY
"EACH DAY HE DESCENDS INTO OUR VILLAGES, DESTROYING HOMES AND DEVOURING WHOMEVER HE SEES.
"TOWNS ARE IN RUINS. MEN FEAR TO GO OUT INTO THE FIELDS, AND WOMEN WILL NOT VENTURE TO THE RIVERS TO FETCH WATER."
WE BEG FOR YOUR HELP, PRINCE YAMATO-DAKE.
I HAVE SUBDUED THE LAND FOR A HUNDRED *RI** AROUND! IT IS UNTHINKABLE THAT SUCH A MONSTER CAN EXIST IN THE HEART OF OUR LANDS.
*1 RI=3.9 KM.
I WILL LEAVE AT FIRST LIGHT TO CONQUER THIS EVIL BEAST.
THANK YOU, MY LORD! THANK YOU!

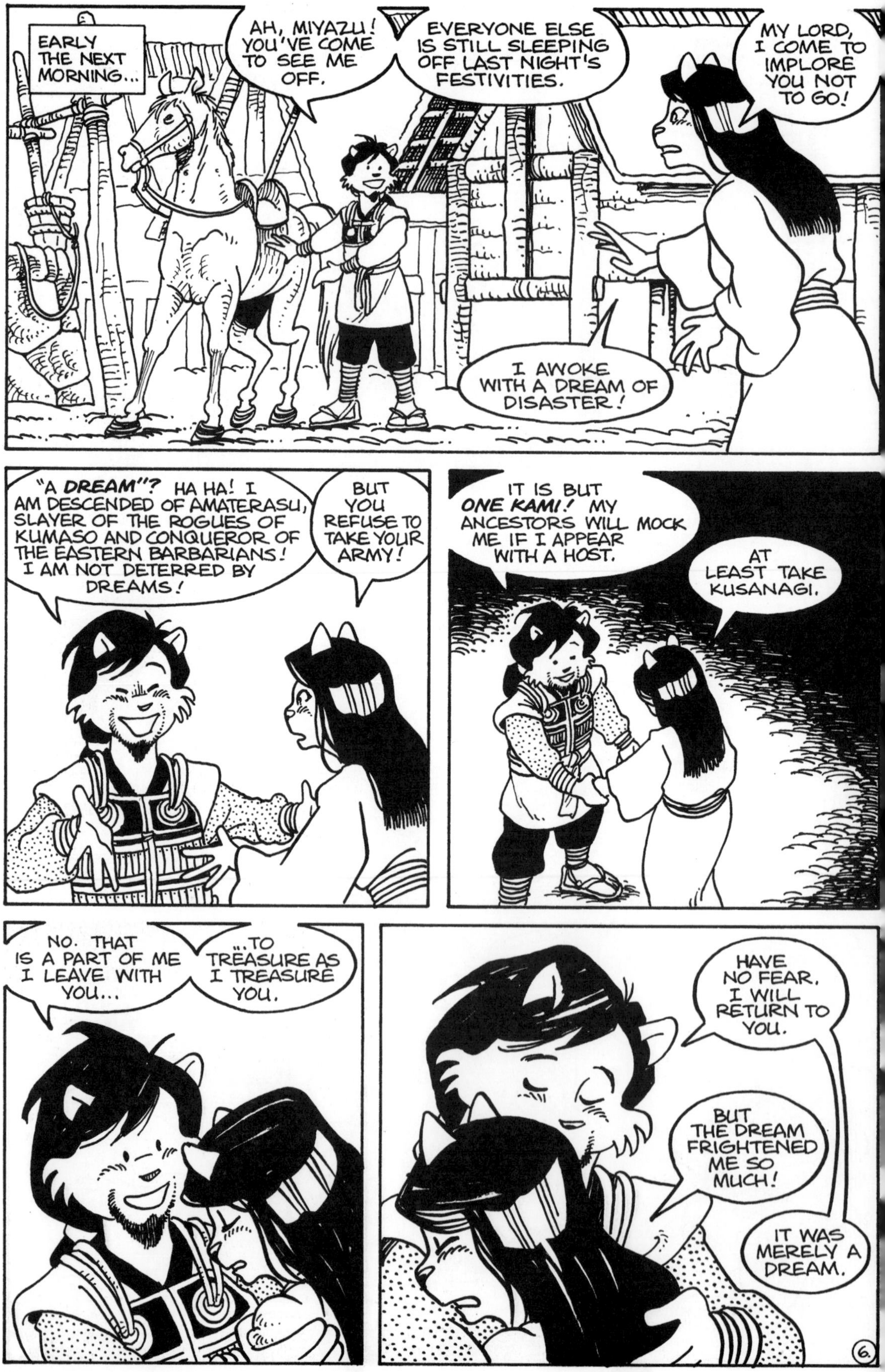
EARLY THE NEXT MORNING...
AH, MIYAZU! YOU'VE COME TO SEE ME OFF.
EVERYONE ELSE IS STILL SLEEPING OFF LAST NIGHT'S FESTIVITIES.
MY LORD, I COME TO IMPLORE YOU NOT TO GO!
I AWOKE WITH A DREAM OF DISASTER!
"A DREAM"? HA HA! I AM DESCENDED OF AMATERASU, SLAYER OF THE ROGUES OF KUMASO AND CONQUEROR OF THE EASTERN BARBARIANS! I AM NOT DETERRED BY DREAMS!
BUT YOU REFUSE TO TAKE YOUR ARMY!
IT IS BUT ONE KAMI! MY ANCESTORS WILL MOCK ME IF I APPEAR WITH A HOST.
AT LEAST TAKE KUSANAGI.
NO. THAT IS A PART OF ME I LEAVE WITH YOU...
...TO TREASURE AS I TREASURE YOU.
HAVE NO FEAR. I WILL RETURN TO YOU.
BUT THE DREAM FRIGHTENED ME SO MUCH!
IT WAS MERELY A DREAM.
6.

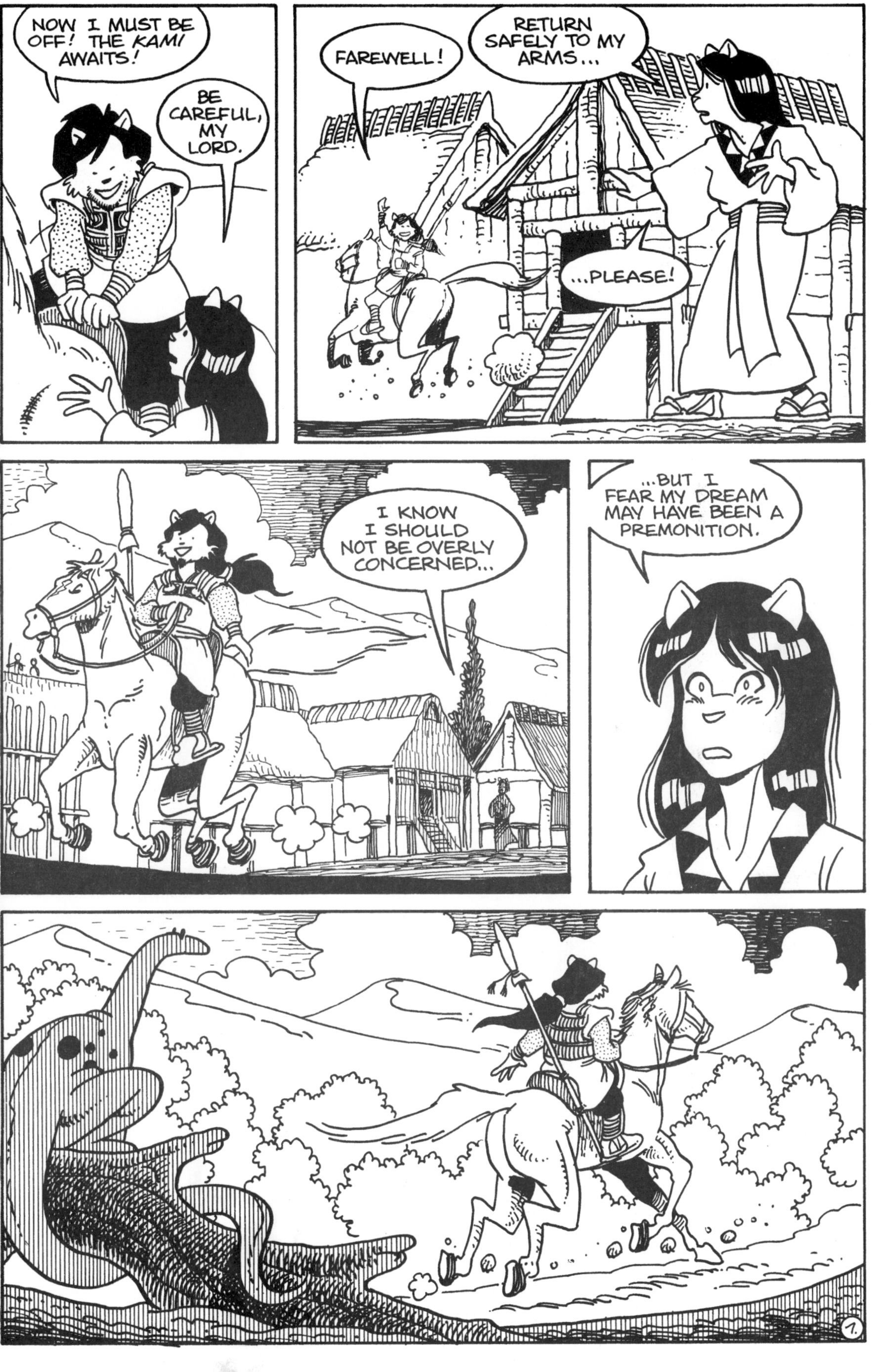
NOW I MUST BE OFF! THE KAMI AWAITS!
BE CAREFUL, MY LORD.
FAREWELL!
RETURN SAFELY TO MY ARMS...
...PLEASE!
I KNOW I SHOULD NOT BE OVERLY CONCERNED...
...BUT I FEAR MY DREAM MAY HAVE BEEN A PREMONITION.
1.

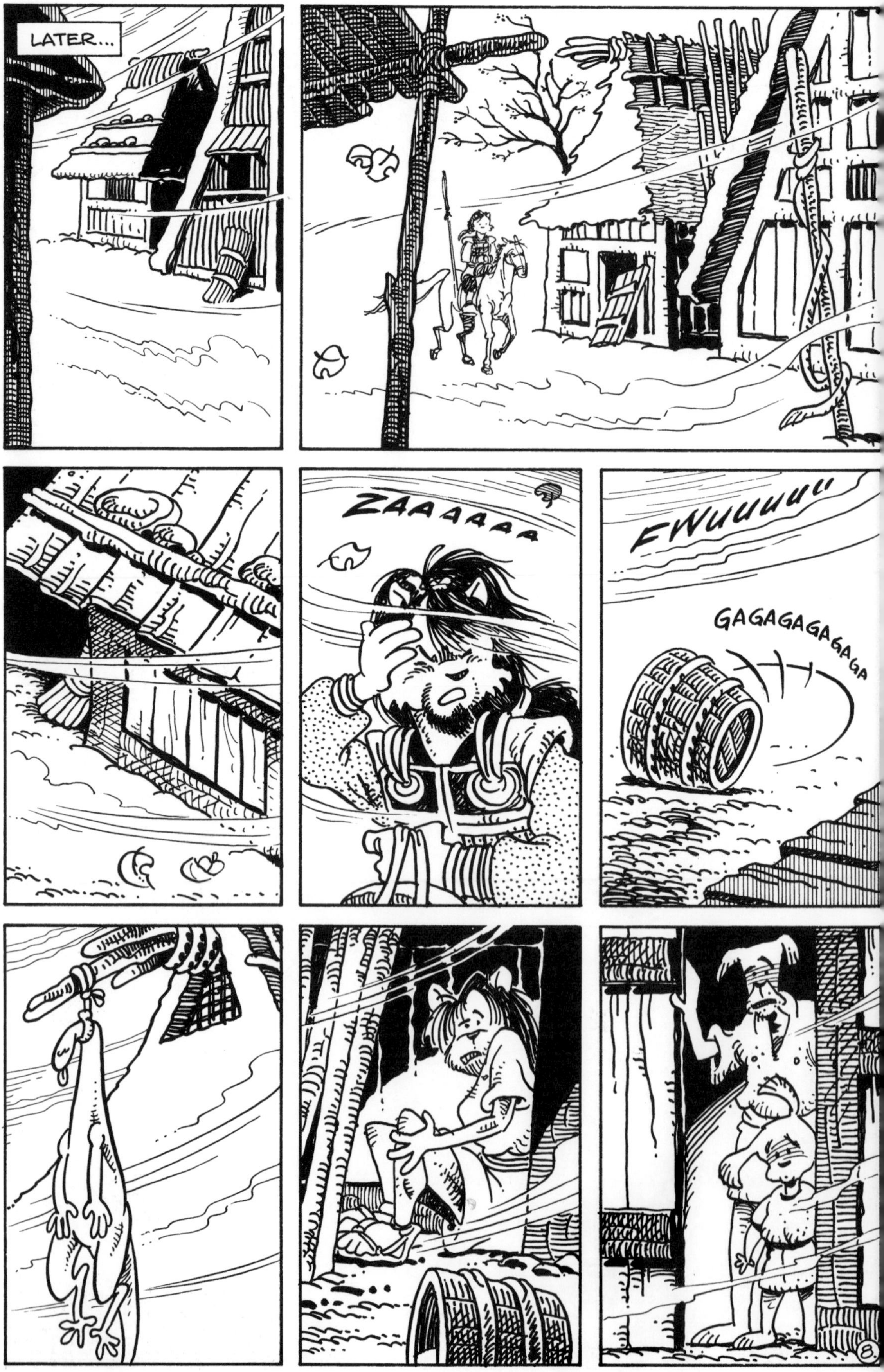
LATER...
ZAAAAAAA
FWUUUUUU
GAGAGAGAGAGAGA
8

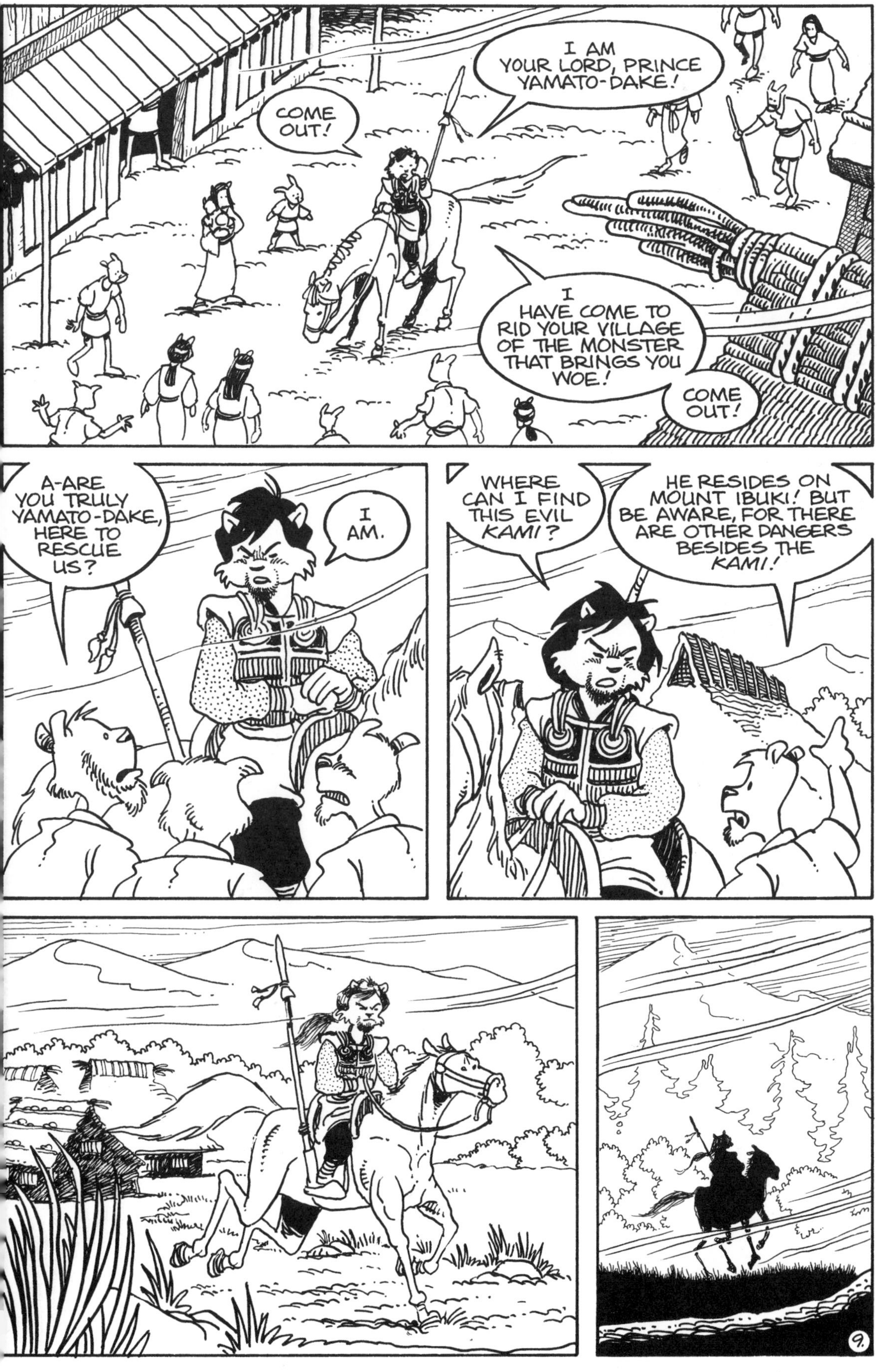
COME OUT!
I AM YOUR LORD, PRINCE YAMATO-DAKE!
I HAVE COME TO RID YOUR VILLAGE OF THE MONSTER THAT BRINGS YOU WOE!
COME OUT!
A-ARE YOU TRULY YAMATO-DAKE, HERE TO RESCUE US?
I AM.
WHERE CAN I FIND THIS EVIL *KAMI*?
HE RESIDES ON MOUNT IBUKI! BUT BE AWARE, FOR THERE ARE OTHER DANGERS BESIDES THE *KAMI*!
9.

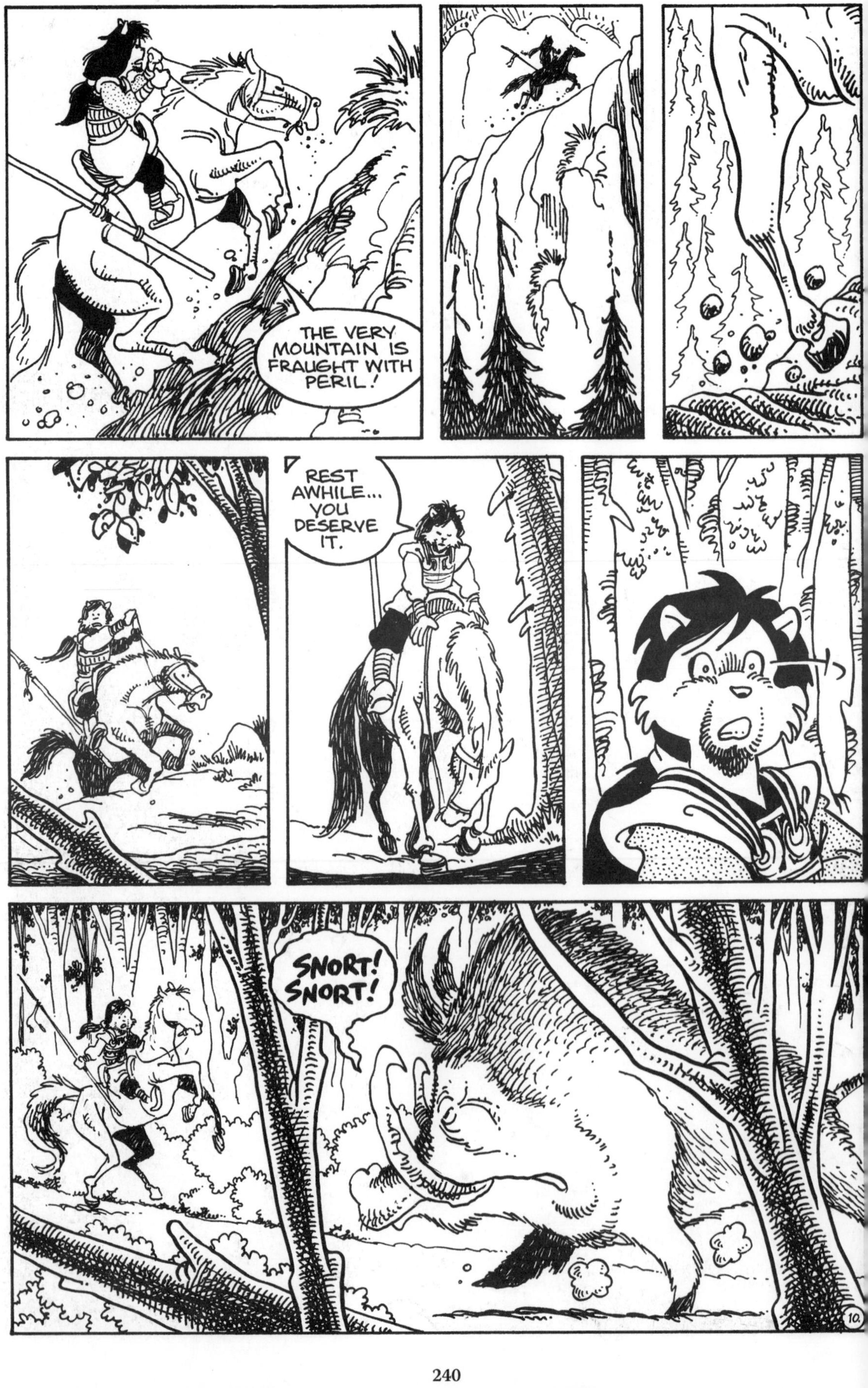
THE VERY MOUNTAIN IS FRAUGHT WITH PERIL!
REST AWHILE... YOU DESERVE IT.
SNORT! SNORT!
10.

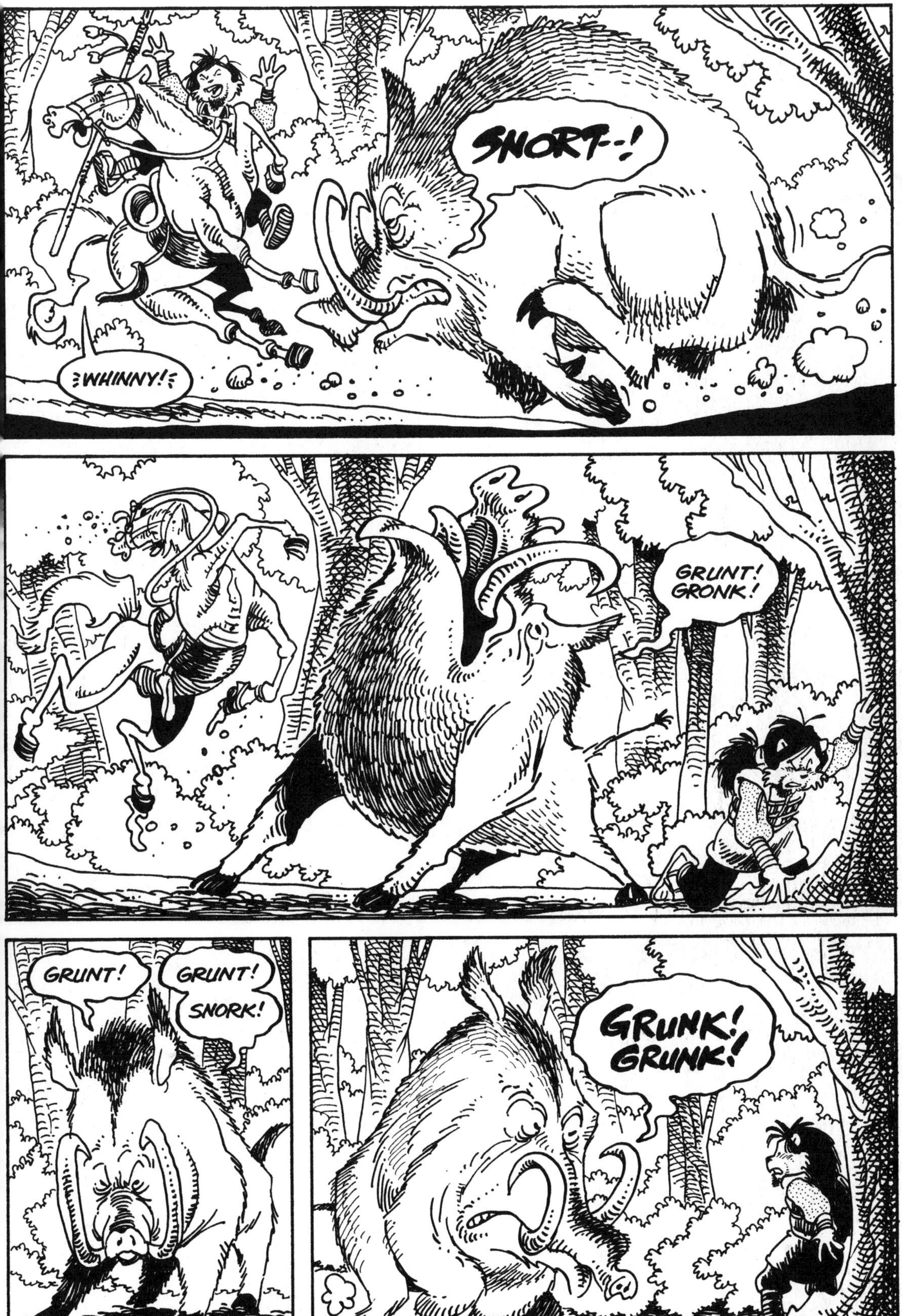
SNORT--!
WHINNY!
GRUNT! GRONK!
GRUNT!
GRUNT! SNORK!
GRUNK! GRUNK!
11.

CRASH!
GRONK!
HIYAHH
THUD! THUD!
12.

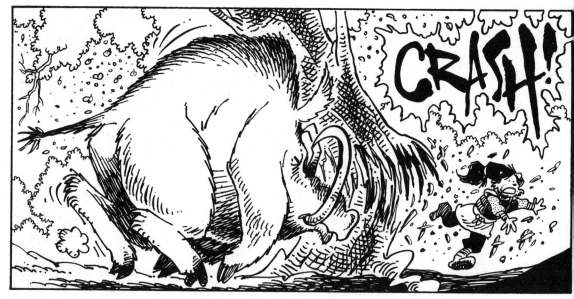

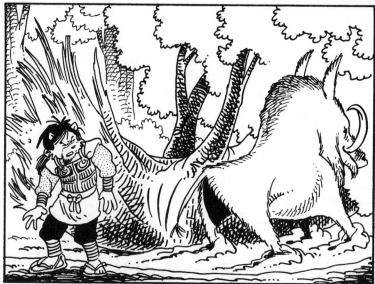

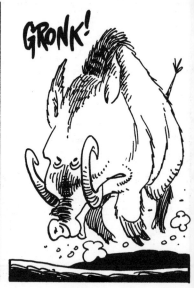

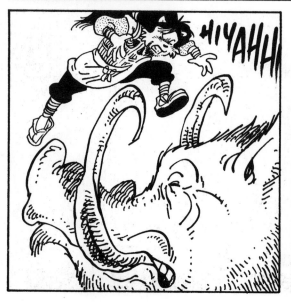

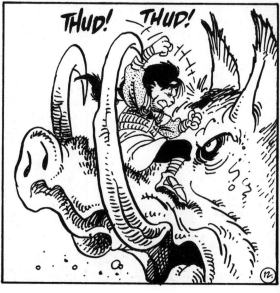

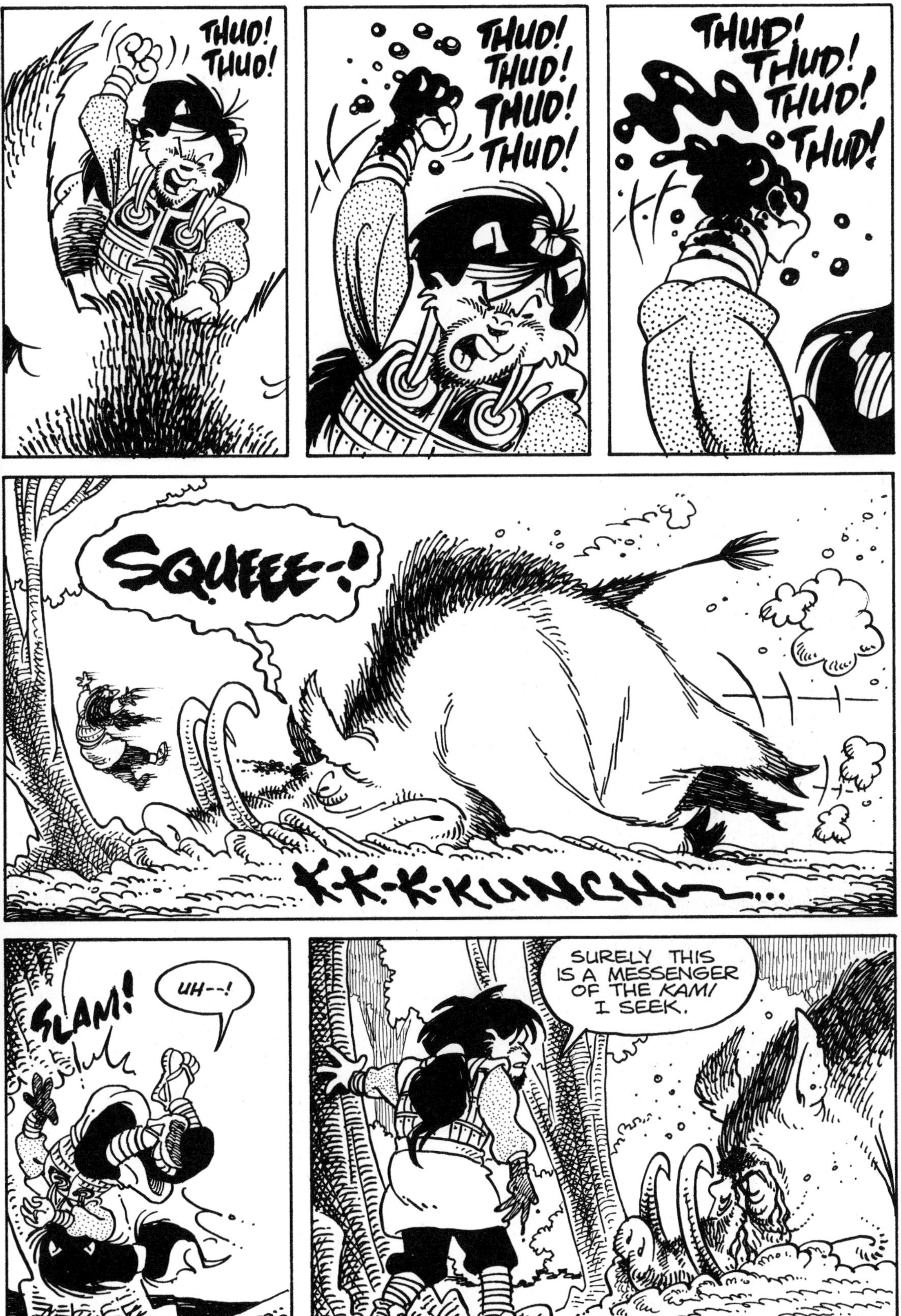
THUD! THUD!
THUD! THUD! THUD! THUD!
THUD! THUD! THUD! THUD!
SQUEEE--!
K-K-K-KUNCH...
SLAM!
UH--!
SURELY THIS IS A MESSENGER OF THE *KAMI* I SEEK.
13

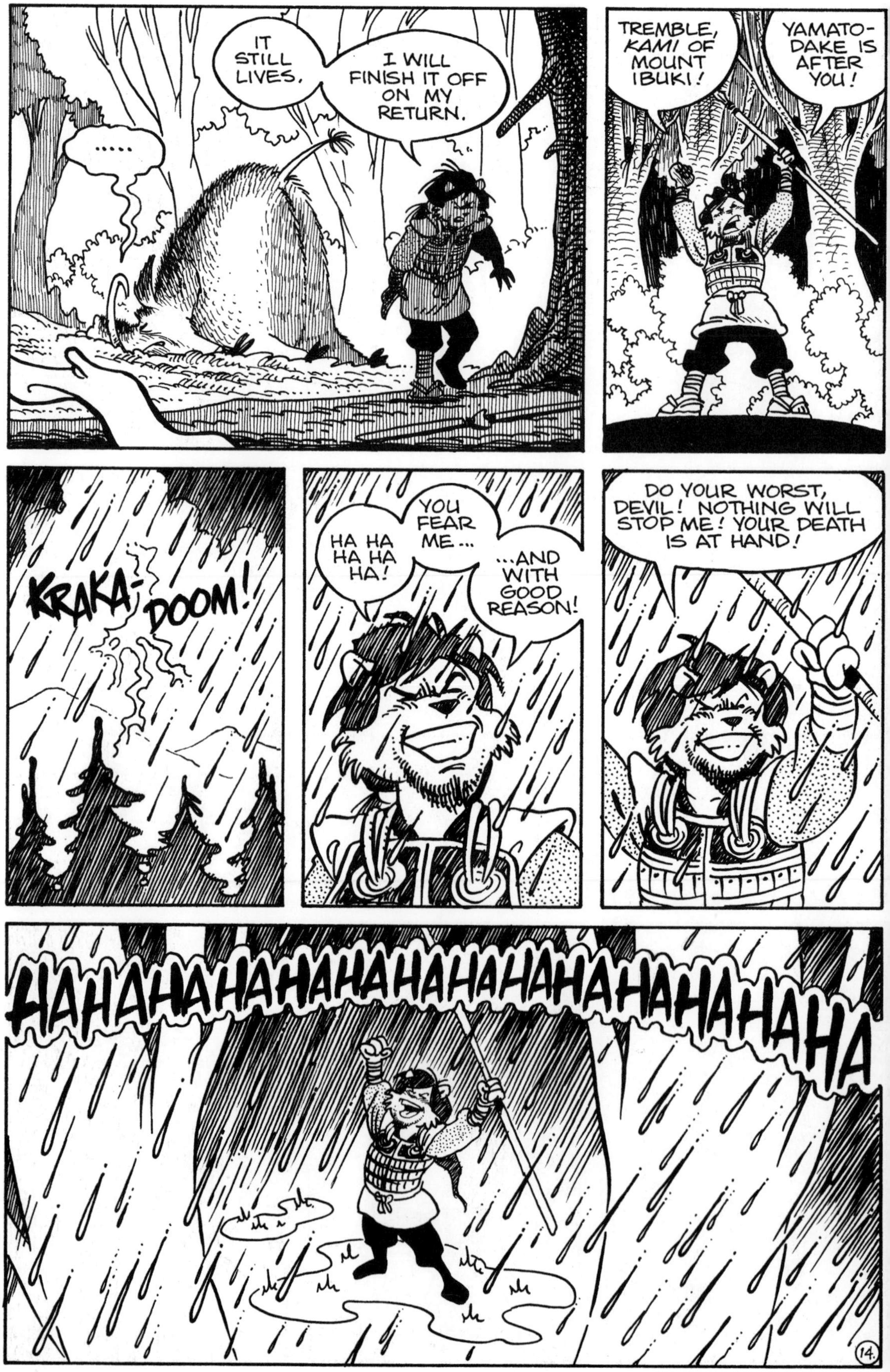
.....
IT STILL LIVES.
I WILL FINISH IT OFF ON MY RETURN.
TREMBLE, KAMI OF MOUNT IBUKI!
YAMATO-DAKE IS AFTER YOU!
KRAKA-DOOM!
HA HA HA HA HA!
YOU FEAR ME...
...AND WITH GOOD REASON!
DO YOUR WORST, DEVIL! NOTHING WILL STOP ME! YOUR DEATH IS AT HAND!
HAHAHAHAHAHAHAHAHAHAHAHAHAHAHAHAHA
14.

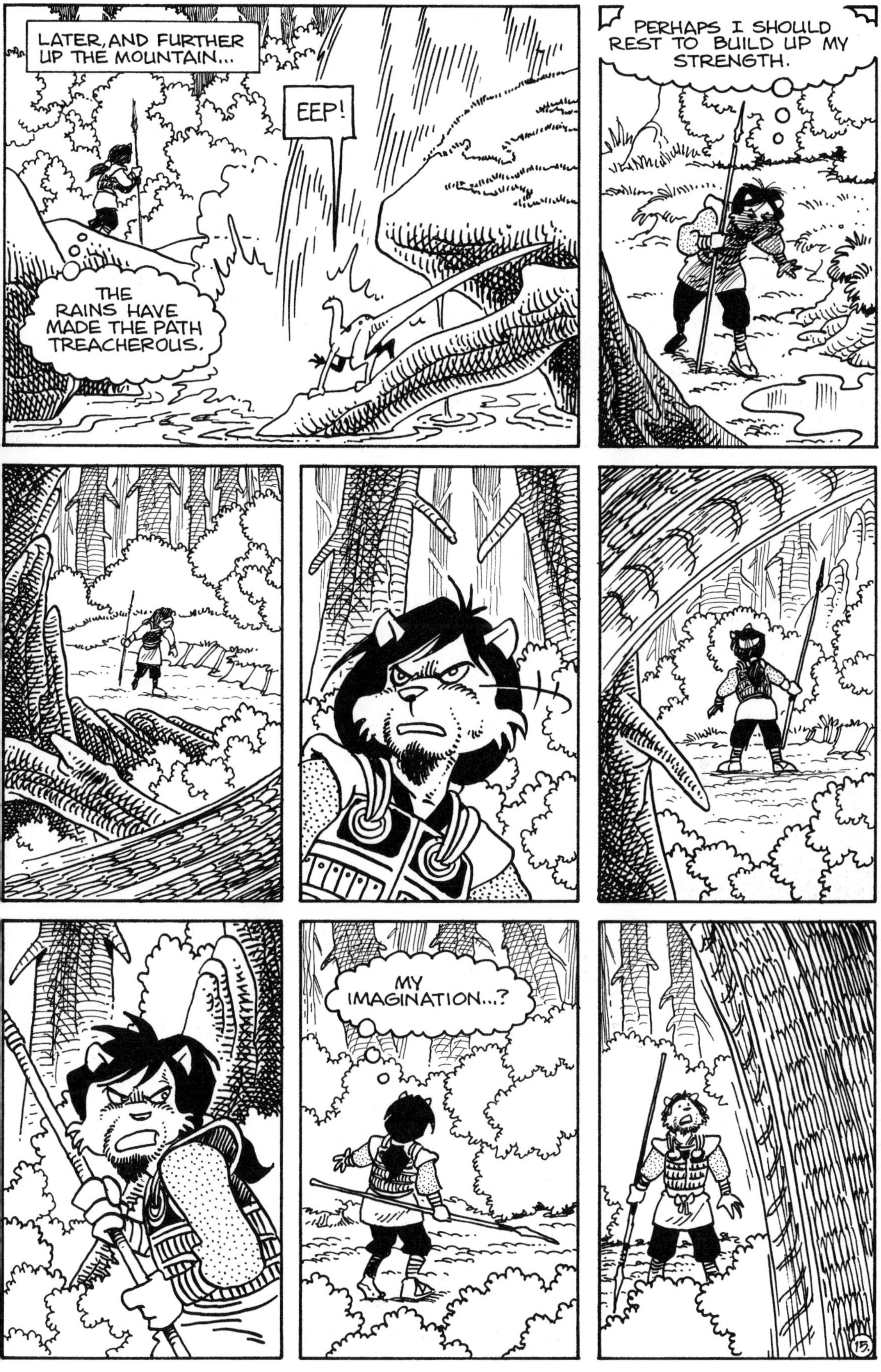
LATER, AND FURTHER UP THE MOUNTAIN...
THE RAINS HAVE MADE THE PATH TREACHEROUS.
EEP!
PERHAPS I SHOULD REST TO BUILD UP MY STRENGTH.
MY IMAGINATION...?
15.

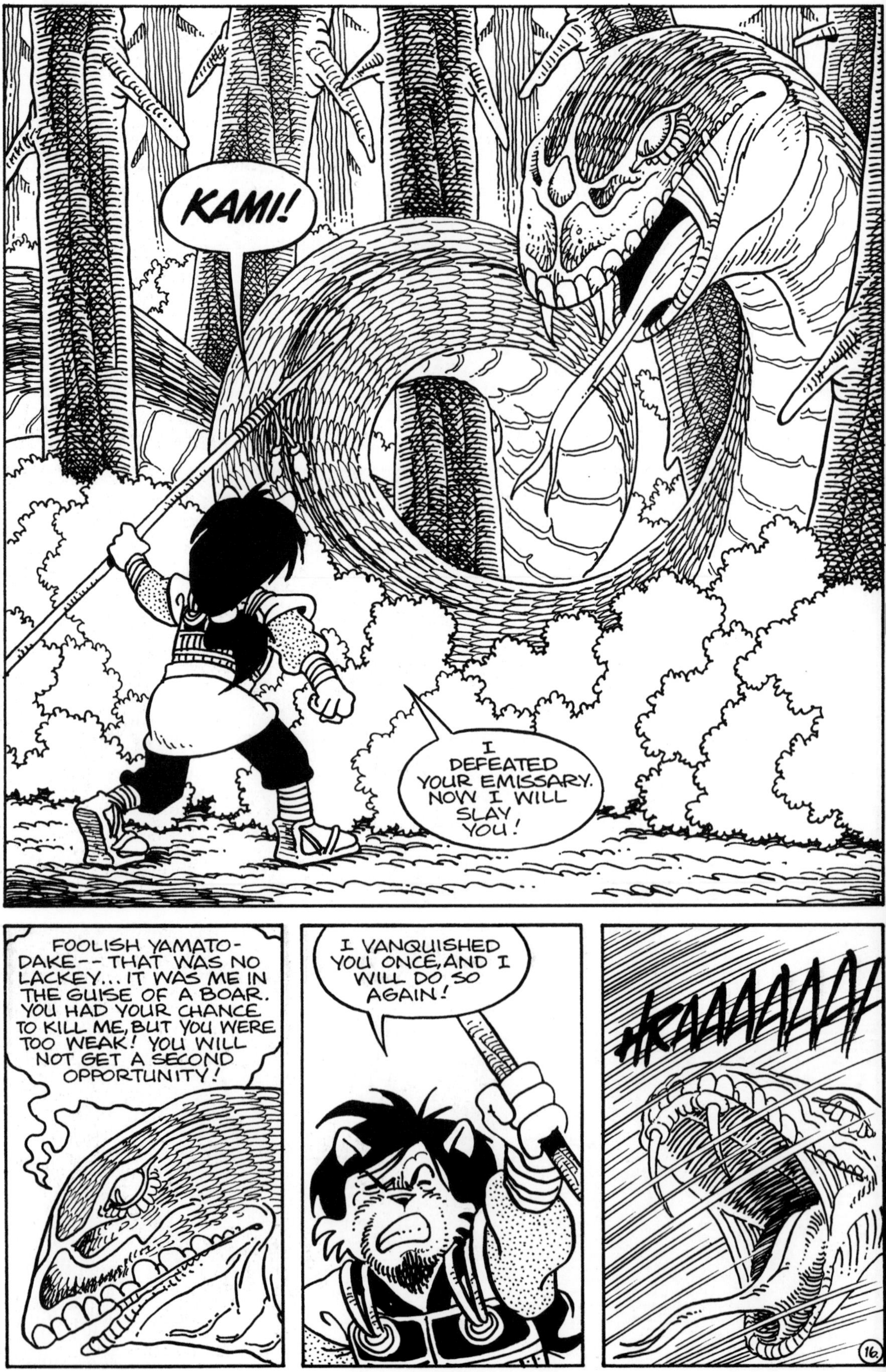
KAMI!
I DEFEATED YOUR EMISSARY. NOW I WILL SLAY YOU!
FOOLISH YAMATO-DAKE-- THAT WAS NO LACKEY... IT WAS ME IN THE GUISE OF A BOAR. YOU HAD YOUR CHANCE TO KILL ME, BUT YOU WERE TOO WEAK! YOU WILL NOT GET A SECOND OPPORTUNITY!
I VANQUISHED YOU ONCE, AND I WILL DO SO AGAIN!
HRAAAAAAA!
16.

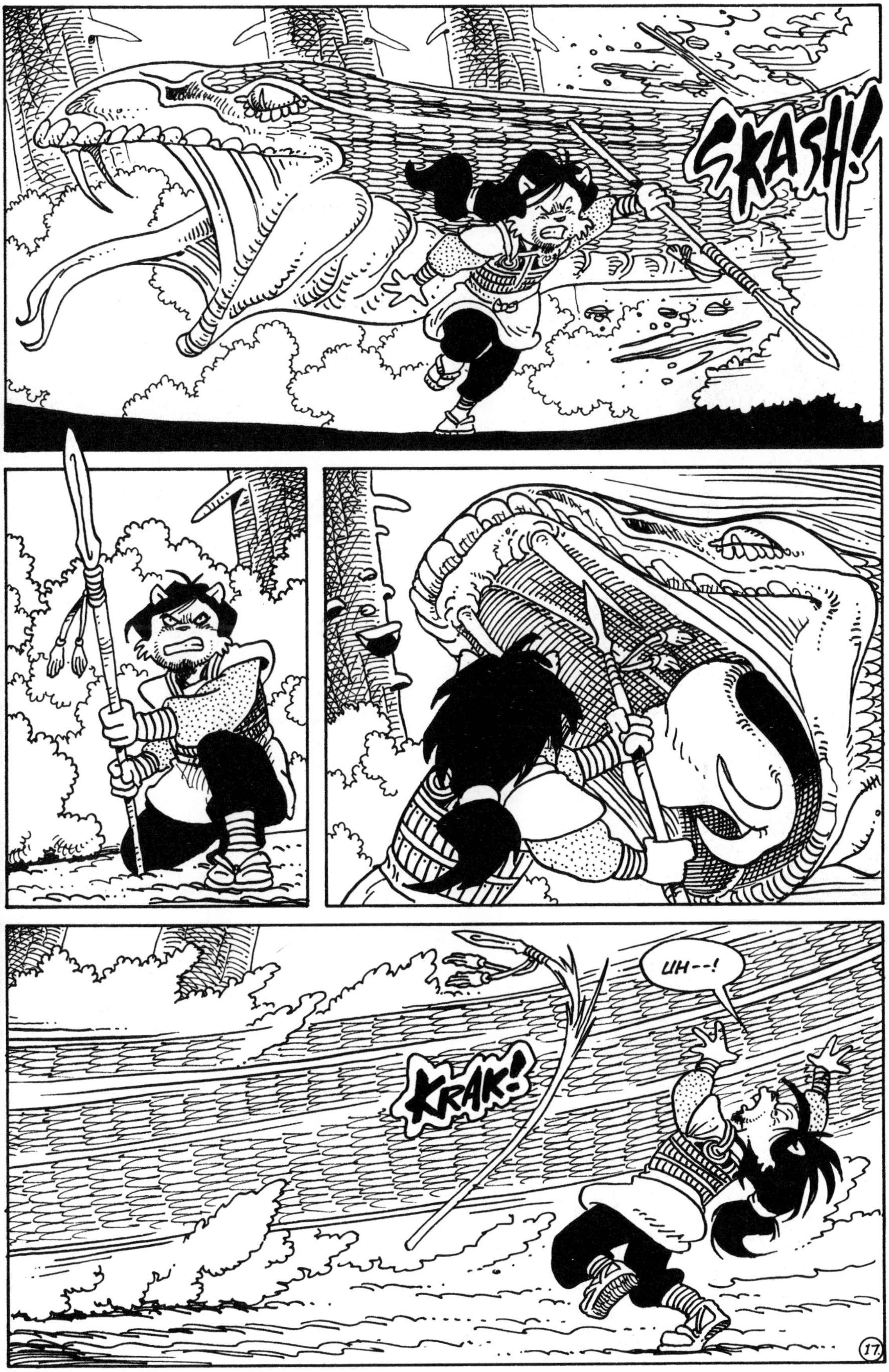
SKASH!
UH--!
KRAK!
17

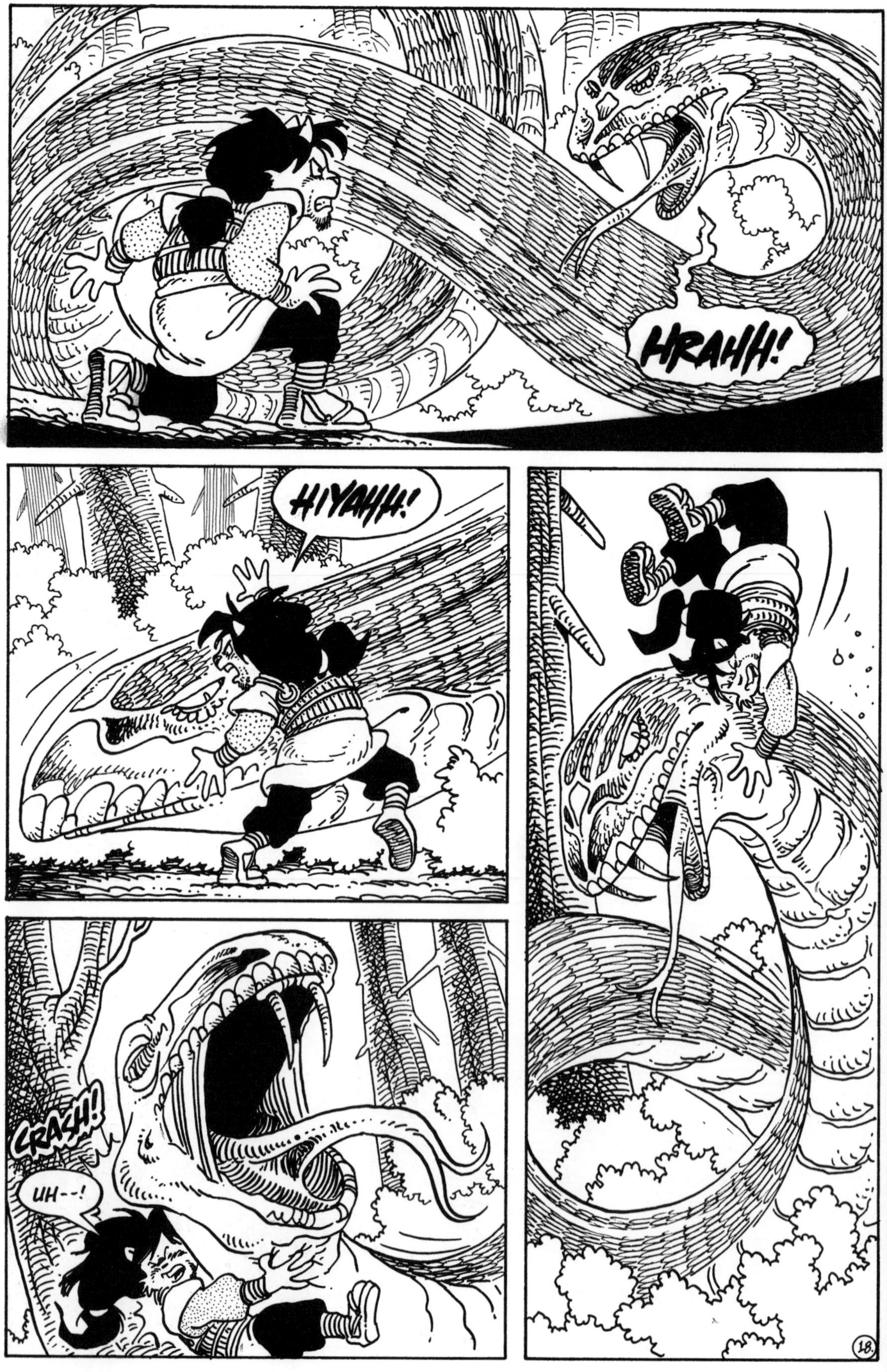
HRAHH!
HIYAHH!
CRASH!
UH--!
18

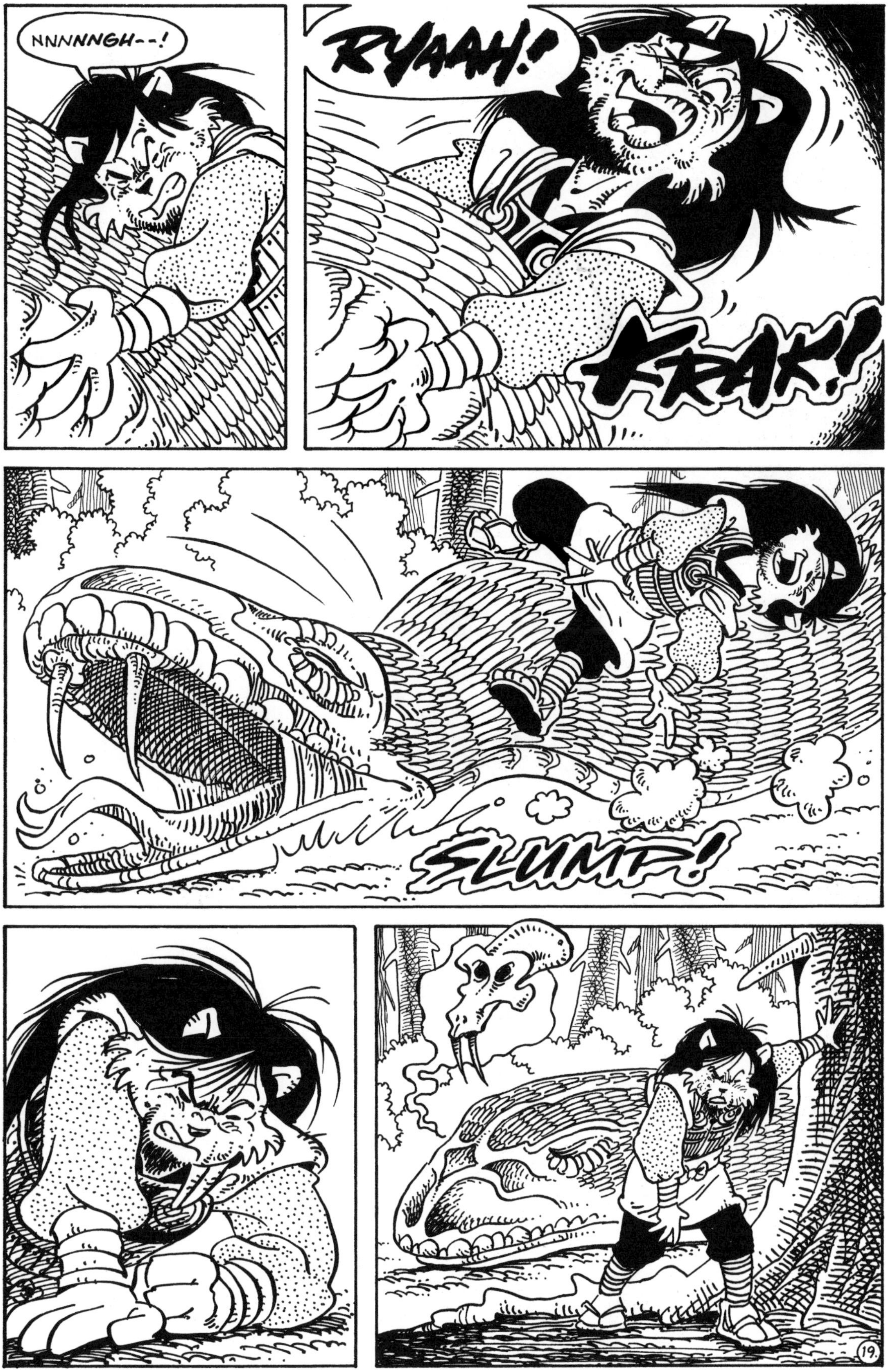
NNNNNGH--!
RYAAH!
KRAK!
SLUMP!
19

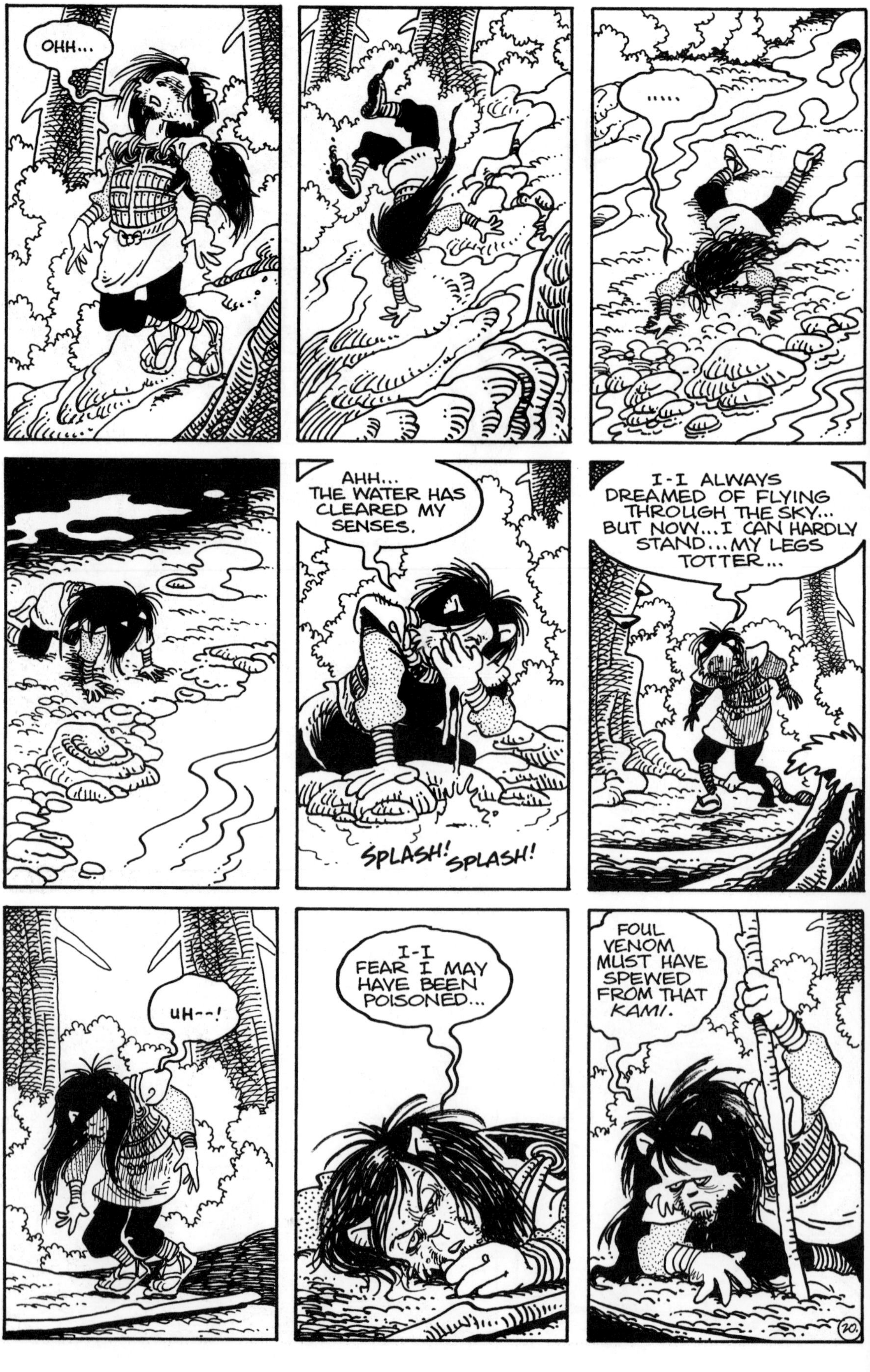
OHH...
.....
AHH... THE WATER HAS CLEARED MY SENSES.
SPLASH! SPLASH!
I-I ALWAYS DREAMED OF FLYING THROUGH THE SKY... BUT NOW... I CAN HARDLY STAND... MY LEGS TOTTER...
UH--!
I-I FEAR I MAY HAVE BEEN POISONED...
FOUL VENOM MUST HAVE SPEWED FROM THAT *KAMI*.
20.

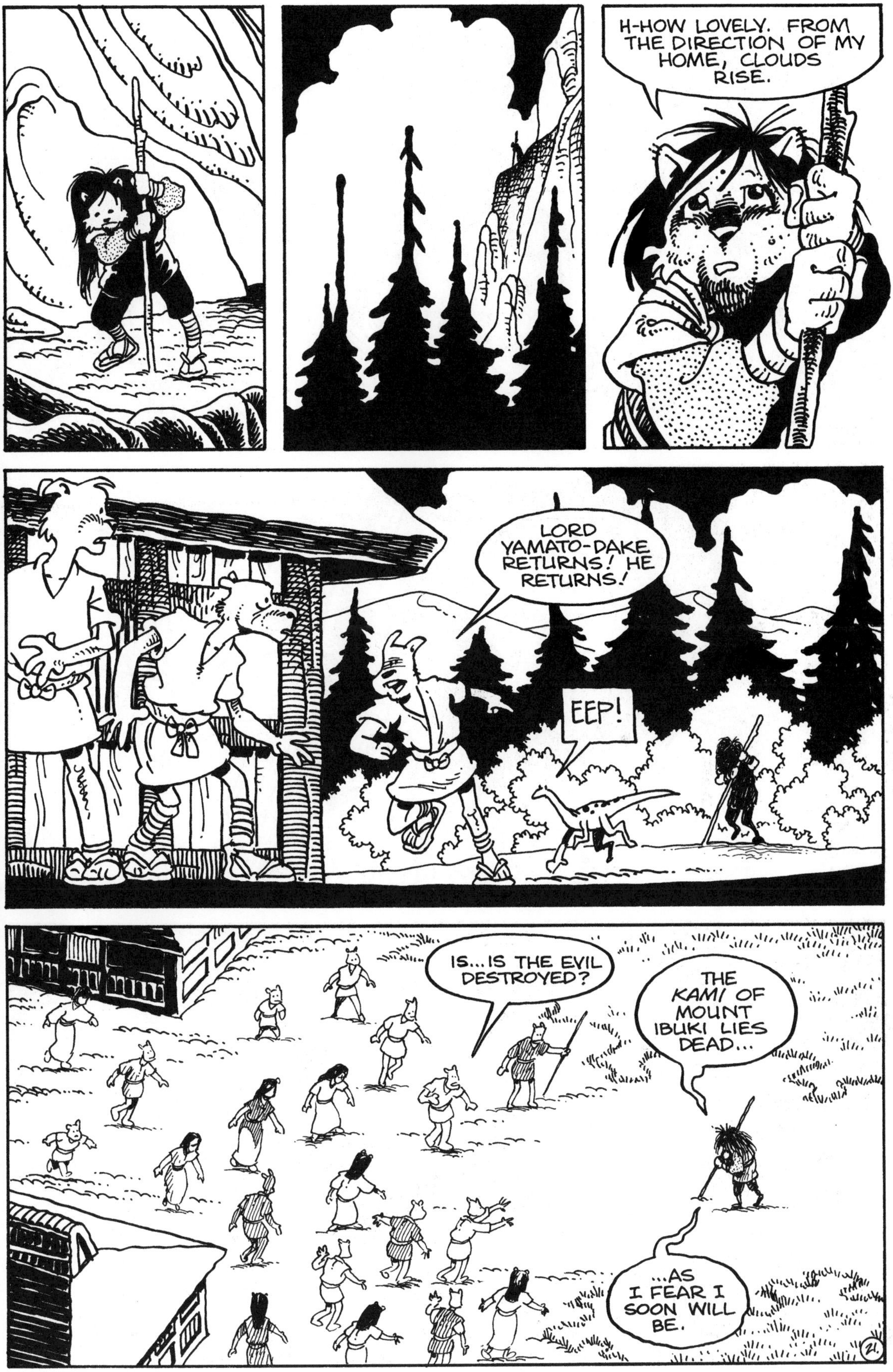

H-HOW LOVELY. FROM THE DIRECTION OF MY HOME, CLOUDS RISE.
LORD YAMATO-DAKE RETURNS! HE RETURNS!
EEP!
IS...IS THE EVIL DESTROYED?
THE *KAMI* OF MOUNT IBUKI LIES DEAD...
...AS I FEAR I SOON WILL BE.
21.

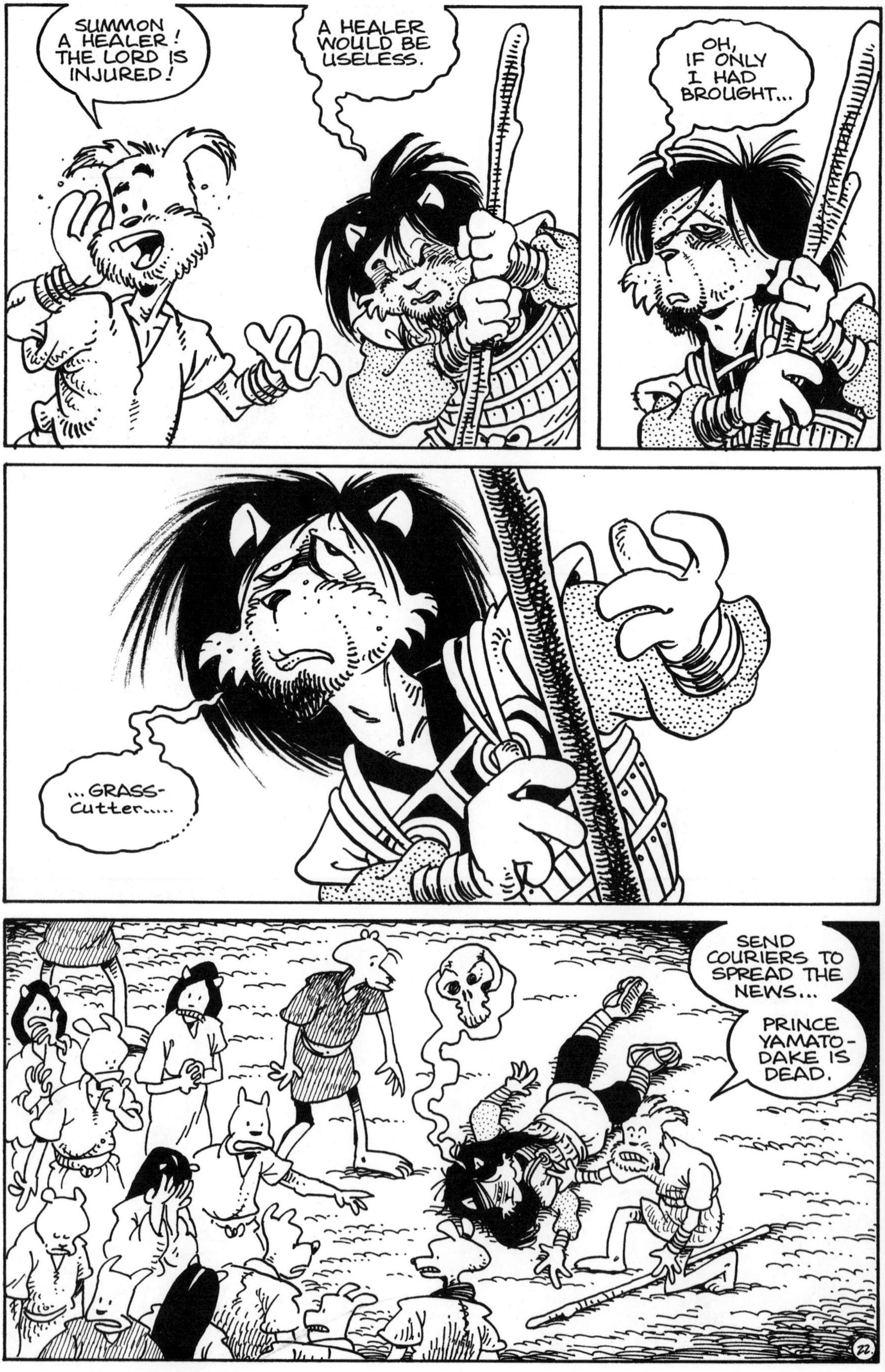
SUMMON A HEALER! THE LORD IS INJURED!
A HEALER WOULD BE USELESS.
OH, IF ONLY I HAD BROUGHT...
...GRASS-Cutter.....
SEND COURIERS TO SPREAD THE NEWS...
PRINCE YAMATO-DAKE IS DEAD.
22.

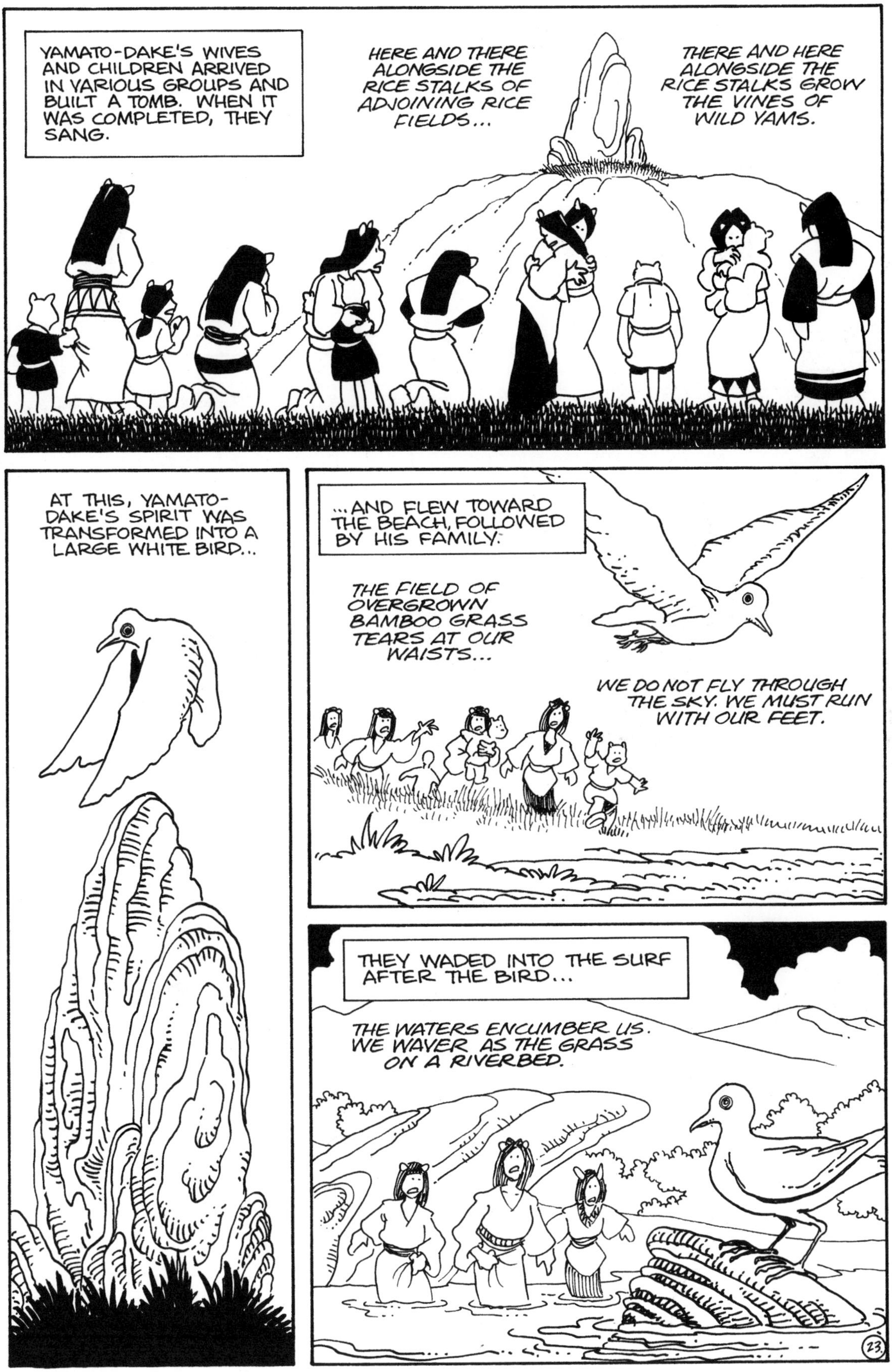

YAMATO-DAKE'S WIVES AND CHILDREN ARRIVED IN VARIOUS GROUPS AND BUILT A TOMB. WHEN IT WAS COMPLETED, THEY SANG.
HERE AND THERE ALONGSIDE THE RICE STALKS OF ADJOINING RICE FIELDS...
THERE AND HERE ALONGSIDE THE RICE STALKS GROW THE VINES OF WILD YAMS.
AT THIS, YAMATO-DAKE'S SPIRIT WAS TRANSFORMED INTO A LARGE WHITE BIRD...
...AND FLEW TOWARD THE BEACH, FOLLOWED BY HIS FAMILY.
THE FIELD OF OVERGROWN BAMBOO GRASS TEARS AT OUR WAISTS...
WE DO NOT FLY THROUGH THE SKY. WE MUST RUN WITH OUR FEET.
THEY WADED INTO THE SURF AFTER THE BIRD...
THE WATERS ENCUMBER US. WE WAVER AS THE GRASS ON A RIVERBED.
23

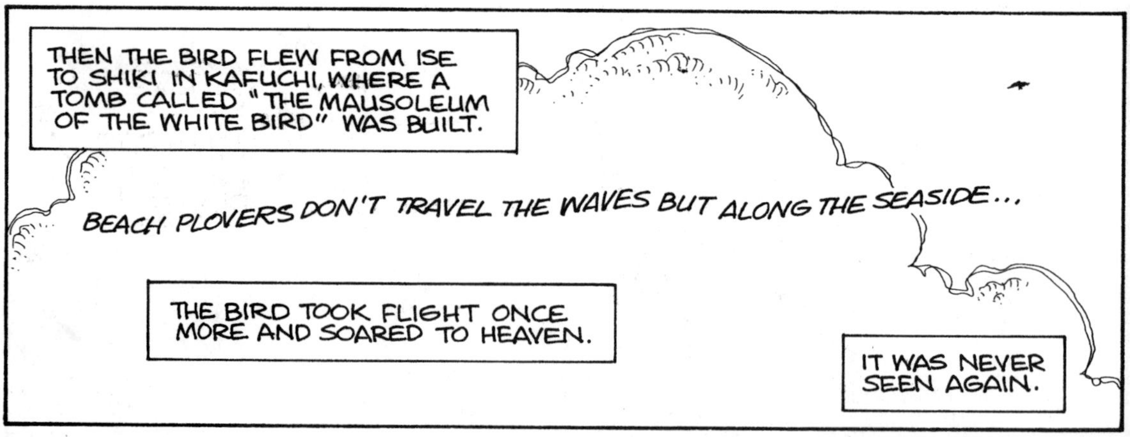
THEN THE BIRD FLEW FROM ISE TO SHIKI IN KAFUCHI, WHERE A TOMB CALLED "THE MAUSOLEUM OF THE WHITE BIRD" WAS BUILT.
BEACH PLOVERS DON'T TRAVEL THE WAVES BUT ALONG THE SEASIDE...
THE BIRD TOOK FLIGHT ONCE MORE AND SOARED TO HEAVEN.
IT WAS NEVER SEEN AGAIN.

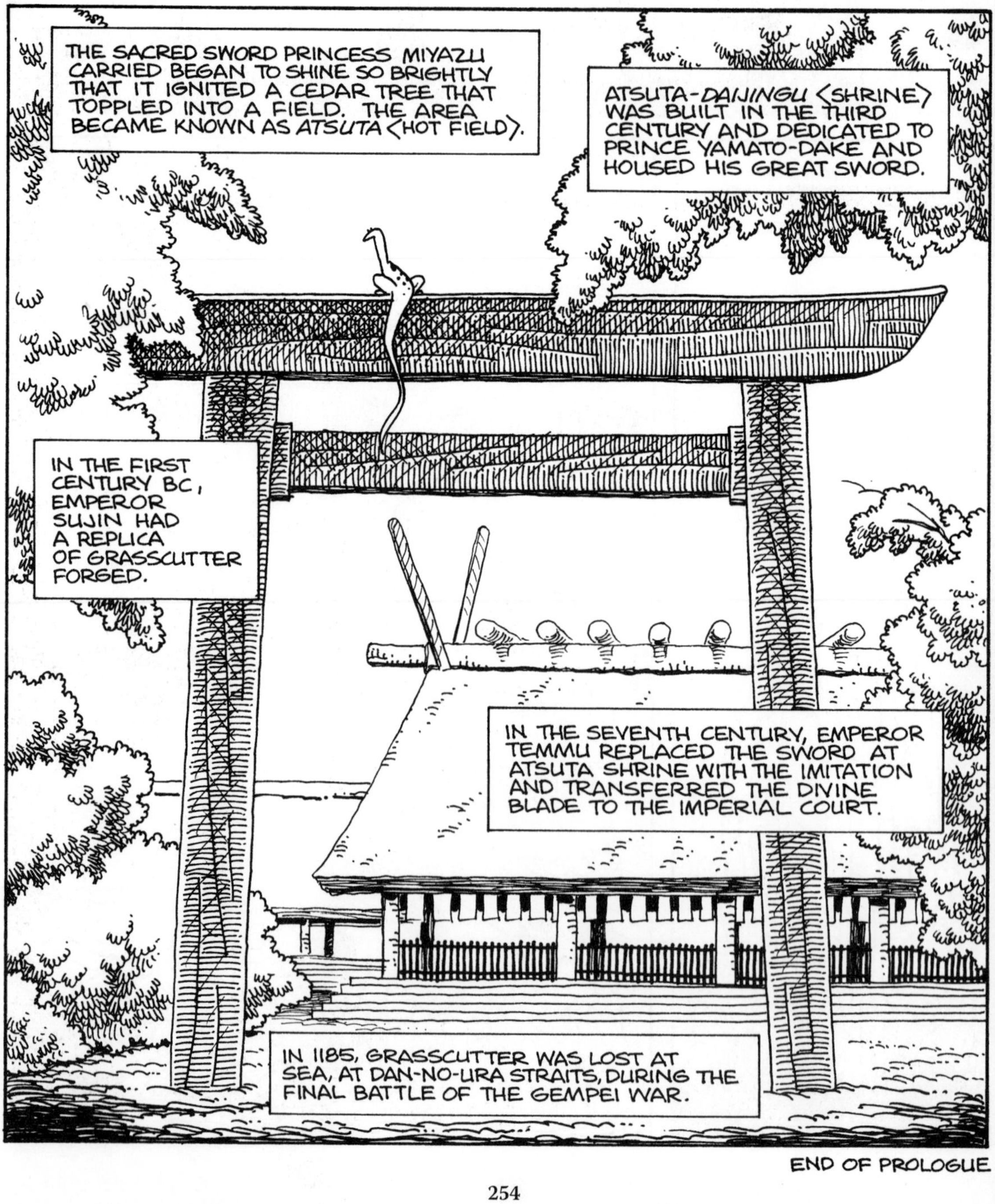
THE SACRED SWORD PRINCESS MIYAZU CARRIED BEGAN TO SHINE SO BRIGHTLY THAT IT IGNITED A CEDAR TREE THAT TOPPLED INTO A FIELD. THE AREA BECAME KNOWN AS *ATSUTA* <HOT FIELD>.
ATSUTA-*DAIJINGU* <SHRINE> WAS BUILT IN THE THIRD CENTURY AND DEDICATED TO PRINCE YAMATO-DAKE AND HOUSED HIS GREAT SWORD.
IN THE FIRST CENTURY BC, EMPEROR SUJIN HAD A REPLICA OF GRASSCUTTER FORGED.
IN THE SEVENTH CENTURY, EMPEROR TEMMU REPLACED THE SWORD AT ATSUTA SHRINE WITH THE IMITATION AND TRANSFERRED THE DIVINE BLADE TO THE IMPERIAL COURT.
IN 1185, GRASSCUTTER WAS LOST AT SEA, AT DAN-NO-URA STRAITS, DURING THE FINAL BATTLE OF THE GEMPEI WAR.

END OF PROLOGUE

Chapter 1: A Whisper of Wings

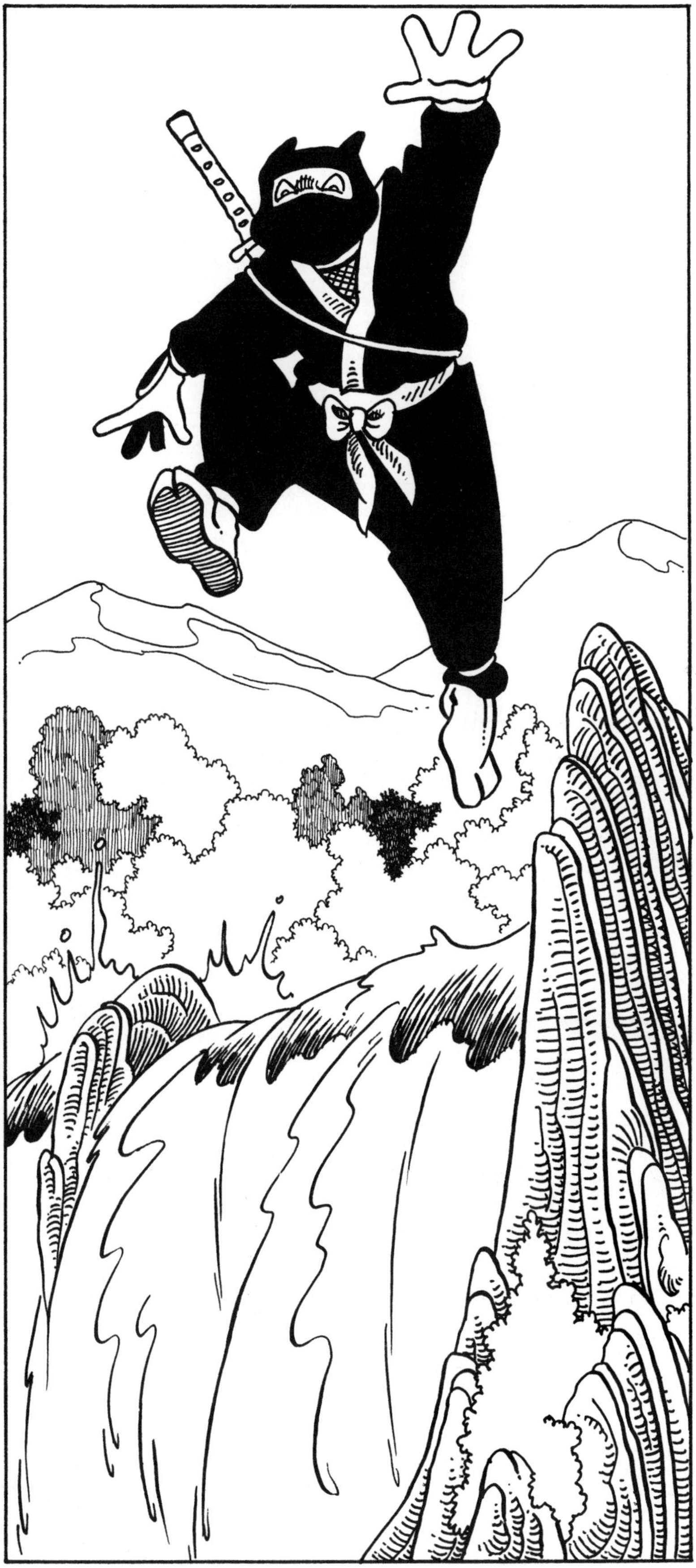

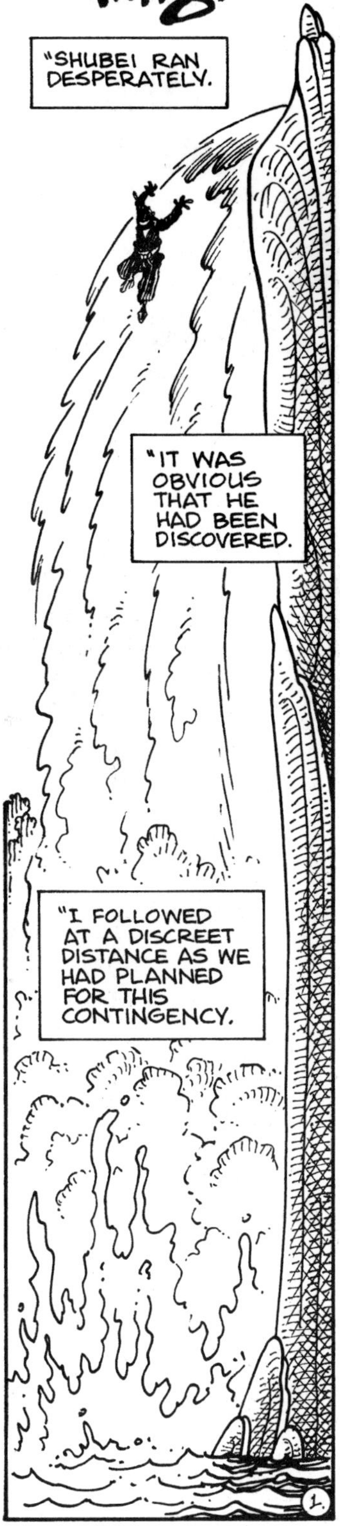
"SHUBEI RAN DESPERATELY.
"IT WAS OBVIOUS THAT HE HAD BEEN DISCOVERED.
"I FOLLOWED AT A DISCREET DISTANCE AS WE HAD PLANNED FOR THIS CONTINGENCY.
1.

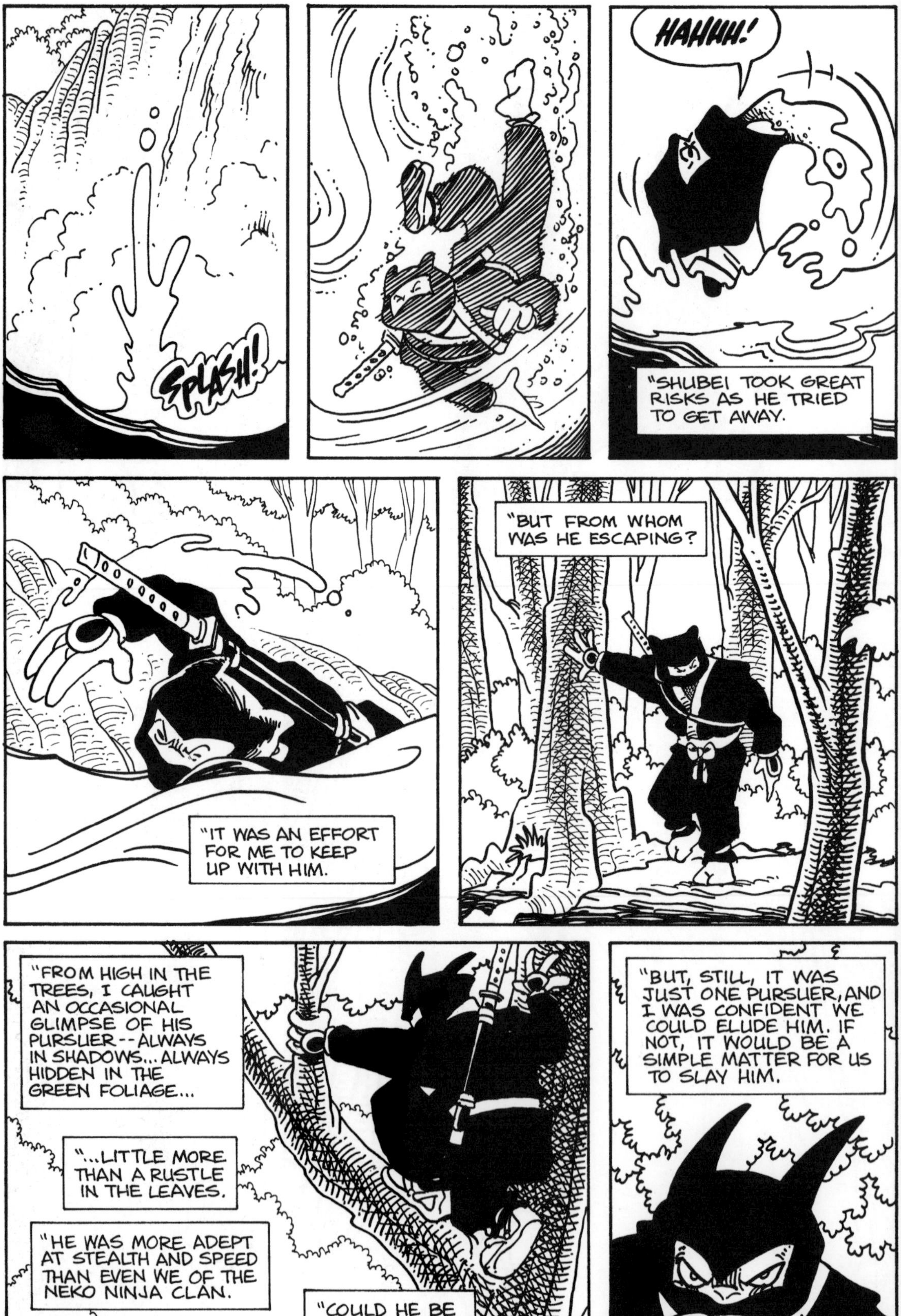
SPLASH!
HAHHH!
"SHUBEI TOOK GREAT RISKS AS HE TRIED TO GET AWAY.
"IT WAS AN EFFORT FOR ME TO KEEP UP WITH HIM.
"BUT FROM WHOM WAS HE ESCAPING?
"FROM HIGH IN THE TREES, I CAUGHT AN OCCASIONAL GLIMPSE OF HIS PURSUER--ALWAYS IN SHADOWS...ALWAYS HIDDEN IN THE GREEN FOLIAGE...
"...LITTLE MORE THAN A RUSTLE IN THE LEAVES.
"HE WAS MORE ADEPT AT STEALTH AND SPEED THAN EVEN WE OF THE NEKO NINJA CLAN.
"COULD HE BE A *NINJA** OF A RIVAL CLAN?
*SPY
"BUT, STILL, IT WAS JUST ONE PURSUER, AND I WAS CONFIDENT WE COULD ELUDE HIM. IF NOT, IT WOULD BE A SIMPLE MATTER FOR US TO SLAY HIM.
2.

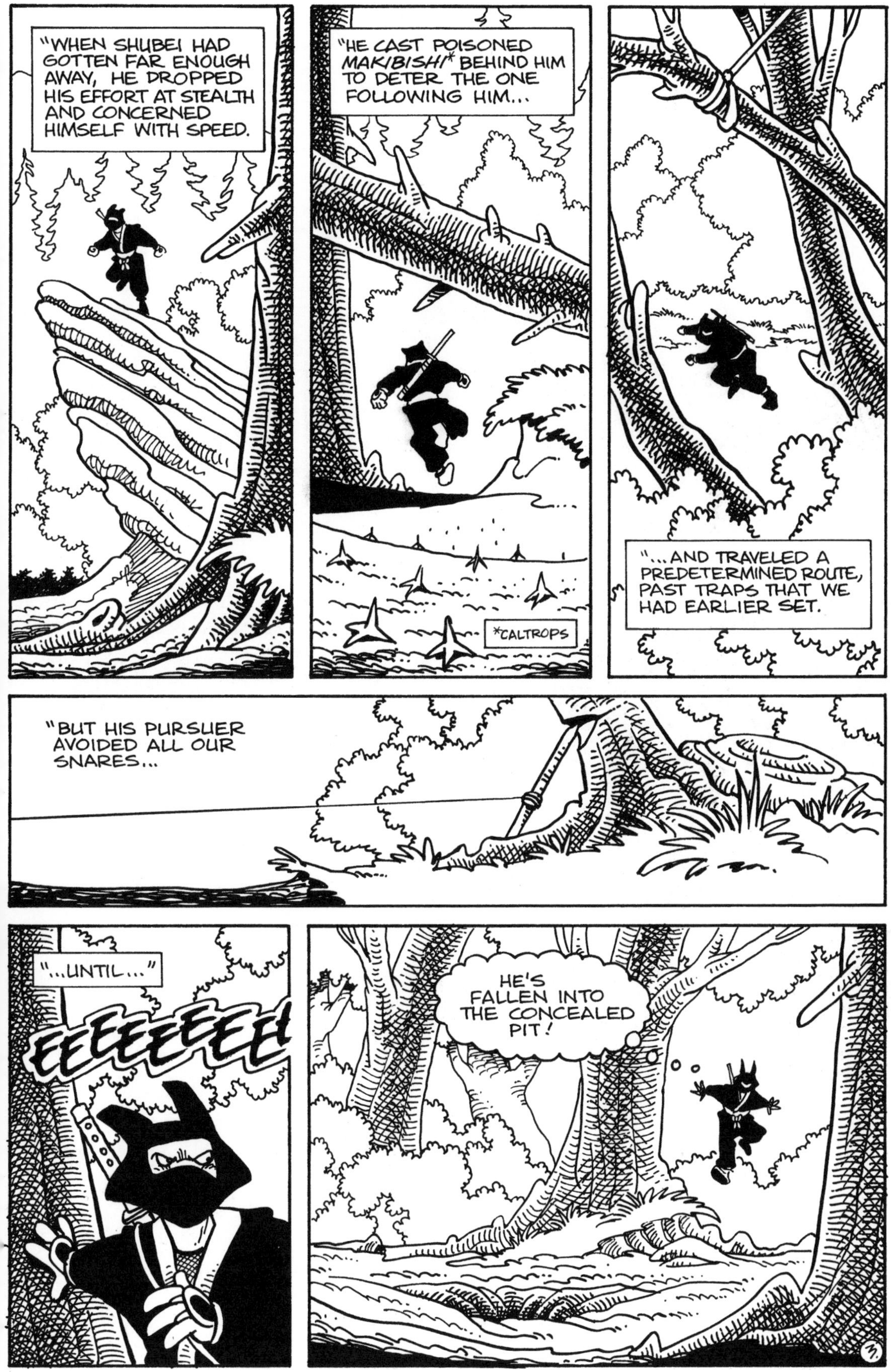
"WHEN SHUBEI HAD GOTTEN FAR ENOUGH AWAY, HE DROPPED HIS EFFORT AT STEALTH AND CONCERNED HIMSELF WITH SPEED.
"HE CAST POISONED *MAKIBISHI** BEHIND HIM TO DETER THE ONE FOLLOWING HIM...
*CALTROPS
"...AND TRAVELED A PREDETERMINED ROUTE, PAST TRAPS THAT WE HAD EARLIER SET.
"BUT HIS PURSUER AVOIDED ALL OUR SNARES...
"...UNTIL..."
EEEEEEEEE
HE'S FALLEN INTO THE CONCEALED PIT!
3.

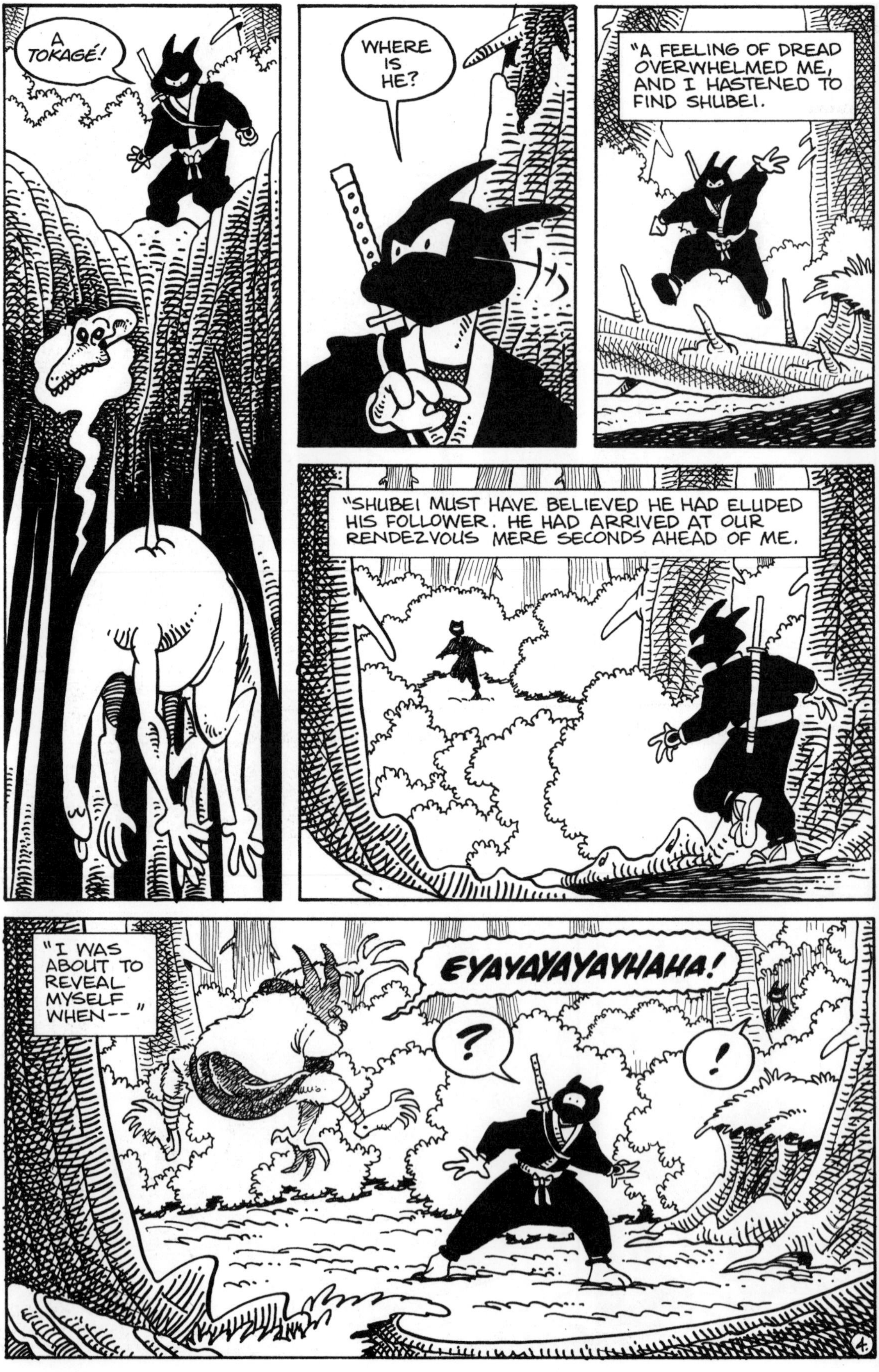
A TOKAGÉ!
WHERE IS HE?
"A FEELING OF DREAD OVERWHELMED ME, AND I HASTENED TO FIND SHUBEI.
"SHUBEI MUST HAVE BELIEVED HE HAD ELUDED HIS FOLLOWER. HE HAD ARRIVED AT OUR RENDEZVOUS MERE SECONDS AHEAD OF ME.
"I WAS ABOUT TO REVEAL MYSELF WHEN--"
EYAYAYAYAYHAHA!
?
!
4.

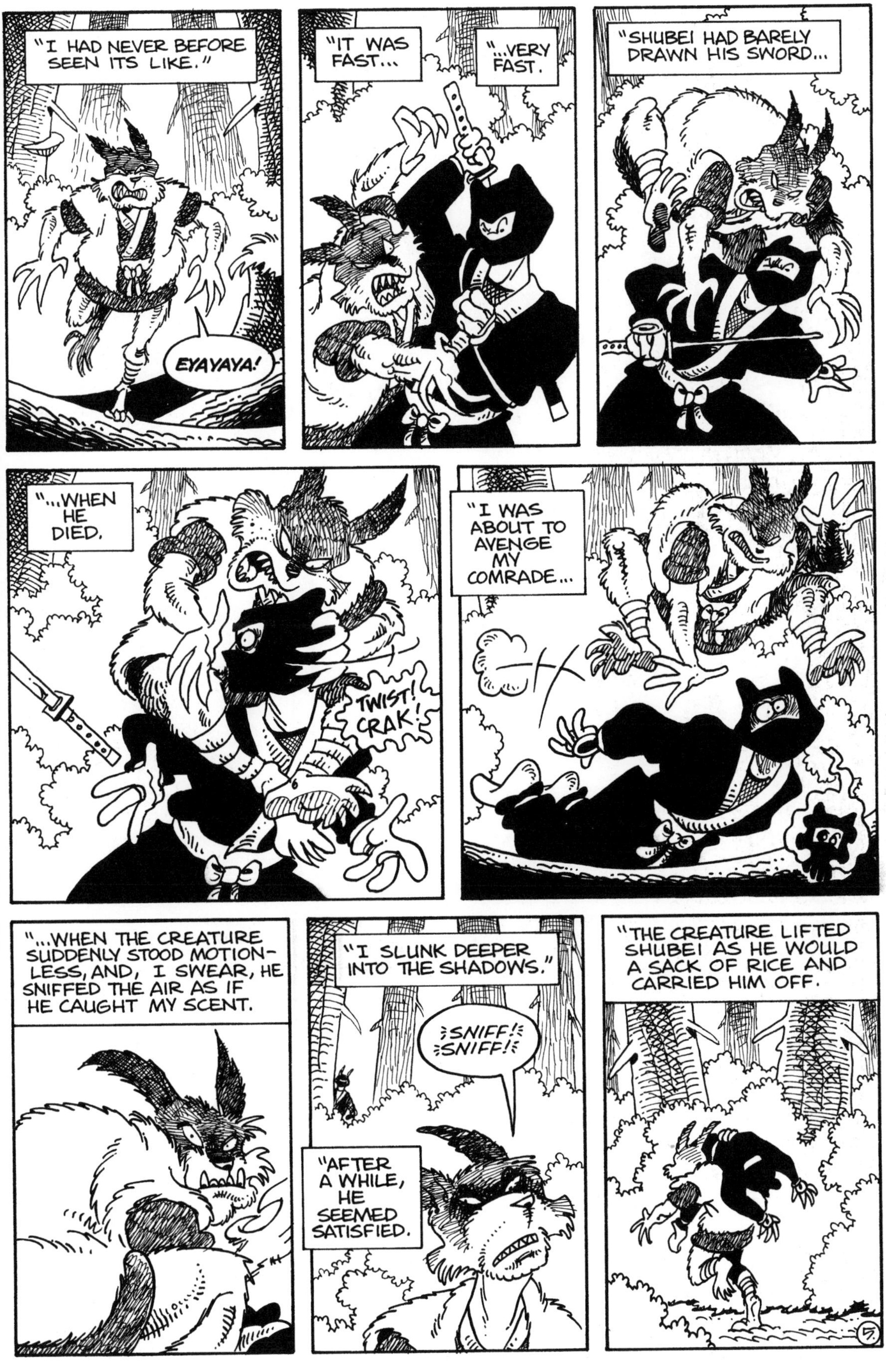
"I HAD NEVER BEFORE SEEN ITS LIKE."
EYAYAYA!
"IT WAS FAST...
"...VERY FAST.
"SHUBEI HAD BARELY DRAWN HIS SWORD...
"...WHEN HE DIED.
TWIST! CRAK!
"I WAS ABOUT TO AVENGE MY COMRADE...
"...WHEN THE CREATURE SUDDENLY STOOD MOTIONLESS, AND, I SWEAR, HE SNIFFED THE AIR AS IF HE CAUGHT MY SCENT.
"I SLUNK DEEPER INTO THE SHADOWS."
SNIFF! SNIFF!
"AFTER A WHILE, HE SEEMED SATISFIED.
"THE CREATURE LIFTED SHUBEI AS HE WOULD A SACK OF RICE AND CARRIED HIM OFF.
7.

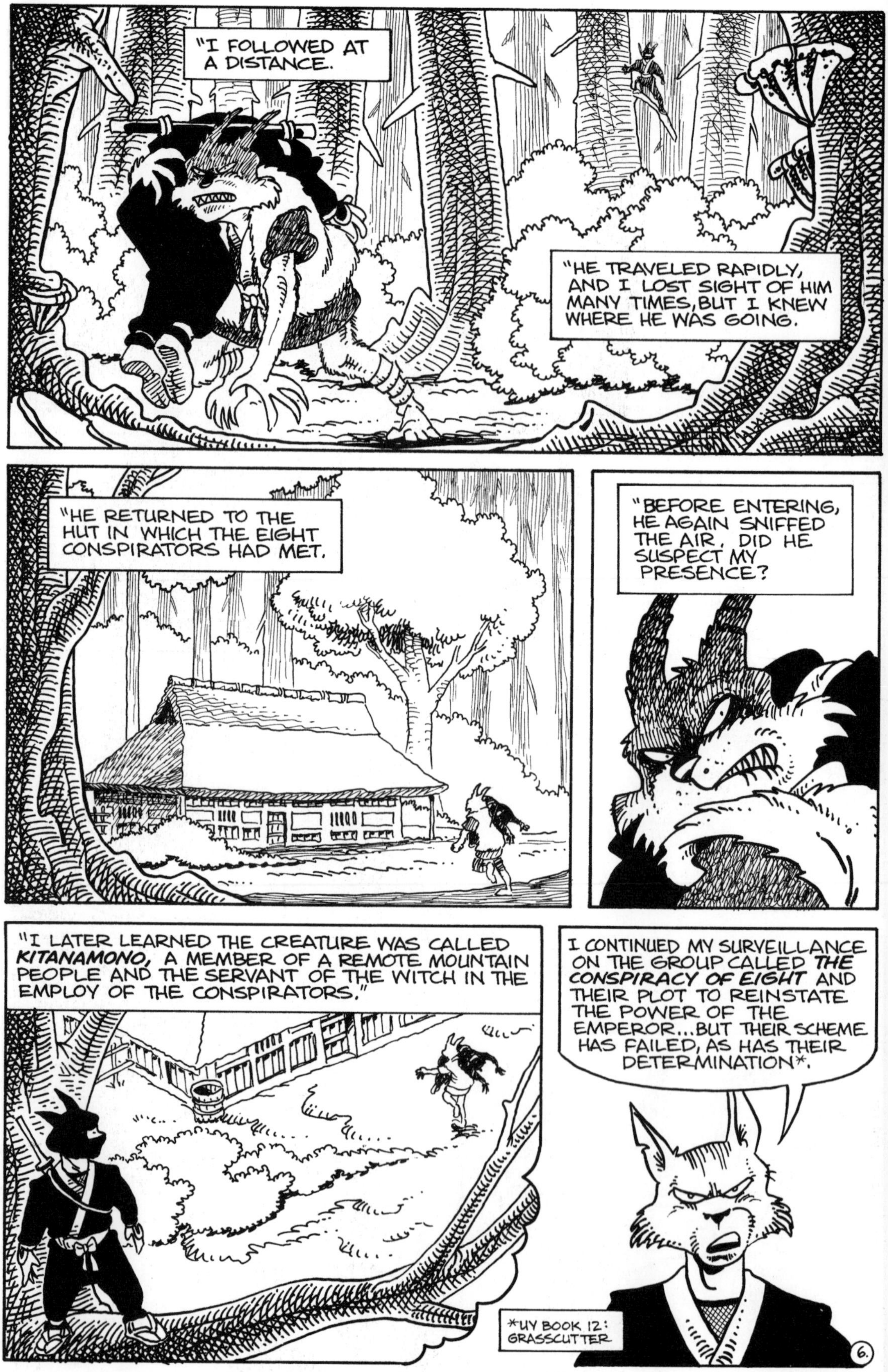
"I FOLLOWED AT A DISTANCE.
"HE TRAVELED RAPIDLY, AND I LOST SIGHT OF HIM MANY TIMES, BUT I KNEW WHERE HE WAS GOING.
"HE RETURNED TO THE HUT IN WHICH THE EIGHT CONSPIRATORS HAD MET.
"BEFORE ENTERING, HE AGAIN SNIFFED THE AIR. DID HE SUSPECT MY PRESENCE?
"I LATER LEARNED THE CREATURE WAS CALLED **KITANAMONO**, A MEMBER OF A REMOTE MOUNTAIN PEOPLE AND THE SERVANT OF THE WITCH IN THE EMPLOY OF THE CONSPIRATORS."
I CONTINUED MY SURVEILLANCE ON THE GROUP CALLED **THE CONSPIRACY OF EIGHT** AND THEIR PLOT TO REINSTATE THE POWER OF THE EMPEROR...BUT THEIR SCHEME HAS FAILED, AS HAS THEIR DETERMINATION*.
*UY BOOK 12: GRASSCUTTER
6.

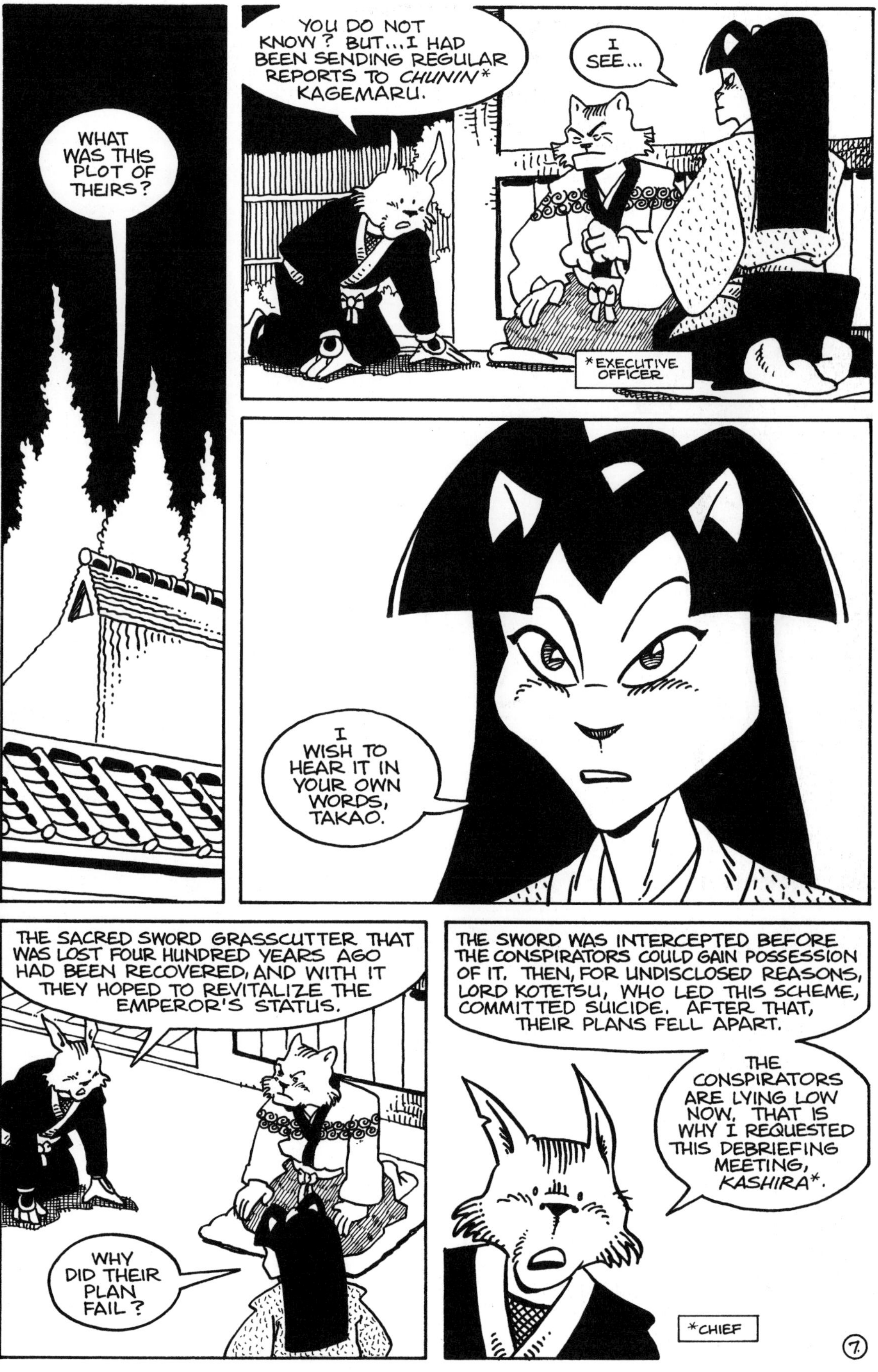
WHAT WAS THIS PLOT OF THEIRS?
YOU DO NOT KNOW? BUT...I HAD BEEN SENDING REGULAR REPORTS TO *CHUNIN** KAGEMARU.
I SEE...
*EXECUTIVE OFFICER
I WISH TO HEAR IT IN YOUR OWN WORDS, TAKAO.
THE SACRED SWORD GRASSCUTTER THAT WAS LOST FOUR HUNDRED YEARS AGO HAD BEEN RECOVERED, AND WITH IT THEY HOPED TO REVITALIZE THE EMPEROR'S STATUS.
WHY DID THEIR PLAN FAIL?
THE SWORD WAS INTERCEPTED BEFORE THE CONSPIRATORS COULD GAIN POSSESSION OF IT. THEN, FOR UNDISCLOSED REASONS, LORD KOTETSU, WHO LED THIS SCHEME, COMMITTED SUICIDE. AFTER THAT, THEIR PLANS FELL APART.
THE CONSPIRATORS ARE LYING LOW NOW. THAT IS WHY I REQUESTED THIS DEBRIEFING MEETING, *KASHIRA**.
*CHIEF
7

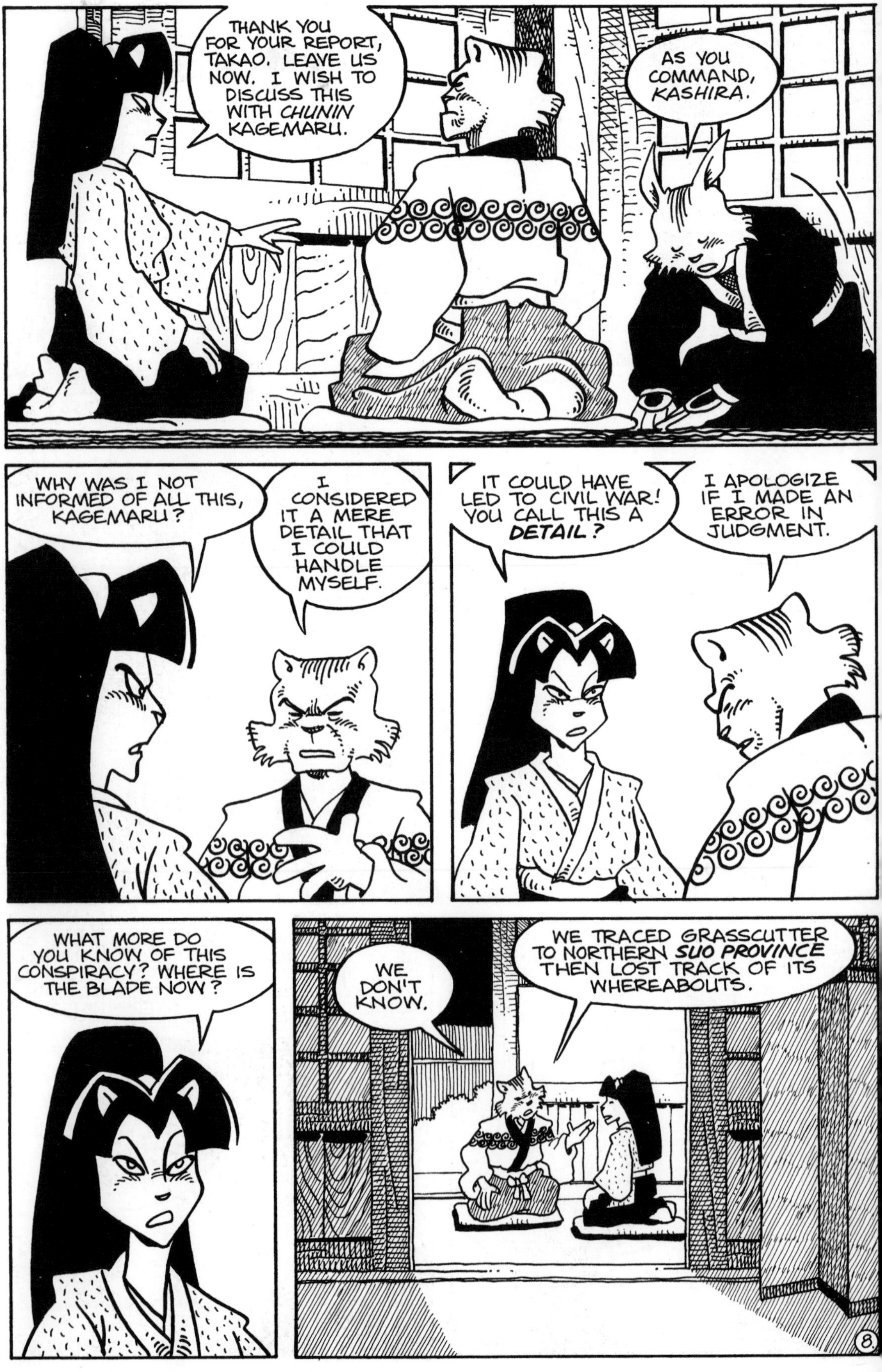
THANK YOU FOR YOUR REPORT, TAKAO. LEAVE US NOW. I WISH TO DISCUSS THIS WITH CHUNIN KAGEMARU.
AS YOU COMMAND, KASHIRA.
WHY WAS I NOT INFORMED OF ALL THIS, KAGEMARU?
I CONSIDERED IT A MERE DETAIL THAT I COULD HANDLE MYSELF.
IT COULD HAVE LED TO CIVIL WAR! YOU CALL THIS A DETAIL?
I APOLOGIZE IF I MADE AN ERROR IN JUDGMENT.
WHAT MORE DO YOU KNOW OF THIS CONSPIRACY? WHERE IS THE BLADE NOW?
WE DON'T KNOW.
WE TRACED GRASSCUTTER TO NORTHERN SUO PROVINCE THEN LOST TRACK OF ITS WHEREABOUTS.
8

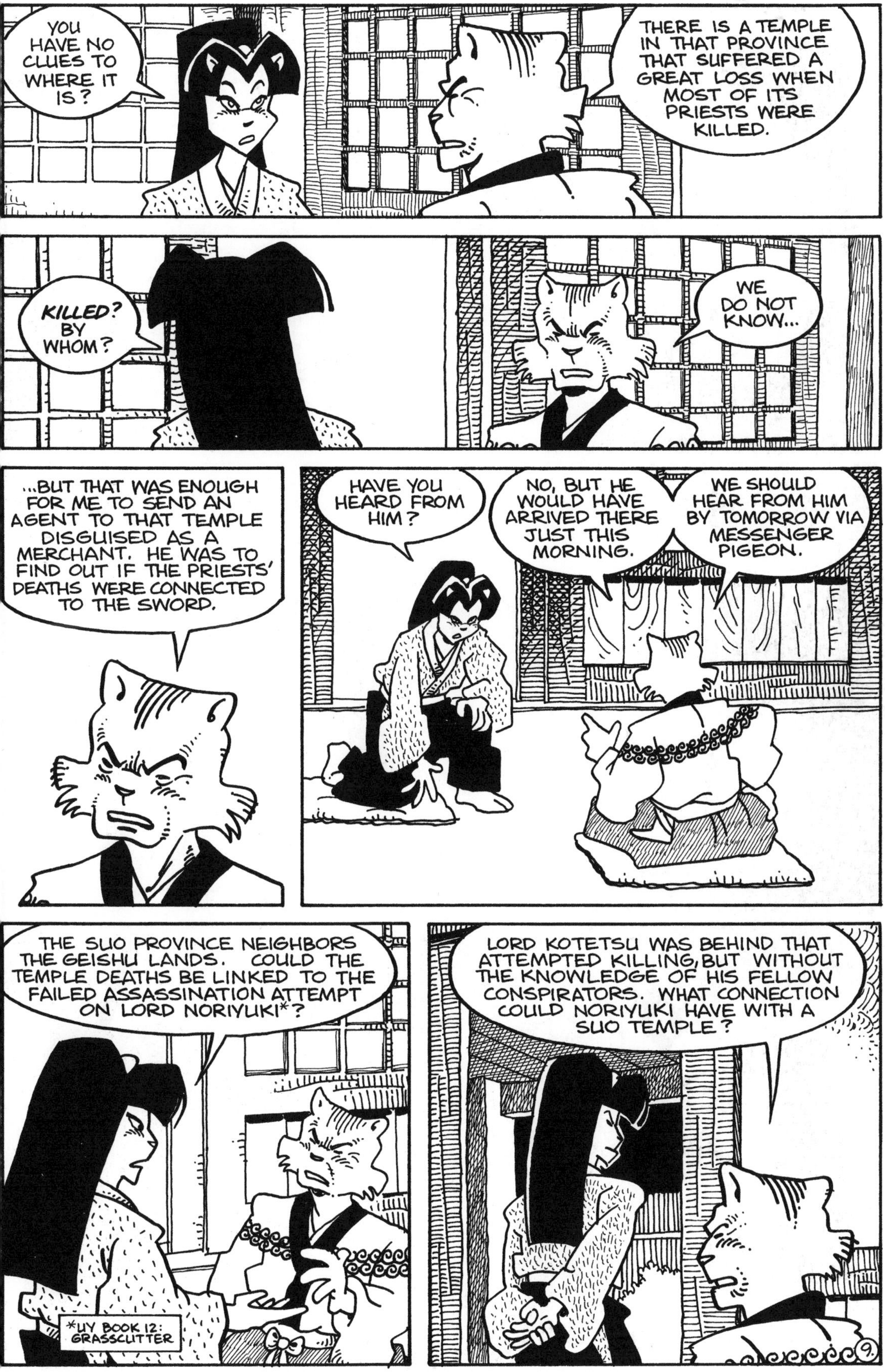
YOU HAVE NO CLUES TO WHERE IT IS?
THERE IS A TEMPLE IN THAT PROVINCE THAT SUFFERED A GREAT LOSS WHEN MOST OF ITS PRIESTS WERE KILLED.
KILLED? BY WHOM?
WE DO NOT KNOW...
...BUT THAT WAS ENOUGH FOR ME TO SEND AN AGENT TO THAT TEMPLE DISGUISED AS A MERCHANT. HE WAS TO FIND OUT IF THE PRIESTS' DEATHS WERE CONNECTED TO THE SWORD.
HAVE YOU HEARD FROM HIM?
NO, BUT HE WOULD HAVE ARRIVED THERE JUST THIS MORNING.
WE SHOULD HEAR FROM HIM BY TOMORROW VIA MESSENGER PIGEON.
THE SUO PROVINCE NEIGHBORS THE GEISHU LANDS. COULD THE TEMPLE DEATHS BE LINKED TO THE FAILED ASSASSINATION ATTEMPT ON LORD NORIYUKI*?
*UY BOOK 12: GRASSCUTTER
LORD KOTETSU WAS BEHIND THAT ATTEMPTED KILLING, BUT WITHOUT THE KNOWLEDGE OF HIS FELLOW CONSPIRATORS. WHAT CONNECTION COULD NORIYUKI HAVE WITH A SUO TEMPLE?
9.

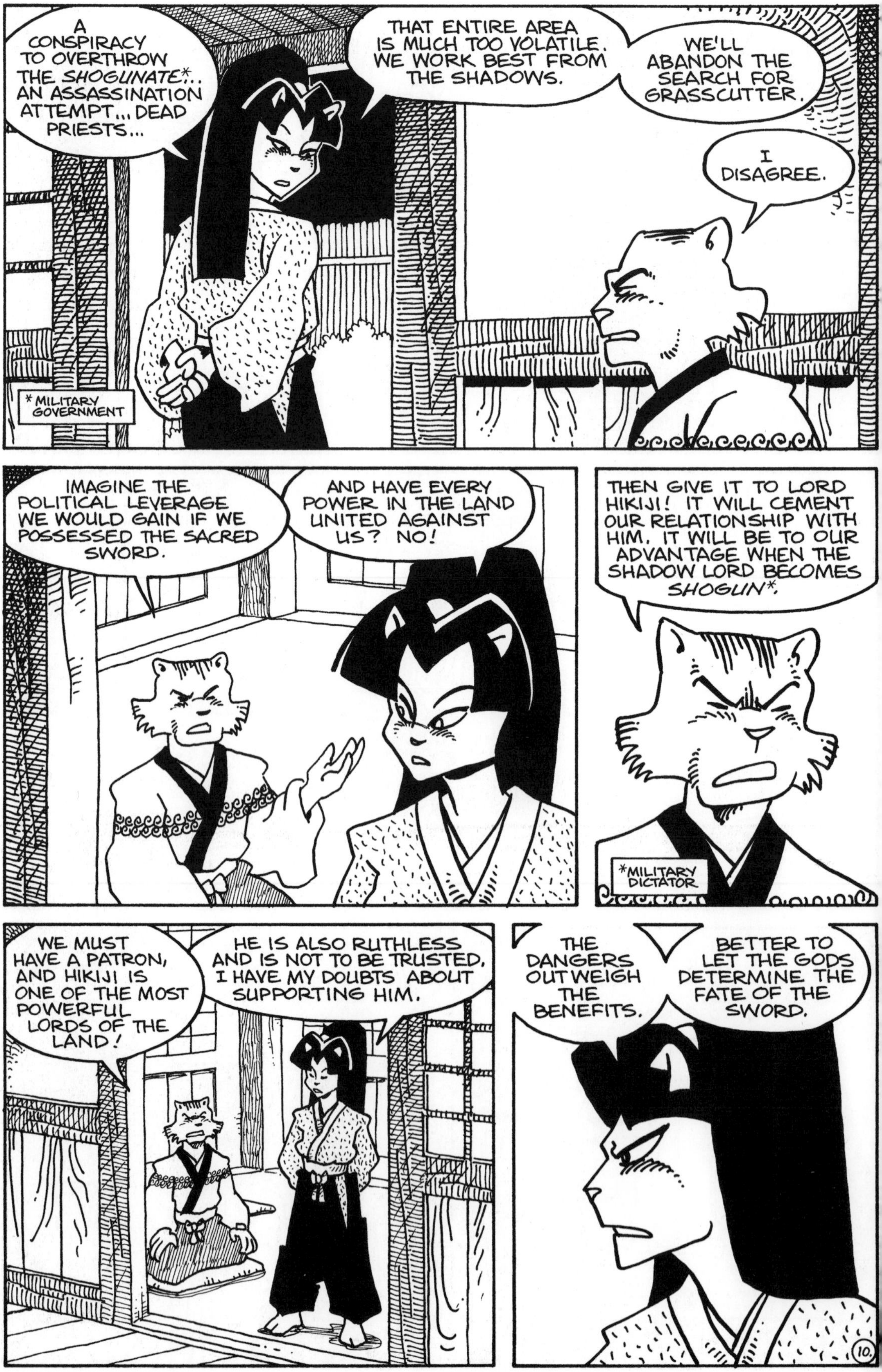
A CONSPIRACY TO OVERTHROW THE *SHOGUNATE**... AN ASSASSINATION ATTEMPT... DEAD PRIESTS...
*MILITARY GOVERNMENT
THAT ENTIRE AREA IS MUCH TOO VOLATILE. WE WORK BEST FROM THE SHADOWS.
WE'LL ABANDON THE SEARCH FOR GRASSCUTTER.
I DISAGREE.
IMAGINE THE POLITICAL LEVERAGE WE WOULD GAIN IF WE POSSESSED THE SACRED SWORD.
AND HAVE EVERY POWER IN THE LAND UNITED AGAINST US? NO!
THEN GIVE IT TO LORD HIKIJI! IT WILL CEMENT OUR RELATIONSHIP WITH HIM. IT WILL BE TO OUR ADVANTAGE WHEN THE SHADOW LORD BECOMES *SHOGUN**.
*MILITARY DICTATOR
WE MUST HAVE A PATRON, AND HIKIJI IS ONE OF THE MOST POWERFUL LORDS OF THE LAND!
HE IS ALSO RUTHLESS AND IS NOT TO BE TRUSTED. I HAVE MY DOUBTS ABOUT SUPPORTING HIM.
THE DANGERS OUTWEIGH THE BENEFITS.
BETTER TO LET THE GODS DETERMINE THE FATE OF THE SWORD.
10.

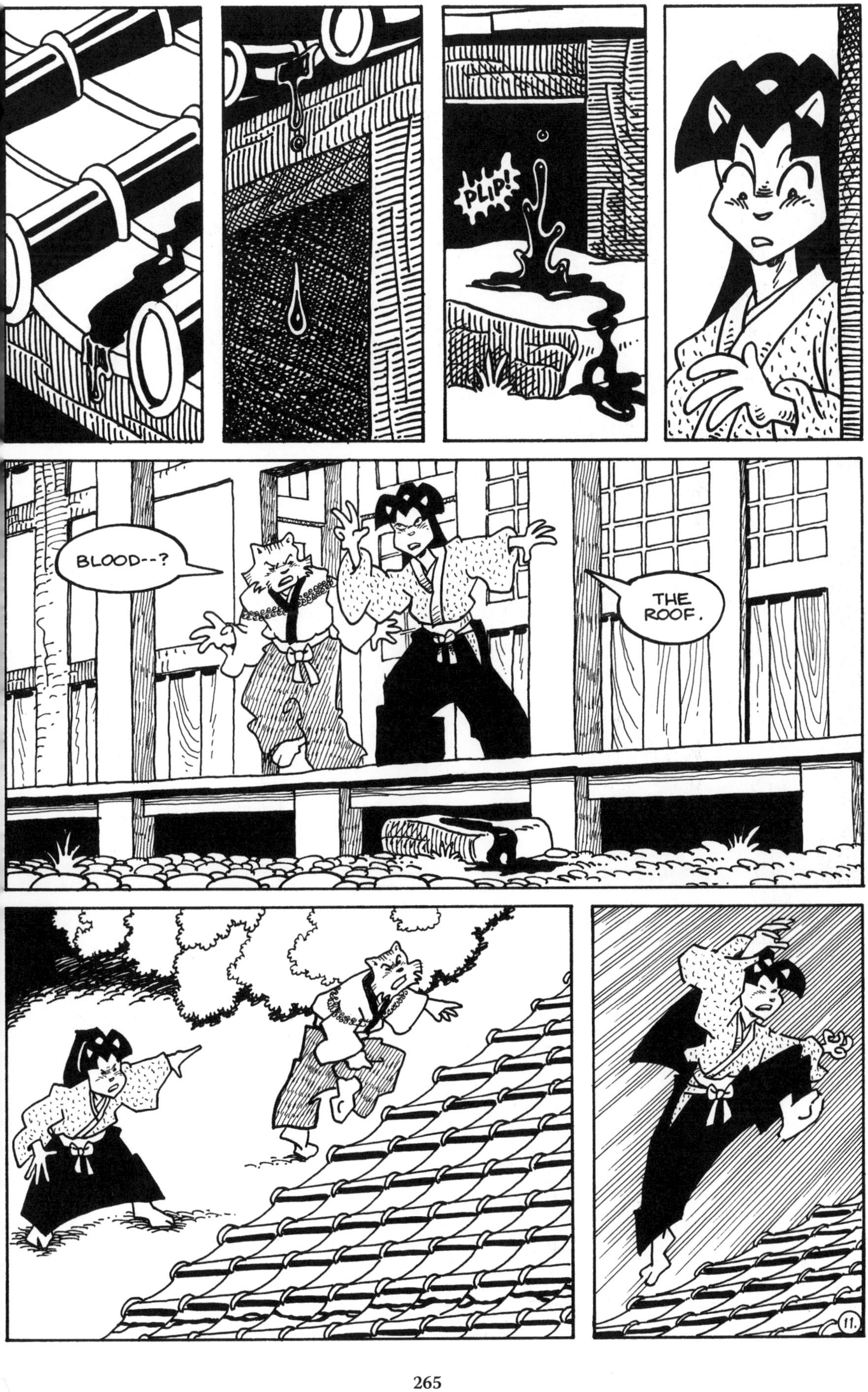
PLIP!
BLOOD--?
THE ROOF.
11.

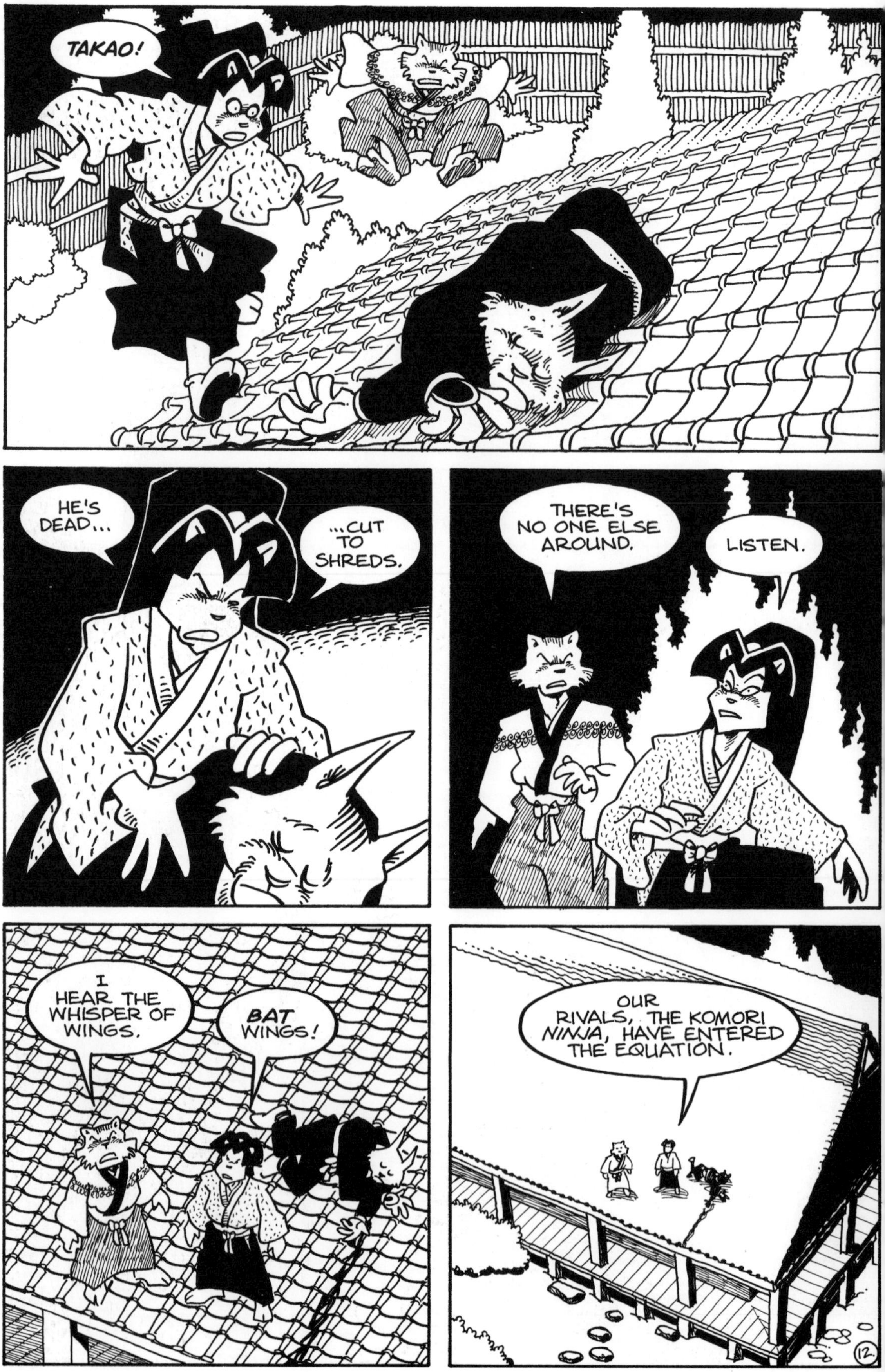
TAKAO!
HE'S DEAD...
...CUT TO SHREDS.
THERE'S NO ONE ELSE AROUND.
LISTEN.
I HEAR THE WHISPER OF WINGS.
BAT WINGS!
OUR RIVALS, THE KOMORI NINJA, HAVE ENTERED THE EQUATION.
12.

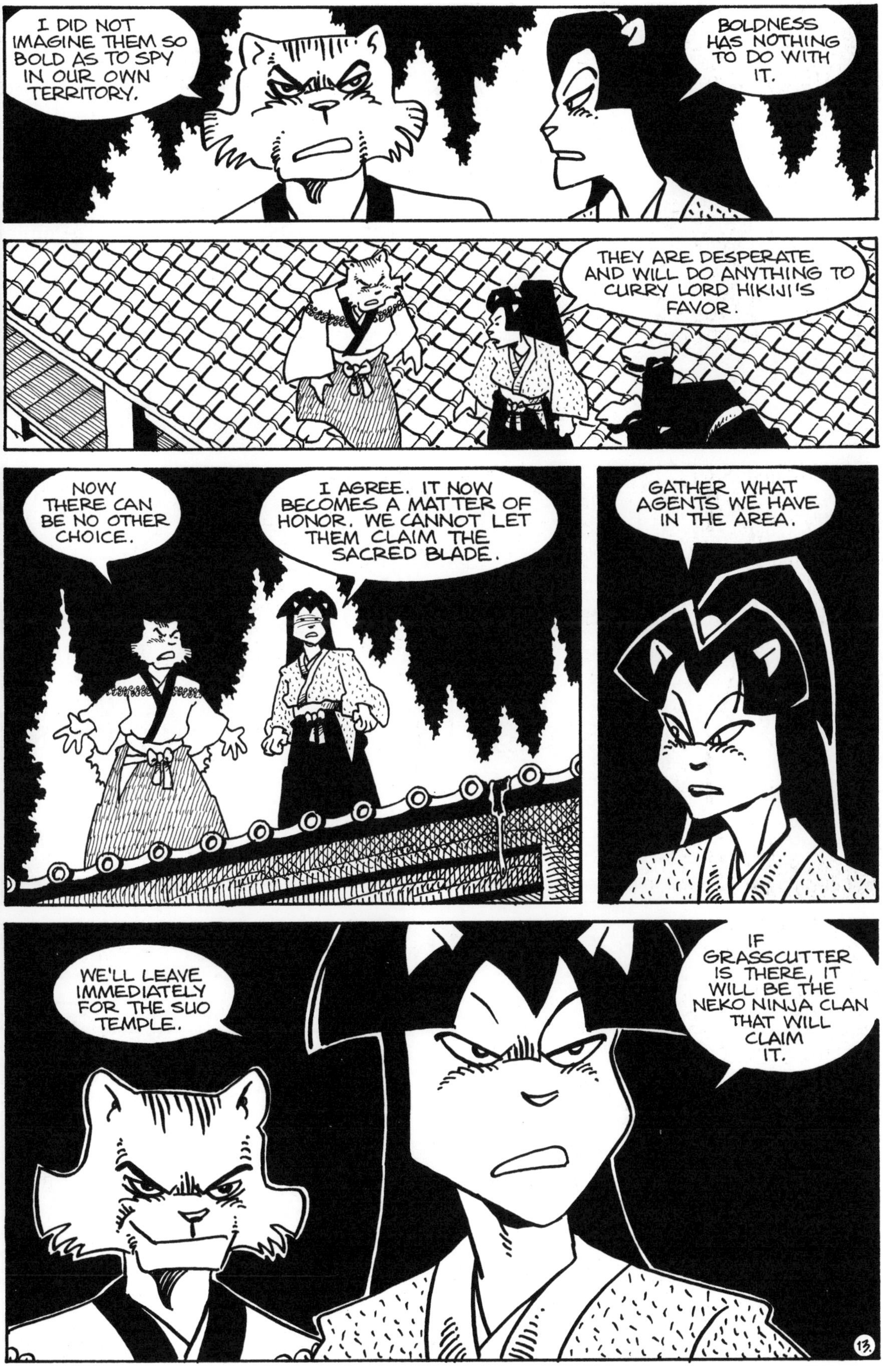
I DID NOT IMAGINE THEM SO BOLD AS TO SPY IN OUR OWN TERRITORY.
BOLDNESS HAS NOTHING TO DO WITH IT.
THEY ARE DESPERATE AND WILL DO ANYTHING TO CURRY LORD HIKIJI'S FAVOR.
NOW THERE CAN BE NO OTHER CHOICE.
I AGREE. IT NOW BECOMES A MATTER OF HONOR. WE CANNOT LET THEM CLAIM THE SACRED BLADE.
GATHER WHAT AGENTS WE HAVE IN THE AREA.
WE'LL LEAVE IMMEDIATELY FOR THE SUO TEMPLE.
IF GRASSCUTTER IS THERE, IT WILL BE THE NEKO NINJA CLAN THAT WILL CLAIM IT.
13.

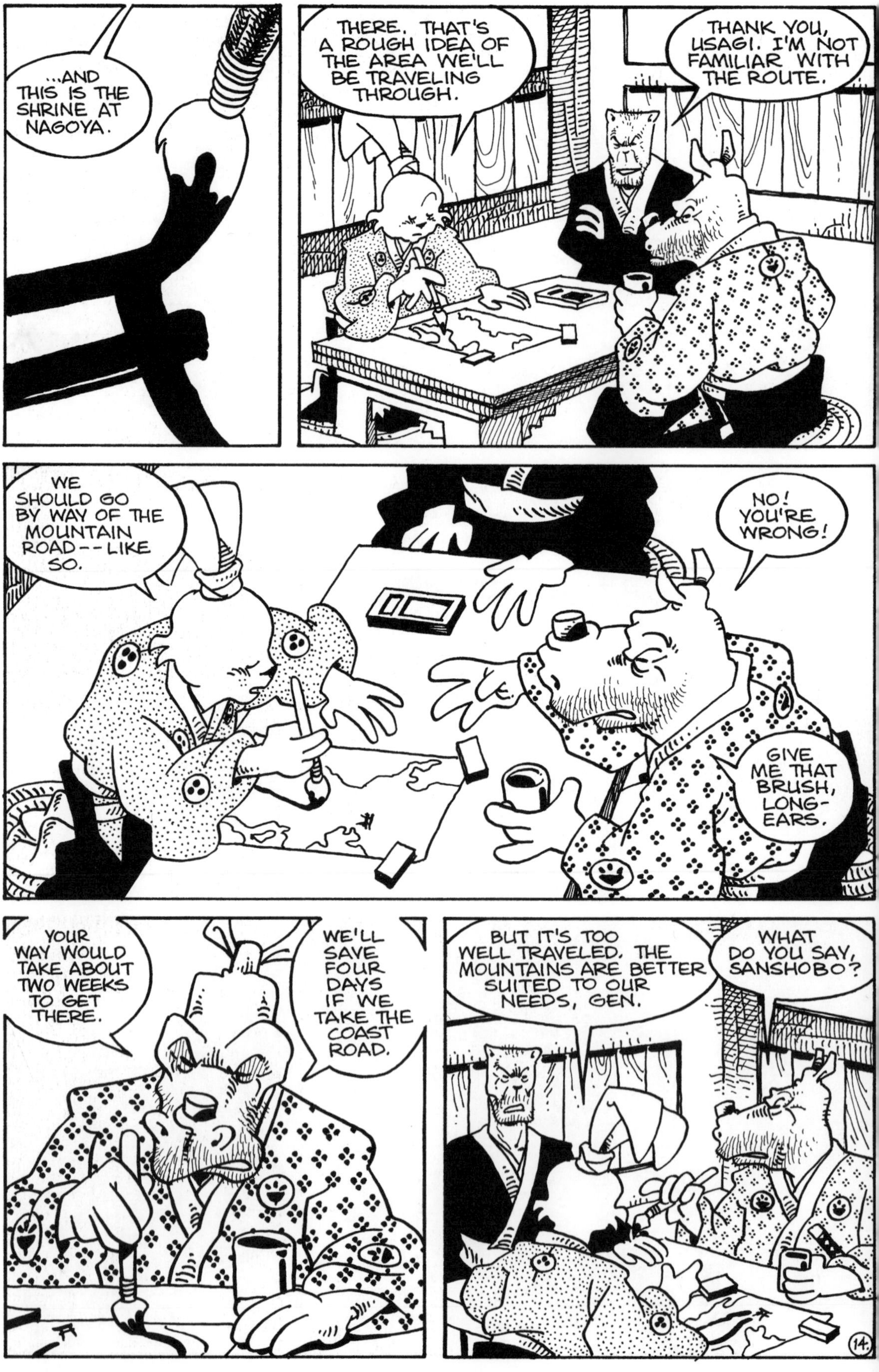
...AND THIS IS THE SHRINE AT NAGOYA.
THERE. THAT'S A ROUGH IDEA OF THE AREA WE'LL BE TRAVELING THROUGH.
THANK YOU, USAGI. I'M NOT FAMILIAR WITH THE ROUTE.
WE SHOULD GO BY WAY OF THE MOUNTAIN ROAD--LIKE SO.
NO! YOU'RE WRONG!
GIVE ME THAT BRUSH, LONG-EARS.
YOUR WAY WOULD TAKE ABOUT TWO WEEKS TO GET THERE.
WE'LL SAVE FOUR DAYS IF WE TAKE THE COAST ROAD.
BUT IT'S TOO WELL TRAVELED. THE MOUNTAINS ARE BETTER SUITED TO OUR NEEDS, GEN.
WHAT DO YOU SAY, SANSHOBO?
14.

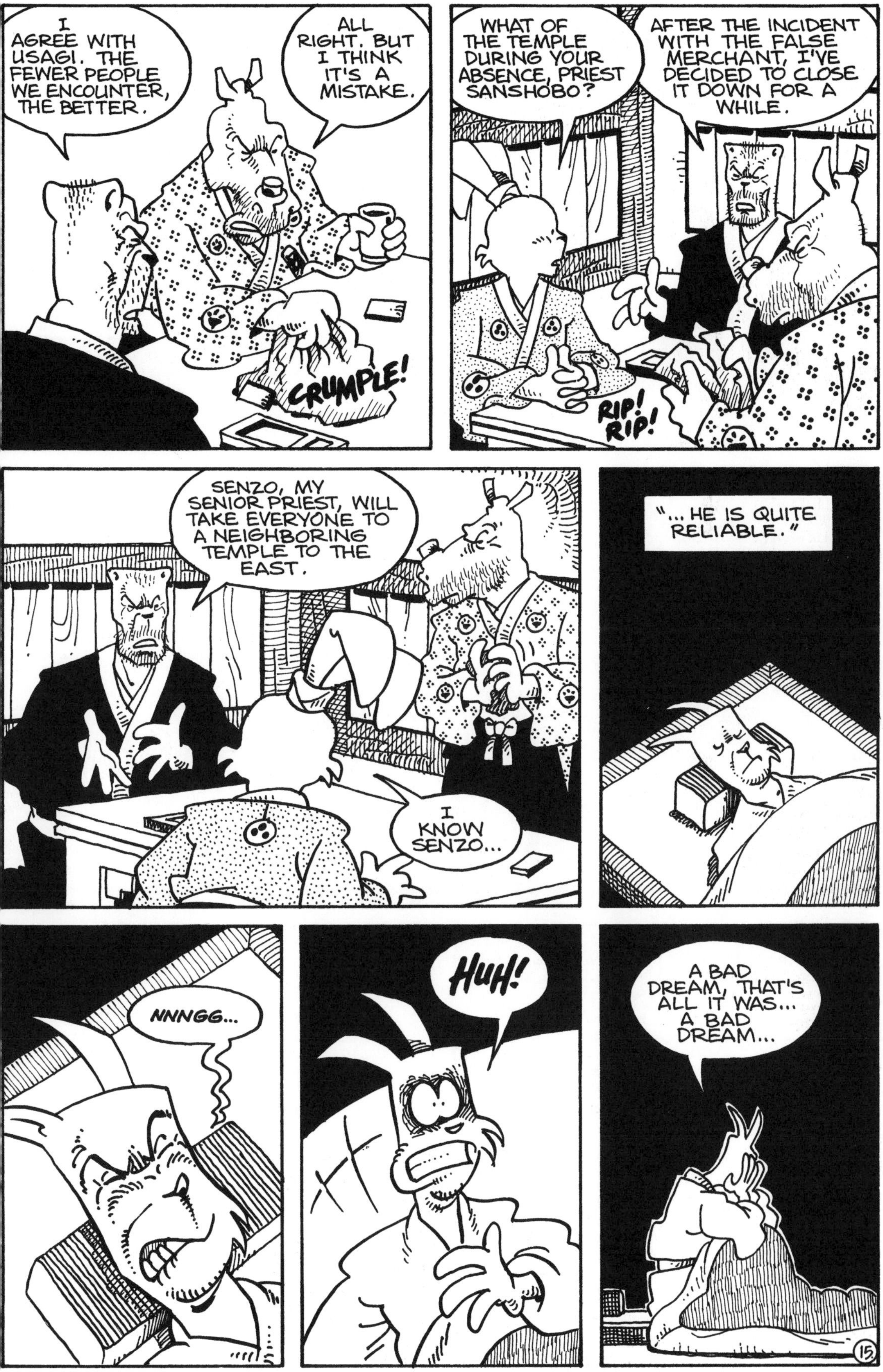
I AGREE WITH USAGI. THE FEWER PEOPLE WE ENCOUNTER, THE BETTER.
ALL RIGHT. BUT I THINK IT'S A MISTAKE.
CRUMPLE!
WHAT OF THE TEMPLE DURING YOUR ABSENCE, PRIEST SANSHOBO?
AFTER THE INCIDENT WITH THE FALSE MERCHANT, I'VE DECIDED TO CLOSE IT DOWN FOR A WHILE.
RIP! RIP!
SENZO, MY SENIOR PRIEST, WILL TAKE EVERYONE TO A NEIGHBORING TEMPLE TO THE EAST.
I KNOW SENZO...
"...HE IS QUITE RELIABLE."
NNNGG...
HUH!
A BAD DREAM, THAT'S ALL IT WAS... A BAD DREAM...
15

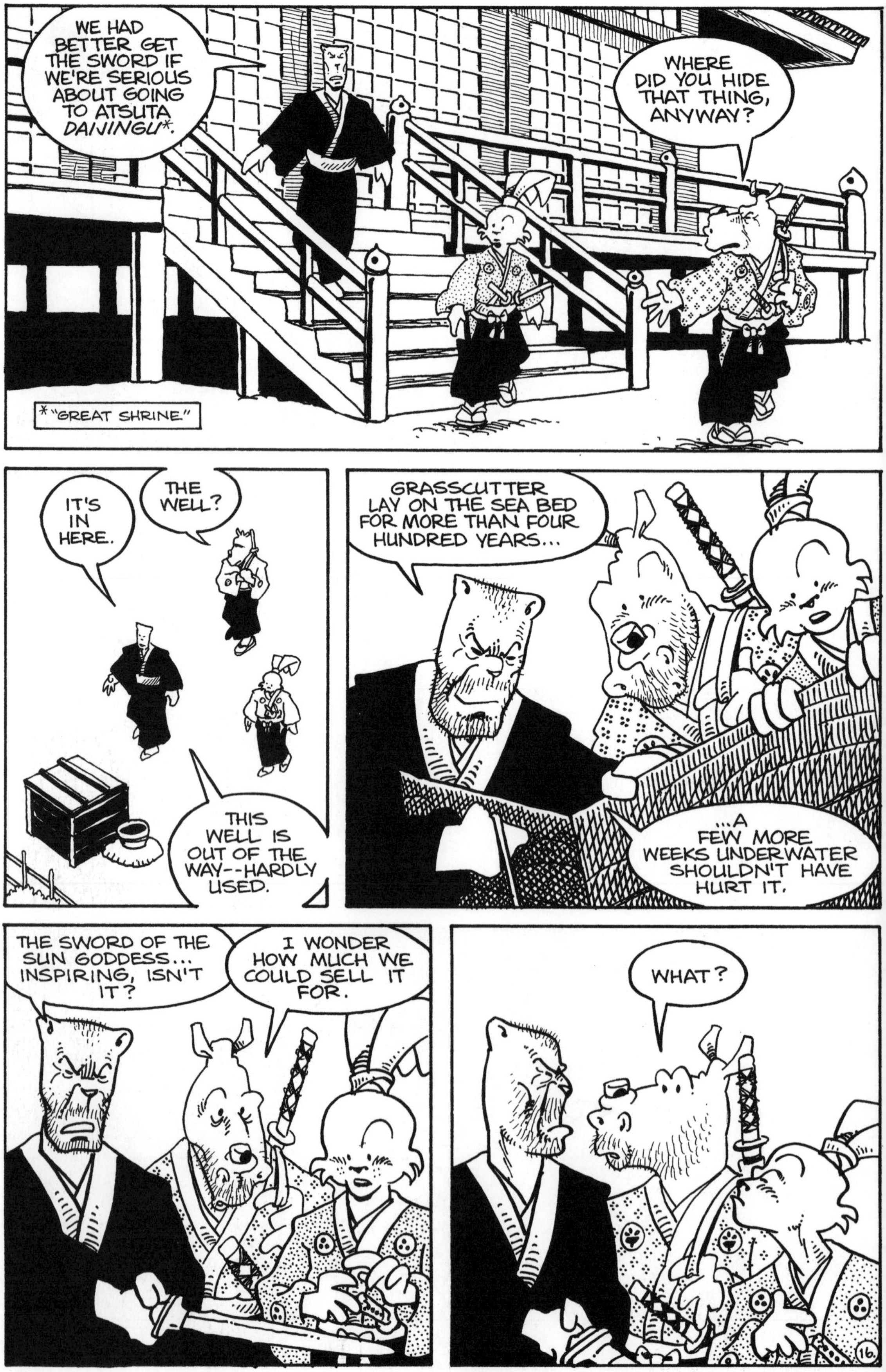
WE HAD BETTER GET THE SWORD IF WE'RE SERIOUS ABOUT GOING TO ATSUTA DAIJINGU*.
WHERE DID YOU HIDE THAT THING, ANYWAY?
*"GREAT SHRINE."
IT'S IN HERE.
THE WELL?
THIS WELL IS OUT OF THE WAY--HARDLY USED.
GRASSCUTTER LAY ON THE SEA BED FOR MORE THAN FOUR HUNDRED YEARS...
...A FEW MORE WEEKS UNDERWATER SHOULDN'T HAVE HURT IT.
THE SWORD OF THE SUN GODDESS... INSPIRING, ISN'T IT?
I WONDER HOW MUCH WE COULD SELL IT FOR.
WHAT?
16.

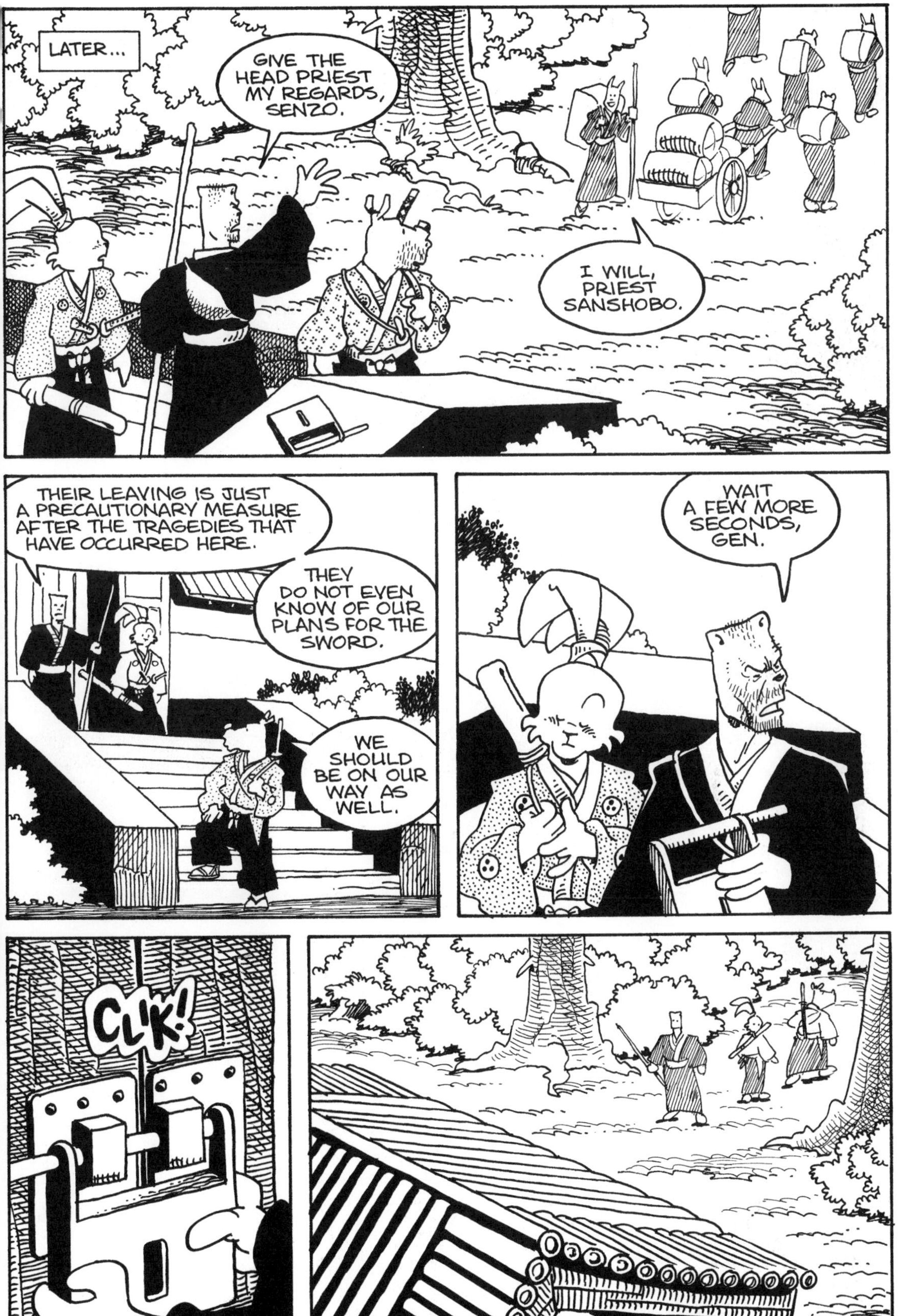
LATER...
GIVE THE HEAD PRIEST MY REGARDS, SENZO.
I WILL, PRIEST SANSHOBO.
THEIR LEAVING IS JUST A PRECAUTIONARY MEASURE AFTER THE TRAGEDIES THAT HAVE OCCURRED HERE.
THEY DO NOT EVEN KNOW OF OUR PLANS FOR THE SWORD.
WE SHOULD BE ON OUR WAY AS WELL.
WAIT A FEW MORE SECONDS, GEN.
CLIK!
17

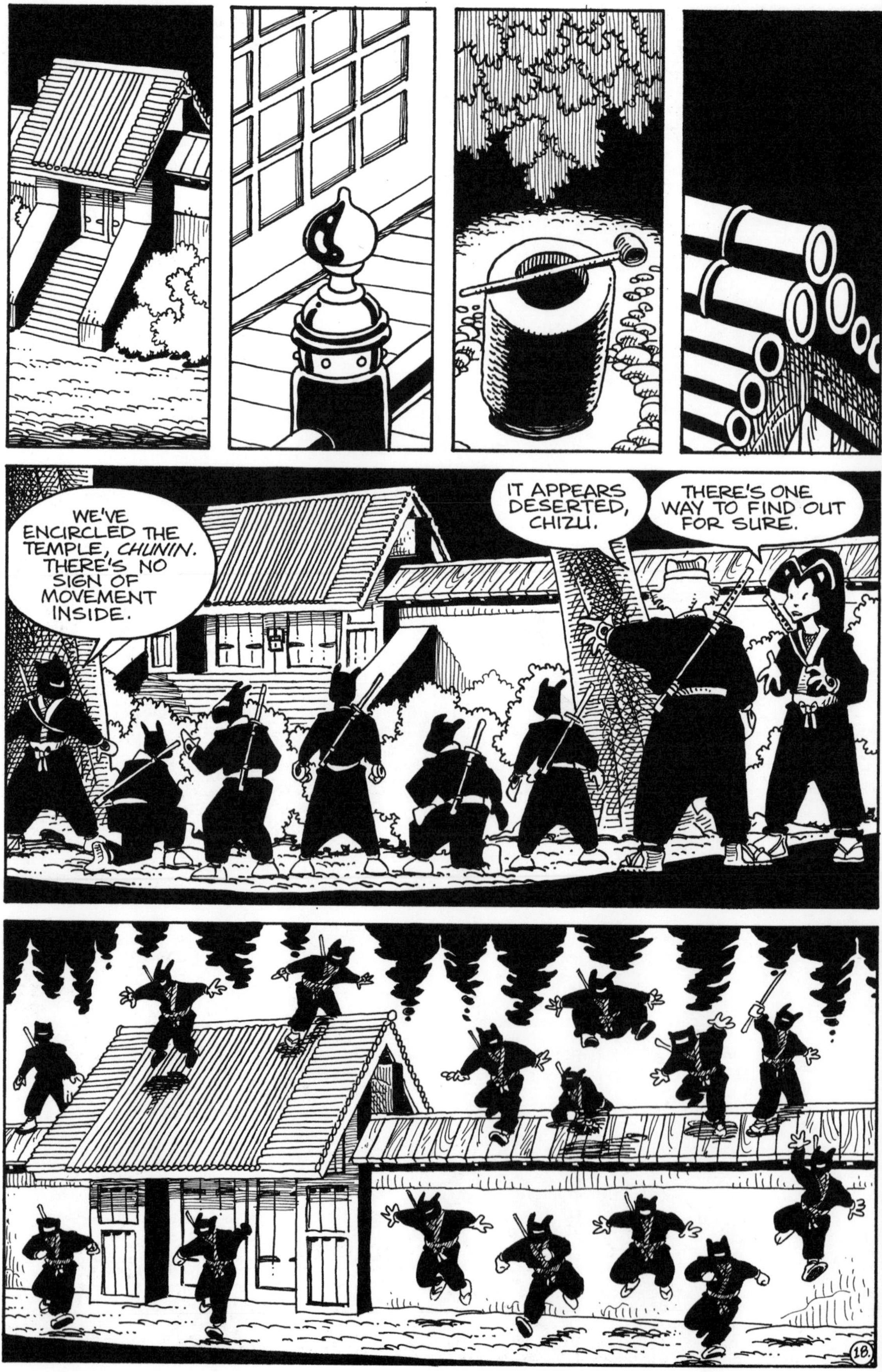
WE'VE ENCIRCLED THE TEMPLE, *CHUNIN*. THERE'S NO SIGN OF MOVEMENT INSIDE.
IT APPEARS DESERTED, CHIZU.
THERE'S ONE WAY TO FIND OUT FOR SURE.
18.

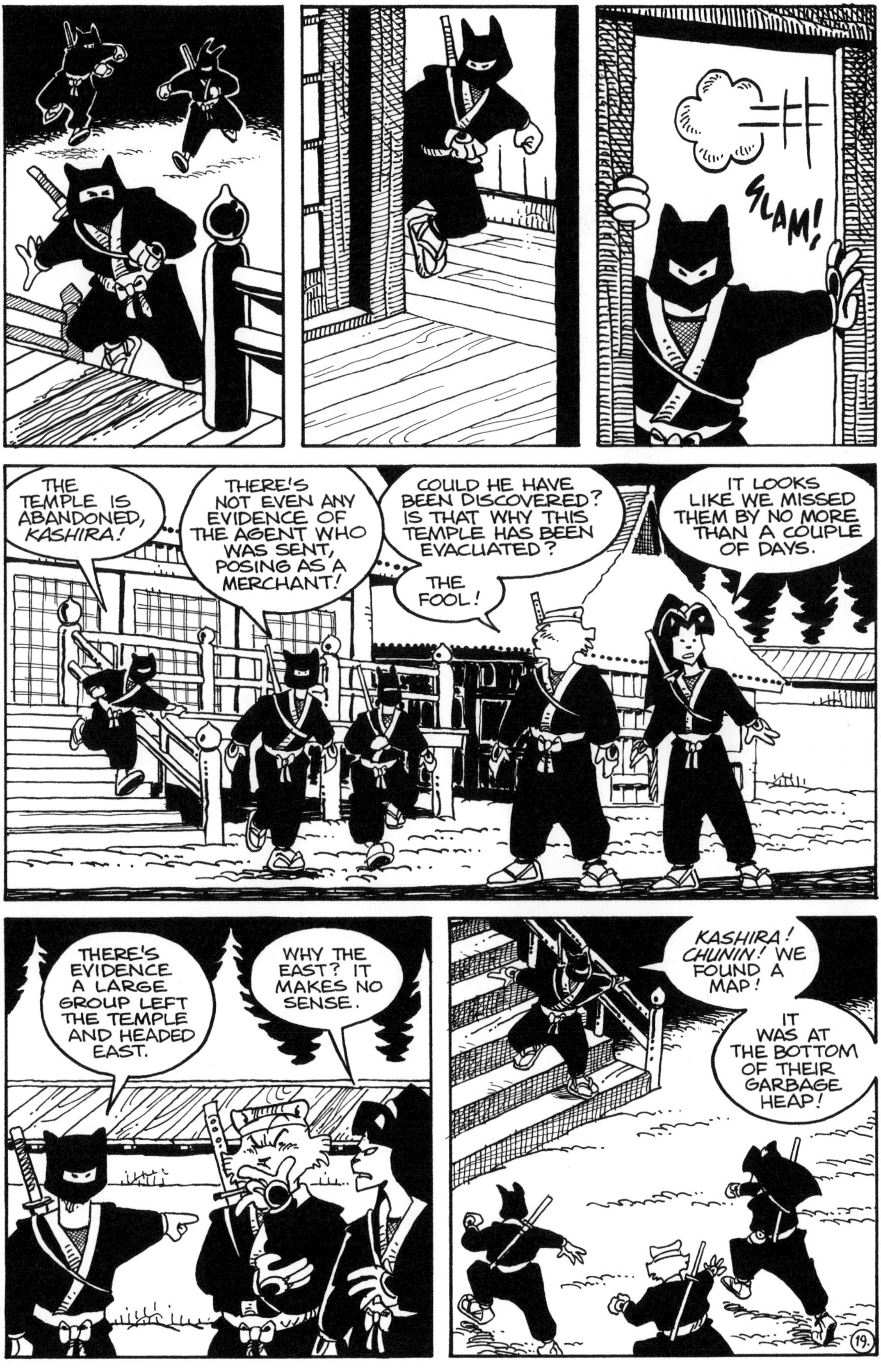
SLAM!
THE TEMPLE IS ABANDONED, KASHIRA!
THERE'S NOT EVEN ANY EVIDENCE OF THE AGENT WHO WAS SENT, POSING AS A MERCHANT!
COULD HE HAVE BEEN DISCOVERED? IS THAT WHY THIS TEMPLE HAS BEEN EVACUATED?
THE FOOL!
IT LOOKS LIKE WE MISSED THEM BY NO MORE THAN A COUPLE OF DAYS.
THERE'S EVIDENCE A LARGE GROUP LEFT THE TEMPLE AND HEADED EAST.
WHY THE EAST? IT MAKES NO SENSE.
KASHIRA! CHUNIN! WE FOUND A MAP!
IT WAS AT THE BOTTOM OF THEIR GARBAGE HEAP!
19.

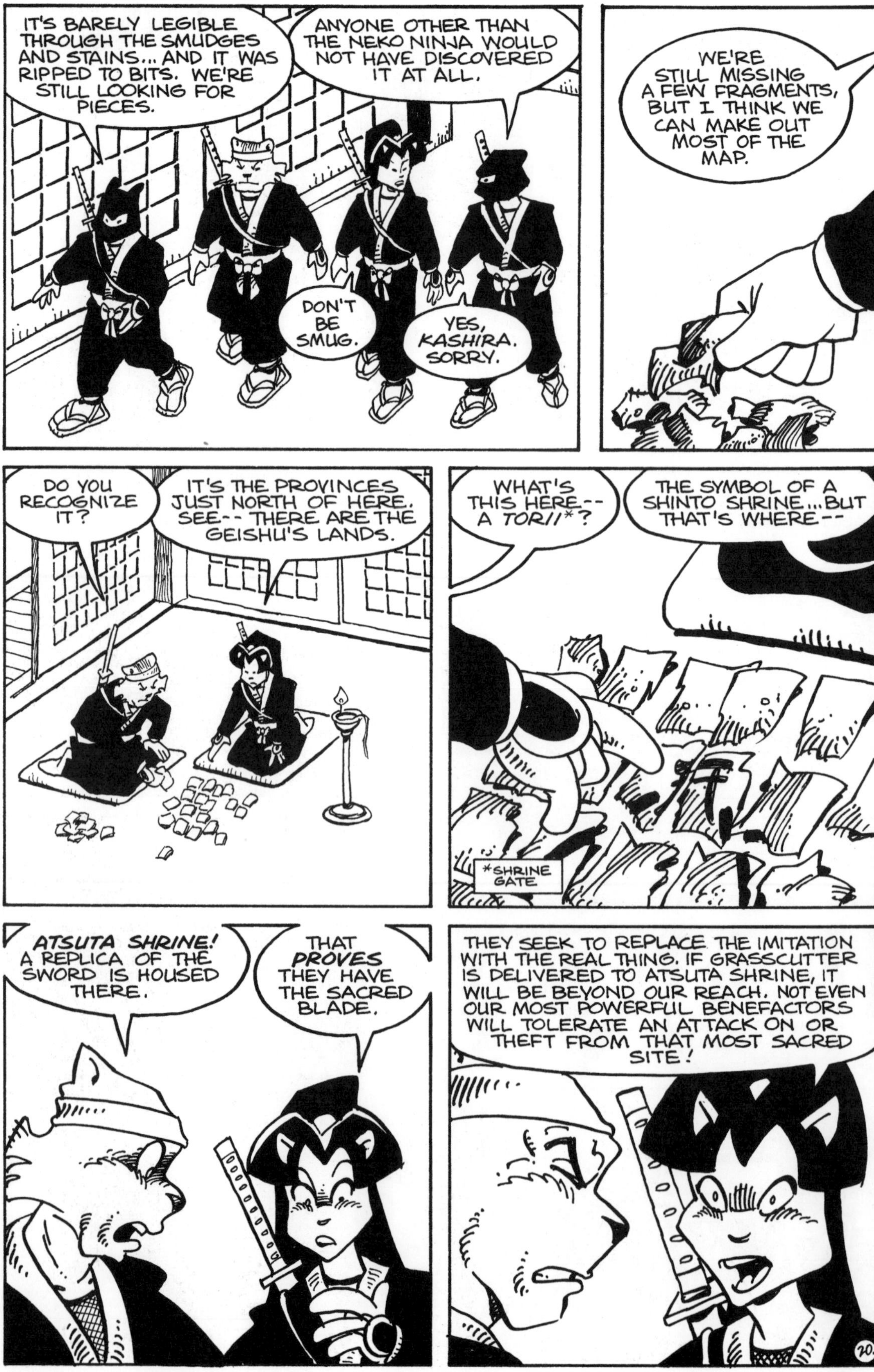
IT'S BARELY LEGIBLE THROUGH THE SMUDGES AND STAINS... AND IT WAS RIPPED TO BITS. WE'RE STILL LOOKING FOR PIECES.
ANYONE OTHER THAN THE NEKO NINJA WOULD NOT HAVE DISCOVERED IT AT ALL.
DON'T BE SMUG.
YES, KASHIRA. SORRY.
WE'RE STILL MISSING A FEW FRAGMENTS, BUT I THINK WE CAN MAKE OUT MOST OF THE MAP.
DO YOU RECOGNIZE IT?
IT'S THE PROVINCES JUST NORTH OF HERE. SEE-- THERE ARE THE GEISHU'S LANDS.
WHAT'S THIS HERE-- A TORII*?
THE SYMBOL OF A SHINTO SHRINE...BUT THAT'S WHERE--
*SHRINE GATE
ATSUTA SHRINE! A REPLICA OF THE SWORD IS HOUSED THERE.
THAT PROVES THEY HAVE THE SACRED BLADE.
THEY SEEK TO REPLACE THE IMITATION WITH THE REAL THING. IF GRASSCUTTER IS DELIVERED TO ATSUTA SHRINE, IT WILL BE BEYOND OUR REACH. NOT EVEN OUR MOST POWERFUL BENEFACTORS WILL TOLERATE AN ATTACK ON OR THEFT FROM THAT MOST SACRED SITE!
20.

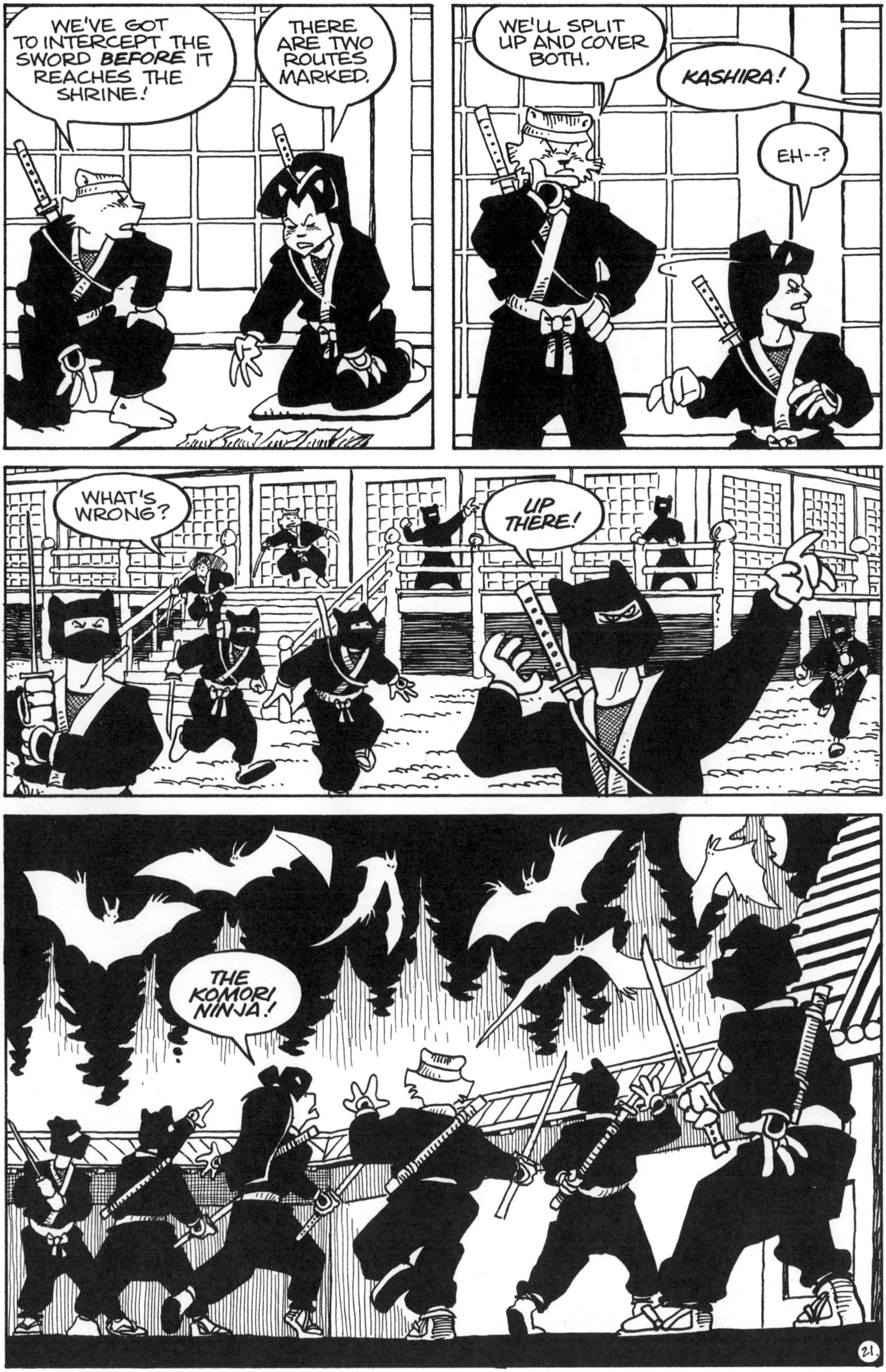
WE'VE GOT TO INTERCEPT THE SWORD BEFORE IT REACHES THE SHRINE!
THERE ARE TWO ROUTES MARKED.
WE'LL SPLIT UP AND COVER BOTH.
KASHIRA!
EH--?
WHAT'S WRONG?
UP THERE!
THE KOMORI NINJA!
21.

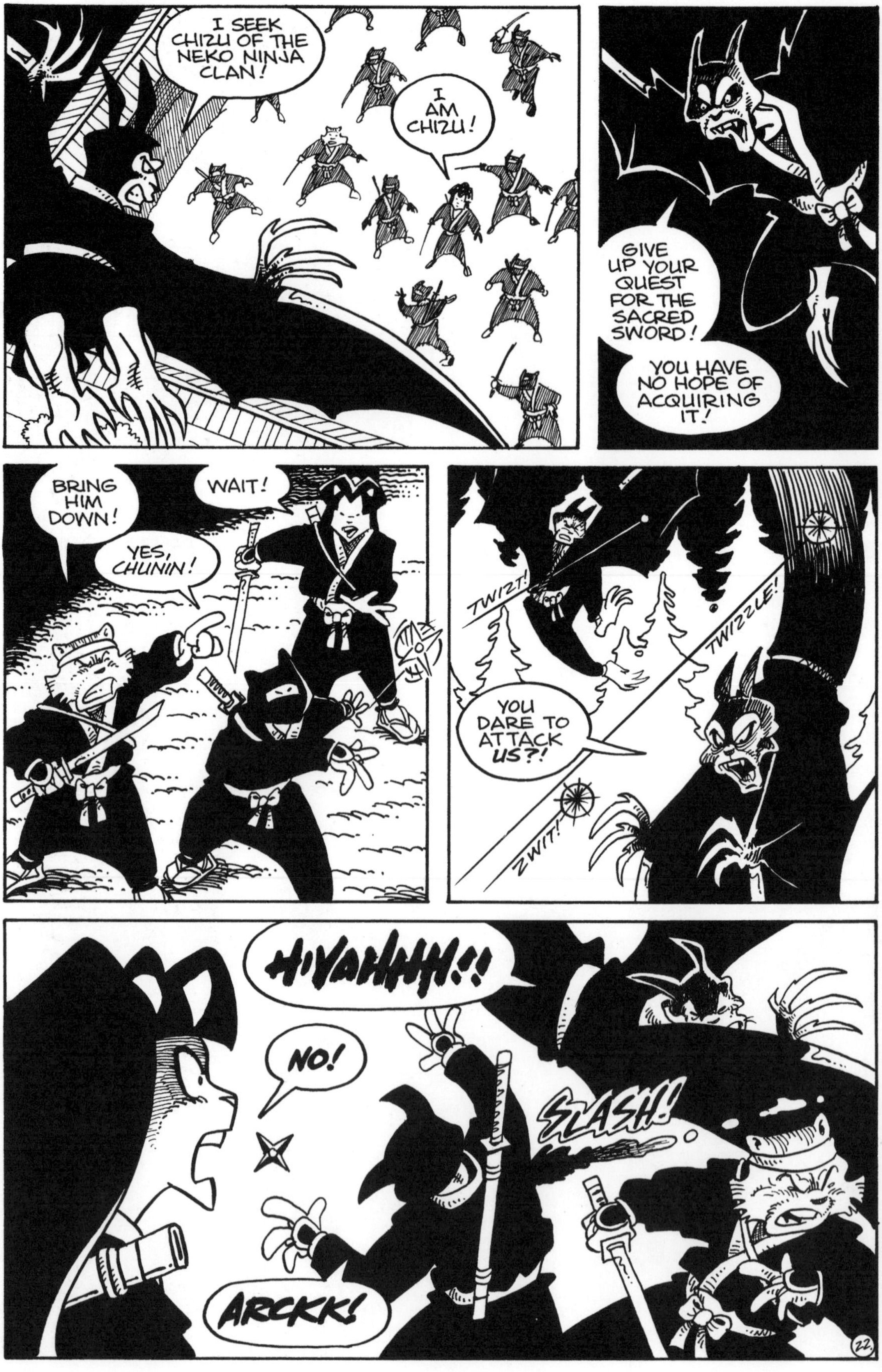

I SEEK CHIZU OF THE NEKO NINJA CLAN!
I AM CHIZU!
GIVE UP YOUR QUEST FOR THE SACRED SWORD!
YOU HAVE NO HOPE OF ACQUIRING IT!
BRING HIM DOWN!
WAIT!
YES, CHUNIN!
TWIZT!
TWIZZLE!
YOU DARE TO ATTACK US?!
ZWIT!
HIYAHHH!!
NO!
SLASH!
ARCKK!
22

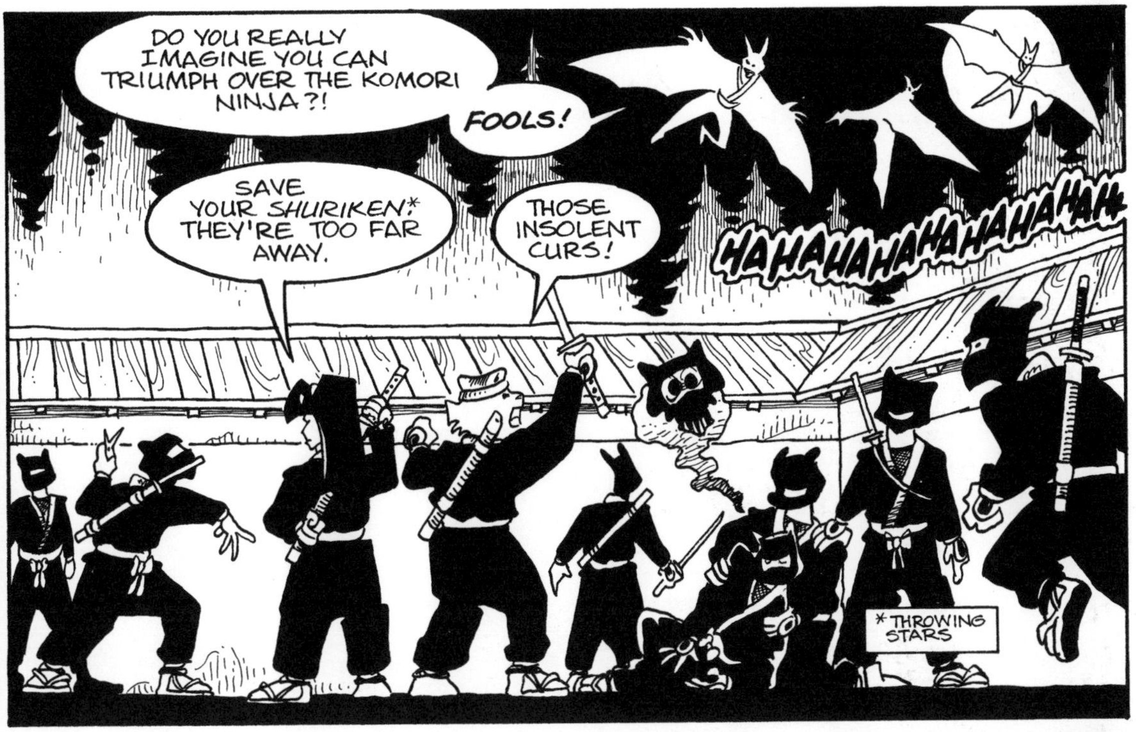
DO YOU REALLY IMAGINE YOU CAN TRIUMPH OVER THE KOMORI NINJA?!
FOOLS!
HAHAHAHAHAHAHAHAHAH
SAVE YOUR SHURIKEN!* THEY'RE TOO FAR AWAY.
THOSE INSOLENT CURS!
*THROWING STARS

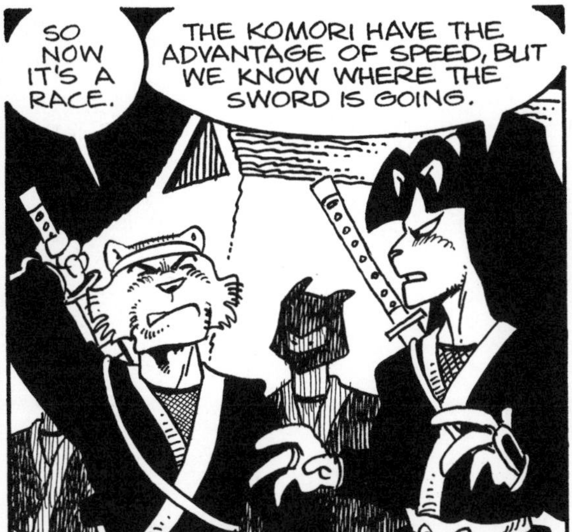
SO NOW IT'S A RACE.
THE KOMORI HAVE THE ADVANTAGE OF SPEED, BUT WE KNOW WHERE THE SWORD IS GOING.

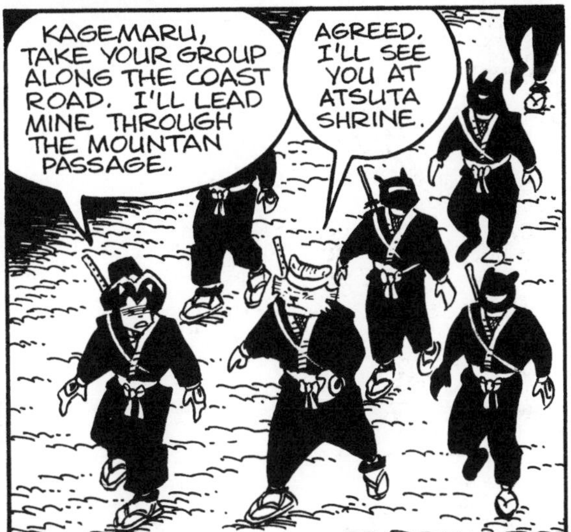
KAGEMARU, TAKE YOUR GROUP ALONG THE COAST ROAD. I'LL LEAD MINE THROUGH THE MOUNTAN PASSAGE.
AGREED. I'LL SEE YOU AT ATSUTA SHRINE.

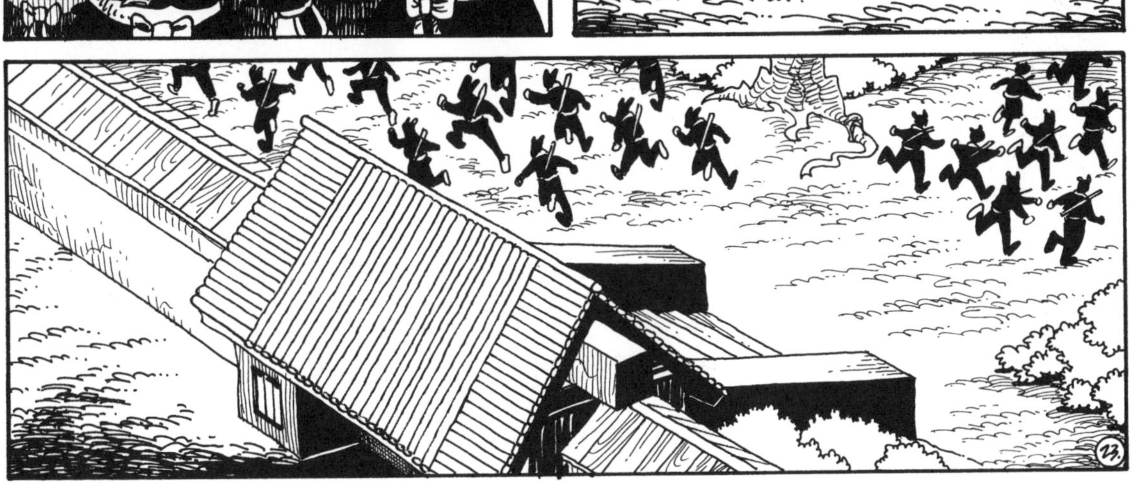
23.

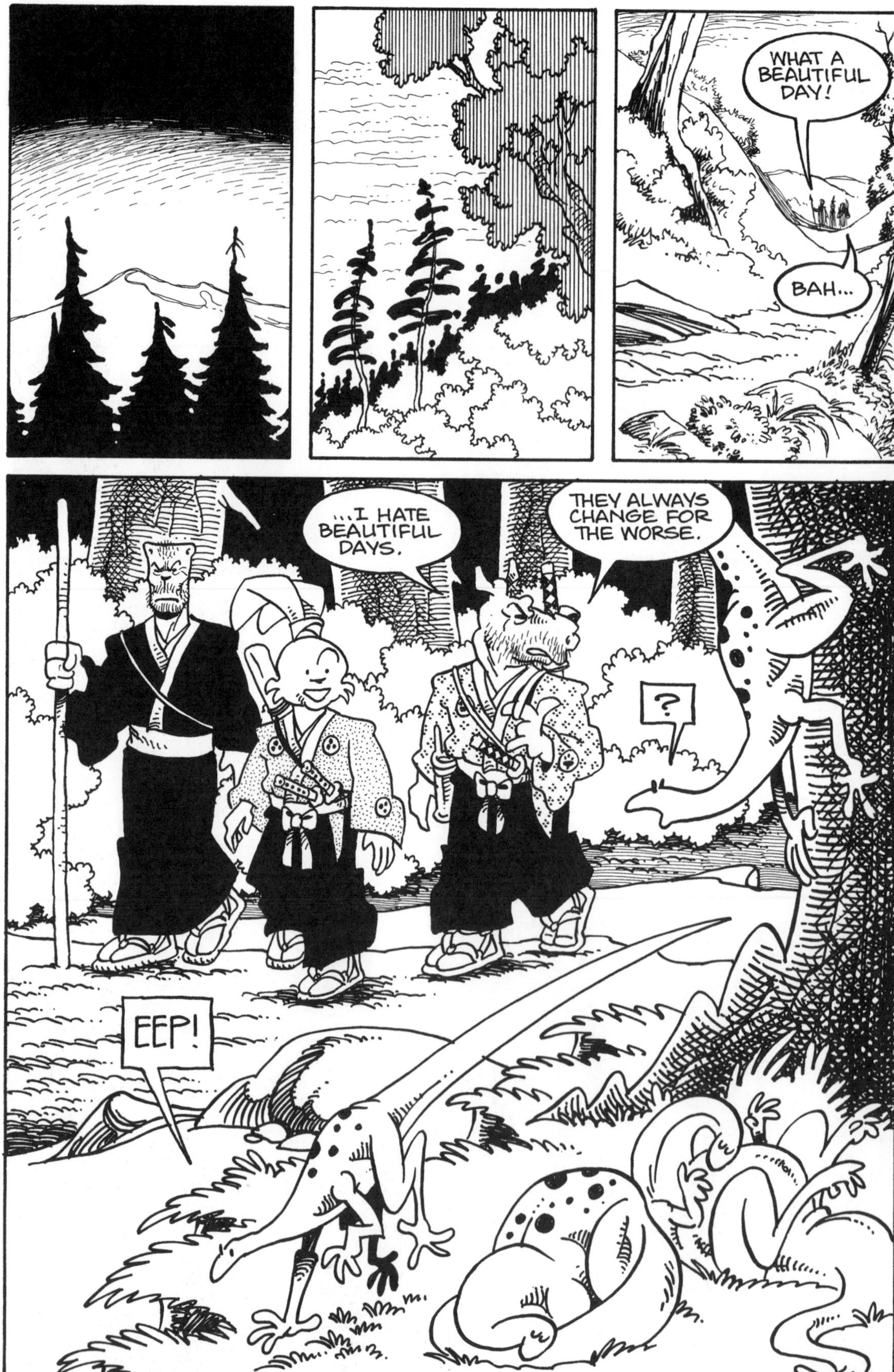
WHAT A BEAUTIFUL DAY!
BAH...
...I HATE BEAUTIFUL DAYS.
THEY ALWAYS CHANGE FOR THE WORSE.
?
EEP!

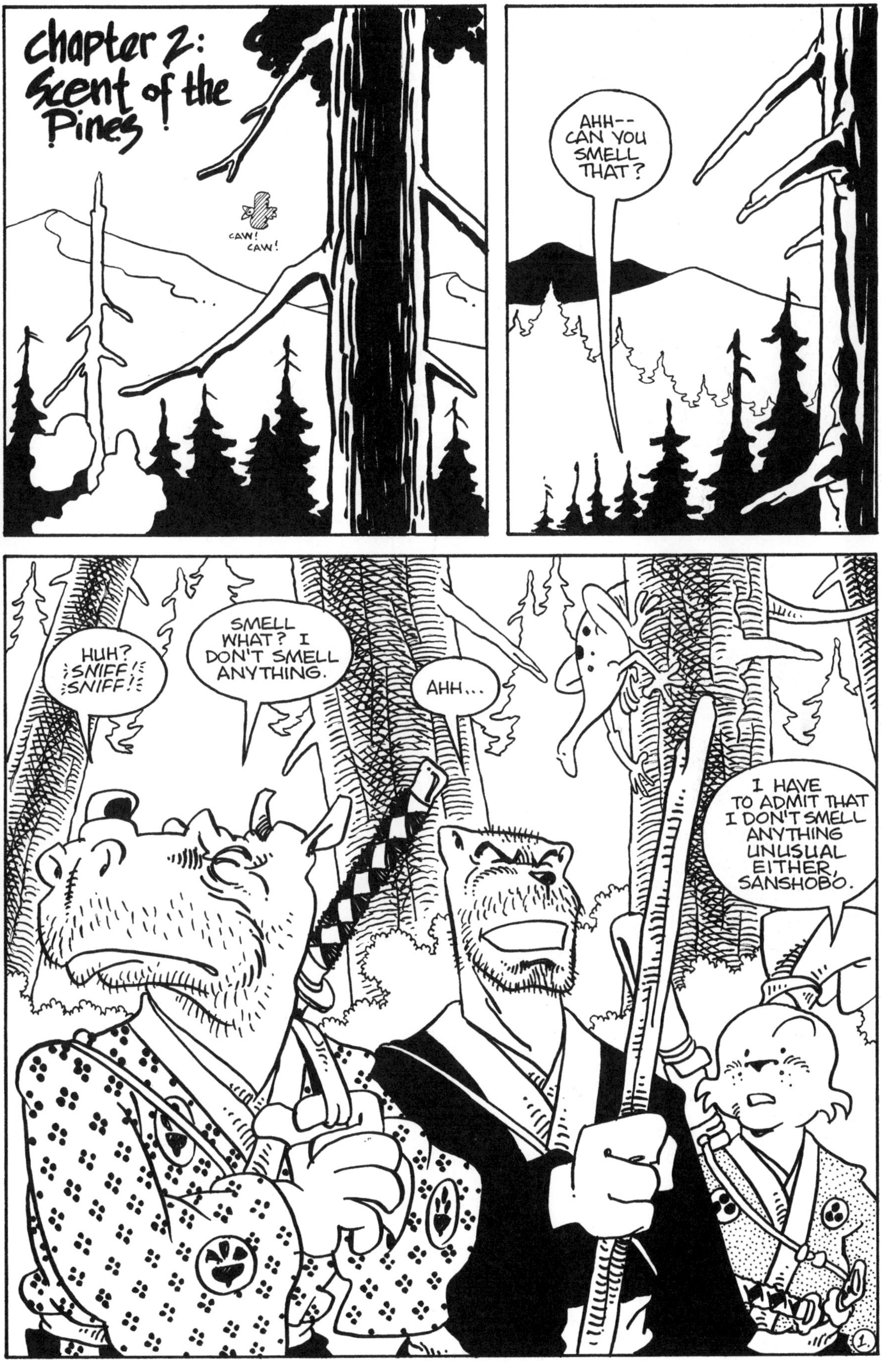
chapter 2: Scent of the Pines!
CAW! CAW!
AHH-- CAN YOU SMELL THAT?
HUH? SNIFF! SNIFF!
SMELL WHAT? I DON'T SMELL ANYTHING.
AHH...
I HAVE TO ADMIT THAT I DON'T SMELL ANYTHING UNUSUAL EITHER, SANSHOBO.
1.

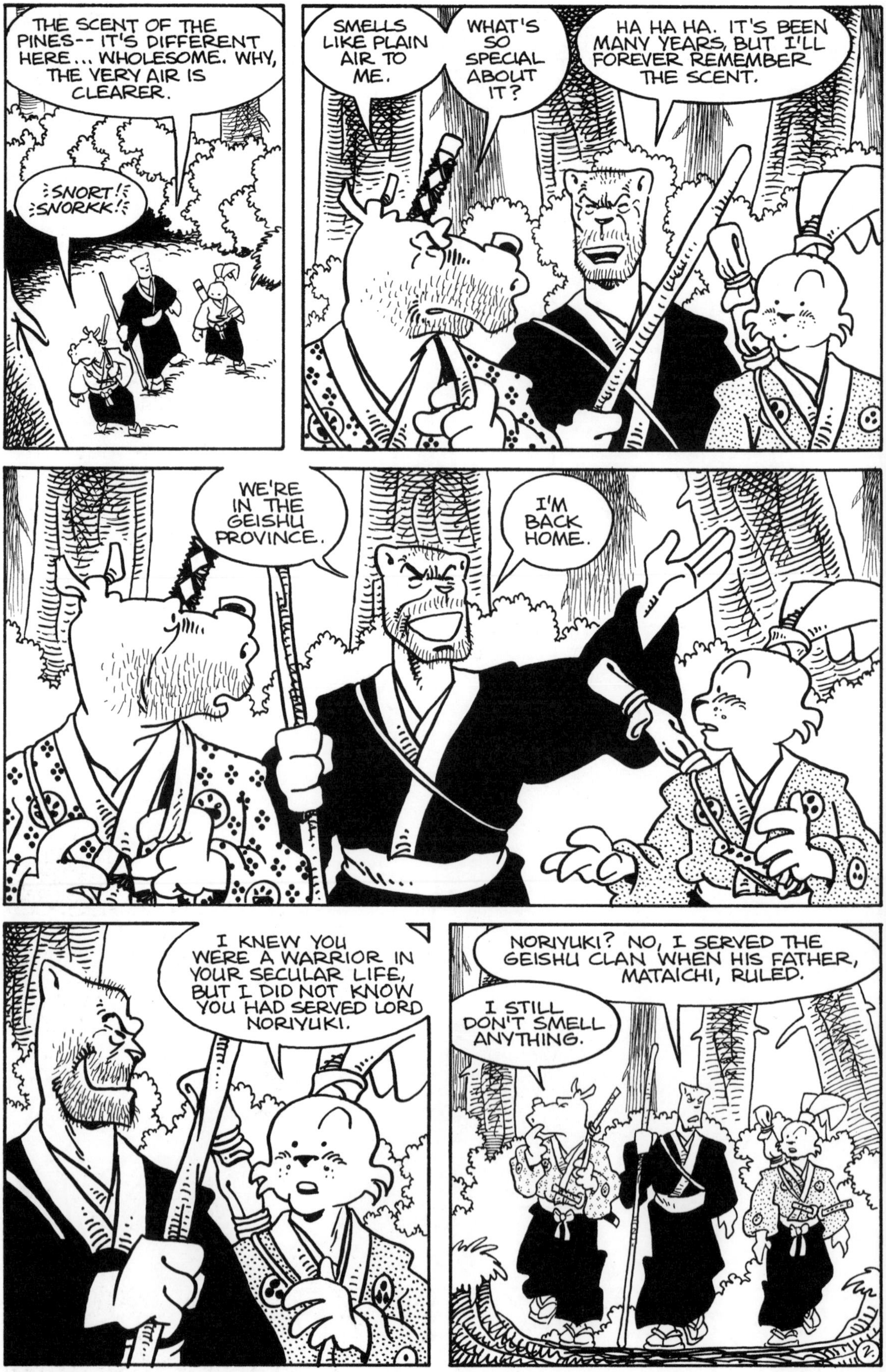
THE SCENT OF THE PINES-- IT'S DIFFERENT HERE... WHOLESOME. WHY, THE VERY AIR IS CLEARER.
SNORT! SNORKK!
SMELLS LIKE PLAIN AIR TO ME.
WHAT'S SO SPECIAL ABOUT IT?
HA HA HA. IT'S BEEN MANY YEARS, BUT I'LL FOREVER REMEMBER THE SCENT.
WE'RE IN THE GEISHU PROVINCE.
I'M BACK HOME.
I KNEW YOU WERE A WARRIOR IN YOUR SECULAR LIFE, BUT I DID NOT KNOW YOU HAD SERVED LORD NORIYUKI.
NORIYUKI? NO, I SERVED THE GEISHU CLAN WHEN HIS FATHER, MATAICHI, RULED.
I STILL DON'T SMELL ANYTHING.
2.

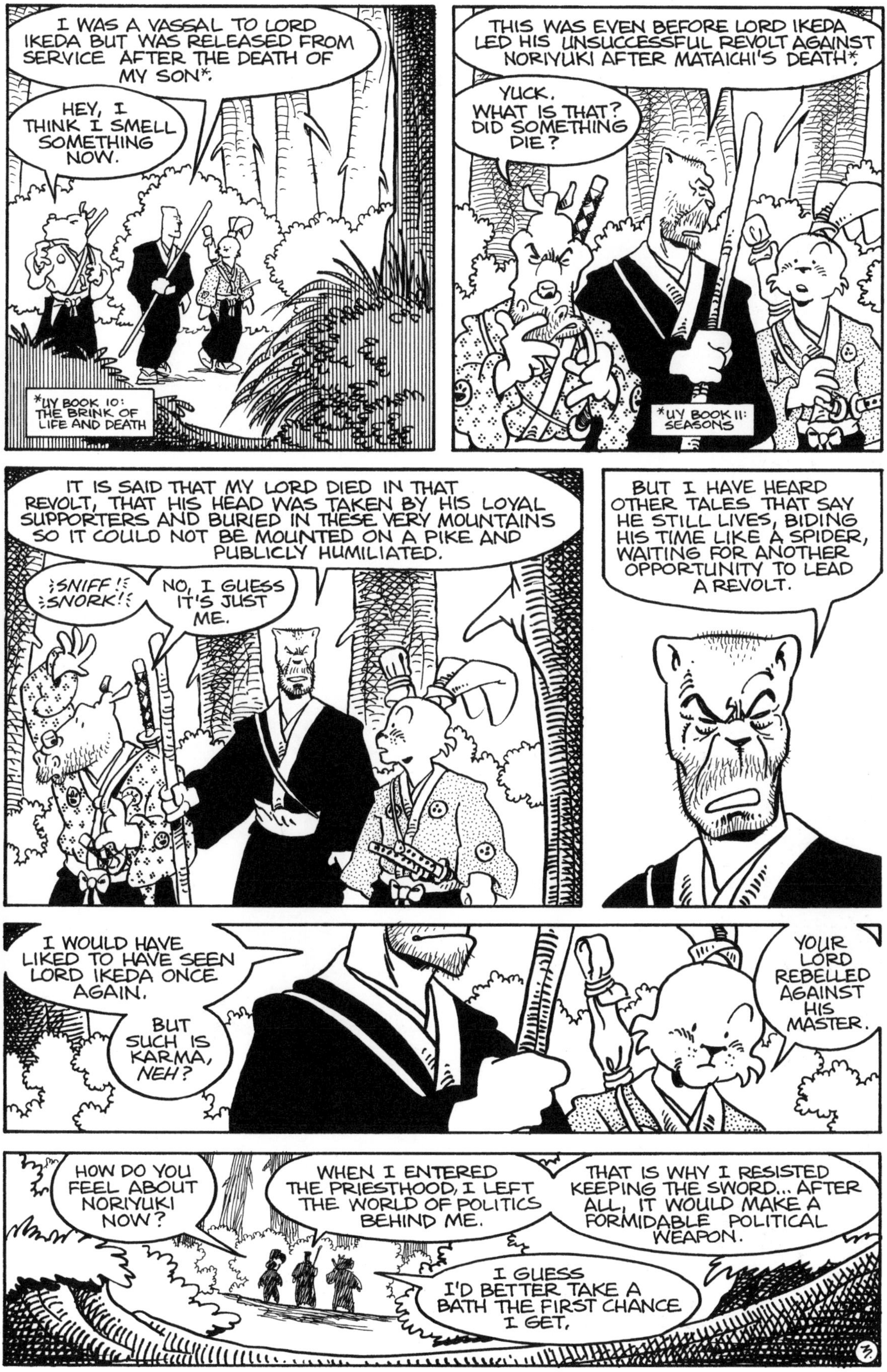
I WAS A VASSAL TO LORD IKEDA BUT WAS RELEASED FROM SERVICE AFTER THE DEATH OF MY SON*.
HEY, I THINK I SMELL SOMETHING NOW.
*UY BOOK 10: THE BRINK OF LIFE AND DEATH
THIS WAS EVEN BEFORE LORD IKEDA LED HIS UNSUCCESSFUL REVOLT AGAINST NORIYUKI AFTER MATAICHI'S DEATH*.
YUCK. WHAT IS THAT? DID SOMETHING DIE?
*UY BOOK 11: SEASONS
IT IS SAID THAT MY LORD DIED IN THAT REVOLT, THAT HIS HEAD WAS TAKEN BY HIS LOYAL SUPPORTERS AND BURIED IN THESE VERY MOUNTAINS SO IT COULD NOT BE MOUNTED ON A PIKE AND PUBLICLY HUMILIATED.
SNIFF! SNORK!
NO, I GUESS IT'S JUST ME.
BUT I HAVE HEARD OTHER TALES THAT SAY HE STILL LIVES, BIDING HIS TIME LIKE A SPIDER, WAITING FOR ANOTHER OPPORTUNITY TO LEAD A REVOLT.
I WOULD HAVE LIKED TO HAVE SEEN LORD IKEDA ONCE AGAIN.
BUT SUCH IS KARMA, NEH?
YOUR LORD REBELLED AGAINST HIS MASTER.
HOW DO YOU FEEL ABOUT NORIYUKI NOW?
WHEN I ENTERED THE PRIESTHOOD, I LEFT THE WORLD OF POLITICS BEHIND ME.
THAT IS WHY I RESISTED KEEPING THE SWORD... AFTER ALL, IT WOULD MAKE A FORMIDABLE POLITICAL WEAPON.
I GUESS I'D BETTER TAKE A BATH THE FIRST CHANCE I GET.
3.

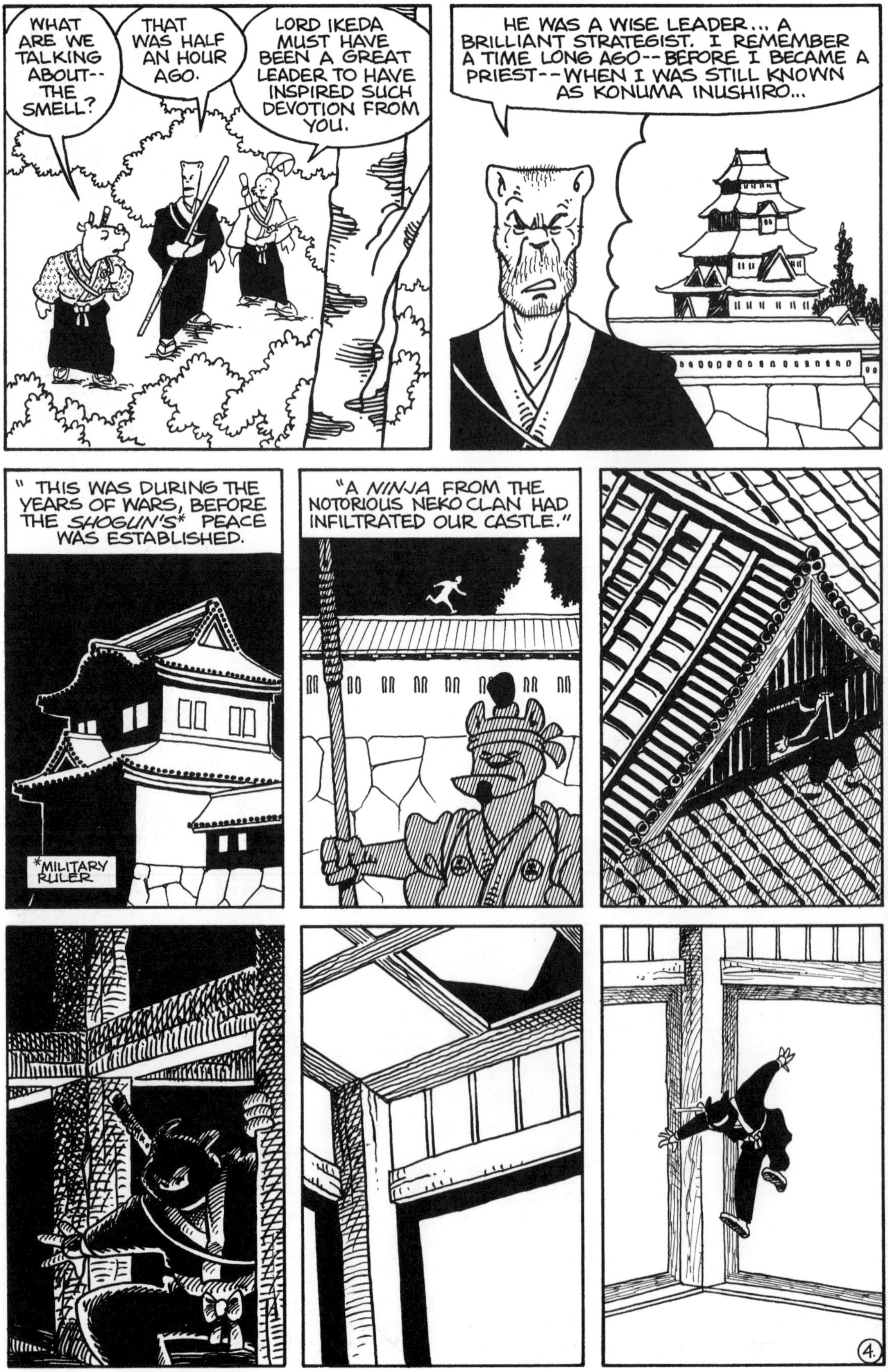
WHAT ARE WE TALKING ABOUT-- THE SMELL?
THAT WAS HALF AN HOUR AGO.
LORD IKEDA MUST HAVE BEEN A GREAT LEADER TO HAVE INSPIRED SUCH DEVOTION FROM YOU.
HE WAS A WISE LEADER... A BRILLIANT STRATEGIST. I REMEMBER A TIME LONG AGO--BEFORE I BECAME A PRIEST--WHEN I WAS STILL KNOWN AS KONUMA INUSHIRO...
" THIS WAS DURING THE YEARS OF WARS, BEFORE THE *SHOGUN'S** PEACE WAS ESTABLISHED.
*MILITARY RULER
"A *NINJA* FROM THE NOTORIOUS NEKO CLAN HAD INFILTRATED OUR CASTLE."
4.

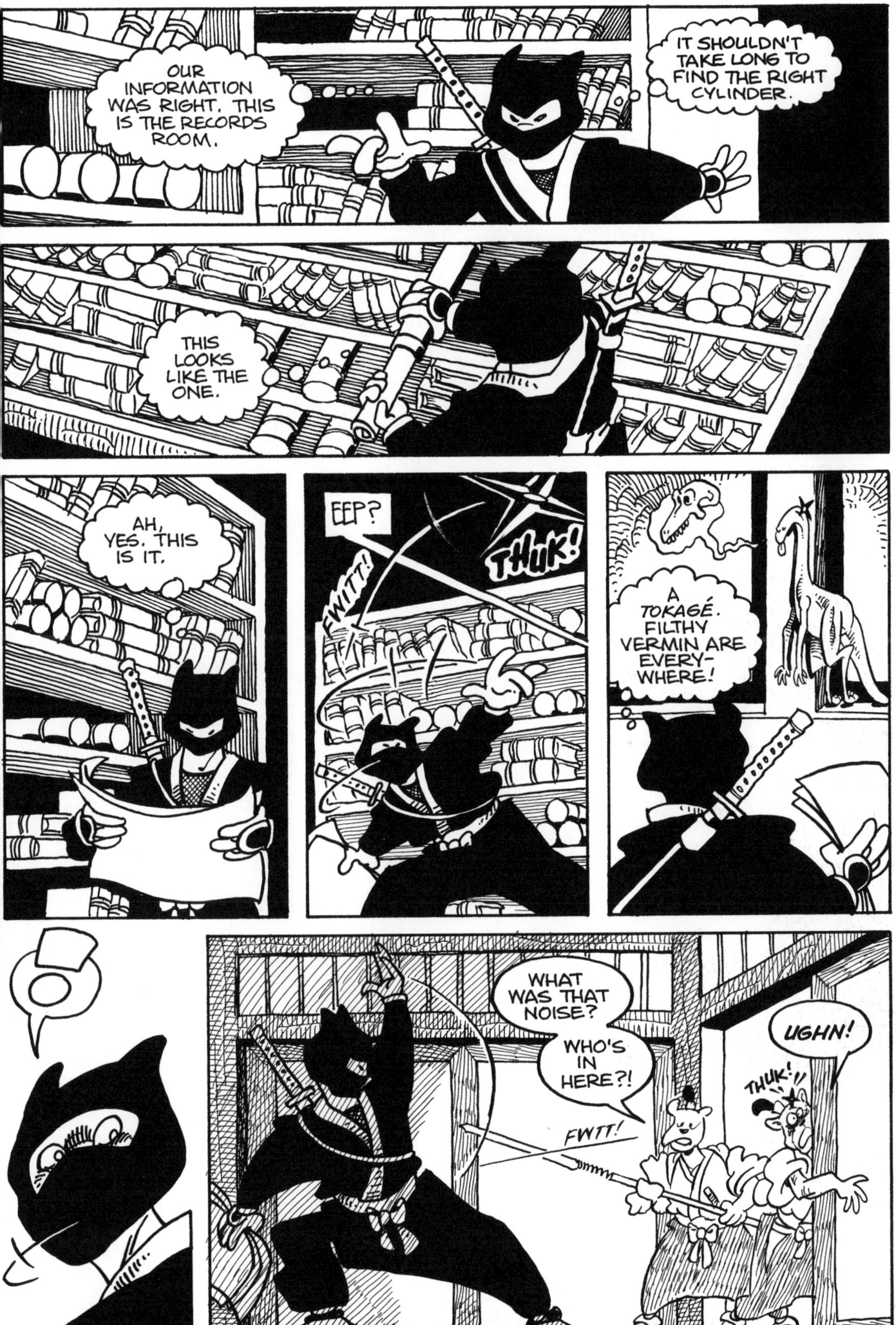
OUR INFORMATION WAS RIGHT. THIS IS THE RECORDS ROOM.
IT SHOULDN'T TAKE LONG TO FIND THE RIGHT CYLINDER.
THIS LOOKS LIKE THE ONE.
AH, YES. THIS IS IT.
EEP?
THUK!
FWITT!
A *TOKAGÉ*. FILTHY VERMIN ARE EVERY-WHERE!
!
WHAT WAS THAT NOISE?
WHO'S IN HERE?!
FWTT!
THUK!
UGHN!
5.

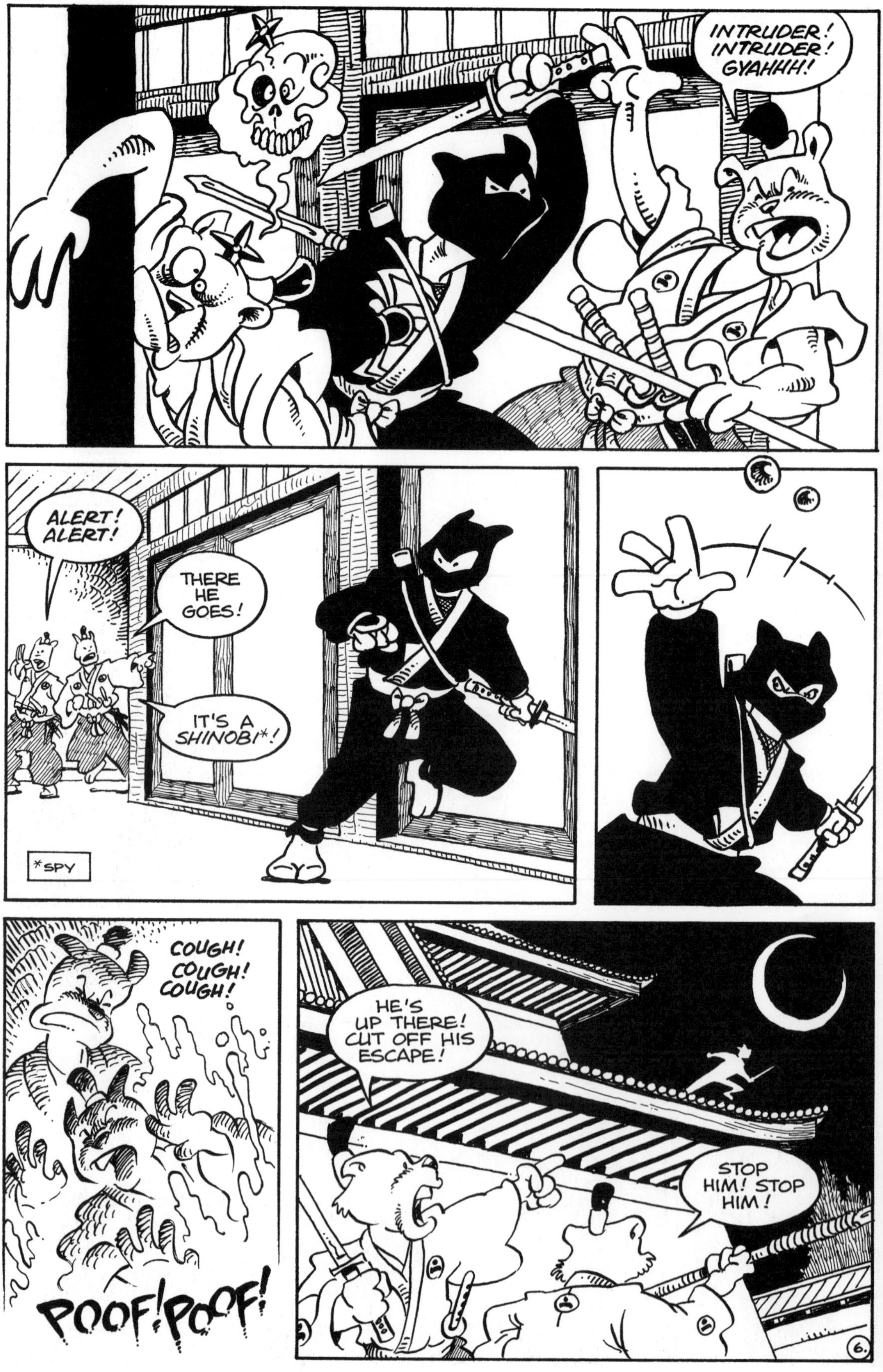

INTRUDER! INTRUDER! GYAHHH!
ALERT! ALERT!
THERE HE GOES!
IT'S A SHINOBI*!
*SPY
COUGH! COUGH! COUGH!
POOF! POOF!
HE'S UP THERE! CUT OFF HIS ESCAPE!
STOP HIM! STOP HIM!
6.

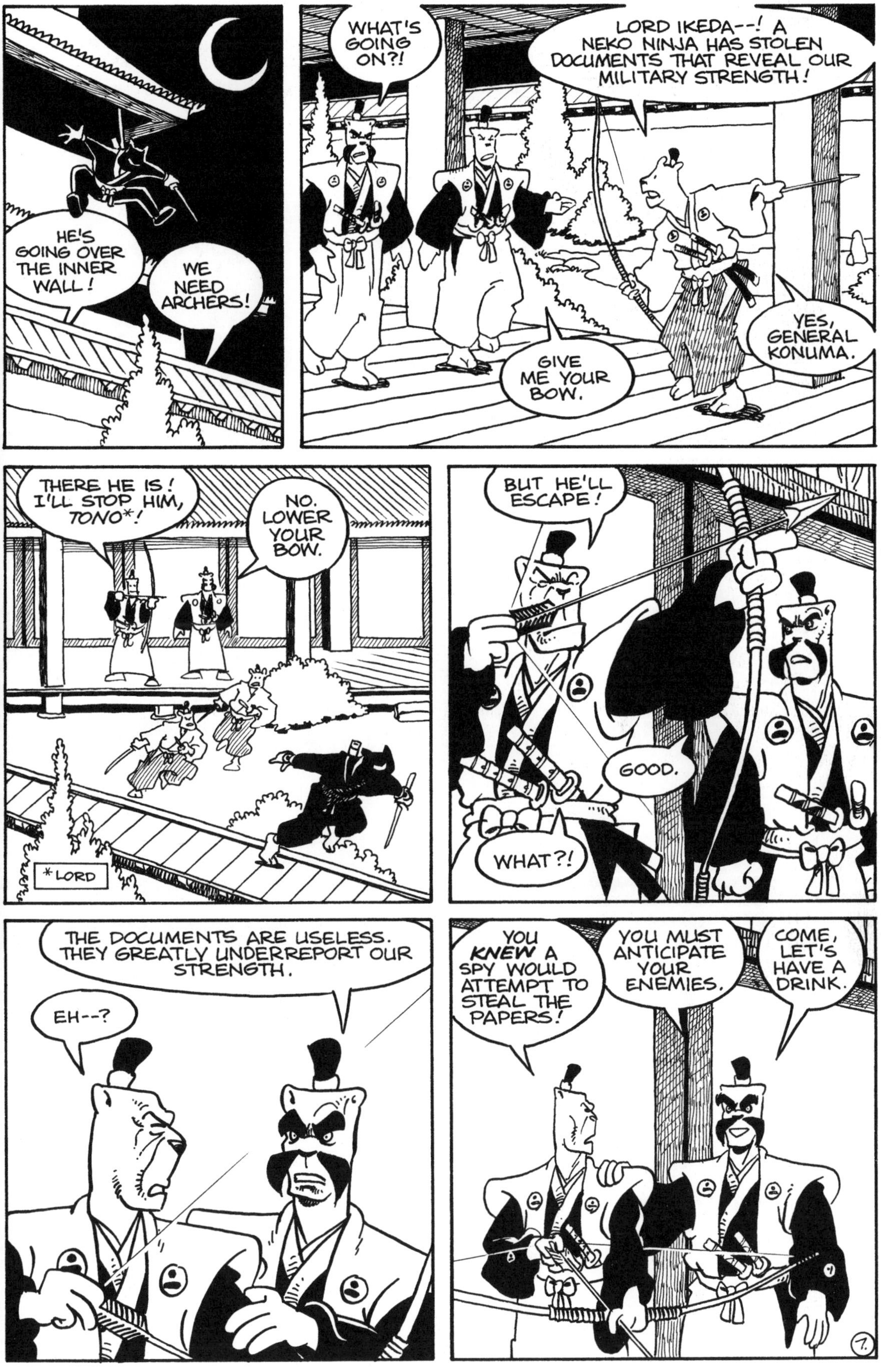
HE'S GOING OVER THE INNER WALL!
WE NEED ARCHERS!
WHAT'S GOING ON?!
LORD IKEDA--! A NEKO NINJA HAS STOLEN DOCUMENTS THAT REVEAL OUR MILITARY STRENGTH!
GIVE ME YOUR BOW.
YES, GENERAL KONUMA.
THERE HE IS! I'LL STOP HIM, TONO*!
NO. LOWER YOUR BOW.
*LORD
BUT HE'LL ESCAPE!
GOOD.
WHAT?!
THE DOCUMENTS ARE USELESS. THEY GREATLY UNDERREPORT OUR STRENGTH.
EH--?
YOU **KNEW** A SPY WOULD ATTEMPT TO STEAL THE PAPERS!
YOU MUST ANTICIPATE YOUR ENEMIES.
COME, LET'S HAVE A DRINK.
7.

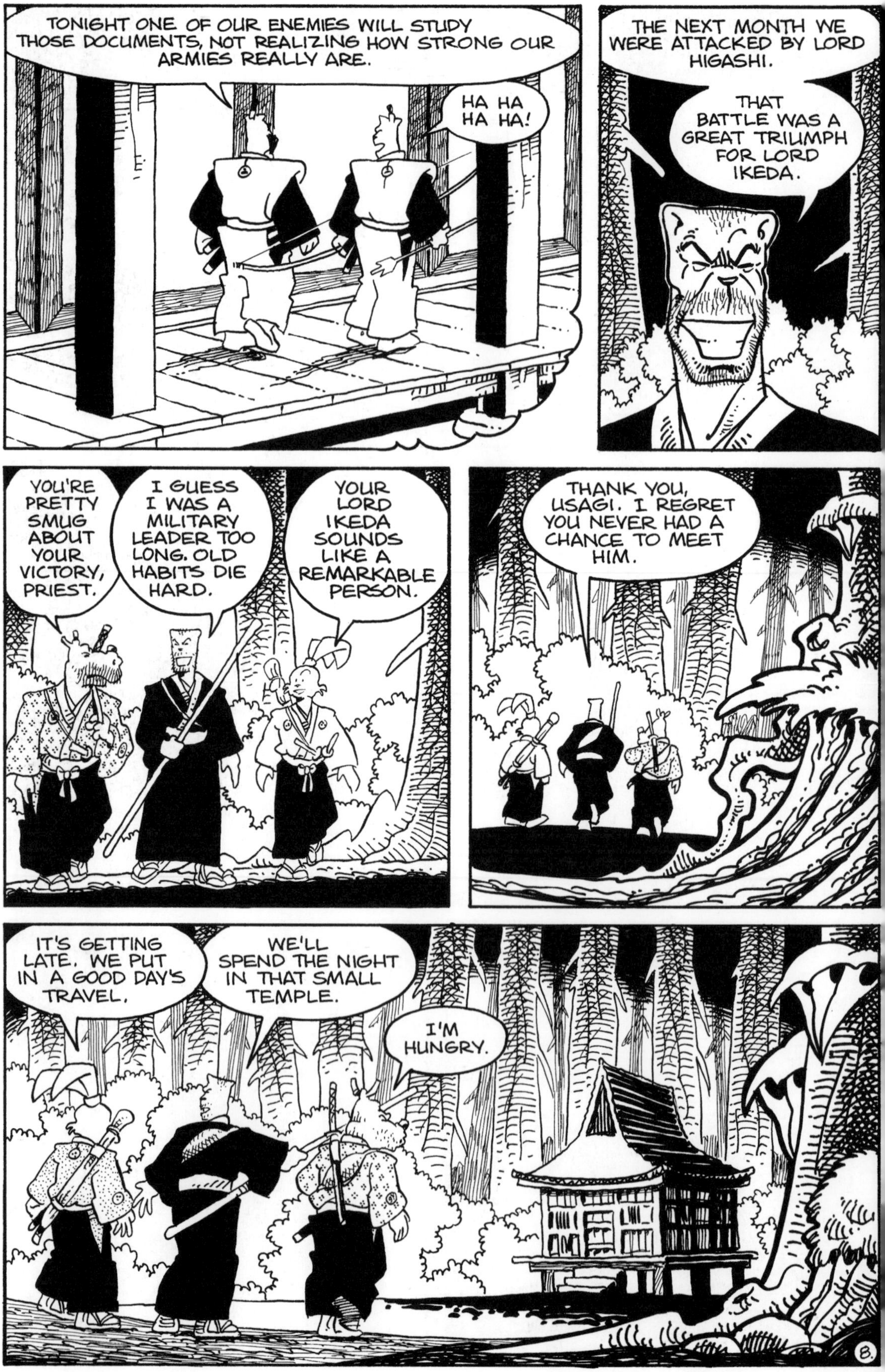
TONIGHT ONE OF OUR ENEMIES WILL STUDY THOSE DOCUMENTS, NOT REALIZING HOW STRONG OUR ARMIES REALLY ARE.
HA HA HA HA!
THE NEXT MONTH WE WERE ATTACKED BY LORD HIGASHI.
THAT BATTLE WAS A GREAT TRIUMPH FOR LORD IKEDA.
YOU'RE PRETTY SMUG ABOUT YOUR VICTORY, PRIEST.
I GUESS I WAS A MILITARY LEADER TOO LONG. OLD HABITS DIE HARD.
YOUR LORD IKEDA SOUNDS LIKE A REMARKABLE PERSON.
THANK YOU, USAGI. I REGRET YOU NEVER HAD A CHANCE TO MEET HIM.
IT'S GETTING LATE. WE PUT IN A GOOD DAY'S TRAVEL.
WE'LL SPEND THE NIGHT IN THAT SMALL TEMPLE.
I'M HUNGRY.
8.

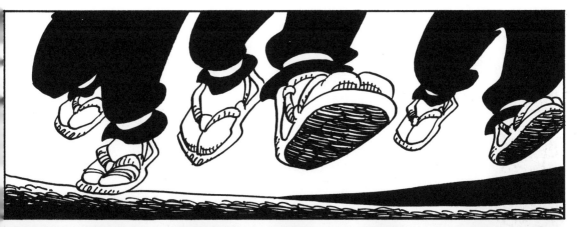

HERE ARE THE THREE SETS OF FOOTPRINTS AGAIN. THEY'RE ONLY A FEW HOURS AHEAD OF US NOW, KASHIRA*.

THEY ARE TRAVELING QUICKLY BUT NOT BOTHERING TO COVER THEIR TRACKS. I DON'T THINK THEY SUSPECT WE'RE ON THEIR HEELS.

EXCELLENT.

*CHIEF

9.

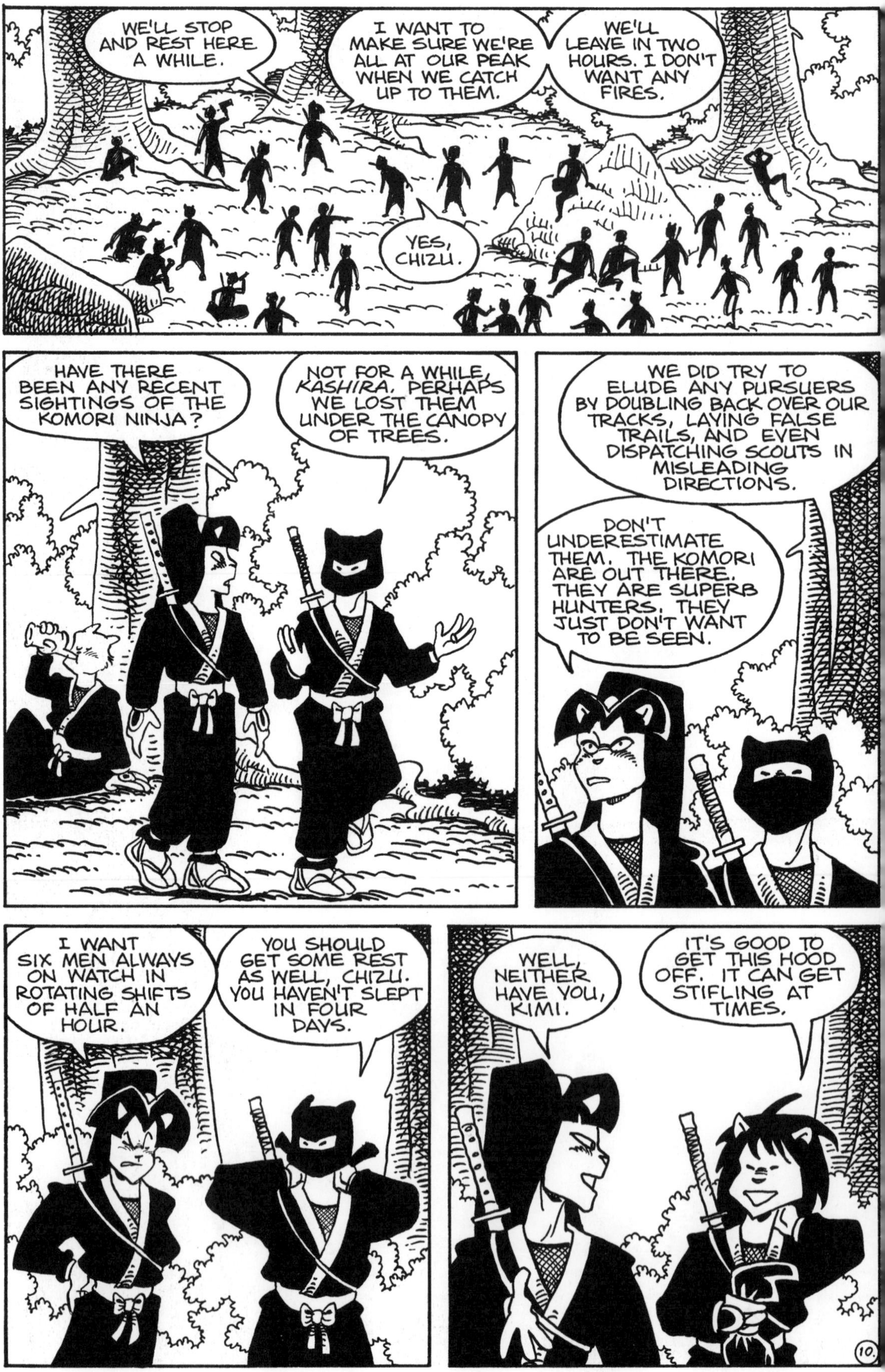
WE'LL STOP AND REST HERE A WHILE.
I WANT TO MAKE SURE WE'RE ALL AT OUR PEAK WHEN WE CATCH UP TO THEM.
WE'LL LEAVE IN TWO HOURS. I DON'T WANT ANY FIRES.
YES, CHIZU.
HAVE THERE BEEN ANY RECENT SIGHTINGS OF THE KOMORI NINJA?
NOT FOR A WHILE, *KASHIRA*. PERHAPS WE LOST THEM UNDER THE CANOPY OF TREES.
WE DID TRY TO ELUDE ANY PURSUERS BY DOUBLING BACK OVER OUR TRACKS, LAYING FALSE TRAILS, AND EVEN DISPATCHING SCOUTS IN MISLEADING DIRECTIONS.
DON'T UNDERESTIMATE THEM. THE KOMORI ARE OUT THERE. THEY ARE SUPERB HUNTERS. THEY JUST DON'T WANT TO BE SEEN.
I WANT SIX MEN ALWAYS ON WATCH IN ROTATING SHIFTS OF HALF AN HOUR.
YOU SHOULD GET SOME REST AS WELL, CHIZU. YOU HAVEN'T SLEPT IN FOUR DAYS.
WELL, NEITHER HAVE YOU, KIMI.
IT'S GOOD TO GET THIS HOOD OFF. IT CAN GET STIFLING AT TIMES.
10.

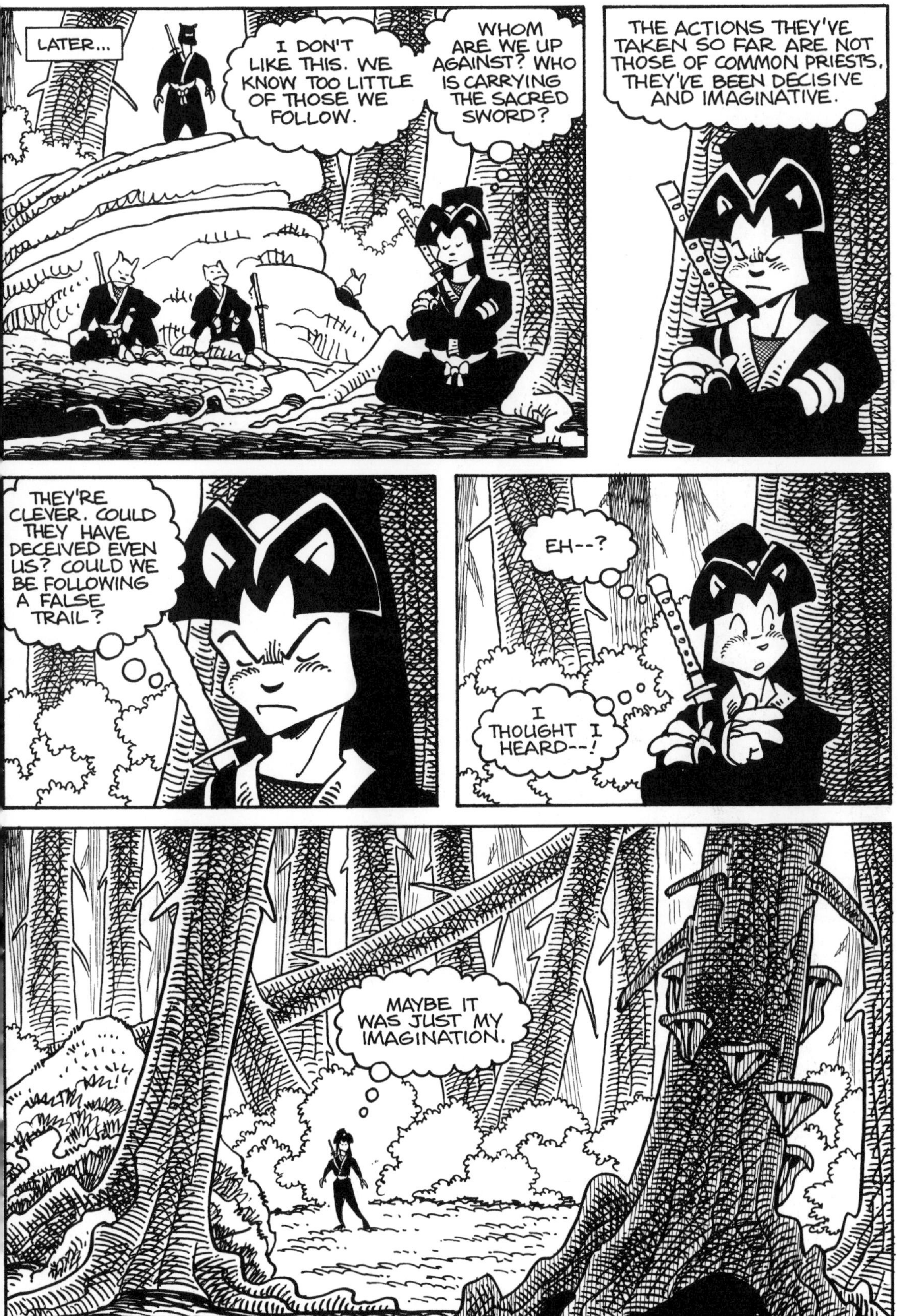
LATER...
I DON'T LIKE THIS. WE KNOW TOO LITTLE OF THOSE WE FOLLOW.
WHOM ARE WE UP AGAINST? WHO IS CARRYING THE SACRED SWORD?
THE ACTIONS THEY'VE TAKEN SO FAR ARE NOT THOSE OF COMMON PRIESTS. THEY'VE BEEN DECISIVE AND IMAGINATIVE.
THEY'RE CLEVER. COULD THEY HAVE DECEIVED EVEN US? COULD WE BE FOLLOWING A FALSE TRAIL?
EH--?
I THOUGHT I HEARD--!
MAYBE IT WAS JUST MY IMAGINATION.
11.

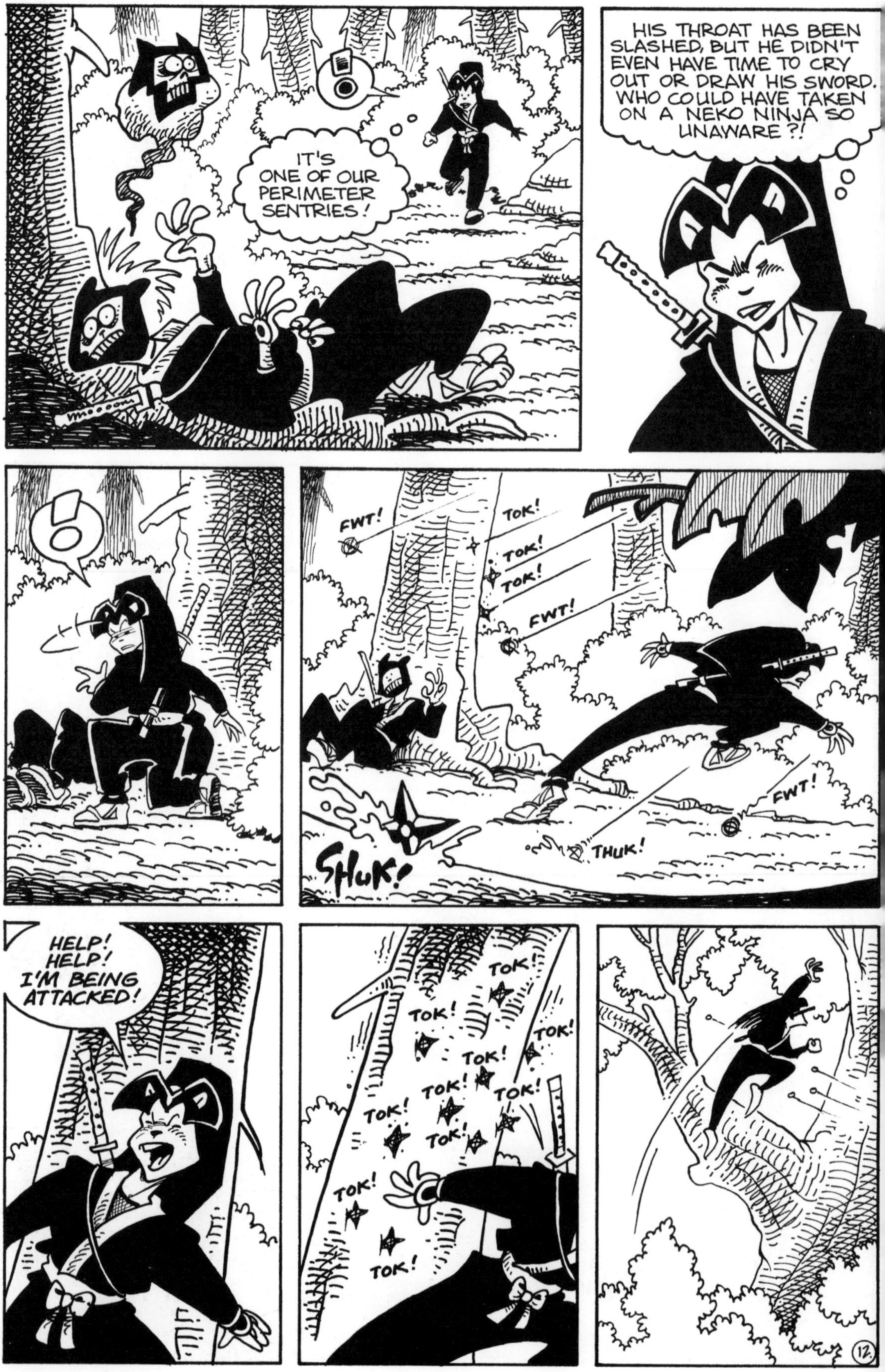
IT'S ONE OF OUR PERIMETER SENTRIES!
HIS THROAT HAS BEEN SLASHED, BUT HE DIDN'T EVEN HAVE TIME TO CRY OUT OR DRAW HIS SWORD. WHO COULD HAVE TAKEN ON A NEKO NINJA SO UNAWARE?!
!
FWT!
TOK!
TOK!
TOK!
FWT!
FWT!
THUK!
SHUK!
HELP! HELP! I'M BEING ATTACKED!
TOK!
TOK!
TOK!
TOK!
TOK!
TOK!
TOK!
TOK!
TOK!
TOK!
12.

THERE--!

SWIT!
SWIT!
SWIT!

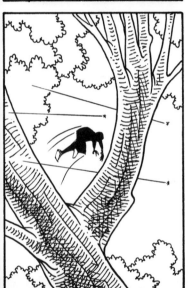

SHWUUUUUUWWWW

SHWOOP!
SHWOOP!
SHWOOP!

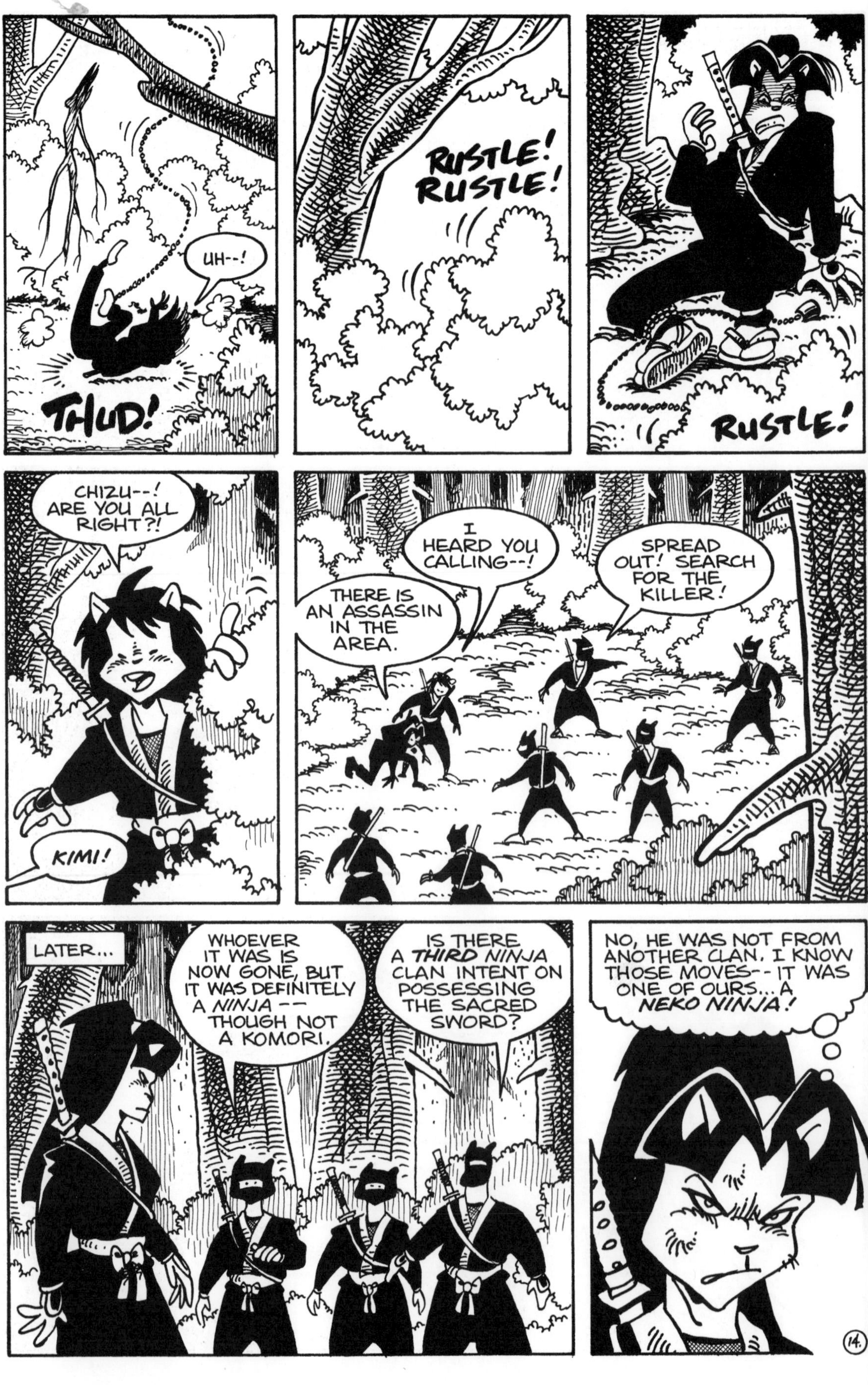
UH--!
THUD!
RUSTLE! RUSTLE!
RUSTLE!
CHIZU--! ARE YOU ALL RIGHT?!
KIMI!
THERE IS AN ASSASSIN IN THE AREA.
I HEARD YOU CALLING--!
SPREAD OUT! SEARCH FOR THE KILLER!
LATER...
WHOEVER IT WAS IS NOW GONE, BUT IT WAS DEFINITELY A *NINJA* -- THOUGH NOT A KOMORI.
IS THERE A *THIRD NINJA* CLAN INTENT ON POSSESSING THE SACRED SWORD?
NO, HE WAS NOT FROM ANOTHER CLAN. I KNOW THOSE MOVES-- IT WAS ONE OF OURS... A *NEKO NINJA*!
14.

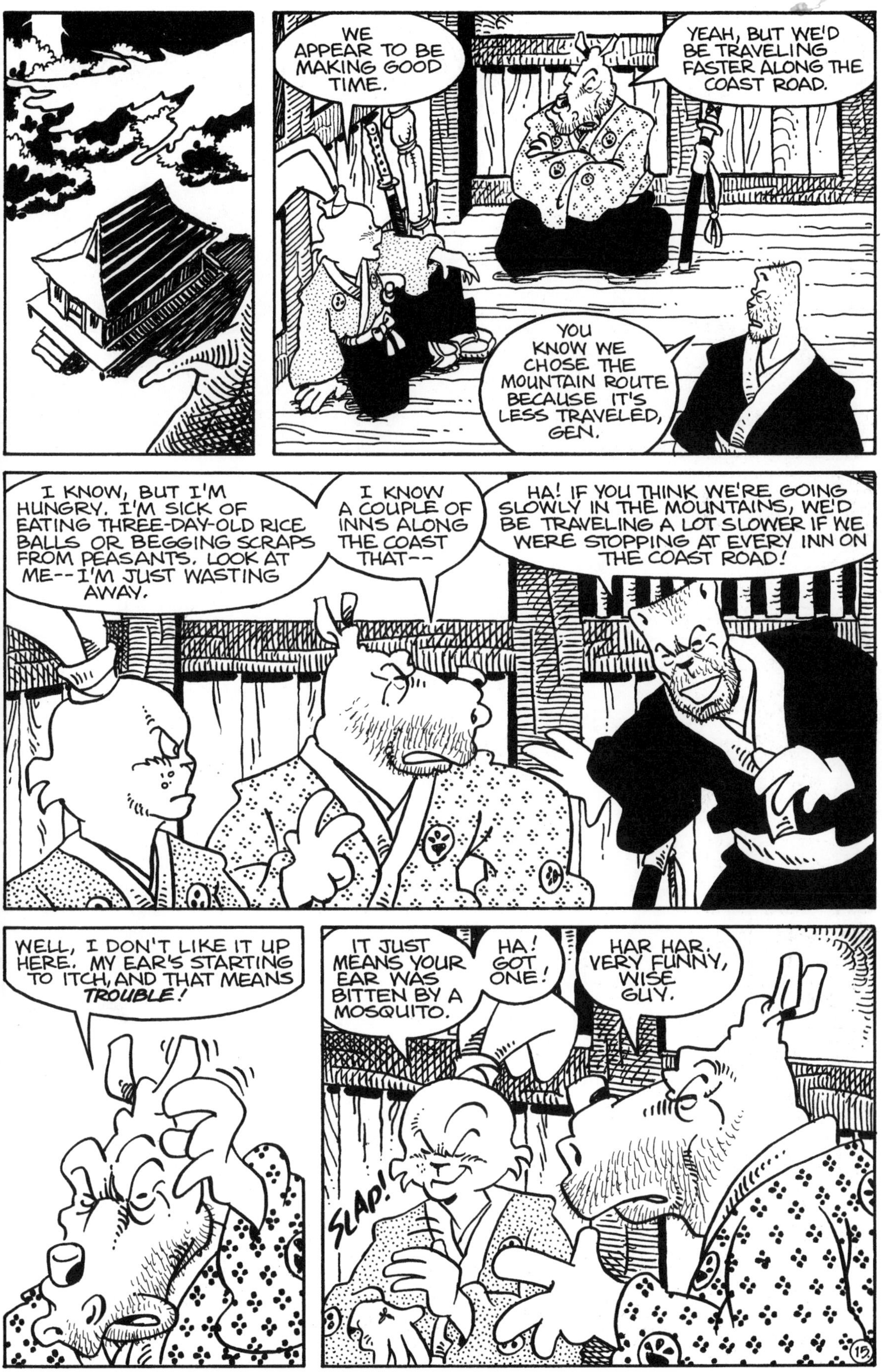
WE APPEAR TO BE MAKING GOOD TIME.
YEAH, BUT WE'D BE TRAVELING FASTER ALONG THE COAST ROAD.
YOU KNOW WE CHOSE THE MOUNTAIN ROUTE BECAUSE IT'S LESS TRAVELED, GEN.
I KNOW, BUT I'M HUNGRY. I'M SICK OF EATING THREE-DAY-OLD RICE BALLS OR BEGGING SCRAPS FROM PEASANTS. LOOK AT ME-- I'M JUST WASTING AWAY.
I KNOW A COUPLE OF INNS ALONG THE COAST THAT--
HA! IF YOU THINK WE'RE GOING SLOWLY IN THE MOUNTAINS, WE'D BE TRAVELING A LOT SLOWER IF WE WERE STOPPING AT EVERY INN ON THE COAST ROAD!
WELL, I DON'T LIKE IT UP HERE. MY EAR'S STARTING TO ITCH, AND THAT MEANS *TROUBLE!*
IT JUST MEANS YOUR EAR WAS BITTEN BY A MOSQUITO.
SLAP!
HA! GOT ONE!
HAR HAR. VERY FUNNY, WISE GUY.
15

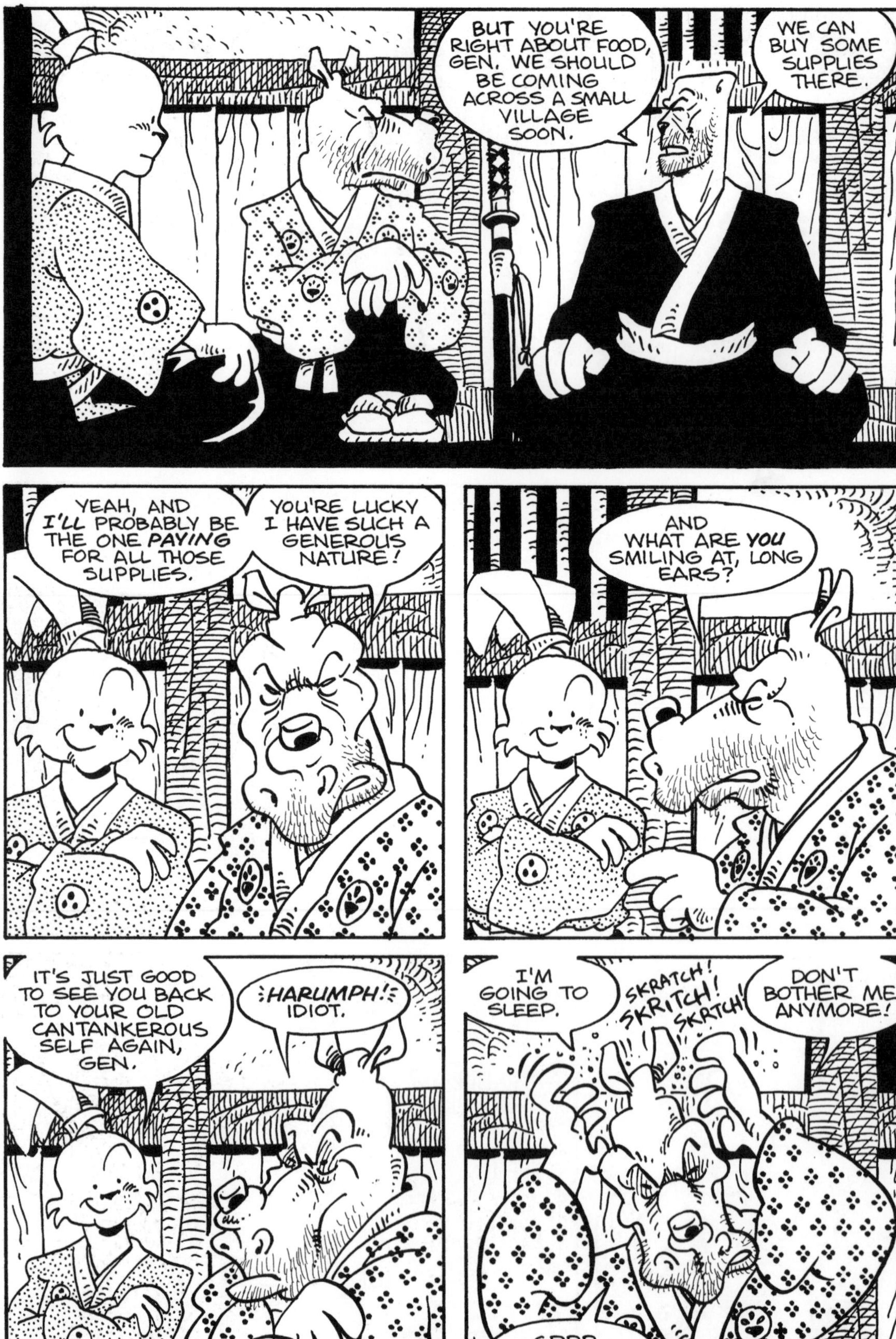
BUT YOU'RE RIGHT ABOUT FOOD, GEN. WE SHOULD BE COMING ACROSS A SMALL VILLAGE SOON.
WE CAN BUY SOME SUPPLIES THERE.
YEAH, AND I'LL PROBABLY BE THE ONE PAYING FOR ALL THOSE SUPPLIES.
YOU'RE LUCKY I HAVE SUCH A GENEROUS NATURE!
AND WHAT ARE YOU SMILING AT, LONG EARS?
IT'S JUST GOOD TO SEE YOU BACK TO YOUR OLD CANTANKEROUS SELF AGAIN, GEN.
HARUMPH! IDIOT.
I'M GOING TO SLEEP.
SKRATCH! SKRITCH! SKRTCH!
DON'T BOTHER ME ANYMORE!
GRRR... CONFOUNDED ITCHING!
16.

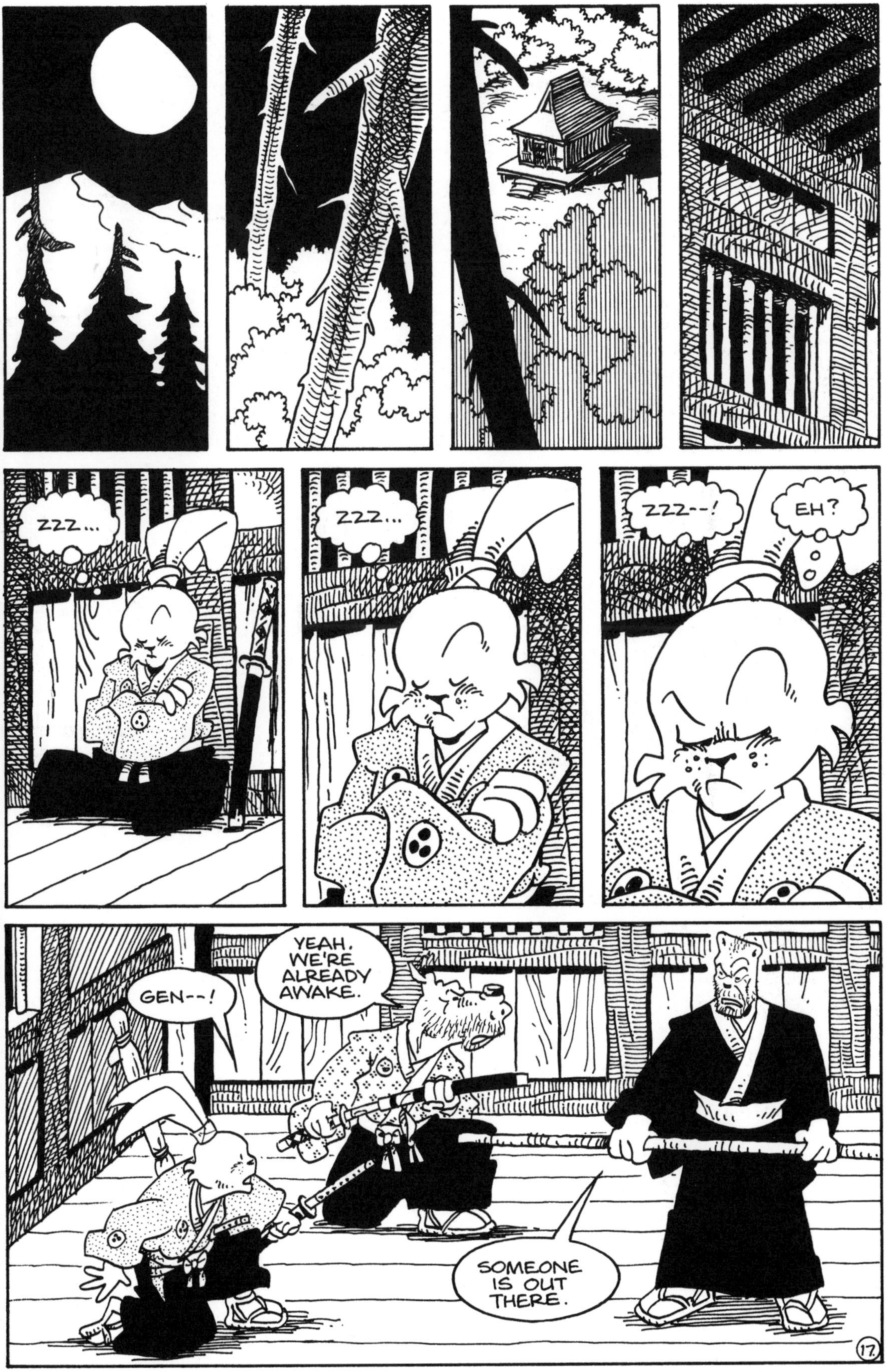
ZZZ...
ZZZ...
ZZZ--!
EH?
GEN--!
YEAH, WE'RE ALREADY AWAKE.
SOMEONE IS OUT THERE.
17

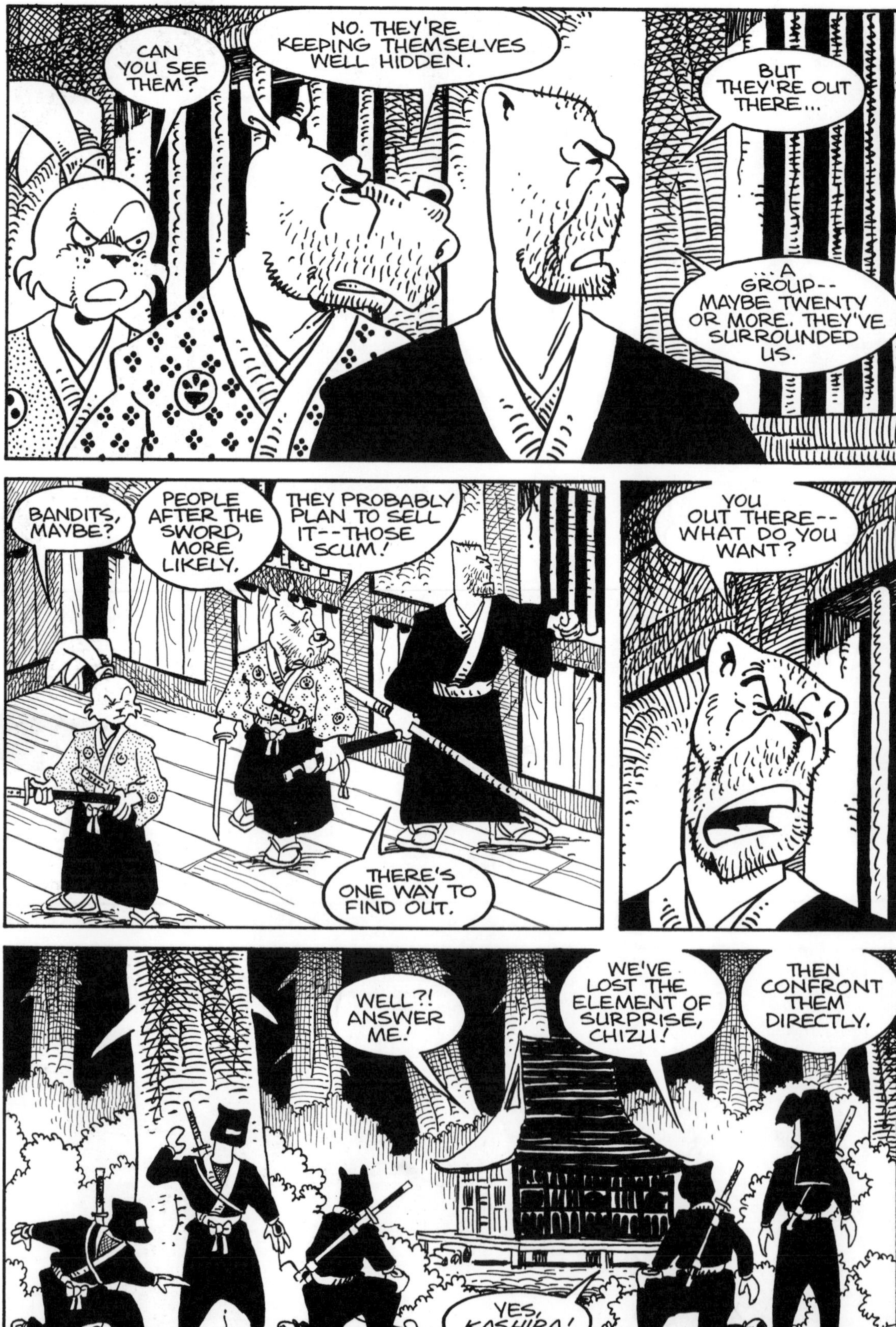
CAN YOU SEE THEM?
NO. THEY'RE KEEPING THEMSELVES WELL HIDDEN.
BUT THEY'RE OUT THERE...
...A GROUP-- MAYBE TWENTY OR MORE. THEY'VE SURROUNDED US.
BANDITS, MAYBE?
PEOPLE AFTER THE SWORD, MORE LIKELY.
THEY PROBABLY PLAN TO SELL IT--THOSE SCUM!
THERE'S ONE WAY TO FIND OUT.
YOU OUT THERE-- WHAT DO YOU WANT?
WELL?! ANSWER ME!
YES, KASHIRA!
WE'VE LOST THE ELEMENT OF SURPRISE, CHIZU!
THEN CONFRONT THEM DIRECTLY.
18.

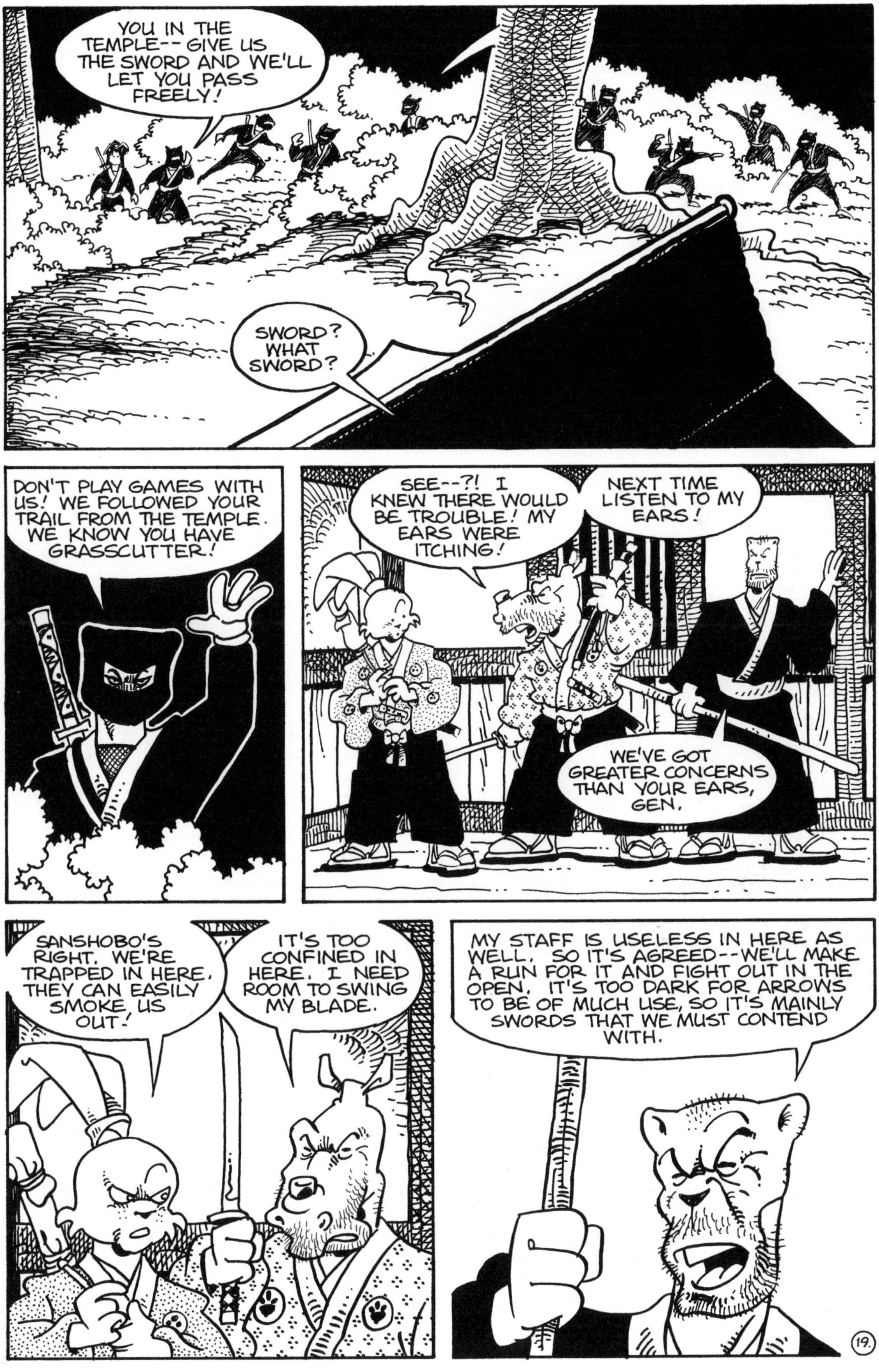
YOU IN THE TEMPLE-- GIVE US THE SWORD AND WE'LL LET YOU PASS FREELY!
SWORD? WHAT SWORD?
DON'T PLAY GAMES WITH US! WE FOLLOWED YOUR TRAIL FROM THE TEMPLE. WE KNOW YOU HAVE GRASSCUTTER!
SEE--?! I KNEW THERE WOULD BE TROUBLE! MY EARS WERE ITCHING!
NEXT TIME LISTEN TO MY EARS!
WE'VE GOT GREATER CONCERNS THAN YOUR EARS, GEN.
SANSHOBO'S RIGHT. WE'RE TRAPPED IN HERE. THEY CAN EASILY SMOKE US OUT!
IT'S TOO CONFINED IN HERE. I NEED ROOM TO SWING MY BLADE.
MY STAFF IS USELESS IN HERE AS WELL, SO IT'S AGREED--WE'LL MAKE A RUN FOR IT AND FIGHT OUT IN THE OPEN. IT'S TOO DARK FOR ARROWS TO BE OF MUCH USE, SO IT'S MAINLY SWORDS THAT WE MUST CONTEND WITH.
19.

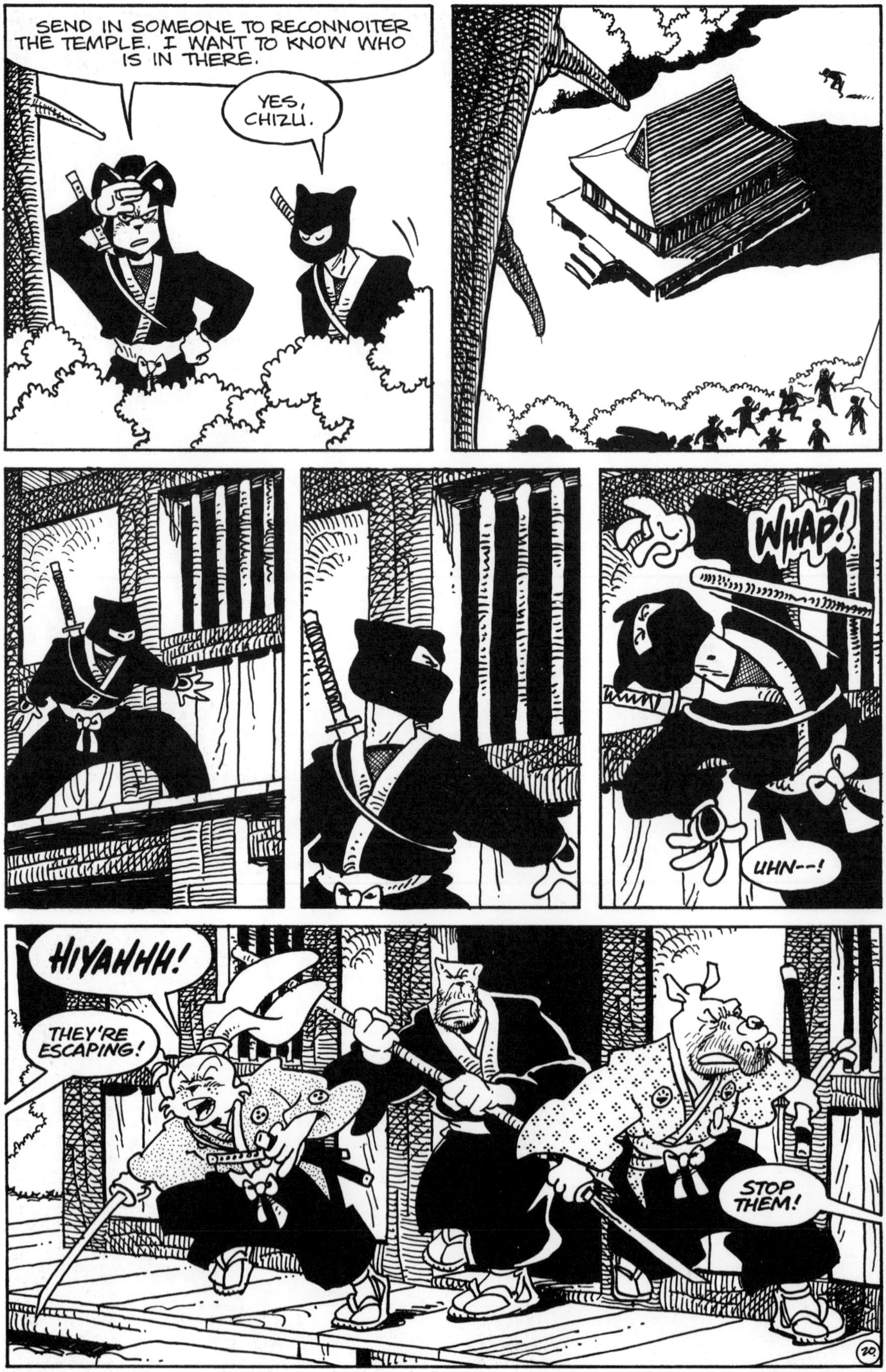
SEND IN SOMEONE TO RECONNOITER THE TEMPLE. I WANT TO KNOW WHO IS IN THERE.
YES, CHIZU.
WHAP!
UHN--!
HIYAHHH!
THEY'RE ESCAPING!
STOP THEM!
20.

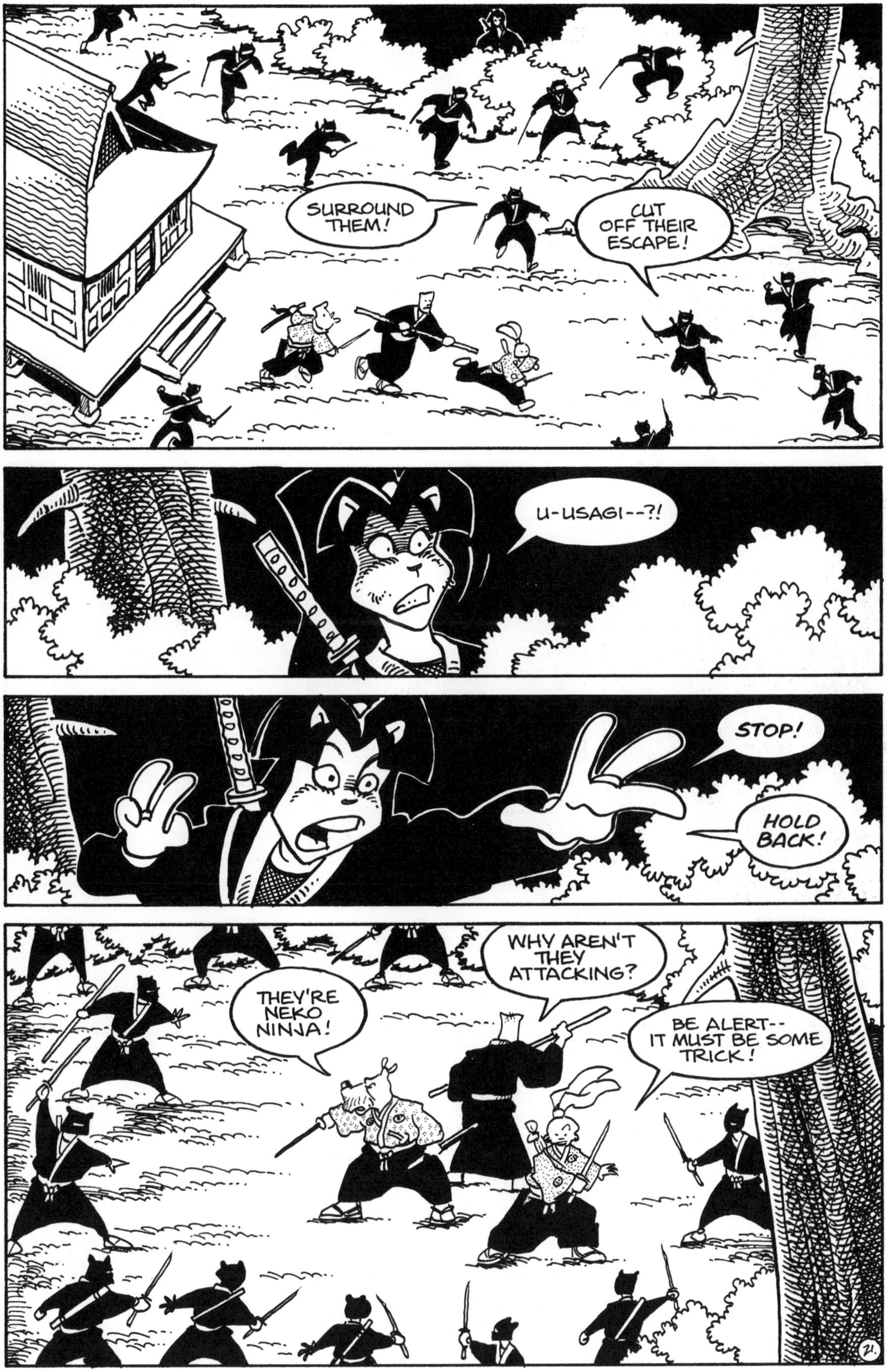
SURROUND THEM!
CUT OFF THEIR ESCAPE!
U-USAGI--?!
STOP!
HOLD BACK!
WHY AREN'T THEY ATTACKING?
THEY'RE NEKO NINJA!
BE ALERT-- IT MUST BE SOME TRICK!
21.

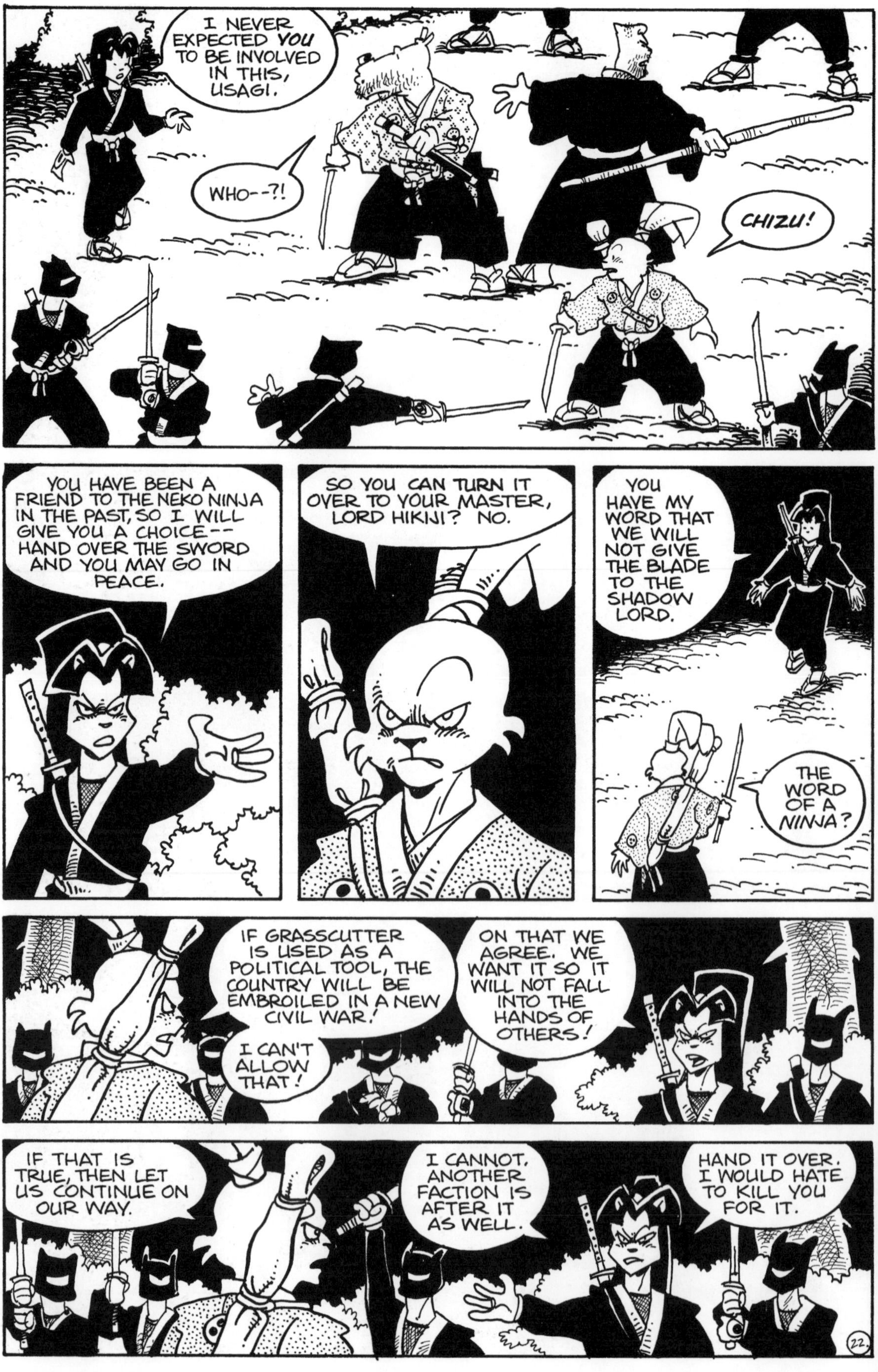

I NEVER EXPECTED YOU TO BE INVOLVED IN THIS, USAGI.
WHO--?!
CHIZU!
YOU HAVE BEEN A FRIEND TO THE NEKO NINJA IN THE PAST, SO I WILL GIVE YOU A CHOICE--HAND OVER THE SWORD AND YOU MAY GO IN PEACE.
SO YOU CAN TURN IT OVER TO YOUR MASTER, LORD HIKIJI? NO.
YOU HAVE MY WORD THAT WE WILL NOT GIVE THE BLADE TO THE SHADOW LORD.
THE WORD OF A NINJA?
IF GRASSCUTTER IS USED AS A POLITICAL TOOL, THE COUNTRY WILL BE EMBROILED IN A NEW CIVIL WAR!
I CAN'T ALLOW THAT!
ON THAT WE AGREE. WE WANT IT SO IT WILL NOT FALL INTO THE HANDS OF OTHERS!
IF THAT IS TRUE, THEN LET US CONTINUE ON OUR WAY.
I CANNOT. ANOTHER FACTION IS AFTER IT AS WELL.
HAND IT OVER. I WOULD HATE TO KILL YOU FOR IT.
22.

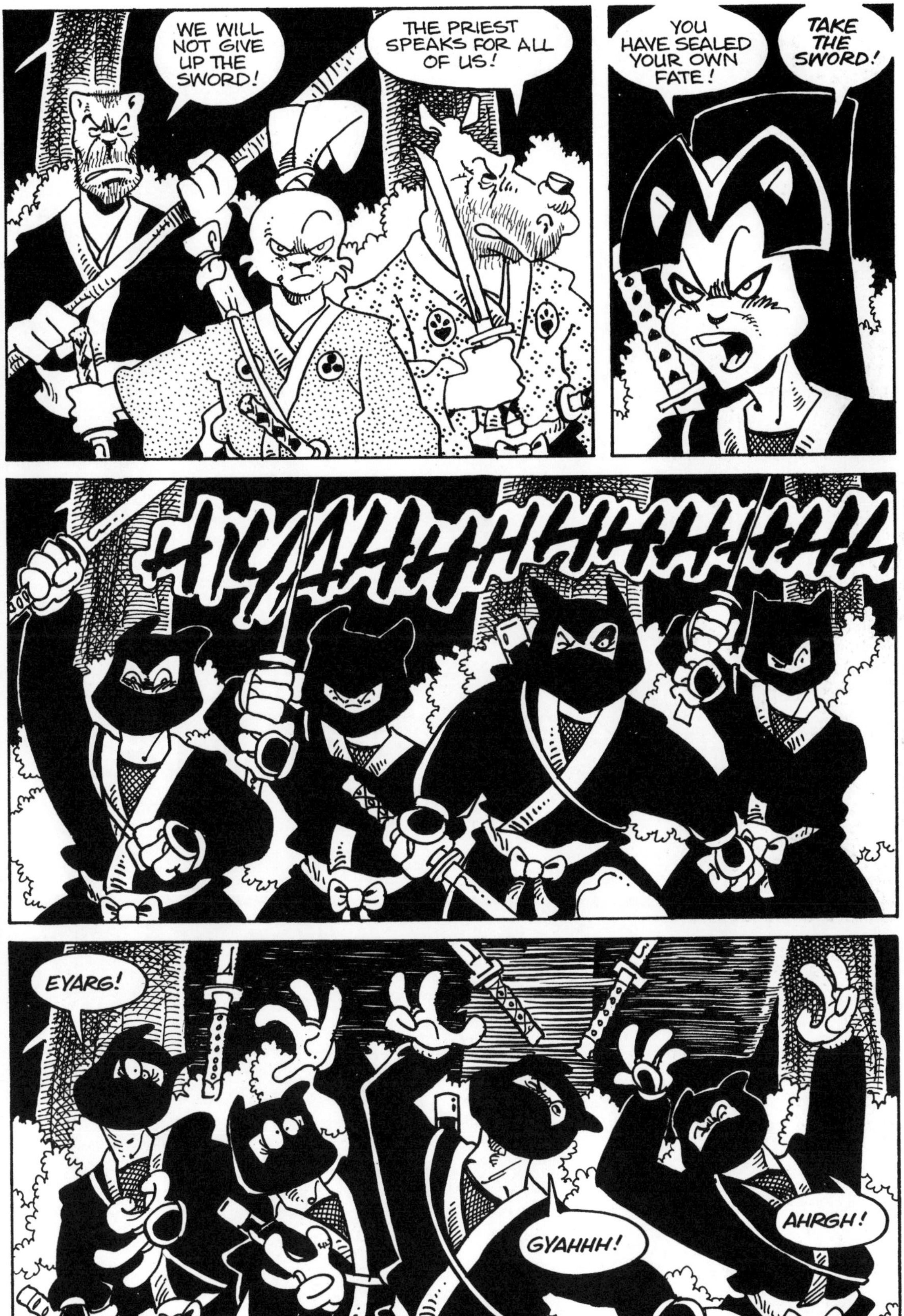
WE WILL NOT GIVE UP THE SWORD!
THE PRIEST SPEAKS FOR ALL OF US!
YOU HAVE SEALED YOUR OWN FATE!
TAKE THE SWORD!
HIYAHHHHHHHHHH
EYARG!
OOGH!
GYAHHH!
AHRGH!
23

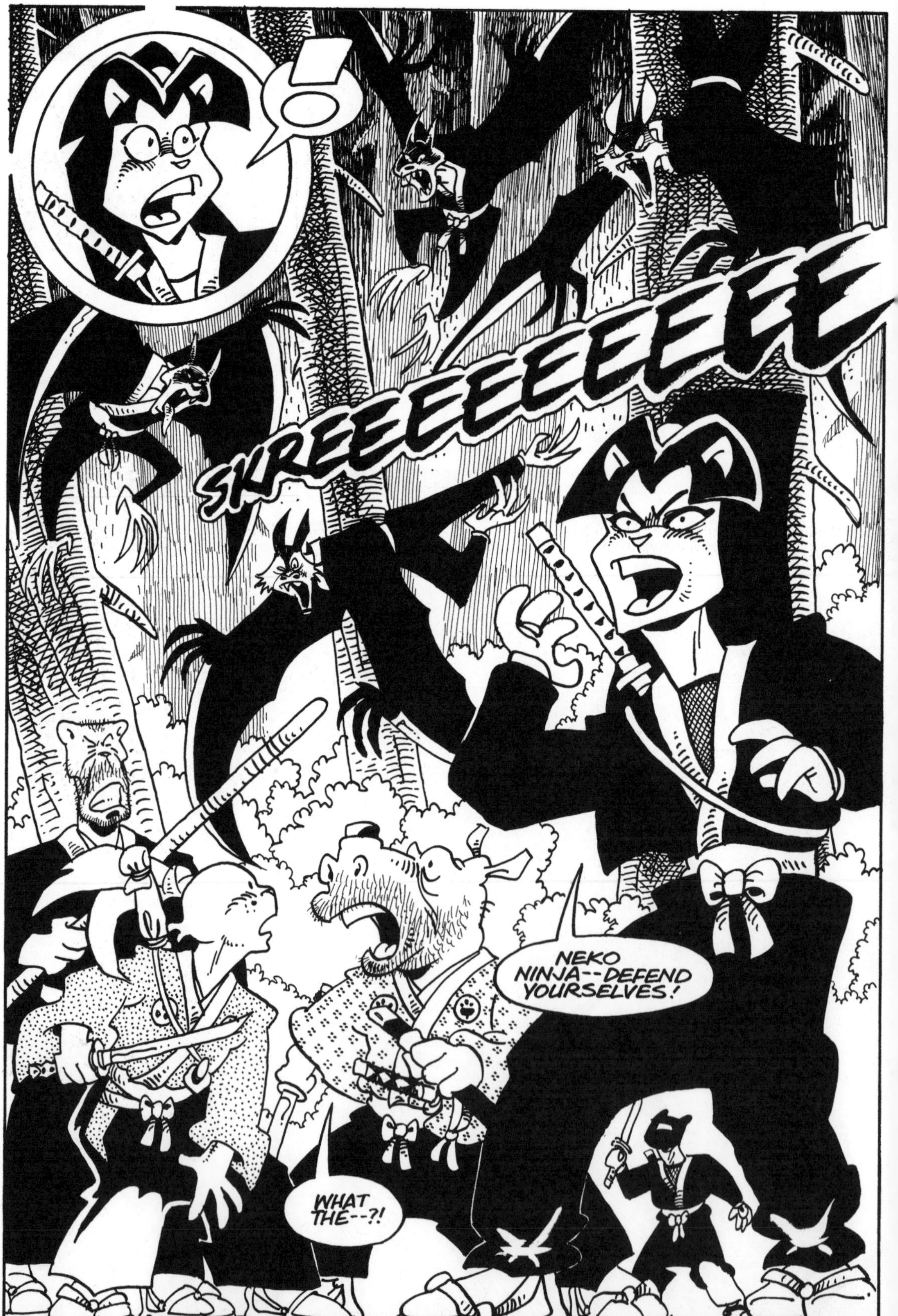
!
SKREEEEEEEEEEEE
NEKO NINJA--DEFEND YOURSELVES!
WHAT THE--?!

CHAPTER 3
THE HUNGER FOR DEATH

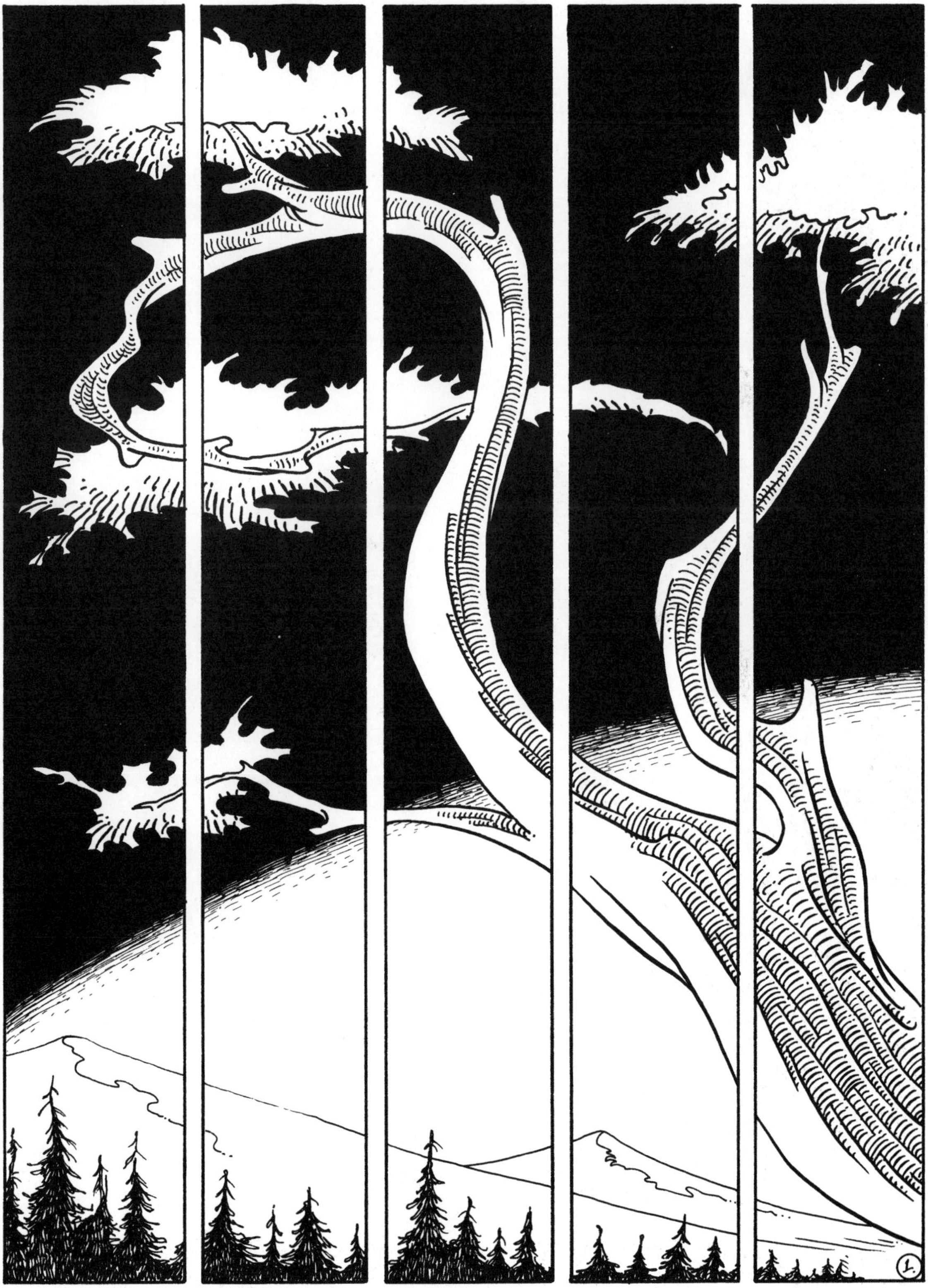
1.

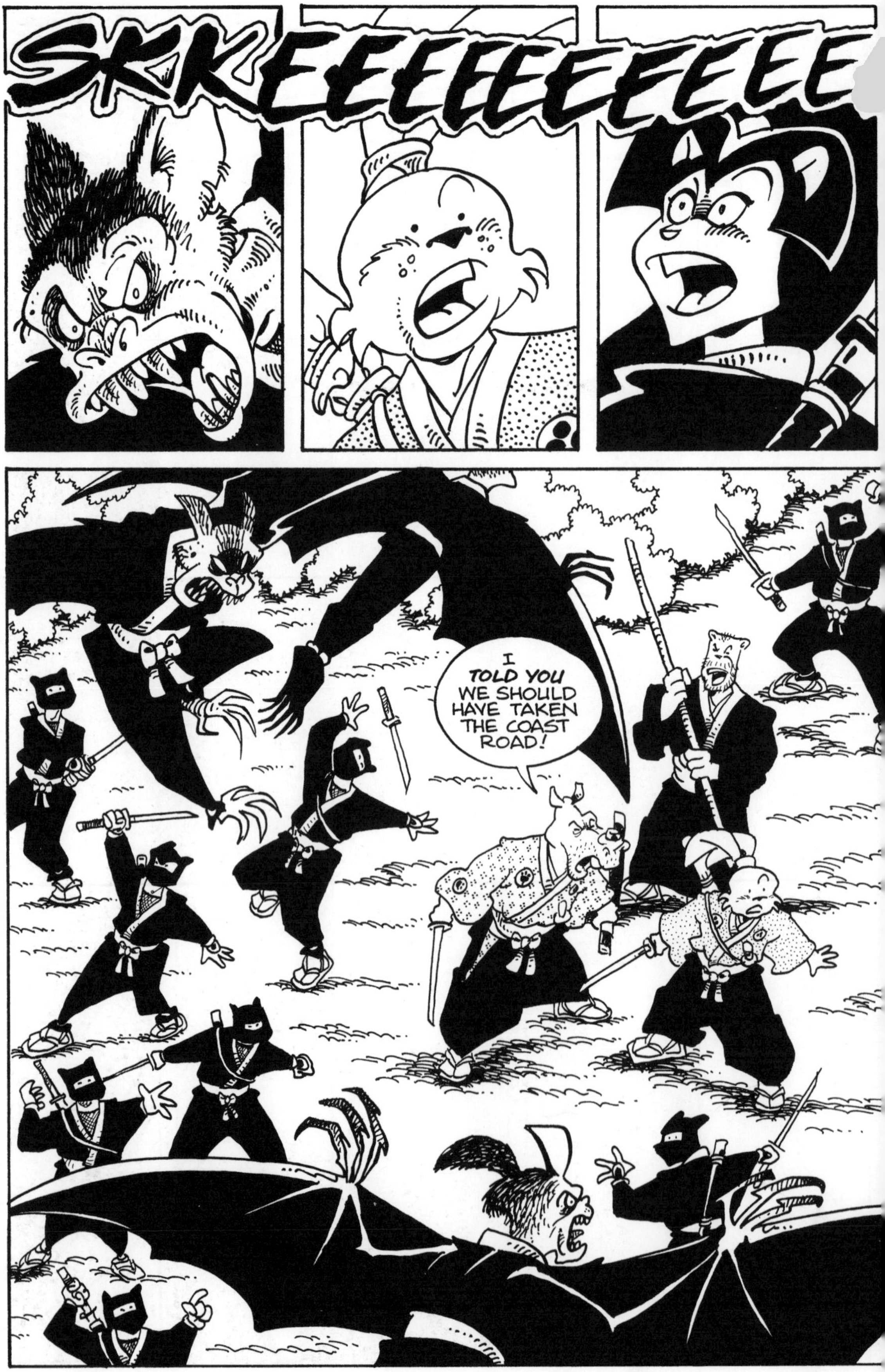
SKREEEEEEEEEEE
I TOLD YOU WE SHOULD HAVE TAKEN THE COAST ROAD!

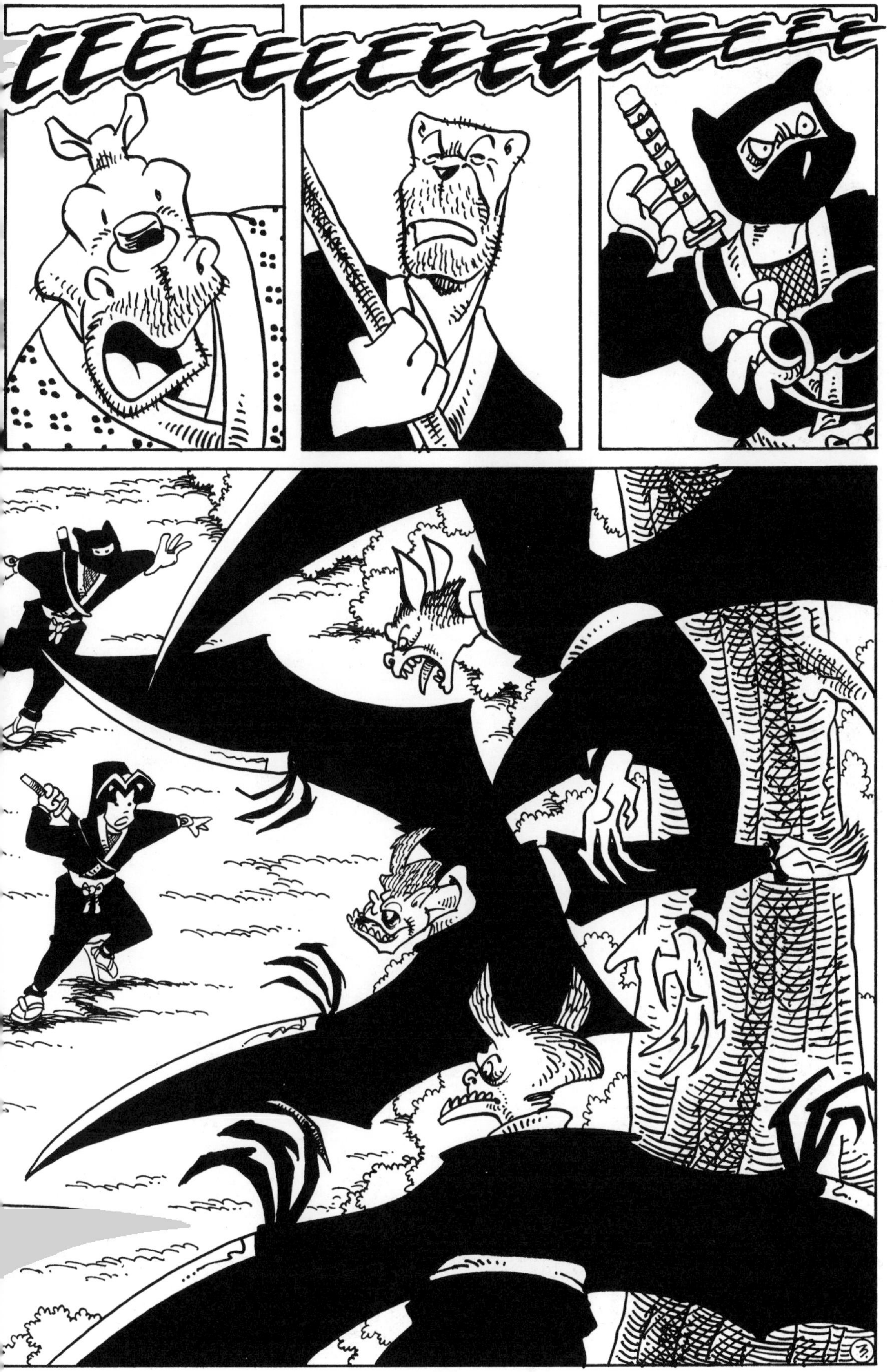
EEEEEEEEEEEEEEEE

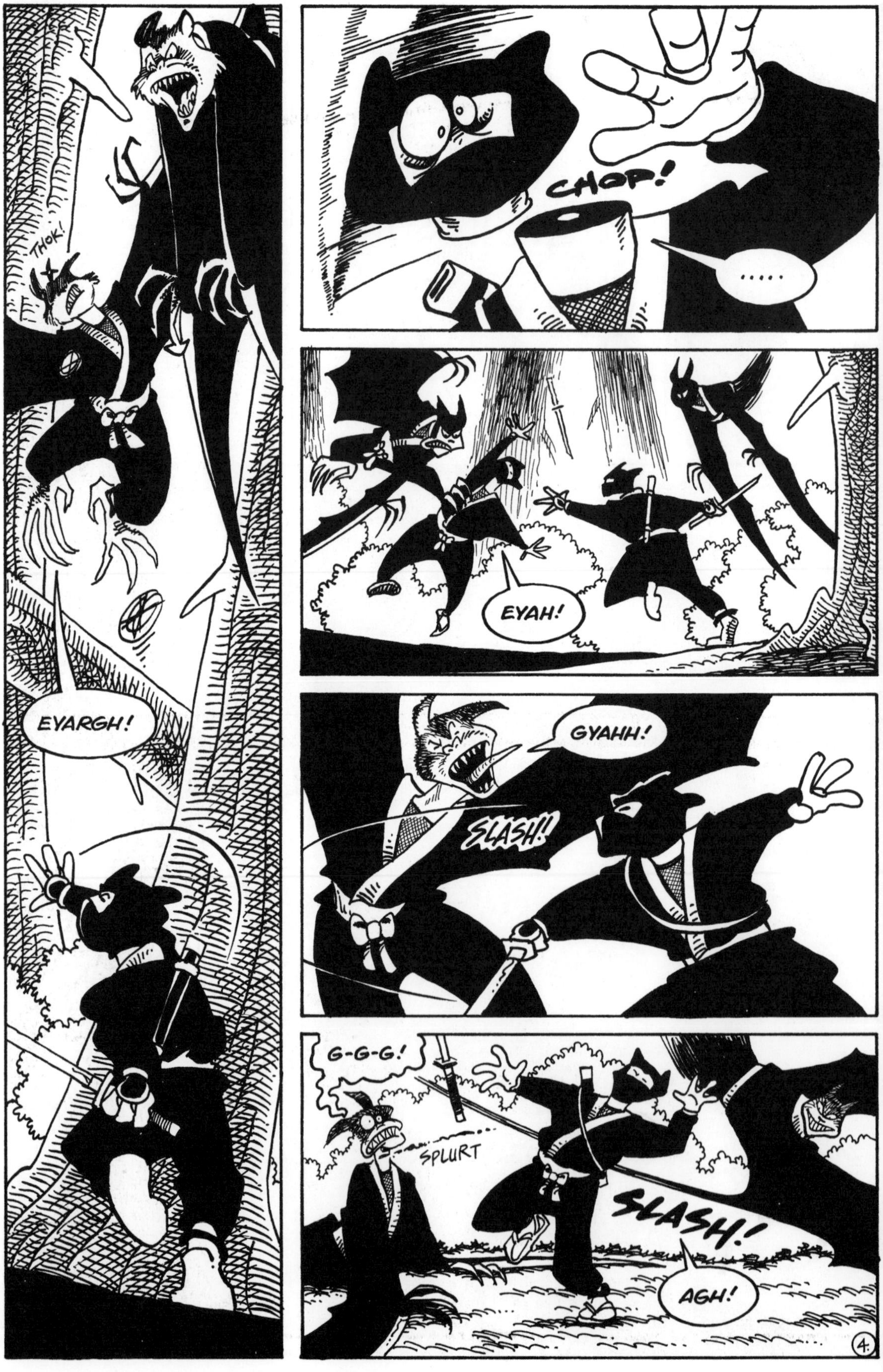
THOK!
EYARGH!
CHOP!
.....
EYAH!
GYAHH!
SLASH!
G-G-G!
SPLURT
SLASH!
AGH!
4.

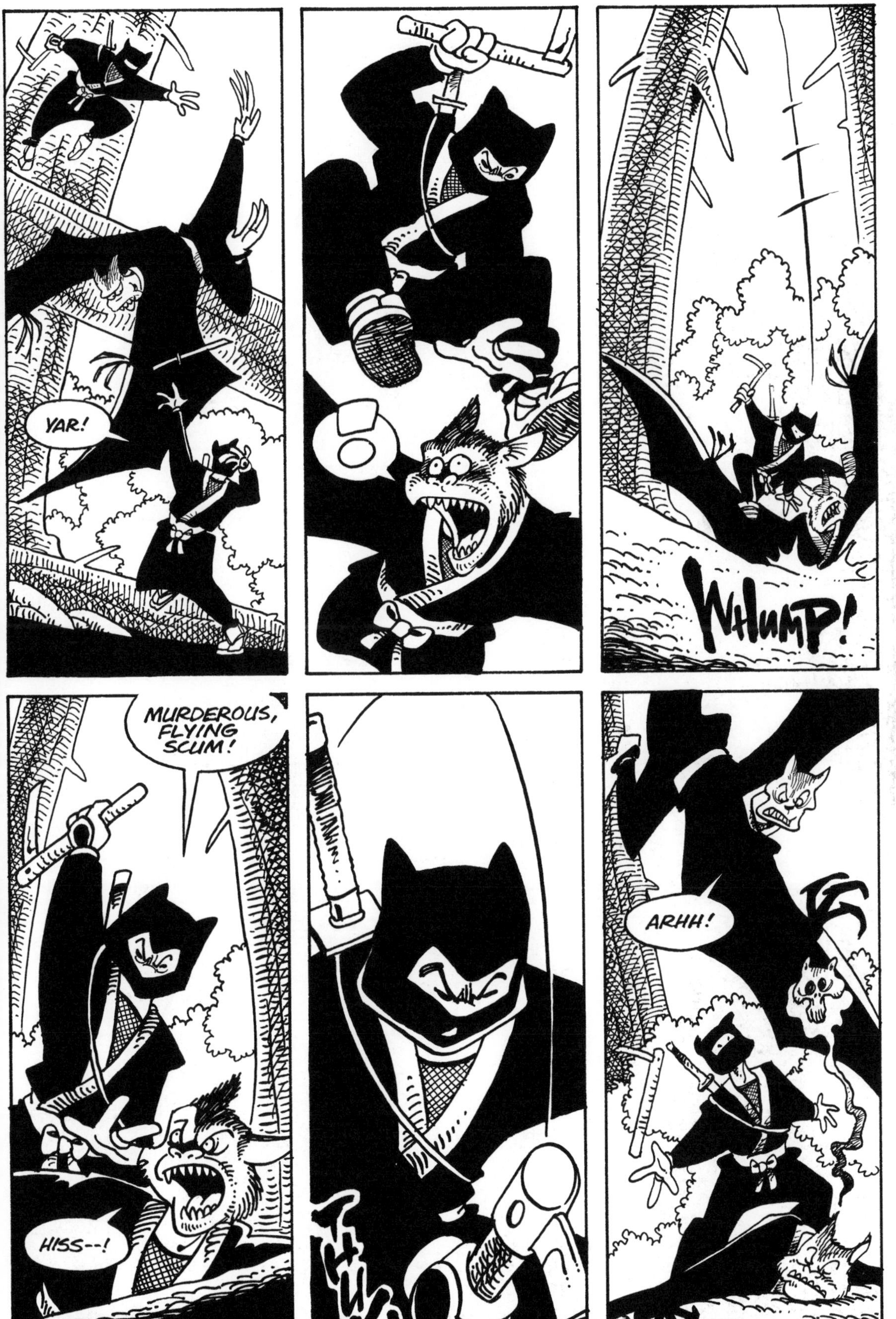
YAR!
WHUMP!
MURDEROUS, FLYING SCUM!
HISS--!
THUK!
ARHH!
5.

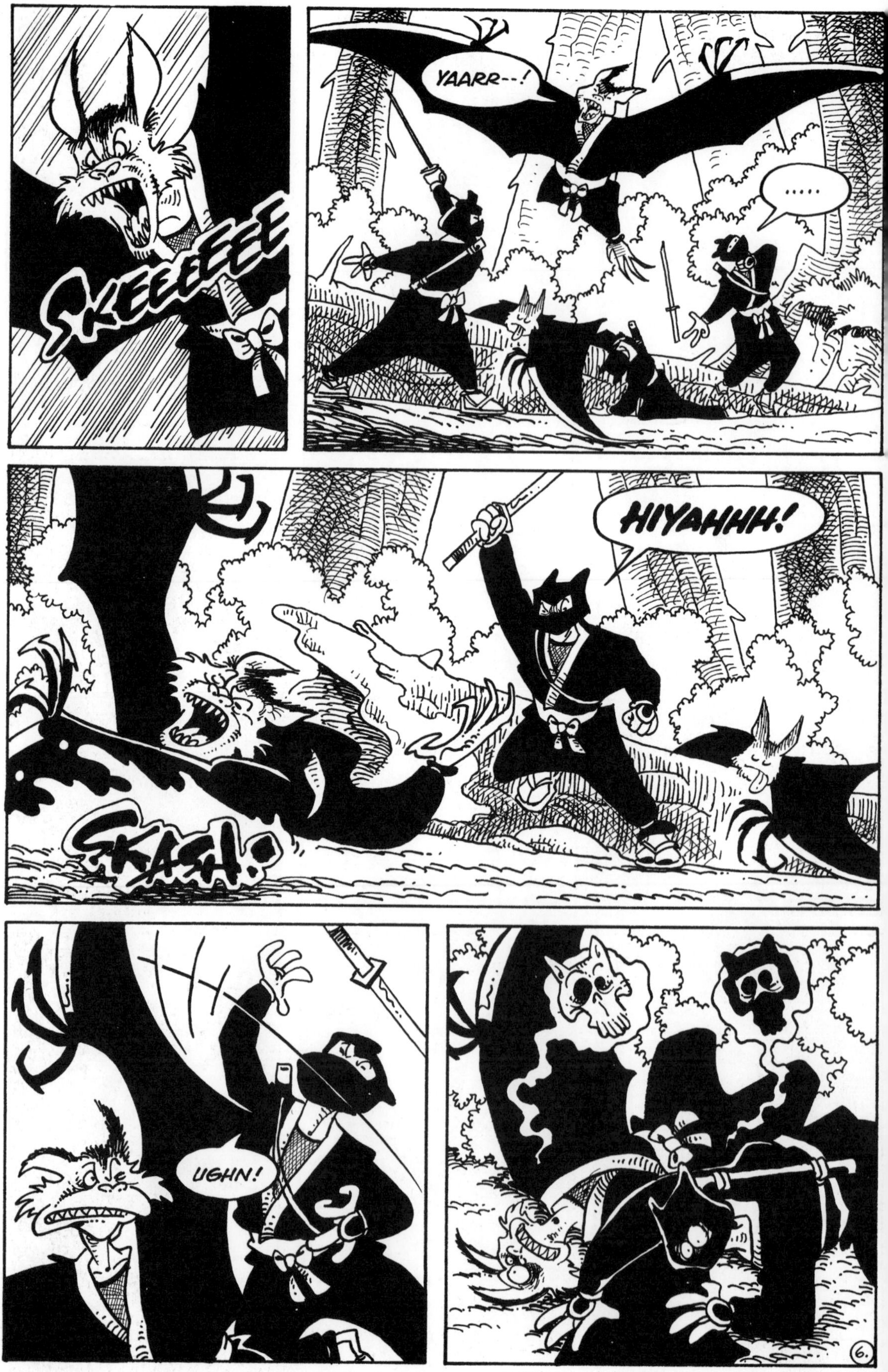
SKEEEEEE
YAARR--!
.....
HIYAHHH!
SKASH!
UGHN!
6.

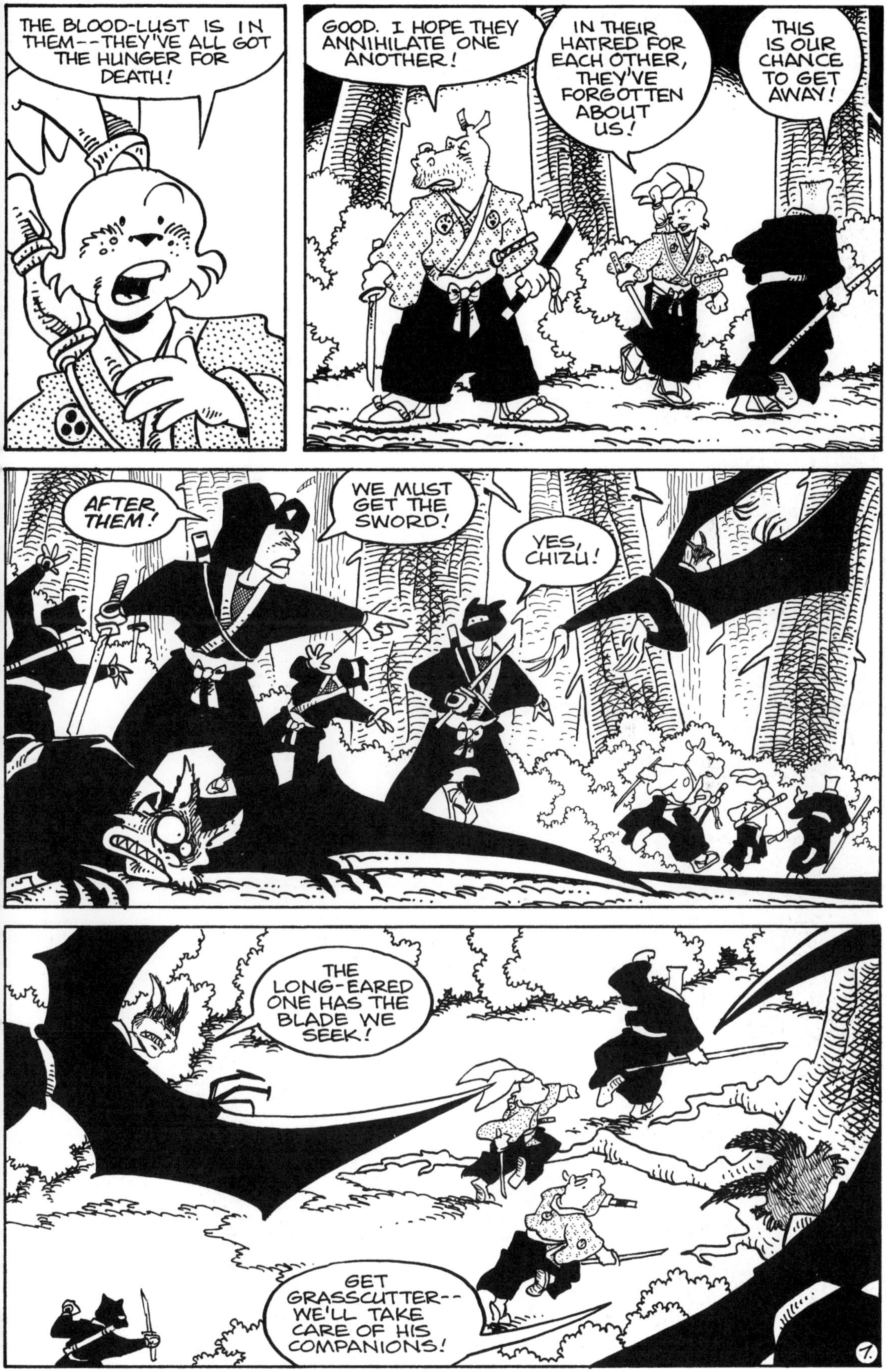
THE BLOOD-LUST IS IN THEM--THEY'VE ALL GOT THE HUNGER FOR DEATH!
GOOD. I HOPE THEY ANNIHILATE ONE ANOTHER!
IN THEIR HATRED FOR EACH OTHER, THEY'VE FORGOTTEN ABOUT US!
THIS IS OUR CHANCE TO GET AWAY!
AFTER THEM!
WE MUST GET THE SWORD!
YES, CHIZU!
THE LONG-EARED ONE HAS THE BLADE WE SEEK!
GET GRASSCUTTER--WE'LL TAKE CARE OF HIS COMPANIONS!
7.

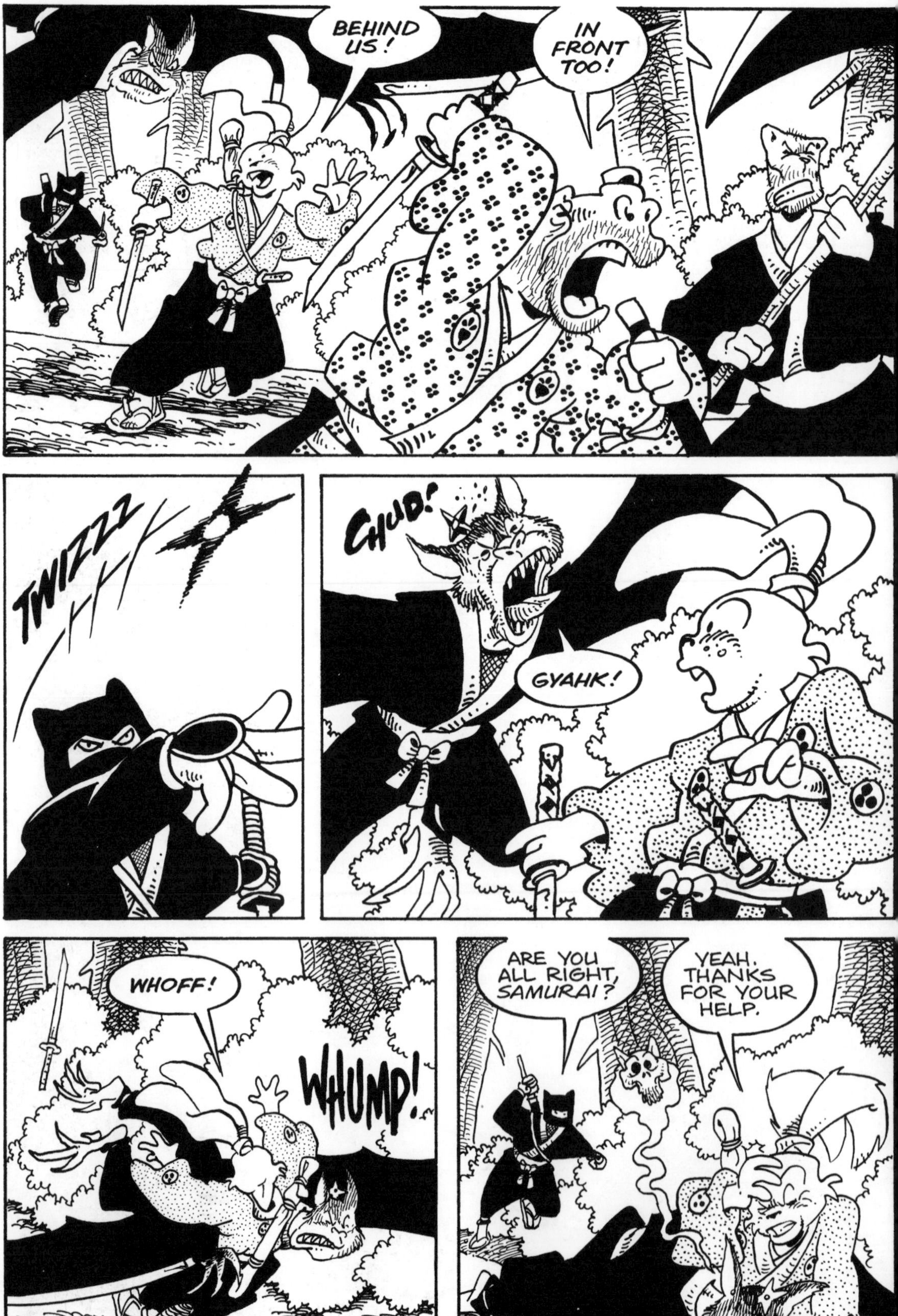
BEHIND US!
IN FRONT TOO!
TWIZZZ
CHUD!
GYAHK!
WHOFF!
WHUMP!
ARE YOU ALL RIGHT, SAMURAI?
YEAH. THANKS FOR YOUR HELP.
8.

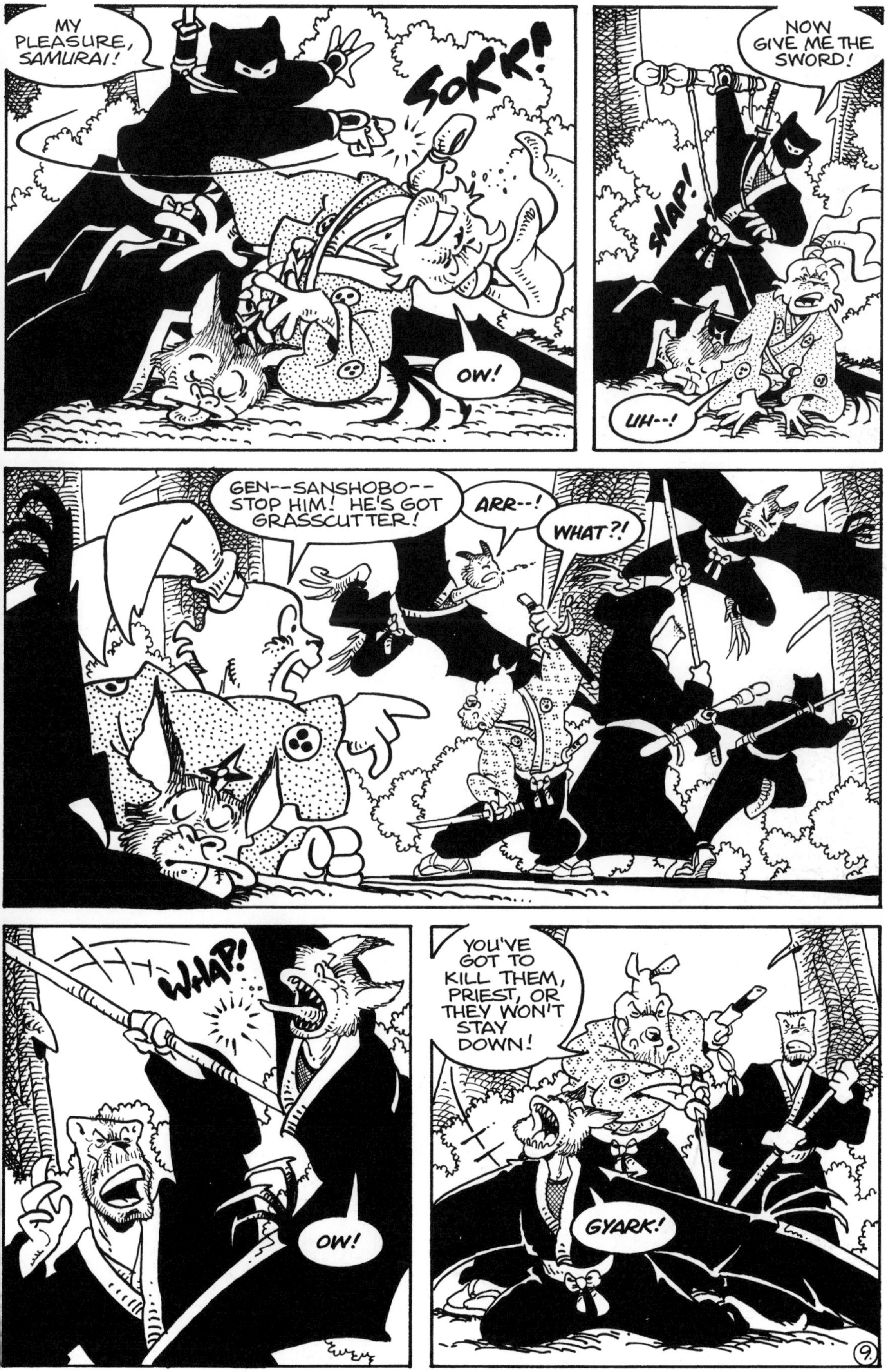
MY PLEASURE, SAMURAI!
SOKK!
OW!
NOW GIVE ME THE SWORD!
SWAP!
UH--!
GEN--SANSHOBO-- STOP HIM! HE'S GOT GRASSCUTTER!
ARR--!
WHAT?!
WHAP!
OW!
YOU'VE GOT TO KILL THEM, PRIEST, OR THEY WON'T STAY DOWN!
GYARK!
9.

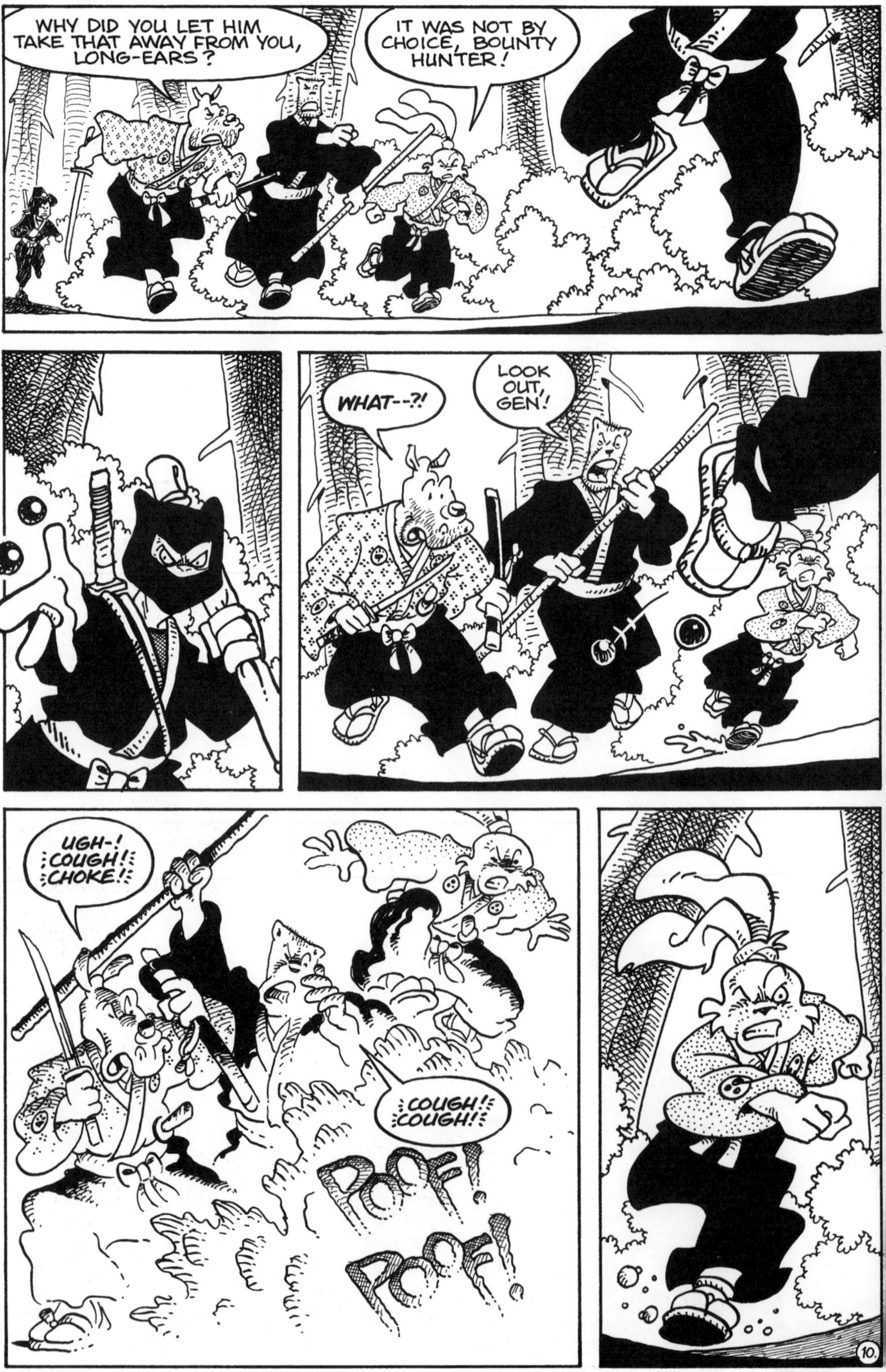
WHY DID YOU LET HIM TAKE THAT AWAY FROM YOU, LONG-EARS?
IT WAS NOT BY CHOICE, BOUNTY HUNTER!
WHAT--?!
LOOK OUT, GEN!
UGH-! COUGH! CHOKE!
COUGH! COUGH!
POOF!
POOF!
10.

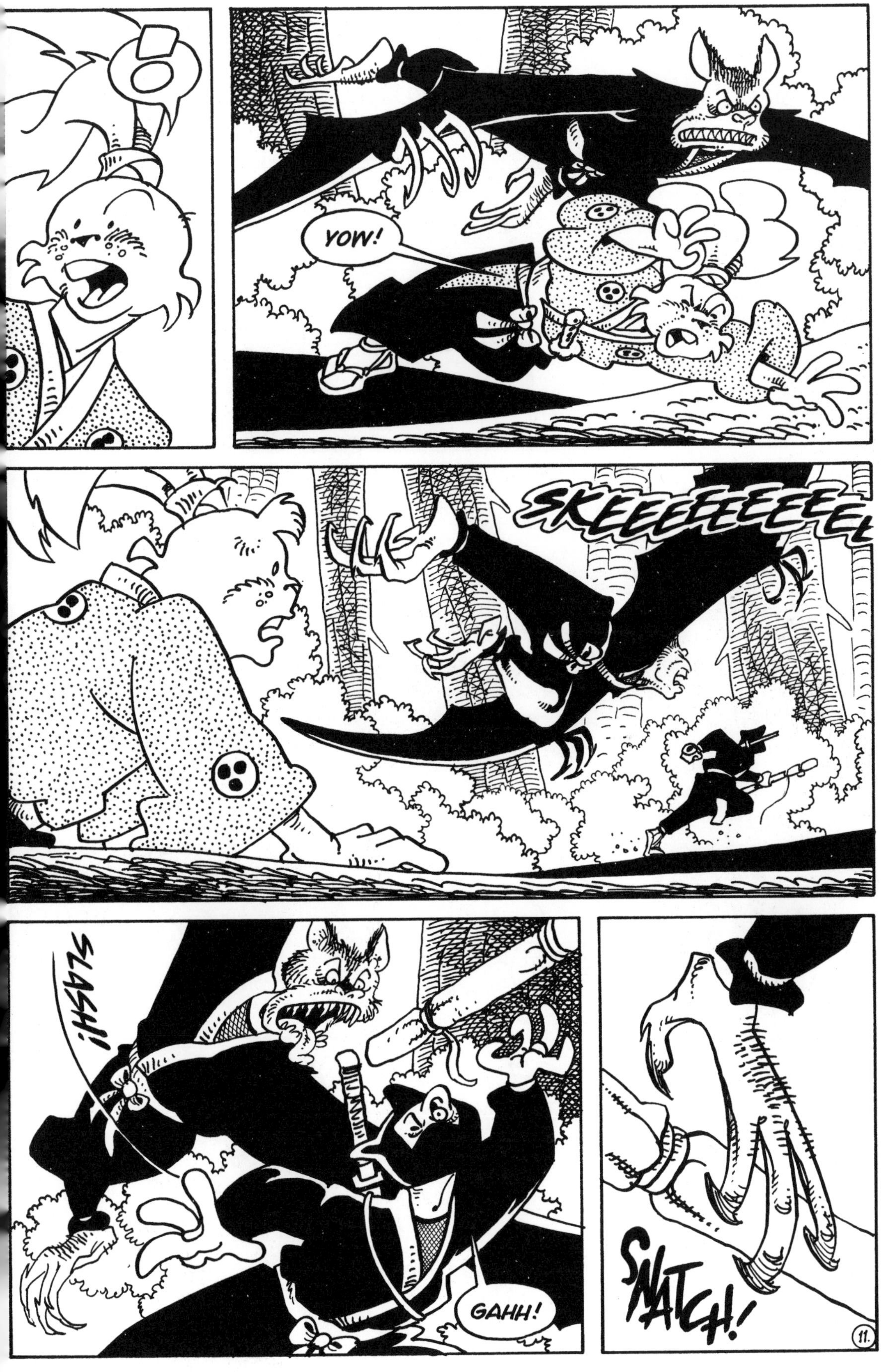
YOW!
SKEEEEEEEEL
SLASH!
GAHH!
SNATCH!
11.

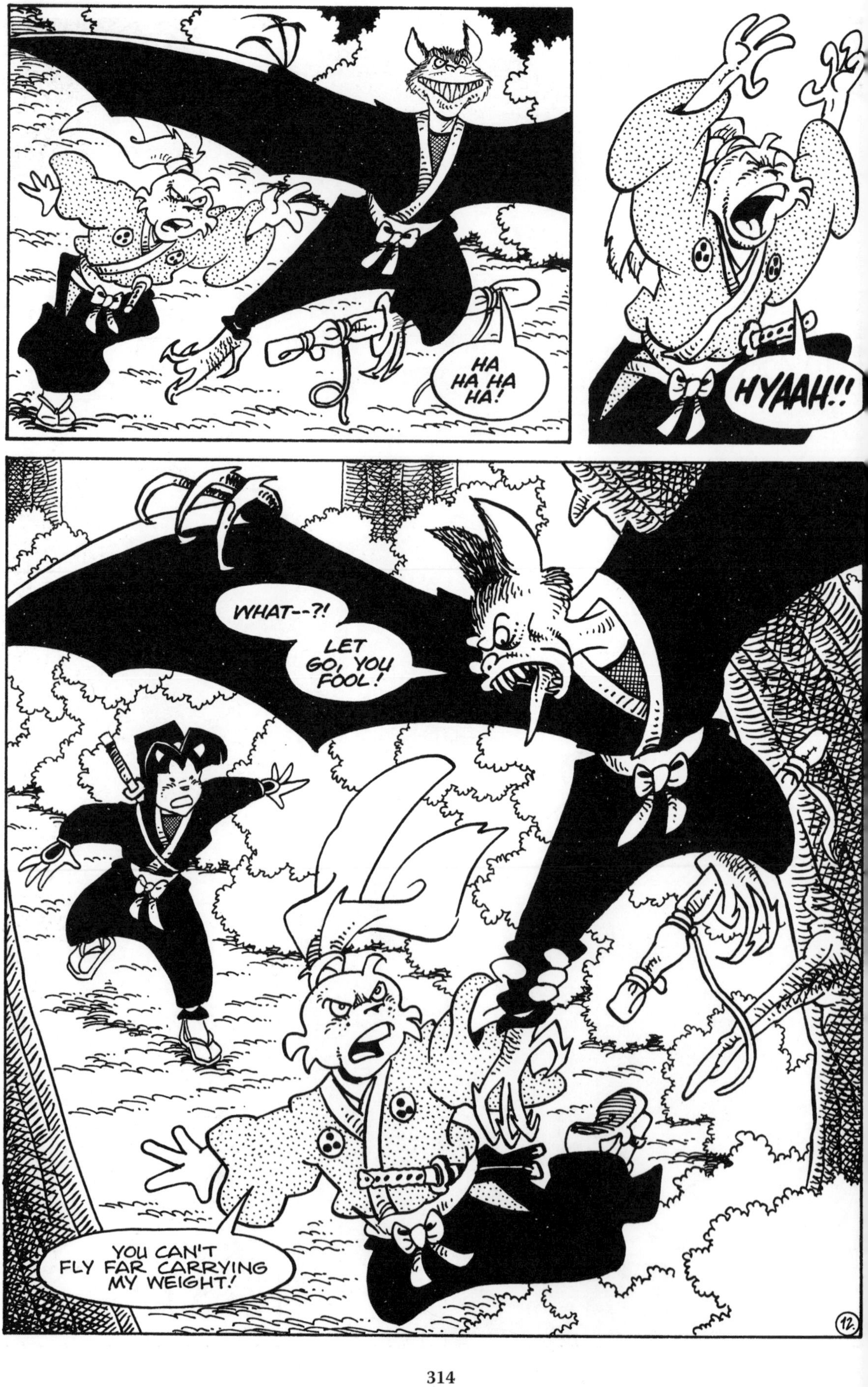
HA HA HA HA!
HYAAH!!
WHAT--?!
LET GO, YOU FOOL!
YOU CAN'T FLY FAR CARRYING MY WEIGHT!
12.

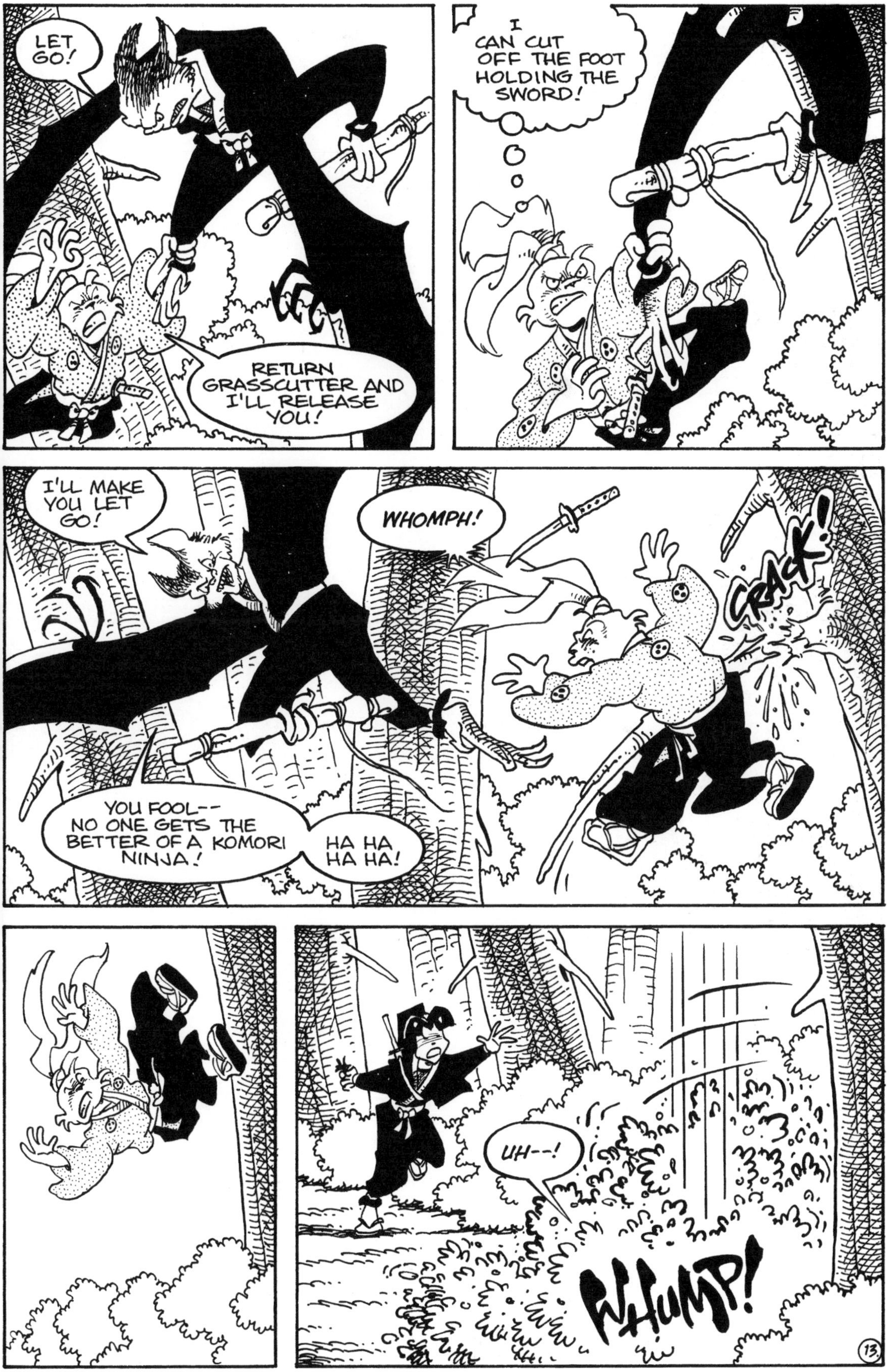
LET GO!
RETURN GRASSCUTTER AND I'LL RELEASE YOU!
I CAN CUT OFF THE FOOT HOLDING THE SWORD!
I'LL MAKE YOU LET GO!
WHOMPH!
CRACK!
YOU FOOL-- NO ONE GETS THE BETTER OF A KOMORI NINJA!
HA HA HA HA!
UH--!
WHUMP!
13

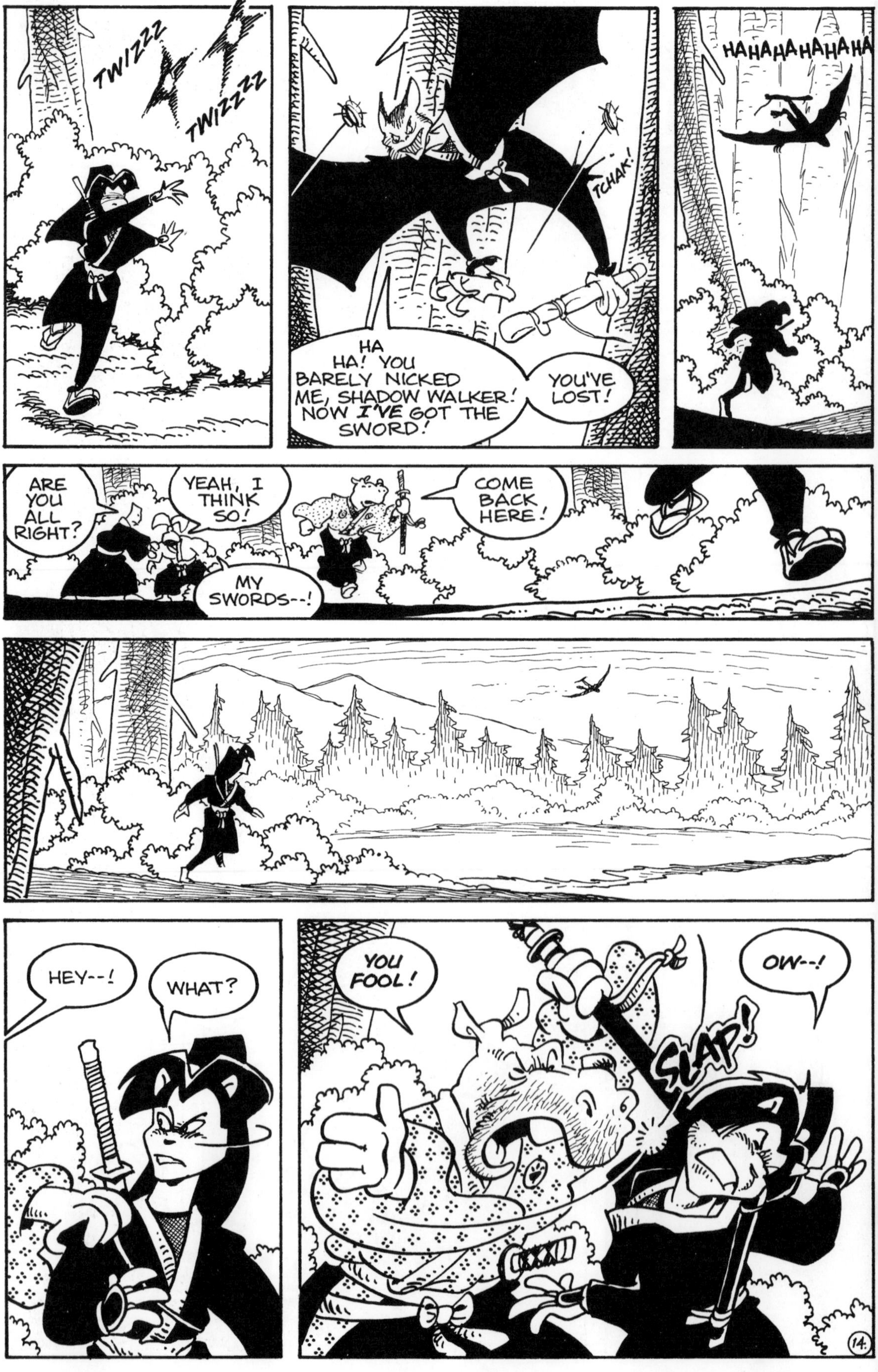
TWIZZZ
TWIZZZZ
TCHAK!
HA HA! YOU BARELY NICKED ME, SHADOW WALKER! NOW I'VE GOT THE SWORD!
YOU'VE LOST!
HAHAHAHAHAHAHA
ARE YOU ALL RIGHT?
YEAH, I THINK SO!
MY SWORDS--!
COME BACK HERE!
HEY--!
WHAT?
YOU FOOL!
SLAP!
OW--!
14.

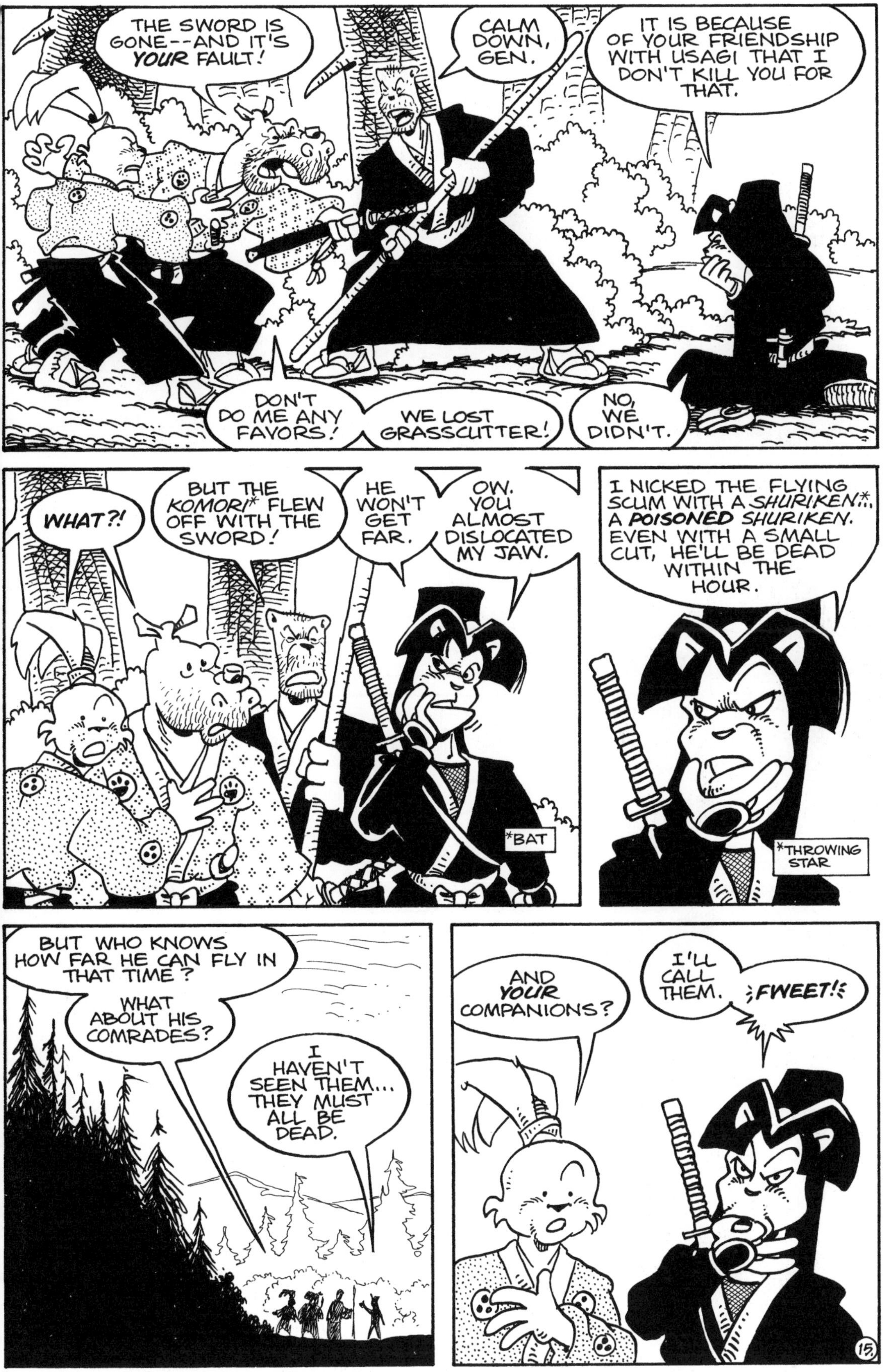
THE SWORD IS GONE--AND IT'S YOUR FAULT!
CALM DOWN, GEN.
IT IS BECAUSE OF YOUR FRIENDSHIP WITH USAGI THAT I DON'T KILL YOU FOR THAT.
DON'T DO ME ANY FAVORS!
WE LOST GRASSCUTTER!
NO, WE DIDN'T.
WHAT?!
BUT THE KOMORI* FLEW OFF WITH THE SWORD!
HE WON'T GET FAR.
OW. YOU ALMOST DISLOCATED MY JAW.
*BAT
I NICKED THE FLYING SCUM WITH A SHURIKEN*... A POISONED SHURIKEN. EVEN WITH A SMALL CUT, HE'LL BE DEAD WITHIN THE HOUR.
*THROWING STAR
BUT WHO KNOWS HOW FAR HE CAN FLY IN THAT TIME?
WHAT ABOUT HIS COMRADES?
I HAVEN'T SEEN THEM... THEY MUST ALL BE DEAD.
AND YOUR COMPANIONS?
I'LL CALL THEM.
FWEET!
15

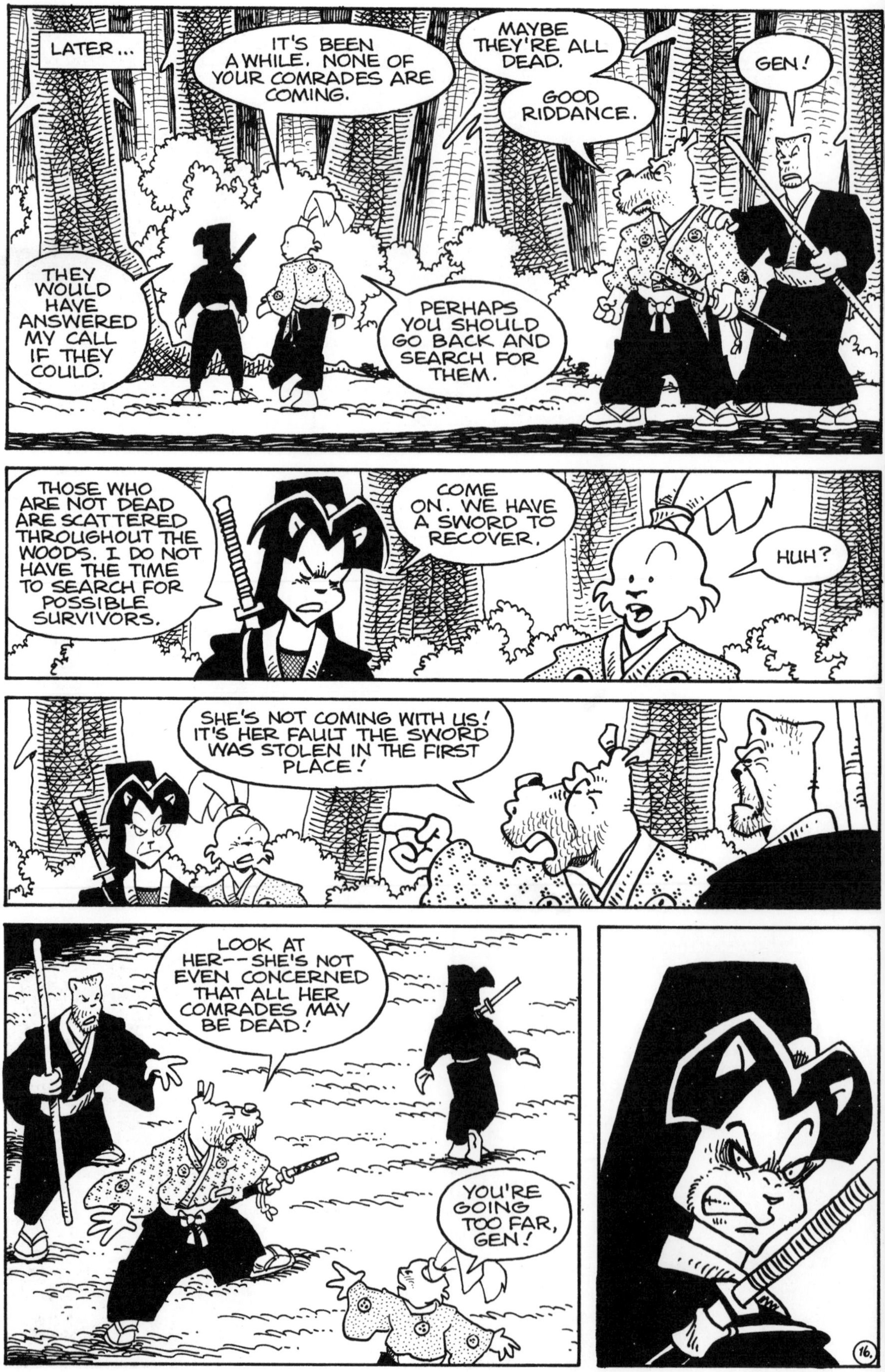
LATER...
IT'S BEEN A WHILE. NONE OF YOUR COMRADES ARE COMING.
MAYBE THEY'RE ALL DEAD.
GOOD RIDDANCE.
GEN!
THEY WOULD HAVE ANSWERED MY CALL IF THEY COULD.
PERHAPS YOU SHOULD GO BACK AND SEARCH FOR THEM.
THOSE WHO ARE NOT DEAD ARE SCATTERED THROUGHOUT THE WOODS. I DO NOT HAVE THE TIME TO SEARCH FOR POSSIBLE SURVIVORS.
COME ON. WE HAVE A SWORD TO RECOVER.
HUH?
SHE'S NOT COMING WITH US! IT'S HER FAULT THE SWORD WAS STOLEN IN THE FIRST PLACE!
LOOK AT HER--SHE'S NOT EVEN CONCERNED THAT ALL HER COMRADES MAY BE DEAD!
YOU'RE GOING TOO FAR, GEN!
16.

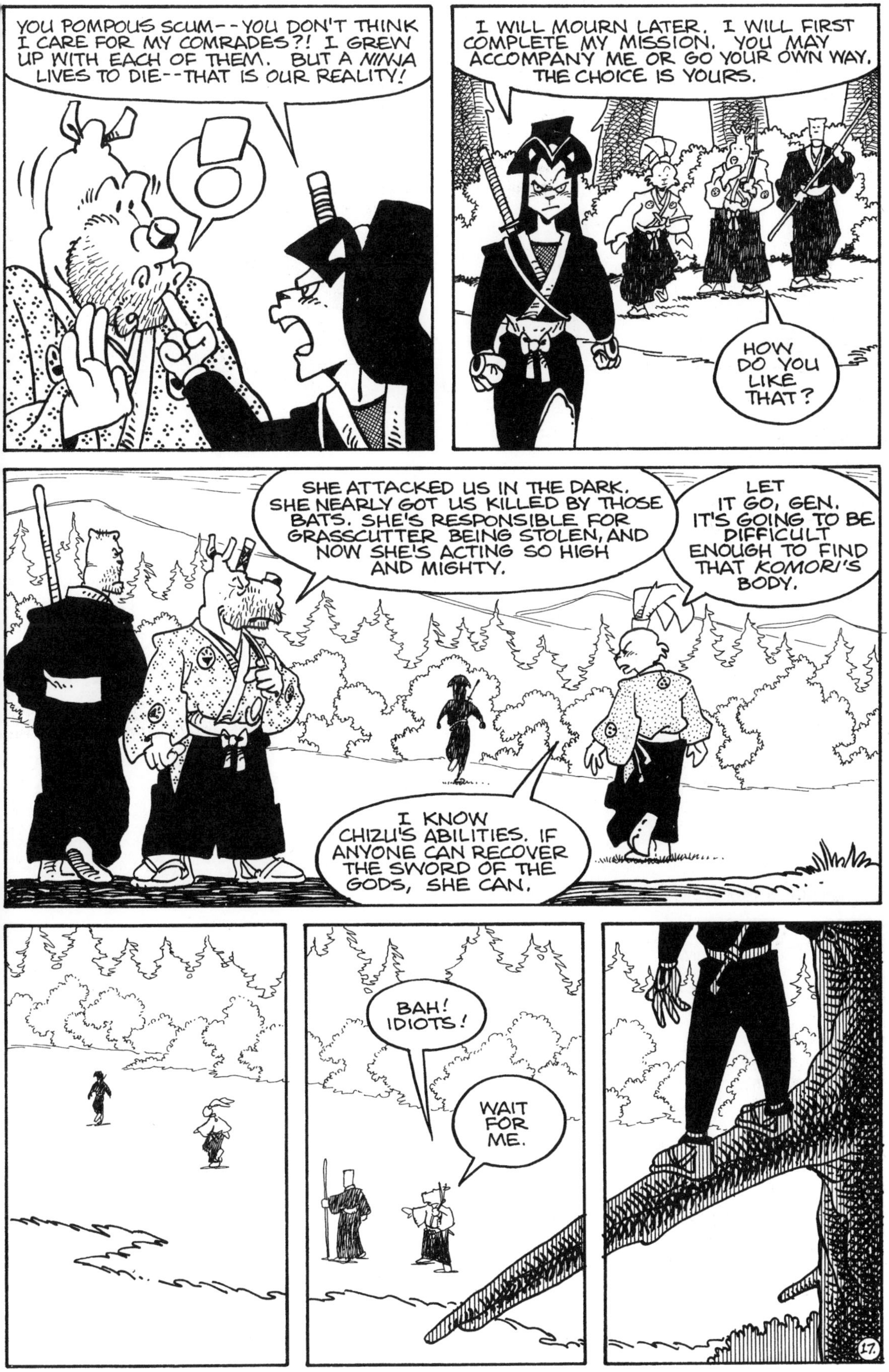
YOU POMPOUS SCUM--YOU DON'T THINK I CARE FOR MY COMRADES?! I GREW UP WITH EACH OF THEM. BUT A *NINJA* LIVES TO DIE--THAT IS OUR REALITY!
!
I WILL MOURN LATER. I WILL FIRST COMPLETE MY MISSION. YOU MAY ACCOMPANY ME OR GO YOUR OWN WAY. THE CHOICE IS YOURS.
HOW DO YOU LIKE THAT?
SHE ATTACKED US IN THE DARK. SHE NEARLY GOT US KILLED BY THOSE BATS. SHE'S RESPONSIBLE FOR GRASSCUTTER BEING STOLEN, AND NOW SHE'S ACTING SO HIGH AND MIGHTY.
LET IT GO, GEN. IT'S GOING TO BE DIFFICULT ENOUGH TO FIND THAT *KOMORI*'S BODY.
I KNOW CHIZU'S ABILITIES. IF ANYONE CAN RECOVER THE SWORD OF THE GODS, SHE CAN.
BAH! IDIOTS!
WAIT FOR ME.
17.

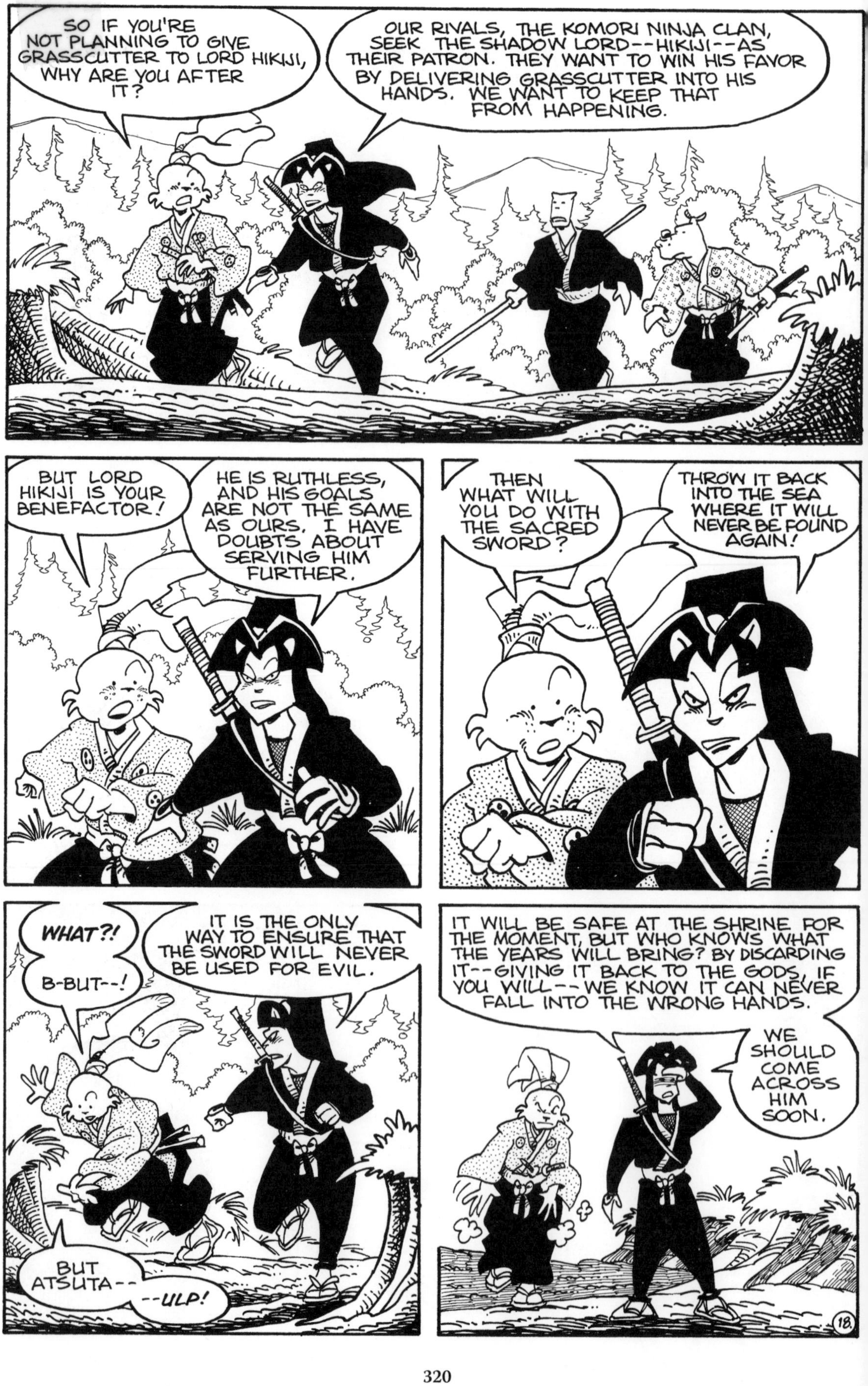
SO IF YOU'RE NOT PLANNING TO GIVE GRASSCUTTER TO LORD HIKIJI, WHY ARE YOU AFTER IT?
OUR RIVALS, THE KOMORI NINJA CLAN, SEEK THE SHADOW LORD--HIKIJI--AS THEIR PATRON. THEY WANT TO WIN HIS FAVOR BY DELIVERING GRASSCUTTER INTO HIS HANDS. WE WANT TO KEEP THAT FROM HAPPENING.
BUT LORD HIKIJI IS YOUR BENEFACTOR!
HE IS RUTHLESS, AND HIS GOALS ARE NOT THE SAME AS OURS. I HAVE DOUBTS ABOUT SERVING HIM FURTHER.
THEN WHAT WILL YOU DO WITH THE SACRED SWORD?
THROW IT BACK INTO THE SEA WHERE IT WILL NEVER BE FOUND AGAIN!
WHAT?!
B-BUT--!
IT IS THE ONLY WAY TO ENSURE THAT THE SWORD WILL NEVER BE USED FOR EVIL.
BUT ATSUTA--
--ULP!
IT WILL BE SAFE AT THE SHRINE FOR THE MOMENT, BUT WHO KNOWS WHAT THE YEARS WILL BRING? BY DISCARDING IT--GIVING IT BACK TO THE GODS, IF YOU WILL--WE KNOW IT CAN NEVER FALL INTO THE WRONG HANDS.
WE SHOULD COME ACROSS HIM SOON.
18

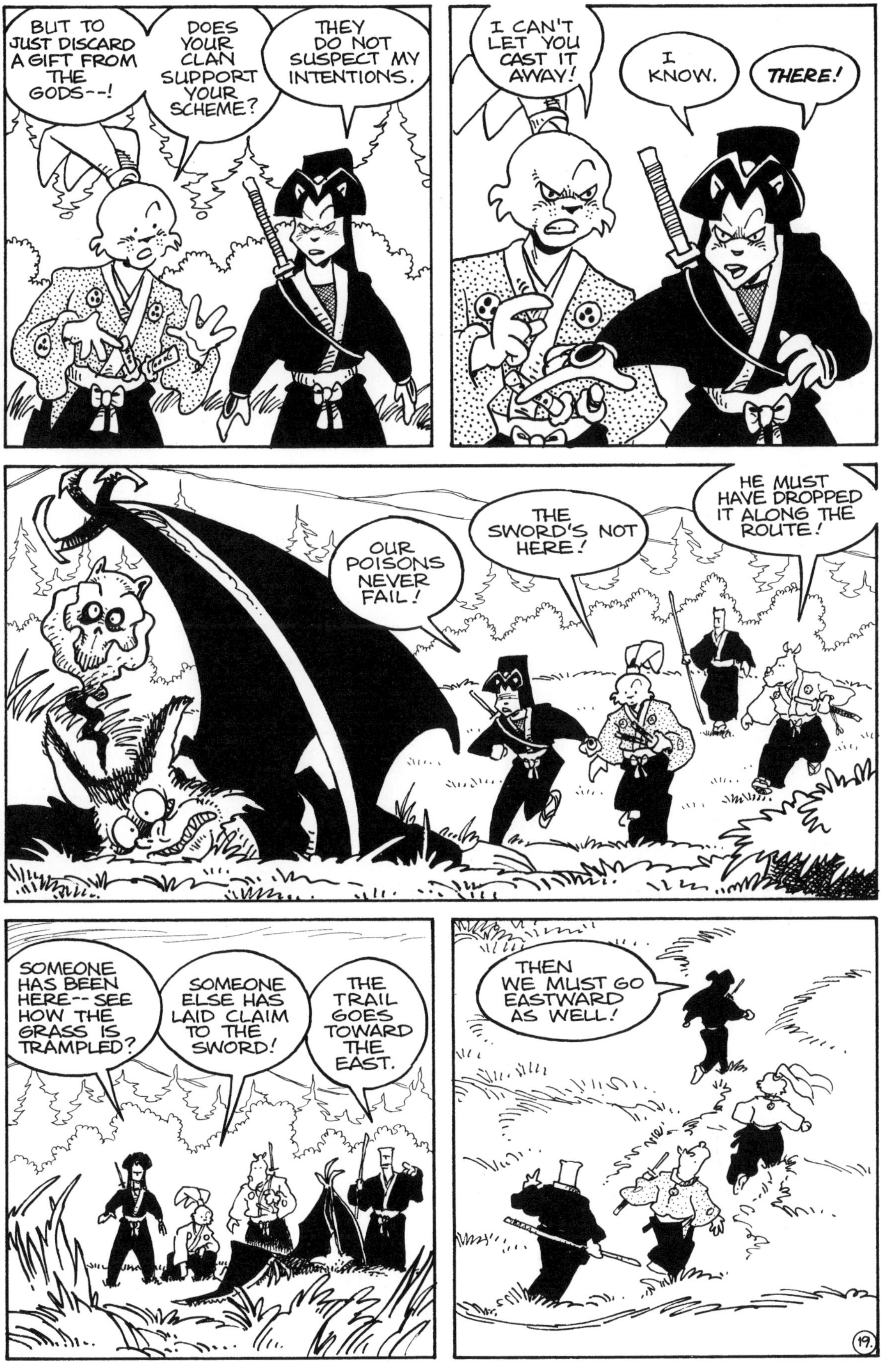
BUT TO JUST DISCARD A GIFT FROM THE GODS--!
DOES YOUR CLAN SUPPORT YOUR SCHEME?
THEY DO NOT SUSPECT MY INTENTIONS.
I CAN'T LET YOU CAST IT AWAY!
I KNOW.
THERE!
OUR POISONS NEVER FAIL!
THE SWORD'S NOT HERE!
HE MUST HAVE DROPPED IT ALONG THE ROUTE!
SOMEONE HAS BEEN HERE--SEE HOW THE GRASS IS TRAMPLED?
SOMEONE ELSE HAS LAID CLAIM TO THE SWORD!
THE TRAIL GOES TOWARD THE EAST.
THEN WE MUST GO EASTWARD AS WELL!
19.

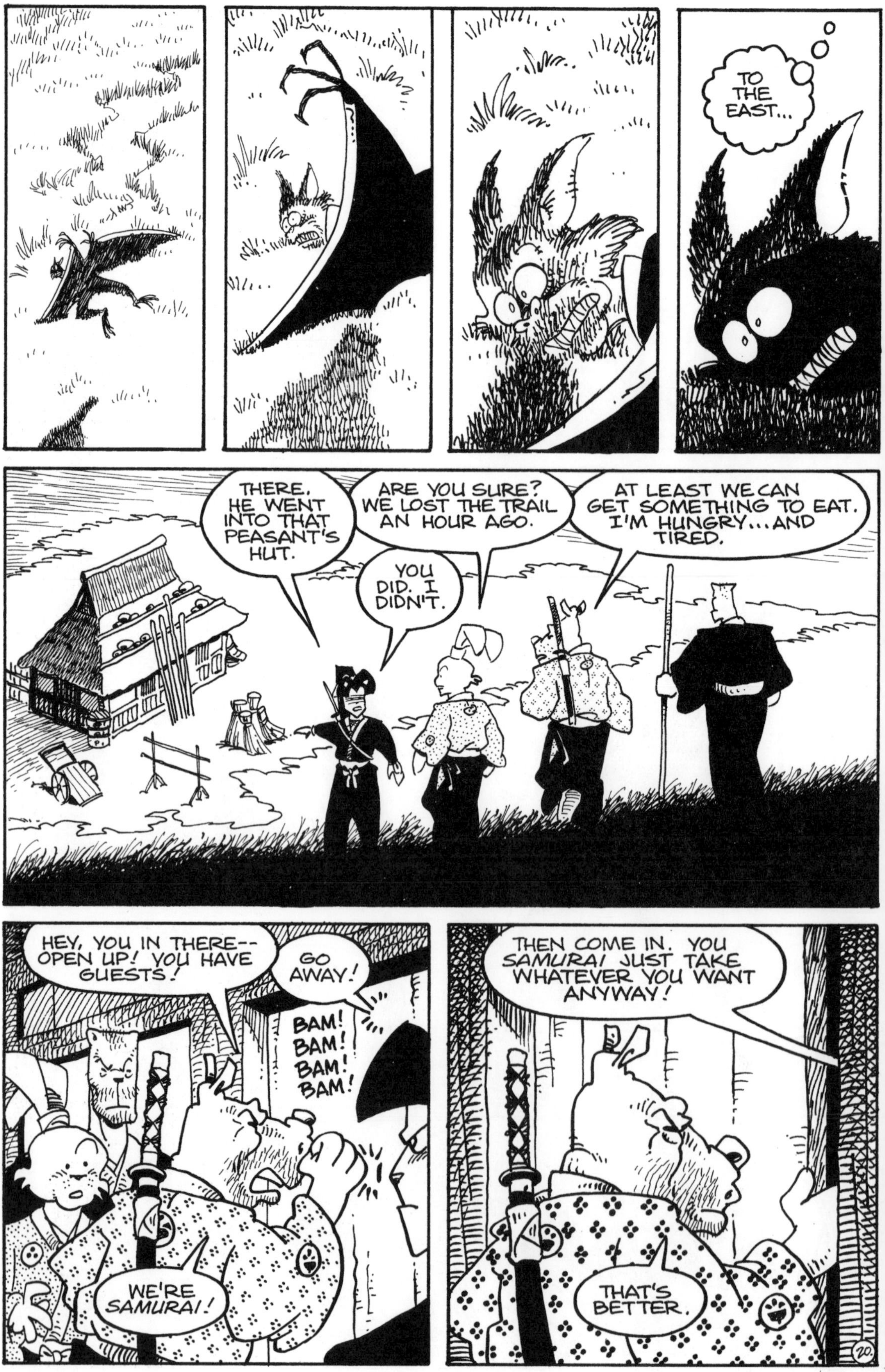
TO THE EAST...
THERE. HE WENT INTO THAT PEASANT'S HUT.
ARE YOU SURE? WE LOST THE TRAIL AN HOUR AGO.
YOU DID. I DIDN'T.
AT LEAST WE CAN GET SOMETHING TO EAT. I'M HUNGRY...AND TIRED.
HEY, YOU IN THERE-- OPEN UP! YOU HAVE GUESTS!
GO AWAY!
BAM! BAM! BAM! BAM!
WE'RE *SAMURAI*!
THEN COME IN. YOU *SAMURAI* JUST TAKE WHATEVER YOU WANT ANYWAY!
THAT'S BETTER.
20.

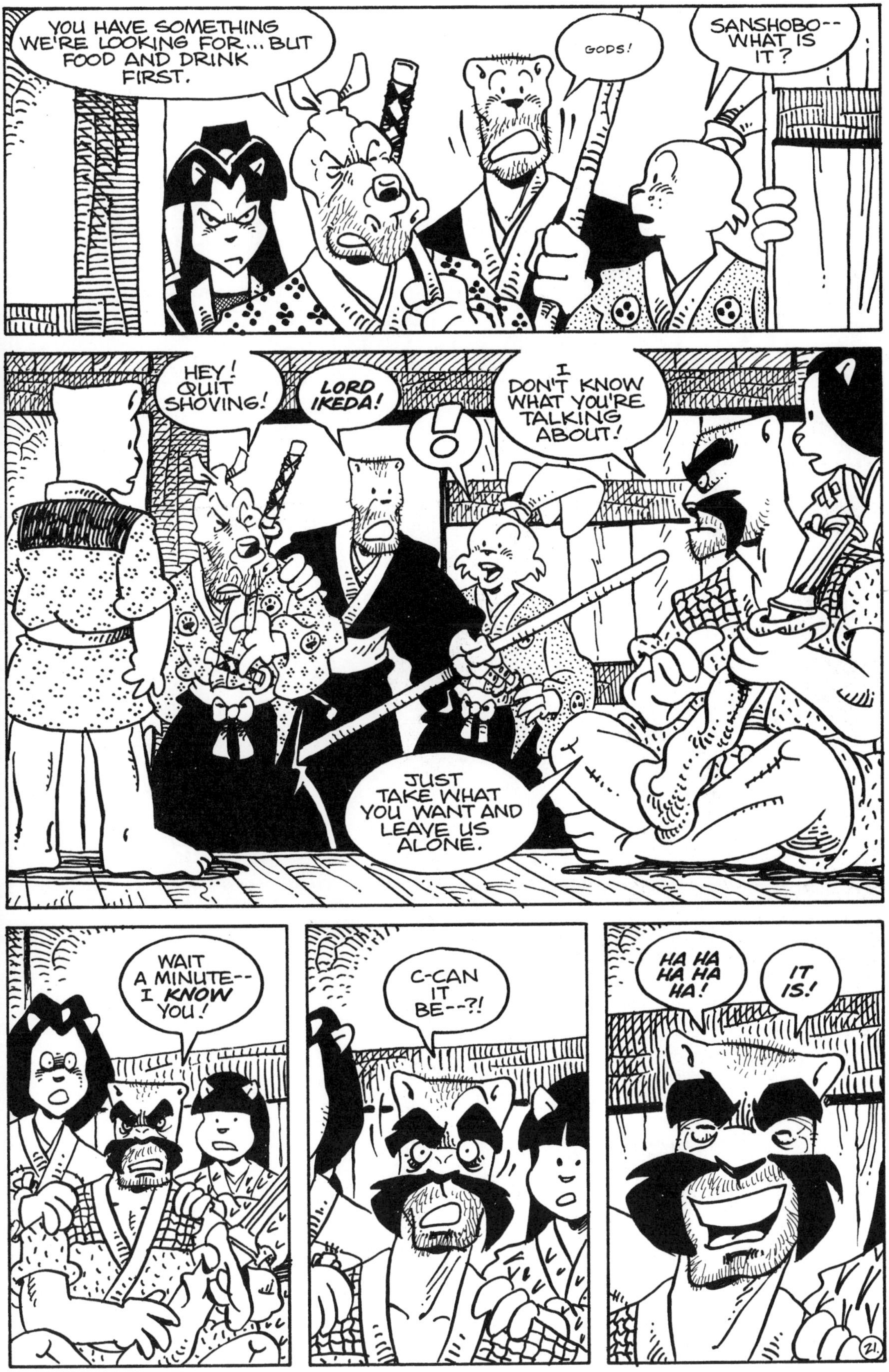
YOU HAVE SOMETHING WE'RE LOOKING FOR... BUT FOOD AND DRINK FIRST.
GODS!
SANSHOBO-- WHAT IS IT?
HEY! QUIT SHOVING!
LORD IKEDA!
!
I DON'T KNOW WHAT YOU'RE TALKING ABOUT!
JUST TAKE WHAT YOU WANT AND LEAVE US ALONE.
WAIT A MINUTE-- I KNOW YOU!
C-CAN IT BE--?!
HA HA HA HA HA!
IT IS!
21.

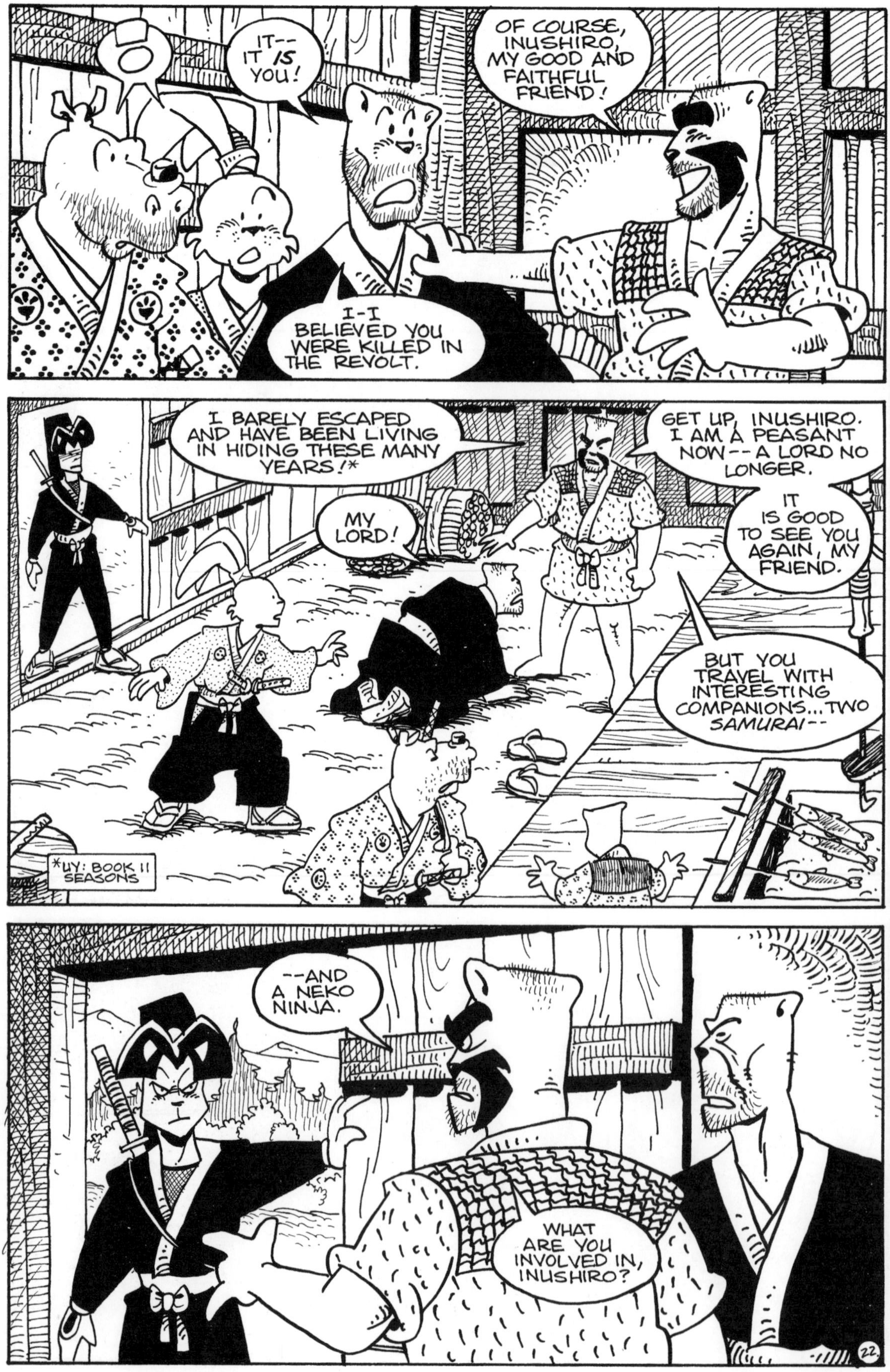
!
IT-- IT *IS* YOU!
OF COURSE, INUSHIRO, MY GOOD AND FAITHFUL FRIEND!
I-I BELIEVED YOU WERE KILLED IN THE REVOLT.
I BARELY ESCAPED AND HAVE BEEN LIVING IN HIDING THESE MANY YEARS!*
MY LORD!
GET UP, INUSHIRO. I AM A PEASANT NOW--A LORD NO LONGER.
IT IS GOOD TO SEE YOU AGAIN, MY FRIEND.
BUT YOU TRAVEL WITH INTERESTING COMPANIONS...TWO *SAMURAI*--
*UY: BOOK 11 SEASONS
--AND A NEKO NINJA.
WHAT ARE YOU INVOLVED IN, INUSHIRO?
22.

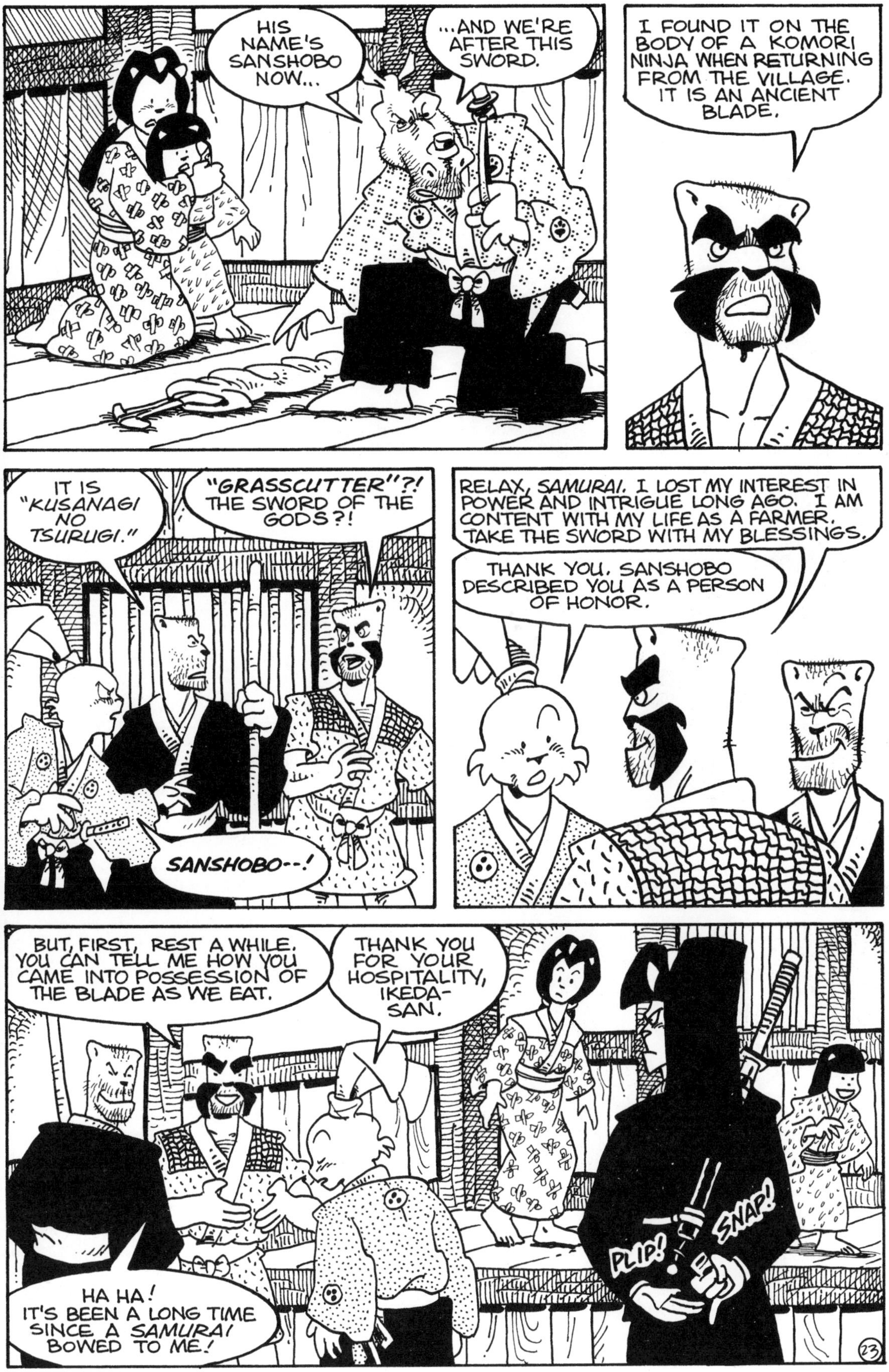
HIS NAME'S SANSHOBO NOW...
...AND WE'RE AFTER THIS SWORD.
I FOUND IT ON THE BODY OF A KOMORI NINJA WHEN RETURNING FROM THE VILLAGE. IT IS AN ANCIENT BLADE.
IT IS "KUSANAGI NO TSURUGI."
"GRASSCUTTER"?! THE SWORD OF THE GODS?!
SANSHOBO--!
RELAX, SAMURAI. I LOST MY INTEREST IN POWER AND INTRIGUE LONG AGO. I AM CONTENT WITH MY LIFE AS A FARMER. TAKE THE SWORD WITH MY BLESSINGS.
THANK YOU. SANSHOBO DESCRIBED YOU AS A PERSON OF HONOR.
BUT, FIRST, REST A WHILE. YOU CAN TELL ME HOW YOU CAME INTO POSSESSION OF THE BLADE AS WE EAT.
THANK YOU FOR YOUR HOSPITALITY, IKEDA-SAN.
HA HA! IT'S BEEN A LONG TIME SINCE A SAMURAI BOWED TO ME!
SNAP!
PLIP!
23

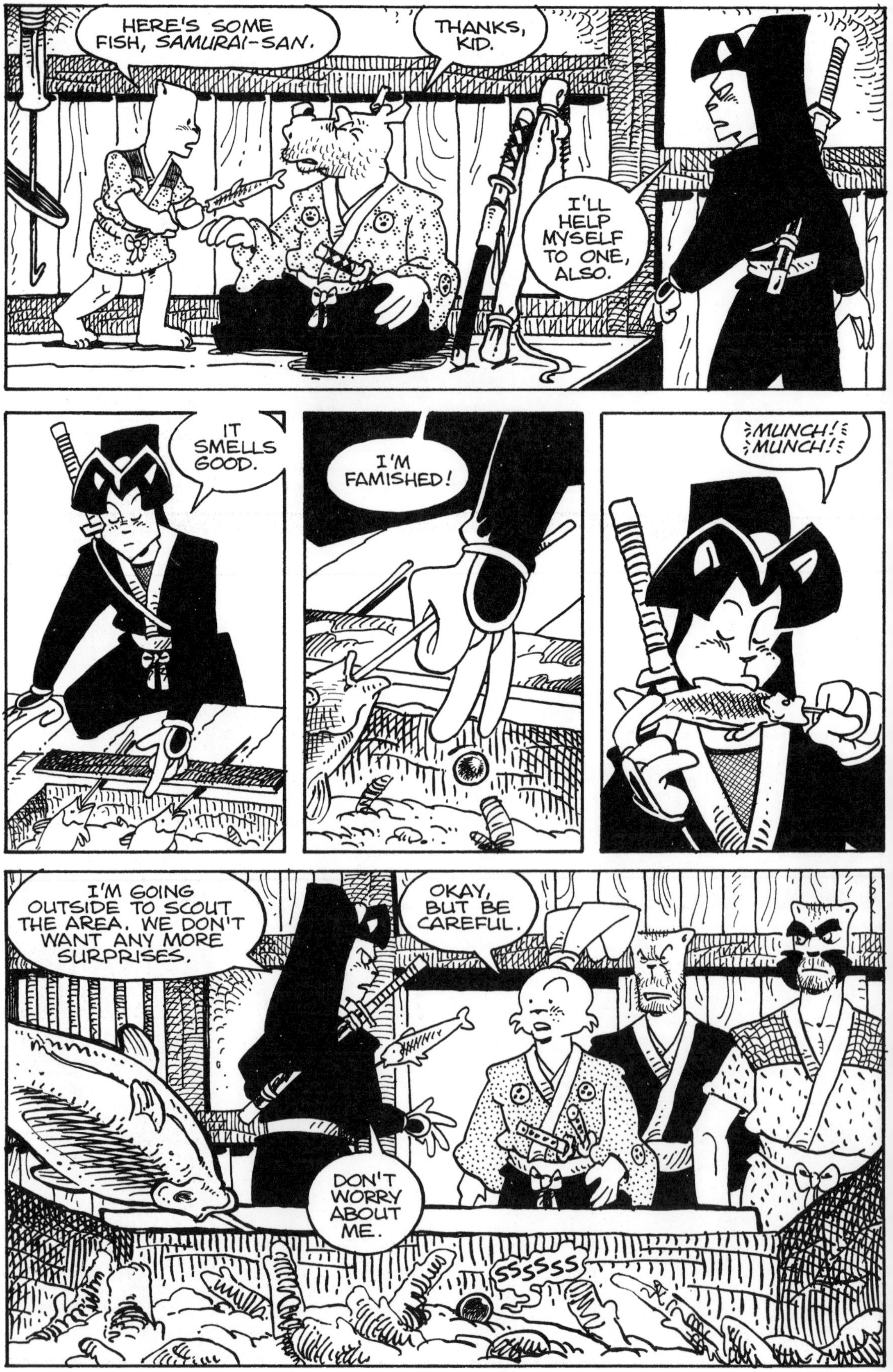
HERE'S SOME FISH, SAMURAI-SAN.
THANKS, KID.
I'LL HELP MYSELF TO ONE, ALSO.
IT SMELLS GOOD.
I'M FAMISHED!
MUNCH! MUNCH!
I'M GOING OUTSIDE TO SCOUT THE AREA. WE DON'T WANT ANY MORE SURPRISES.
OKAY, BUT BE CAREFUL.
DON'T WORRY ABOUT ME.
SSSSSS

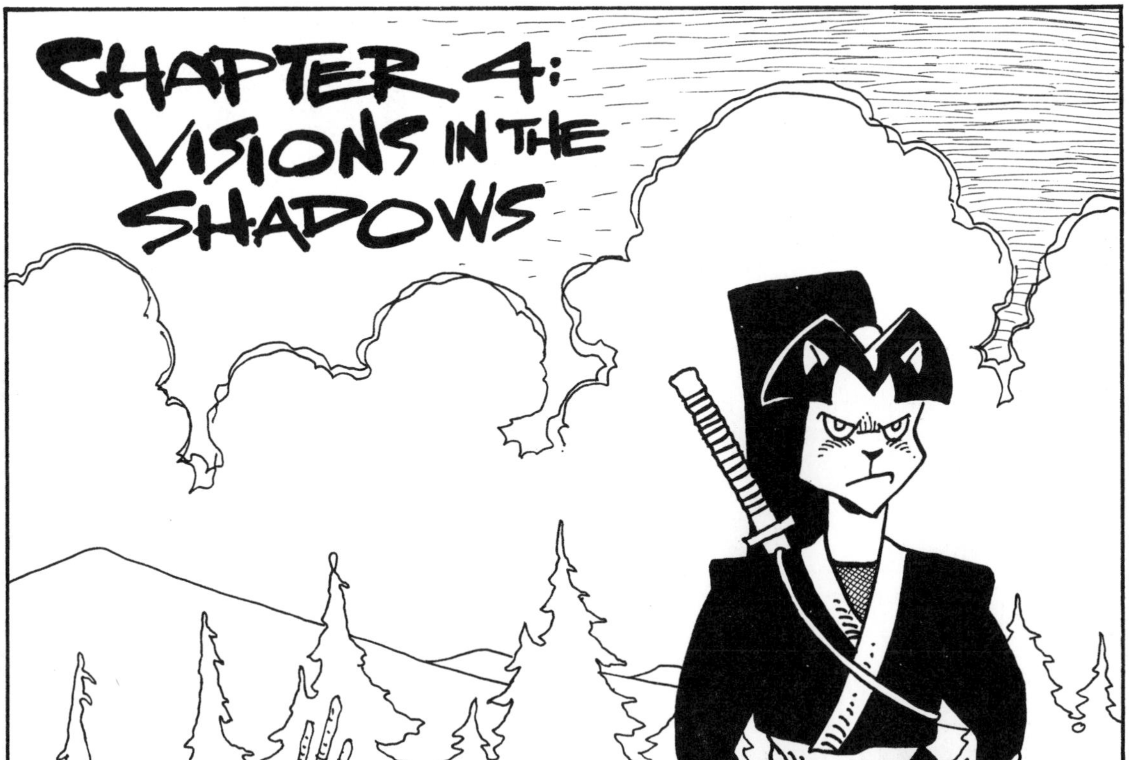
CHAPTER 4:
VISIONS IN THE SHADOWS

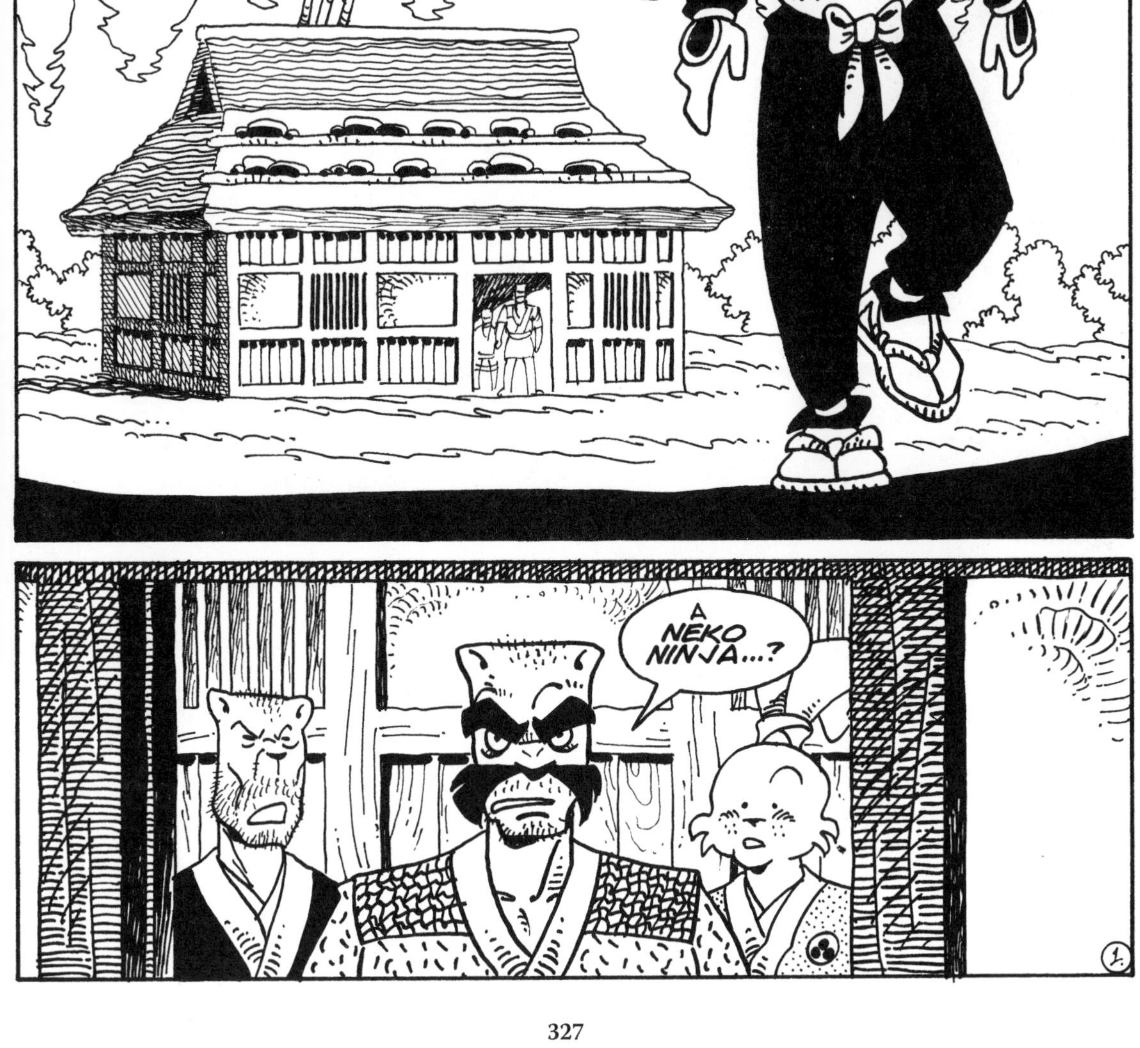
A NEKO NINJA...?
1.

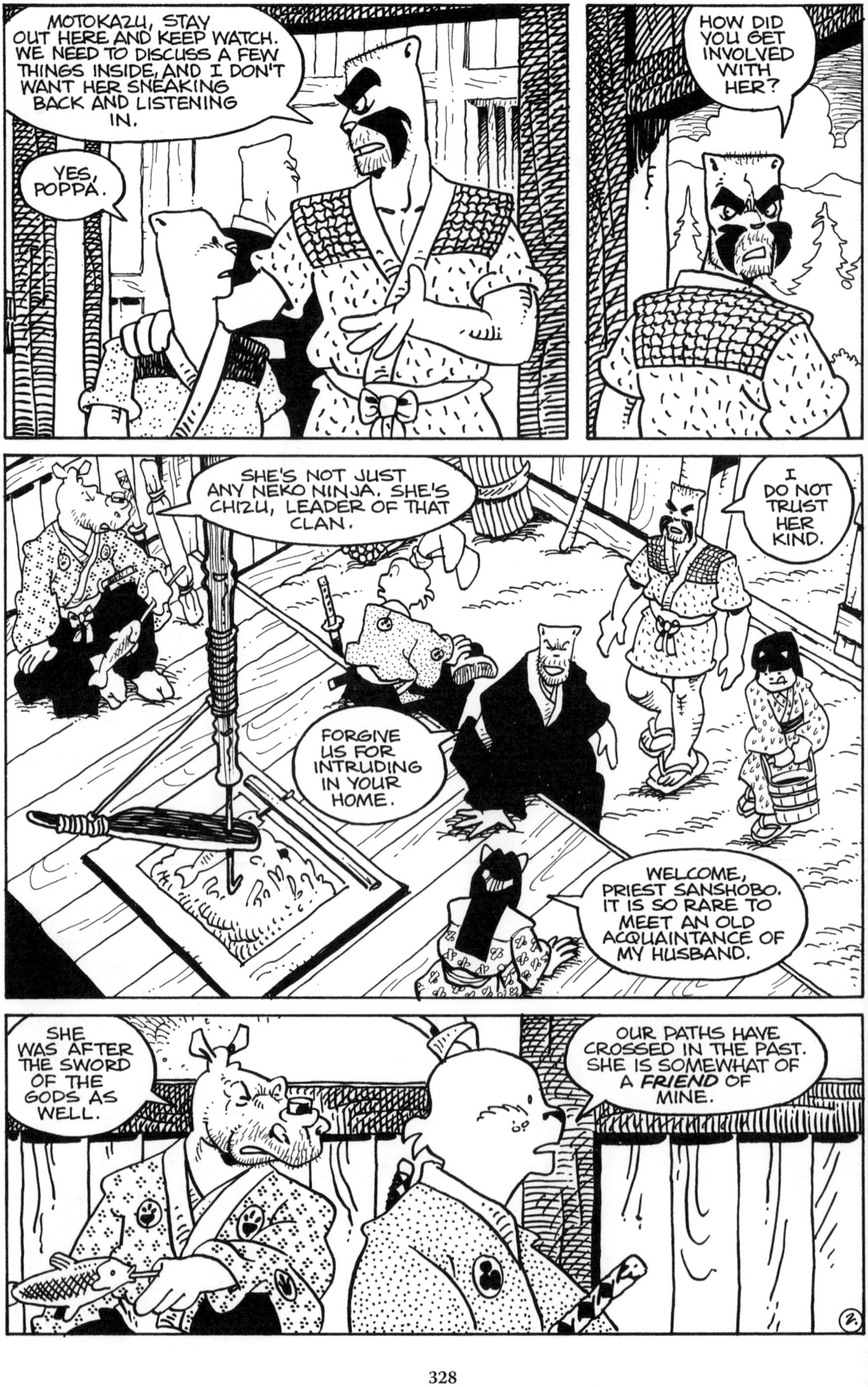
MOTOKAZU, STAY OUT HERE AND KEEP WATCH. WE NEED TO DISCUSS A FEW THINGS INSIDE, AND I DON'T WANT HER SNEAKING BACK AND LISTENING IN.
YES, POPPA.
HOW DID YOU GET INVOLVED WITH HER?
SHE'S NOT JUST ANY NEKO NINJA. SHE'S CHIZU, LEADER OF THAT CLAN.
I DO NOT TRUST HER KIND.
FORGIVE US FOR INTRUDING IN YOUR HOME.
WELCOME, PRIEST SANSHOBO. IT IS SO RARE TO MEET AN OLD ACQUAINTANCE OF MY HUSBAND.
SHE WAS AFTER THE SWORD OF THE GODS AS WELL.
OUR PATHS HAVE CROSSED IN THE PAST. SHE IS SOMEWHAT OF A FRIEND OF MINE.
2.

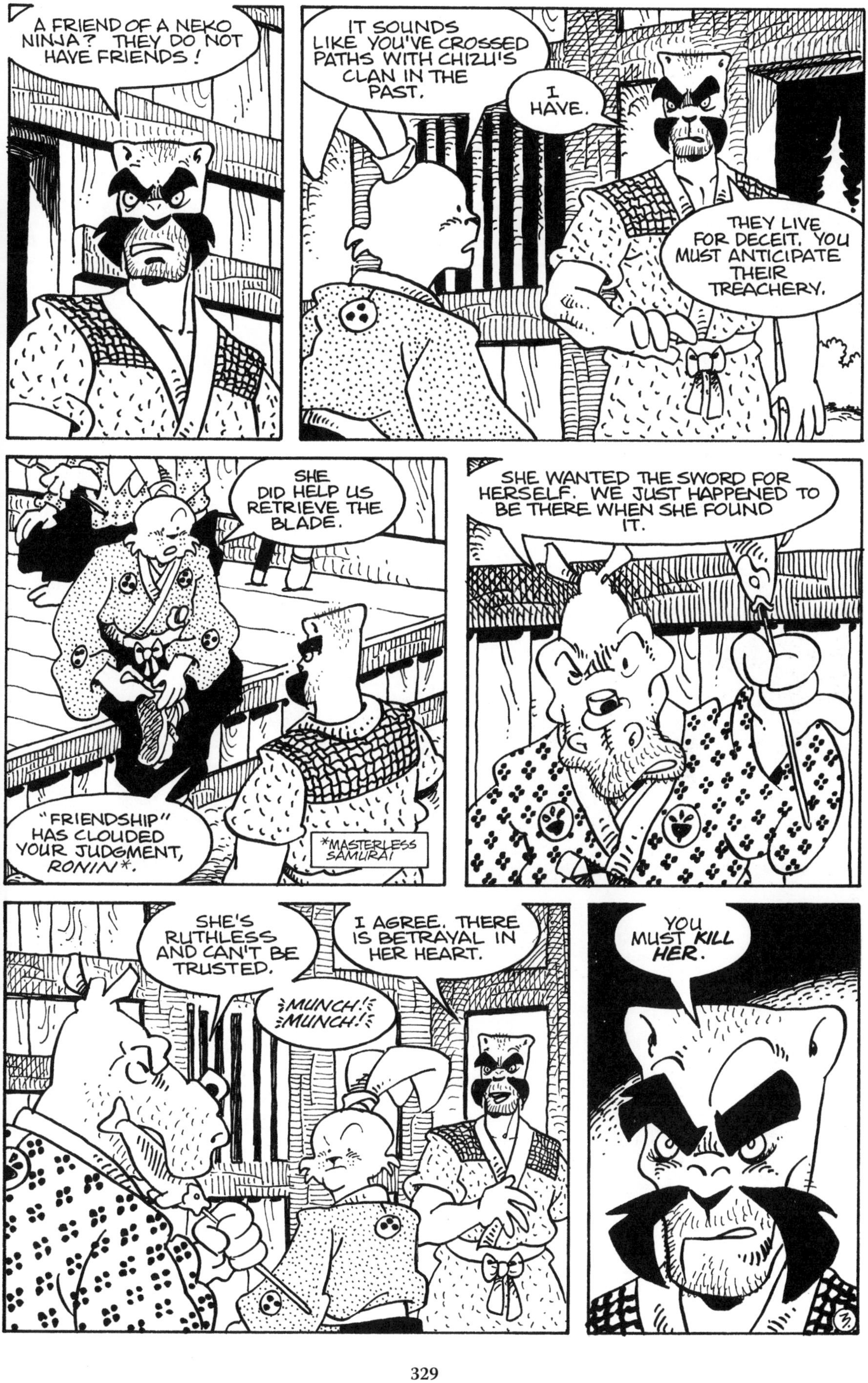
A FRIEND OF A NEKO NINJA? THEY DO NOT HAVE FRIENDS!
IT SOUNDS LIKE YOU'VE CROSSED PATHS WITH CHIZU'S CLAN IN THE PAST.
I HAVE.
THEY LIVE FOR DECEIT. YOU MUST ANTICIPATE THEIR TREACHERY.
SHE DID HELP US RETRIEVE THE BLADE.
"FRIENDSHIP" HAS CLOUDED YOUR JUDGMENT, RONIN*.
*MASTERLESS SAMURAI
SHE WANTED THE SWORD FOR HERSELF. WE JUST HAPPENED TO BE THERE WHEN SHE FOUND IT.
SHE'S RUTHLESS AND CAN'T BE TRUSTED.
MUNCH! MUNCH!
I AGREE. THERE IS BETRAYAL IN HER HEART.
YOU MUST KILL HER.
3

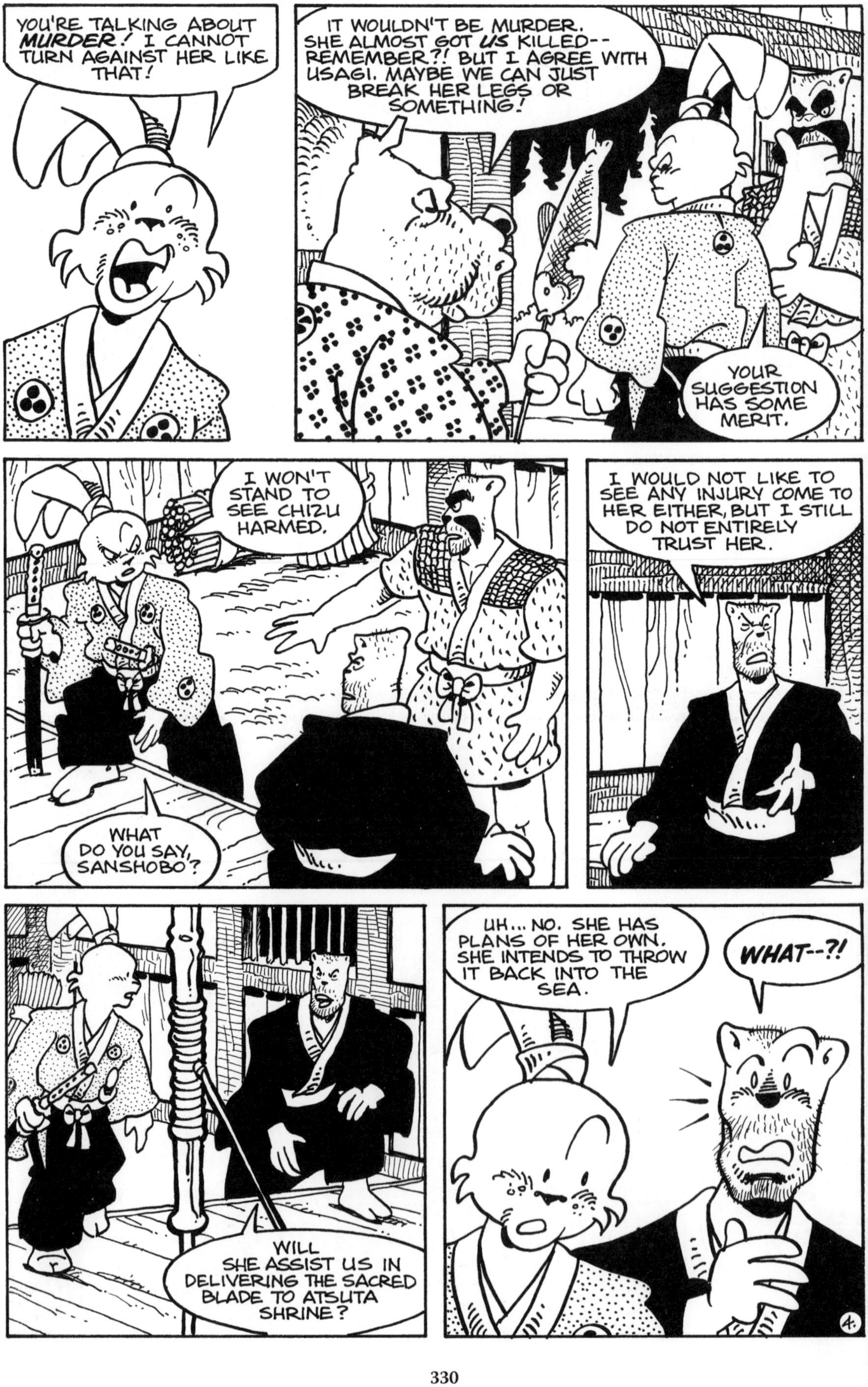
YOU'RE TALKING ABOUT MURDER! I CANNOT TURN AGAINST HER LIKE THAT!
IT WOULDN'T BE MURDER. SHE ALMOST GOT US KILLED-- REMEMBER?! BUT I AGREE WITH USAGI. MAYBE WE CAN JUST BREAK HER LEGS OR SOMETHING!
YOUR SUGGESTION HAS SOME MERIT.
I WON'T STAND TO SEE CHIZU HARMED.
WHAT DO YOU SAY, SANSHOBO?
I WOULD NOT LIKE TO SEE ANY INJURY COME TO HER EITHER, BUT I STILL DO NOT ENTIRELY TRUST HER.
WILL SHE ASSIST US IN DELIVERING THE SACRED BLADE TO ATSUTA SHRINE?
UH... NO. SHE HAS PLANS OF HER OWN. SHE INTENDS TO THROW IT BACK INTO THE SEA.
WHAT--?!
4.

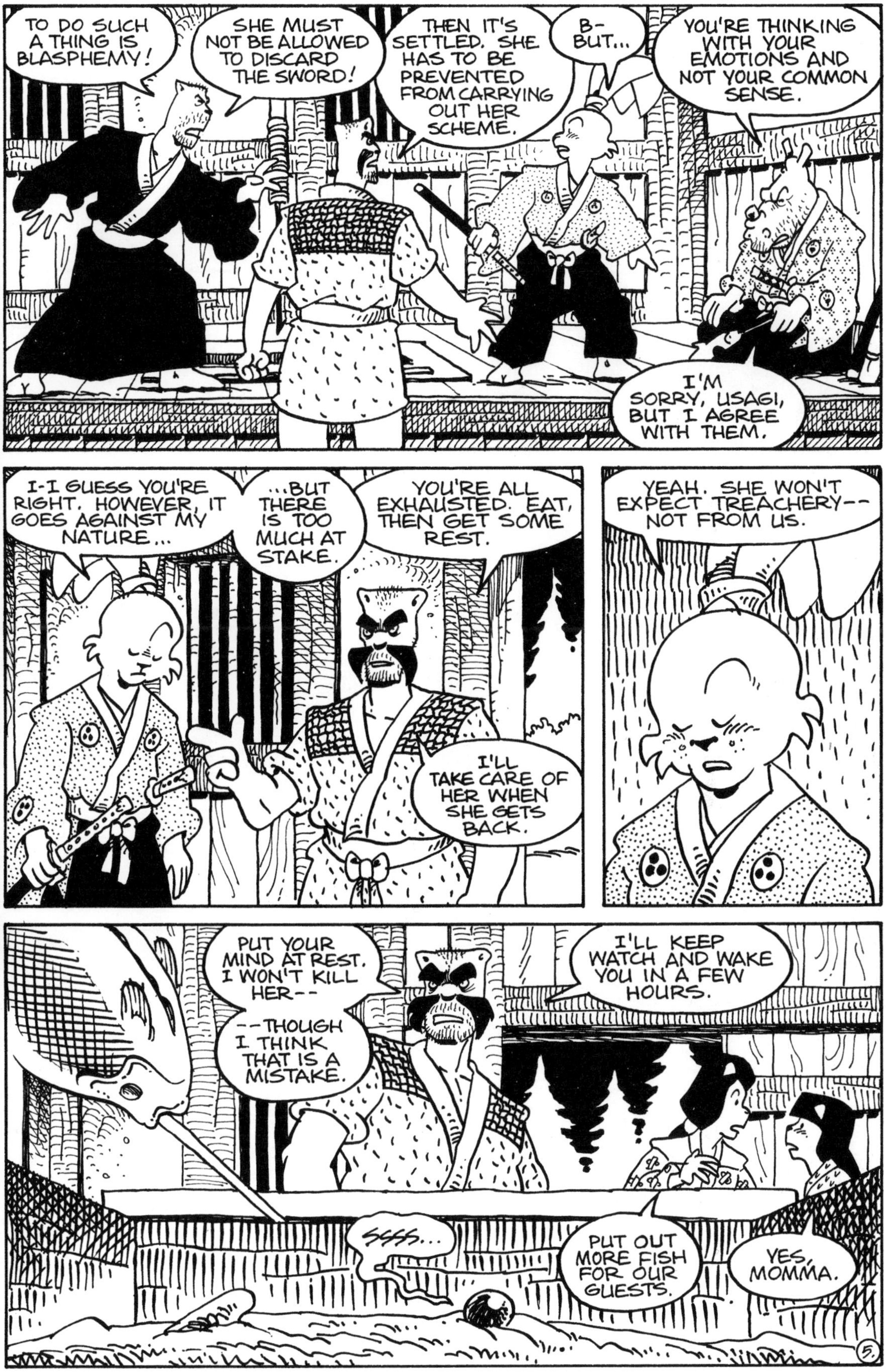
TO DO SUCH A THING IS BLASPHEMY!
SHE MUST NOT BE ALLOWED TO DISCARD THE SWORD!
THEN IT'S SETTLED. SHE HAS TO BE PREVENTED FROM CARRYING OUT HER SCHEME.
B- BUT...
YOU'RE THINKING WITH YOUR EMOTIONS AND NOT YOUR COMMON SENSE.
I'M SORRY, USAGI, BUT I AGREE WITH THEM.
I-I GUESS YOU'RE RIGHT. HOWEVER, IT GOES AGAINST MY NATURE...
...BUT THERE IS TOO MUCH AT STAKE.
YOU'RE ALL EXHAUSTED. EAT, THEN GET SOME REST.
I'LL TAKE CARE OF HER WHEN SHE GETS BACK.
YEAH. SHE WON'T EXPECT TREACHERY-- NOT FROM US.
PUT YOUR MIND AT REST. I WON'T KILL HER--
--THOUGH I THINK THAT IS A MISTAKE.
I'LL KEEP WATCH AND WAKE YOU IN A FEW HOURS.
SSSS...
PUT OUT MORE FISH FOR OUR GUESTS.
YES, MOMMA.
5

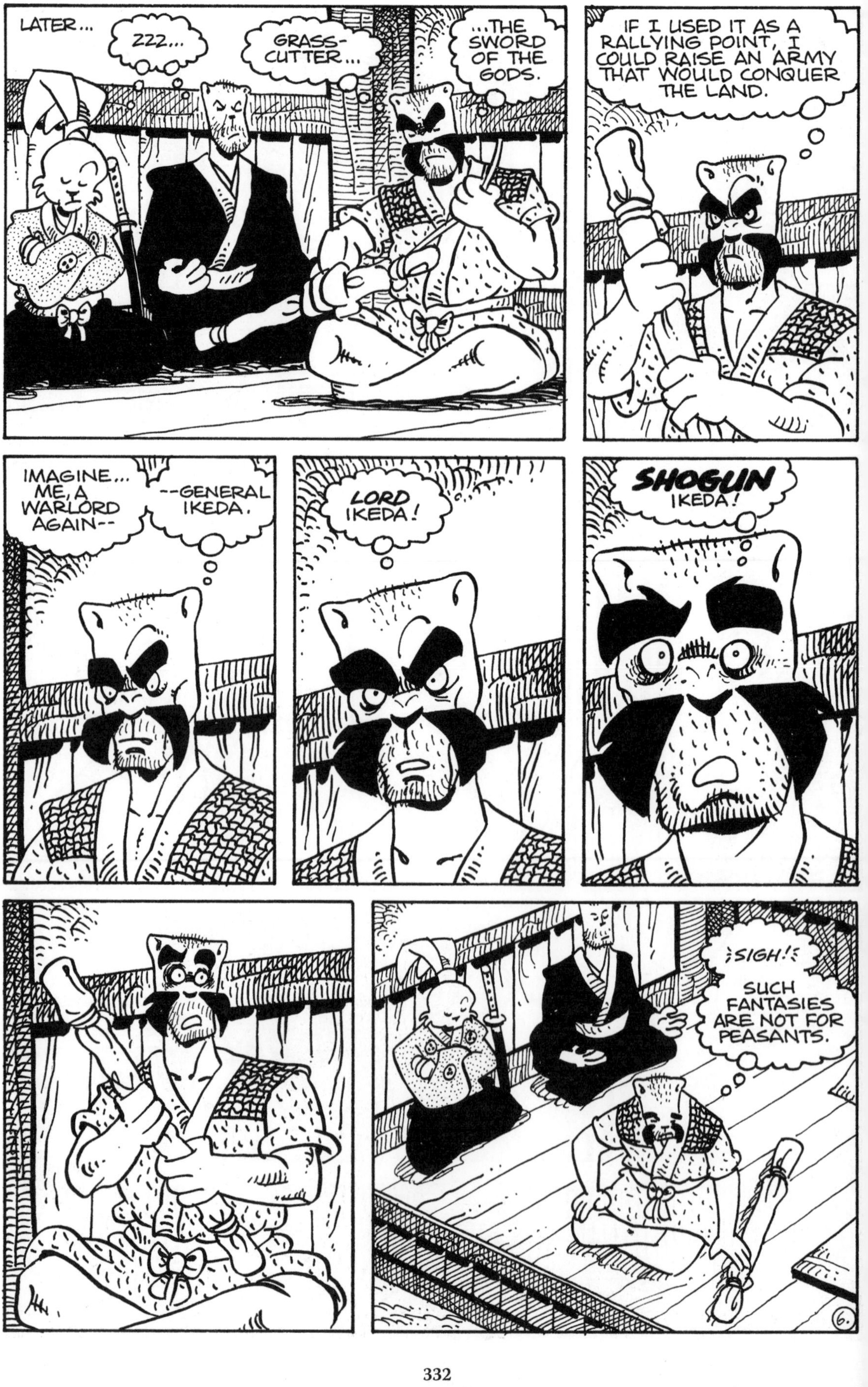
LATER...
ZZZ...
GRASS-CUTTER...
...THE SWORD OF THE GODS.
IF I USED IT AS A RALLYING POINT, I COULD RAISE AN ARMY THAT WOULD CONQUER THE LAND.
IMAGINE... ME, A WARLORD AGAIN--
--GENERAL IKEDA.
LORD IKEDA!
SHOGUN IKEDA!
SIGH!
SUCH FANTASIES ARE NOT FOR PEASANTS.
6.

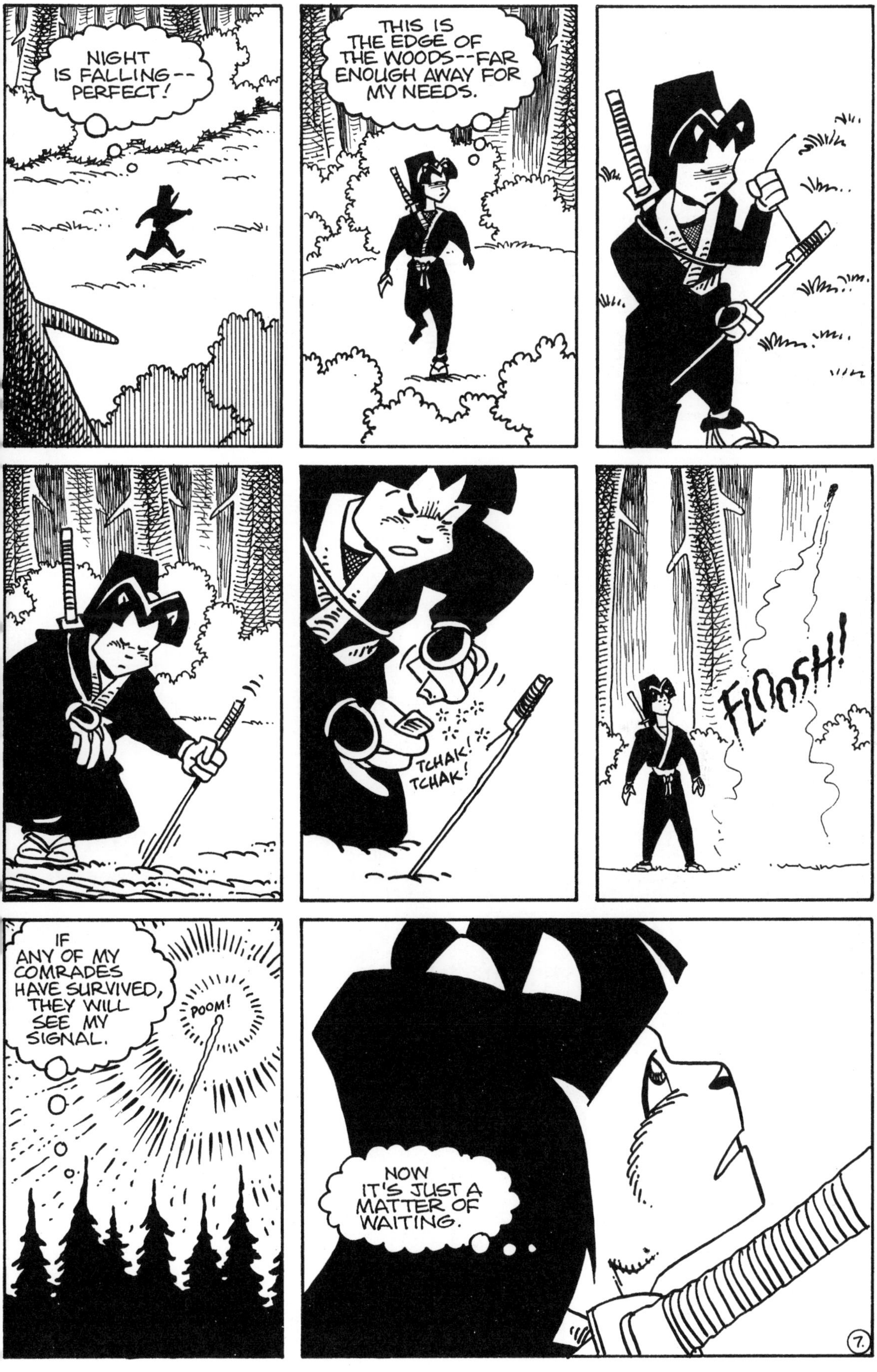
NIGHT IS FALLING-- PERFECT!
THIS IS THE EDGE OF THE WOODS--FAR ENOUGH AWAY FOR MY NEEDS.
TCHAK! TCHAK!
FLOOSH!
IF ANY OF MY COMRADES HAVE SURVIVED, THEY WILL SEE MY SIGNAL.
POOM!
NOW IT'S JUST A MATTER OF WAITING.
7.

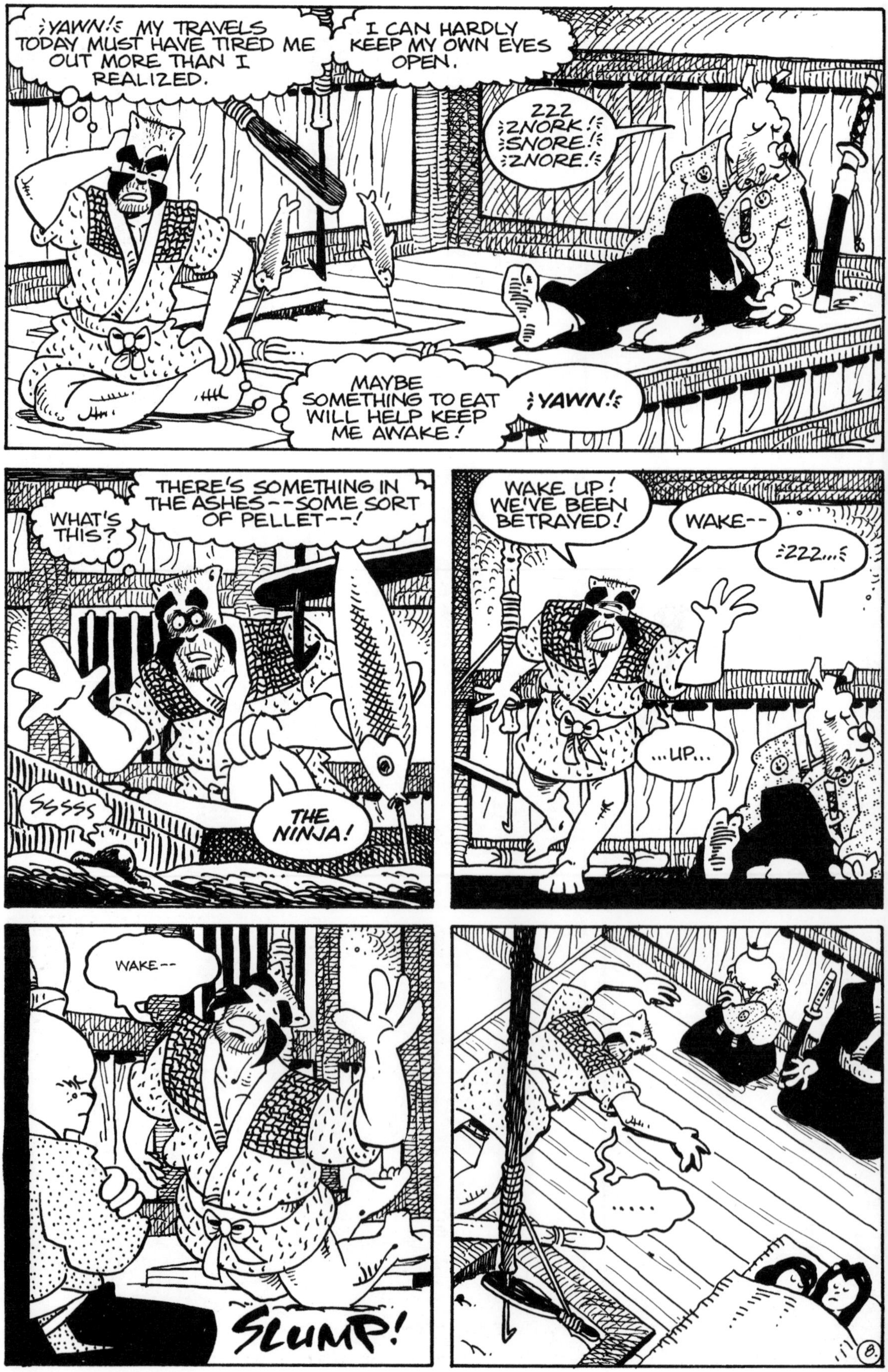
¡YAWN!¡ MY TRAVELS TODAY MUST HAVE TIRED ME OUT MORE THAN I REALIZED.
I CAN HARDLY KEEP MY OWN EYES OPEN.
ZZZ ¡ZNORK!¡ ¡SNORE!¡ ¡ZNORE!¡
MAYBE SOMETHING TO EAT WILL HELP KEEP ME AWAKE!
¡YAWN!¡
WHAT'S THIS?
THERE'S SOMETHING IN THE ASHES--SOME SORT OF PELLET--!
SSSSS
THE NINJA!
WAKE UP! WE'VE BEEN BETRAYED!
WAKE--
¡ZZZ...¡
...UP...
WAKE--
SLUMP!
.....
8.

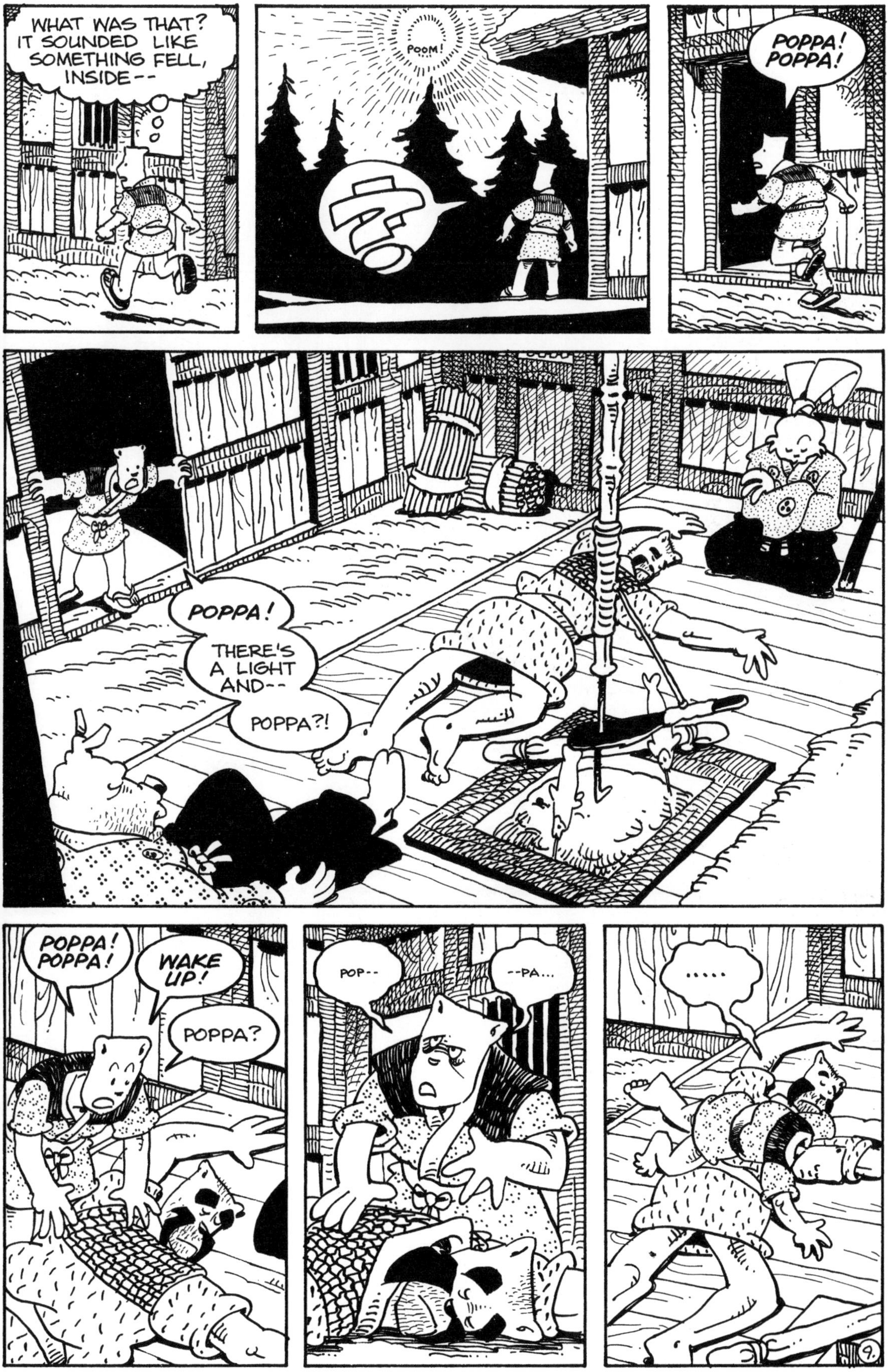
WHAT WAS THAT? IT SOUNDED LIKE SOMETHING FELL, INSIDE--
POOM!
POPPA! POPPA!
POPPA!
THERE'S A LIGHT AND--
POPPA?!
POPPA! POPPA!
WAKE UP!
POPPA?
POP--
--PA...
.....
9.

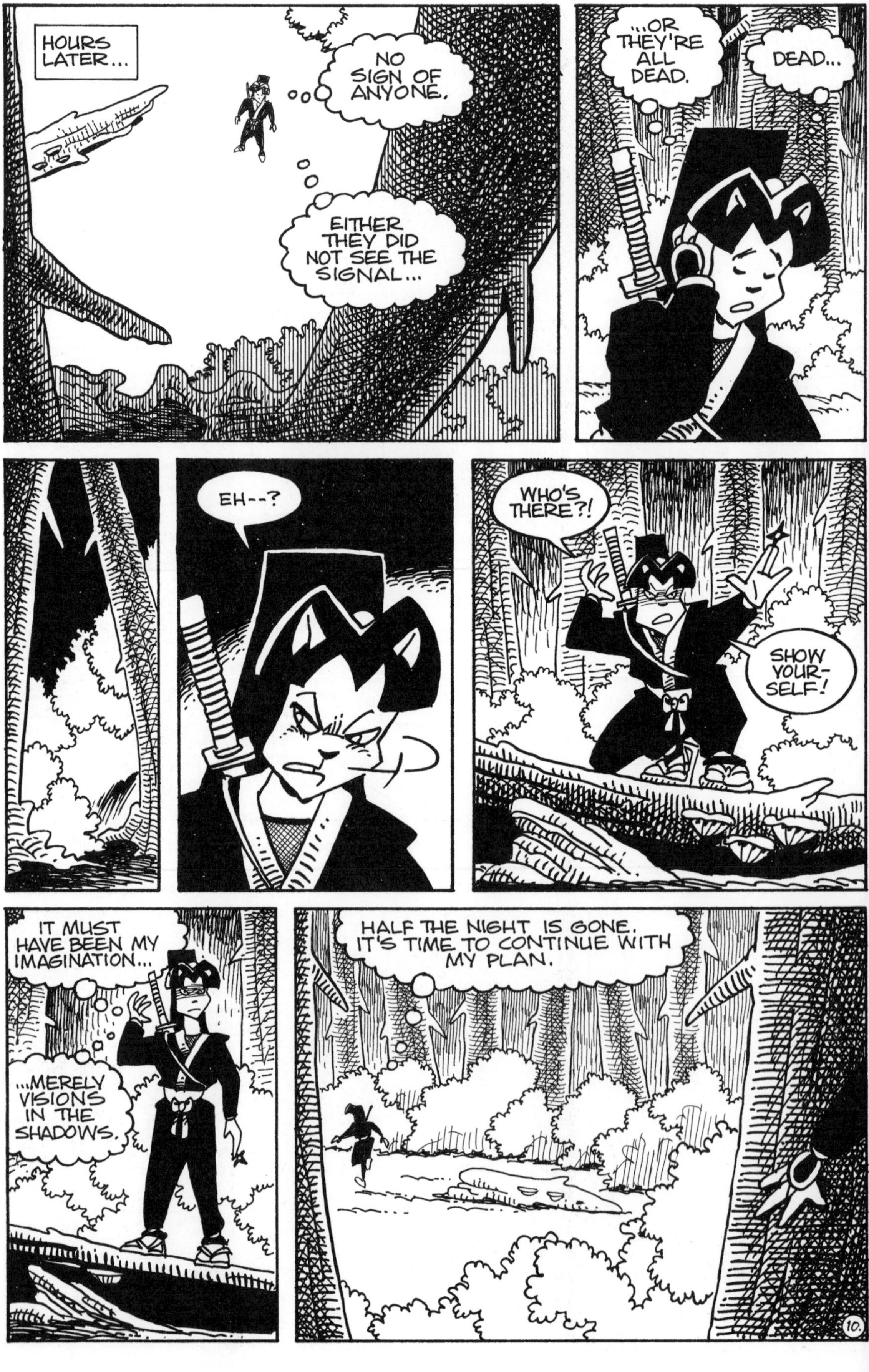
HOURS LATER...
NO SIGN OF ANYONE.
EITHER THEY DID NOT SEE THE SIGNAL...
...OR THEY'RE ALL DEAD.
DEAD...
EH--?
WHO'S THERE?!
SHOW YOUR-SELF!
IT MUST HAVE BEEN MY IMAGINATION...
...MERELY VISIONS IN THE SHADOWS.
HALF THE NIGHT IS GONE. IT'S TIME TO CONTINUE WITH MY PLAN.
10.

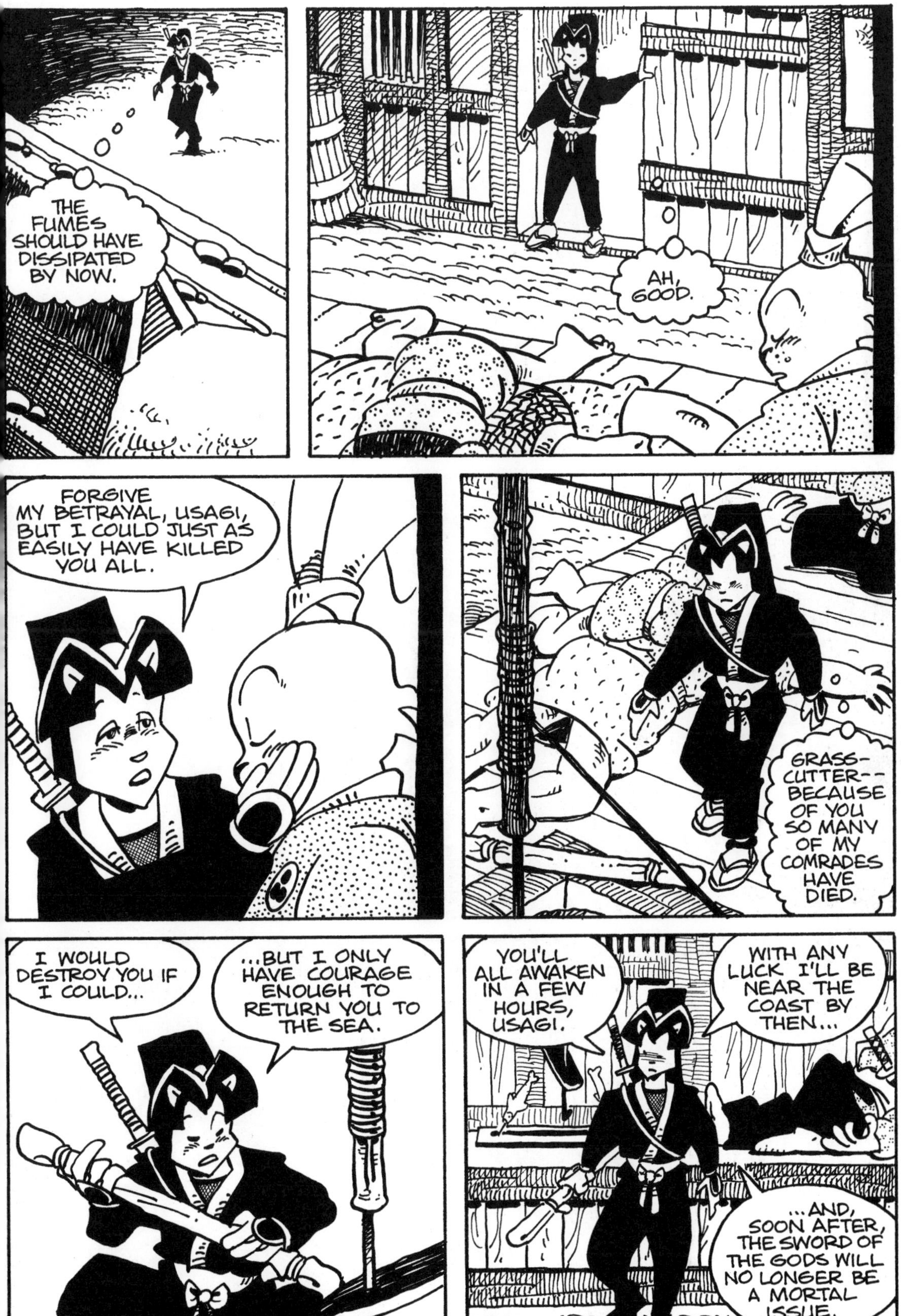
THE FUMES SHOULD HAVE DISSIPATED BY NOW.
AH, GOOD.
FORGIVE MY BETRAYAL, USAGI, BUT I COULD JUST AS EASILY HAVE KILLED YOU ALL.
GRASS-CUTTER-- BECAUSE OF YOU SO MANY OF MY COMRADES HAVE DIED.
I WOULD DESTROY YOU IF I COULD...
...BUT I ONLY HAVE COURAGE ENOUGH TO RETURN YOU TO THE SEA.
YOU'LL ALL AWAKEN IN A FEW HOURS, USAGI.
WITH ANY LUCK I'LL BE NEAR THE COAST BY THEN...
...AND, SOON AFTER, THE SWORD OF THE GODS WILL NO LONGER BE A MORTAL ISSUE.
11.

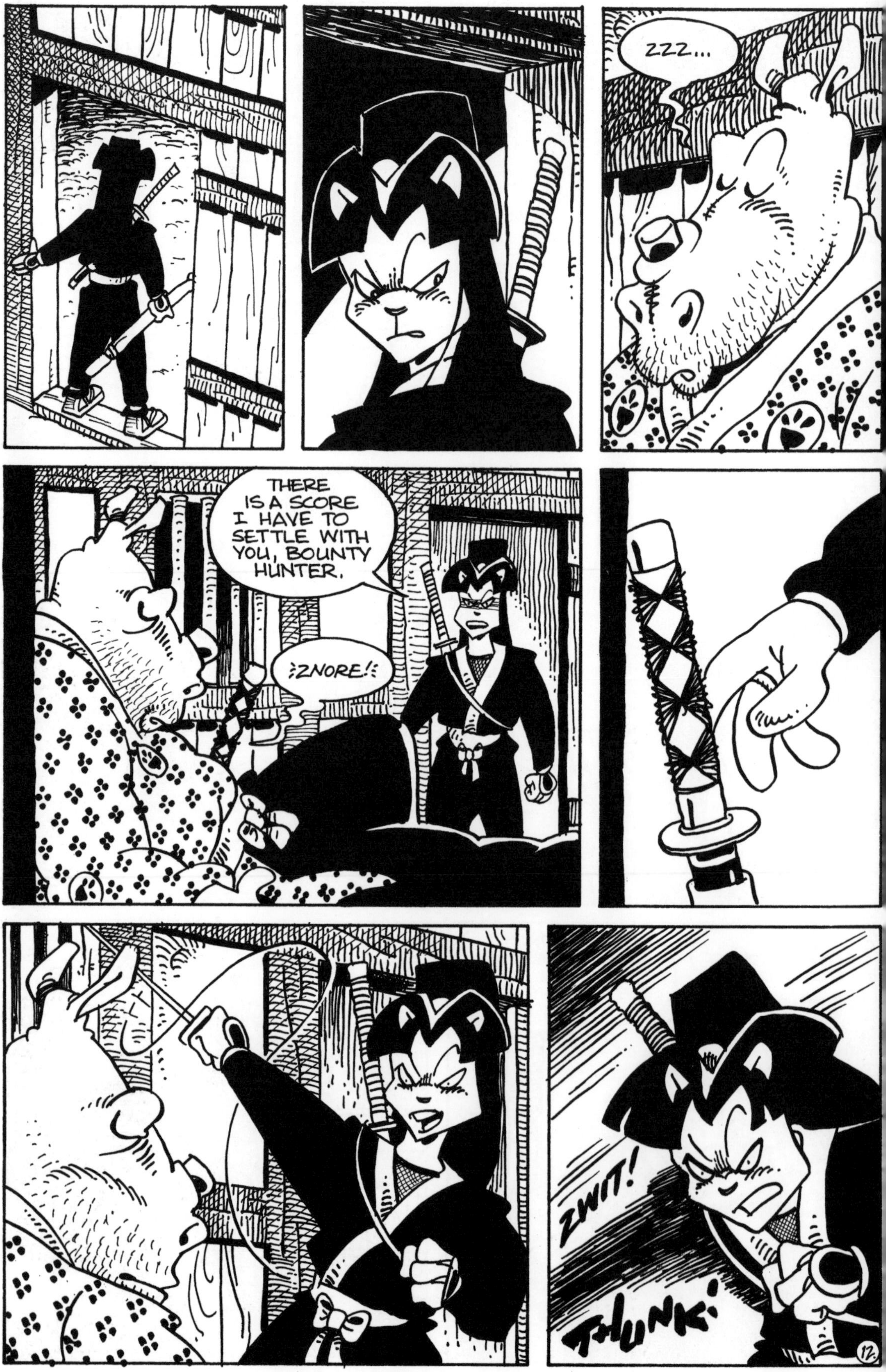
ZZZ...
THERE IS A SCORE I HAVE TO SETTLE WITH YOU, BOUNTY HUNTER.
ZNORE!
ZWIT!
THUNK!
12.

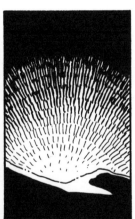

.....

UH...

SANSHOBO--! SANSHOBO, WAKE UP!

UH... WHAT...?

IT'S MORNING!

339

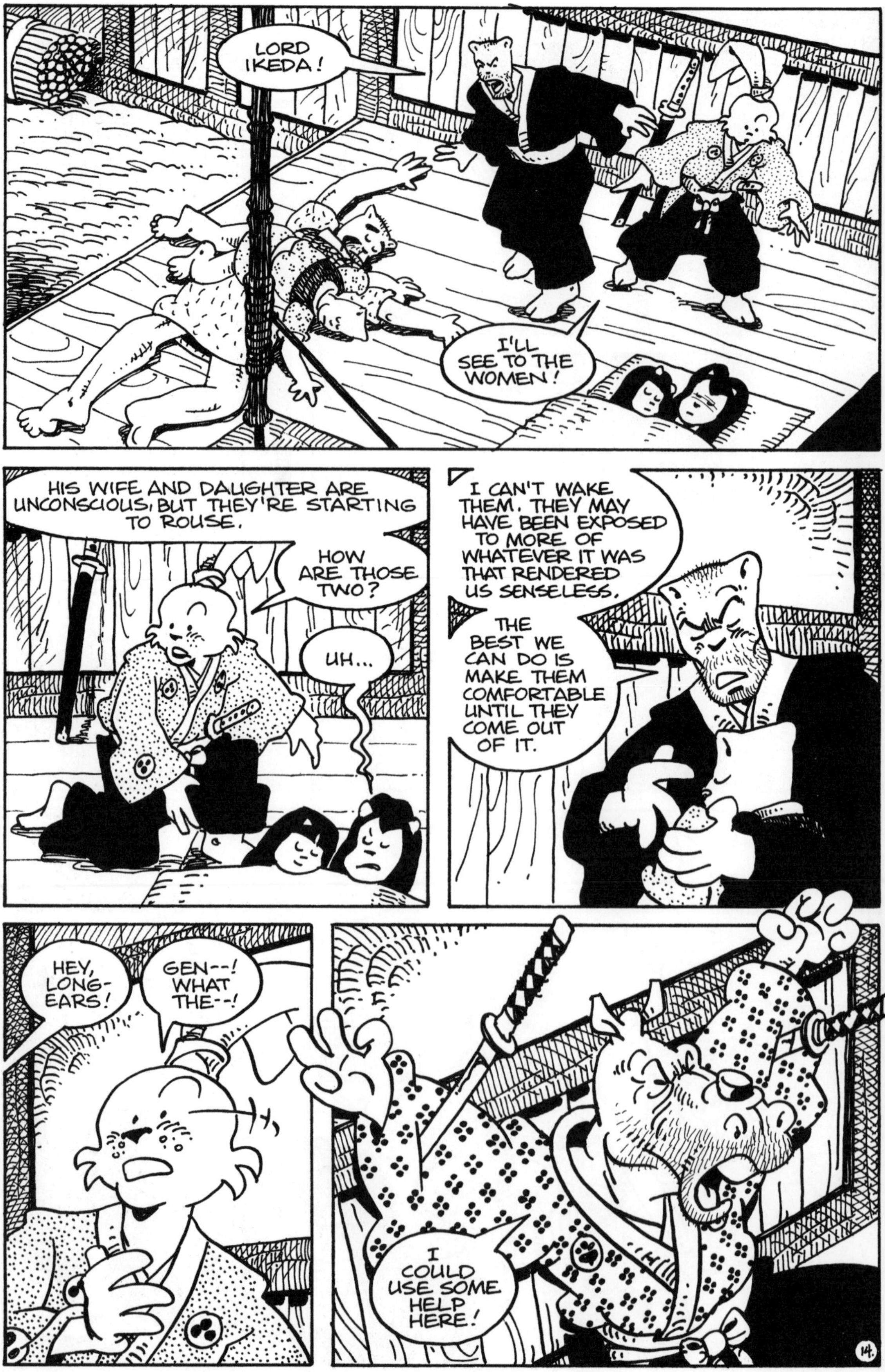
LORD IKEDA!
I'LL SEE TO THE WOMEN!
HIS WIFE AND DAUGHTER ARE UNCONSCIOUS, BUT THEY'RE STARTING TO ROUSE.
HOW ARE THOSE TWO?
UH...
I CAN'T WAKE THEM. THEY MAY HAVE BEEN EXPOSED TO MORE OF WHATEVER IT WAS THAT RENDERED US SENSELESS.
THE BEST WE CAN DO IS MAKE THEM COMFORTABLE UNTIL THEY COME OUT OF IT.
HEY, LONG-EARS!
GEN--! WHAT THE--!
I COULD USE SOME HELP HERE!
14.

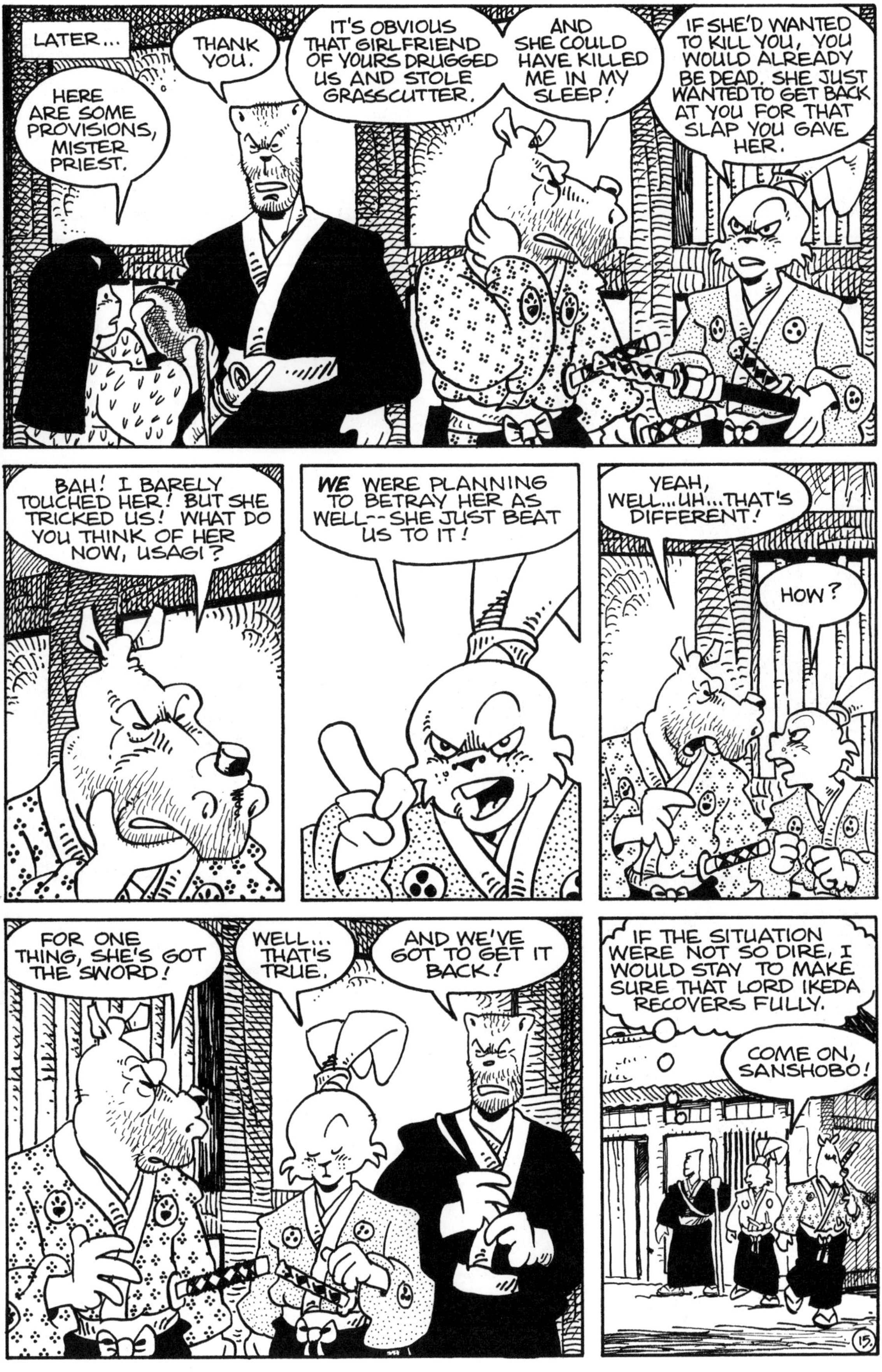
LATER...
HERE ARE SOME PROVISIONS, MISTER PRIEST.
THANK YOU.
IT'S OBVIOUS THAT GIRLFRIEND OF YOURS DRUGGED US AND STOLE GRASSCUTTER.
AND SHE COULD HAVE KILLED ME IN MY SLEEP!
IF SHE'D WANTED TO KILL YOU, YOU WOULD ALREADY BE DEAD. SHE JUST WANTED TO GET BACK AT YOU FOR THAT SLAP YOU GAVE HER.
BAH! I BARELY TOUCHED HER! BUT SHE TRICKED US! WHAT DO YOU THINK OF HER NOW, USAGI?
WE WERE PLANNING TO BETRAY HER AS WELL--SHE JUST BEAT US TO IT!
YEAH, WELL...UH...THAT'S DIFFERENT!
HOW?
FOR ONE THING, SHE'S GOT THE SWORD!
WELL... THAT'S TRUE.
AND WE'VE GOT TO GET IT BACK!
IF THE SITUATION WERE NOT SO DIRE, I WOULD STAY TO MAKE SURE THAT LORD IKEDA RECOVERS FULLY.
COME ON, SANSHOBO!
15

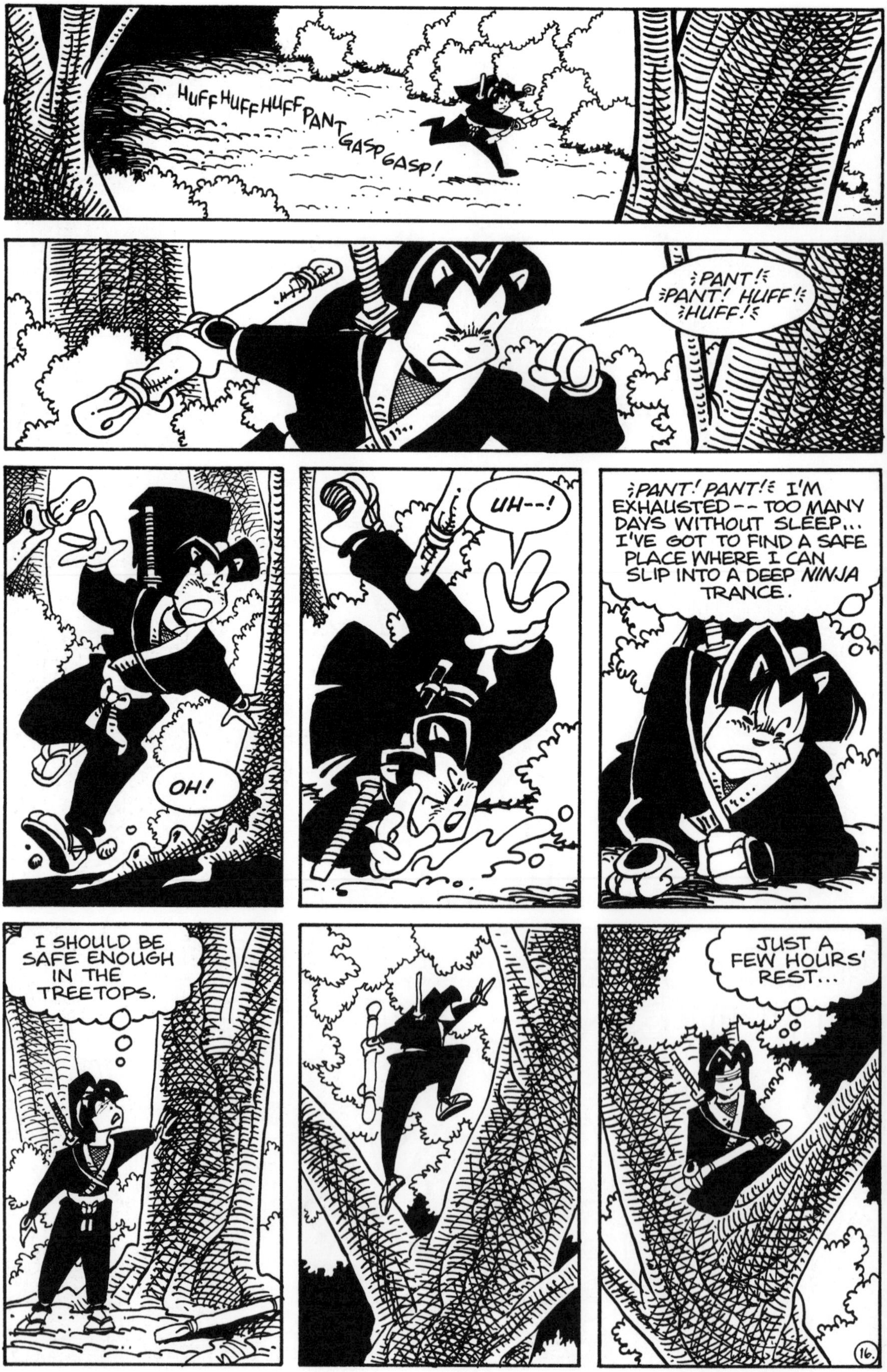
HUFF HUFF HUFF PANT GASP GASP!
PANT! PANT! HUFF! HUFF!
OH!
UH--!
PANT! PANT! I'M EXHAUSTED -- TOO MANY DAYS WITHOUT SLEEP... I'VE GOT TO FIND A SAFE PLACE WHERE I CAN SLIP INTO A DEEP *NINJA* TRANCE.
I SHOULD BE SAFE ENOUGH IN THE TREETOPS.
JUST A FEW HOURS' REST...
16.

FWITT!

FWITT!

FWITT!

TOK!

TOK!

TOK!

THE MYSTERIOUS *NINJA* ASSASSIN IS BACK.

I *MUST* BE WEARY. HE ALMOST CAUGHT ME UNAWARES.

WHERE IS HE?

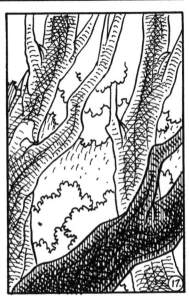

17.

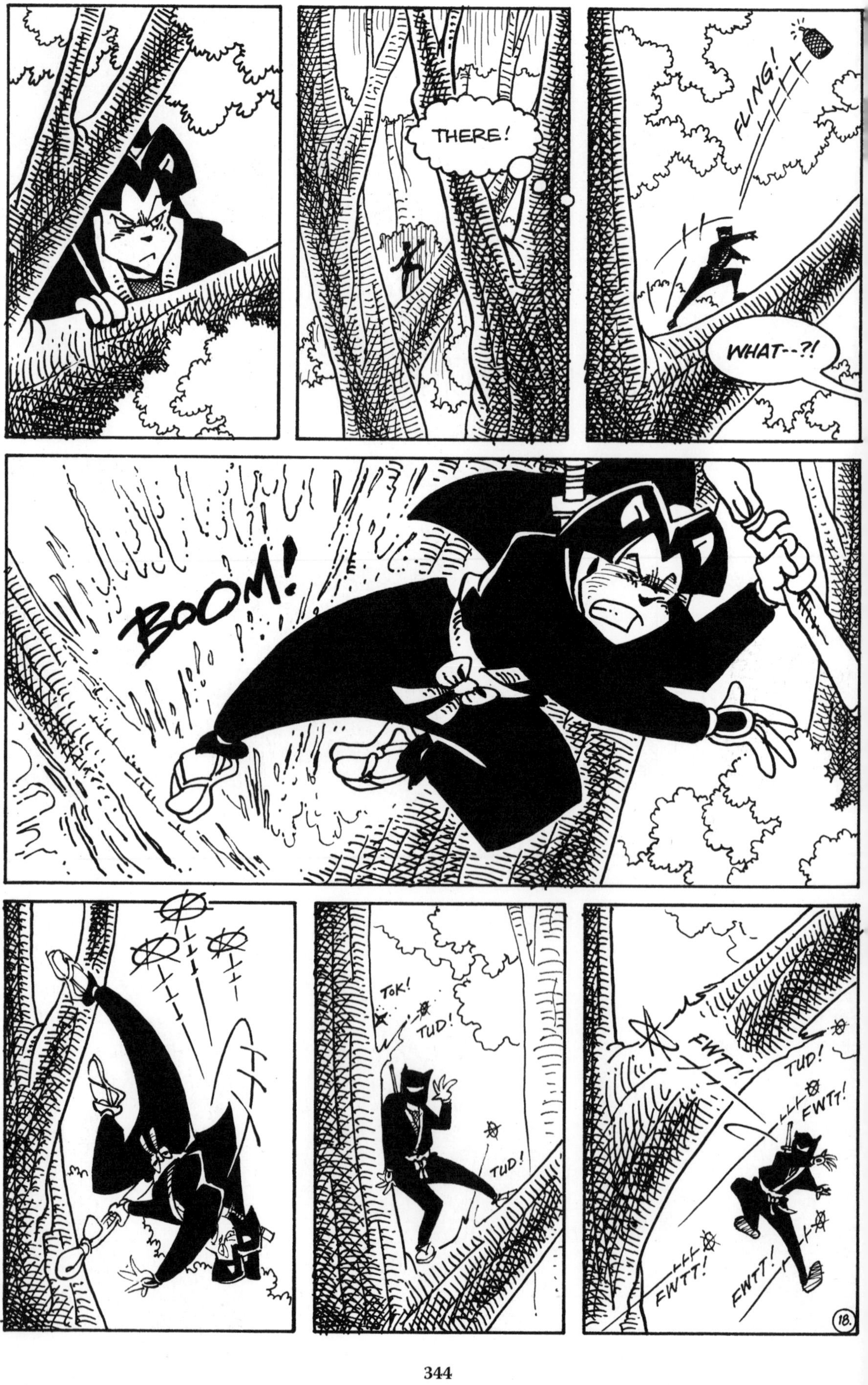

THERE!
FLING!
WHAT--?!
BOOM!
TOK!
TUD!
TUD!
FWTT!
TUD!
FWTT!
FWTT!
FWTT!
18.

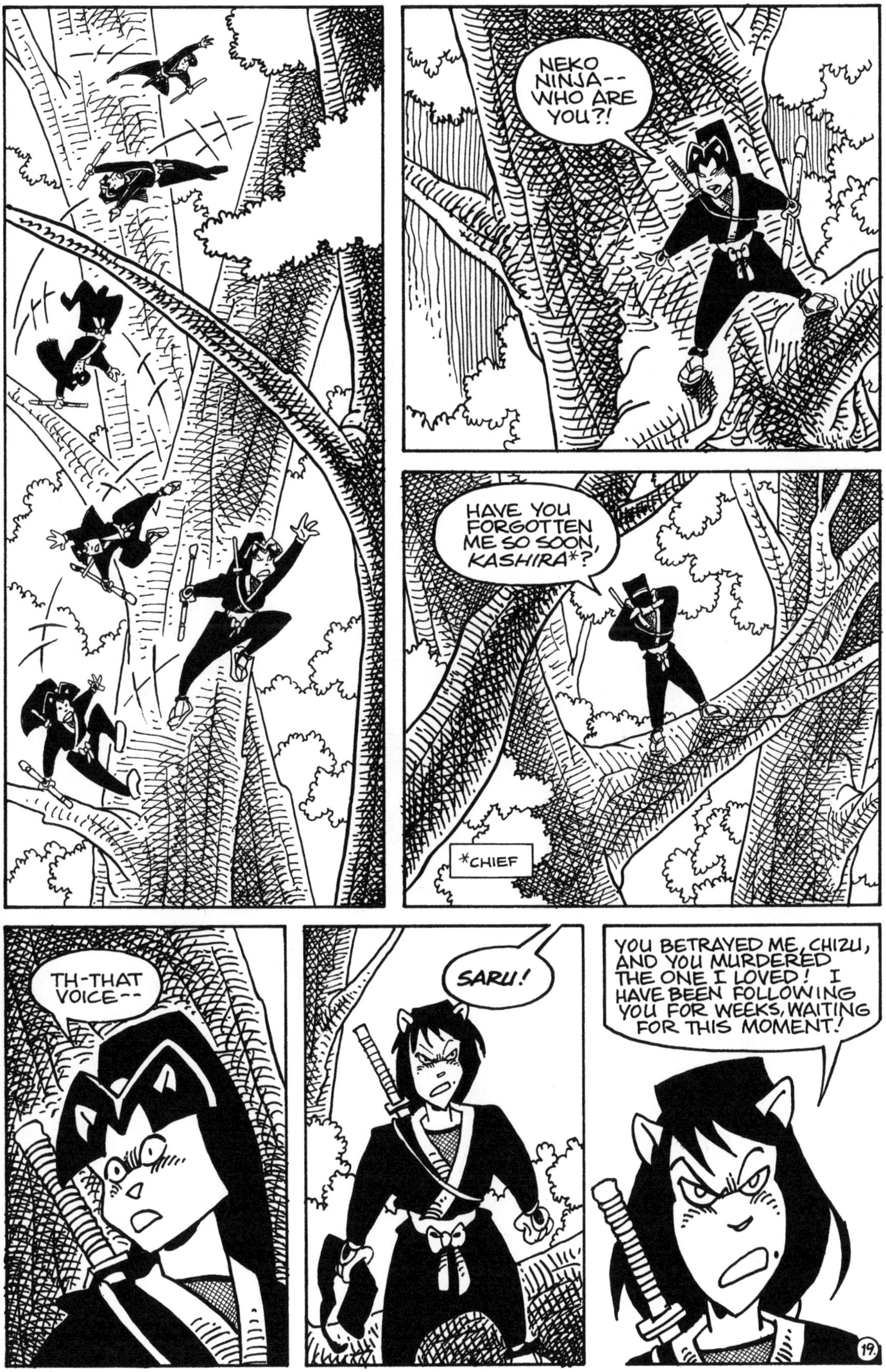
NEKO NINJA-- WHO ARE YOU?!
HAVE YOU FORGOTTEN ME SO SOON, *KASHIRA**?
*CHIEF
TH-THAT VOICE--
SARU!
YOU BETRAYED ME, CHIZU, AND YOU MURDERED THE ONE I LOVED! I HAVE BEEN FOLLOWING YOU FOR WEEKS, WAITING FOR THIS MOMENT!
19.

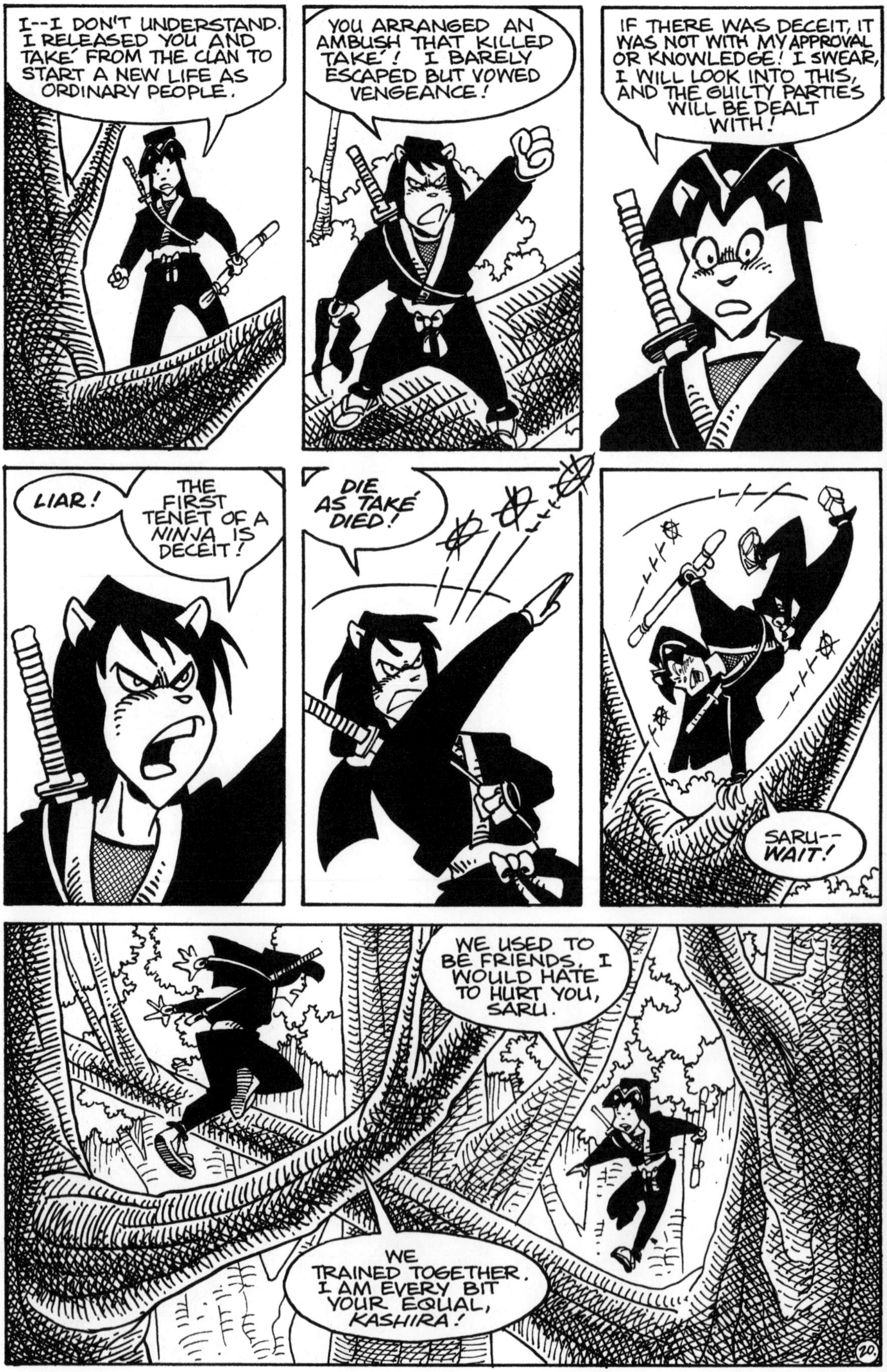
I--I DON'T UNDERSTAND. I RELEASED YOU AND TAKÉ FROM THE CLAN TO START A NEW LIFE AS ORDINARY PEOPLE.
YOU ARRANGED AN AMBUSH THAT KILLED TAKÉ! I BARELY ESCAPED BUT VOWED VENGEANCE!
IF THERE WAS DECEIT, IT WAS NOT WITH MY APPROVAL OR KNOWLEDGE! I SWEAR, I WILL LOOK INTO THIS, AND THE GUILTY PARTIES WILL BE DEALT WITH!
LIAR!
THE FIRST TENET OF A *NINJA* IS DECEIT!
DIE AS TAKÉ DIED!
SARU-- WAIT!
WE USED TO BE FRIENDS. I WOULD HATE TO HURT YOU, SARU.
WE TRAINED TOGETHER. I AM EVERY BIT YOUR EQUAL, *KASHIRA*!
20.

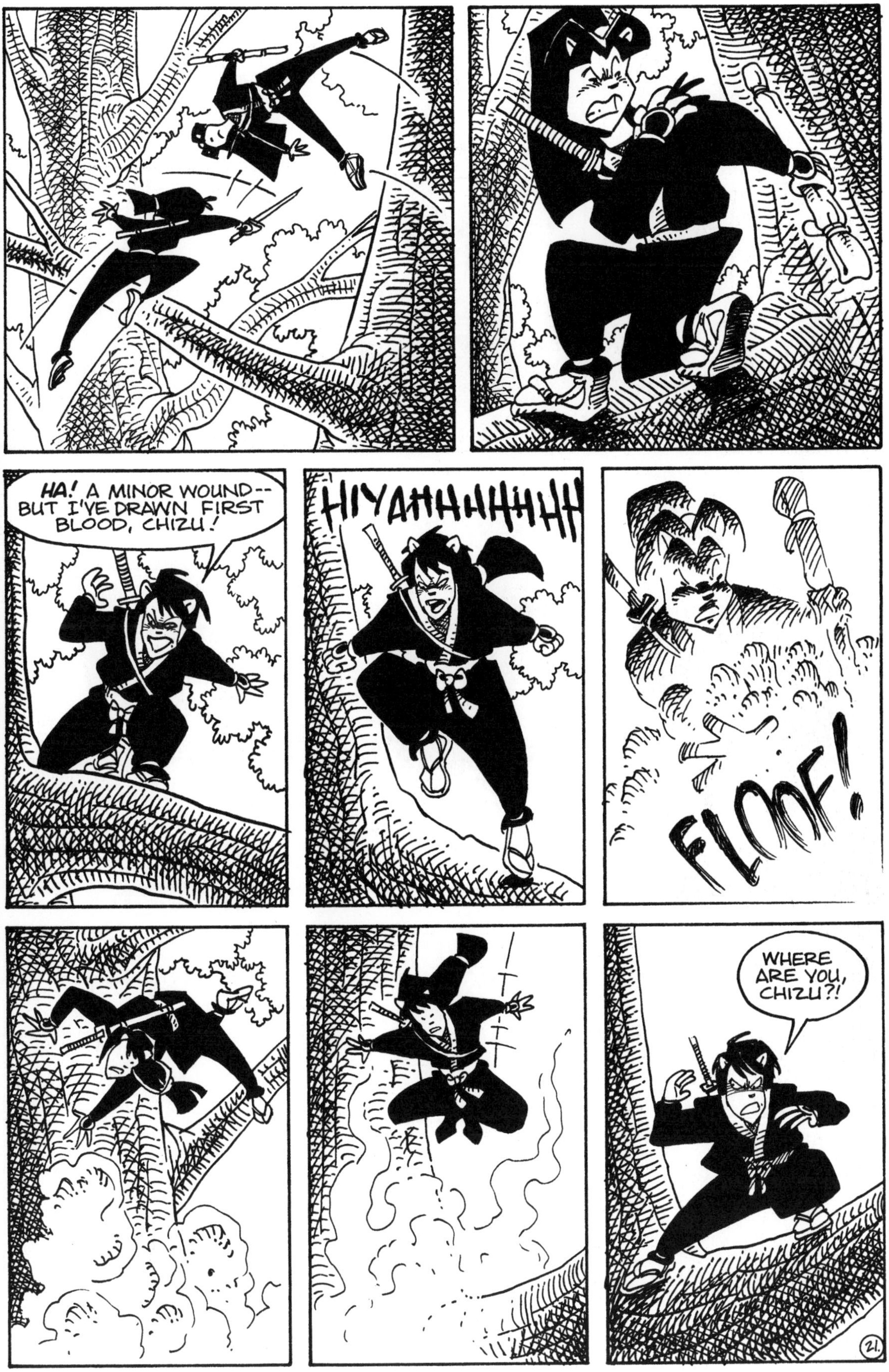
HA! A MINOR WOUND-- BUT I'VE DRAWN FIRST BLOOD, CHIZU!
HIYAHHHHHHH
FLOOF!
WHERE ARE YOU, CHIZU?!
21.

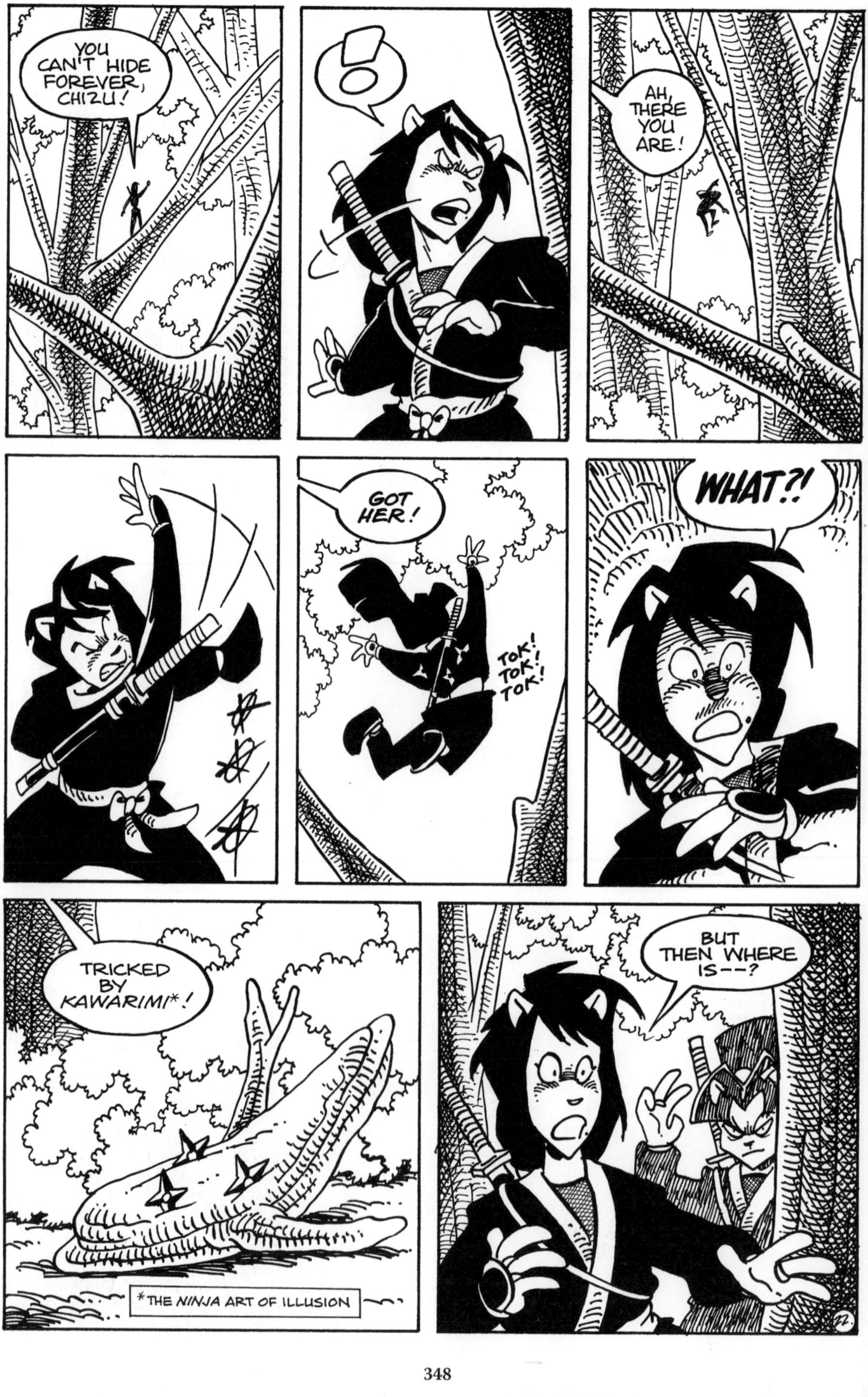
YOU CAN'T HIDE FOREVER, CHIZU!
!
AH, THERE YOU ARE!
GOT HER!
TOK! TOK! TOK!
WHAT?!
TRICKED BY *KAWARIMI**!
BUT THEN WHERE IS--?
*THE *NINJA* ART OF ILLUSION
22.

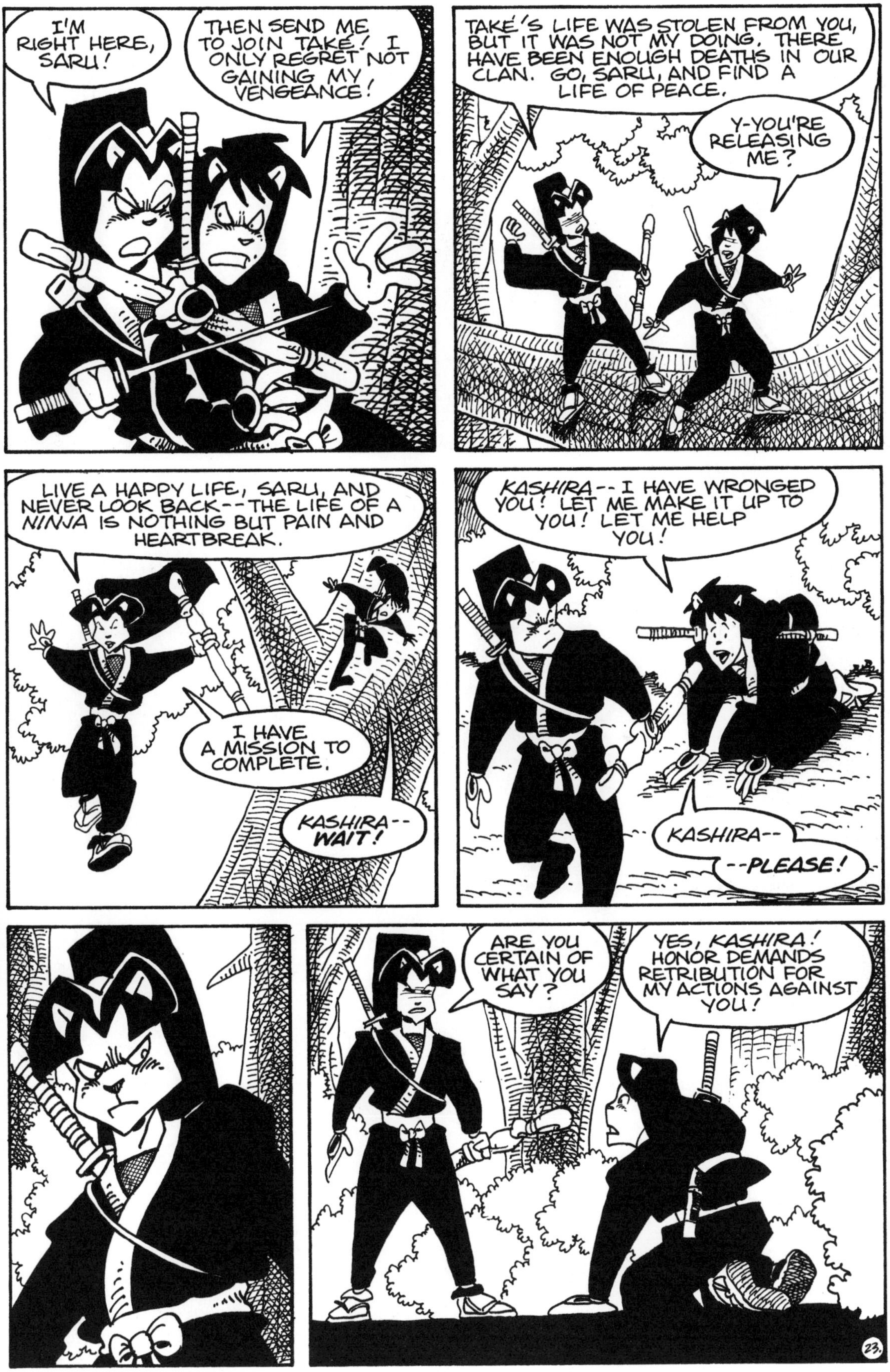
I'M RIGHT HERE, SARU!
THEN SEND ME TO JOIN TAKÉ! I ONLY REGRET NOT GAINING MY VENGEANCE!
TAKÉ'S LIFE WAS STOLEN FROM YOU, BUT IT WAS NOT MY DOING. THERE HAVE BEEN ENOUGH DEATHS IN OUR CLAN. GO, SARU, AND FIND A LIFE OF PEACE.
Y-YOU'RE RELEASING ME?
LIVE A HAPPY LIFE, SARU, AND NEVER LOOK BACK--THE LIFE OF A *NINJA* IS NOTHING BUT PAIN AND HEARTBREAK.
I HAVE A MISSION TO COMPLETE.
KASHIRA--**WAIT!**
KASHIRA--I HAVE WRONGED YOU! LET ME MAKE IT UP TO YOU! LET ME HELP YOU!
KASHIRA--
--**PLEASE!**
ARE YOU CERTAIN OF WHAT YOU SAY?
YES, *KASHIRA*! HONOR DEMANDS RETRIBUTION FOR MY ACTIONS AGAINST YOU!
23.

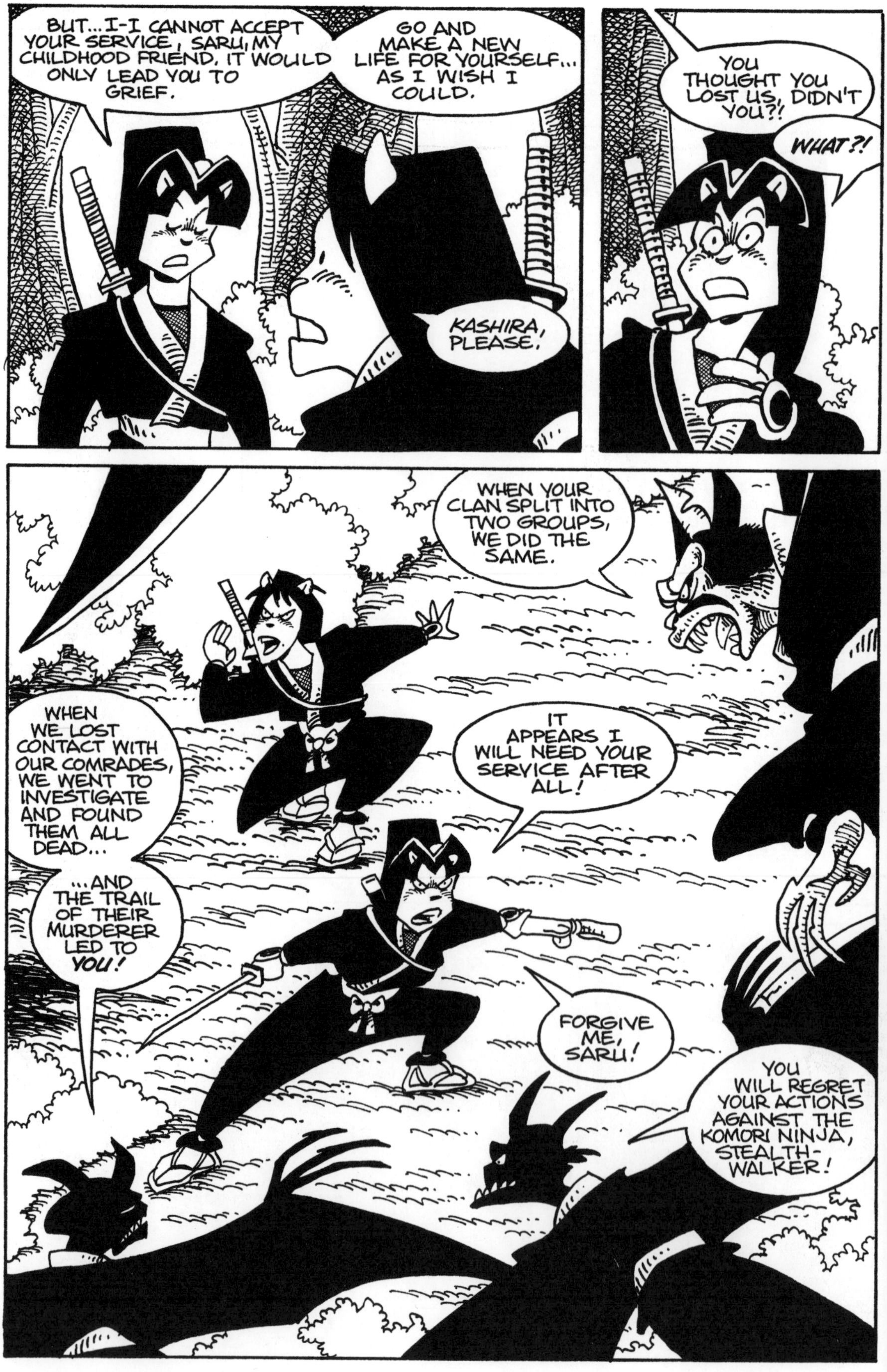
BUT...I-I CANNOT ACCEPT YOUR SERVICE, SARU, MY CHILDHOOD FRIEND. IT WOULD ONLY LEAD YOU TO GRIEF.
GO AND MAKE A NEW LIFE FOR YOURSELF... AS I WISH I COULD.
KASHIRA, PLEASE!
YOU THOUGHT YOU LOST US, DIDN'T YOU?!
WHAT?!
WHEN YOUR CLAN SPLIT INTO TWO GROUPS, WE DID THE SAME.
WHEN WE LOST CONTACT WITH OUR COMRADES, WE WENT TO INVESTIGATE AND FOUND THEM ALL DEAD...
...AND THE TRAIL OF THEIR MURDERER LED TO YOU!
IT APPEARS I WILL NEED YOUR SERVICE AFTER ALL!
FORGIVE ME, SARU!
YOU WILL REGRET YOUR ACTIONS AGAINST THE KOMORI NINJA, STEALTH-WALKER!

CHAPTER 5
THE FEEL OF SALT

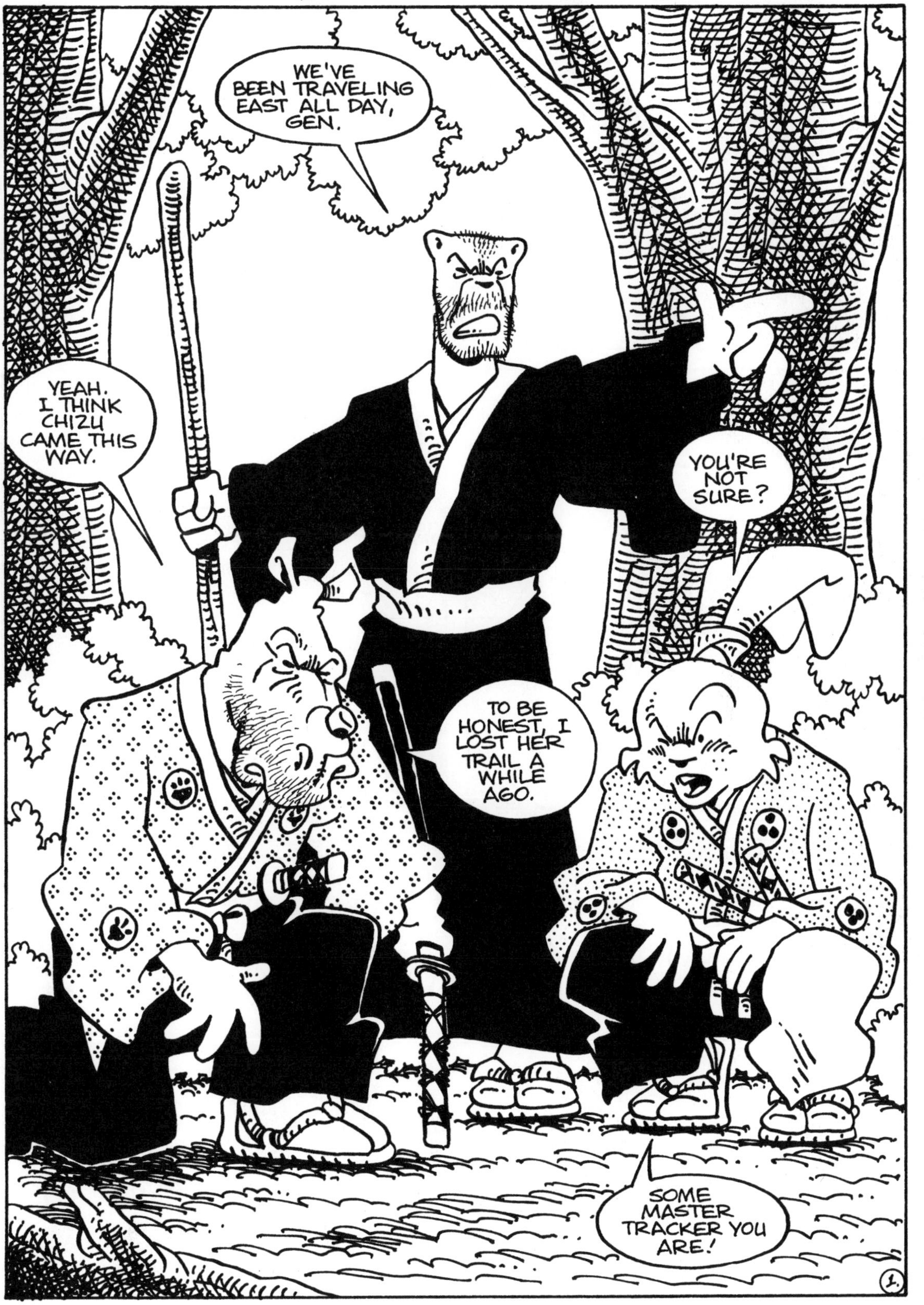
WE'VE BEEN TRAVELING EAST ALL DAY, GEN.
YEAH. I THINK CHIZU CAME THIS WAY.
YOU'RE NOT SURE?
TO BE HONEST, I LOST HER TRAIL A WHILE AGO.
SOME MASTER TRACKER YOU ARE!
1.

SHE'S A *NINJA*. THEY CAN RUN THROUGH A BED OF DRIED LEAVES WITHOUT DISTURBING A ONE.

ARE YOU SURE SHE WAS GOING THIS WAY?

HER PLAN WAS TO THROW THE SACRED SWORD INTO THE SEA-- TO THE EAST.

SHE WAS PROBABLY LYING. REMEMBER WHAT IKEDA SAID--THOSE *NINJA* LIVE FOR TREACHERY.

BUT HE DOESN'T KNOW HER LIKE I DO.

YEAH, SOME FRIEND. SHE DRUGGED US AND STOLE GRASSCUTTER. SHE PROBABLY ESCAPED IN A DIFFERENT DIRECTION ENTIRELY AND WE'RE ON A FOOL'S ERRAND.

WE MAY AS WELL CONTINUE ON OUR WAY.

COME ON, SANSHOBO.

HEY, ARE YOU COMING, PRIEST?

EH?

UH...SORRY. I WAS...UH... PREOCCUPIED.

CONCERNED ABOUT LORD IKEDA? THE EFFECTS OF THE DRUG SHOULD HAVE WORN OFF BY NOW.

COME ON--WE'RE WASTING TIME.

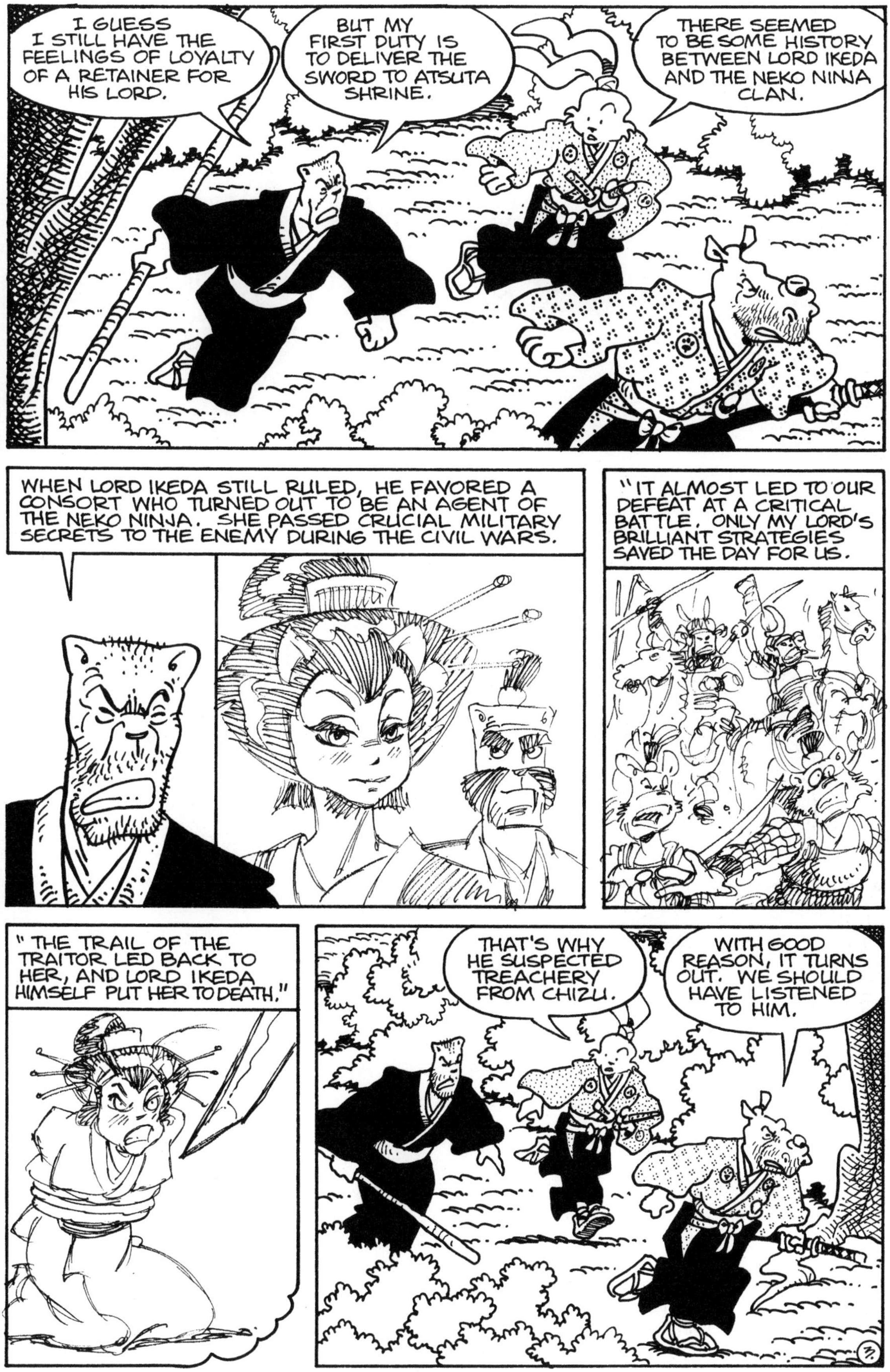
I GUESS I STILL HAVE THE FEELINGS OF LOYALTY OF A RETAINER FOR HIS LORD.
BUT MY FIRST DUTY IS TO DELIVER THE SWORD TO ATSUTA SHRINE.
THERE SEEMED TO BE SOME HISTORY BETWEEN LORD IKEDA AND THE NEKO NINJA CLAN.
WHEN LORD IKEDA STILL RULED, HE FAVORED A CONSORT WHO TURNED OUT TO BE AN AGENT OF THE NEKO NINJA. SHE PASSED CRUCIAL MILITARY SECRETS TO THE ENEMY DURING THE CIVIL WARS.
"IT ALMOST LED TO OUR DEFEAT AT A CRITICAL BATTLE. ONLY MY LORD'S BRILLIANT STRATEGIES SAVED THE DAY FOR US.
"THE TRAIL OF THE TRAITOR LED BACK TO HER, AND LORD IKEDA HIMSELF PUT HER TO DEATH."
THAT'S WHY HE SUSPECTED TREACHERY FROM CHIZU.
WITH GOOD REASON, IT TURNS OUT. WE SHOULD HAVE LISTENED TO HIM.
31

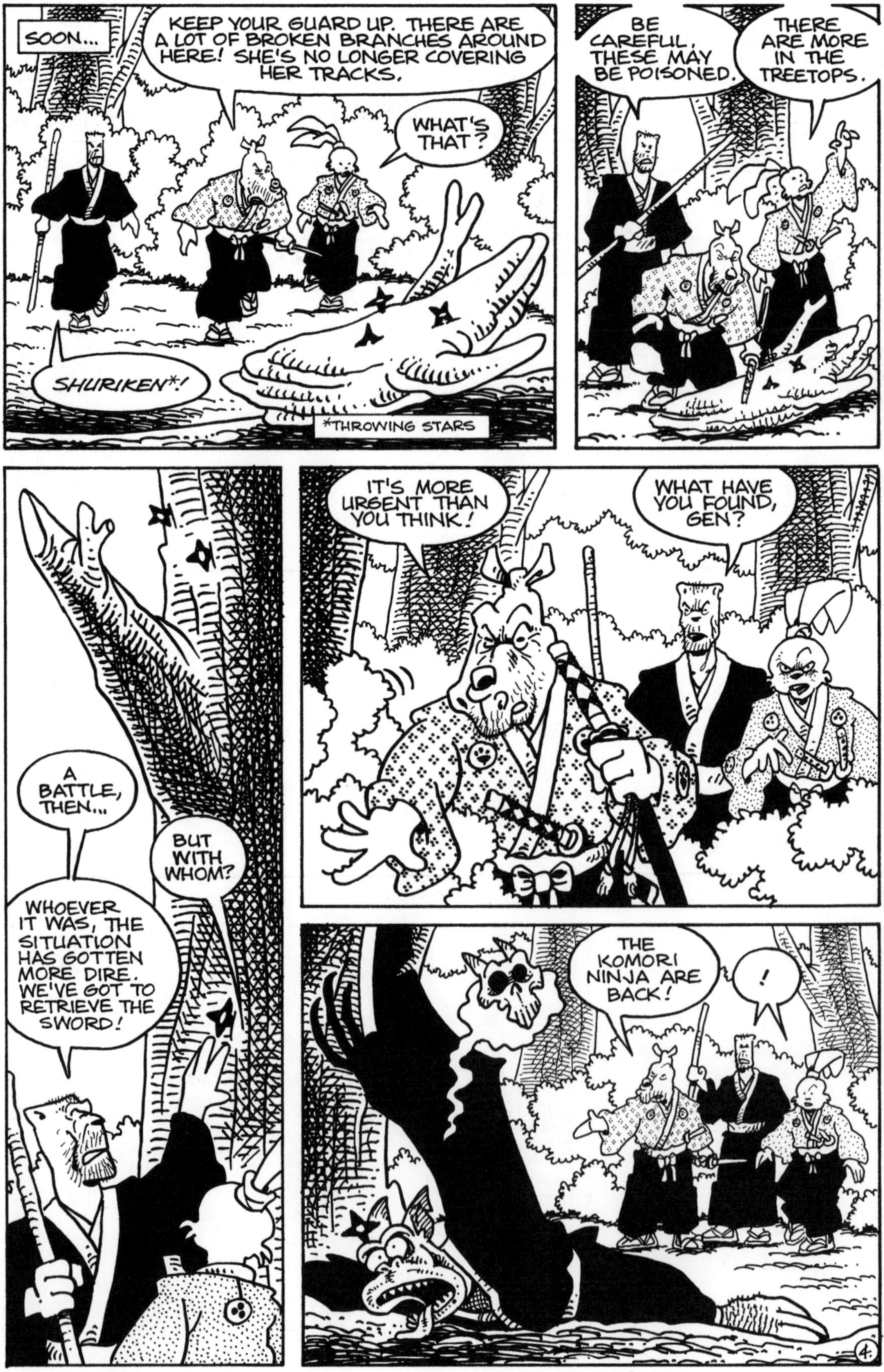
SOON...
KEEP YOUR GUARD UP. THERE ARE A LOT OF BROKEN BRANCHES AROUND HERE! SHE'S NO LONGER COVERING HER TRACKS.
WHAT'S THAT?
SHURIKEN*!
*THROWING STARS
BE CAREFUL, THESE MAY BE POISONED.
THERE ARE MORE IN THE TREETOPS.
A BATTLE, THEN...
BUT WITH WHOM?
WHOEVER IT WAS, THE SITUATION HAS GOTTEN MORE DIRE. WE'VE GOT TO RETRIEVE THE SWORD!
IT'S MORE URGENT THAN YOU THINK!
WHAT HAVE YOU FOUND, GEN?
THE KOMORI NINJA ARE BACK!
!
4.

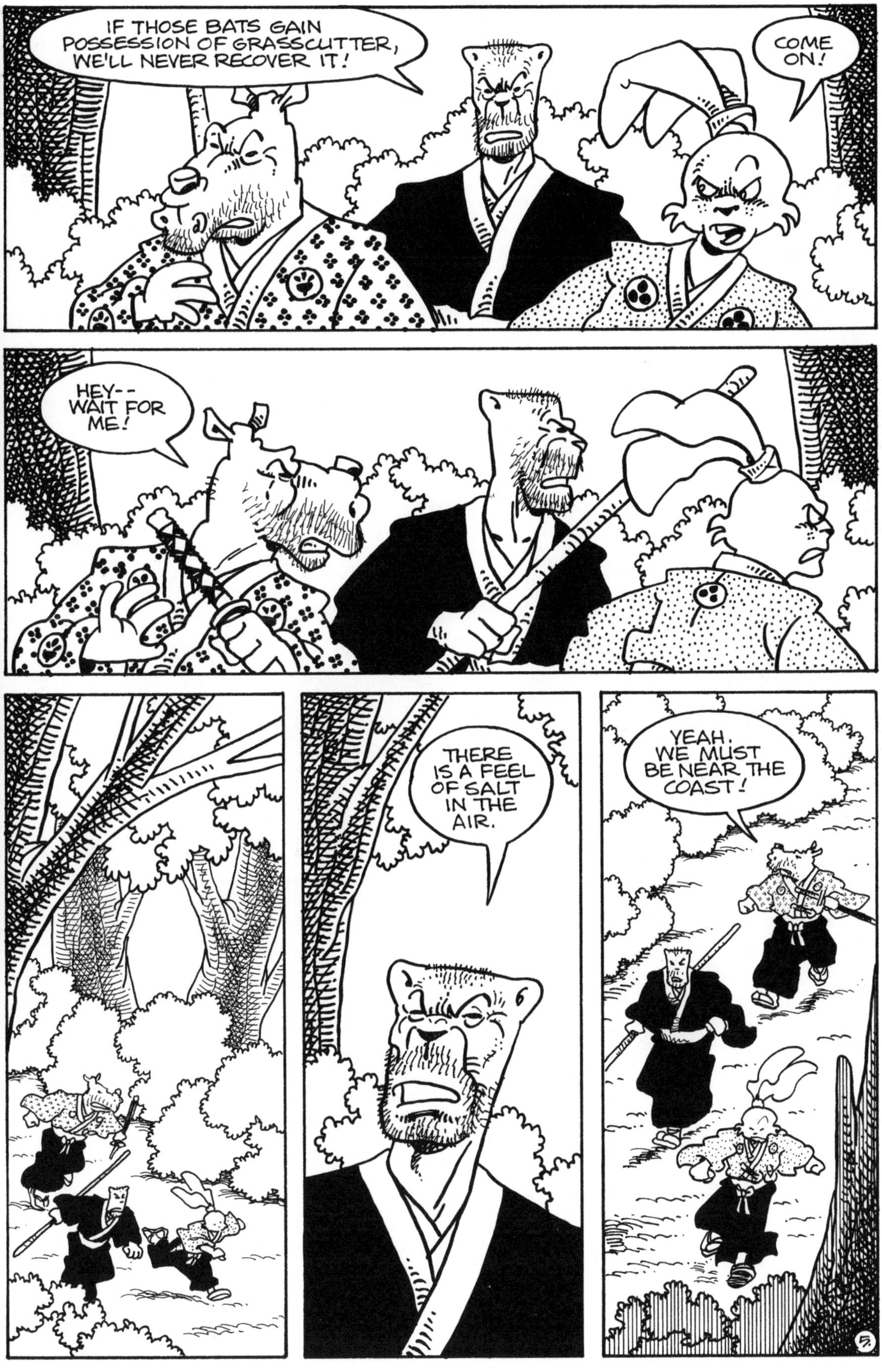
IF THOSE BATS GAIN POSSESSION OF GRASSCUTTER, WE'LL NEVER RECOVER IT!
COME ON!
HEY-- WAIT FOR ME!
THERE IS A FEEL OF SALT IN THE AIR.
YEAH. WE MUST BE NEAR THE COAST!

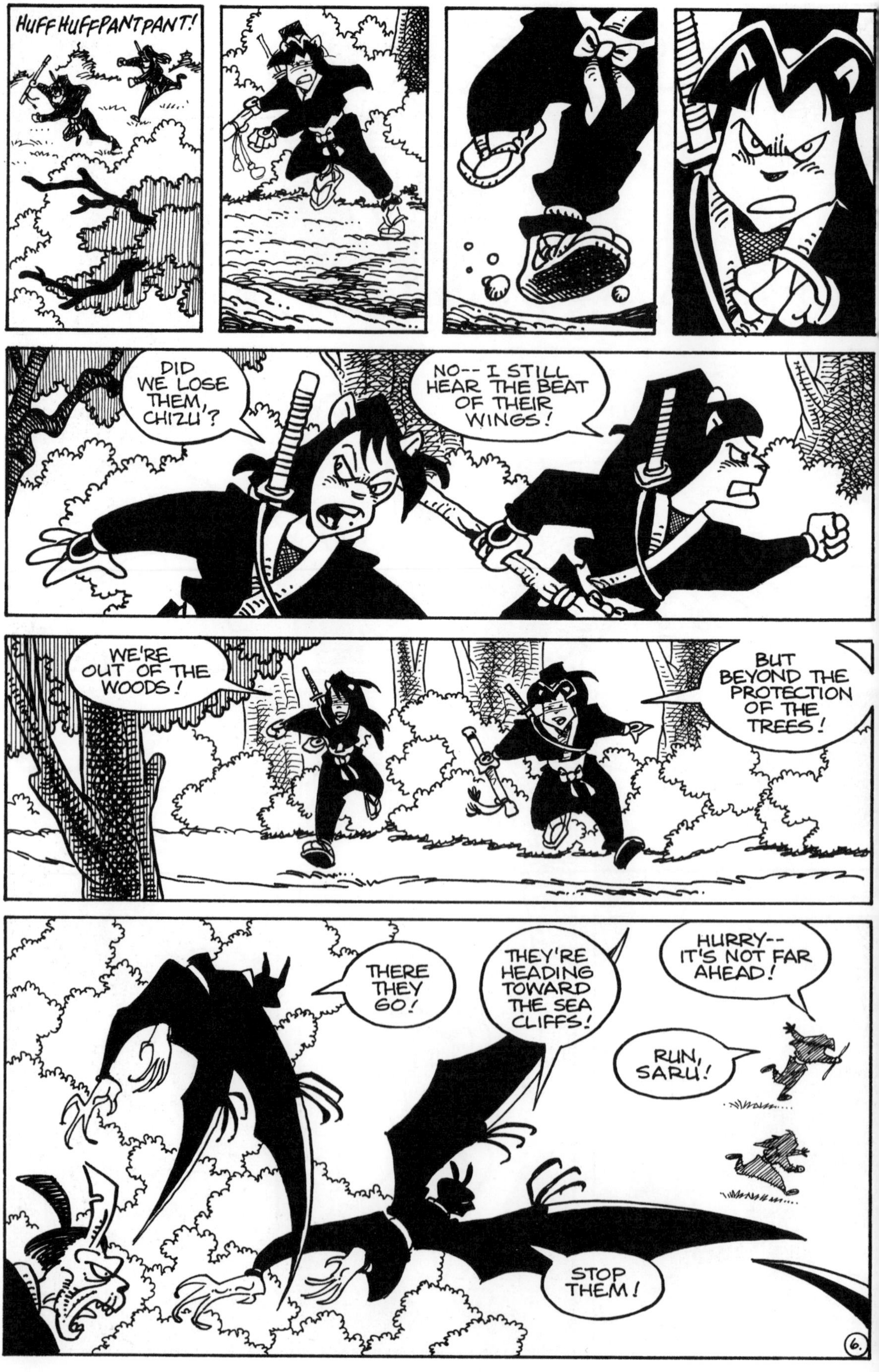
HUFF HUFF PANT PANT!
DID WE LOSE THEM, CHIZU?
NO-- I STILL HEAR THE BEAT OF THEIR WINGS!
WE'RE OUT OF THE WOODS!
BUT BEYOND THE PROTECTION OF THE TREES!
THERE THEY GO!
THEY'RE HEADING TOWARD THE SEA CLIFFS!
HURRY-- IT'S NOT FAR AHEAD!
RUN, SARU!
STOP THEM!
6.

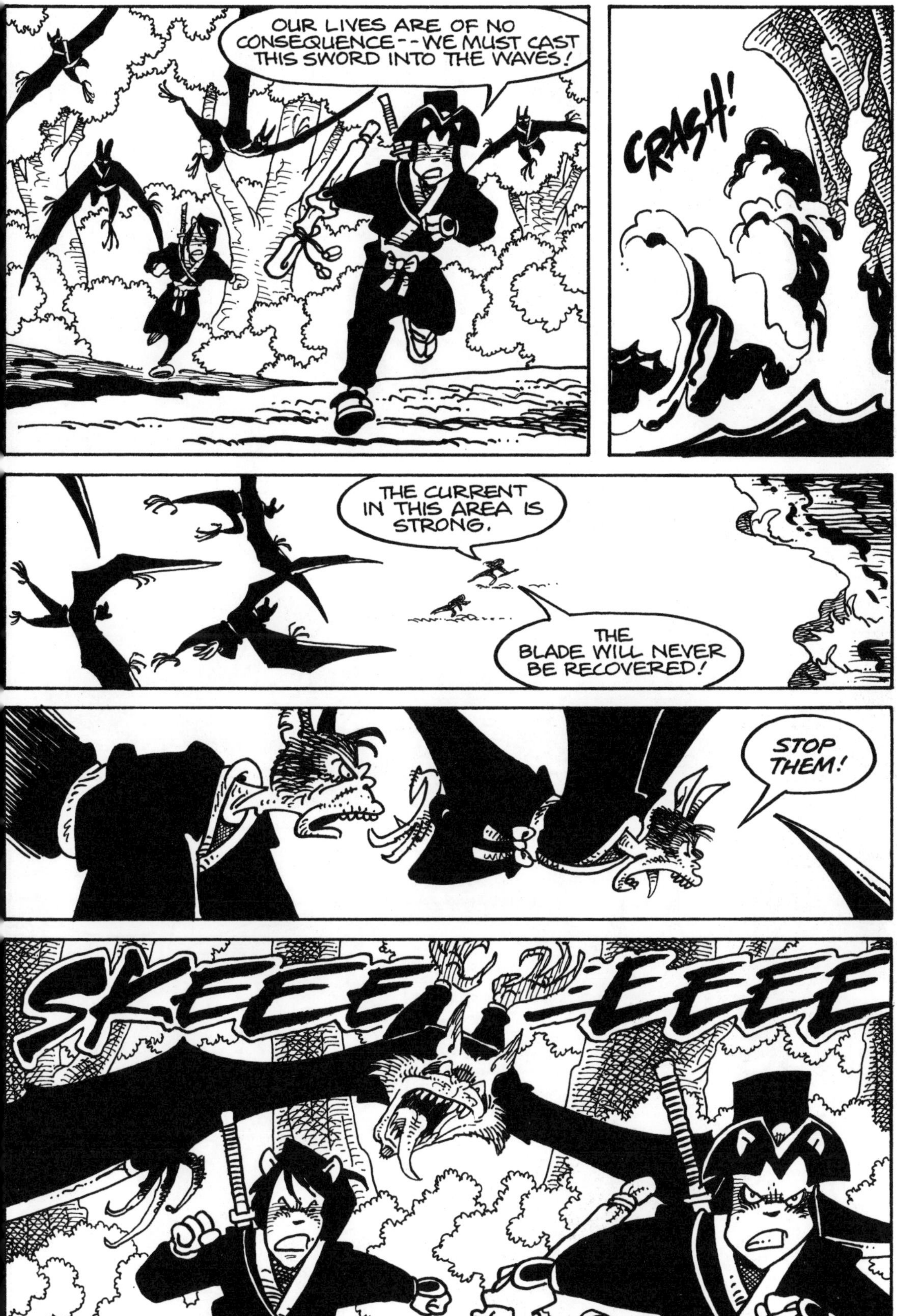
OUR LIVES ARE OF NO CONSEQUENCE--WE MUST CAST THIS SWORD INTO THE WAVES!
CRASH!
THE CURRENT IN THIS AREA IS STRONG.
THE BLADE WILL NEVER BE RECOVERED!
STOP THEM!
SKEEE--EEEE
7.

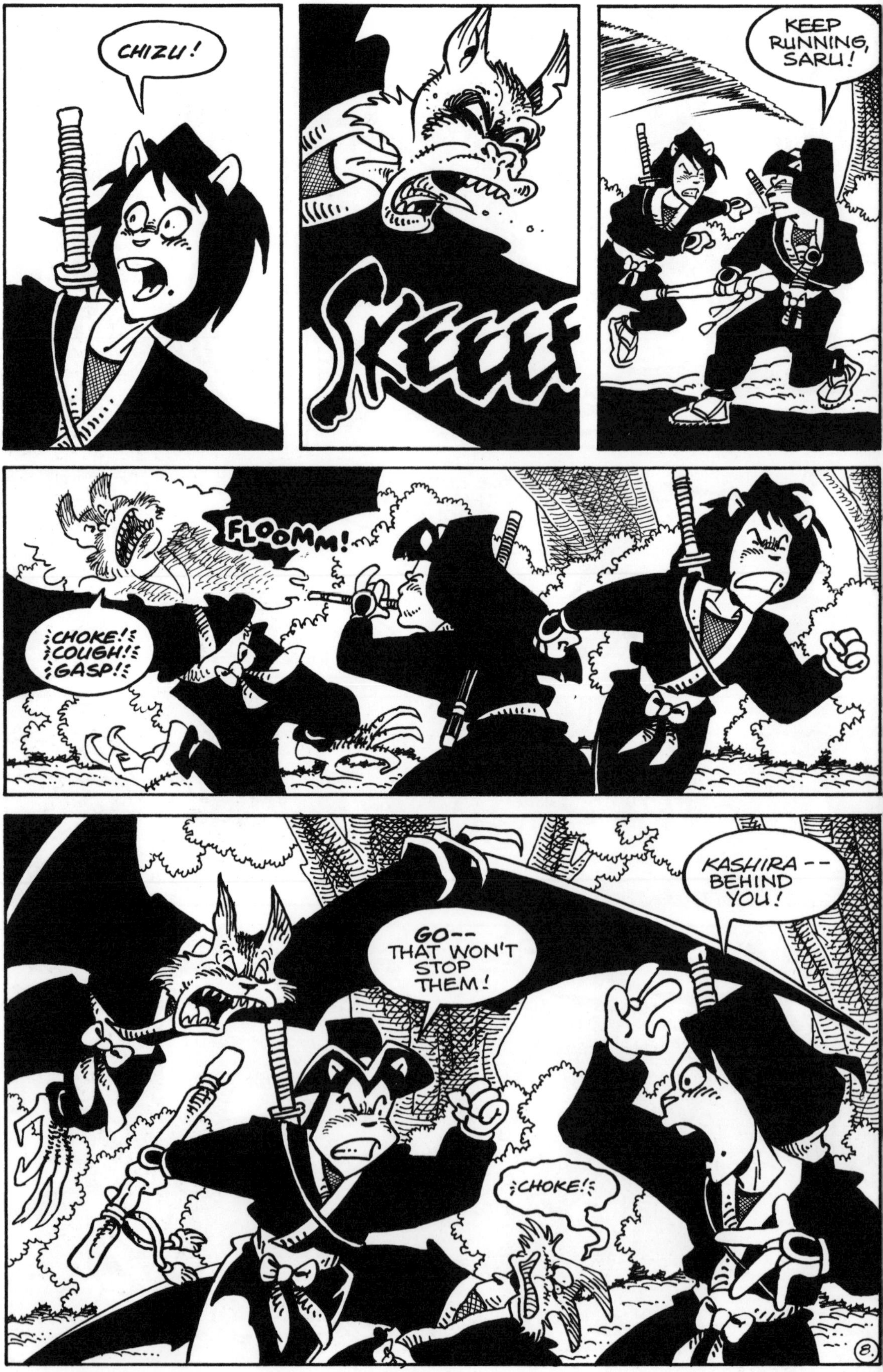
CHIZU!
SKEEEE
KEEP RUNNING, SARU!
FLOOMM!
CHOKE! COUGH! GASP!
GO-- THAT WON'T STOP THEM!
KASHIRA -- BEHIND YOU!
CHOKE!
8.

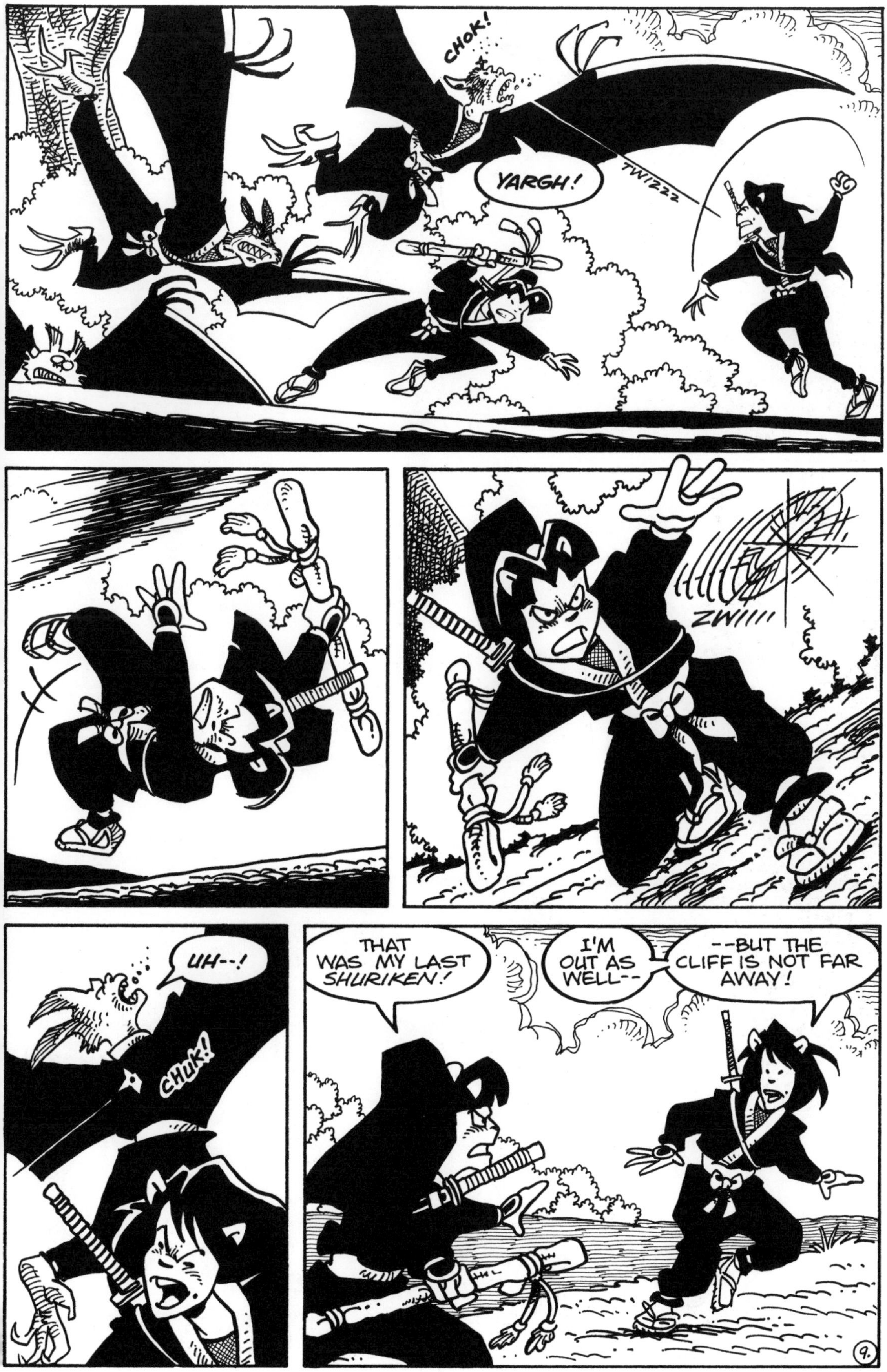
CHOK!
YARGH!
TWIZZZ
ZWIIII
UH--!
CHUK!
THAT WAS MY LAST SHURIKEN!
I'M OUT AS WELL--
--BUT THE CLIFF IS NOT FAR AWAY!
9.

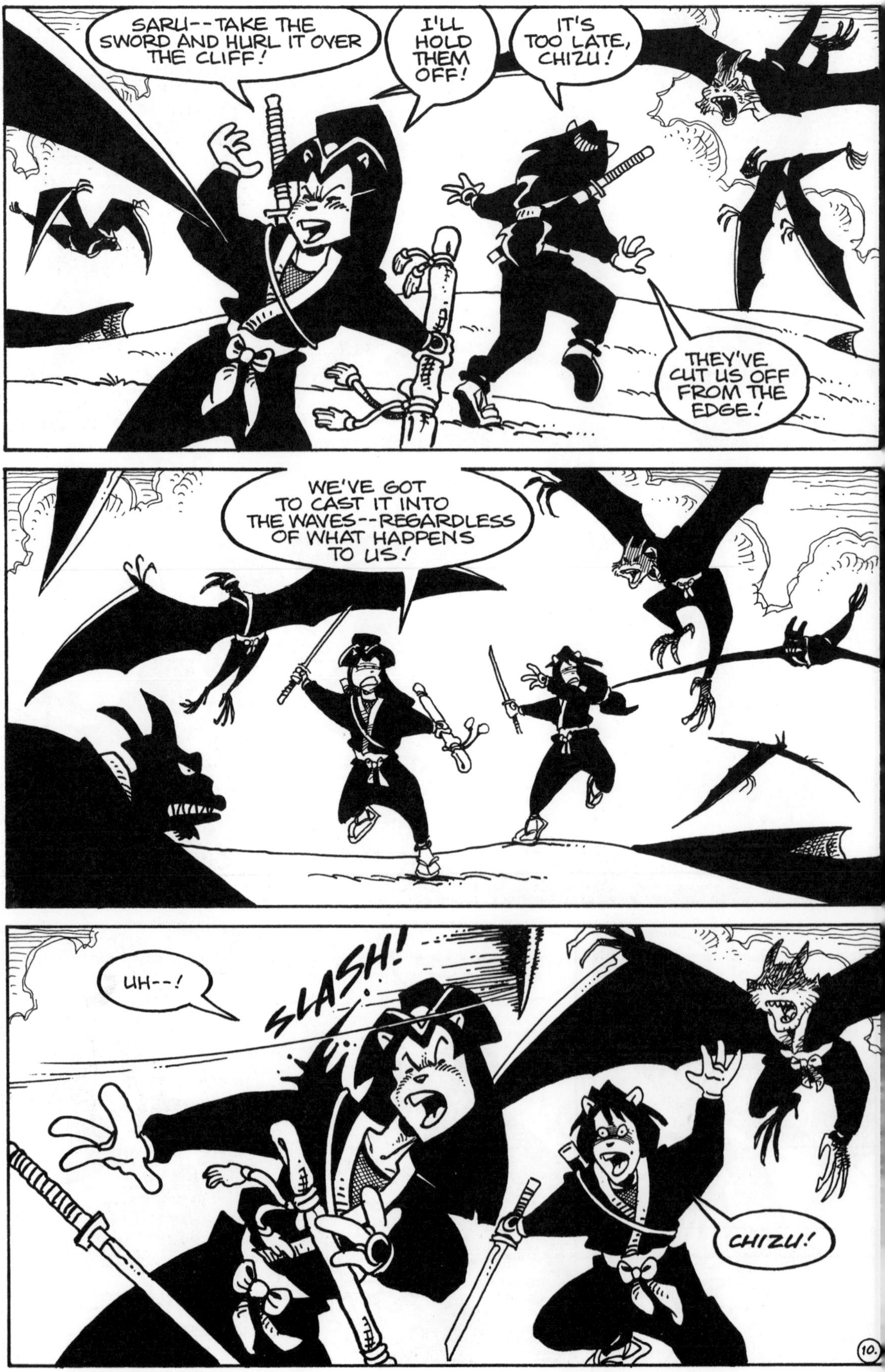
SARU--TAKE THE SWORD AND HURL IT OVER THE CLIFF!
I'LL HOLD THEM OFF!
IT'S TOO LATE, CHIZU!
THEY'VE CUT US OFF FROM THE EDGE!
WE'VE GOT TO CAST IT INTO THE WAVES--REGARDLESS OF WHAT HAPPENS TO US!
UH--!
SLASH!
CHIZU!
10.

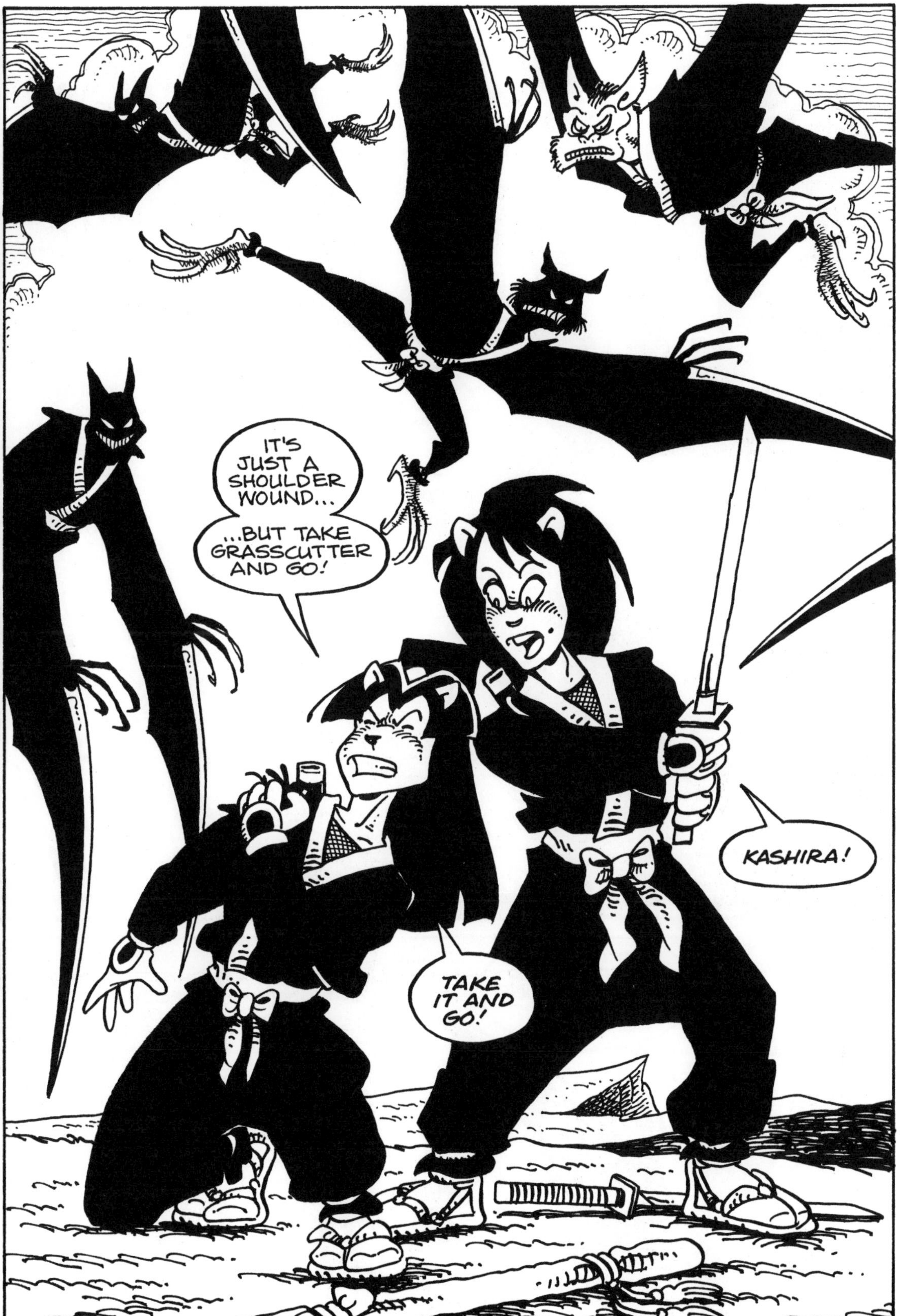
IT'S JUST A SHOULDER WOUND...
...BUT TAKE GRASSCUTTER AND GO!
KASHIRA!
TAKE IT AND GO!
11.

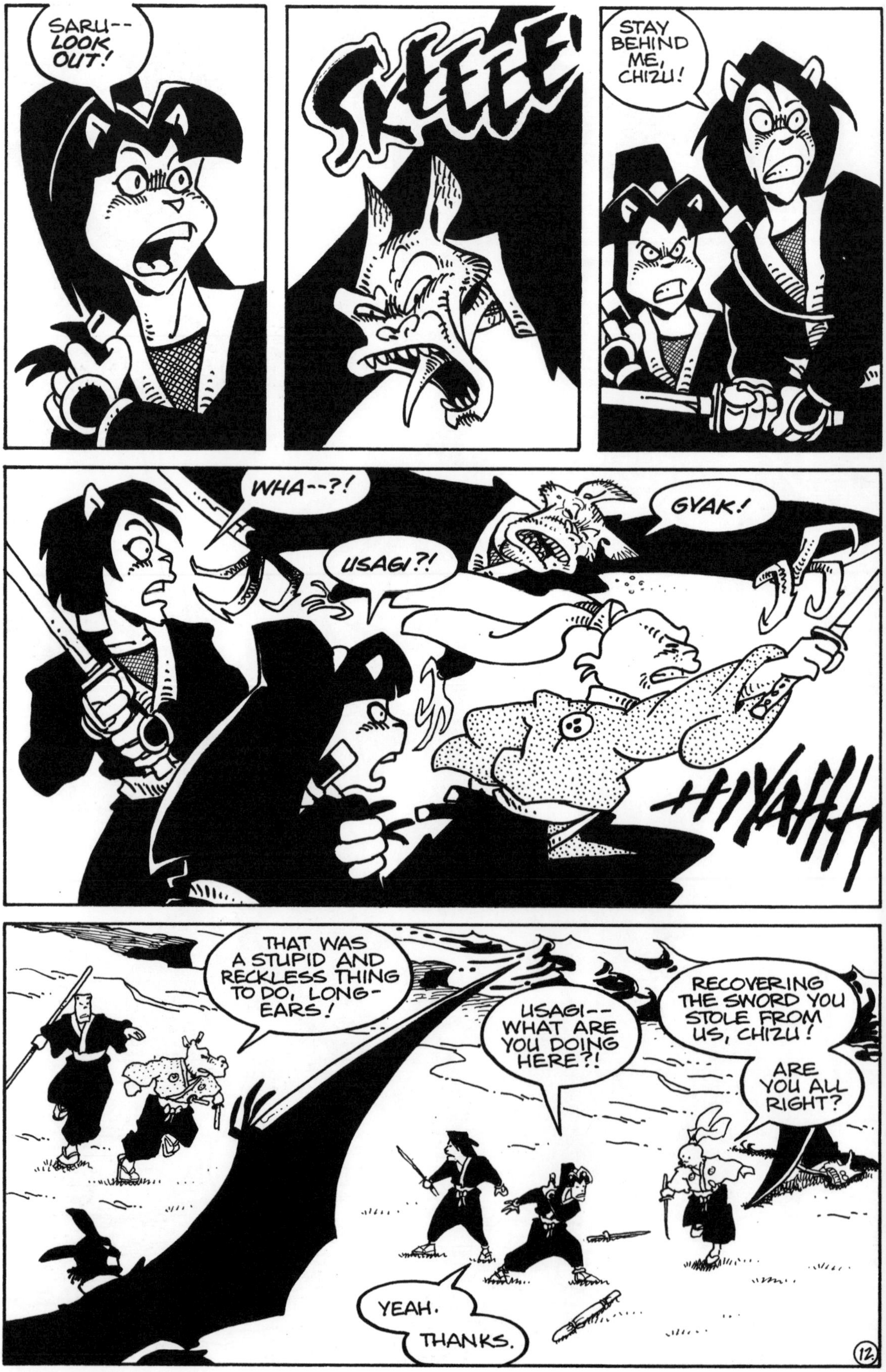
SARU-- LOOK OUT!
SKEEEE!
STAY BEHIND ME, CHIZU!
WHA--?!
USAGI?!
GYAK!
HIYAHH
THAT WAS A STUPID AND RECKLESS THING TO DO, LONG-EARS!
USAGI-- WHAT ARE YOU DOING HERE?!
RECOVERING THE SWORD YOU STOLE FROM US, CHIZU!
ARE YOU ALL RIGHT?
YEAH.
THANKS.
12

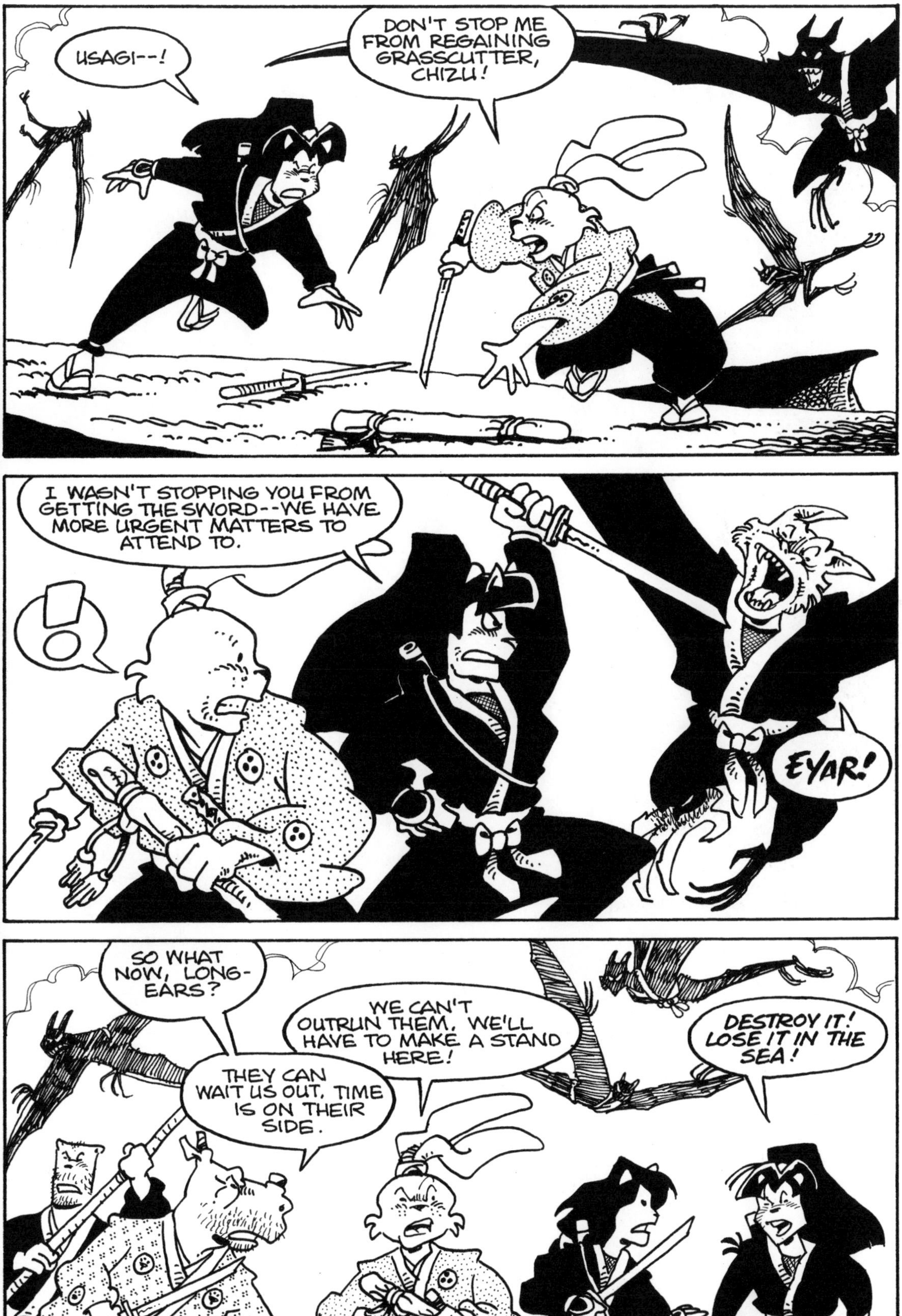
USAGI--!
DON'T STOP ME FROM REGAINING GRASSCUTTER, CHIZU!
I WASN'T STOPPING YOU FROM GETTING THE SWORD--WE HAVE MORE URGENT MATTERS TO ATTEND TO.
!
EYAR!
SO WHAT NOW, LONG-EARS?
THEY CAN WAIT US OUT. TIME IS ON THEIR SIDE.
WE CAN'T OUTRUN THEM. WE'LL HAVE TO MAKE A STAND HERE!
DESTROY IT! LOSE IT IN THE SEA!
13.

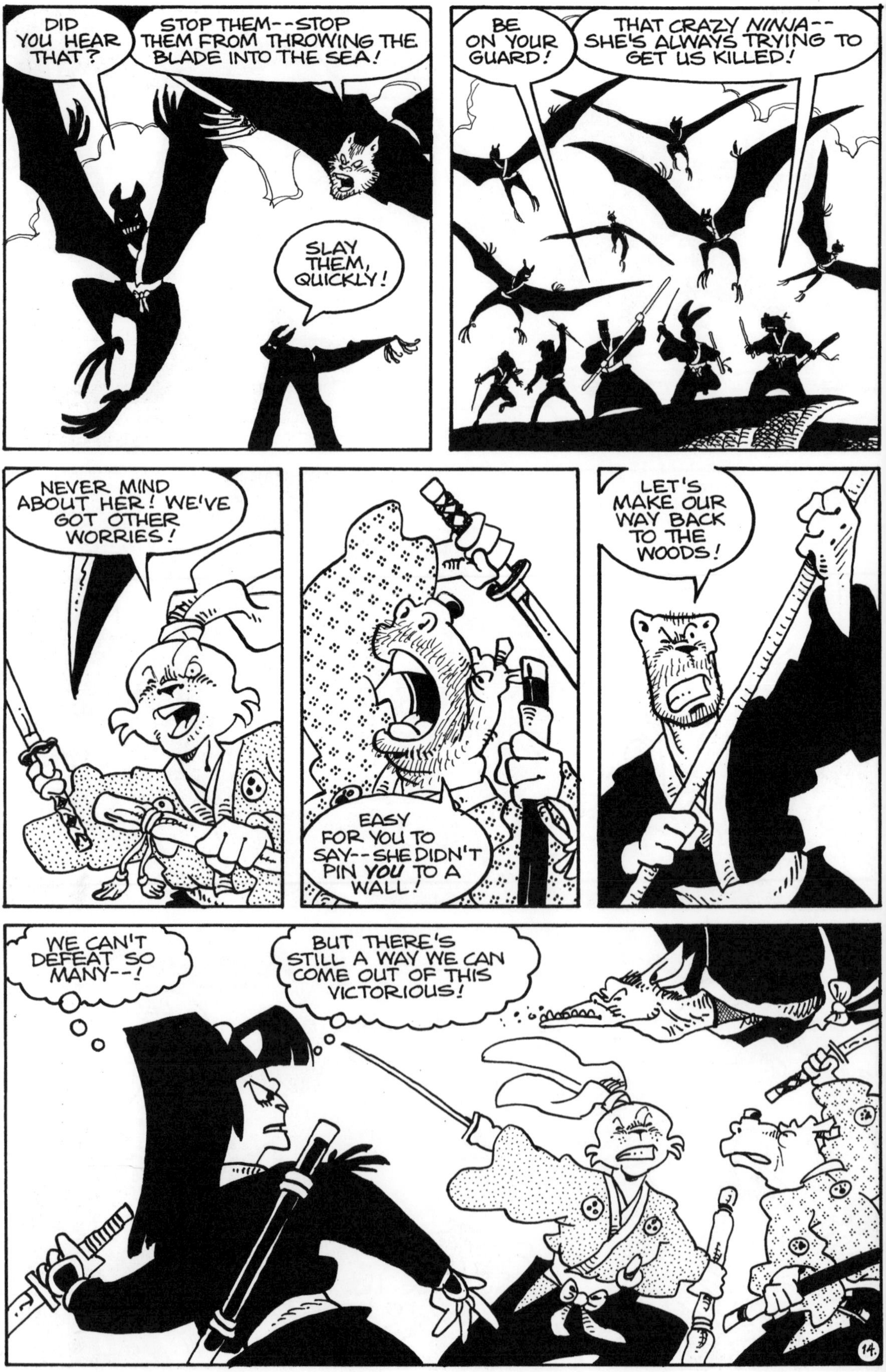

DID YOU HEAR THAT?
STOP THEM--STOP THEM FROM THROWING THE BLADE INTO THE SEA!
SLAY THEM, QUICKLY!
BE ON YOUR GUARD!
THAT CRAZY *NINJA*--SHE'S ALWAYS TRYING TO GET US KILLED!
NEVER MIND ABOUT HER! WE'VE GOT OTHER WORRIES!
EASY FOR YOU TO SAY--SHE DIDN'T PIN ***YOU*** TO A WALL!
LET'S MAKE OUR WAY BACK TO THE WOODS!
WE CAN'T DEFEAT SO MANY--!
BUT THERE'S STILL A WAY WE CAN COME OUT OF THIS VICTORIOUS!
14.

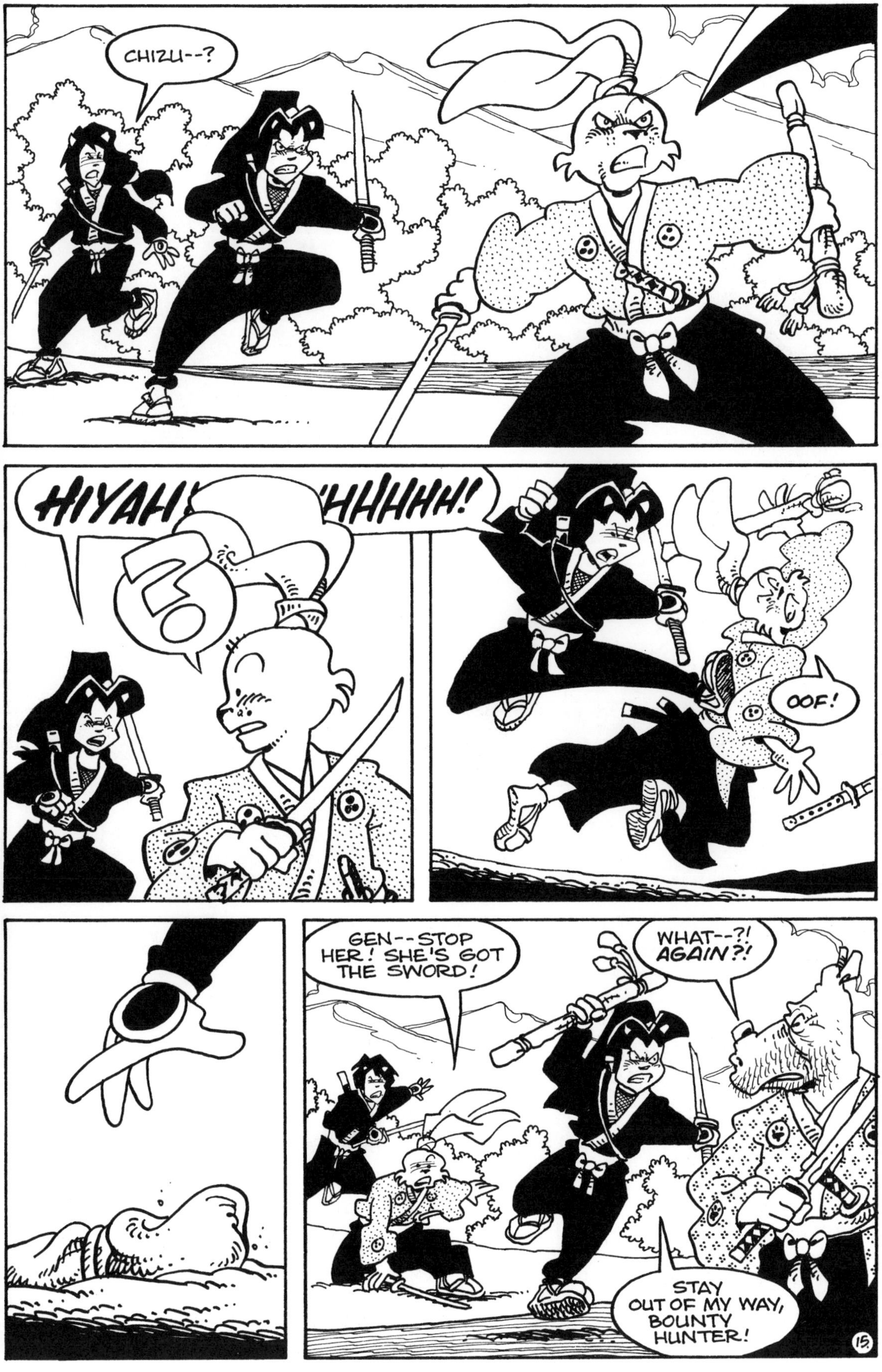

CHIZU--?
HIYAH! ...HHHHH!
?
OOF!
GEN--STOP HER! SHE'S GOT THE SWORD!
WHAT--?! AGAIN?!
STAY OUT OF MY WAY, BOUNTY HUNTER!
15

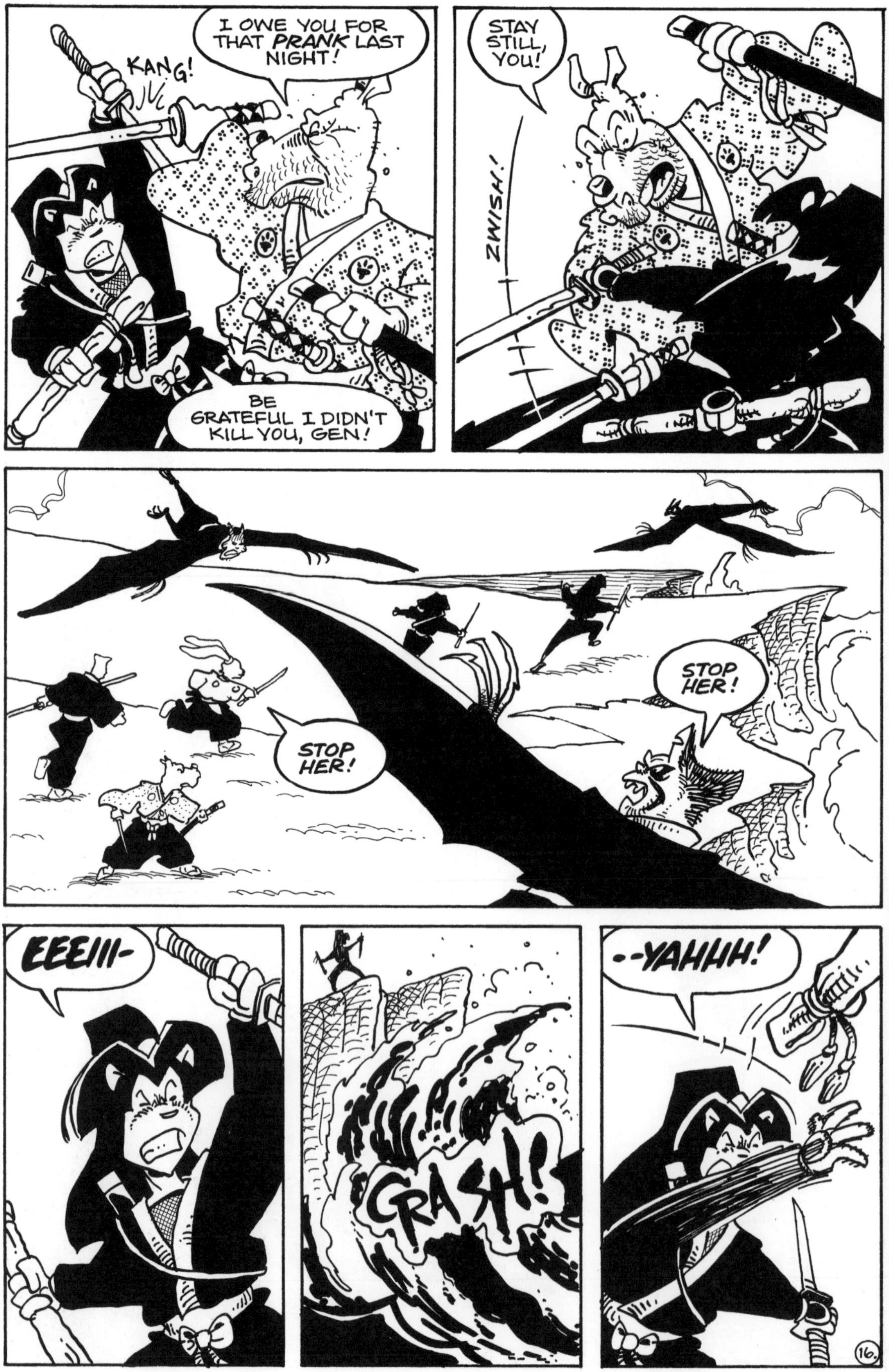

KANG!
I OWE YOU FOR THAT PRANK LAST NIGHT!
BE GRATEFUL I DIDN'T KILL YOU, GEN!
STAY STILL, YOU!
ZWISH!
STOP HER!
STOP HER!
EEEIII-
CRASH!
--YAHHH!
16.

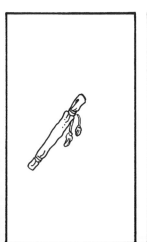
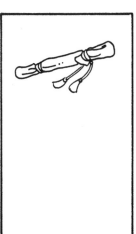
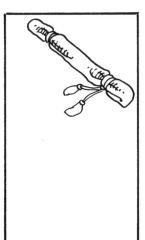
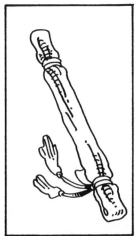

SKEEEE

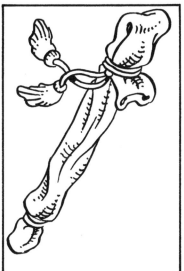

SNATCH!

NO!

HA HA HA HA HA! YOU'RE BEATEN, SHADOW WALKER!

WE, OF THE KOMORI NINJA, WILL ALWAYS WIN OUT IN THE END!

17.

WHAT--?!
HIYAAHHHHHH!!
SARU--!
AHHHHHHH
MY DEATH WILL ATONE FOR MY DISLOYALTY TO YOU, CHIZU!
LET GO OF ME, YOU FOOL!
18.

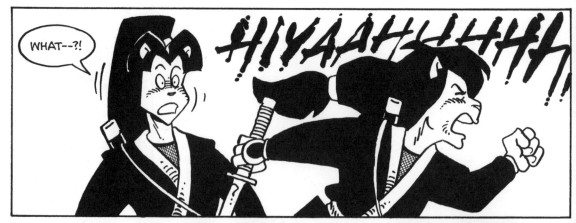

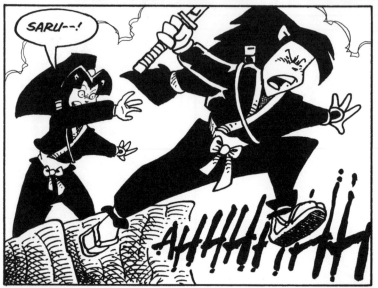

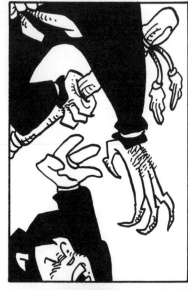

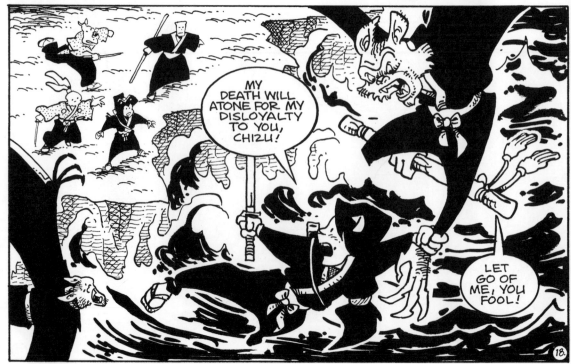

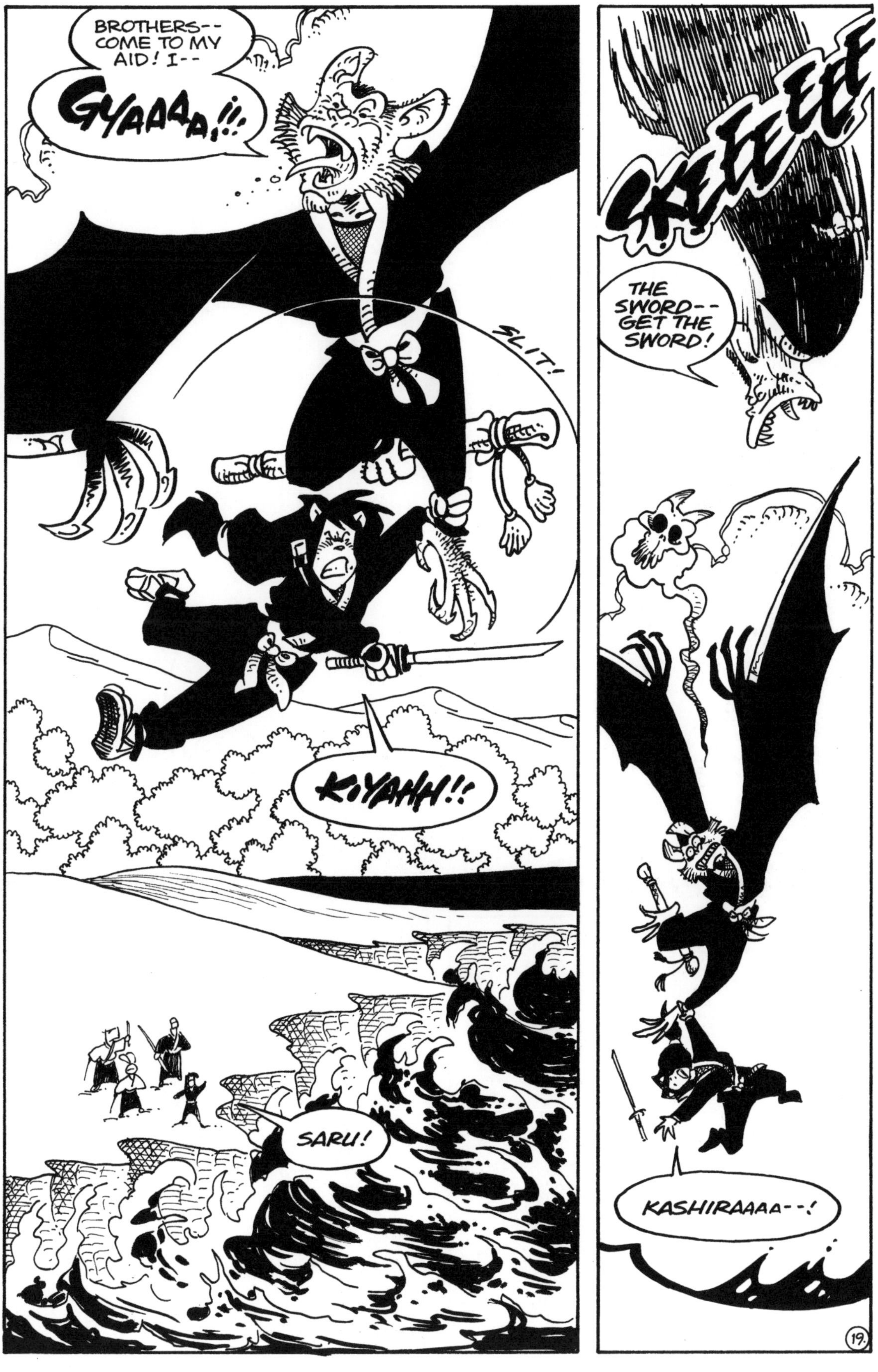
BROTHERS-- COME TO MY AID! I--
GYAAAA!!!
SLIT!
KIYAHH!!
SARU!
SKEEEEEE
THE SWORD-- GET THE SWORD!
KASHIRAAAA--!
19.

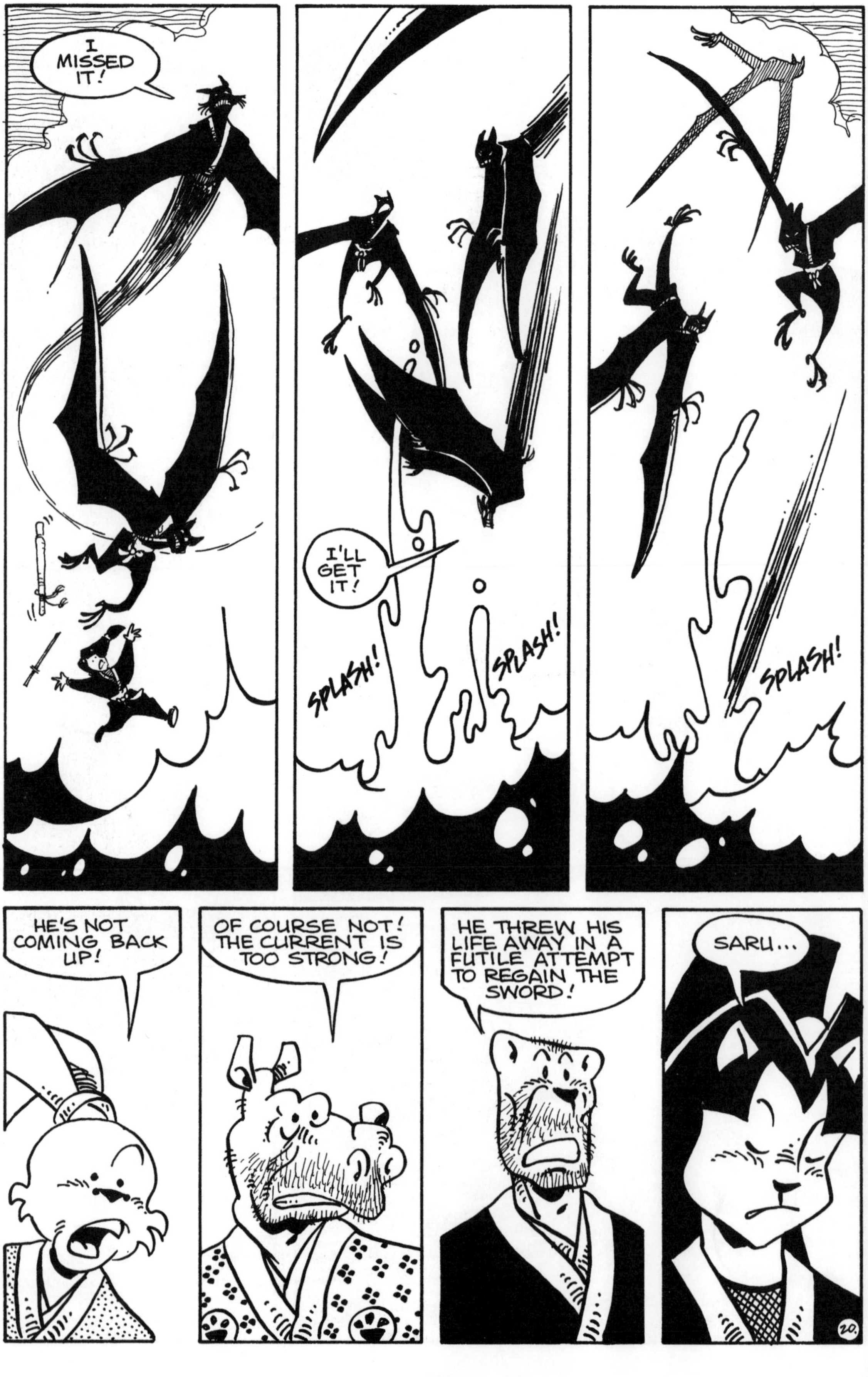
I MISSED IT!
I'LL GET IT!
SPLASH!
SPLASH!
SPLASH!
HE'S NOT COMING BACK UP!
OF COURSE NOT! THE CURRENT IS TOO STRONG!
HE THREW HIS LIFE AWAY IN A FUTILE ATTEMPT TO REGAIN THE SWORD!
SARU...
20.

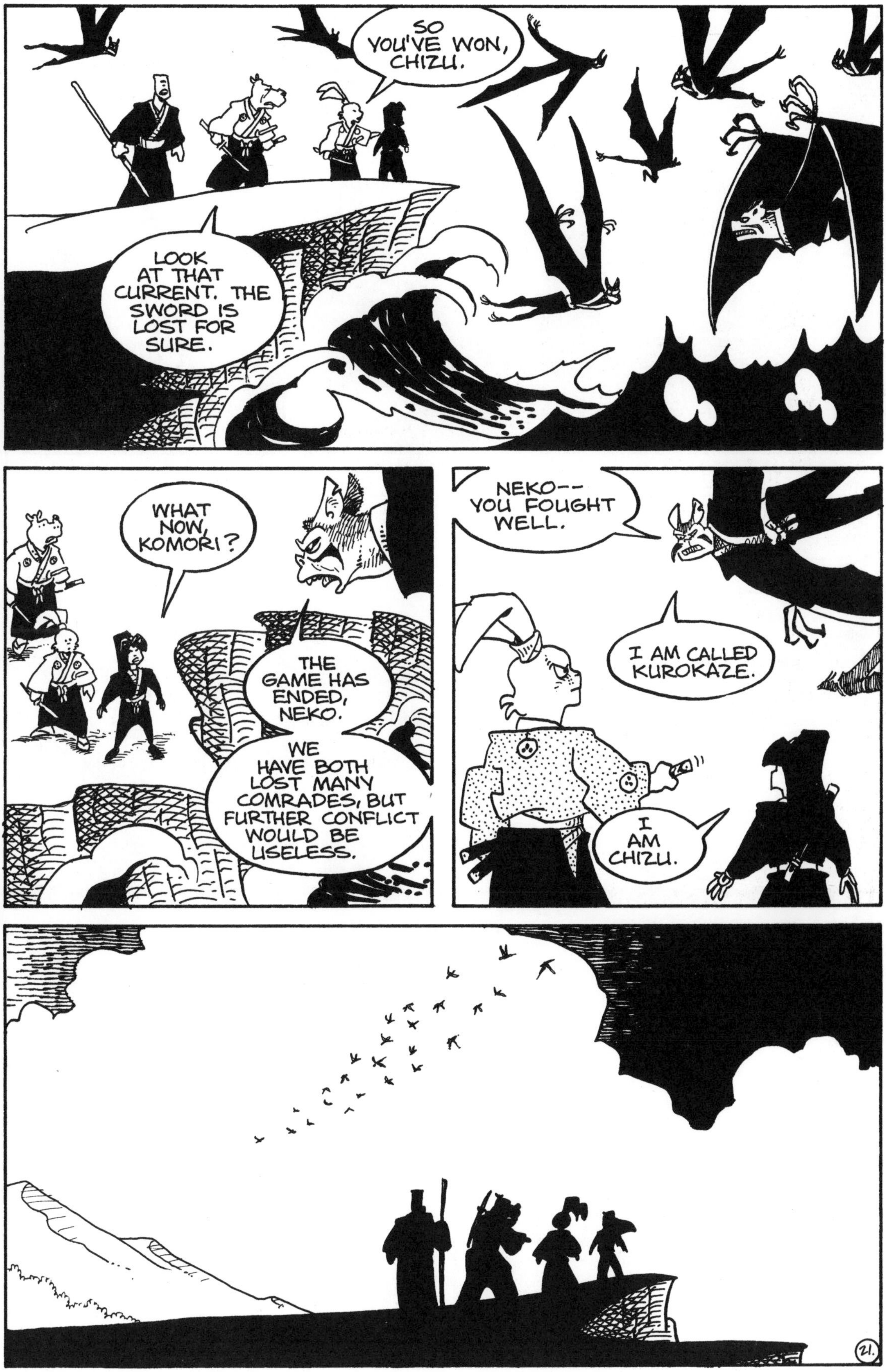
SO YOU'VE WON, CHIZU.
LOOK AT THAT CURRENT. THE SWORD IS LOST FOR SURE.
WHAT NOW, KOMORI?
THE GAME HAS ENDED, NEKO.
WE HAVE BOTH LOST MANY COMRADES, BUT FURTHER CONFLICT WOULD BE USELESS.
NEKO-- YOU FOUGHT WELL.
I AM CALLED KUROKAZE.
I AM CHIZU.
21.

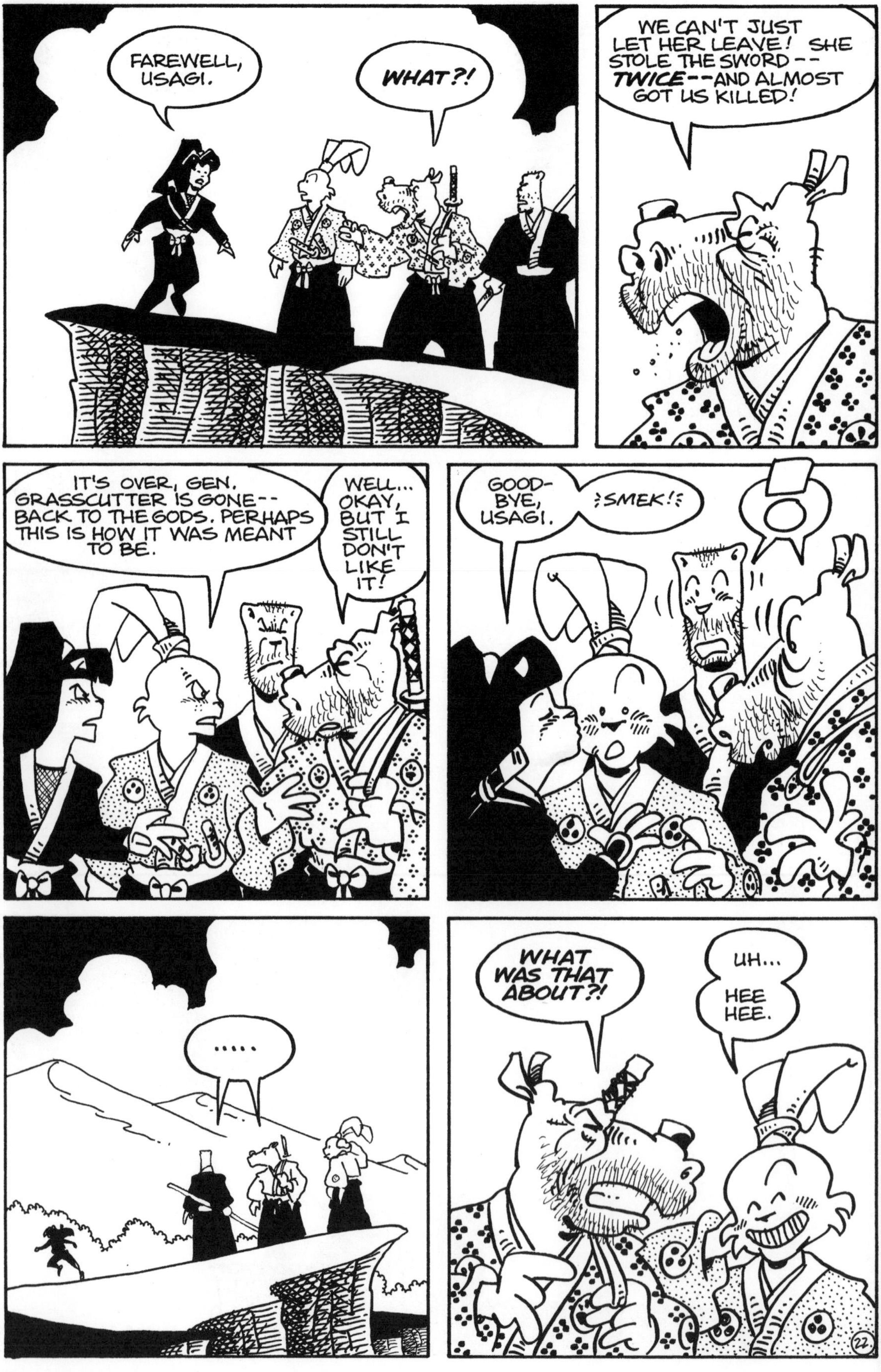
FAREWELL, USAGI.
WHAT?!
WE CAN'T JUST LET HER LEAVE! SHE STOLE THE SWORD -- TWICE -- AND ALMOST GOT US KILLED!
IT'S OVER, GEN. GRASSCUTTER IS GONE-- BACK TO THE GODS. PERHAPS THIS IS HOW IT WAS MEANT TO BE.
WELL... OKAY, BUT I STILL DON'T LIKE IT!
GOOD-BYE, USAGI.
SMEK!
!
.....
WHAT WAS THAT ABOUT?!
UH...
HEE HEE.
22

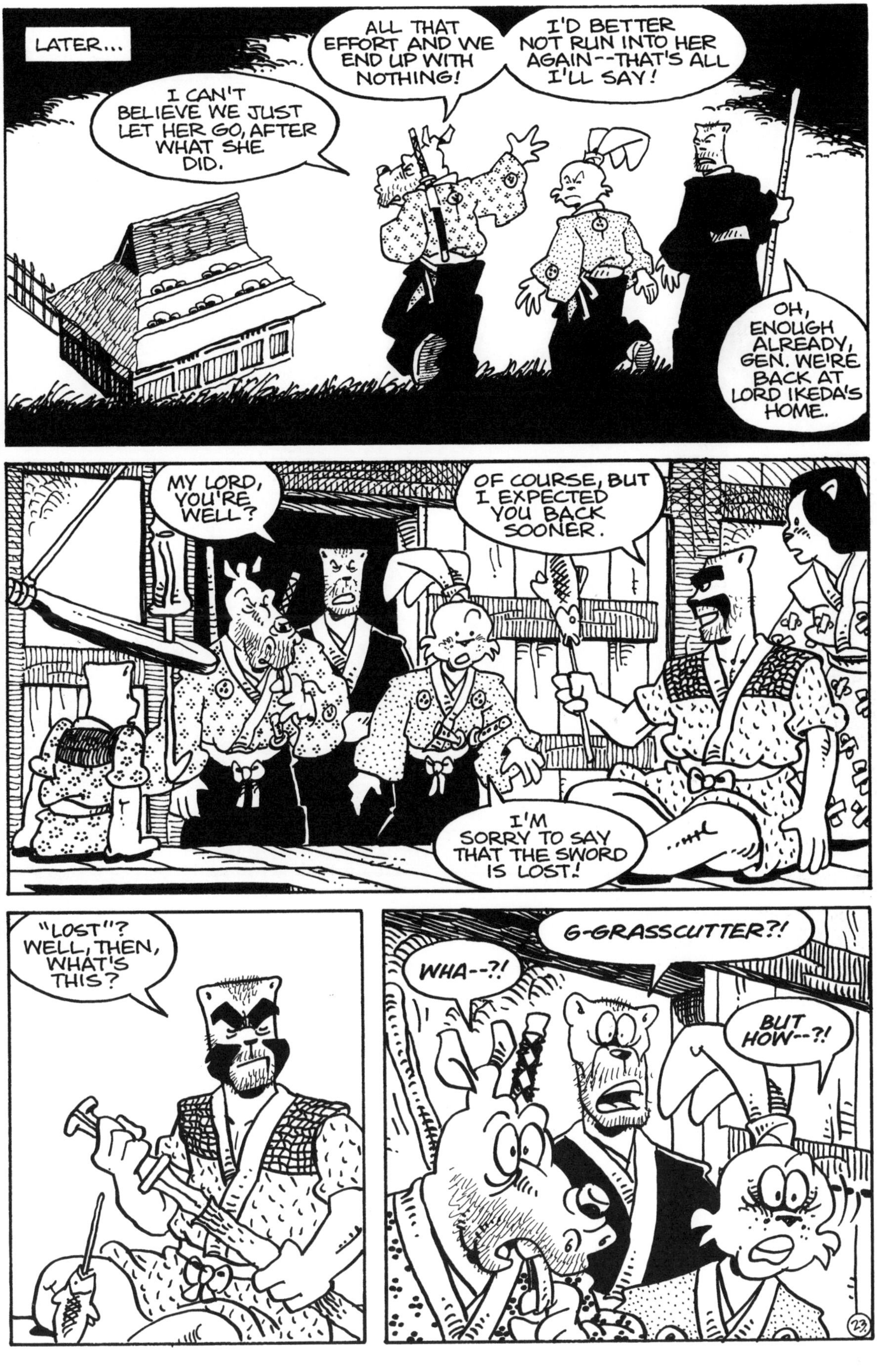
LATER...
I CAN'T BELIEVE WE JUST LET HER GO, AFTER WHAT SHE DID.
ALL THAT EFFORT AND WE END UP WITH NOTHING!
I'D BETTER NOT RUN INTO HER AGAIN--THAT'S ALL I'LL SAY!
OH, ENOUGH ALREADY, GEN. WE'RE BACK AT LORD IKEDA'S HOME.
MY LORD, YOU'RE WELL?
OF COURSE, BUT I EXPECTED YOU BACK SOONER.
I'M SORRY TO SAY THAT THE SWORD IS LOST!
"LOST"? WELL, THEN, WHAT'S THIS?
WHA--?!
G-GRASSCUTTER?!
BUT HOW--?!
23

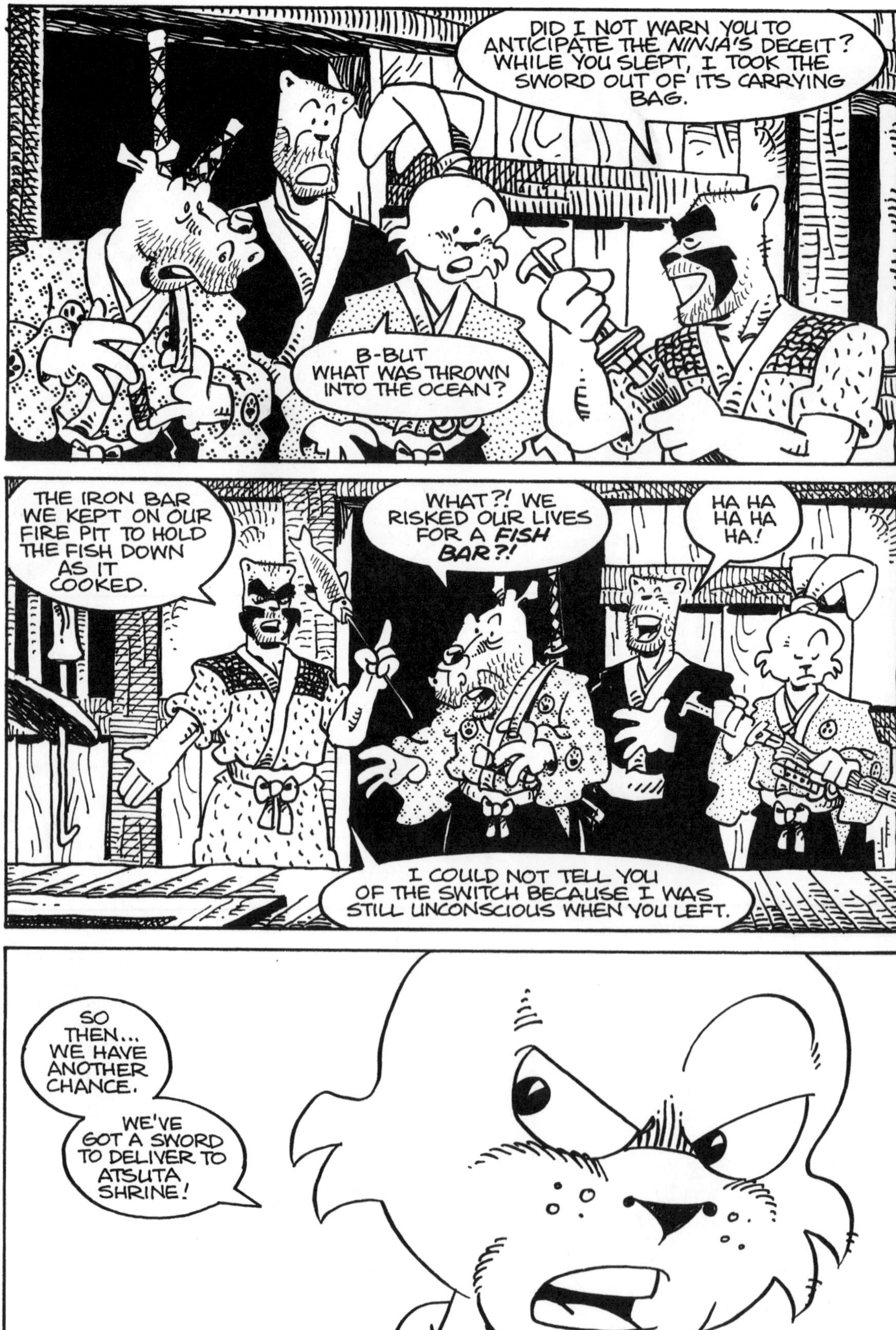
DID I NOT WARN YOU TO ANTICIPATE THE *NINJA'S* DECEIT? WHILE YOU SLEPT, I TOOK THE SWORD OUT OF ITS CARRYING BAG.
B-BUT WHAT WAS THROWN INTO THE OCEAN?
THE IRON BAR WE KEPT ON OUR FIRE PIT TO HOLD THE FISH DOWN AS IT COOKED.
WHAT?! WE RISKED OUR LIVES FOR A ***FISH BAR?!***
HA HA HA HA HA!
I COULD NOT TELL YOU OF THE SWITCH BECAUSE I WAS STILL UNCONSCIOUS WHEN YOU LEFT.
SO THEN... WE HAVE ANOTHER CHANCE.
WE'VE GOT A SWORD TO DELIVER TO ATSUTA SHRINE!

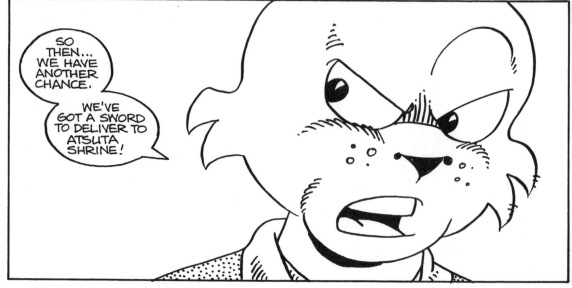

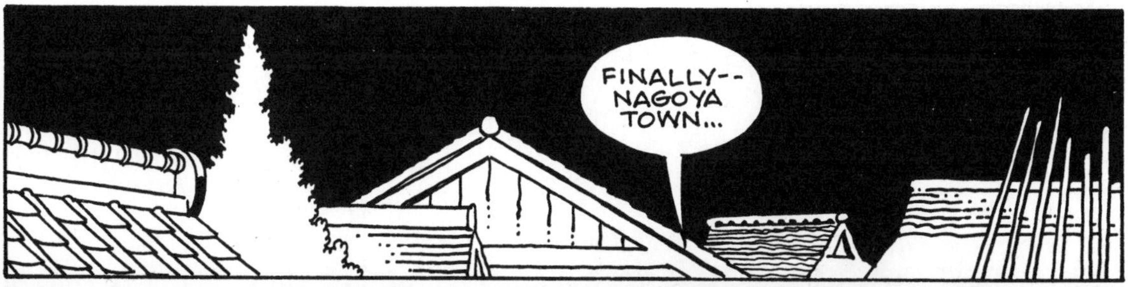
FINALLY-- NAGOYA TOWN...

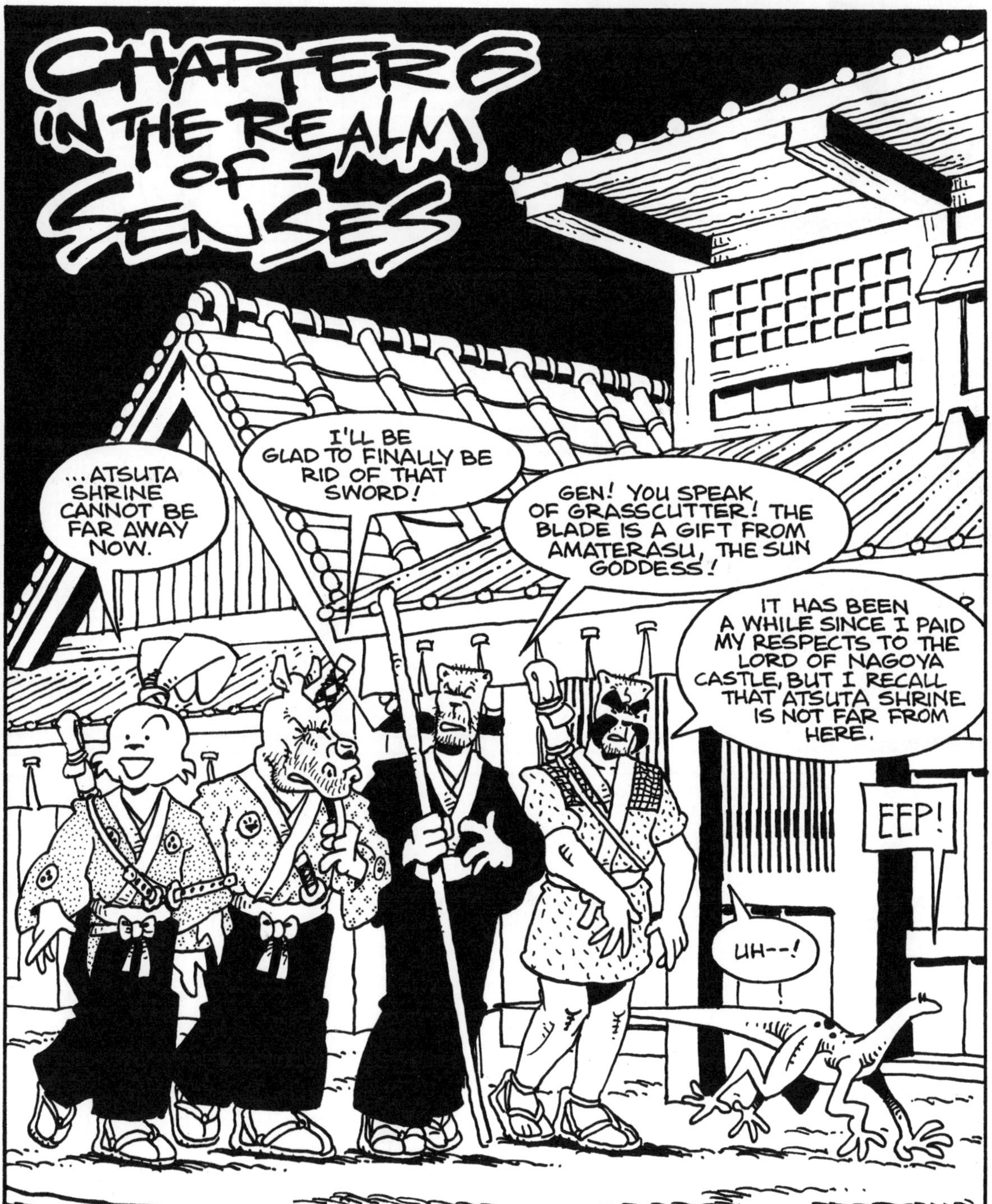
CHAPTER 6
IN THE REALM OF SENSES
...ATSUTA SHRINE CANNOT BE FAR AWAY NOW.
I'LL BE GLAD TO FINALLY BE RID OF THAT SWORD!
GEN! YOU SPEAK OF GRASSCUTTER! THE BLADE IS A GIFT FROM AMATERASU, THE SUN GODDESS!
IT HAS BEEN A WHILE SINCE I PAID MY RESPECTS TO THE LORD OF NAGOYA CASTLE, BUT I RECALL THAT ATSUTA SHRINE IS NOT FAR FROM HERE.
EEP!
UH--!

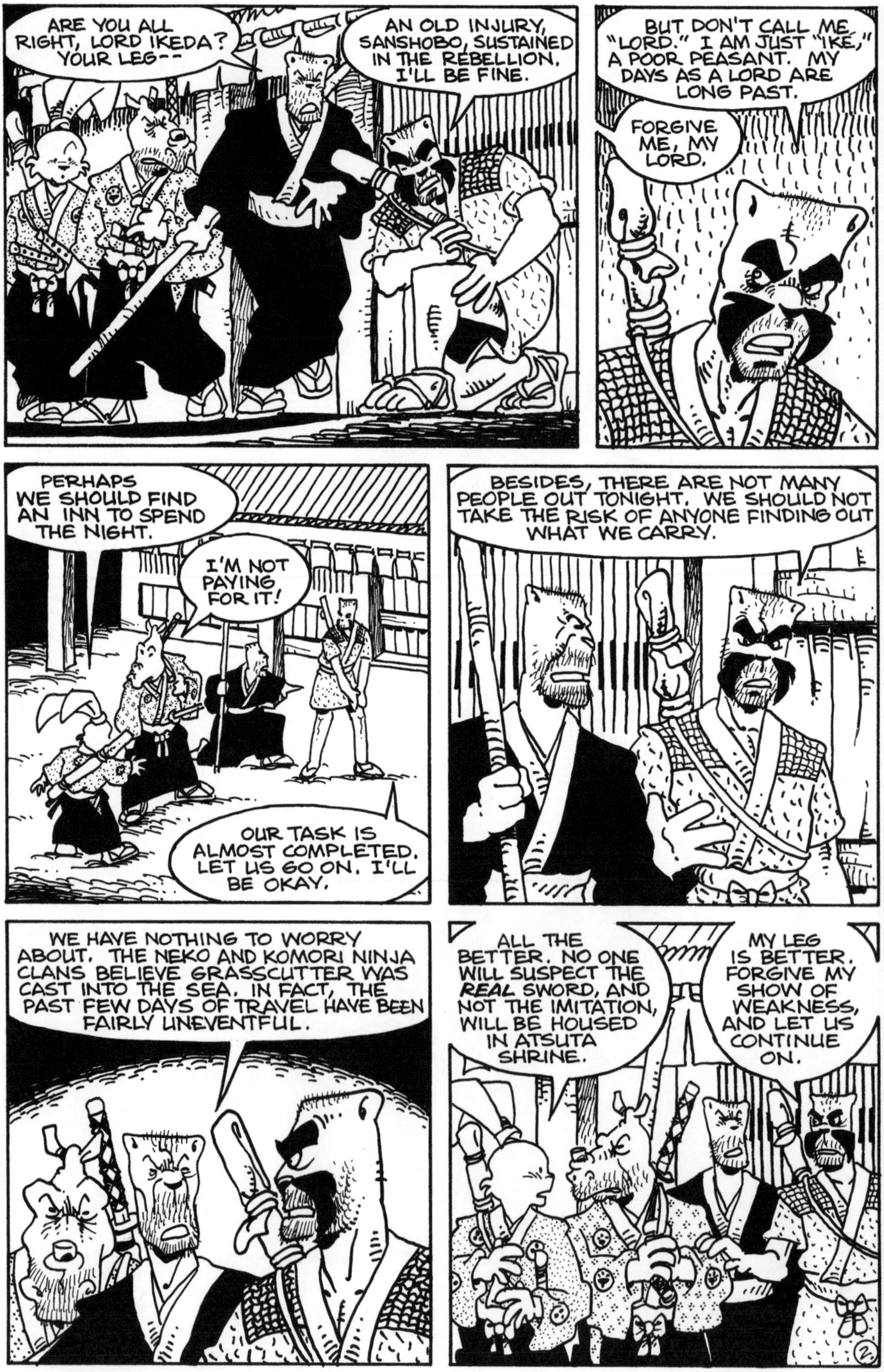
ARE YOU ALL RIGHT, LORD IKEDA? YOUR LEG--
AN OLD INJURY, SANSHOBO, SUSTAINED IN THE REBELLION. I'LL BE FINE.
BUT DON'T CALL ME "LORD." I AM JUST "IKE," A POOR PEASANT. MY DAYS AS A LORD ARE LONG PAST.
FORGIVE ME, MY LORD.
PERHAPS WE SHOULD FIND AN INN TO SPEND THE NIGHT.
I'M NOT PAYING FOR IT!
OUR TASK IS ALMOST COMPLETED. LET US GO ON. I'LL BE OKAY.
BESIDES, THERE ARE NOT MANY PEOPLE OUT TONIGHT. WE SHOULD NOT TAKE THE RISK OF ANYONE FINDING OUT WHAT WE CARRY.
WE HAVE NOTHING TO WORRY ABOUT. THE NEKO AND KOMORI NINJA CLANS BELIEVE GRASSCUTTER WAS CAST INTO THE SEA. IN FACT, THE PAST FEW DAYS OF TRAVEL HAVE BEEN FAIRLY UNEVENTFUL.
ALL THE BETTER. NO ONE WILL SUSPECT THE *REAL* SWORD, AND NOT THE IMITATION, WILL BE HOUSED IN ATSUTA SHRINE.
MY LEG IS BETTER. FORGIVE MY SHOW OF WEAKNESS, AND LET US CONTINUE ON.
2

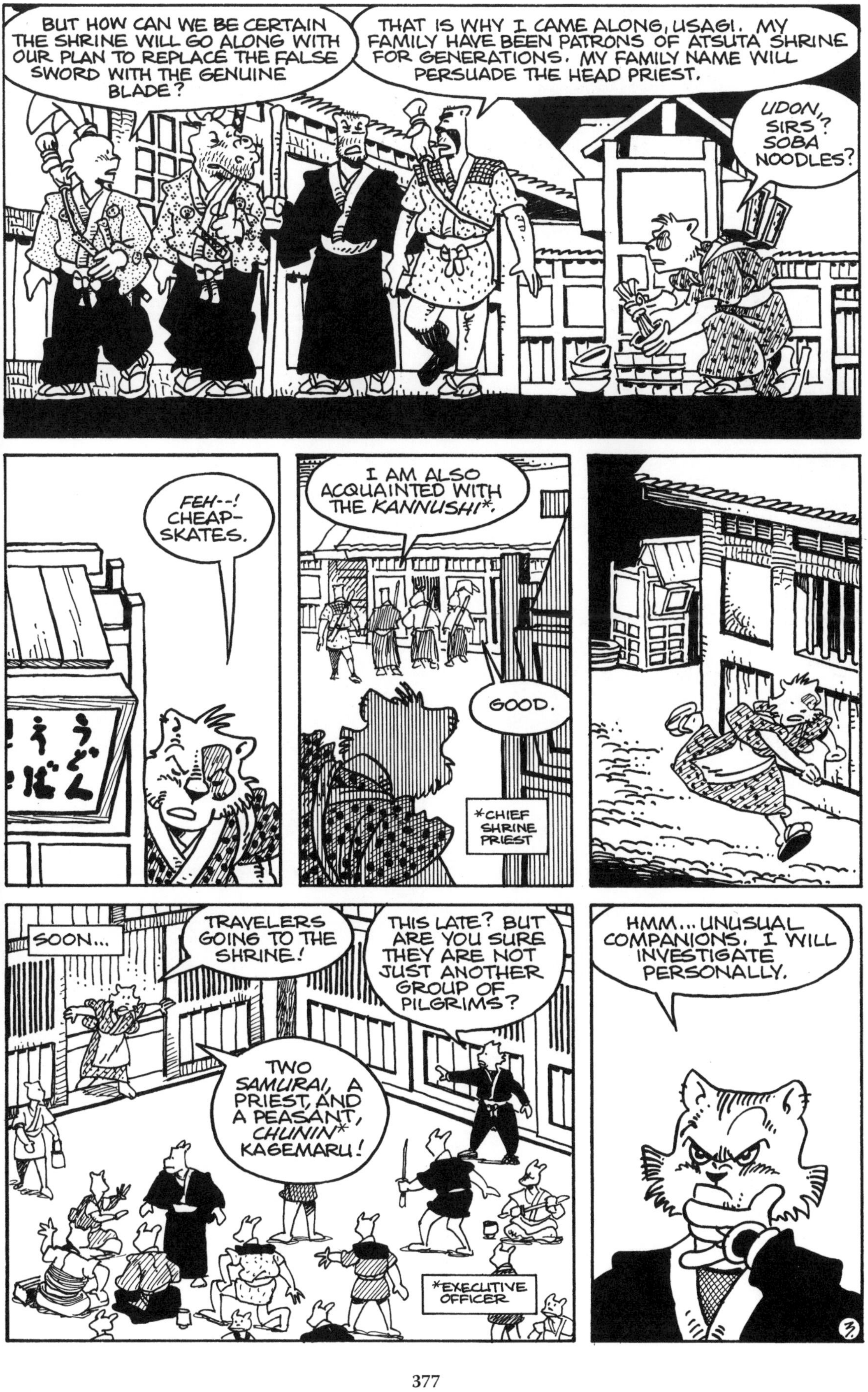
BUT HOW CAN WE BE CERTAIN THE SHRINE WILL GO ALONG WITH OUR PLAN TO REPLACE THE FALSE SWORD WITH THE GENUINE BLADE?
THAT IS WHY I CAME ALONG, USAGI. MY FAMILY HAVE BEEN PATRONS OF ATSUTA SHRINE FOR GENERATIONS. MY FAMILY NAME WILL PERSUADE THE HEAD PRIEST.
UDON, SIRS? SOBA NOODLES?
FEH--! CHEAP-SKATES.
I AM ALSO ACQUAINTED WITH THE *KANNUSHI**.
GOOD.
*CHIEF SHRINE PRIEST
SOON...
TRAVELERS GOING TO THE SHRINE!
THIS LATE? BUT ARE YOU SURE THEY ARE NOT JUST ANOTHER GROUP OF PILGRIMS?
TWO *SAMURAI*, A PRIEST, AND A PEASANT, *CHUNIN** KAGEMARU!
*EXECUTIVE OFFICER
HMM... UNUSUAL COMPANIONS. I WILL INVESTIGATE PERSONALLY.

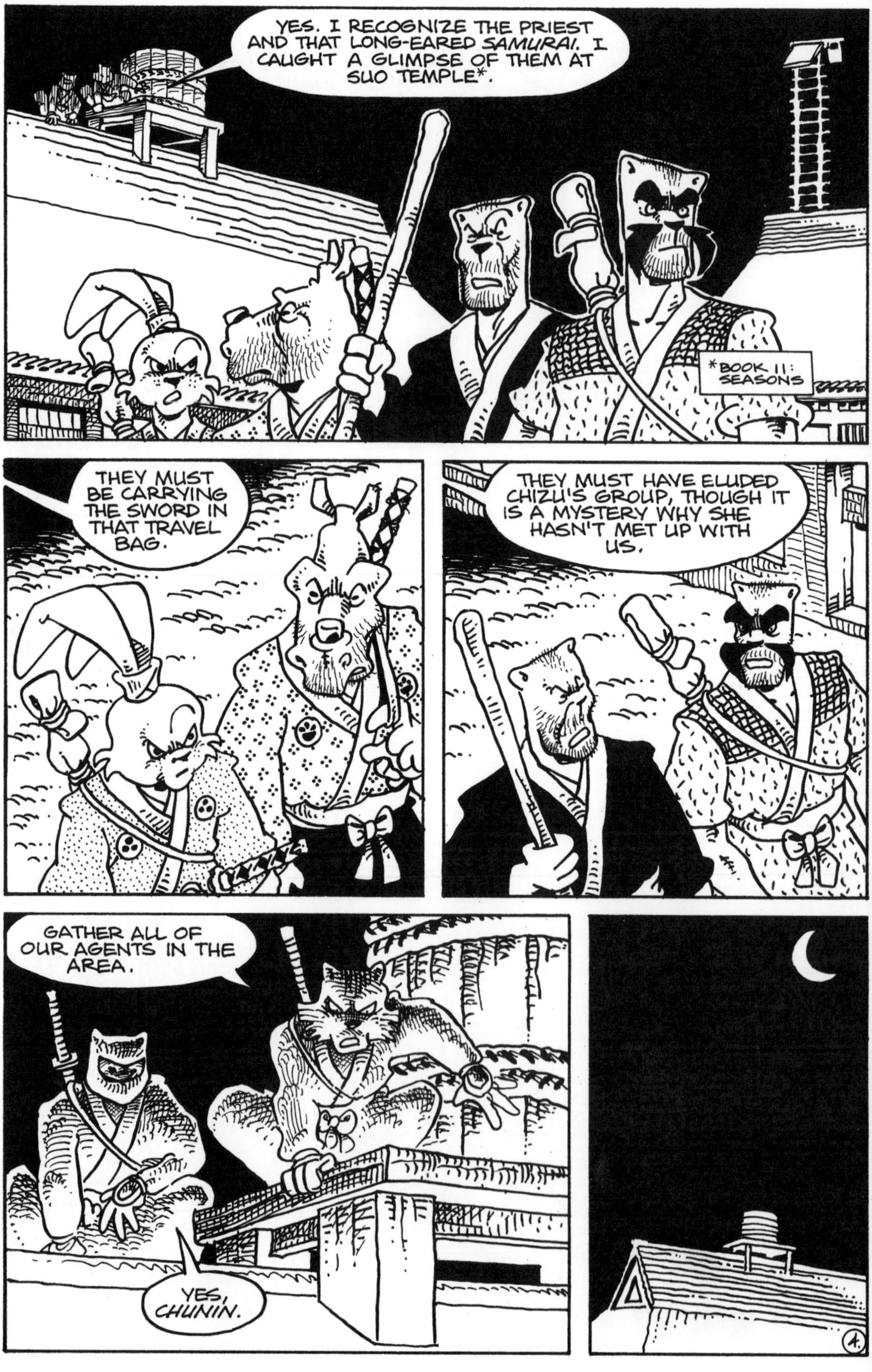

YES. I RECOGNIZE THE PRIEST AND THAT LONG-EARED *SAMURAI*. I CAUGHT A GLIMPSE OF THEM AT SUO TEMPLE*.
*BOOK 11: SEASONS
THEY MUST BE CARRYING THE SWORD IN THAT TRAVEL BAG.
THEY MUST HAVE ELUDED CHIZU'S GROUP, THOUGH IT IS A MYSTERY WHY SHE HASN'T MET UP WITH US.
GATHER ALL OF OUR AGENTS IN THE AREA.
YES, *CHUNIN*.

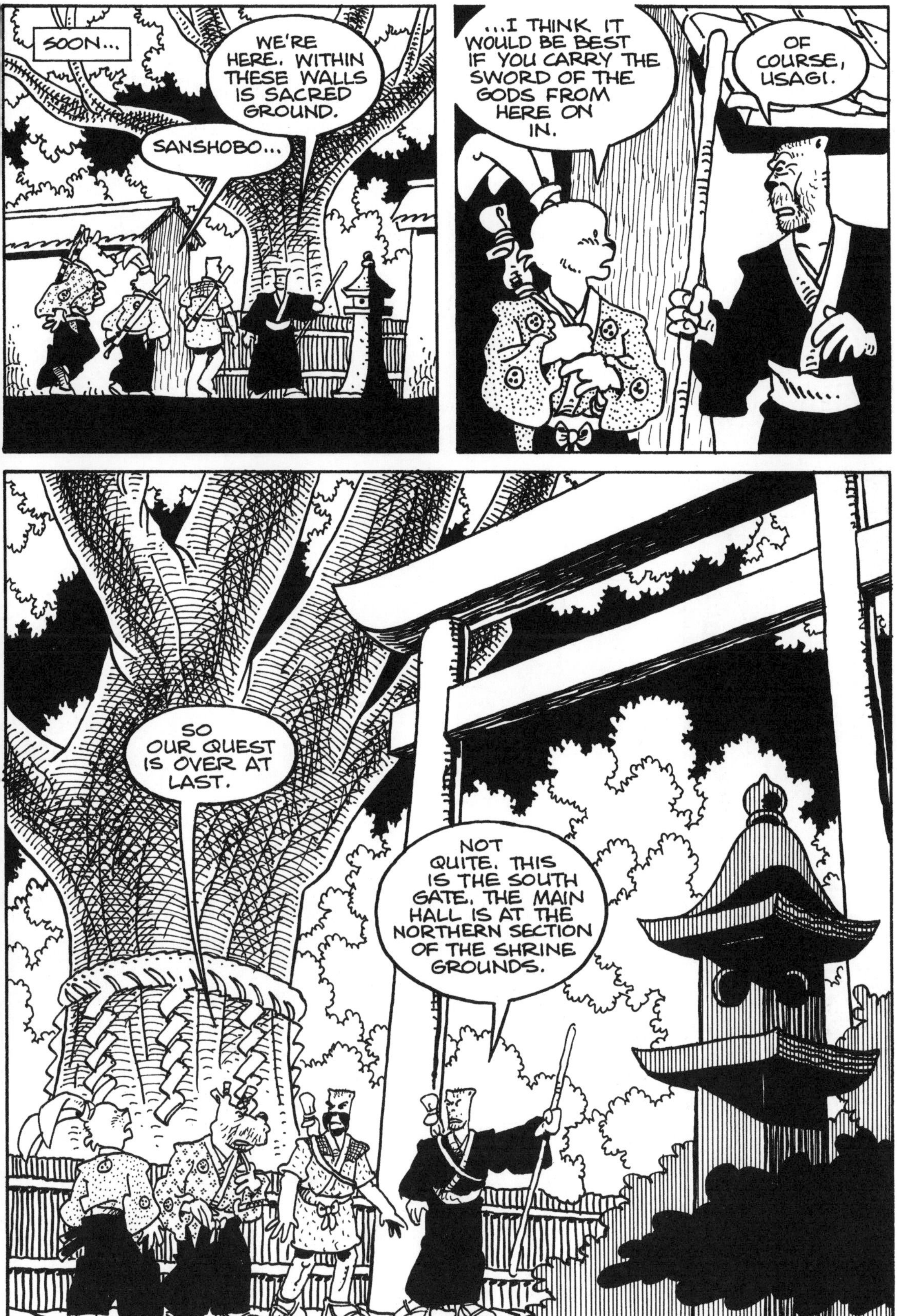
SOON...
SANSHOBO...
WE'RE HERE. WITHIN THESE WALLS IS SACRED GROUND.
...I THINK IT WOULD BE BEST IF YOU CARRY THE SWORD OF THE GODS FROM HERE ON IN.
OF COURSE, USAGI.
SO OUR QUEST IS OVER AT LAST.
NOT QUITE. THIS IS THE SOUTH GATE. THE MAIN HALL IS AT THE NORTHERN SECTION OF THE SHRINE GROUNDS.
5.

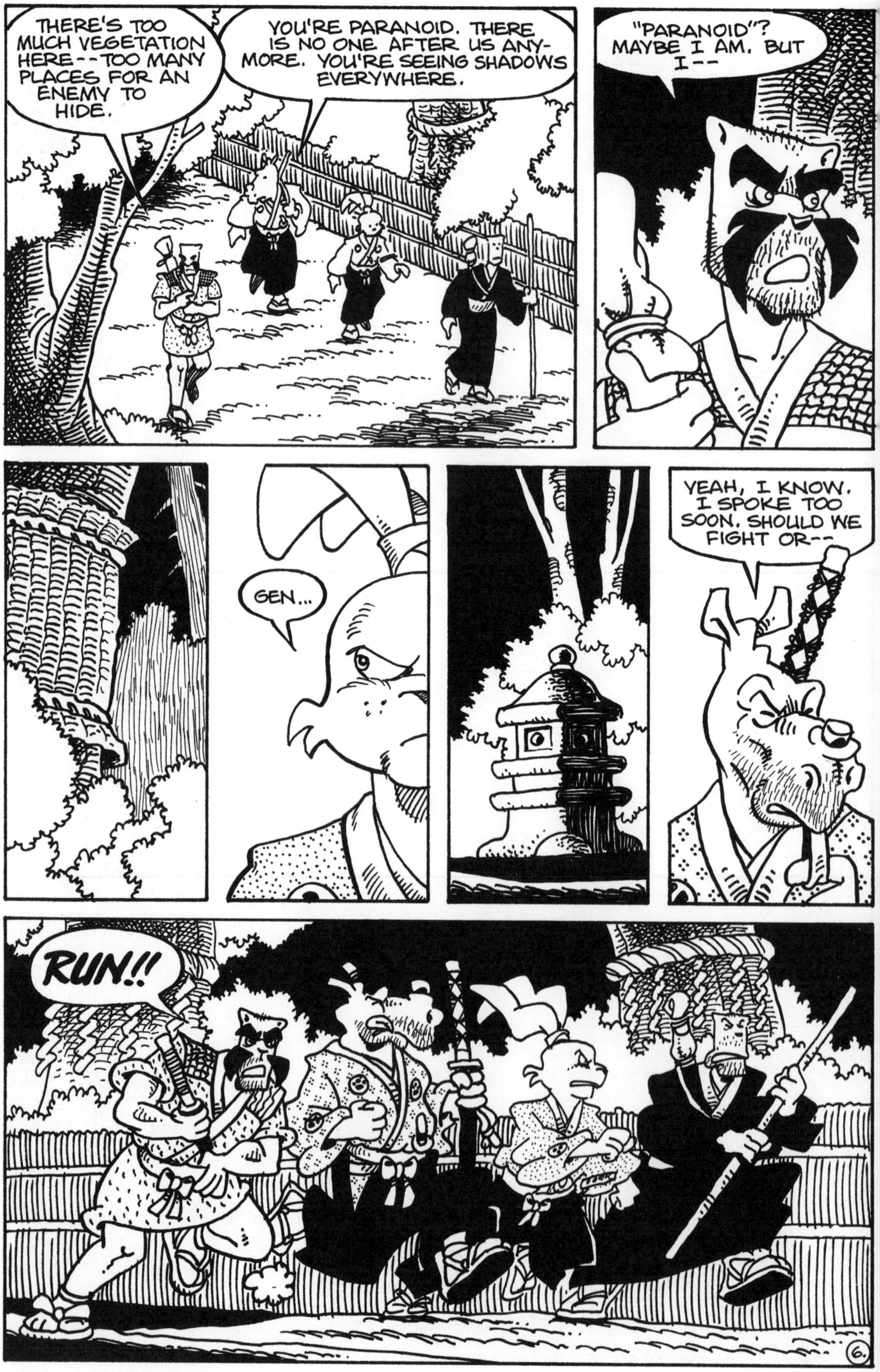
THERE'S TOO MUCH VEGETATION HERE--TOO MANY PLACES FOR AN ENEMY TO HIDE.
YOU'RE PARANOID. THERE IS NO ONE AFTER US ANY-MORE. YOU'RE SEEING SHADOWS EVERYWHERE.
"PARANOID"? MAYBE I AM. BUT I--
GEN...
YEAH, I KNOW. I SPOKE TOO SOON. SHOULD WE FIGHT OR--
RUN!!
6.

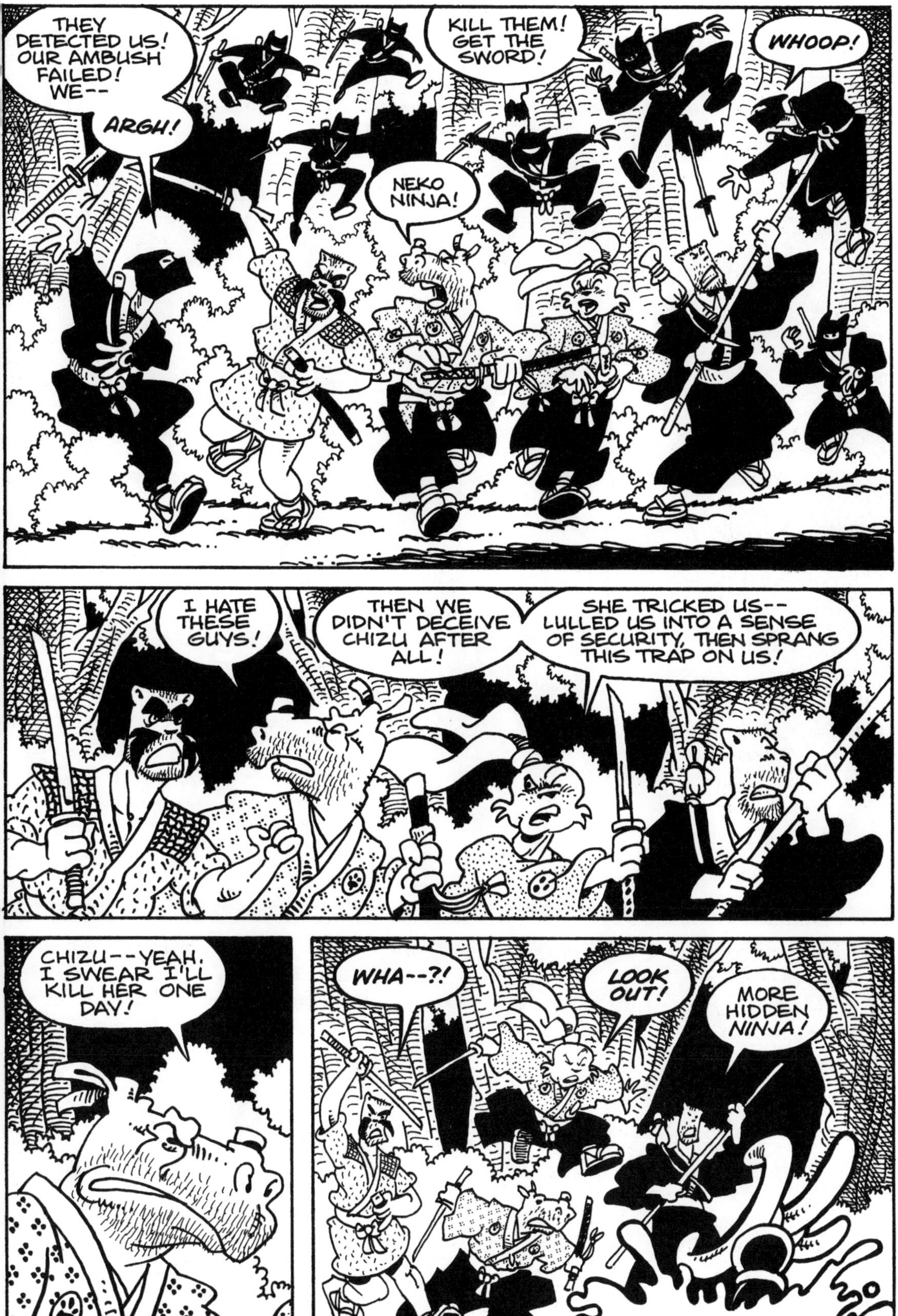
THEY DETECTED US! OUR AMBUSH FAILED! WE--
ARGH!
KILL THEM! GET THE SWORD!
WHOOP!
NEKO NINJA!
I HATE THESE GUYS!
THEN WE DIDN'T DECEIVE CHIZU AFTER ALL!
SHE TRICKED US-- LULLED US INTO A SENSE OF SECURITY, THEN SPRANG THIS TRAP ON US!
CHIZU--YEAH. I SWEAR I'LL KILL HER ONE DAY!
WHA--?!
LOOK OUT!
MORE HIDDEN NINJA!
7.

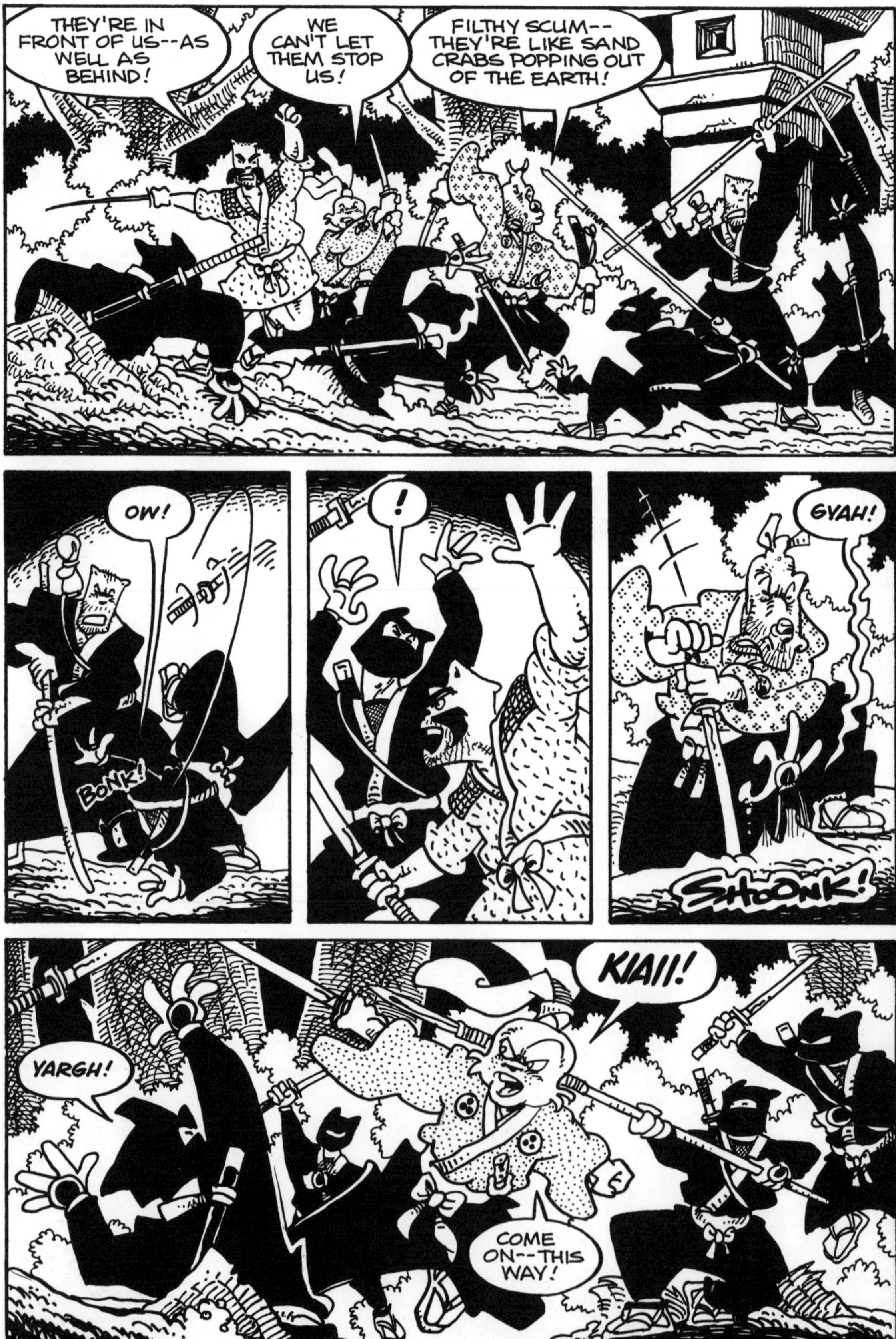
THEY'RE IN FRONT OF US--AS WELL AS BEHIND!
WE CAN'T LET THEM STOP US!
FILTHY SCUM-- THEY'RE LIKE SAND CRABS POPPING OUT OF THE EARTH!
OW!
BONK!
!
GYAH!
SHOONK!
YARGH!
KIAII!
COME ON--THIS WAY!
8.

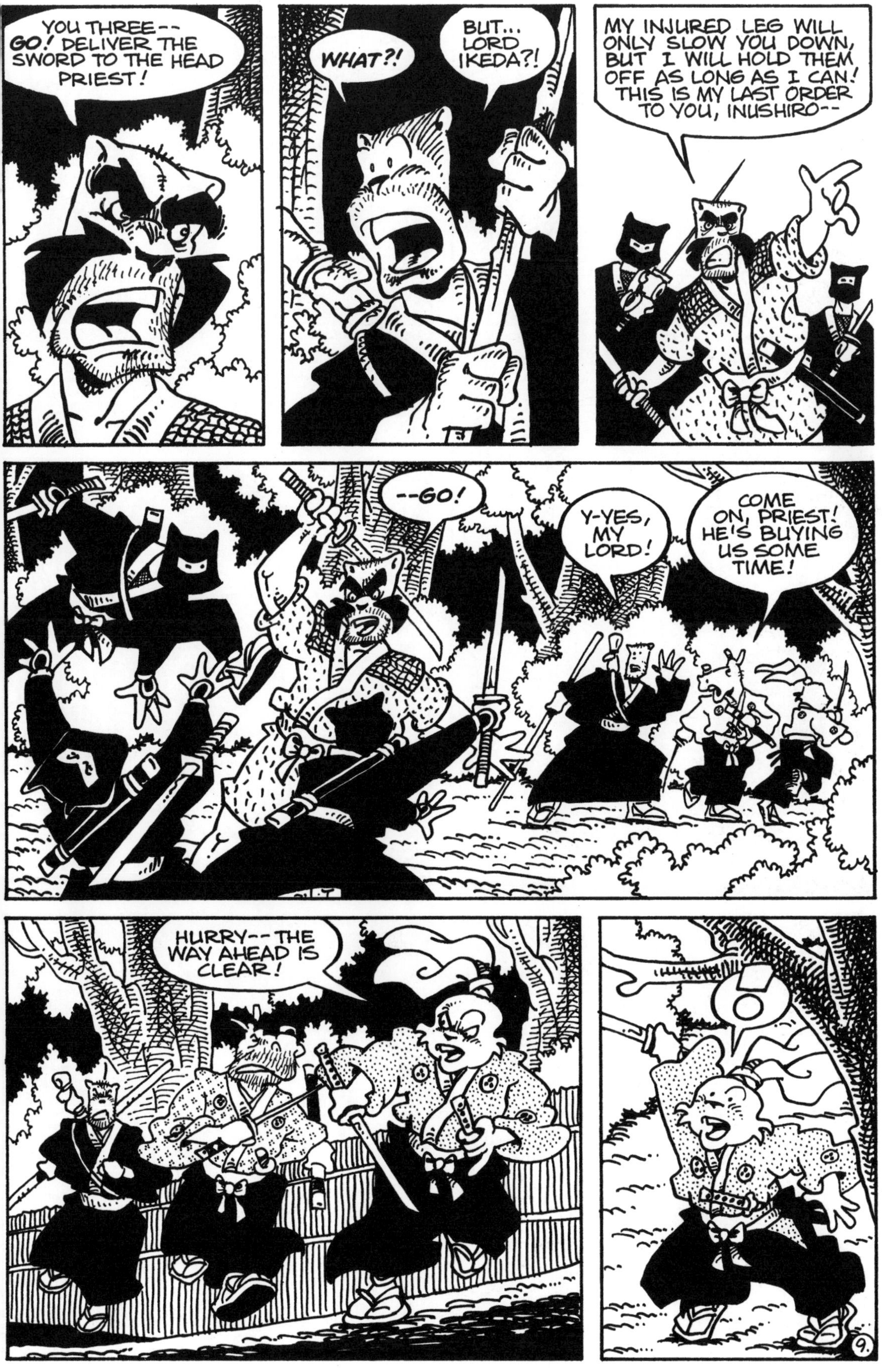
YOU THREE-- GO! DELIVER THE SWORD TO THE HEAD PRIEST!
WHAT?!
BUT... LORD IKEDA?!
MY INJURED LEG WILL ONLY SLOW YOU DOWN, BUT I WILL HOLD THEM OFF AS LONG AS I CAN! THIS IS MY LAST ORDER TO YOU, INUSHIRO--
--GO!
Y-YES, MY LORD!
COME ON, PRIEST! HE'S BUYING US SOME TIME!
HURRY-- THE WAY AHEAD IS CLEAR!
9.

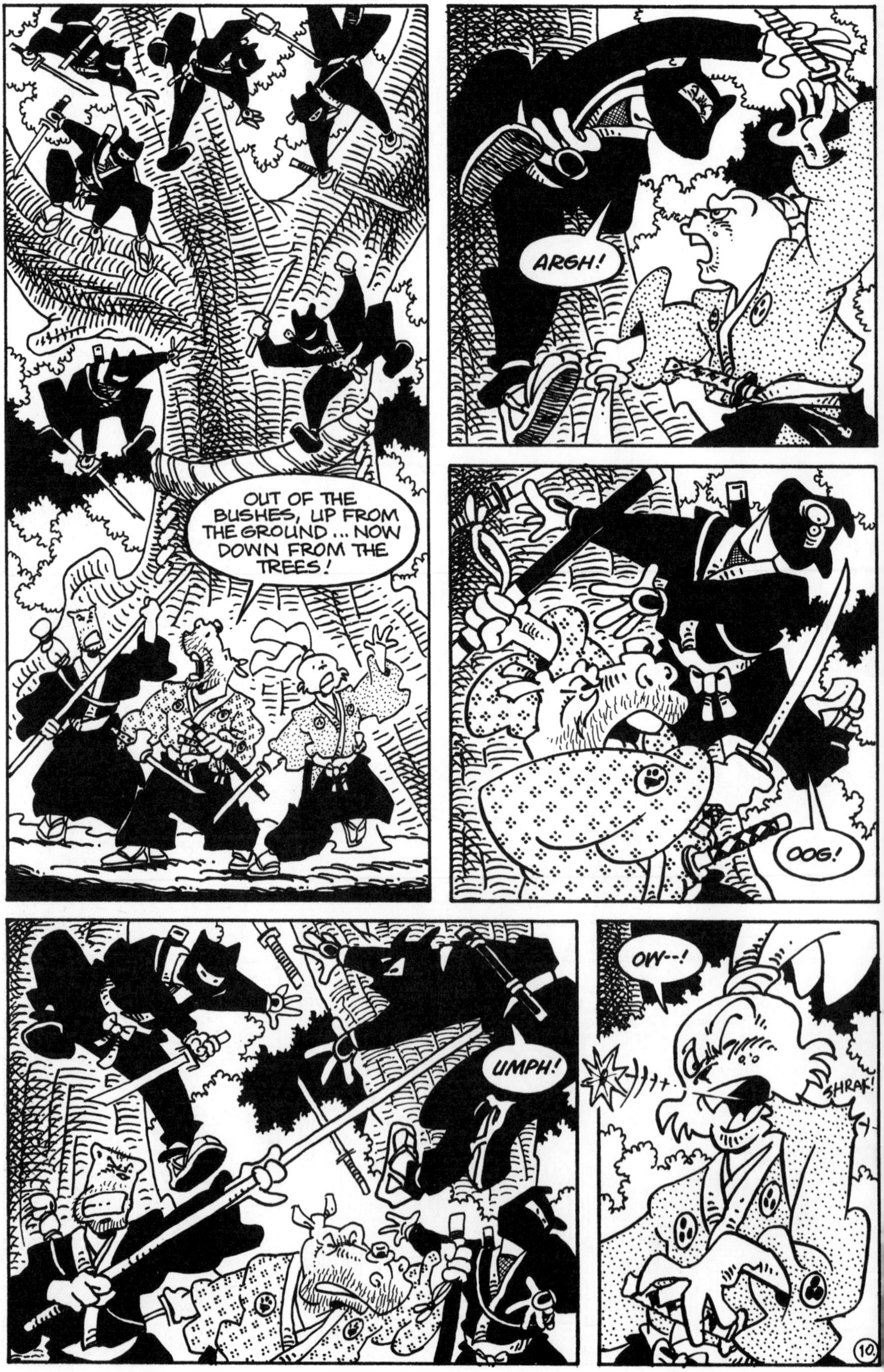

OUT OF THE BUSHES, UP FROM THE GROUND ... NOW DOWN FROM THE TREES!
ARGH!
OOG!
UMPH!
OW--!
SHRAK!
10.

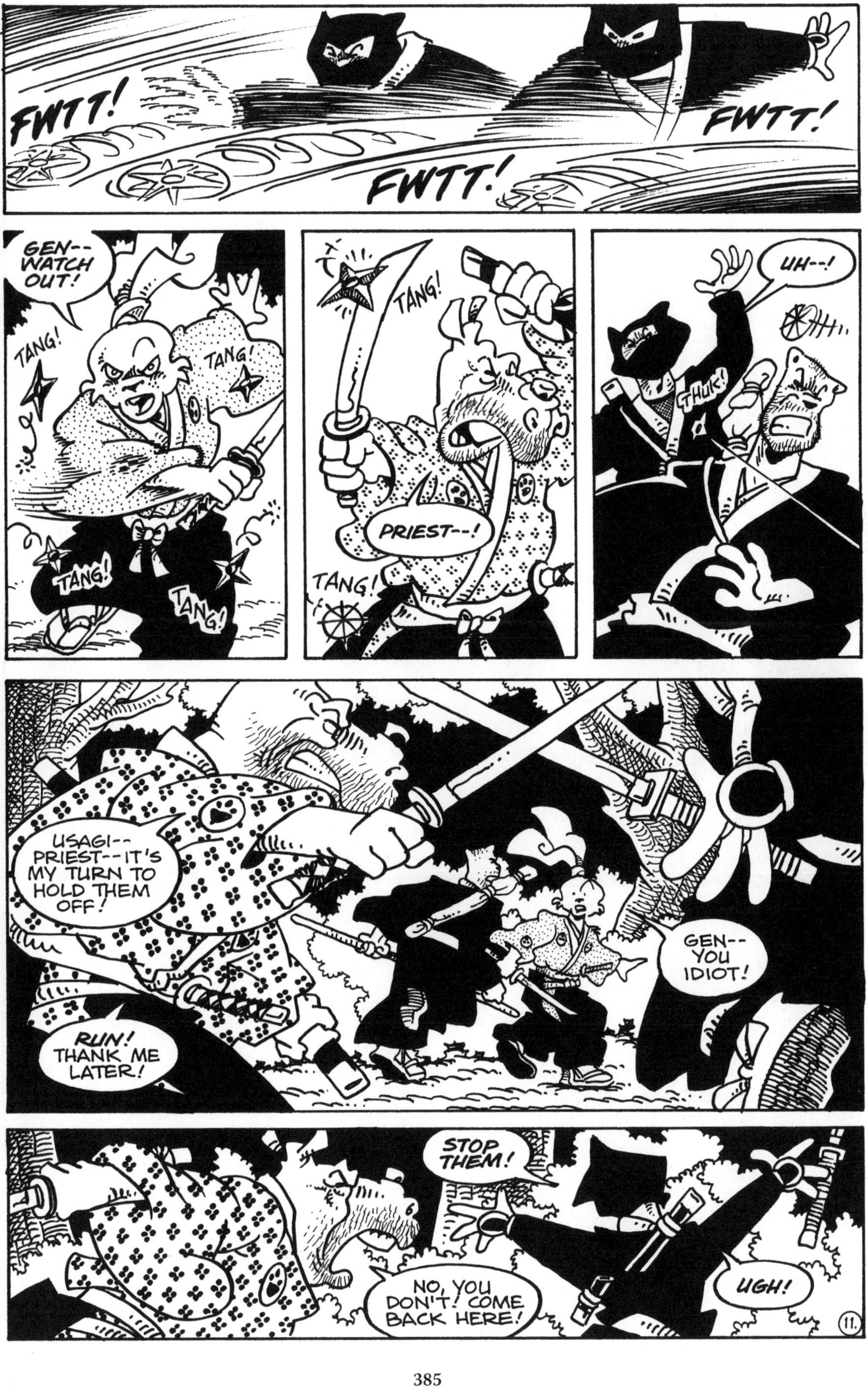
FWTT!
FWTT!
FWTT!
GEN-- WATCH OUT!
TANG!
TANG!
TANG!
TANG!
TANG!
TANG!
PRIEST--!
TANG!
UH--!
THUK!
USAGI-- PRIEST--IT'S MY TURN TO HOLD THEM OFF!
RUN! THANK ME LATER!
GEN-- YOU IDIOT!
STOP THEM!
NO, YOU DON'T! COME BACK HERE!
UGH!
11.

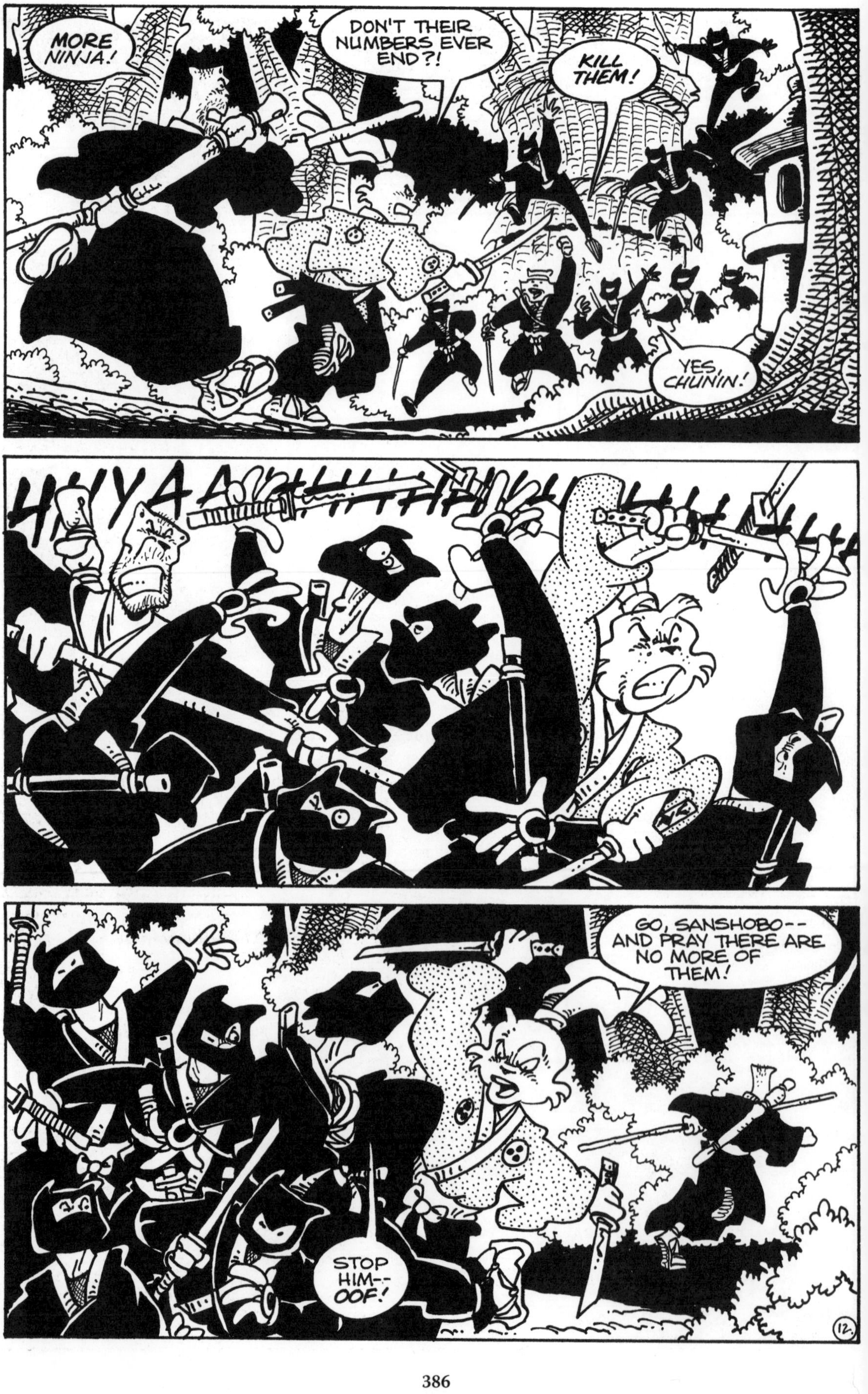
MORE NINJA!
DON'T THEIR NUMBERS EVER END?!
KILL THEM!
YES, CHUNIN!
HIIYAA
GO, SANSHOBO-- AND PRAY THERE ARE NO MORE OF THEM!
STOP HIM-- OOF!
12.

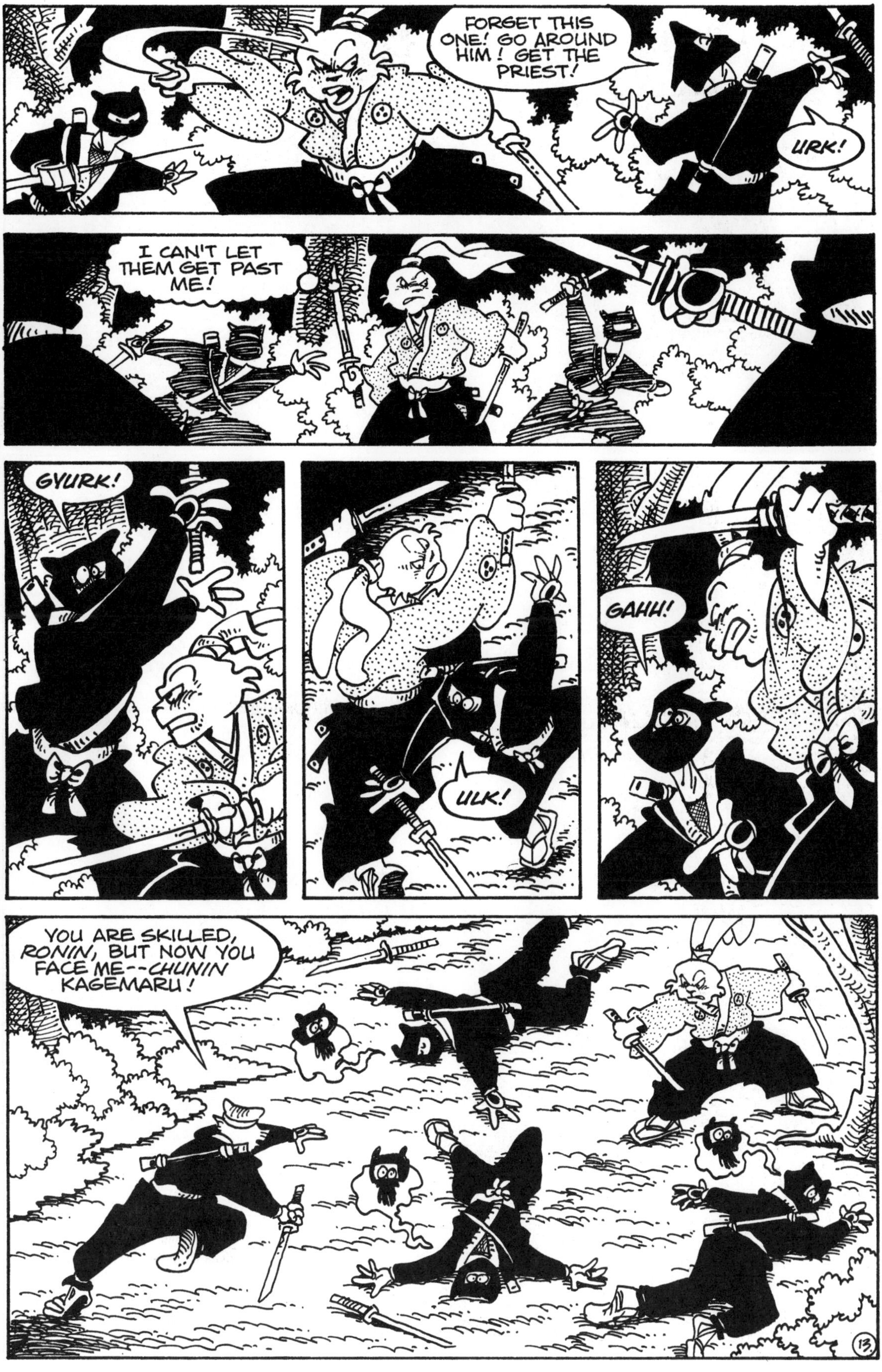
FORGET THIS ONE! GO AROUND HIM! GET THE PRIEST!
URK!
I CAN'T LET THEM GET PAST ME!
GYURK!
ULK!
GAHH!
YOU ARE SKILLED, *RONIN*, BUT NOW YOU FACE ME--*CHUNIN* KAGEMARU!
13

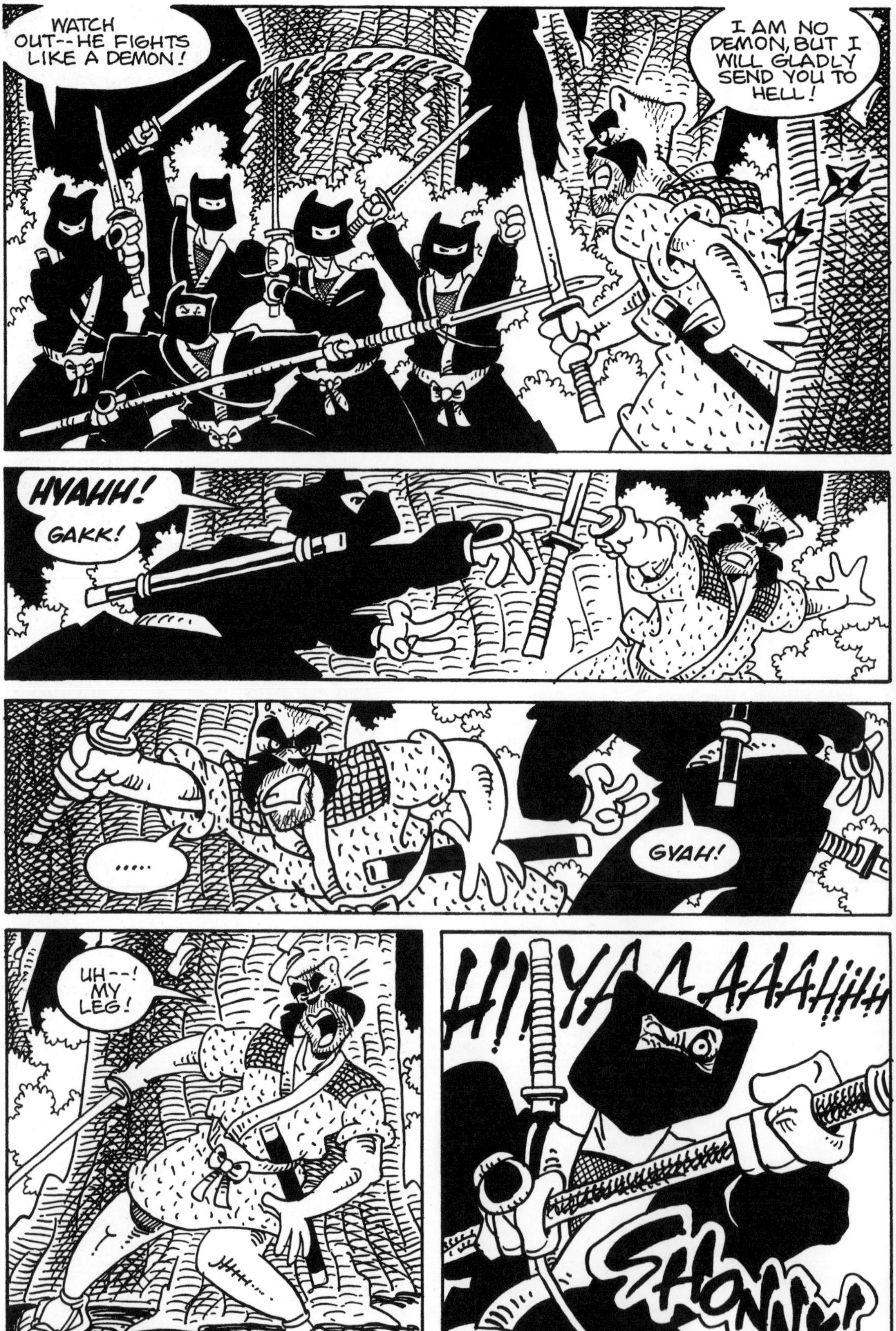
WATCH OUT--HE FIGHTS LIKE A DEMON!
I AM NO DEMON, BUT I WILL GLADLY SEND YOU TO HELL!
HYAHH!
GAKK!
.....
GYAH!
UH--! MY LEG!
HIYAAAAHHHH!
SHONNK!
14.

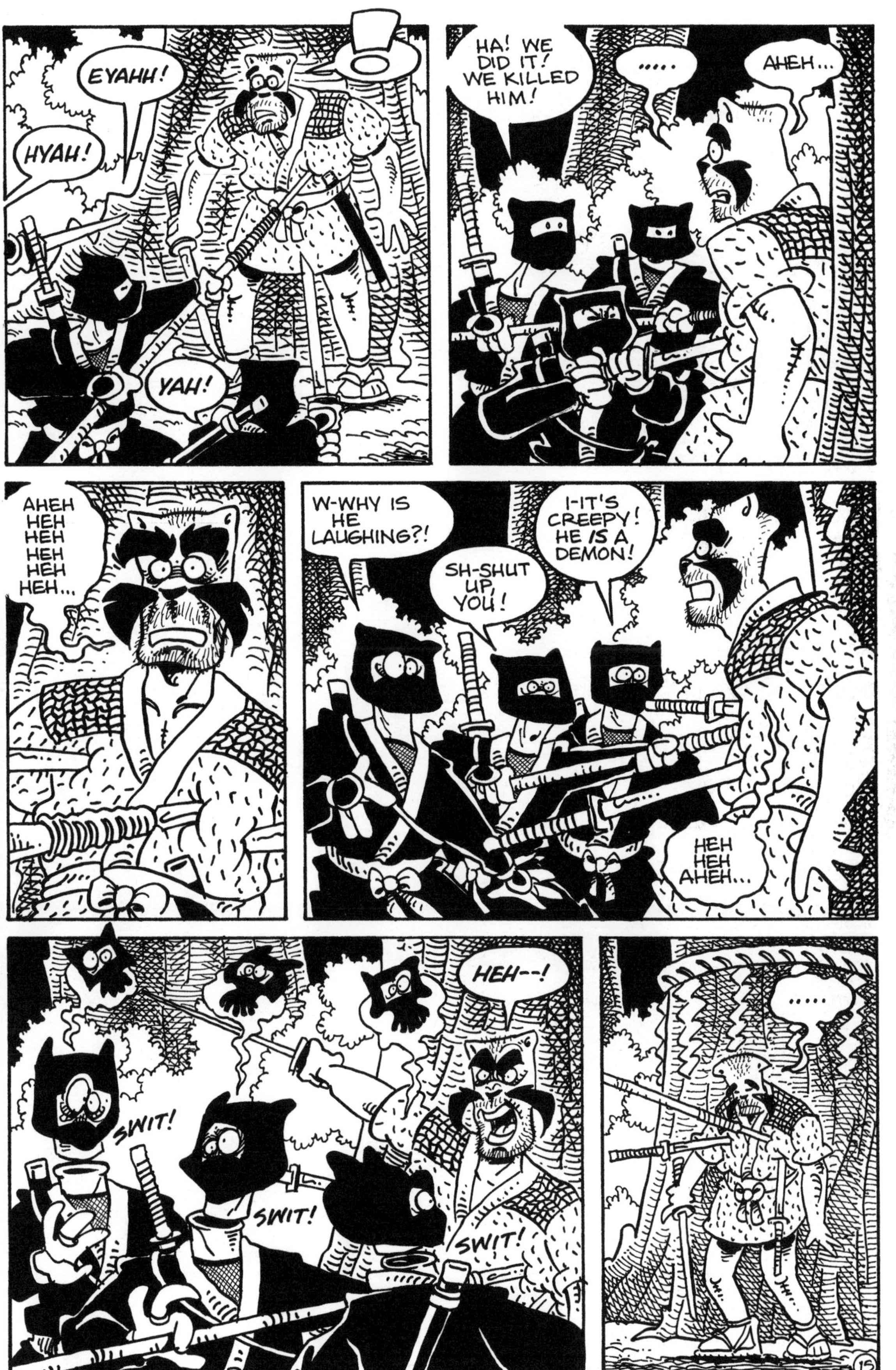
EYAHH!
HYAH!
YAH!
HA! WE DID IT! WE KILLED HIM!
.....
AHEH...
AHEH HEH HEH HEH HEH HEH...
W-WHY IS HE LAUGHING?!
SH-SHUT UP, YOU!
I-IT'S CREEPY! HE IS A DEMON!
HEH HEH AHEH...
HEH--!
SWIT!
SWIT!
SWIT!
.....
15

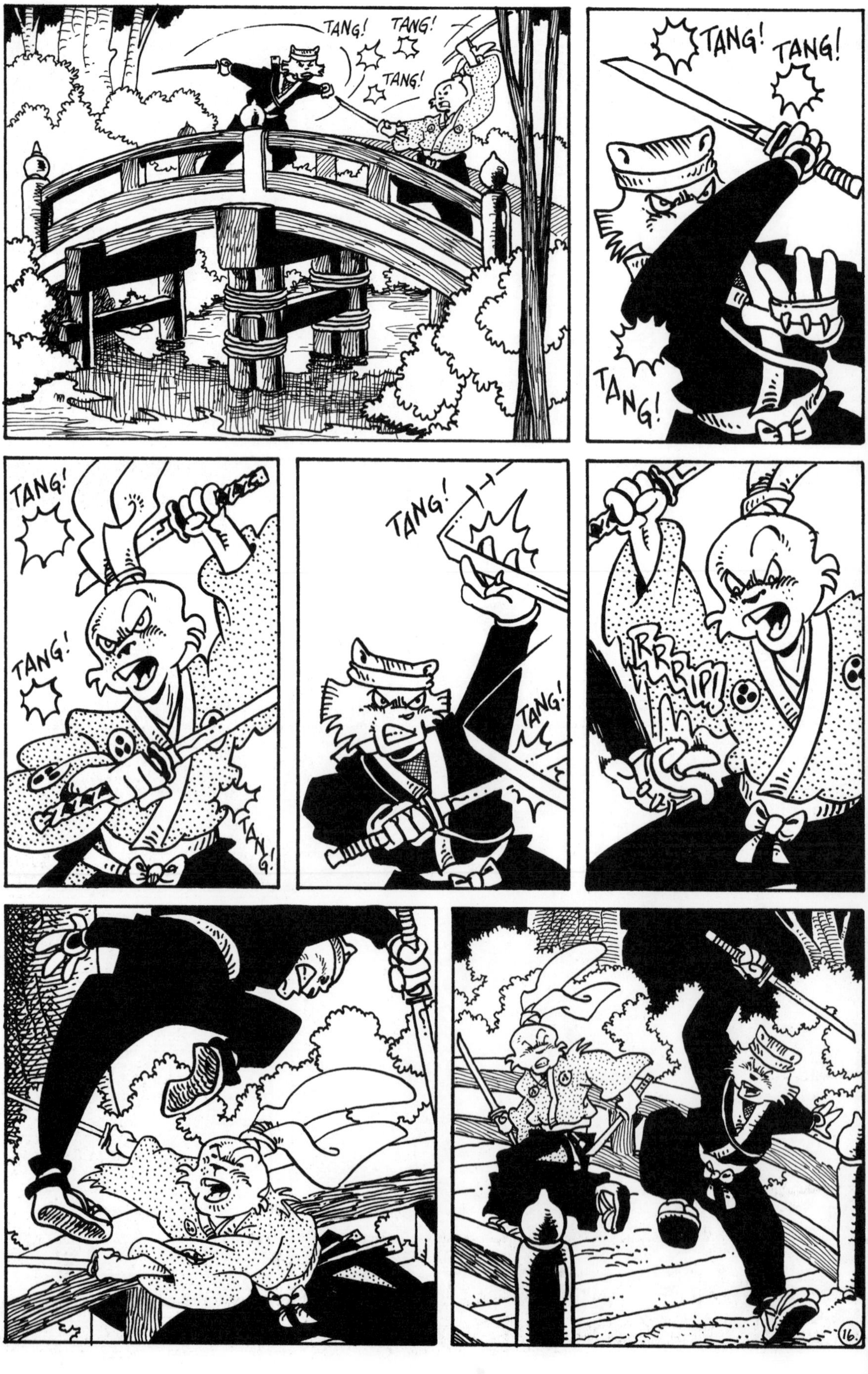

TANG!
TANG!
TANG!
TANG!
TANG!
TANG!
TANG!
TANG!
TANG!
TANG!
TANG!
RRRRIP!!
16.

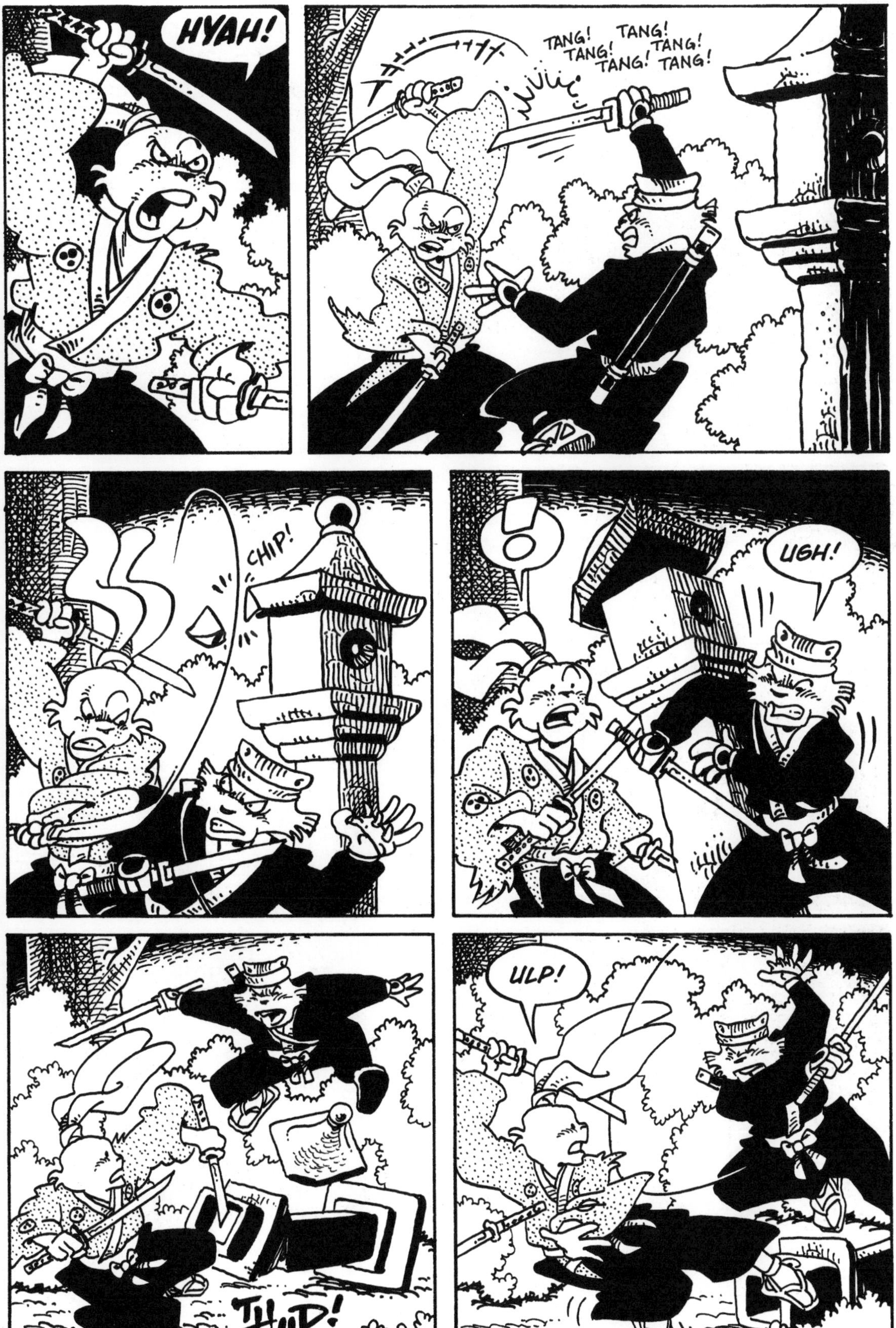
HYAH!
TANG! TANG! TANG! TANG! TANG! TANG! TANG!
CHIP!
!
UGH!
THUD!
ULP!
17

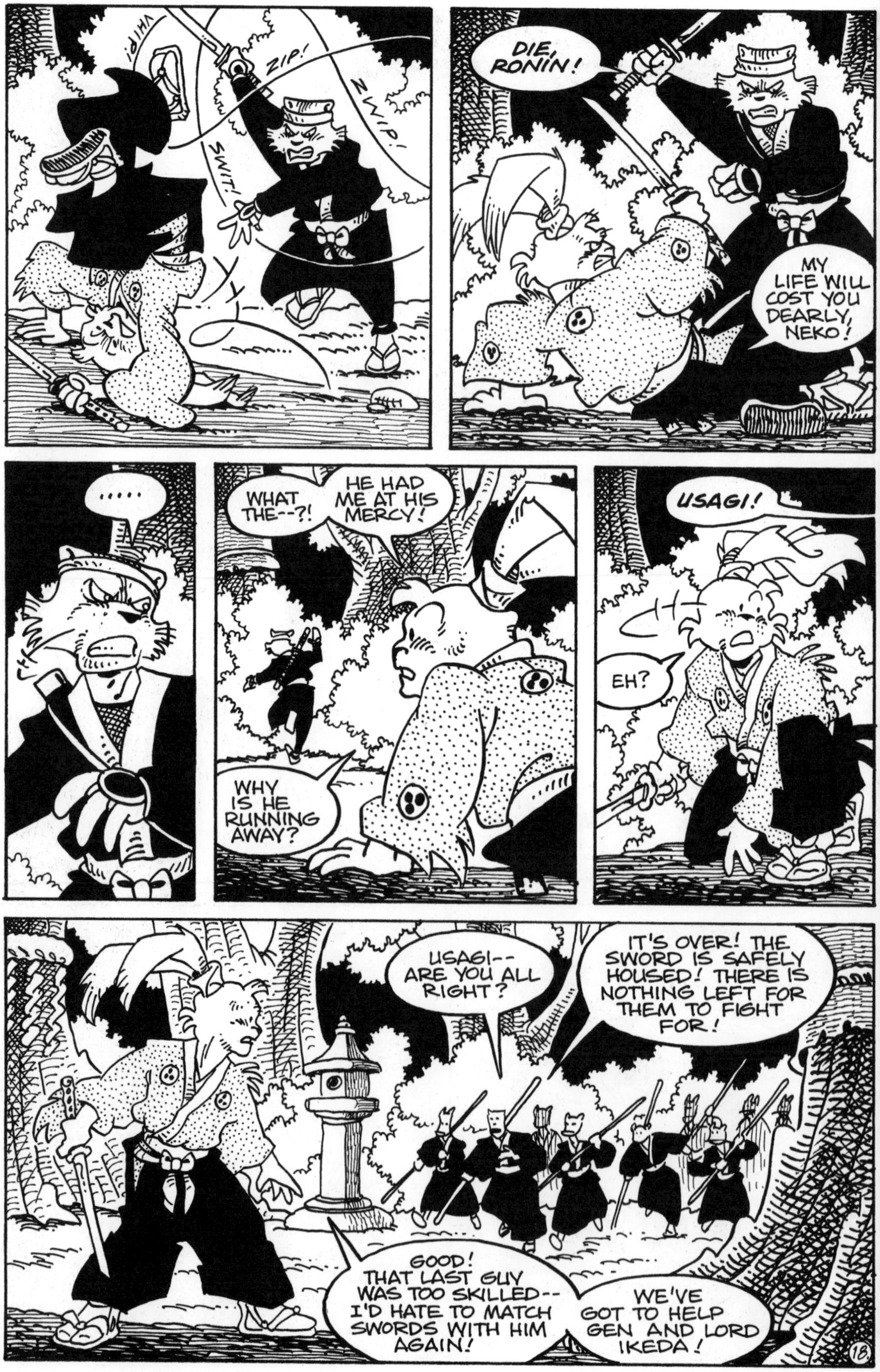
WHIP!
ZIP!
ZWIP!
SWIT!
DIE, RONIN!
MY LIFE WILL COST YOU DEARLY, NEKO!
......
WHAT THE--?!
HE HAD ME AT HIS MERCY!
WHY IS HE RUNNING AWAY?
USAGI!
EH?
USAGI-- ARE YOU ALL RIGHT?
IT'S OVER! THE SWORD IS SAFELY HOUSED! THERE IS NOTHING LEFT FOR THEM TO FIGHT FOR!
GOOD! THAT LAST GUY WAS TOO SKILLED-- I'D HATE TO MATCH SWORDS WITH HIM AGAIN!
WE'VE GOT TO HELP GEN AND LORD IKEDA!
18

PANT! GASP! CAN'T KEEP THIS UP MUCH LONGER!
HUFF! HUFF! GASP! PANT!
FWEET!
THE SIGNAL!
PHEW!
GASP! YEAH. PANT! NEVER BEEN GASP! BETTER.
GEN--ARE YOU OKAY?
LORD IKEDA!
19.

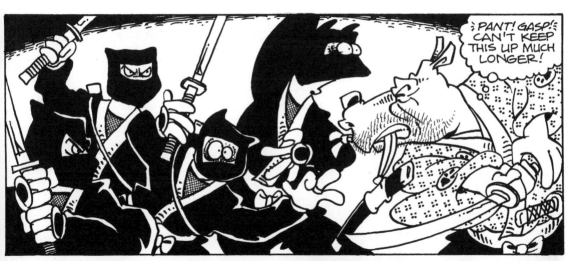

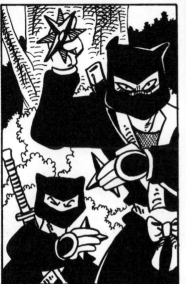

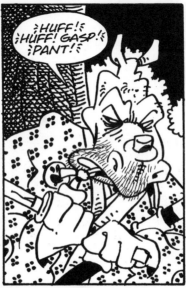

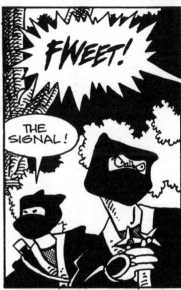

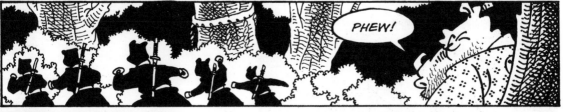

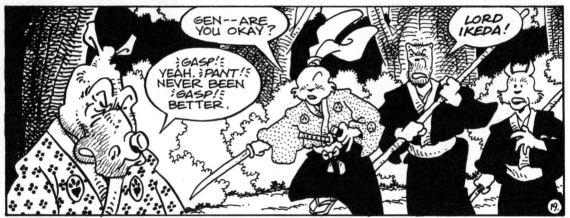

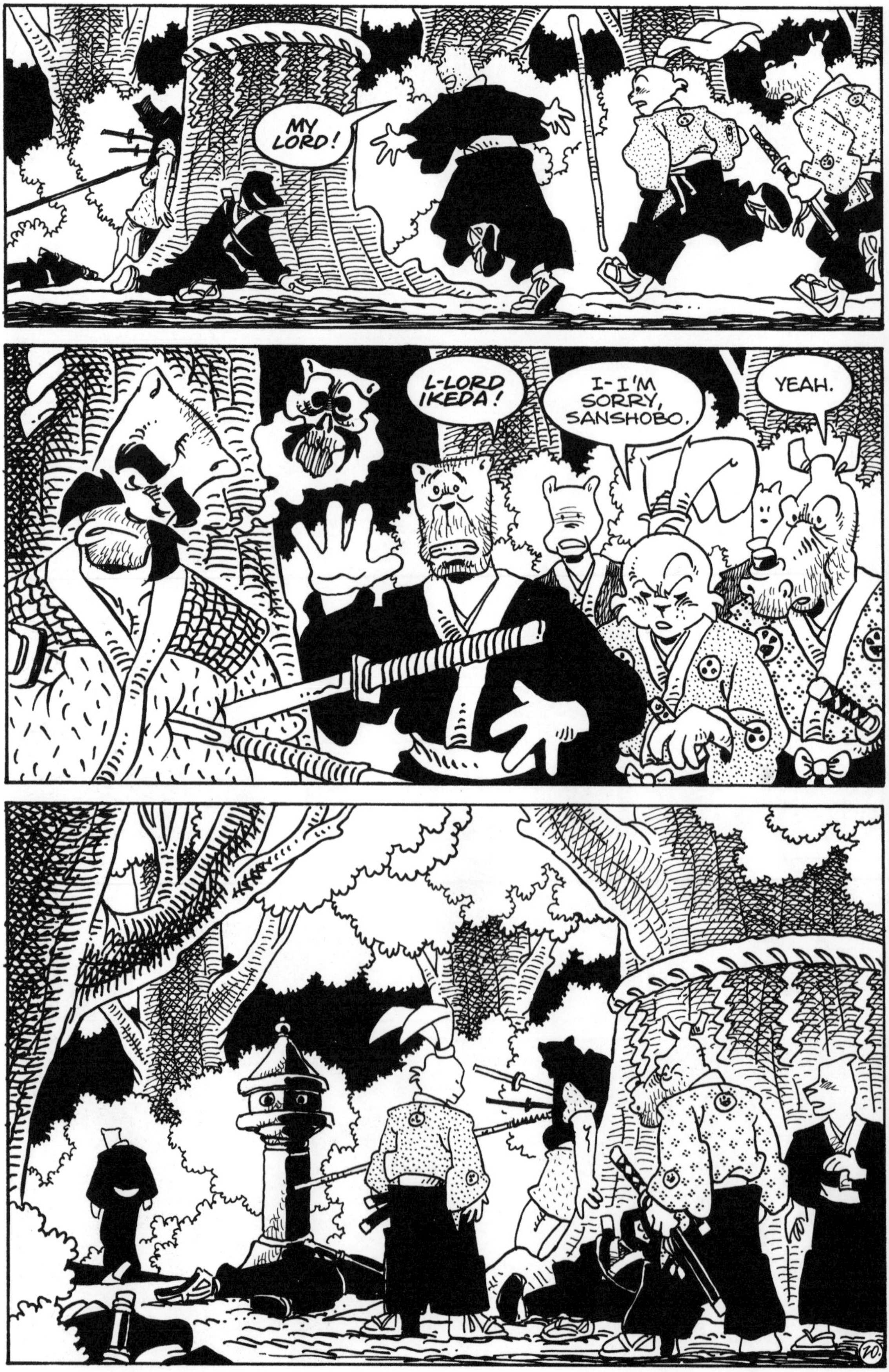
MY LORD!
L-LORD IKEDA!
I-I'M SORRY, SANSHOBO.
YEAH.

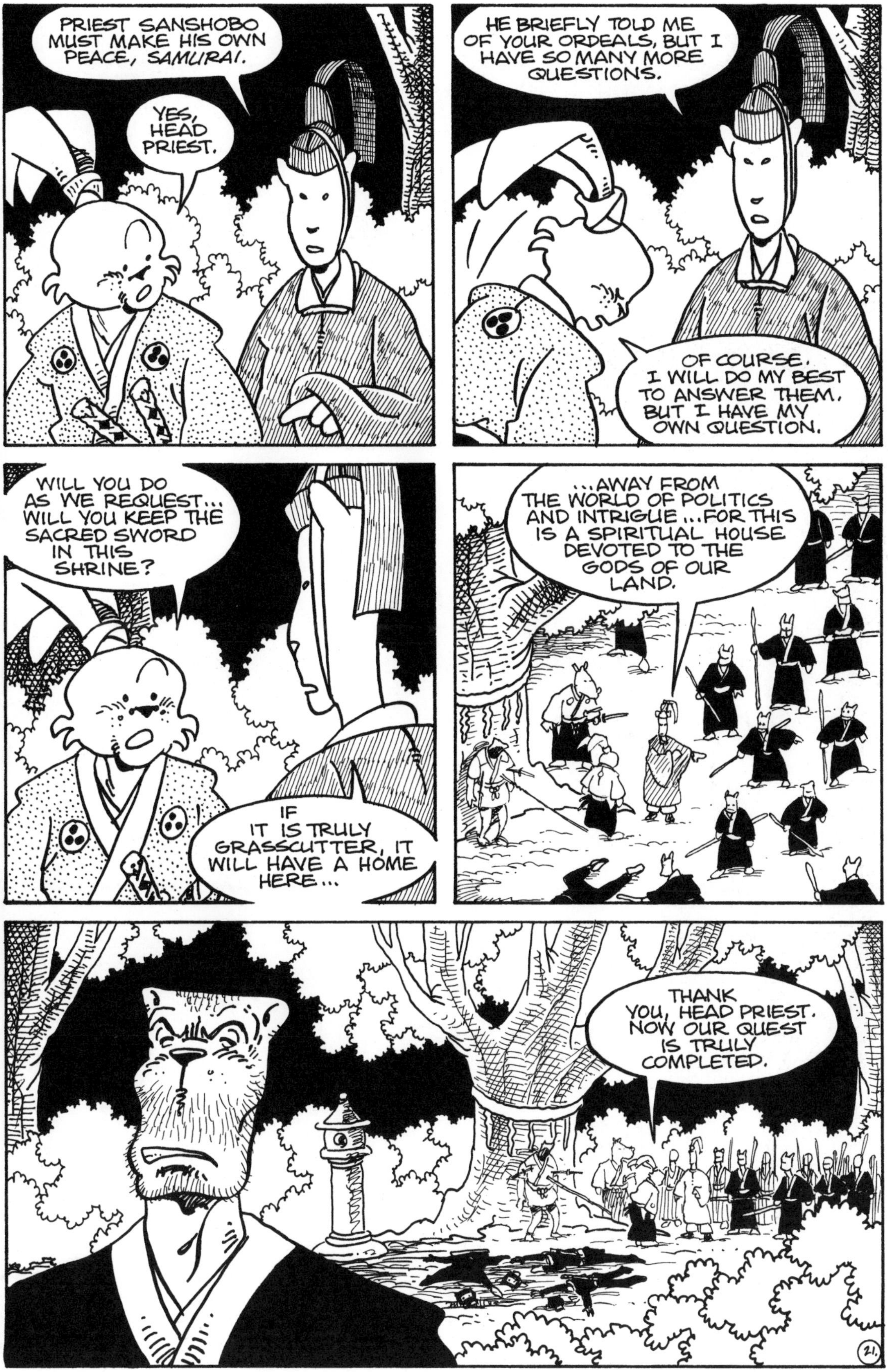
PRIEST SANSHOBO MUST MAKE HIS OWN PEACE, SAMURAI.
YES, HEAD PRIEST.
HE BRIEFLY TOLD ME OF YOUR ORDEALS, BUT I HAVE SO MANY MORE QUESTIONS.
OF COURSE. I WILL DO MY BEST TO ANSWER THEM. BUT I HAVE MY OWN QUESTION.
WILL YOU DO AS WE REQUEST... WILL YOU KEEP THE SACRED SWORD IN THIS SHRINE?
IF IT IS TRULY GRASSCUTTER, IT WILL HAVE A HOME HERE...
...AWAY FROM THE WORLD OF POLITICS AND INTRIGUE...FOR THIS IS A SPIRITUAL HOUSE DEVOTED TO THE GODS OF OUR LAND.
THANK YOU, HEAD PRIEST. NOW OUR QUEST IS TRULY COMPLETED.
21.

EPILOGUE I

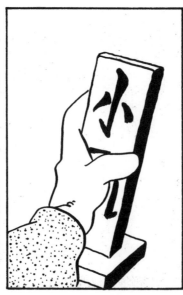

KASHIRA...?

YES, KIMI?

SHUNICHI HAS DIED.

I HAD HOPED HIS INJURIES WOULD NOT BE FATAL. I WILL SET OUT A MEMORIAL PLAQUE FOR HIM.

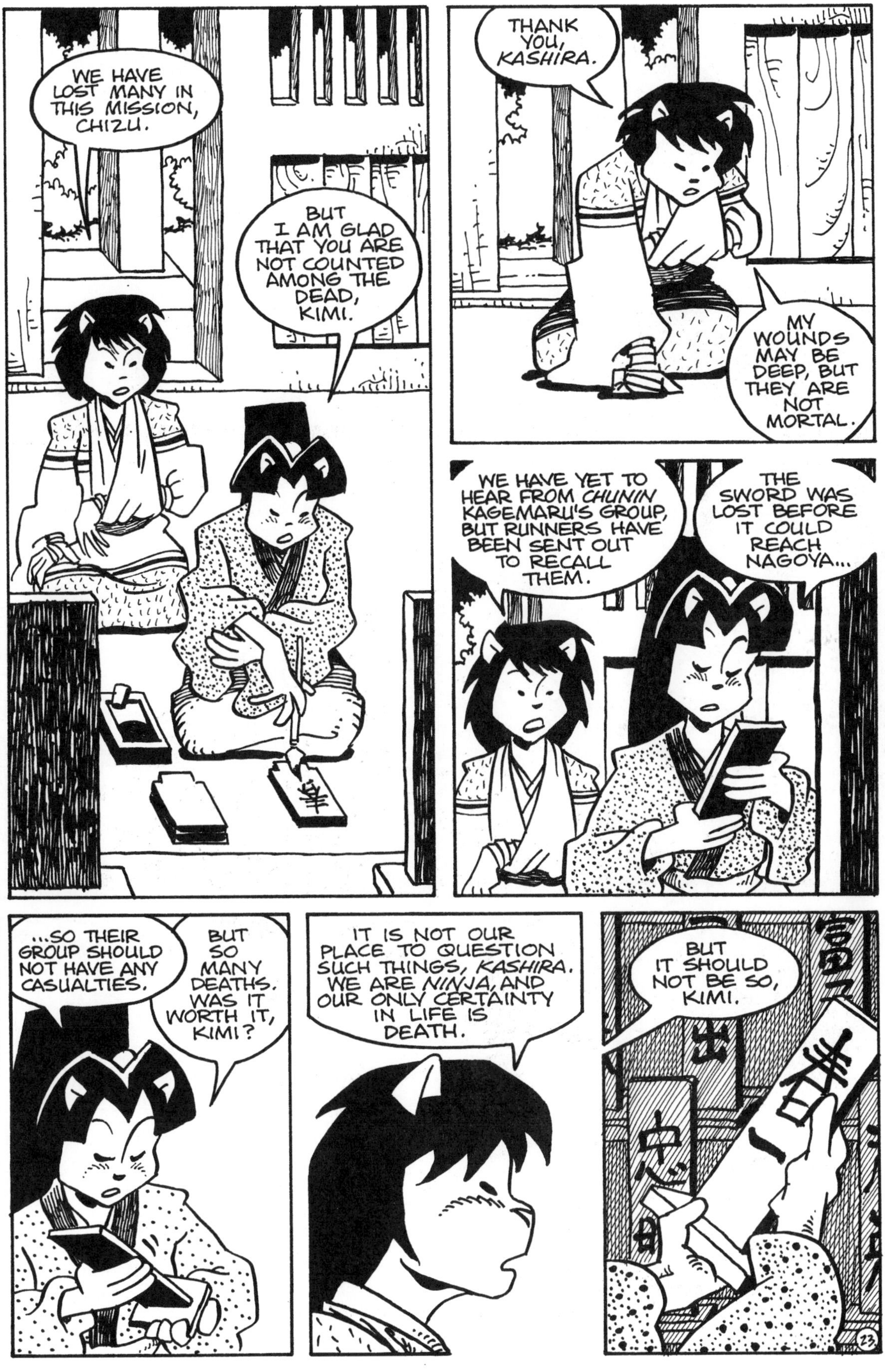
WE HAVE LOST MANY IN THIS MISSION, CHIZU.
BUT I AM GLAD THAT YOU ARE NOT COUNTED AMONG THE DEAD, KIMI.
THANK YOU, KASHIRA.
MY WOUNDS MAY BE DEEP, BUT THEY ARE NOT MORTAL.
WE HAVE YET TO HEAR FROM CHUNIN KAGEMARU'S GROUP, BUT RUNNERS HAVE BEEN SENT OUT TO RECALL THEM.
THE SWORD WAS LOST BEFORE IT COULD REACH NAGOYA...
...SO THEIR GROUP SHOULD NOT HAVE ANY CASUALTIES.
BUT SO MANY DEATHS. WAS IT WORTH IT, KIMI?
IT IS NOT OUR PLACE TO QUESTION SUCH THINGS, KASHIRA. WE ARE NINJA, AND OUR ONLY CERTAINTY IN LIFE IS DEATH.
BUT IT SHOULD NOT BE SO, KIMI.
23

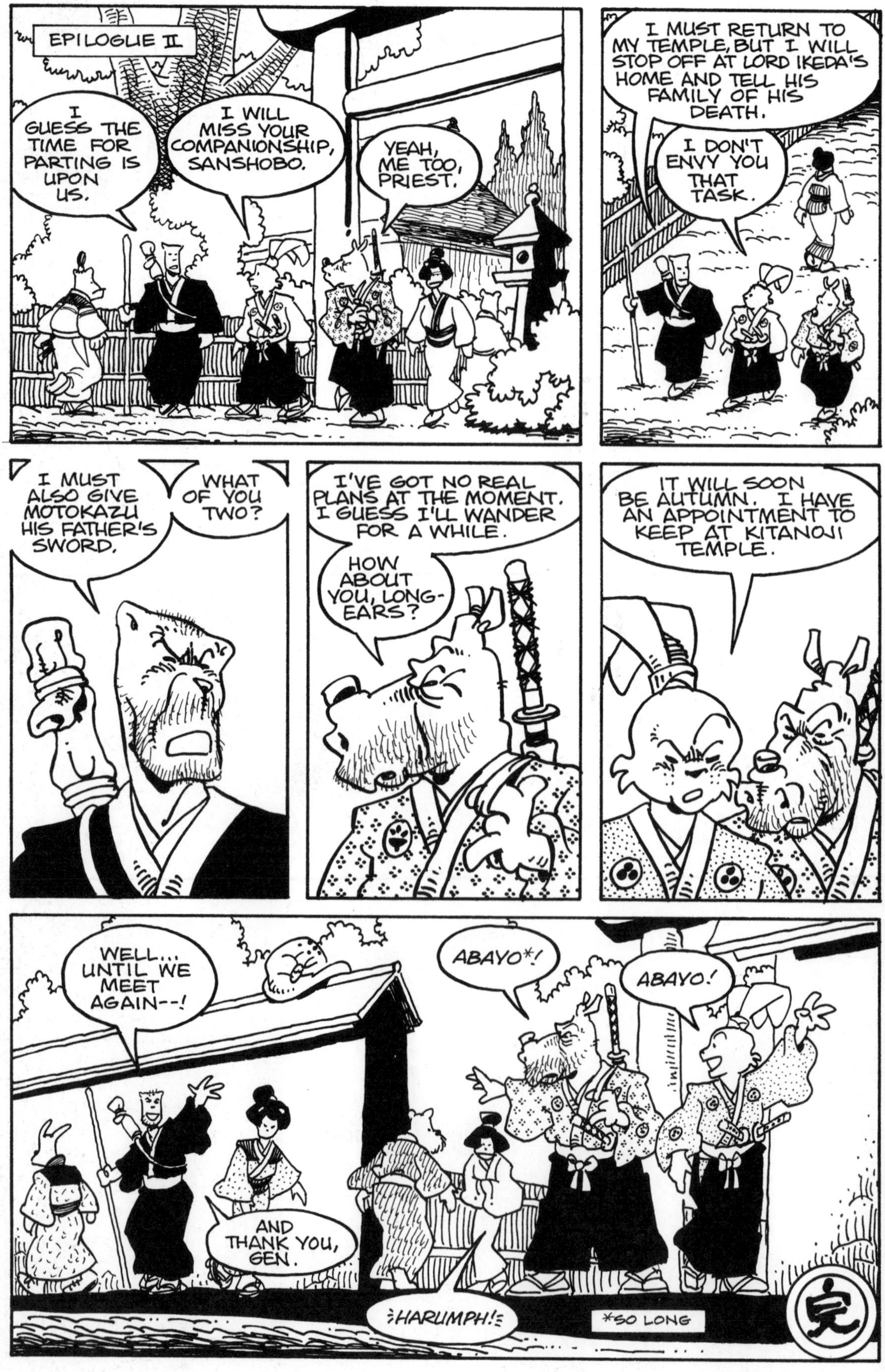
EPILOGUE II
I GUESS THE TIME FOR PARTING IS UPON US.
I WILL MISS YOUR COMPANIONSHIP, SANSHOBO.
YEAH, ME TOO, PRIEST.
I MUST RETURN TO MY TEMPLE, BUT I WILL STOP OFF AT LORD IKEDA'S HOME AND TELL HIS FAMILY OF HIS DEATH.
I DON'T ENVY YOU THAT TASK.
I MUST ALSO GIVE MOTOKAZU HIS FATHER'S SWORD.
WHAT OF YOU TWO?
I'VE GOT NO REAL PLANS AT THE MOMENT. I GUESS I'LL WANDER FOR A WHILE.
HOW ABOUT YOU, LONG-EARS?
IT WILL SOON BE AUTUMN. I HAVE AN APPOINTMENT TO KEEP AT KITANOJI TEMPLE.
WELL... UNTIL WE MEET AGAIN--!
AND THANK YOU, GEN.
ABAYO*!
ABAYO!
HARUMPH!
*SO LONG
完

THE SHROUDED MOON

INTRODUCTION

I WAS EXTREMELY SURPRISED and pleased when Stan Sakai asked me to write the introduction to *The Shrouded Moon*, this latest collected volume of *Usagi Yojimbo*. Stan's Federal Express pickup-and-delivery person probably has more to do with the production of *Usagi Yojimbo* than I do, but his schedule was probably too busy for him to write an intro.

However, it occurs to me that I've actually had a *lot* to do with *Usagi Yojimbo* over the years. In fact, I may be the single person most responsible for convincing Stan to pursue what would become a stellar career in comic books—at least, instead of him becoming yet another overlooked talent working on animated cartoons.

I first met Stan in 1979, when he was one of an entourage of Hawaiian cartoonists visiting the San Diego Comic-Con (now known as Comic-Con International), led by Oahu's much-loved cartoon *sensei*, Dave Thorne. The following year, Dave's group (including young Stan) returned to the convention, as well as taking a side trip to Los Angeles. There, they dropped by Hanna-Barbera Productions, where I was working in the layout department on new *Flintstones* TV cartoons. I was delighted to give my new friends an insider's tour of the studio, where my coworkers greeted the newcomers with the same sort of poo flinging (thankfully, not literally) that's usually unleashed upon unsuspecting visitors to a zoo's monkey house! Years later, Stan confided in me that the sight of dozens of animators laboring in identical cubicles is what convinced him that the one career he definitely *didn't* want to pursue was making animated cartoons!

And—other than cocreating a backup story ("Digger Duckbill" in Fantagraphics' *Usagi Yojimbo* #13, with Mark Evanier) back when Stan often spotlighted work by his cartoonist friends—I'm proud to claim I've had yet another effect on everyone's favorite rabbit *ronin*.

For decades, in addition to my own cartooning career in comic books, animation, and advertising, I've collected and studied what I refer to as "Oddball Comics." These include mainstream comic books of all genres that, due to various nutty aspects, make one wonder how they ever got published in the first place! One of the most popular—and certainly most ridiculous—categories of Oddball Comics that I've identified are funnybooks bearing what I call "fish-in-the-face" covers. These four-color oddities feature cover scenes of people (usually bad guys) getting hit smack-dab in the face with a fish! Apparently, Stan's a big fin, er, fan of these fish-in-the-face covers, too, as his cover of *Usagi Yojimbo* #49—reprinted within this volume—attests. And if you think that's a fluke (ow!), check out my guest appearance on pages 13 through 16 of "Three Seasons." (Stan's portrayed me as that thug with the crewcut and the aloha-print kimono!)

Finally, here are some observations about Stan himself. When I first met him, his work certainly showed great promise. But I can think of no one in comics who has worked harder than Stan to bring his level of writing, drawing, and sheer storytelling to the heights of excellence he delivers with each new issue of *Usagi Yojimbo*. I'm equally impressed with Stan's ability to produce consistently outstanding work with the flawless self-discipline of a samurai. At our traditional Friday-afternoon cartoonist lunches, many of our gang relate sob stories about creative blocks, clueless bosses, layoffs, or missed deadlines. Meanwhile, with a little smile on his face, Stan calmly hands out copies of the latest *Usagi*! Amazingly, Stan is also able to maintain a full life away from the drawing board as a wonderful husband and father. Everyone who knows Stan seems to respect and admire him; he's certainly the most "balanced" person I've ever met. (As for his rotten side, well, you'll just have to wait for the FedEx man's introduction to the next *Usagi Yojimbo* collection to spill the beans about that!)

We're all lucky to have Stan's *Usagi Yojimbo* to enjoy on a regular basis, but I'm especially lucky to have Stan as one of my best friends. And that's better than getting a fish in the face any day!

SCOTT SHAW!
SEPTEMBER 27, 2002

SHOWDOWN

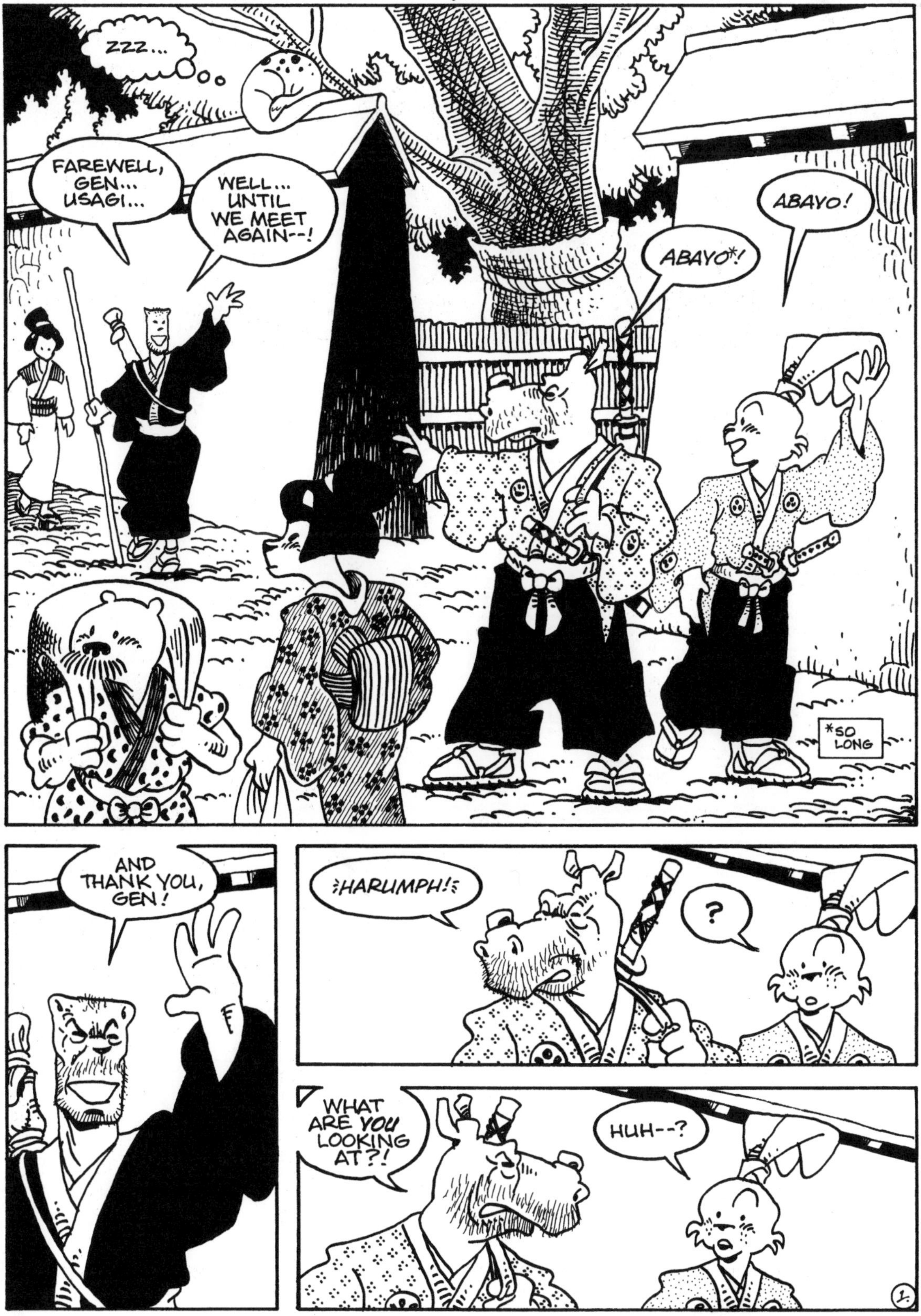
ZZZ...
FAREWELL, GEN... USAGI...
WELL... UNTIL WE MEET AGAIN--!
ABAYO*!
ABAYO!
*SO LONG
AND THANK YOU, GEN!
HARUMPH!
?
WHAT ARE *YOU* LOOKING AT?!
HUH--?

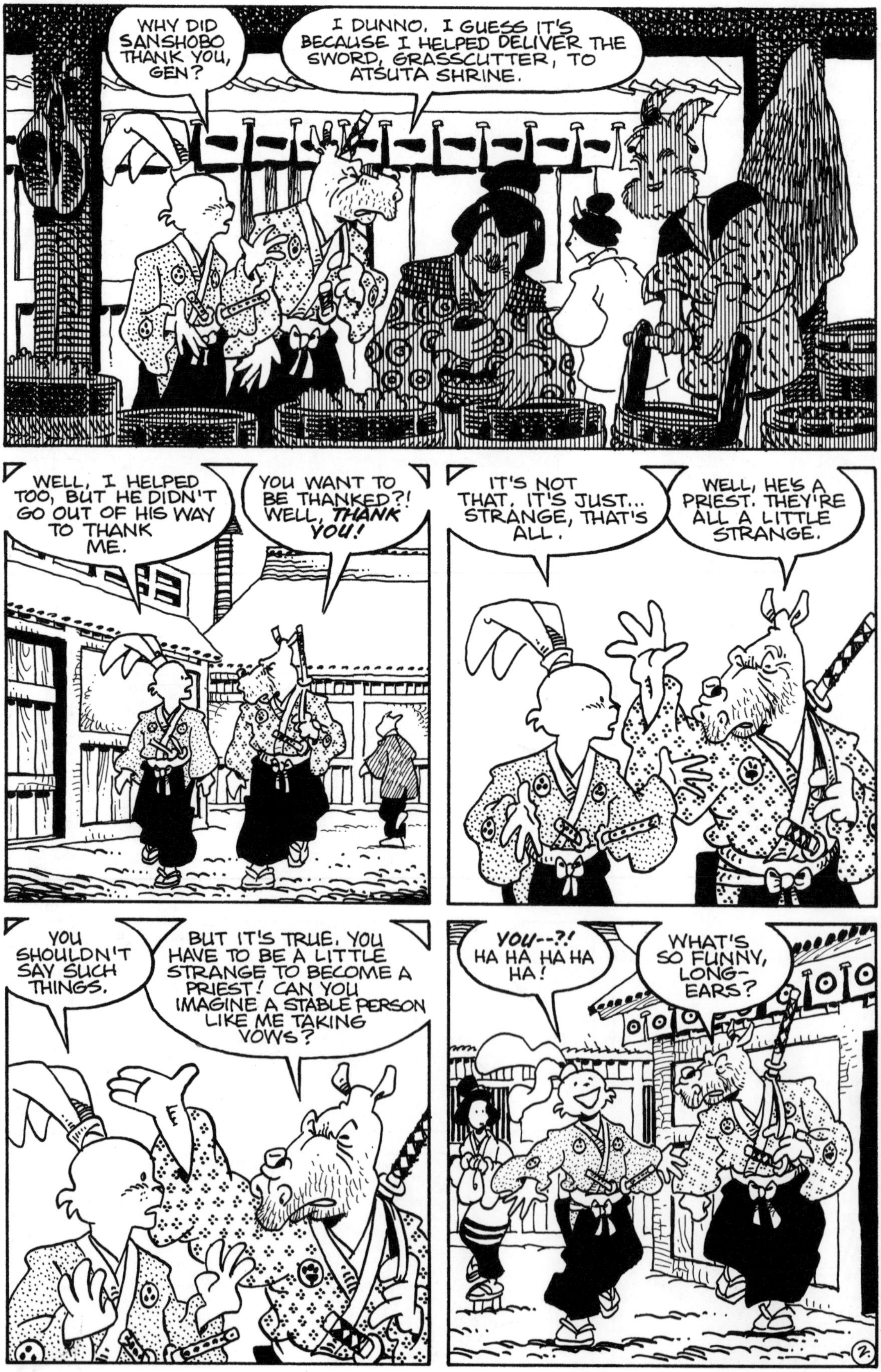

WHY DID SANSHOBO THANK YOU, GEN?
I DUNNO. I GUESS IT'S BECAUSE I HELPED DELIVER THE SWORD, GRASSCUTTER, TO ATSUTA SHRINE.
WELL, I HELPED TOO, BUT HE DIDN'T GO OUT OF HIS WAY TO THANK ME.
YOU WANT TO BE THANKED?! WELL, *THANK YOU!*
IT'S NOT THAT. IT'S JUST... STRANGE, THAT'S ALL.
WELL, HE'S A PRIEST. THEY'RE ALL A LITTLE STRANGE.
YOU SHOULDN'T SAY SUCH THINGS.
BUT IT'S TRUE. YOU HAVE TO BE A LITTLE STRANGE TO BECOME A PRIEST! CAN YOU IMAGINE A STABLE PERSON LIKE ME TAKING VOWS?
YOU--?! HA HA HA HA HA!
WHAT'S SO FUNNY, LONG-EARS?
2.

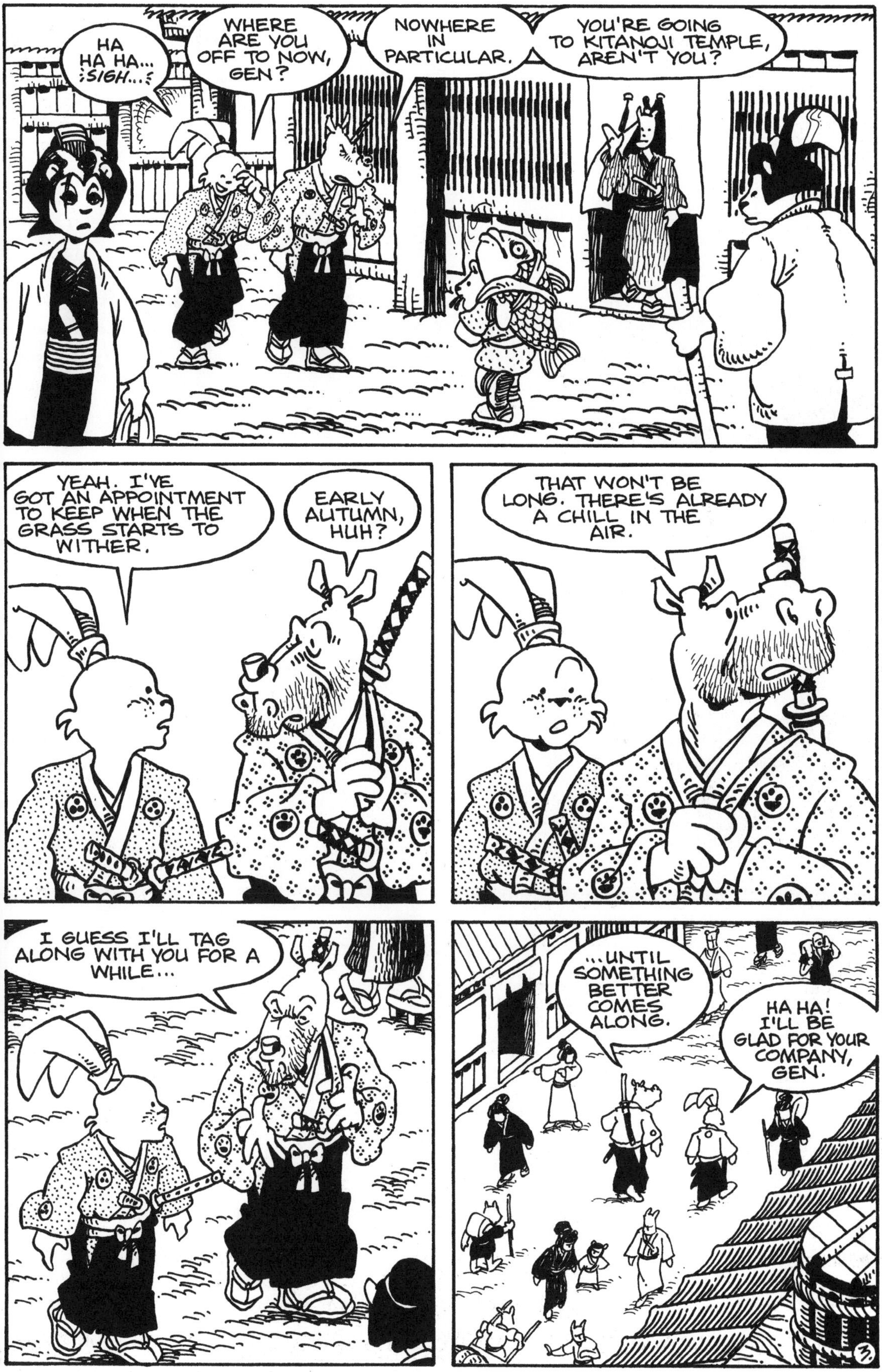

HA HA HA... SIGH...
WHERE ARE YOU OFF TO NOW, GEN?
NOWHERE IN PARTICULAR.
YOU'RE GOING TO KITANOJI TEMPLE, AREN'T YOU?
YEAH. I'VE GOT AN APPOINTMENT TO KEEP WHEN THE GRASS STARTS TO WITHER.
EARLY AUTUMN, HUH?
THAT WON'T BE LONG. THERE'S ALREADY A CHILL IN THE AIR.
I GUESS I'LL TAG ALONG WITH YOU FOR A WHILE...
...UNTIL SOMETHING BETTER COMES ALONG.
HA HA! I'LL BE GLAD FOR YOUR COMPANY, GEN.
3

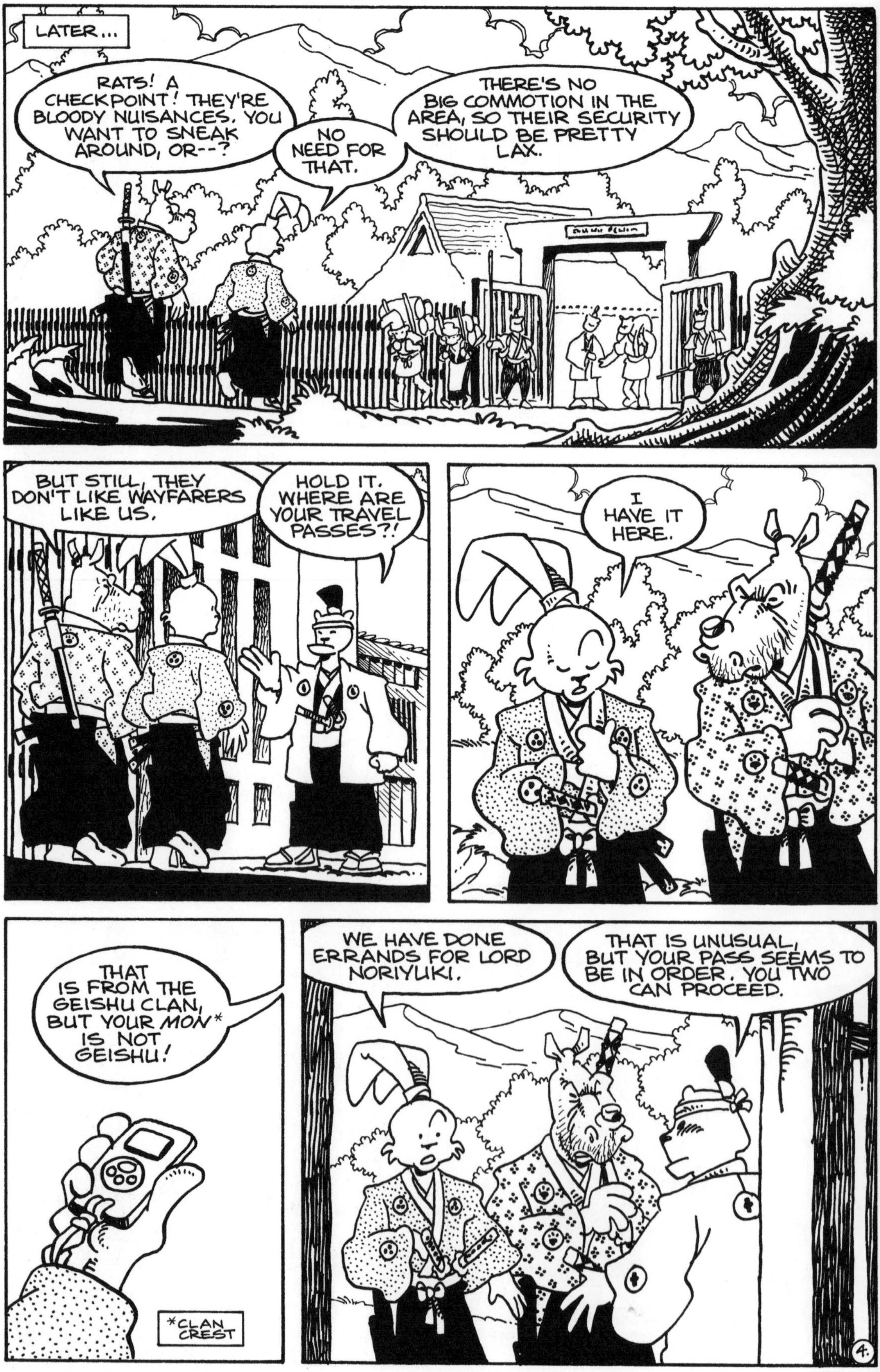
LATER...
RATS! A CHECKPOINT! THEY'RE BLOODY NUISANCES. YOU WANT TO SNEAK AROUND, OR--?
NO NEED FOR THAT.
THERE'S NO BIG COMMOTION IN THE AREA, SO THEIR SECURITY SHOULD BE PRETTY LAX.
BUT STILL, THEY DON'T LIKE WAYFARERS LIKE US.
HOLD IT. WHERE ARE YOUR TRAVEL PASSES?!
I HAVE IT HERE.
THAT IS FROM THE GEISHU CLAN, BUT YOUR *MON** IS NOT GEISHU!
*CLAN CREST
WE HAVE DONE ERRANDS FOR LORD NORIYUKI.
THAT IS UNUSUAL, BUT YOUR PASS SEEMS TO BE IN ORDER. YOU TWO CAN PROCEED.
4.

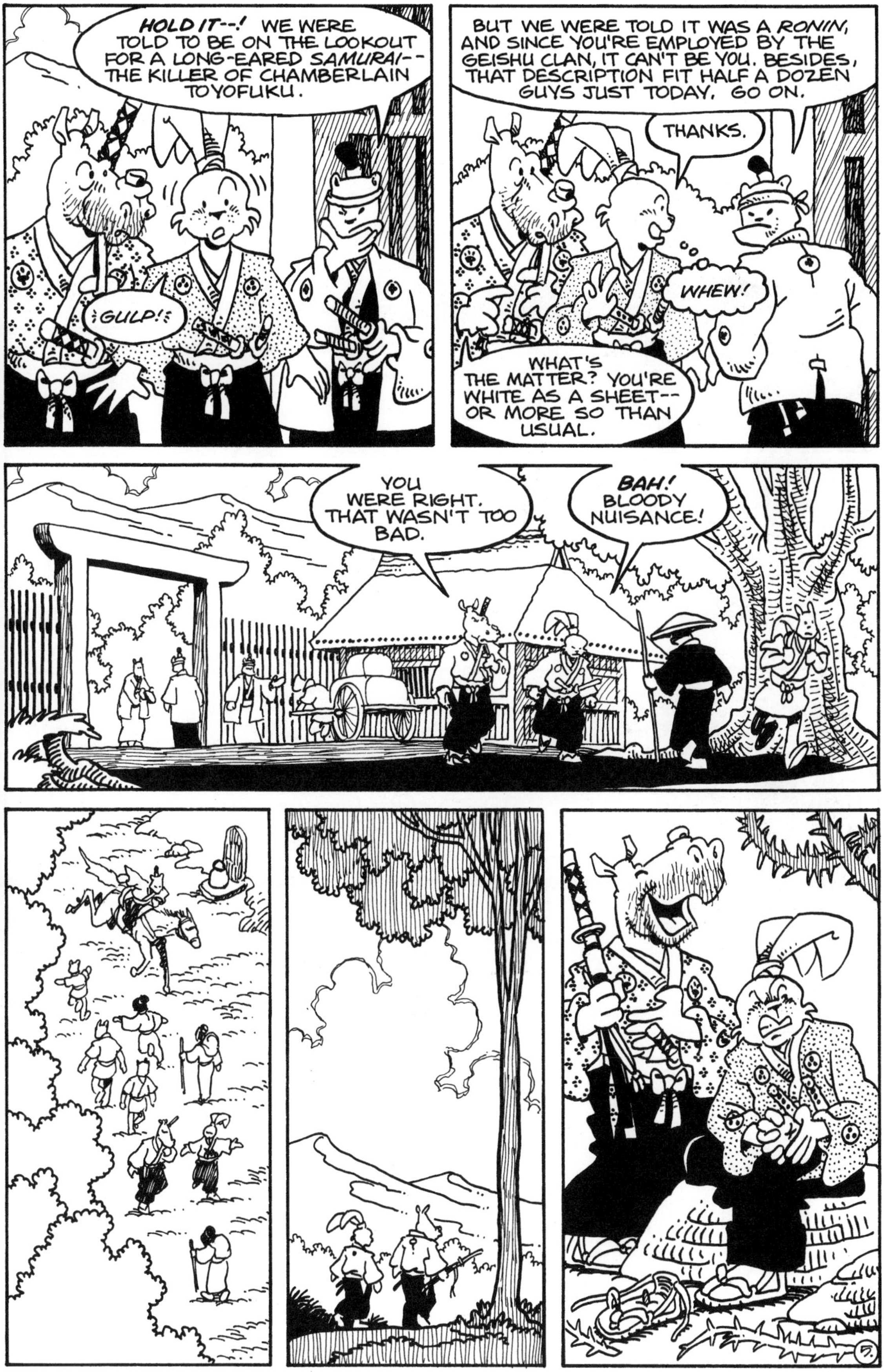
HOLD IT--! WE WERE TOLD TO BE ON THE LOOKOUT FOR A LONG-EARED SAMURAI-- THE KILLER OF CHAMBERLAIN TOYOFUKU.
GULP!
BUT WE WERE TOLD IT WAS A RONIN, AND SINCE YOU'RE EMPLOYED BY THE GEISHU CLAN, IT CAN'T BE YOU. BESIDES, THAT DESCRIPTION FIT HALF A DOZEN GUYS JUST TODAY. GO ON.
THANKS.
WHEW!
WHAT'S THE MATTER? YOU'RE WHITE AS A SHEET-- OR MORE SO THAN USUAL.
YOU WERE RIGHT. THAT WASN'T TOO BAD.
BAH! BLOODY NUISANCE!

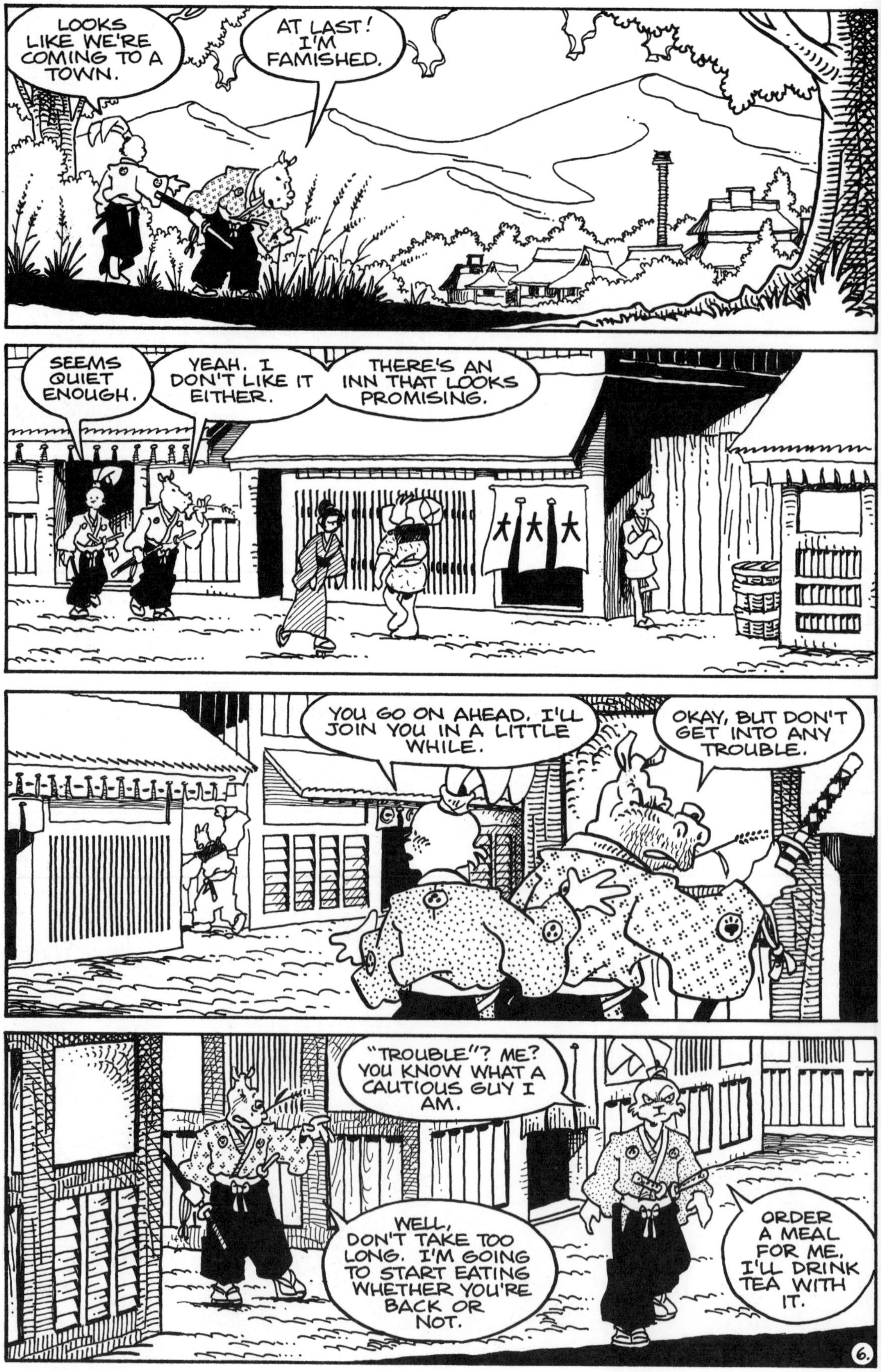

LOOKS LIKE WE'RE COMING TO A TOWN.
AT LAST! I'M FAMISHED.
SEEMS QUIET ENOUGH.
YEAH. I DON'T LIKE IT EITHER.
THERE'S AN INN THAT LOOKS PROMISING.
YOU GO ON AHEAD. I'LL JOIN YOU IN A LITTLE WHILE.
OKAY, BUT DON'T GET INTO ANY TROUBLE.
"TROUBLE"? ME? YOU KNOW WHAT A CAUTIOUS GUY I AM.
WELL, DON'T TAKE TOO LONG. I'M GOING TO START EATING WHETHER YOU'RE BACK OR NOT.
ORDER A MEAL FOR ME. I'LL DRINK TEA WITH IT.
6.

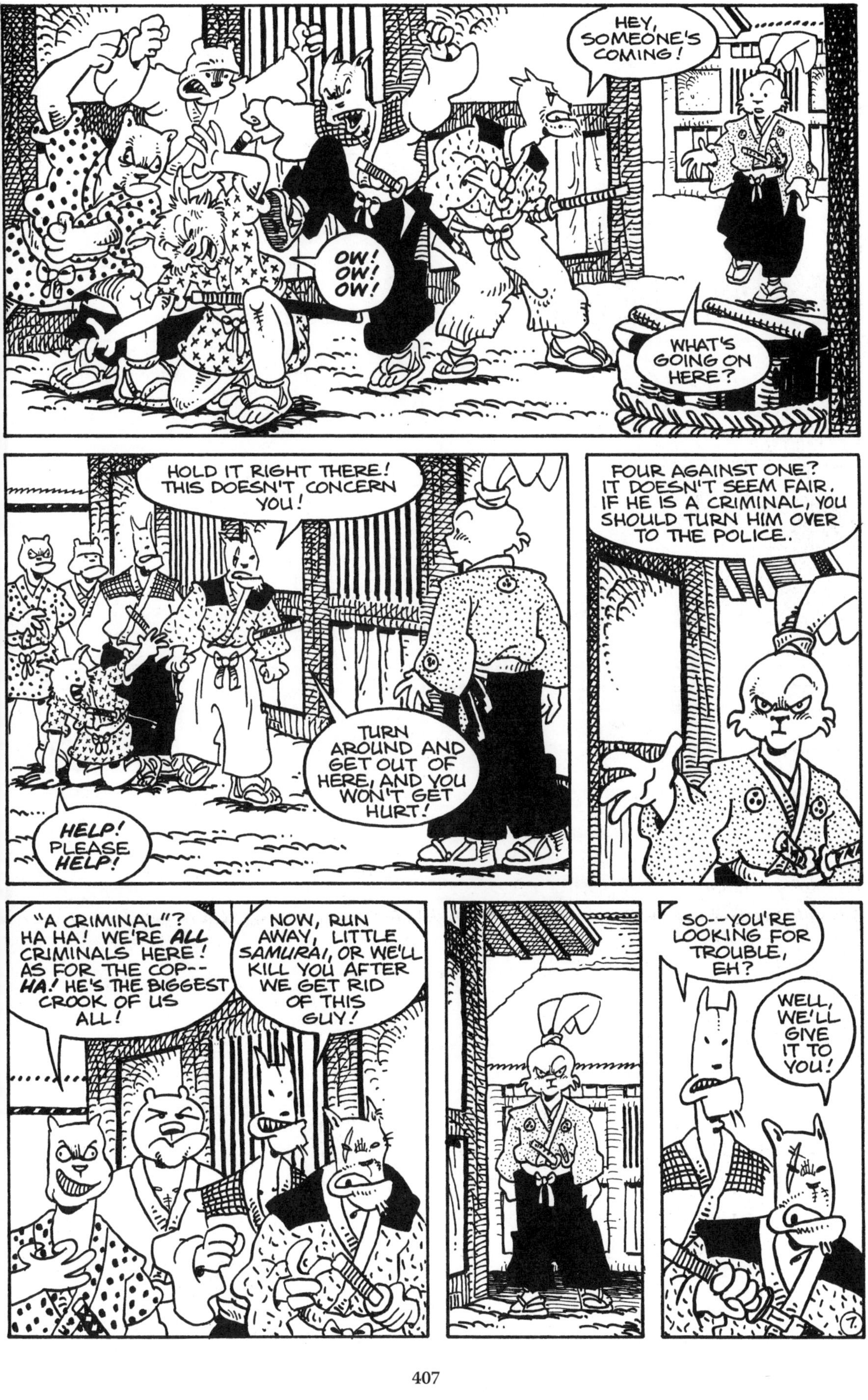
HEY, SOMEONE'S COMING!
OW! OW! OW!
WHAT'S GOING ON HERE?
HOLD IT RIGHT THERE! THIS DOESN'T CONCERN YOU!
TURN AROUND AND GET OUT OF HERE, AND YOU WON'T GET HURT!
HELP! PLEASE HELP!
FOUR AGAINST ONE? IT DOESN'T SEEM FAIR. IF HE IS A CRIMINAL, YOU SHOULD TURN HIM OVER TO THE POLICE.
"A CRIMINAL"? HA HA! WE'RE ALL CRIMINALS HERE! AS FOR THE COP-- HA! HE'S THE BIGGEST CROOK OF US ALL!
NOW, RUN AWAY, LITTLE SAMURAI, OR WE'LL KILL YOU AFTER WE GET RID OF THIS GUY!
SO--YOU'RE LOOKING FOR TROUBLE, EH?
WELL, WE'LL GIVE IT TO YOU!
7.

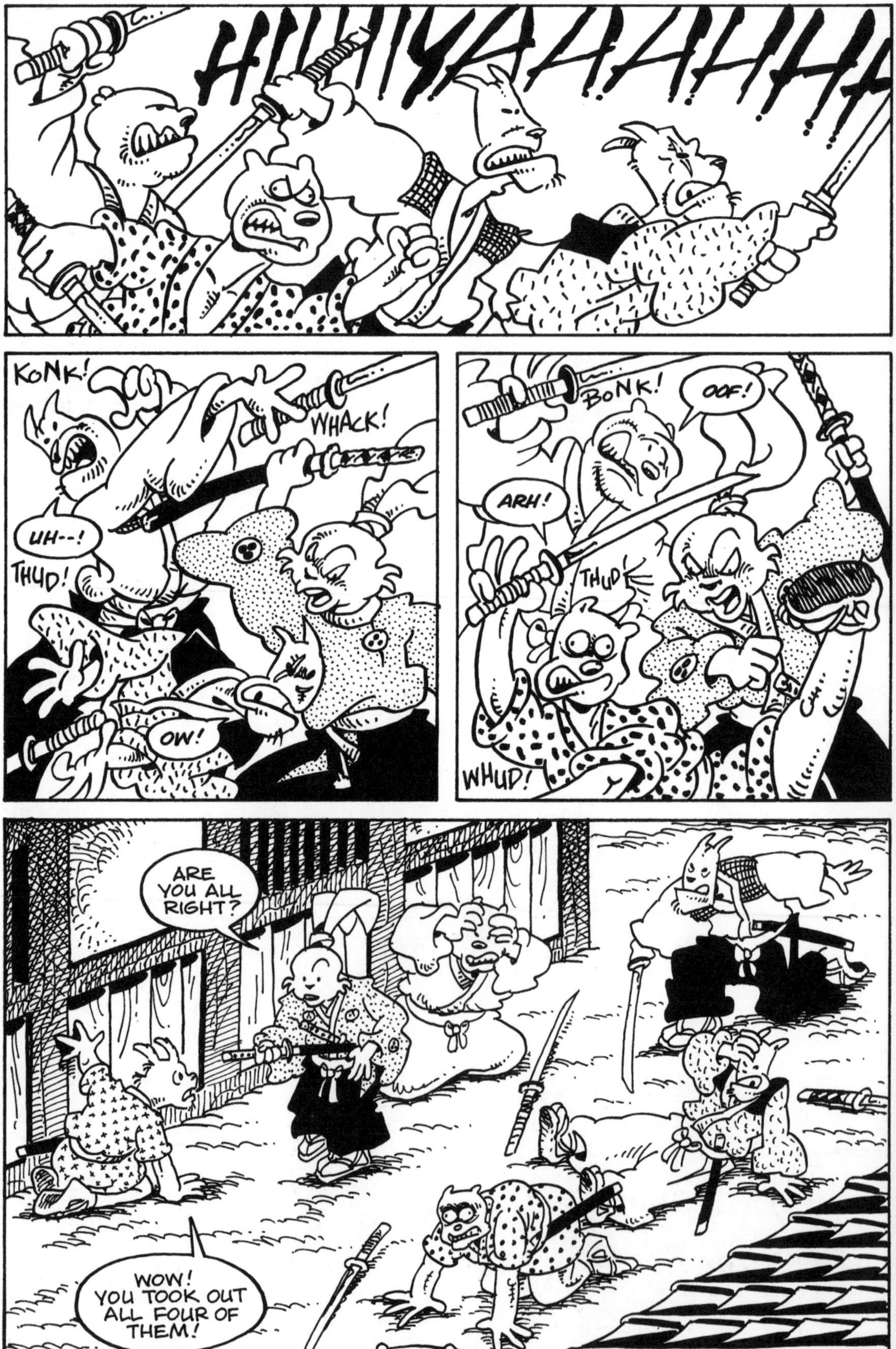
HIIIIYAAAAHHHA
KONK!
WHACK!
UH--!
THUD!
OW!
BONK!
OOF!
ARH!
THUD!
WHUD!
ARE YOU ALL RIGHT?
WOW! YOU TOOK OUT ALL FOUR OF THEM!
8.

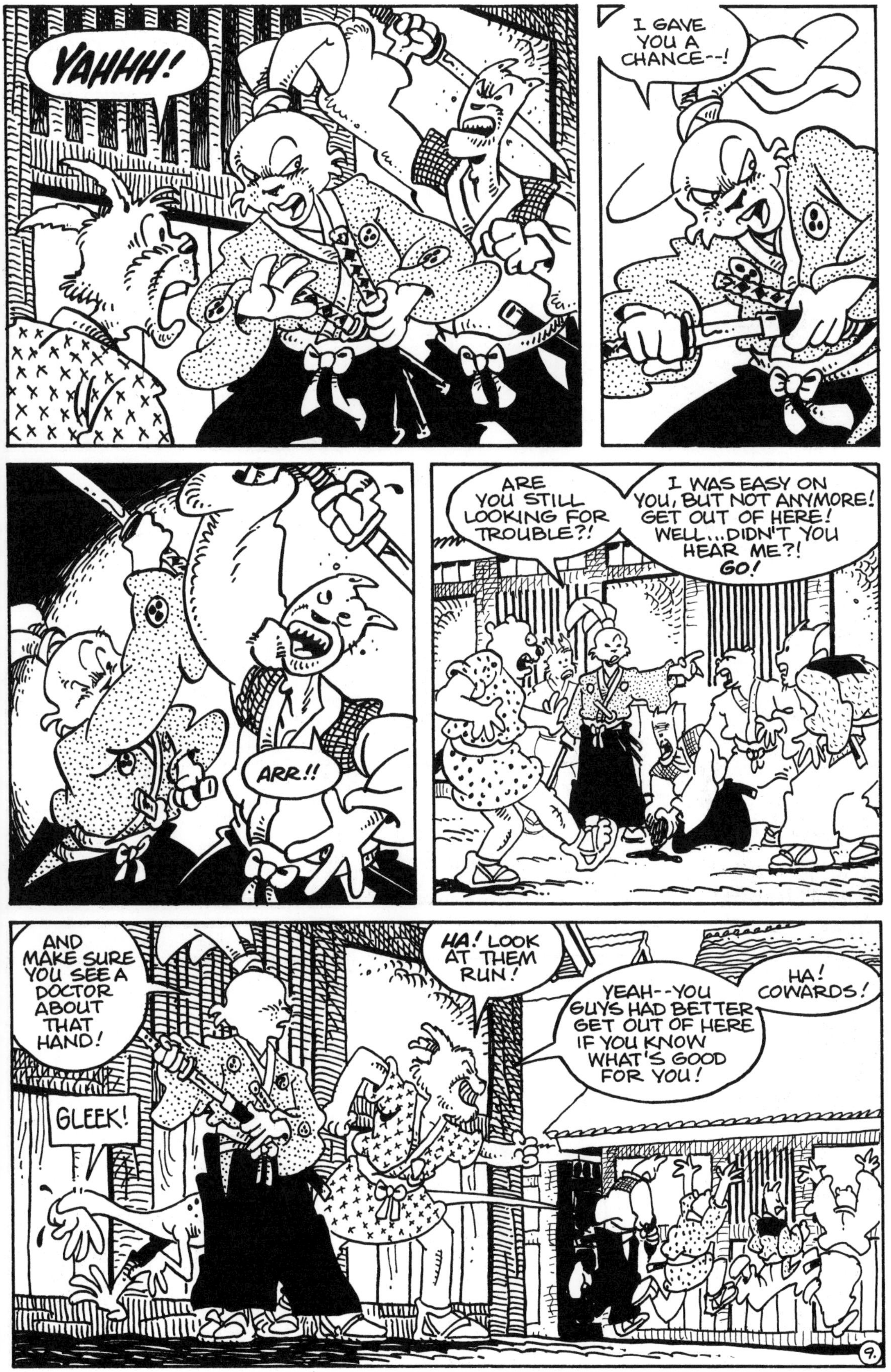
YAHHH!
I GAVE YOU A CHANCE--!
ARR!!
ARE YOU STILL LOOKING FOR TROUBLE?!
I WAS EASY ON YOU, BUT NOT ANYMORE! GET OUT OF HERE! WELL...DIDN'T YOU HEAR ME?! GO!
AND MAKE SURE YOU SEE A DOCTOR ABOUT THAT HAND!
GLEEK!
HA! LOOK AT THEM RUN!
YEAH--YOU GUYS HAD BETTER GET OUT OF HERE IF YOU KNOW WHAT'S GOOD FOR YOU!
HA! COWARDS!
9.

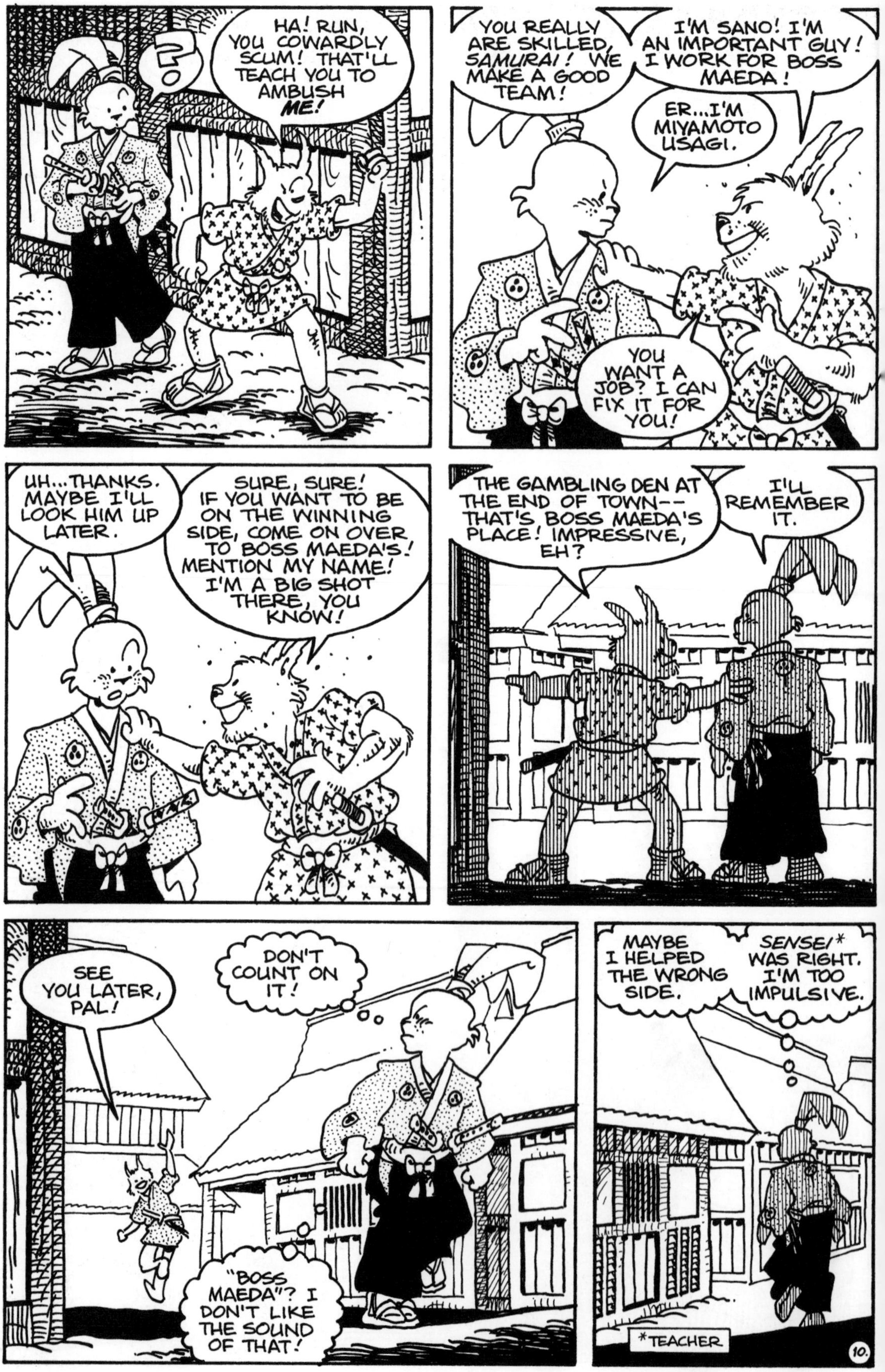
?
HA! RUN, YOU COWARDLY SCUM! THAT'LL TEACH YOU TO AMBUSH *ME!*
YOU REALLY ARE SKILLED, *SAMURAI!* WE MAKE A GOOD TEAM!
I'M SANO! I'M AN IMPORTANT GUY! I WORK FOR BOSS MAEDA!
ER...I'M MIYAMOTO USAGI.
YOU WANT A JOB? I CAN FIX IT FOR YOU!
UH...THANKS. MAYBE I'LL LOOK HIM UP LATER.
SURE, SURE! IF YOU WANT TO BE ON THE WINNING SIDE, COME ON OVER TO BOSS MAEDA'S! MENTION MY NAME! I'M A BIG SHOT THERE, YOU KNOW!
THE GAMBLING DEN AT THE END OF TOWN-- THAT'S BOSS MAEDA'S PLACE! IMPRESSIVE, EH?
I'LL REMEMBER IT.
SEE YOU LATER, PAL!
DON'T COUNT ON IT!
"BOSS MAEDA"? I DON'T LIKE THE SOUND OF THAT!
MAYBE I HELPED THE WRONG SIDE.
*SENSEI** WAS RIGHT. I'M TOO IMPULSIVE.
*TEACHER
10.

I'M BACK.

YEAH. I CAN SEE THAT.

SHOJI, HERE, WAS FILLING ME IN ON WHAT'S GOING ON IN THIS TOWN.

¡SLURP!¡

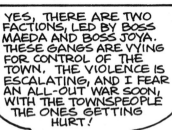

YES, THERE ARE TWO FACTIONS, LED BY BOSS MAEDA AND BOSS JOYA. THESE GANGS ARE VYING FOR CONTROL OF THE TOWN. THE VIOLENCE IS ESCALATING, AND I FEAR AN ALL-OUT WAR SOON, WITH THE TOWNSPEOPLE THE ONES GETTING HURT!

WHY HAVEN'T YOU CALLED IN THE AUTHORITIES?

AH, I'M FAMISHED.

THE GOVERNMENT DOESN'T CARE AS LONG AS THEY GET THEIR TAX MONEY. BESIDES, WHENEVER AN INSPECTOR ARRIVES, THEY CHANGE THEIR ACT AND BECOME AS FRIENDS.

IT'S NOT RIGHT FOR PEOPLE TO LIVE IN FEAR.

YEAH, BUT WHAT CAN WE DO ABOUT IT?

WELL...

OH, NO! I SEE THAT LOOK IN YOUR EYES! YOU'RE GOING TO BUTT IN AGAIN, AREN'T YOU? YOU'RE ALWAYS STICKING YOUR NOSE IN WHERE IT DOESN'T BELONG!

BUT...

NO "BUTS"!

⑪

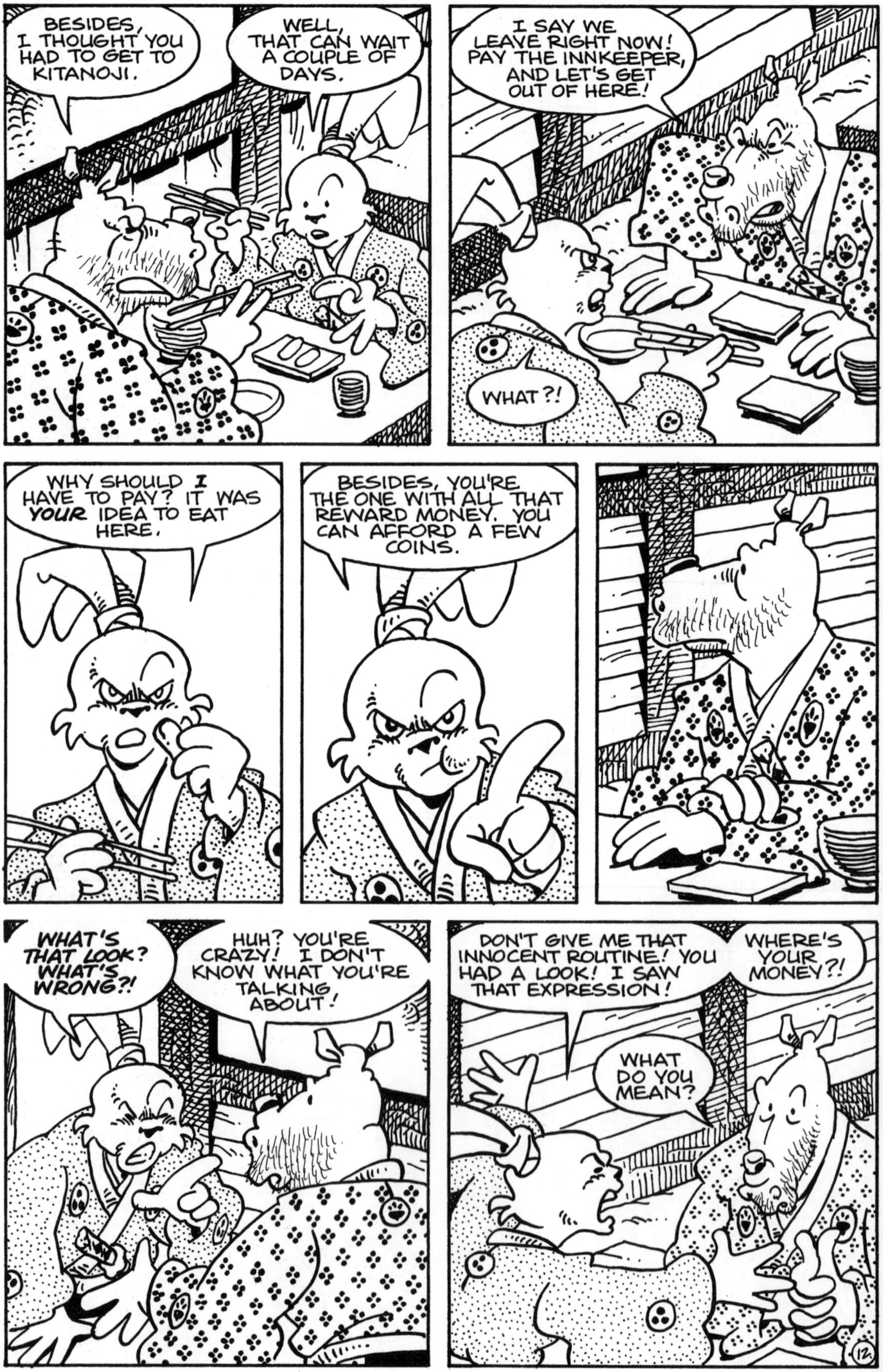
BESIDES, I THOUGHT YOU HAD TO GET TO KITANOJI.
WELL, THAT CAN WAIT A COUPLE OF DAYS.
I SAY WE LEAVE RIGHT NOW! PAY THE INNKEEPER, AND LET'S GET OUT OF HERE!
WHAT?!
WHY SHOULD *I* HAVE TO PAY? IT WAS *YOUR* IDEA TO EAT HERE.
BESIDES, YOU'RE THE ONE WITH ALL THAT REWARD MONEY. YOU CAN AFFORD A FEW COINS.
WHAT'S THAT LOOK? WHAT'S WRONG?!
HUH? YOU'RE CRAZY! I DON'T KNOW WHAT YOU'RE TALKING ABOUT!
DON'T GIVE ME THAT INNOCENT ROUTINE! YOU HAD A LOOK! I SAW THAT EXPRESSION!
WHERE'S YOUR MONEY?!
WHAT DO YOU MEAN?
12

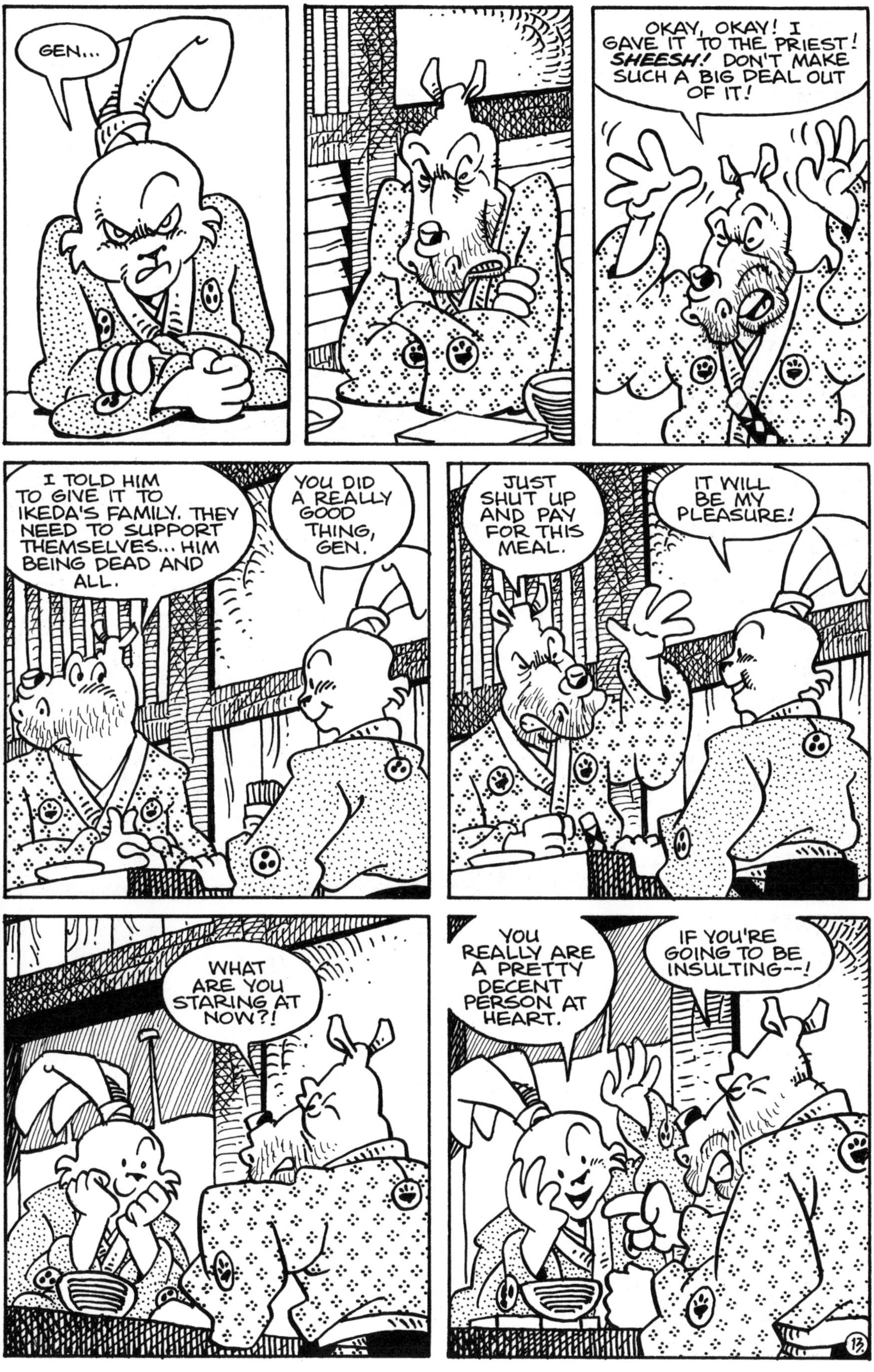
GEN...
OKAY, OKAY! I GAVE IT TO THE PRIEST! SHEESH! DON'T MAKE SUCH A BIG DEAL OUT OF IT!
I TOLD HIM TO GIVE IT TO IKEDA'S FAMILY. THEY NEED TO SUPPORT THEMSELVES... HIM BEING DEAD AND ALL.
YOU DID A REALLY GOOD THING, GEN.
JUST SHUT UP AND PAY FOR THIS MEAL.
IT WILL BE MY PLEASURE!
WHAT ARE YOU STARING AT NOW?!
YOU REALLY ARE A PRETTY DECENT PERSON AT HEART.
IF YOU'RE GOING TO BE INSULTING--!
13

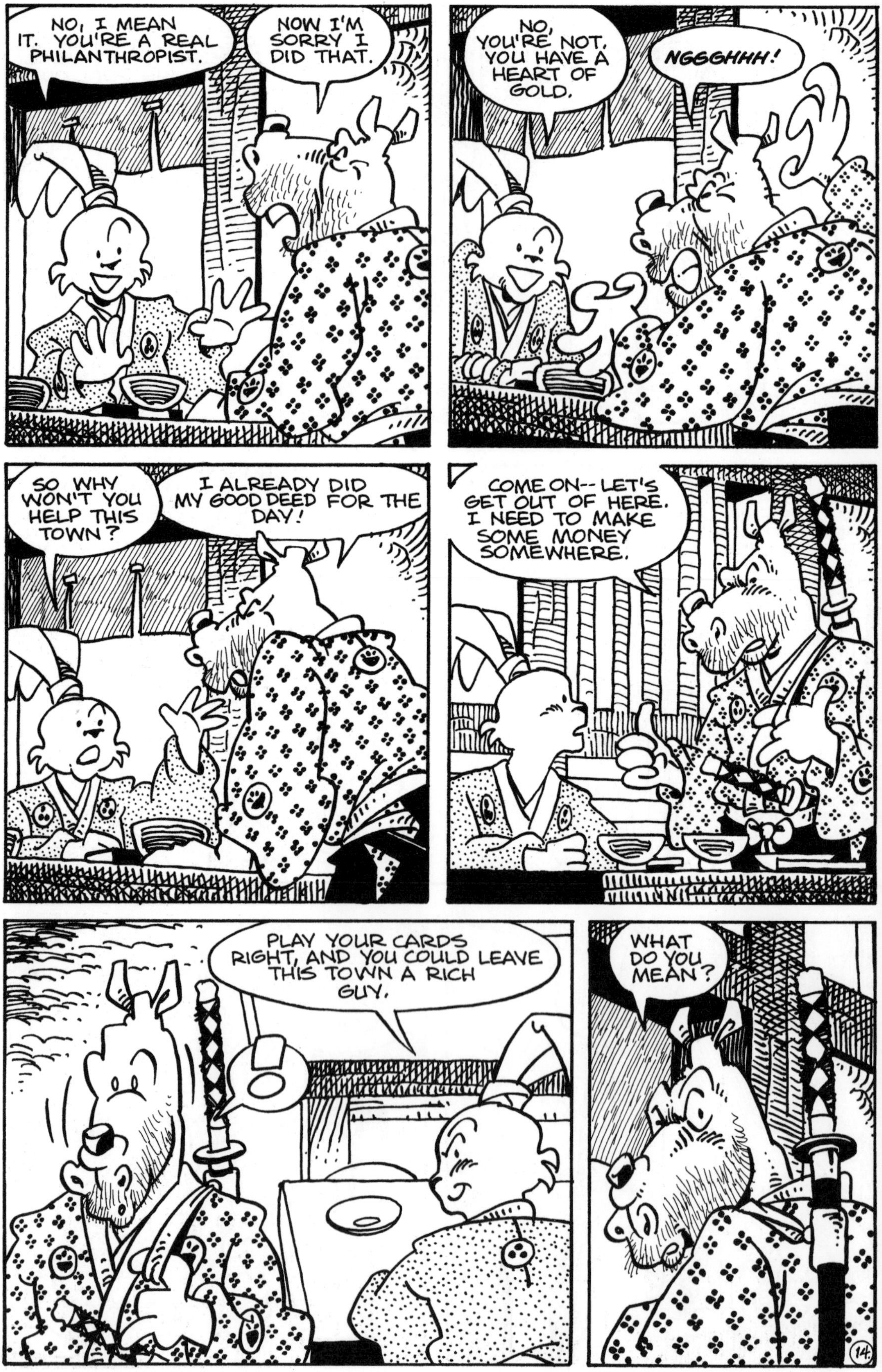
NO, I MEAN IT. YOU'RE A REAL PHILANTHROPIST.
NOW I'M SORRY I DID THAT.
NO, YOU'RE NOT, YOU HAVE A HEART OF GOLD.
NGGGHHH!
SO WHY WON'T YOU HELP THIS TOWN?
I ALREADY DID MY GOOD DEED FOR THE DAY!
COME ON-- LET'S GET OUT OF HERE. I NEED TO MAKE SOME MONEY SOMEWHERE.
PLAY YOUR CARDS RIGHT, AND YOU COULD LEAVE THIS TOWN A RICH GUY.
!
WHAT DO YOU MEAN?
14.

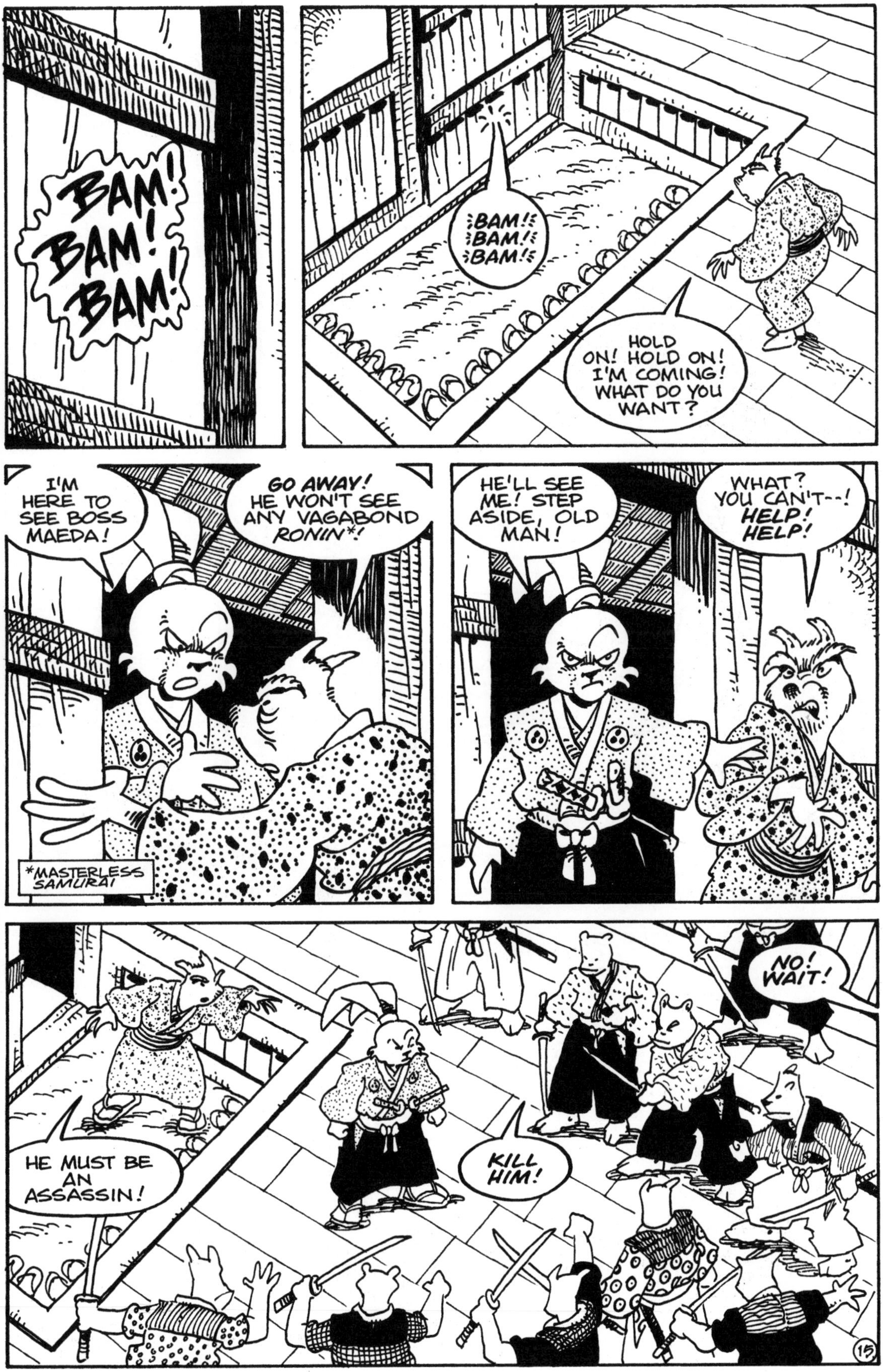
BAM! BAM! BAM!
BAM!! BAM!! BAM!!
HOLD ON! HOLD ON! I'M COMING! WHAT DO YOU WANT?
I'M HERE TO SEE BOSS MAEDA!
GO AWAY! HE WON'T SEE ANY VAGABOND RONIN*!
*MASTERLESS SAMURAI
HE'LL SEE ME! STEP ASIDE, OLD MAN!
WHAT? YOU CAN'T--! HELP! HELP!
NO! WAIT!
HE MUST BE AN ASSASSIN!
KILL HIM!
15

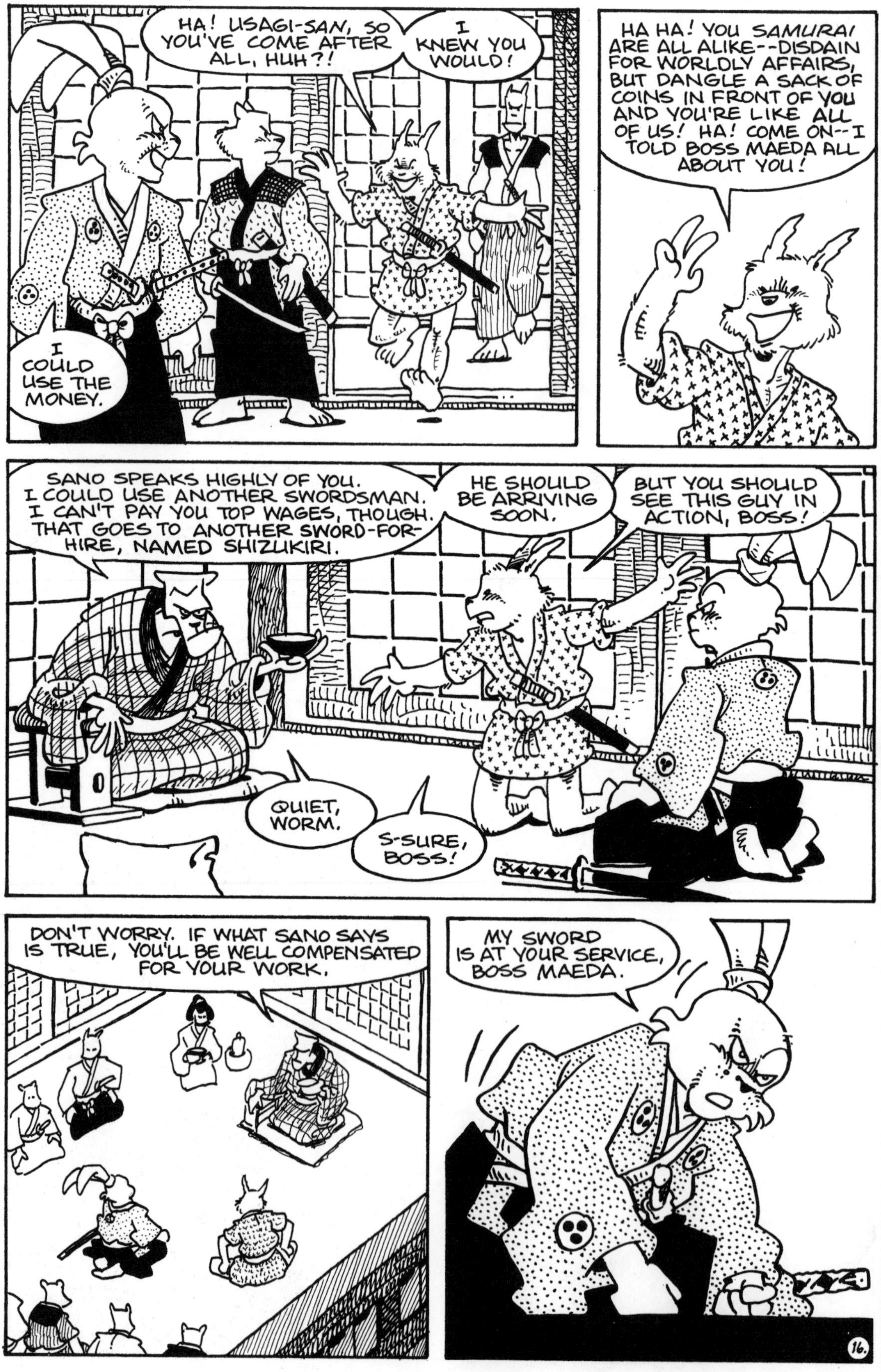
HA! USAGI-SAN, SO YOU'VE COME AFTER ALL, HUH?!
I KNEW YOU WOULD!
I COULD USE THE MONEY.
HA HA! YOU SAMURAI ARE ALL ALIKE--DISDAIN FOR WORLDLY AFFAIRS, BUT DANGLE A SACK OF COINS IN FRONT OF YOU AND YOU'RE LIKE ALL OF US! HA! COME ON--I TOLD BOSS MAEDA ALL ABOUT YOU!
SANO SPEAKS HIGHLY OF YOU. I COULD USE ANOTHER SWORDSMAN. I CAN'T PAY YOU TOP WAGES, THOUGH. THAT GOES TO ANOTHER SWORD-FOR-HIRE, NAMED SHIZUKIRI.
HE SHOULD BE ARRIVING SOON.
BUT YOU SHOULD SEE THIS GUY IN ACTION, BOSS!
QUIET, WORM.
S-SURE, BOSS!
DON'T WORRY. IF WHAT SANO SAYS IS TRUE, YOU'LL BE WELL COMPENSATED FOR YOUR WORK.
MY SWORD IS AT YOUR SERVICE, BOSS MAEDA.
16.

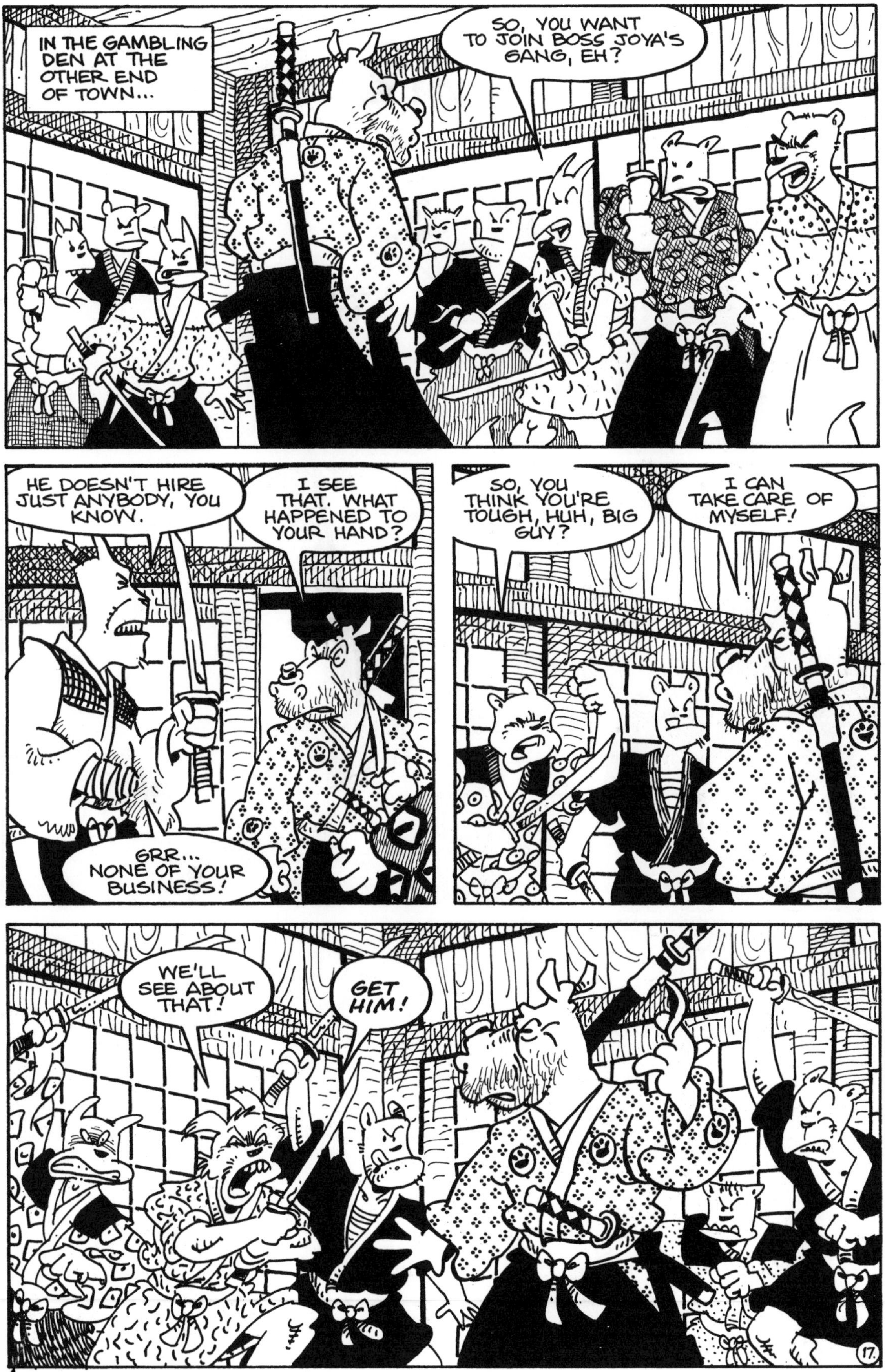

IN THE GAMBLING DEN AT THE OTHER END OF TOWN...
SO, YOU WANT TO JOIN BOSS JOYA'S GANG, EH?
HE DOESN'T HIRE JUST ANYBODY, YOU KNOW.
I SEE THAT. WHAT HAPPENED TO YOUR HAND?
GRR... NONE OF YOUR BUSINESS!
SO, YOU THINK YOU'RE TOUGH, HUH, BIG GUY?
I CAN TAKE CARE OF MYSELF!
WE'LL SEE ABOUT THAT!
GET HIM!
17

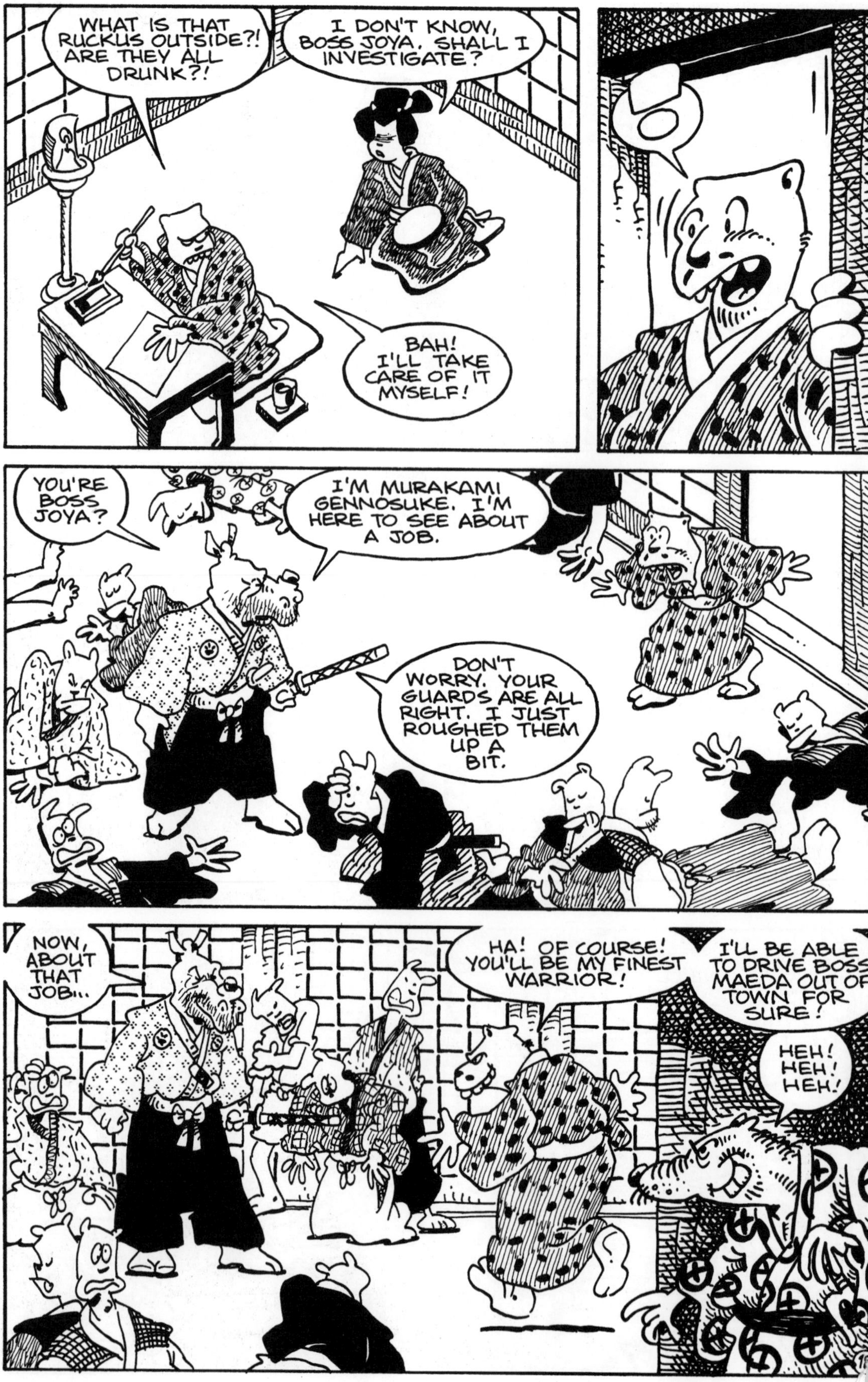
WHAT IS THAT RUCKUS OUTSIDE?! ARE THEY ALL DRUNK?!
I DON'T KNOW, BOSS JOYA. SHALL I INVESTIGATE?
BAH! I'LL TAKE CARE OF IT MYSELF!
YOU'RE BOSS JOYA?
I'M MURAKAMI GENNOSUKE. I'M HERE TO SEE ABOUT A JOB.
DON'T WORRY. YOUR GUARDS ARE ALL RIGHT. I JUST ROUGHED THEM UP A BIT.
NOW, ABOUT THAT JOB...
HA! OF COURSE! YOU'LL BE MY FINEST WARRIOR!
I'LL BE ABLE TO DRIVE BOSS MAEDA OUT OF TOWN FOR SURE!
HEH! HEH! HEH!
13

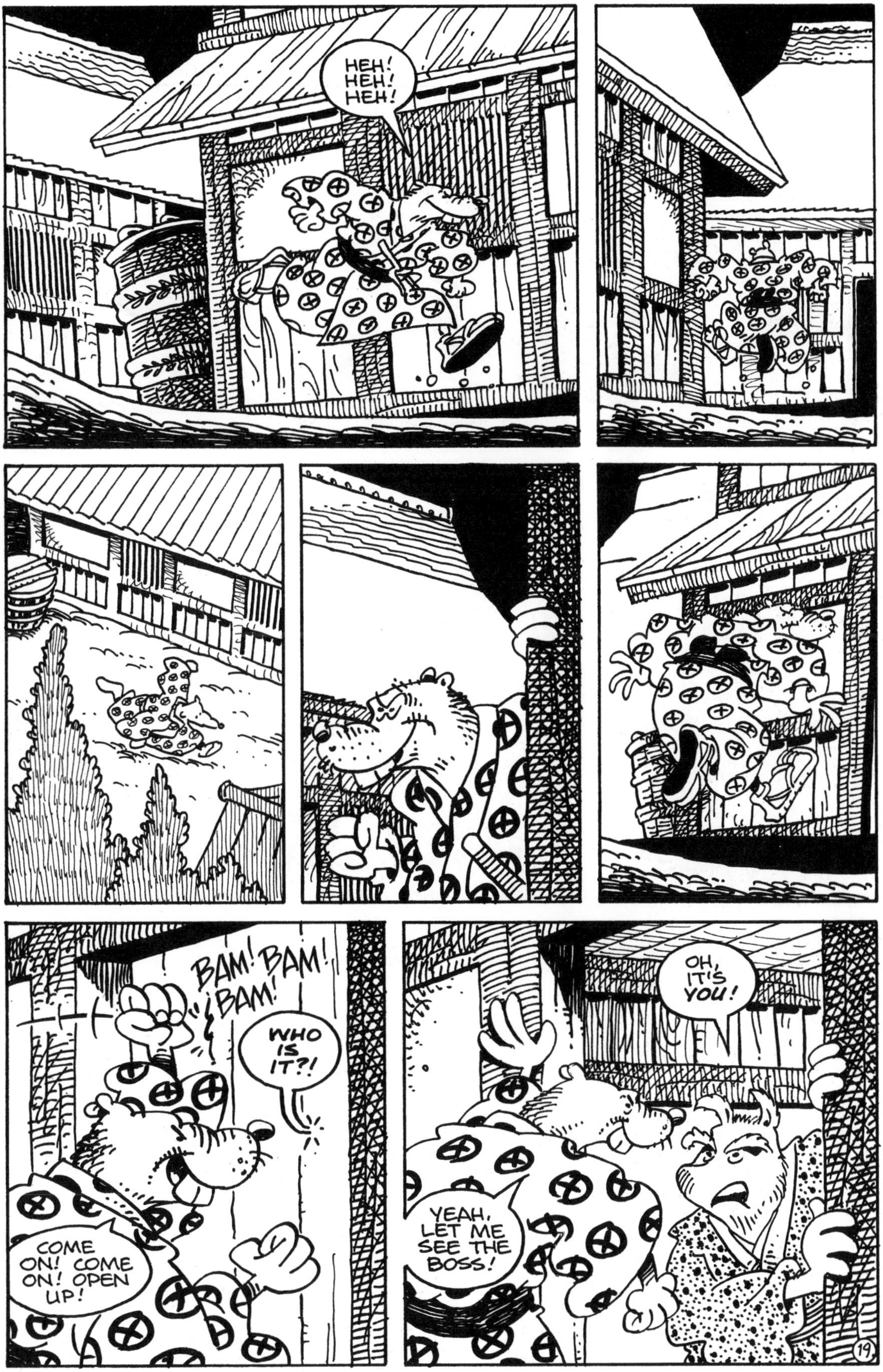
HEH! HEH! HEH!
BAM! BAM! BAM!
WHO IS IT?!
COME ON! COME ON! OPEN UP!
OH, IT'S YOU!
YEAH, LET ME SEE THE BOSS!
19

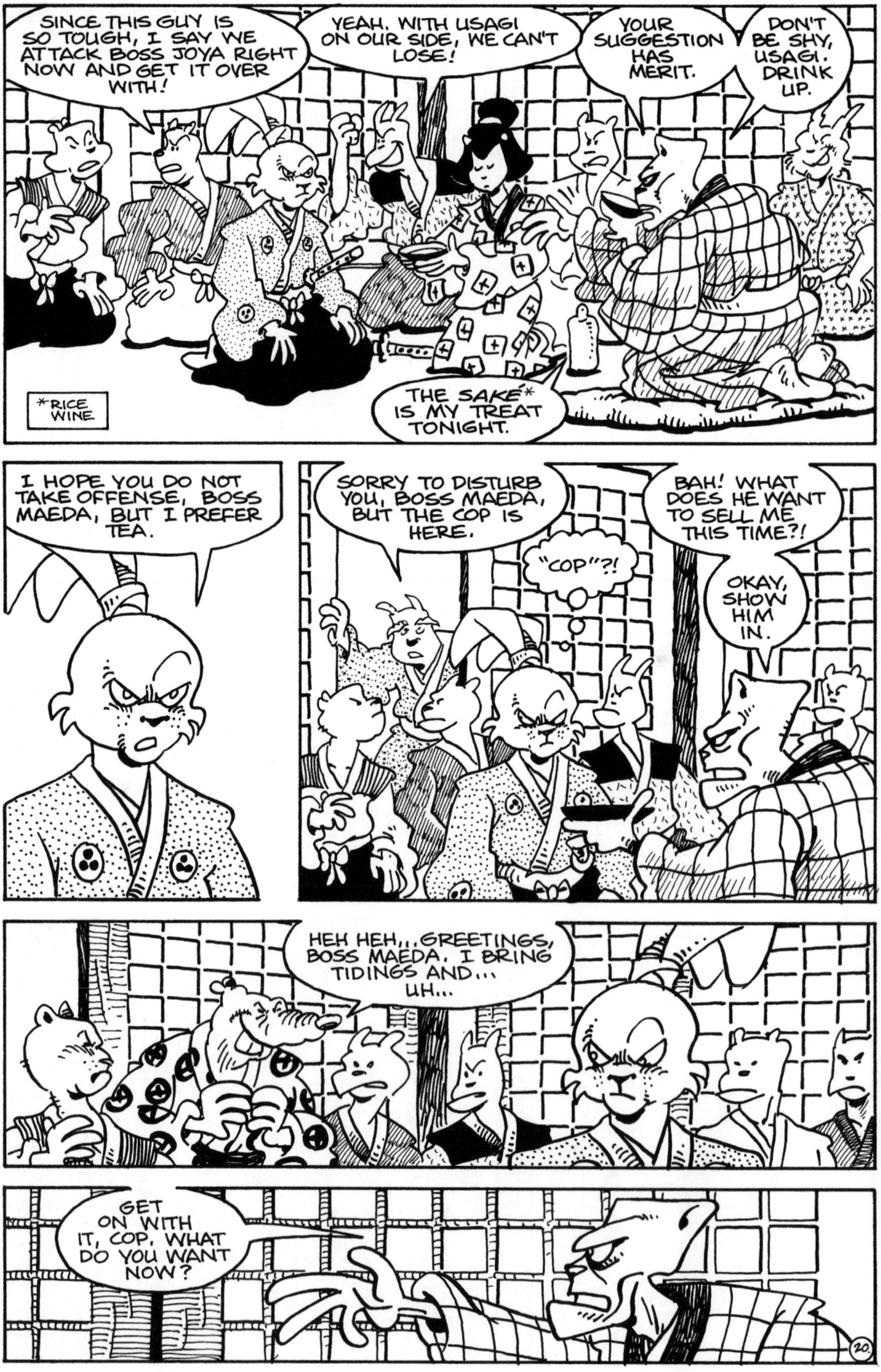
SINCE THIS GUY IS SO TOUGH, I SAY WE ATTACK BOSS JOYA RIGHT NOW AND GET IT OVER WITH!
YEAH. WITH USAGI ON OUR SIDE, WE CAN'T LOSE!
YOUR SUGGESTION HAS MERIT.
DON'T BE SHY, USAGI. DRINK UP.
THE SAKE* IS MY TREAT TONIGHT.
*RICE WINE
I HOPE YOU DO NOT TAKE OFFENSE, BOSS MAEDA, BUT I PREFER TEA.
SORRY TO DISTURB YOU, BOSS MAEDA, BUT THE COP IS HERE.
"COP"?!
BAH! WHAT DOES HE WANT TO SELL ME THIS TIME?!
OKAY, SHOW HIM IN.
HEH HEH... GREETINGS, BOSS MAEDA. I BRING TIDINGS AND... UH...
GET ON WITH IT, COP. WHAT DO YOU WANT NOW?
20.

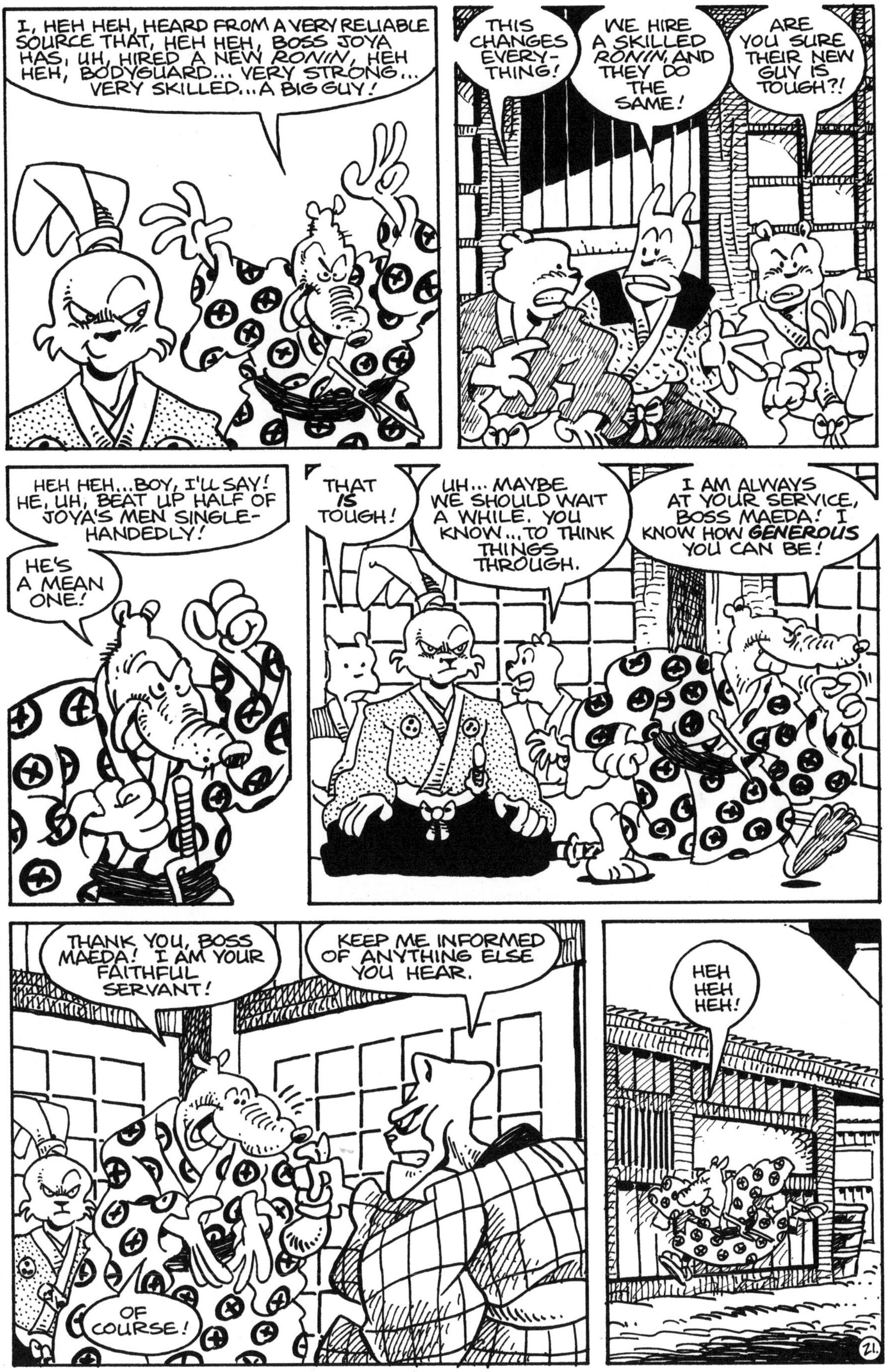
I, HEH HEH, HEARD FROM A VERY RELIABLE SOURCE THAT, HEH HEH, BOSS JOYA HAS, UH, HIRED A NEW *RONIN*, HEH HEH, BODYGUARD... VERY STRONG... VERY SKILLED...A BIG GUY!
THIS CHANGES EVERYTHING!
WE HIRE A SKILLED *RONIN*, AND THEY DO THE SAME!
ARE YOU SURE THEIR NEW GUY IS TOUGH?!
HEH HEH...BOY, I'LL SAY! HE, UH, BEAT UP HALF OF JOYA'S MEN SINGLE-HANDEDLY!
HE'S A MEAN ONE!
THAT **IS** TOUGH!
UH... MAYBE WE SHOULD WAIT A WHILE. YOU KNOW...TO THINK THINGS THROUGH.
I AM ALWAYS AT YOUR SERVICE, BOSS MAEDA! I KNOW HOW **GENEROUS** YOU CAN BE!
THANK YOU, BOSS MAEDA! I AM YOUR FAITHFUL SERVANT!
KEEP ME INFORMED OF ANYTHING ELSE YOU HEAR.
OF COURSE!
HEH HEH HEH!
21.

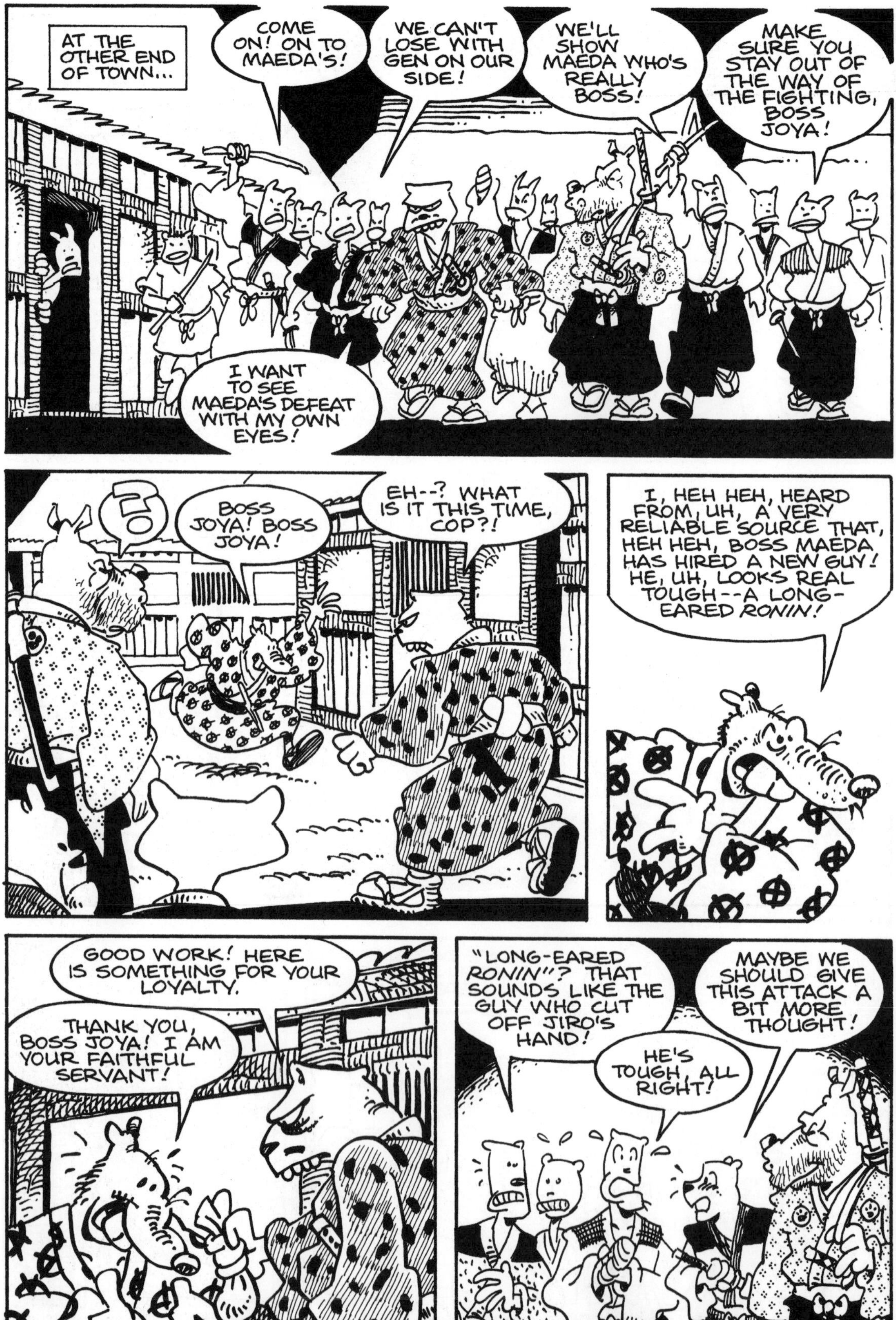
AT THE OTHER END OF TOWN...
COME ON! ON TO MAEDA'S!
WE CAN'T LOSE WITH GEN ON OUR SIDE!
WE'LL SHOW MAEDA WHO'S REALLY BOSS!
MAKE SURE YOU STAY OUT OF THE WAY OF THE FIGHTING, BOSS JOYA!
I WANT TO SEE MAEDA'S DEFEAT WITH MY OWN EYES!
BOSS JOYA! BOSS JOYA!
EH--? WHAT IS IT THIS TIME, COP?!
I, HEH HEH, HEARD FROM, UH, A VERY RELIABLE SOURCE THAT, HEH HEH, BOSS MAEDA HAS HIRED A NEW GUY! HE, UH, LOOKS REAL TOUGH--A LONG-EARED RONIN!
GOOD WORK! HERE IS SOMETHING FOR YOUR LOYALTY.
THANK YOU, BOSS JOYA! I AM YOUR FAITHFUL SERVANT!
"LONG-EARED RONIN"? THAT SOUNDS LIKE THE GUY WHO CUT OFF JIRO'S HAND!
HE'S TOUGH, ALL RIGHT!
MAYBE WE SHOULD GIVE THIS ATTACK A BIT MORE THOUGHT!
22.

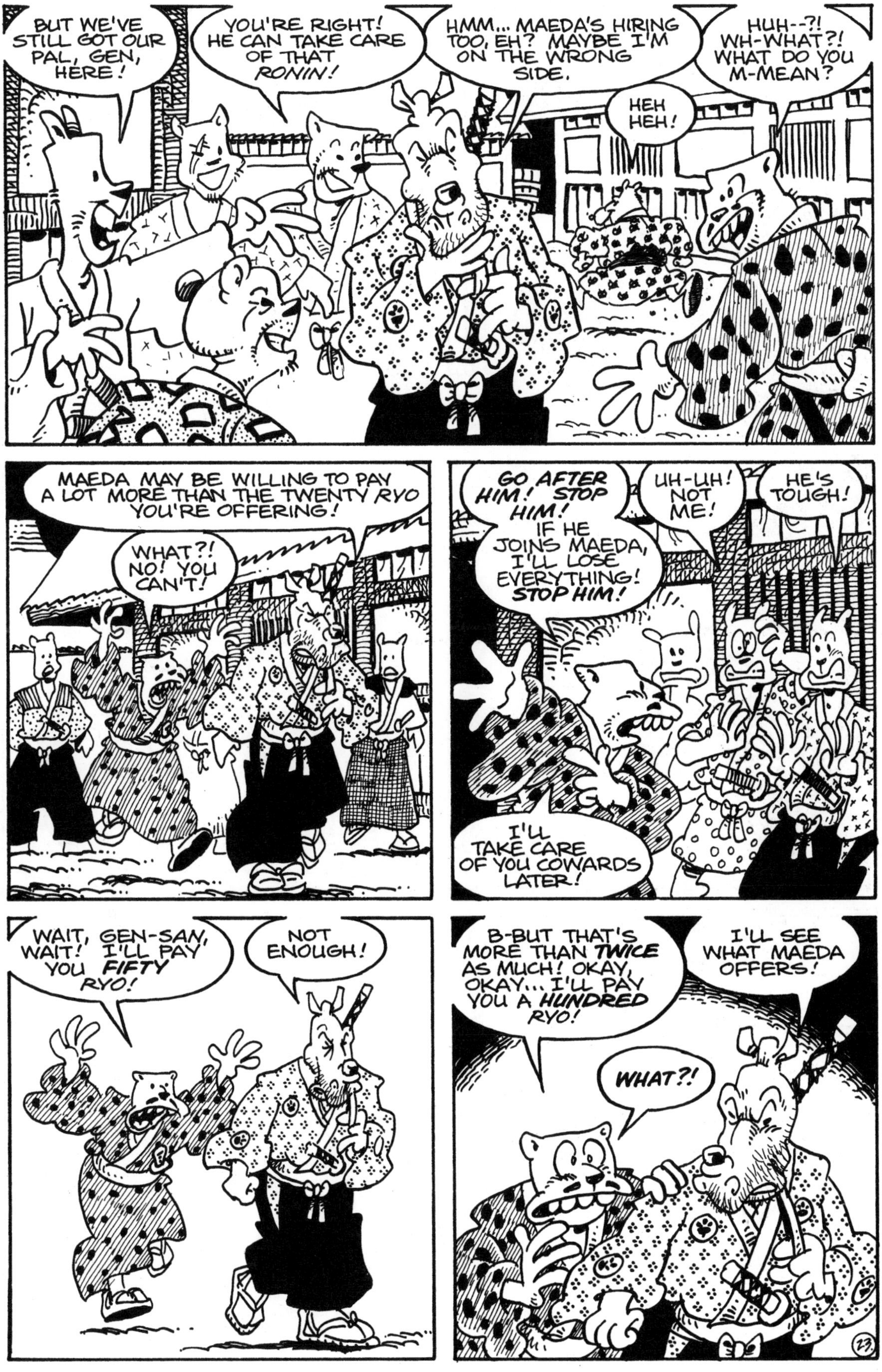

BUT WE'VE STILL GOT OUR PAL, GEN, HERE!
YOU'RE RIGHT! HE CAN TAKE CARE OF THAT RONIN!
HMM... MAEDA'S HIRING TOO, EH? MAYBE I'M ON THE WRONG SIDE.
HEH HEH!
HUH--?! WH-WHAT?! WHAT DO YOU M-MEAN?
MAEDA MAY BE WILLING TO PAY A LOT MORE THAN THE TWENTY RYO YOU'RE OFFERING!
WHAT?! NO! YOU CAN'T!
GO AFTER HIM! STOP HIM! IF HE JOINS MAEDA, I'LL LOSE EVERYTHING! STOP HIM!
UH-UH! NOT ME!
HE'S TOUGH!
I'LL TAKE CARE OF YOU COWARDS LATER!
WAIT, GEN-SAN, WAIT! I'LL PAY YOU FIFTY RYO!
NOT ENOUGH!
B-BUT THAT'S MORE THAN TWICE AS MUCH! OKAY, OKAY... I'LL PAY YOU A HUNDRED RYO!
I'LL SEE WHAT MAEDA OFFERS!
WHAT?!
23

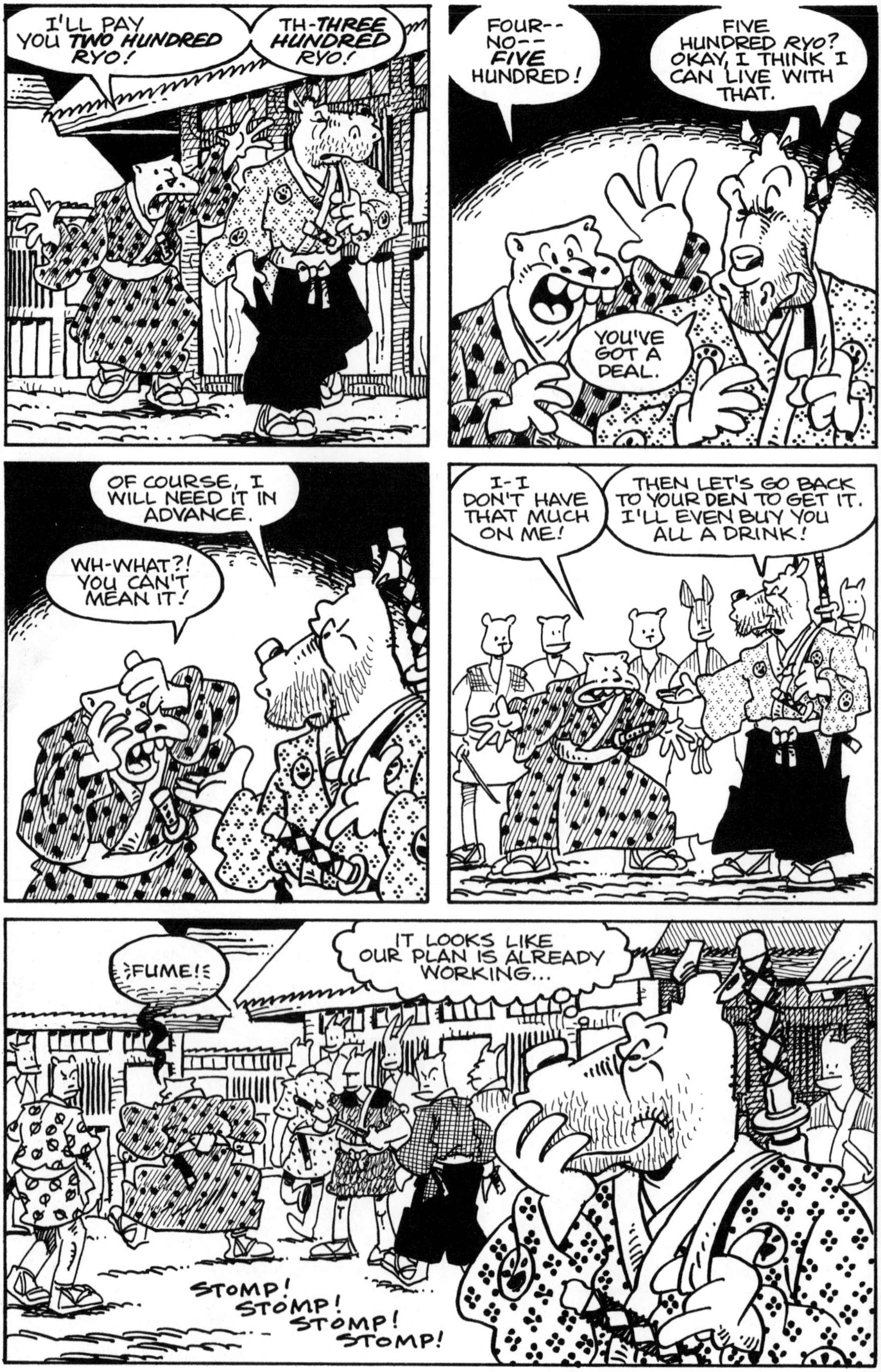
I'LL PAY YOU **TWO HUNDRED** *RYO*!
TH-***THREE HUNDRED*** *RYO*!
FOUR-- NO-- ***FIVE*** HUNDRED!
FIVE HUNDRED *RYO*? OKAY, I THINK I CAN LIVE WITH THAT.
YOU'VE GOT A DEAL.
OF COURSE, I WILL NEED IT IN ADVANCE.
WH-WHAT?! YOU CAN'T MEAN IT!
I-I DON'T HAVE THAT MUCH ON ME!
THEN LET'S GO BACK TO YOUR **DEN** TO GET IT. I'LL EVEN BUY YOU ALL A DRINK!
FUME!
IT LOOKS LIKE OUR PLAN IS ALREADY WORKING...
STOMP! STOMP! STOMP! STOMP!

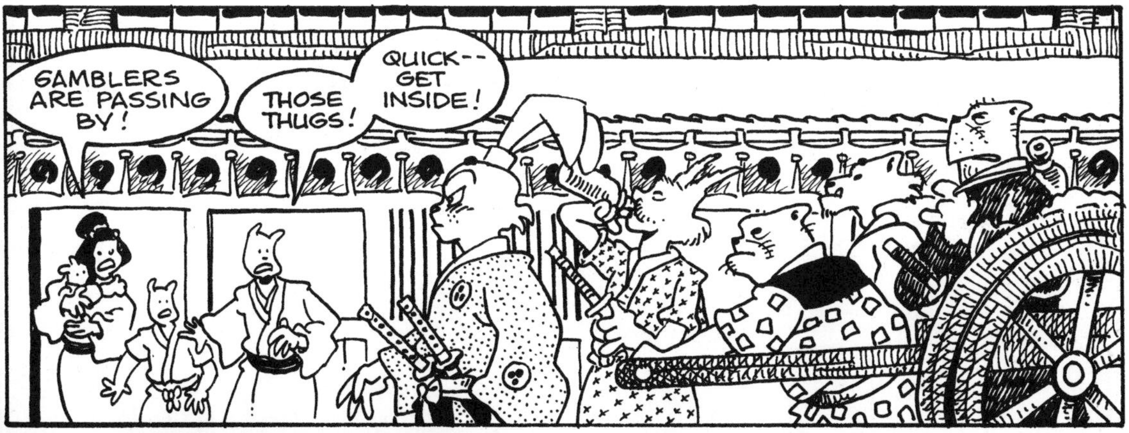
GAMBLERS ARE PASSING BY!
THOSE THUGS!
QUICK-- GET INSIDE!

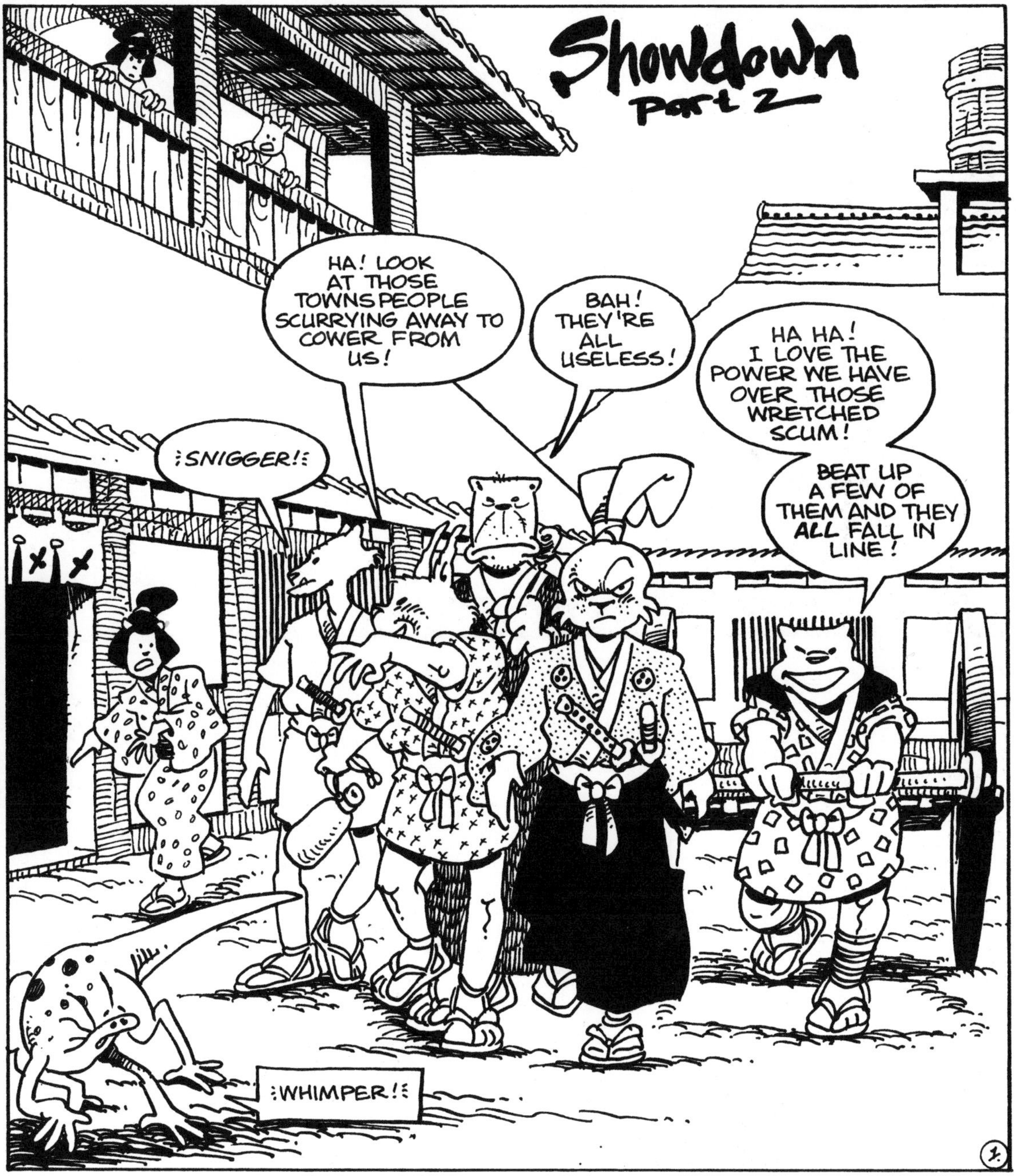
Showdown
Part 2
HA! LOOK AT THOSE TOWNSPEOPLE SCURRYING AWAY TO COWER FROM US!
BAH! THEY'RE ALL USELESS!
HA HA! I LOVE THE POWER WE HAVE OVER THOSE WRETCHED SCUM!
BEAT UP A FEW OF THEM AND THEY ALL FALL IN LINE!
:SNIGGER!:
:WHIMPER!:
1

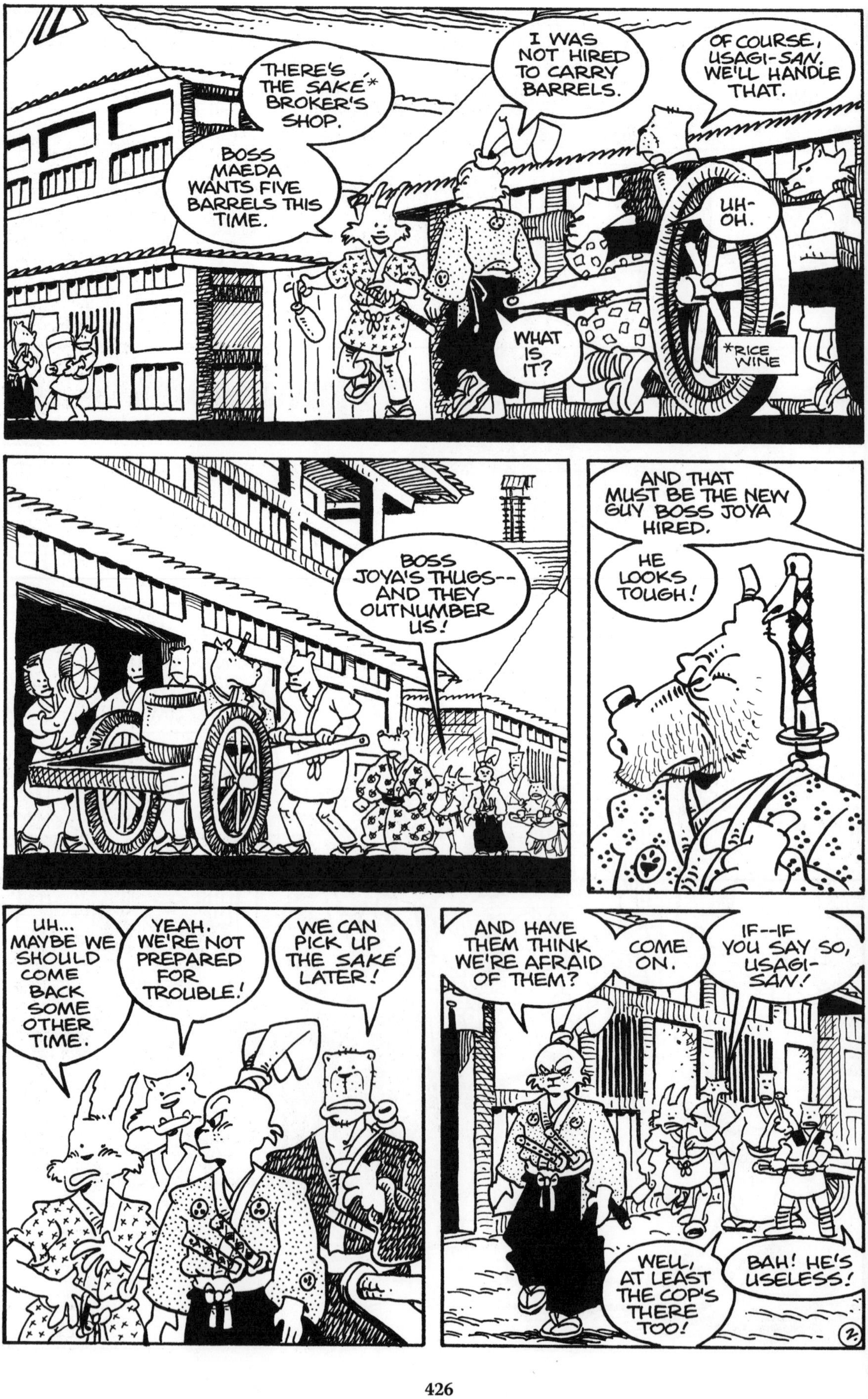
THERE'S THE *SAKE** BROKER'S SHOP.
BOSS MAEDA WANTS FIVE BARRELS THIS TIME.
I WAS NOT HIRED TO CARRY BARRELS.
OF COURSE, USAGI-*SAN*. WE'LL HANDLE THAT.
UH-OH.
WHAT IS IT?
*RICE WINE
BOSS JOYA'S THUGS--AND THEY OUTNUMBER US!
AND THAT MUST BE THE NEW GUY BOSS JOYA HIRED.
HE LOOKS TOUGH!
UH... MAYBE WE SHOULD COME BACK SOME OTHER TIME.
YEAH. WE'RE NOT PREPARED FOR TROUBLE!
WE CAN PICK UP THE *SAKE* LATER!
AND HAVE THEM THINK WE'RE AFRAID OF THEM?
COME ON.
IF--IF YOU SAY SO, USAGI-*SAN*!
WELL, AT LEAST THE COP'S THERE TOO!
BAH! HE'S USELESS!
2.

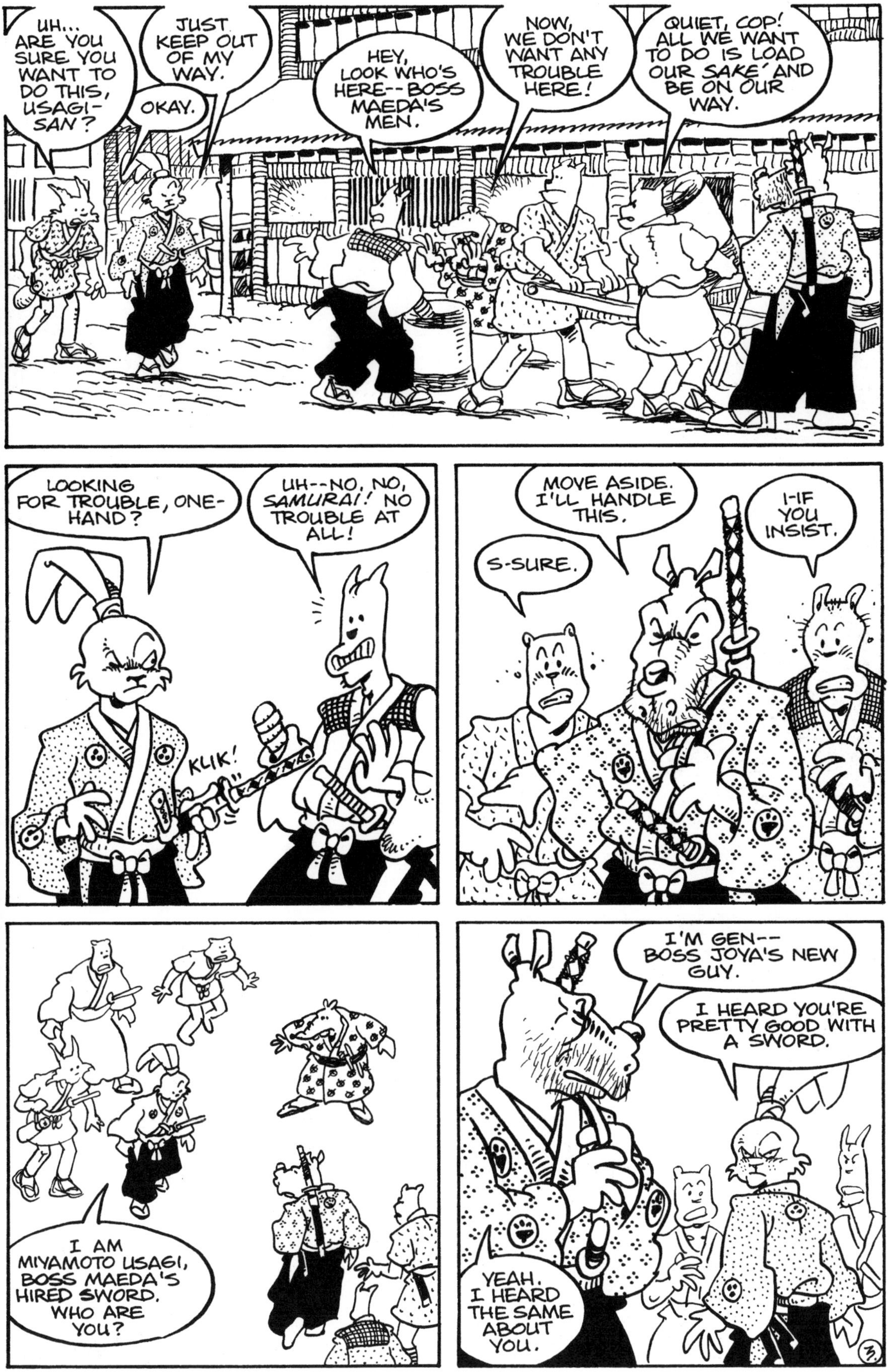
UH... ARE YOU SURE YOU WANT TO DO THIS, USAGI-SAN?
JUST KEEP OUT OF MY WAY.
OKAY.
HEY, LOOK WHO'S HERE--BOSS MAEDA'S MEN.
NOW, WE DON'T WANT ANY TROUBLE HERE!
QUIET, COP! ALL WE WANT TO DO IS LOAD OUR SAKE AND BE ON OUR WAY.
LOOKING FOR TROUBLE, ONE-HAND?
UH--NO, NO, SAMURAI! NO TROUBLE AT ALL!
KLIK!
MOVE ASIDE. I'LL HANDLE THIS.
S-SURE.
I-IF YOU INSIST.
I AM MIYAMOTO USAGI, BOSS MAEDA'S HIRED SWORD. WHO ARE YOU?
I'M GEN--BOSS JOYA'S NEW GUY.
I HEARD YOU'RE PRETTY GOOD WITH A SWORD.
YEAH. I HEARD THE SAME ABOUT YOU.
3.

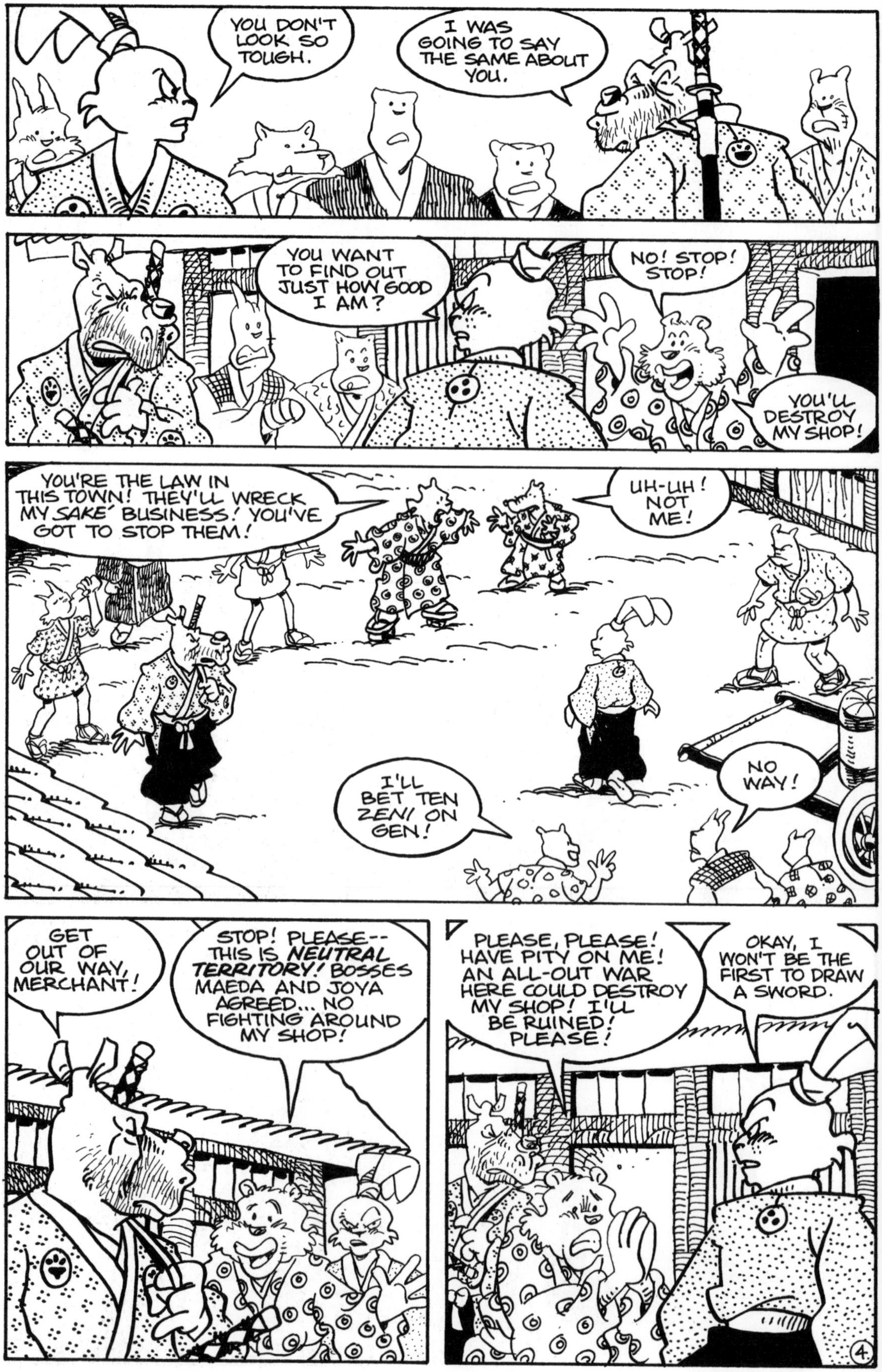
YOU DON'T LOOK SO TOUGH.
I WAS GOING TO SAY THE SAME ABOUT YOU.
YOU WANT TO FIND OUT JUST HOW GOOD I AM?
NO! STOP! STOP!
YOU'LL DESTROY MY SHOP!
YOU'RE THE LAW IN THIS TOWN! THEY'LL WRECK MY SAKE' BUSINESS! YOU'VE GOT TO STOP THEM!
UH-UH! NOT ME!
I'LL BET TEN ZENI ON GEN!
NO WAY!
GET OUT OF OUR WAY, MERCHANT!
STOP! PLEASE-- THIS IS NEUTRAL TERRITORY! BOSSES MAEDA AND JOYA AGREED... NO FIGHTING AROUND MY SHOP!
PLEASE, PLEASE! HAVE PITY ON ME! AN ALL-OUT WAR HERE COULD DESTROY MY SHOP! I'LL BE RUINED! PLEASE!
OKAY, I WON'T BE THE FIRST TO DRAW A SWORD.
4

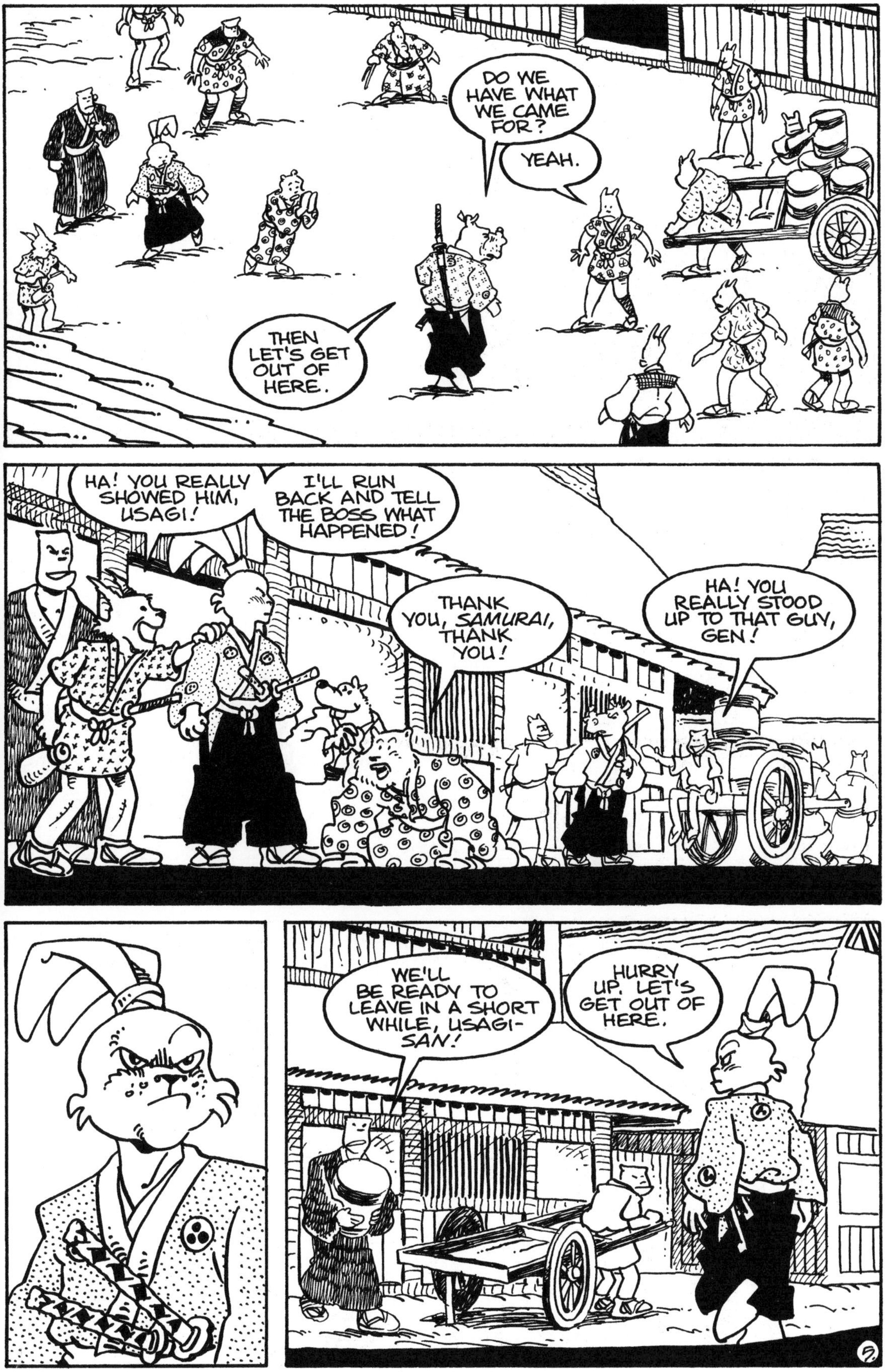
DO WE HAVE WHAT WE CAME FOR?
YEAH.
THEN LET'S GET OUT OF HERE.
HA! YOU REALLY SHOWED HIM, USAGI!
I'LL RUN BACK AND TELL THE BOSS WHAT HAPPENED!
THANK YOU, *SAMURAI*, THANK YOU!
HA! YOU REALLY STOOD UP TO THAT GUY, GEN!
WE'LL BE READY TO LEAVE IN A SHORT WHILE, USAGI-*SAN*!
HURRY UP. LET'S GET OUT OF HERE.
5

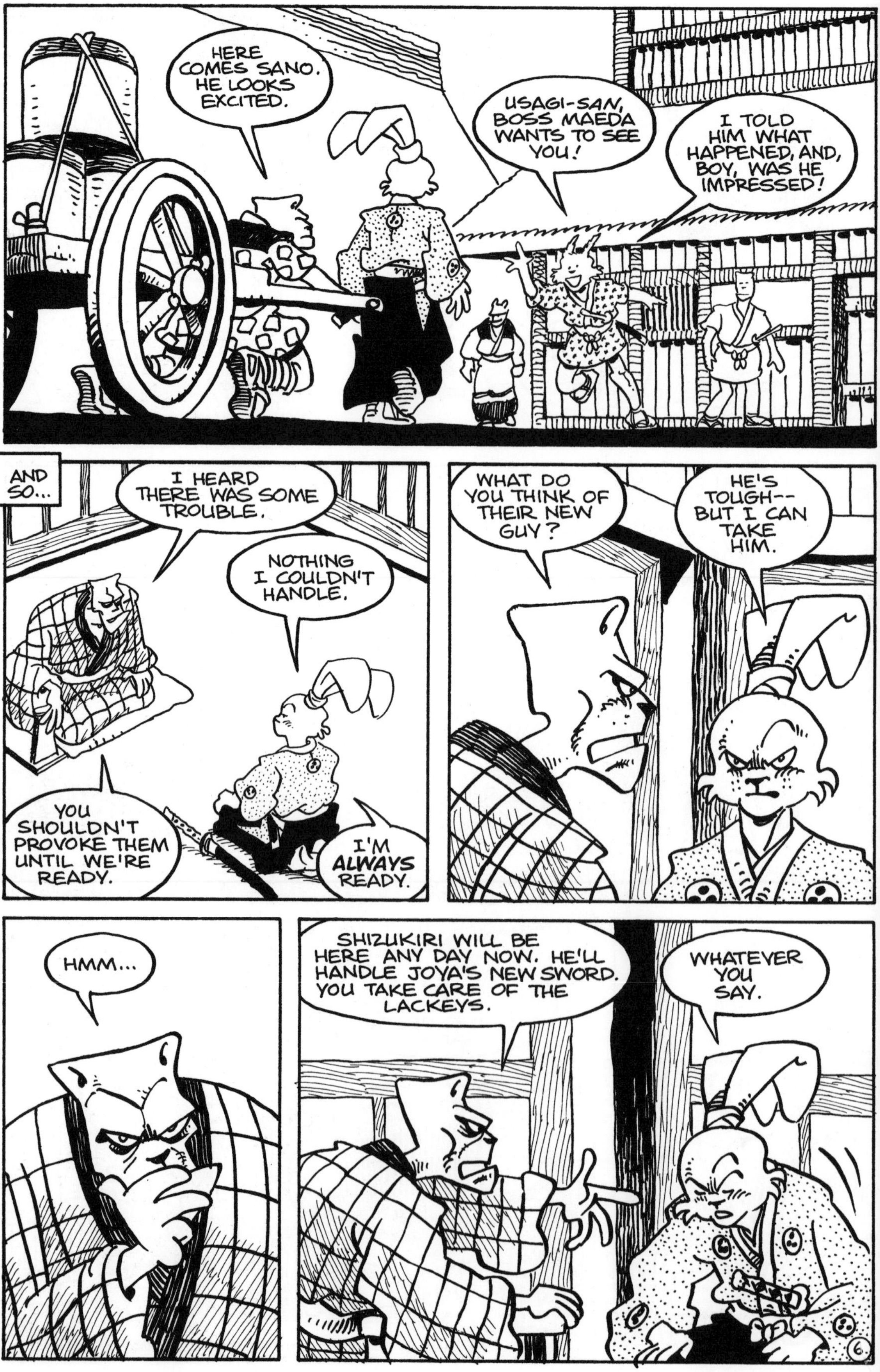

HERE COMES SANO. HE LOOKS EXCITED.
USAGI-SAN, BOSS MAEDA WANTS TO SEE YOU!
I TOLD HIM WHAT HAPPENED, AND, BOY, WAS HE IMPRESSED!
AND SO...
I HEARD THERE WAS SOME TROUBLE.
NOTHING I COULDN'T HANDLE.
YOU SHOULDN'T PROVOKE THEM UNTIL WE'RE READY.
I'M ALWAYS READY.
WHAT DO YOU THINK OF THEIR NEW GUY?
HE'S TOUGH-- BUT I CAN TAKE HIM.
HMM...
SHIZUKIRI WILL BE HERE ANY DAY NOW. HE'LL HANDLE JOYA'S NEW SWORD. YOU TAKE CARE OF THE LACKEYS.
WHATEVER YOU SAY.
6.

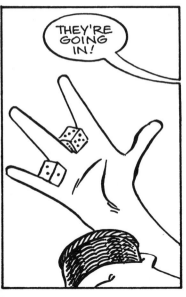

THEY'RE GOING IN!

GARA GARA GARA

PLACE YOUR BETS!

SPAK

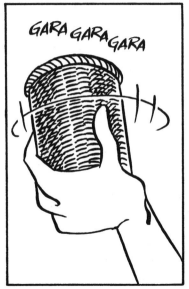

HAN*!

HAN!

CHO**!

HAN! PLEASE MAKE IT HAN! THIS IS ALL I HAVE LEFT! HAN! HAN!

CHO!

ME TOO! CHO!

HAN!

*ODD **EVEN

CHO!

¡GULP!

THEY'RE GOING IN!

WE WIN AGAIN, USAGI-SAN! I'LL KEEP FOLLOWING YOUR LEAD, AND YOU'LL MAKE ME A RICH GUY!

HAN!

⑦

431

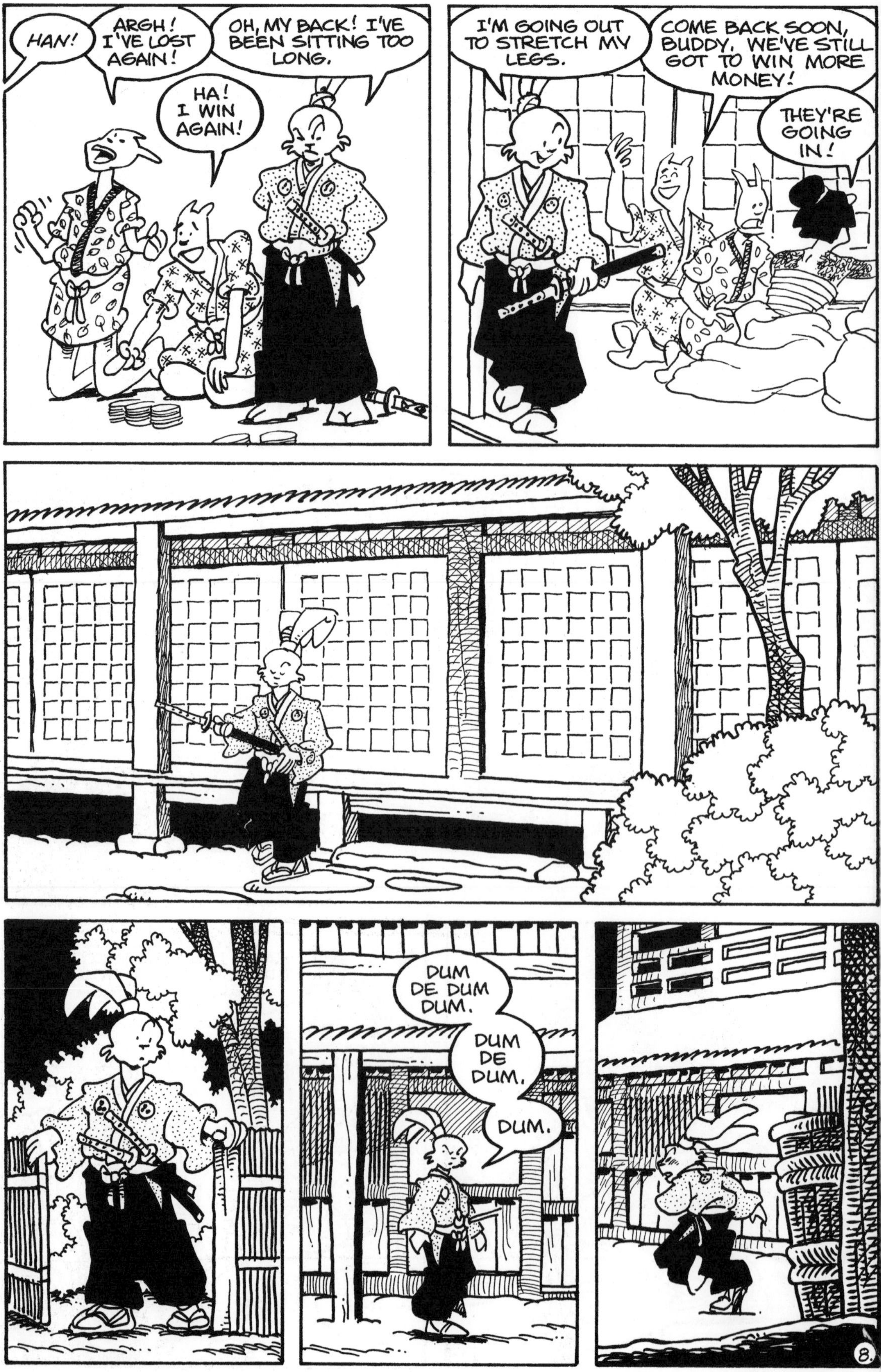
HAN!
ARGH! I'VE LOST AGAIN!
OH, MY BACK! I'VE BEEN SITTING TOO LONG.
HA! I WIN AGAIN!
I'M GOING OUT TO STRETCH MY LEGS.
COME BACK SOON, BUDDY. WE'VE STILL GOT TO WIN MORE MONEY!
THEY'RE GOING IN!
DUM DE DUM DUM.
DUM DE DUM.
DUM.
8.

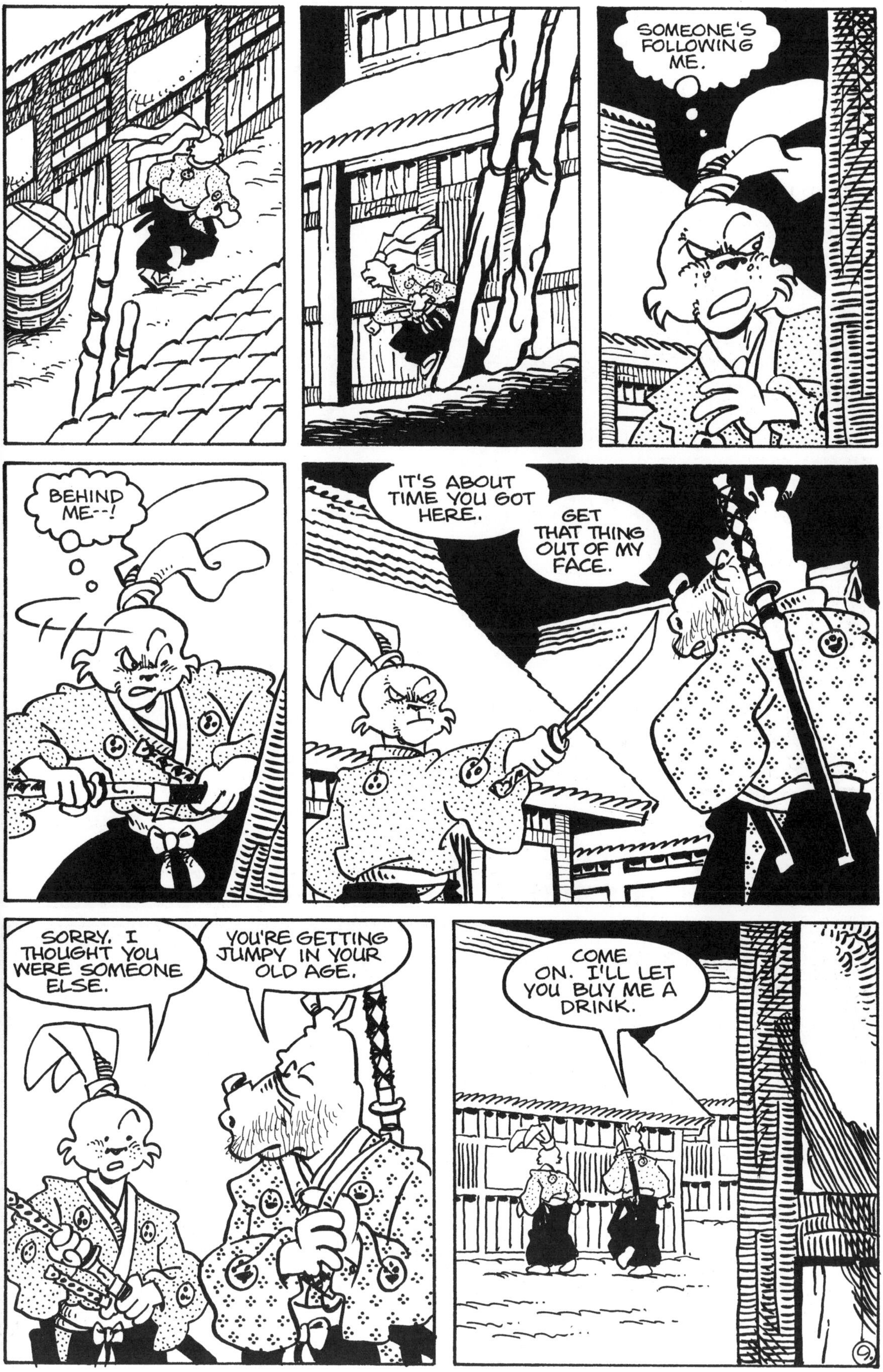
SOMEONE'S FOLLOWING ME.
BEHIND ME--!
IT'S ABOUT TIME YOU GOT HERE.
GET THAT THING OUT OF MY FACE.
SORRY. I THOUGHT YOU WERE SOMEONE ELSE.
YOU'RE GETTING JUMPY IN YOUR OLD AGE.
COME ON. I'LL LET YOU BUY ME A DRINK.
9

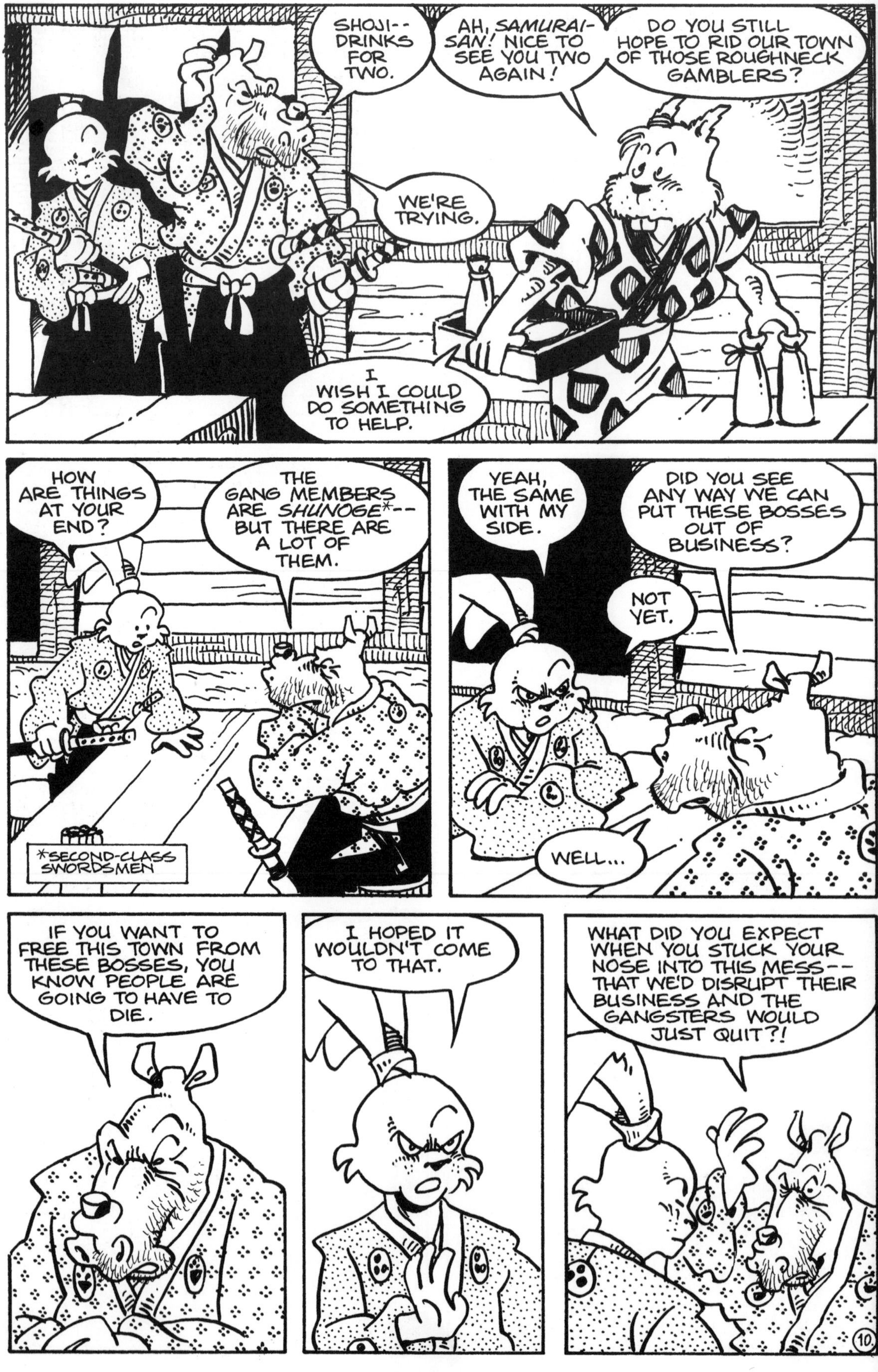
SHOJI-- DRINKS FOR TWO.
AH, SAMURAI-SAN! NICE TO SEE YOU TWO AGAIN!
DO YOU STILL HOPE TO RID OUR TOWN OF THOSE ROUGHNECK GAMBLERS?
WE'RE TRYING.
I WISH I COULD DO SOMETHING TO HELP.
HOW ARE THINGS AT YOUR END?
THE GANG MEMBERS ARE SHUNOGE*-- BUT THERE ARE A LOT OF THEM.
*SECOND-CLASS SWORDSMEN
YEAH, THE SAME WITH MY SIDE.
DID YOU SEE ANY WAY WE CAN PUT THESE BOSSES OUT OF BUSINESS?
NOT YET.
WELL...
IF YOU WANT TO FREE THIS TOWN FROM THESE BOSSES, YOU KNOW PEOPLE ARE GOING TO HAVE TO DIE.
I HOPED IT WOULDN'T COME TO THAT.
WHAT DID YOU EXPECT WHEN YOU STUCK YOUR NOSE INTO THIS MESS-- THAT WE'D DISRUPT THEIR BUSINESS AND THE GANGSTERS WOULD JUST QUIT?!
10

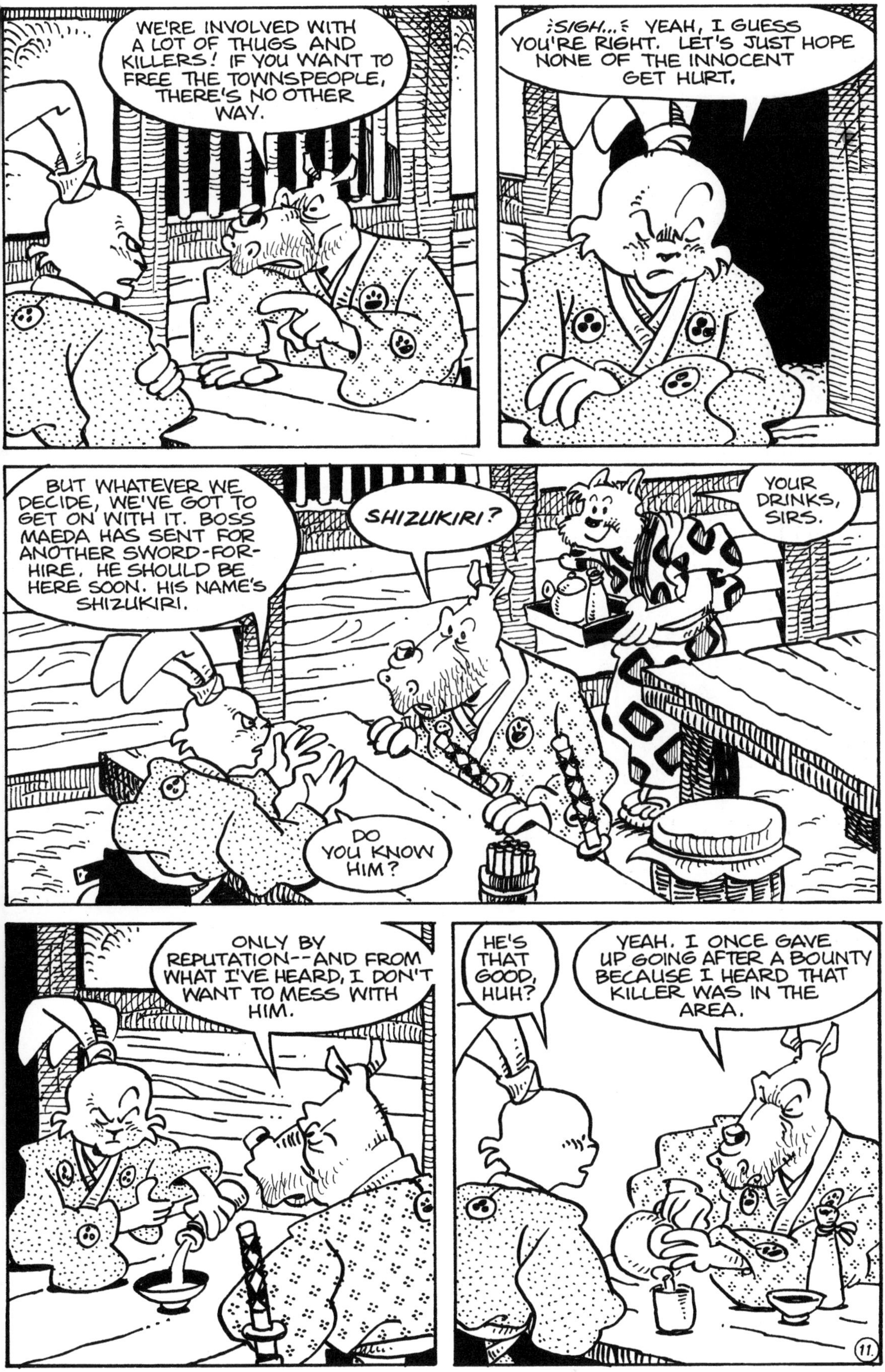
WE'RE INVOLVED WITH A LOT OF THUGS AND KILLERS! IF YOU WANT TO FREE THE TOWNSPEOPLE, THERE'S NO OTHER WAY.
:SIGH...: YEAH, I GUESS YOU'RE RIGHT. LET'S JUST HOPE NONE OF THE INNOCENT GET HURT.
BUT WHATEVER WE DECIDE, WE'VE GOT TO GET ON WITH IT. BOSS MAEDA HAS SENT FOR ANOTHER SWORD-FOR-HIRE. HE SHOULD BE HERE SOON. HIS NAME'S SHIZUKIRI.
SHIZUKIRI?
YOUR DRINKS, SIRS.
DO YOU KNOW HIM?
ONLY BY REPUTATION--AND FROM WHAT I'VE HEARD, I DON'T WANT TO MESS WITH HIM.
HE'S THAT GOOD, HUH?
YEAH. I ONCE GAVE UP GOING AFTER A BOUNTY BECAUSE I HEARD THAT KILLER WAS IN THE AREA.
11.

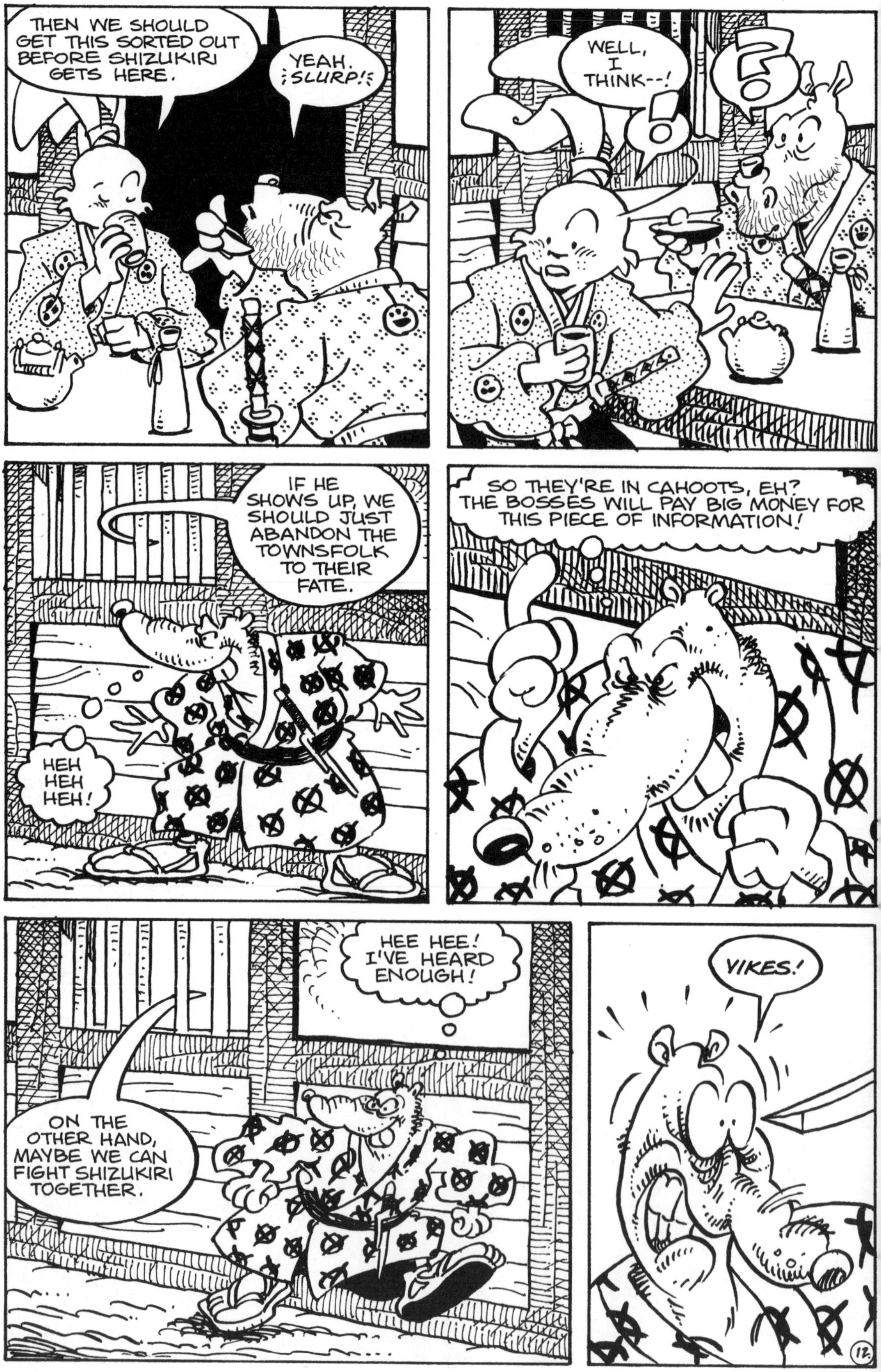
THEN WE SHOULD GET THIS SORTED OUT BEFORE SHIZUKIRI GETS HERE.
YEAH. SLURP!
WELL, I THINK--!
!
?
IF HE SHOWS UP, WE SHOULD JUST ABANDON THE TOWNSFOLK TO THEIR FATE.
HEH HEH HEH!
SO THEY'RE IN CAHOOTS, EH? THE BOSSES WILL PAY BIG MONEY FOR THIS PIECE OF INFORMATION!
HEE HEE! I'VE HEARD ENOUGH!
ON THE OTHER HAND, MAYBE WE CAN FIGHT SHIZUKIRI TOGETHER.
YIKES!
12.

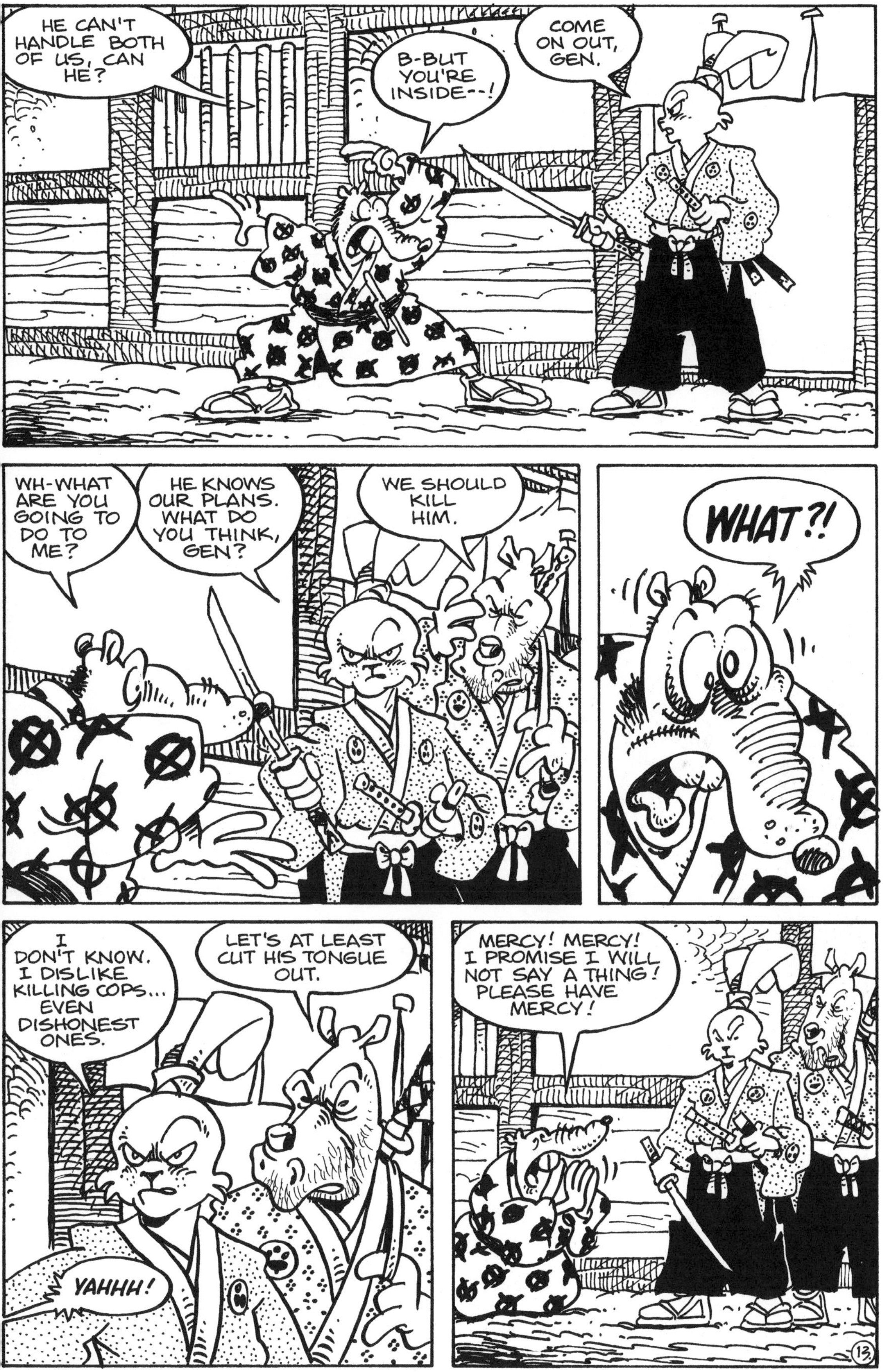
HE CAN'T HANDLE BOTH OF US, CAN HE?
B-BUT YOU'RE INSIDE--!
COME ON OUT, GEN.
WH-WHAT ARE YOU GOING TO DO TO ME?
HE KNOWS OUR PLANS. WHAT DO YOU THINK, GEN?
WE SHOULD KILL HIM.
WHAT?!
I DON'T KNOW. I DISLIKE KILLING COPS... EVEN DISHONEST ONES.
LET'S AT LEAST CUT HIS TONGUE OUT.
YAHHH!
MERCY! MERCY! I PROMISE I WILL NOT SAY A THING! PLEASE HAVE MERCY!
13

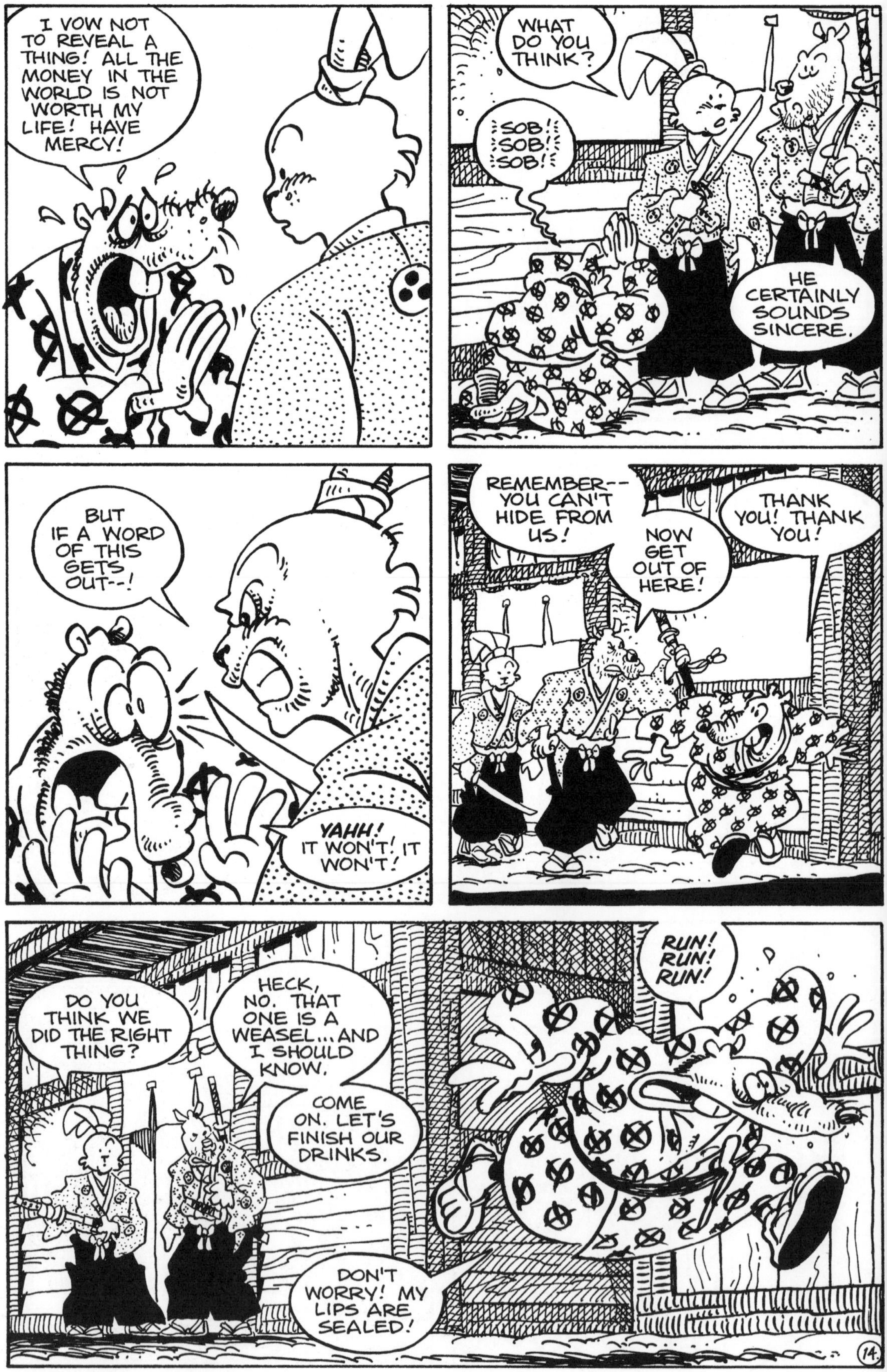
I VOW NOT TO REVEAL A THING! ALL THE MONEY IN THE WORLD IS NOT WORTH MY LIFE! HAVE MERCY!
WHAT DO YOU THINK?
SOB! SOB! SOB!
HE CERTAINLY SOUNDS SINCERE.
BUT IF A WORD OF THIS GETS OUT--!
YAHH! IT WON'T! IT WON'T!
REMEMBER-- YOU CAN'T HIDE FROM US!
NOW GET OUT OF HERE!
THANK YOU! THANK YOU!
DO YOU THINK WE DID THE RIGHT THING?
HECK, NO. THAT ONE IS A WEASEL...AND I SHOULD KNOW.
COME ON. LET'S FINISH OUR DRINKS.
RUN! RUN! RUN!
DON'T WORRY! MY LIPS ARE SEALED!
14.

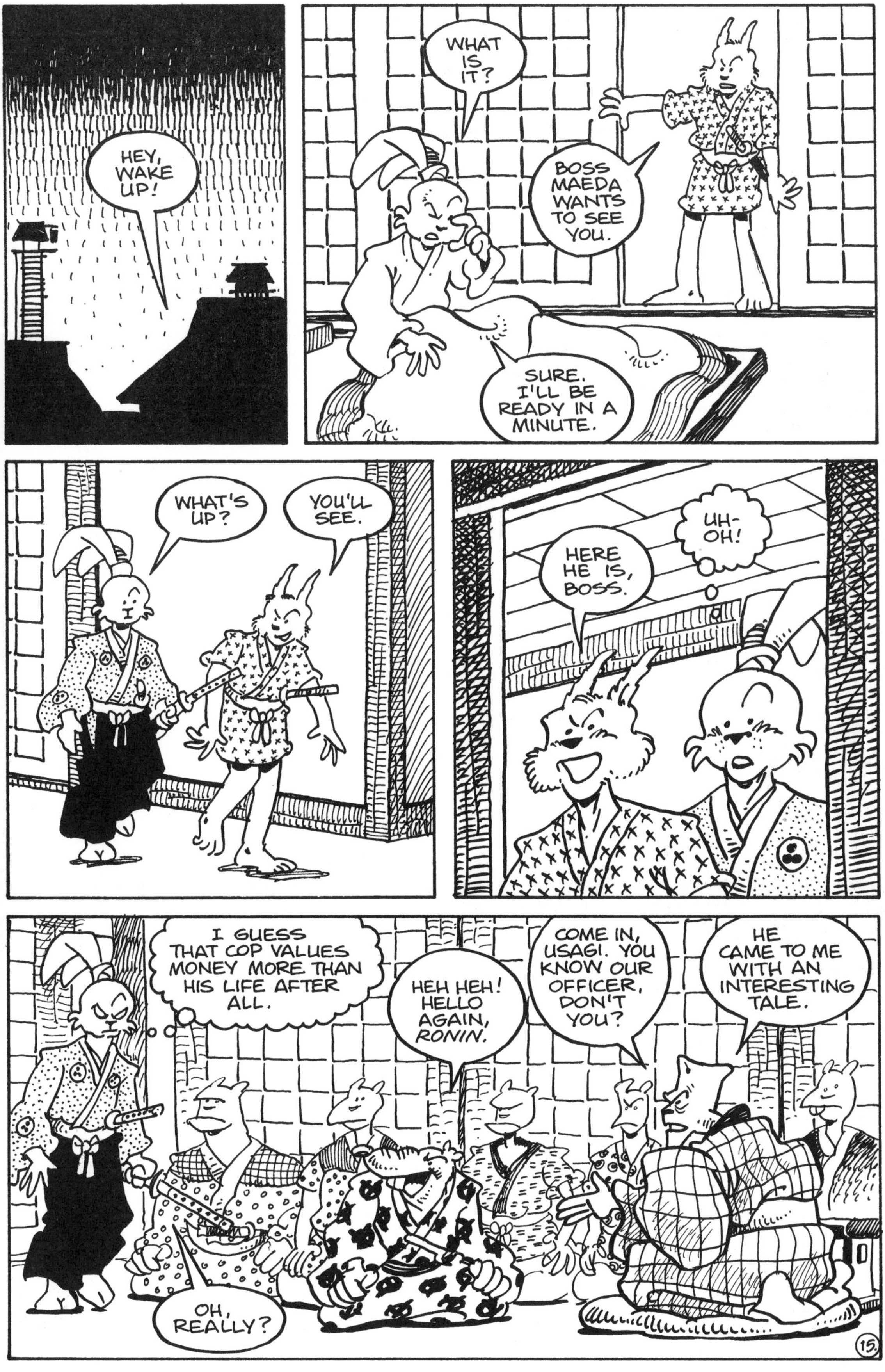
HEY, WAKE UP!
WHAT IS IT?
BOSS MAEDA WANTS TO SEE YOU.
SURE. I'LL BE READY IN A MINUTE.
WHAT'S UP?
YOU'LL SEE.
HERE HE IS, BOSS.
UH-OH!
I GUESS THAT COP VALUES MONEY MORE THAN HIS LIFE AFTER ALL.
HEH HEH! HELLO AGAIN, *RONIN*.
COME IN, USAGI. YOU KNOW OUR OFFICER, DON'T YOU?
HE CAME TO ME WITH AN INTERESTING TALE.
OH, REALLY?
15

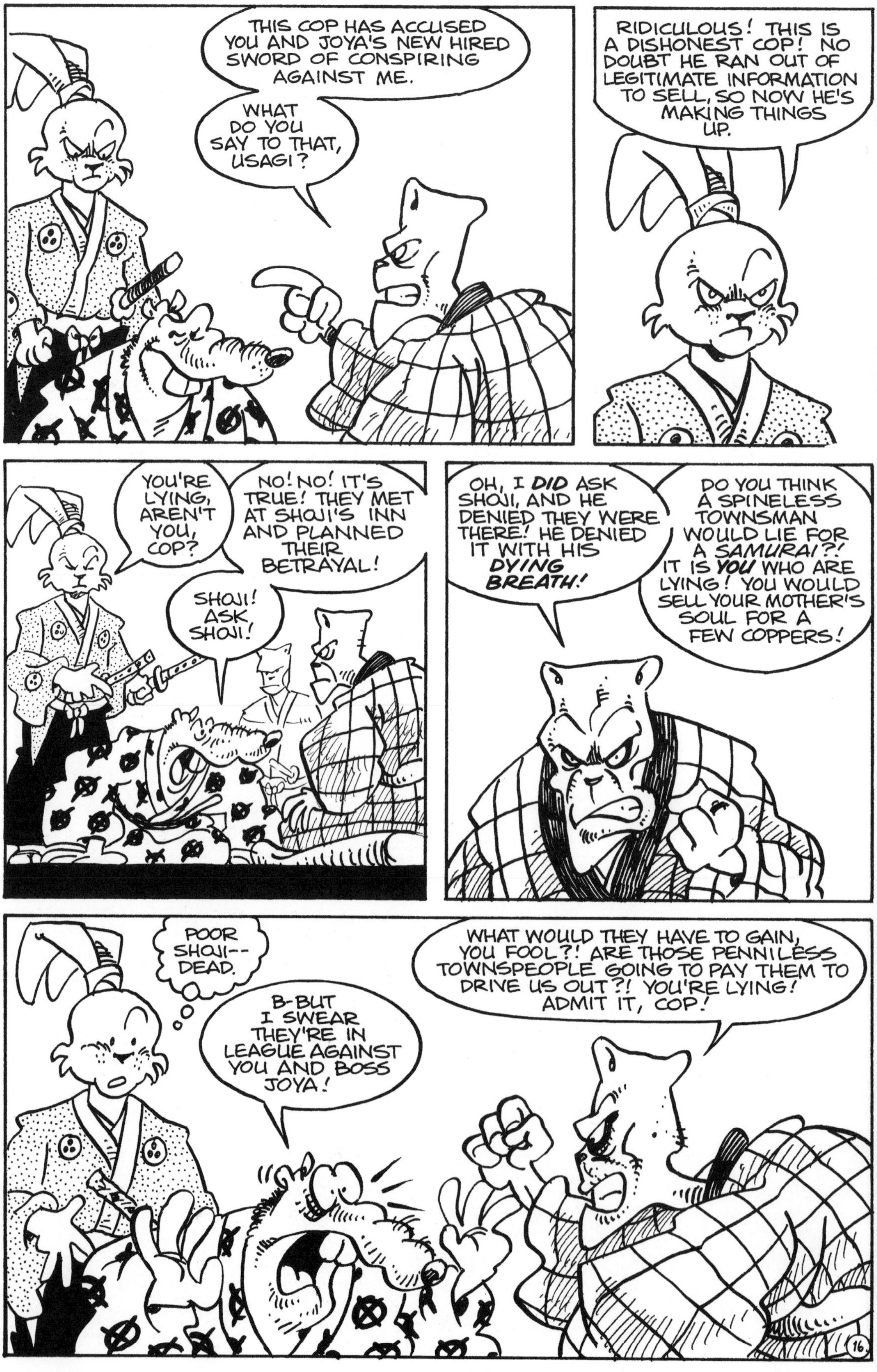
THIS COP HAS ACCUSED YOU AND JOYA'S NEW HIRED SWORD OF CONSPIRING AGAINST ME.
WHAT DO YOU SAY TO THAT, USAGI?
RIDICULOUS! THIS IS A DISHONEST COP! NO DOUBT HE RAN OUT OF LEGITIMATE INFORMATION TO SELL, SO NOW HE'S MAKING THINGS UP.
YOU'RE LYING, AREN'T YOU, COP?
NO! NO! IT'S TRUE! THEY MET AT SHOJI'S INN AND PLANNED THEIR BETRAYAL!
SHOJI! ASK SHOJI!
OH, I *DID* ASK SHOJI, AND HE DENIED THEY WERE THERE! HE DENIED IT WITH HIS ***DYING BREATH!***
DO YOU THINK A SPINELESS TOWNSMAN WOULD LIE FOR A *SAMURAI?!* IT IS ***YOU*** WHO ARE LYING! YOU WOULD SELL YOUR MOTHER'S SOUL FOR A FEW COPPERS!
POOR SHOJI-- DEAD.
B-BUT I SWEAR THEY'RE IN LEAGUE AGAINST YOU AND BOSS JOYA!
WHAT WOULD THEY HAVE TO GAIN, YOU FOOL?! ARE THOSE PENNILESS TOWNSPEOPLE GOING TO PAY THEM TO DRIVE US OUT?! YOU'RE LYING! ADMIT IT, COP!
16

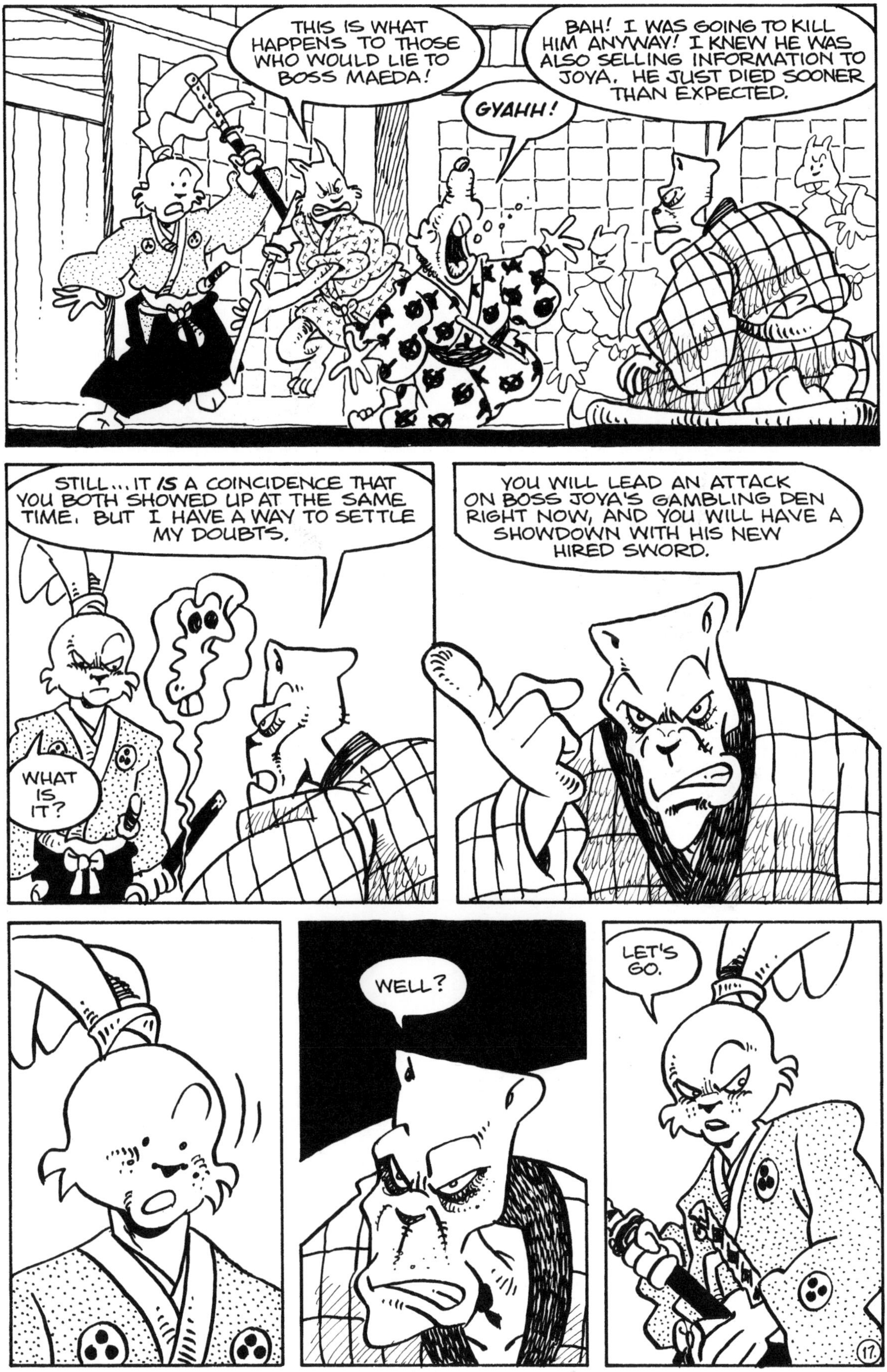
THIS IS WHAT HAPPENS TO THOSE WHO WOULD LIE TO BOSS MAEDA!
GYAHH!
BAH! I WAS GOING TO KILL HIM ANYWAY! I KNEW HE WAS ALSO SELLING INFORMATION TO JOYA. HE JUST DIED SOONER THAN EXPECTED.
STILL... IT IS A COINCIDENCE THAT YOU BOTH SHOWED UP AT THE SAME TIME. BUT I HAVE A WAY TO SETTLE MY DOUBTS.
WHAT IS IT?
YOU WILL LEAD AN ATTACK ON BOSS JOYA'S GAMBLING DEN RIGHT NOW, AND YOU WILL HAVE A SHOWDOWN WITH HIS NEW HIRED SWORD.
WELL?
LET'S GO.
17.

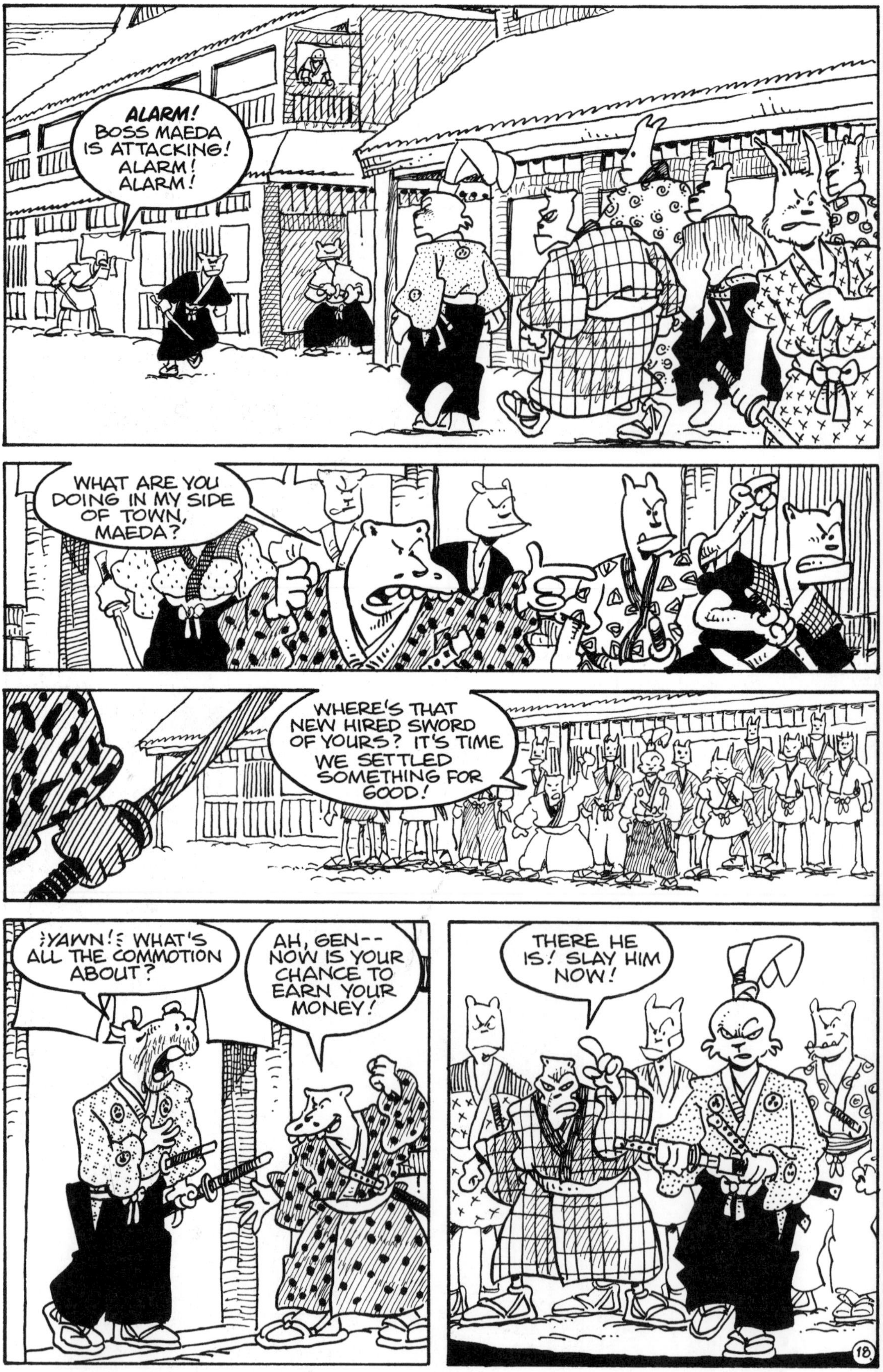
ALARM! BOSS MAEDA IS ATTACKING! ALARM! ALARM!
WHAT ARE YOU DOING IN MY SIDE OF TOWN, MAEDA?
WHERE'S THAT NEW HIRED SWORD OF YOURS? IT'S TIME WE SETTLED SOMETHING FOR GOOD!
YAWN! WHAT'S ALL THE COMMOTION ABOUT?
AH, GEN-- NOW IS YOUR CHANCE TO EARN YOUR MONEY!
THERE HE IS! SLAY HIM NOW!
18

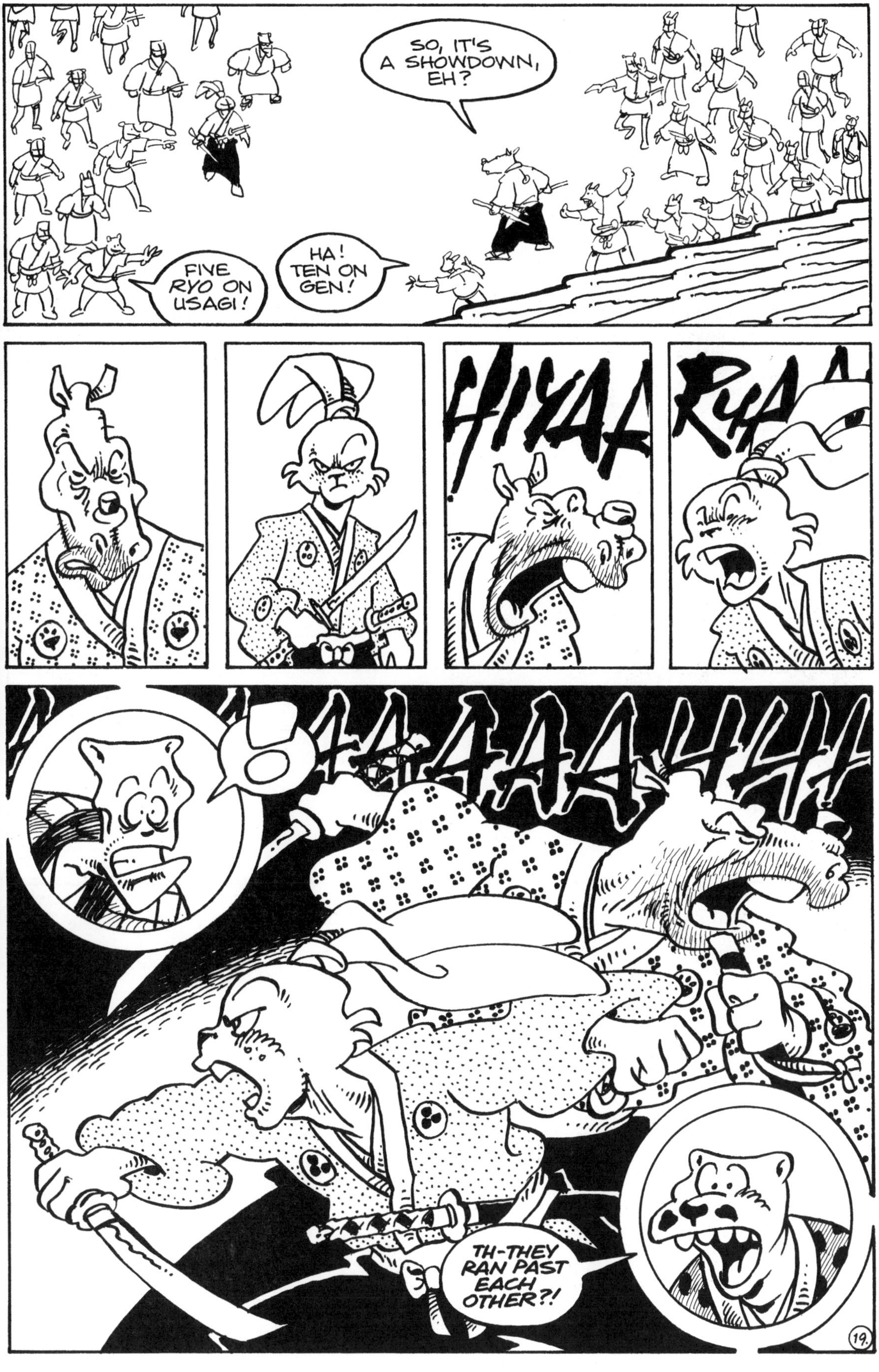
SO, IT'S A SHOWDOWN, EH?
FIVE RYO ON USAGI!
HA! TEN ON GEN!
HIYAA
RYA
AAAAAAAAHH!
TH-THEY RAN PAST EACH OTHER?!
19

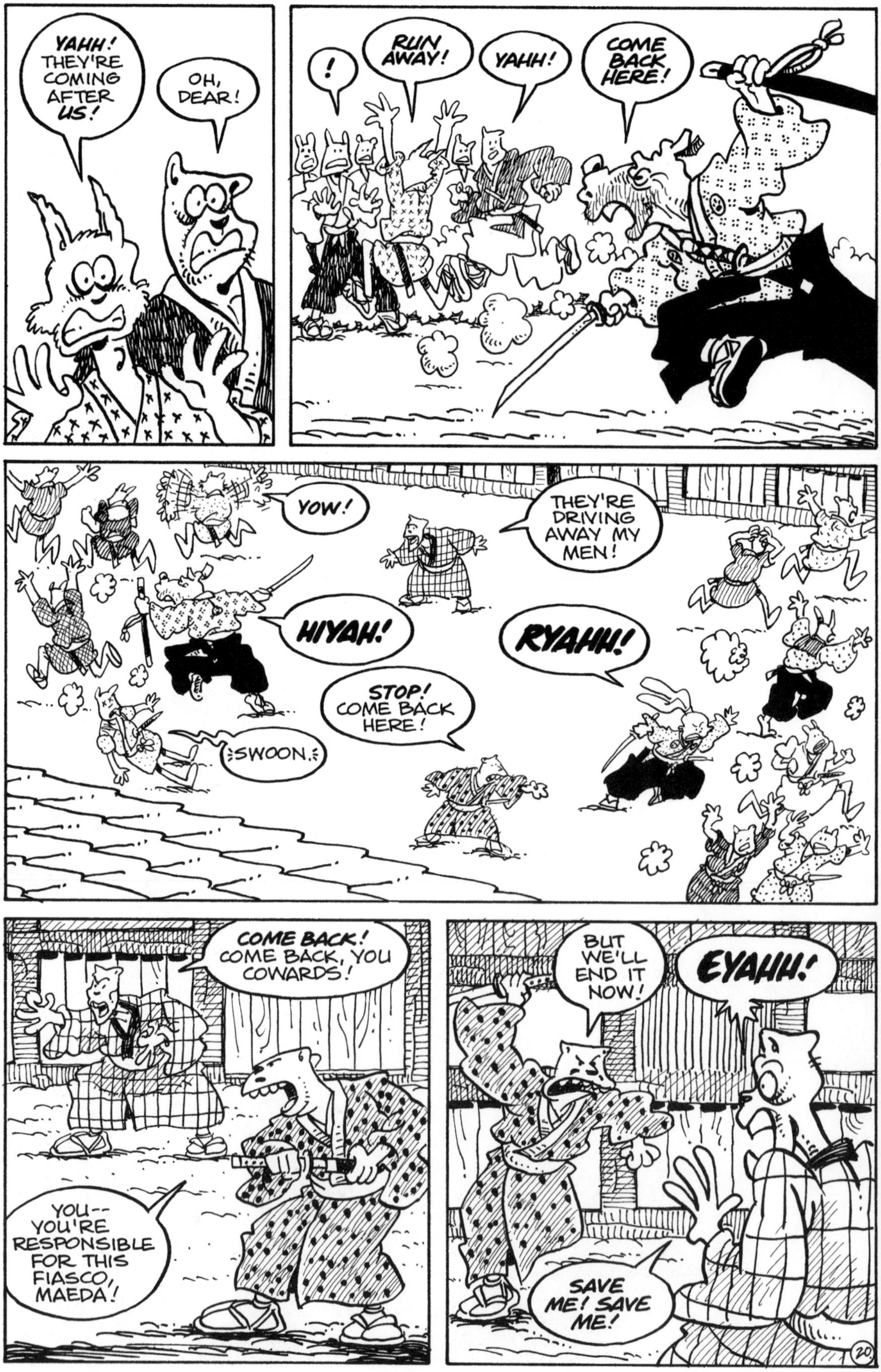
YAHH! THEY'RE COMING AFTER US!
OH, DEAR!
!
RUN AWAY!
YAHH!
COME BACK HERE!
YOW!
THEY'RE DRIVING AWAY MY MEN!
HIYAH!
RYAHH!
STOP! COME BACK HERE!
SWOON.
COME BACK! COME BACK, YOU COWARDS!
YOU-- YOU'RE RESPONSIBLE FOR THIS FIASCO, MAEDA!
BUT WE'LL END IT NOW!
EYAHH!
SAVE ME! SAVE ME!
20

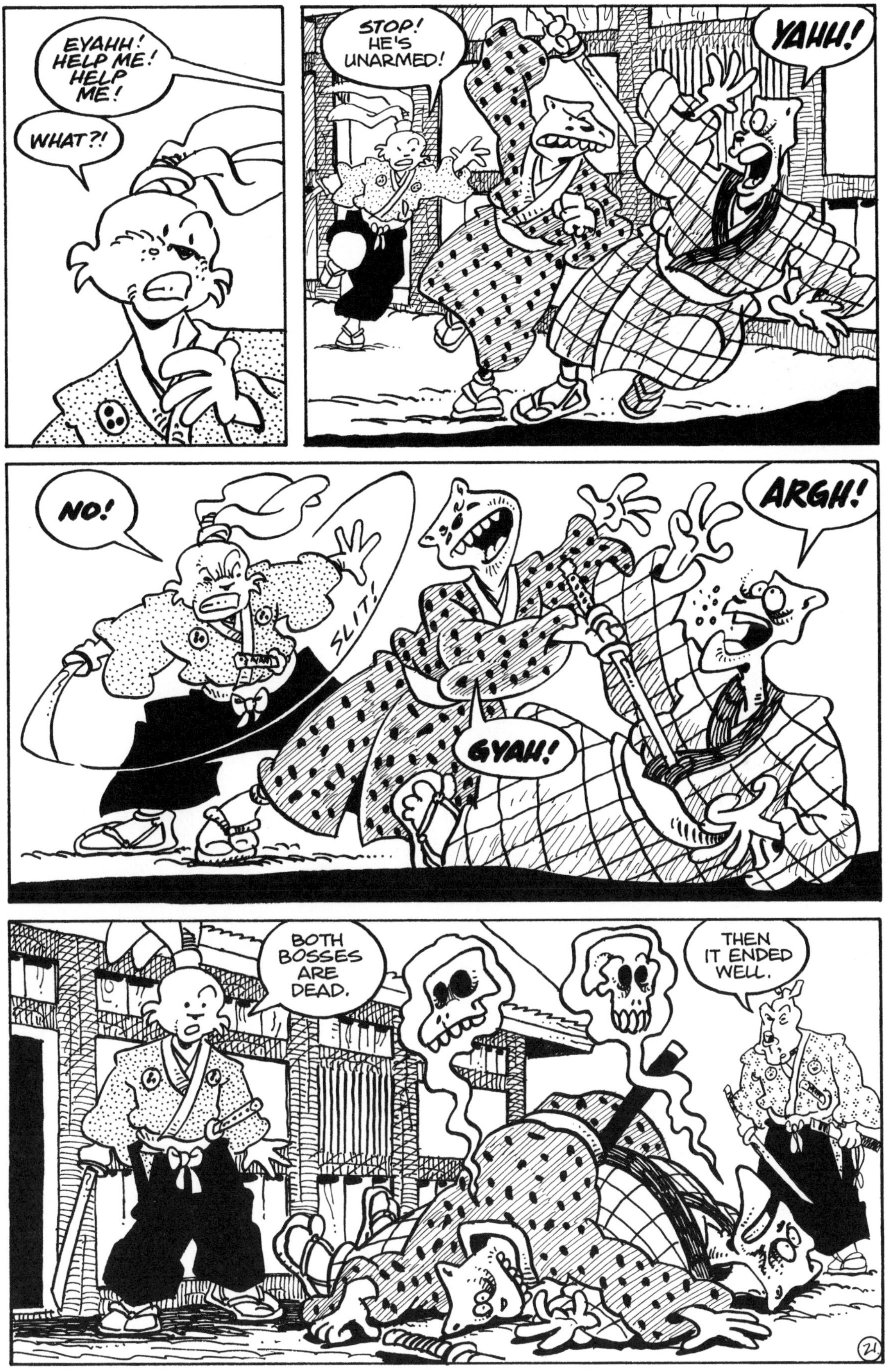
EYAHH! HELP ME! HELP ME!
WHAT?!
STOP! HE'S UNARMED!
YAHH!
NO!
SLIT!
ARGH!
GYAH!
BOTH BOSSES ARE DEAD.
THEN IT ENDED WELL.
21

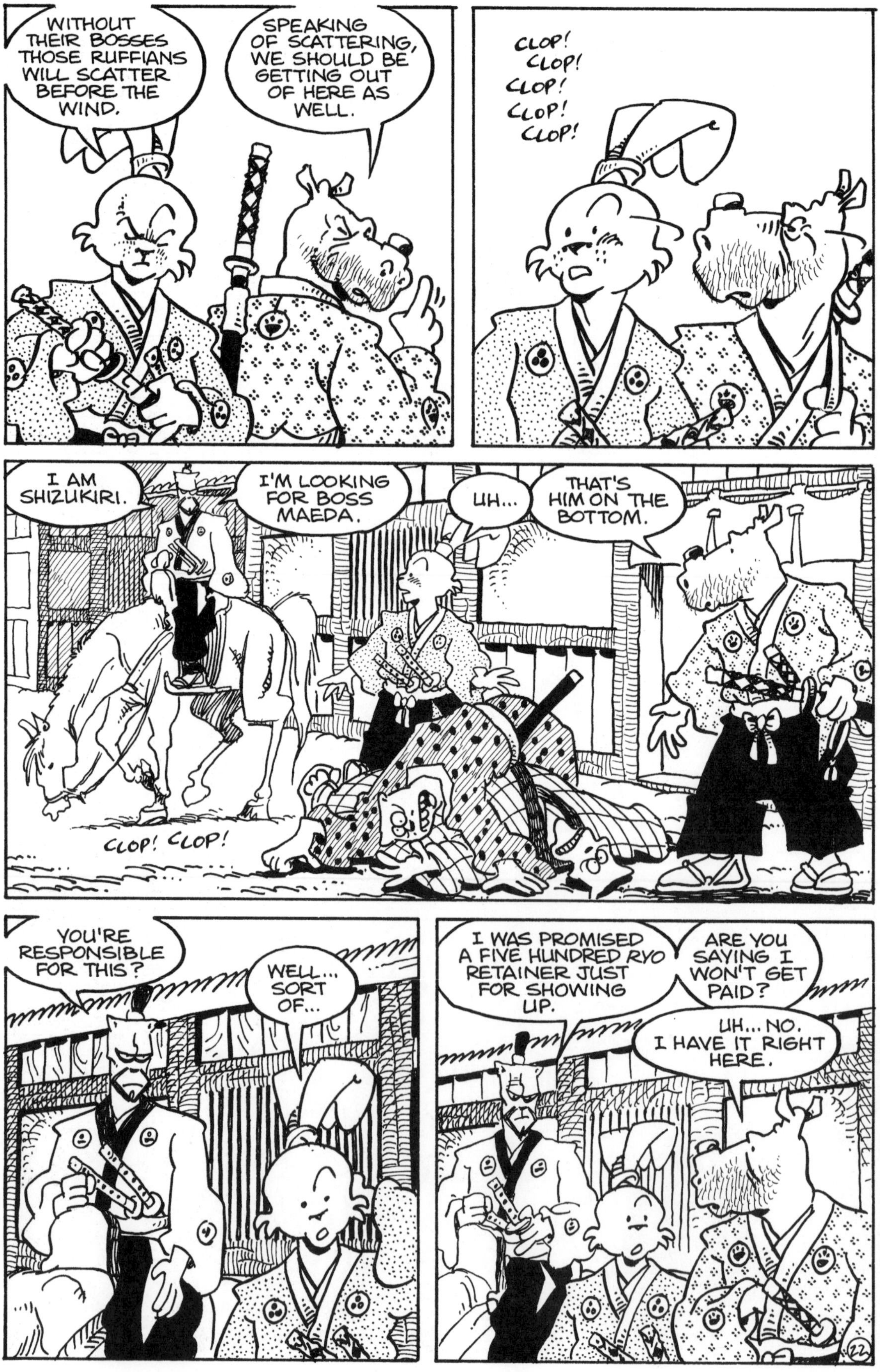

WITHOUT THEIR BOSSES THOSE RUFFIANS WILL SCATTER BEFORE THE WIND.
SPEAKING OF SCATTERING, WE SHOULD BE GETTING OUT OF HERE AS WELL.
CLOP! CLOP! CLOP! CLOP! CLOP!
I AM SHIZUKIRI.
I'M LOOKING FOR BOSS MAEDA.
UH...
THAT'S HIM ON THE BOTTOM.
CLOP! CLOP!
YOU'RE RESPONSIBLE FOR THIS?
WELL... SORT OF...
I WAS PROMISED A FIVE HUNDRED RYO RETAINER JUST FOR SHOWING UP.
ARE YOU SAYING I WON'T GET PAID?
UH... NO. I HAVE IT RIGHT HERE.
22

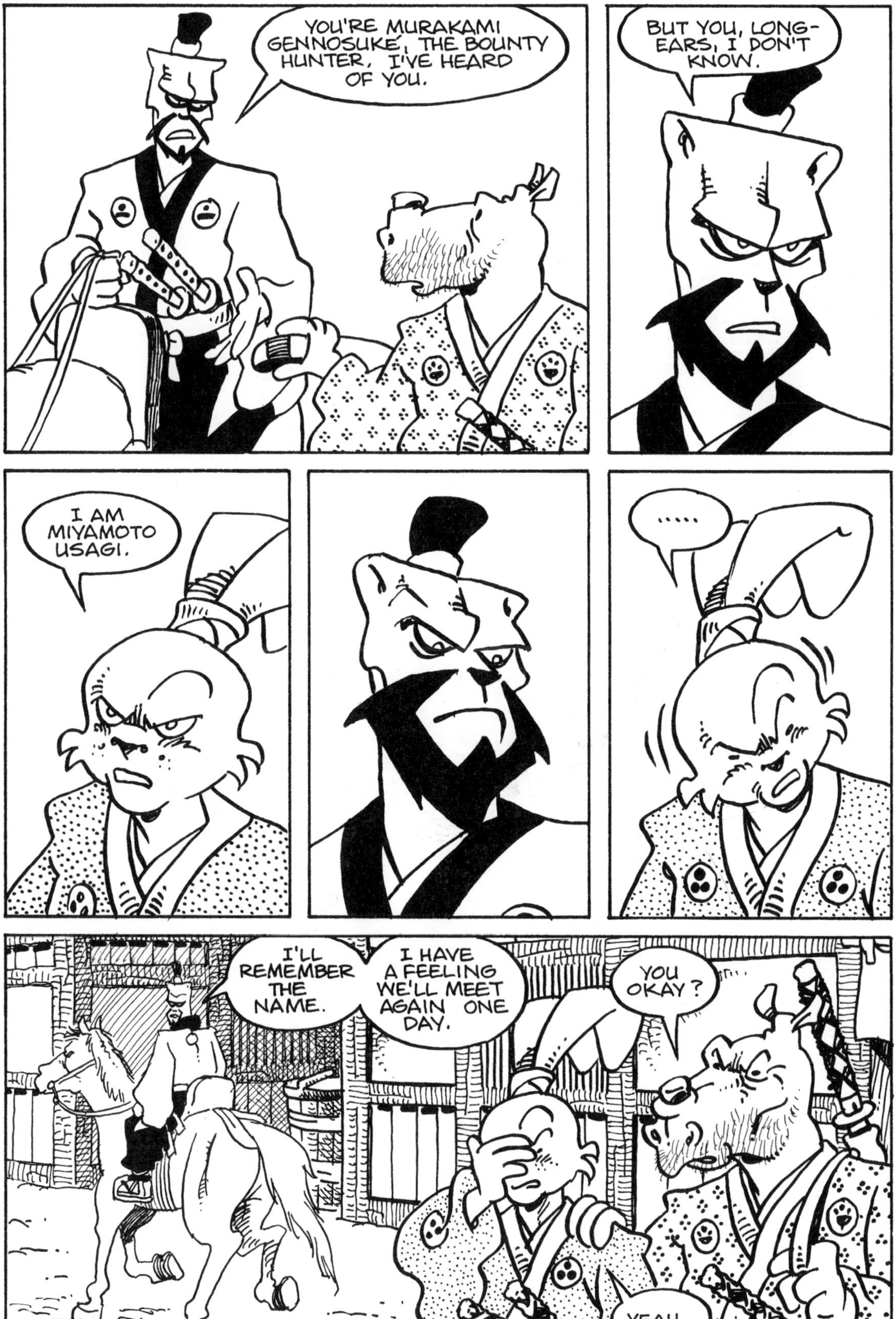
YOU'RE MURAKAMI GENNOSUKE, THE BOUNTY HUNTER, I'VE HEARD OF YOU.
BUT YOU, LONG-EARS, I DON'T KNOW.
I AM MIYAMOTO USAGI.
.....
I'LL REMEMBER THE NAME.
I HAVE A FEELING WE'LL MEET AGAIN ONE DAY.
YOU OKAY?
YEAH...
23

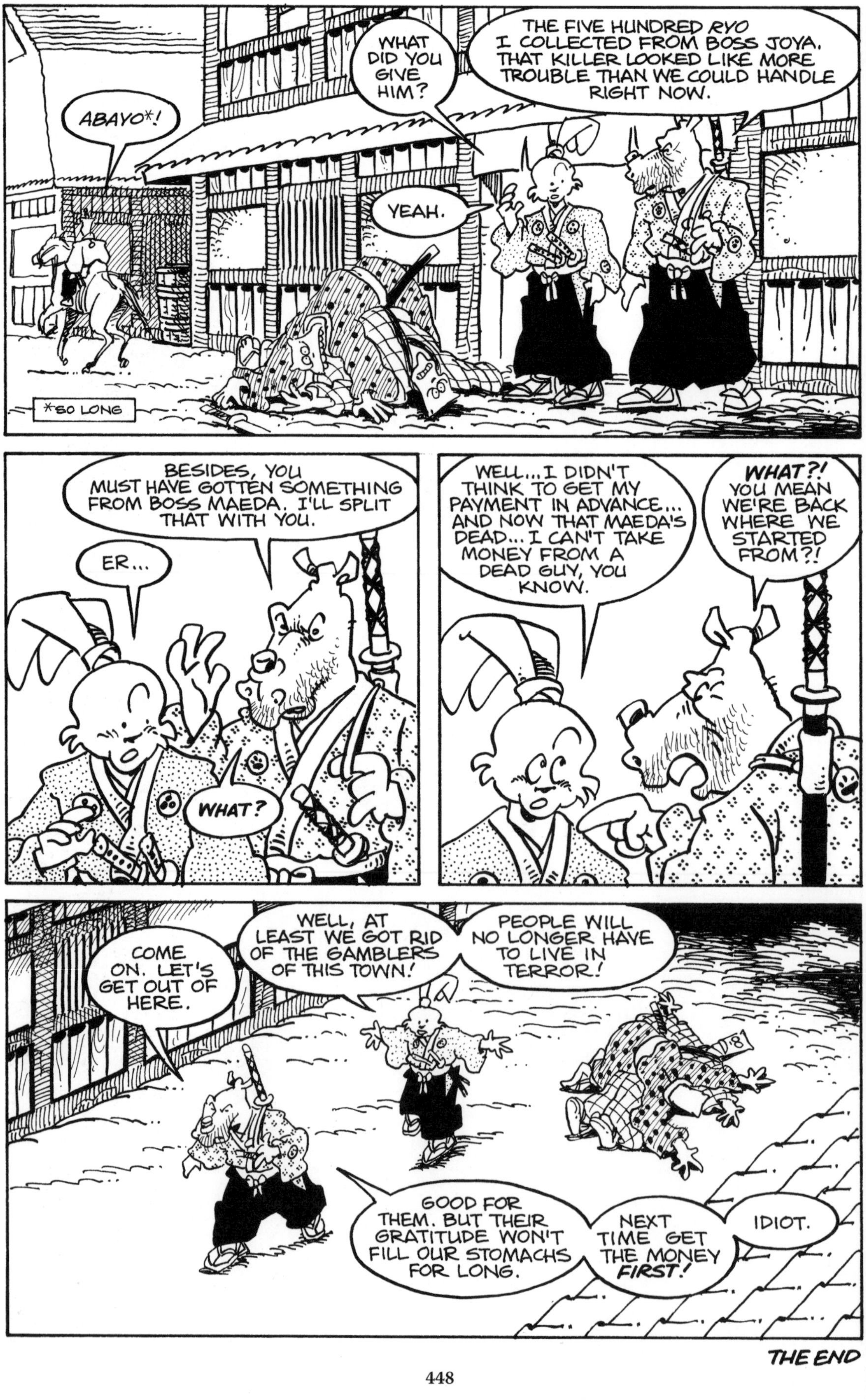
ABAYO*!
*SO LONG
WHAT DID YOU GIVE HIM?
THE FIVE HUNDRED *RYO* I COLLECTED FROM BOSS JOYA. THAT KILLER LOOKED LIKE MORE TROUBLE THAN WE COULD HANDLE RIGHT NOW.
YEAH.
BESIDES, YOU MUST HAVE GOTTEN SOMETHING FROM BOSS MAEDA. I'LL SPLIT THAT WITH YOU.
ER...
WHAT?
WELL... I DIDN'T THINK TO GET MY PAYMENT IN ADVANCE... AND NOW THAT MAEDA'S DEAD... I CAN'T TAKE MONEY FROM A DEAD GUY, YOU KNOW.
WHAT?! YOU MEAN WE'RE BACK WHERE WE STARTED FROM?!
COME ON. LET'S GET OUT OF HERE.
WELL, AT LEAST WE GOT RID OF THE GAMBLERS OF THIS TOWN!
PEOPLE WILL NO LONGER HAVE TO LIVE IN TERROR!
GOOD FOR THEM. BUT THEIR GRATITUDE WON'T FILL OUR STOMACHS FOR LONG.
NEXT TIME GET THE MONEY ***FIRST!***
IDIOT.

THE END

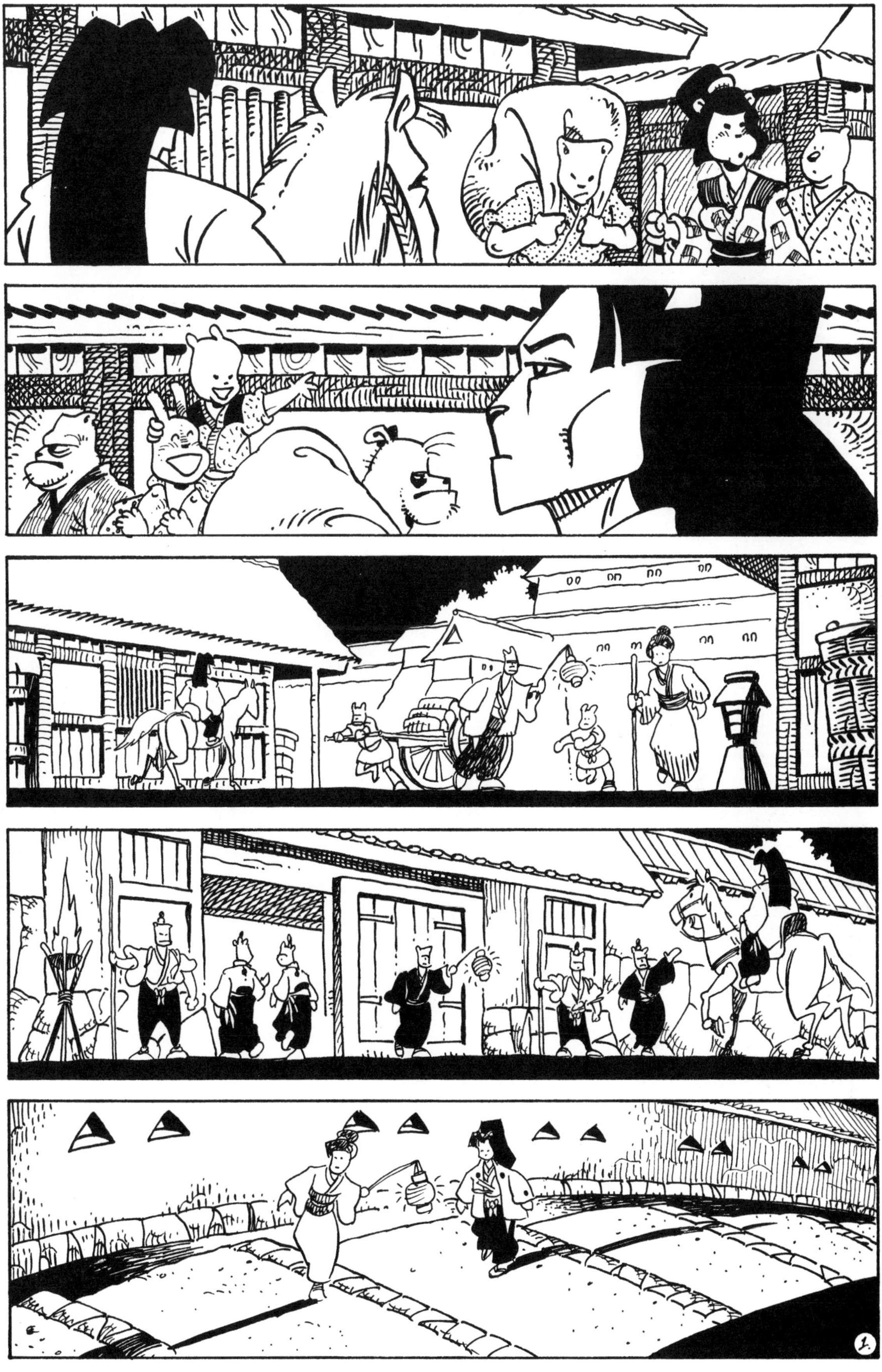

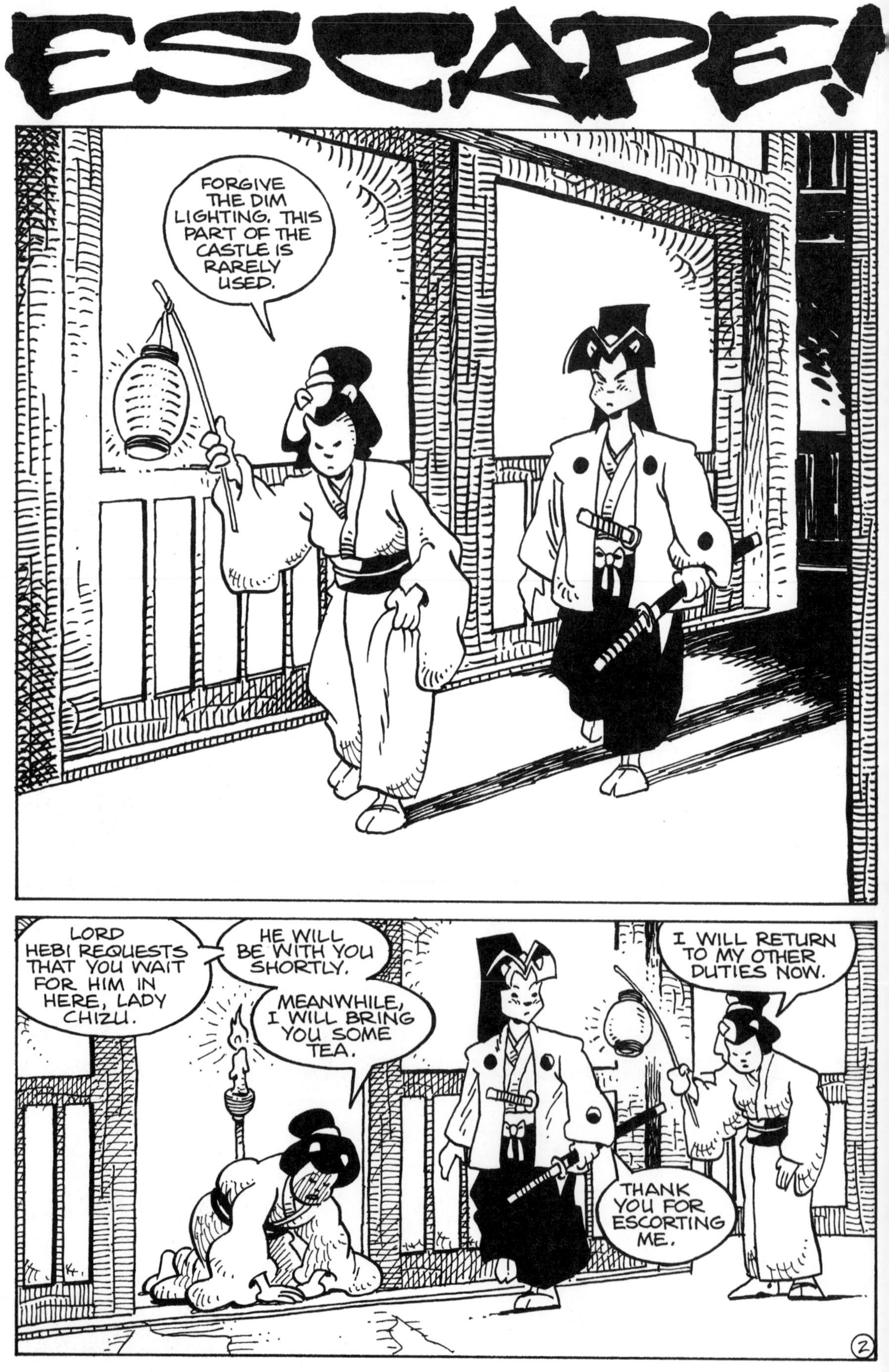
ESCAPE!
FORGIVE THE DIM LIGHTING. THIS PART OF THE CASTLE IS RARELY USED.
LORD HEBI REQUESTS THAT YOU WAIT FOR HIM IN HERE, LADY CHIZU.
HE WILL BE WITH YOU SHORTLY.
MEANWHILE, I WILL BRING YOU SOME TEA.
I WILL RETURN TO MY OTHER DUTIES NOW.
THANK YOU FOR ESCORTING ME.
2

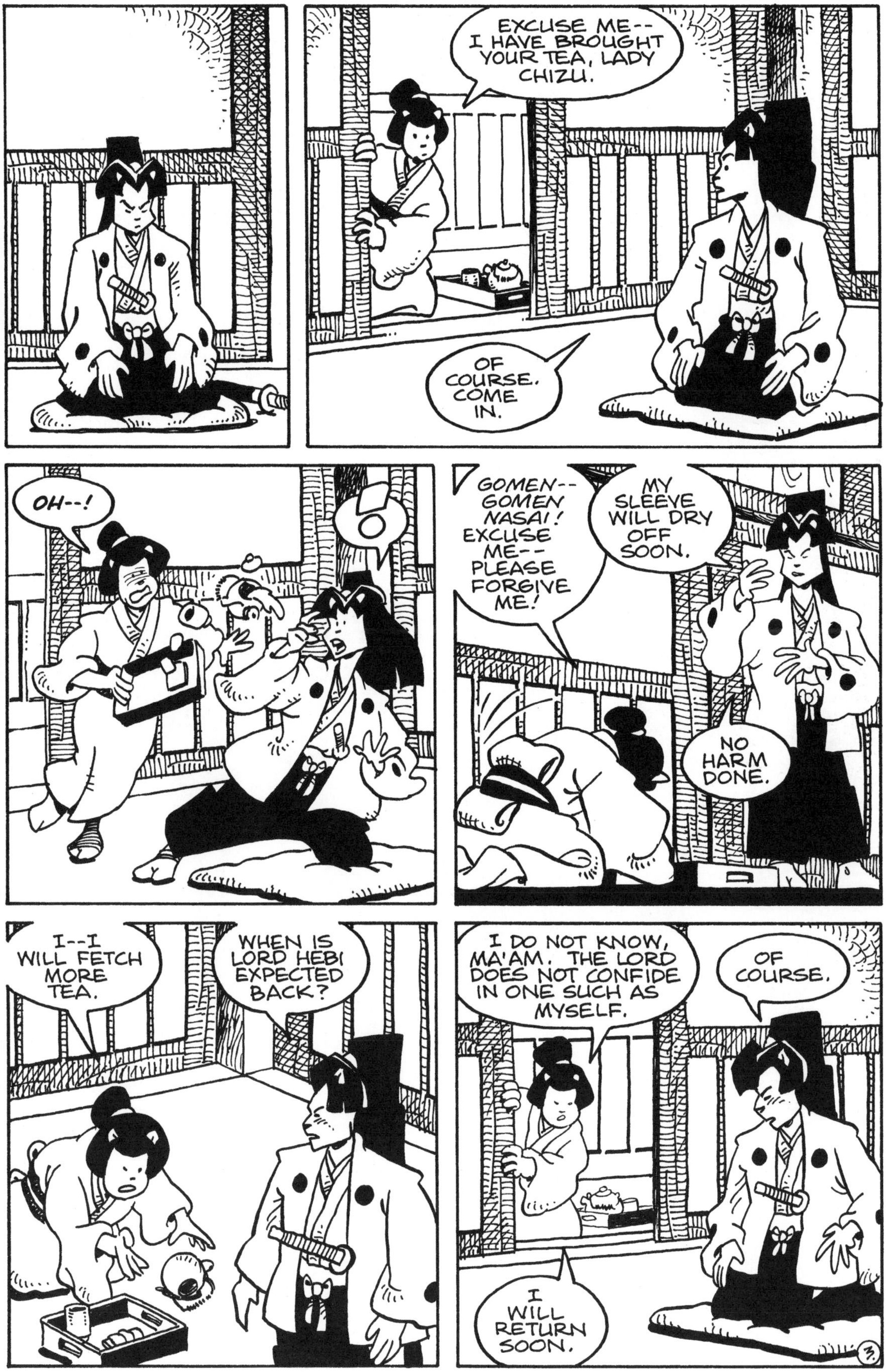
EXCUSE ME-- I HAVE BROUGHT YOUR TEA, LADY CHIZU.
OF COURSE. COME IN.
OH--!
!
GOMEN-- GOMEN NASAI! EXCUSE ME-- PLEASE FORGIVE ME!
MY SLEEVE WILL DRY OFF SOON.
NO HARM DONE.
I--I WILL FETCH MORE TEA.
WHEN IS LORD HEBI EXPECTED BACK?
I DO NOT KNOW, MA'AM. THE LORD DOES NOT CONFIDE IN ONE SUCH AS MYSELF.
OF COURSE.
I WILL RETURN SOON.
3.

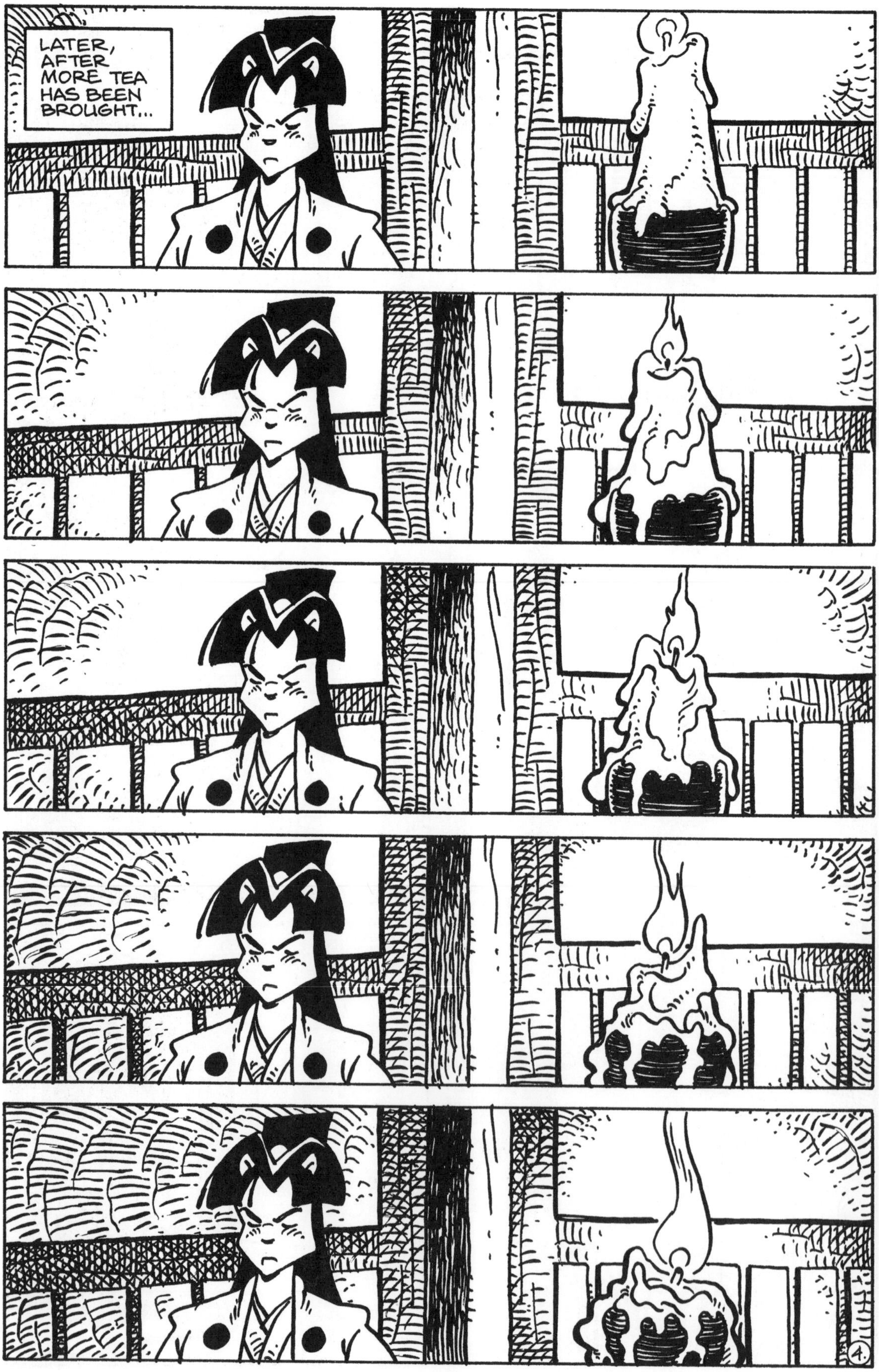
LATER, AFTER MORE TEA HAS BEEN BROUGHT...

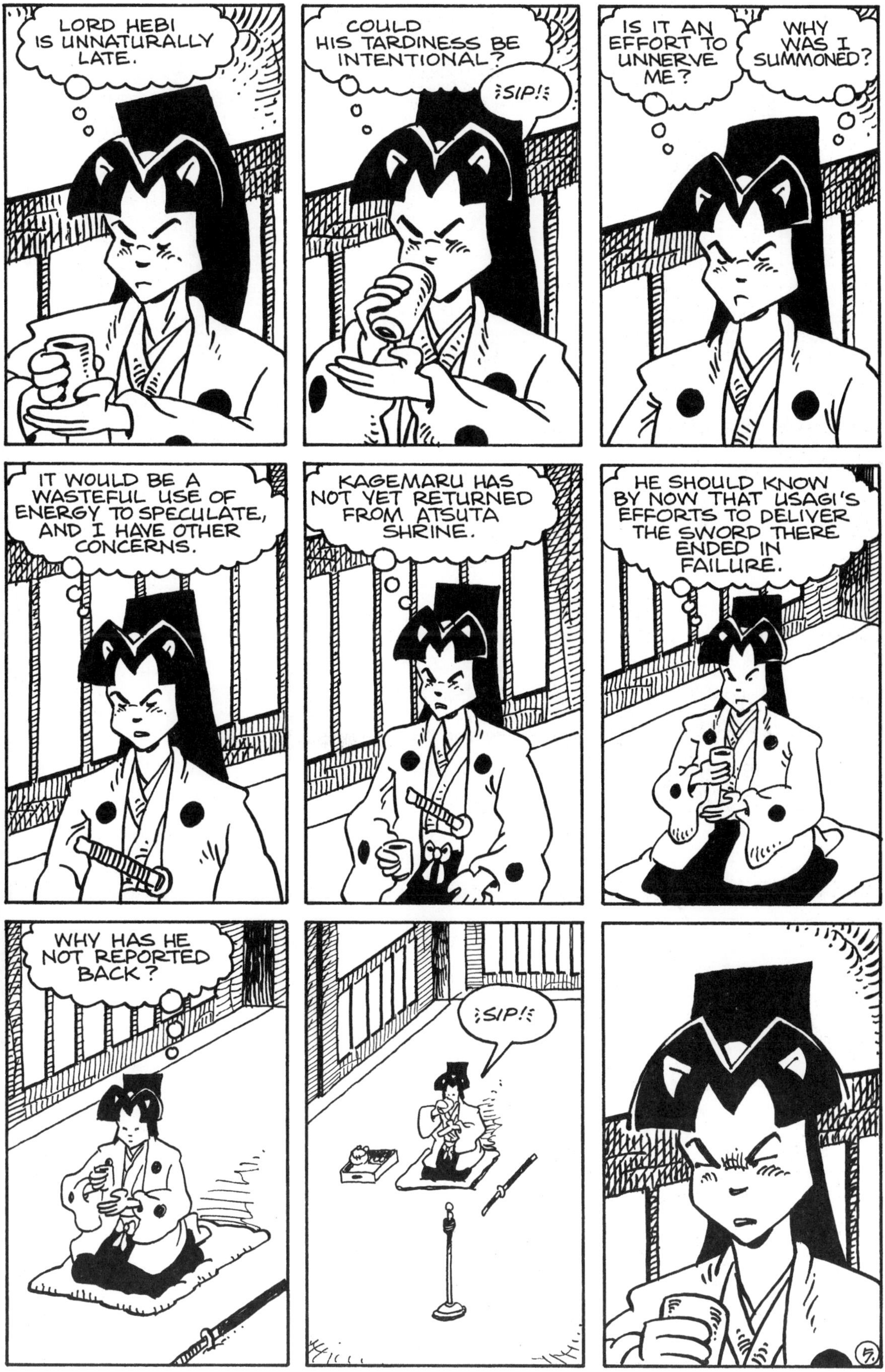
LORD HEBI IS UNNATURALLY LATE.
COULD HIS TARDINESS BE INTENTIONAL?
SIP!
IS IT AN EFFORT TO UNNERVE ME?
WHY WAS I SUMMONED?
IT WOULD BE A WASTEFUL USE OF ENERGY TO SPECULATE, AND I HAVE OTHER CONCERNS.
KAGEMARU HAS NOT YET RETURNED FROM ATSUTA SHRINE.
HE SHOULD KNOW BY NOW THAT USAGI'S EFFORTS TO DELIVER THE SWORD THERE ENDED IN FAILURE.
WHY HAS HE NOT REPORTED BACK?
SIP!
5

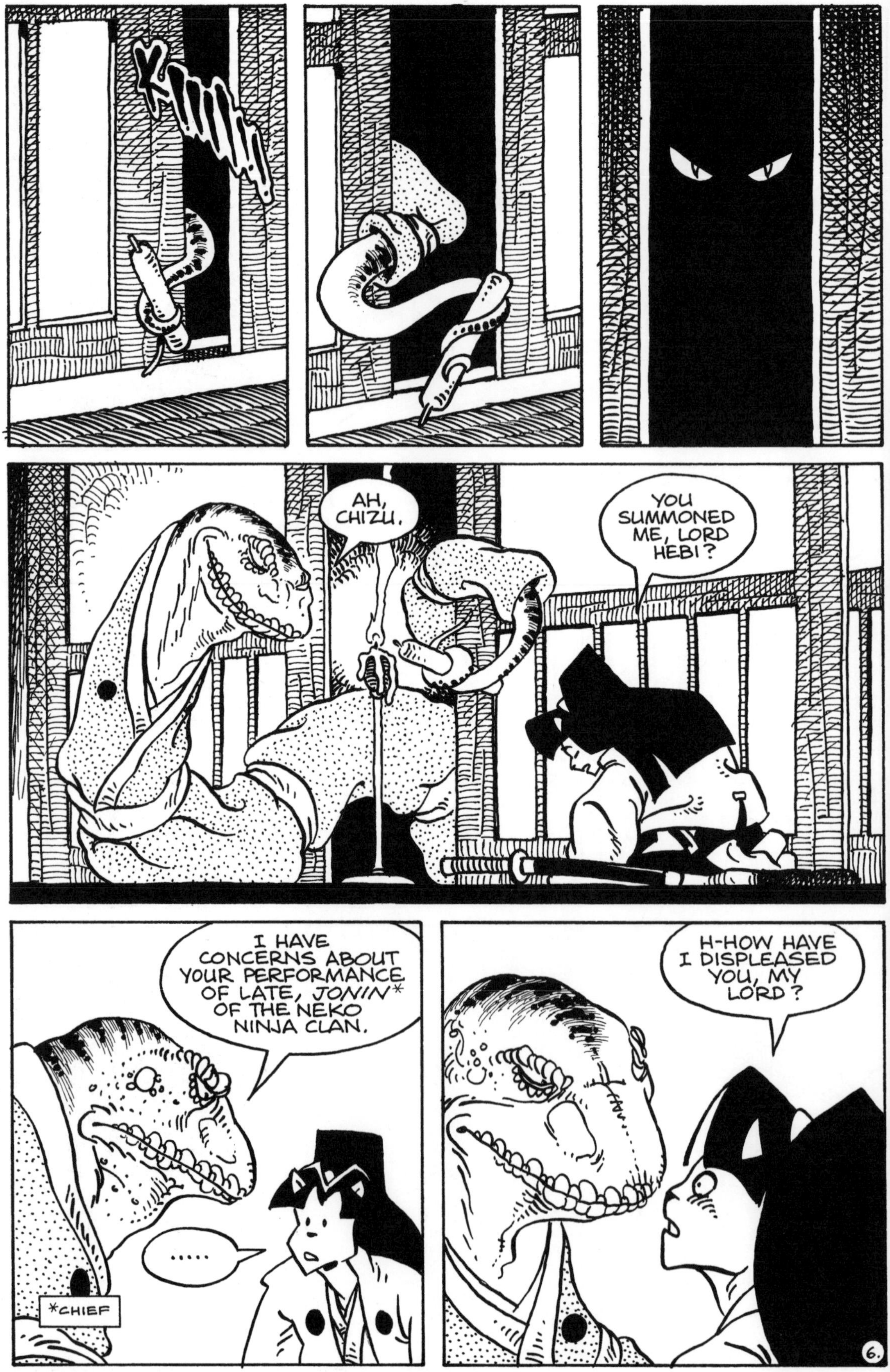
AH, CHIZU.
YOU SUMMONED ME, LORD HEBI?
I HAVE CONCERNS ABOUT YOUR PERFORMANCE OF LATE, JONIN* OF THE NEKO NINJA CLAN.
.....
*CHIEF
H-HOW HAVE I DISPLEASED YOU, MY LORD?
6.

I HEARD THAT YOU HAD OBTAINED A FORMULA FOR A POWERFUL EXPLOSIVE BLACK POWDER BUT FAILED TO NOTIFY ME OR OUR LORD HIKIJI.*

WHO HAS ACCUSED ME OF SUCH A THING?

*UY BOOK 10: THE BRINK OF LIFE & DEATH

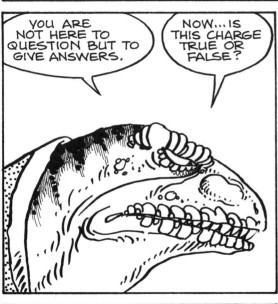

YOU ARE NOT HERE TO QUESTION BUT TO GIVE ANSWERS.

NOW... IS THIS CHARGE TRUE OR FALSE?

IT IS TRUE, LORD HEBI. BUT I FIRST WISHED TO TEST THE POWDER BEFORE INFORMING YOU. IT TURNED OUT TO BE TOO UNSTABLE. IT KILLED MANY OF THE KOMORI NINJA WHO STOLE IT FROM ME.

I HAVE ALSO HEARD THAT YOU HELD A LIST OF CONSPIRATORS AGAINST THE GOVERNMENT AND AGAIN FAILED TO INFORM US.* IS THIS TRUE?

*UY BOOK 11: SEASONS

YES, BUT UPON INVESTIGATION IT WAS FOUND THAT THE LIST WAS FALSE-- MERELY A RUSE TO IMPLICATE CERTAIN NOBLES IN TREASON.

⑦

455

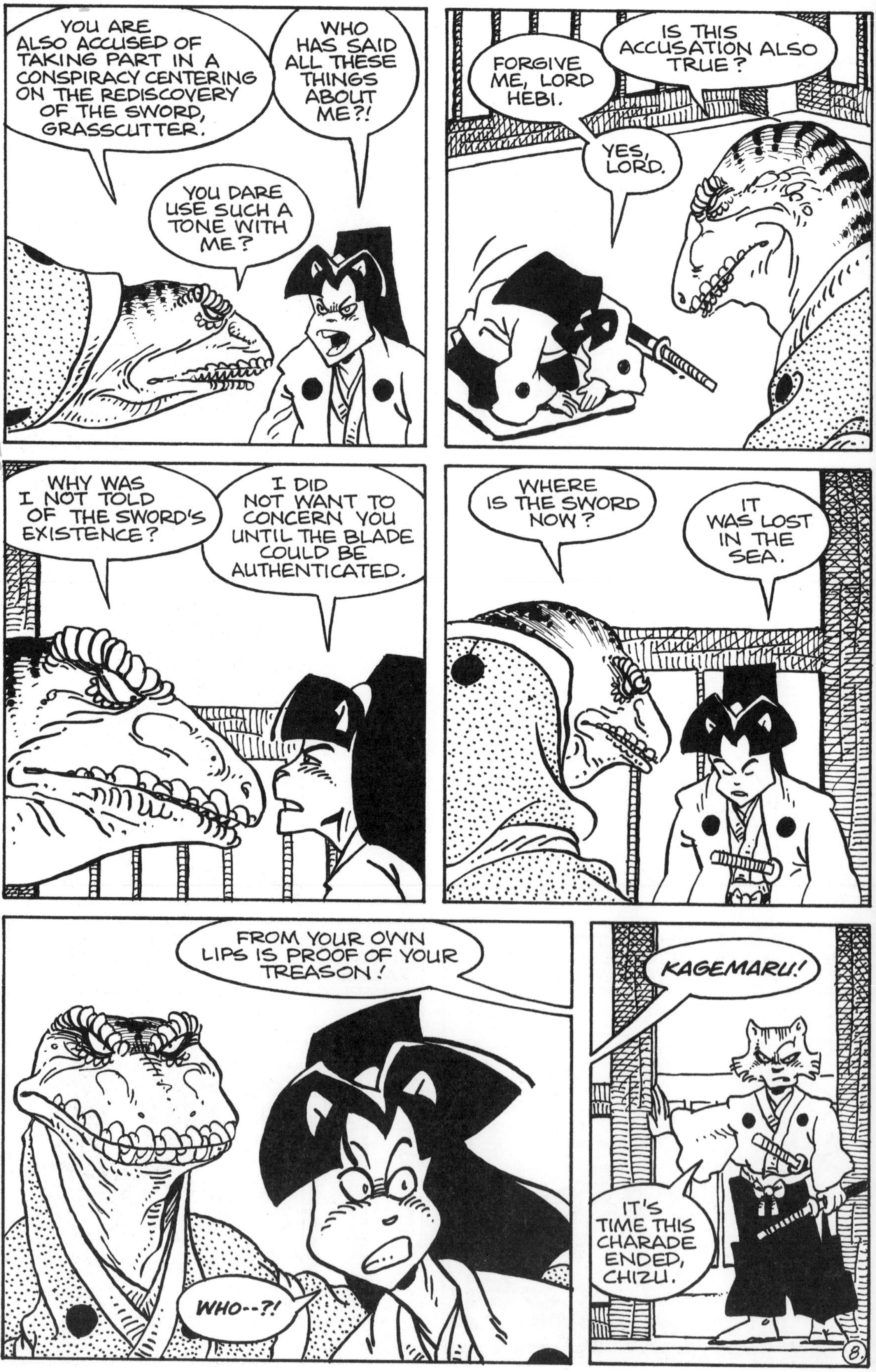
YOU ARE ALSO ACCUSED OF TAKING PART IN A CONSPIRACY CENTERING ON THE REDISCOVERY OF THE SWORD, GRASSCUTTER.
WHO HAS SAID ALL THESE THINGS ABOUT ME?!
YOU DARE USE SUCH A TONE WITH ME?
IS THIS ACCUSATION ALSO TRUE?
FORGIVE ME, LORD HEBI.
YES, LORD.
WHY WAS I NOT TOLD OF THE SWORD'S EXISTENCE?
I DID NOT WANT TO CONCERN YOU UNTIL THE BLADE COULD BE AUTHENTICATED.
WHERE IS THE SWORD NOW?
IT WAS LOST IN THE SEA.
FROM YOUR OWN LIPS IS PROOF OF YOUR TREASON!
WHO--?!
KAGEMARU!
IT'S TIME THIS CHARADE ENDED, CHIZU.
8

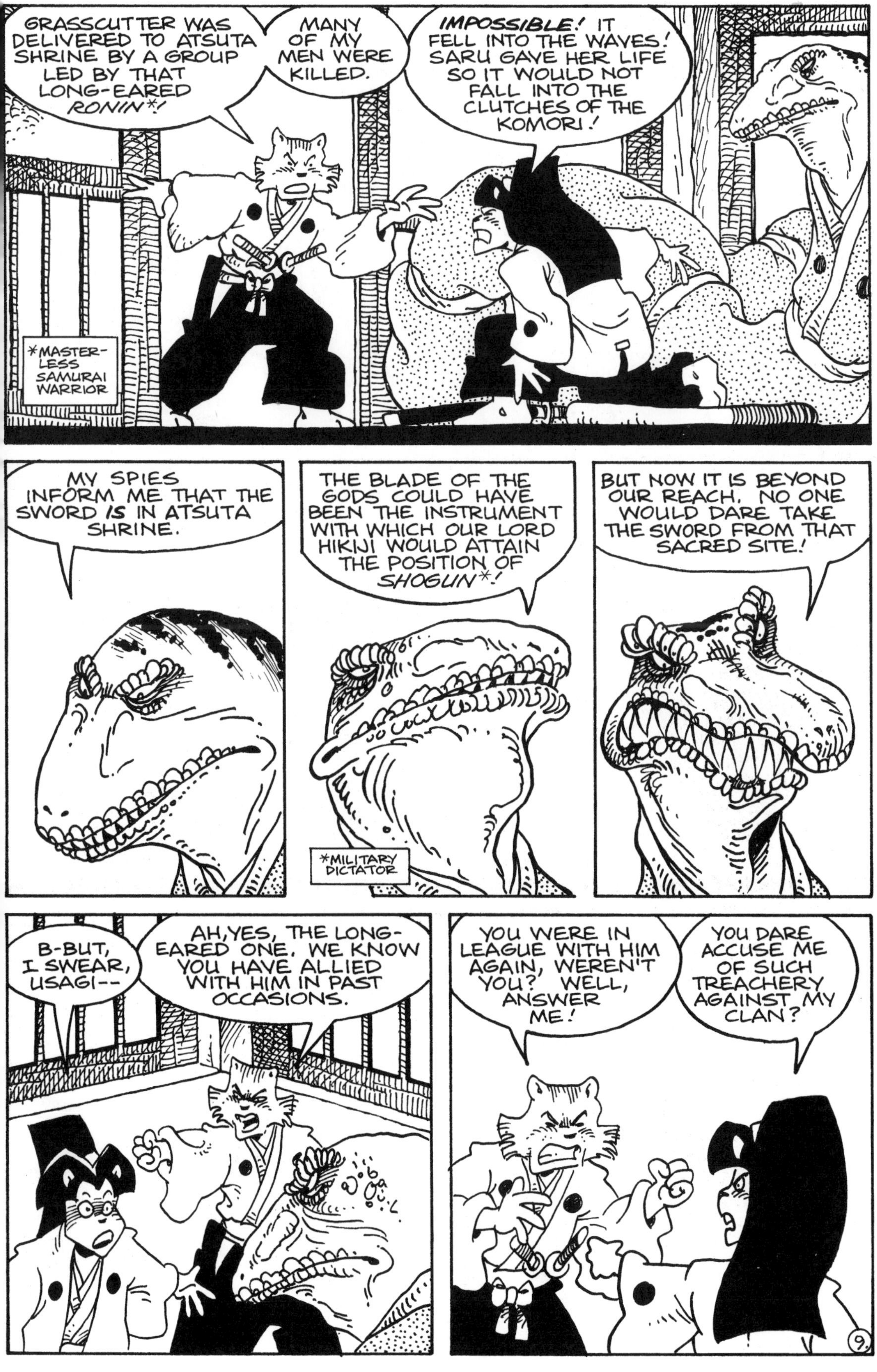
GRASSCUTTER WAS DELIVERED TO ATSUTA SHRINE BY A GROUP LED BY THAT LONG-EARED *RONIN**!
MANY OF MY MEN WERE KILLED.
IMPOSSIBLE! IT FELL INTO THE WAVES! SARU GAVE HER LIFE SO IT WOULD NOT FALL INTO THE CLUTCHES OF THE KOMORI!
*MASTER-LESS SAMURAI WARRIOR
MY SPIES INFORM ME THAT THE SWORD *IS* IN ATSUTA SHRINE.
THE BLADE OF THE GODS COULD HAVE BEEN THE INSTRUMENT WITH WHICH OUR LORD HIKIJI WOULD ATTAIN THE POSITION OF *SHOGUN**!
*MILITARY DICTATOR
BUT NOW IT IS BEYOND OUR REACH. NO ONE WOULD DARE TAKE THE SWORD FROM THAT SACRED SITE!
B-BUT, I SWEAR, USAGI--
AH, YES, THE LONG-EARED ONE. WE KNOW YOU HAVE ALLIED WITH HIM IN PAST OCCASIONS.
YOU WERE IN LEAGUE WITH HIM AGAIN, WEREN'T YOU? WELL, ANSWER ME!
YOU DARE ACCUSE ME OF SUCH TREACHERY AGAINST MY CLAN?
9.

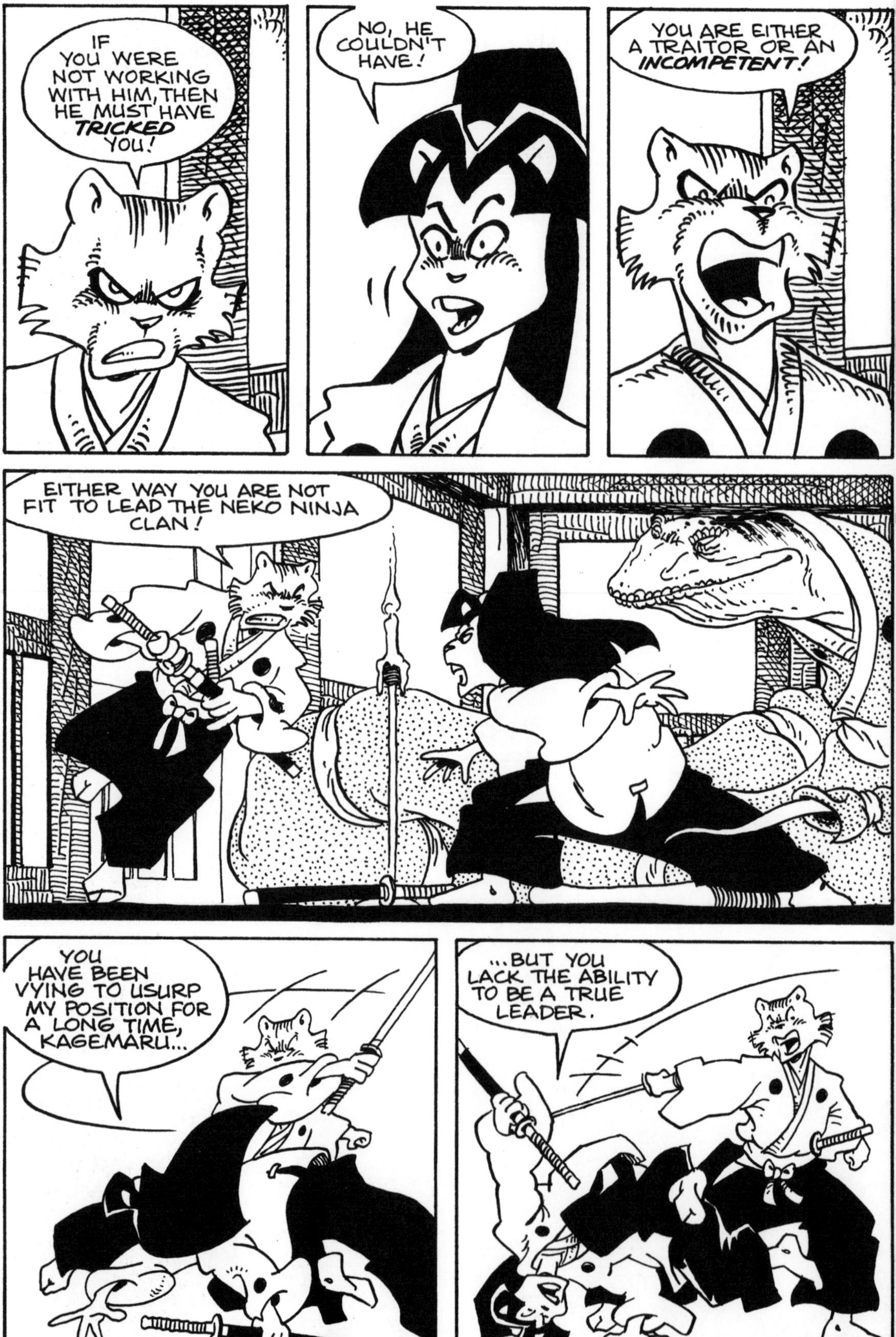
IF YOU WERE NOT WORKING WITH HIM, THEN HE MUST HAVE TRICKED YOU!
NO, HE COULDN'T HAVE!
YOU ARE EITHER A TRAITOR OR AN INCOMPETENT!
EITHER WAY YOU ARE NOT FIT TO LEAD THE NEKO NINJA CLAN!
YOU HAVE BEEN VYING TO USURP MY POSITION FOR A LONG TIME, KAGEMARU...
...BUT YOU LACK THE ABILITY TO BE A TRUE LEADER.
10.

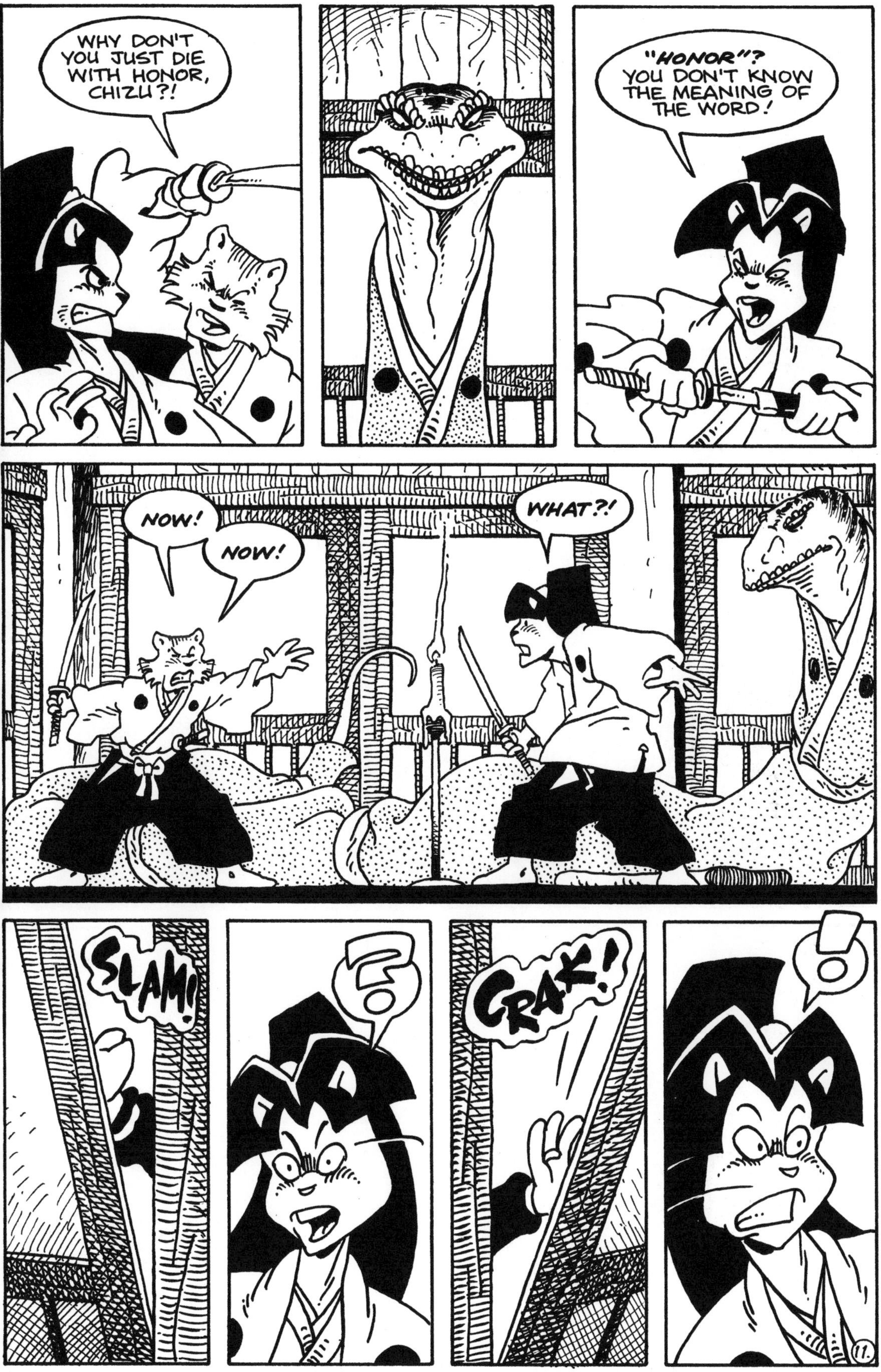

WHY DON'T YOU JUST DIE WITH HONOR, CHIZU?!
"HONOR"? YOU DON'T KNOW THE MEANING OF THE WORD!
NOW!
NOW!
WHAT?!
SLAM!
?
CRAK!
!
11.

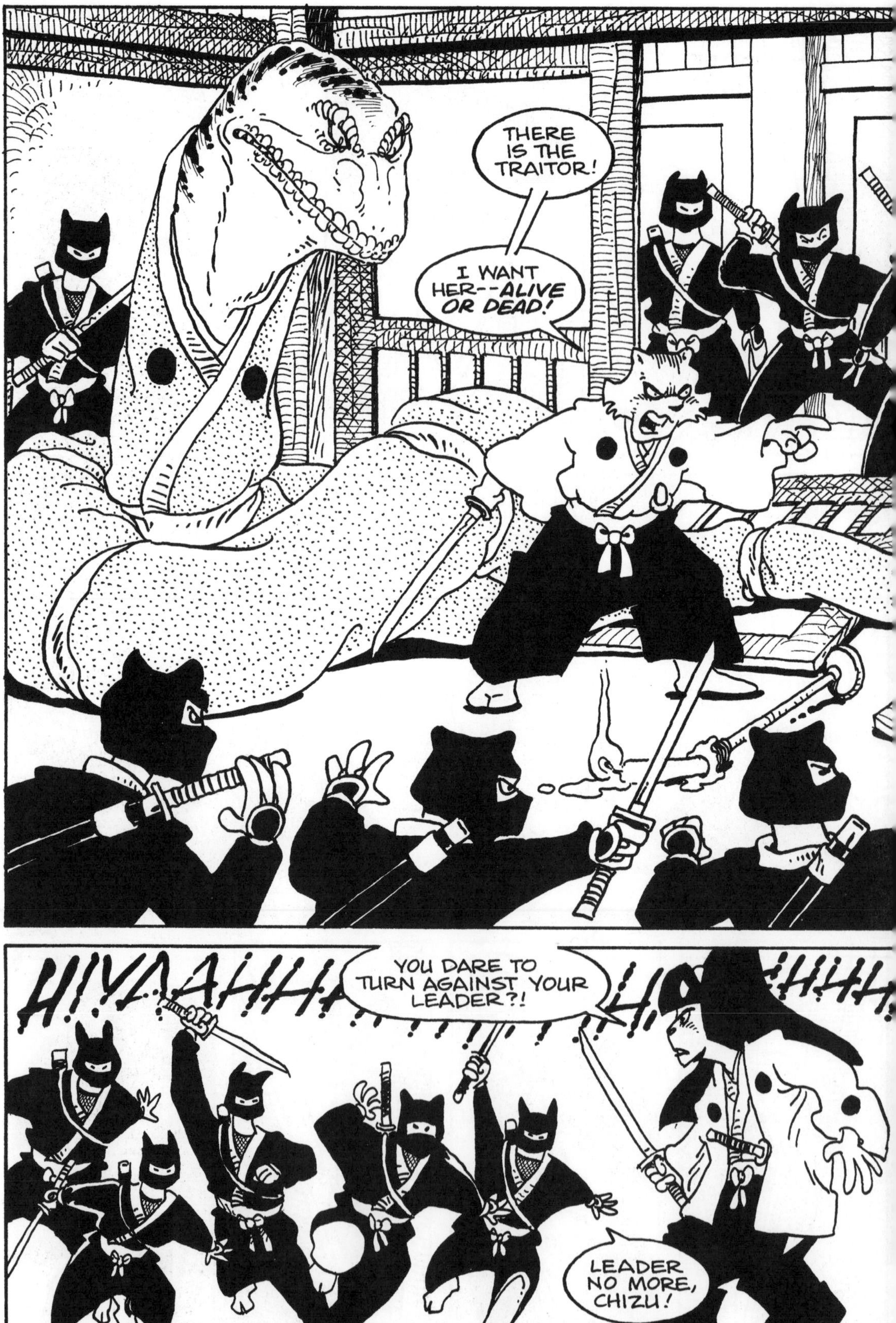
THERE IS THE TRAITOR!
I WANT HER--*ALIVE OR DEAD!*
HIYAAHHH
YOU DARE TO TURN AGAINST YOUR LEADER?!
LEADER NO MORE, CHIZU!
12

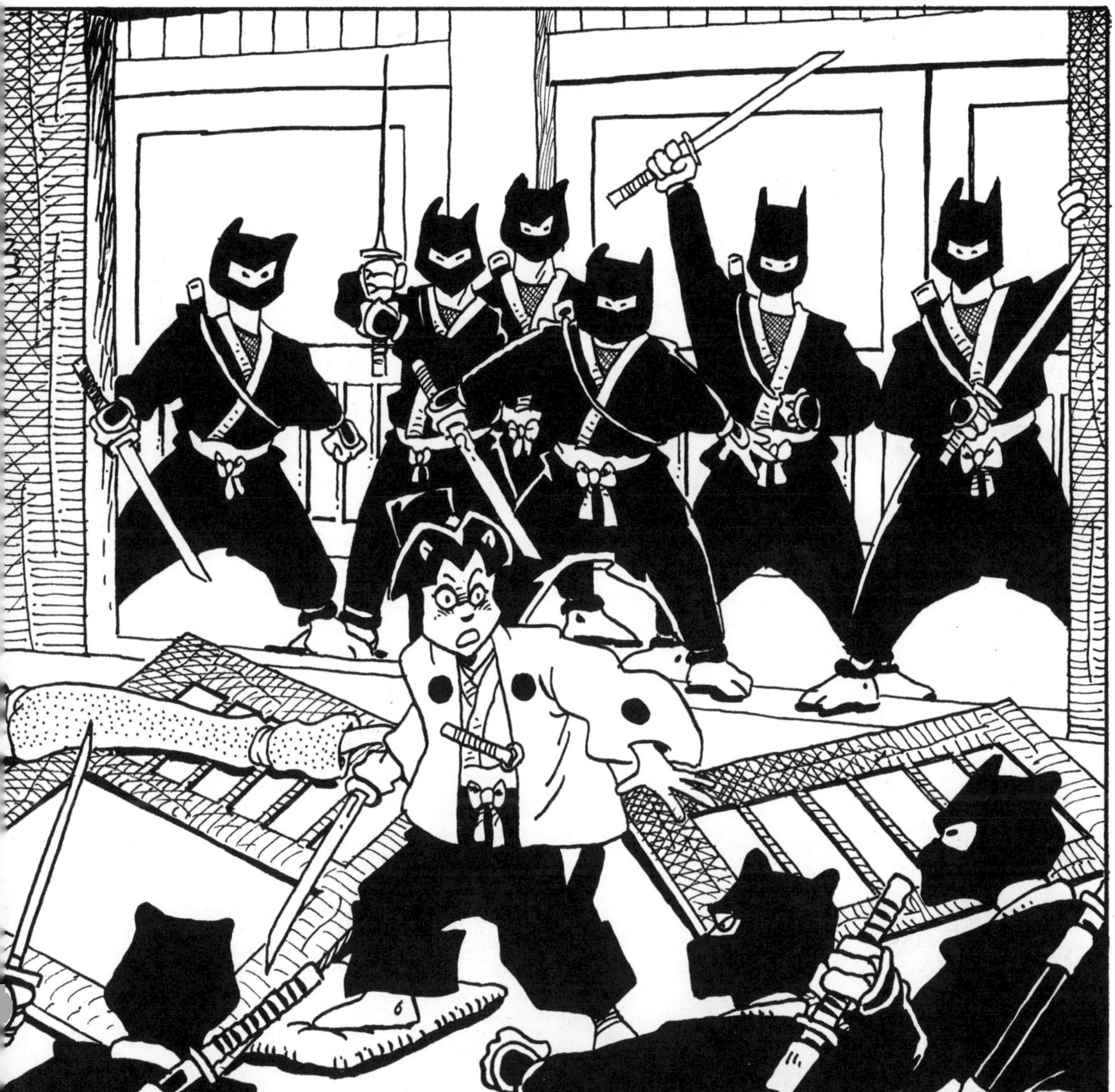

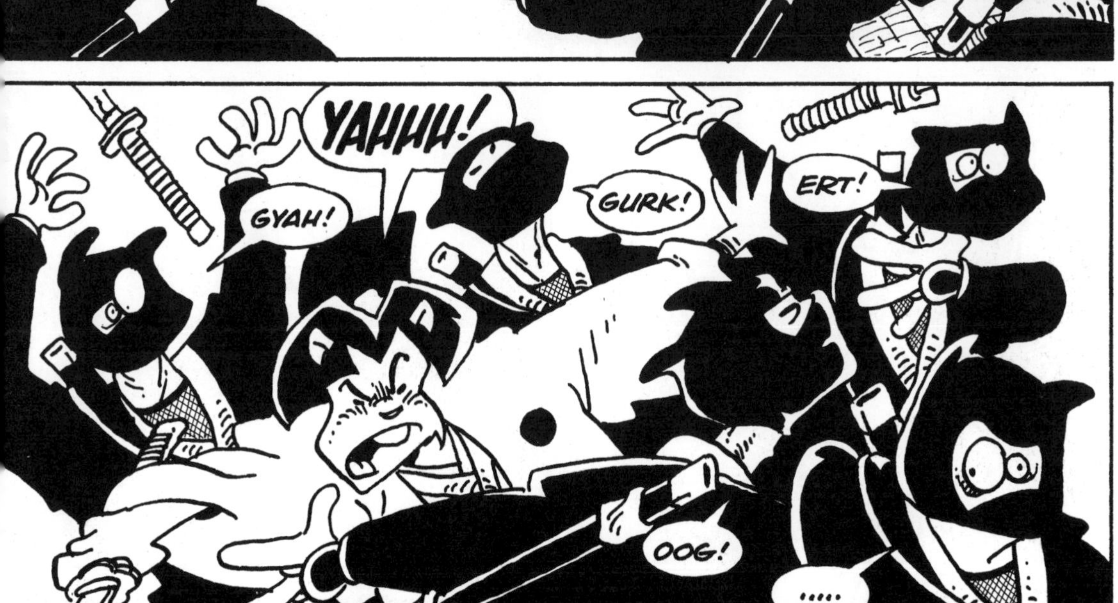
YAHHH!
GYAH!
GURK!
ERT!
OOG!
.....
13.

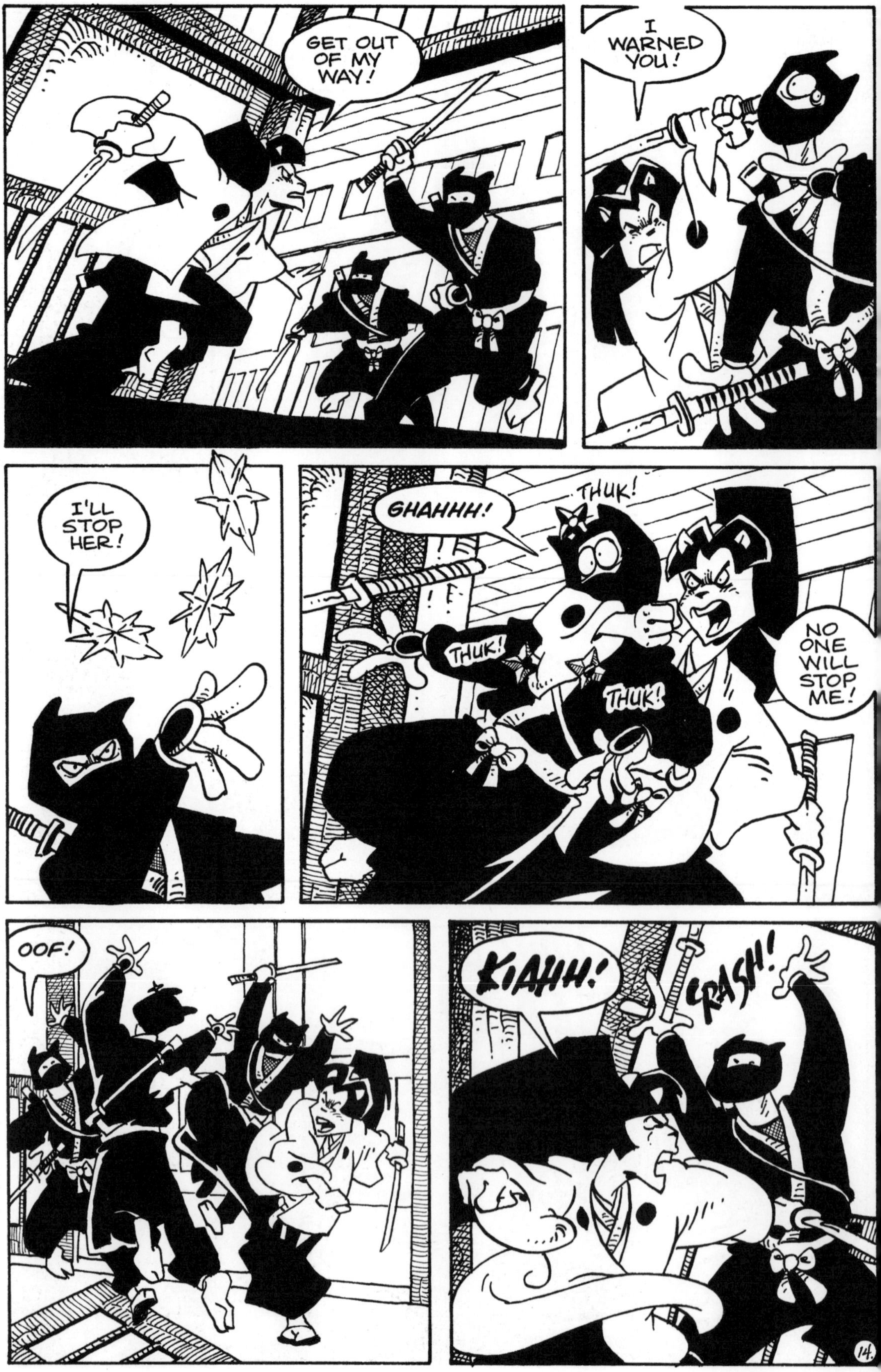
GET OUT OF MY WAY!
I WARNED YOU!
I'LL STOP HER!
GHAHHH!
THUK!
THUK!
THUK!
NO ONE WILL STOP ME!
OOF!
KIAHH!
CRASH!
14.

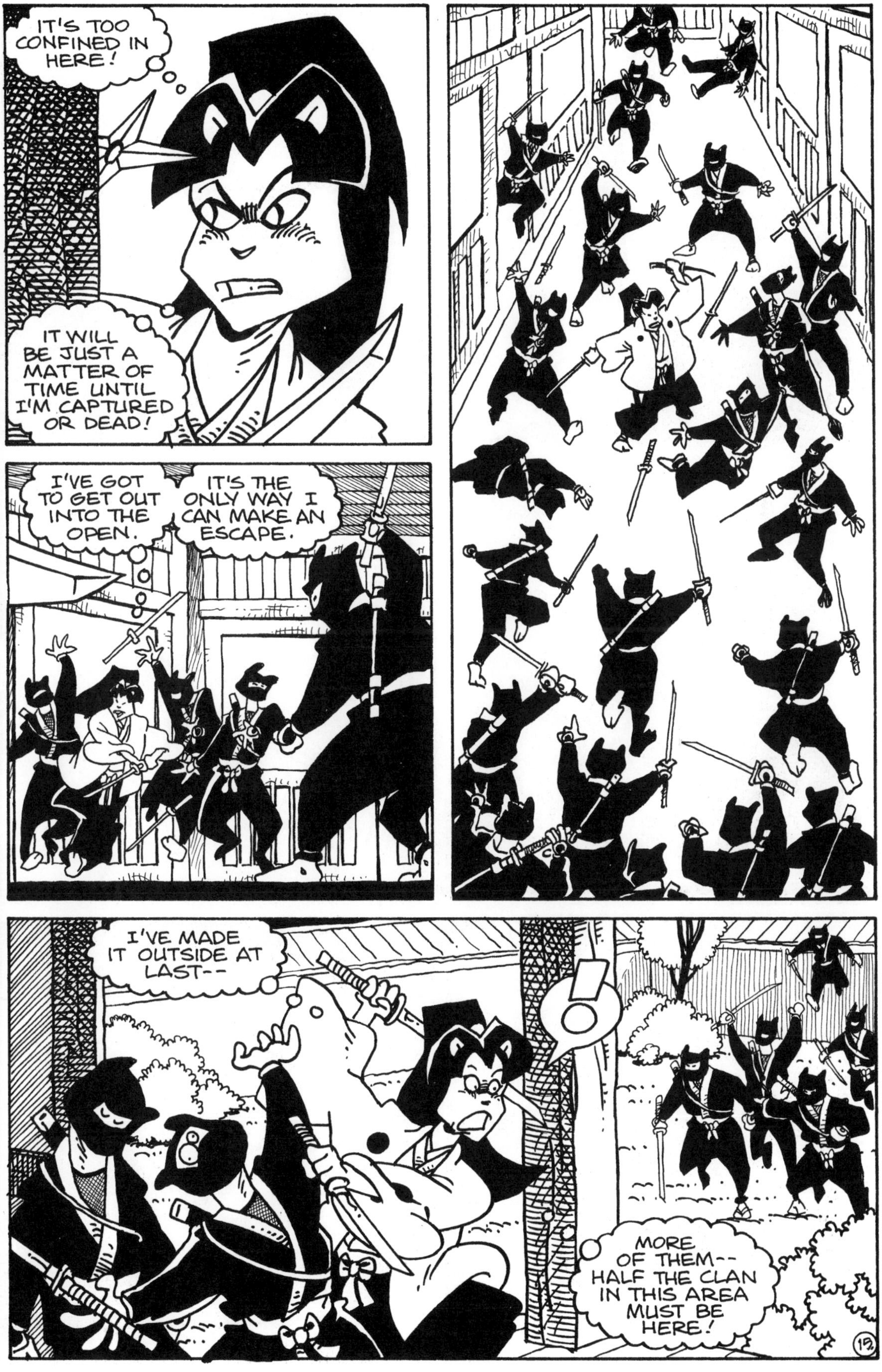
IT'S TOO CONFINED IN HERE!
IT WILL BE JUST A MATTER OF TIME UNTIL I'M CAPTURED OR DEAD!
I'VE GOT TO GET OUT INTO THE OPEN.
IT'S THE ONLY WAY I CAN MAKE AN ESCAPE.
I'VE MADE IT OUTSIDE AT LAST--
!
MORE OF THEM-- HALF THE CLAN IN THIS AREA MUST BE HERE!
15

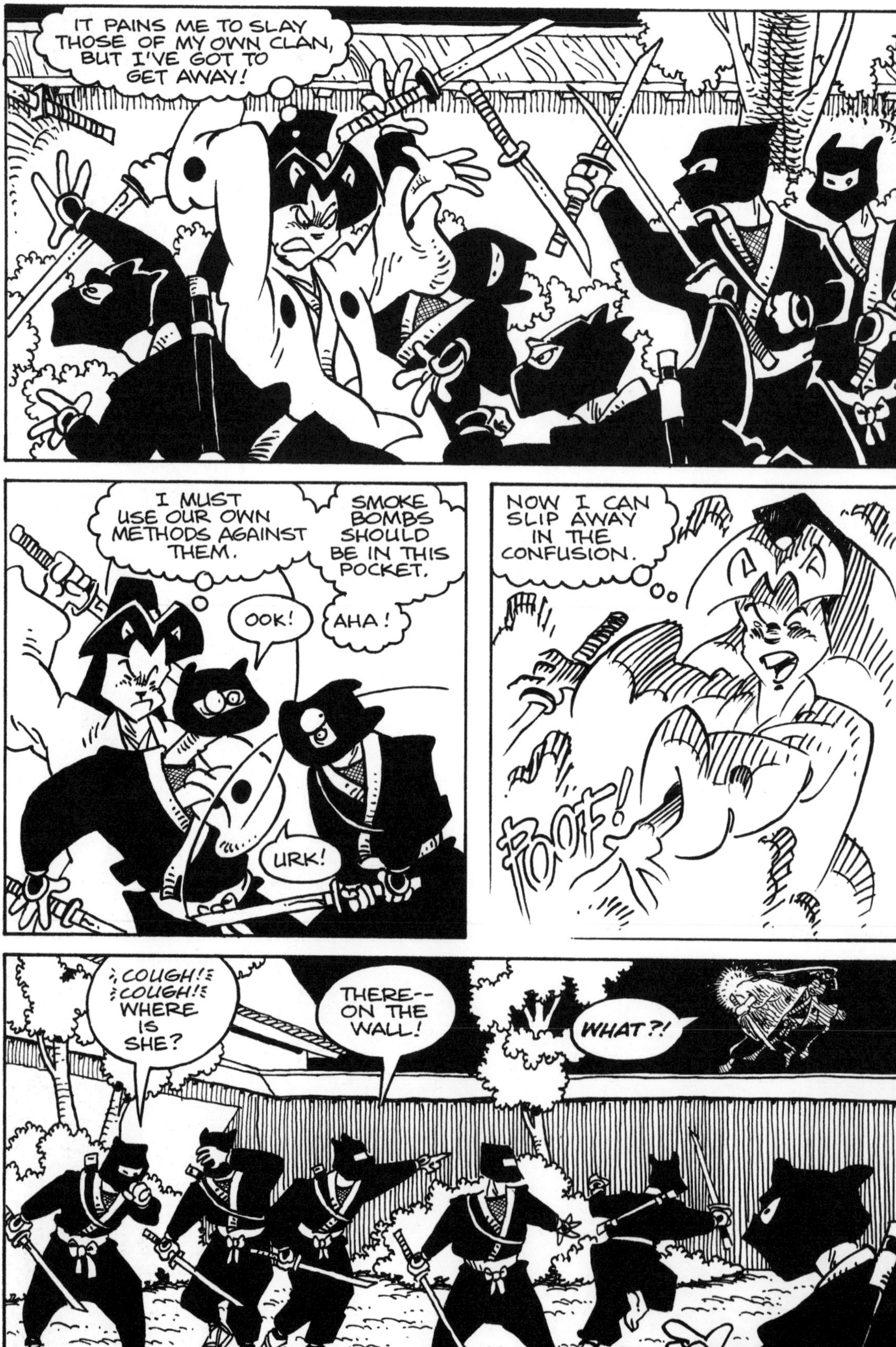
IT PAINS ME TO SLAY THOSE OF MY OWN CLAN, BUT I'VE GOT TO GET AWAY!
I MUST USE OUR OWN METHODS AGAINST THEM.
SMOKE BOMBS SHOULD BE IN THIS POCKET.
OOK!
AHA!
URK!
NOW I CAN SLIP AWAY IN THE CONFUSION.
POOF!
COUGH! COUGH! WHERE IS SHE?
THERE-- ON THE WALL!
WHAT?!
16.

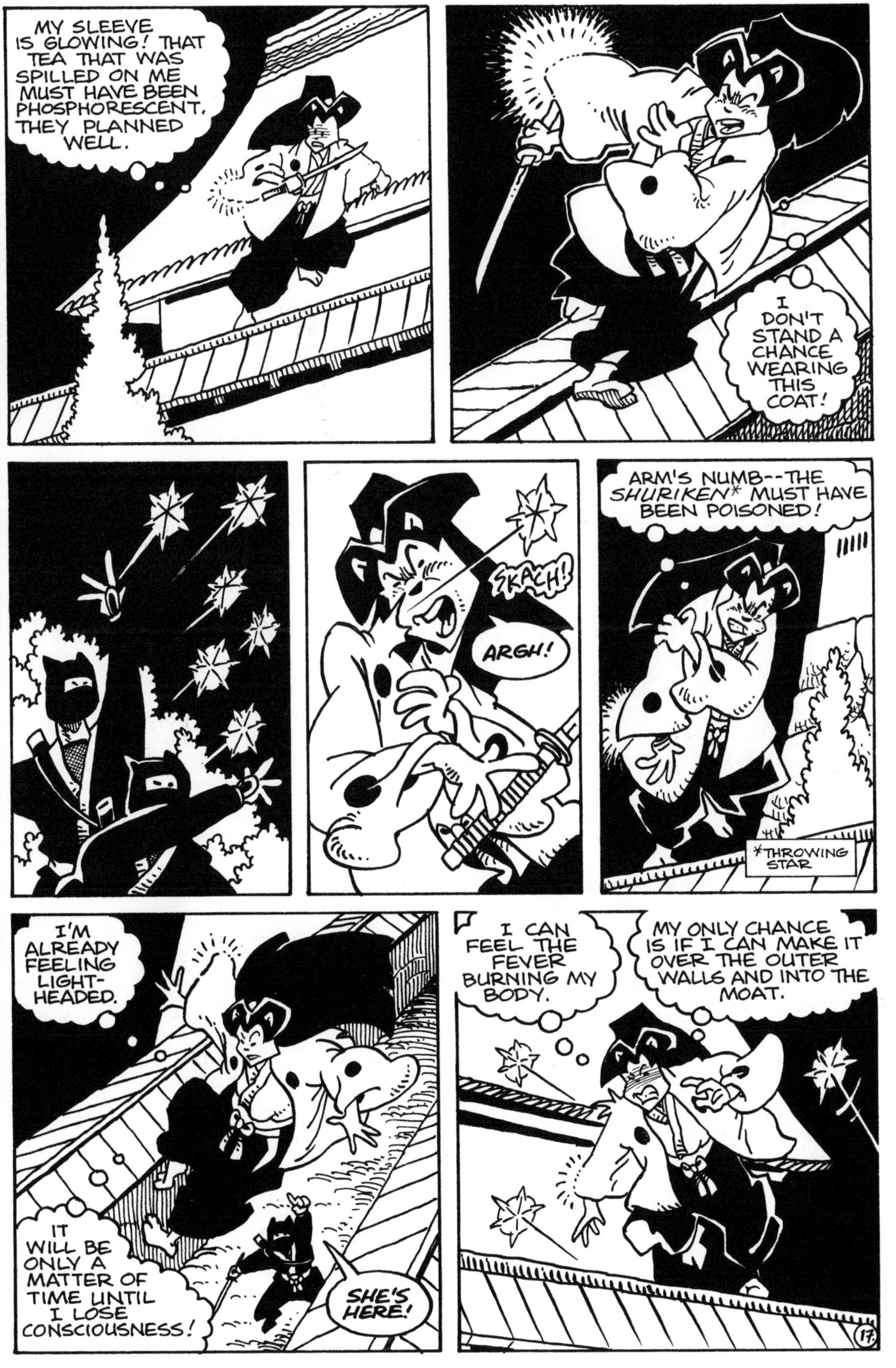

MY SLEEVE IS GLOWING! THAT TEA THAT WAS SPILLED ON ME MUST HAVE BEEN PHOSPHORESCENT. THEY PLANNED WELL.
I DON'T STAND A CHANCE WEARING THIS COAT!
SKACH!
ARGH!
ARM'S NUMB--THE SHURIKEN* MUST HAVE BEEN POISONED!
*THROWING STAR
I'M ALREADY FEELING LIGHT-HEADED.
IT WILL BE ONLY A MATTER OF TIME UNTIL I LOSE CONSCIOUSNESS!
SHE'S HERE!
I CAN FEEL THE FEVER BURNING MY BODY.
MY ONLY CHANCE IS IF I CAN MAKE IT OVER THE OUTER WALLS AND INTO THE MOAT.
17

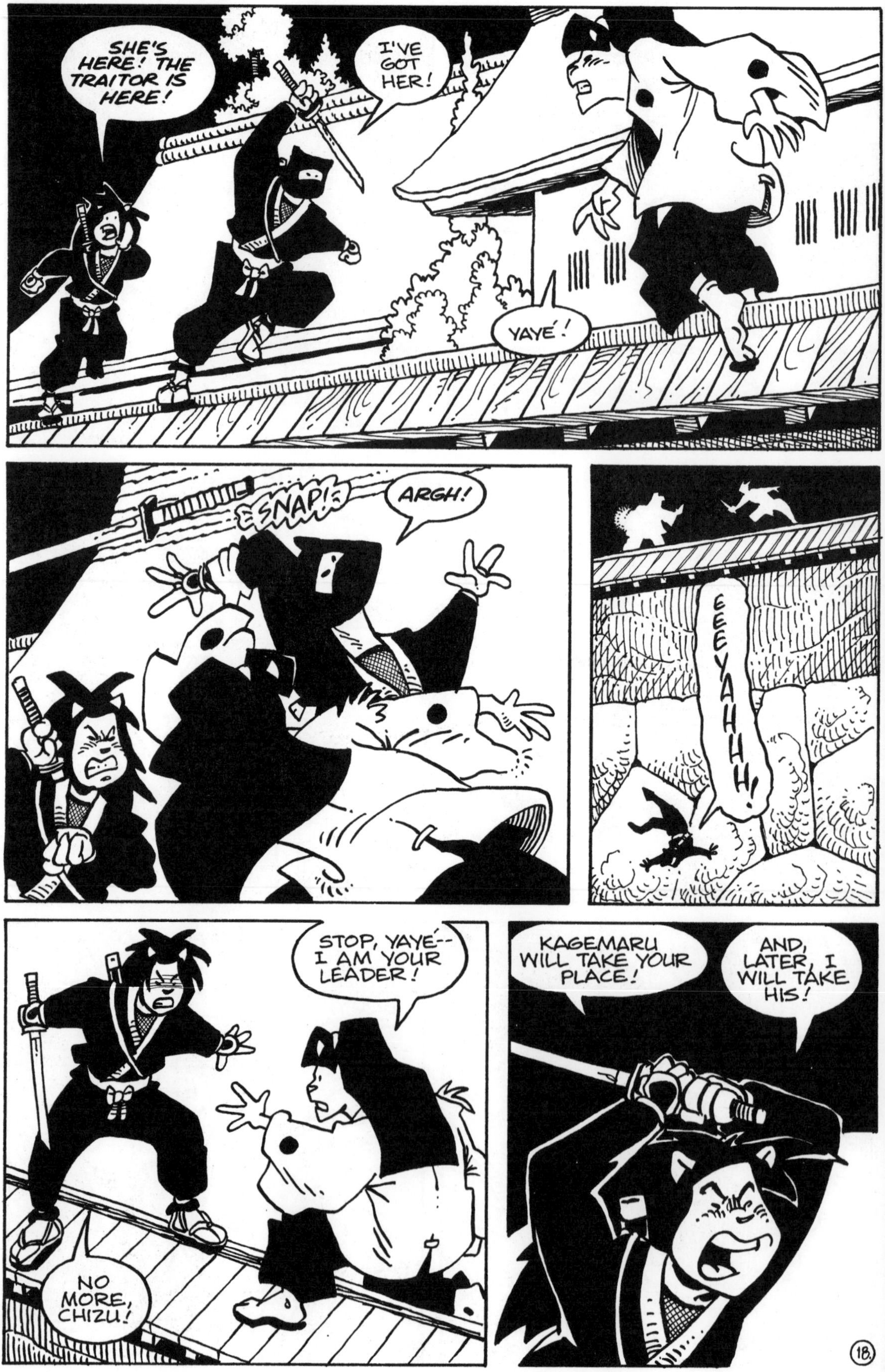

SHE'S HERE! THE TRAITOR IS HERE!
I'VE GOT HER!
YAYE!
SNAP!
ARGH!
EEEYAHHHH!
STOP, YAYE-- I AM YOUR LEADER!
NO MORE, CHIZU!
KAGEMARU WILL TAKE YOUR PLACE!
AND, LATER, I WILL TAKE HIS!
18.

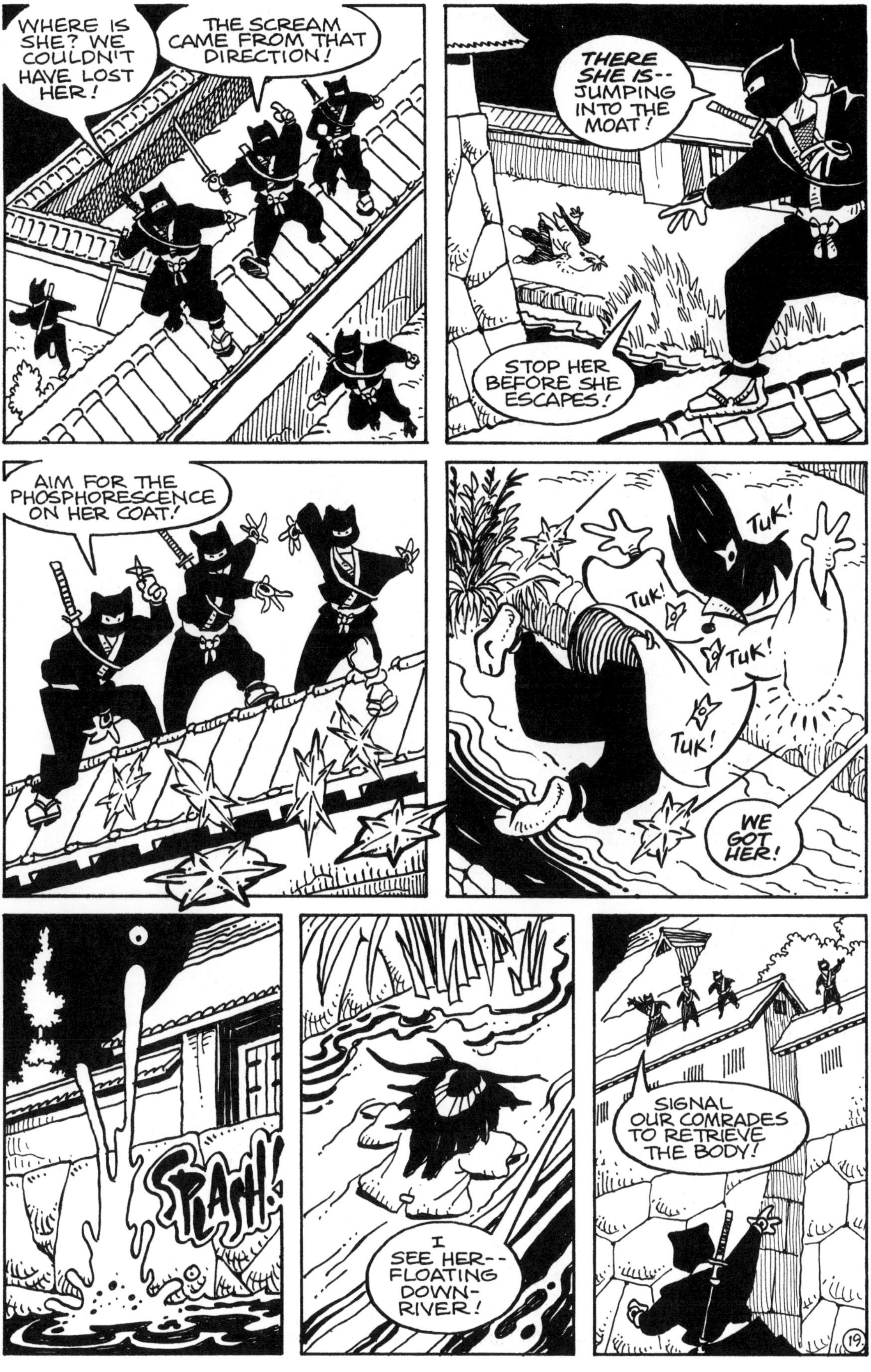
WHERE IS SHE? WE COULDN'T HAVE LOST HER!
THE SCREAM CAME FROM THAT DIRECTION!
THERE SHE IS-- JUMPING INTO THE MOAT!
STOP HER BEFORE SHE ESCAPES!
AIM FOR THE PHOSPHORESCENCE ON HER COAT!
TUK!
TUK!
TUK!
TUK!
WE GOT HER!
SPLASH!
I SEE HER-- FLOATING DOWN-RIVER!
SIGNAL OUR COMRADES TO RETRIEVE THE BODY!
19.

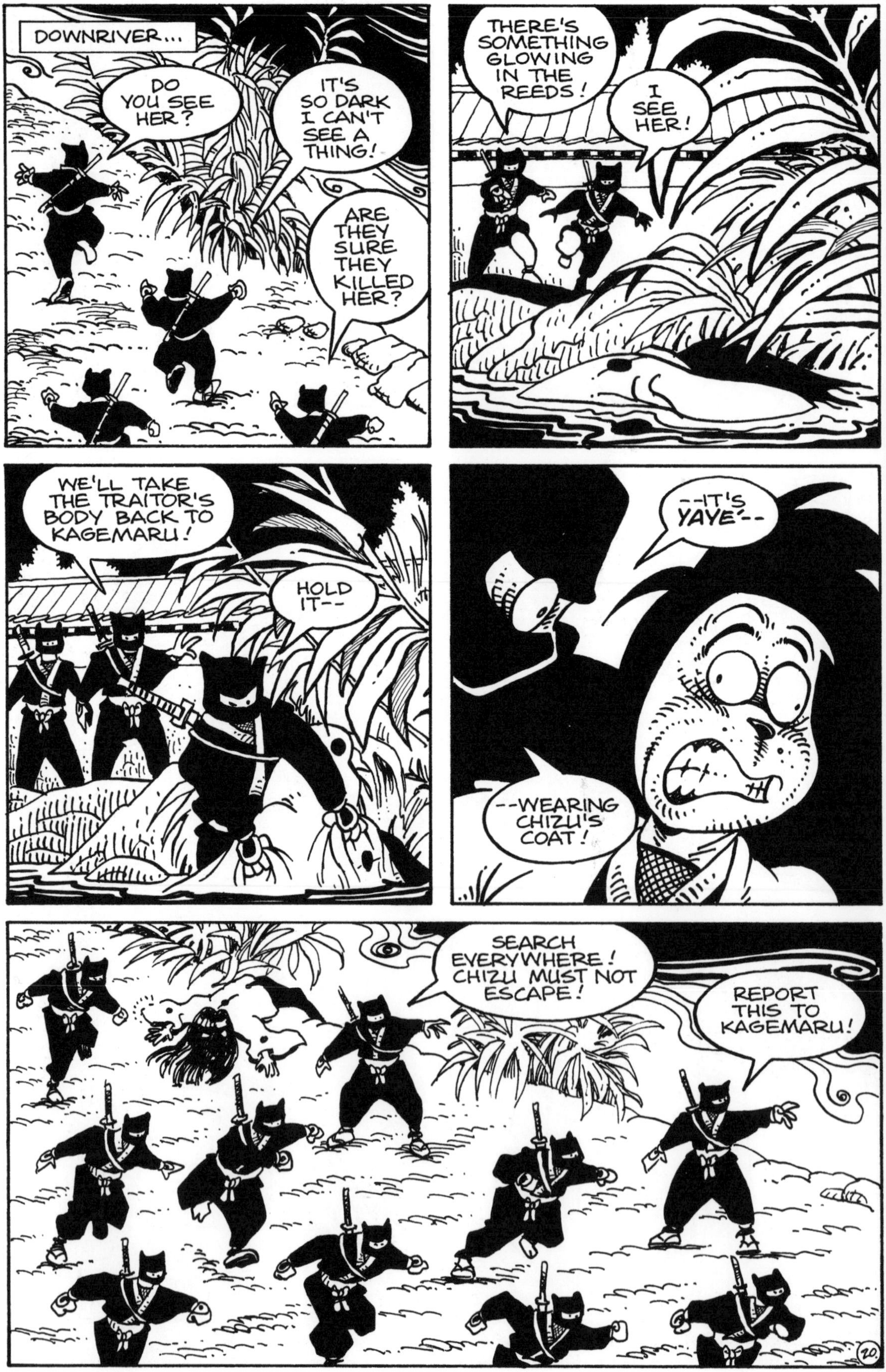
DOWNRIVER...
DO YOU SEE HER?
IT'S SO DARK I CAN'T SEE A THING!
ARE THEY SURE THEY KILLED HER?
THERE'S SOMETHING GLOWING IN THE REEDS!
I SEE HER!
WE'LL TAKE THE TRAITOR'S BODY BACK TO KAGEMARU!
HOLD IT--
--IT'S YAYE--
--WEARING CHIZU'S COAT!
SEARCH EVERYWHERE! CHIZU MUST NOT ESCAPE!
REPORT THIS TO KAGEMARU!
20.

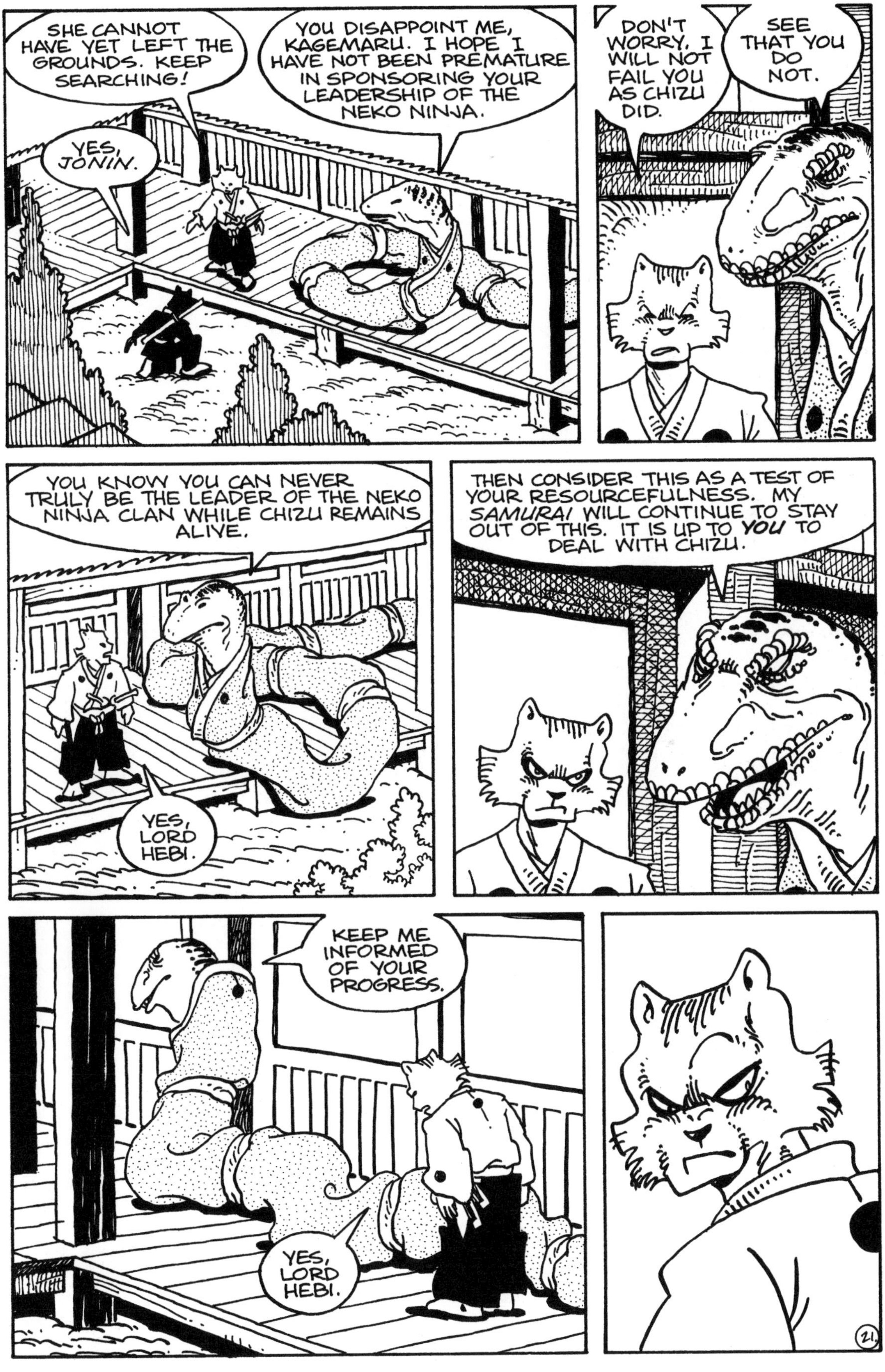
SHE CANNOT HAVE YET LEFT THE GROUNDS. KEEP SEARCHING!
YOU DISAPPOINT ME, KAGEMARU. I HOPE I HAVE NOT BEEN PREMATURE IN SPONSORING YOUR LEADERSHIP OF THE NEKO NINJA.
YES, JONIN.
DON'T WORRY. I WILL NOT FAIL YOU AS CHIZU DID.
SEE THAT YOU DO NOT.
YOU KNOW YOU CAN NEVER TRULY BE THE LEADER OF THE NEKO NINJA CLAN WHILE CHIZU REMAINS ALIVE.
YES, LORD HEBI.
THEN CONSIDER THIS AS A TEST OF YOUR RESOURCEFULNESS. MY SAMURAI WILL CONTINUE TO STAY OUT OF THIS. IT IS UP TO YOU TO DEAL WITH CHIZU.
KEEP ME INFORMED OF YOUR PROGRESS.
YES, LORD HEBI.
21

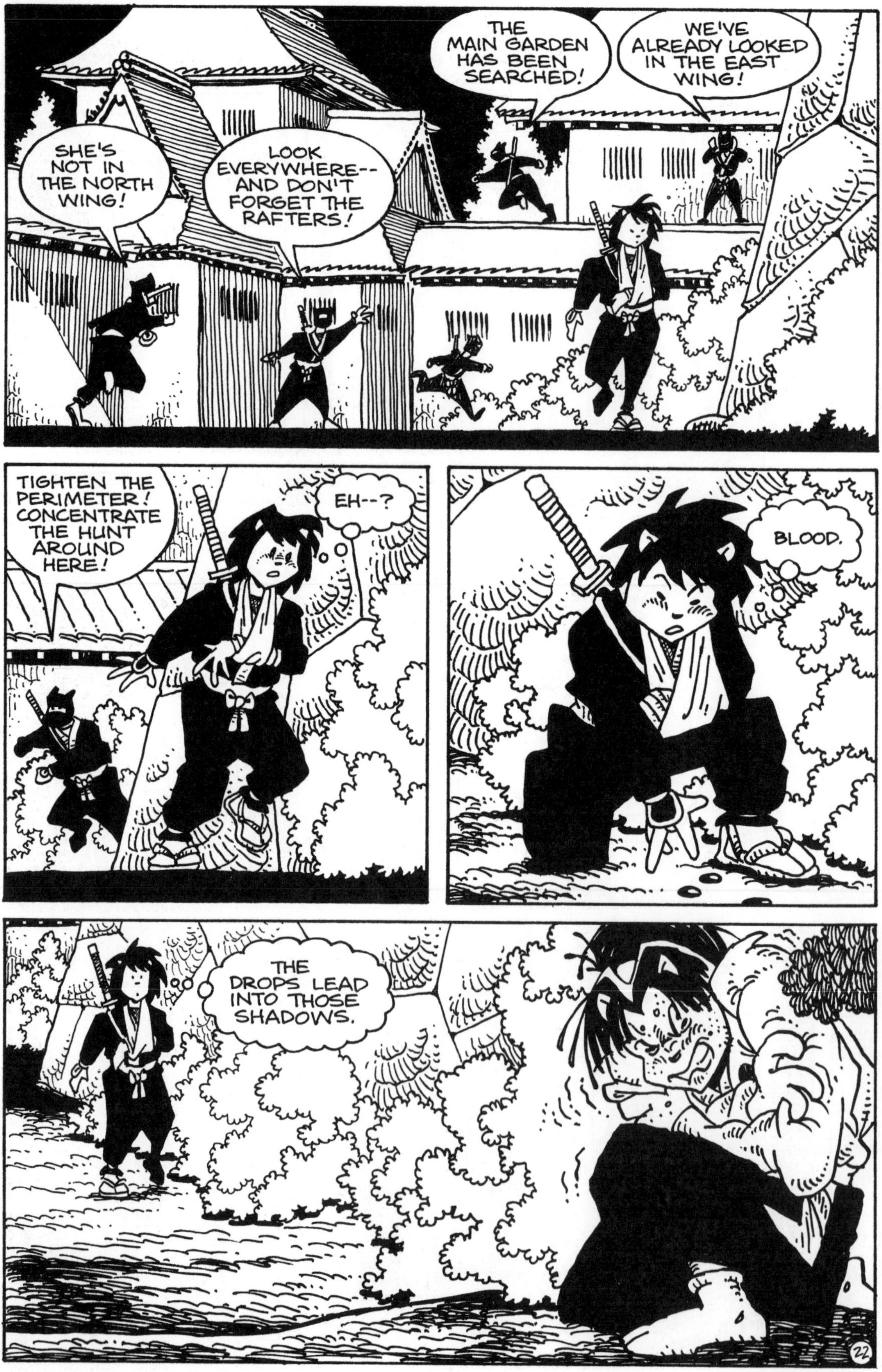
SHE'S NOT IN THE NORTH WING!
LOOK EVERYWHERE-- AND DON'T FORGET THE RAFTERS!
THE MAIN GARDEN HAS BEEN SEARCHED!
WE'VE ALREADY LOOKED IN THE EAST WING!
TIGHTEN THE PERIMETER! CONCENTRATE THE HUNT AROUND HERE!
EH--?
BLOOD.
THE DROPS LEAD INTO THOSE SHADOWS.
22

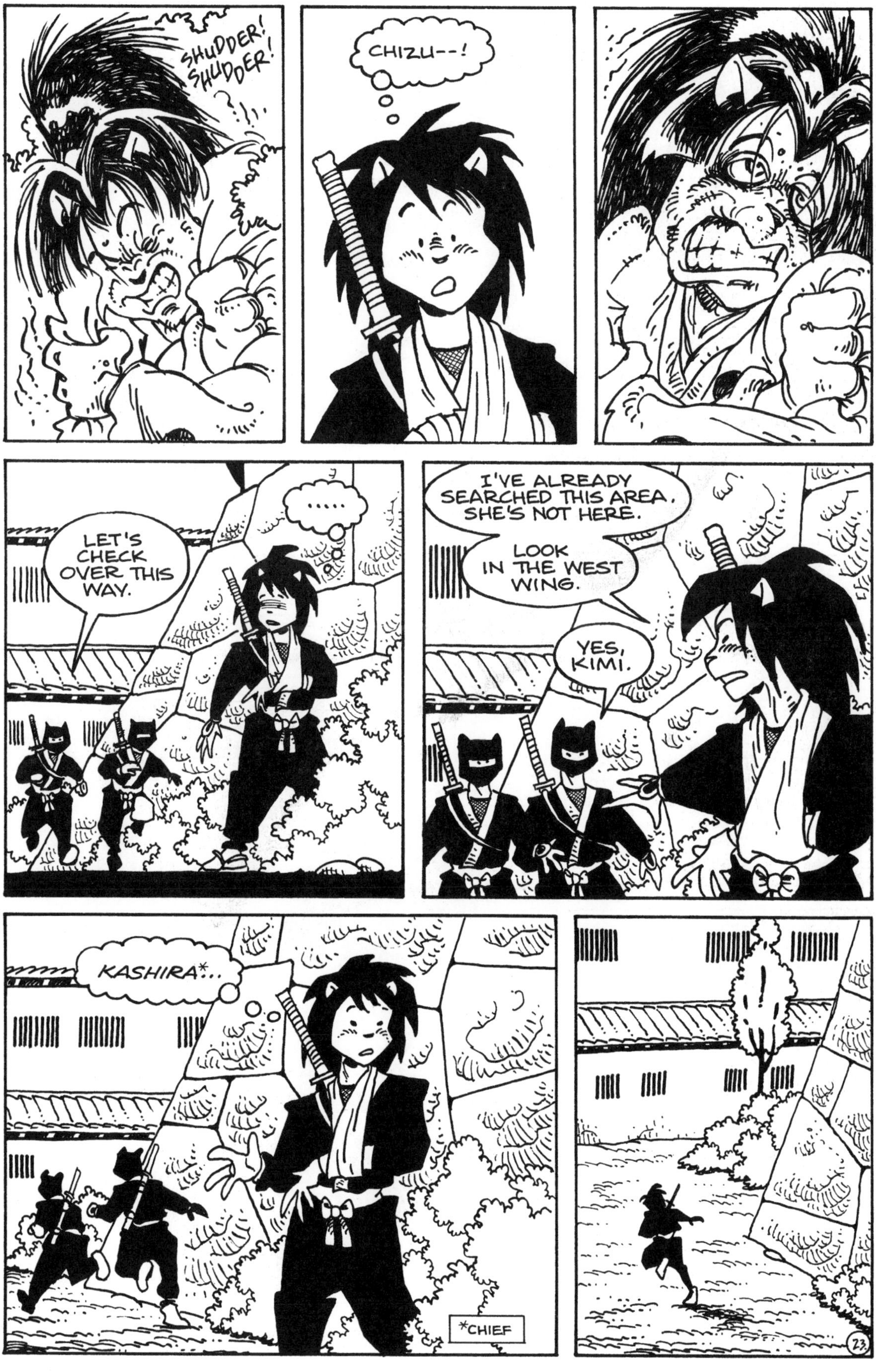
SHUDDER! SHUDDER!
CHIZU--!
LET'S CHECK OVER THIS WAY.
.....
I'VE ALREADY SEARCHED THIS AREA. SHE'S NOT HERE.
LOOK IN THE WEST WING.
YES, KIMI.
KASHIRA*...
*CHIEF
23

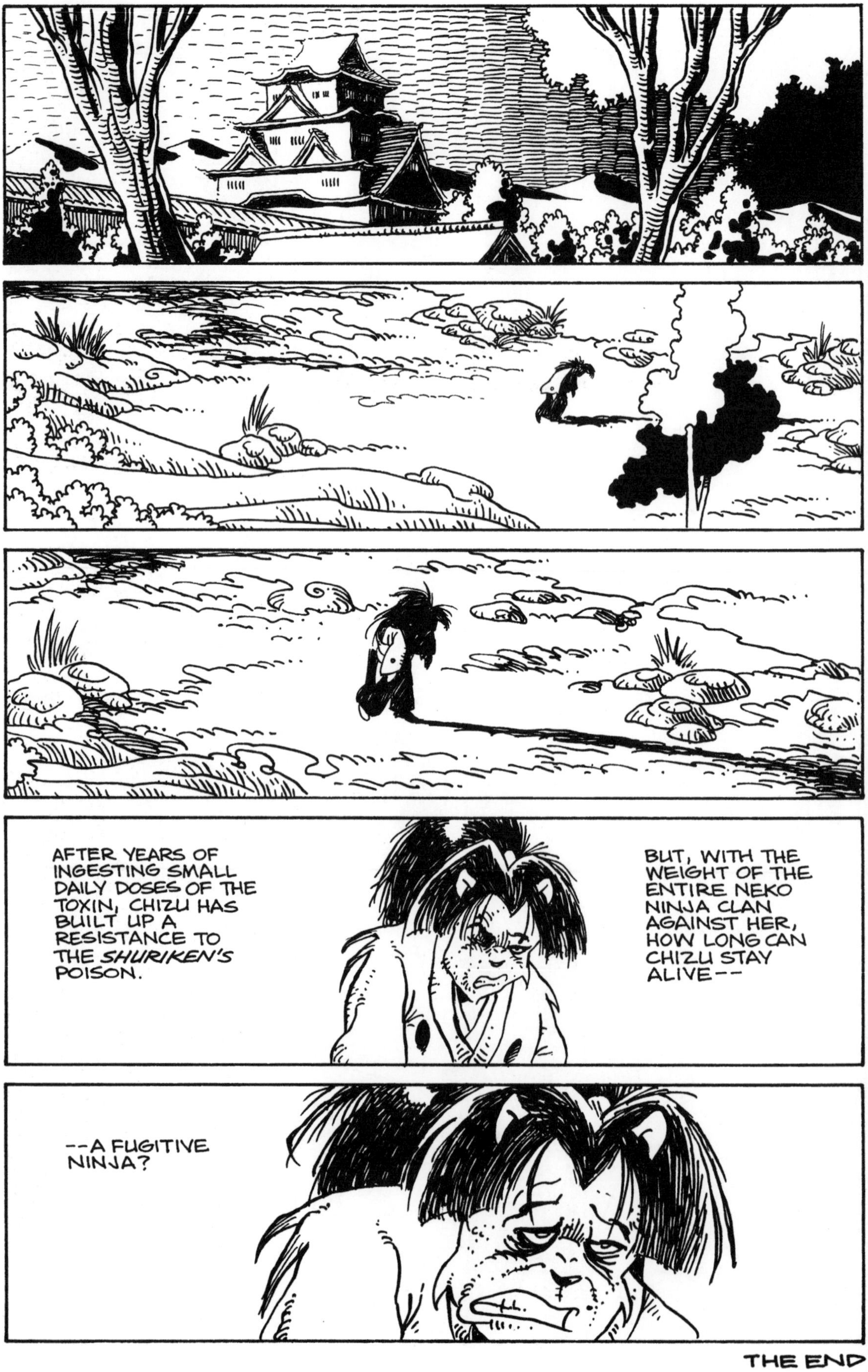
AFTER YEARS OF INGESTING SMALL DAILY DOSES OF THE TOXIN, CHIZU HAS BUILT UP A RESISTANCE TO THE *SHURIKEN'S* POISON.
BUT, WITH THE WEIGHT OF THE ENTIRE NEKO NINJA CLAN AGAINST HER, HOW LONG CAN CHIZU STAY ALIVE--
--A FUGITIVE NINJA?
THE END

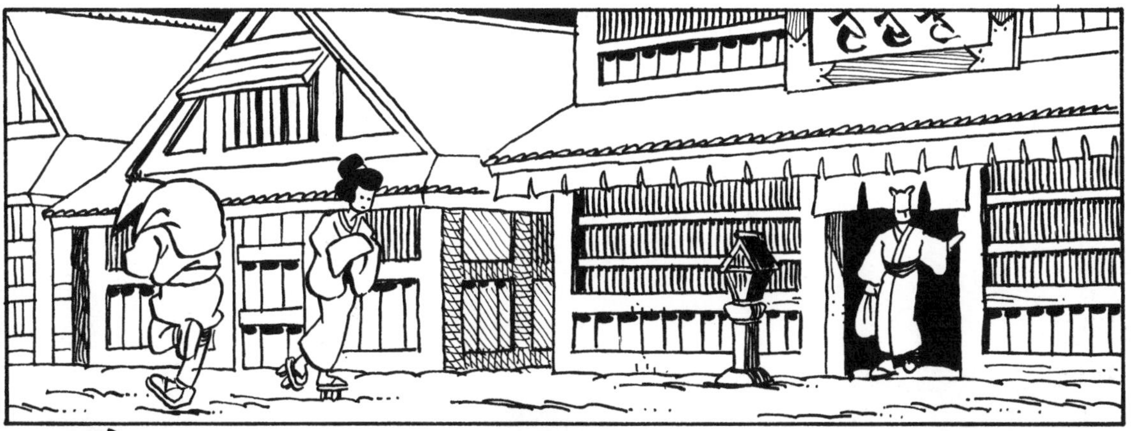

Three Seasons

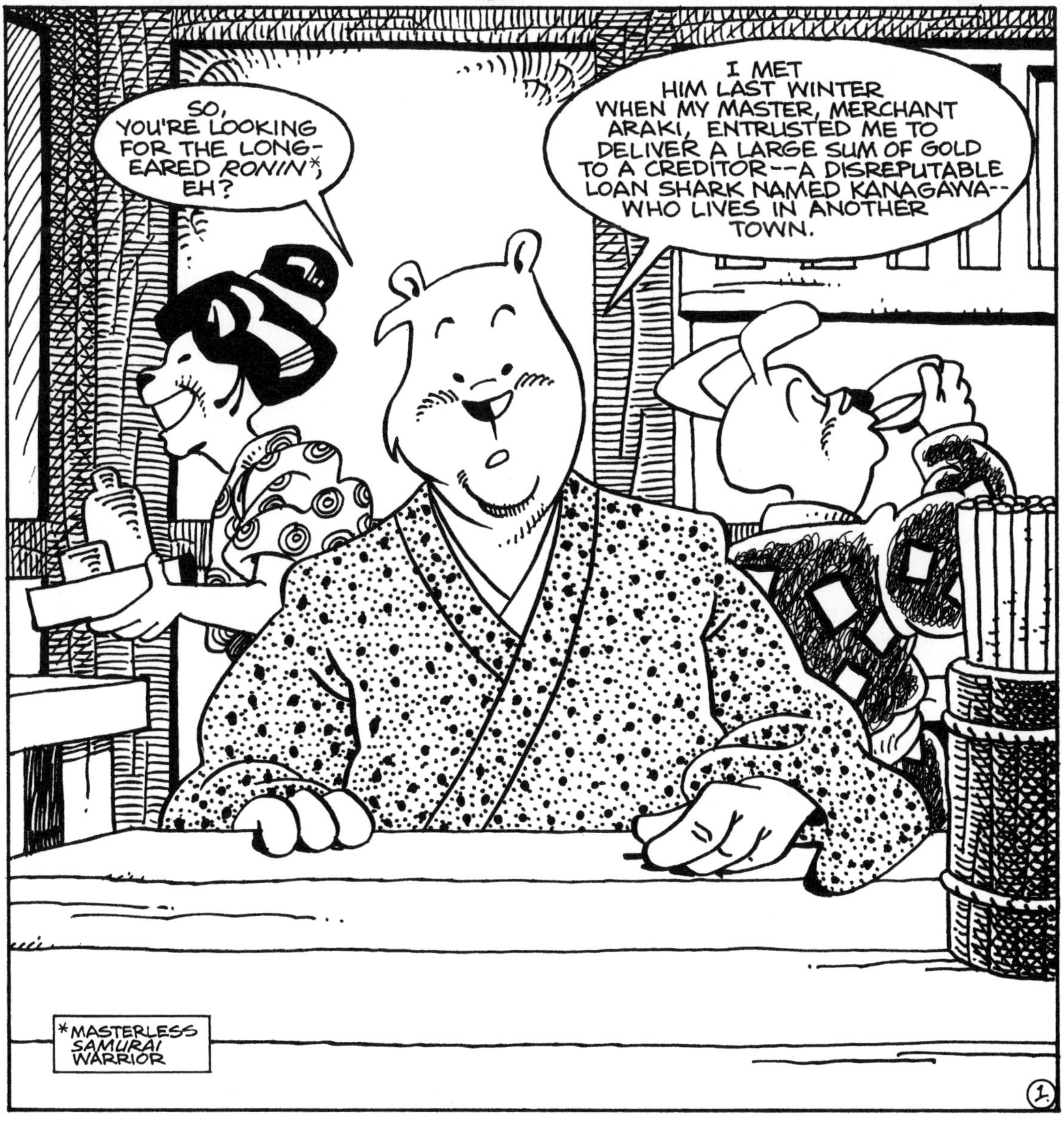
SO, YOU'RE LOOKING FOR THE LONG-EARED *RONIN**, EH?
I MET HIM LAST WINTER WHEN MY MASTER, MERCHANT ARAKI, ENTRUSTED ME TO DELIVER A LARGE SUM OF GOLD TO A CREDITOR--A DISREPUTABLE LOAN SHARK NAMED KANAGAWA--WHO LIVES IN ANOTHER TOWN.
*MASTERLESS SAMURAI WARRIOR
1

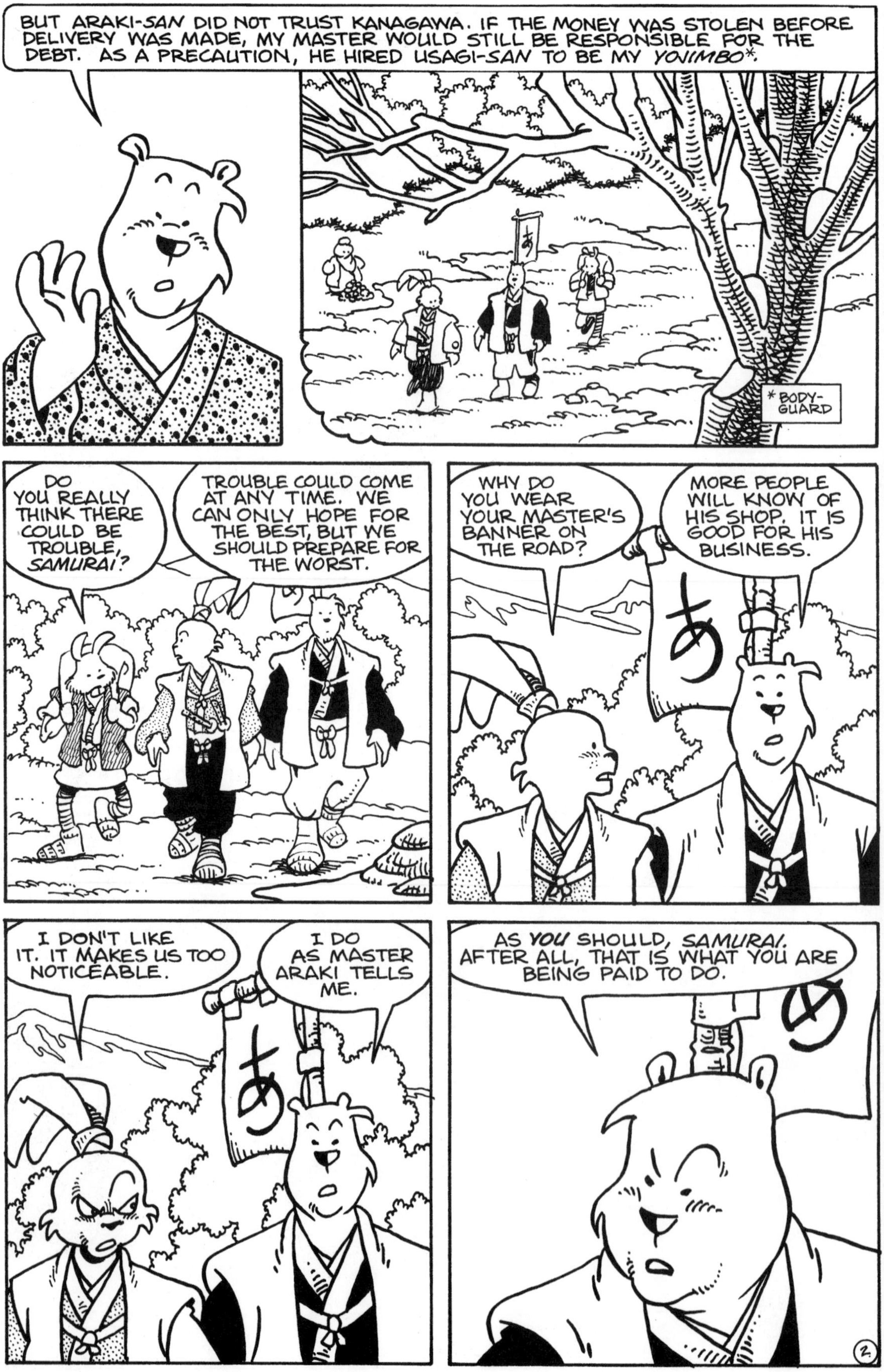
BUT ARAKI-*SAN* DID NOT TRUST KANAGAWA. IF THE MONEY WAS STOLEN BEFORE DELIVERY WAS MADE, MY MASTER WOULD STILL BE RESPONSIBLE FOR THE DEBT. AS A PRECAUTION, HE HIRED USAGI-*SAN* TO BE MY *YOJIMBO**.
* BODY-GUARD
DO YOU REALLY THINK THERE COULD BE TROUBLE, *SAMURAI*?
TROUBLE COULD COME AT ANY TIME. WE CAN ONLY HOPE FOR THE BEST, BUT WE SHOULD PREPARE FOR THE WORST.
WHY DO YOU WEAR YOUR MASTER'S BANNER ON THE ROAD?
MORE PEOPLE WILL KNOW OF HIS SHOP. IT IS GOOD FOR HIS BUSINESS.
I DON'T LIKE IT. IT MAKES US TOO NOTICEABLE.
I DO AS MASTER ARAKI TELLS ME.
AS ***YOU*** SHOULD, *SAMURAI*. AFTER ALL, THAT IS WHAT YOU ARE BEING PAID TO DO.
2

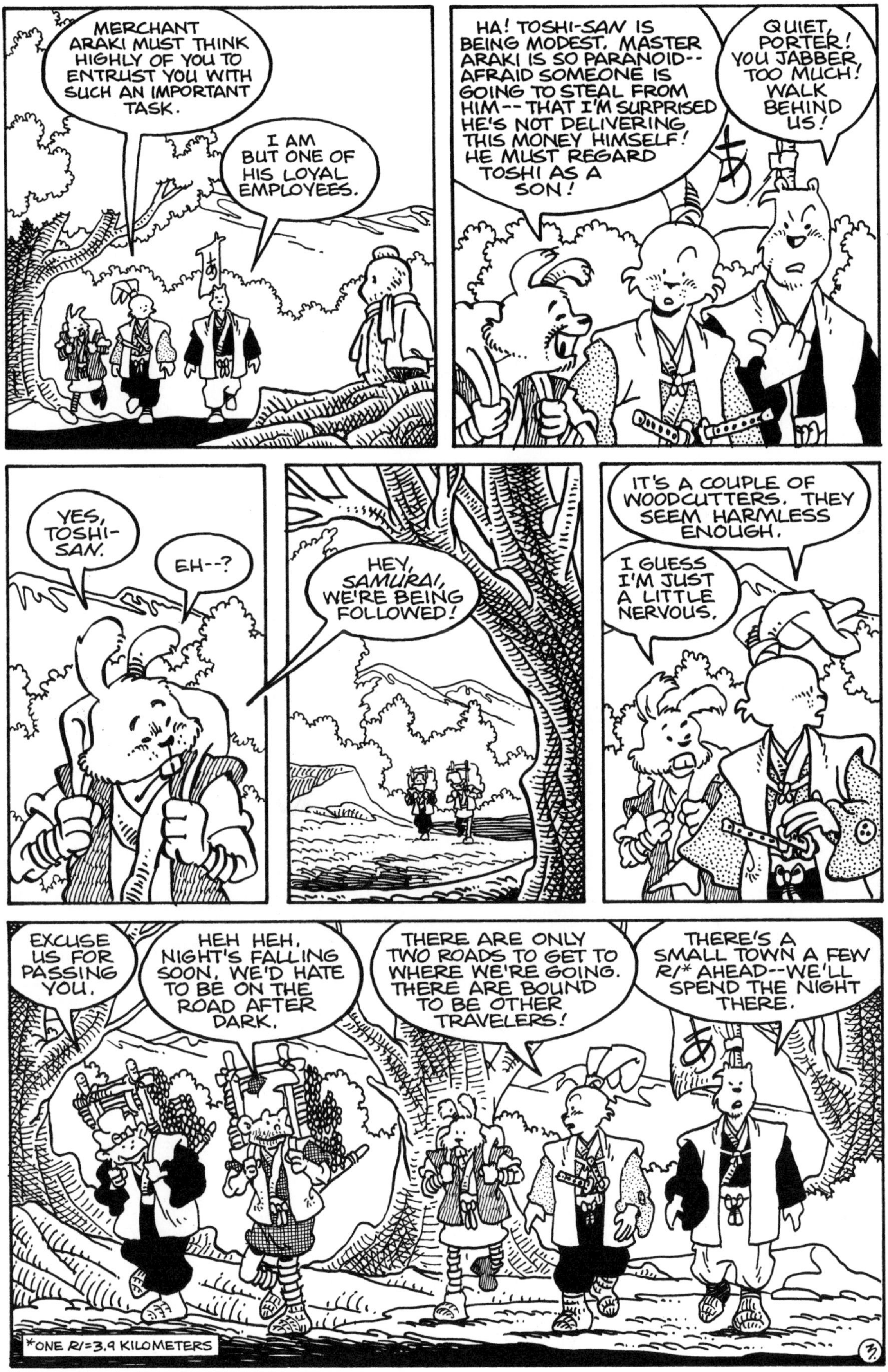
MERCHANT ARAKI MUST THINK HIGHLY OF YOU TO ENTRUST YOU WITH SUCH AN IMPORTANT TASK.
I AM BUT ONE OF HIS LOYAL EMPLOYEES.
HA! TOSHI-SAN IS BEING MODEST. MASTER ARAKI IS SO PARANOID-- AFRAID SOMEONE IS GOING TO STEAL FROM HIM--THAT I'M SURPRISED HE'S NOT DELIVERING THIS MONEY HIMSELF! HE MUST REGARD TOSHI AS A SON!
QUIET, PORTER! YOU JABBER TOO MUCH! WALK BEHIND US!
YES, TOSHI-SAN.
EH--?
HEY, SAMURAI, WE'RE BEING FOLLOWED!
IT'S A COUPLE OF WOODCUTTERS. THEY SEEM HARMLESS ENOUGH.
I GUESS I'M JUST A LITTLE NERVOUS.
EXCUSE US FOR PASSING YOU.
HEH HEH. NIGHT'S FALLING SOON. WE'D HATE TO BE ON THE ROAD AFTER DARK.
THERE ARE ONLY TWO ROADS TO GET TO WHERE WE'RE GOING. THERE ARE BOUND TO BE OTHER TRAVELERS!
THERE'S A SMALL TOWN A FEW RI* AHEAD--WE'LL SPEND THE NIGHT THERE.
*ONE RI=3.9 KILOMETERS
3

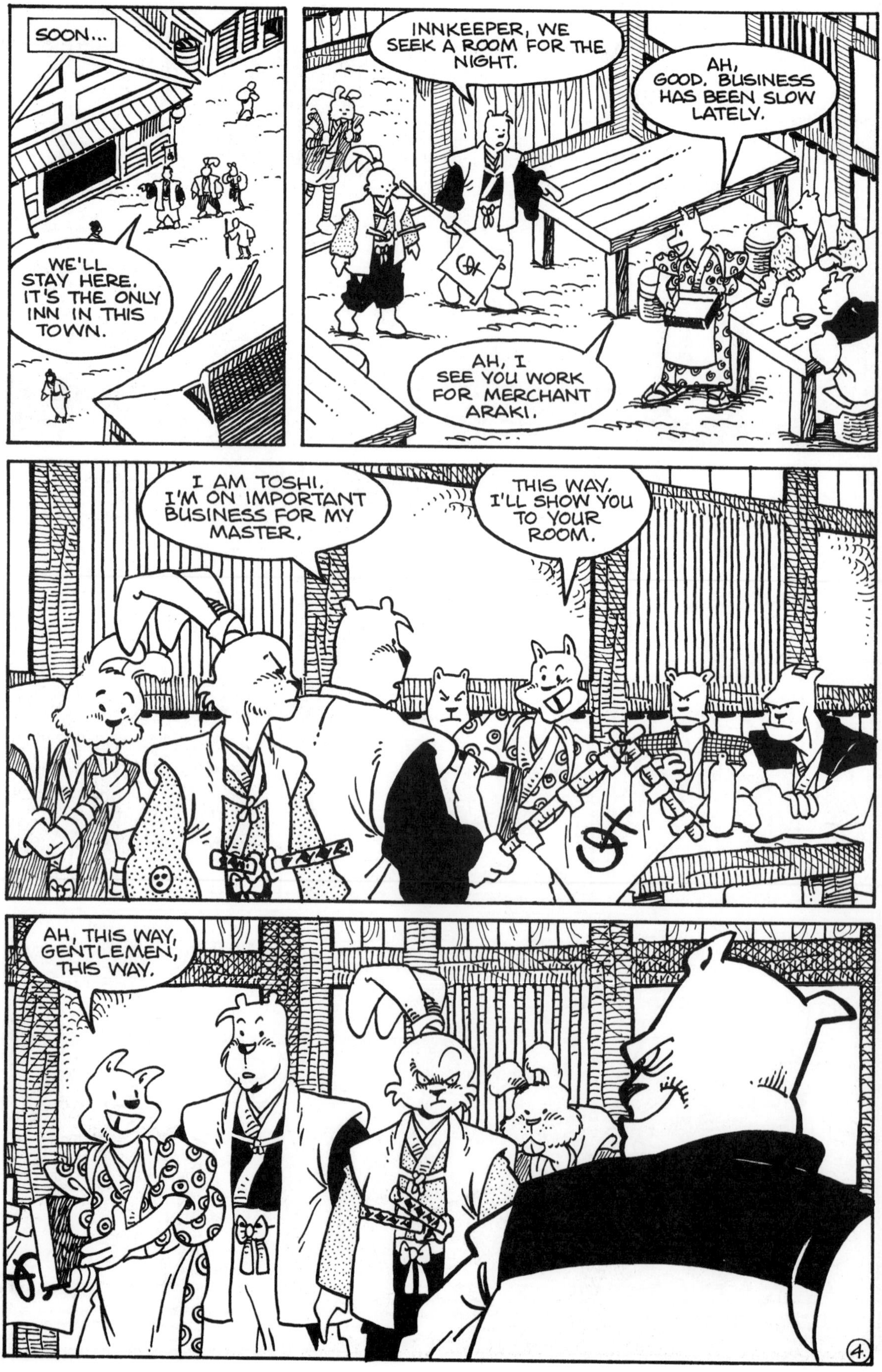
SOON...
WE'LL STAY HERE. IT'S THE ONLY INN IN THIS TOWN.
INNKEEPER, WE SEEK A ROOM FOR THE NIGHT.
AH, GOOD. BUSINESS HAS BEEN SLOW LATELY.
AH, I SEE YOU WORK FOR MERCHANT ARAKI.
I AM TOSHI. I'M ON IMPORTANT BUSINESS FOR MY MASTER.
THIS WAY. I'LL SHOW YOU TO YOUR ROOM.
AH, THIS WAY, GENTLEMEN, THIS WAY.
4.

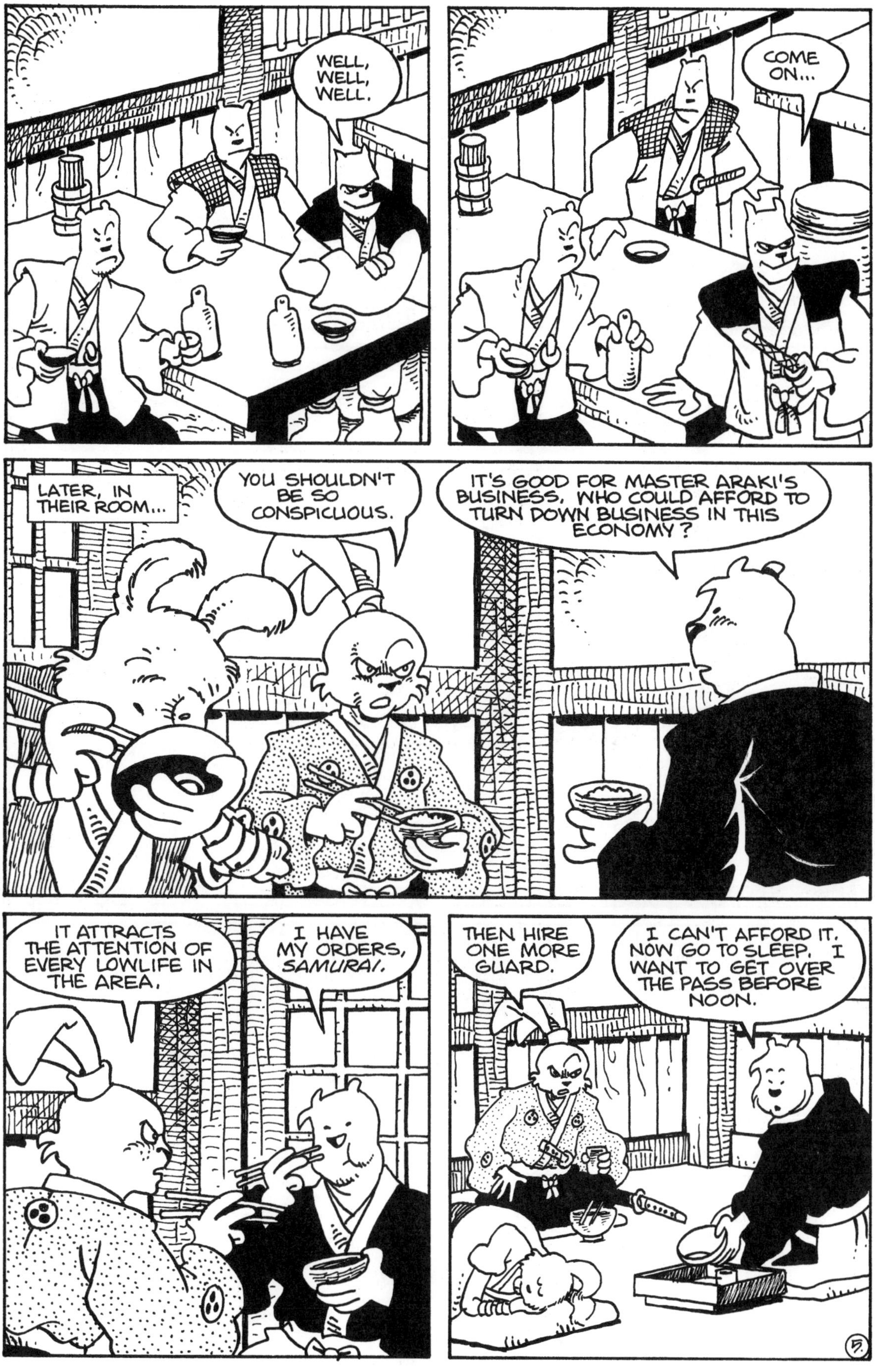

WELL, WELL, WELL.
COME ON...
LATER, IN THEIR ROOM...
YOU SHOULDN'T BE SO CONSPICUOUS.
IT'S GOOD FOR MASTER ARAKI'S BUSINESS. WHO COULD AFFORD TO TURN DOWN BUSINESS IN THIS ECONOMY?
IT ATTRACTS THE ATTENTION OF EVERY LOWLIFE IN THE AREA.
I HAVE MY ORDERS, *SAMURAI*.
THEN HIRE ONE MORE GUARD.
I CAN'T AFFORD IT. NOW GO TO SLEEP. I WANT TO GET OVER THE PASS BEFORE NOON.

ABOUT NOON THE NEXT DAY...

IT'S NOT FAR NOW, SAMURAI! ALL YOUR WORRIES WERE FOR NAUGHT.

WE HAVE YET TO REACH OUR DESTINATION, TOSHI-SAN.

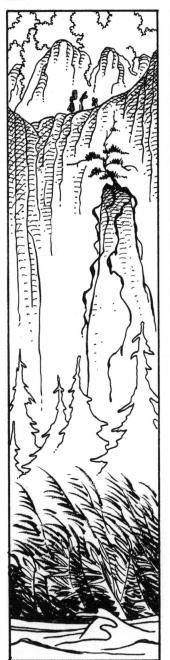

IT'S ABOUT TIME YOU GOT HERE. WE WERE GETTING COLD.

WHAT?

IT'S THOSE GUYS FROM THE INN!

THERE ARE MORE OF THEM BEHIND US!

WE KNOW YOU'RE CARRYING GOLD IN THAT CHEST!

GIVE IT UP!

6.

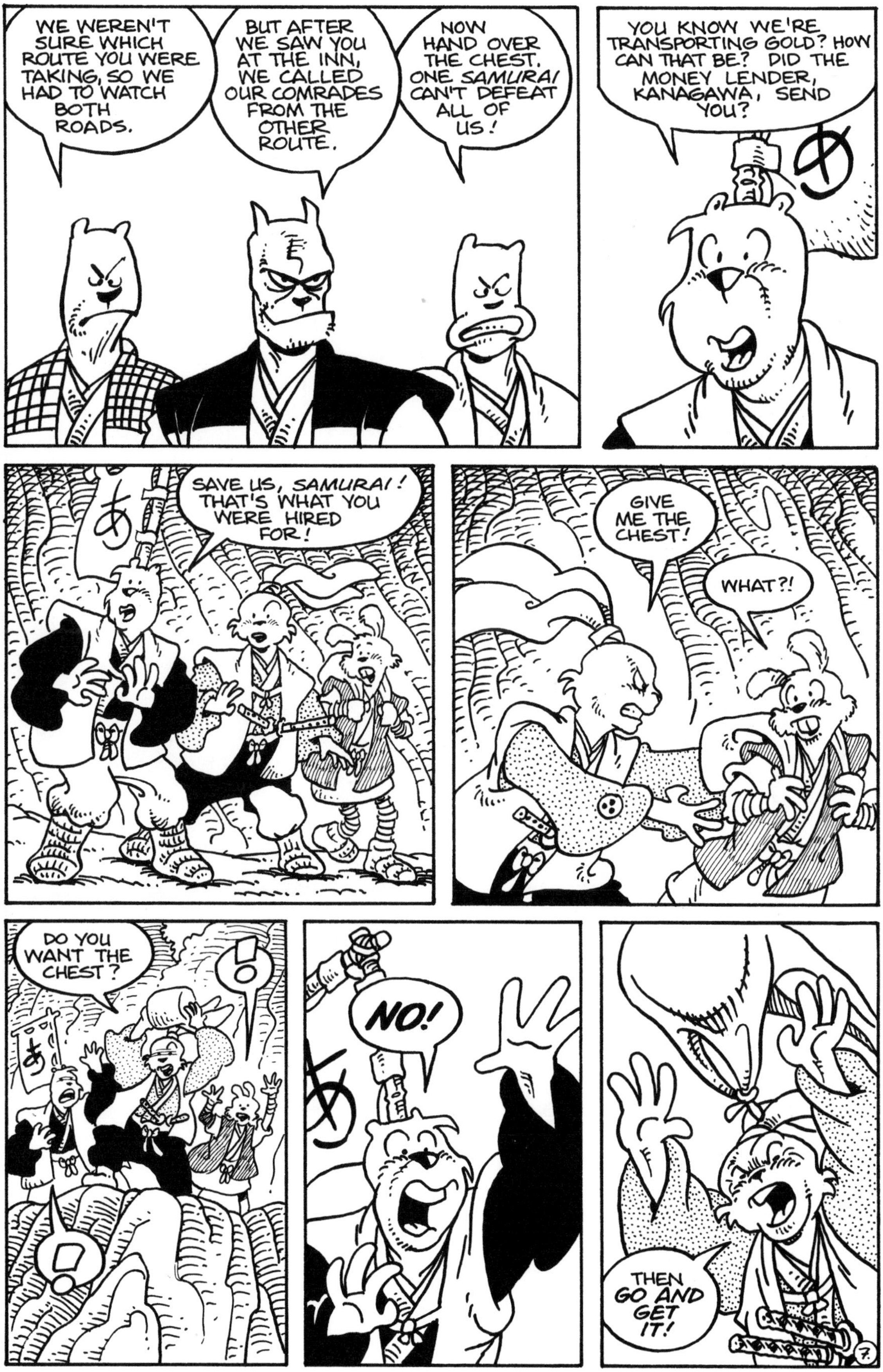
WE WEREN'T SURE WHICH ROUTE YOU WERE TAKING, SO WE HAD TO WATCH BOTH ROADS.
BUT AFTER WE SAW YOU AT THE INN, WE CALLED OUR COMRADES FROM THE OTHER ROUTE.
NOW HAND OVER THE CHEST. ONE SAMURAI CAN'T DEFEAT ALL OF US!
YOU KNOW WE'RE TRANSPORTING GOLD? HOW CAN THAT BE? DID THE MONEY LENDER, KANAGAWA, SEND YOU?
SAVE US, SAMURAI! THAT'S WHAT YOU WERE HIRED FOR!
GIVE ME THE CHEST!
WHAT?!
DO YOU WANT THE CHEST?
!
!
NO!
THEN GO AND GET IT!
7.

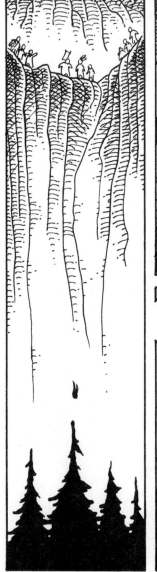

DOWN THE TRAIL--HURRY, BEFORE SOMEONE ELSE FINDS IT!

IMAGINE A YOJIMBO SO AFRAID, HE WOULD DISCARD THE TREASURE HE WAS GUARDING!

HURRY!

COWARD! MASTER ARAKI ENTRUSTED US WITH THAT CHEST!

WOULD IT HAVE BEEN BETTER IF THEY'D DISCOVERED THERE IS NO GOLD IN THAT CHEST?

WH- WHAT?!

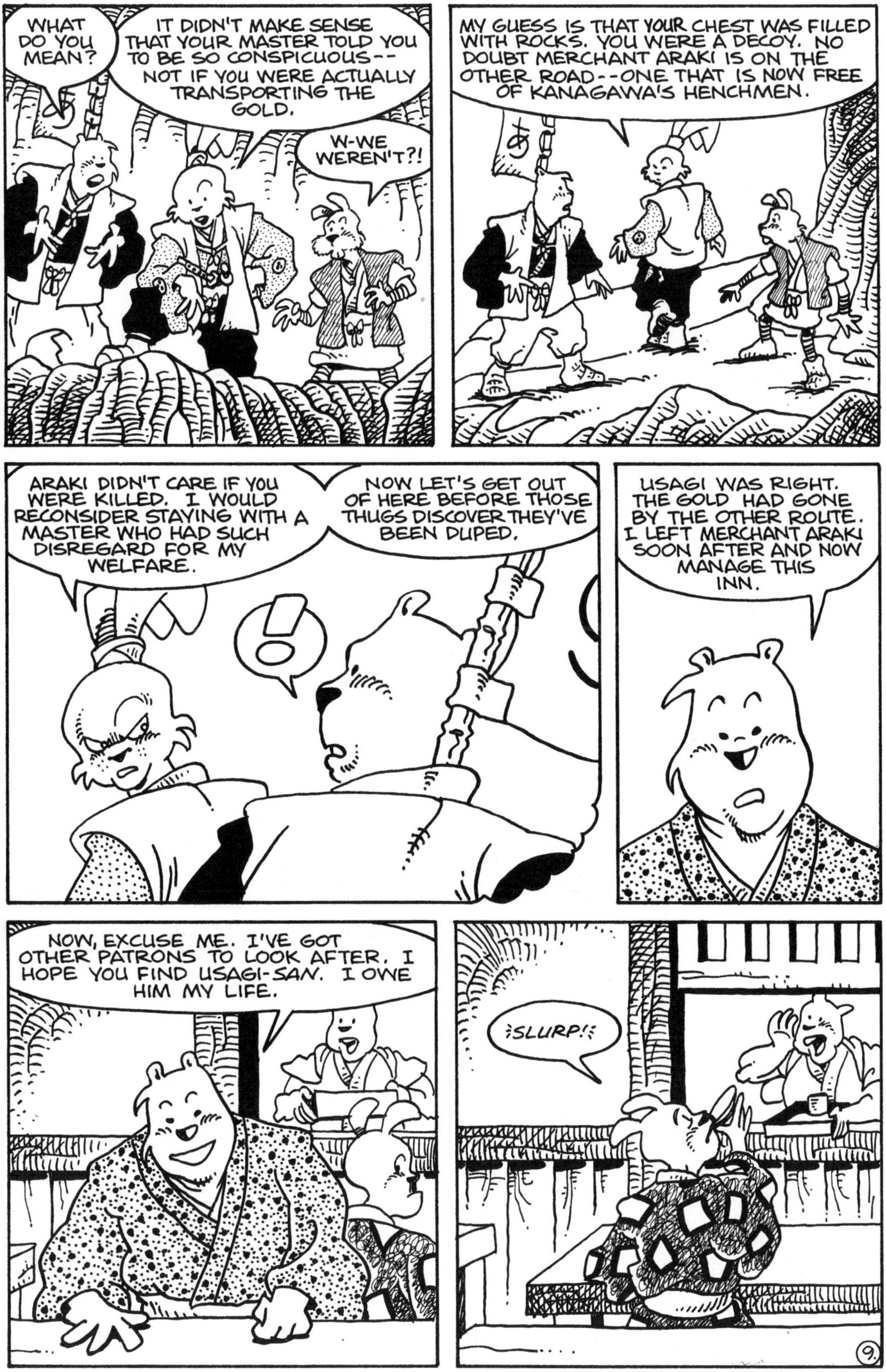
WHAT DO YOU MEAN?
IT DIDN'T MAKE SENSE THAT YOUR MASTER TOLD YOU TO BE SO CONSPICUOUS-- NOT IF YOU WERE ACTUALLY TRANSPORTING THE GOLD.
W-WE WEREN'T?!
MY GUESS IS THAT YOUR CHEST WAS FILLED WITH ROCKS. YOU WERE A DECOY. NO DOUBT MERCHANT ARAKI IS ON THE OTHER ROAD--ONE THAT IS NOW FREE OF KANAGAWA'S HENCHMEN.
ARAKI DIDN'T CARE IF YOU WERE KILLED. I WOULD RECONSIDER STAYING WITH A MASTER WHO HAD SUCH DISREGARD FOR MY WELFARE.
NOW LET'S GET OUT OF HERE BEFORE THOSE THUGS DISCOVER THEY'VE BEEN DUPED.
!
USAGI WAS RIGHT. THE GOLD HAD GONE BY THE OTHER ROUTE. I LEFT MERCHANT ARAKI SOON AFTER AND NOW MANAGE THIS INN.
NOW, EXCUSE ME. I'VE GOT OTHER PATRONS TO LOOK AFTER. I HOPE YOU FIND USAGI-SAN. I OWE HIM MY LIFE.
SLURP!
9.

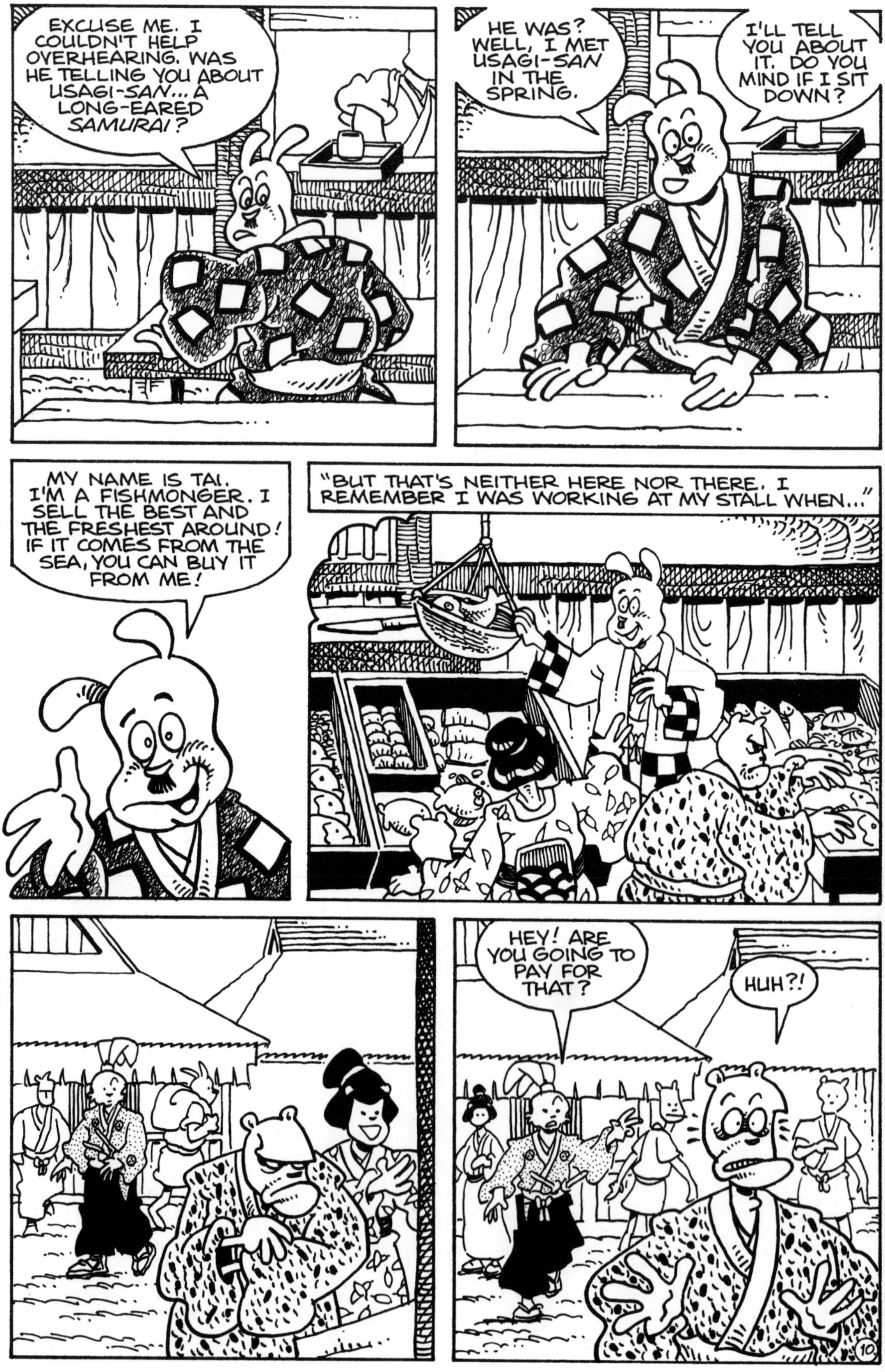
EXCUSE ME. I COULDN'T HELP OVERHEARING. WAS HE TELLING YOU ABOUT USAGI-SAN... A LONG-EARED SAMURAI?
HE WAS? WELL, I MET USAGI-SAN IN THE SPRING.
I'LL TELL YOU ABOUT IT. DO YOU MIND IF I SIT DOWN?
MY NAME IS TAI. I'M A FISHMONGER. I SELL THE BEST AND THE FRESHEST AROUND! IF IT COMES FROM THE SEA, YOU CAN BUY IT FROM ME!
"BUT THAT'S NEITHER HERE NOR THERE. I REMEMBER I WAS WORKING AT MY STALL WHEN..."
HEY! ARE YOU GOING TO PAY FOR THAT?
HUH?!
10

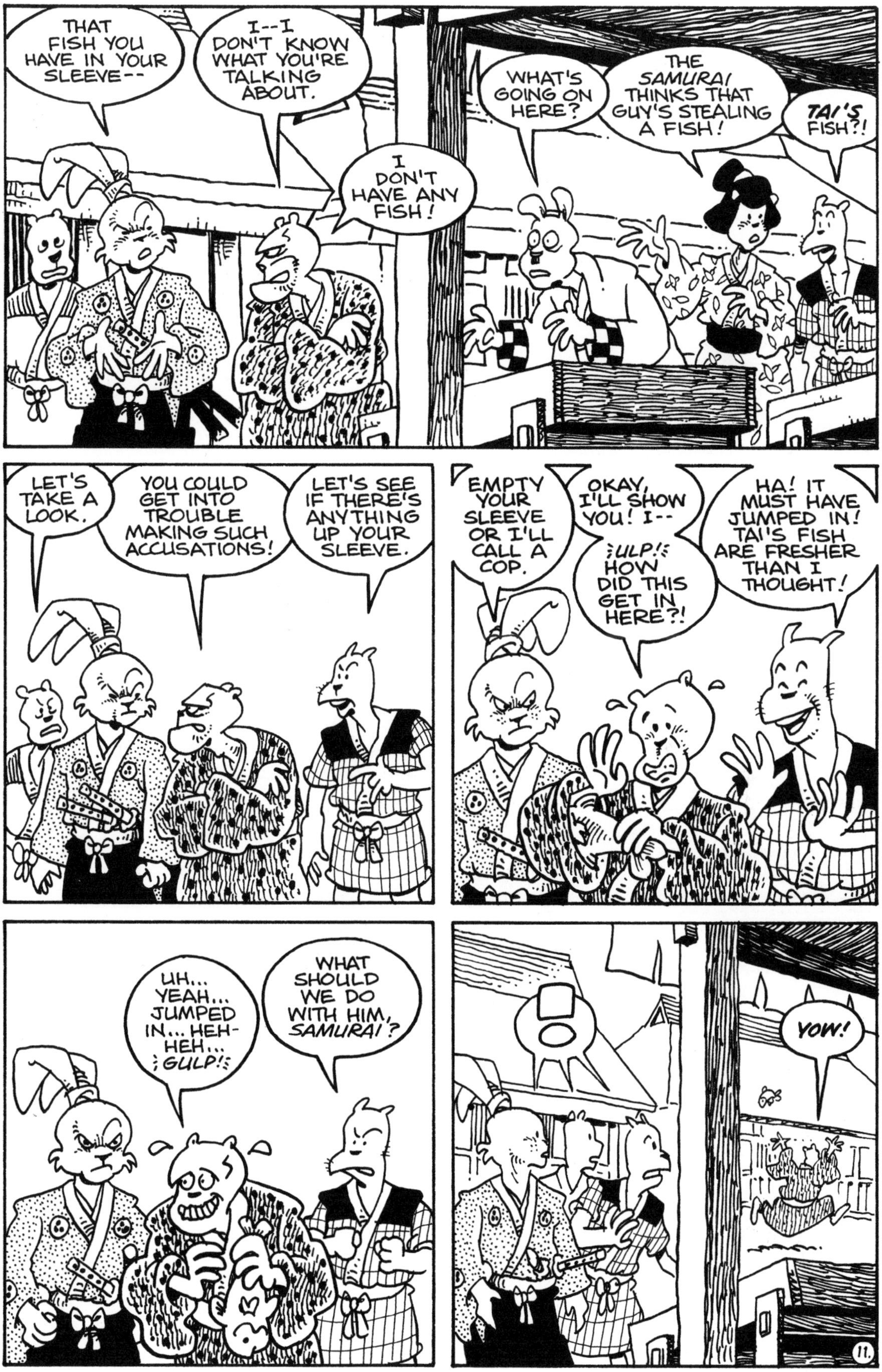
THAT FISH YOU HAVE IN YOUR SLEEVE--
I--I DON'T KNOW WHAT YOU'RE TALKING ABOUT.
I DON'T HAVE ANY FISH!
WHAT'S GOING ON HERE?
THE SAMURAI THINKS THAT GUY'S STEALING A FISH!
TAI'S FISH?!
LET'S TAKE A LOOK.
YOU COULD GET INTO TROUBLE MAKING SUCH ACCUSATIONS!
LET'S SEE IF THERE'S ANYTHING UP YOUR SLEEVE.
EMPTY YOUR SLEEVE OR I'LL CALL A COP.
OKAY, I'LL SHOW YOU! I--
ULP! HOW DID THIS GET IN HERE?!
HA! IT MUST HAVE JUMPED IN! TAI'S FISH ARE FRESHER THAN I THOUGHT!
UH... YEAH... JUMPED IN... HEH-HEH... GULP!
WHAT SHOULD WE DO WITH HIM, SAMURAI?
YOW!
11.

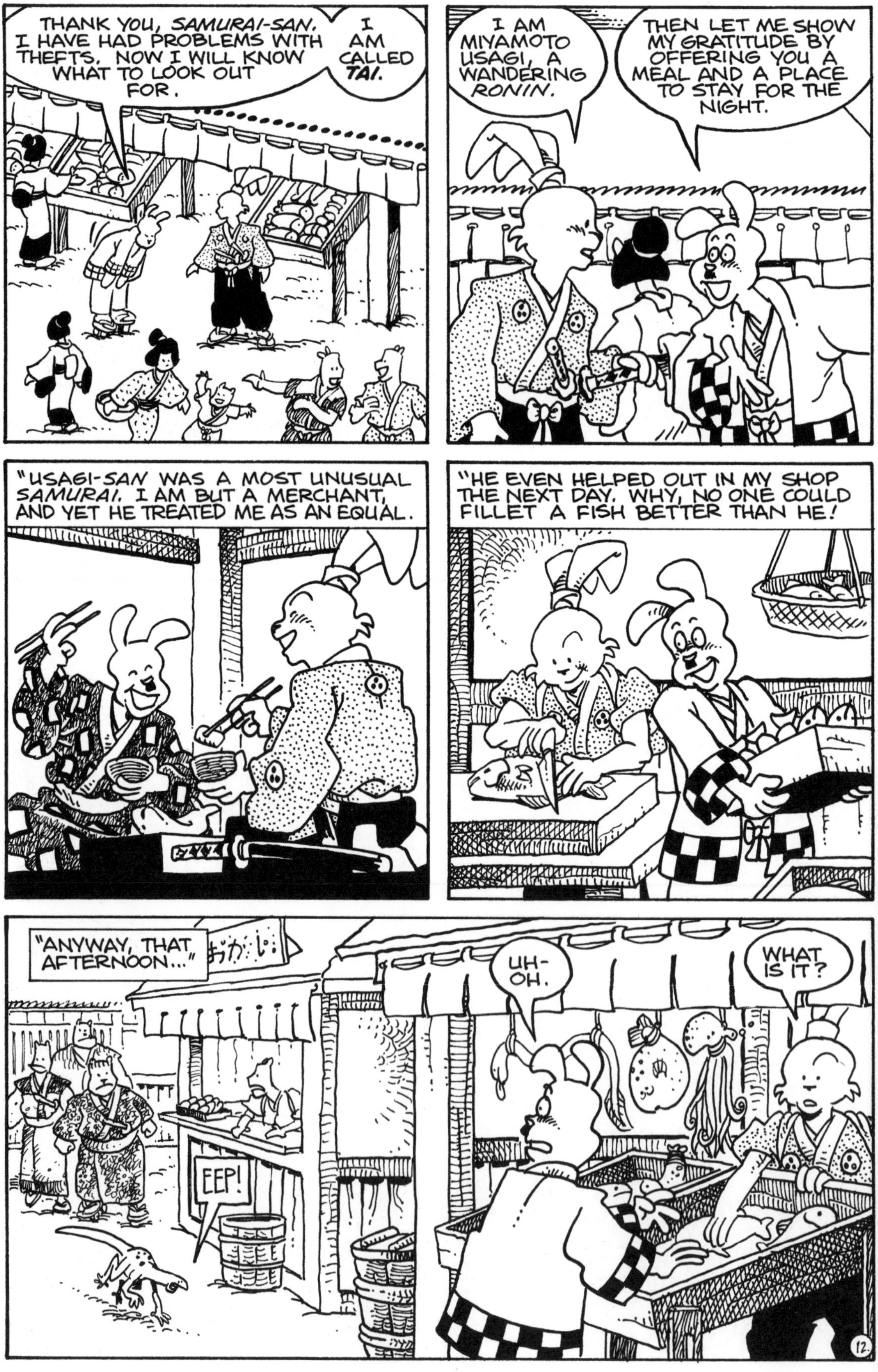
THANK YOU, SAMURAI-SAN. I HAVE HAD PROBLEMS WITH THEFTS. NOW I WILL KNOW WHAT TO LOOK OUT FOR.
I AM CALLED TAI.
I AM MIYAMOTO USAGI, A WANDERING RONIN.
THEN LET ME SHOW MY GRATITUDE BY OFFERING YOU A MEAL AND A PLACE TO STAY FOR THE NIGHT.
"USAGI-SAN WAS A MOST UNUSUAL SAMURAI. I AM BUT A MERCHANT, AND YET HE TREATED ME AS AN EQUAL.
"HE EVEN HELPED OUT IN MY SHOP THE NEXT DAY. WHY, NO ONE COULD FILLET A FISH BETTER THAN HE!
"ANYWAY, THAT AFTERNOON..."
EEP!
UH-OH.
WHAT IS IT?
12.

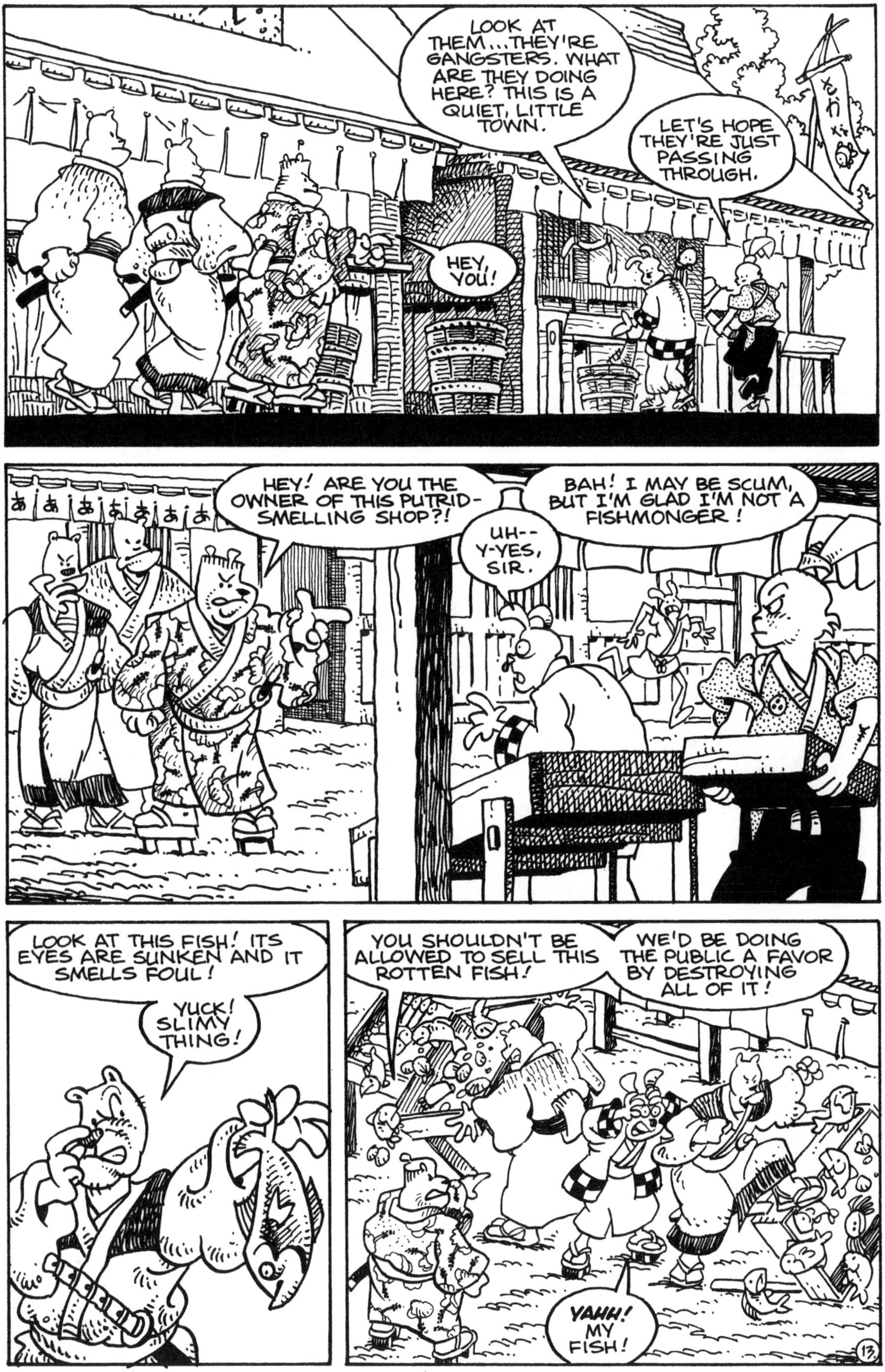
LOOK AT THEM...THEY'RE GANGSTERS. WHAT ARE THEY DOING HERE? THIS IS A QUIET, LITTLE TOWN.
LET'S HOPE THEY'RE JUST PASSING THROUGH.
HEY, YOU!
HEY! ARE YOU THE OWNER OF THIS PUTRID-SMELLING SHOP?!
UH-- Y-YES, SIR.
BAH! I MAY BE SCUM, BUT I'M GLAD I'M NOT A FISHMONGER!
LOOK AT THIS FISH! ITS EYES ARE SUNKEN AND IT SMELLS FOUL!
YUCK! SLIMY THING!
YOU SHOULDN'T BE ALLOWED TO SELL THIS ROTTEN FISH!
WE'D BE DOING THE PUBLIC A FAVOR BY DESTROYING ALL OF IT!
YAHH! MY FISH!
13

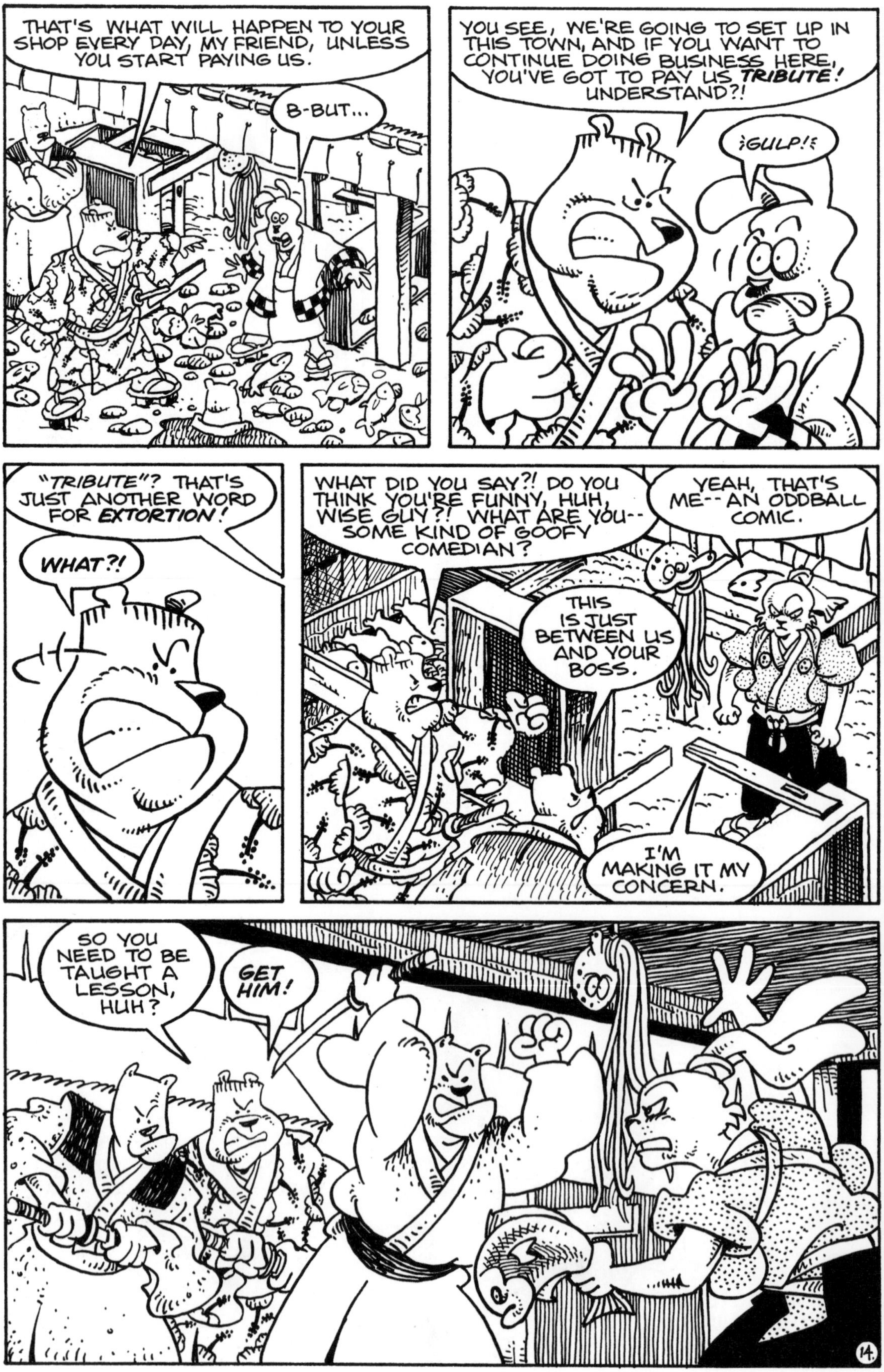
THAT'S WHAT WILL HAPPEN TO YOUR SHOP EVERY DAY, MY FRIEND, UNLESS YOU START PAYING US.
B-BUT...
YOU SEE, WE'RE GOING TO SET UP IN THIS TOWN, AND IF YOU WANT TO CONTINUE DOING BUSINESS HERE, YOU'VE GOT TO PAY US TRIBUTE! UNDERSTAND?!
GULP!
"TRIBUTE"? THAT'S JUST ANOTHER WORD FOR EXTORTION!
WHAT?!
WHAT DID YOU SAY?! DO YOU THINK YOU'RE FUNNY, HUH, WISE GUY?! WHAT ARE YOU-- SOME KIND OF GOOFY COMEDIAN?
YEAH, THAT'S ME--AN ODDBALL COMIC.
THIS IS JUST BETWEEN US AND YOUR BOSS.
I'M MAKING IT MY CONCERN.
SO YOU NEED TO BE TAUGHT A LESSON, HUH?
GET HIM!
14.

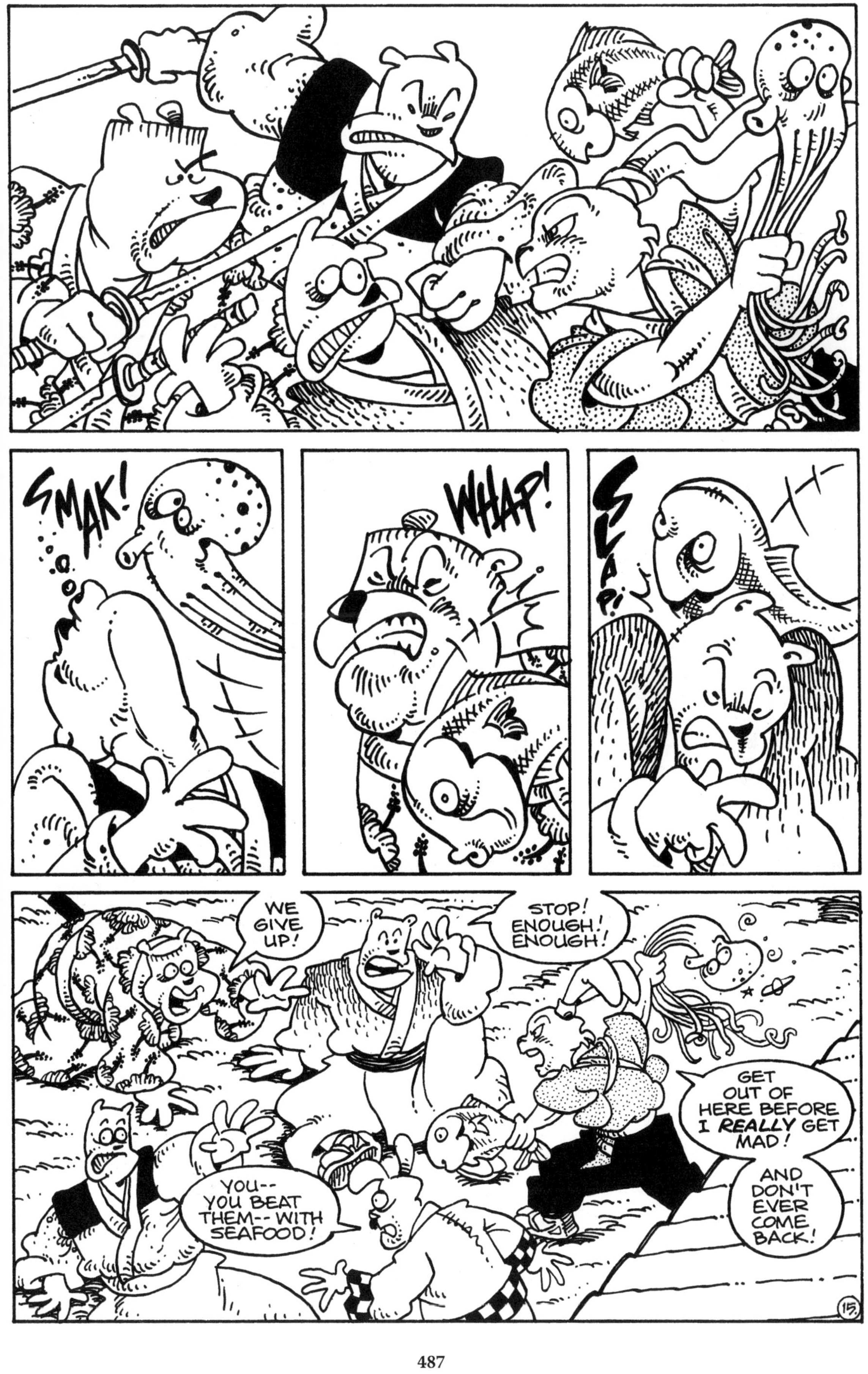
SMAK!
WHAP!
SLAP!
WE GIVE UP!
STOP! ENOUGH! ENOUGH!
GET OUT OF HERE BEFORE I *REALLY* GET MAD!
AND DON'T EVER COME BACK!
YOU-- YOU BEAT THEM-- WITH SEAFOOD!
15

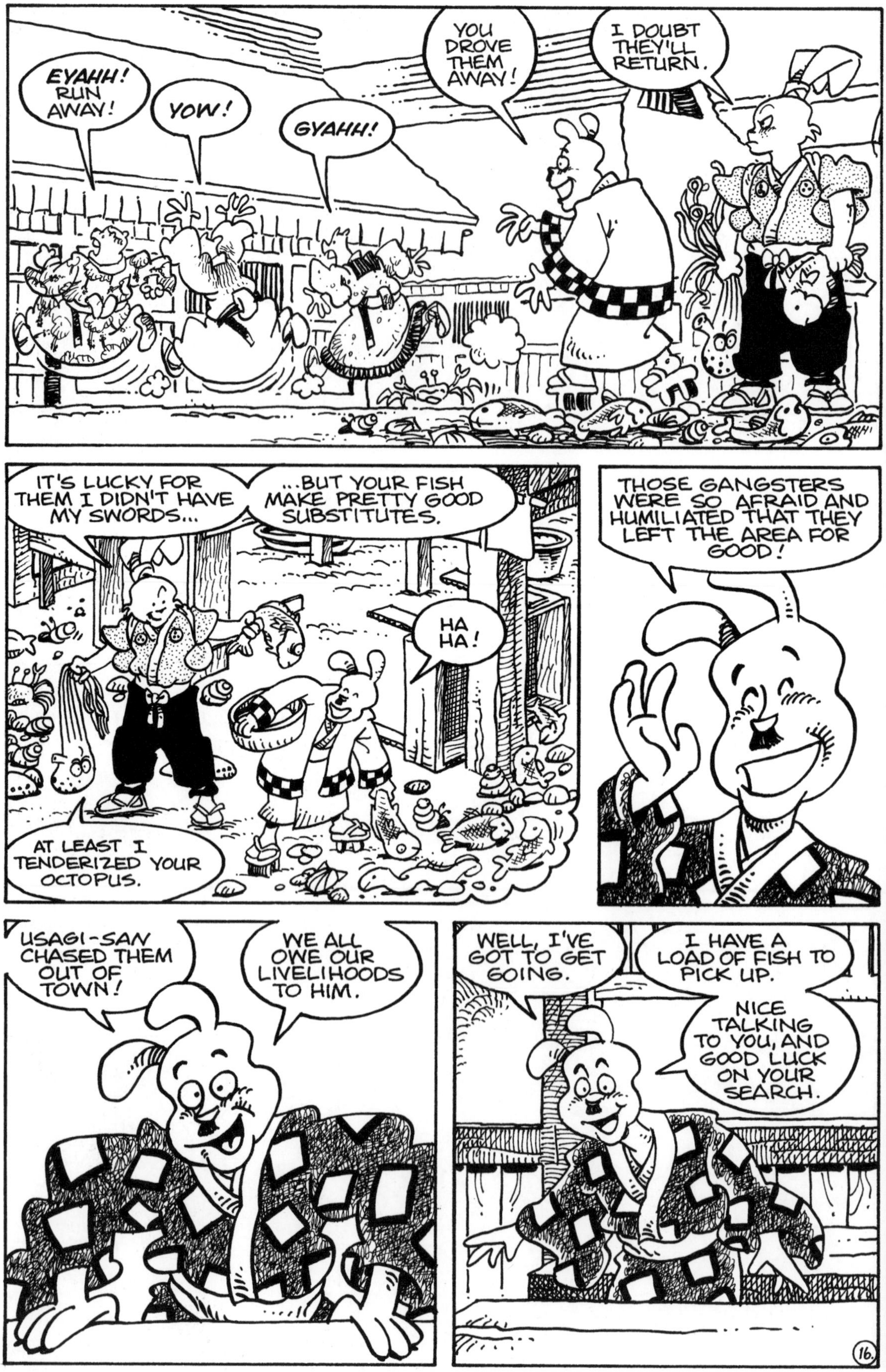
EYAHH! RUN AWAY!
YOW!
GYAHH!
YOU DROVE THEM AWAY!
I DOUBT THEY'LL RETURN.
IT'S LUCKY FOR THEM I DIDN'T HAVE MY SWORDS...
...BUT YOUR FISH MAKE PRETTY GOOD SUBSTITUTES.
HA HA!
AT LEAST I TENDERIZED YOUR OCTOPUS.
THOSE GANGSTERS WERE SO AFRAID AND HUMILIATED THAT THEY LEFT THE AREA FOR GOOD!
USAGI-SAN CHASED THEM OUT OF TOWN!
WE ALL OWE OUR LIVELIHOODS TO HIM.
WELL, I'VE GOT TO GET GOING.
I HAVE A LOAD OF FISH TO PICK UP.
NICE TALKING TO YOU, AND GOOD LUCK ON YOUR SEARCH.
16.

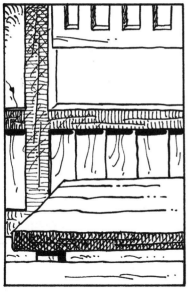

UH...

OKAY IF I SIT DOWN?

I HEARD YOU WERE ASKING ABOUT THAT LONG-EARED *SAMURAI.* I--I MET HIM JUST A FEW DAYS AGO.

I SHOULDN'T BE TELLING YOU THIS, BUT I'VE GOT TO TELL SOMEONE. YOU KNOW HOW IT IS. BESIDES, YOU DON'T LOOK LIKE THE TYPE OF PERSON WHO WOULD TURN ME IN. HEH HEH. I'M REFORMED NOW, ANYWAY.

I DON'T WANT TO TELL YOU MY NAME, BUT MY FATHER IS A POOR FARMER LIVING IN THE NEXT PROVINCE.

"BUT THAT KIND OF DIRTY LIFE, WORKING HARD IN THE FIELDS, WAS NOT FOR ME.

SPLAT!

17.

489

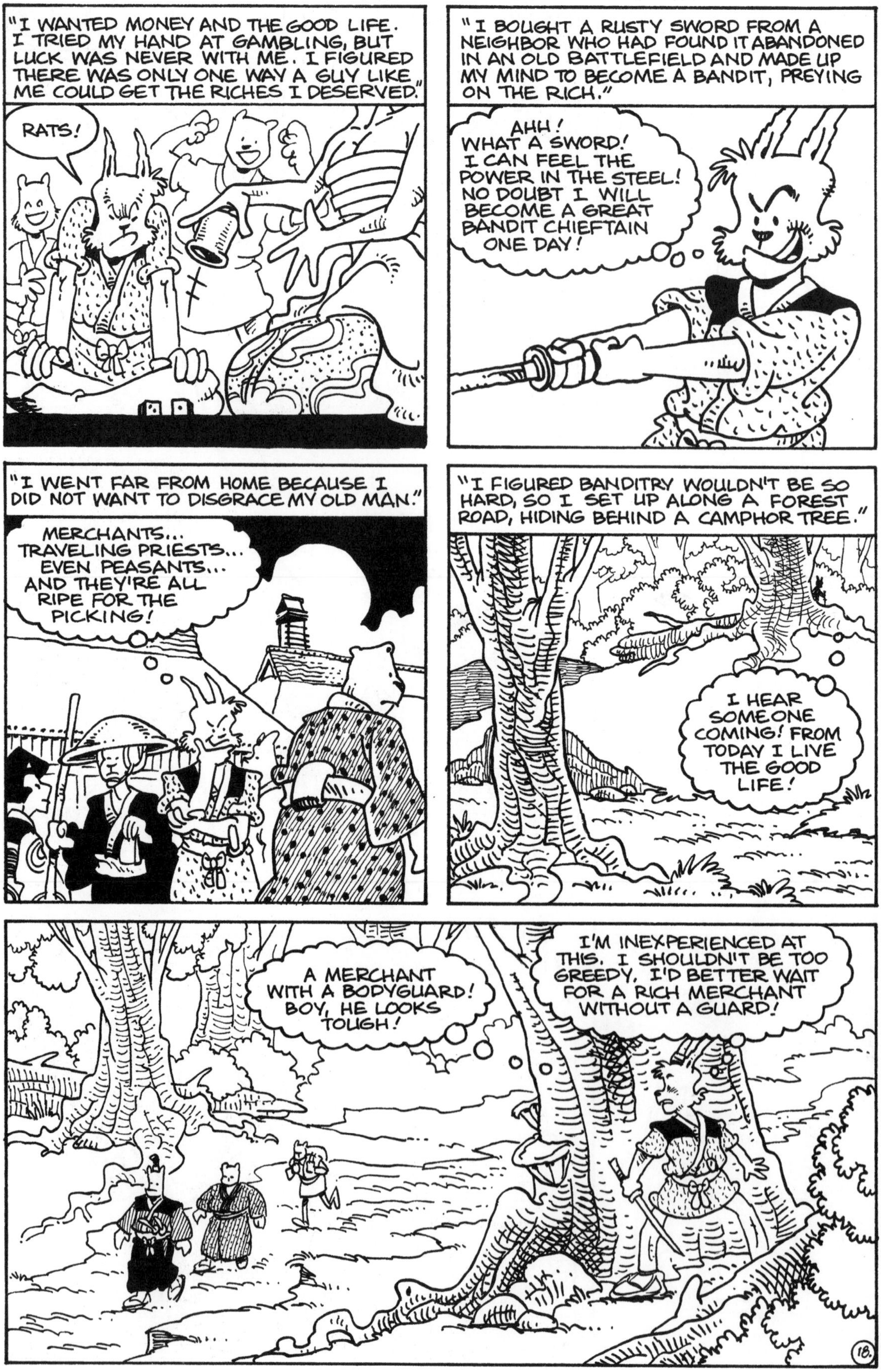
"I WANTED MONEY AND THE GOOD LIFE. I TRIED MY HAND AT GAMBLING, BUT LUCK WAS NEVER WITH ME. I FIGURED THERE WAS ONLY ONE WAY A GUY LIKE ME COULD GET THE RICHES I DESERVED."
RATS!
"I BOUGHT A RUSTY SWORD FROM A NEIGHBOR WHO HAD FOUND IT ABANDONED IN AN OLD BATTLEFIELD AND MADE UP MY MIND TO BECOME A BANDIT, PREYING ON THE RICH."
AHH! WHAT A SWORD! I CAN FEEL THE POWER IN THE STEEL! NO DOUBT I WILL BECOME A GREAT BANDIT CHIEFTAIN ONE DAY!
"I WENT FAR FROM HOME BECAUSE I DID NOT WANT TO DISGRACE MY OLD MAN."
MERCHANTS... TRAVELING PRIESTS... EVEN PEASANTS... AND THEY'RE ALL RIPE FOR THE PICKING!
"I FIGURED BANDITRY WOULDN'T BE SO HARD, SO I SET UP ALONG A FOREST ROAD, HIDING BEHIND A CAMPHOR TREE."
I HEAR SOMEONE COMING! FROM TODAY I LIVE THE GOOD LIFE!
A MERCHANT WITH A BODYGUARD! BOY, HE LOOKS TOUGH!
I'M INEXPERIENCED AT THIS. I SHOULDN'T BE TOO GREEDY, I'D BETTER WAIT FOR A RICH MERCHANT WITHOUT A GUARD!
18.

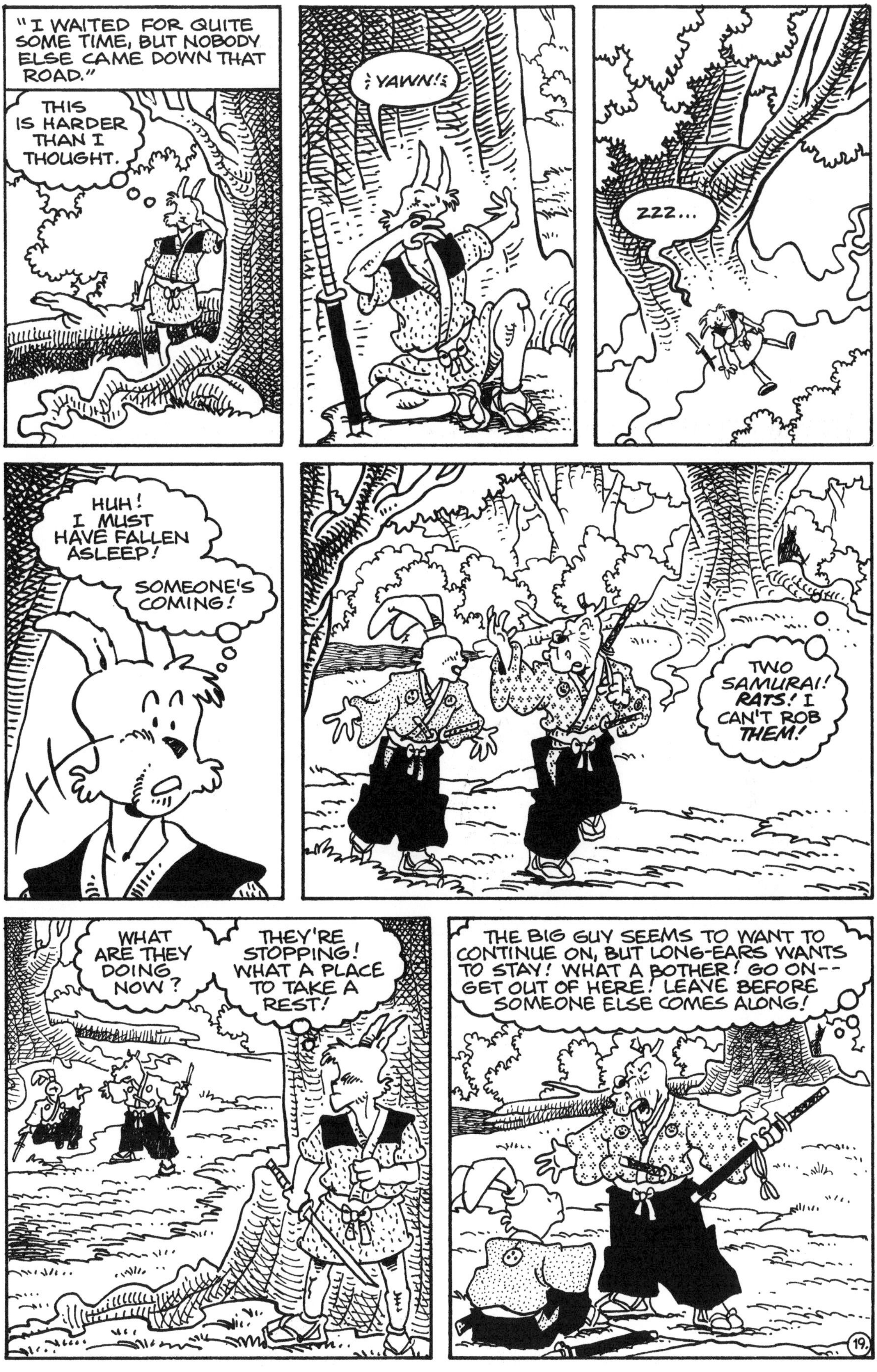
"I WAITED FOR QUITE SOME TIME, BUT NOBODY ELSE CAME DOWN THAT ROAD."
THIS IS HARDER THAN I THOUGHT.
YAWN!
ZZZ...
HUH! I MUST HAVE FALLEN ASLEEP!
SOMEONE'S COMING!
TWO SAMURAI! RATS! I CAN'T ROB THEM!
WHAT ARE THEY DOING NOW?
THEY'RE STOPPING! WHAT A PLACE TO TAKE A REST!
THE BIG GUY SEEMS TO WANT TO CONTINUE ON, BUT LONG-EARS WANTS TO STAY! WHAT A BOTHER! GO ON-- GET OUT OF HERE! LEAVE BEFORE SOMEONE ELSE COMES ALONG!
19.

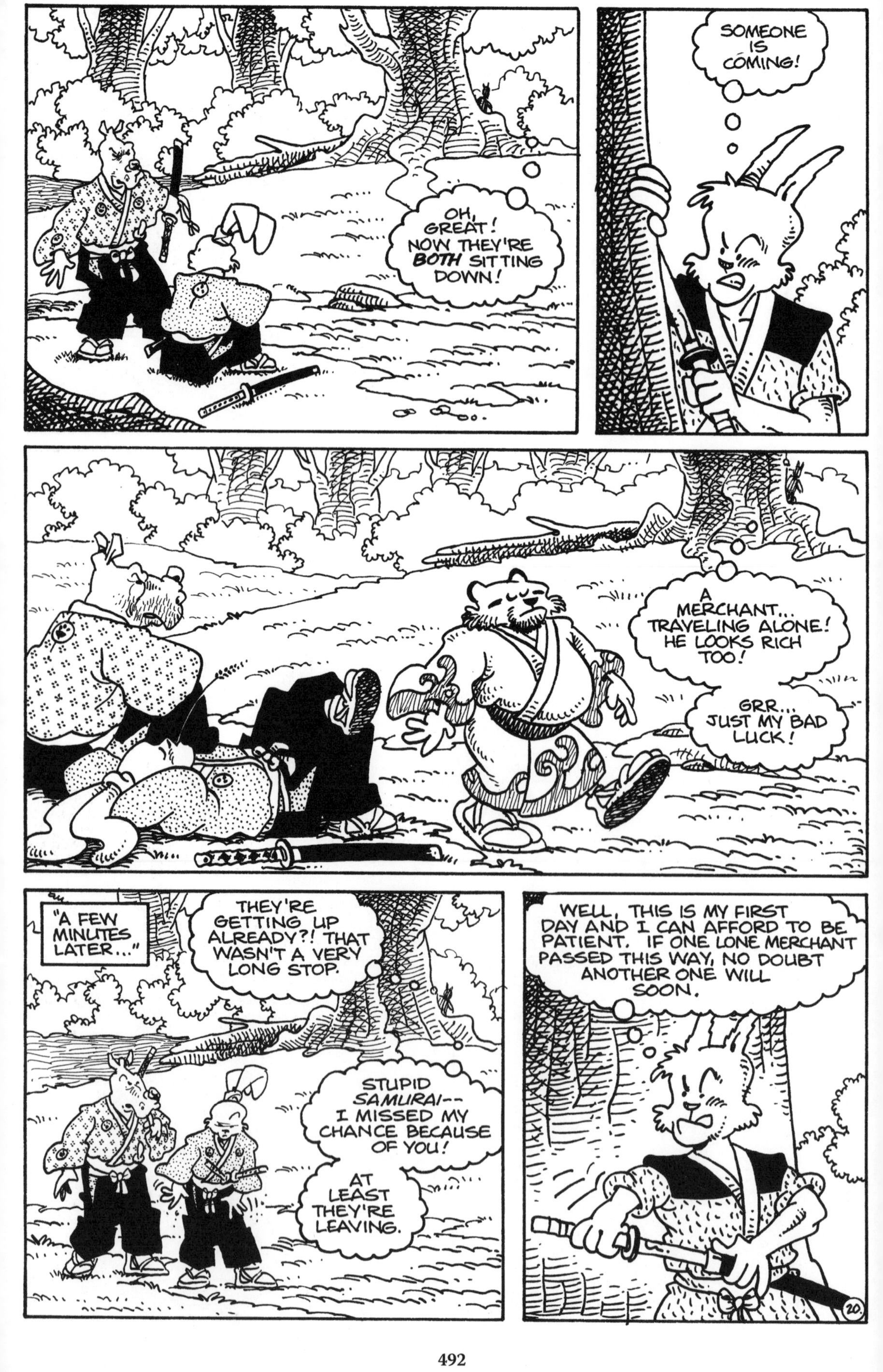
OH, GREAT! NOW THEY'RE *BOTH* SITTING DOWN!
SOMEONE IS COMING!
A MERCHANT... TRAVELING ALONE! HE LOOKS RICH TOO!
GRR... JUST MY BAD LUCK!
"A FEW MINUTES LATER..."
THEY'RE GETTING UP ALREADY?! THAT WASN'T A VERY LONG STOP.
STUPID *SAMURAI*-- I MISSED MY CHANCE BECAUSE OF YOU!
AT LEAST THEY'RE LEAVING.
WELL, THIS IS MY FIRST DAY AND I CAN AFFORD TO BE PATIENT. IF ONE LONE MERCHANT PASSED THIS WAY, NO DOUBT ANOTHER ONE WILL SOON.
20.

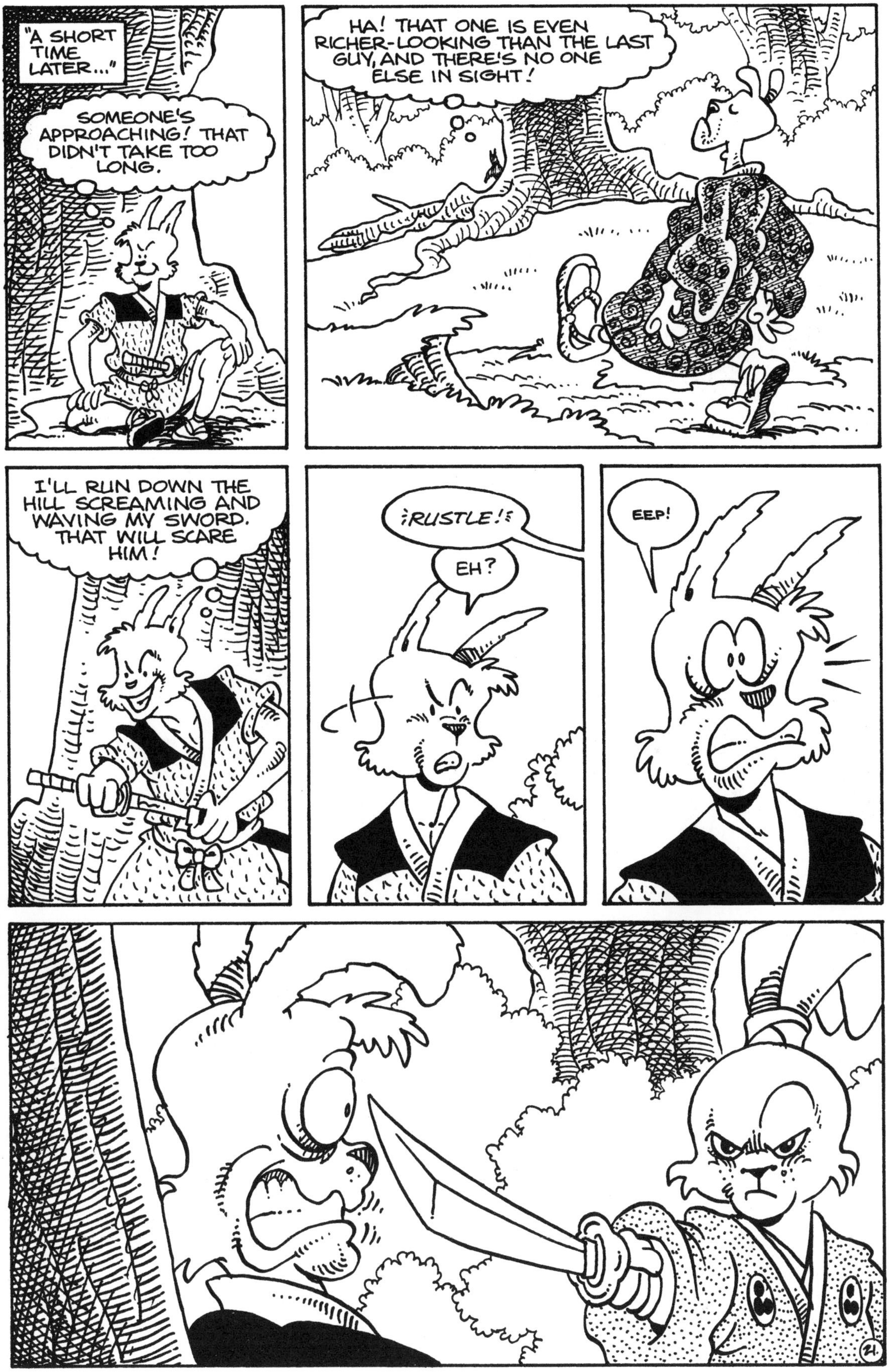
"A SHORT TIME LATER..."
SOMEONE'S APPROACHING! THAT DIDN'T TAKE TOO LONG.
HA! THAT ONE IS EVEN RICHER-LOOKING THAN THE LAST GUY, AND THERE'S NO ONE ELSE IN SIGHT!
I'LL RUN DOWN THE HILL SCREAMING AND WAVING MY SWORD. THAT WILL SCARE HIM!
¡RUSTLE!
EH?
EEP!
21.

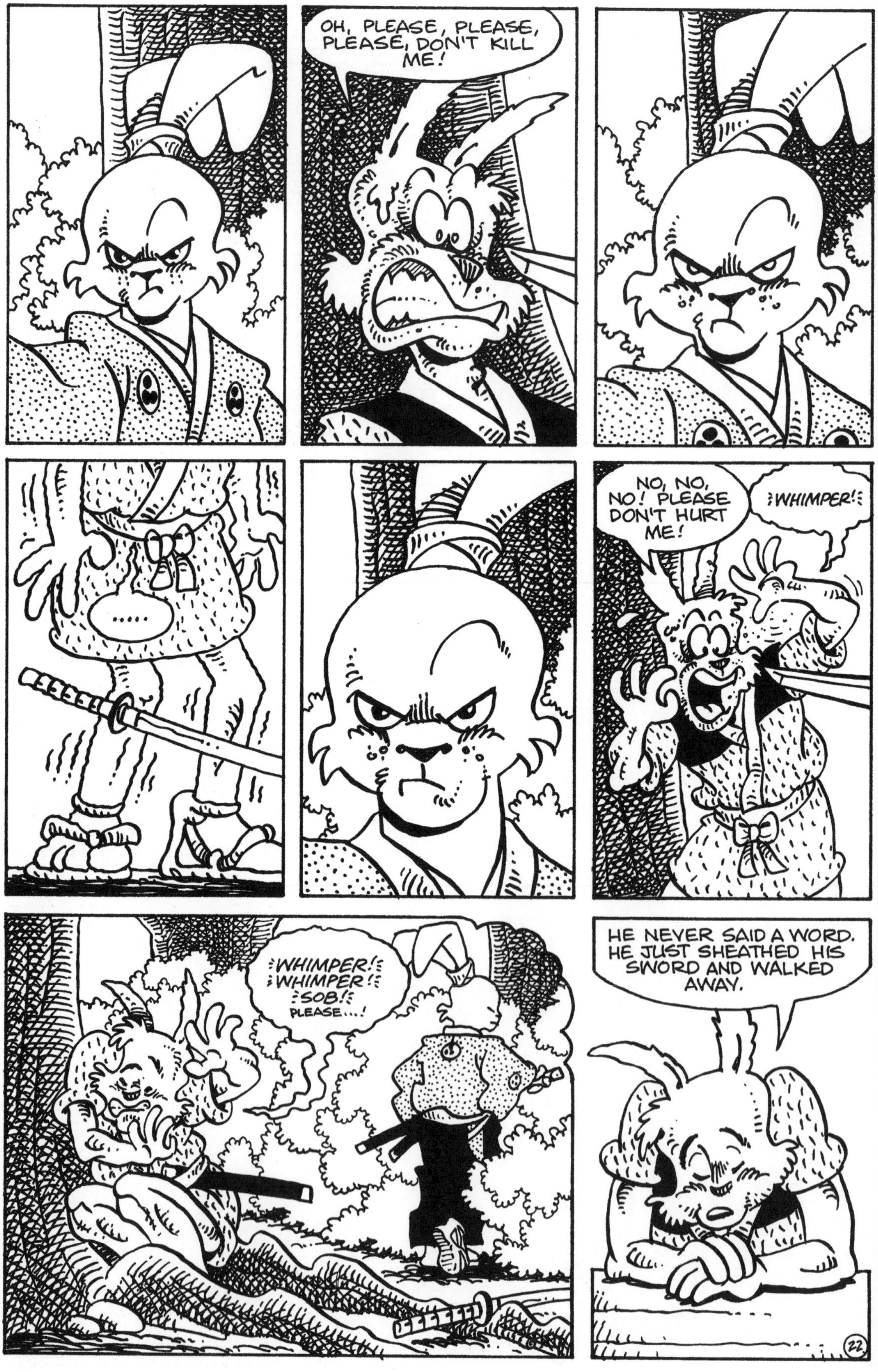
OH, PLEASE, PLEASE, PLEASE, DON'T KILL ME!
.....
NO, NO, NO! PLEASE DON'T HURT ME!
WHIMPER!
WHIMPER! WHIMPER! SOB! PLEASE...!
HE NEVER SAID A WORD. HE JUST SHEATHED HIS SWORD AND WALKED AWAY.
22

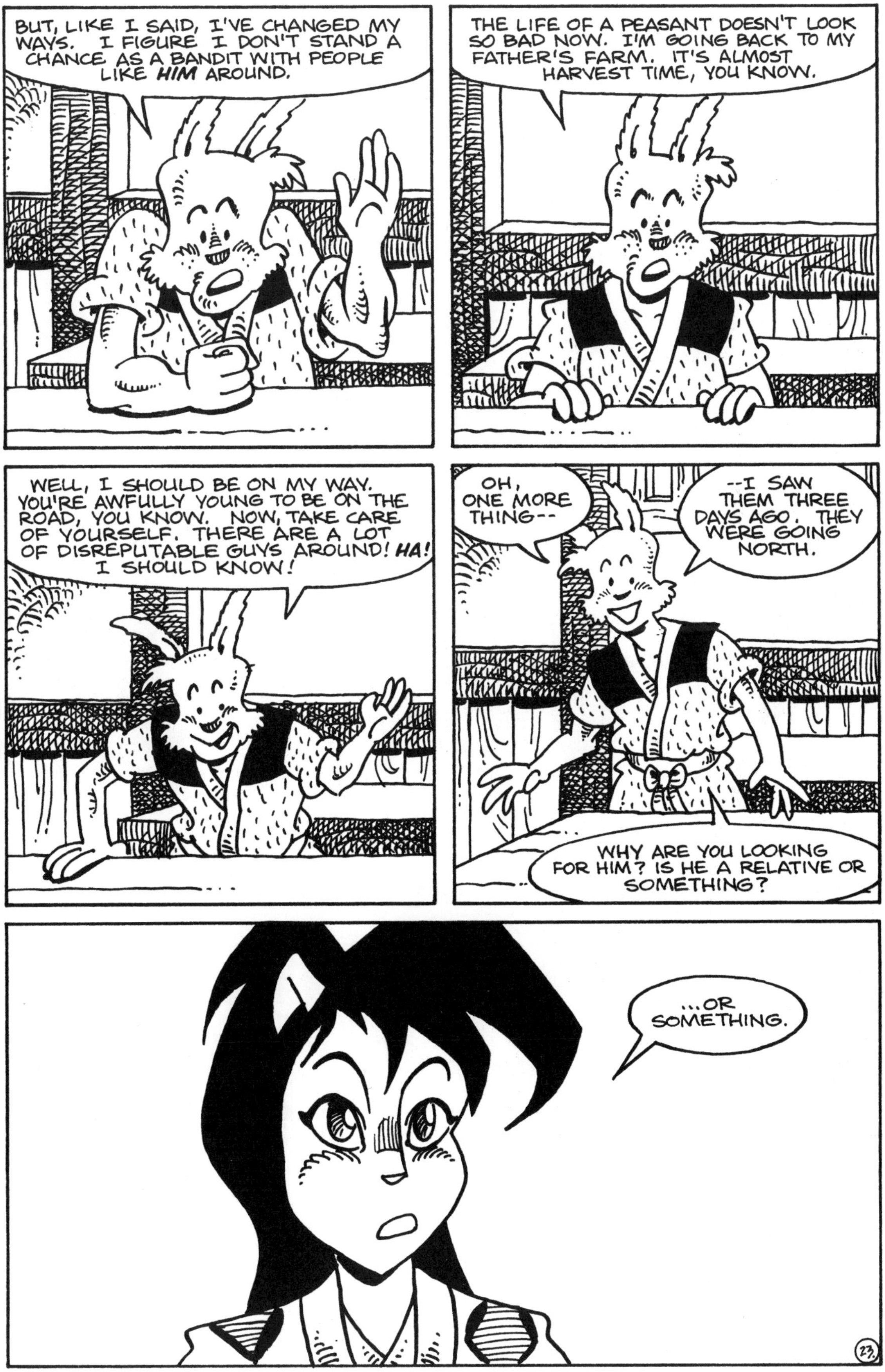
BUT, LIKE I SAID, I'VE CHANGED MY WAYS. I FIGURE I DON'T STAND A CHANCE AS A BANDIT WITH PEOPLE LIKE *HIM* AROUND.
THE LIFE OF A PEASANT DOESN'T LOOK SO BAD NOW. I'M GOING BACK TO MY FATHER'S FARM. IT'S ALMOST HARVEST TIME, YOU KNOW.
WELL, I SHOULD BE ON MY WAY. YOU'RE AWFULLY YOUNG TO BE ON THE ROAD, YOU KNOW. NOW, TAKE CARE OF YOURSELF. THERE ARE A LOT OF DISREPUTABLE GUYS AROUND! *HA!* I SHOULD KNOW!
OH, ONE MORE THING--
--I SAW THEM THREE DAYS AGO. THEY WERE GOING NORTH.
WHY ARE YOU LOOKING FOR HIM? IS HE A RELATIVE OR SOMETHING?
...OR SOMETHING.
23

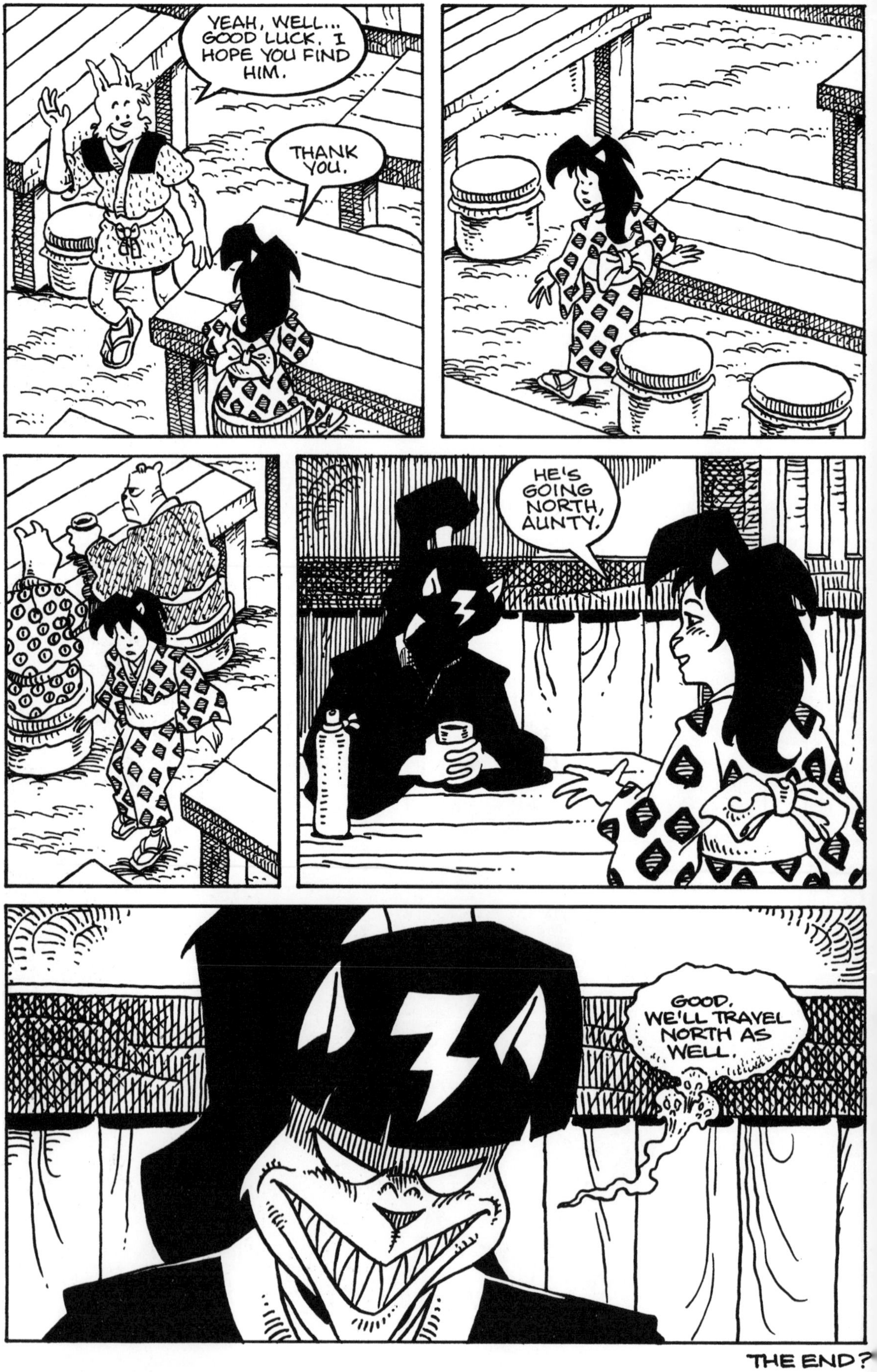

YEAH, WELL... GOOD LUCK. I HOPE YOU FIND HIM.
THANK YOU.
HE'S GOING NORTH, AUNTY.
GOOD. WE'LL TRAVEL NORTH AS WELL.
THE END?

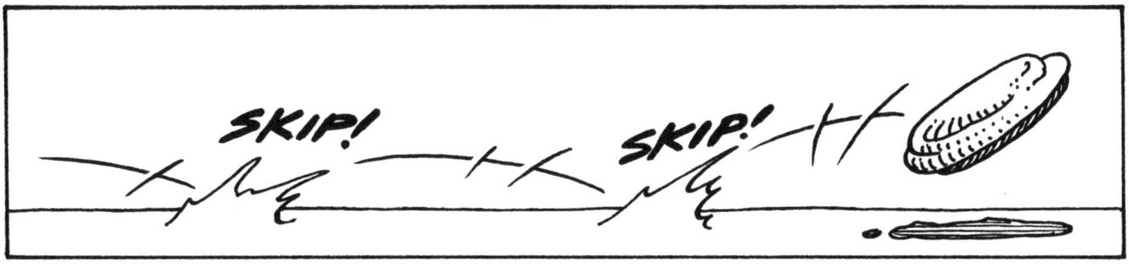
SKIP!
SKIP!

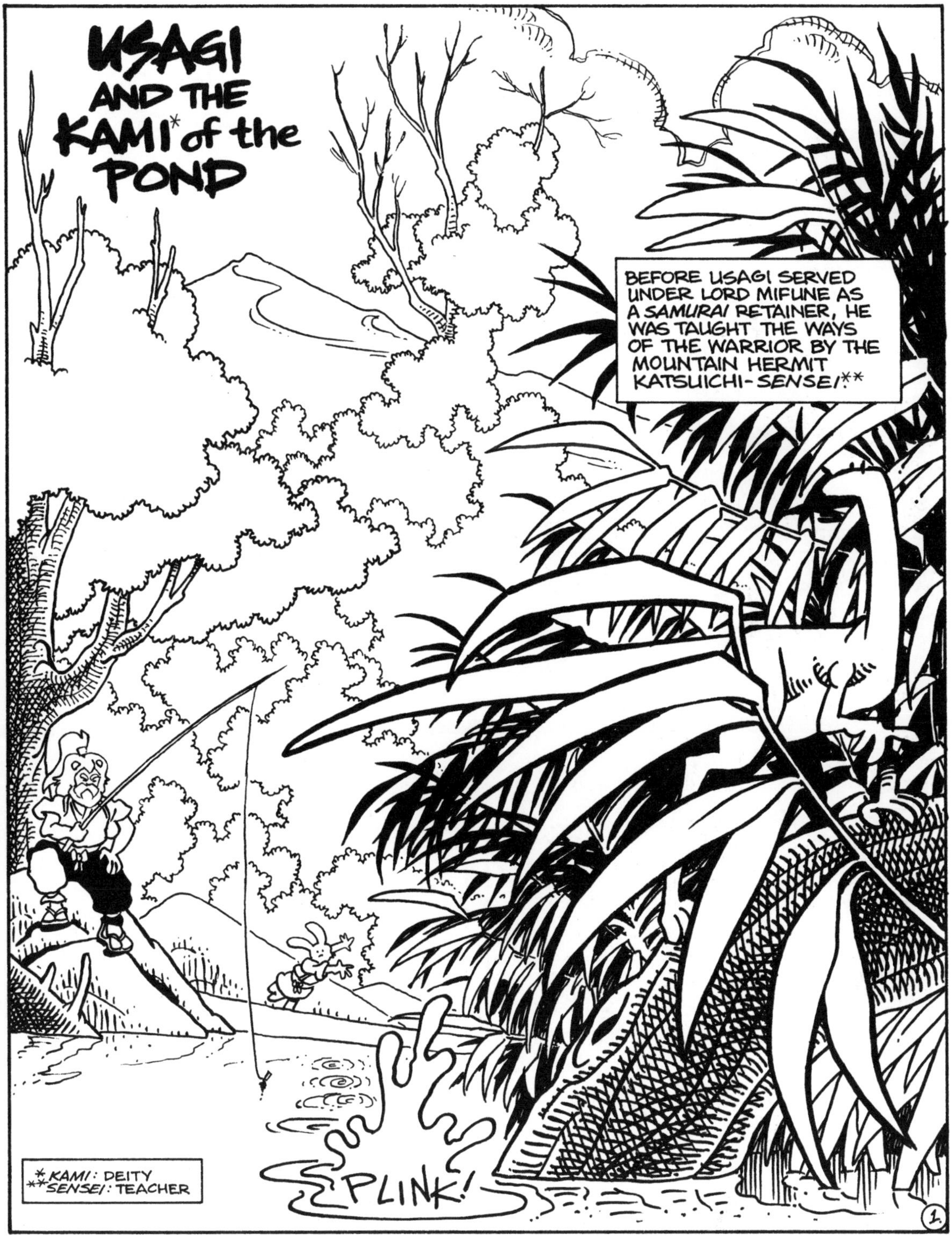
USAGI AND THE KAMI* of the POND
BEFORE USAGI SERVED UNDER LORD MIFUNE AS A *SAMURAI* RETAINER, HE WAS TAUGHT THE WAYS OF THE WARRIOR BY THE MOUNTAIN HERMIT KATSUICHI-*SENSEI*!**
PLINK!
*KAMI: DEITY
**SENSEI: TEACHER
1

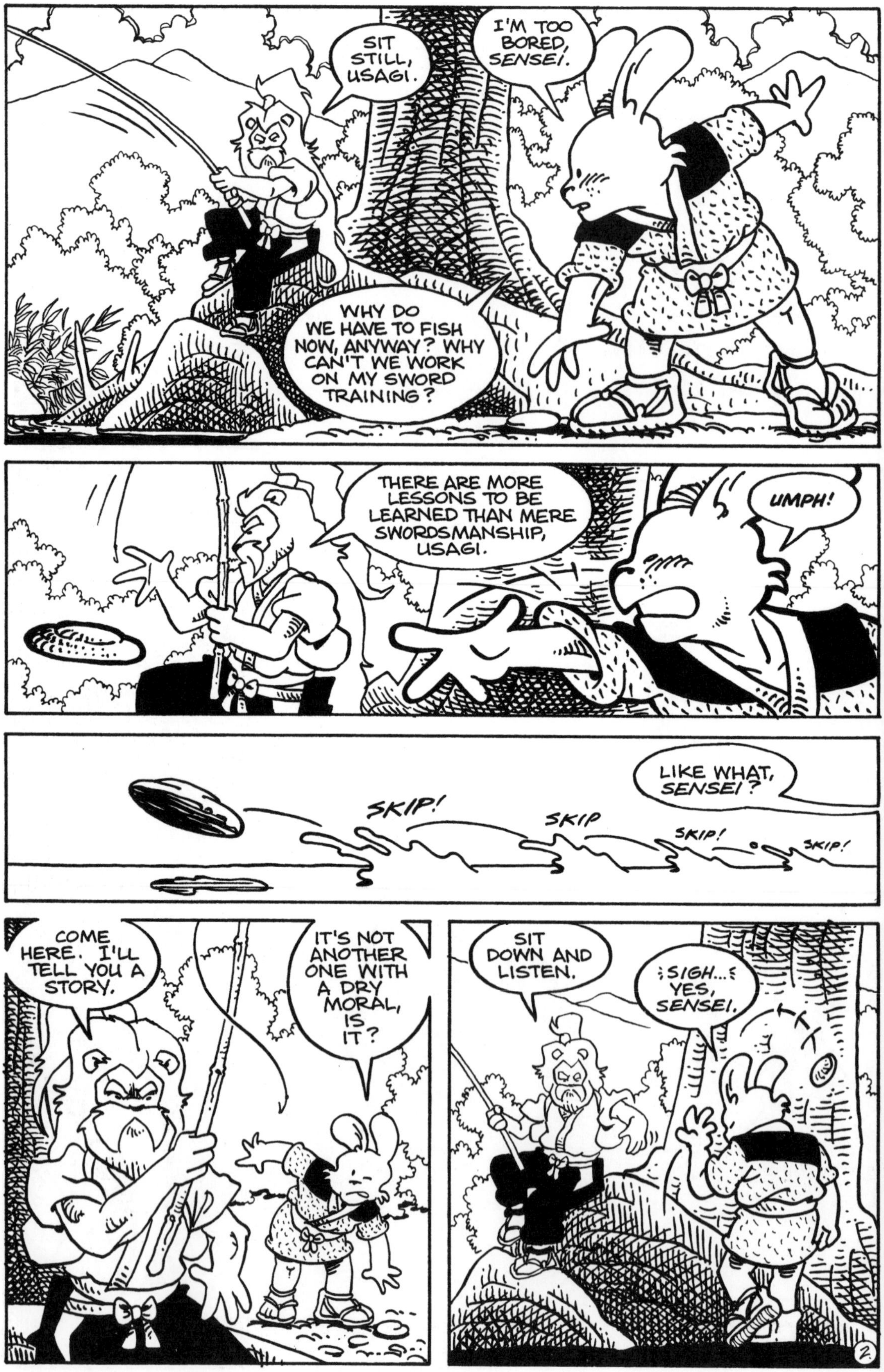
SIT STILL, USAGI.
I'M TOO BORED, SENSEI.
WHY DO WE HAVE TO FISH NOW, ANYWAY? WHY CAN'T WE WORK ON MY SWORD TRAINING?
THERE ARE MORE LESSONS TO BE LEARNED THAN MERE SWORDSMANSHIP, USAGI.
UMPH!
SKIP!
SKIP
SKIP!
SKIP!
LIKE WHAT, SENSEI?
COME HERE. I'LL TELL YOU A STORY.
IT'S NOT ANOTHER ONE WITH A DRY MORAL, IS IT?
SIT DOWN AND LISTEN.
SIGH... YES, SENSEI.
2

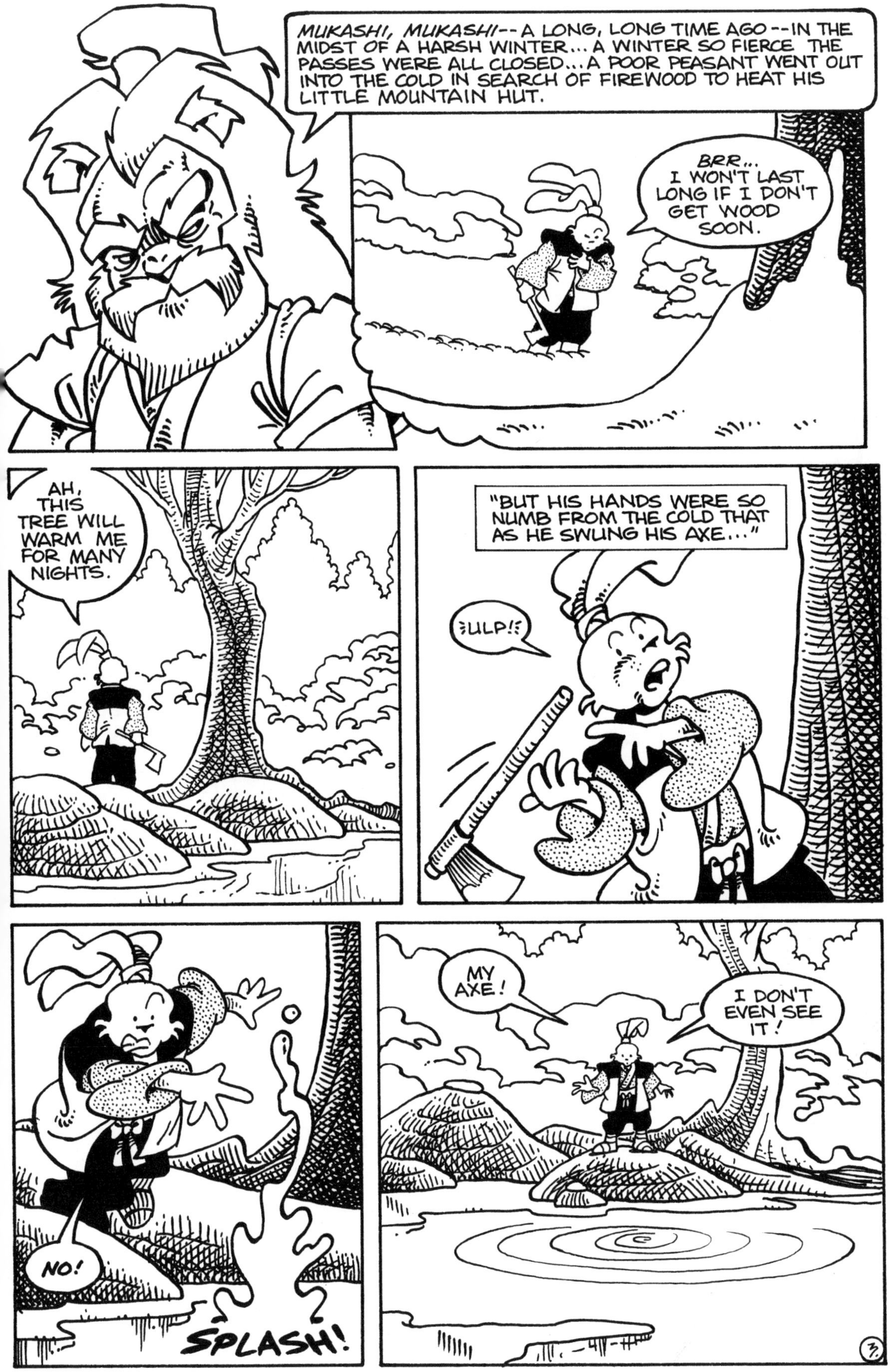
MUKASHI, MUKASHI--A LONG, LONG TIME AGO--IN THE MIDST OF A HARSH WINTER... A WINTER SO FIERCE THE PASSES WERE ALL CLOSED... A POOR PEASANT WENT OUT INTO THE COLD IN SEARCH OF FIREWOOD TO HEAT HIS LITTLE MOUNTAIN HUT.
BRR... I WON'T LAST LONG IF I DON'T GET WOOD SOON.
AH, THIS TREE WILL WARM ME FOR MANY NIGHTS.
"BUT HIS HANDS WERE SO NUMB FROM THE COLD THAT AS HE SWUNG HIS AXE..."
ULP!
NO!
SPLASH!
MY AXE!
I DON'T EVEN SEE IT!
3.

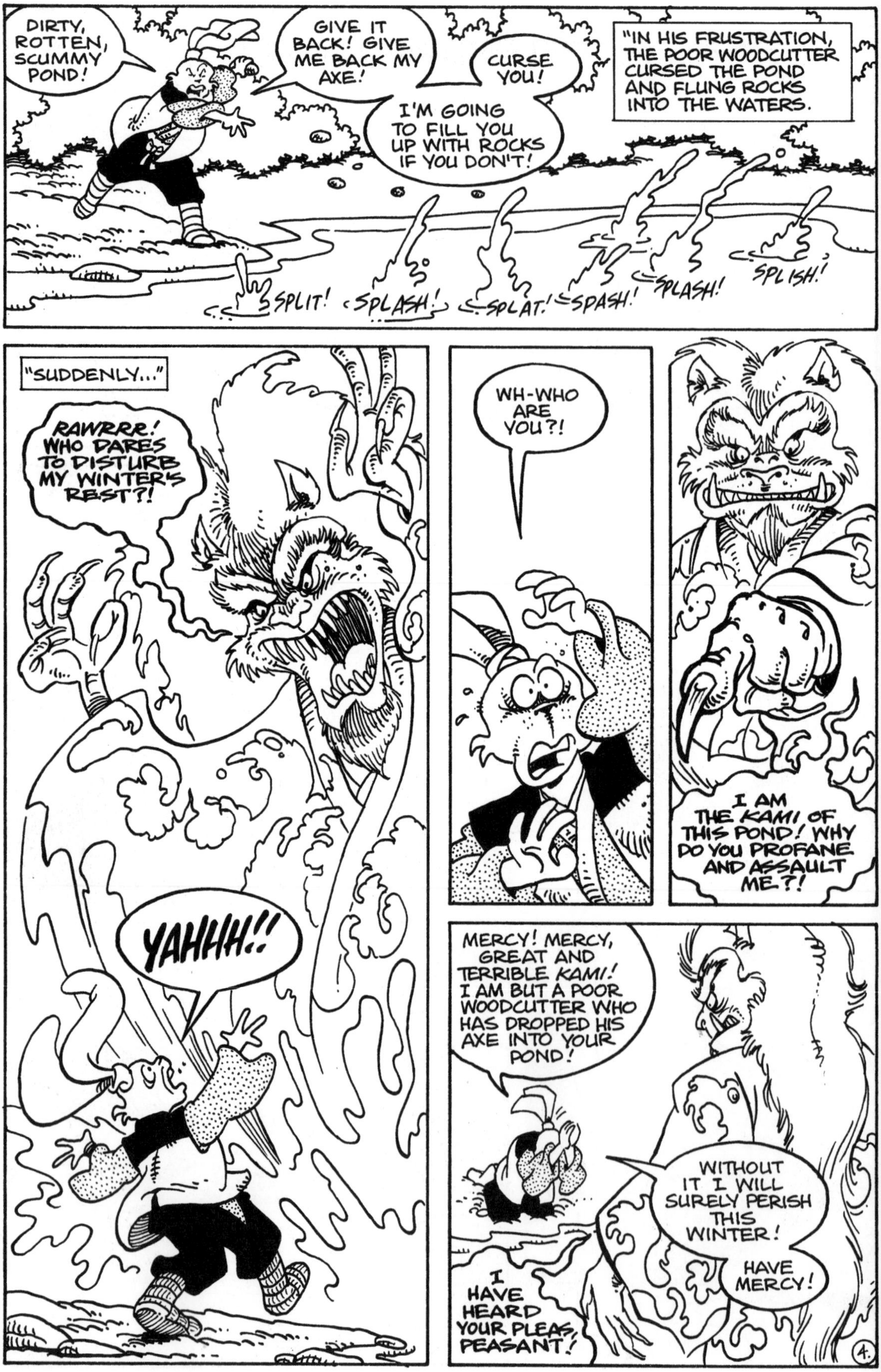

DIRTY, ROTTEN, SCUMMY POND!
GIVE IT BACK! GIVE ME BACK MY AXE!
CURSE YOU!
I'M GOING TO FILL YOU UP WITH ROCKS IF YOU DON'T!
"IN HIS FRUSTRATION, THE POOR WOODCUTTER CURSED THE POND AND FLUNG ROCKS INTO THE WATERS.
SPLIT!
SPLASH!
SPLAT!
SPASH!
SPLASH!
SPLISH!
"SUDDENLY..."
RAWRRR! WHO DARES TO DISTURB MY WINTER'S REST?!
YAHHH!!
WH-WHO ARE YOU?!
I AM THE *KAMI* OF THIS POND! WHY DO YOU PROFANE AND ASSAULT ME?!
MERCY! MERCY, GREAT AND TERRIBLE *KAMI*! I AM BUT A POOR WOODCUTTER WHO HAS DROPPED HIS AXE INTO YOUR POND!
WITHOUT IT I WILL SURELY PERISH THIS WINTER!
HAVE MERCY!
I HAVE HEARD YOUR PLEAS, PEASANT!
4.

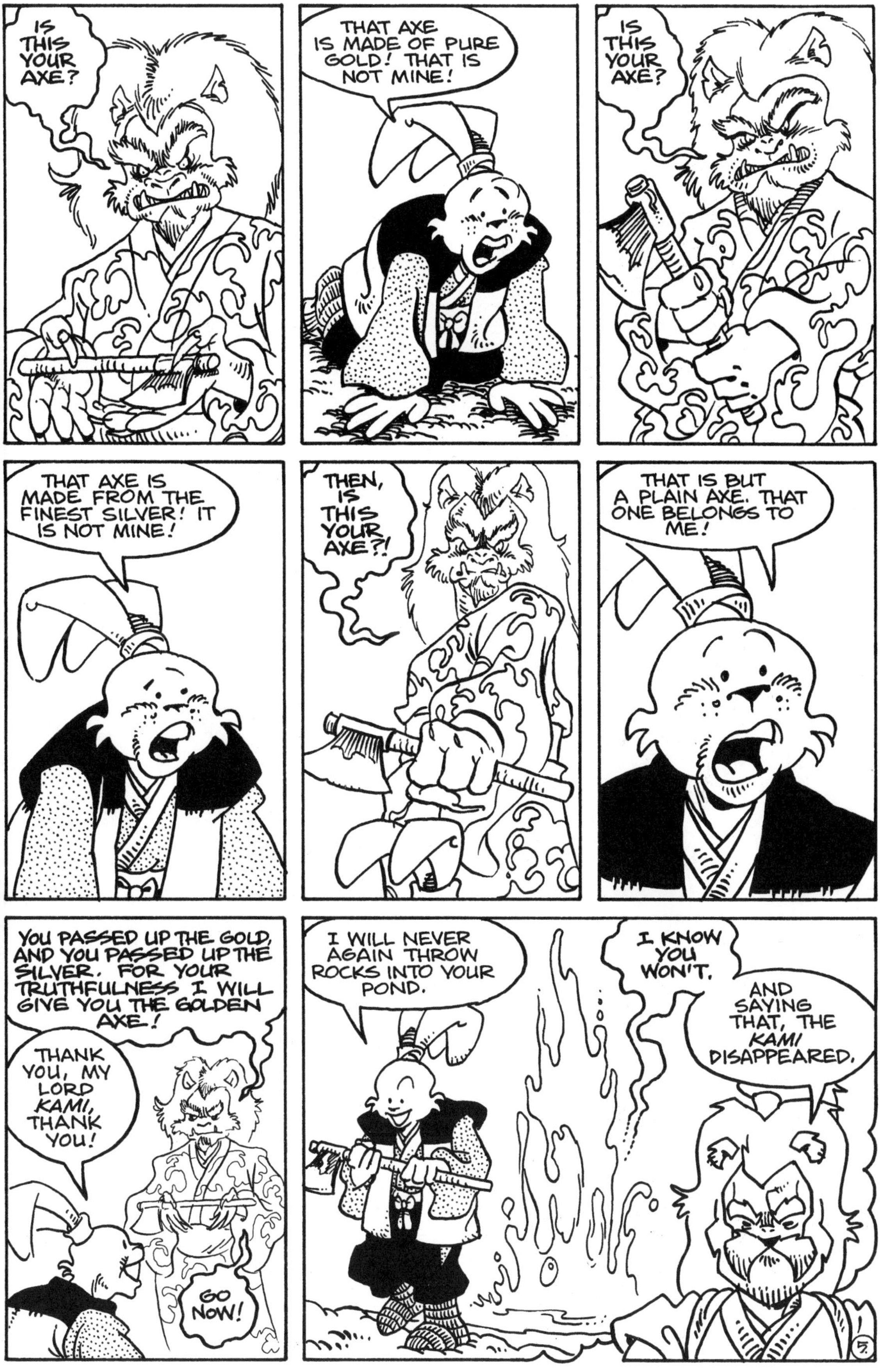
IS THIS YOUR AXE?
THAT AXE IS MADE OF PURE GOLD! THAT IS NOT MINE!
IS THIS YOUR AXE?
THAT AXE IS MADE FROM THE FINEST SILVER! IT IS NOT MINE!
THEN, IS THIS YOUR AXE?!
THAT IS BUT A PLAIN AXE. THAT ONE BELONGS TO ME!
YOU PASSED UP THE GOLD, AND YOU PASSED UP THE SILVER. FOR YOUR TRUTHFULNESS I WILL GIVE YOU THE GOLDEN AXE!
THANK YOU, MY LORD *KAMI*, THANK YOU!
GO NOW!
I WILL NEVER AGAIN THROW ROCKS INTO YOUR POND.
I KNOW YOU WON'T.
AND SAYING THAT, THE *KAMI* DISAPPEARED.
5.

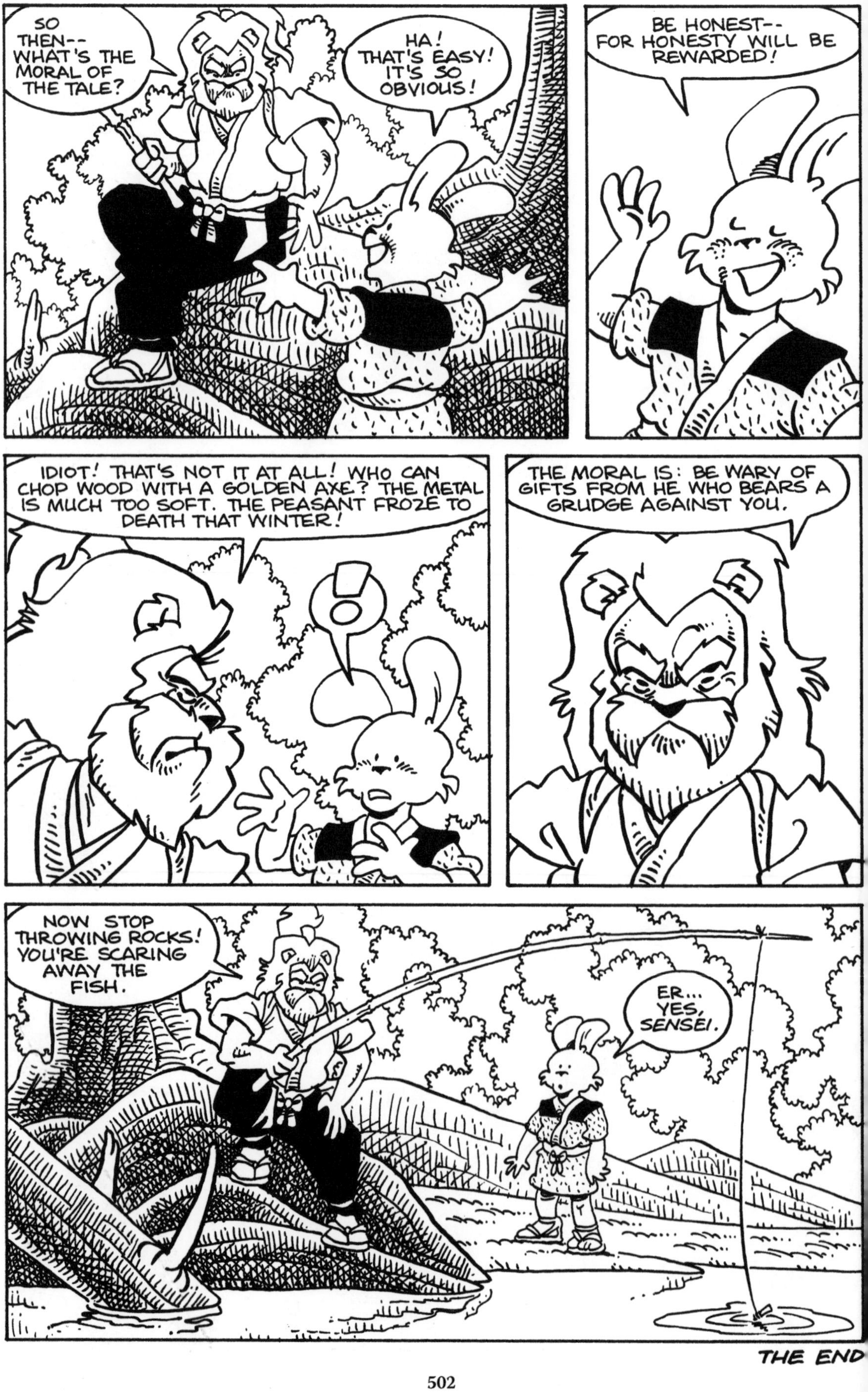
SO THEN-- WHAT'S THE MORAL OF THE TALE?
HA! THAT'S EASY! IT'S SO OBVIOUS!
BE HONEST-- FOR HONESTY WILL BE REWARDED!
IDIOT! THAT'S NOT IT AT ALL! WHO CAN CHOP WOOD WITH A GOLDEN AXE? THE METAL IS MUCH TOO SOFT. THE PEASANT FROZE TO DEATH THAT WINTER!
!
THE MORAL IS: BE WARY OF GIFTS FROM HE WHO BEARS A GRUDGE AGAINST YOU.
NOW STOP THROWING ROCKS! YOU'RE SCARING AWAY THE FISH.
ER... YES, SENSEI.
THE END

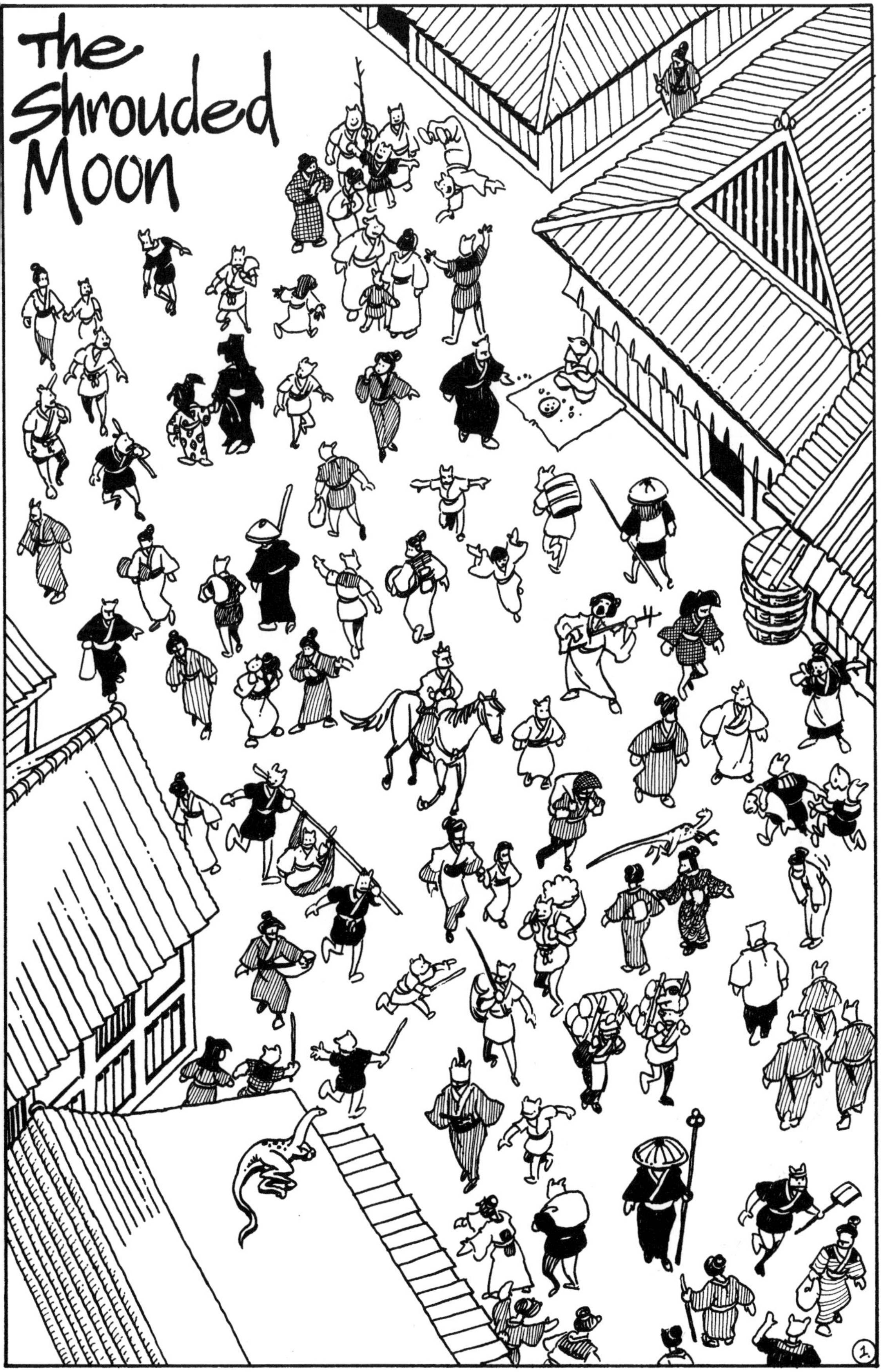
The Shrouded Moon
1

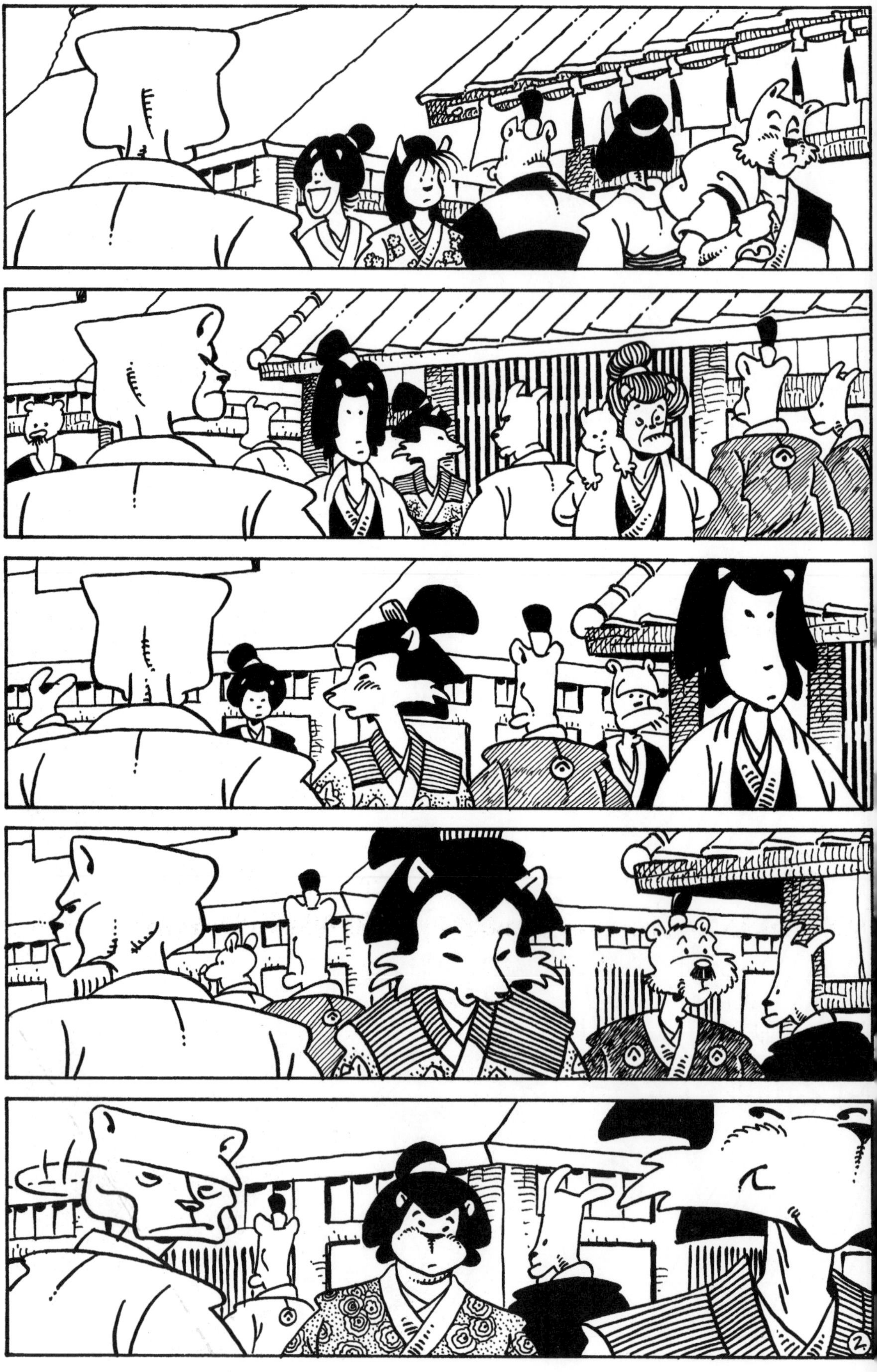

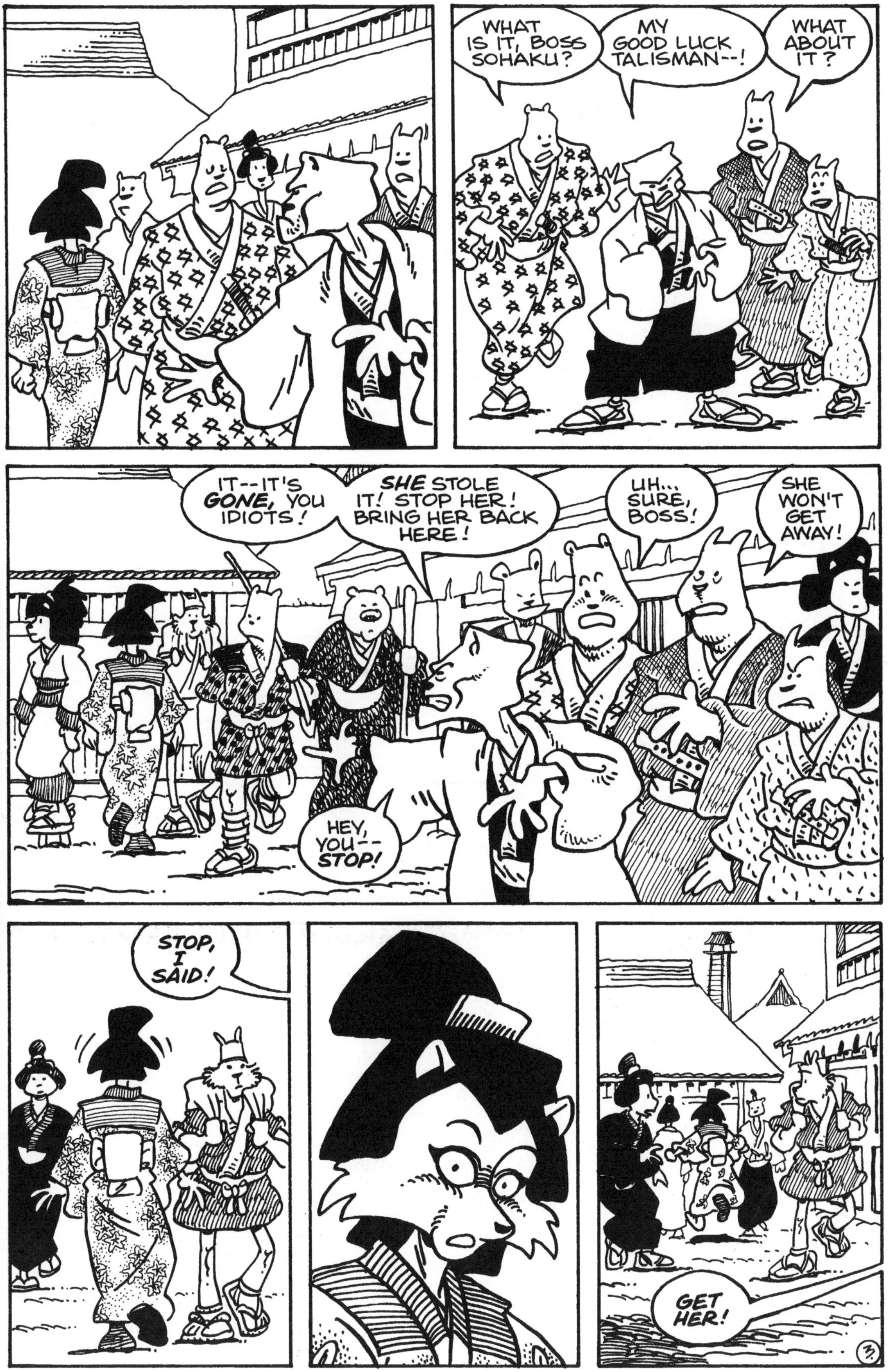
WHAT IS IT, BOSS SOHAKU?
MY GOOD LUCK TALISMAN--!
WHAT ABOUT IT?
IT--IT'S **GONE,** YOU IDIOTS!
SHE STOLE IT! STOP HER! BRING HER BACK HERE!
UH... SURE, BOSS!
SHE WON'T GET AWAY!
HEY, YOU-- **STOP!**
STOP, I SAID!
GET HER!
3

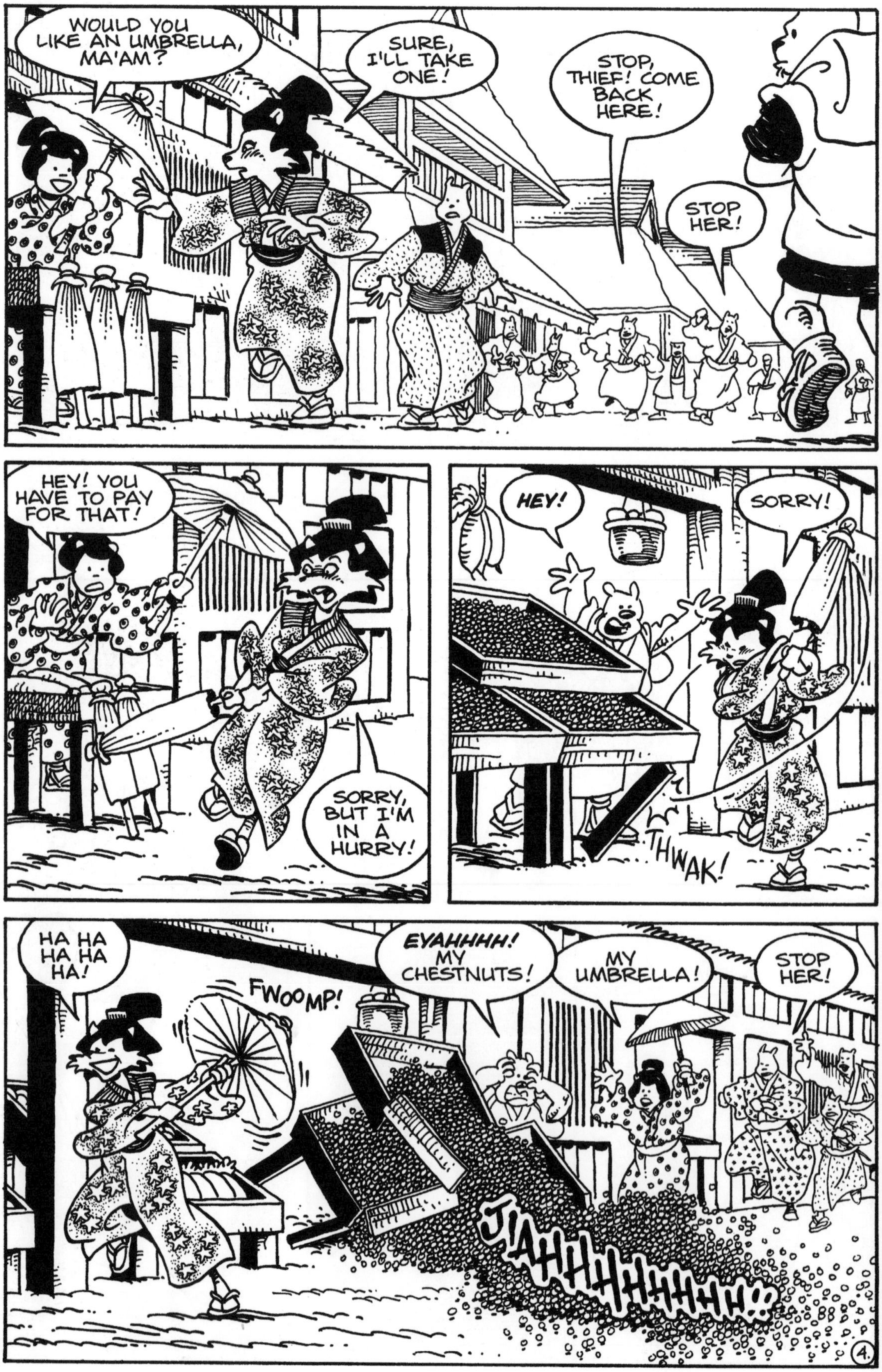

WOULD YOU LIKE AN UMBRELLA, MA'AM?
SURE, I'LL TAKE ONE!
STOP, THIEF! COME BACK HERE!
STOP HER!
HEY! YOU HAVE TO PAY FOR THAT!
SORRY, BUT I'M IN A HURRY!
HEY!
SORRY!
THWAK!
HA HA HA HA HA!
FWOOMP!
EYAHHHH! MY CHESTNUTS!
MY UMBRELLA!
STOP HER!
JIAHHHHHHHHHH!!
4.

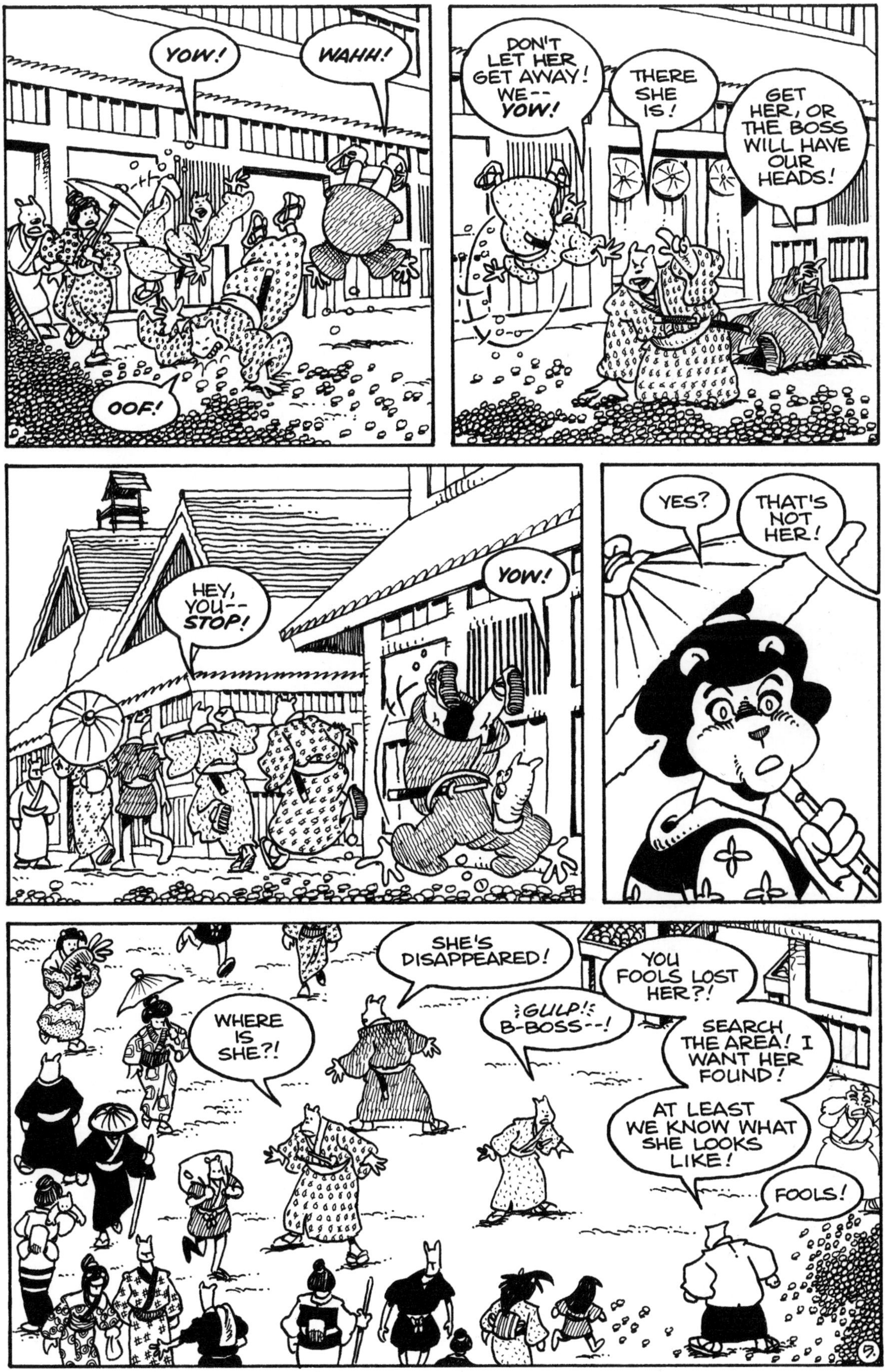

YOW!
WAHH!
OOF!
DON'T LET HER GET AWAY! WE-- YOW!
THERE SHE IS!
GET HER, OR THE BOSS WILL HAVE OUR HEADS!
HEY, YOU-- STOP!
YOW!
YES?
THAT'S NOT HER!
WHERE IS SHE?!
SHE'S DISAPPEARED!
GULP! B-BOSS--!
YOU FOOLS LOST HER?!
SEARCH THE AREA! I WANT HER FOUND!
AT LEAST WE KNOW WHAT SHE LOOKS LIKE!
FOOLS!

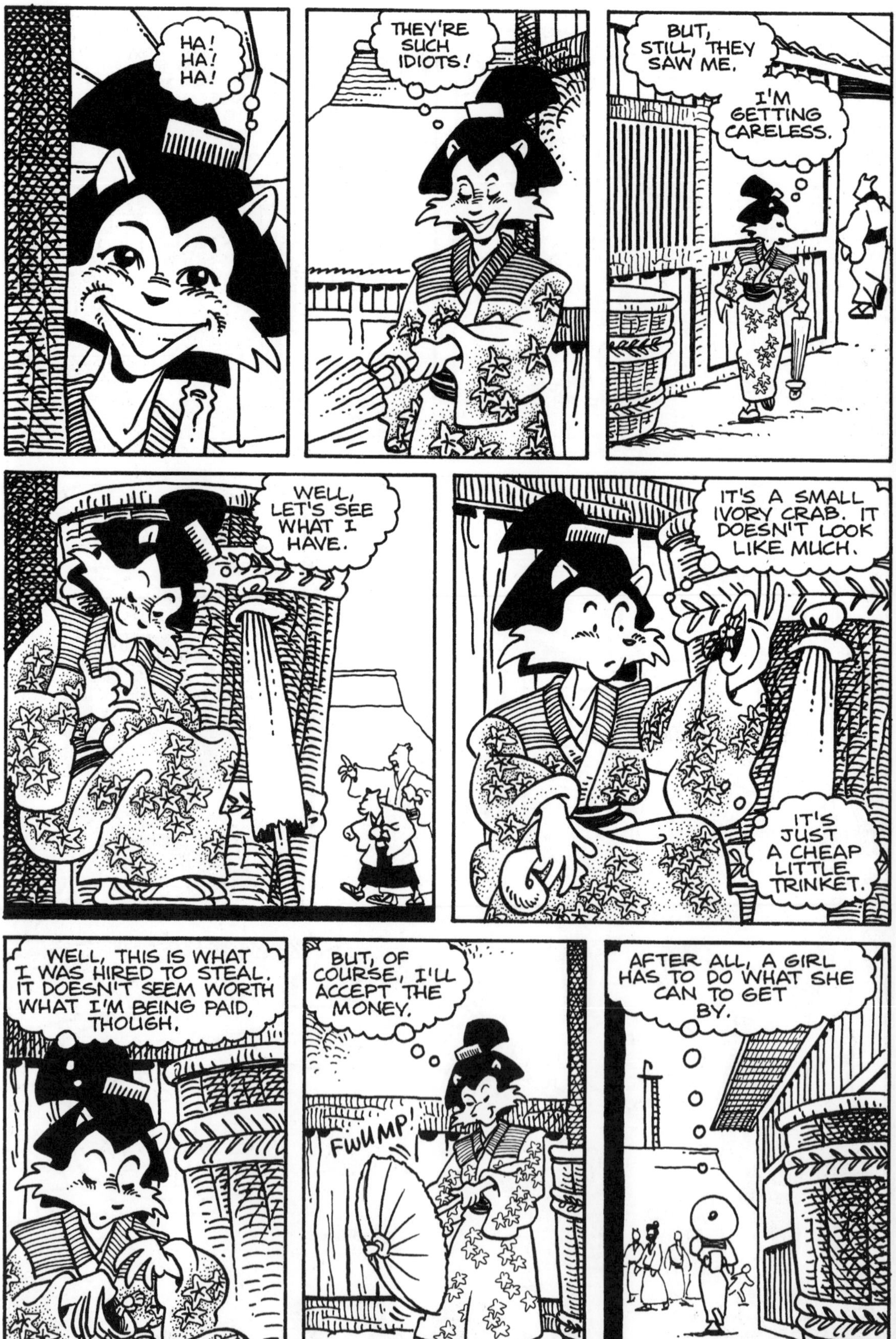
HA! HA! HA!
THEY'RE SUCH IDIOTS!
BUT, STILL, THEY SAW ME.
I'M GETTING CARELESS.
WELL, LET'S SEE WHAT I HAVE.
IT'S A SMALL IVORY CRAB. IT DOESN'T LOOK LIKE MUCH.
IT'S JUST A CHEAP LITTLE TRINKET.
WELL, THIS IS WHAT I WAS HIRED TO STEAL. IT DOESN'T SEEM WORTH WHAT I'M BEING PAID, THOUGH.
BUT, OF COURSE, I'LL ACCEPT THE MONEY.
FWUMP!
AFTER ALL, A GIRL HAS TO DO WHAT SHE CAN TO GET BY.
6.

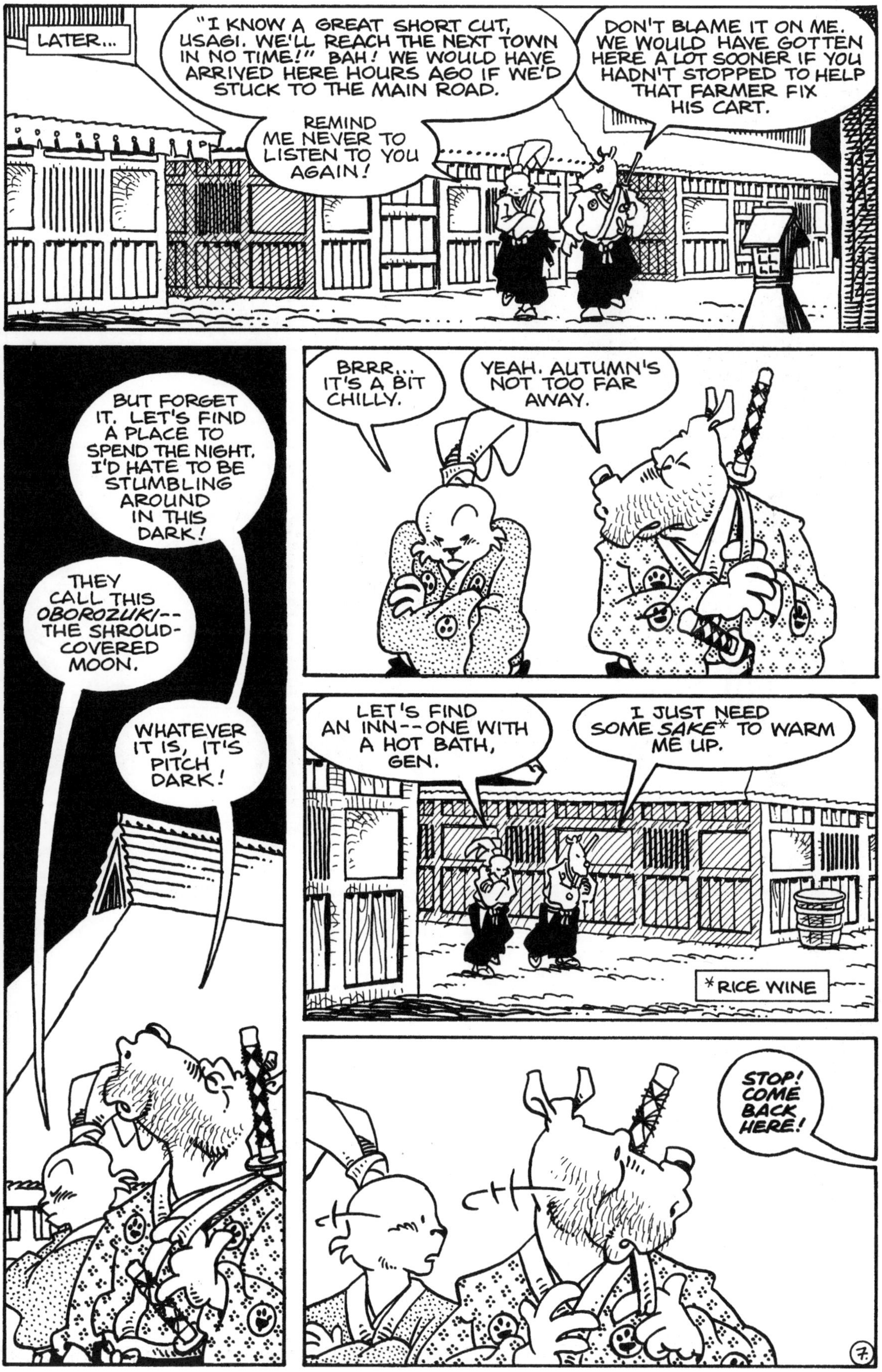
LATER...
"I KNOW A GREAT SHORT CUT, USAGI. WE'LL REACH THE NEXT TOWN IN NO TIME!" BAH! WE WOULD HAVE ARRIVED HERE HOURS AGO IF WE'D STUCK TO THE MAIN ROAD.
REMIND ME NEVER TO LISTEN TO YOU AGAIN!
DON'T BLAME IT ON ME. WE WOULD HAVE GOTTEN HERE A LOT SOONER IF YOU HADN'T STOPPED TO HELP THAT FARMER FIX HIS CART.
BUT FORGET IT. LET'S FIND A PLACE TO SPEND THE NIGHT. I'D HATE TO BE STUMBLING AROUND IN THIS DARK!
THEY CALL THIS *OBOROZUKI*-- THE SHROUD-COVERED MOON.
WHATEVER IT IS, IT'S PITCH DARK!
BRRR... IT'S A BIT CHILLY.
YEAH. AUTUMN'S NOT TOO FAR AWAY.
LET'S FIND AN INN--ONE WITH A HOT BATH, GEN.
I JUST NEED SOME *SAKE** TO WARM ME UP.
*RICE WINE
STOP! COME BACK HERE!
7.

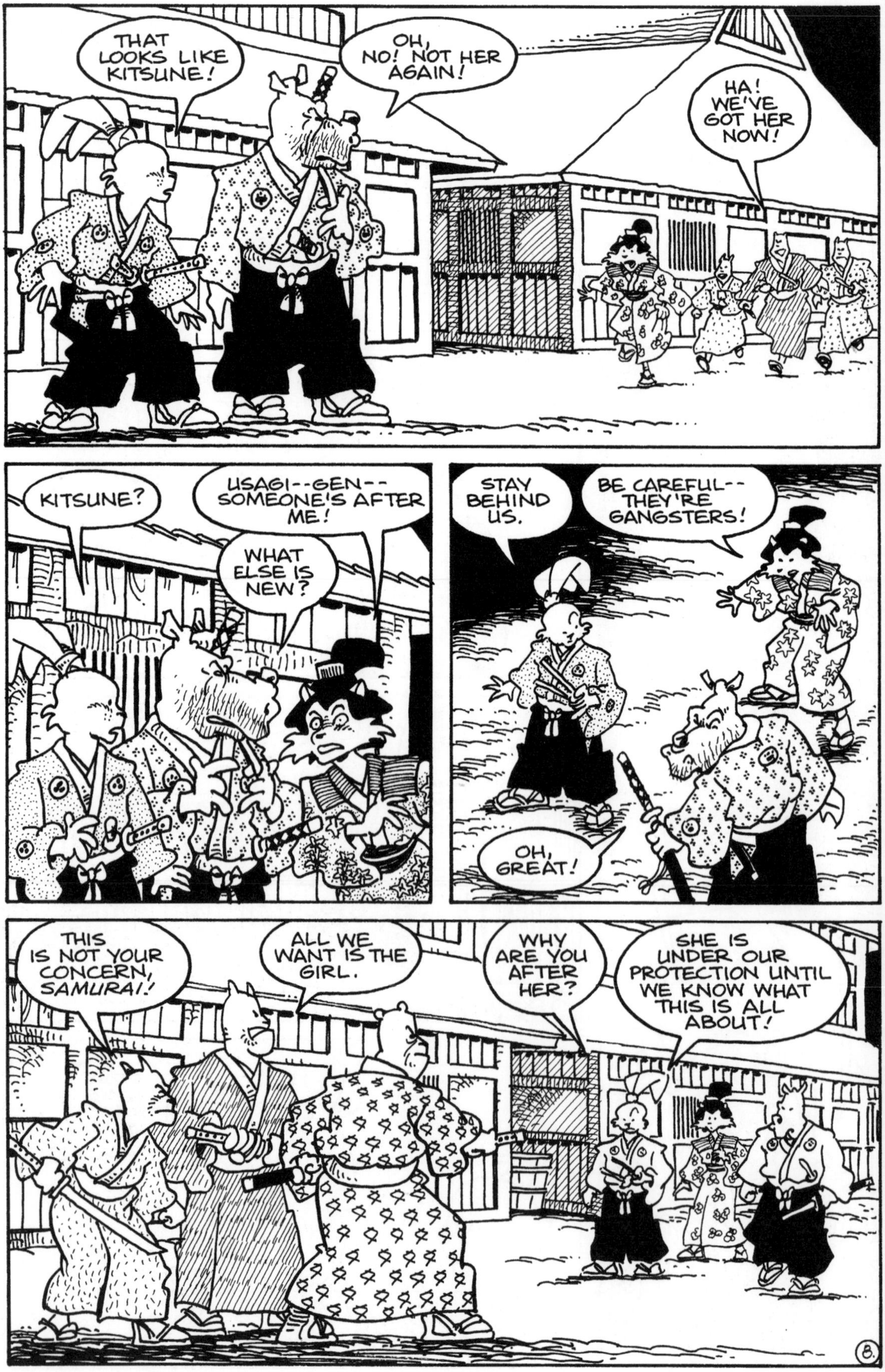
THAT LOOKS LIKE KITSUNE!
OH, NO! NOT HER AGAIN!
HA! WE'VE GOT HER NOW!
KITSUNE?
USAGI--GEN--SOMEONE'S AFTER ME!
WHAT ELSE IS NEW?
STAY BEHIND US.
BE CAREFUL--THEY'RE GANGSTERS!
OH, GREAT!
THIS IS NOT YOUR CONCERN, SAMURAI!
ALL WE WANT IS THE GIRL.
WHY ARE YOU AFTER HER?
SHE IS UNDER OUR PROTECTION UNTIL WE KNOW WHAT THIS IS ALL ABOUT!
8.

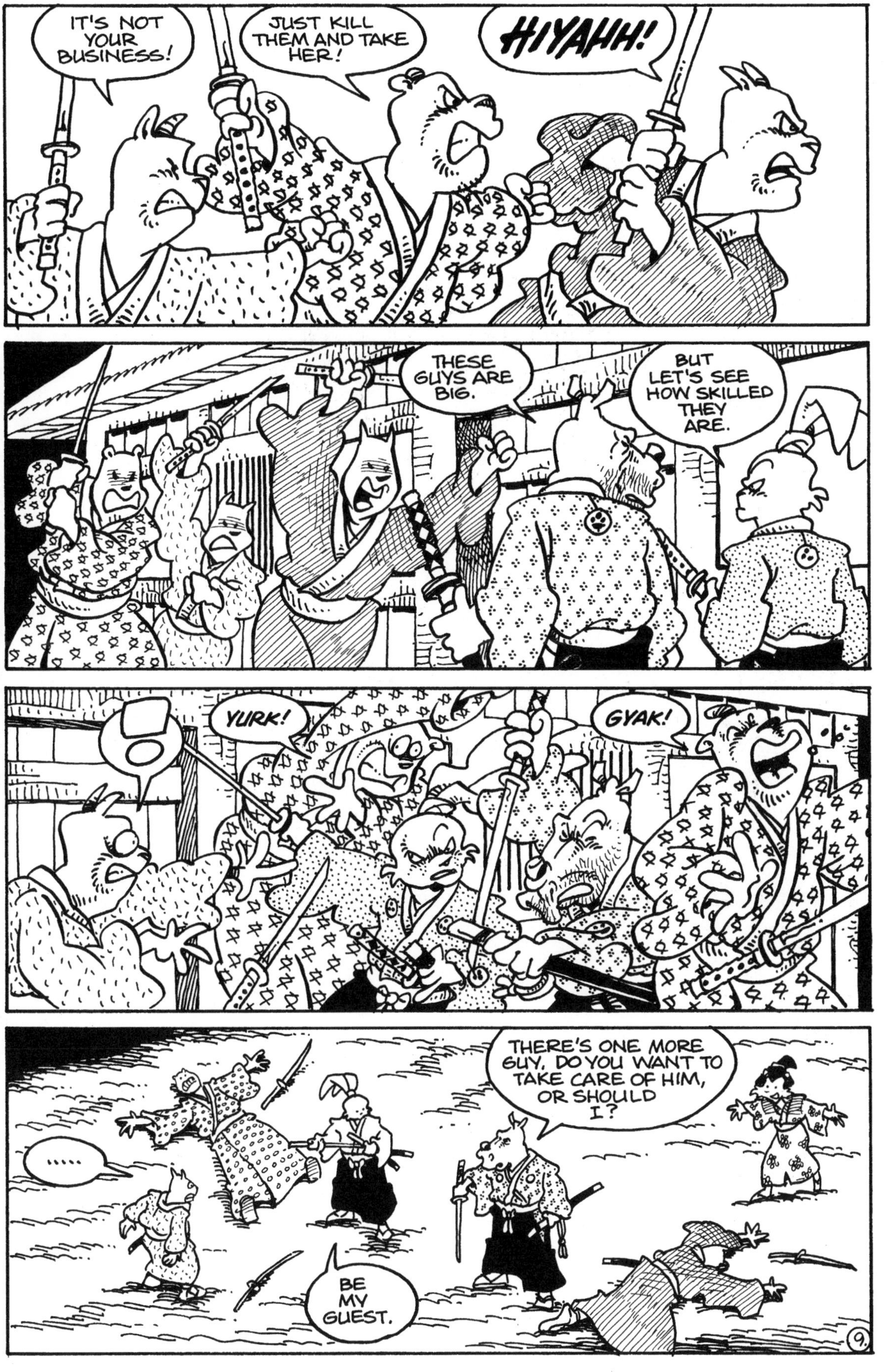
IT'S NOT YOUR BUSINESS!
JUST KILL THEM AND TAKE HER!
HIYAHH!
THESE GUYS ARE BIG.
BUT LET'S SEE HOW SKILLED THEY ARE.
YURK!
GYAK!
.....
THERE'S ONE MORE GUY, DO YOU WANT TO TAKE CARE OF HIM, OR SHOULD I?
BE MY GUEST.
9

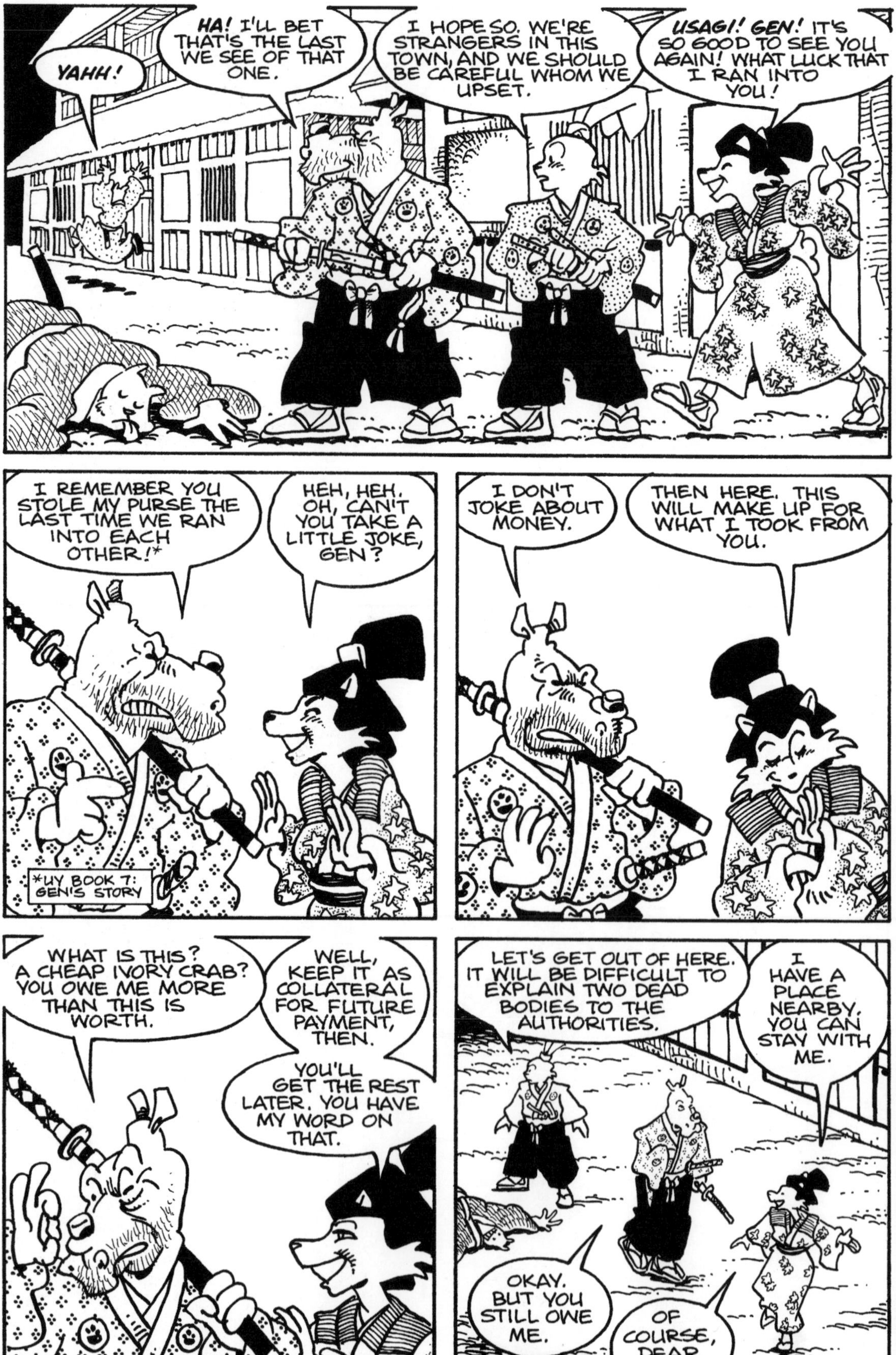
YAHH!
HA! I'LL BET THAT'S THE LAST WE SEE OF THAT ONE.
I HOPE SO. WE'RE STRANGERS IN THIS TOWN, AND WE SHOULD BE CAREFUL WHOM WE UPSET.
USAGI! GEN! IT'S SO GOOD TO SEE YOU AGAIN! WHAT LUCK THAT I RAN INTO YOU!
I REMEMBER YOU STOLE MY PURSE THE LAST TIME WE RAN INTO EACH OTHER!*
HEH, HEH. OH, CAN'T YOU TAKE A LITTLE JOKE, GEN?
*UY BOOK 7: GEN'S STORY
I DON'T JOKE ABOUT MONEY.
THEN HERE. THIS WILL MAKE UP FOR WHAT I TOOK FROM YOU.
WHAT IS THIS? A CHEAP IVORY CRAB? YOU OWE ME MORE THAN THIS IS WORTH.
WELL, KEEP IT AS COLLATERAL FOR FUTURE PAYMENT, THEN.
YOU'LL GET THE REST LATER. YOU HAVE MY WORD ON THAT.
LET'S GET OUT OF HERE. IT WILL BE DIFFICULT TO EXPLAIN TWO DEAD BODIES TO THE AUTHORITIES.
I HAVE A PLACE NEARBY. YOU CAN STAY WITH ME.
OKAY. BUT YOU STILL OWE ME.
OF COURSE, DEAR GEN.
10

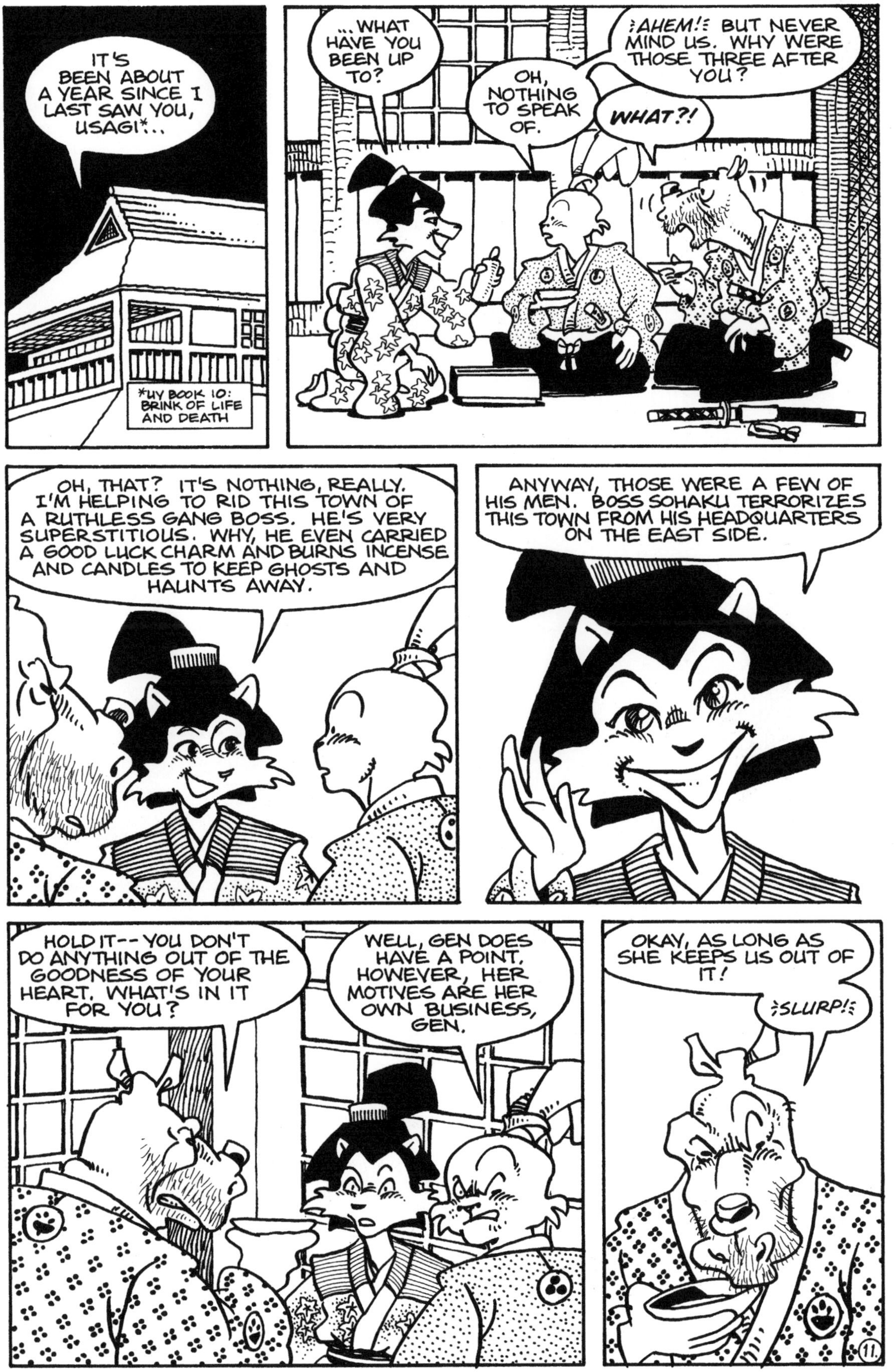
IT'S BEEN ABOUT A YEAR SINCE I LAST SAW YOU, USAGI*...
*UY BOOK 10: BRINK OF LIFE AND DEATH
...WHAT HAVE YOU BEEN UP TO?
OH, NOTHING TO SPEAK OF.
WHAT?!
:AHEM!: BUT NEVER MIND US. WHY WERE THOSE THREE AFTER YOU?
OH, THAT? IT'S NOTHING, REALLY. I'M HELPING TO RID THIS TOWN OF A RUTHLESS GANG BOSS. HE'S VERY SUPERSTITIOUS. WHY, HE EVEN CARRIED A GOOD LUCK CHARM AND BURNS INCENSE AND CANDLES TO KEEP GHOSTS AND HAUNTS AWAY.
ANYWAY, THOSE WERE A FEW OF HIS MEN. BOSS SOHAKU TERRORIZES THIS TOWN FROM HIS HEADQUARTERS ON THE EAST SIDE.
HOLD IT-- YOU DON'T DO ANYTHING OUT OF THE GOODNESS OF YOUR HEART. WHAT'S IN IT FOR YOU?
WELL, GEN DOES HAVE A POINT. HOWEVER, HER MOTIVES ARE HER OWN BUSINESS, GEN.
OKAY, AS LONG AS SHE KEEPS US OUT OF IT!
:SLURP!:
11.

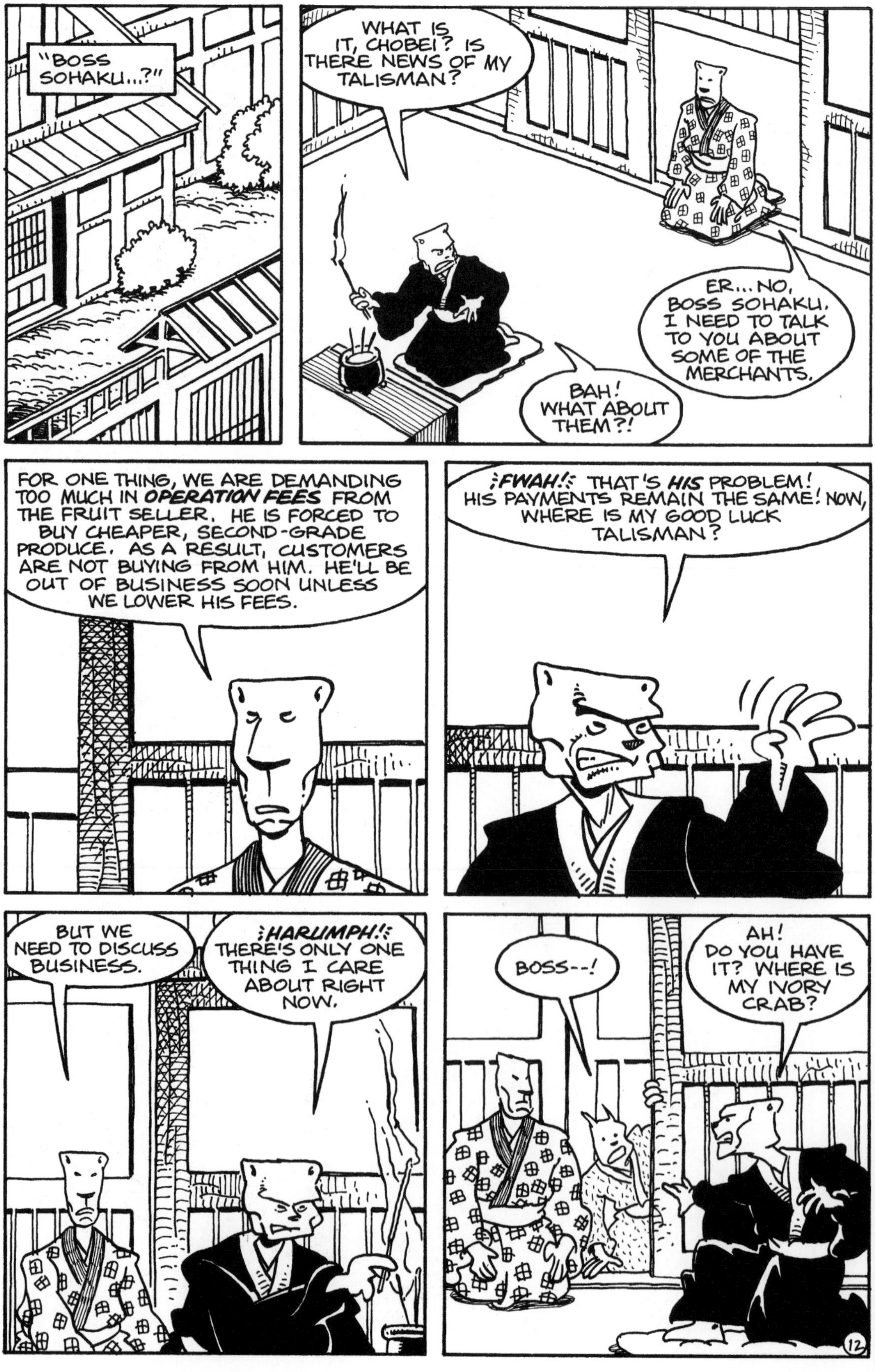
"BOSS SOHAKU...?"
WHAT IS IT, CHOBEI? IS THERE NEWS OF MY TALISMAN?
ER... NO, BOSS SOHAKU. I NEED TO TALK TO YOU ABOUT SOME OF THE MERCHANTS.
BAH! WHAT ABOUT THEM?!
FOR ONE THING, WE ARE DEMANDING TOO MUCH IN OPERATION FEES FROM THE FRUIT SELLER. HE IS FORCED TO BUY CHEAPER, SECOND-GRADE PRODUCE. AS A RESULT, CUSTOMERS ARE NOT BUYING FROM HIM. HE'LL BE OUT OF BUSINESS SOON UNLESS WE LOWER HIS FEES.
FWAH! THAT'S HIS PROBLEM! HIS PAYMENTS REMAIN THE SAME! NOW, WHERE IS MY GOOD LUCK TALISMAN?
BUT WE NEED TO DISCUSS BUSINESS.
HARUMPH! THERE'S ONLY ONE THING I CARE ABOUT RIGHT NOW.
BOSS--!
AH! DO YOU HAVE IT? WHERE IS MY IVORY CRAB?
12

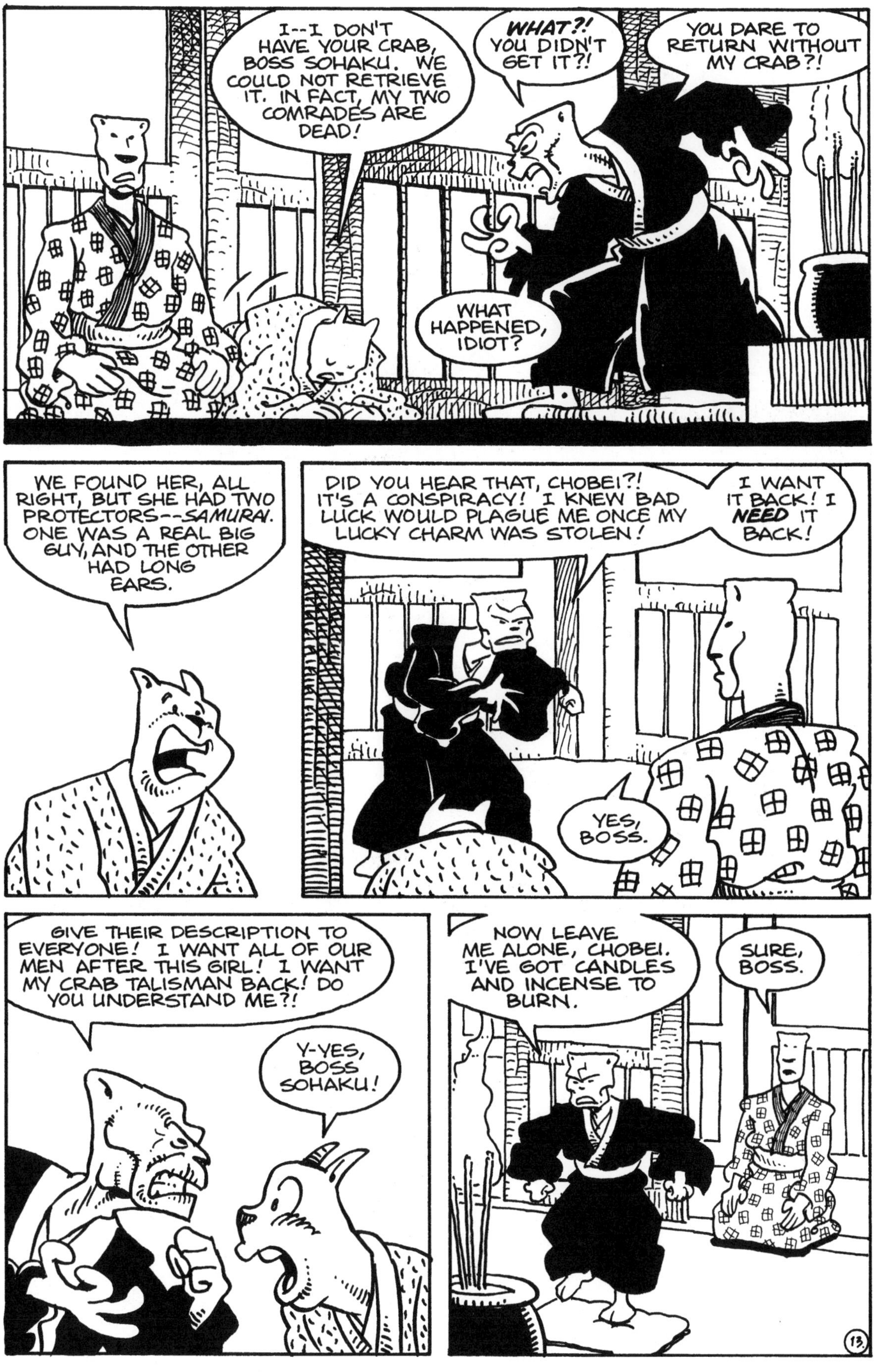

I--I DON'T HAVE YOUR CRAB, BOSS SOHAKU. WE COULD NOT RETRIEVE IT. IN FACT, MY TWO COMRADES ARE DEAD!
WHAT?! YOU DIDN'T GET IT?!
YOU DARE TO RETURN WITHOUT MY CRAB?!
WHAT HAPPENED, IDIOT?
WE FOUND HER, ALL RIGHT, BUT SHE HAD TWO PROTECTORS--SAMURAI. ONE WAS A REAL BIG GUY, AND THE OTHER HAD LONG EARS.
DID YOU HEAR THAT, CHOBEI?! IT'S A CONSPIRACY! I KNEW BAD LUCK WOULD PLAGUE ME ONCE MY LUCKY CHARM WAS STOLEN!
I WANT IT BACK! I NEED IT BACK!
YES, BOSS.
GIVE THEIR DESCRIPTION TO EVERYONE! I WANT ALL OF OUR MEN AFTER THIS GIRL! I WANT MY CRAB TALISMAN BACK! DO YOU UNDERSTAND ME?!
Y-YES, BOSS SOHAKU!
NOW LEAVE ME ALONE, CHOBEI. I'VE GOT CANDLES AND INCENSE TO BURN.
SURE, BOSS.
13

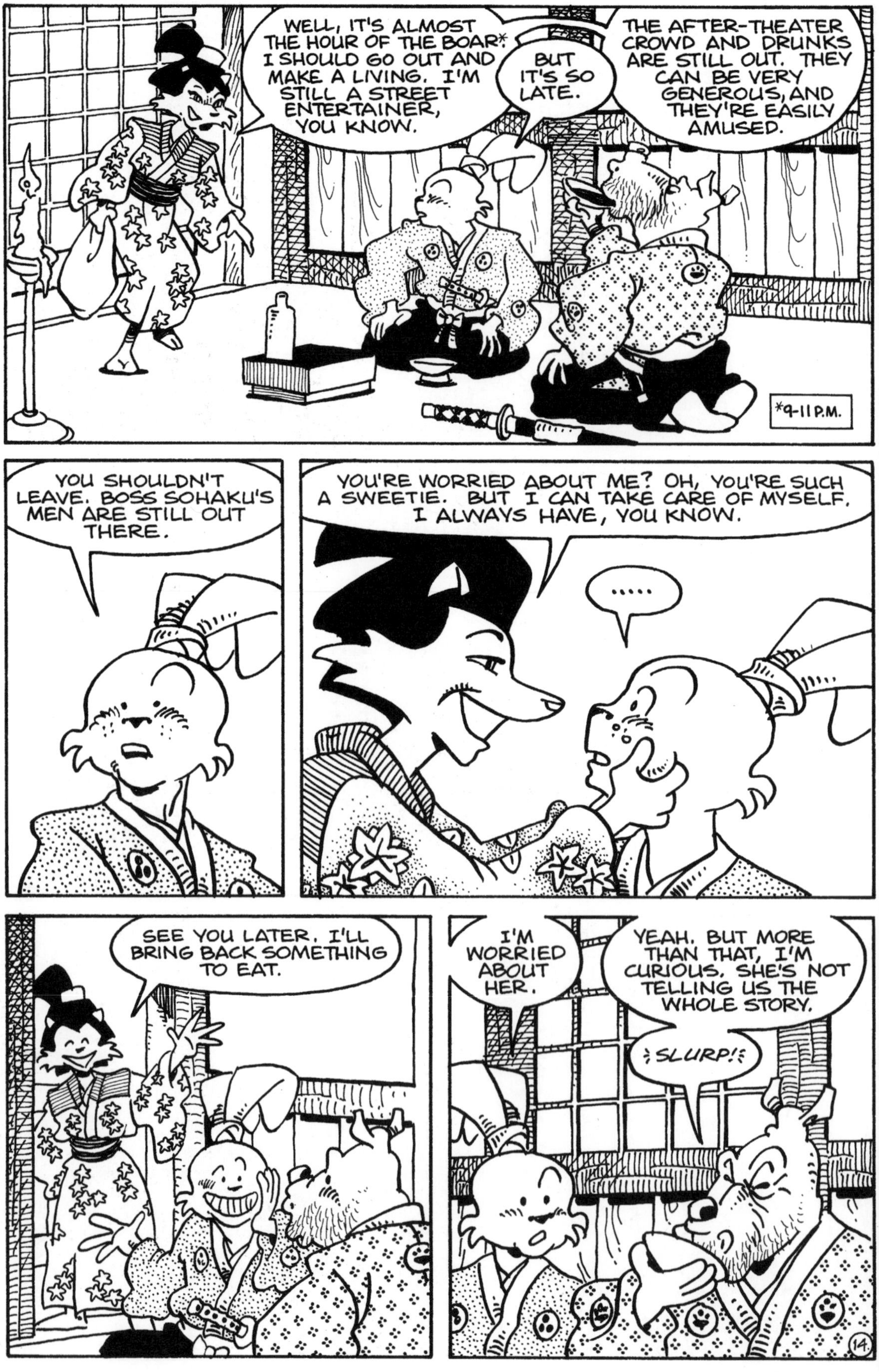
WELL, IT'S ALMOST THE HOUR OF THE BOAR* I SHOULD GO OUT AND MAKE A LIVING. I'M STILL A STREET ENTERTAINER, YOU KNOW.
BUT IT'S SO LATE.
THE AFTER-THEATER CROWD AND DRUNKS ARE STILL OUT. THEY CAN BE VERY GENEROUS, AND THEY'RE EASILY AMUSED.
*9-11 P.M.
YOU SHOULDN'T LEAVE. BOSS SOHAKU'S MEN ARE STILL OUT THERE.
YOU'RE WORRIED ABOUT ME? OH, YOU'RE SUCH A SWEETIE. BUT I CAN TAKE CARE OF MYSELF. I ALWAYS HAVE, YOU KNOW.
.....
SEE YOU LATER. I'LL BRING BACK SOMETHING TO EAT.
I'M WORRIED ABOUT HER.
YEAH. BUT MORE THAN THAT, I'M CURIOUS. SHE'S NOT TELLING US THE WHOLE STORY.
SLURP!
14

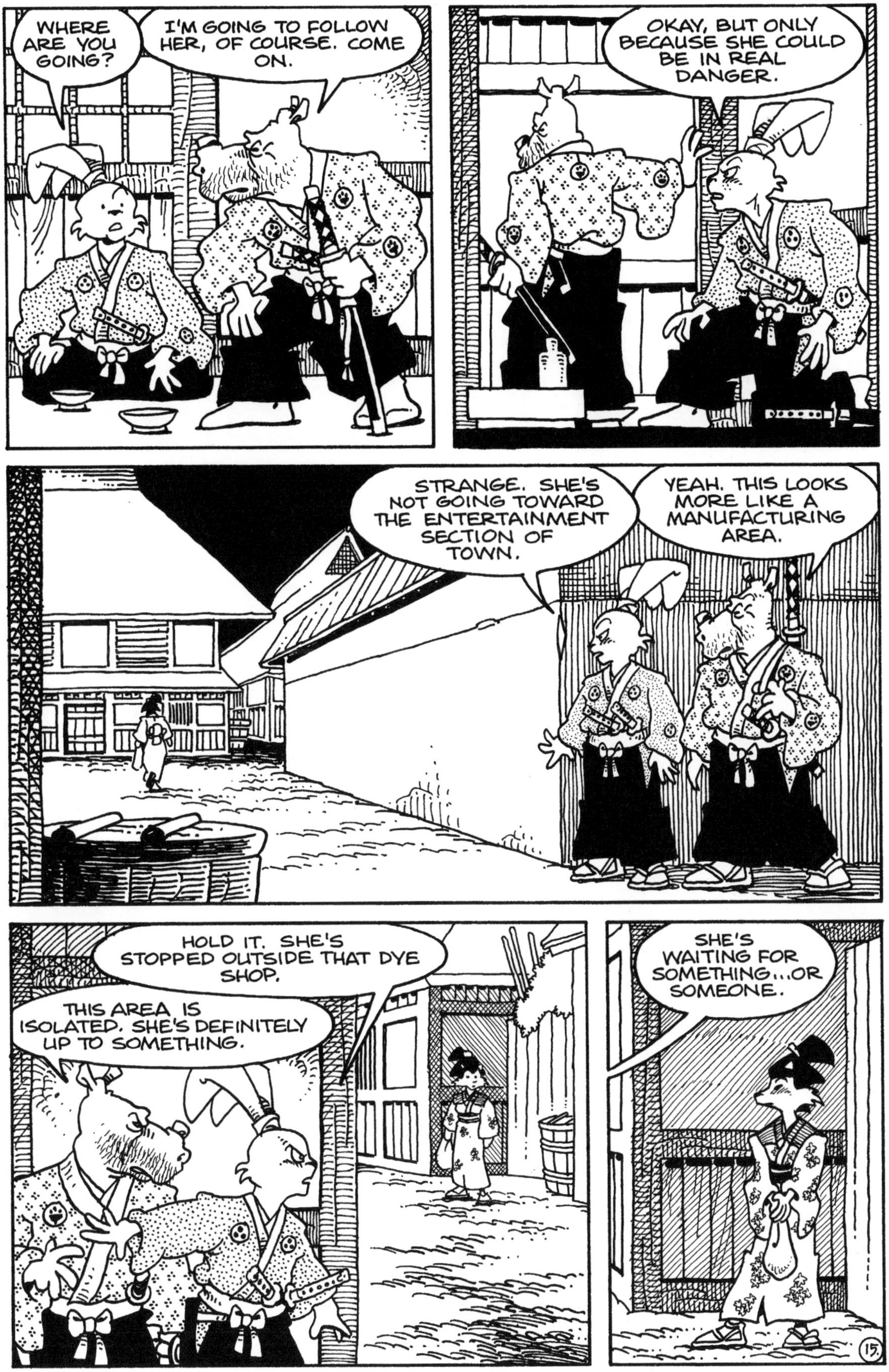
WHERE ARE YOU GOING?
I'M GOING TO FOLLOW HER, OF COURSE. COME ON.
OKAY, BUT ONLY BECAUSE SHE COULD BE IN REAL DANGER.
STRANGE. SHE'S NOT GOING TOWARD THE ENTERTAINMENT SECTION OF TOWN.
YEAH. THIS LOOKS MORE LIKE A MANUFACTURING AREA.
HOLD IT. SHE'S STOPPED OUTSIDE THAT DYE SHOP.
THIS AREA IS ISOLATED. SHE'S DEFINITELY UP TO SOMETHING.
SHE'S WAITING FOR SOMETHING...OR SOMEONE.
15

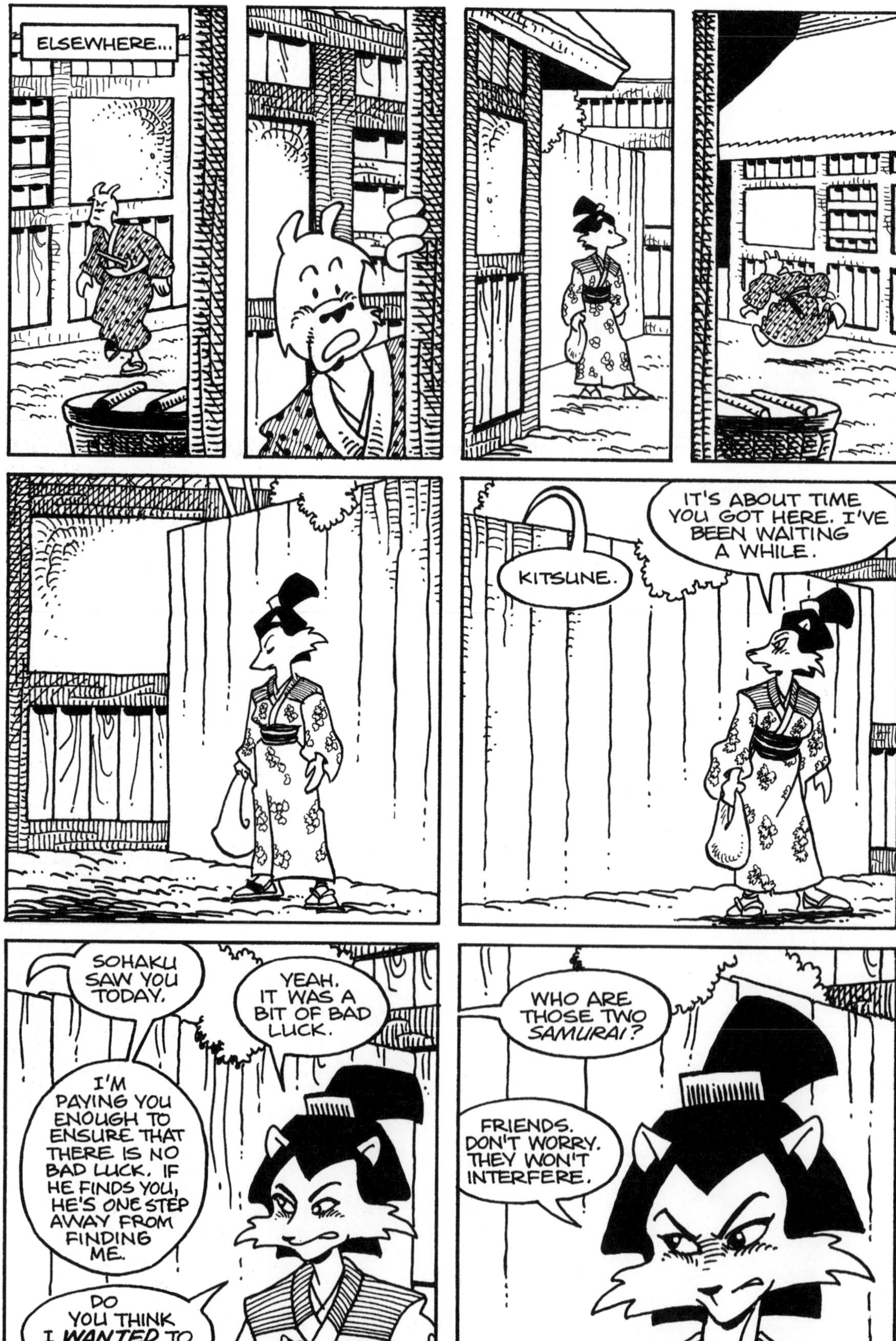
ELSEWHERE...
KITSUNE.
IT'S ABOUT TIME YOU GOT HERE. I'VE BEEN WAITING A WHILE.
SOHAKU SAW YOU TODAY.
YEAH. IT WAS A BIT OF BAD LUCK.
I'M PAYING YOU ENOUGH TO ENSURE THAT THERE IS NO BAD LUCK. IF HE FINDS YOU, HE'S ONE STEP AWAY FROM FINDING ME.
DO YOU THINK I *WANTED* TO BE SEEN?
WHO ARE THOSE TWO *SAMURAI*?
FRIENDS. DON'T WORRY. THEY WON'T INTERFERE.
16.

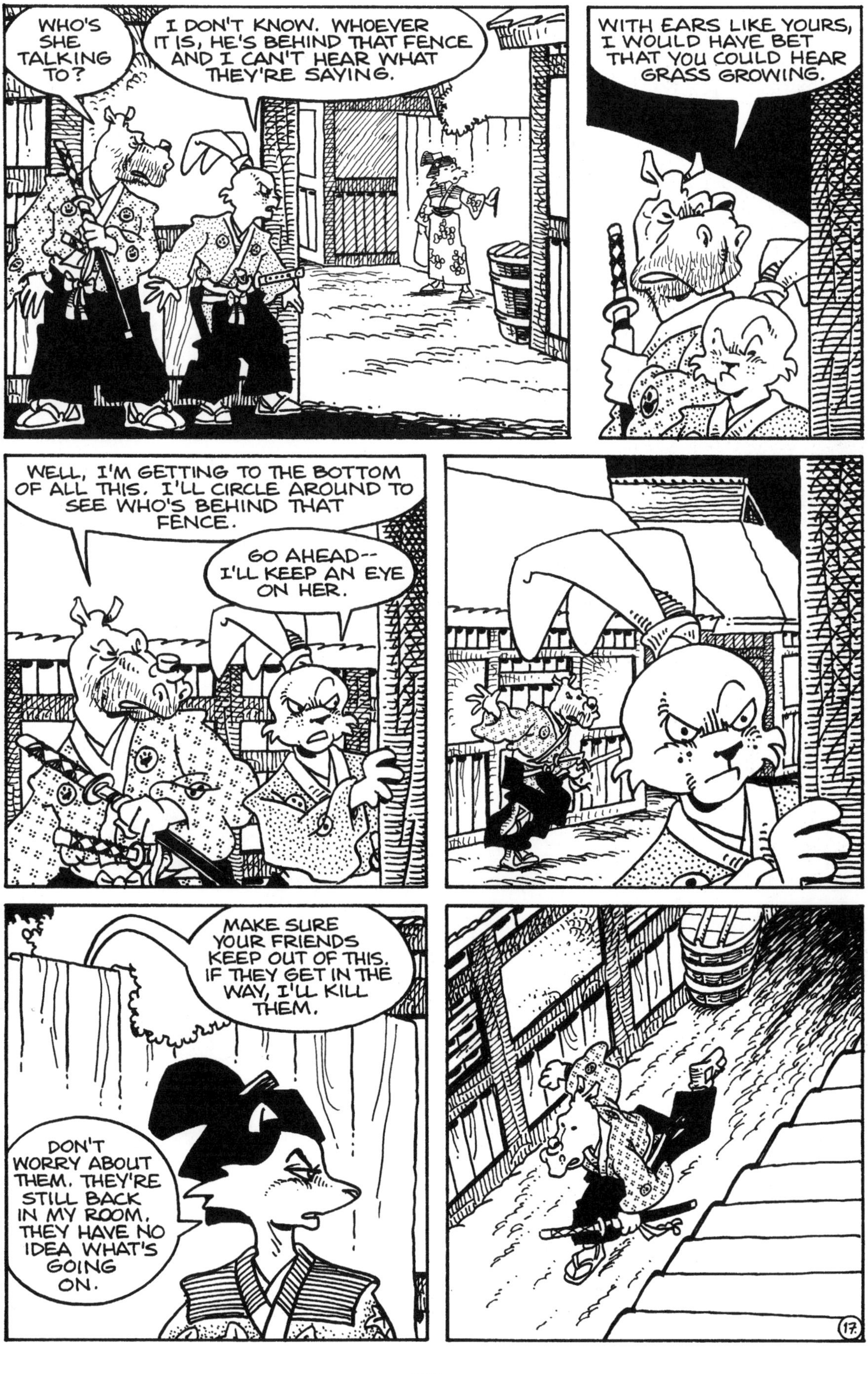
WHO'S SHE TALKING TO?
I DON'T KNOW. WHOEVER IT IS, HE'S BEHIND THAT FENCE AND I CAN'T HEAR WHAT THEY'RE SAYING.
WITH EARS LIKE YOURS, I WOULD HAVE BET THAT YOU COULD HEAR GRASS GROWING.
WELL, I'M GETTING TO THE BOTTOM OF ALL THIS. I'LL CIRCLE AROUND TO SEE WHO'S BEHIND THAT FENCE.
GO AHEAD-- I'LL KEEP AN EYE ON HER.
MAKE SURE YOUR FRIENDS KEEP OUT OF THIS. IF THEY GET IN THE WAY, I'LL KILL THEM.
DON'T WORRY ABOUT THEM. THEY'RE STILL BACK IN MY ROOM. THEY HAVE NO IDEA WHAT'S GOING ON.
17

WHERE IS THE CHARM?

I DON'T HAVE IT WITH ME. I GAVE IT TO A FRIEND FOR SAFE-KEEPING.

WHY?

IF I HANDED IT OVER TO YOU NOW, MY USEFULNESS-- AND MAYBE MY LIFE--WOULD COME TO AN END. GIVE ME THE REST OF MY PAYMENT FIRST. DID YOU BRING IT?

HA HA! YOU'RE JUST AS SHREWD AS I WAS TOLD.

I TRY.

SO... WHAT DO WE DO NOW?

WE'LL MEET AGAIN TOMORROW NIGHT. I'LL BRING THE MONEY, YOU'LL BRING THE IVORY.

AGREED.

AND, KITSUNE-- NO TRICKS.

UNTIL TOMORROW, THEN.

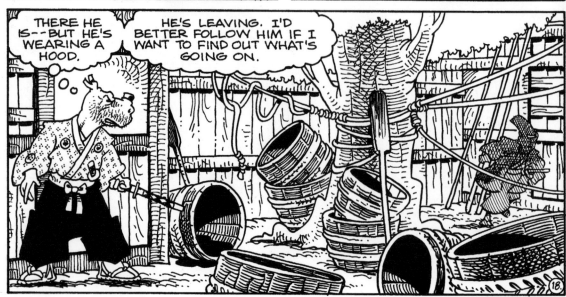

THERE HE IS--BUT HE'S WEARING A HOOD.

HE'S LEAVING. I'D BETTER FOLLOW HIM IF I WANT TO FIND OUT WHAT'S GOING ON.

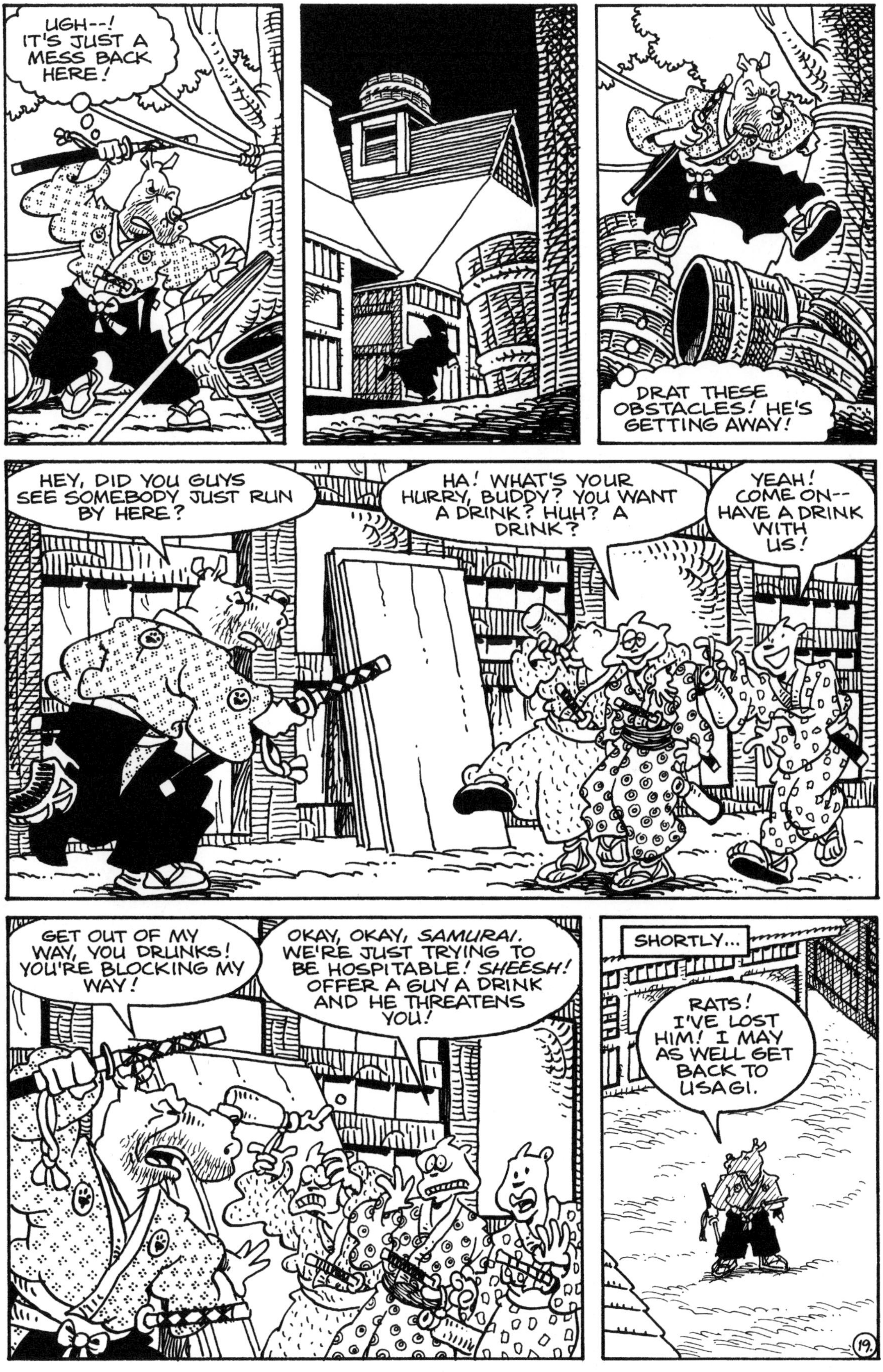
UGH--! IT'S JUST A MESS BACK HERE!
DRAT THESE OBSTACLES! HE'S GETTING AWAY!
HEY, DID YOU GUYS SEE SOMEBODY JUST RUN BY HERE?
HA! WHAT'S YOUR HURRY, BUDDY? YOU WANT A DRINK? HUH? A DRINK?
YEAH! COME ON-- HAVE A DRINK WITH US!
GET OUT OF MY WAY, YOU DRUNKS! YOU'RE BLOCKING MY WAY!
OKAY, OKAY, *SAMURAI*. WE'RE JUST TRYING TO BE HOSPITABLE! *SHEESH!* OFFER A GUY A DRINK AND HE THREATENS YOU!
SHORTLY...
RATS! I'VE LOST HIM! I MAY AS WELL GET BACK TO USAGI.
19.

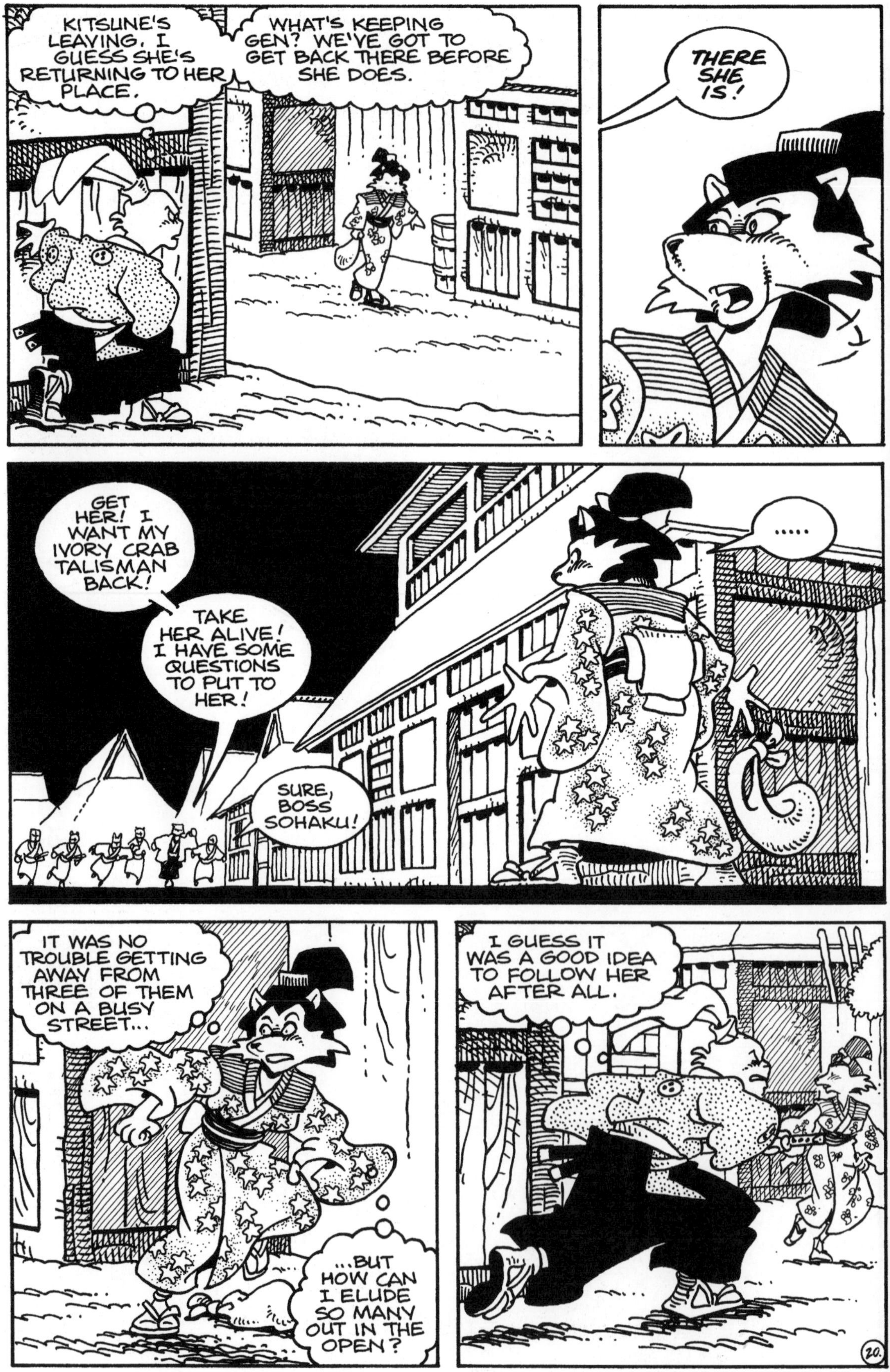

KITSUNE'S LEAVING. I GUESS SHE'S RETURNING TO HER PLACE.
WHAT'S KEEPING GEN? WE'VE GOT TO GET BACK THERE BEFORE SHE DOES.
THERE SHE IS!
GET HER! I WANT MY IVORY CRAB TALISMAN BACK!
TAKE HER ALIVE! I HAVE SOME QUESTIONS TO PUT TO HER!
SURE, BOSS SOHAKU!
.....
IT WAS NO TROUBLE GETTING AWAY FROM THREE OF THEM ON A BUSY STREET...
...BUT HOW CAN I ELUDE SO MANY OUT IN THE OPEN?
I GUESS IT WAS A GOOD IDEA TO FOLLOW HER AFTER ALL.
20.

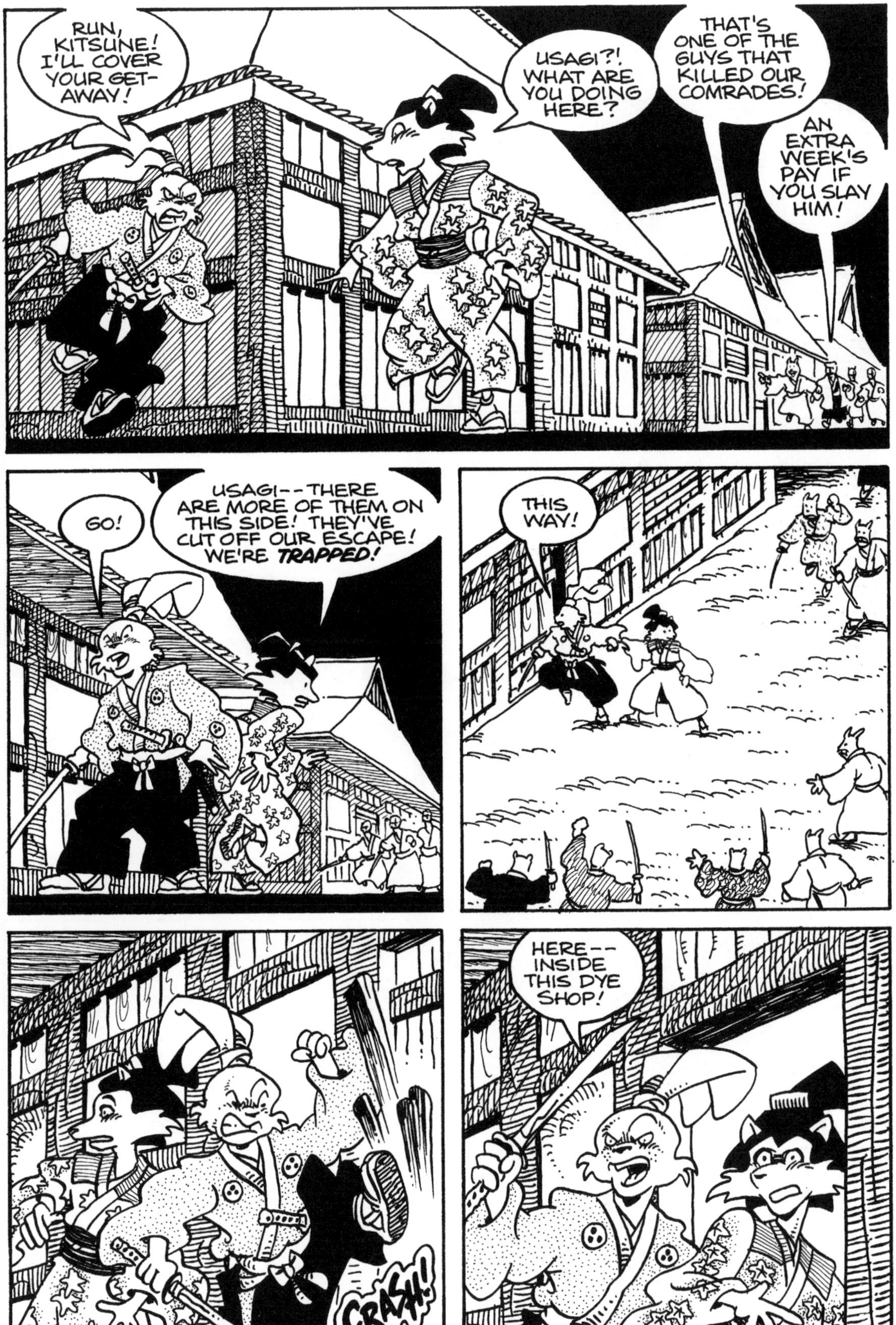
RUN, KITSUNE! I'LL COVER YOUR GET-AWAY!
USAGI?! WHAT ARE YOU DOING HERE?
THAT'S ONE OF THE GUYS THAT KILLED OUR COMRADES!
AN EXTRA WEEK'S PAY IF YOU SLAY HIM!
GO!
USAGI--THERE ARE MORE OF THEM ON THIS SIDE! THEY'VE CUT OFF OUR ESCAPE! WE'RE TRAPPED!
THIS WAY!
CRASH!
HERE--INSIDE THIS DYE SHOP!
21.

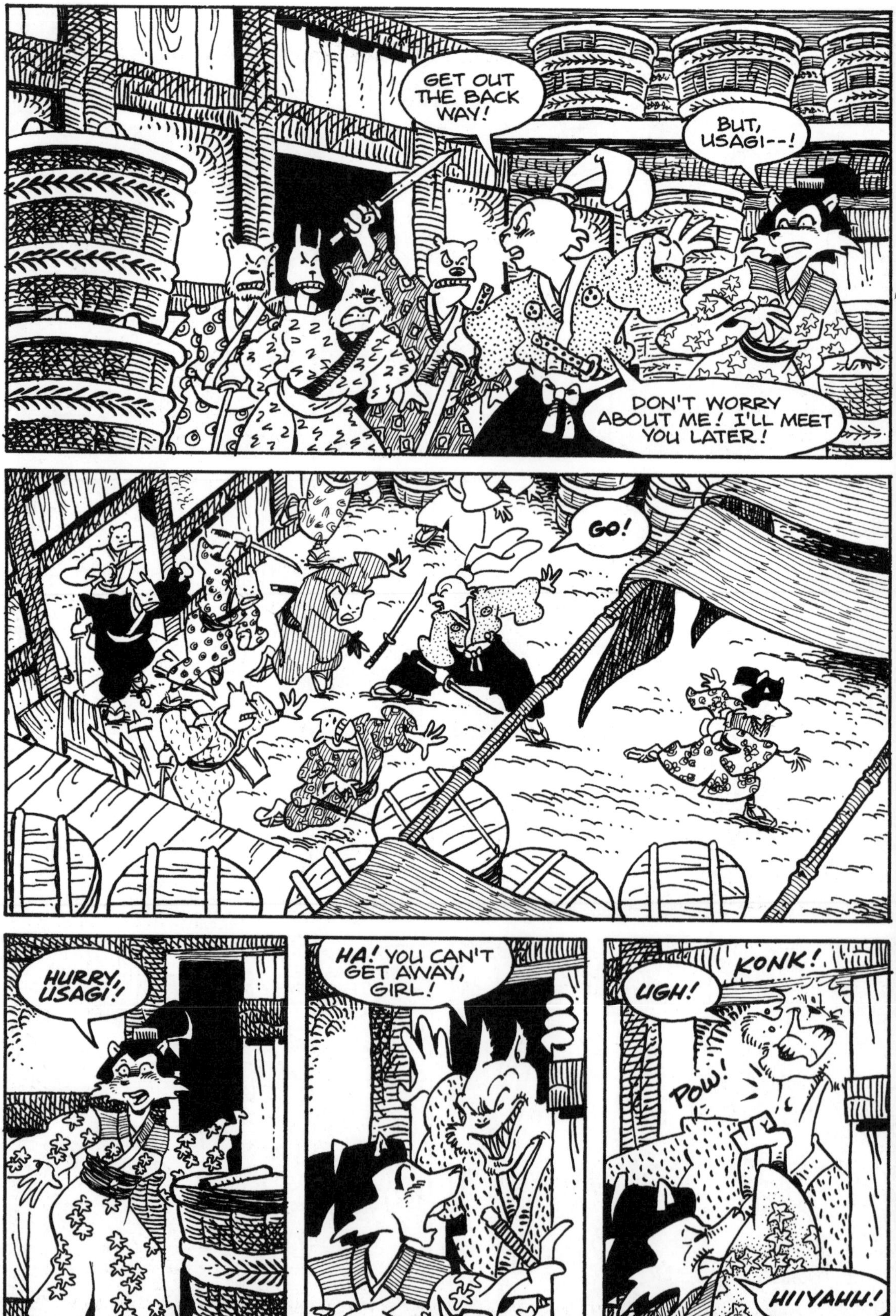

GET OUT THE BACK WAY!
BUT, USAGI--!
DON'T WORRY ABOUT ME! I'LL MEET YOU LATER!
GO!
HURRY, USAGI!
HA! YOU CAN'T GET AWAY, GIRL!
KONK!
UGH!
POW!
HIIYAHH!
22

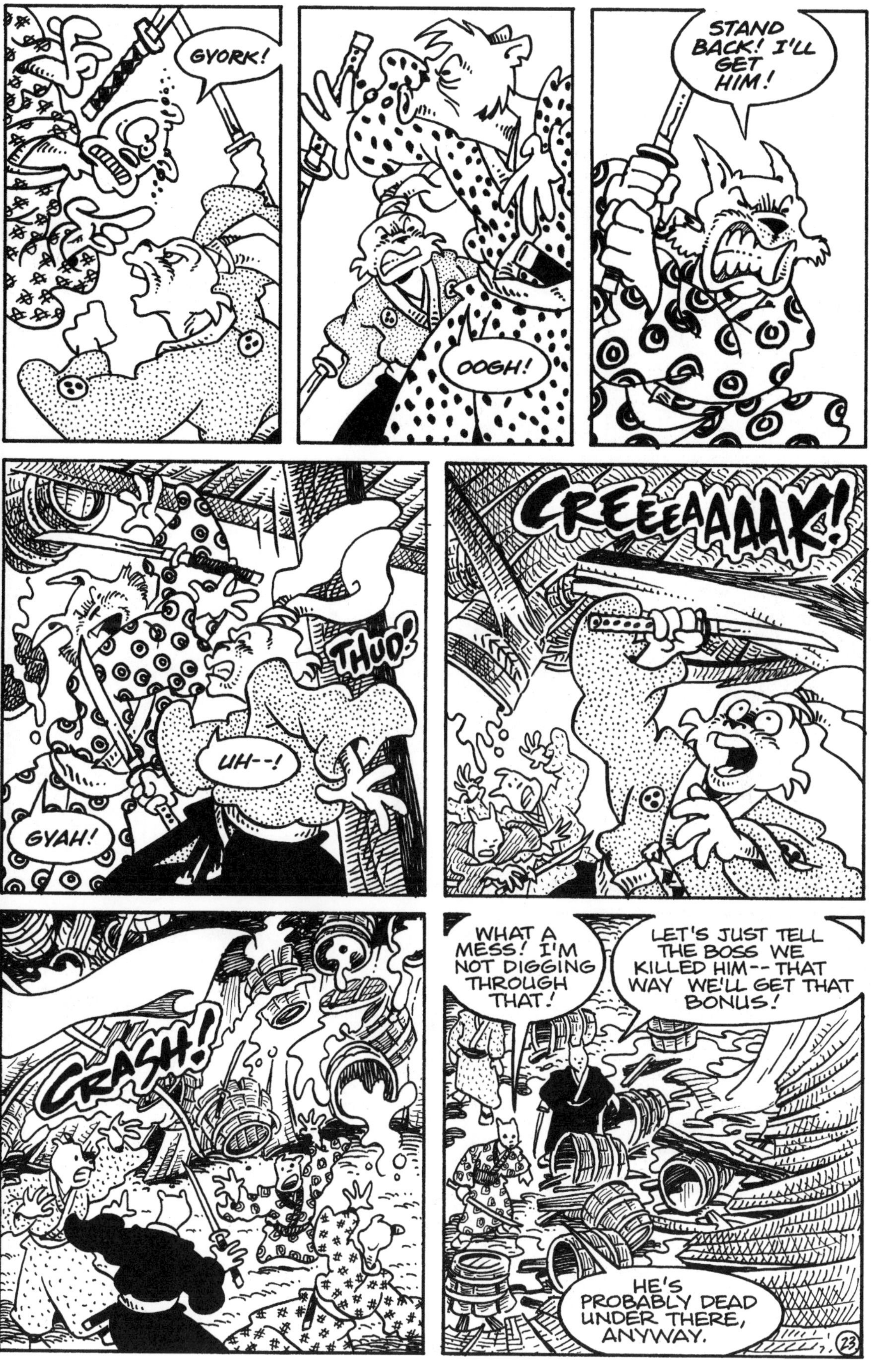
GYORK!
OOGH!
STAND BACK! I'LL GET HIM!
THUD!
UH--!
GYAH!
CREEEAAAAK!
CRASH!
WHAT A MESS! I'M NOT DIGGING THROUGH THAT!
LET'S JUST TELL THE BOSS WE KILLED HIM--THAT WAY WE'LL GET THAT BONUS!
HE'S PROBABLY DEAD UNDER THERE, ANYWAY.
23

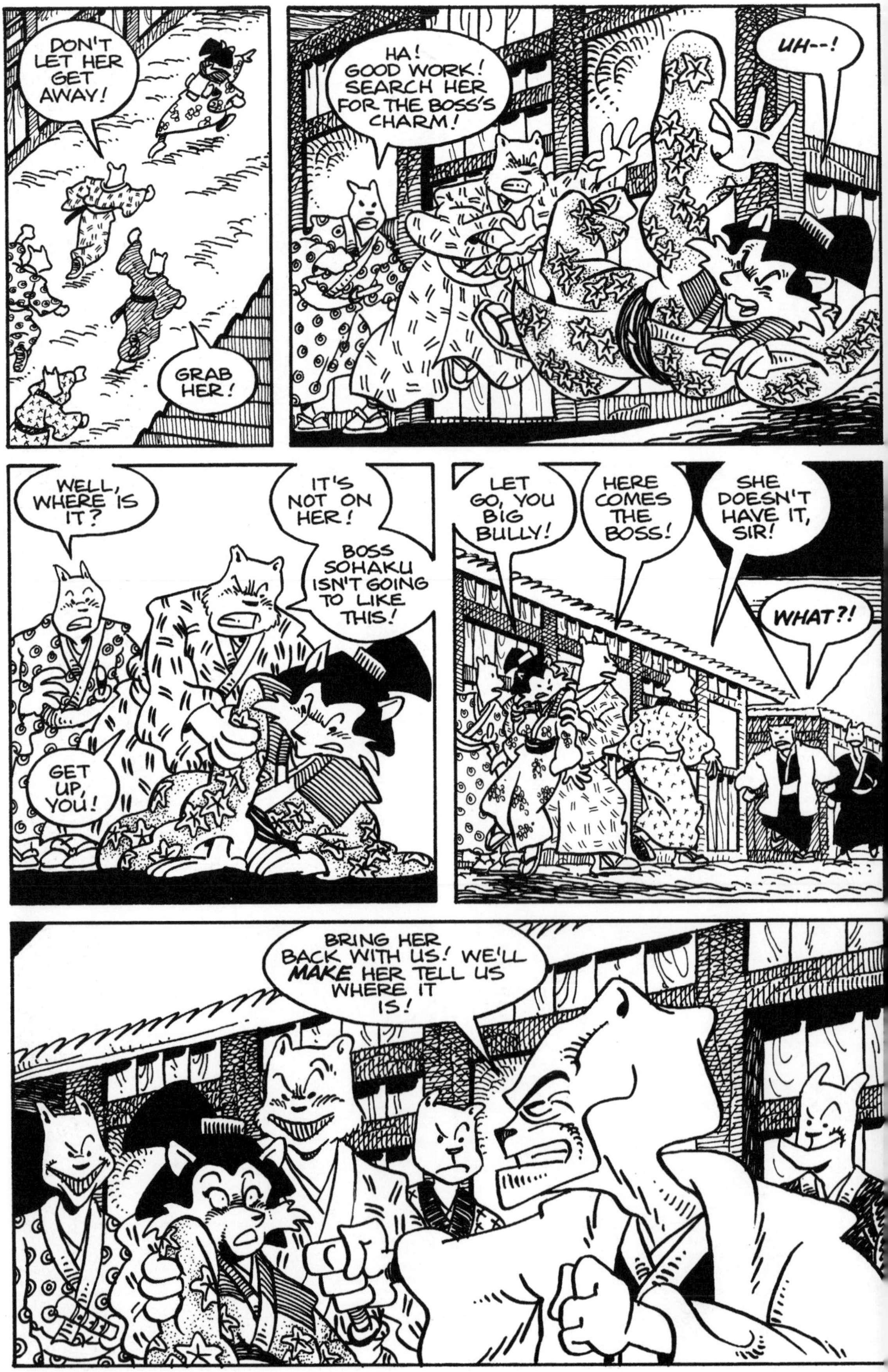

DON'T LET HER GET AWAY!
GRAB HER!
HA! GOOD WORK! SEARCH HER FOR THE BOSS'S CHARM!
UH--!
WELL, WHERE IS IT?
IT'S NOT ON HER!
BOSS SOHAKU ISN'T GOING TO LIKE THIS!
GET UP, YOU!
LET GO, YOU BIG BULLY!
HERE COMES THE BOSS!
SHE DOESN'T HAVE IT, SIR!
WHAT?!
BRING HER BACK WITH US! WE'LL MAKE HER TELL US WHERE IT IS!

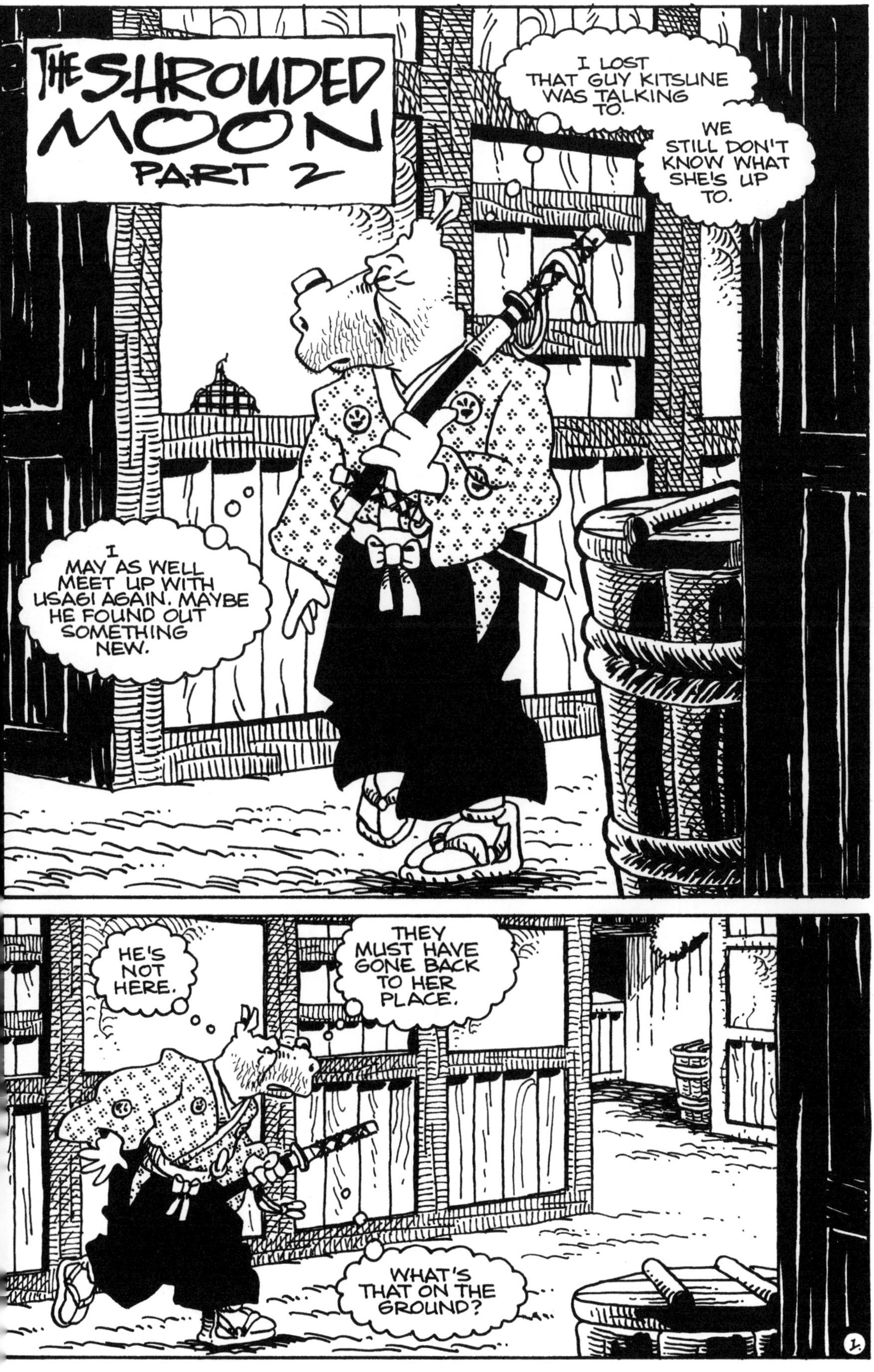
THE SHROUDED MOON
PART 2
I LOST THAT GUY KITSUNE WAS TALKING TO.
WE STILL DON'T KNOW WHAT SHE'S UP TO.
I MAY AS WELL MEET UP WITH USAGI AGAIN. MAYBE HE FOUND OUT SOMETHING NEW.
HE'S NOT HERE.
THEY MUST HAVE GONE BACK TO HER PLACE.
WHAT'S THAT ON THE GROUND?
1.

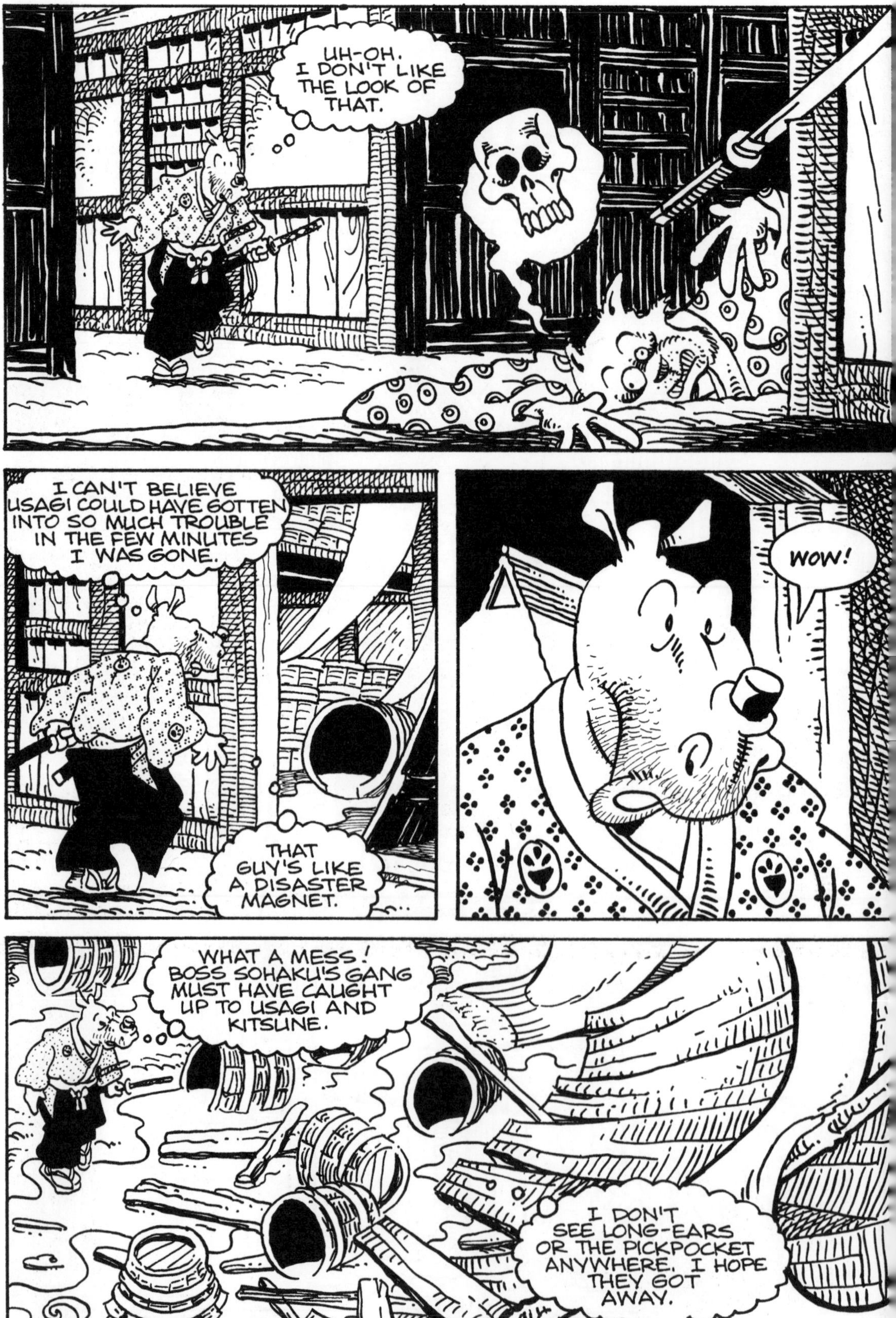
UH-OH. I DON'T LIKE THE LOOK OF THAT.
I CAN'T BELIEVE USAGI COULD HAVE GOTTEN INTO SO MUCH TROUBLE IN THE FEW MINUTES I WAS GONE.
THAT GUY'S LIKE A DISASTER MAGNET.
WOW!
WHAT A MESS! BOSS SOHAKU'S GANG MUST HAVE CAUGHT UP TO USAGI AND KITSUNE.
I DON'T SEE LONG-EARS OR THE PICKPOCKET ANYWHERE. I HOPE THEY GOT AWAY.
2.

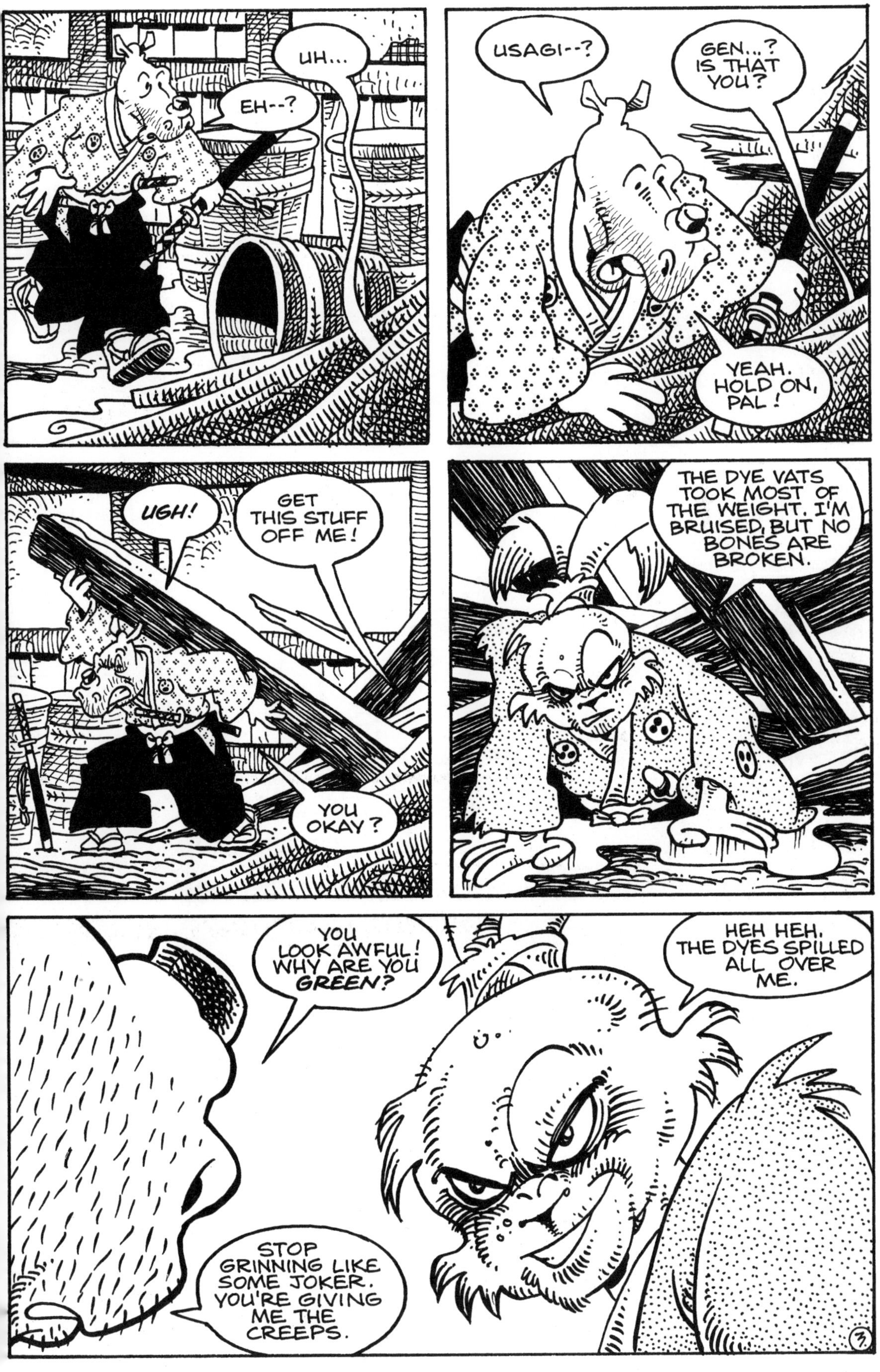
UH...
EH--?
USAGI--?
GEN...? IS THAT YOU?
YEAH. HOLD ON, PAL!
UGH!
GET THIS STUFF OFF ME!
YOU OKAY?
THE DYE VATS TOOK MOST OF THE WEIGHT. I'M BRUISED, BUT NO BONES ARE BROKEN.
YOU LOOK AWFUL! WHY ARE YOU *GREEN?*
HEH HEH. THE DYES SPILLED ALL OVER ME.
STOP GRINNING LIKE SOME JOKER. YOU'RE GIVING ME THE CREEPS.
3

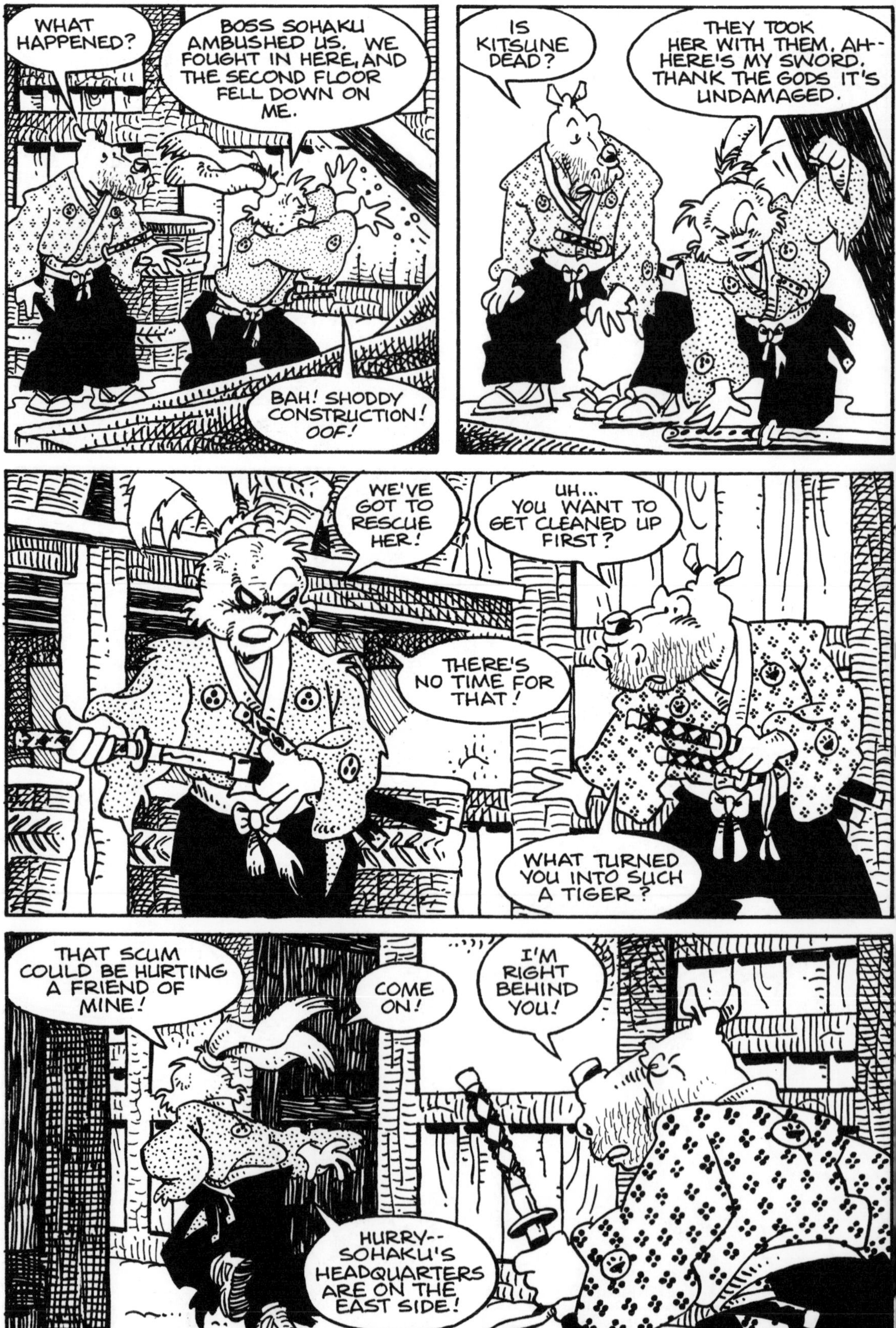
WHAT HAPPENED?
BOSS SOHAKU AMBUSHED US. WE FOUGHT IN HERE, AND THE SECOND FLOOR FELL DOWN ON ME.
BAH! SHODDY CONSTRUCTION! OOF!
IS KITSUNE DEAD?
THEY TOOK HER WITH THEM. AH-- HERE'S MY SWORD. THANK THE GODS IT'S UNDAMAGED.
WE'VE GOT TO RESCUE HER!
UH... YOU WANT TO GET CLEANED UP FIRST?
THERE'S NO TIME FOR THAT!
WHAT TURNED YOU INTO SUCH A TIGER?
THAT SCUM COULD BE HURTING A FRIEND OF MINE!
COME ON!
I'M RIGHT BEHIND YOU!
HURRY-- SOHAKU'S HEADQUARTERS ARE ON THE EAST SIDE!
4.

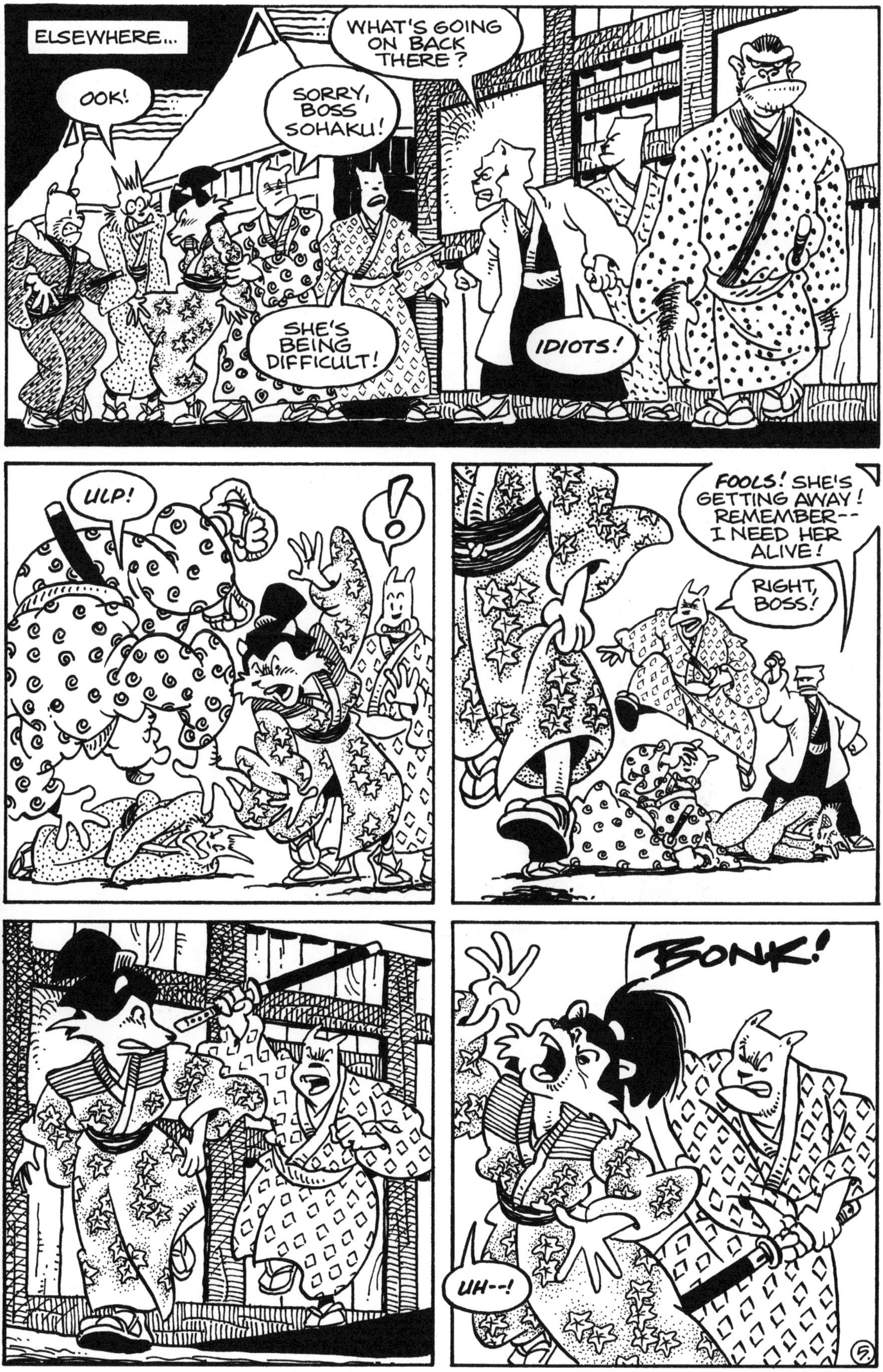
ELSEWHERE...
OOK!
SORRY, BOSS SOHAKU!
WHAT'S GOING ON BACK THERE?
SHE'S BEING DIFFICULT!
IDIOTS!
ULP!
!
FOOLS! SHE'S GETTING AWAY! REMEMBER-- I NEED HER ALIVE!
RIGHT, BOSS!
BONK!
UH--!
5

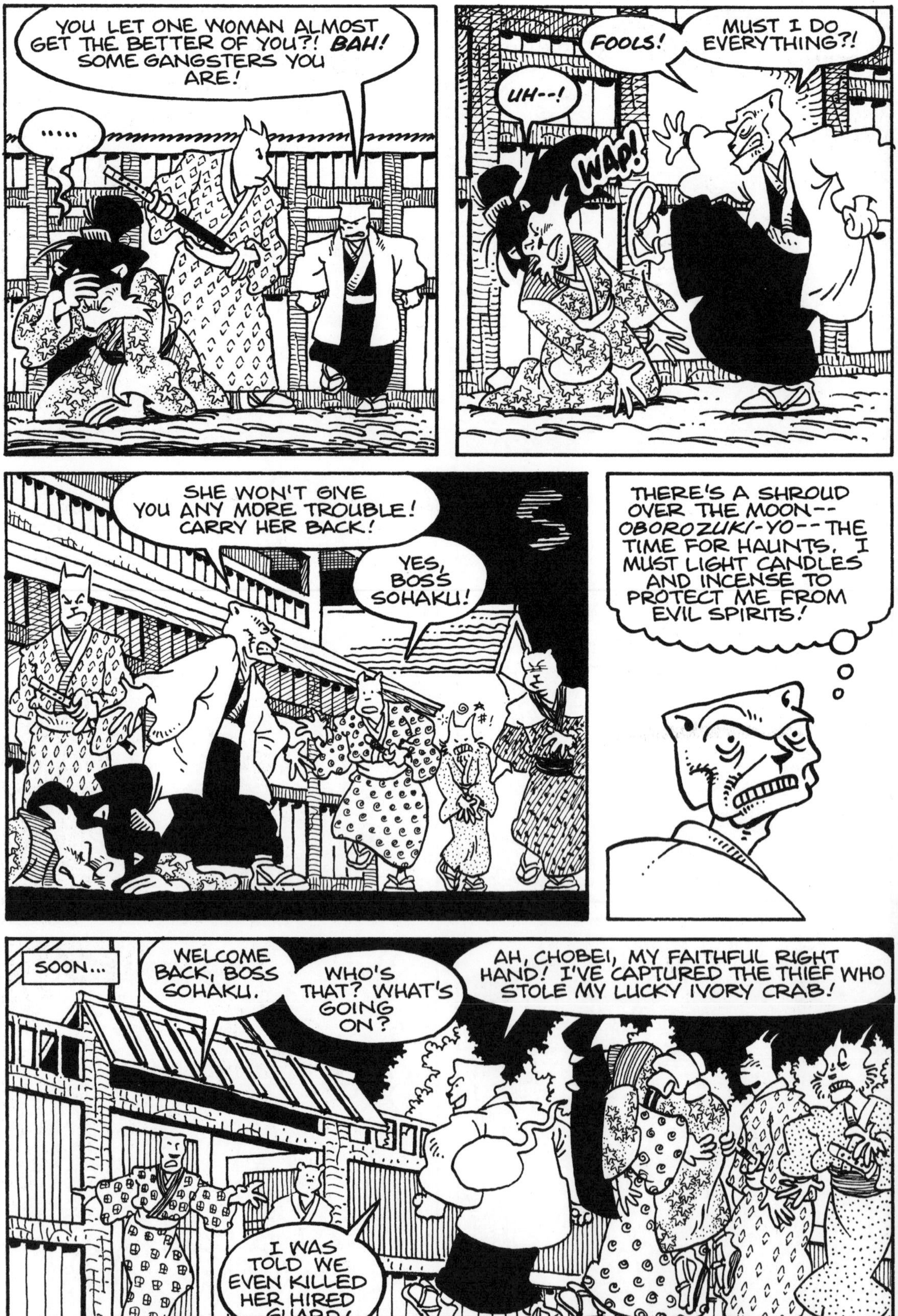
YOU LET ONE WOMAN ALMOST GET THE BETTER OF YOU?! BAH! SOME GANGSTERS YOU ARE!
.....
FOOLS!
MUST I DO EVERYTHING?!
UH--!
WAP!
SHE WON'T GIVE YOU ANY MORE TROUBLE! CARRY HER BACK!
YES, BOSS SOHAKU!
THERE'S A SHROUD OVER THE MOON-- OBOROZUKI-YO-- THE TIME FOR HAUNTS. I MUST LIGHT CANDLES AND INCENSE TO PROTECT ME FROM EVIL SPIRITS!
SOON...
WELCOME BACK, BOSS SOHAKU.
WHO'S THAT? WHAT'S GOING ON?
AH, CHOBEI, MY FAITHFUL RIGHT HAND! I'VE CAPTURED THE THIEF WHO STOLE MY LUCKY IVORY CRAB!
I WAS TOLD WE EVEN KILLED HER HIRED GUARD!
6.

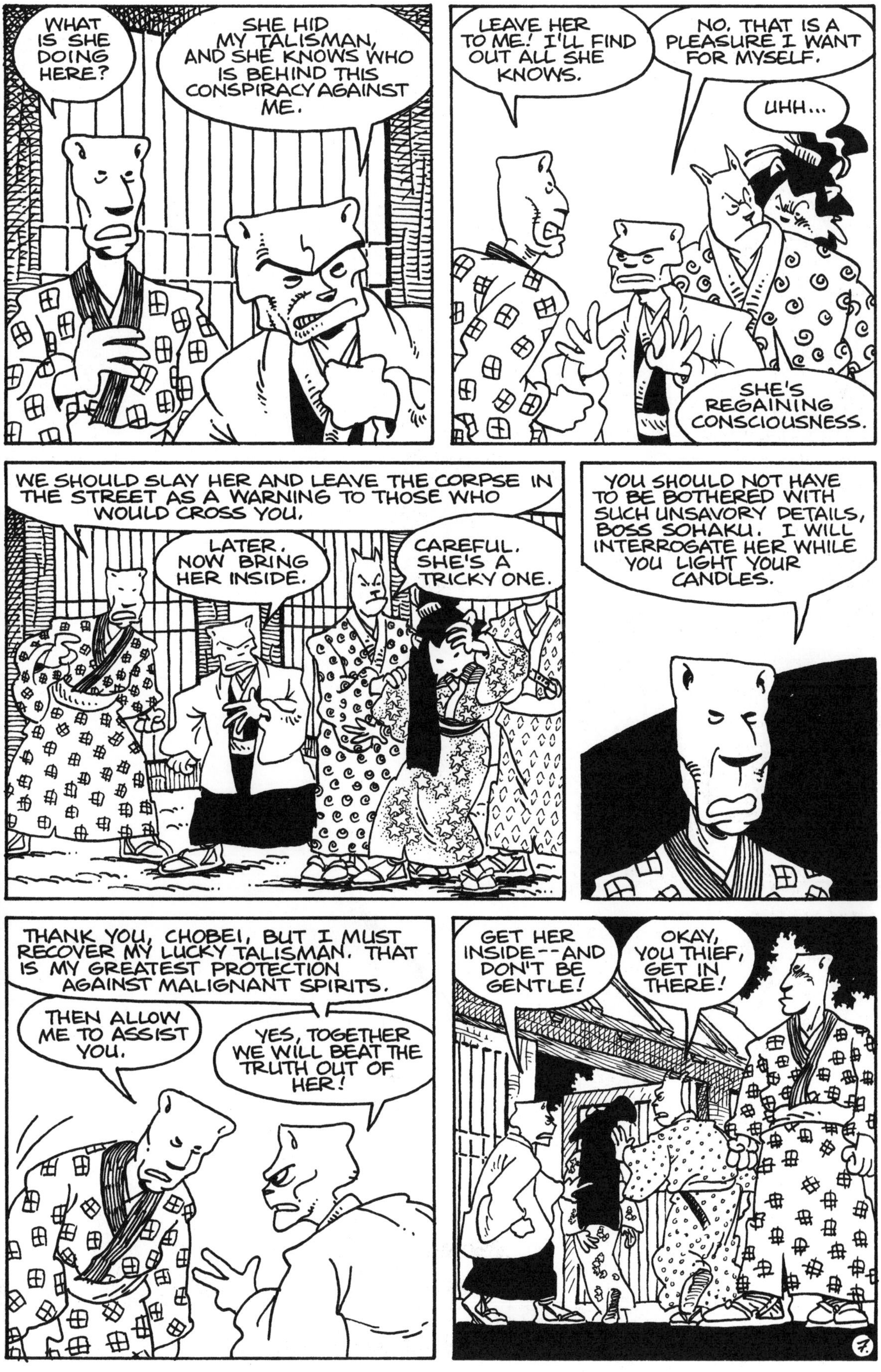
WHAT IS SHE DOING HERE?
SHE HID MY TALISMAN, AND SHE KNOWS WHO IS BEHIND THIS CONSPIRACY AGAINST ME.
LEAVE HER TO ME! I'LL FIND OUT ALL SHE KNOWS.
NO. THAT IS A PLEASURE I WANT FOR MYSELF.
UHH...
SHE'S REGAINING CONSCIOUSNESS.
WE SHOULD SLAY HER AND LEAVE THE CORPSE IN THE STREET AS A WARNING TO THOSE WHO WOULD CROSS YOU.
LATER. NOW BRING HER INSIDE.
CAREFUL. SHE'S A TRICKY ONE.
YOU SHOULD NOT HAVE TO BE BOTHERED WITH SUCH UNSAVORY DETAILS, BOSS SOHAKU. I WILL INTERROGATE HER WHILE YOU LIGHT YOUR CANDLES.
THANK YOU, CHOBEI, BUT I MUST RECOVER MY LUCKY TALISMAN. THAT IS MY GREATEST PROTECTION AGAINST MALIGNANT SPIRITS.
THEN ALLOW ME TO ASSIST YOU.
YES, TOGETHER WE WILL BEAT THE TRUTH OUT OF HER!
GET HER INSIDE--AND DON'T BE GENTLE!
OKAY, YOU THIEF, GET IN THERE!
7.

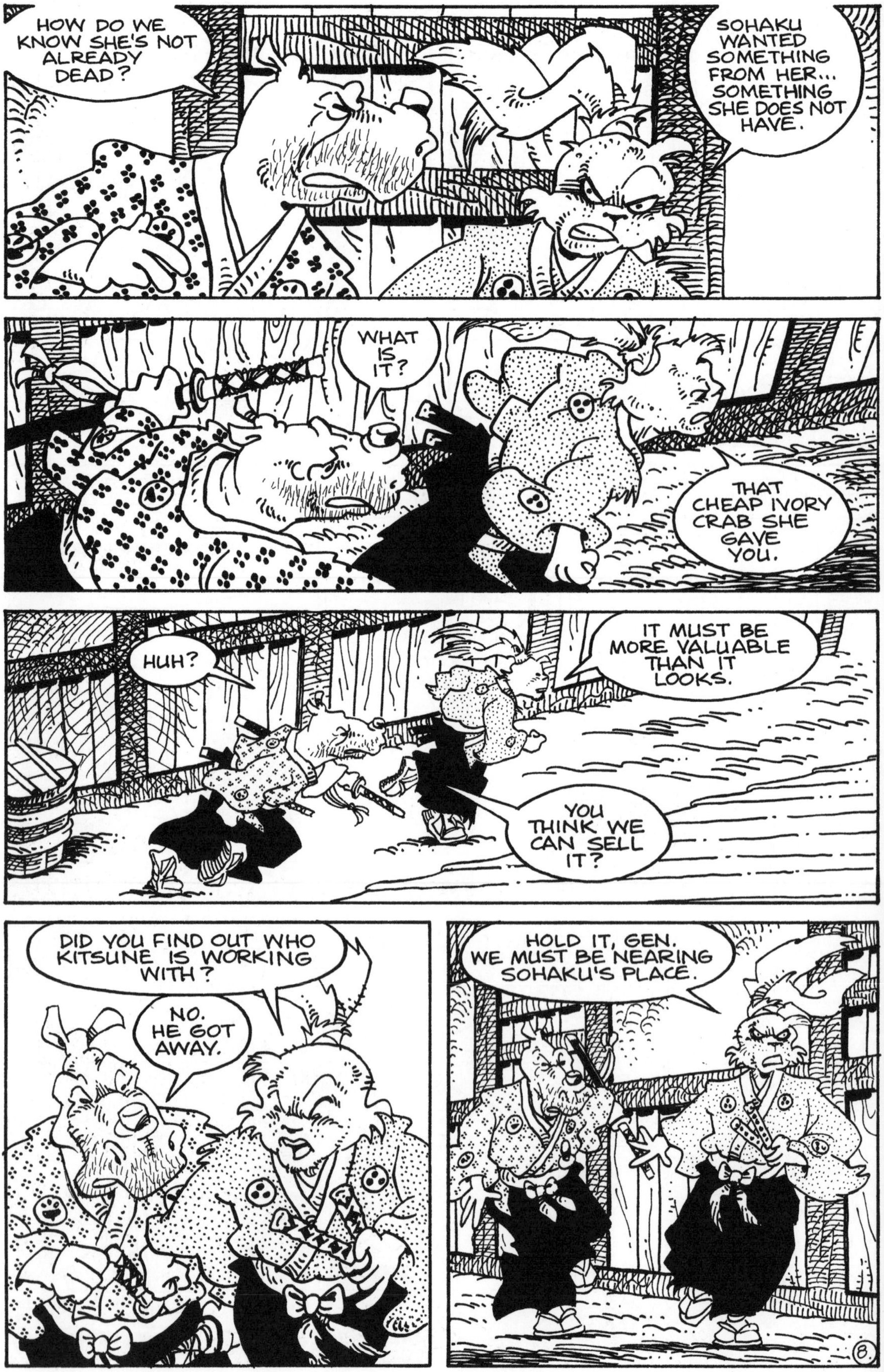
HOW DO WE KNOW SHE'S NOT ALREADY DEAD?
SOHAKU WANTED SOMETHING FROM HER... SOMETHING SHE DOES NOT HAVE.
WHAT IS IT?
THAT CHEAP IVORY CRAB SHE GAVE YOU.
HUH?
IT MUST BE MORE VALUABLE THAN IT LOOKS.
YOU THINK WE CAN SELL IT?
DID YOU FIND OUT WHO KITSUNE IS WORKING WITH?
NO. HE GOT AWAY.
HOLD IT, GEN. WE MUST BE NEARING SOHAKU'S PLACE.
8.

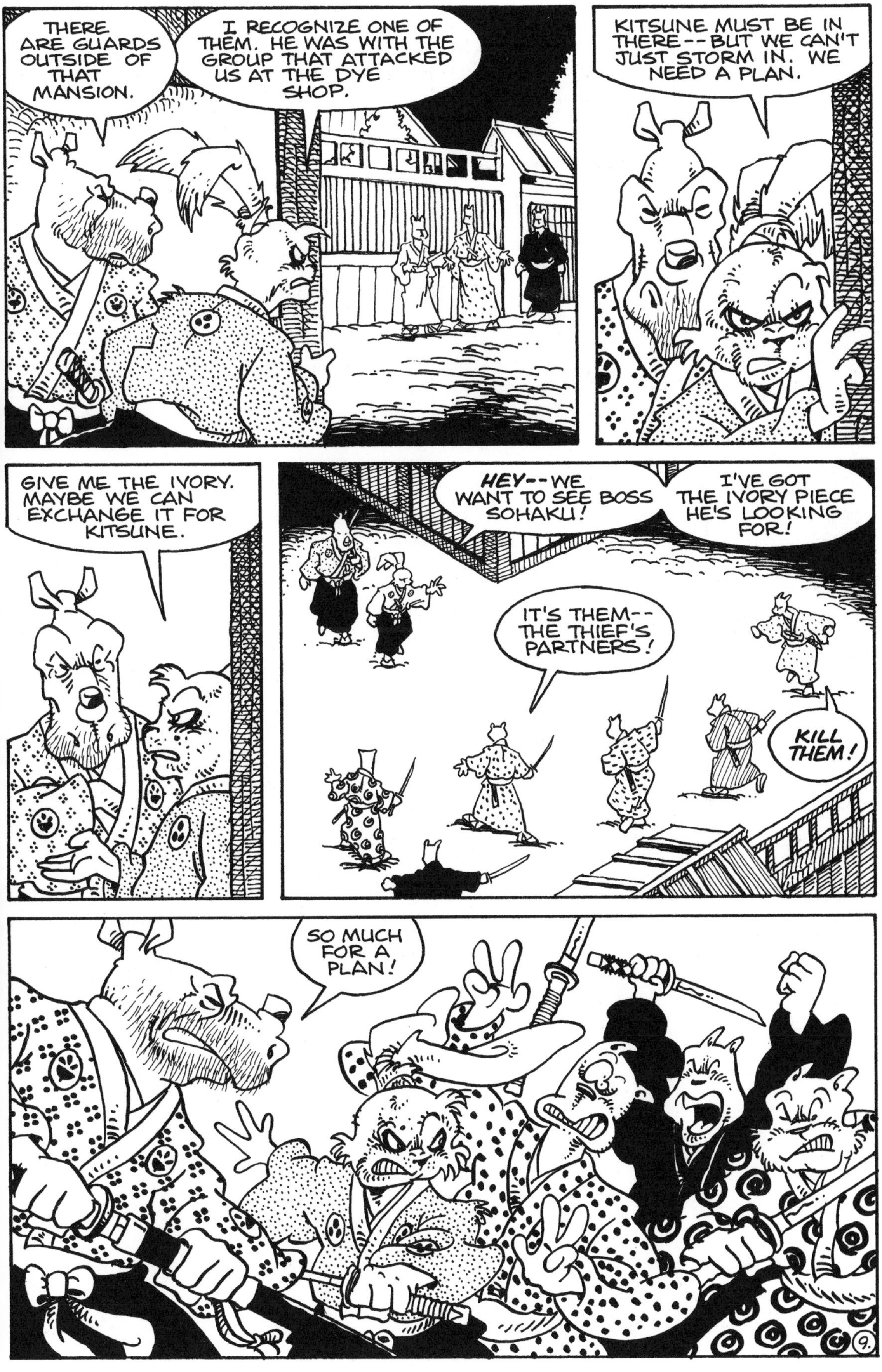
THERE ARE GUARDS OUTSIDE OF THAT MANSION.
I RECOGNIZE ONE OF THEM. HE WAS WITH THE GROUP THAT ATTACKED US AT THE DYE SHOP.
KITSUNE MUST BE IN THERE--BUT WE CAN'T JUST STORM IN. WE NEED A PLAN.
GIVE ME THE IVORY. MAYBE WE CAN EXCHANGE IT FOR KITSUNE.
HEY--WE WANT TO SEE BOSS SOHAKU!
I'VE GOT THE IVORY PIECE HE'S LOOKING FOR!
IT'S THEM--THE THIEF'S PARTNERS!
KILL THEM!
SO MUCH FOR A PLAN!
9.

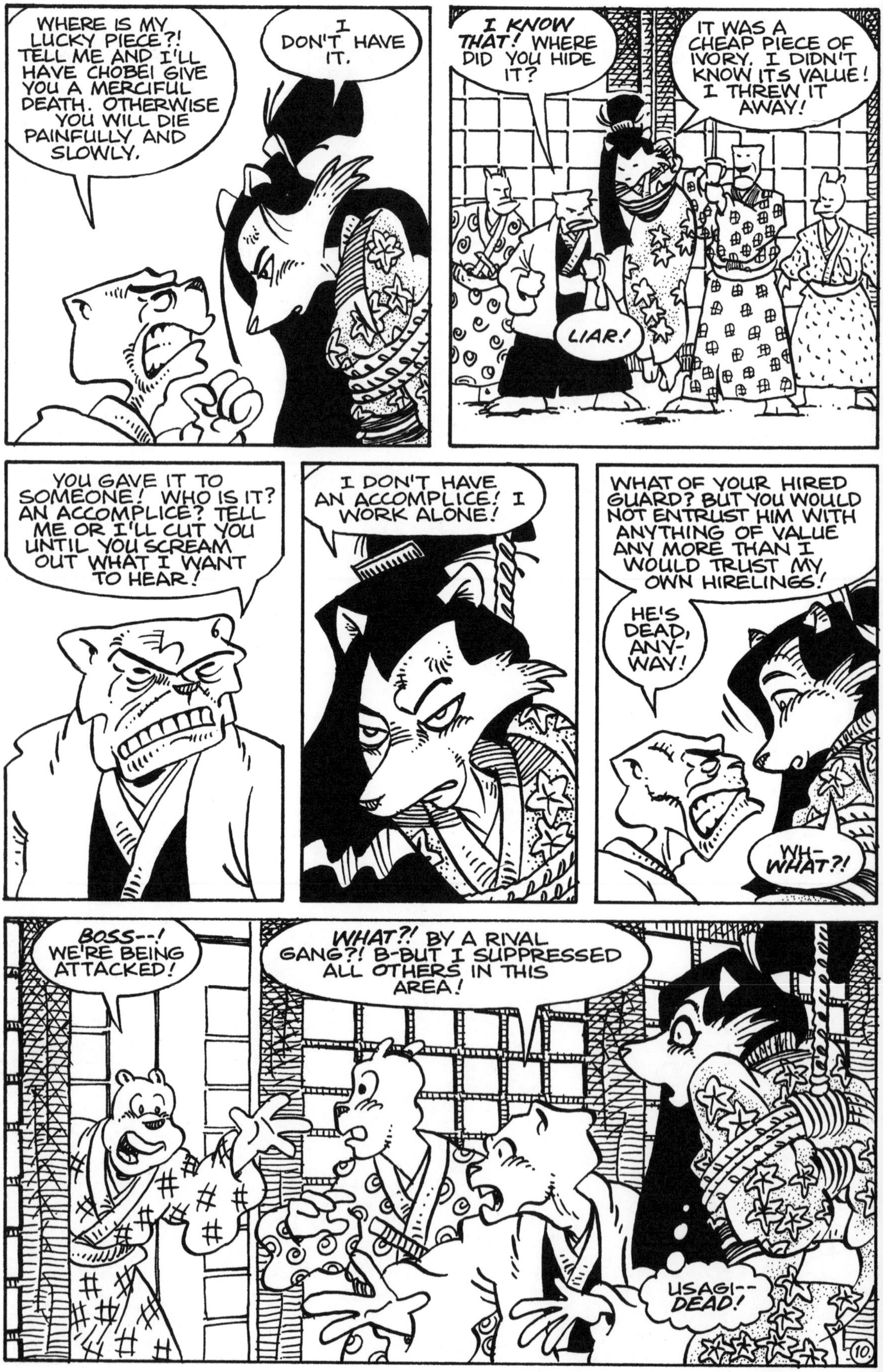
WHERE IS MY LUCKY PIECE?! TELL ME AND I'LL HAVE CHOBEI GIVE YOU A MERCIFUL DEATH. OTHERWISE YOU WILL DIE PAINFULLY AND SLOWLY.
I DON'T HAVE IT.
I KNOW THAT! WHERE DID YOU HIDE IT?
IT WAS A CHEAP PIECE OF IVORY. I DIDN'T KNOW ITS VALUE! I THREW IT AWAY!
LIAR!
YOU GAVE IT TO SOMEONE! WHO IS IT? AN ACCOMPLICE? TELL ME OR I'LL CUT YOU UNTIL YOU SCREAM OUT WHAT I WANT TO HEAR!
I DON'T HAVE AN ACCOMPLICE! I WORK ALONE!
WHAT OF YOUR HIRED GUARD? BUT YOU WOULD NOT ENTRUST HIM WITH ANYTHING OF VALUE ANY MORE THAN I WOULD TRUST MY OWN HIRELINGS!
HE'S DEAD, ANYWAY!
WH- WHAT?!
BOSS--! WE'RE BEING ATTACKED!
WHAT?! BY A RIVAL GANG?! B-BUT I SUPPRESSED ALL OTHERS IN THIS AREA!
USAGI-- DEAD!
10

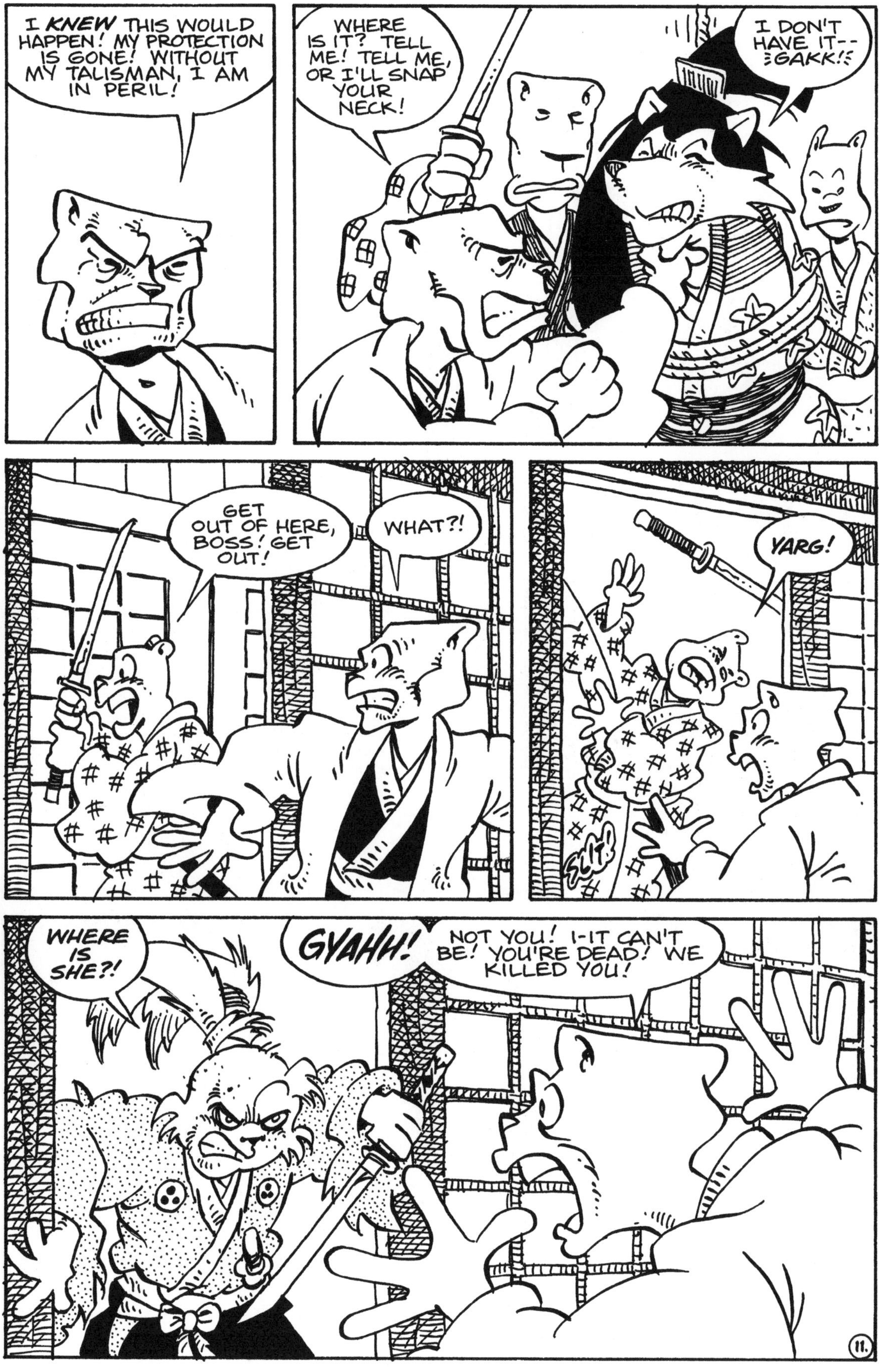

I KNEW THIS WOULD HAPPEN! MY PROTECTION IS GONE! WITHOUT MY TALISMAN, I AM IN PERIL!
WHERE IS IT? TELL ME! TELL ME, OR I'LL SNAP YOUR NECK!
I DON'T HAVE IT-- GAKK!
GET OUT OF HERE, BOSS! GET OUT!
WHAT?!
YARG!
SLIT!
WHERE IS SHE?!
GYAHH!
NOT YOU! I-IT CAN'T BE! YOU'RE DEAD! WE KILLED YOU!
11.

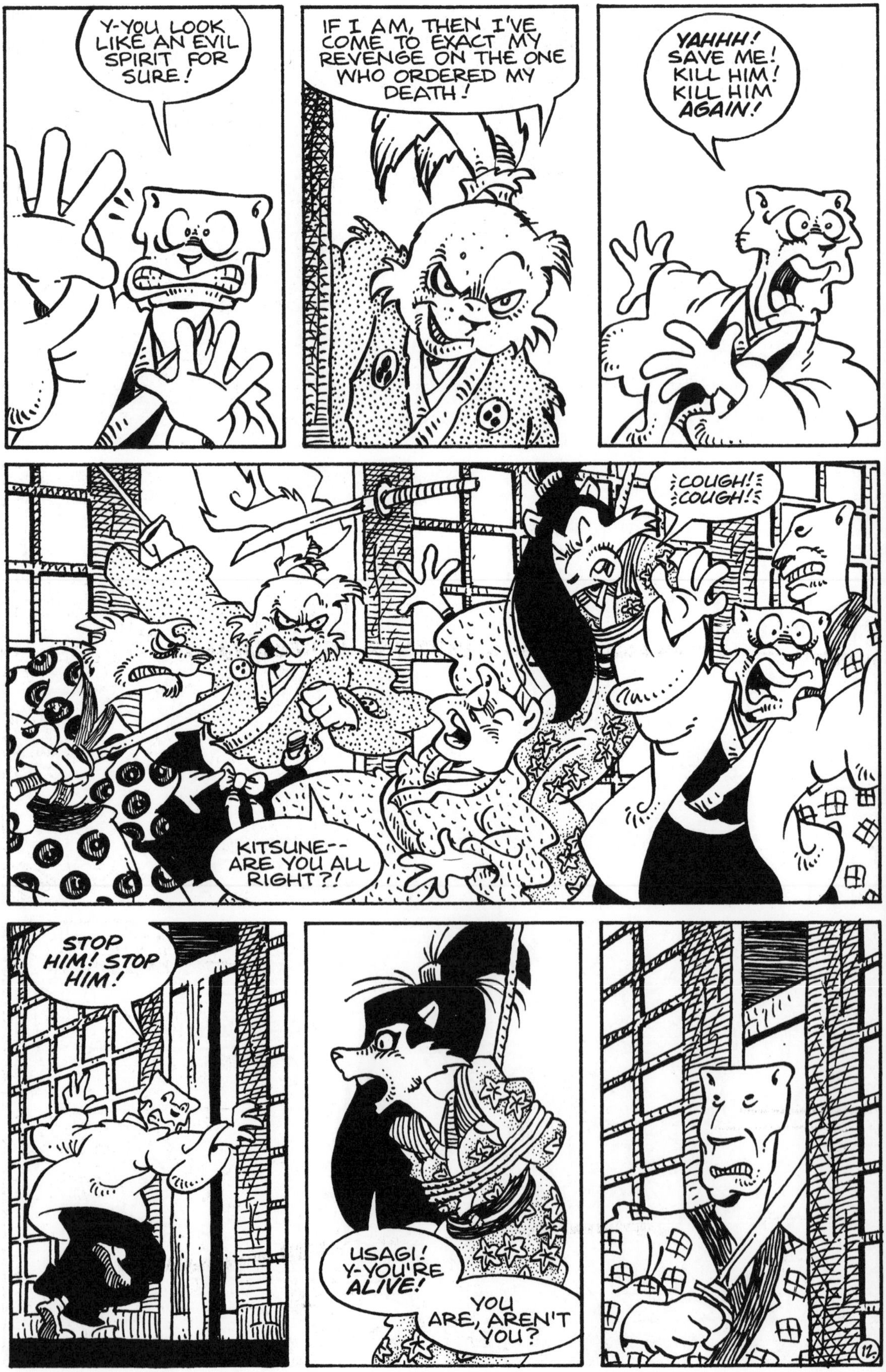

Y-YOU LOOK LIKE AN EVIL SPIRIT FOR SURE!
IF I AM, THEN I'VE COME TO EXACT MY REVENGE ON THE ONE WHO ORDERED MY DEATH!
YAHHH! SAVE ME! KILL HIM! KILL HIM AGAIN!
COUGH! COUGH!
KITSUNE-- ARE YOU ALL RIGHT?!
STOP HIM! STOP HIM!
USAGI! Y-YOU'RE ALIVE!
YOU ARE, AREN'T YOU?
12.

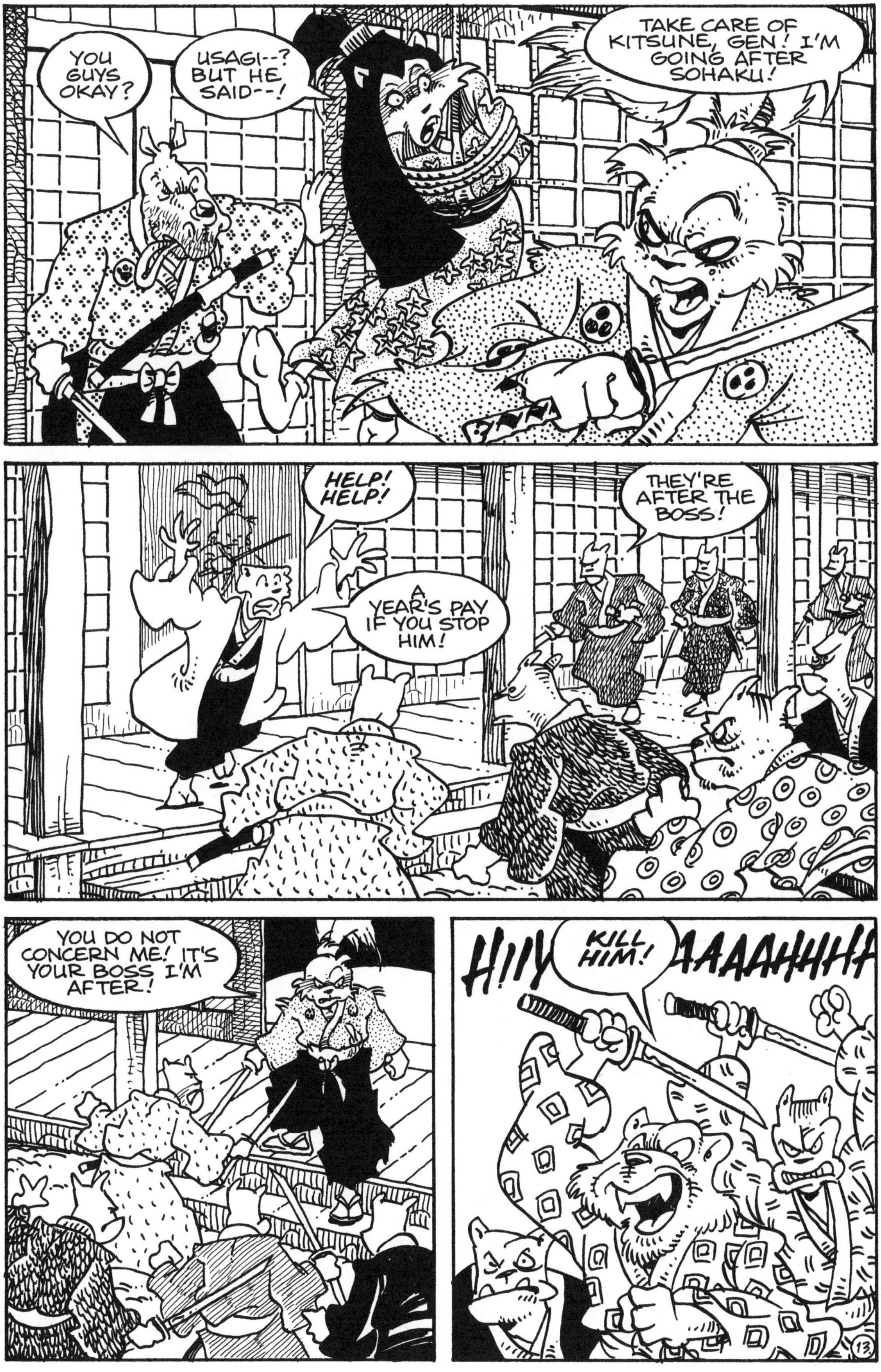

YOU GUYS OKAY?
USAGI--? BUT HE SAID--!
TAKE CARE OF KITSUNE, GEN! I'M GOING AFTER SOHAKU!
HELP! HELP!
A YEAR'S PAY IF YOU STOP HIM!
THEY'RE AFTER THE BOSS!
YOU DO NOT CONCERN ME! IT'S YOUR BOSS I'M AFTER!
HIIY
KILL HIM!
AAAAHHHA
13

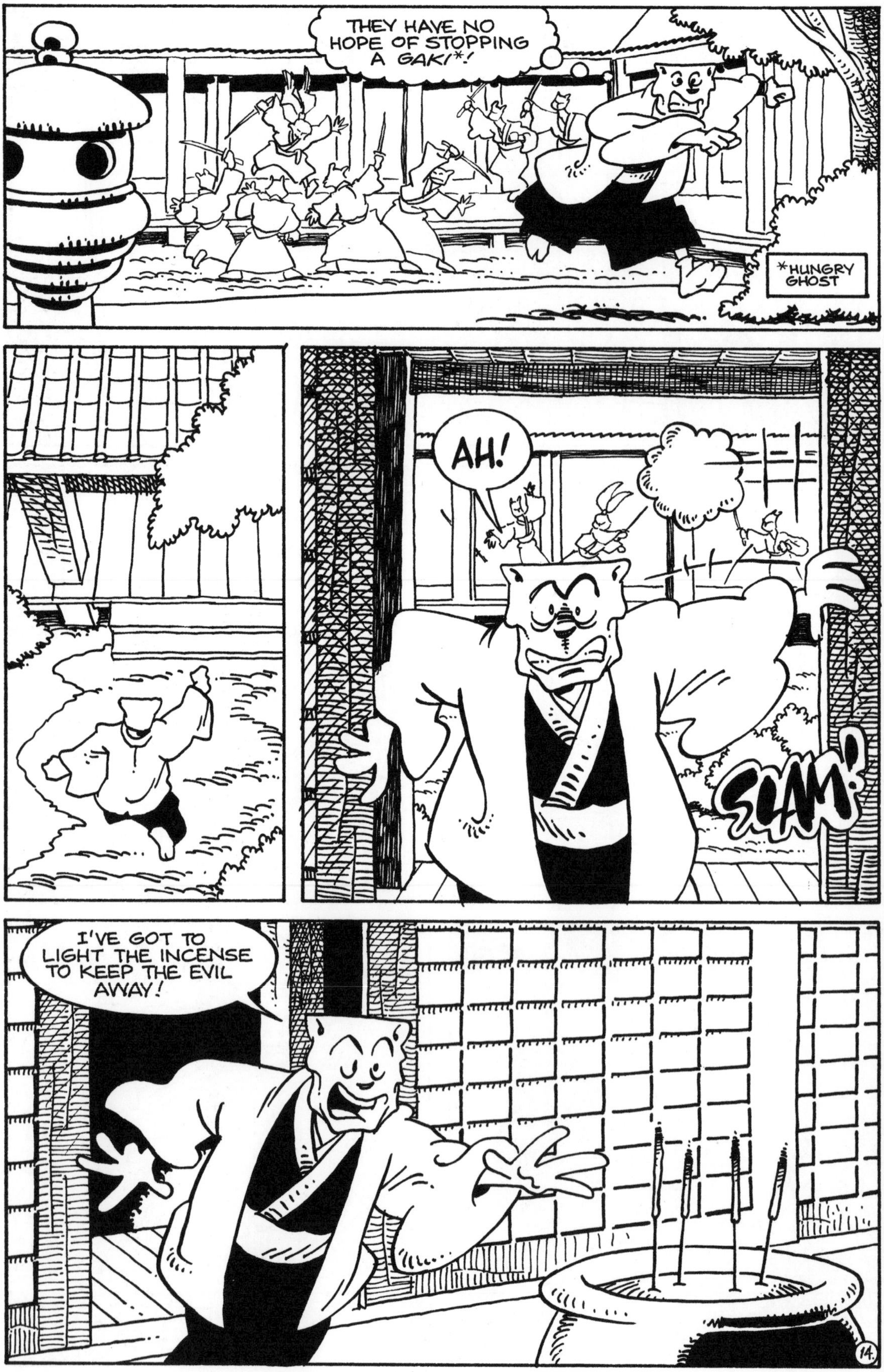
THEY HAVE NO HOPE OF STOPPING A GAKI*!
*HUNGRY GHOST
AH!
SLAM!
I'VE GOT TO LIGHT THE INCENSE TO KEEP THE EVIL AWAY!
14.

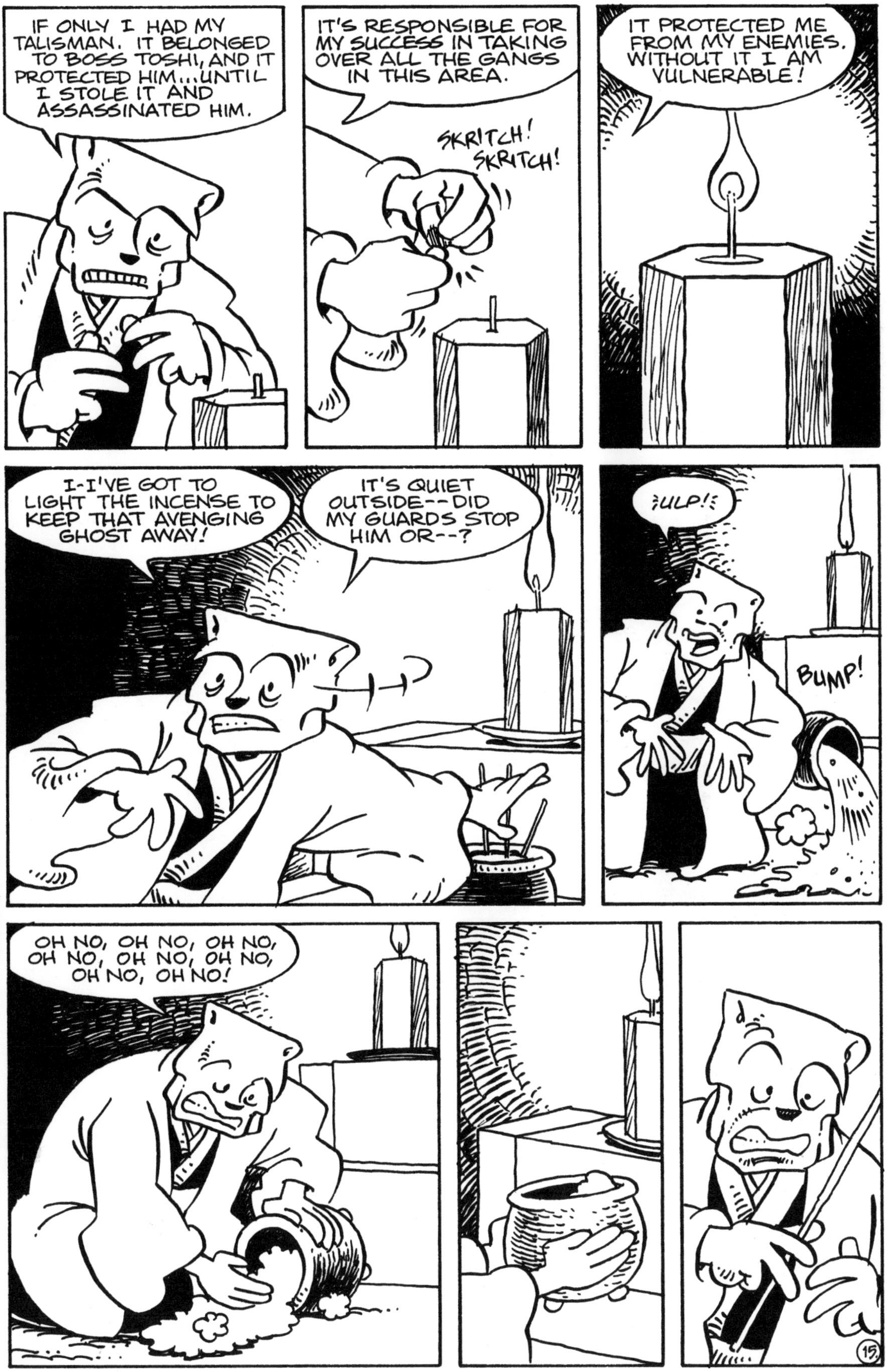

IF ONLY I HAD MY TALISMAN. IT BELONGED TO BOSS TOSHI, AND IT PROTECTED HIM...UNTIL I STOLE IT AND ASSASSINATED HIM.
IT'S RESPONSIBLE FOR MY SUCCESS IN TAKING OVER ALL THE GANGS IN THIS AREA.
SKRITCH! SKRITCH!
IT PROTECTED ME FROM MY ENEMIES. WITHOUT IT I AM VULNERABLE!
I-I'VE GOT TO LIGHT THE INCENSE TO KEEP THAT AVENGING GHOST AWAY!
IT'S QUIET OUTSIDE--DID MY GUARDS STOP HIM OR--?
ULP!
BUMP!
OH NO, OH NO, OH NO, OH NO, OH NO, OH NO, OH NO, OH NO!
15

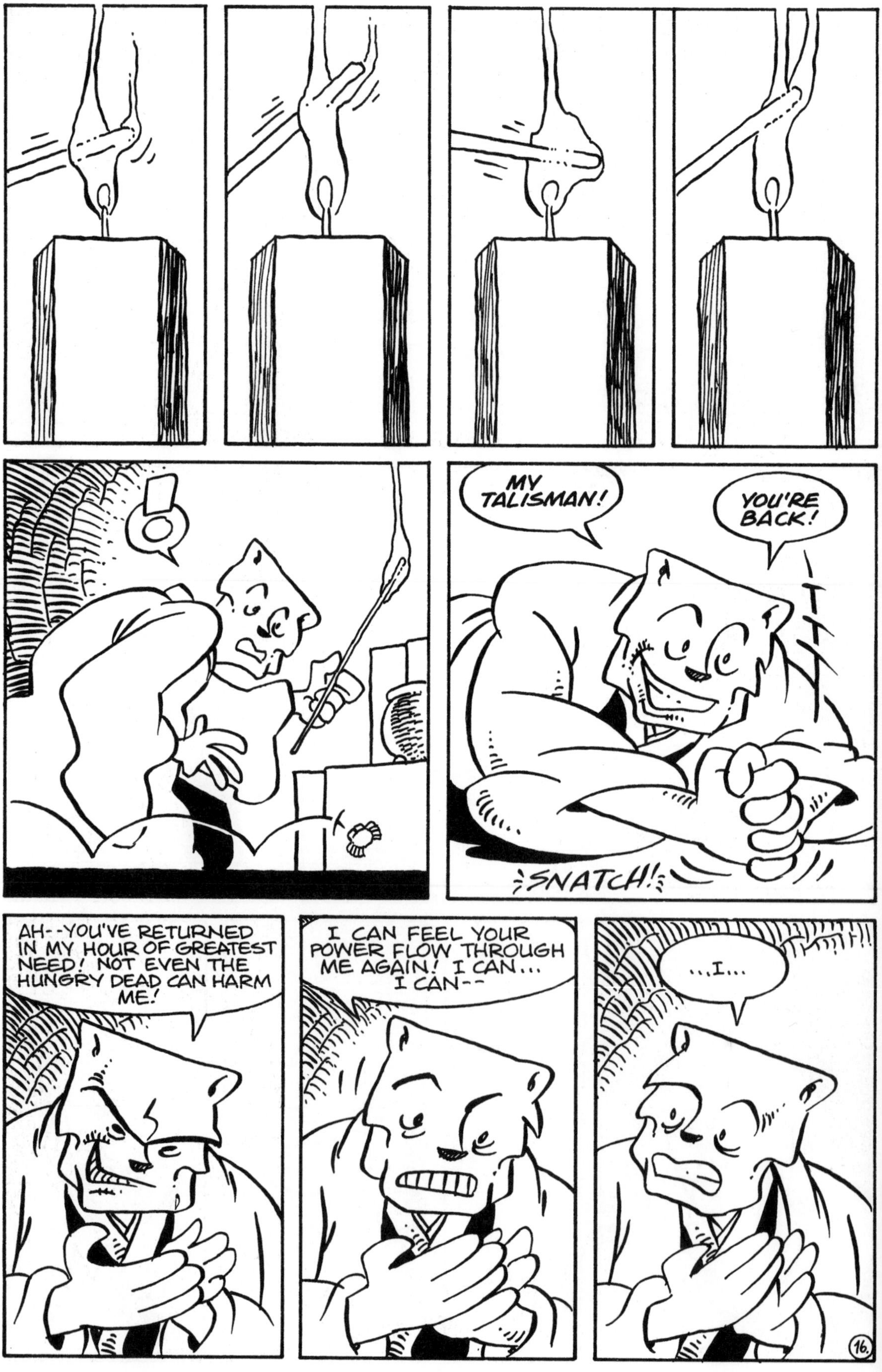
!
MY TALISMAN!
YOU'RE BACK!
SNATCH!
AH--YOU'VE RETURNED IN MY HOUR OF GREATEST NEED! NOT EVEN THE HUNGRY DEAD CAN HARM ME!
I CAN FEEL YOUR POWER FLOW THROUGH ME AGAIN! I CAN... I CAN--
...I...
16.

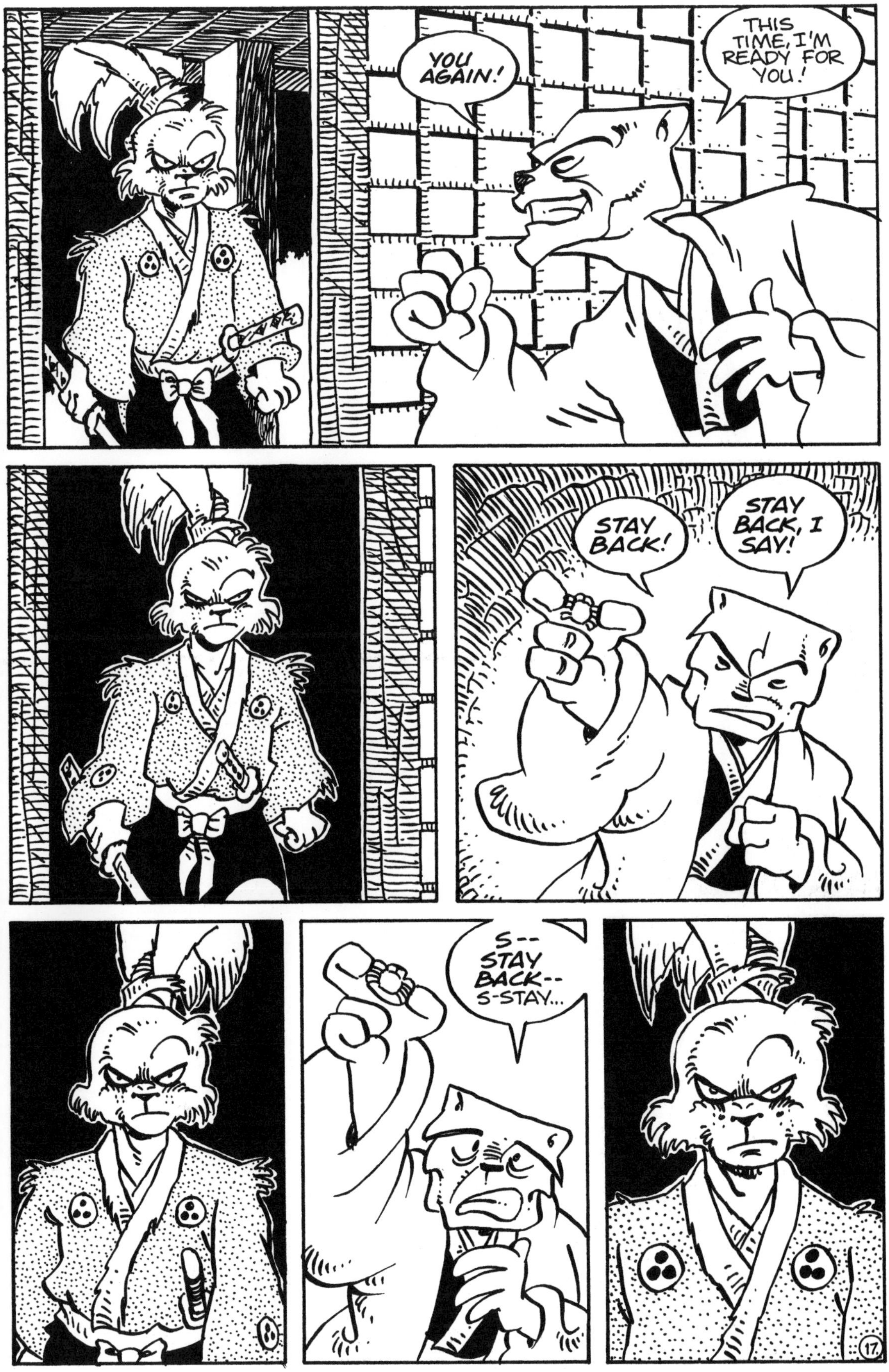

YOU AGAIN!
THIS TIME, I'M READY FOR YOU!
STAY BACK!
STAY BACK, I SAY!
S-- STAY BACK-- S-STAY...
17

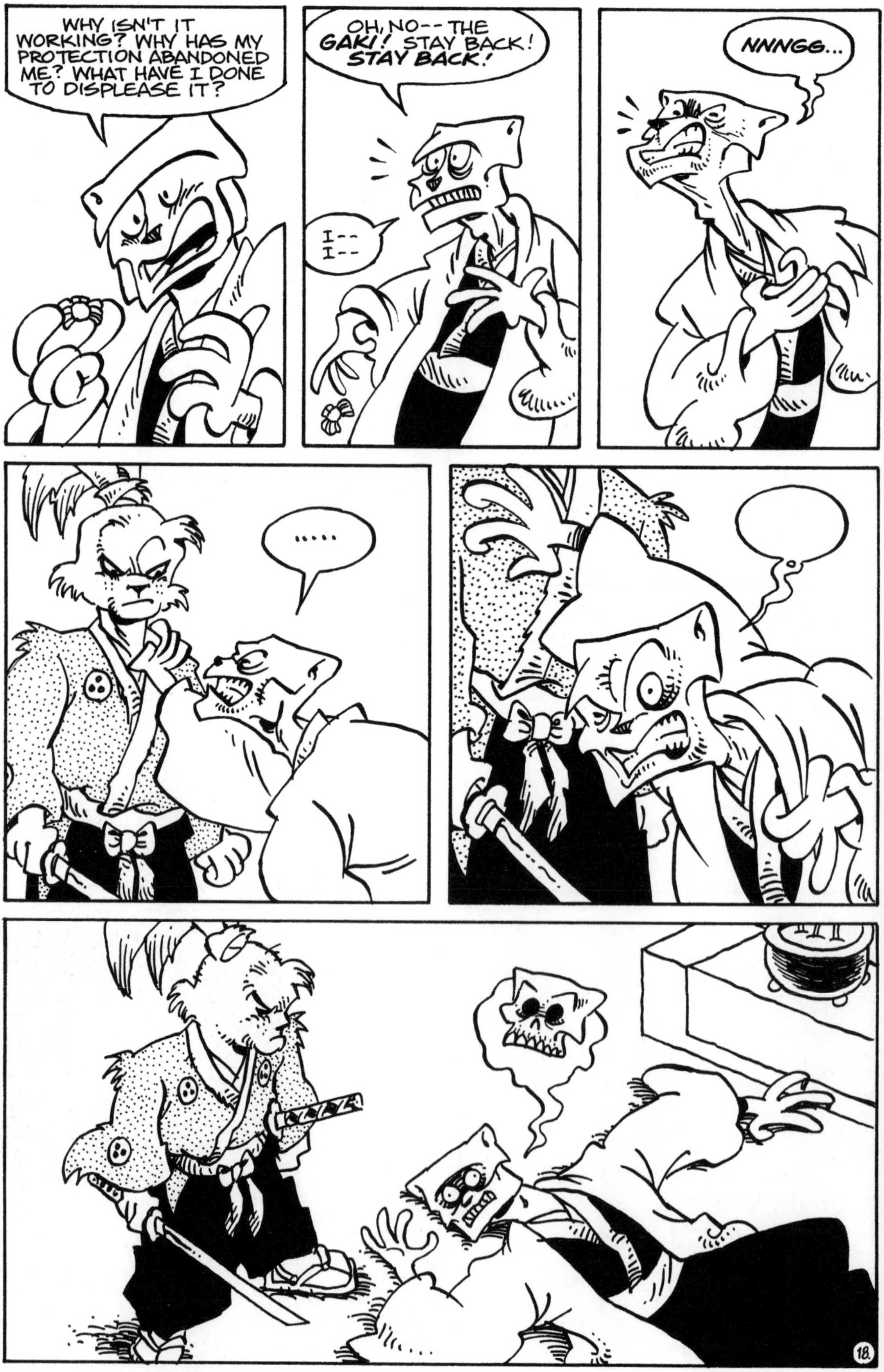
WHY ISN'T IT WORKING? WHY HAS MY PROTECTION ABANDONED ME? WHAT HAVE I DONE TO DISPLEASE IT?
OH, NO-- THE GAKI! STAY BACK! STAY BACK!
I-- I--
NNNGG...
.....
18.

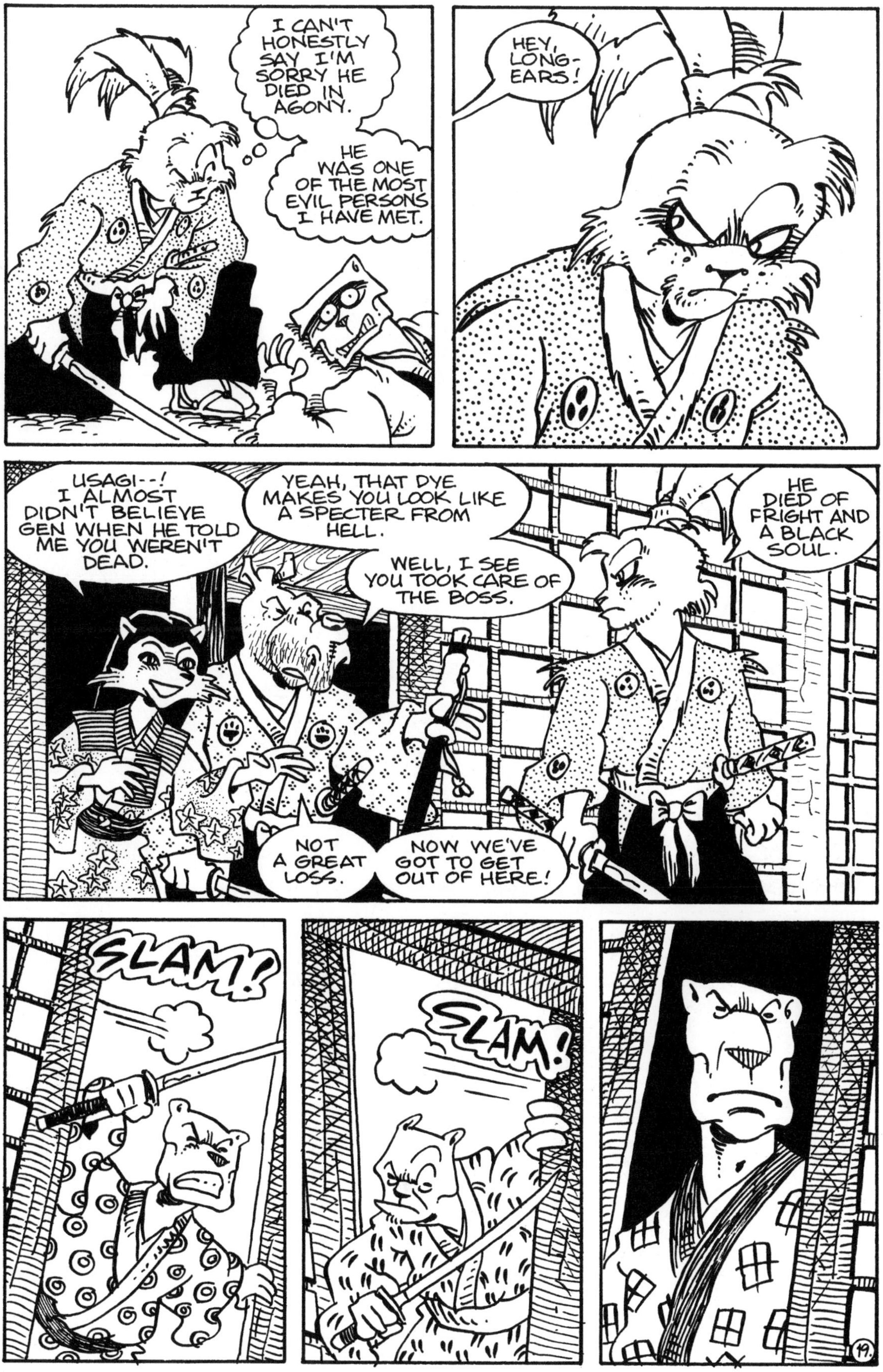
I CAN'T HONESTLY SAY I'M SORRY HE DIED IN AGONY.
HE WAS ONE OF THE MOST EVIL PERSONS I HAVE MET.
HEY, LONG-EARS!
USAGI--! I ALMOST DIDN'T BELIEVE GEN WHEN HE TOLD ME YOU WEREN'T DEAD.
YEAH, THAT DYE MAKES YOU LOOK LIKE A SPECTER FROM HELL.
WELL, I SEE YOU TOOK CARE OF THE BOSS.
HE DIED OF FRIGHT AND A BLACK SOUL.
NOT A GREAT LOSS.
NOW WE'VE GOT TO GET OUT OF HERE!
SLAM!
SLAM!
19.

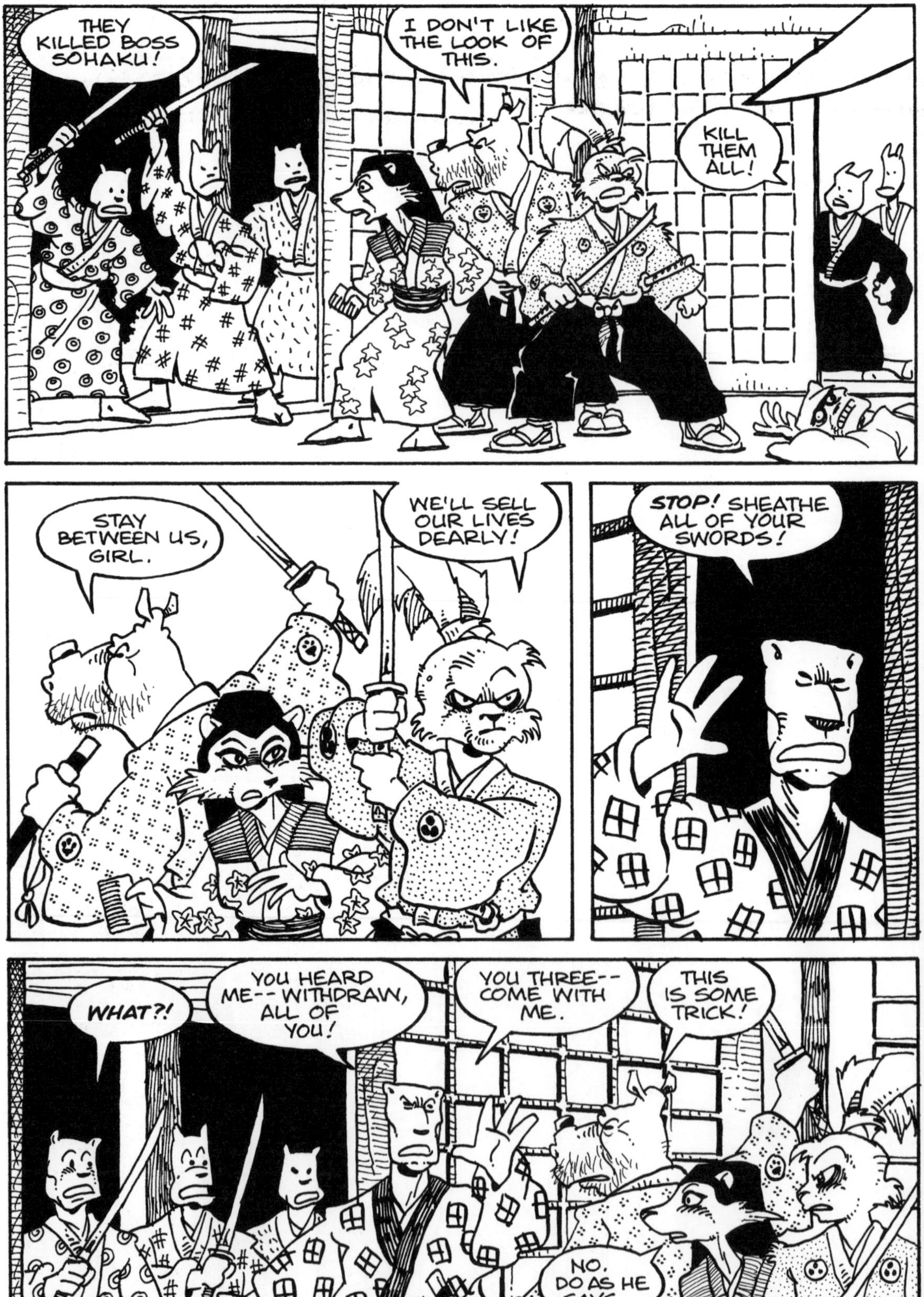
THEY KILLED BOSS SOHAKU!
I DON'T LIKE THE LOOK OF THIS.
KILL THEM ALL!
STAY BETWEEN US, GIRL.
WE'LL SELL OUR LIVES DEARLY!
STOP! SHEATHE ALL OF YOUR SWORDS!
WHAT?!
YOU HEARD ME-- WITHDRAW, ALL OF YOU!
YOU THREE-- COME WITH ME.
THIS IS SOME TRICK!
NO. DO AS HE SAYS.
20.

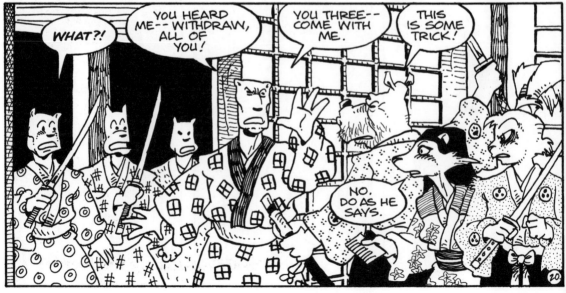

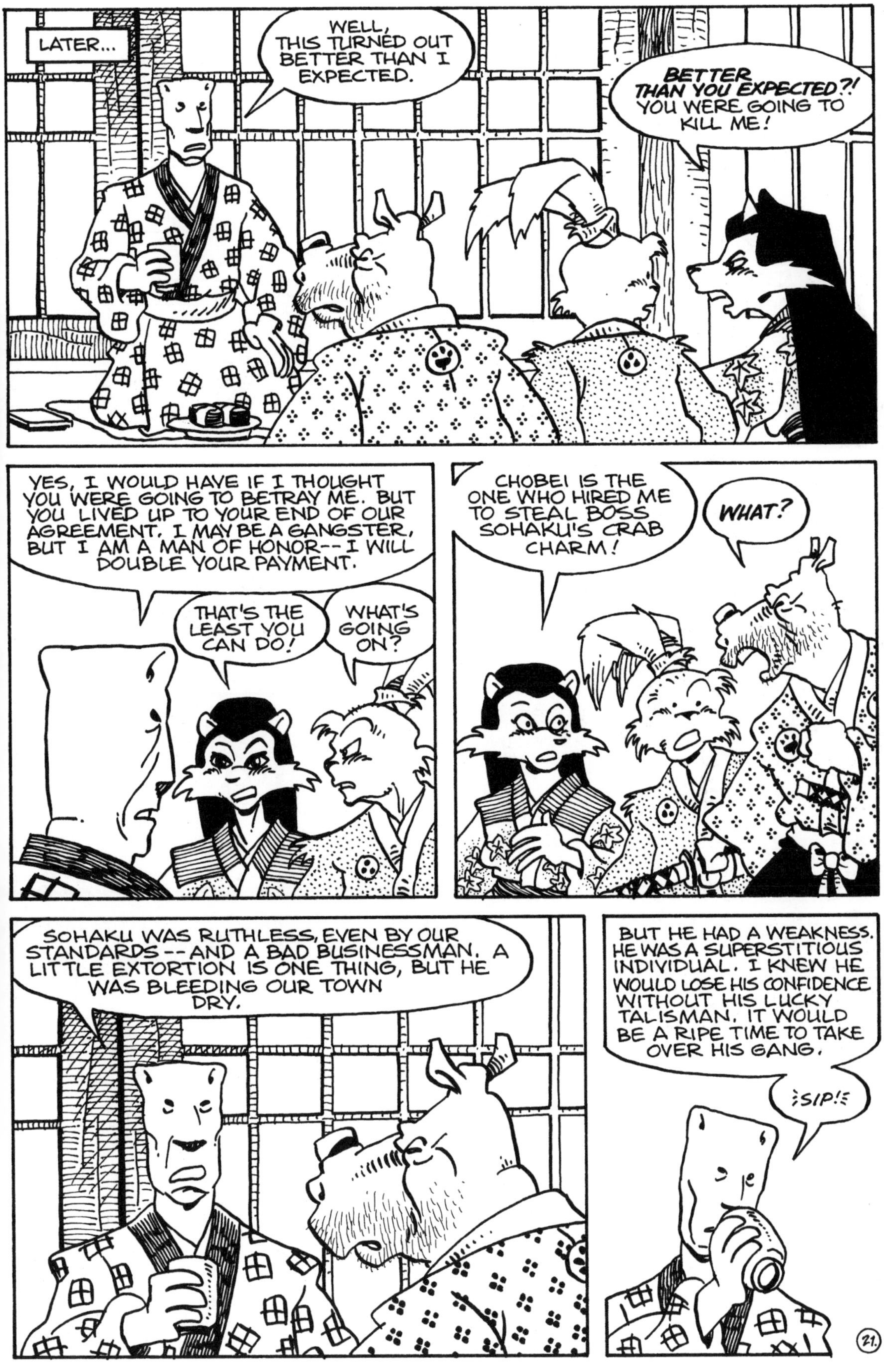
LATER...
WELL, THIS TURNED OUT BETTER THAN I EXPECTED.
BETTER THAN YOU EXPECTED?! YOU WERE GOING TO KILL ME!
YES, I WOULD HAVE IF I THOUGHT YOU WERE GOING TO BETRAY ME. BUT YOU LIVED UP TO YOUR END OF OUR AGREEMENT. I MAY BE A GANGSTER, BUT I AM A MAN OF HONOR-- I WILL DOUBLE YOUR PAYMENT.
THAT'S THE LEAST YOU CAN DO!
WHAT'S GOING ON?
CHOBEI IS THE ONE WHO HIRED ME TO STEAL BOSS SOHAKU'S CRAB CHARM!
WHAT?
SOHAKU WAS RUTHLESS, EVEN BY OUR STANDARDS--AND A BAD BUSINESSMAN. A LITTLE EXTORTION IS ONE THING, BUT HE WAS BLEEDING OUR TOWN DRY.
BUT HE HAD A WEAKNESS. HE WAS A SUPERSTITIOUS INDIVIDUAL. I KNEW HE WOULD LOSE HIS CONFIDENCE WITHOUT HIS LUCKY TALISMAN. IT WOULD BE A RIPE TIME TO TAKE OVER HIS GANG.
SIP!
21.

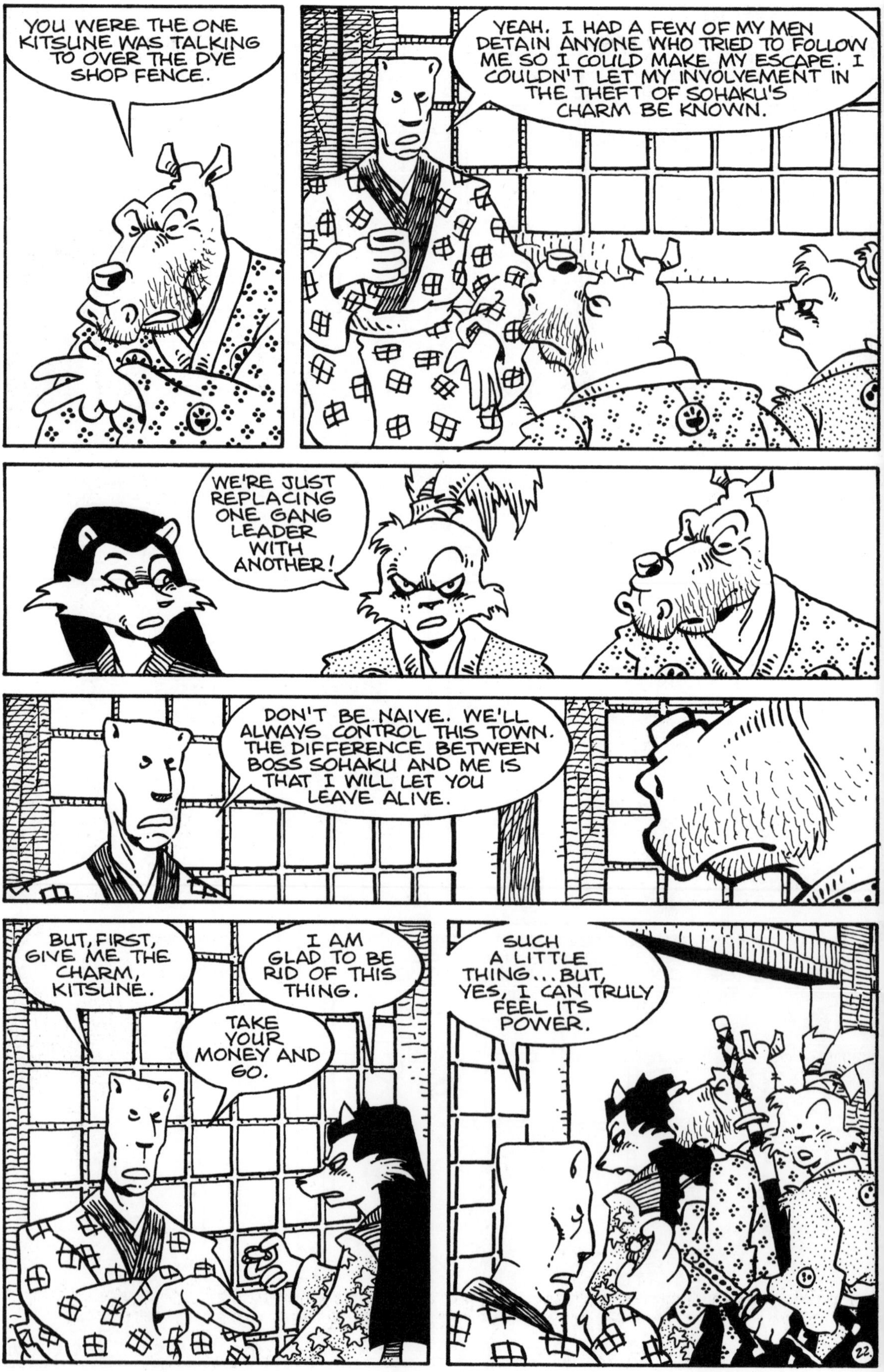
YOU WERE THE ONE KITSUNE WAS TALKING TO OVER THE DYE SHOP FENCE.
YEAH. I HAD A FEW OF MY MEN DETAIN ANYONE WHO TRIED TO FOLLOW ME SO I COULD MAKE MY ESCAPE. I COULDN'T LET MY INVOLVEMENT IN THE THEFT OF SOHAKU'S CHARM BE KNOWN.
WE'RE JUST REPLACING ONE GANG LEADER WITH ANOTHER!
DON'T BE NAIVE. WE'LL ALWAYS CONTROL THIS TOWN. THE DIFFERENCE BETWEEN BOSS SOHAKU AND ME IS THAT I WILL LET YOU LEAVE ALIVE.
BUT, FIRST, GIVE ME THE CHARM, KITSUNE.
I AM GLAD TO BE RID OF THIS THING.
TAKE YOUR MONEY AND GO.
SUCH A LITTLE THING... BUT, YES, I CAN TRULY FEEL ITS POWER.
22.

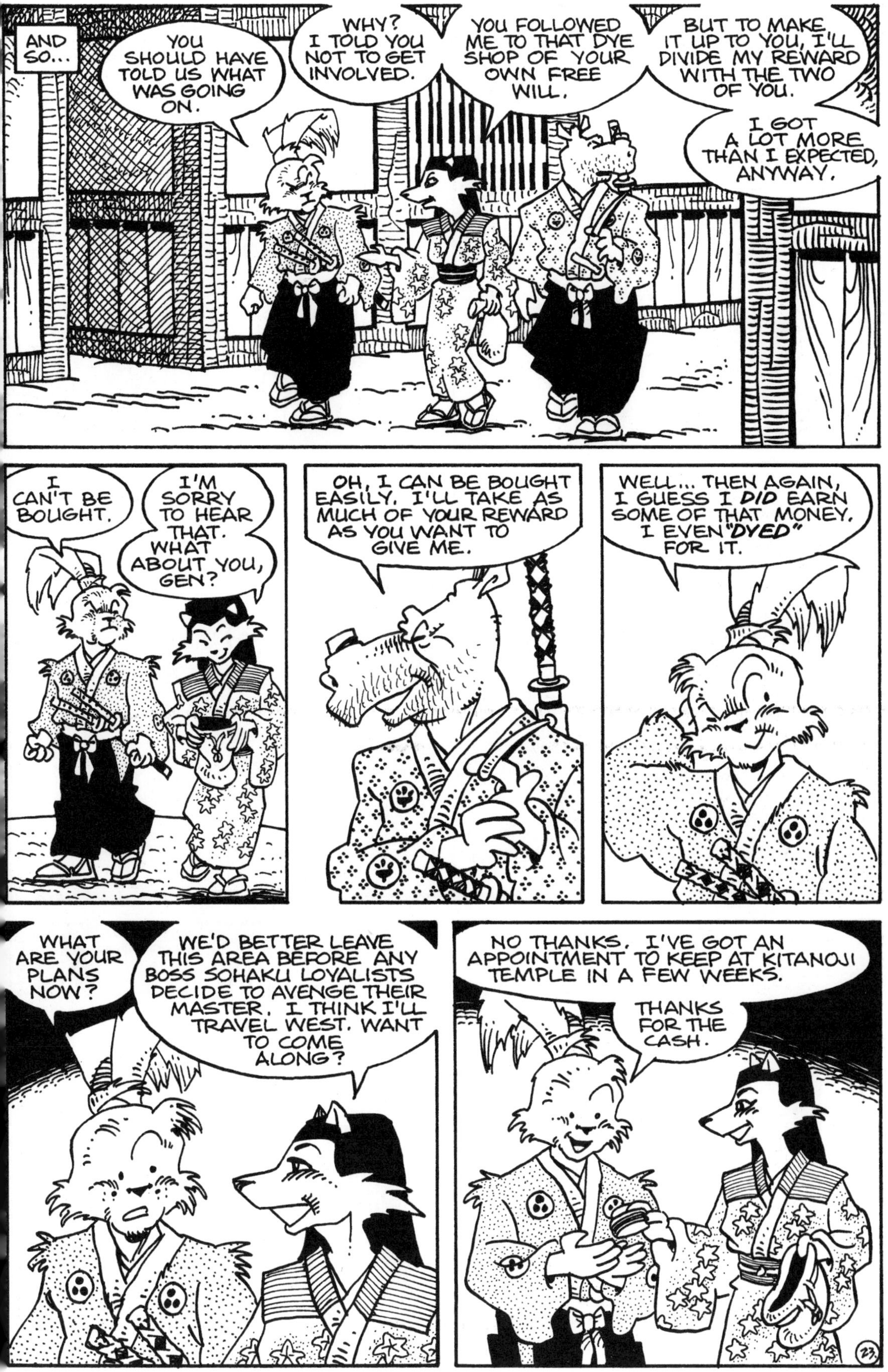
AND SO...
YOU SHOULD HAVE TOLD US WHAT WAS GOING ON.
WHY? I TOLD YOU NOT TO GET INVOLVED.
YOU FOLLOWED ME TO THAT DYE SHOP OF YOUR OWN FREE WILL.
BUT TO MAKE IT UP TO YOU, I'LL DIVIDE MY REWARD WITH THE TWO OF YOU.
I GOT A LOT MORE THAN I EXPECTED, ANYWAY.
I CAN'T BE BOUGHT.
I'M SORRY TO HEAR THAT. WHAT ABOUT YOU, GEN?
OH, I CAN BE BOUGHT EASILY. I'LL TAKE AS MUCH OF YOUR REWARD AS YOU WANT TO GIVE ME.
WELL... THEN AGAIN, I GUESS I DID EARN SOME OF THAT MONEY. I EVEN "DYED" FOR IT.
WHAT ARE YOUR PLANS NOW?
WE'D BETTER LEAVE THIS AREA BEFORE ANY BOSS SOHAKU LOYALISTS DECIDE TO AVENGE THEIR MASTER. I THINK I'LL TRAVEL WEST. WANT TO COME ALONG?
NO THANKS. I'VE GOT AN APPOINTMENT TO KEEP AT KITANOJI TEMPLE IN A FEW WEEKS.
THANKS FOR THE CASH.
23.

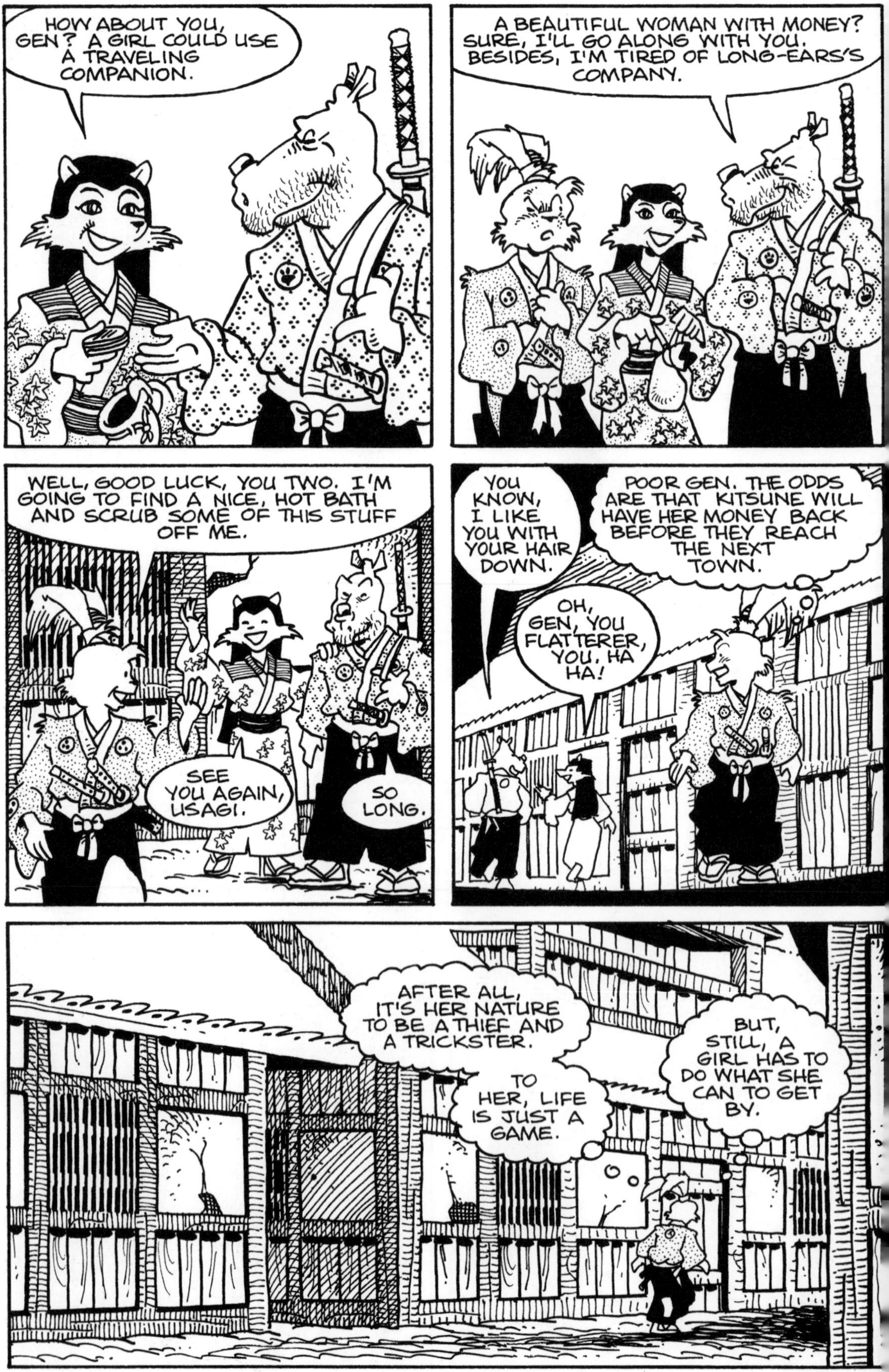
HOW ABOUT YOU, GEN? A GIRL COULD USE A TRAVELING COMPANION.
A BEAUTIFUL WOMAN WITH MONEY? SURE, I'LL GO ALONG WITH YOU. BESIDES, I'M TIRED OF LONG-EARS'S COMPANY.
WELL, GOOD LUCK, YOU TWO. I'M GOING TO FIND A NICE, HOT BATH AND SCRUB SOME OF THIS STUFF OFF ME.
SEE YOU AGAIN, USAGI.
SO LONG.
YOU KNOW, I LIKE YOU WITH YOUR HAIR DOWN.
POOR GEN. THE ODDS ARE THAT KITSUNE WILL HAVE HER MONEY BACK BEFORE THEY REACH THE NEXT TOWN.
OH, GEN, YOU FLATTERER, YOU. HA HA!
AFTER ALL, IT'S HER NATURE TO BE A THIEF AND A TRICKSTER.
TO HER, LIFE IS JUST A GAME.
BUT, STILL, A GIRL HAS TO DO WHAT SHE CAN TO GET BY.
THE END

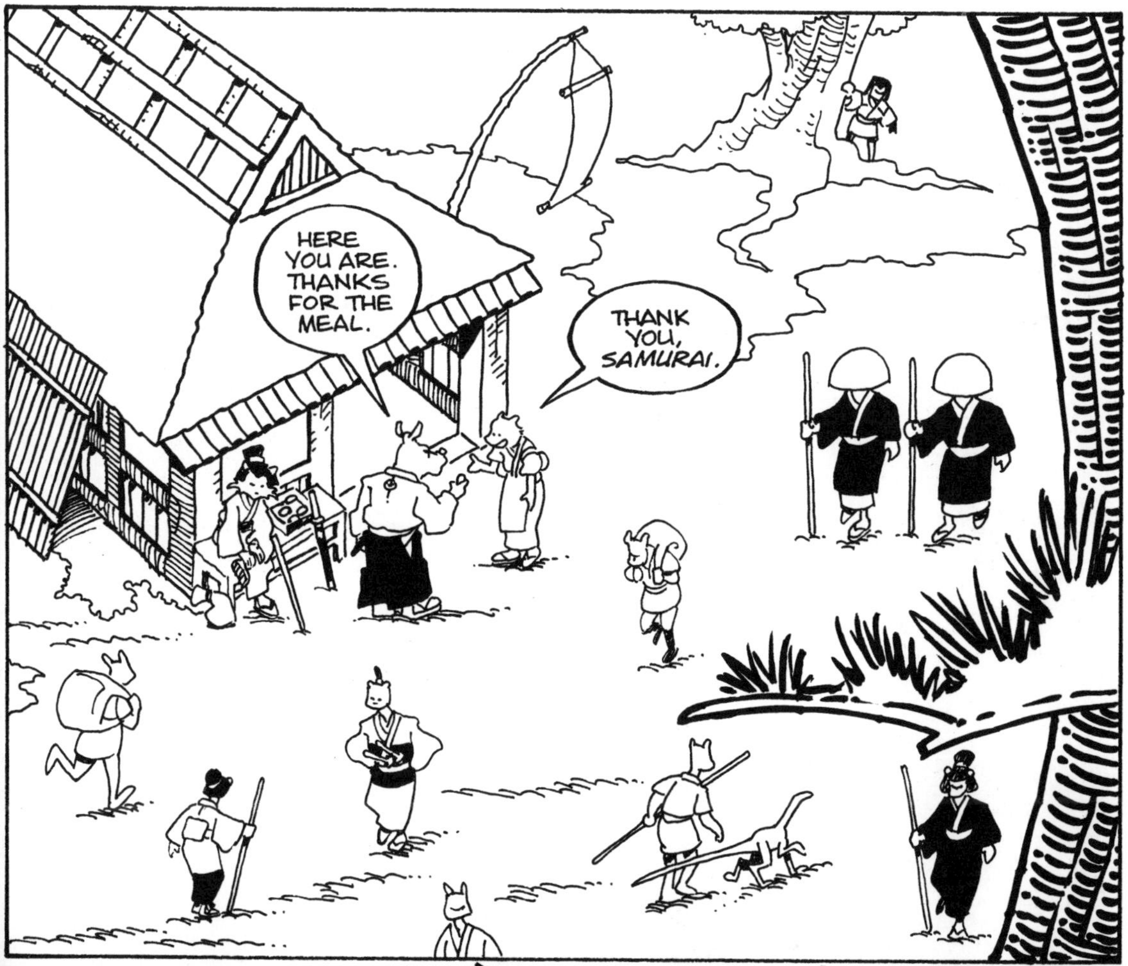
HERE YOU ARE. THANKS FOR THE MEAL.
THANK YOU, SAMURAI.

KITSUNE'S TALE

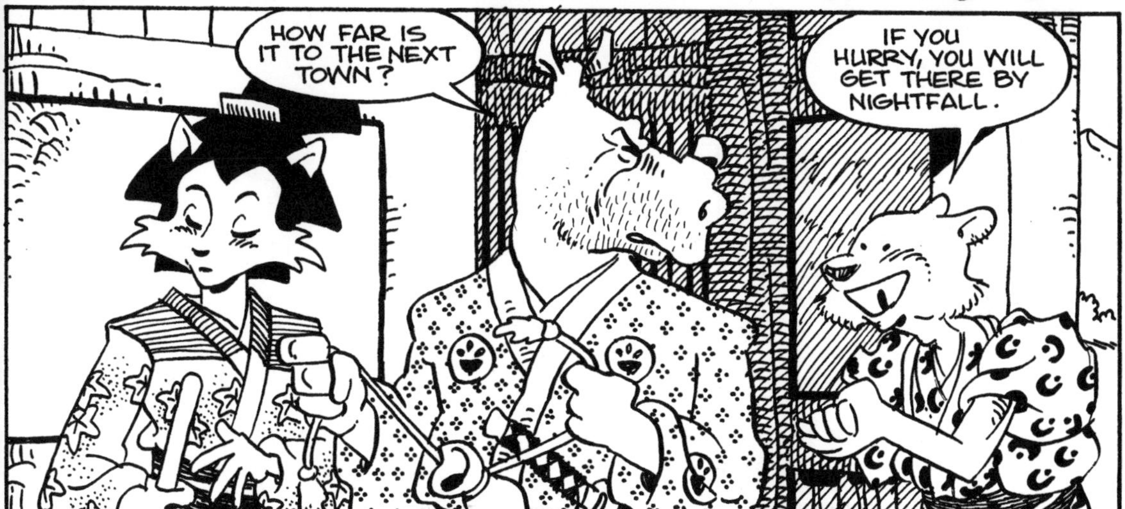
HOW FAR IS IT TO THE NEXT TOWN?
IF YOU HURRY, YOU WILL GET THERE BY NIGHTFALL.

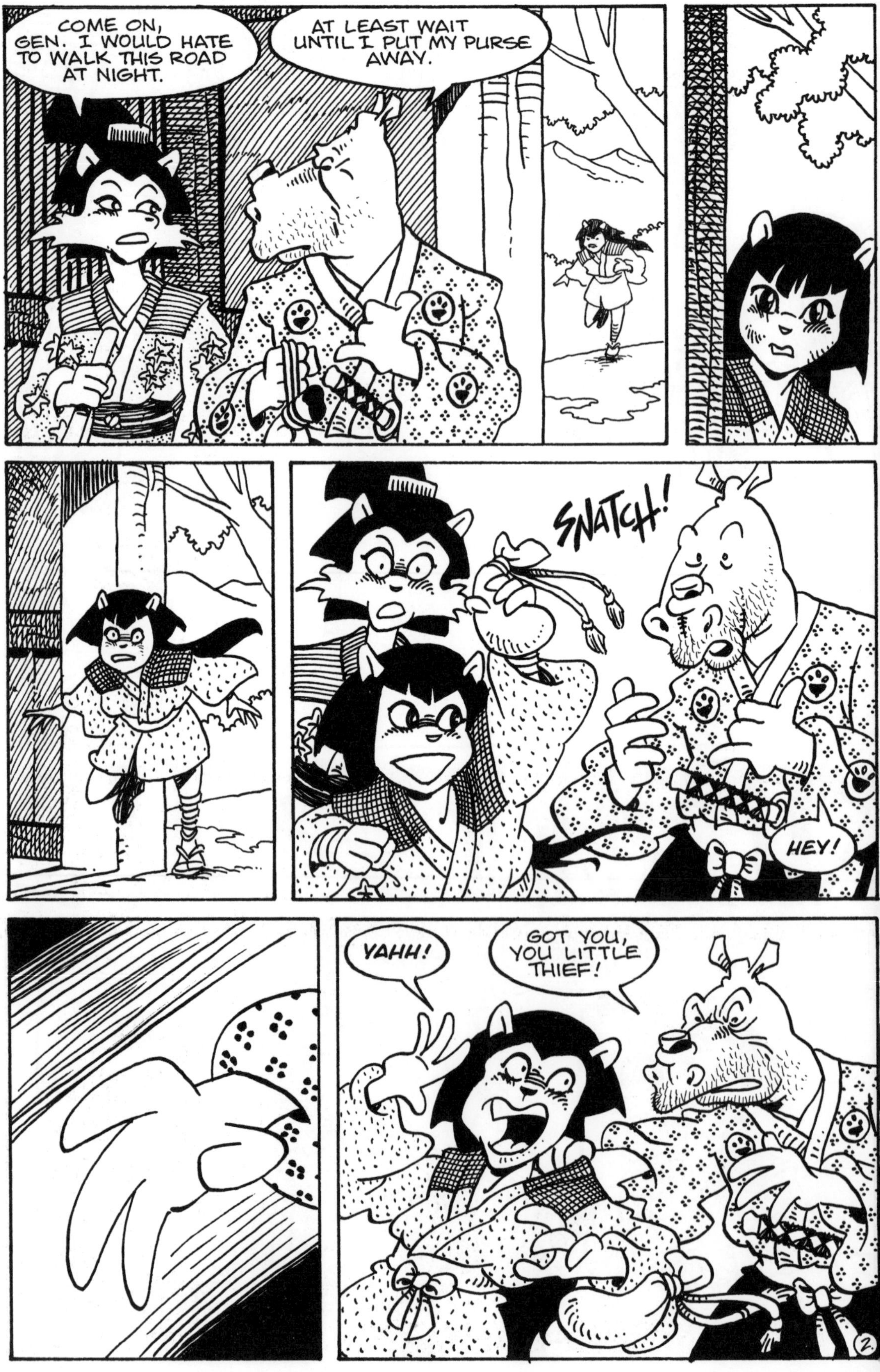
COME ON, GEN. I WOULD HATE TO WALK THIS ROAD AT NIGHT.
AT LEAST WAIT UNTIL I PUT MY PURSE AWAY.
SNATCH!
HEY!
YAHH!
GOT YOU, YOU LITTLE THIEF!
2.

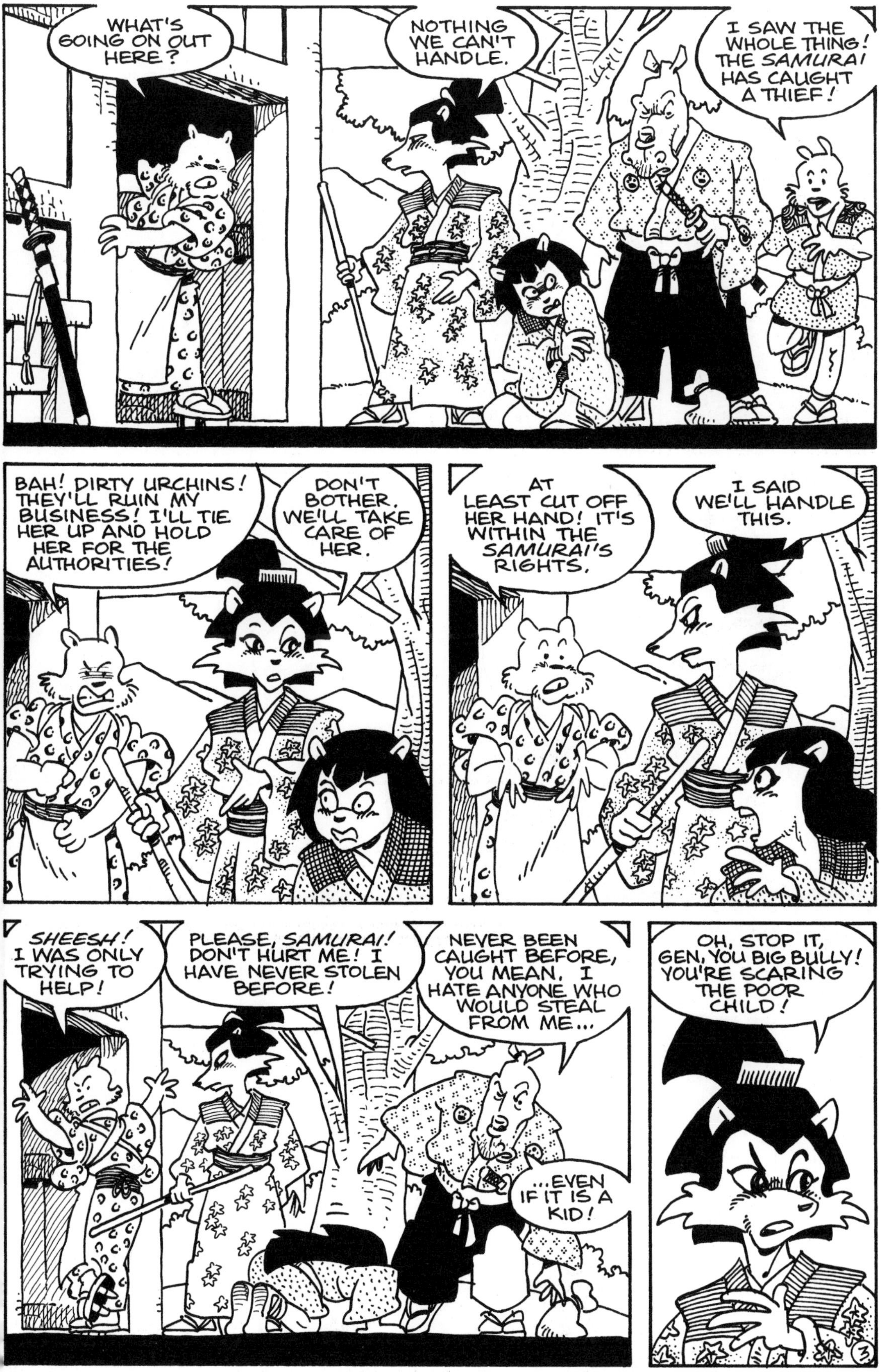

WHAT'S GOING ON OUT HERE?
NOTHING WE CAN'T HANDLE.
I SAW THE WHOLE THING! THE SAMURAI HAS CAUGHT A THIEF!
BAH! DIRTY URCHINS! THEY'LL RUIN MY BUSINESS! I'LL TIE HER UP AND HOLD HER FOR THE AUTHORITIES!
DON'T BOTHER. WE'LL TAKE CARE OF HER.
AT LEAST CUT OFF HER HAND! IT'S WITHIN THE SAMURAI'S RIGHTS.
I SAID WE'LL HANDLE THIS.
SHEESH! I WAS ONLY TRYING TO HELP!
PLEASE, SAMURAI! DON'T HURT ME! I HAVE NEVER STOLEN BEFORE!
NEVER BEEN CAUGHT BEFORE, YOU MEAN. I HATE ANYONE WHO WOULD STEAL FROM ME...
...EVEN IF IT IS A KID!
OH, STOP IT, GEN, YOU BIG BULLY! YOU'RE SCARING THE POOR CHILD!
3

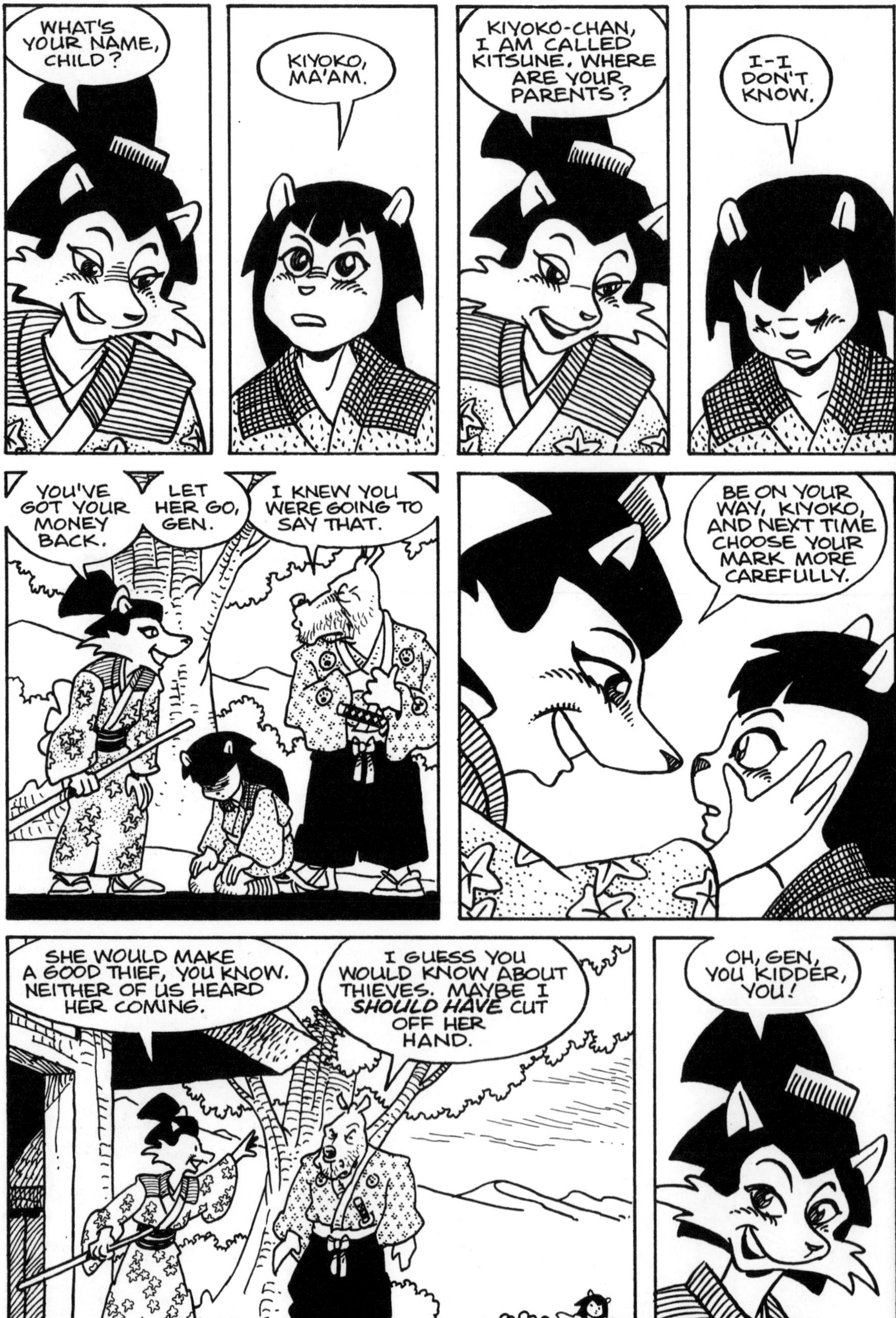
WHAT'S YOUR NAME, CHILD?
KIYOKO, MA'AM.
KIYOKO-CHAN, I AM CALLED KITSUNE. WHERE ARE YOUR PARENTS?
I-I DON'T KNOW.
YOU'VE GOT YOUR MONEY BACK.
LET HER GO, GEN.
I KNEW YOU WERE GOING TO SAY THAT.
BE ON YOUR WAY, KIYOKO, AND NEXT TIME CHOOSE YOUR MARK MORE CAREFULLY.
SHE WOULD MAKE A GOOD THIEF, YOU KNOW. NEITHER OF US HEARD HER COMING.
I GUESS YOU WOULD KNOW ABOUT THIEVES. MAYBE I *SHOULD HAVE* CUT OFF HER HAND.
OH, GEN, YOU KIDDER, YOU!
4.

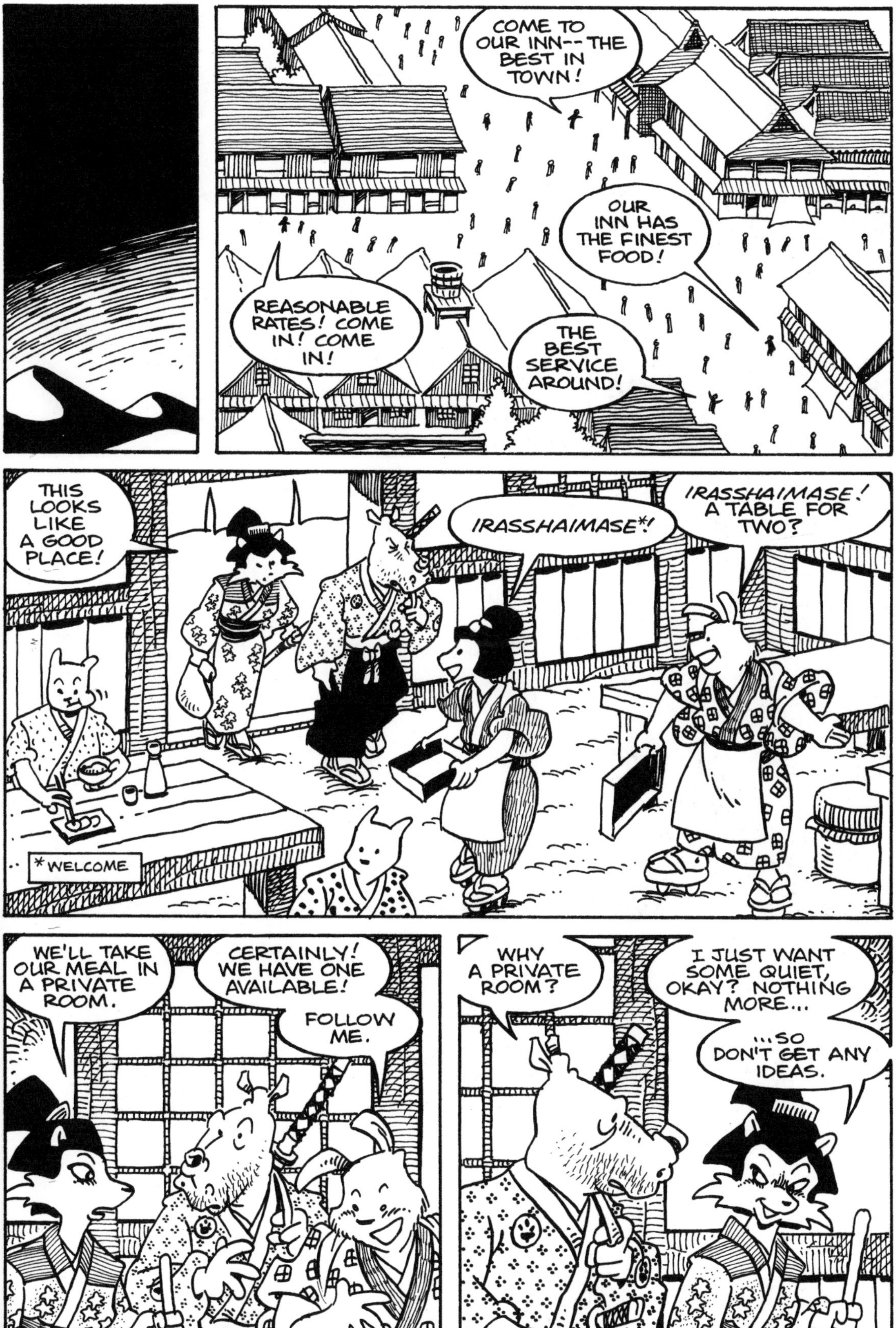
COME TO OUR INN--THE BEST IN TOWN!
OUR INN HAS THE FINEST FOOD!
REASONABLE RATES! COME IN! COME IN!
THE BEST SERVICE AROUND!
THIS LOOKS LIKE A GOOD PLACE!
IRASSHAIMASE*!
IRASSHAIMASE! A TABLE FOR TWO?
*WELCOME
WE'LL TAKE OUR MEAL IN A PRIVATE ROOM.
CERTAINLY! WE HAVE ONE AVAILABLE!
FOLLOW ME.
WHY A PRIVATE ROOM?
I JUST WANT SOME QUIET, OKAY? NOTHING MORE...
...SO DON'T GET ANY IDEAS.
5.

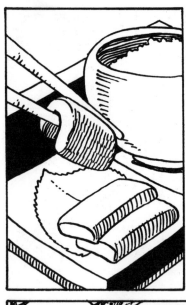

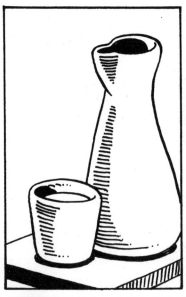

YOU'RE NOT EATING.

WHAT'S THE MATTER?

MUNCH! MUNCH!

I'M NOT HUNGRY, THAT'S ALL.

GOOD. MORE FOR ME THEN.

YOU'VE BEEN ACTING MOODIER SINCE WE LEFT THAT ROADSIDE INN. THAT LITTLE THIEF REALLY GOT TO YOU, DIDN'T SHE?

SHE JUST GOT ME THINKING OF SOMEONE, THAT'S ALL... A PERSON I HAD ALL BUT FORGOTTEN.

6

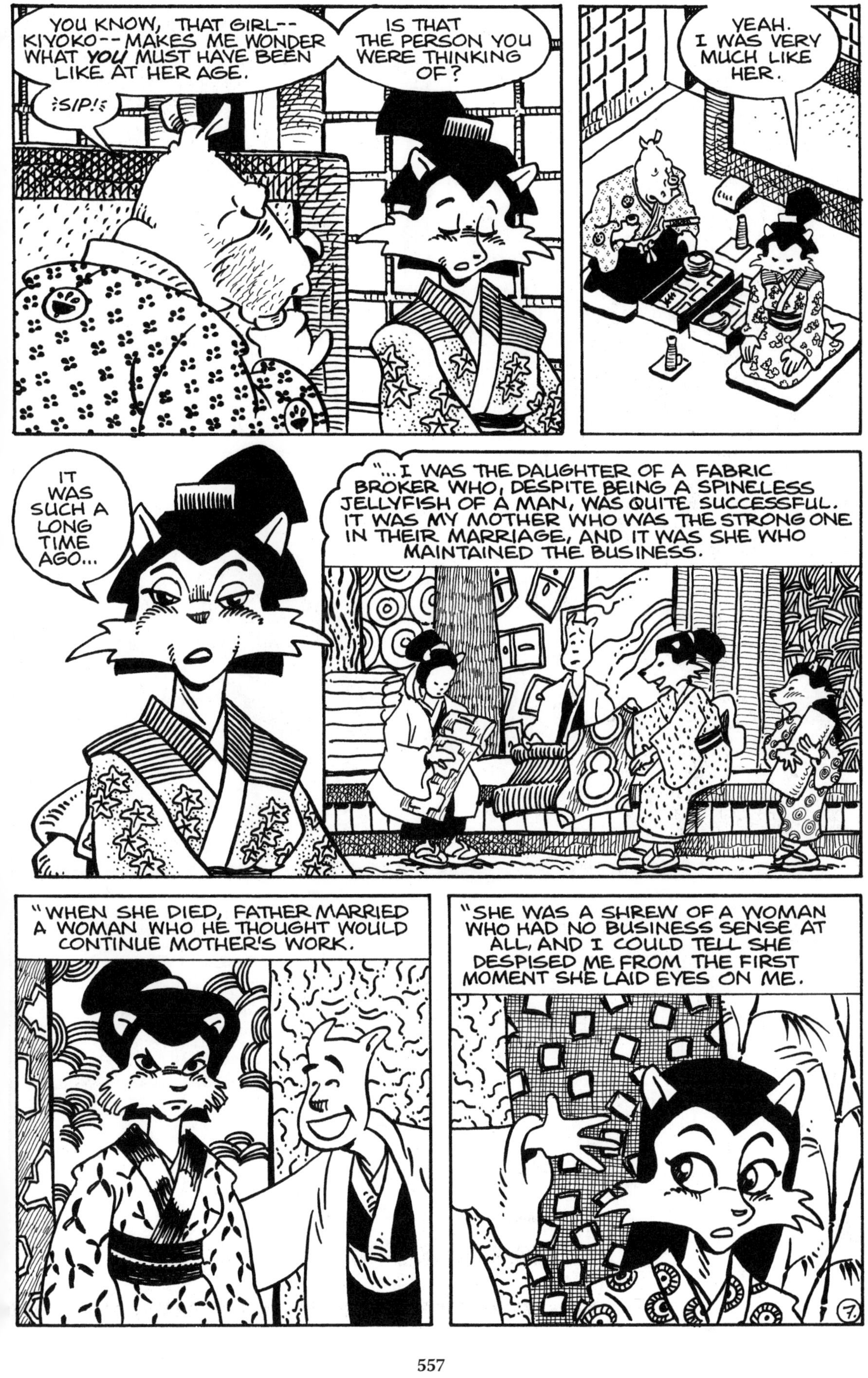
YOU KNOW, THAT GIRL-- KIYOKO--MAKES ME WONDER WHAT *YOU* MUST HAVE BEEN LIKE AT HER AGE.
:SIP!:
IS THAT THE PERSON YOU WERE THINKING OF?
YEAH. I WAS VERY MUCH LIKE HER.
IT WAS SUCH A LONG TIME AGO...
"...I WAS THE DAUGHTER OF A FABRIC BROKER WHO, DESPITE BEING A SPINELESS JELLYFISH OF A MAN, WAS QUITE SUCCESSFUL. IT WAS MY MOTHER WHO WAS THE STRONG ONE IN THEIR MARRIAGE, AND IT WAS SHE WHO MAINTAINED THE BUSINESS.
"WHEN SHE DIED, FATHER MARRIED A WOMAN WHO HE THOUGHT WOULD CONTINUE MOTHER'S WORK.
"SHE WAS A SHREW OF A WOMAN WHO HAD NO BUSINESS SENSE AT ALL, AND I COULD TELL SHE DESPISED ME FROM THE FIRST MOMENT SHE LAID EYES ON ME.
7.

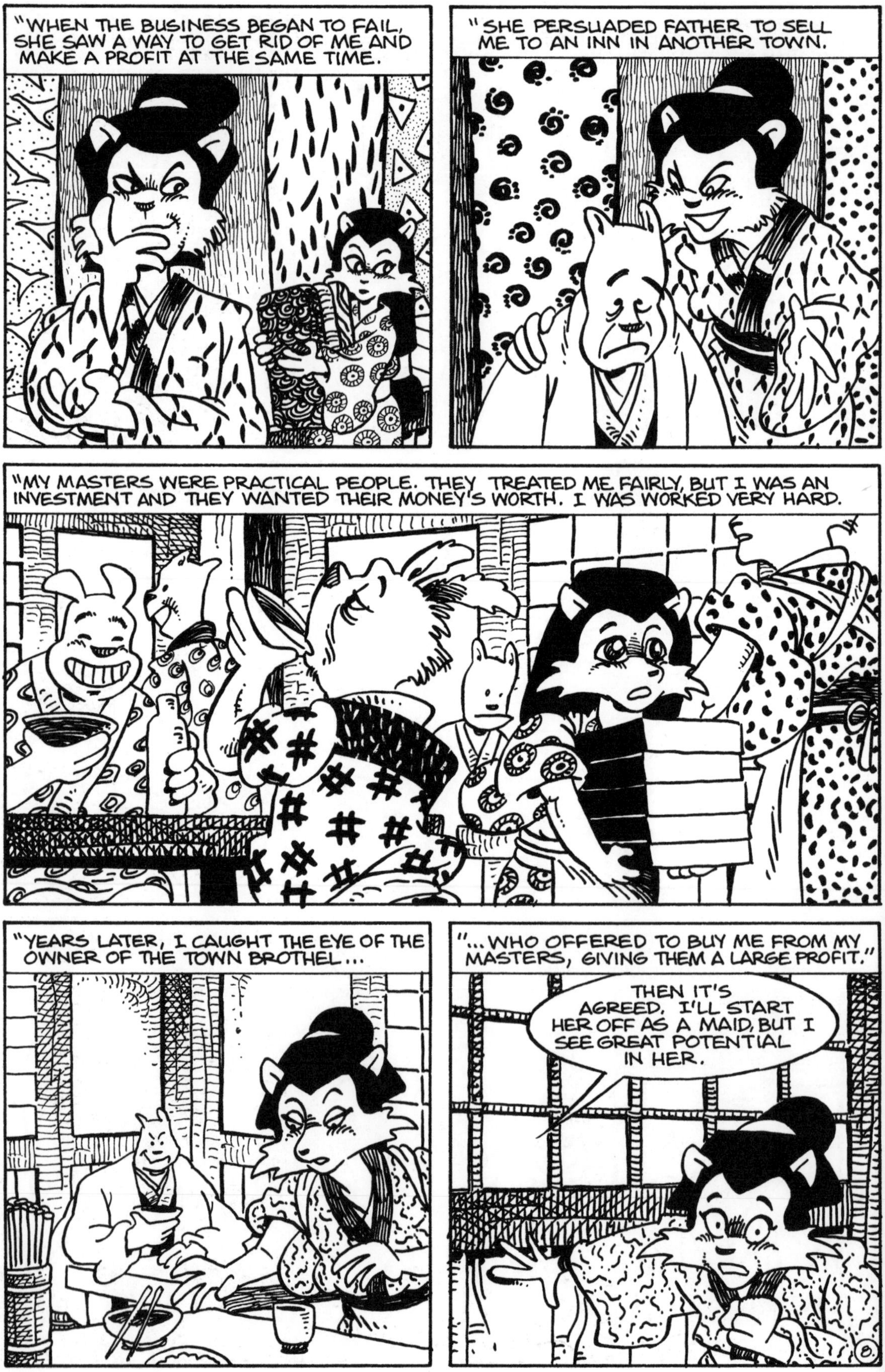
"WHEN THE BUSINESS BEGAN TO FAIL, SHE SAW A WAY TO GET RID OF ME AND MAKE A PROFIT AT THE SAME TIME.
"SHE PERSUADED FATHER TO SELL ME TO AN INN IN ANOTHER TOWN.
"MY MASTERS WERE PRACTICAL PEOPLE. THEY TREATED ME FAIRLY, BUT I WAS AN INVESTMENT AND THEY WANTED THEIR MONEY'S WORTH. I WAS WORKED VERY HARD.
"YEARS LATER, I CAUGHT THE EYE OF THE OWNER OF THE TOWN BROTHEL...
"...WHO OFFERED TO BUY ME FROM MY MASTERS, GIVING THEM A LARGE PROFIT."
THEN IT'S AGREED. I'LL START HER OFF AS A MAID, BUT I SEE GREAT POTENTIAL IN HER.

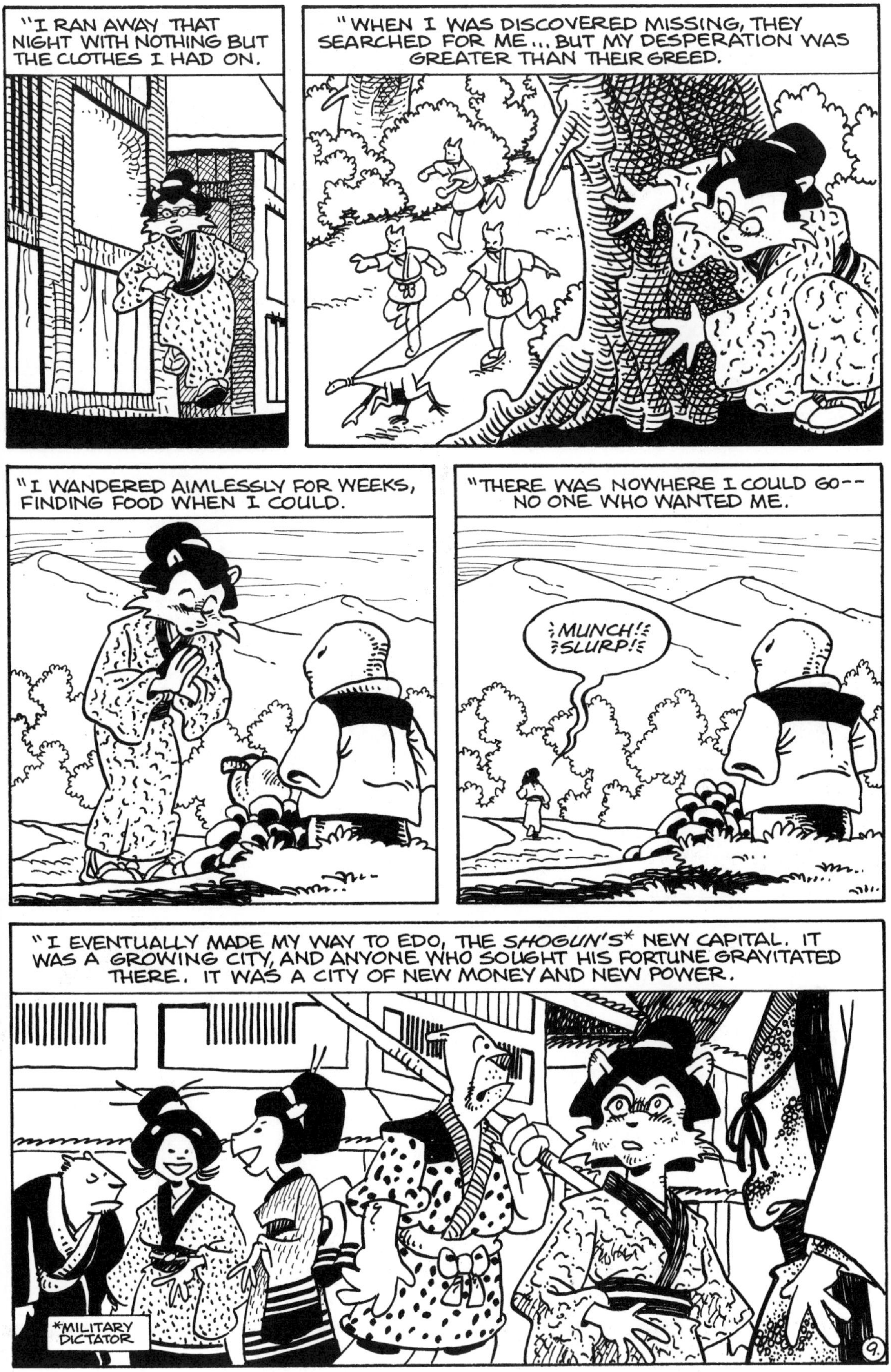
"I RAN AWAY THAT NIGHT WITH NOTHING BUT THE CLOTHES I HAD ON.
"WHEN I WAS DISCOVERED MISSING, THEY SEARCHED FOR ME... BUT MY DESPERATION WAS GREATER THAN THEIR GREED.
"I WANDERED AIMLESSLY FOR WEEKS, FINDING FOOD WHEN I COULD.
"THERE WAS NOWHERE I COULD GO-- NO ONE WHO WANTED ME.
MUNCH! SLURP!
"I EVENTUALLY MADE MY WAY TO EDO, THE SHOGUN'S* NEW CAPITAL. IT WAS A GROWING CITY, AND ANYONE WHO SOUGHT HIS FORTUNE GRAVITATED THERE. IT WAS A CITY OF NEW MONEY AND NEW POWER.
*MILITARY DICTATOR
9.

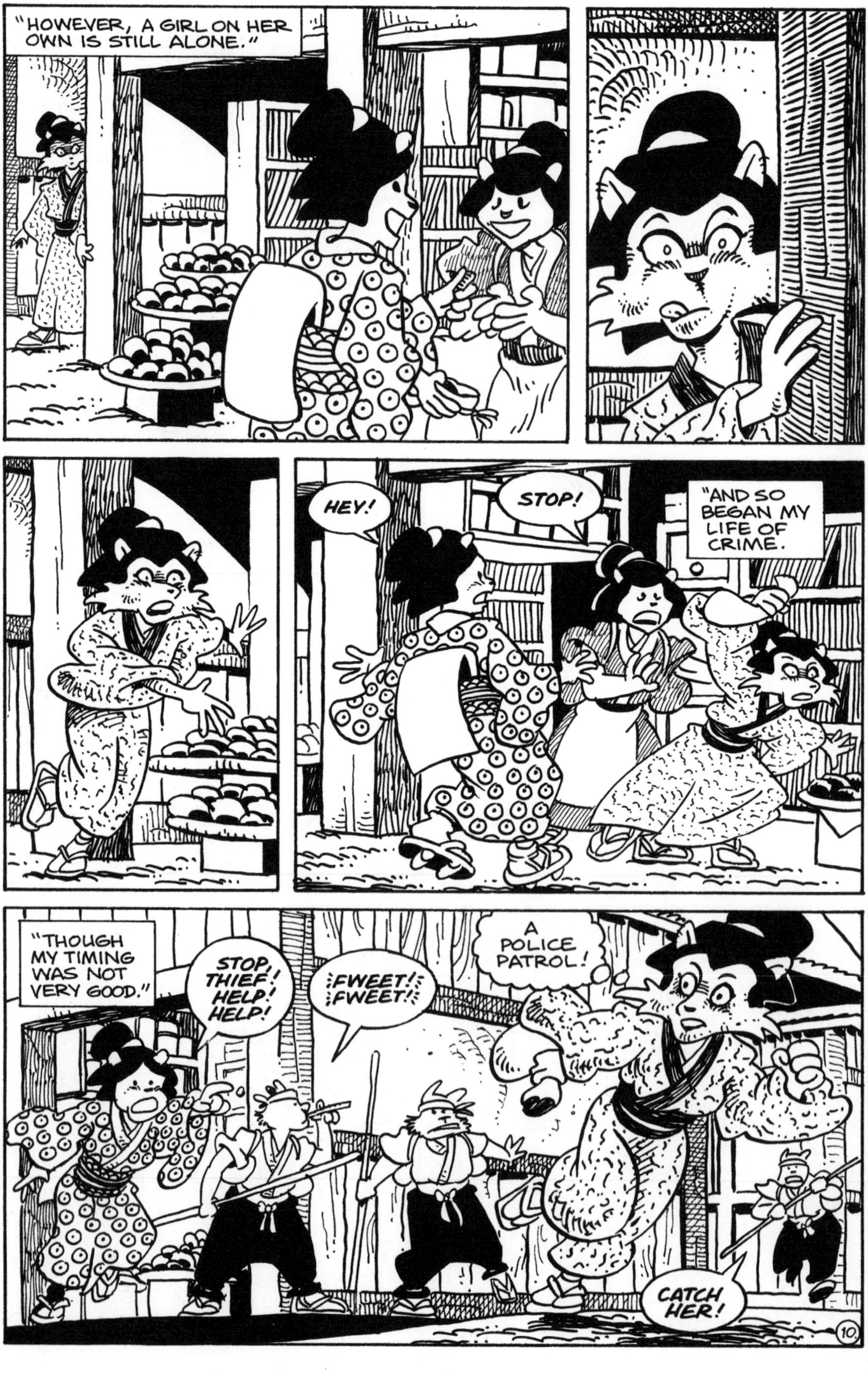
"HOWEVER, A GIRL ON HER OWN IS STILL ALONE."
HEY!
STOP!
"AND SO BEGAN MY LIFE OF CRIME.
"THOUGH MY TIMING WAS NOT VERY GOOD."
STOP THIEF! HELP! HELP!
FWEET! FWEET!
A POLICE PATROL!
CATCH HER!
10

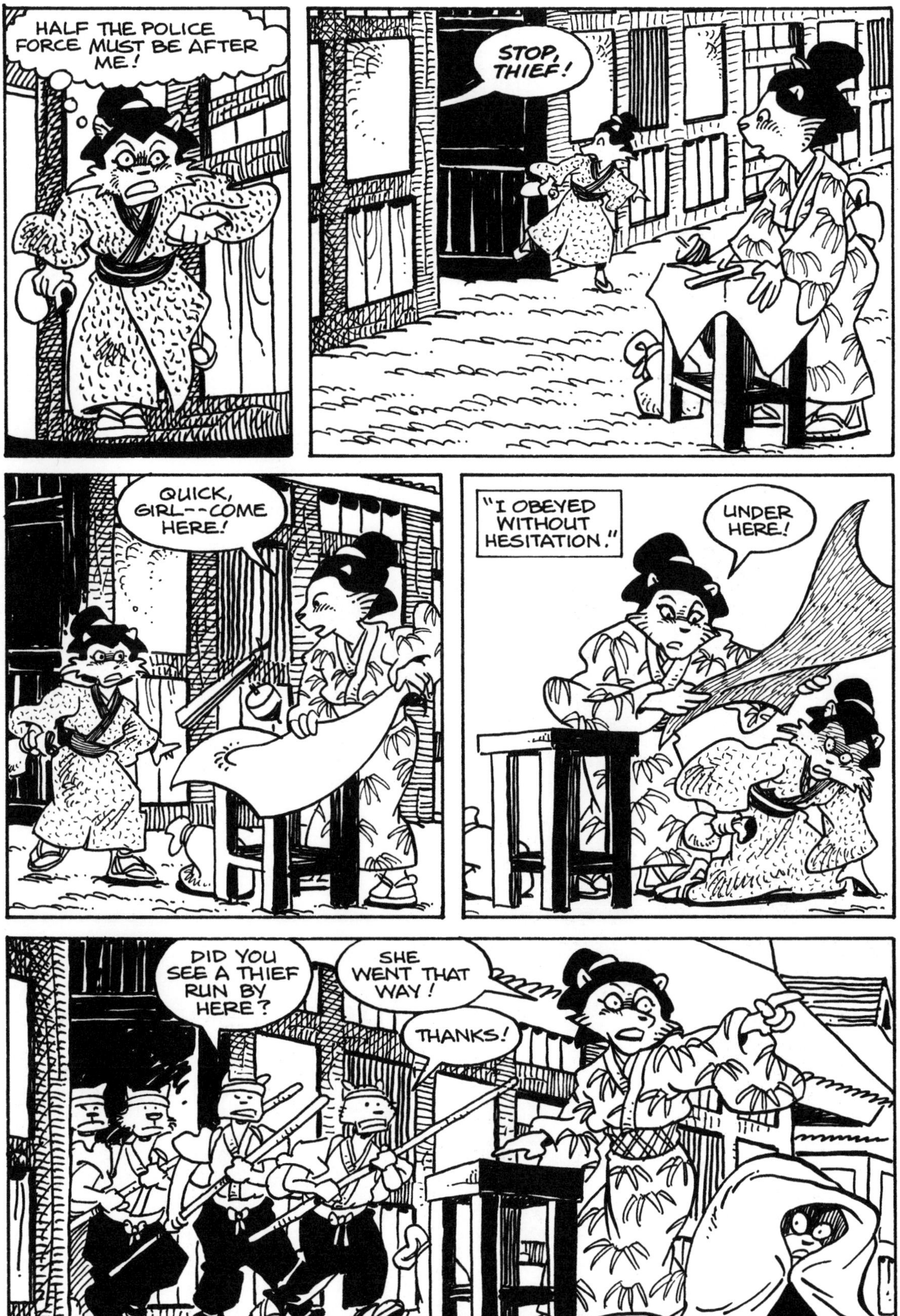
HALF THE POLICE FORCE MUST BE AFTER ME!
STOP, THIEF!
QUICK, GIRL--COME HERE!
"I OBEYED WITHOUT HESITATION."
UNDER HERE!
DID YOU SEE A THIEF RUN BY HERE?
SHE WENT THAT WAY!
THANKS!
11.

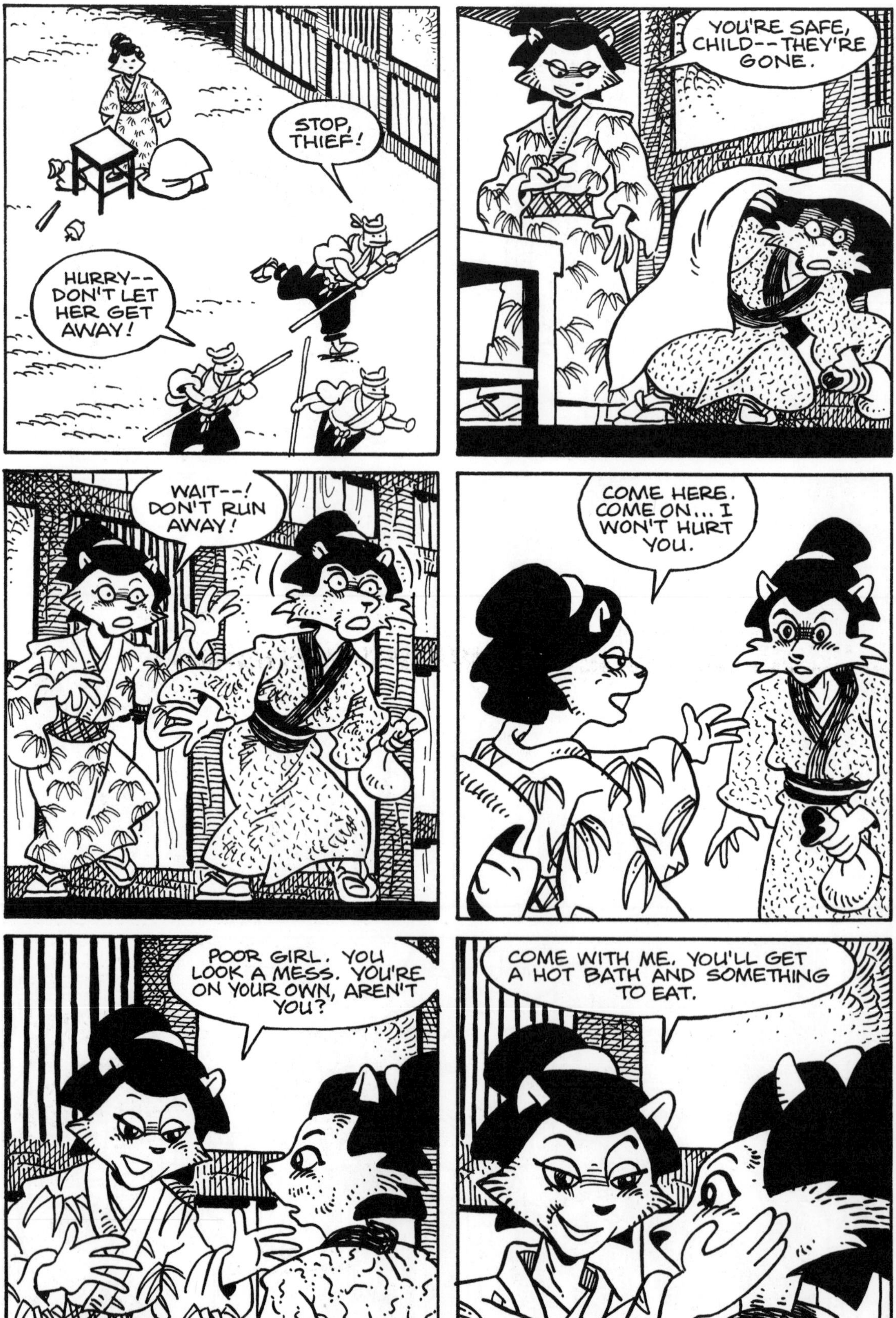
STOP, THIEF!
HURRY-- DON'T LET HER GET AWAY!
YOU'RE SAFE, CHILD-- THEY'RE GONE.
WAIT--! DON'T RUN AWAY!
COME HERE. COME ON... I WON'T HURT YOU.
POOR GIRL. YOU LOOK A MESS. YOU'RE ON YOUR OWN, AREN'T YOU?
COME WITH ME. YOU'LL GET A HOT BATH AND SOMETHING TO EAT.
12.

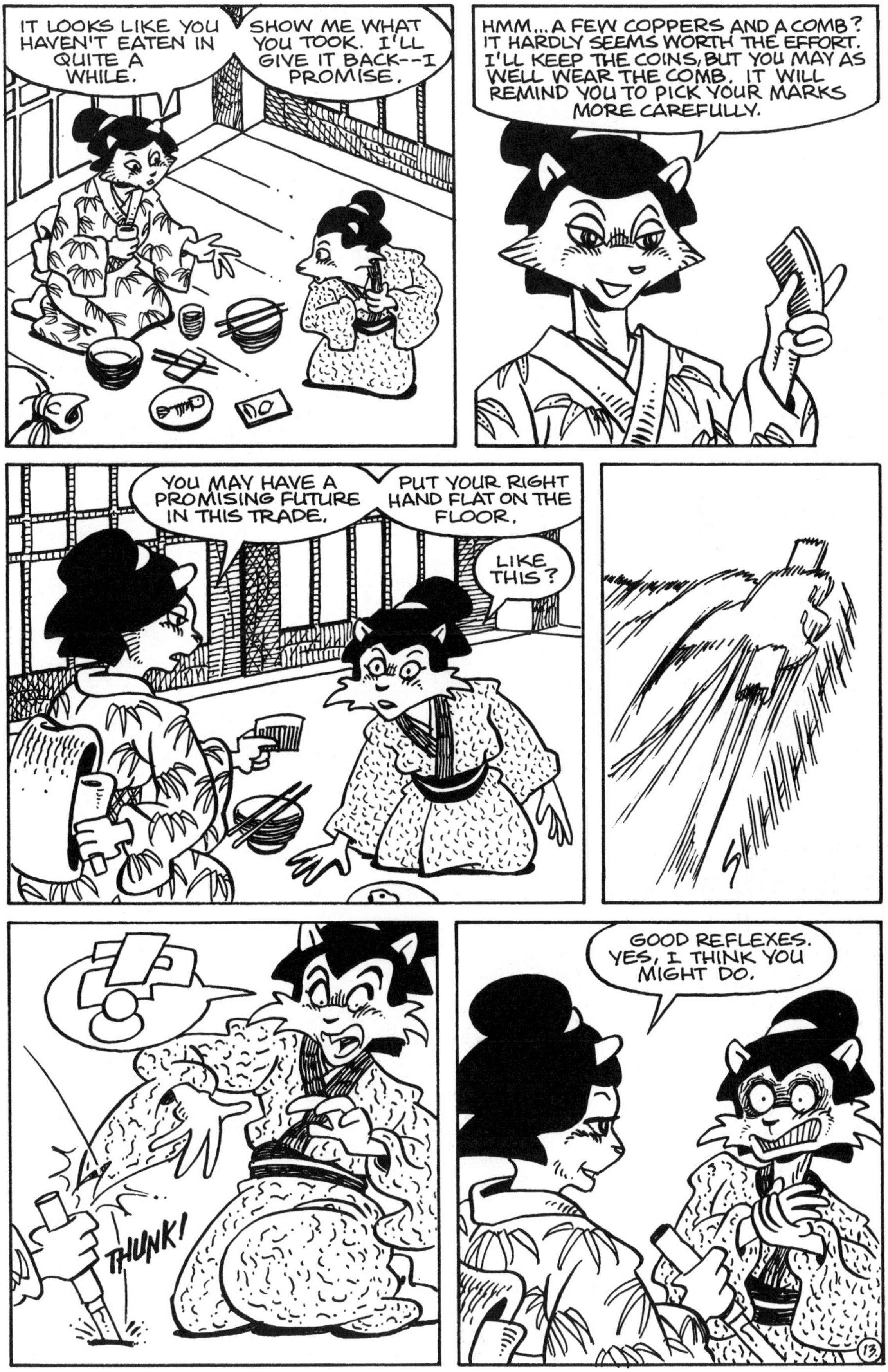
IT LOOKS LIKE YOU HAVEN'T EATEN IN QUITE A WHILE.
SHOW ME WHAT YOU TOOK. I'LL GIVE IT BACK--I PROMISE.
HMM... A FEW COPPERS AND A COMB? IT HARDLY SEEMS WORTH THE EFFORT. I'LL KEEP THE COINS, BUT YOU MAY AS WELL WEAR THE COMB. IT WILL REMIND YOU TO PICK YOUR MARKS MORE CAREFULLY.
YOU MAY HAVE A PROMISING FUTURE IN THIS TRADE.
PUT YOUR RIGHT HAND FLAT ON THE FLOOR.
LIKE THIS?
SHHHHHHH
THUNK!
GOOD REFLEXES. YES, I THINK YOU MIGHT DO.
13

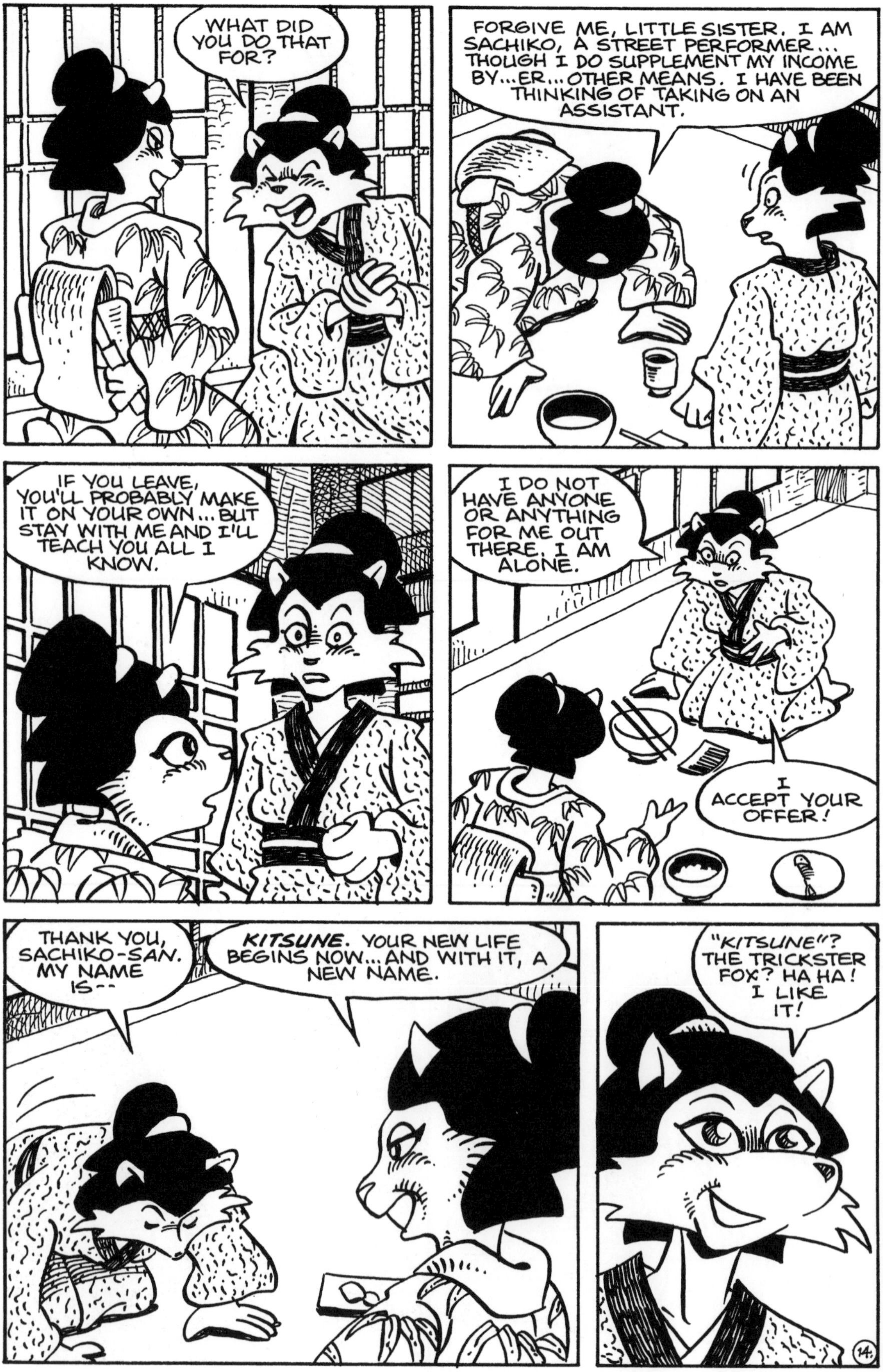
WHAT DID YOU DO THAT FOR?
FORGIVE ME, LITTLE SISTER. I AM SACHIKO, A STREET PERFORMER... THOUGH I DO SUPPLEMENT MY INCOME BY...ER...OTHER MEANS. I HAVE BEEN THINKING OF TAKING ON AN ASSISTANT.
IF YOU LEAVE, YOU'LL PROBABLY MAKE IT ON YOUR OWN... BUT STAY WITH ME AND I'LL TEACH YOU ALL I KNOW.
I DO NOT HAVE ANYONE OR ANYTHING FOR ME OUT THERE. I AM ALONE.
I ACCEPT YOUR OFFER!
THANK YOU, SACHIKO-SAN. MY NAME IS--
KITSUNE. YOUR NEW LIFE BEGINS NOW...AND WITH IT, A NEW NAME.
"KITSUNE"? THE TRICKSTER FOX? HA HA! I LIKE IT!
14.

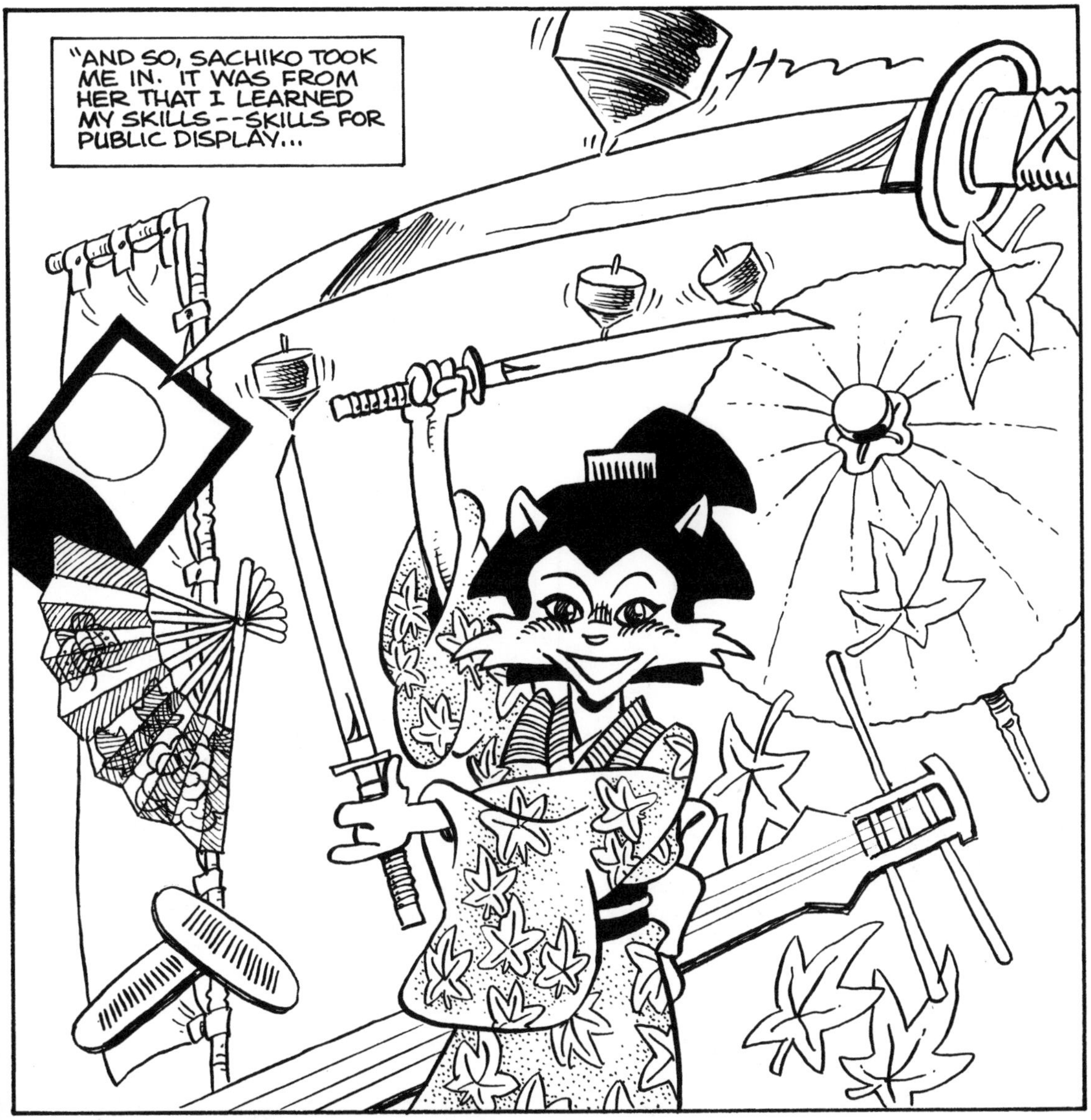
"AND SO, SACHIKO TOOK ME IN. IT WAS FROM HER THAT I LEARNED MY SKILLS--SKILLS FOR PUBLIC DISPLAY...

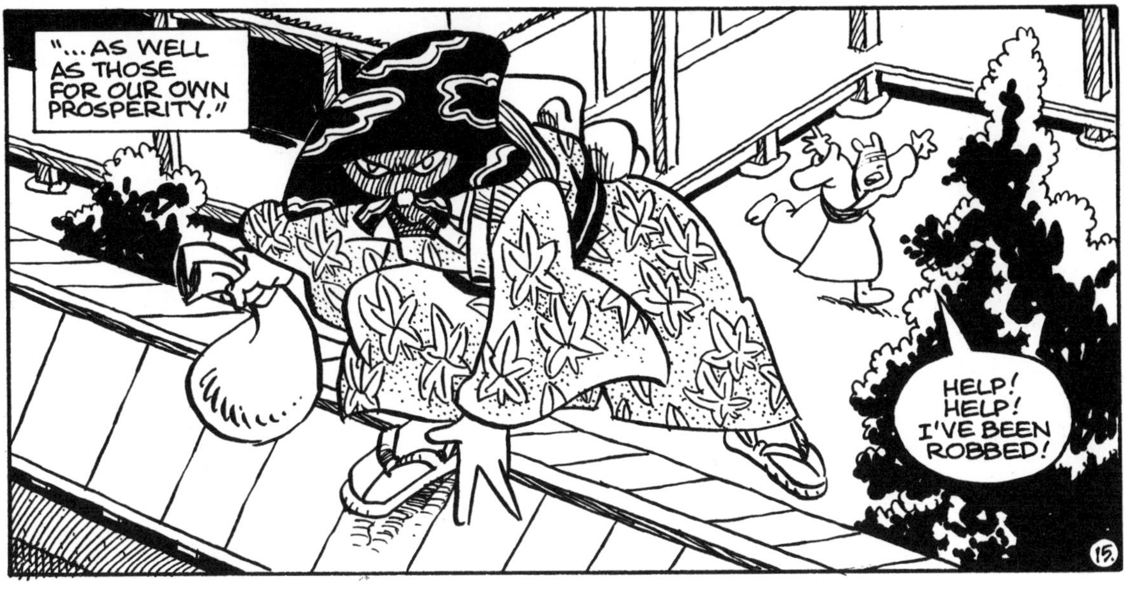
"...AS WELL AS THOSE FOR OUR OWN PROSPERITY."
HELP! HELP! I'VE BEEN ROBBED!
15

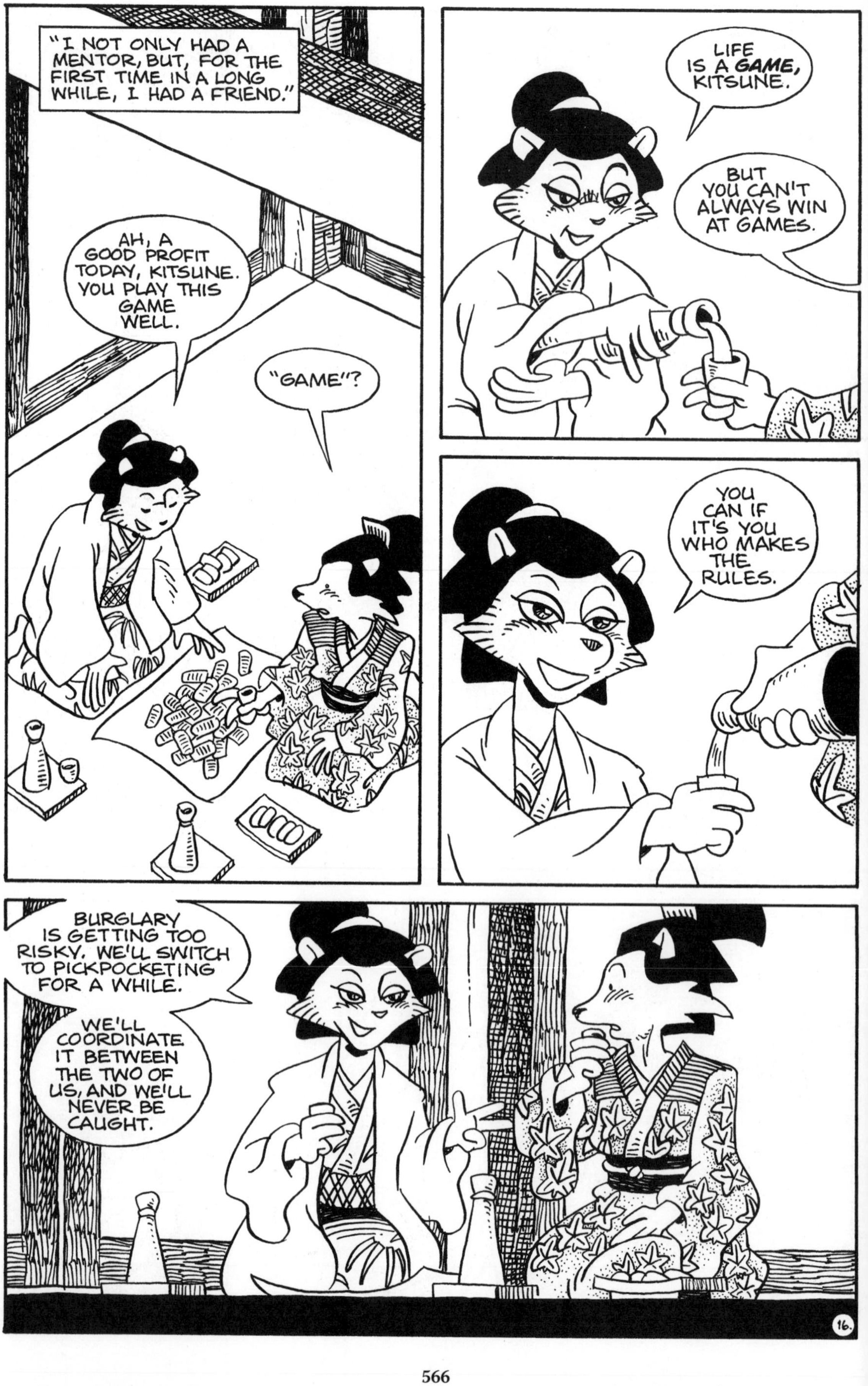
"I NOT ONLY HAD A MENTOR, BUT, FOR THE FIRST TIME IN A LONG WHILE, I HAD A FRIEND."
AH, A GOOD PROFIT TODAY, KITSUNE. YOU PLAY THIS GAME WELL.
"GAME"?
LIFE IS A **GAME,** KITSUNE.
BUT YOU CAN'T ALWAYS WIN AT GAMES.
YOU CAN IF IT'S YOU WHO MAKES THE RULES.
BURGLARY IS GETTING TOO RISKY. WE'LL SWITCH TO PICKPOCKETING FOR A WHILE.
WE'LL COORDINATE IT BETWEEN THE TWO OF US, AND WE'LL NEVER BE CAUGHT.
16.

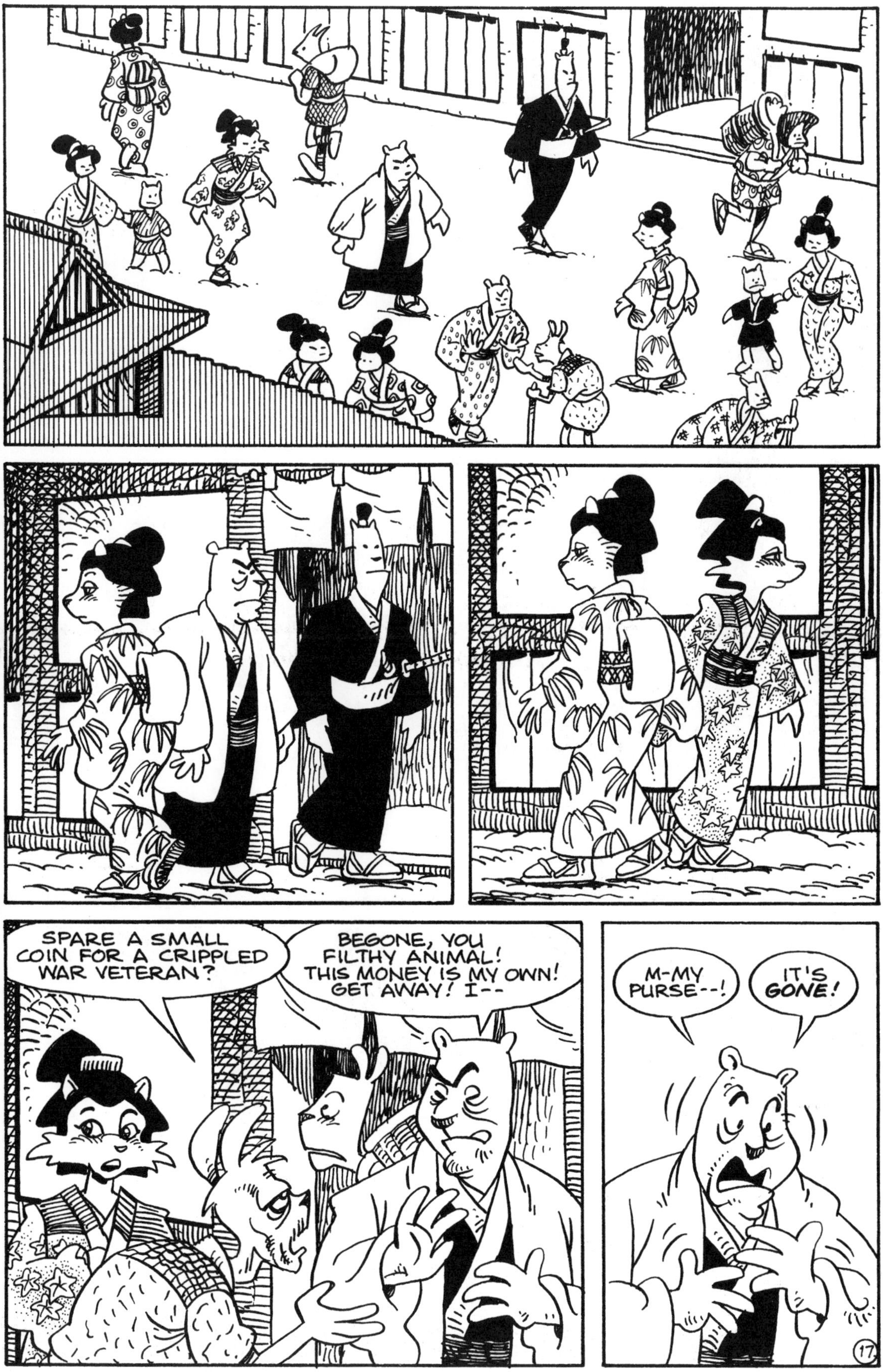
SPARE A SMALL COIN FOR A CRIPPLED WAR VETERAN?
BEGONE, YOU FILTHY ANIMAL! THIS MONEY IS MY OWN! GET AWAY! I--
M-MY PURSE--!
IT'S **GONE**!
17

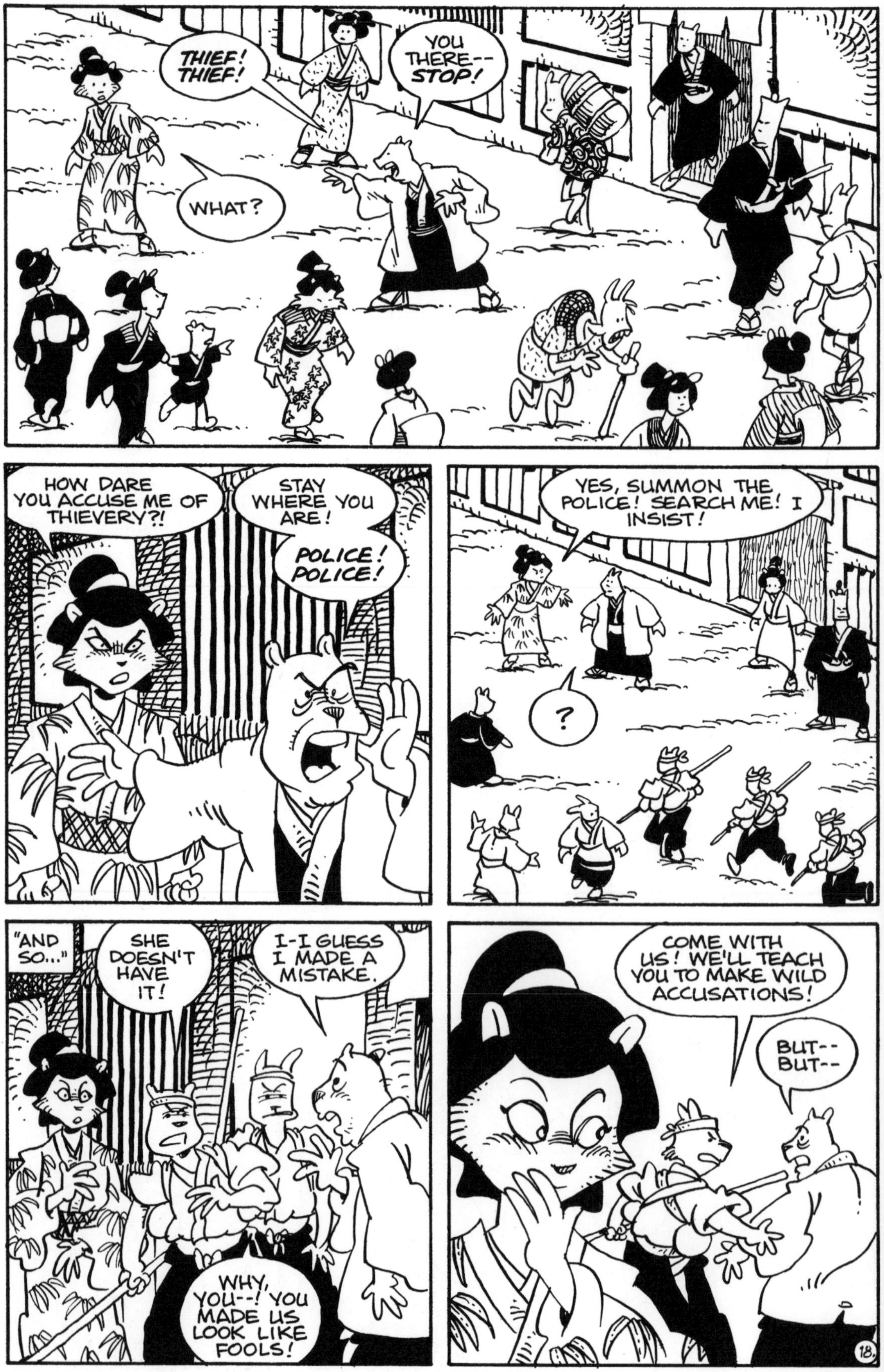
THIEF! THIEF!
YOU THERE-- STOP!
WHAT?
HOW DARE YOU ACCUSE ME OF THIEVERY?!
STAY WHERE YOU ARE!
POLICE! POLICE!
YES, SUMMON THE POLICE! SEARCH ME! I INSIST!
?
"AND SO..."
SHE DOESN'T HAVE IT!
I-I GUESS I MADE A MISTAKE.
WHY, YOU--! YOU MADE US LOOK LIKE FOOLS!
COME WITH US! WE'LL TEACH YOU TO MAKE WILD ACCUSATIONS!
BUT-- BUT--
18

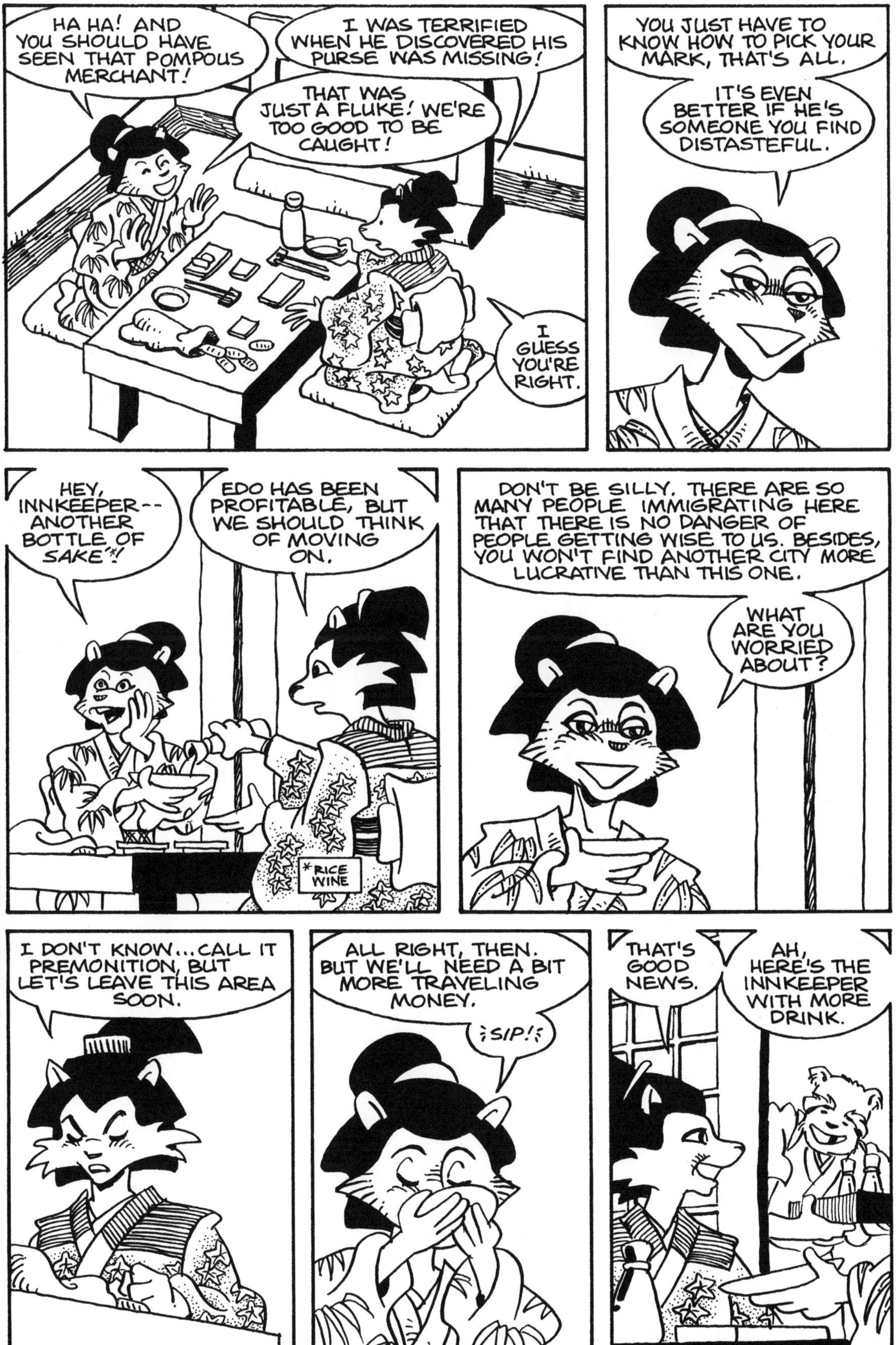
HA HA! AND YOU SHOULD HAVE SEEN THAT POMPOUS MERCHANT!
I WAS TERRIFIED WHEN HE DISCOVERED HIS PURSE WAS MISSING!
THAT WAS JUST A FLUKE! WE'RE TOO GOOD TO BE CAUGHT!
I GUESS YOU'RE RIGHT.
YOU JUST HAVE TO KNOW HOW TO PICK YOUR MARK, THAT'S ALL.
IT'S EVEN BETTER IF HE'S SOMEONE YOU FIND DISTASTEFUL.
HEY, INNKEEPER-- ANOTHER BOTTLE OF SAKE*!
EDO HAS BEEN PROFITABLE, BUT WE SHOULD THINK OF MOVING ON.
*RICE WINE
DON'T BE SILLY. THERE ARE SO MANY PEOPLE IMMIGRATING HERE THAT THERE IS NO DANGER OF PEOPLE GETTING WISE TO US. BESIDES, YOU WON'T FIND ANOTHER CITY MORE LUCRATIVE THAN THIS ONE.
WHAT ARE YOU WORRIED ABOUT?
I DON'T KNOW...CALL IT PREMONITION, BUT LET'S LEAVE THIS AREA SOON.
ALL RIGHT, THEN. BUT WE'LL NEED A BIT MORE TRAVELING MONEY.
SIP!
THAT'S GOOD NEWS.
AH, HERE'S THE INNKEEPER WITH MORE DRINK.
19.

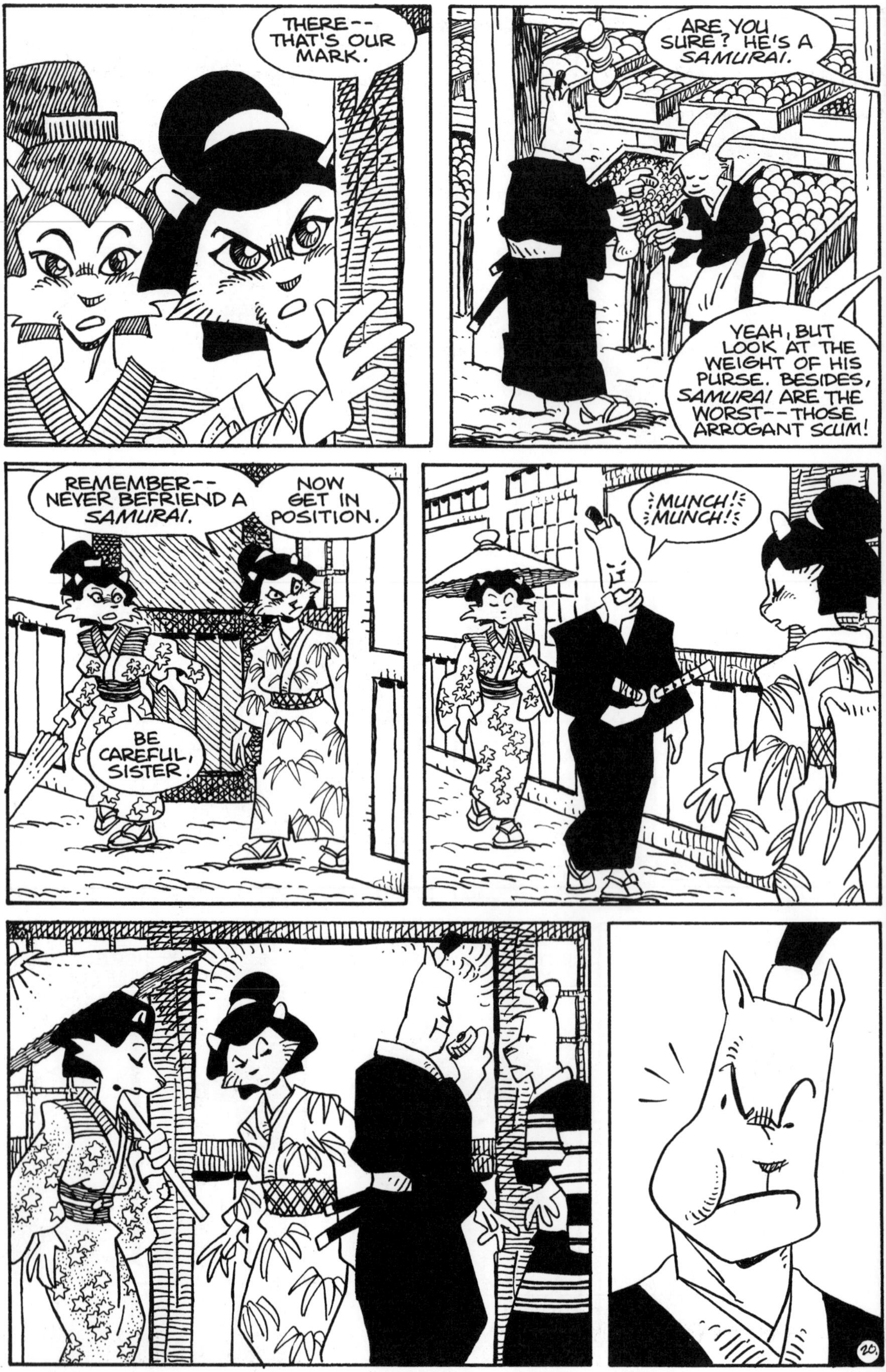
THERE--THAT'S OUR MARK.
ARE YOU SURE? HE'S A SAMURAI.
YEAH, BUT LOOK AT THE WEIGHT OF HIS PURSE. BESIDES, SAMURAI ARE THE WORST--THOSE ARROGANT SCUM!
REMEMBER--NEVER BEFRIEND A SAMURAI.
NOW GET IN POSITION.
BE CAREFUL, SISTER.
MUNCH! MUNCH!
20.

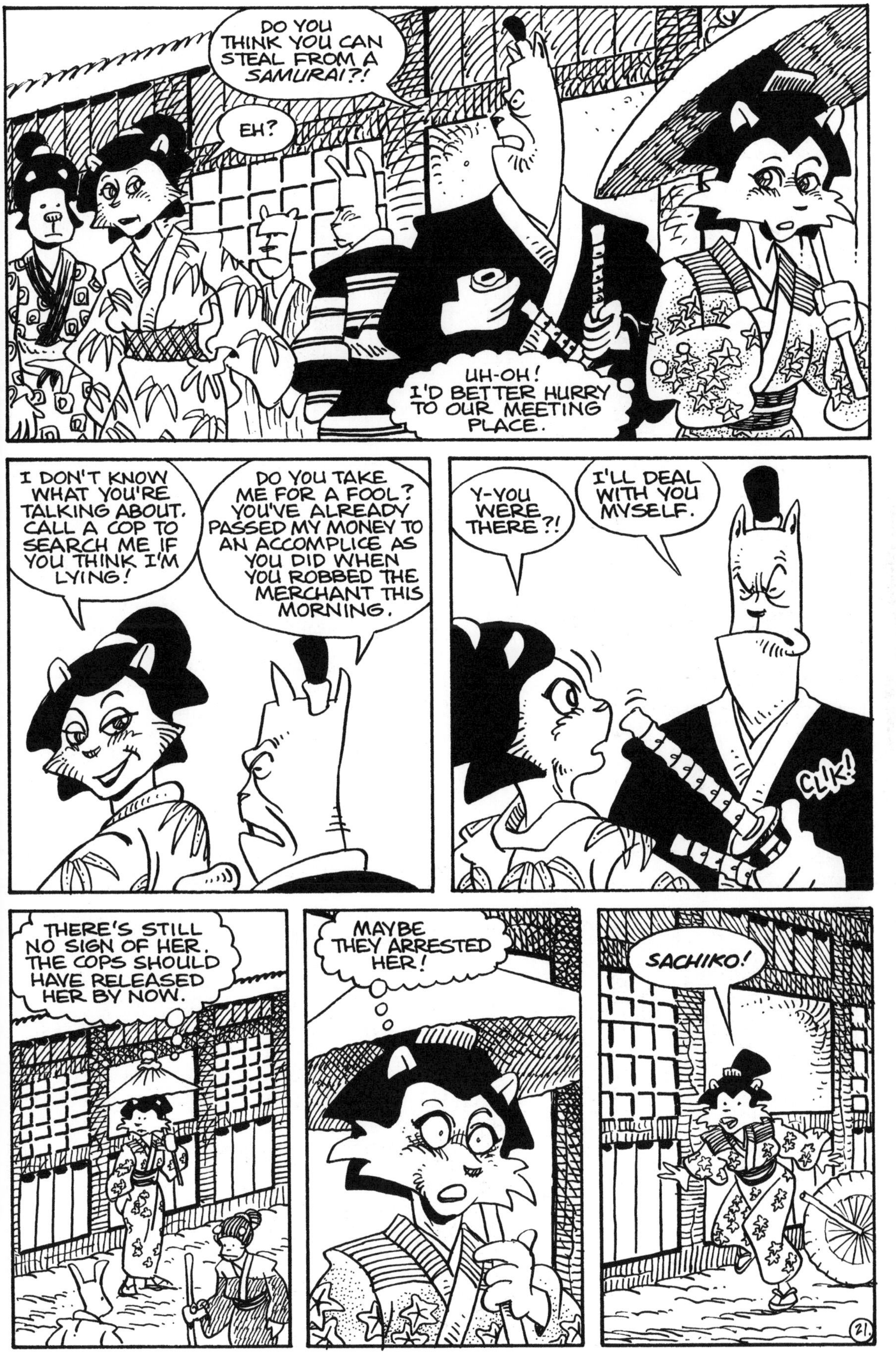
DO YOU THINK YOU CAN STEAL FROM A *SAMURAI*?!
EH?
UH-OH! I'D BETTER HURRY TO OUR MEETING PLACE.
I DON'T KNOW WHAT YOU'RE TALKING ABOUT. CALL A COP TO SEARCH ME IF YOU THINK I'M LYING!
DO YOU TAKE ME FOR A FOOL? YOU'VE ALREADY PASSED MY MONEY TO AN ACCOMPLICE AS YOU DID WHEN YOU ROBBED THE MERCHANT THIS MORNING.
Y-YOU WERE THERE?!
I'LL DEAL WITH YOU MYSELF.
CLIK!
THERE'S STILL NO SIGN OF HER. THE COPS SHOULD HAVE RELEASED HER BY NOW.
MAYBE THEY ARRESTED HER!
SACHIKO!
21.

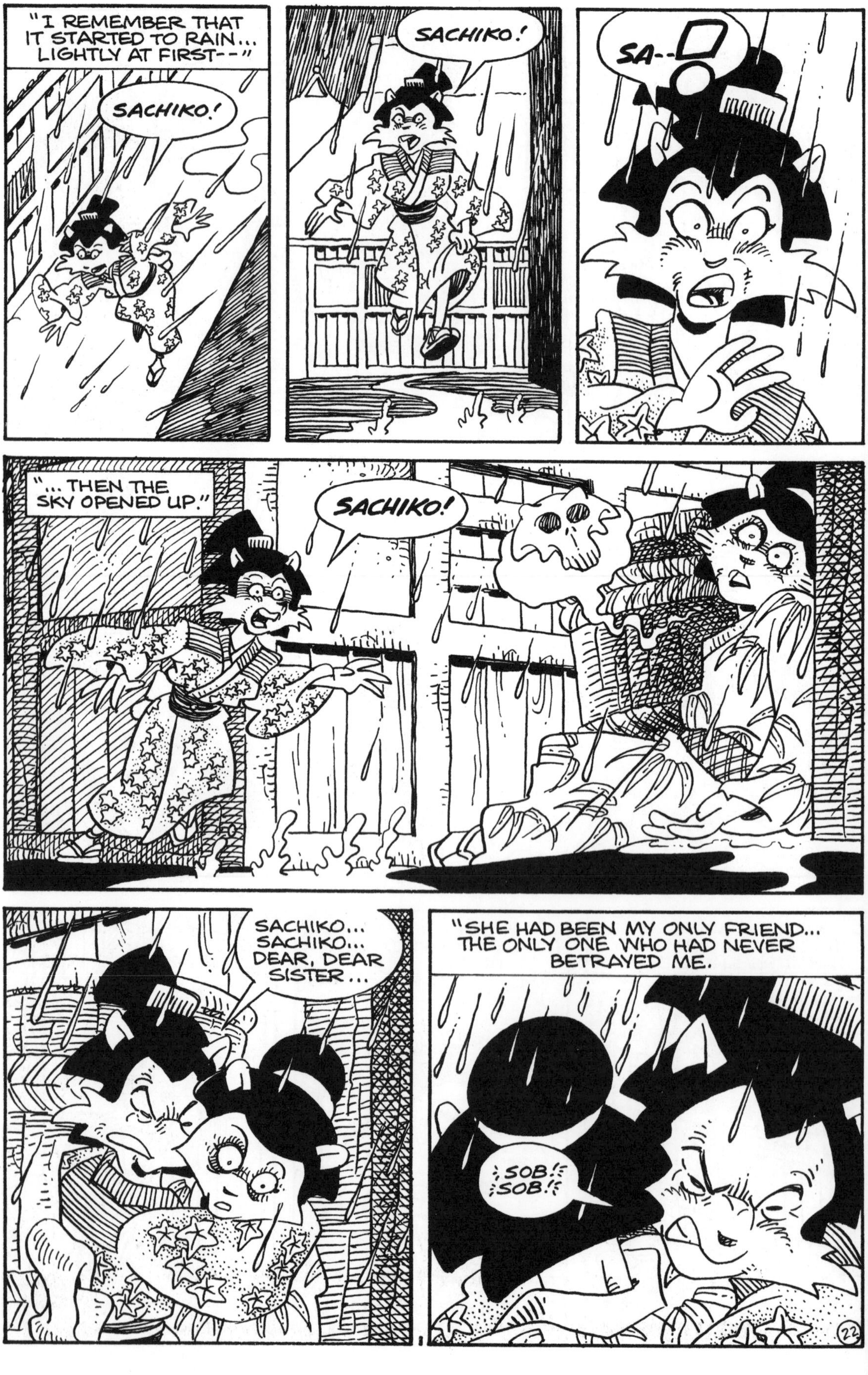
"I REMEMBER THAT IT STARTED TO RAIN... LIGHTLY AT FIRST--"
SACHIKO!
SACHIKO!
SA--
"...THEN THE SKY OPENED UP."
SACHIKO!
SACHIKO... SACHIKO... DEAR, DEAR SISTER...
"SHE HAD BEEN MY ONLY FRIEND... THE ONLY ONE WHO HAD NEVER BETRAYED ME.
SOB! SOB!
22

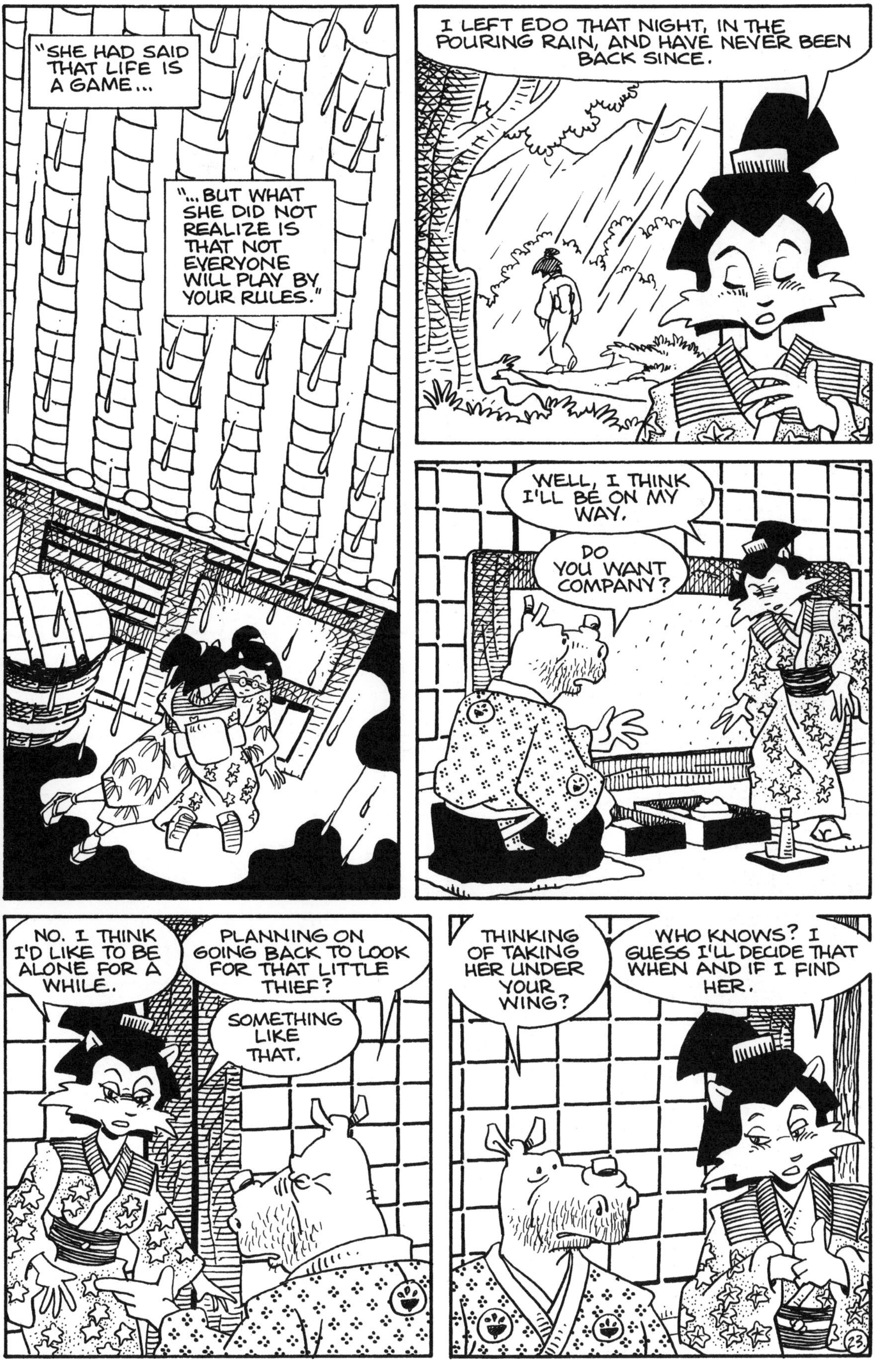
"SHE HAD SAID THAT LIFE IS A GAME...
"...BUT WHAT SHE DID NOT REALIZE IS THAT NOT EVERYONE WILL PLAY BY YOUR RULES."
I LEFT EDO THAT NIGHT, IN THE POURING RAIN, AND HAVE NEVER BEEN BACK SINCE.
WELL, I THINK I'LL BE ON MY WAY.
DO YOU WANT COMPANY?
NO. I THINK I'D LIKE TO BE ALONE FOR A WHILE.
PLANNING ON GOING BACK TO LOOK FOR THAT LITTLE THIEF?
SOMETHING LIKE THAT.
THINKING OF TAKING HER UNDER YOUR WING?
WHO KNOWS? I GUESS I'LL DECIDE THAT WHEN AND IF I FIND HER.
23

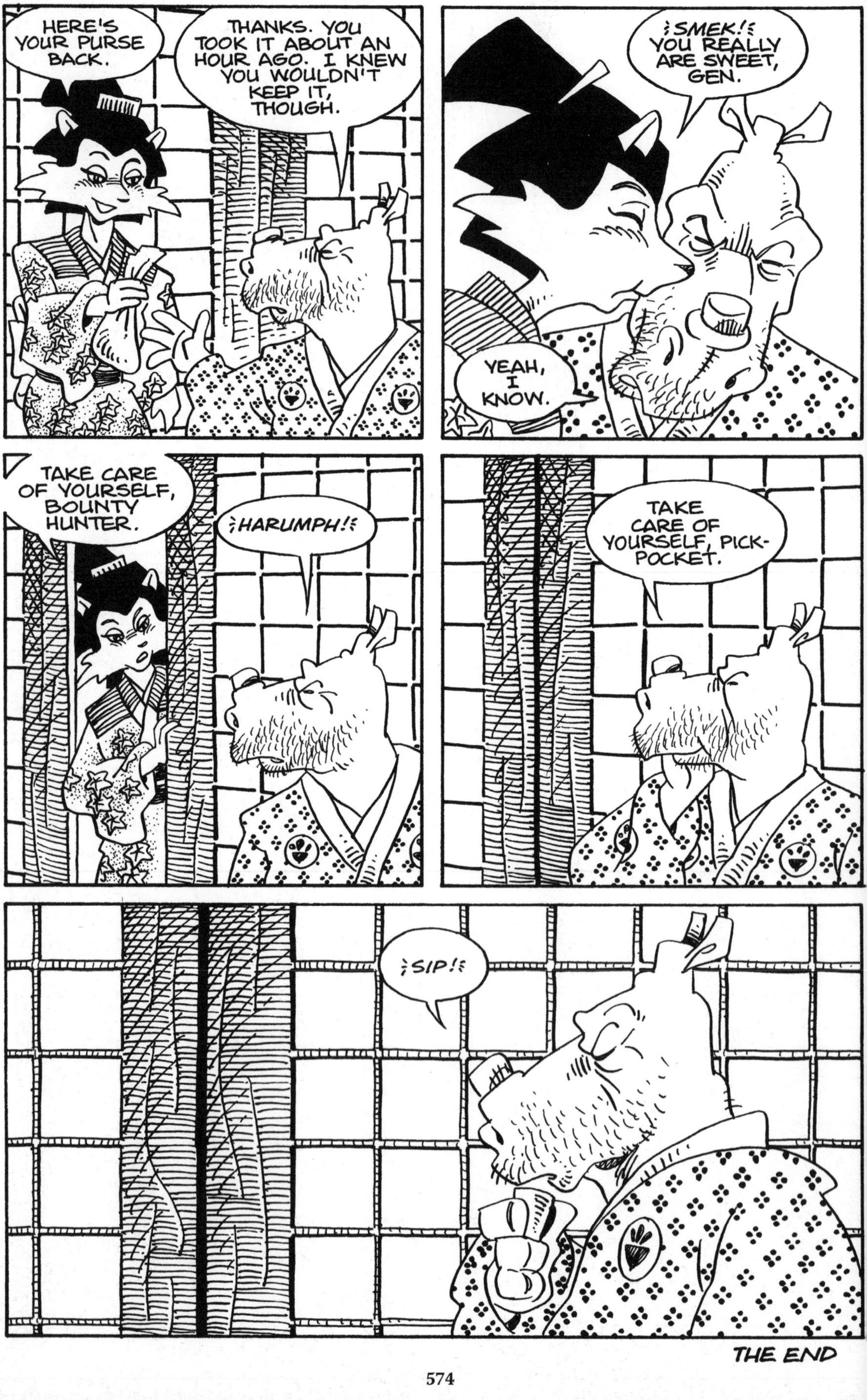
HERE'S YOUR PURSE BACK.
THANKS. YOU TOOK IT ABOUT AN HOUR AGO. I KNEW YOU WOULDN'T KEEP IT, THOUGH.
SMEK! YOU REALLY ARE SWEET, GEN.
YEAH, I KNOW.
TAKE CARE OF YOURSELF, BOUNTY HUNTER.
HARUMPH!
TAKE CARE OF YOURSELF, PICK-POCKET.
SIP!

THE END

STORY NOTES by Stan Sakai

The Inn on Moon Shadow Hill

Japan has an incredibly rich tradition of folklore. Usagi has encountered a few of the more maleficent *obake* (haunts), such as the *kappa*, the *obakéneko*, the *tengu*, and the *nue*, and will, no doubt, meet up with a few more.

"The Inn on Moon Shadow Hill," however, focuses on some of the weirder of the Japanese monsters of folklore. I grew up hearing of some of these creatures in Hawaii, which has a huge Japanese American population. A *mujina* (faceless woman) was purported to have haunted the women's restroom at the old Waialae Drive-In Theatre in Honolulu. She really didn't do anything. The story usually unfolds as a woman goes into the restroom and sees a girl combing her long hair. She sees a reflection of her face in the mirror . . . only there is no face, just a smooth, egg-like shape. The girl may or may not have feet . . . a trait common to many Japanese ghosts. The drive-in is no longer there, having been torn down to make way for a subdivision.

Many *obakemono* seem to be fairly benign, such as the *rokuroshikubi* (long-neck woman) or the *sasosho* (that hairy foot with the eye) . . . and what's with that walking umbrella (*bakegasa*)?

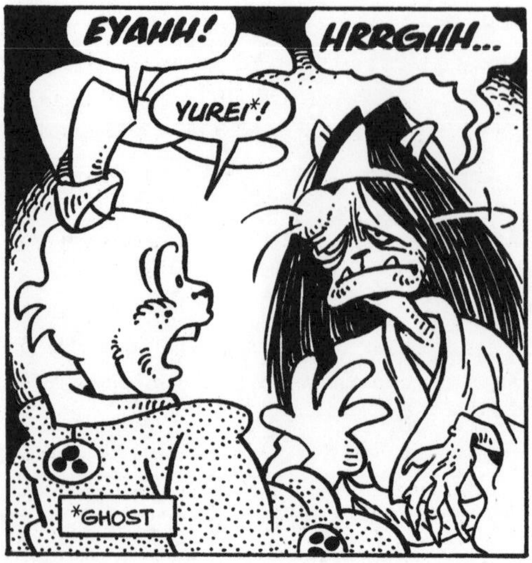
EYAHH!
YUREI*!
HRRGHH...
*GHOST

For another story of a *mujina* and other strange tales, I suggest *Kwaidan*, by Lafcadio Hearn (New York: Dover Publications, 1968).

A Potter's Tale

Many believe Japan to have the oldest ceramics tradition in the world. Based on carbon dating, it goes as far back as 10,000 BC with the Jomon—or "cord marked"—pottery.

Unlike in the West, in Japan ceramics is admired as a fine art, on a par with painting and sculpture, as well as for its utilitarian purposes. A single teacup crafted by a master potter could command as high a price as 25,000 *koku* by feudal lords. (A *koku* is the amount of rice needed to feed a man for a full year.)

Different areas are known for their unique pottery. Mashiko, a village northeast of Tokyo, is renowned for sturdy pieces of glazed stoneware. Shigaraki is famous for large storage jars. The Arita district of Kyushu, Japan's southernmost island, is known for its fine porcelain and is considered the nation's ceramics capital.

Toyotomi, the great unifier of Japan during the later sixteenth century, led an unsuccessful invasion of Korea, and many Korean artisans were taken back to Japan. The Arita porcelain industry was founded by these Korean artisans. Today, the wares from the Arita kilns are known as Imari ware, after the port from which they are shipped.

The major difference between ceramics and porcelain has to do with the materials used and the firing temperatures. Ceramic pieces consist primarily of clay and are baked at 1,000°C. Porcelain is made of finely crushed quartz, feldspar, and kaolin, and is fired above 1,300°C.

The Dawns of Tradition (Japan: Nissan Motor Co., 1983) has a wonderful overview and focuses on two schools, with beautiful photographs of potters at work. In *Japan Day by Day*, by Edward S. Morse (Atlanta: Cherokee Publishing, 1990) the author describes

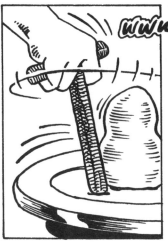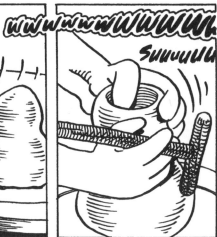

in detail visits to several schools and kilns. Many of the visuals came from two films: *Ugetsu monogatari* (1953), directed by Kenji Mizoguchi, a beautifully photographed ghost story about two peasants who try to seek their fortune; and a *National Geographic* presentation titled *Living Treasures of Japan*, which profiles several artisans working in various traditional arts, such as cloth making, sword making, and, of course, pottery.

THE MYSTERY
OF THE DEMON MASK

In Japan, the board game *go* is attributed to the Chinese emperor Shun (2255–2206 BC). Legend has it that it was invented to strengthen the weak mind of his son Shang Kiun. It was brought to the Japanese islands around the year AD 735 with the return of the envoy Kibi Daijin. It became a game for the warrior class, and by the thirteenth century it was played by everyone from the greatest generals to the meanest foot soldiers. Boards were carried on campaigns, and when the day's fighting was done the soldiers would retire to fight another type of battle. All three of the great generals, Nobunaga, Hideyoshi, and Ieyasu, were devotees of *go*. Private and state-endorsed *go* academies were founded, and the highest-ranked masters of the land appeared

annually to "combat" before the shogun. This ceremony was referred to as *go zen go* (playing the game before the exalted presence). The custom was maintained until the fall of the shogunate in 1868.

Go has been likened to Western chess. However, whereas chess concerns a single battle, *go* is an entire campaign and so a severe loss on a portion of the board does not mean a loss of the game. The player can take to another part of the field and may even secure a decisive advantage. Battles occur in various parts of the board as positions are besieged and armies are cut off and captured in an effort to acquire the most territory and surround the most vacant spaces possible. A typical game can take an hour or two, but, as in chess, a championship game may be played over a period of days. There is record of such a game lasting nine days. It is said that a player would have to play ten thousand games to reach the lowest professional rank. At a rate of one game a day, that would be about twenty-seven years.

The board, or *ban*, is a solid block of wood, always stained yellow. The feet are cut to resemble the *kuchinashi* fruit and are supposed to restrain onlookers from offering comments (*kuchinashi* means "without a mouth"). The top of the board is painted with thin, black lines, nineteen on each side, dividing it into squares. The intersections of these lines are called *me* or *moku*. Disk-shaped stones are placed on these intersections.

THERE.
CLIK!
THE GAME IS OVER. I CLAIM THE GREATER TERRITORY!
HUH?
YOU WIN!
BY ONE STONE.

Stones are picked from *tsubo* boxes and, with the middle and index fingers, placed on the board so they give a cheerful little "click."

The game comes to an end when the opposing armies are in absolute contact. The whole board need not be covered.

For people living in wood-and-paper homes, fire was a big concern. It did not take much to set a house on fire, and any strong wind could quickly spread it out of control.

There were some twenty major fires in Edo from 1600 to 1866. One of the most destructive was in 1657; 108,000 people died and half the city was laid waste.

Many precautions were taken to prevent the spread of fire. Large barrels of water and buckets were kept on streets, and many streets themselves were wide enough to act as firebreaks. Fire towers were erected throughout the city. They were equipped with bells or alarm boards. The location and ferocity of the fires were indicated by the number and strength of the strokes hitting the alarm.

Firefighters were organized by the *daimyo* (lord) to protect his castle and the homes of his retainers and by merchants to protect their own interests. Firefighters were called *tobi-no-mono* or *hikeshi*. The term *tobi-no-mono* refers to the hook used by firefighters, which was shaped like a bird's beak (*tobi* refers to the Siberian black kite; *mono* means "person"). *Hikeshi* is a more descriptive term (*hi* means "fire"; *keshi* means "to extinguish"). The *daimyo*'s firefighters wore protective leather clothing with hooded helmets, whereas the town's *tobi* wore heavy cotton clothing and were mainly composed of carpenters, roofers, and other construction experts. Large mallets and poles were used to knock down walls, bamboo ladders enabled the firefighters to climb, and hooks tore down burning roofs. Manually operated wooden pumps were introduced in the mid-eighteenth century to shoot streams of water through bamboo pipes. Each company of *tobi* had a standard: a geometric shape mounted on a pole. The standard-bearer took a position as close to the fire as possible, sometimes even on the roof of a burning building. The owner of the saved building would pay a fee to those companies whose standards were represented and who put out the blaze.

Reference for the game *go* came from *The Game of Go: The National Game of Japan,* by Arthur Smith (Rutland, VT/Tokyo: Charles E. Tuttle, 1956); additional information came from the website of the American Go Association. References for the firefighting scene were from *Mukashi no shobo ima no shobo* (The history of firefighting in Japan), by Tadayoshi Yamamoto (Tokyo: Fukuinkan-Shoten, 1981), a wonderful picture book depicting firefighters from the Edo period to the present; *Everyday Life in Traditional Japan*, by Charles J. Dunn (Rutland, VT/ Tokyo: Charles E. Tuttle, 1969), which describes the structure of the fire department; *Kabuki Costume*, by Ruth M. Shaver, with illustrations by Soma Akira and Ota Gako (Rutland, VT/Tokyo: Charles E. Tuttle, 1966), which describes in detail the *tobi* and his uniform; and *Japan Day by Day*, by Edward S. Morse (Boston: Houghton Mifflin, 1945), which gives fascinating accounts of three fires witnessed by the author, including one extinguished by traditional means and another using a foreign-type water pump.

KUMO

Spider goblins, sometimes called earth spiders, are not uncommon in Japanese folklore.

Minamoto no Yorimitsu (AD 944–1021) had fallen ill and was brought medicine every midnight by an unfamiliar youth. As his illness worsened, he began to suspect the servant of some evil. One night he attacked the boy, who fled, but not before throwing a sticky spider web at him, entwining him. Yorimitsu's four loyal lieutenants tracked the servant to a cave, where, in his true guise of a spider goblin, he battled them. The monster was killed, and Yorimitsu immediately recovered.

In another story, Kurogumo-oji (Prince Black Spider) was taught magic by the spider goblin of Katsurayama to prepare himself for an assassination attempt.

There are two major inspirations for the creation of Sasuké:

Chung K'uei vowed to the Chinese emperor Kao-tsu that he would free the world of demons and monsters. His legend was imported to Japan during the Kamakura period (AD 1185–1392), and he was integrated into Japanese folklore as Shoki (the Japanese reading of Chung K'uei's name). Early woodcut prints depict Shoki as a huge, bearded figure dressed as a Chinese scholar with a double-edged sword, subduing demons.

The other source was Sarutobi Sasuke, a legendary ninja whose exploits are shrouded in mystery and magic. Sasuke, a farmer's son, studied *ninjutsu*, the art of invisibility, under the mountain hermit Tozawa Hakuunsai. Japanese folklore took the art of invisibility literally and imbued the ninja with magical powers such as transformation, weather manipulation, and, of course, invisibility. Toads and frogs are often associated with these ninja-wizards. They have the ability to hypnotize and to belch deadly gas from their mouths.

References: *Japanese Ghosts and Demons*, by Stephen Addiss (New York: George Braziller, 1985); *Japanese Mythology*, by Juliet Piggott (New York: Hamlyn Publishing Group, 1969); and *Ninja: The True Story of Japan's Secret Warrior Cult*, by Stephen Turnbull (UK: Firebird Books, 1991), which gives a comprehensive look at the ninja of history as well as of folklore.

GRASSCUTTER II

The tenth emperor, Sujin, ascended to the throne in the first century BC. By this time, society had developed to the point where a clear distinction had to be made between worldly and spiritual affairs. Sujin established a shrine at Kasanui Village in Yamato Province dedicated to Amaterasu, the sun goddess, and installed there the sacred mirror and sword. The emperor ordered replicas of them made, which he kept in the Imperial Palace.

His successor, Suinin, established a new shrine in Ise Province and transferred the mirror and sword and a third treasure, a jewel, to be housed there. His daughter was given charge of Ise Shrine.

Yamato-Dake is the most famous hero of legendary times. He was the third son of Emperor Keiko. He was initially named Wousu (Little Mortar) and had an elder twin named Oousu (Big Mortar), whom he killed before being sent to quell the Kumaso rebels at the age of sixteen.

Before the start of a later campaign, Yamato-Dake paid his respects to the Grand Shrine at Ise and was given the sword Ame-no-Murakumo-no-Tsurugi by his aunt. He renamed it Kusanagi-no-Tsurugi (The Grass-Cutting Sword) after it saved his life in an open field.

There are many variations of the story of Yamato-Dake and the *kami* of Mt. Ibuki. In one, the hero is unable to slay either the boar or the snake but is repulsed from the mountain by a violent ice rain and later dies, seemingly from fatigue. In another, he goes to a hot spring after the killing of the serpent and regains his health and strength. The events I've recounted are probably the most familiar and are found in *The Kojiki: Records of Ancient Matters*, the oldest history of the Japanese people, written in AD 712 by Yasumaro, as dictated by Hiyeda no Are by order of Emperor Temmu.

The hot spring Yamato-Dake came to after meeting the *kami* is now called Isame no Shimizu, "Clear Water Where He Came to His Senses." The area where he could hardly stand is Tagino, or "Totter." And when exhaustion finally took him, he walked with a stick at Tsuetsuki-zake, or "Slope with a Walking Stick."

His consorts sang four songs at the prince's funeral. These four were sung at every emperor's death afterward, until the funeral of Emperor Meiji in AD 1912.

Atsuta Jingu is one of the three major shrines in Japan, along with the Meiji Shrine and the Grand Shrine at Ise. Atsuta is said to be the repository of Kusanagi-no-Tsurugi, the Grass-Cutting Sword, though some believe the original sword was lost in the Battle of Dan-no-Ura Strait during the Genpei War, in the twelfth century.

The shrine grounds cover 190,000 square meters of thickly wooded area in the middle of Nagoya. Some of the trees there are over a thousand years old. The shrine is also home to sixty annual festivals and ten religious events, including the Atsuta Jingu Hono Tanren, a festival for swordsmiths.

Kusanagi is actually housed in the *honden*, or main inner shrine, along with many other treasures. Only priests and *miko* (shrine maidens) are allowed to approach the *honden*.

A few historians believe that the sword kept at the shrine no longer exists, that it was destroyed in an Allied bombing raid in World War II. The present shrine was built on the old site in 1955.

AHH... THE WATER HAS CLEARED MY SENSES.
SPLASH! SPLASH!
I-I ALWAYS DREAMED OF FLYING THROUGH THE SKY... BUT NOW...I CAN HARDLY STAND...MY LEGS TOTTER...
FOUL VENOM MUST HAVE SPEWED FROM THAT *KAMI*.

References for Yamato-Dake came from *The Kojiki*, translated by Basil Hall Chamberlain (Rutland, VT/ Tokyo: Charles E. Tuttle, 1981); *Legends of the Samurai*, by Hiroaki Sato (Woodstock, NY: Overlook Press, 1995); *Myths and Legends of Japan*, by F. Hadland Davis (Mineola, NY: Dover Publications, 1992); *The Japanese Fairy Book*, compiled by Yei Theodora Ozaki (Rutland, VT/Tokyo: Charles E. Tuttle, 1970); *Myths and Legends Series: China and Japan* by Donald A. Mackenzie (London: Bracken Books, 1985); *A History of the Japanese People from the Earliest Times to the End of the Meiji Era*, by Capt. F. Brinkley (New York: Encyclopedia Britannica, 1915); and *Japan, a Country Founded by "Mother": An Outline History*, by Hajime Hoshi (Tokyo: Columbia University Club, 1937).

References for the Japanese culture during that era came from *Early Samurai: AD 200–1500*, by Anthony Bryant and Angus McBride (Oxford: Osprey Press, 1991); *Cultural Atlas of Japan*, by Martin Collcutt, Marius Jansen, and Isao Kumakura (New York: Facts on File, 1988); and *Step into . . . Ancient Japan*, by Fiona Macdonald (New York: Anness Publishing, 1999).

References for chapter 6, "In the Realm of Senses," came from *Japan, a Country Founded by "Mother"* and *Japan Handbook*, by J. D. Bisignani (Chico, CA: Moon Publications, 1983). Reference for the *kannushi* was found in *A Look into Japan*, published in 1985 by the Japan Travel Bureau, and additional reference came from *Nagoya Visitors Guide, Live Map of Nagoya*, and *Sightseeing Spot Guide to Nagoya and Inuyama*, published by the Nagoya Convention and Visitors Bureau. I would also like to acknowledge the help of the Usagi Yojimbo Dojo website members, who scoured the Internet for visuals and information on Atsuta Shrine.

The Shrouded Moon

Crabs, or *kani*, have both good and bad connotations in Japanese tradition.

According to legend, crabs once appeared at a seaside village which had never seen any such creatures before.

IT'S A SMALL IVORY CRAB. IT DOESN'T LOOK LIKE MUCH.
IT'S JUST A CHEAP LITTLE TRINKET.

The villagers thought they surely must be supernatural creatures, so they caught the crabs and hung them over their doorways to keep themselves from being harmed. That night, the evil spirit of the village descended on them but, upon seeing the strange creatures, became afraid and left the area. Dried crab shells became a protection against evil.

On the other hand, crabs were also looked upon with malice. Their sideways walking was compared to the twisted dealings of deceitful people. Western script was referred to as "crab writing" because it is written horizontally.

The Buddhist tradition looked upon the crab's hibernation as a metaphor for the period of rest between one's reincarnations. A crab on a lotus flower or pod is a decidedly Buddhist symbol.

Two remarkable Japanese crabs are the giant crab of Hokkaido, whose body width can measure fifty centimeters, and the tiny *Heike gani*, with the faces of defeated warriors embossed on its shell.

Stan

GALLERY

Stan Sakai's cover art for the issues collected in this volume.
Colors by Tom Luth, except on painted covers and where noted.

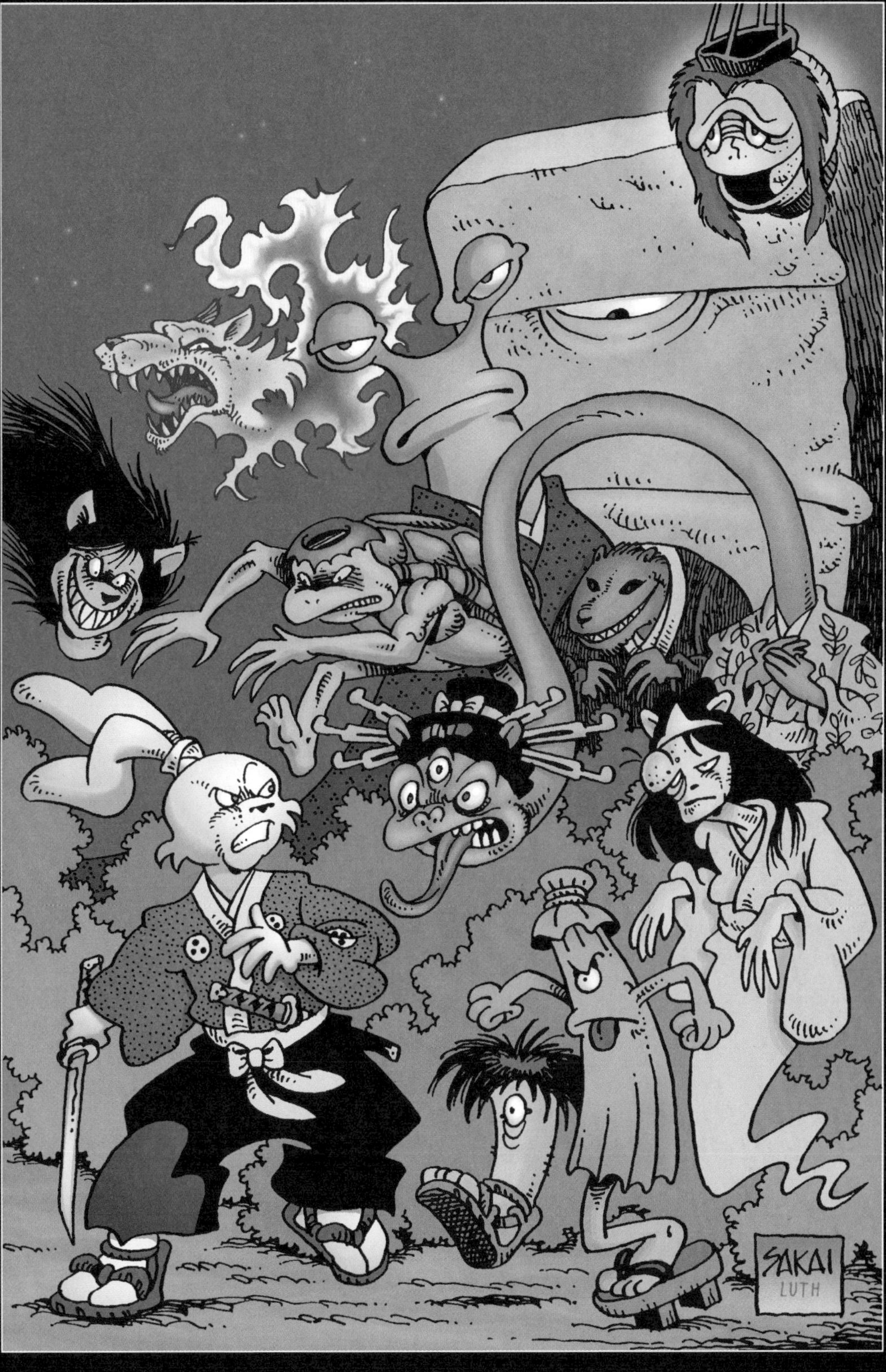
SAKAI
LUTH

Usagi Yojimbo Volume Three #31

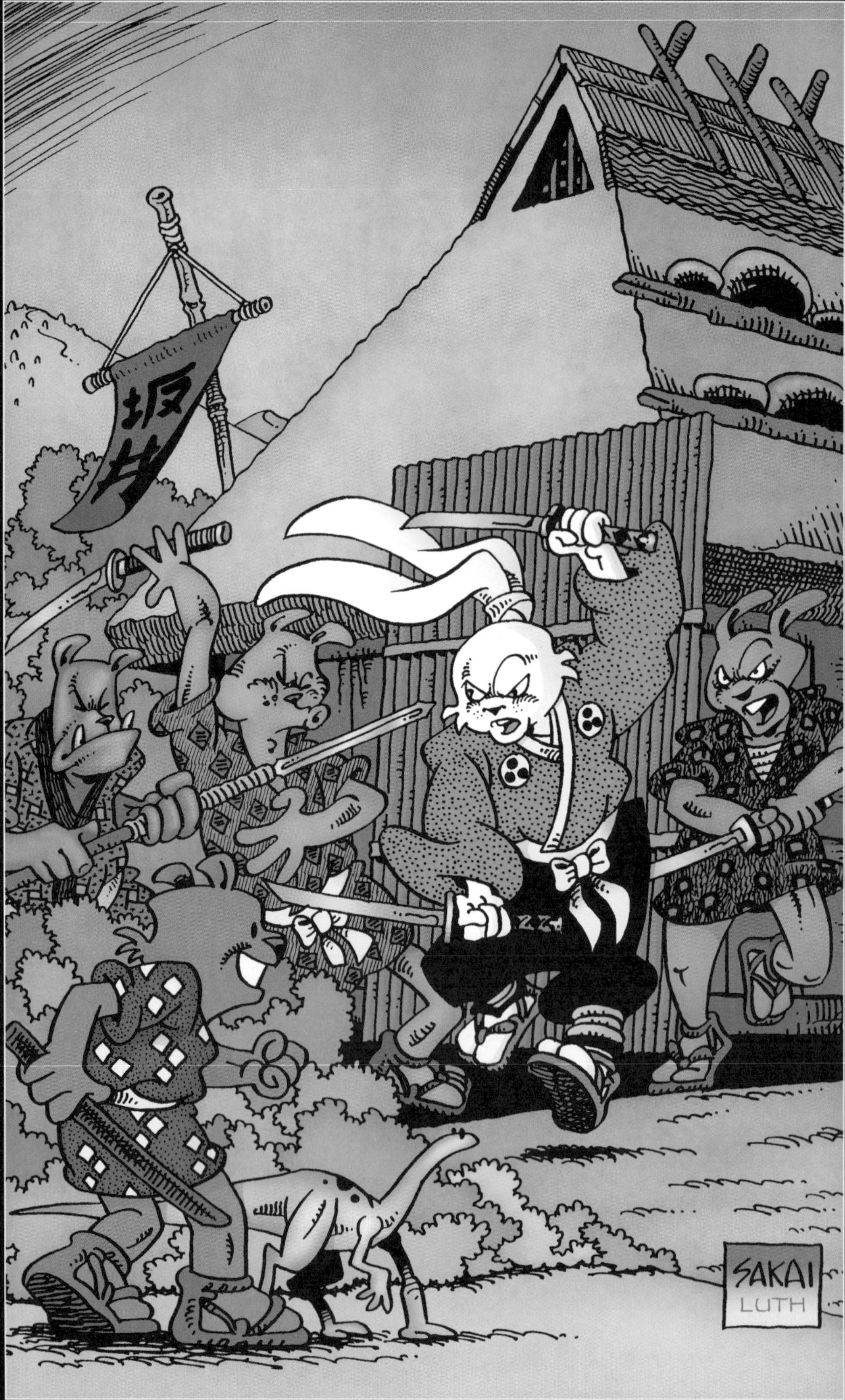
SAKAI
LUTH

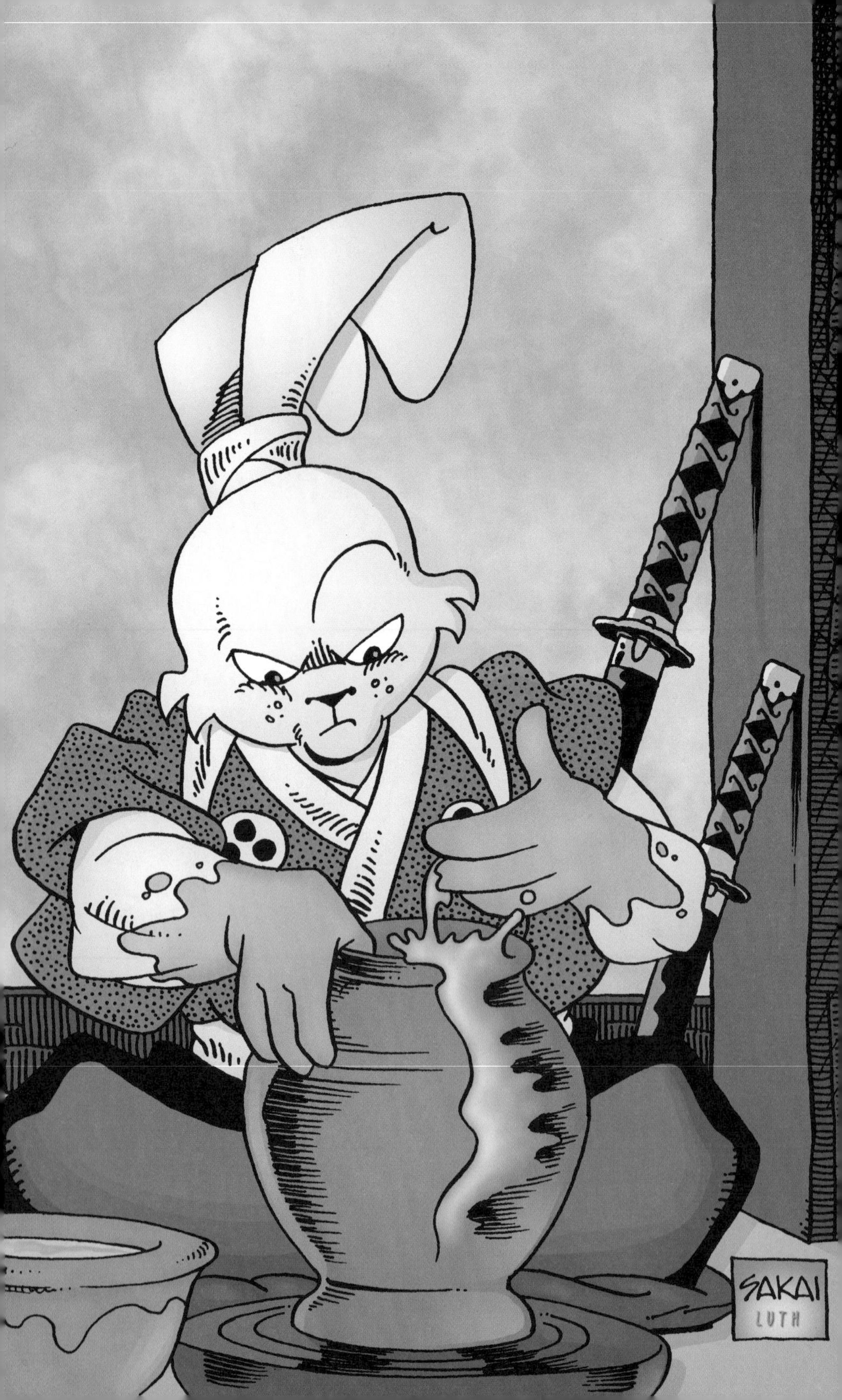
SAKAI
LUTH

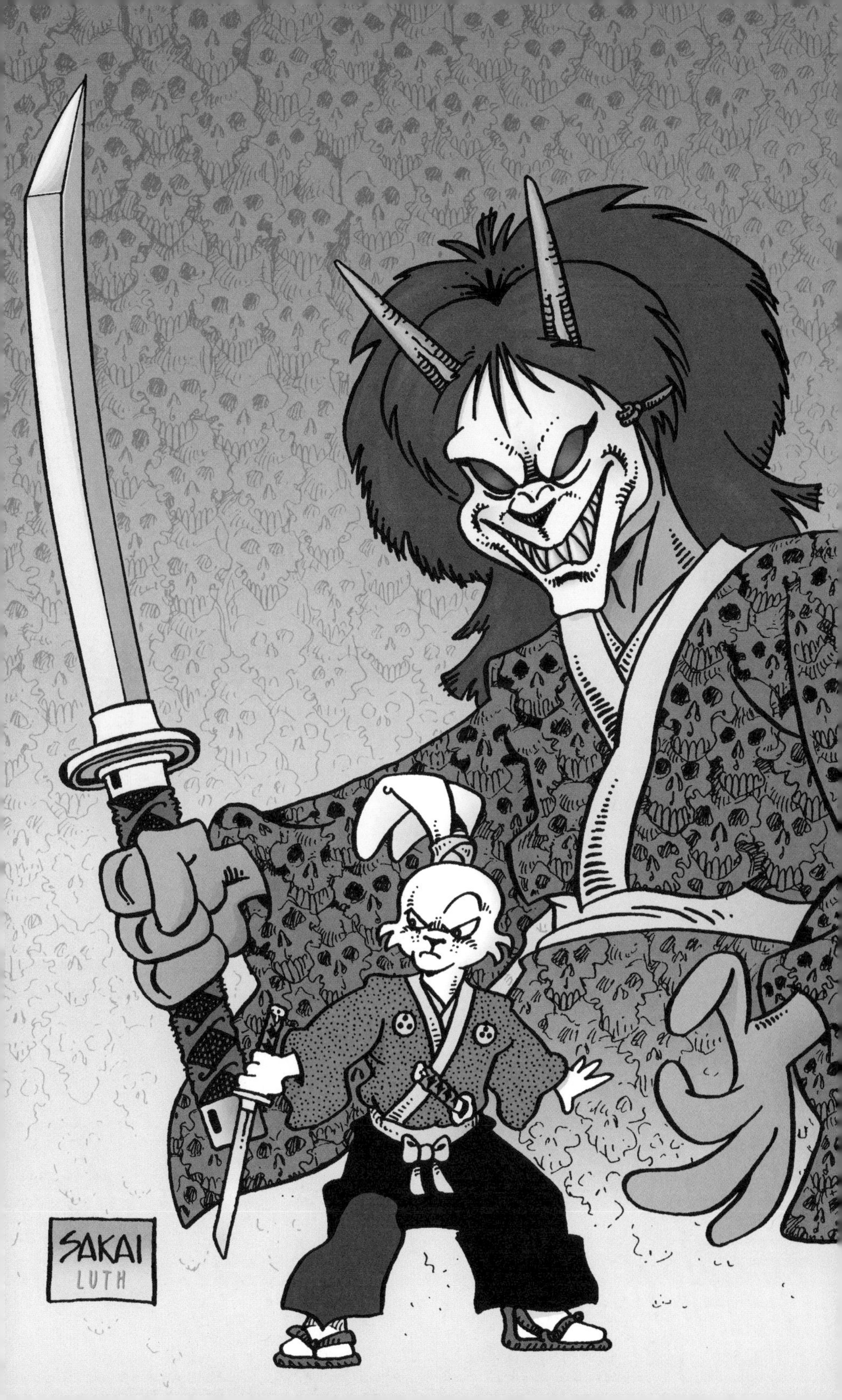
SAKAI
LUTH

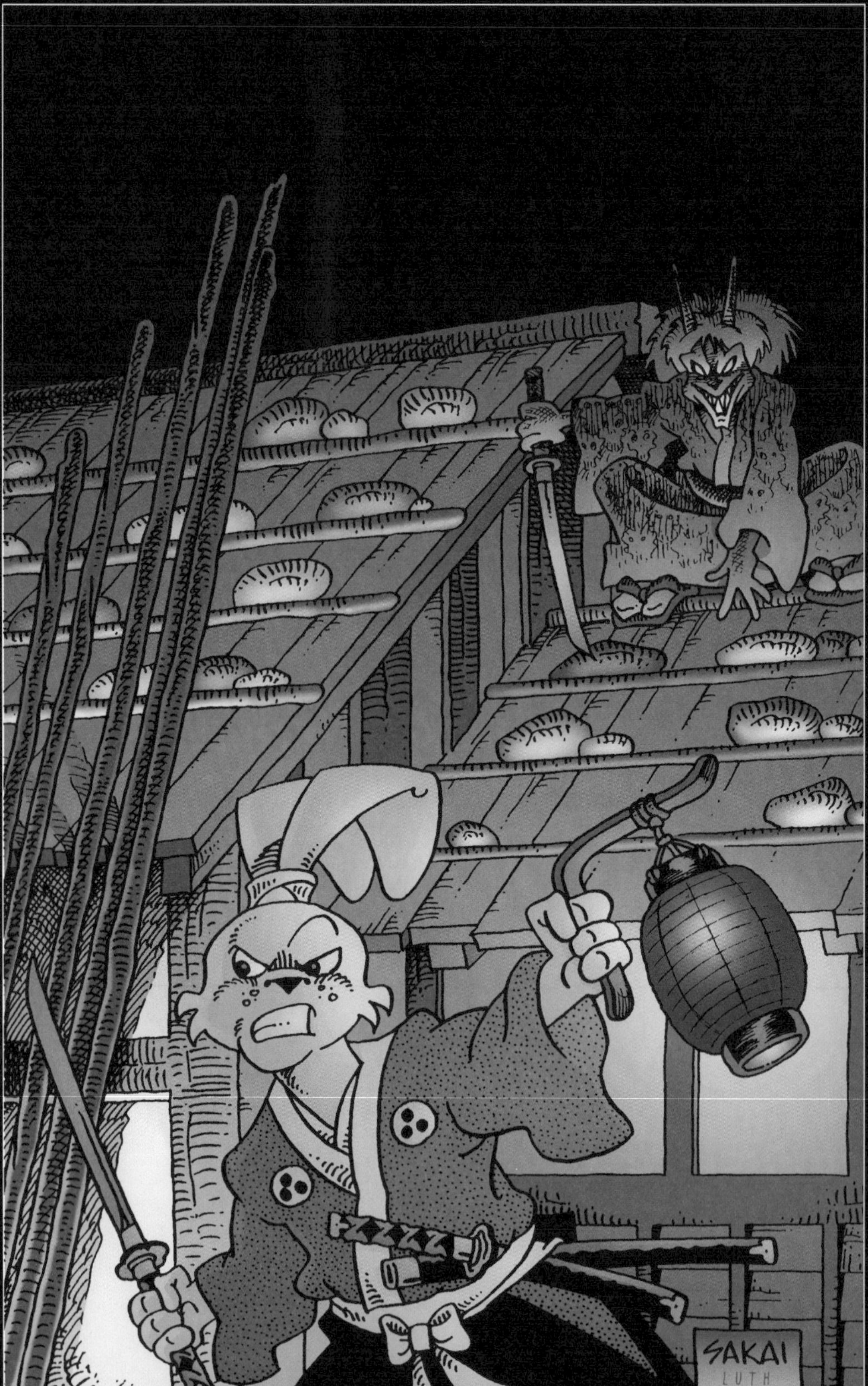
SAKAI
LUTH

Usagi Yojimbo Volume Three #35

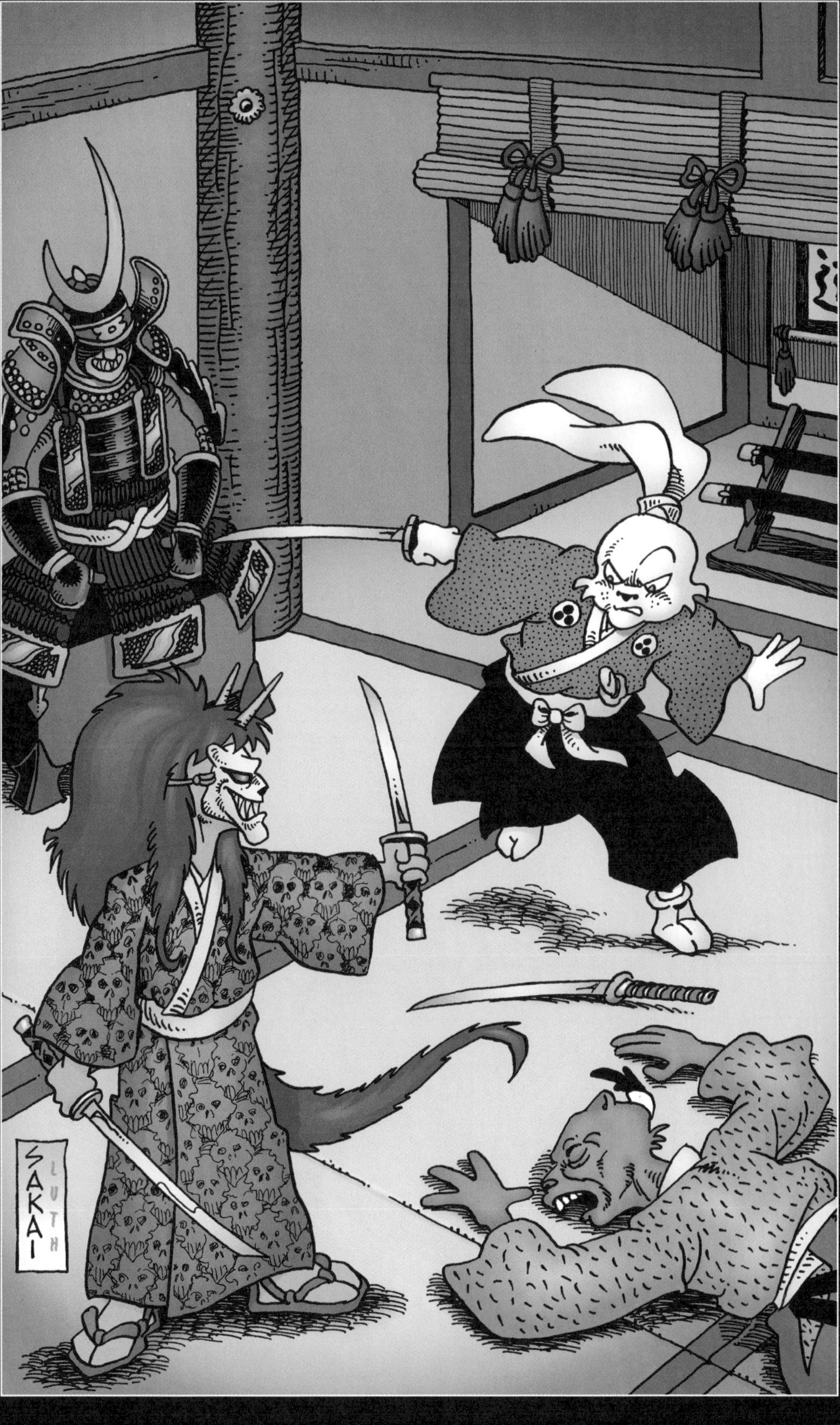
SAKAI
LUTH

Usagi Yojimbo Volume Three #36

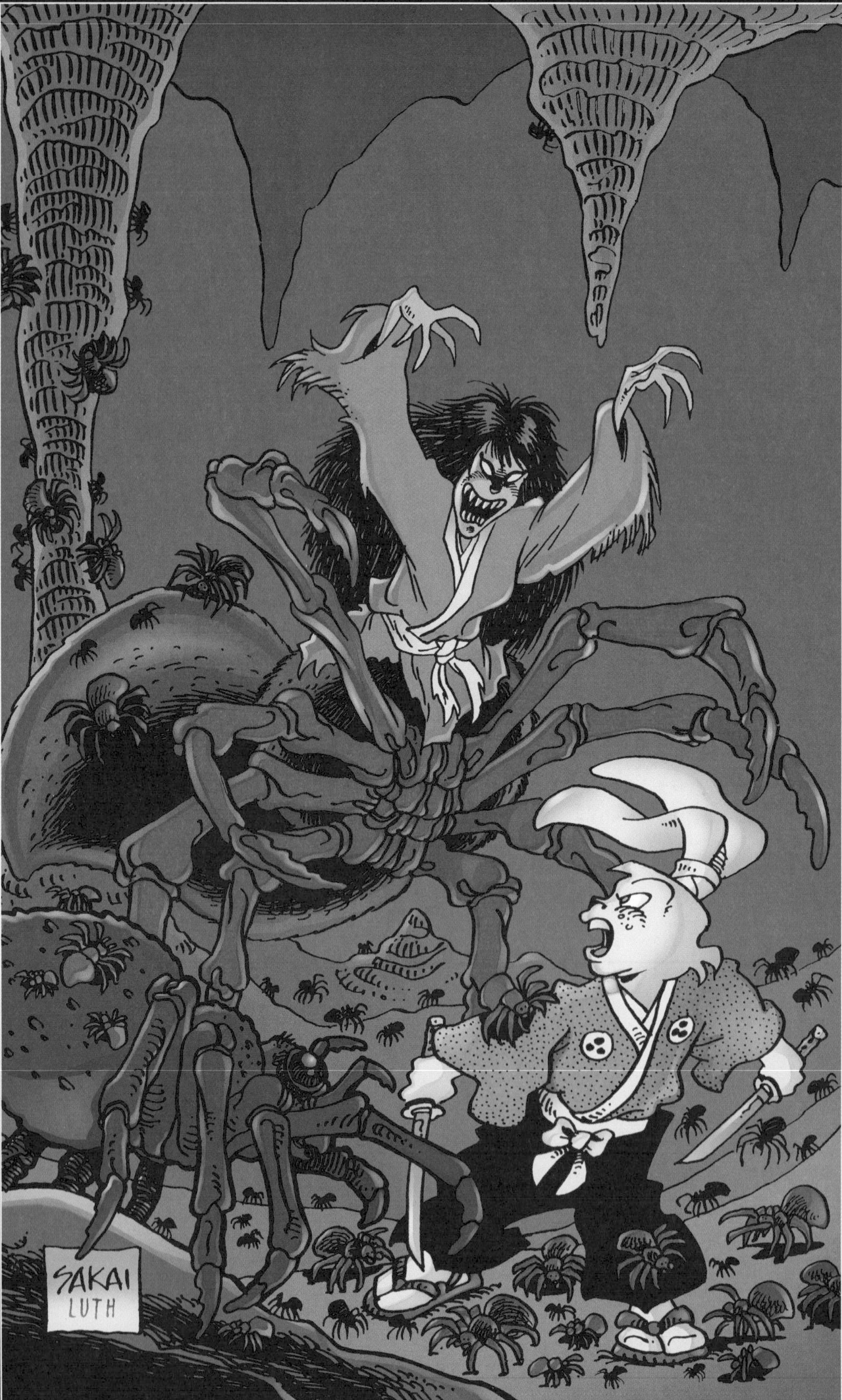
SAKAI
LUTH

Usagi Yojimbo Volume Three #37

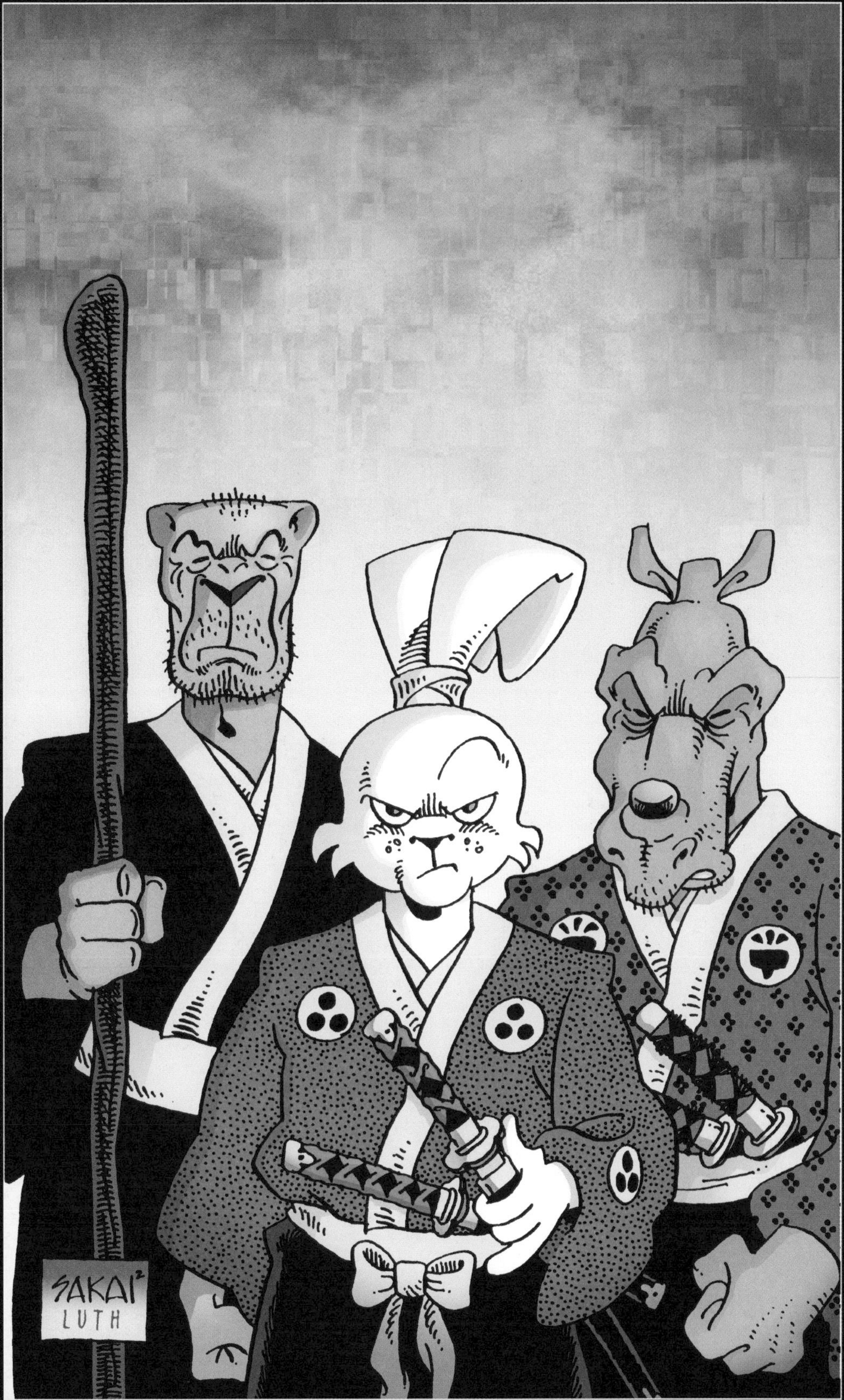
SAKAI
LUTH

Usagi Yojimbo Volume Three #38

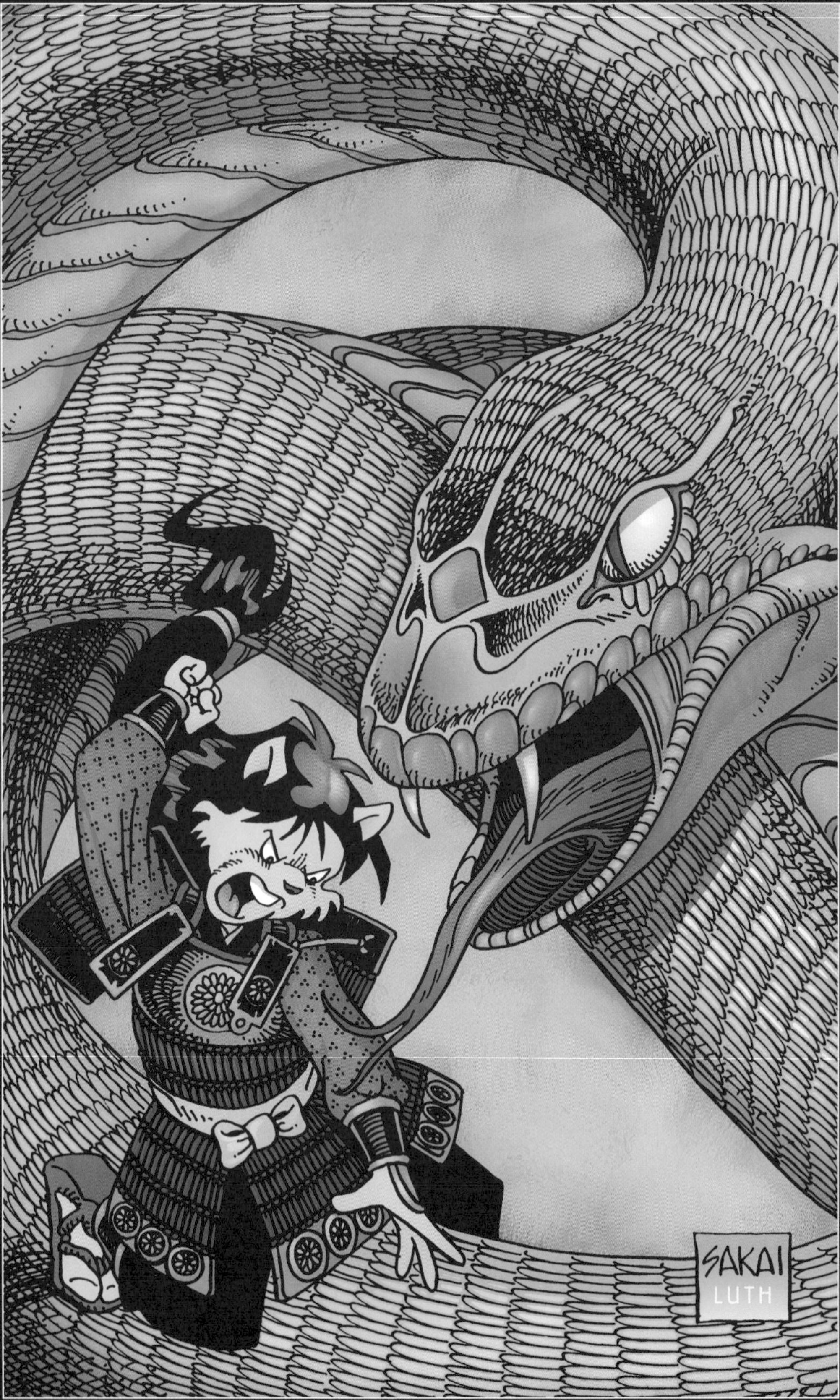
SAKAI
LUTH

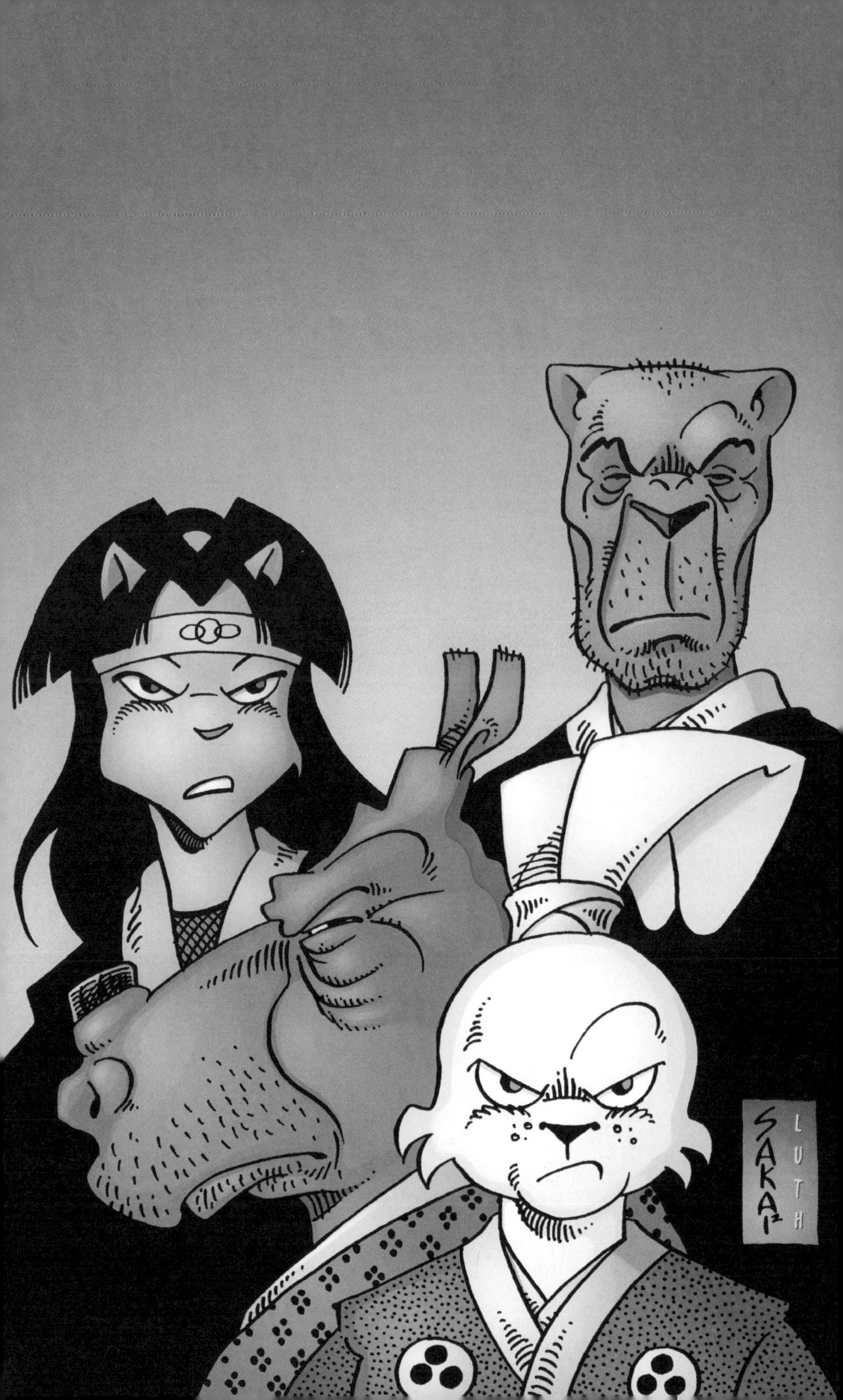
SAKAI
LUTH

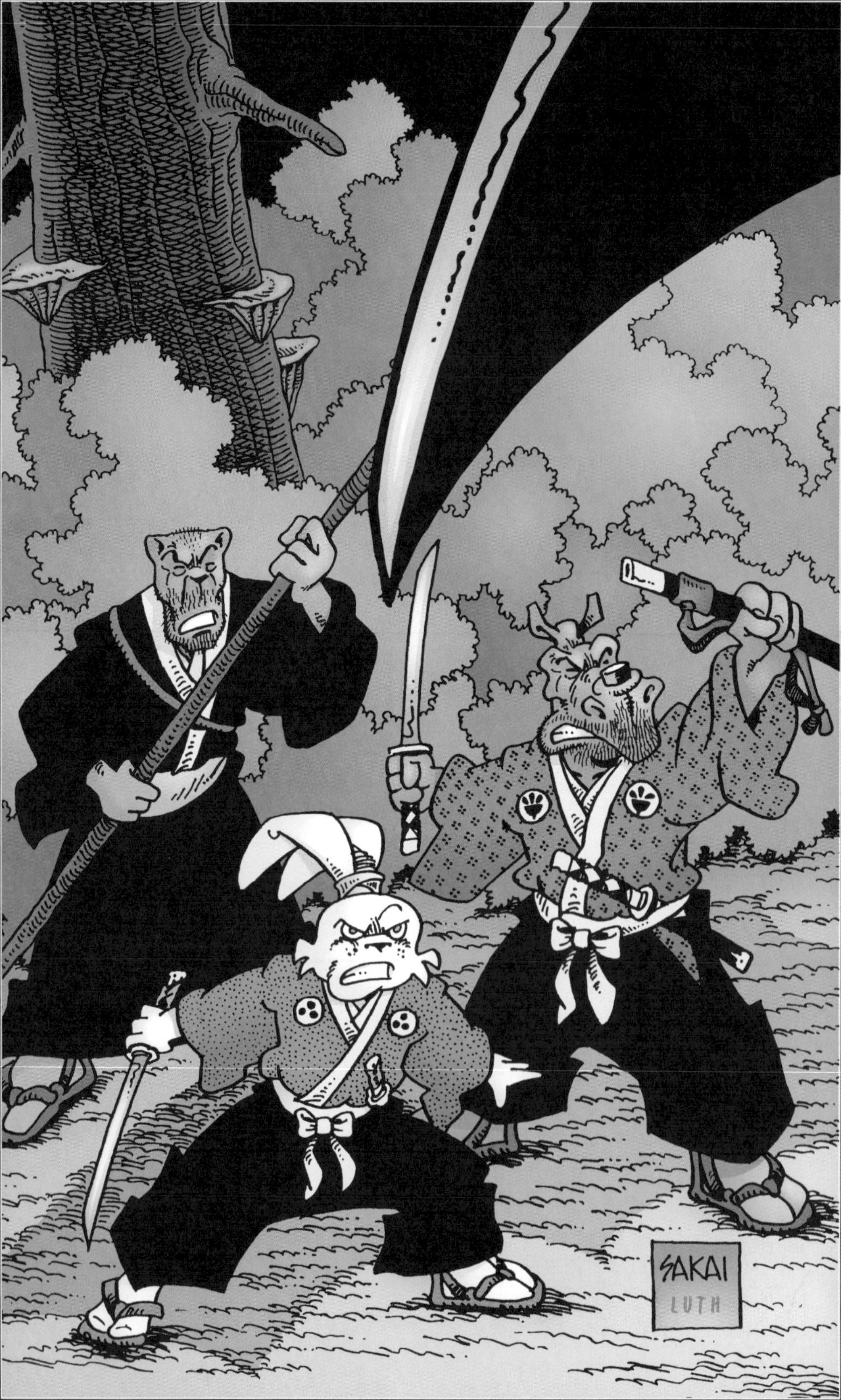
SAKAI
LUTH

Usagi Yojimbo Volume Three #41

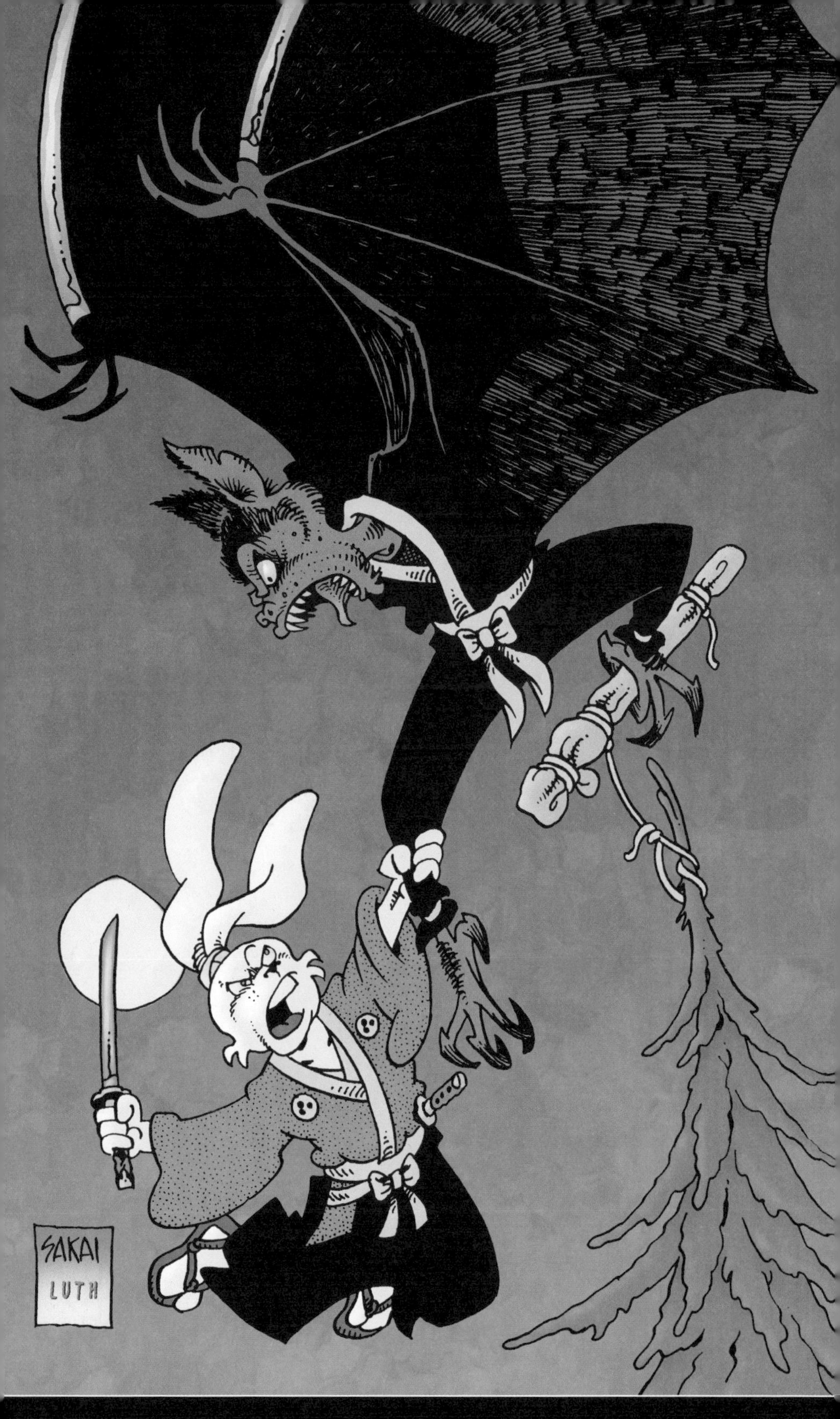
SAKAI
LUTH

Usagi Yojimbo Volume Three #42

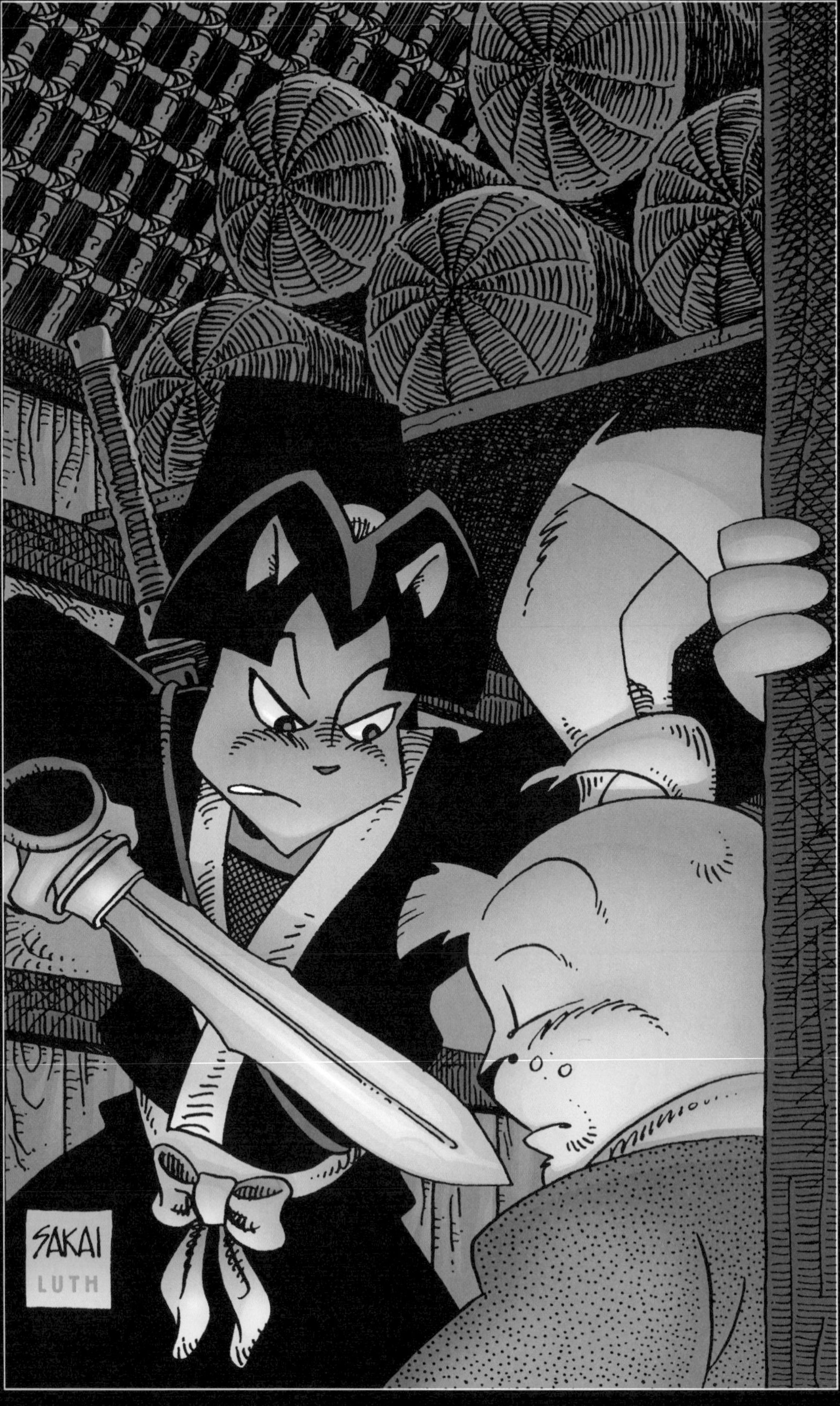
SAKAI
LUTH

Usagi Yojimbo Volume Three #43

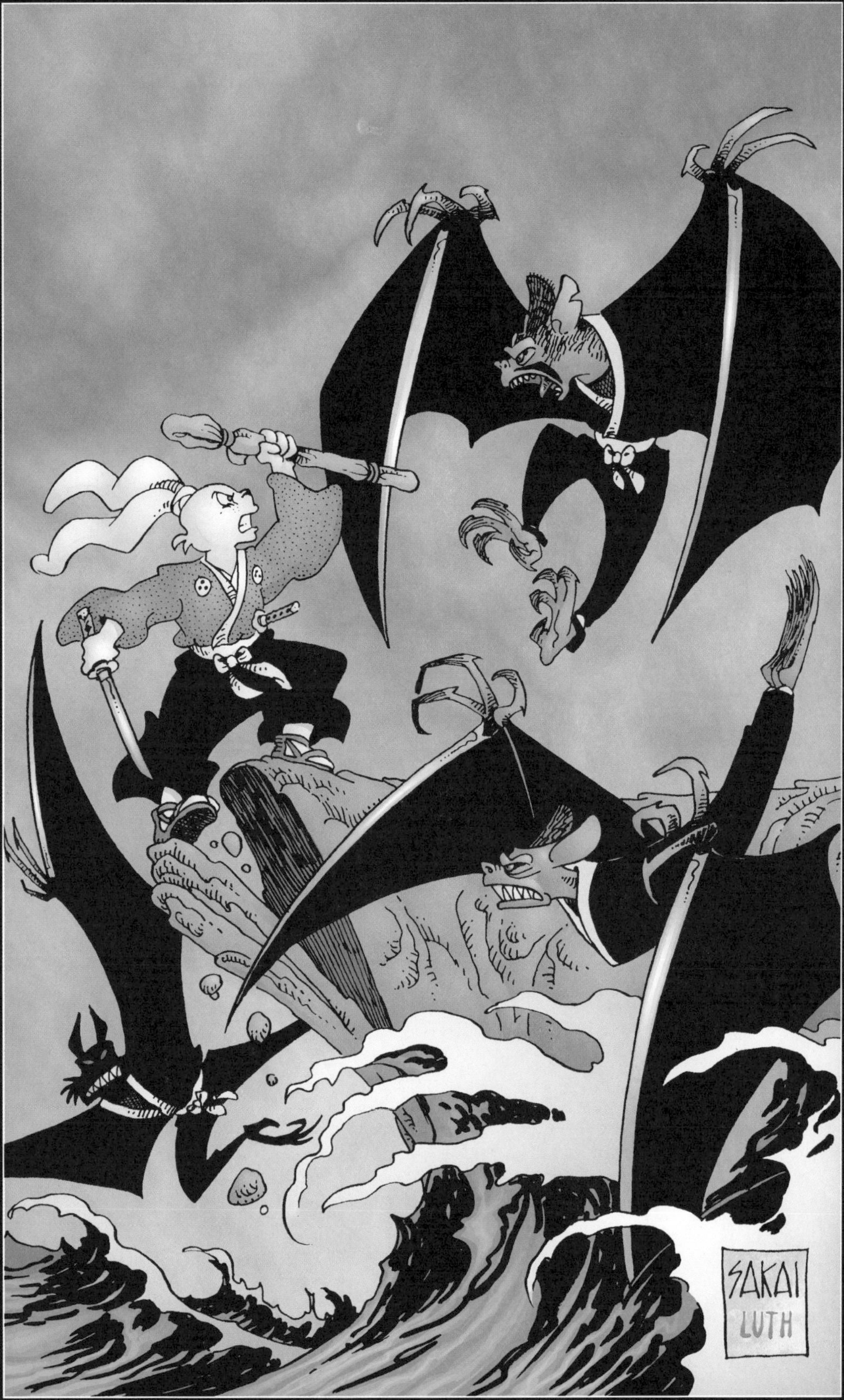
SAKAI
LUTH

Usagi Yojimbo Volume Three #44

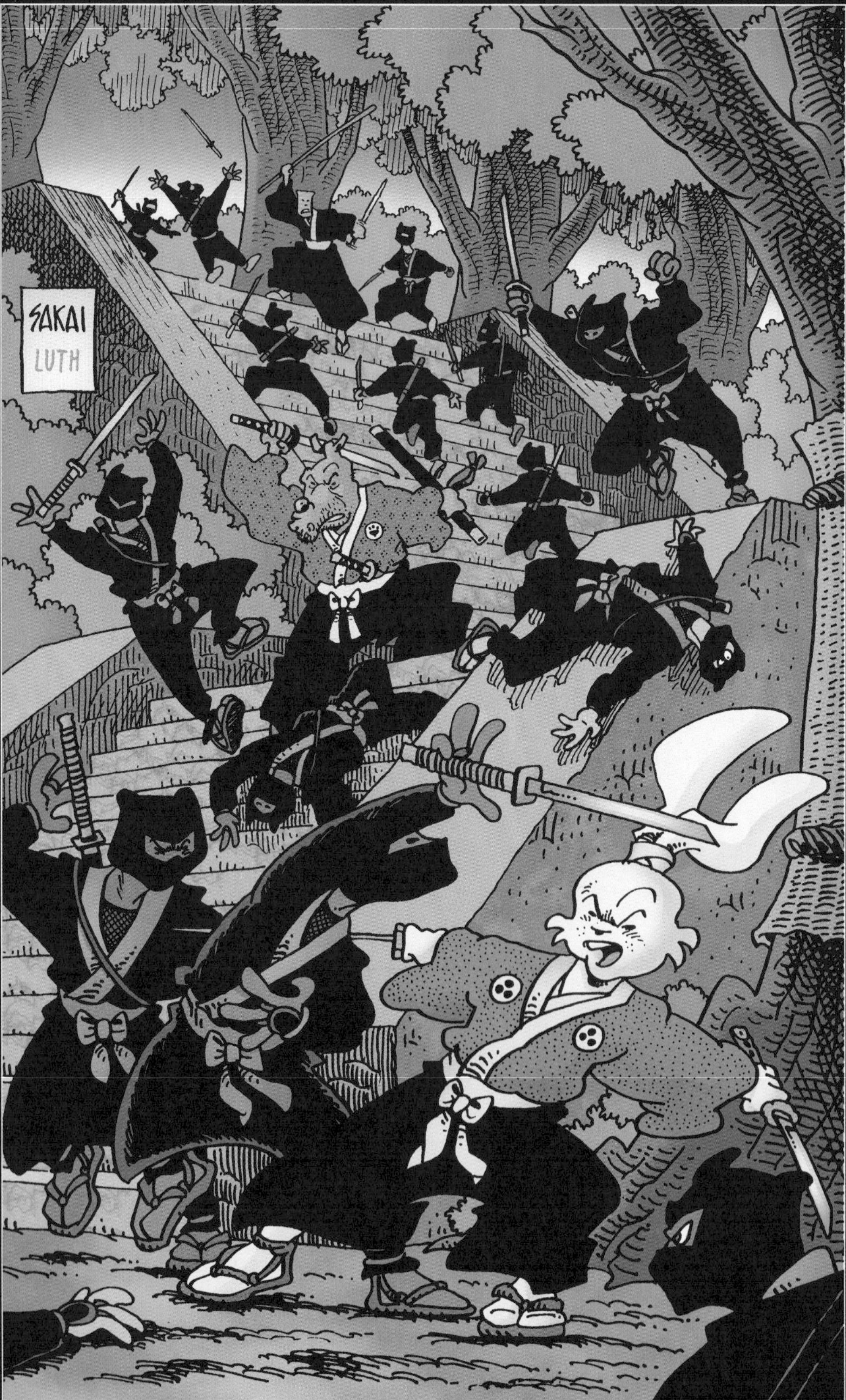
SAKAI
LUTH

Usagi Yojimbo Volume Three #45

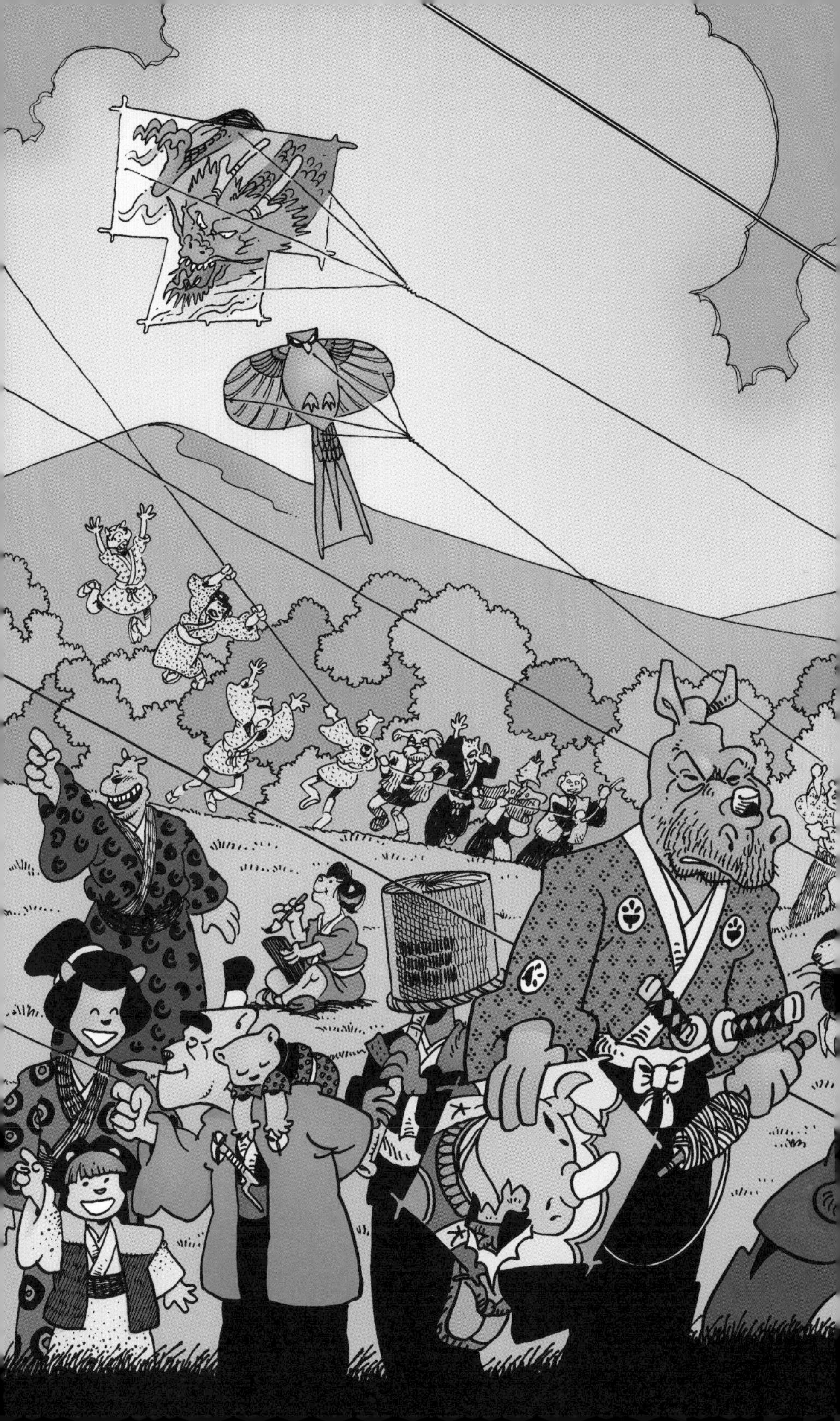

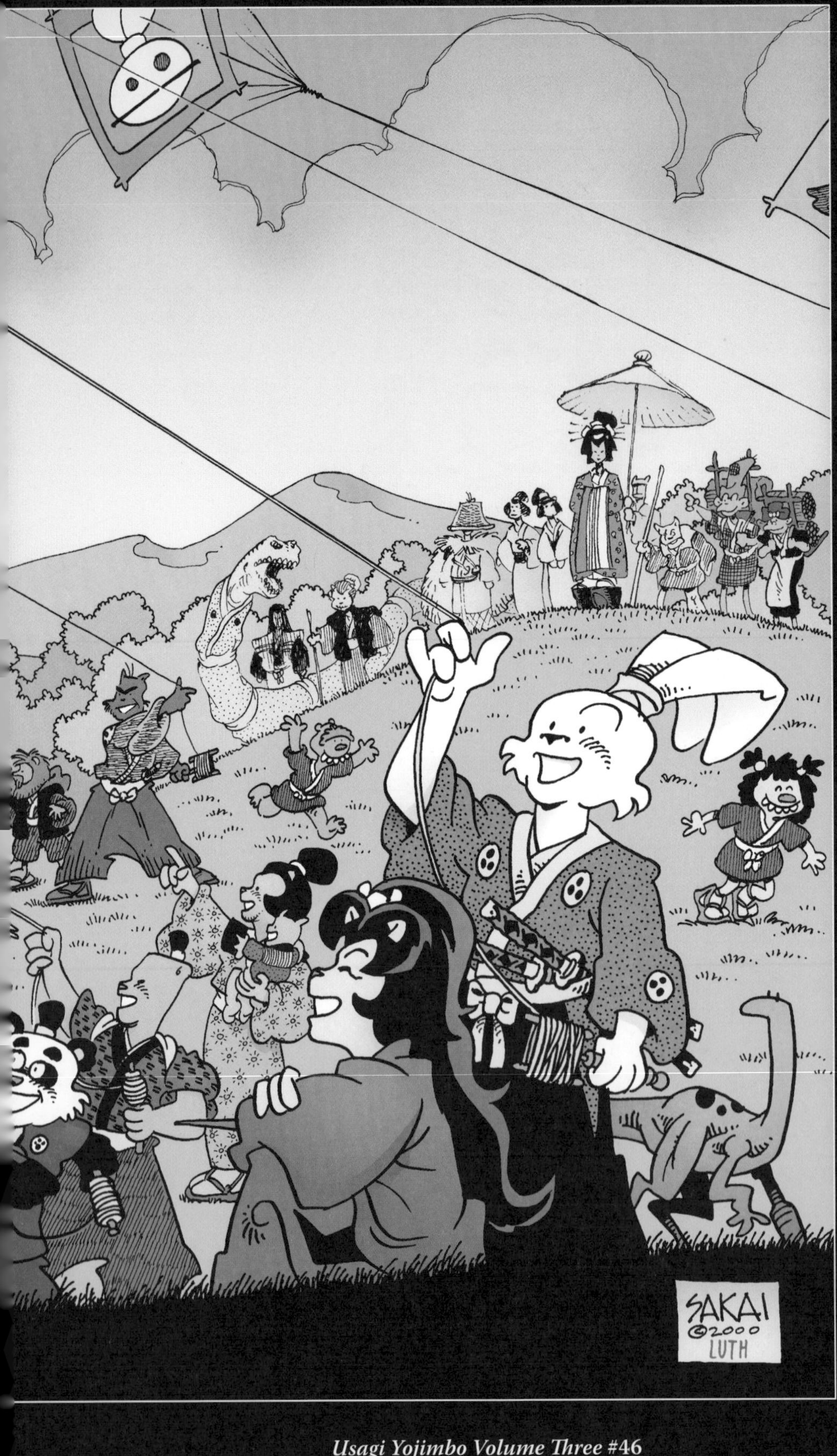
SAKAI
©2000
LUTH

Usagi Yojimbo Volume Three #46

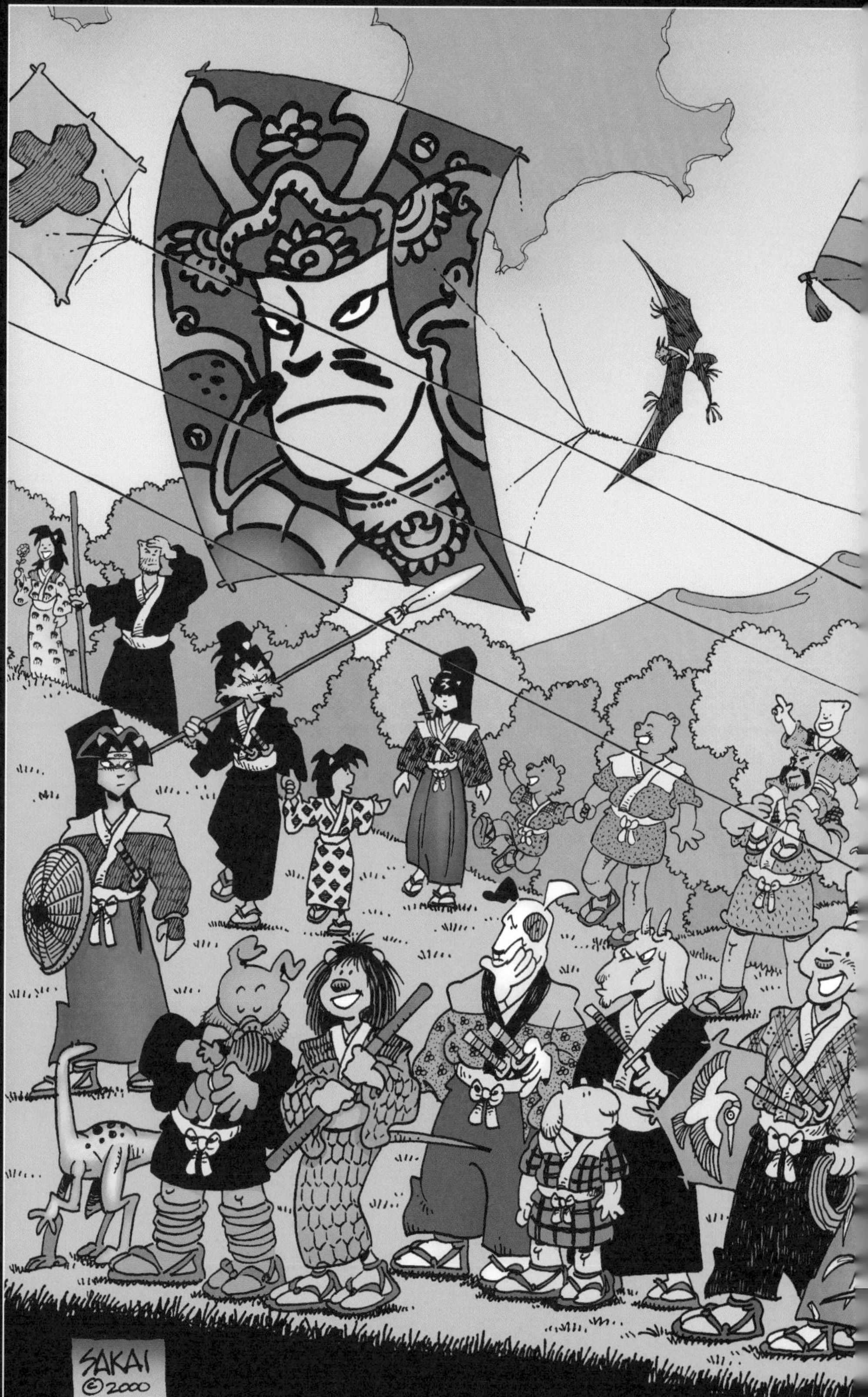
SAKAI
©2000
LUTH

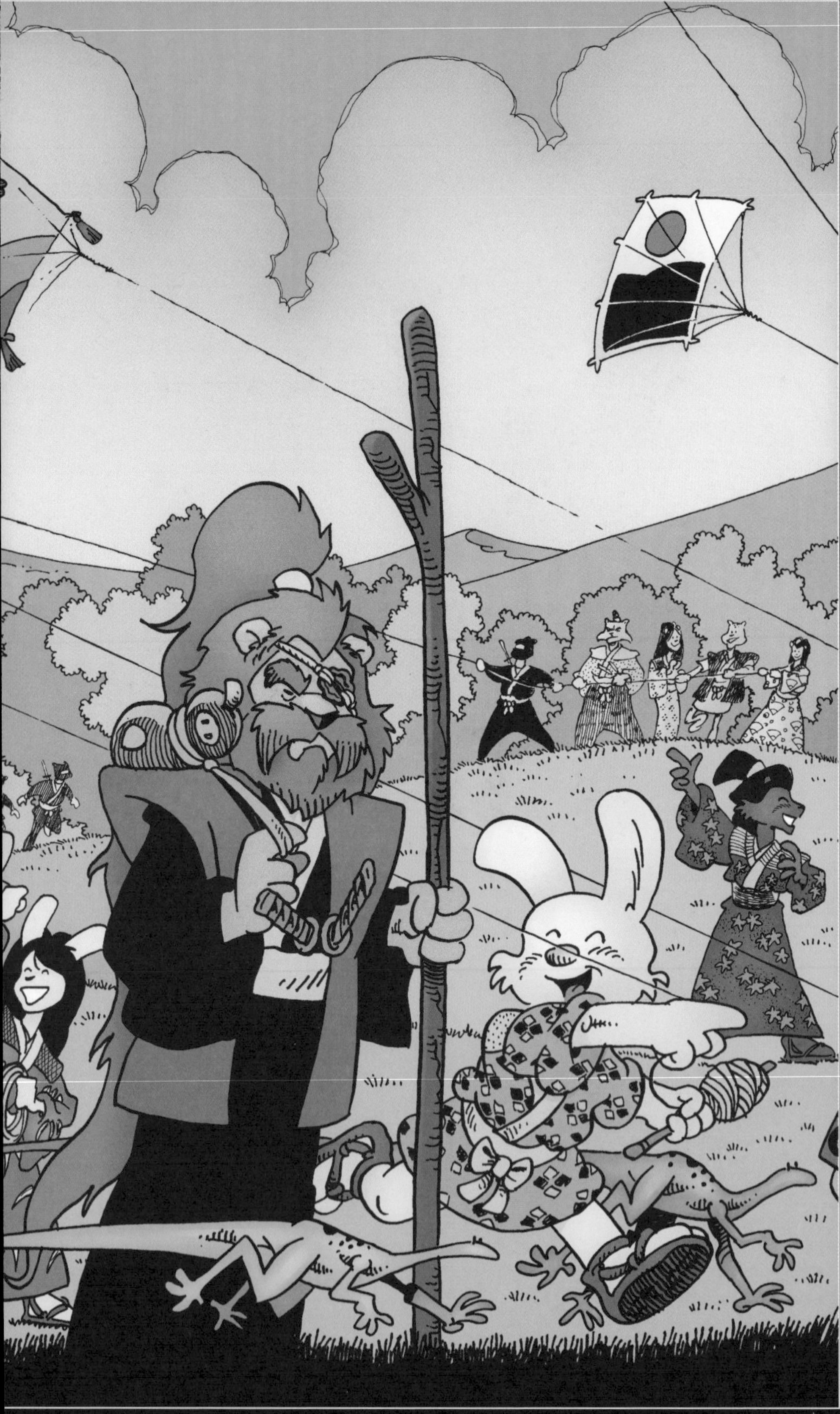

Usagi Yojimbo Volume Three #47

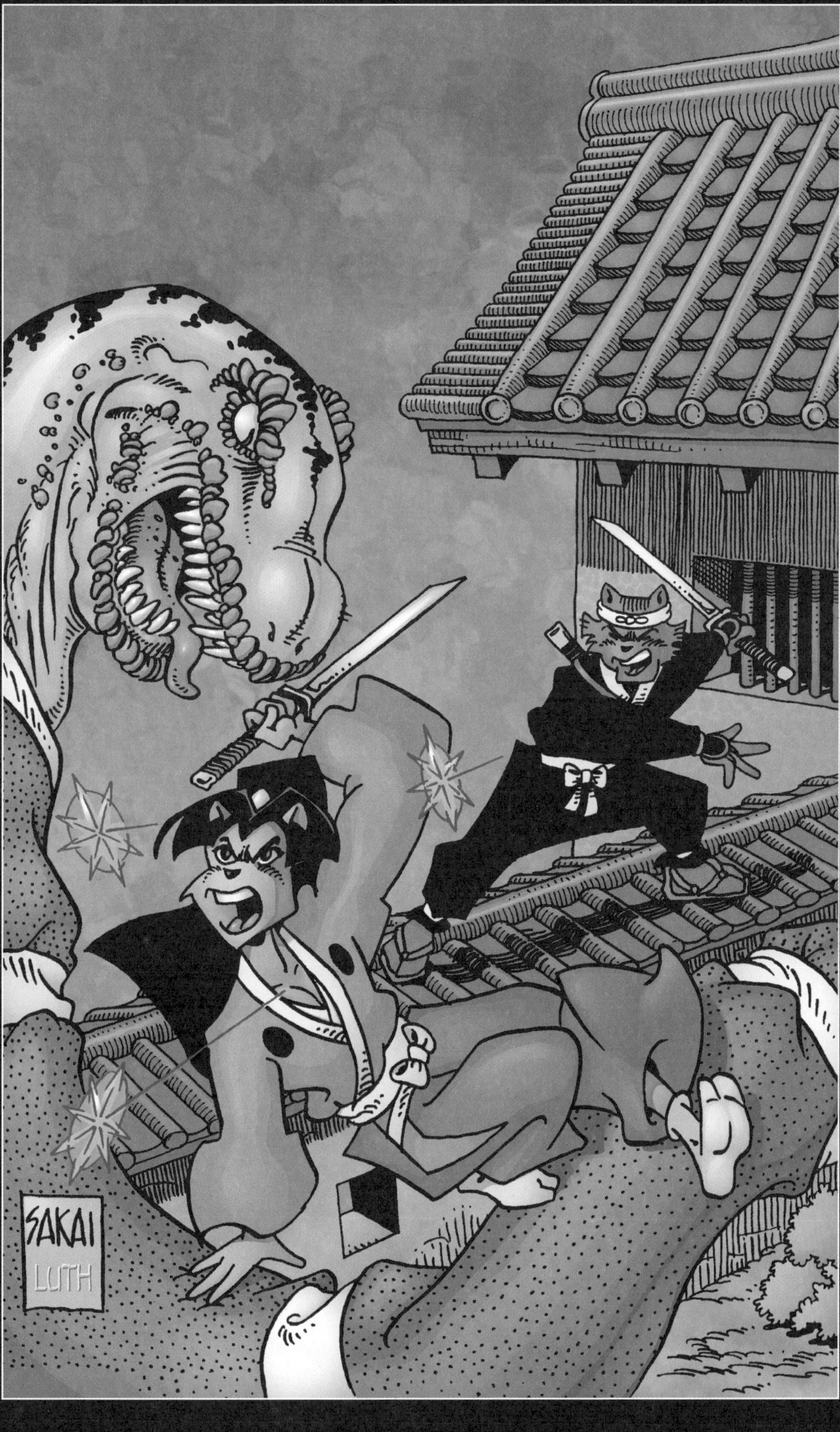
SAKAI
LUTH
Usagi Yojimbo Volume Three #48

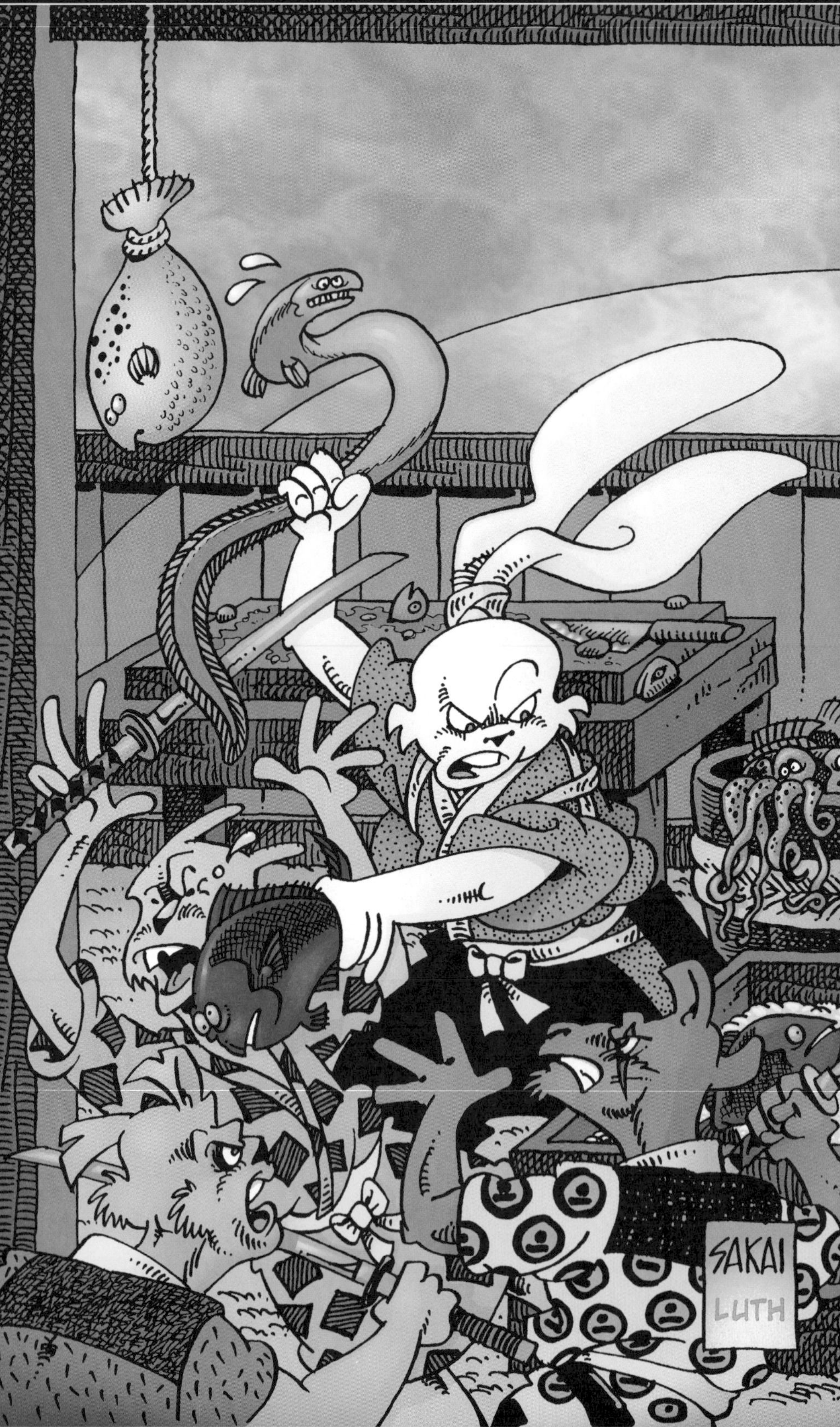
SAKAI
LUTH

Usagi Yojimbo Volume Three #49

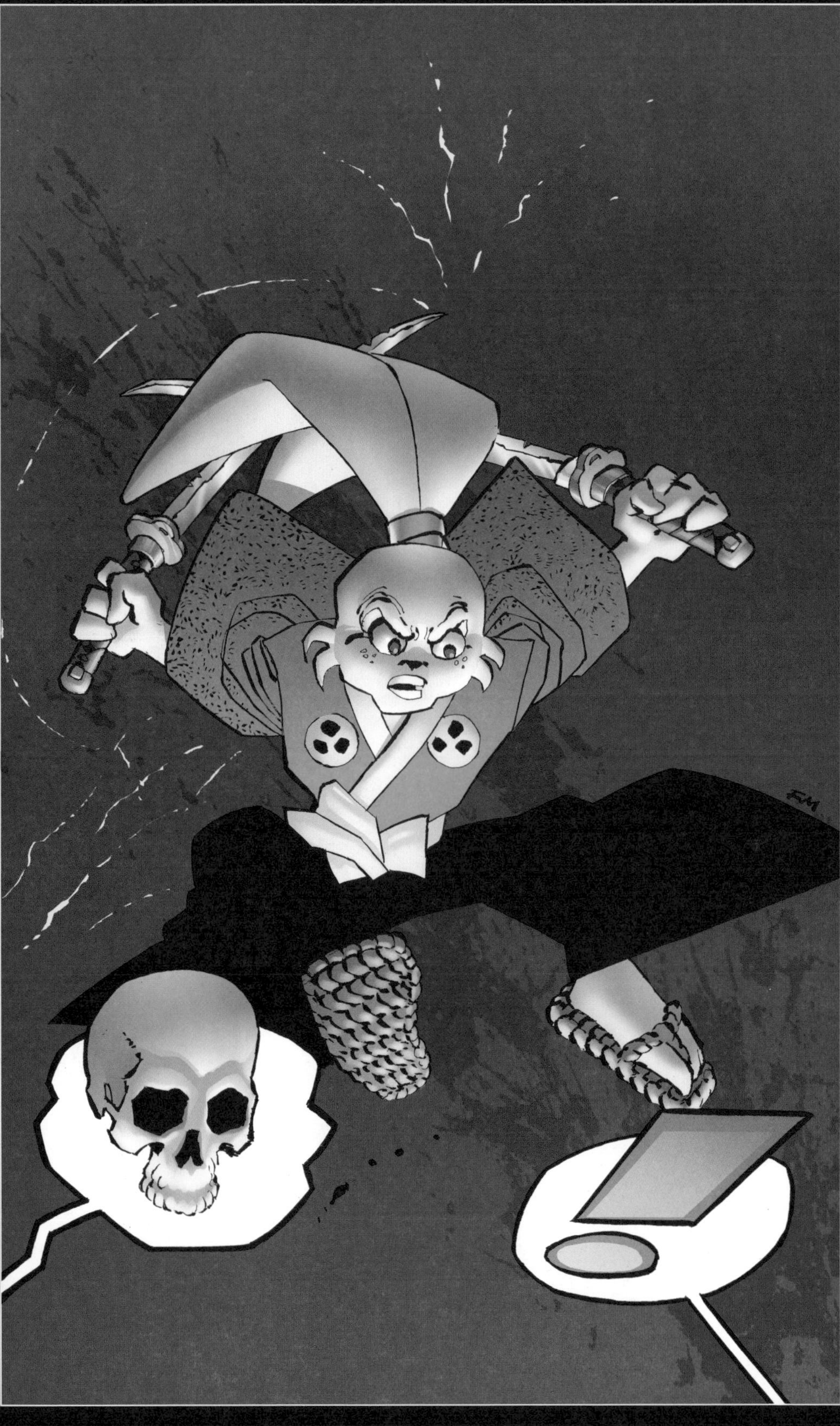

Dark Horse Maverick 2001, art by Frank Miller, colors by Laura Martin

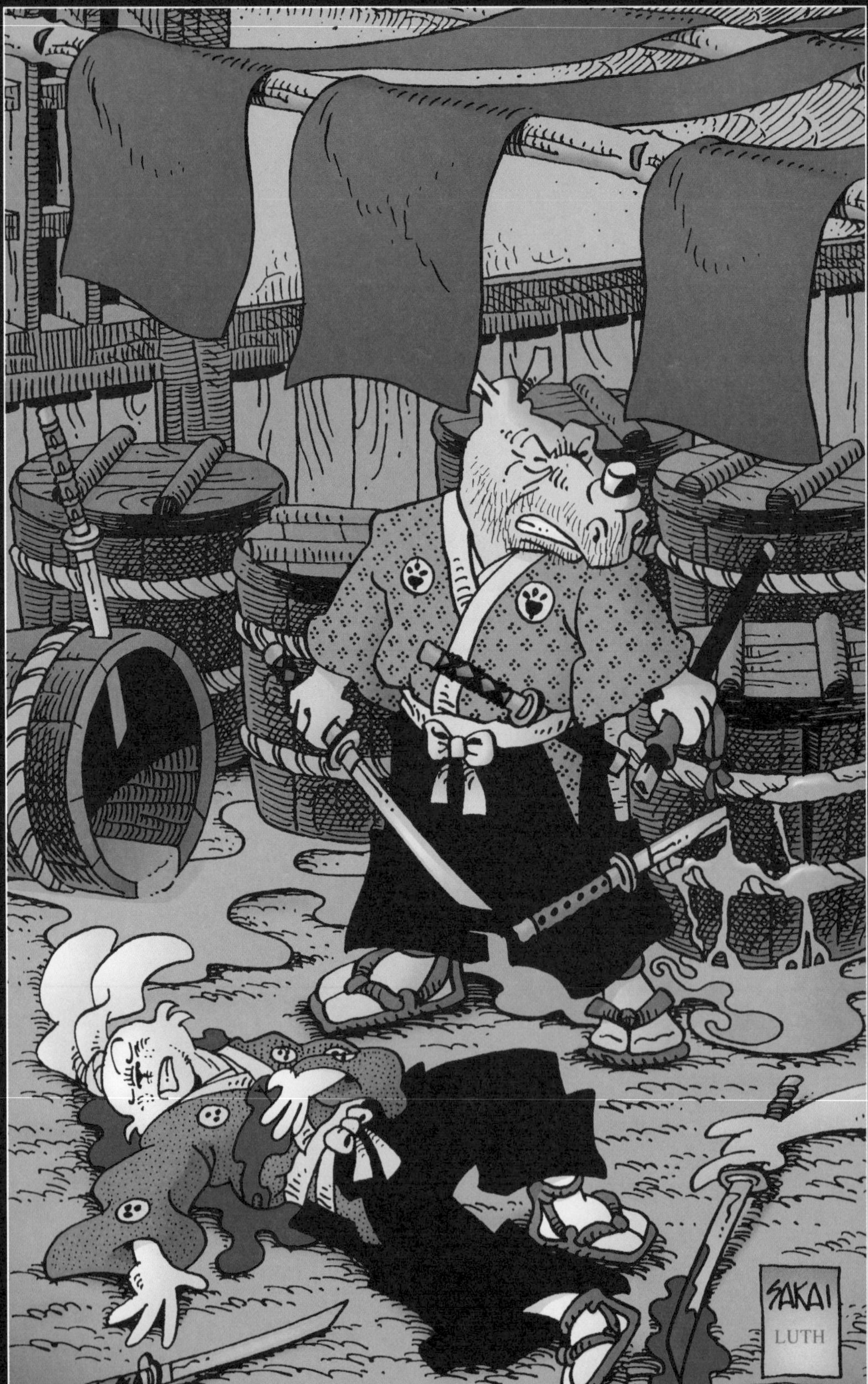
SAKAI
LUTH

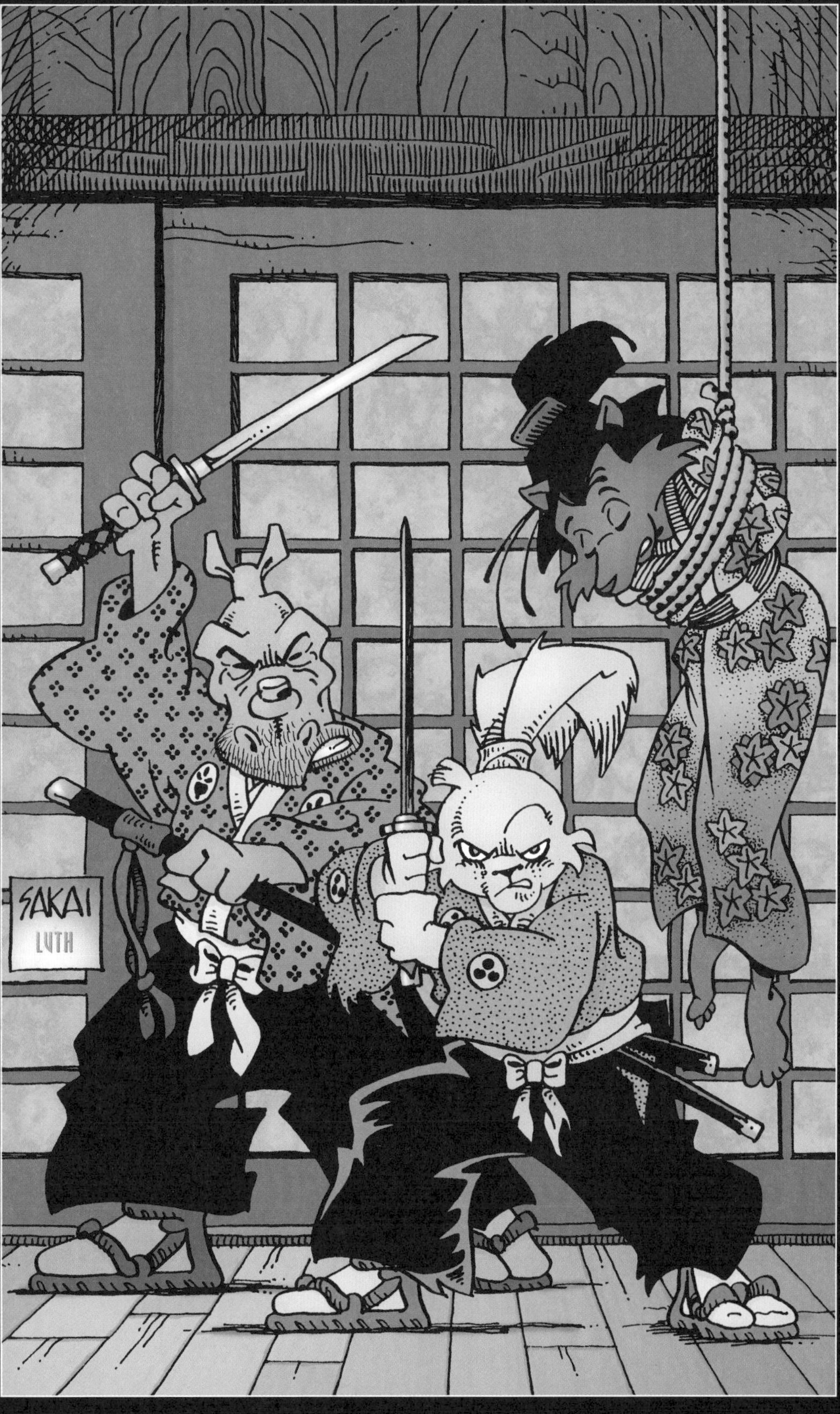
SAKAI
LUTH

Usagi Yojimbo Volume Three #51

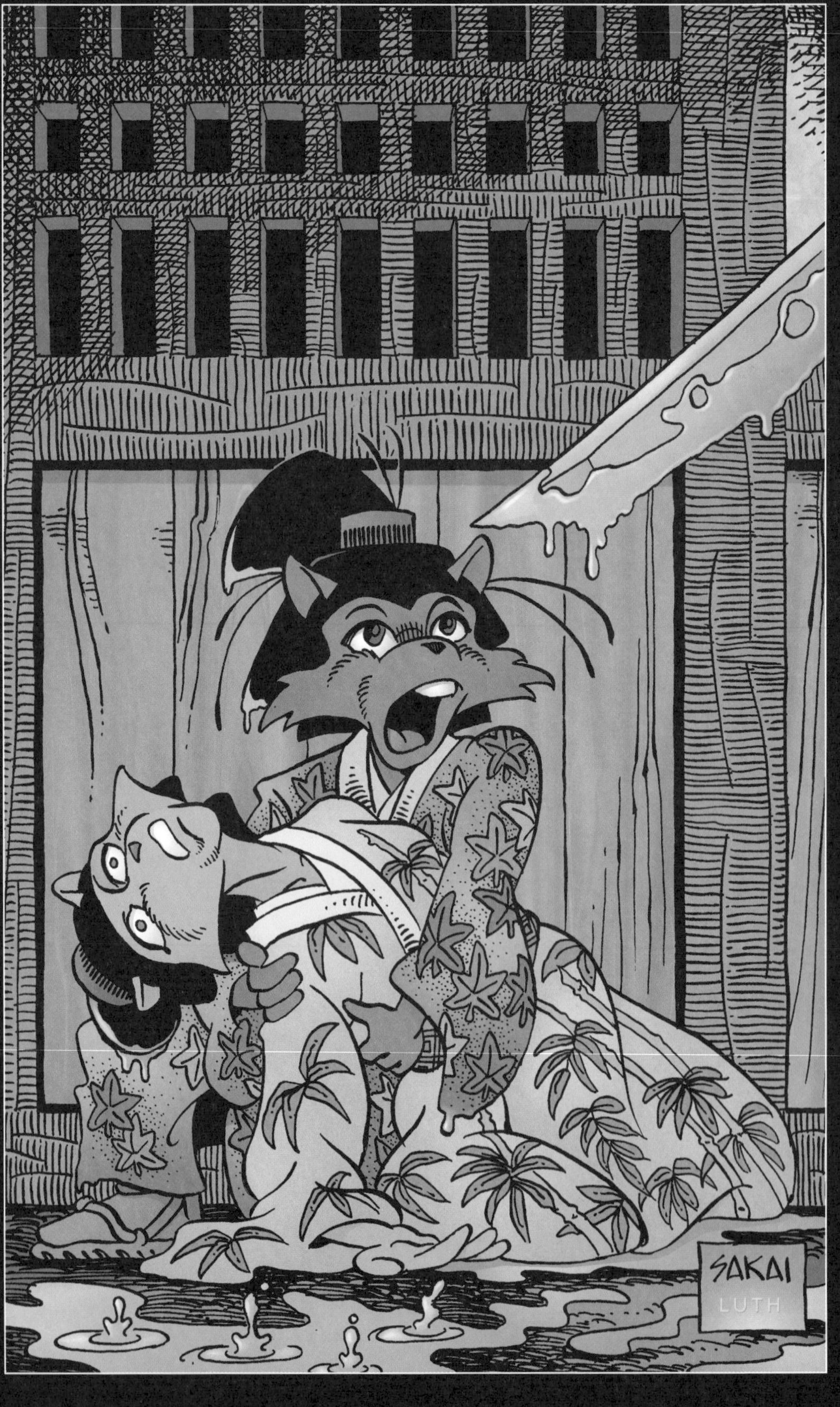
SAKAI
LUTH

Usagi Yojimbo Volume Three #52

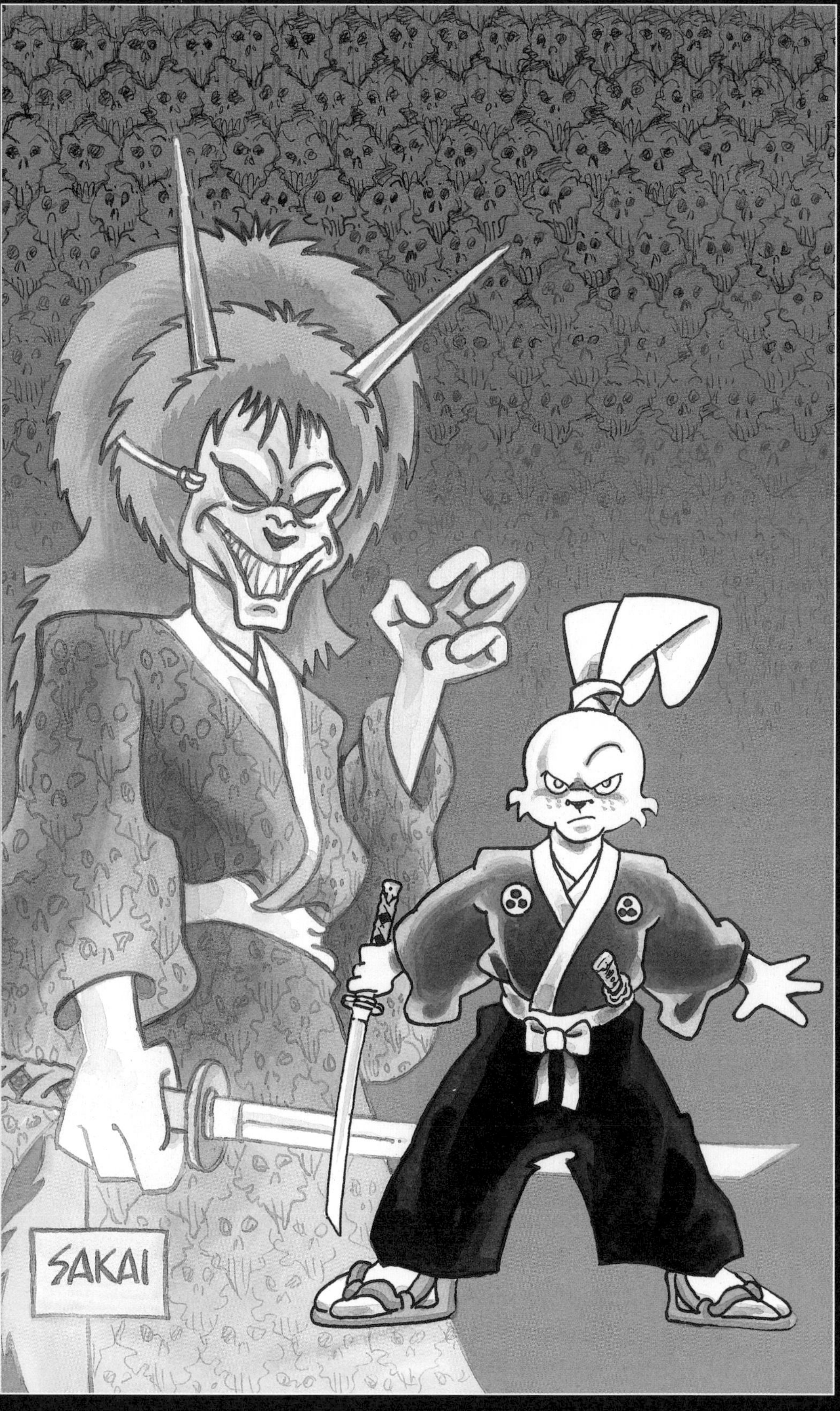
SAKAI

Usagi Yojimbo Book 14: *Demon Mask*

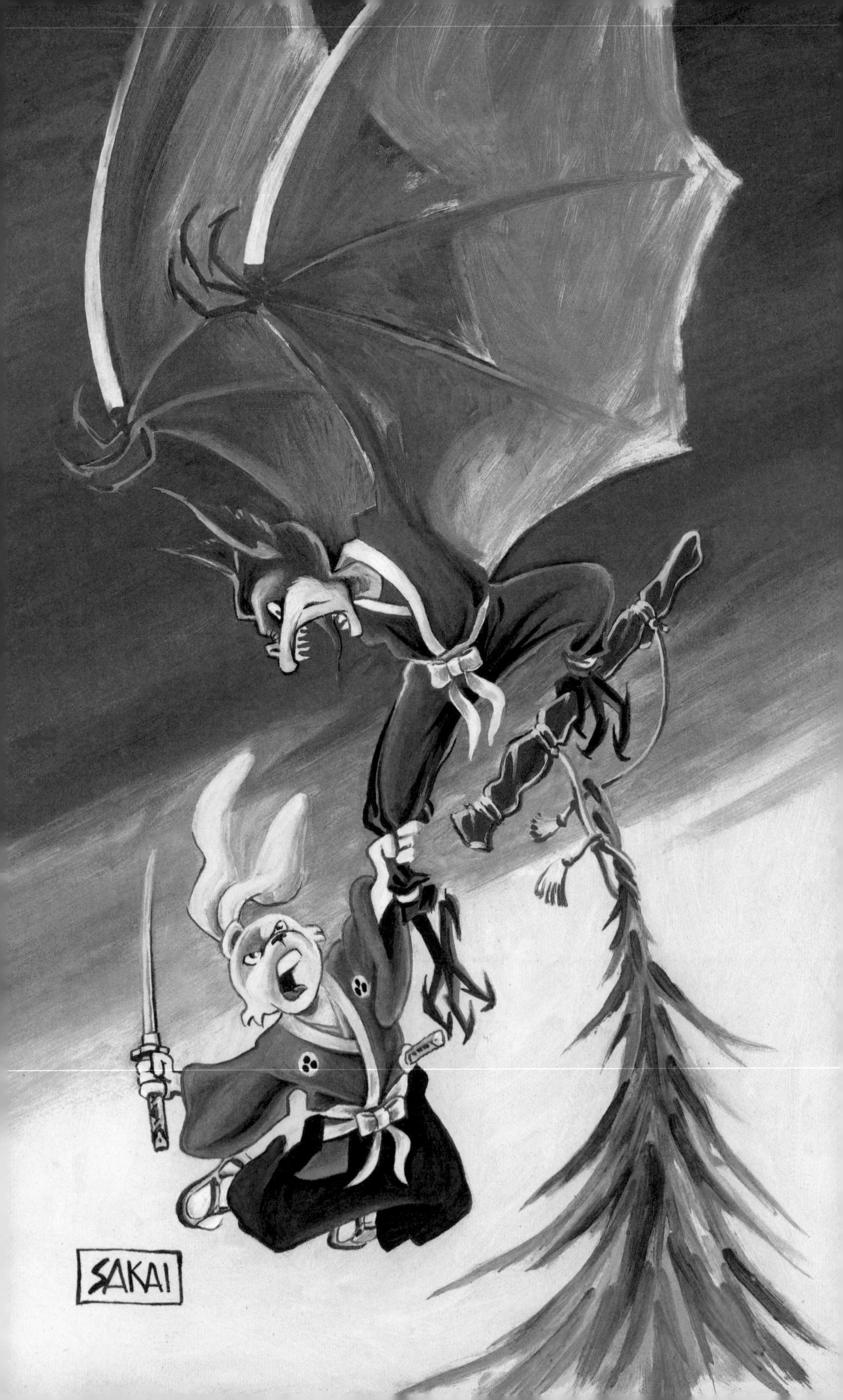
SAKAI

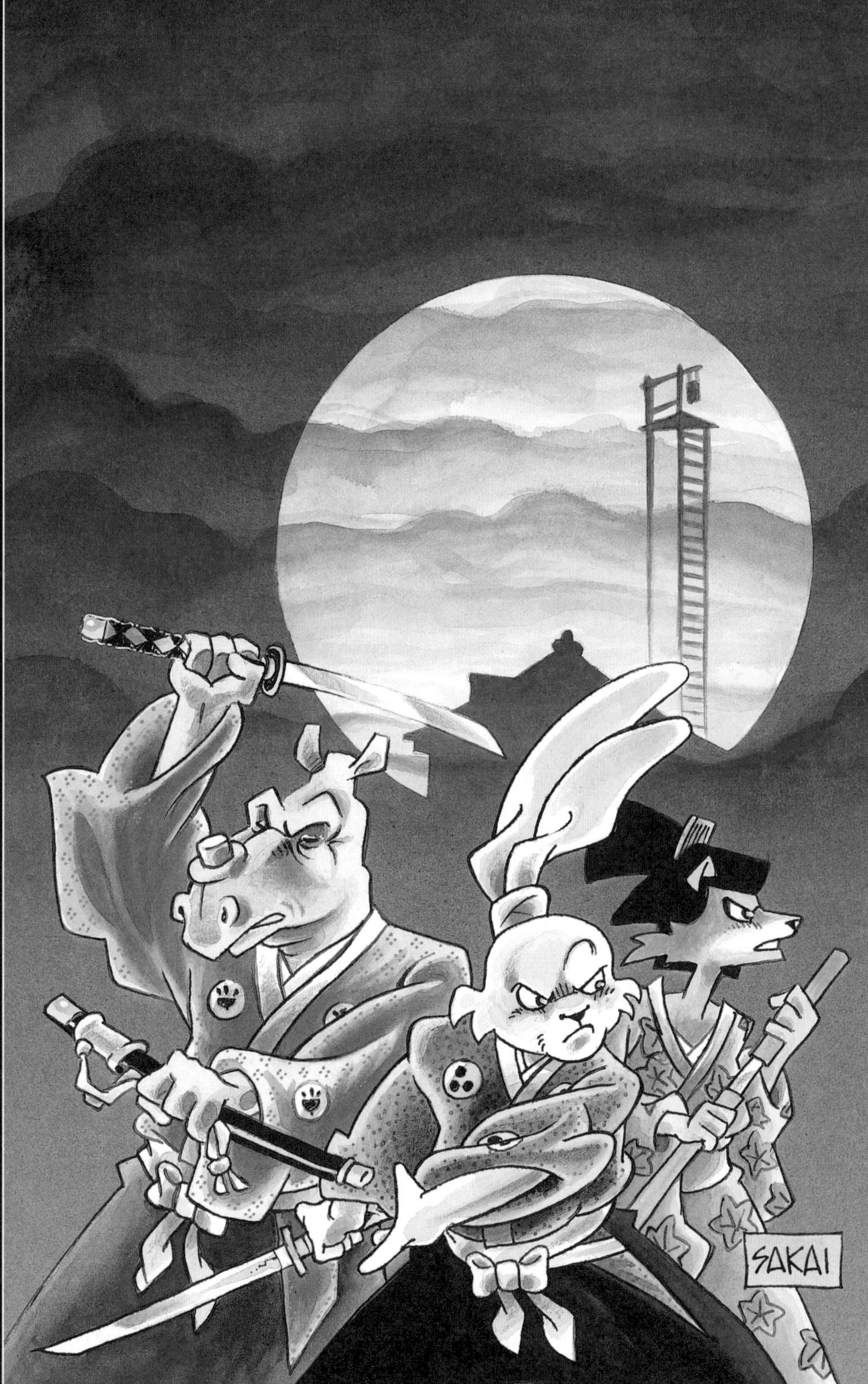
SAKAI

Usagi Yojimbo Book 16: *The Shrouded Moon*

ABOUT THE AUTHOR

Stan at Miyajima, Japan. Photo by Sharon Sakai.

STAN SAKAI was born in Kyoto, Japan, grew up in Hawaii, and now lives in California. He has two children, Hannah and Matthew. Stan received a fine arts degree from the University of Hawaii and furthered his studies at the Art Center College of Design in Pasadena, California.

Stan's creation *Usagi Yojimbo* first appeared in comics in 1984. Since then, Usagi has been on television as a guest of the Teenage Mutant Ninja Turtles and has been made into toys, seen on clothing, and featured in a series of graphic novel collections.

In 1991, Stan created *Space Usagi*, a series dealing with samurai in a futuristic setting, featuring the adventures of a descendant of the original Usagi.

Stan is also an award-winning letterer for his work on Sergio Aragonés's *Groo*, the *Spider-Man* Sunday newspaper strips, and *Usagi Yojimbo*.

Stan is the recipient of a Parents' Choice Award, an Inkpot Award, an American Library Association Award, a Harvey Award, five Spanish Haxtur Awards, several Eisner Awards, and an Inkwell Award. In 2002 he won the prestigious National Cartoonists Society Award in the Comic Book division, and in 2011 Stan received the Cultural Ambassador Award from the Japanese American National Museum.

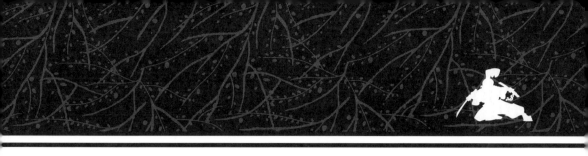

Akiko™ © Mark Crilley.

Mark Crilley

613

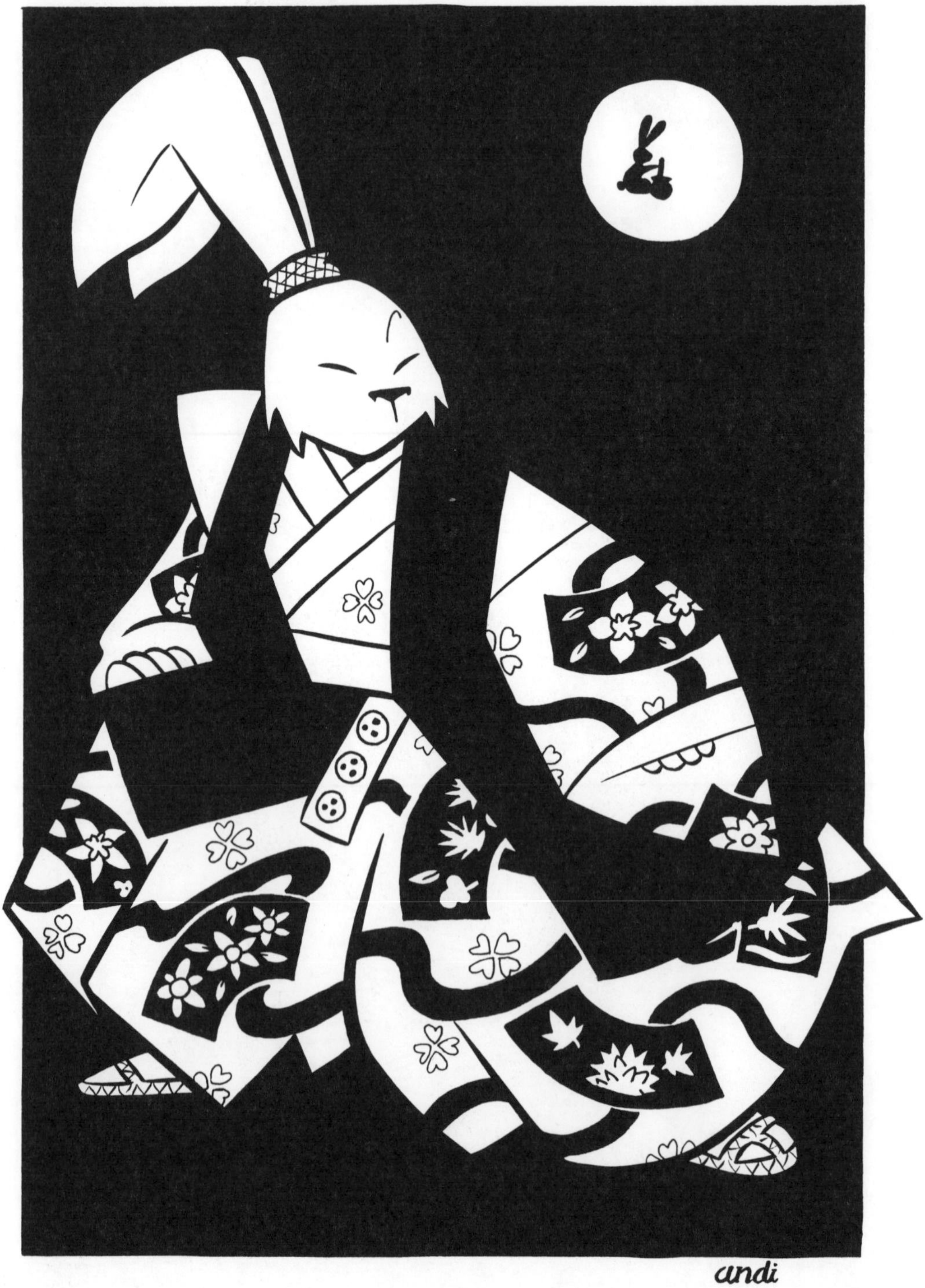
andi

Andi Watson

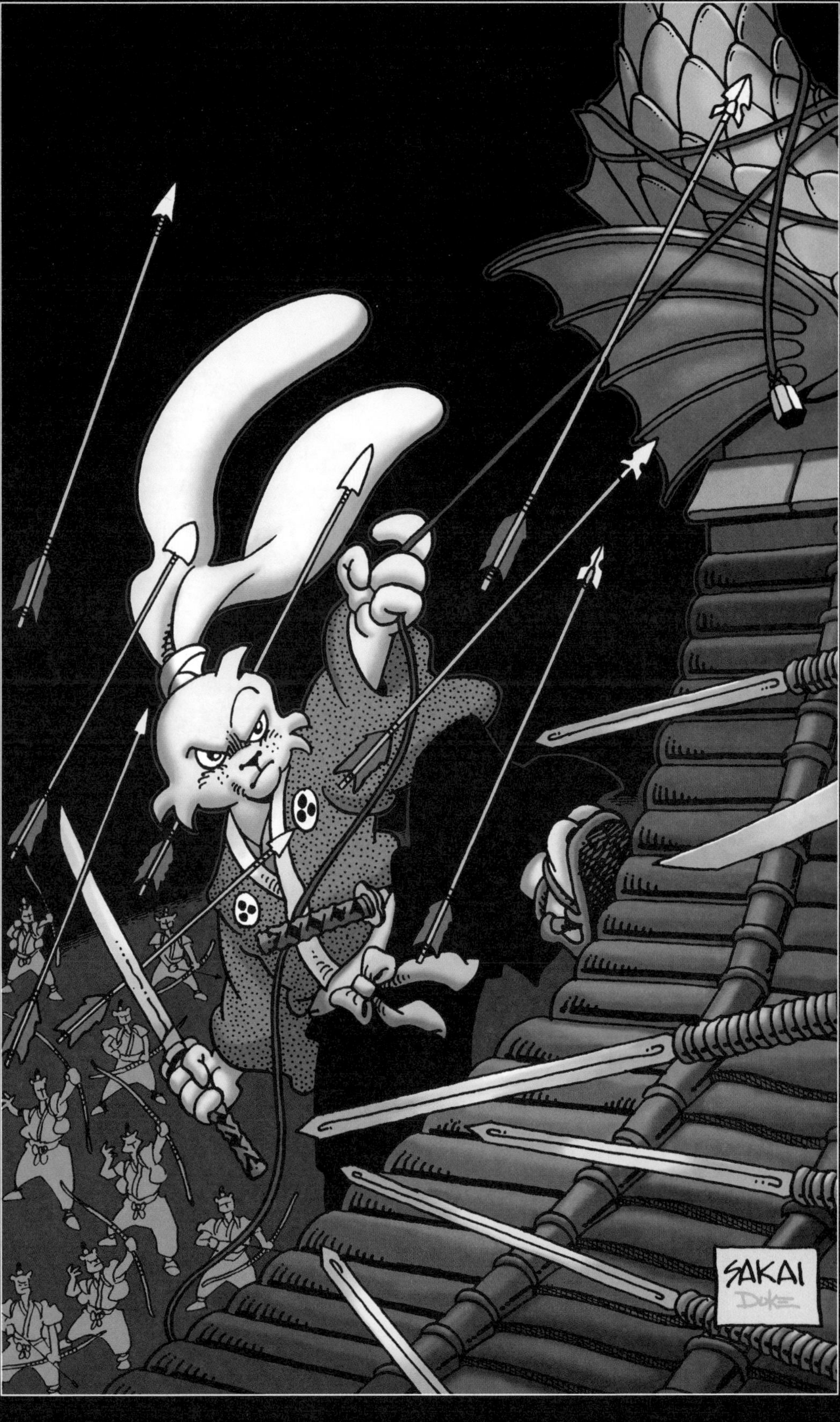
SAKAI
DUKE

Bonus cover: *The Art of Usagi Yojimbo* #2, colors by Pat Duke